Running Case Features

Closing Cases

Strategic Management

Strategic Management

An Integrated Approach

EIGHTH EDITION

Charles W. L. Hill
UNIVERSITY OF WASHINGTON

Gareth R. Jones
TEXAS A&M UNIVERSITY

Houghton Mifflin Company   Boston   New York

For my children, Elizabeth, Charlotte, and Michelle
Charles W. L. Hill

For Nicholas and Julia and Morgan and Nia
Gareth R. Jones

Executive Publisher: George Hoffman
Executive Editor: Lisé Johnson
Senior Marketing Manager: Nicole Hamm
Development Editor: Suzanna Smith
Senior Project Editor: Carol Merrigan
Art and Design Manager: Jill Haber
Cover Design Director: Tony Saizon
Senior Photo Editor: Jennifer Meyer Dare
Senior Composition Buyer: Chuck Dutton
New Title Project Manager: James Lonergan
Editorial Assistant: Kathryn White
Marketing Assistant: Tom DiGiano

Cover image: Jason Hawkes, www.jasonhawkes.com

Printed in the U.S.A.

Library of Congress Control Number: 2007934813

Instructor's examination copy:
ISBN-10: 0-547-00497-4
ISBN-13: 978-0-547-00497-6

For orders, use student text ISBNs:
ISBN-10: 0-618-89469-1
ISBN-13: 978-0-618-89469-7

2   3   4   5   6   7   8   9–DOW–11   10   09   08

Brief Contents

Contents

2   External Analysis: The Identification of Opportunities and Threats   41

Part 2   The Nature of Competitive Advantage

3   Internal Analysis: Distinctive Competencies, Competitive Advantage, and Profitability   75

4 Building Competitive Advantage Through Functional-Level Strategy

Part 3   Strategies

5   Building Competitive Advantage Through Business-Level Strategy   149

6 Business-Level Strategy and the Industry Environment   186

7 Strategy and Technology   228

8   Strategy in the Global Environment   262

9 Corporate-Level Strategy: Horizontal Integration, Vertical Integration, and Strategic Outsourcing   302

10   Corporate-Level Strategy: Formulating and Implementing Related and Unrelated Diversification   331

Part 4   Implementing Strategy

11   Corporate Performance, Governance, and Business Ethics   366

12 Implementing Strategy in Companies That Compete in a Single Industry 401

13 Implementing Strategy in Companies That Compete Across Industries and Countries

442

Part 5 Cases in Strategic Management
Introduction: Analyzing a Case Study and Writing a Case Study Analysis

C1

Cases

Section C: Ethics Cases

Preface

Since the seventh edition was published, this book has strengthened its position as the most widely used strategic management textbook on the market. This tells us that we continue to meet the expectations of existing users and attract many new users to our book. It is clear that most strategy instructors share with us a concern for currency in the text and its examples to ensure that cutting-edge issues and new developments in strategic management are continually addressed.

Just as in the last edition, our objective in writing the eighth edition has been to maintain all that was good about prior editions, while refining our approach to discussing established strategic management issues and adding new material to the text to present a more complete, clear, and current account of strategic management as we move steadily into the twenty-first century. We believe that the result is a book that is more closely aligned with the needs of today's professors and students and with the realities of competition in the new global environment.

Comprehensive and Up-to-Date Coverage

We have updated many of the features running throughout the chapters, including all new Opening Cases and Running Cases. For the Running Cases, Dell has replaced Wal-Mart as the focus company. In this edition, we have made no changes to the number or sequencing of our chapters. However, we have made many significant changes inside each chapter to refine and update our presentation of strategic management. Continuing real-world changes in strategic management practices such as the increased use of cost reduction strategies like global outsourcing, ethical issues, and lean production, and a continued emphasis on the business model as the driver of differentiation and competitive advantage, have led to many changes in our approach. To emphasize the importance of ethical decision making in strategic management, we have included a new feature in the end matter of every chapter that introduces concept-specific ethical dilemmas that could develop in a real-world business setting.

Throughout the revision process, we have been careful to preserve the *balanced and integrated* nature of our account of strategic management. As we have continued to add new material, we have also shortened or deleted coverage of out-of-date or less important models and concepts to help students identify and focus on the core concepts and issues in the field. We have also paid close attention to retaining the book's readability.

Finally, it is important to emphasize that we have overhauled the case selection. Twenty-nine of the thirty-four end-of-text cases are completely new, with the remaining five cases being heavily revised based on new data. As always, we have used a tight screen to filter out irrelevant cases, and we believe that the selection we offer is the best on the market.

Practicing Strategic Management: An Interactive Approach

We have received a lot of positive feedback about the usefulness of the end-of-chapter exercises and assignments in the Practicing Strategic Management sections in our book. They offer a wide range of hands-on learning experiences for students. Following the Chapter Summary and Discussion Questions, each chapter contains the following exercises and assignments:

- *Small Group Exercise.* This short (20-minute) experiential exercise asks students to divide into groups and discuss a scenario concerning some aspect of strategic management. For example, the scenario in Chapter 11 asks students to identify the stakeholders of their educational institution and evaluate how stakeholders' claims are being and should be met.

- *Ethics Exercise.* The ethics exercise has replaced the Exploring the Web feature (now online). This feature has been developed to highlight the importance of ethical decision making in today's business environment. With today's current examples of poor decision making (as seen in Enron, Tyco, and WorldCom, to name a few), we hope to equip students with the tools they need to be strong ethical leaders.

- *Article File.* As in the last edition, this exercise requires students to search business magazines to identify a company that is facing a particular strategic management problem. For instance, students are asked to locate and research a company pursuing a low-cost or a differentiation strategy, and to describe this company's strategy, its advantages and disadvantages, and the core competencies required to pursue it. Students' presentations of their findings lead to lively class discussions.

- *Strategic Management Project.* In small groups, students choose a company to study for the whole semester and then analyze the company using the series of questions provided at the end of every chapter. For example, students might select Ford Motor Co. and, using the series of chapter questions, collect information on Ford's top managers, mission, ethical position, domestic and global strategy and structure, and so on. Students write a case study of their company and present it to the class at the end of the semester. In the past, we also had students present one or more of the cases in the book early in the semester, but now in our classes, we treat the students' own projects as the major class assignment and their case presentations as the climax of the semester's learning experience.

- *Closing Case Study.* A short closing case provides an opportunity for a short class discussion of a chapter-related theme.

In creating these exercises, it is not our intention to suggest that they should *all* be used for *every* chapter. For example, over a semester, an instructor might combine a group Strategic Management Project with five to six Article File assignments and five to six Exploring the Web exercises, while doing eight to ten Small Group Exercises in class.

We have found that our interactive approach to teaching strategic management appeals to students. It also greatly improves the quality of their learning experience. Our approach is more fully discussed in the *Instructor's Resource Manual.*

Strategic Management Cases

The thirty-four cases that we have selected for this edition will appeal, we are certain, to students and professors alike, both because these cases are intrinsically interesting and because of the number of strategic management issues they illuminate. The organizations discussed in the cases range from large, well-known companies, for which students can do research to update the information, to small, entrepreneurial businesses that illustrate the uncertainty and challenge of the strategic management process. In addition, the selections include many international cases, and most of the other cases contain some element of global strategy. Refer to the Contents for a complete listing of the cases with brief descriptions.

To help students learn how to effectively analyze and write a case study, we continue to include a special section on this subject. It has a checklist and an explanation of areas to consider, suggested research tools, and tips on financial analysis.

We feel that our entire selection of cases is unrivaled in breadth and depth, and we are grateful to the other case authors who have contributed to this edition:

Isaac Cohen, *San Jose State University*

William P. Barnett, *Stanford Graduate School of Business*

Mike Harkey, *Stanford Graduate School of Business*

Robert A. Burgelman, *Stanford Graduate School of Business*

Aneesha Capur, *Stanford Graduate School of Business*

David B. Yoffie, *Harvard Business School*

Michael Slind, *Harvard Business School*

Patricia Harasta, *Bentley College*

Alan N. Hoffman, *Bentley College*

Vivek Gupta, *ICFAI Center for Management Research*

Vinay Kumar, *ICFAI Center for Management Research*

Shengjun Liu, *University of Western Ontario*

Darryl Davis, *New York University*

Tom Davis, *New York University*

Sara Moodie, *New York University*

Melissa A. Schilling, *New York University*

Suresh Kotha, *University of Washington*

Sandip Basu, *University of Washington*

Robert J. Mockler, *St. John's University*

Christopher A. Bartlett, *Harvard Business School*

Anne T. Lawrence, *San Jose State University*

Teaching and Learning Aids

Taken together, the teaching and learning features of *Strategic Management* provide a package that is unsurpassed in its coverage and that supports the integrated approach that we have taken throughout the book.

For the Instructor

- The **Instructor's Resource Manual: Theory** has been completely revised. For each chapter, we provide a clearly focused synopsis, a list of teaching objectives, a comprehensive lecture outline, suggested answers to discussion questions, and comments on the end-of-chapter activities. Each chapter-opening case, Strategy in Action boxed feature, and chapter-closing case has a synopsis and a corresponding teaching note to help guide class discussion.

- The **HMTesting CD** has been revised and offers a set of comprehensive true/false and multiple-choice questions, and new essay questions for each chapter in the book. The mix of questions has been adjusted to provide fewer fact-based or simple memorization items and to provide more items that rely on synthesis or application. Also, more items now reflect real or hypothetical situations in organizations. Every question is keyed to the teaching objectives in the *Instructor's Resource Manual* and includes an answer and page reference to the textbook.

- The **Instructor's Resource Manual: Cases** includes a complete list of case discussion questions as well as a comprehensive teaching note for each case, which gives a complete analysis of case issues. It is written in a user-friendly question-and-answer format.

- The **video program** highlights many issues of interest and can be used to spark class discussion. It offers a compilation of footage from the Videos for Humanities series.

- An extensive **website** contains many features to aid instructors, including downloadable files for the text and case materials from the *Instructor's Resource Manuals*, the downloadable Premium and Basic PowerPoint slides, the Video Guide, and sample syllabi. Additional materials on the student website may also be of use to instructors.

- **Eduspace®,** powered by Blackboard®, is a course management tool that includes chapter outlines, chapter summaries, audio chapter summaries and quizzes, all questions from the textbook with suggested answers, Debate Issues, ACE self-test questions, auto-graded quizzes, Premium and Basic PowerPoint slides, Classroom Response System content, links to content on the websites, video activities, and test pools. A Course Materials Guide is available to help instructor organization.

- **Blackboard®/Web CT®** includes course material, chapter outlines, chapter summaries, audio chapter summaries and quizzes, all questions from the textbook with suggested answers, Premium and Basic PowerPoint slides, Classroom Response System content, links to content on the websites, video activities, and Test Bank content.

For the Student

- The student **website** includes chapter overviews, Internet exercises, ACE self-tests, audio summaries and quizzes, case discussion questions to help guide student case analysis, glossaries, flashcards for studying the key terms, a section with guidelines on how to do case study analysis, and much more.

Acknowledgments

This book is the product of far more than two authors. We are grateful to Lisé Johnson, our sponsor; Suzanna Smith, our editor; and Nicole Hamm, our marketing manager, for their help in promoting and developing the book and for providing us with timely feedback and information from professors and reviewers, which allowed us to shape the book to meet the needs of its intended market. We are also grateful to Carol Merrigan and Kristen Truncellito, project editors, for their adept handling of production. We are also grateful to the case authors for allowing us to use their materials. We also want to thank the departments of management at the University of Washington and Texas A&M University for providing the setting and atmosphere in which the book could be written, and the students of these universities who reacted to and provided input for many of our ideas. In addition, the following reviewers of this and earlier editions gave us valuable suggestions for improving the manuscript from its original version to its current form:

Ken Armstrong, *Anderson University*

Richard Babcock, *University of San Francisco*

Kunal Banerji, *West Virginia University*

Kevin Banning, *Auburn University – Montgomery*

Glenn Bassett, *University of Bridgeport*

Thomas H. Berliner, *The University of Texas at Dallas*

Bonnie Bollinger, *Ivy Technical Community College*

Richard G. Brandenburg, *University of Vermont*

Steven Braund, *University of Hull*

Philip Bromiley, *University of Minnesota*

Geoffrey Brooks, *Western Oregon State College*

Amanda Budde, *University of Hawaii*

Lowell Busenitz, *University of Houston*

Charles J. Capps III, *Sam Houston State University*

Don Caruth, *Texas A&M Commerce*

Gene R. Conaster, *Golden State University*

Steven W. Congden, *University of Hartford*

Catherine M. Daily, *Ohio State University*

Robert DeFillippi, *Suffolk University Sawyer School of Management*

Helen Deresky, *SUNY – Plattsburgh*

Gerald E. Evans, *The University of Montana*

John Fahy, *Trinity College, Dublin*

Patricia Feltes, *Southwest Missouri State University*

Bruce Fern, *New York University*

Mark Fiegener, *Oregon State University*

Chuck Foley, *Columbus State Community College*

Isaac Fox, *Washington State University*

Craig Galbraith, *University of North Carolina at Wilmington*

Scott R. Gallagher, *Rutgers University*

Eliezer Geisler, *Northeastern Illinois University*

Gretchen Gemeinhardt, *University of Houston*

Lynn Godkin, *Lamar University*

Sanjay Goel, *University of Minnesota – Duluth*

Robert L. Goldberg, *Northeastern University*

James Grinnell, *Merrimack College*

Russ Hagberg, *Northern Illinois University*

Allen Harmon, *University of Minnesota – Duluth*

David Hoopes, *California State University – Dominguez Hills*

Todd Hostager, *University of Wisconsin – Eau Claire*

Graham L. Hubbard, *University of Minnesota*

Tammy G. Hunt, *University of North Carolina at Wilmington*

James Gaius Ibe, *Morris College*

W. Grahm Irwin, *Miami University*

Homer Johnson, *Loyola University – Chicago*

Jonathan L. Johnson, *University of Arkansas – Walton College of Business Administration*

Marios Katsioloudes, *St. Joseph's University*

Robert Keating, *University of North Carolina at Wilmington*

Geoffrey King, *California State University – Fullerton*

John Kraft, *University of Florida*

Rico Lam, *University of Oregon*

Robert J. Litschert, *Virginia Polytechnic Institute and State University*

Franz T. Lohrke, *Louisiana State University*

Paul Mallette, *Colorado State University*

Daniel Marrone, *SUNY Farmingdale*

Lance A. Masters, *California State University – San Bernardino*

Robert N. McGrath, *Embry-Riddle Aeronautical University*

Charles Mercer, *Drury College*

Van Miller, *University of Dayton*

Tom Morris, *University of San Diego*

Joanna Mulholland, *West Chester University of Pennsylvania*

John Nebeck, *Viterbo University*

Richard Neubert, *University of Tennessee – Knoxville*

Francine Newth, *Providence College*

Don Okhomina, *Fayetteville State University*

Phaedon P. Papadopoulos, *Houston Baptist University*

John Pappalardo, *Keene State College*

Paul R. Reed, *Sam Houston State University*

Rhonda K. Reger, *Arizona State University*

Malika Richards, *Indiana University*

Simon Rodan, *San Jose State*

Stuart Rosenberg, *Dowling College*

Douglas Ross, *Towson University*

Ronald Sanchez, *University of Illinois*

Joseph A. Schenk, *University of Dayton*

Brian Shaffer, *University of Kentucky*

Leonard Sholtis, *Eastern Michigan University*

Pradip K. Shukla, *Chapman University*

Mel Sillmon, *University of Michigan – Dearborn*

Dennis L. Smart, *University of Nebraska at Omaha*

Barbara Spencer, *Clemson University*

Lawrence Steenberg, *University of Evansville*

Kim A. Stewart, *University of Denver*

Ted Takamura, *Warner Pacific College*

Scott Taylor, *Florida Metropolitan University*
Bobby Vaught, *Southwest Missouri State*
Robert P. Vichas, *Florida Atlantic University*
Edward Ward, *St. Cloud State University*
Kenneth Wendeln, *Indiana University*
Daniel L. White, *Drexel University*
Edgar L. Williams, Jr., *Norfolk State University*
Jun Zhao, *Governors State University*

Charles W. L. Hill
Gareth R. Jones

Strategic Management

Strategic Leadership: Managing the Strategy-Making Process for Competitive Advantage

Dell Computer

Dell Computer has enjoyed a decade of very high profitability. Between 1998 and 2006, its average return on invested capital (ROIC) was a staggering 48.3%, far ahead of the profitability of competing manufacturers of personal computers (see Figure 1.1). Moreover, while the profitability of its competitors fell sharply during 2001–2004, reflecting a tough selling environment in the personal computer industry, Dell managed to maintain a very high ROIC. Clearly, Dell has had a sustained competitive advantage over its rivals. Where did this come from?

An answer can be found in Dell's business model: selling directly to retail customers. Michael Dell reasoned that by cutting out wholesalers and retailers, he would obtain the profit they would otherwise receive and could give part of the profit back to customers in the form of lower prices. Initially, Dell did its direct selling through mailings and telephone contacts, but since the mid-1990s, much of its sales have been made through its website. Dell's sophisticated website allows customers to mix and match product features such as microprocessors, memory, monitors, internal hard drives, CD and DVD drives, keyboard and mouse format, and so on, to customize their own computer systems. The ability to customize orders kept retail customers coming back to Dell and helped to drive sales to a record $55.9 billion in 2004.

Another reason for Dell's high performance is the way it manages its supply chain to minimize the costs of holding inventory. Dell has about 200 suppliers, over half of them located outside the United States. Dell uses the Internet to feed real-time information about order flow to its suppliers so they have up-to-the-minute information about demand trends for the components they produce, along with volume expectations for the upcoming four to twelve weeks. Dell's suppliers use this information to adjust their own production schedules, manufacturing just enough components for Dell's needs and shipping them by the most appropriate mode so that they arrive just in time for production. This tight coordination is pushed back even further down the supply chain because Dell shares this information with its suppliers' biggest suppliers.

Dell's goal is to coordinate its supply chain to such an extent that it drives all inventories out of the supply chain, apart from those actually in transit between suppliers and Dell, effectively replacing inventory with information. Dell has succeeded in driving down inventory to the lowest

FIGURE 1.1

Profitability of U.S. Personal Computer Makers

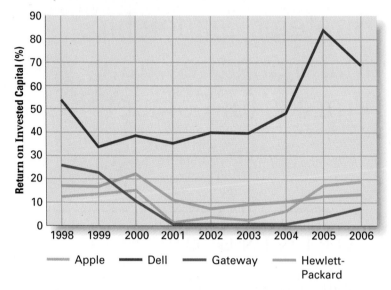

Source: Value Line Calculations. Data for 2006 are estimates based on three quarters.

level in the industry. In mid-2006, it was turning its inventory over every five days, compared to an average of forty-one days at key competitor Hewlett-Packard. This is a major source of competitive advantage in the computer industry, where component costs account for 75% of revenues and typically fall by 1% per week due to rapid obsolescence.

Despite its high profitability, between mid-2005 and mid-2006, Dell's stock lost half its market value, sliding from $42 a share to $22. There were several reasons for this. First, after years of trying, three of Dell's competitors, Acer, Hewlett-Packard, and Lenovo, had reduced their cost structure and become more competitive with Dell, enabling them to match Dell on prices and still make profits. Second, by 2005, the consumer market for PCs in developed nations had become mature. To keep growing, Dell tried to expand its share of the business market—but here it faces tough competition from Hewlett-Packard, which can offer business users a wider range of products, and extensive consulting services and

after-sales service and support, all things that business users value highly. Third, Dell's growth had been hurt by poor customer service. Dell had outsourced customer service to India in an attempt to reduce costs, only to find that poor service alienated its customers. Even though Dell moved customer service for business users back to the United States, some damage had already been done, and this only served to emphasize the difference between Dell and HP in the minds of business customers. Fourth, in an attempt to gain market share from competitors, Dell cut prices in 2005 and 2006, but it gained little in sales volume, made less profit per computer, and experienced only sluggish profit growth for 2006.

Many investors, deciding that Dell's years of rapid profit growth might be over, sold the stock. Looking forward, analysts think that Dell's profitability, as measured by ROIC, will decline from over 60% in 2006 to 30% by 2009 as competitors like Acer, Lenovo, and Hewlett-Packard start to match Dell's cost structure, and differentiate themselves from Dell in ways that users value.[1]

Why do some companies succeed while others fail? Why has Dell Computer been able to do so well in the fiercely competitive personal computer industry, while competitors like Gateway have struggled to make money? In the airline industry, how is it that Southwest Airlines has managed to keep increasing its revenues and profits through both good times and bad, while rivals such as US Airways and United Airlines have had to seek bankruptcy protection? What explains the persistent growth and profitability of Nucor Steel, now the largest steel maker in America, during a period when many of its once larger rivals disappeared into bankruptcy?

In this book, we argue that the strategies that a company's managers pursue have a major impact on its performance relative to its competitors. A **strategy** is a set of related actions that managers take to increase their company's performance. For most, if not all, companies, achieving superior performance relative to rivals is the ultimate challenge. If a company's strategies result in superior performance, it is said to have a competitive advantage. Dell Computer's strategies produced superior performance during the late 1990s and first half of the 2000s; as a result, Dell enjoyed a competitive advantage over its rivals. How did Dell achieve this competitive advantage? As explained in the Opening Case, it was due to the successful pursuit of a number of strategies by Dell's managers. These strategies enabled the company to lower its cost structure, charge low prices, gain market share, and become more profitable than its rivals. We will return to the example of Dell several times throughout this book in a Running Case that examines various aspects of Dell strategy and performance.

This book identifies and describes the strategies that managers can pursue to achieve superior performance and provide their company with a competitive advantage. One of its central aims is to give you a thorough understanding of the analytical techniques and skills necessary to identify and implement strategies successfully. The first step toward achieving this objective is to describe in more detail what superior performance and competitive advantage mean and to explain the pivotal role that managers play in leading the strategy-making process.

Strategic leadership is about how to most effectively manage a company's strategy-making process to create competitive advantage. The strategy-making process is the process by which managers select and then implement a set of strategies that aim to achieve a competitive advantage. **Strategy formulation** is the task of selecting strategies, whereas **strategy implementation** is the task of putting strategies into action, which includes designing, delivering, and supporting products; improving the efficiency and effectiveness of operations; and designing a company's organization structure, control systems, and culture. Paraphrasing the well-known saying that "success is 10% inspiration and 90% perspiration," in the strategic management arena we might say that "success is 10% formulation and 90% implementation." The task of selecting strategies is relatively easy (but requires good analysis and some inspiration); the hard part is putting those strategies into effect.

By the end of this chapter, you will understand how strategic leaders can manage the strategy-making process by formulating and implementing strategies that enable a company to achieve a competitive advantage and superior performance. Moreover, you will learn how the strategy-making process can go wrong and what managers can do to make this process more effective.

Strategic Leadership, Competitive Advantage, and Superior Performance

Strategic leadership is concerned with managing the strategy-making process to increase the performance of a company, thereby increasing the value of the enterprise to its owners, its shareholders. As shown in Figure 1.2, to increase shareholder value, managers must pursue strategies that increase the profitability of the company and ensure that profits grow (for more details, see the Appendix to this chapter). To do this, a company must be able to outperform its rivals; it must have a competitive advantage.

● **Superior Performance**   Maximizing shareholder value is the ultimate goal of profit-making companies, for two reasons. First, shareholders provide a company with the risk capital that enables managers to buy the resources needed to produce and sell goods and services. **Risk capital** is capital that cannot be recovered if a company fails and goes bankrupt. In the case of Dell, for example, shareholders provided the company with capital to build its assembly plants, invest in information systems, build its order taking and customer support system, and so on. Had Dell failed, its shareholders would have lost their money; their shares would have been worthless. Thus, shareholders will not provide risk capital unless they believe that managers are committed to pursuing strategies that give them a good return on their capital investment. Second, shareholders are the legal owners of a corporation, and their shares therefore represent a claim on the profits generated by a company. Thus, managers have an obligation to invest those profits in ways that maximize shareholder value. Of course, as explained later in this book, managers must behave in a legal, ethical, and socially responsible manner while working to maximize shareholder value.

By **shareholder value**, we mean the returns that shareholders earn from purchasing shares in a company. These returns come from two sources: (a) capital appreciation in the value of a company's shares and (b) dividend payments. For example, between January 2 and December 31, 2003, the value of one share in the bank JPMorgan increased from $23.96 to $35.78, which represents a capital appreciation of $11.82. In addition, JPMorgan paid out a dividend of $1.30 a share during 2003. Thus, if an investor had bought one share of JPMorgan on January 2 and held on to it for the entire year, her return would have been $13.12 ($11.82 + $1.30), an impressive 54.8% return on her investment. One reason JPMorgan's shareholders did so well during 2003 was that investors came to believe that managers were pursuing strategies that would both increase the long-term profitability of the company and significantly grow its profits in the future.

FIGURE 1.2

Determinants of Shareholder Value

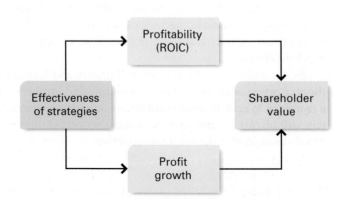

One way of measuring the **profitability** of a company is by the return that it makes on the capital invested in the enterprise.[2] The return on invested capital (ROIC) that a company earns is defined as its net profit over the capital invested in the firm (profit/capital invested). By net profit, we mean net income after tax. By capital, we mean the sum of money invested in the company: that is, stockholders' equity plus debt owed to creditors. So defined, profitability is the result of how efficiently and effectively managers use the capital at their disposal to produce goods and services that satisfy customer needs. A company that uses its capital efficiently and effectively makes a positive return on invested capital.

The **profit growth** of a company can be measured by the increase in net profit over time. A company can grow its profits if it sells products in markets that are growing rapidly, gains market share from rivals, increases the amount it sells to existing customers, expands overseas, or diversifies profitably into new lines of business. For example, between 1996 and 2005, Dell increased its net profit from $531 million to $3.825 billion. It was able to do this because the company had a low cost structure, which enabled it to take market share from rivals such as Gateway, Hewlett-Packard, and IBM. In addition, the entire PC industry was growing at a healthy pace during this period, further boosting Dell's profits.

Together, profitability and profit growth are the principal drivers of shareholder value (see the Appendix to this chapter for details). To both boost profitability and grow profits over time, managers must formulate and implement strategies that give their company a competitive advantage over rivals. Dell's strategies achieved this until 2005. As a result, investors who purchased Dell stock on January 1, 1996, at $1.11 a share, and held that position until December 30, 2005, when the stock was worth $29.95, would have made a 2,700% return on their investment! However, as noted in the Opening Case, now Dell is finding it increasingly difficult to achieve profit growth and high profitability. Indeed, Dell's net profits shrank between 2005 and 2006. As a result, the shares traded as low as $18.95 in 2006, even though the company remained very profitable. To get the share price up, managers at Dell need to pursue strategies that reignite profit growth while maintaining the company's historically high profitability.

One of the key challenges managers face is to simultaneously generate high profitability and increase the profits of the company. As Dell's managers have discovered since 2005, companies that have high profitability but whose profits are not growing will not be as highly valued by shareholders as a company that has both high profitability and rapid profit growth (see the Appendix for details). At the same time, managers need to be aware that if they grow profits but profitability declines, that too will not be as highly valued by shareholders. What shareholders want to see, and what managers must try to deliver through strategic leadership, is *profitable growth*: that is, high profitability and sustainable profit growth. This is not easy, but some of the most successful enterprises of our era have achieved it—companies such as Microsoft, Intel, and Wal-Mart, and until 2005 at least, Dell.

● Competitive Advantage and a Company's Business Model

Managers do not make strategic decisions in a competitive vacuum. Their company is competing against other companies for customers. Competition is a rough-and-tumble process in which only the most efficient and effective companies win out. It is a race without end. To maximize shareholder value, managers must formulate and implement strategies that enable their company to outperform rivals—that give it a competitive advantage. A company is said to have a **competitive advantage** over its rivals when its profitability is greater than the average profitability and profit growth of other companies competing for the same set of customers. The higher its profitability relative to rivals, the greater its competitive advantage will be. A company has a **sustained competitive advantage** when its strategies enable it to maintain above-average profitability for a number of years. As discussed in the Opening Case, Dell had a significant and sustained competitive advantage over rivals such as Gateway and Hewlett-Packard between 1996 and 2004. That competitive advantage may now be starting to dissipate.

If a company has a sustained competitive advantage, it is likely to gain market share from its rivals and thus grow its profits more rapidly than those of rivals. In turn, competitive advantage will also lead to higher profit growth than that shown by rivals.

The key to understanding competitive advantage is appreciating how the different strategies managers pursue over time can create activities that fit together to make a company unique or different from its rivals and able to consistently outperform them. A **business model** is managers' conception of how the set of strategies their company pursues should mesh together into a congruent whole, enabling the company to gain a competitive advantage and achieve superior profitability and profit growth. In essence, a business model is a kind of mental model, or gestalt, of how the various strategies and capital investments made by a company should fit together to generate above-average profitability and profit growth. A business model encompasses the totality of how a company will:

- Select its customers
- Define and differentiate its product offerings
- Create value for its customers
- Acquire and keep customers
- Produce goods or services
- Lower costs
- Deliver those goods and services to the market
- Organize activities within the company
- Configure its resources
- Achieve and sustain a high level of profitability
- Grow the business over time

The business model at Dell Computer, for example, is based on the idea that costs can be lowered by selling directly to consumers and avoiding using a distribution channel (see the Opening Case). The cost savings that are attained as a result of this model are passed to consumers in the form of lower prices, which has enabled Dell to gain market share from rivals. Over time, this business model proved superior to the established business model in the industry, which involved selling computers through retailers.

Dell outperformed close rivals, like Gateway, who adopted the same basic direct-selling business model because Dell implemented its business model more effectively. Most important, Dell did a much better job of using the Internet to coordinate its supply chain and to match orders for computers to the delivery of inventory from suppliers, so that it increased its inventory turnover and reduced its costs.

The business model that managers develop may not only lead to higher profitability and thus competitive advantage at a certain point in time, but it may also help the firm to grow its profits over time, thereby maximizing shareholder value while maintaining or even increasing profitability. Dell's business model was so efficient and effective that it enabled the company to take market share from rivals and thereby increase its profits over time.

● **Industry Differences in Performance**

It is important to recognize that in addition to its business model and associated strategies, a company's performance is also determined by the characteristics of the industry in which it competes. Different industries are characterized by different competitive conditions. In some, demand is growing rapidly, and in others it is contracting. Some might be beset by excess capacity and persistent price wars, others by excess demand and rising prices. In some, technological change might be revolutionizing competition. Others might be characterized by a lack of technological change. In some industries, high profitability among incumbent companies might induce new companies to enter the industry, and these new entrants might depress prices and profits in the industry. In other industries, new entry might be difficult, and periods of high profitability might persist for a considerable time. Thus, the different competitive conditions prevailing in different industries might lead to differences in profitability and profit growth. For example, average profitability might be higher in some industries and lower in other industries because competitive conditions vary from industry to industry.

Figure 1.3 shows the average profitability, measured by ROIC, among companies in several different industries between 2002 and 2006. The drug industry had a favorable competitive environment: demand for drugs was high and competition was generally not based on price. Just the opposite was the case in the air transport industry, which was extremely price competitive. Exactly how industries differ is discussed in detail in Chapter 2. For now, the important point to remember is that the profitability and profit growth of a company are determined by two main factors: its relative success in its industry and the overall performance of its industry relative to other industries.[3]

● **Performance in Nonprofit Enterprises**

A final point concerns the concept of superior performance in the nonprofit sector. By definition, nonprofit enterprises such as government agencies, universities, and charities are not in "business" to make profits. Nevertheless, they are expected to use their resources efficiently and operate effectively, and their managers set goals to measure their performance. The performance goal for a business school might be to

FIGURE 1.3

Return on Invested Capital in Selected Industries, 2002–2006

Source: Value Line Investment Survey.

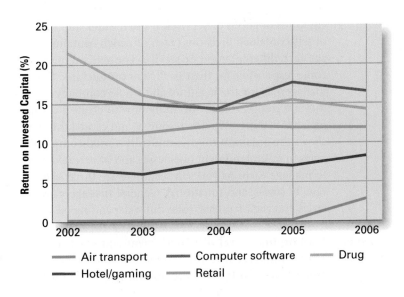

get its programs ranked among the best in the nation. The performance goal for a charity might be to prevent childhood illnesses in poor countries. The performance goal for a government agency might be to improve its services while not exceeding its budget. The managers of nonprofits need to map out strategies to attain these goals. They also need to understand that nonprofits compete with each other for scarce resources, just as businesses do. For example, charities compete for scarce donations, and their managers must plan and develop strategies that lead to high performance and demonstrate a track record of meeting performance goals. A successful strategy gives potential donors a compelling message about why they should contribute additional donations. Thus, planning and thinking strategically are as important for managers in the nonprofit sector as they are for managers in profit-seeking firms.

Strategic Managers

Managers are the linchpin in the strategy-making process. It is individual managers who must take responsibility for formulating strategies to attain a competitive advantage and for putting those strategies into effect. They must lead the strategy-making process. The strategies that made Dell Computer so successful were not chosen by some abstract entity known as the company; they were chosen by the company's founder, Michael Dell, and the managers he hired. Dell's success, like the success of any company, was based in large part on how well the company's managers performed their strategic roles. In this section, we look at the strategic roles of different managers. Later in the chapter, we discuss strategic leadership, which is how managers can effectively lead the strategy-making process.

In most companies, there are two main types of managers: **general managers**, who bear responsibility for the overall performance of the company or for one of its major self-contained subunits or divisions, and **functional managers**, who are responsible for supervising a particular function, that is, a task, activity, or operation, such as accounting, marketing, research and development (R&D), information technology, or logistics.

A company is a collection of functions or departments that work together to bring a particular good or service to the market. If a company provides several different kinds of goods or services, it often duplicates these functions and creates a series of self-contained divisions (each of which contains its own set of functions) to manage each different good or service. The general managers of these divisions then become responsible for their particular product line. The overriding concern of general managers is for the health of the whole company or division under their direction; they are responsible for deciding how to create a competitive advantage and achieve high profitability with the resources and capital they have at their disposal. Figure 1.4 shows the organization of a **multidivisional company**, that is, a company that competes in several different businesses and has created a separate self-contained division to manage each. As you can see, there are three main levels of management: corporate, business, and functional. General managers are found at the first two of these levels, but their strategic roles differ depending on their sphere of responsibility.

● **Corporate-Level Managers**   The corporate level of management consists of the chief executive officer (CEO), other senior executives, and corporate staff. These individuals occupy the apex of decision making within the organization. The CEO is the principal general manager. In

FIGURE 1.4

Levels of Strategic
Management

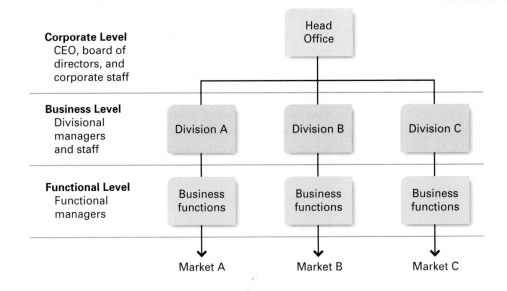

Corporate Level
CEO, board of
directors, and
corporate staff

Business Level
Divisional
managers
and staff

Functional Level
Functional
managers

consultation with other senior executives, the role of corporate-level managers is to oversee the development of strategies for the whole organization. This role includes defining the goals of the organization, determining what businesses it should be in, allocating resources among the different businesses, formulating and implementing strategies that span individual businesses, and providing leadership for the entire organization.

Consider General Electric as an example. GE is active in a wide range of businesses, including lighting equipment, major appliances, motor and transportation equipment, turbine generators, construction and engineering services, industrial electronics, medical systems, aerospace, aircraft engines, and financial services. The main strategic responsibilities of its CEO, Jeffrey Immelt, are setting overall strategic goals, allocating resources among the different business areas, deciding whether the firm should divest itself of any of its businesses, and determining whether it should acquire any new ones. In other words, it is up to Immelt to develop strategies that span individual businesses; his concern is with building and managing the corporate portfolio of businesses to maximize corporate profitability.

It is not his specific responsibility to develop strategies for competing in the individual business areas, such as financial services. The development of such strategies is the responsibility of the general managers in these different businesses, or business-level managers. However, it is Immelt's responsibility to probe the strategic thinking of business-level managers to make sure that they are pursuing robust business models and strategies that will contribute toward the maximization of GE's long-run profitability, to coach and motivate those managers, to reward them for attaining or exceeding goals, and to hold them accountable for poor performance.

Corporate-level managers also provide a link between the people who oversee the strategic development of a firm and those who own it (the shareholders). Corporate-level managers, and particularly the CEO, can be viewed as the agents of shareholders.[4] It is their responsibility to ensure that the corporate and business strategies that the company pursues are consistent with maximizing profitability and profit growth. If they are not, then ultimately the CEO is likely to be called to account by the shareholders.

● **Business-Level Managers**

A **business unit** is a self-contained division (with its own functions—for example, finance, purchasing, production, and marketing departments) that provides a product or service for a particular market. The principal general manager at the business level, or the business-level manager, is the head of the division. The strategic role of these managers is to translate the general statements of direction and intent that come from the corporate level into concrete strategies for individual businesses. Whereas corporate-level general managers are concerned with strategies that span individual businesses, business-level general managers are concerned with strategies that are specific to a particular business. At GE, a major corporate goal is to be first or second in every business in which the corporation competes. Then the general managers in each division work out for their business the details of a business model that is consistent with this objective.

● **Functional-Level Managers**

Functional-level managers are responsible for the specific business functions or operations (human resources, purchasing, product development, customer service, and so on) that constitute a company or one of its divisions. Thus, a functional manager's sphere of responsibility is generally confined to one organizational activity, whereas general managers oversee the operation of a whole company or division. Although they are not responsible for the overall performance of the organization, functional managers nevertheless have a major strategic role: to develop functional strategies in their area that help fulfill the strategic objectives set by business- and corporate-level general managers.

In GE's aerospace business, for instance, manufacturing managers are responsible for developing manufacturing strategies consistent with corporate objectives. Moreover, functional managers provide most of the information that makes it possible for business- and corporate-level general managers to formulate realistic and attainable strategies. Indeed, because they are closer to the customer than is the typical general manager, functional managers themselves may generate important ideas that subsequently become major strategies for the company. Thus, it is important for general managers to listen closely to the ideas of their functional managers. An equally great responsibility for managers at the operational level is strategy implementation: the execution of corporate- and business-level plans.

The Strategy-Making Process

We can now turn our attention to the process by which managers formulate and implement strategies. Many writers have emphasized that strategy is the outcome of a formal planning process and that top management plays the most important role in this process.[5] Although this view has some basis in reality, it is not the whole story. As we shall see later in the chapter, valuable strategies often emerge from deep within the organization without prior planning. Nevertheless, a consideration of formal, rational planning is a useful starting point for our journey into the world of strategy. Accordingly, we consider what might be described as a typical formal strategic planning model for making strategy.

● **A Model of the Strategic Planning Process**

The formal strategic planning process has five main steps:

1. Select the corporate mission and major corporate goals.

2. Analyze the organization's external competitive environment to identify opportunities and threats.

3. Analyze the organization's internal operating environment to identify the organization's strengths and weaknesses.

4. Select strategies that build on the organization's strengths and correct its weaknesses in order to take advantage of external opportunities and counter external threats. These strategies should be consistent with the mission and major goals of the organization. They should be congruent and constitute a viable business model.

5. Implement the strategies.

The task of analyzing the organization's external and internal environments and then selecting appropriate strategies constitutes strategy formulation. In contrast, as noted earlier, strategy implementation involves putting the strategies (or plan) into action. This includes taking actions consistent with the selected strategies of the company at the corporate, business, and functional levels; allocating roles and responsibilities among managers (typically through the design of organization structure); allocating resources (including capital and money); setting short-term objectives; and designing the organization's control and reward systems. These steps are illustrated in Figure 1.5 (which can also be viewed as a plan for the rest of this book).

Each step in Figure 1.5 constitutes a sequential step in the strategic planning process. At step 1, each round or cycle of the planning process begins with a statement of the corporate mission and major corporate goals. This statement is shaped by the existing business model of the company. The mission statement is followed by the foundation of strategic thinking: external analysis, internal analysis, and strategic choice. The strategy-making process ends with the design of the organizational structure and the culture and control systems necessary to implement the organization's chosen strategy. This chapter discusses how to select a corporate mission and choose major goals. Other parts of strategic planning are reserved for later chapters, as indicated in Figure 1.5.

Some organizations go through a new cycle of the strategic planning process every year. This does not necessarily mean that managers choose a new strategy each year. In many instances, the result is simply to modify and reaffirm a strategy and structure already in place. The strategic plans generated by the planning process generally look out over a period of one to five years, with the plan being updated, or rolled forward, every year. In most organizations, the results of the annual strategic planning process are used as input into the budgetary process for the coming year so that strategic planning is used to shape resource allocation within the organization.

● Mission Statement

The first component of the strategic management process is crafting the organization's mission statement, which provides the framework or context within which strategies are formulated. A mission statement has four main components: a statement of the raison d'être of a company or organization—its reason for existence—which is normally referred to as the mission; a statement of some desired future state, usually referred to as the vision; a statement of the key values that the organization is committed to; and a statement of major goals.

THE MISSION A company's **mission** describes what the company does. For example, the mission of Kodak is to provide "customers with the solutions they need to capture, store, process, output, and communicate images—anywhere, anytime."[6] In other words, Kodak exists to provide imaging solutions to consumers. In its mission statement, Ford Motor Company describes itself as a company that is "passionately committed

FIGURE 1.5

Main Components of
the Strategic Planning
Process

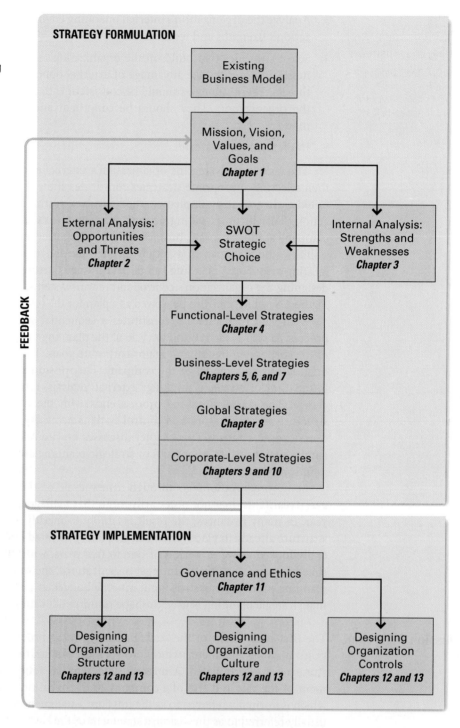

to providing personal mobility for people around the world. . . . We anticipate consumer need and deliver outstanding products and services that improve people's lives."[7] In short, Ford is a company that exists to satisfy consumer needs for personal mobility; that is its mission. Both of these missions focus on the customer needs that the company is trying to satisfy rather than on particular products (imaging and personal

FIGURE 1.6

Defining the Business

Source: D. F. Abell, *Defining the Business: The Starting Point of Strategic Planning* (Englewood Cliffs, N.J.: Prentice-Hall, 1980), p. 7.

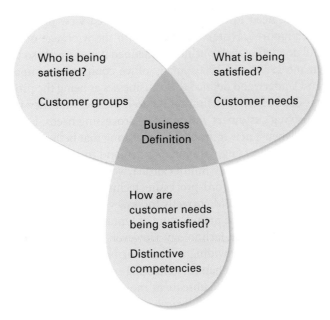

mobility rather than conventional film or cameras and automobiles). These are customer-oriented rather than product-oriented missions.

An important first step in the process of formulating a mission is to come up with a definition of the organization's business. Essentially, the definition answers these questions: "What is our business? What will it be? What should it be?"[8] The responses guide the formulation of the mission. To answer the question, "What is our business?" a company should define its business in terms of three dimensions: who is being satisfied (what customer groups), what is being satisfied (what customer needs), and how customers' needs are being satisfied (by what skills, knowledge, or distinctive competencies).[9] Figure 1.6 illustrates these dimensions.

This approach stresses the need for a *customer-oriented* rather than a *product-oriented* business definition. A product-oriented business definition focuses on the characteristics of the products sold and the markets served, not on which kinds of customer needs the products are satisfying. Such an approach obscures the company's true mission because a product is only the physical manifestation of applying a particular skill to satisfy a particular need for a particular customer group. In practice, that need may be served in many different ways, and a broad customer-oriented business definition that identifies these ways can safeguard companies from being caught unaware by major shifts in demand.

By helping anticipate demand shifts, a customer-oriented mission statement can also assist companies in capitalizing on changes in their environment. It can help answer the question, "What will our business be?" Kodak's mission statement—to provide "customers with the solutions they need to capture, store, process, output, and communicate images"—is a customer-oriented statement that focuses on customer needs rather than a particular product (or solution) for satisfying those needs, such as chemical film processing. For this reason, it is helping to drive Kodak's current investments in digital imaging technologies, which are now fast replacing its traditional business based on chemical film processing.

The need to take a customer-oriented view of a company's business has often been ignored. History is littered with the wreckage of once-great corporations that did not define their business or defined it incorrectly so that ultimately they declined. In the 1950s and 1960s, many office equipment companies such as Smith Corona and Underwood defined their businesses as being the production of typewriters. This product-oriented definition ignored the fact that they were really in the business of satisfying customers' information-processing needs. Unfortunately for those companies, when a new technology came along that better served customer needs for information processing (computers), demand for typewriters plummeted. The last great typewriter company, Smith Corona, went bankrupt in 1996, a victim of the success of computer-based word-processing technology.

In contrast, IBM correctly foresaw what its business would be. In the 1950s, IBM was a leader in the manufacture of typewriters and mechanical tabulating equipment using punch-card technology. However, unlike many of its competitors, IBM defined its business as providing a means for *information processing and storage*, rather than just supplying mechanical tabulating equipment and typewriters.[10] Given this definition, the company's subsequent moves into computers, software systems, office systems, and printers seem logical.

VISION The vision of a company lays out some desired future state; it articulates, often in bold terms, what the company would like to achieve. Nokia, the world's largest manufacturer of mobile (wireless) phones, operates with a very simple but powerful vision: "If it can go mobile, it will!" This vision implies that not only will voice telephony go mobile (it already has), but so will a host of other services based on data, such as imaging and Internet browsing. This vision has led Nokia to develop multimedia mobile handsets that not only can be used for voice communication but that also take pictures, browse the Internet, play games, and manipulate personal and corporate information.

VALUES The values of a company state how managers and employees should conduct themselves, how they should do business, and what kind of organization they should build to help a company achieve its mission. Insofar as they help drive and shape behavior within a company, values are commonly seen as the bedrock of a company's organizational culture: the set of values, norms, and standards that control how employees work to achieve an organization's mission and goals. An organization's culture is commonly seen as an important source of its competitive advantage.[11] (We discuss the issue of organization culture in depth in Chapter 12.) For example, Nucor Steel is one of the most productive and profitable steel firms in the world. Its competitive advantage is based in part on the extremely high productivity of its work force, which the company maintains is a direct result of its cultural values, which in turn determine how it treats its employees. These values are as follow:

- "Management is obligated to manage Nucor in such a way that employees will have the opportunity to earn according to their productivity."
- "Employees should be able to feel confident that if they do their jobs properly, they will have a job tomorrow."
- "Employees have the right to be treated fairly and must believe that they will be."
- "Employees must have an avenue of appeal when they believe they are being treated unfairly."[12]

At Nucor, values emphasizing pay for performance, job security, and fair treatment for employees help to create an atmosphere within the company that leads to high employee productivity. In turn, this has helped to give Nucor one of the lowest cost structures in its industry, which helps to explain the company's profitability in a very price-competitive business.

In one study of organizational values, researchers identified a set of values associated with high-performing organizations that help companies achieve superior financial performance through their impact on employee behavior.[13] These values included respect for the interests of key organizational stakeholders: individuals or groups that have an interest, claim, or stake in the company, in what it does, and in how well it performs.[14] They include stockholders, bondholders, employees, customers, the communities in which the company does business, and the general public. One study found that deep respect for the interests of customers, employees, suppliers, and shareholders was associated with high performance.[15] The study also noted that the encouragement of leadership and entrepreneurial behavior by mid- and lower-level managers and a willingness to support change efforts within the organization contributed to high performance. Companies that emphasize such values consistently throughout their organization include Hewlett-Packard, Wal-Mart, and PepsiCo. The same study identified the values of poorly performing companies—values that, as might be expected, are not articulated in company mission statements: (1) arrogance, particularly to ideas from outside the company; (2) a lack of respect for key stakeholders; and (3) a history of resisting change efforts and "punishing" mid- and lower-level managers who showed "too much leadership." General Motors was held up as an example of one such organization. According to the authors of this study, a mid- or lower-level manager who showed too much leadership and initiative there was not promoted!

MAJOR GOALS Having stated the mission, vision, and key values, strategic managers can take the next step in the formulation of a mission statement: establishing major goals. A goal is a precise and measurable desired future state that a company attempts to realize. In this context, the purpose of goals is to specify with precision what must be done if the company is to attain its mission or vision.

Well-constructed goals have four main characteristics:[16]

- They are precise and measurable. Measurable goals give managers a yardstick or standard against which they can judge their performance.

- They address crucial issues. To maintain focus, managers should select a limited number of major goals to assess the performance of the company. The goals that are selected should be crucial or important ones.

- They are challenging but realistic. They give all employees an incentive to look for ways of improving the operations of an organization. If a goal is unrealistic in the challenges it poses, employees may give up; a goal that is too easy may fail to motivate managers and other employees.[17]

- They specify a time period in which the goals should be achieved, when that is appropriate. Time constraints tell employees that success requires a goal to be attained by a given date, not after that date. Deadlines can inject a sense of urgency into goal attainment and act as a motivator. However, not all goals require time constraints.

Well-constructed goals also provide a means by which the performance of managers can be evaluated.

As noted earlier, although most companies operate with a variety of goals, the central goal of most corporations is to maximize shareholder returns, and doing this requires both high profitability and sustained profit growth. Thus, most companies operate with goals for profitability and profit growth. However, it is important that top managers do not make the mistake of overemphasizing current profitability to the detriment of long-term profitability and profit growth.[18] The overzealous pursuit of current profitability to maximize short-term ROIC can encourage such misguided managerial actions as cutting expenditures judged to be nonessential in the short run—for instance, expenditures for research and development, marketing, and new capital investments. Although cutting current expenditure increases current profitability, the resulting underinvestment, lack of innovation, and diminished marketing can jeopardize long-run profitability and profit growth. These expenditures are vital if a company is to pursue its long-term mission and sustain its competitive advantage and profitability over time. Despite these negative consequences, managers may make such decisions because the adverse effects of a short-run orientation may not materialize and become apparent to shareholders for several years, or because they are under extreme pressure to hit short-term profitability goals.[19] It is also worth noting that pressures to maximize short-term profitability may drive managers to act unethically. This apparently occurred during the late 1990s at Enron Corporation, Tyco, WorldCom, and Computer Associates, where managers systematically inflated profits by manipulating financial accounts in a manner that misrepresented the true performance of the firm to shareholders. (Chapter 11 provides a detailed discussion of the issues.)

To guard against short-run behavior, managers need to ensure that they adopt goals whose attainment will increase the long-run performance and competitiveness of their enterprise. Long-term goals are related to such issues as product development, customer satisfaction, and efficiency, and they emphasize specific objectives or targets concerning such details as employee and capital productivity, product quality, innovation, customer satisfaction and customer service. At Dell Computer, for example, the goal of replacing inventory with information is to focus management attention on what can be done to increase inventory turnover and thus reduce costs.

● External Analysis

The second component of the strategic management process is an analysis of the organization's external operating environment. The essential purpose of the external analysis is to identify strategic opportunities and threats in the organization's operating environment that will affect how it pursues its mission. Strategy in Action 1.1 describes how an analysis of opportunities and threats in the external environment led to a strategic shift at Time Inc.

Three interrelated environments should be examined when undertaking an external analysis: the industry environment in which the company operates, the country or national environment, and the wider socioeconomic or macroenvironment. Analyzing the industry environment requires an assessment of the competitive structure of the company's industry, including the competitive position of the company and its major rivals. It also requires analysis of the nature, stage, dynamics, and history of the industry. Because many markets are now global markets, analyzing the industry environment also means assessing the impact of globalization on competition within an industry. Such an analysis may reveal that a company should move some production facilities to another nation, that it should aggressively expand in emerging markets such as China, or that it should beware of new competition from emerging nations. Analyzing the macroenvironment consists of examining macroeconomic, social, government, legal, international, and technological factors that may affect the company and its industry. We look at external analysis in Chapter 2.

Strategy in Action   1.1

Strategic Analysis at Time Inc.

Time Inc., the magazine publishing division of media conglomerate Time Warner, has a venerable history. Its magazine titles include *Time, Fortune, Sports Illustrated,* and *People,* all long-time leaders in their respective categories. By the mid 2000s, however, Time Inc. recognized that it needed to change its strategy. In 2005, circulation at *Time* was off by 12%; *Fortune,* by 10%; and *Sports Illustrated,* by 17%.

An external analysis revealed what was going on. The readership of Time's magazines was aging. Increasingly, younger readers were getting what they wanted from the Web. This was both a *threat* for Time Inc., since its Web offerings were not strong, and an *opportunity,* since with the right offerings Time Inc. could capture this audience. Time also realized that advertising dollars were migrating rapidly to the Web, and if the company was going to hold onto its share, its Web offerings had to be every bit as good as its print offerings.

An internal analysis revealed why, despite multiple attempts, Time had failed to capitalize on the opportunities offered by the emergence of the Web. Although Time had tremendous *strengths,* including powerful brands and strong reporting, development of its Web offerings had been hindered by a serious *weakness*—an editorial culture that regarded Web publishing as a backwater. At *People,* for example, the online operation used to be "like a distant moon" according to managing editor Martha Nelson. Managers at Time Inc. had also been worried that Web offerings would cannibalize print offerings and help to accelerate the decline in the circulation of magazines, with dire financial consequences for the company. As a result of this culture, efforts to move publications onto the Web were underfunded or were stymied by a lack of management attention and commitment.

It was Martha Nelson at *People* who in 2003 showed the way forward for the company. Her *strategy* for overcoming the *weakness* at Time Inc., and better exploiting *opportunities* on the Web, started with merging the print and online newsrooms at *People,* removing the distinction between them. Then she relaunched the magazine's online site, made major editorial commitments to Web publishing, stated that original content should appear on the Web, and emphasized the importance of driving traffic to the site and earning advertising revenues. Over the next two years, page views at People.com increased fivefold.

Ann Moore, the CEO at Time Inc., formalized this strategy in 2005, mandating that all print offerings should follow the lead of People.com, integrating print and online newsrooms and investing significantly more resources in Web publishing. To drive this home, Time hired several well-known bloggers to write for its online publications. The goal of Moore's strategy was to neutralize the cultural *weakness* that had hindered online efforts in the past at Time Inc. and to direct resources toward Web publishing.

In 2006, Time made another strategic move designed to exploit the opportunities associated with the Web when it started a partnership with the twenty-four-hour news channel, CNN, putting all of its financial magazines onto a site that is jointly owned, CNNMoney.com. The site, which offers free access to *Fortune, Money,* and *Business 2.0,* quickly took the third spot in online financial websites behind Yahoo finance and MSN. This was followed with a redesigned website for *Sports Illustrated* that has rolled out video downloads for iPods and mobile phones.

To drive home the shift to Web-centric publishing, in late 2006, Time announced another change in strategy—it would sell off eighteen magazine titles that, while good performers, did not appear to have much traction on the Web. Ann Moore stated that going forward Time would be focusing its energy, resources, and investments on the company's largest and most profitable brands, brands that have demonstrated an ability to draw large audiences in digital form.[a]

● **Internal Analysis**   Internal analysis, the third component of the strategic planning process, focuses on reviewing the resources, capabilities, and competencies of a company. The goal is to identify the strengths and weaknesses of the company. For example, as described in Strategy in Action 1.1, an internal analysis at Time Inc. revealed that while the company had strong well-known brands such as *Fortune*, *Money*, *Sports Illustrated*, and *People* (a strength), and a strong reporting capabilities (another strength), it suffered from a lack of editorial commitment to online publishing (a weakness). We consider internal analysis in Chapter 3.

● **SWOT Analysis and the Business Model**   The next component of strategic thinking requires the generation of a series of strategic alternatives, or choices of future strategies to pursue, given the company's internal strengths and weaknesses and its external opportunities and threats. The comparison of **s**trengths, **w**eaknesses, **o**pportunities, and **t**hreats is normally referred to as a **SWOT analysis**.[20] The central purpose is to identify the strategies to exploit external opportunities, counter threats, build on and protect company strengths, and eradicate weaknesses.

At Time Inc., managers saw the move of readership to the Web as both an *opportunity* that they must exploit and a *threat* to Time's established print magazines. They recognized that Time's well-known brands and strong reporting capabilities were *strengths* that would serve it well online, but that an editorial culture that marginalized online publishing was a *weakness* that had to be fixed. The *strategies* that managers at Time Inc. came up with included merging the print and online newsrooms to remove distinctions between them; investing significant financial resources in online sites; and entering into a partnership with CNN, which already had a strong online presence.

More generally, the goal of a SWOT analysis is to create, affirm, or fine-tune a company-specific business model that will best align, fit, or match a company's resources and capabilities to the demands of the environment in which it operates. Managers compare and contrast the various alternative possible strategies against each other and then identify the set of strategies that will create and sustain a competitive advantage. These strategies can be divided into four main categories:

- *Functional-level strategies*, directed at improving the effectiveness of operations within a company, such as manufacturing, marketing, materials management, product development, and customer service. We review functional-level strategies in Chapter 4.

- *Business-level strategies*, which encompasses the business's overall competitive theme, the way it positions itself in the marketplace to gain a competitive advantage, and the different positioning strategies that can be used in different industry settings—for example, cost leadership, differentiation, focusing on a particular niche or segment of the industry, or some combination of these. We review business-level strategies in Chapters 5, 6 and 7.

- *Global strategies*, which addresses how to expand operations outside the home country to grow and prosper in a world where competitive advantage is determined at a global level. We review global strategies in Chapter 8.

- *Corporate-level strategies*, which answer the primary questions: What business or businesses should we be in to maximize the long-run profitability and profit growth of the organization, and how should we enter and increase our presence in these businesses to gain a competitive advantage? We review corporate-level strategies in Chapters 9 and 10.

The strategies identified through a SWOT analysis should be congruent with each other. Thus, functional-level strategies should be consistent with, or support, the company's business-level strategy and global strategy. Moreover, as we explain later in this book, corporate-level strategies should support business-level strategies. When taken together, the various strategies pursued by a company constitute a viable business model. In essence, a SWOT analysis is a methodology for choosing between competing business models and for fine-tuning the business model that managers choose. For example, when Microsoft entered the videogame market with its Xbox offering, it had to settle on the best business model for competing in this market. Microsoft used a SWOT type of analysis to compare alternatives and settled on a "razor and razor blades" business model in which the Xbox console is priced below cost to build sales (the "razor"), while profits are made from royalties on the sale of games for the Xbox (the "blades").

● Strategy Implementation

Having chosen a set of congruent strategies to achieve a competitive advantage and increase performance, managers must put those strategies into action: strategy has to be implemented. Strategy implementation involves taking actions at the functional, business, and corporate levels to execute a strategic plan. Implementation can include, for example, putting quality improvement programs into place, changing the way a product is designed, positioning the product differently in the marketplace, segmenting the marketing and offering different versions of the product to different consumer groups, implementing price increases or decreases, expanding through mergers and acquisitions, or downsizing the company by closing down or selling off parts of the company. These and other topics are discussed in detail in Chapters 4 through 10.

Strategy implementation also entails designing the best organization structure and the best culture and control systems to put a chosen strategy into action. In addition, senior managers need to put a governance system in place to make sure that all within the organization act in a manner that is not only consistent with maximizing profitability and profit growth but also legal and ethical. In this book, we look at the topic of governance and ethics in Chapter 11; we discuss the organization structure, culture, and controls required to implement business-level strategies in Chapter 12; and the structure, culture, and controls required to implement corporate-level strategies in Chapter 13.

● The Feedback Loop

The feedback loop in Figure 1.5 indicates that strategic planning is ongoing; it never ends. Once a strategy has been implemented, its execution must be monitored to determine the extent to which strategic goals and objectives are actually being achieved and to what degree competitive advantage is being created and sustained. This information and knowledge pass back to the corporate level through feedback loops and become the input for the next round of strategy formulation and implementation. Top managers can then decide whether to reaffirm the existing business model and the existing strategies and goals or suggest changes for the future. For example, if a strategic goal proves too optimistic, the next time, a more conservative goal is set. Or feedback may reveal that the business model is not working, so managers may seek ways to change it. In essence, this is what happened at Time Inc. (see Strategy in Action 1.1). This may also be what is now happening at Dell Computer (see the Opening Case). Dell's business model, which worked so well for so long, now seems to be faltering, and to reestablish its competitive advantage in the personal computer industry, Dell's managers may well have to make strategic changes.

Strategy as an Emergent Process

The basic planning model suggests that a company's strategies are the result of a plan, that the strategic planning process itself is rational and highly structured, and that the process is orchestrated by top management. Several scholars have criticized the formal planning model for three main reasons: the unpredictability of the real world, the role that lower-level managers can play in the strategic management process, and the fact that many successful strategies are often the result of serendipity, not rational strategizing. They have advocated an alternative view of strategy making.[21]

● **Strategy Making in an Unpredictable World**

Critics of formal planning systems argue that we live in a world in which uncertainty, complexity, and ambiguity dominate, and in which small chance events can have a large and unpredictable impact on outcomes.[22] In such circumstances, they claim, even the most carefully thought-out strategic plans are prone to being rendered useless by rapid and unforeseen change. In an unpredictable world, there is a premium on being able to respond quickly to changing circumstances and to alter the strategies of the organization accordingly. The dramatic rise of Google, for example, with its business model based revenues earned from advertising links associated with search results (the so-called pay-per-click business model), disrupted the online advertising industry in 2003–2004. Nobody foresaw this development or planned for it, but they had to respond to it, and rapidly. Companies with a strong online advertising presence, including Yahoo.com and Microsoft's MSN network, rapidly changed their strategies to adapt to the threat posed by Google. Specifically, both developed their own search engines and copied Google's pay-per-click business model. According to critics of formal systems, such a flexible approach to strategy making is not possible within the framework of a traditional strategic planning process, with its implicit assumption that an organization's strategies need to be reviewed only during the annual strategic planning exercise.

● **Autonomous Action: Strategy Making by Lower-Level Managers**

Another criticism leveled at the rational planning model of strategy is that too much importance is attached to the role of top management, particularly the CEO.[23] An alternative view now gaining wide acceptance is that individual managers deep within an organization can and often do exert a profound influence over the strategic direction of the firm.[24] Writing with Robert Burgelman of Stanford University, Andy Grove, the former CEO of Intel, noted that many important strategic decisions at Intel were initiated not by top managers but by the autonomous action of lower-level managers deep within Intel who, on their own initiative, formulated new strategies and worked to persuade top-level managers to alter the strategic priorities of the firm.[25] These strategic decisions included the decision to exit an important market (the DRAM memory chip market) and to develop a certain class of microprocessors (RISC-based microprocessors) in direct contrast to the stated strategy of Intel's top managers. Similarly, the original prototype for Microsoft's first Xbox videogame system was developed by four lower-level engineering employees on their own initiative. They then successfully lobbied top managers to dedicate resources toward commercializing their prototype. Another example of autonomous action, this one at Starbucks, is given in Strategy in Action 1.2.

Autonomous action may be particularly important in helping established companies deal with the uncertainty created by the arrival of a radical new technology that changes the dominant paradigm in an industry.[26] Top managers usually rise to

Strategy in Action   1.2

Starbucks's Music Business

Anyone who has walked into a Starbucks cannot help but notice that, in addition to various coffee beverages and food, the company also sells music CDs. Most Starbucks stores now have racks displaying about twenty CDs. Reports suggest that when Starbucks decides to carry a CD, it typically ranks among the top four retailers selling it. The interesting thing about Starbucks's entry into music retailing is that it was not the result of a formal planning process. The company's journey into music retailing started in the late 1980s when Tim Jones, then the manager of a Starbucks in Seattle's University Village, started to bring his own tapes of music compilations into the store to play. Soon Jones was getting requests for copies from customers. Jones told this to Starbucks's CEO, Howard Schultz, and suggested that Starbucks start to sell its own music. At first, Schultz was skeptical but after repeated lobbying efforts by Jones, he eventually took up the suggestion. Today, Starbucks not only sells CDs, it is also moving into music downloading with its "Hear Music" Starbucks stores, where customers can listen to music from Starbucks's 200,000-song online music library while sipping their coffee and can burn their own CDs.[b]

preeminence by successfully executing the established strategy of the firm. Therefore, they may have an emotional commitment to the status quo and are often unable to see things from a different perspective. In this sense, they are a conservative force that promotes inertia. Lower-level managers, however, are less likely to have the same commitment to the status quo and have more to gain from promoting new technologies and strategies. They may be the first ones to recognize new strategic opportunities and lobby for strategic change. As described in Strategy in Action 1.3, this seems to have been the case at discount stockbroker, Charles Schwab, which had to adjust to the arrival of the Web in the 1990s.

● **Serendipity and Strategy**

Business history is replete with examples of accidental events that help to push companies in new and profitable directions. What these examples suggest is that many successful strategies are not the result of well-thought-out plans but of serendipity, that is, of stumbling across good things unexpectedly. One such example occurred at 3M during the 1960s. At that time, 3M was producing fluorocarbons for sale as coolant liquid in air conditioning equipment. One day, a researcher working with fluorocarbons in a 3M lab spilled some of the liquid on her shoes. Later that day when she spilled coffee over her shoes, she watched with interest as the coffee formed into little beads of liquid and then ran off her shoes without leaving a stain. Reflecting on this phenomenon, she realized that a fluorocarbon-based liquid might turn out to be useful for protecting fabrics from liquid stains, and so the idea for Scotch Guard was born. Subsequently, Scotch Guard became one of 3M's most profitable products and took the company into the fabric protection business, an area it had never planned to participate in.[27]

Serendipitous discoveries and events can open all sorts of profitable avenues for a company. But some companies have missed profitable opportunities because serendipitous discoveries or events were inconsistent with their prior (planned) conception of what their strategy should be. In one of the classic examples of such myopia, a century ago, the telegraph company Western Union turned down an opportunity to purchase

Strategy in Action

A Strategic Shift at Charles Schwab

In the mid-1990s, Charles Schwab was the most successful discount stockbroker in the world. Over twenty years, it had gained share from full-service brokers like Merrill Lynch by offering deep discounts on the commissions charged for stock trades. Although Schwab had a nationwide network of branches, most customers executed their trades through a telephone system called Telebroker. Others used online proprietary software, Street Smart, which had to be purchased from Schwab. It was a business model that worked well—then along came E*Trade.

E*Trade was a discount broker started in 1994 by Bill Porter, a physicist and inventor, to take advantage of the opportunity created by the rapid emergence of the World Wide Web. E*Trade launched the first dedicated website for online trading. E*Trade had no branches, no brokers, and no telephone system for taking orders, and thus it had a very low-cost structure. Customers traded stocks over the company's website. Due to its low-cost structure, E*Trade was able to announce a flat $14.95 commission on stock trades, a figure significantly below Schwab's average commission, which at the time was $65. It was clear from the outset that E*Trade and other online brokers, such as Ameritrade, who soon followed, offered a direct threat to Schwab. Not only were their cost structures and commission rates considerably below Schwab's, but the ease, speed, and flexibility of trading stocks over the Web suddenly made Schwab's Street Smart trading software seem limited and its telephone system antiquated.

Deep within Schwab, William Pearson, a young software specialist who had worked on the development of Street Smart, immediately saw the transformational power of the Web. Pearson believed that Schwab needed to develop its own Web-based software, and quickly. Try as he might, though, Pearson could not get the attention of his supervisor. He tried a number of other executives but found support hard to come by. Eventually he approached Anne Hennegar, a former Schwab manager who now worked as a consultant to the company. Hennegar suggest that Pearson meet with Tom Seip, an executive vice president at Schwab who was known for his ability to think outside the box. Hennegar approached Seip on Pearson's behalf, and Seip responded positively, asking her to set up a meeting. Hennegar and Pearson turned up expecting to meet just Seip, but to their surprise in walked Charles Schwab; his chief operating officer, David Pottruck; and the vice presidents in charge of strategic planning and the electronic brokerage arena.

As the group watched Pearson's demo of how a Web-based system would look and work, they became increasingly excited. It was clear to those in the room that a Web-based system using real-time information, personalization, customization, and interactivity all advanced Schwab's commitment to empowering customers. By the end of the meeting, Pearson had received a green light to start work on the project. A year later, Schwab launched its own Web-based offering, eSchwab, which enabled Schwab clients to execute stock trades for a low flat-rate commission. eSchwab went on to become the core of the company's offering, enabling it to stave off competition from deep discount brokers like E*Trade.[c]

the rights to an invention made by Alexander Graham Bell. The invention was the telephone, a technology that subsequently made the telegraph obsolete.

● Intended and Emergent Strategies

Henry Mintzberg's model of strategy development provides a more encompassing view of what strategy actually is. According to this model, illustrated in Figure 1.7, a company's realized strategy is the product of whatever planned strategies are actually put into action (the company's deliberate strategies) and of any unplanned, or emergent, strategies. In Mintzberg's view, many planned strategies are not implemented because of unpredicted changes in the environment (they are unrealized). Emergent strategies are the unplanned responses to unforeseen circumstances. They arise from

FIGURE 1.7

Emergent and
Deliberate Strategies

Data Source: Adapted from
H. Mintzberg and A. McGugh,
*Administrative Science
Quarterly,* Vol. 30. No. 2,
June 1985.

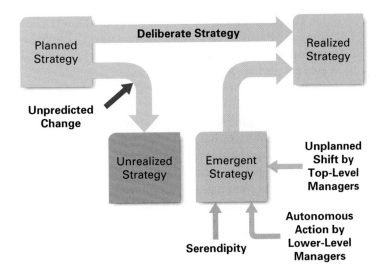

autonomous action by individual managers deep within the organization, from serendipitous discoveries or events, or from an unplanned strategic shift by top-level managers in response to changed circumstances. They are not the product of formal top-down planning mechanisms.

Mintzberg maintains that emergent strategies are often successful and may be more appropriate than intended strategies. In the classic description of this process, Richard Pascale described how this was the case for the entry of Honda Motor Co. into the U.S. motorcycle market.[28] When a number of Honda executives arrived in Los Angeles from Japan in 1959 to establish a U.S. operation, their original aim (intended strategy) was to focus on selling 250-cc and 350-cc machines to confirmed motorcycle enthusiasts rather than 50-cc Honda Cubs, which were a big hit in Japan. Their instinct told them that the Honda 50s were not suitable for the U.S. market, where everything was bigger and more luxurious than in Japan.

However, sales of the 250-cc and 350-cc bikes were sluggish, and the bikes themselves were plagued by mechanical failure. It looked as if Honda's strategy was going to fail. At the same time, the Japanese executives who were using the Honda 50s to run errands around Los Angeles were attracting a lot of attention. One day, they got a call from a Sears, Roebuck buyer who wanted to sell the 50-cc bikes to a broad market of Americans who were not necessarily motorcycle enthusiasts. The Honda executives were hesitant to sell the small bikes for fear of alienating serious bikers, who might then associate Honda with "wimpy" machines. In the end, however, they were pushed into doing so by the failure of the 250-cc and 350-cc models.

Honda had stumbled onto a previously untouched market segment that was to prove huge: the average American who had never owned a motorbike. Honda had also found an untried channel of distribution: general retailers rather than specialty motorbike stores. By 1964, nearly one out of every two motorcycles sold in the United States was a Honda.

The conventional explanation for Honda's success is that the company redefined the U.S. motorcycle industry with a brilliantly conceived intended strategy. The fact was that Honda's intended strategy was a near-disaster. The strategy that emerged did so not through planning but through unplanned action in response to unforeseen circumstances. Nevertheless, credit should be given to the Japanese management for recognizing the strength of the emergent strategy and for pursuing it with vigor.

The critical point demonstrated by the Honda example is that successful strategies can often emerge within an organization without prior planning and in response to unforeseen circumstances. As Mintzberg has noted, strategies can take root wherever people have the capacity to learn and the resources to support that capacity.

In practice, the strategies of most organizations are probably a combination of the intended (planned) and the emergent. The message for management is that it needs to recognize the process of emergence and to intervene when appropriate, killing off bad emergent strategies but nurturing potentially good ones.[29] To make such decisions, managers must be able to judge the worth of emergent strategies. They must be able to think strategically. Although emergent strategies arise from within the organization without prior planning—that is, without going through the steps illustrated in Figure 1.5 in a sequential fashion—top management still has to evaluate emergent strategies. Such evaluation involves comparing each emergent strategy with the organization's goals, external environmental opportunities and threats, and internal strengths and weaknesses. The objective is to assess whether the emergent strategy fits the company's needs and capabilities. In addition, Mintzberg stresses that an organization's capability to produce emergent strategies is a function of the kind of corporate culture that the organization's structure and control systems foster. In other words, the different components of the strategic management process are just as important from the perspective of emergent strategies as they are from the perspective of intended strategies.

Strategic Planning in Practice

Despite criticisms, research suggests that formal planning systems do help managers make better strategic decisions. A study that analyzed the results of twenty-six previously published studies came to the conclusion that, on average, strategic planning has a positive impact on company performance.[30] Another study of strategic planning in 656 firms found that formal planning methodologies and emergent strategies both form part of a good strategy formulation process, particularly in an unstable environment.[31] For strategic planning to work, it is important that top-level managers plan not just in the context of the current competitive environment but also in the context of the future competitive environment. To try to forecast what that future will look like, managers can use scenario planning techniques to plan for different possible futures. They can also involve operating managers in the planning process and seek to shape the future competitive environment by emphasizing strategic intent.

● **Scenario Planning**   One reason that strategic planning may fail over the long run is that strategic managers, in their initial enthusiasm for planning techniques, may forget that the future is inherently unpredictable. Even the best-laid plans can fall apart if unforeseen contingencies occur, and that happens all the time in the real world. The recognition that uncertainty makes it difficult to forecast the future accurately led planners at Royal Dutch Shell to pioneer the scenario approach to planning.[32] **Scenario planning** involves formulating plans that are based upon what-if scenarios about the future. In the typical scenario planning exercise, some scenarios are optimistic and some are pessimistic. Teams of managers are asked to develop specific strategies to cope with each scenario. A set of indicators is chosen to be used as signposts to track trends and identify the probability that any particular scenario is coming to pass. The idea is to get managers to understand the dynamic and complex nature of their environment, to think through problems in a strategic fashion, and to generate a range of strategic options that might be pursued under different circumstances.[33] The scenario approach to planning has spread rapidly among large companies. One survey found that over 50 percent of the *Fortune 500* companies use some form of scenario-planning methods.[34]

The oil company Royal Dutch Shell has perhaps done more than most to pioneer the concept of scenario planning, and its experience demonstrates the power of the approach.[35] Shell has been using scenario planning since the 1980s. Today, it uses two main scenarios to refine its strategic planning. The scenarios relate to future demand for oil. One, called "Dynamics as Usual," sees a gradual shift from carbon fuels such as oil to natural gas and eventually to renewable energy. The second scenario, "The Spirit of the Coming Age," looks at the possibility that a technological revolution will lead to a rapid shift to new energy sources.[36] Shell is making investments that will ensure the profitability of the company whichever scenario comes to pass, and it is carefully tracking technological and market trends for signs of which scenario is becoming more likely over time.

The great virtue of the scenario approach to planning is that it can push managers to think outside the box, to anticipate what they might have to do in different situations, and to learn that the world is a complex and unpredictable place that places a premium on flexibility rather than on inflexible plans based on assumptions about the future that may turn out to be incorrect. As a result of scenario planning, organizations might pursue one dominant strategy related to the scenario that is judged to be most likely, but they make some investments that will pay off if other scenarios come to the fore (see Figure 1.8). Thus, the current strategy of Shell is based on the assumption that the world will only gradually shift way from carbon-based fuels (its "Dynamics as Usual" scenario), but the company is also hedging its bets by investing in new energy technologies and mapping out a strategy to pursue should its second scenario come to pass.

● **Decentralized Planning**   A mistake that some companies have made in constructing their strategic planning process has been to treat planning as an exclusively top management responsibility. This ivory tower approach can result in strategic plans formulated in a vacuum by top managers who have little understanding or appreciation of current operating realities. Consequently, top managers may formulate strategies that do more harm than good.

FIGURE 1.8

Scenario Planning

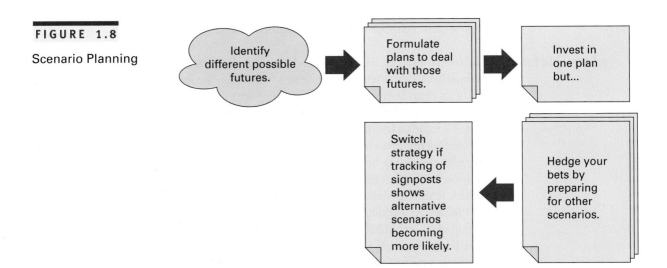

For example, when demographic data indicated that houses and families were shrinking, planners at GE's appliance group concluded that smaller appliances were the wave of the future. Because they had little contact with home builders and retailers, they did not realize that kitchens and bathrooms were the two rooms that were not shrinking. Nor did they appreciate that working women wanted big refrigerators to cut down on trips to the supermarket. GE ended up wasting a lot of time designing small appliances with limited demand.

The ivory tower concept of planning can also lead to tensions between corporate-, business-, and functional-level managers. The experience of GE's appliance group is again illuminating. Many of the corporate managers in the planning group were recruited from consulting firms or top-flight business schools. Many of the functional managers took this pattern of recruitment to mean that corporate managers did not think they were smart enough to think through strategic problems for themselves. They felt shut out of the decision-making process, which they believed to be unfairly constituted. Out of this perceived lack of procedural justice grew an us-versus-them mindset that quickly escalated into hostility. As a result, even when the planners were right, operating managers would not listen to them. For example, the planners correctly recognized the importance of the globalization of the appliance market and the emerging Japanese threat. However, operating managers, who then saw Sears, Roebuck as the competition, paid them little heed. Finally, ivory tower planning ignores the important strategic role of autonomous action by lower-level managers and serendipity.

Correcting the ivory tower approach to planning requires recognizing that successful strategic planning encompasses managers at all levels of the corporation. Much of the best planning can and should be done by business and functional managers who are closest to the facts; in other words, planning should be decentralized. The role of corporate-level planners should be that of facilitators who help business and functional managers do the planning by setting the broad strategic goals of the organization and providing the resources required to identify the strategies that might be required to attain those goals.

It is not enough to involve lower-level managers in the strategic planning process, however; they also need to perceive that the decision-making process is fair, a concept that Chan Kim and Renée Mauborgne refer to as procedural justice.[37] If people perceive the decision-making process to be unjust, they are less likely to be committed to any resulting decisions and to cooperate voluntarily in activities designed to implement those decisions. Consequently, the strategy chosen might fail for lack of support among those who must implement it at the operating level.

● Strategic Intent

The formal strategic planning model has been characterized as the fit model of strategy making because it attempts to achieve a fit between the internal resources and capabilities of an organization and the external opportunities and threats in the industry environment. Gary Hamel and C. K. Prahalad have criticized the fit model because it can lead to a mindset in which management focuses too much on the degree of fit between the existing resources of a company and current environmental opportunities, and not enough on building new resources and capabilities to create and exploit future opportunities.[38] Strategies formulated with only the present in mind, argue Prahalad and Hamel, tend to be more concerned with today's problems than with tomorrow's opportunities. As a result, companies that rely exclusively on the fit approach to strategy formulation are unlikely to be able to build and maintain a competitive advantage. This is particularly true in a dynamic competitive environment, where new competitors are continually arising and new ways of doing business are constantly being invented.

As Prahalad and Hamel note, again and again, companies using the fit approach have been surprised by the ascent of competitors that initially seemed to lack the resources and capabilities needed to make them a real threat. This happened to Xerox, which ignored the rise of Canon and Ricoh in the photocopier market until they had become serious global competitors; to General Motors, which initially overlooked the threat posed by Toyota and Honda in the 1970s; and to Caterpillar, which ignored the danger Komatsu posed to its heavy earthmoving business until it was almost too late to respond.

The secret of the success of companies like Toyota, Canon, and Komatsu, according to Prahalad and Hamel, is that they all had bold ambitions that outstripped their existing resources and capabilities. All wanted to achieve global leadership, and they set out to build the resources and capabilities that would enable them to attain this goal. Consequently, top management created an obsession with winning at all levels of the organization that they sustained over a ten- to twenty-year quest for global leadership. Prahalad and Hamel refer to this type of obsession as **strategic intent**. They stress that strategic intent is more than simply unfettered ambition. It encompasses an active management process that includes "focusing the organization's attention on the essence of winning; motivating people by communicating the value of the target; leaving room for individual and team contributions; sustaining enthusiasm by providing new operational definitions as circumstances change; and using intent consistently to guide resource allocations."[39]

Thus, underlying the concept of strategic intent is the notion that strategic planning should be based on setting an ambitious vision and ambitious goals that stretch a company and then finding ways to build the resources and capabilities necessary to attain that vision and those goals. As Prahalad and Hamel note, in practice, the two approaches to strategy formulation are not mutually exclusive. All the components of the strategic planning process that we discussed earlier (see Figure 1.5) are important.

In addition, say Prahalad and Hamel, the strategic management process should begin with a challenging vision, such as attaining global leadership, that stretches the organization. Throughout the subsequent process, the emphasis should be on finding ways (strategies) to develop the resources and capabilities necessary to achieve these goals rather than on exploiting existing strengths to take advantage of existing opportunities. The difference between strategic fit and strategic intent, therefore, may just be one of emphasis. Strategic intent is more internally focused and is concerned with building new resources and capabilities. Strategic fit focuses more on matching existing resources and capabilities to the external environment.

Strategic Decision Making

Even the best-designed strategic planning systems will fail to produce the desired results if managers do not use the information at their disposal effectively. Consequently, it is important that strategic managers learn to make better use of the information they have and understand why they sometimes make poor decisions. One important way in which managers can make better use of their knowledge and information is to understand how common cognitive biases can result in good managers making bad decisions.[40]

● Cognitive Biases and Strategic Decision Making

The rationality of human decisionmakers is bounded by our own cognitive capabilities.[41] We are not supercomputers, and it is difficult for us to absorb and process large amounts of information effectively. As a result, when making decisions, we tend to fall back on certain rules of thumb, or heuristics, that help us to make sense out of a complex and uncertain world. However, sometimes these rules lead to severe and systematic errors in the decision-making process.[42] Systematic errors are those that appear time and time again. They seem to arise from a series of **cognitive biases** in the way that human decisionmakers process information and reach decisions. Because of cognitive biases, many managers end up making poor strategic decisions.

A number of biases have been verified repeatedly in laboratory settings, so we can be reasonably sure that they exist and that we are all prone to them.[43] The **prior hypothesis bias** refers to the fact that decisionmakers who have strong prior beliefs about the relationship between two variables tend to make decisions on the basis of these beliefs, even when presented with evidence that their beliefs are wrong. Moreover, they tend to seek and use information that is consistent with their prior beliefs while ignoring information that contradicts these beliefs. To put this bias in a strategic context, it suggests that a CEO who has a strong prior belief that a certain strategy makes sense might continue to pursue that strategy, despite evidence that it is inappropriate or failing.

Another well-known cognitive bias, **escalating commitment**, occurs when decisionmakers, having already committed significant resources to a project, commit even more resources even if they receive feedback that the project is failing.[44] This may be an irrational response; a more logical response would be to abandon the project and move on (that is, to cut your losses and run), rather than escalate commitment. Feelings of personal responsibility for a project apparently induce decisionmakers to stick with a project despite evidence that it is failing.

A third bias, **reasoning by analogy**, involves the use of simple analogies to make sense out of complex problems. The problem with this heuristic is that the analogy may not be valid. A fourth bias, **representativeness**, is rooted in the tendency to generalize from a small sample or even a single vivid anecdote. This bias violates the statistical law of large numbers, which says that it is inappropriate to generalize from a small sample, let alone from a single case. In many respects, the dot-com boom of the late 1990s was based on reasoning by analogy and representativeness. Prospective entrepreneurs saw some of the early dot-com companies such Amazon and Yahoo! achieve rapid success, at least judged by some metrics. Reasoning by analogy from a very small sample, they assumed that any dot-com could achieve similar success. Many investors reached similar conclusions. The result was a massive wave of start-ups that jumped into the Internet space in an attempt to capitalize on the perceived opportunities. That the vast majority of these companies subsequently went bankrupt is testament to the fact that the analogy was wrong and that the success of the small sample of early entrants was no guarantee that all dot-coms would succeed.

A fifth cognitive bias is referred to as **the illusion of control**: the tendency to overestimate one's ability to control events. General or top managers seem to be particularly prone to this bias: having risen to the top of an organization, they tend to be overconfident about their ability to succeed. According to Richard Roll, such overconfidence leads to what he has termed the hubris hypothesis of takeovers.[45] Roll argues that top managers are typically overconfident about their ability to create value by acquiring another company. Hence, they end up making poor acquisition decisions, often paying far too much for the companies they acquire. Subsequently, servicing the debt taken on to finance such an acquisition makes it all but impossible to make money from the acquisition.

The **availability error** is yet another common bias. The availability error arises from our predisposition to estimate the probability of an outcome based on how easy the outcome is to imagine. For example, more people seem to fear a plane crash than a car accident, and yet statistically one is far more likely to be killed in a car on the way to the airport than in a plane crash. They overweigh the probability of a plane crash because the outcome is easier to imagine, and because plane crashes are more vivid events than car crashes, which affect only small numbers of people at a time. As a result of the availability error, managers might allocate resources to a project whose outcome is easier to imagine rather than to one that might have the highest return.

Groupthink and Strategic Decisions

Because most strategic decisions are made by groups, the group context within which decisions are made is clearly an important variable in determining whether cognitive biases will operate to adversely affect the strategic decision-making process. The psychologist Irvin Janis has argued that many groups are characterized by a process known as groupthink and, as a result, make poor strategic decisions.[46] Groupthink occurs when a group of decisionmakers embarks on a course of action without questioning underlying assumptions. Typically, a group coalesces around a person or policy. It ignores or filters out information that can be used to question the policy and develops after-the-fact rationalizations for its decision. Commitment to the mission or goals becomes based on an emotional rather than an objective assessment of the "correct" course of action. The consequences can be poor decisions.

The phenomenon of groupthink may explain, at least in part, why companies often make poor strategic decisions in spite of sophisticated strategic management. Janis traced many historical fiascoes to defective policymaking by government leaders who received social support from their in-group of advisers. For example, he suggested that President John F. Kennedy's inner circle suffered from groupthink when the members of this group supported the decision to launch the Bay of Pigs invasion of Cuba in 1961, even though available information showed that it would be an unsuccessful venture and would damage U.S. relations with other countries. Janis has observed that groupthink-dominated groups are characterized by strong pressures toward uniformity, which make their members avoid raising controversial issues, questioning weak arguments, or calling a halt to soft-headed thinking. As discussed in Strategy in Action 1.4, the Senate Intelligence Committee believed that groupthink biased CIA and other reports on Iraq's weapons of mass destruction that the Bush administration subsequently used to justify the 2003 invasion of that nation.

Techniques for Improving Decision Making

The existence of cognitive biases and groupthink raises the issue of how to bring critical information to bear on the decision-making mechanism so that a company's strategic decisions are realistic and based on thorough evaluation. Two techniques known to enhance strategic thinking and counteract groupthink and cognitive biases are devil's advocacy and dialectic inquiry.[47]

Devil's advocacy requires the generation of both a plan and a critical analysis of the plan. One member of the decision-making group acts as the devil's advocate, bringing out all the reasons that might make the proposal unacceptable. In this way, decisionmakers can become aware of the possible perils of recommended courses of action.

Dialectic inquiry is more complex because it requires the generation of a plan (a thesis) and a counterplan (an antithesis) that reflect plausible but conflicting courses of action.[48] Strategic managers listen to a debate between advocates of the plan and counterplan and then decide which plan will lead to the higher performance. The purpose of the debate is to reveal the problems with definitions, recommended courses of action, and assumptions of both plans. As a result of this exercise, strategic managers are able to form a new and more encompassing conceptualization of the problem,

Strategy in Action

1.4

Was Intelligence on Iraq Biased by Groupthink?

In October 2002, intelligence agencies in the United States issued a national intelligence estimate on Iraq's efforts to procure and build weapons of mass destruction (WMDs). The report concluded that there was good evidence that Iraq was actively pursuing a nuclear weapons program and, furthermore, had tried to procure uranium for its bomb-making efforts from the African nation of Niger. In addition, the report claimed that Iraq was stockpiling chemical weapons, including mustard, saran, and nerve gas, and was actively pursuing a research program to produce biological weapons, including anthrax and smallpox viruses. The report was used by the Bush administration to help justify the 2003 invasion of Iraq, which culminated in the removal of Saddam Hussein's regime. The report also helped convince the U.S. Senate that Iraq was violating United Nations conditions imposed after the first Gulf War in 1991. On the basis of this intelligence, seventy-five senators voted to authorize the 2003 war.

By late 2003, however, it was becoming increasingly apparent that if there were WMDs in Iraq, they were very few in number and extremely well hidden. Had the prewar intelligence been wrong? In mid-2004, the Senate Intelligence Committee published a report evaluating the information contained in the October 2002 national intelligence estimate. The findings of the Senate report were endorsed by all seventeen members of the committee, nine Republicans and eight Democrats. In total, they constituted a damning indictment of the prewar intelligence provided by the CIA and others to the Bush administration and Congress.

The Senate report concluded that a groupthink dynamic inside American intelligence agencies generated a "collective presumption that Iraq had an active and growing weapons program." This internal bias, according to the senators, prompted analysts, collectors, and managers in the CIA and other agencies to "interpret ambiguous evidence as being conclusively indicative of a WMD program as well as ignore or minimize evidence that Iraq did not have active or expanding weapons of mass destruction programs." As a consequence, most of the key judgments in the October 2002 national intelligence estimate were "either overstated, or were not supported by the underlying intelligence reporting."

One of the most critical parts of the Senate report dealt with the prewar assessment of Iraq's nuclear weapons program. The report stated that the 2002 national intelligence estimate represented a sharp break from previous assessments, which had concluded that Iraq had not reconstituted its nuclear weapons program. The Senate report stated that the CIA made a significant shift in its assessment shortly after Vice President Dick Cheney began stating publicly that Iraq had actively reconstituted its nuclear weapons program. The implication was that the CIA gave the administration the information it thought it wanted rather than accurate information. Moreover, the Senate report claimed that the CIA's leading advocate of the Iraqi nuclear weapons threat withheld evidence from analysts who disagreed with him, misstated the analysis and information produced by others, and distributed misleading information both inside and outside the agency. The committee also concluded that the CIA overstated what it knew about Iraq's attempts to procure uranium from Niger and that it delayed for months examining documents pertaining to those attempts that would later prove to be forgeries.

On the topic of biological weapons, the Senate report concluded that none of the claims about Iraq's biological weapons or capabilities was supported by intelligence and that claims that Iraq had restarted its chemical weapons program were the results of "analytical judgments" and not based on hard evidence. The intelligence on biological weapons came from a single Iraqi defector code-named Curve Ball who was apparently an alcoholic and, in the opinion of the one person who had interviewed him, a Pentagon analyst, "utterly useless as a source." When the same analyst saw information provided by Curve Ball included in a speech that Colin Powell made to the United Nations to justify war with Iraq, he contacted the CIA to express his concerns. A CIA official quickly responded in an email: "Let's keep in mind the fact that this war's going to happen regardless of what Curve Ball said or didn't say. The powers that be probably aren't terribly interested in whether Curve Ball knows what he is talking about."

In sum, the Senate report painted a picture of intelligence institutions that selectively interpreted information to support what they thought administration policy was, while ignoring or dismissing contradictory information—sure signs of groupthink. At the same time, the report concluded that there was no evidence of undue political pressure by policymakers in the administration or Congress. Instead, the committee blamed intelligence leaders "who did not encourage analysts to challenge their assumptions, fully consider alternative arguments, accurately characterize the intelligence reporting, or counsel analysts who lost their objectivity." Be this as it may, an objective observer might also wonder why neither the Senate nor the administration asked hard questions about the quality and source of the intelligence information in the run-up to the war.[d]

which then becomes the final plan (a synthesis). Dialectic inquiry can promote strategic thinking.

Another technique for countering cognitive biases is the outside view, which has been championed by Nobel Prize winner Daniel Kahneman and his associates.[49] The **outside view** requires planners to identify a reference class of analogous past strategic initiatives, determine whether those initiatives succeeded or failed, and evaluate the project at hand against those prior initiatives. According to Kahneman, this technique is particularly useful for countering biases such as the illusion of control (hubris), reasoning by analogy, and representativeness. For example, when considering a potential acquisition, planners should look at the track record of acquisitions made by other enterprises (the reference class), determine if they succeeded or failed, and objectively evaluate the potential acquisition against that reference class. Kahneman argues that such a reality check against a large sample of prior events tends to constrain the inherent optimism of planners and produce more realistic assessments and plans.

Strategic Leadership

One of the key strategic roles of both general and functional managers is to use all their knowledge, energy, and enthusiasm to provide strategic leadership for their subordinates and develop a high-performing organization. Several authors have identified a few key characteristics of good strategic leaders that do lead to high performance: (1) vision, eloquence, and consistency; (2) articulation of a business model; (3) commitment; (4) being well informed; (5) willingness to delegate and empower; (6) astute use of power; and (7) emotional intelligence.[50]

● **Vision, Eloquence, and Consistency**

One of the key tasks of leadership is to give an organization a sense of direction. Strong leaders seem to have a clear and compelling vision of where the organization should go, are eloquent enough to communicate this vision to others within the organization in terms that energize people, and consistently articulate their vision until it becomes part of the organization's culture.[51]

In the political arena, John F. Kennedy, Winston Churchill, Martin Luther King, Jr., and Margaret Thatcher have all been held up as examples of visionary leaders. Think of the impact of Kennedy's sentence, "Ask not what your country can do for you, ask what you can do for your country," of King's "I have a dream" speech, and of Churchill's "we will never surrender." Kennedy and Thatcher were able to use their political office to push for governmental actions that were consistent with their vision.

Churchill's speech galvanized a nation to defend itself against an aggressor, and King was able to pressure the government from outside to make changes in society.

Examples of strong business leaders include Microsoft's Bill Gates; Jack Welch, the former CEO of General Electric; and Sam Walton, Wal-Mart's founder. For years, Bill Gates's vision of a world in which there would be a Windows-based personal computer on every desk was a driving force at Microsoft. More recently, the vision has evolved into one of a world in which Windows-based software can be found on any computing device, from PCs and servers to videogame consoles (Xbox), cell phones, and hand-held computers. At GE, Jack Welch was responsible for articulating the simple but powerful vision that GE should be first or second in every business in which it competed, or it should exit from that business. Similarly, it was Wal-Mart founder Sam Walton who established and articulated the vision that has been central to Wal-Mart's success: passing on cost savings from suppliers and operating efficiencies to customers in the form of everyday low prices.

Articulation of the Business Model

Another key characteristic of good strategic leaders is their ability to identify and articulate the business model the company will use to attain its vision. A business model is managers' conception of how the various strategies that the company pursues fit together into a congruent whole. At Dell Computer, for example, it was Michael Dell who identified and articulated the basic business model of the company: the direct sales business model. The various strategies that Dell has pursued over the years have refined this basic model, creating one that is very robust in terms of its efficiency and effectiveness. Although individual strategies can take root in many different places in an organization, and although their identification is not the exclusive preserve of top management, only strategic leaders have the perspective required to make sure that the various strategies fit together into a congruent whole and form a valid and compelling business model. If strategic leaders lack a clear conception of what the business model of the company is or should be, it is likely that the strategies the firm pursues will not fit together, and the result will be lack of focus and poor performance.

Commitment

Strong leaders demonstrate their commitment to their vision and business model by actions and words, and they often lead by example. Consider Nucor's former CEO, Ken Iverson. Nucor is a very efficient steel maker with perhaps the lowest cost structure in the steel industry. It has turned in thirty years of profitable performance in an industry where most other companies have lost money because of a relentless focus on cost minimization. In his tenure as CEO, Iverson set the example: he answered his own phone, employed only one secretary, drove an old car, flew coach class, and was proud of the fact that his base salary was the lowest of the *Fortune 500* CEOs (Iverson made most of his money from performance-based pay bonuses). This commitment was a powerful signal to employees that Iverson was serious about doing everything possible to minimize costs. It earned him the respect of Nucor employees and made them more willing to work hard. Although Iverson has retired, his legacy lives on in the cost-conscious organization culture that has been built at Nucor, and like all other great leaders, his impact will last beyond his tenure.

Being Well Informed

Effective strategic leaders develop a network of formal and informal sources who keep them well informed about what is going on within their company. At Starbucks for example, the first thing that CEO Jim Donald does every morning is call five to ten stores to talk to the managers and other employees there and get a sense for how their stores are performing. Donald also stops at a local Starbucks every morning on the way to work to buy his morning coffee. This has allowed him to get to know individual employees there very well. Donald finds these informal contacts to be a very useful source of information about how the company is performing.[52]

Similarly, Herb Kelleher at Southwest Airlines was able to find out much about the health of his company by dropping in unannounced on aircraft maintenance facilities and helping workers perform their tasks. Herb Kelleher would also often help airline attendants on Southwest flights, distributing refreshments and talking to customers. One frequent flyer on Southwest Airlines reported sitting next to Kelleher three times in ten years. Each time Kelleher asked him and others sitting nearby how Southwest Airlines was doing in a number of areas, looking for trends and spotting inconsistencies.[53]

Using informal and unconventional ways to gather information is wise because formal channels can be captured by special interests within the organization or by gatekeepers, managers who may misrepresent the true state of affairs to the leader. People like Donald and Kelleher who constantly interact with employees at all levels are better able to build informal information networks than leaders who closet themselves and never interact with lower-level employees.

● Willingness to Delegate and Empower

High-performance leaders are skilled at delegation. They recognize that unless they learn how to delegate effectively, they can quickly become overloaded with responsibilities. They also recognize that empowering subordinates to make decisions is a good motivation tool and often results in decisions being made by those who must implement them. At the same time, astute leaders recognize that they need to maintain control over certain key decisions. Thus, although they will delegate many important decisions to lower-level employees, they will not delegate those that they judge to be of critical importance to the future success of the organization, such as articulating the company's vision and business model.

● The Astute Use of Power

In a now classic article on leadership, Edward Wrapp noted that effective leaders tend to be very astute in their use of power.[54] He argued that strategic leaders must often play the power game with skill and attempt to build consensus for their ideas rather than use their authority to force ideas through; they must act as members of a coalition or its democratic leaders rather than as dictators. Jeffery Pfeffer has articulated a similar vision of the politically astute manager who gets things done in organizations through the intelligent use of power.[55] In Pfeffer's view, power comes from control over resources that are important to the organization: budgets, capital, positions, information, and knowledge. Politically astute managers use these resources to acquire another critical resource: critically placed allies who can help them attain their strategic objectives. Pfeffer stresses that one does not need to be a CEO to assemble power in an organization. Sometimes junior functional managers can build a surprisingly effective power base and use it to influence organizational outcomes.

● Emotional Intelligence

Emotional intelligence is a term that Daniel Goldman coined to describe a bundle of psychological attributes that many strong and effective leaders exhibit:[56]

- Self-awareness—the ability to understand one's own moods, emotions, and drives, as well as their effect on others.

- Self-regulation—the ability to control or redirect disruptive impulses or moods, that is, to think before acting.

- Motivation—a passion for work that goes beyond money or status and a propensity to pursue goals with energy and persistence.

- Empathy—the ability to understand the feelings and viewpoints of subordinates and to take those into account when making decisions.

- Social skills—friendliness with a purpose.

According to Goldman, leaders who possess these attributes—who exhibit a high degree of emotional intelligence—tend to be more effective than those who lack these attributes. Their self-awareness and self-regulation help to elicit the trust and confidence of subordinates. In Goldman's view, people respect leaders who, because they are self-aware, recognize their own limitations and, because they are self-regulating, consider decisions carefully. Goldman also argues that self-aware and self-regulating individuals tend to be more self-confident and therefore better able to cope with ambiguity and more open to change. A strong motivation exhibited in a passion for work can also be infectious, helping to persuade others to join together in pursuit of a common goal or organizational mission. Finally, strong empathy and social skills can help leaders earn the loyalty of subordinates. Empathetic and socially adept individuals tend to be skilled at managing disputes between managers, better able to find common ground and purpose among diverse constituencies, and better able to move people in a desired direction compared to leaders who lack these skills. In short, Goldman argues that the psychological makeup of a leader matters.

Summary of Chapter

1. A strategy is a set of related actions that managers take to increase their company's performance goals.

2. The major goal of companies is to maximize the returns that shareholders get from holding shares in the company. To maximize shareholder value, managers must pursue strategies that result in high and sustained profitability and also in profit growth.

3. The profitability of a company can be measured by the return that it makes on the capital invested in the enterprise. The profit growth of a company can be measured by the growth in earnings per share. Profitability and profit growth are determined by the strategies managers adopt.

4. A company has a competitive advantage over its rivals when it is more profitable than the average for all firms in its industry. It has a sustained competitive advantage when it is able to maintain above-average profitability over a number of years. In general, a company with a competitive advantage will grow its profits more rapidly than its rivals will.

5. General managers are responsible for the overall performance of the organization or for one of its major self-contained divisions. Their overriding strategic concern is for the health of the total organization under their direction.

6. Functional managers are responsible for a particular business function or operation. Although they lack general management responsibilities, they play a very important strategic role.

7. Formal strategic planning models stress that an organization's strategy is the outcome of a rational planning process.

8. The major components of the strategic management process are defining the mission, vision, and major goals of the organization; analyzing the external and internal environments of the organization; choosing a business model and strategies that align an organization's strengths and weaknesses with external environmental opportunities and threats; and adopting organizational structures and control systems to implement the organization's chosen strategies.

9. Strategy can emerge from deep within an organization in the absence of formal plans as lower-level managers respond to unpredicted situations.

10. Strategic planning often fails because executives do not plan for uncertainty and because ivory tower planners lose touch with operating realities.

11. The fit approach to strategic planning has been criticized for focusing too much on the degree of fit between existing resources and current opportunities,

and not enough on building new resources and capabilities to create and exploit future opportunities.

12. Strategic intent refers to an obsession with achieving an objective that stretches the company and requires it to build new resources and capabilities.

13. In spite of systematic planning, companies may adopt poor strategies if their decision-making processes are vulnerable to groupthink and if individual cognitive biases are allowed to intrude into the decision-making process.

14. Devil's advocacy, dialectic inquiry, and the outside view are techniques for enhancing the effectiveness of strategic decision making.

15. Good leaders of the strategy-making process have a number of key attributes: vision, eloquence, and consistency; ability to craft a business model; commitment; being well informed; a willingness to delegate and empower; political astuteness; and emotional intelligence.

Discussion Questions

1. What do we mean by strategy? How is a business model different from a strategy?

2. What do you think are the sources of sustained superior profitability?

3. Between 1997 and 2004, Microsoft's ROIC fell from 32% to 17.5%. Over the same period, Microsoft's profits grew from $3.45 billion to $11.33 billion. How can a company have declining profitability (as measured by ROIC) but growing profits? What do you think explains this situation at Microsoft? For 2004, analysts predicted that Microsoft's ROIC would jump to 35%. Why do you think this was the case? Was it due to any change in the company's strategy?

4. What are the strengths of formal strategic planning? What are its weaknesses?

5. Discuss the accuracy of the following statement: Formal strategic planning systems are irrelevant for firms competing in high-technology industries where the pace of change is so rapid that plans are routinely made obsolete by unforeseen events.

6. Pick the current or a past president of the United States and evaluate his performance against the leadership characteristics discussed in the text. On the basis of this comparison, do you think that the president was/is a good strategic leader? Why?

Practicing Strategic Management

SMALL-GROUP EXERCISE
Designing a Planning System

Break up into groups of three to five each and discuss the following scenario. Appoint one group member as a spokesperson who will communicate the group's findings to the class when called on to do so by the instructor.

You are a group of senior managers working for a fast-growing computer software company. Your product allows users to play interactive role-playing games over the Internet. In the past three years, your company has gone from being a start-up enterprise with ten employees and no revenues to a company with 250 employees and revenues of $60 million. It has been growing so rapidly that you have not had time to create a strategic plan, but now your board of directors is telling you that they want to see a plan, and they want it to drive decision making and resource allocation at the company. They want you

to design a planning process that will have the following attributes:

1. It will be democratic, involving as many key employees as possible in the process.

2. It will help to build a sense of shared vision within the company about how to continue to grow rapidly.

3. It will lead to the generation of three to five key strategies for the company.

4. It will drive the formulation of detailed action plans, and these plans will be subsequently linked to the company's annual operating budget.

Design a planning process to present to your board of directors. Think carefully about who should be included in this process. Be sure to outline the strengths and weaknesses of the approach you choose, and be prepared to justify why your approach might be superior to alternative approaches.

ARTICLE FILE 1

At the end of every chapter in this book is an article file task. The task requires you to search newspapers or magazines in the library for an example of a real company that satisfies the task question or issue.

Your first article file task is to find an example of a company that has recently changed its strategy. Identify whether this change was the outcome of a formal planning process or whether it was an emergent response to unforeseen events occurring in the company's environment.

STRATEGIC MANAGEMENT PROJECT
Module 1

To give you practical insight into the strategic management process, we provide a series of strategic modules; one is at the end of every chapter in this book. Each module asks you to collect and analyze information relating to the material discussed in that chapter. By completing these strategic modules, you will gain a clearer idea of the overall strategic management process.

The first step in this project is to pick a company to study. We recommend that you focus on the same company throughout the book. Remember also that we will be asking you for information about the corporate and international strategy of your company as well as its structure. We strongly recommend that you pick a company for which such information is likely to be available.

There are two approaches that can be used to select a company to study, and your instructor will tell you which one to follow. The first approach is to pick a well-known company that has a lot of information written about it. For example, large publicly held companies such as IBM, Microsoft, and Southwest Airlines are routinely covered in the business and financial press. By going to the library at your university, you should be able to track down a great deal of information on such companies. Many libraries now have comprehensive web-based electronic data search facilities such as *ABI/Inform*, the *Wall Street Journal Index*, the *F&S Index*, and the *Nexis-Lexis* databases. These enable you to identify any article that has been written in the business press on the company of your choice within the past few years. A number of nonelectronic data sources are also available and useful. For example, *F&S Predicasts* publishes an annual list of articles relating to major companies that appeared in the national and international business press. *S&P Industry Surveys* is also a great source for basic industry data, and *Value Line Ratings and Reports* contain good summaries of a firm's financial position and future prospects. Collect full financial information on the company that you pick. This information can be accessed from web-based electronic databases such as the *Edgar* database, which archives all forms that publicly quoted companies have to file with the Securities and Exchange Commission (SEC); for example, 10-K filings can be accessed from the SEC's *Edgar* database. Most SEC forms for public companies can now be accessed from Internet-based financial sites, such as Yahoo!'s finance site (www.finance.yahoo.com/).

A second approach is to pick a smaller company in your city or town to study. Although small companies are not routinely covered in the national business press, they may be covered in the local press. More importantly, this approach can work well if the management of the company will agree to talk to you at length about the strategy and structure of the company. If you happen to know somebody in such a company or if you have worked there at some point, this approach can be very worthwhile. However, we do not recommend this approach unless you can get a substantial amount of guaranteed access to the company of your choice. If in doubt, ask your instructor before making a decision. The key issue is to make sure that you have access to enough interesting information to complete a detailed and comprehensive analysis.

Your assignment for Module 1 is to choose a company to study and to obtain enough information about it to carry out the following instructions and answer the questions:

1. Give a short account of the history of the company, and trace the evolution of its strategy. Try to determine whether the strategic evolution of your company is the product of intended strategies, emergent strategies, or some combination of the two.

2. Identify the mission and major goals of the company.

3. Do a preliminary analysis of the internal strengths and weaknesses of the company and the opportunities and threats that it faces in its environment. On the basis of this analysis, identify the strategies that you think the company should pursue. (You will need to perform a much more detailed analysis later in the book.)

4. Who is the CEO of the company? Evaluate the CEO's leadership capabilities.

ETHICS EXERCISE

Sarah has recently been hired as an assistant manager by Smith & Sons, a midsize retail company located in her small town. Previously, Sarah worked for a smaller retail company that always seemed to be trailing along in Smith & Sons' wake, struggling to make ends meet. Both companies sell commonly used items such as greeting cards, stationery, party decorations, and more. Hoping to open her own retail store someday, Sarah was intrigued by the idea of working for a company that appeared to hold competitive advantage in the area.

John, Smith & Sons' manager and Sarah's superior, put Sarah out on the floor immediately. There she began to meet Smith & Sons' employees—the frontline who was expected to provide customer satisfaction and product information. During her second week on the job, Sarah met Molly, a single mother of two. Being a mother herself, Sarah found she had a lot in common with Molly and the two began to talk. Over the course of their talk, Molly revealed that she was being paid $6 an hour and could barely make ends meet. Sarah knew that her previous employer had been struggling, in part, due to the fact that she

was determined to pay her employees a fair wage. With jobs in short supply in the small town, Sarah resolved to talk with John to find out if something could be done.

That afternoon, Sarah brought the issue to John's attention. "John, I happen to know that some of the other retail firms in the area are raising pay rates in order to be fair to their employees. Don't you think that we should do the same to make certain that we retain our employees and their loyalty?"

John's response shocked Sarah. "How do you think we got to be successful, Sarah—by coddling our employees—by running business into the ground in order to focus on their best interests? No, we pay our employees as little as possible! They're a dime a dozen—if one leaves, another takes her place! Those other retail firms—they'll be going out of business sooner than they realize, and we'll still be here thriving."

1. Identify the ethical dilemma addressed in this case.
2. Do you think that paying low wages really contributes to Smith & Sons' competitive advantage?
3. How might the other companies offering higher wages gain competitive advantage over Smith & Sons?

CLOSING CASE

The Best-Laid Plans—Chrysler Hits the Wall

In 1998, after Germany's Daimler-Benz acquired Chrysler, the third largest U.S. automobile manufacturer, to form DaimlerChrysler, many observers thought that Chrysler would break away from its troubled U.S. brethren, Ford and General Motors, and join ranks with the Japanese automobile makers. The strategic plan was to emphasize bold design, better product quality, and higher productivity by sharing designs and parts between the two companies. Jurgen Schrempp, the CEO of the combined companies, told shareholders to "expect the extraordinary"

and went on to say that DaimlerChrysler "has the size, profitability and reach to take on everyone."

Eight years later, the grand scheme has proved extraordinary, but for all of the wrong reasons. In 2006, Chrysler saw its market share fall to 10.6%, and the company announced that it would lose $1.26 billion in 2006. This shocked shareholders, who had been told a few months earlier that the Chrysler unit would break even in 2006.

What went wrong? First, Schrempp and his planners may have overestimated Chrysler's competitiveness prior to the merger. Chrysler was the most profitable of the three U.S. auto companies in the late 1990s, but the U.S. economy was very strong and the company's core offering of pickup trucks, sport utility vehicles (SUVs), and minivans were the right product for a time of low gas prices. After the merger, the Germans discovered that Chrysler's factories were in worse shape than they had thought, and product quality was poor. Second, sharing design and engineering resources, and parts, between Daimler's Mercedez-Benz models and Chrysler proved to be very difficult. Mercedez was a luxury car maker, Chrysler a mass-market manufacturer, and it would take years to redesign Chrysler cars so that they could use Daimler parts and benefit from Daimler engineering. Nor did Daimler's engineers and managers seem enthusiastic about helping Chrysler, which many saw as a black hole into which a profitable Mercedes-Benz line would pour billions of euros.

To be fair, the new cars that Chrysler did produce, including the 300C sedan and the PT Cruiser, garnered good reviews. Sales of the 300C were strong, but not strong enough to shift the balance of Chrysler's business away from the small-truck segment.

Despite several years of financial struggle, by 2004, it looked as if things might finally be turning round at Chrysler. In 2004 and then again in 2005, the company made good money. The company actually gained market share in 2005. Dieter Zetsche, Chrysler's German CEO, hoped to capitalize on this with the introduction of a new SUV, the seven-seat Jeep Commander. Launched in mid-2005, the timing of the Commander could not have been worse. In 2005, the price of oil surged dramatically as strong demand from developed nations and China combined with tight supplies (which were made worse by supply disruptions caused by Hurricane Katrina). By mid-2006 oil had reached $70 a barrel, up from half that just eighteen months earlier, and gas prices hit $3 a gallon.

To make matters worse, Ford and General Motors, who themselves were hemorrhaging red ink, were engaged in an aggressive price war, offering deep incentives to move their own excess inventory, and Chrysler was forced to match prices or lose much share. Meanwhile, Japanese manufacturers, particularly Toyota and Honda, who had been expanding their U.S. production facilities for fifteen years, were gaining share with their smaller fuel-efficient offerings and popular hybrids.

In September 2006, Chrysler announced that due to a buildup of inventory on dealers' lots, it would cut production by 16%, double the planned figure announced in June 2006. In addition to slumping sales, Thomas LaSorda revealed that the company was facing sharply higher costs for its raw materials and parts, some of which were up as much as 60%. Chrysler was also suffering from high health care costs and pension liabilities to its unionized work force.

Scrambling to fill the gap in its product line, Chrysler announced that it might enter into a partnership with China's Chery Motors to produce small fuel-efficient cars in China, which would then be imported into the United States.[57]

Case Discussion Questions

1. What was the planned strategy at Daimler-Benz for Chrysler in 1988?

2. In retrospect, Daimler-Benz's plans for Chrysler seemed overoptimistic. What decision-making errors might Daimler-Benz have made in its evaluation of Chrysler? How might those errors have been avoided?

3. What opportunities and threats was Chrysler facing in 2005 and 2006? What were Chrysler's strengths and weaknesses? Did its product strategy make sense given these considerations?

4. Why did Chrysler get its forecasts for product sales and earnings so wrong in 2006? What does this teach you about the nature of planning?

5. What must Chrysler do now if it is to regain its footing in this industry?

Appendix to Chapter 1

Enterprise Valuation, ROIC, and Growth

The ultimate goal of strategy is to maximize the value of a company to its shareholders (subject to the important constraints that this is done in a legal, ethical, and socially responsible manner). The two main drivers of enterprise valuation are return on invested capital (ROIC) and the growth rate of profits, g.[58]

ROIC is defined as net operating profits less adjusted taxes (NOPLAT) over the invested capital of the enterprise (IC), where IC is the sum of the company's equity and debt (the method for calculating adjusted taxes need not concern us here). That is:

$$ROIC = NOPLAT/IC$$

where:

$$NOPLAT = \text{revenues} - \text{cost of goods sold}$$
$$- \text{operating expenses}$$
$$- \text{depreciation charges}$$
$$- \text{adjusted taxes}$$

$$IC = \text{value of shareholders' equity} + \text{value of debt}$$

The growth rate of profits, g, can be defined as the percentage increase in net operating profits (NOPLAT) over a given time period. More precisely:

$$g = [(NOPLAT_{t+1} - NOPLAT_t)/NOPLAT_t] \times 100$$

Note that if NOPLAT is increasing over time, earnings per share will also increase so long as (a) the number of shares stays constant, or (b) the number of shares outstanding increases more slowly than NOPLAT.

The valuation of a company can be calculated using discounted cash flow analysis and applying it to future expected free cash flows (free cash flow in a period is defined as NOPLAT − net investments). It can be shown that the valuation of a company so calculated is related to the company's weighted average cost of capital (WACC), which is the cost of the equity and debt that the firm uses to finance its business, and the company's ROIC. Specifically:

- If ROIC > WACC, the company is earning more than its cost of capital and it is creating value.

- If ROIC = WACC, the company is earning its cost of capital and its valuation will be stable.

- If ROIC < WACC, the company is earning less than its cost of capital and it is therefore destroying value.

A company that earns more than its cost of capital is even more valuable if it can grow its net operating profits less adjusted taxes (NOPLAT) over time. Conversely, a firm that is not earning its cost of capital destroys value if it grows its NOPLAT. This critical relationship between ROIC, g, and value is shown in Table A1.

In Table A1, the figures in the cells of the matrix represent the discounted present values of future free cash flows for a company that has a starting NOPLAT of $100, invested capital of $1,000, a cost of capital of 10%, and a twenty-five-year time horizon after which ROIC = cost of capital.

TABLE A1

ROIC, Growth, and Valuation

NOPLAT Growth g	ROIC 7.5%	ROIC 10.0%	ROIC 12.5%	ROIC 15%	ROIC 20%
3%	887	1,000	1,058	1,113	1,170
6%	708	1,000	1,117	1,295	1,442
9%	410	1,000	1,354	1,591	1,886

The important points revealed by this exercise are as follows:

1. A company with an already high ROIC can create more value by increasing its profit growth rate rather than pushing for an even higher ROIC. Thus, a company with an ROIC of 15% and a 3% growth rate can create more value by increasing its profit growth rate from 3% to 9% than it can by increasing ROIC to 20%.

2. A company with a low ROIC destroys value if it grows. Thus, if ROIC = 7.5%, a 9% growth rate for twenty-five years will produce less value than a 3% growth rate. This is because unprofitable growth requires capital investments, the cost of which cannot be covered. Unprofitable growth destroys value.

3. The best of both worlds is high ROIC and high growth.

Very few companies are able to maintain an ROIC > WACC and grow NOPLAT over time, but there are some notable examples, including Dell, Microsoft, and Wal-Mart. Because these companies have generally been able to fund their capital investment needs from internally generated cash flows, they have not had to issue more shares to raise capital. Thus, growth in NOPLAT has translated directly into higher earnings per share for these companies, making their shares more attractive to investors and leading to substantial share-price appreciation. By successfully pursuing strategies that result in a high ROIC and growing NOPLAT, these firms have maximized shareholder value.

External Analysis: The Identification of Opportunities and Threats

---

OPENING CASE

The United States Beer Industry

Over the last few decades, the United States beer industry has been characterized by a very clear trend toward an increase in the concentration of the market. Today, some 80% of all the beer consumed in the United States is produced by just three companies: Anheuser-Busch, SAB-Miller, and Molson Coors, up from 57% of the market in 1980. Anheuser-Busch had almost 50% of the market in 2006, up from just 28.2% in 1980. SAB-Miller (formed in 2002 when South African Breweries merged with Miller Beer) had around 19% of the market, and Molson Coors (formed in 2005 when Canada's Molson merged with Coors) had 11% of the market.

Anheuser Busch, SAB-Miller, and Molson Coors dominate the *mass-market* segment of the industry, where competition revolves around aggressive pricing, brand loyalty, wide distribution, and national advertising spending. In contrast, another segment in the industry, the *premium beer* segment, is served by a large number of microbrewers and importers, the majority of which have a market share of less than 1%. The premium segment focuses on discerning buyers. Producers are engaged in the art of craft brewing. They build their brands around taste and cover higher product costs by charging much higher prices—roughly twice as much for a six-pack as the mass-market brewers. The microbrewers and importers have been gaining share and currently account for around 11% of the total market.

The increase in concentration among mass-market brewers reflects a number of factors. First, consumption of beer in the United States has been gradually declining (even though consumption of premium beer has been increasing). Per-capita consumption of beer peaked at 34 gallons in 1980, fell to a low of 29.1 gallons in 2003, and crept back up to 30 gallons per capita in 2005. The decline in consumption was partly due to the growing popularity of substitutes, particularly wine and spirits. In 1994, Americans consumed 1.75 gallons of wine per capita. By 2005, the figure had risen 2.16 gallons. Consumption of spirits increased from 1.27 gallons per capita in 1994 to 1.34 gallons per capita over the same period.

Second, advertising spending has steadily increased, putting smaller mass-market brewers at a distinct disadvantage. In 1975, the industry was spending $0.18 a case on advertising; by 2002, it was spending $0.40 a case (these figures are in inflation-adjusted or constant dollars). Smaller mass-market brewers couldn't afford the expensive national television advertising campaigns required to match the spending of the largest firms in the industry, and they saw their market share shrink as a result.

Third, due to a combination of technological change in canning and distribution, and increased advertising expenditures, the size that a mass-market brewer has to attain in order to reap all economies of scale—called the *minimum efficient scale* of production—has steadily increased. In 1970, the minimum efficient scale of production was estimated to be 8 million barrels of beer a year, suggesting that a market share of 6.4% was required to reap significant economies of scale. By the early 2000s, the minimum efficient scale had increased to 23 million barrels, implying that a market share of 13.06% was required to reap significant scale economies.

In sum, the combination of declining demand, increasing advertising spending, and an increase in the minimum efficient scale of production put smaller mass-market brewers at a competitive disadvantage. Many sold out to the larger brewers or, in some cases, simply shut down. By the early 2000s, there were only twenty-four mass-market brewers left in the United States, down from eighty-two in 1970. Among the remaining mass-market brewers, Anheuser Busch is the most consistent performer due to its superior economies of scale. The company's return on invested capital (ROIC) has been high, fluctuating in the 17% to 23% range between 1996 and 2006, while net profits grew from $1.1 billion in 1996 to $2 billion in 2006. In contrast, both Coors and Miller, along with most other mass-market brewers, have had mediocre financial performance at best. Coors and Miller merged with Molson and SAB, respectively, in an attempt to gain scale economies.[1]

OVERVIEW

Strategy formulation begins with an analysis of the forces that shape competition in the industry in which a company is based. The goal is to understand the opportunities and threats confronting the firm and to use this understanding to identify strategies that will enable the company to outperform its rivals. **Opportunities** arise when a company can take advantage of conditions in its environment to formulate and implement strategies that enable it to become more profitable. For example, as discussed in the Opening Case, the growth in consumption of premium beer represents an *opportunity* for brewers to expand their sales volume by creating products for the premium segment. **Threats** arise when conditions in the external environment endanger the integrity and profitability of the company's business. Declining beer consumption and the rise in the minimum efficient scale of production have been *threats* to the profitability of all but the very largest mass-market brewers in the beer industry (see the Opening Case).

This chapter begins with an analysis of the industry environment. First, it examines concepts and tools for analyzing the competitive structure of an industry and identifying industry opportunities and threats. Second, it analyzes the competitive implications that arise when groups of companies within an industry pursue similar and different kinds of competitive strategies. Third, it explores the way an industry evolves over time and the accompanying changes in competitive conditions. Fourth, it looks at the way in which forces in the macroenvironment affect industry structure and influence opportunities and threats. By the end of the chapter, you will understand that to succeed, a company must either fit its strategy to the external environment in which it operates or be able to reshape the environment to its advantage through its chosen strategy.

Defining an Industry

An industry can be defined as a group of companies offering products or services that are close substitutes for each other—that is, products or services that satisfy the same basic customer needs. A company's closest competitors, its rivals, are those that serve the same basic customer needs. For example, carbonated drinks, fruit punches, and bottled water can be viewed as close substitutes for each other because they serve the same basic customer needs for refreshing and cold nonalcoholic beverages. Thus, we can talk about the soft drink industry, whose major players are Coca-Cola, PepsiCo, and Cadbury Schweppes. Similarly, desktop computers and notebook computers satisfy the same basic need that customers have for computer hardware on which to run personal productivity software; browse the Internet; send email; play games; and store, display, and manipulate digital images. Thus, we can talk about the personal computer industry, whose major players are Dell, Hewlett-Packard, Lenovo (the Chinese company that purchased IBM's personal computer business), Gateway, and Apple Computer.

The starting point of external analysis is to identify the industry that a company competes in. To do this, managers must begin by looking at the basic customer needs their company is serving—that is, they must take a customer-oriented view of their business as opposed to a product-oriented view (see Chapter 1). An industry is the supply side of a market, and companies in the industry are the suppliers. Customers are the demand side of a market and are the buyers of the industry's products. The basic customer needs that are served by a market define an industry's boundary. It is very important for managers to realize this, for if they define industry boundaries incorrectly, they may be caught flat-footed by the rise of competitors that serve the same basic customer needs with different product offerings. For example, Coca-Cola long saw itself as being in the soda industry—meaning carbonated soft drinks—whereas in fact, it was in the soft drink industry, which includes noncarbonated soft drinks. In the mid-1990s, Coca-Cola was caught by surprise by the rise of customer demand for bottled water and fruit drinks, which began to cut into the demand for sodas. Coca-Cola moved quickly to respond to these threats, introducing its own brand of water, Dasani, and acquiring orange-juice-maker Minute Maid. By defining its industry boundaries too narrowly, Coca-Cola almost missed the rapid rise of the noncarbonated soft drinks segment of the soft drinks market.

● **Industry and Sector**   An important distinction that needs to be made is between an industry and a sector. A sector is a group of closely related industries. For example, as illustrated in Figure 2.1, the computer sector comprises several related industries: the computer component industries (for example, the disk drive industry, the semiconductor industry, and the modem industry), the computer hardware industries (for example, the personal computer industry, the hand-held computer industry, and the mainframe computer industry), and the computer software industry. Industries within a sector may be involved with each other in many different ways. Companies in the computer component industries are the suppliers of firms in the computer hardware industries. Companies in the computer software industry provide important complements to computer hardware: the software programs that customers purchase to run on their hardware. And companies in the personal, hand-held, and mainframe industries are in indirect competition with each other because all provide products that are, to a degree, substitutes for each other.

FIGURE 2.1

The Computer Sector: Industries and Segments

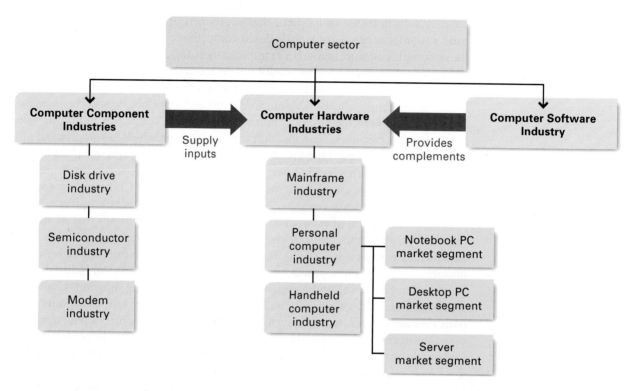

● **Industry and Market Segments**

It is also important to recognize the difference between an industry and the market segments within that industry. Market segments are distinct groups of customers within a market that can be differentiated from each other on the basis of their distinct attributes and specific demands. In the beer industry, for example, there are three main segments—consumers who drink long-established mass-market brands (for example, Budweiser), weight-conscious consumers who drink less filling, low-calorie mass-market brands (for example, Coors Light), and consumers who prefer premium-priced craft beer offered by microbreweries and many importers (see the Opening Case). Similarly, in the personal computer industry, there are different segments where customers desire desktop machines, lightweight portable machines, and servers that sit at the center of a network of personal computers (see Figure 2.1). Personal computer makers recognize the existence of these different segments by producing a range of product offerings that appeal to customers in different segments. Customers in all of these different segments, however, share a common need for PCs on which to run personal software applications.

● **Changing Industry Boundaries**

Industry boundaries may change over time as customer needs evolve or new technologies emerge that enable companies in hitherto unrelated industries to satisfy established customer needs in new ways. We have noted that during the 1990s, as consumers of soft drinks began to develop a taste for bottled water and noncarbonated fruit-based drinks, Coca-Cola found itself in direct competition with the manufacturers of bottled water and fruit-based soft drinks: all were in the same industry.

For an example of how technological change can alter industry boundaries, consider the convergence that is currently taking place between the computer and telecommunications industries. Historically, the telecommunications equipment industry has been considered a distinct entity from the computer hardware industry. However, as telecommunications equipment has moved from traditional analog technology to digital technology, so telecommunications equipment has increasingly come to resemble computers. The result is that the boundaries between these different industries are blurring. A digital wireless phone, for example, is nothing more than a small hand-held computer with a wireless connection, and small hand-held computers often now come with wireless capabilities, transforming them into phones. Thus, Nokia and Motorola, which manufacture wireless phones, are now finding themselves competing directly with Palm, which manufactures hand-held computers.

Industry competitive analysis begins by focusing on the overall industry in which a firm competes before market segments or sector-level issues are considered. Tools that managers can use to perform such industry analysis—Porter's five forces model, strategic group analysis, and industry life cycle analysis—are discussed in the following sections.

Porter's Five Forces Model

Once the boundaries of an industry have been identified, the task facing managers is to analyze competitive forces in the industry environment to identify opportunities and threats. Michael E. Porter's well-known framework, known as the five forces model, helps managers with this analysis.[2] His model, shown in Figure 2.2, focuses on five forces that shape competition within an industry: (1) the risk of entry by potential competitors, (2) the intensity of rivalry among established companies within an industry, (3) the bargaining power of buyers, (4) the bargaining power of suppliers, and (5) the closeness of substitutes to an industry's products.

Porter argues that the stronger each of these forces is, the more limited is the ability of established companies to raise prices and earn greater profits. Within Porter's framework, a strong competitive force can be regarded as a threat because it depresses profits. A weak competitive force can be viewed as an opportunity because it allows a company to earn greater profits. The strength of the five forces may change through

FIGURE 2.2

Porter's Five Forces Model

Source: Adapted and reprinted by permission of Harvard Business Review. From "How Competitive Forces Shape Strategy," by Michael E. Porter, *Harvard Business Review*, March/April 1979, copyright © 1979 by the President and Fellows of Harvard College. All rights reserved.

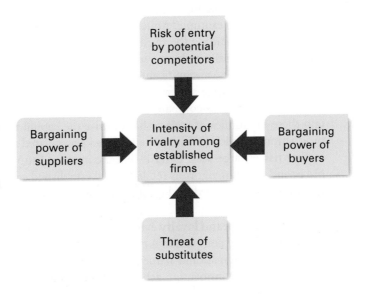

time as industry conditions change. The task facing managers is to recognize how changes in the five forces give rise to new opportunities and threats and to formulate appropriate strategic responses. In addition, it is possible for a company, through its choice of strategy, to alter the strength of one or more of the five forces to its advantage. This is discussed in the following chapters.

• Risk of Entry by Potential Competitors

Potential competitors are companies that are not currently competing in an industry but have the capability to do so if they choose. For example, cable television companies have recently emerged as potential competitors to traditional phone companies. New digital technologies have allowed cable companies to offer telephone service over the same cables that transmit television shows.

Established companies already operating in an industry often attempt to discourage potential competitors from entering the industry because the more companies that enter, the more difficult it becomes for established companies to protect their share of the market and generate profits. A high risk of entry by potential competitors represents a threat to the profitability of established companies. But if the risk of new entry is low, established companies can take advantage of this opportunity to raise prices and earn greater returns.

The risk of entry by potential competitors is a function of the height of barriers to entry, that is, factors that make it costly for companies to enter an industry. The greater the costs that potential competitors must bear to enter an industry, the greater are the barriers to entry and the weaker this competitive force. High entry barriers may keep potential competitors out of an industry even when industry profits are high. Important barriers to entry include economies of scale, brand loyalty, absolute cost advantages, customer switching costs, and government regulation.[3] An important strategy is building barriers to entry (in the case of incumbent firms) or finding ways to circumvent those barriers (in the case of new entrants). We shall discuss this topic in more detail in subsequent chapters.

ECONOMIES OF SCALE **Economies of scale** arise when unit costs fall as a firm expands its output. Sources of scale economies include (1) cost reductions gained through mass-producing a standardized output, (2) discounts on bulk purchases of raw material inputs and component parts, (3) the advantages gained by spreading fixed production costs over a large production volume, and (4) the cost savings associated with spreading marketing and advertising costs over a large volume of output. In the beer industry, for example, Anheuser Busch has been able to reap substantial scale economies by spreading the fixed costs associated with national advertising over its industry-leading sales volume (see the Opening case). If the cost advantages from economies of scale are significant, a new company that enters the industry and produces on a small scale suffers a significant cost disadvantage relative to established companies. If the new company decides to enter on a large scale in an attempt to obtain these economies of scale, it has to raise the capital required to build large-scale production facilities and bear the high risks associated with such an investment. A further risk of large-scale entry is that the increased supply of products will depress prices and result in vigorous retaliation by established companies. For these reasons, the threat of entry is reduced when established companies have economies of scale.

BRAND LOYALTY **Brand loyalty** exists when consumers have a preference for the products of established companies. A company can create brand loyalty through continuous advertising of its brand-name products and company name, patent protection of products, product innovation achieved through company research and development

(R&D) programs, an emphasis on high product quality, and good after-sales service. Significant brand loyalty makes it difficult for new entrants to take market share away from established companies. Thus, it reduces the threat of entry by potential competitors since they may see the task of breaking down well-established customer preferences as too costly. In the mass-market segments of the beer industry, for example, the brand loyalty enjoyed by Anheuser Busch (Budweiser), Molson Coors (Coors), and SAB-Miller (Miller) is such that new entry into these segments of the industry is very difficult. Hence, most new entrants have focused on the premium segment of the industry, where established brands have less of a hold. (For an example of how a company circumvented brand-based barriers to entry in the market for carbonated soft drinks, see Strategy in Action 2.1).

Strategy in Action　2.1

Circumventing Entry Barriers into the Soft Drink Industry

The soft drink industry has long been dominated by two companies, Coca-Cola and PepsiCo. By spending large sums of money on advertising and promotion, both companies have created significant brand loyalty and made it very difficult for new competitors to enter the industry and take market share away from these two giants. When new competitors do try to enter, both companies have responded by cutting prices and thus forcing the new entrant to curtail expansion plans.

However, in the early 1990s, the Cott Corporation, then a small Canadian bottling company, worked out a strategy for entering the soft drink market. Cott's strategy was deceptively simple. The company initially focused on the cola segment of the soft drink market. Cott signed a deal with Royal Crown Cola for exclusive global rights to its cola concentrate. RC Cola was a small player in the U.S. cola market. Its products were recognized as high quality, but RC Cola had never been able to effectively challenge Coke or Pepsi. Next, Cott signed a deal with a Canadian grocery retailer, Loblaw, to provide the retailer with its own private-label brand of cola. Priced low, the Loblaw private-label brand, known as President's Choice, was very successful and took share from both Coke and Pepsi.

Emboldened by this success, Cott decided to try to convince other retailers to carry private-label cola. To retailers, the value proposition was simple because, unlike its major rivals, Cott spent almost nothing on advertising and promotion. This constituted a major source of cost savings, which Cott passed on to retailers in the form of lower prices. For their part, the retailers found that they could significantly undercut the price of Coke and Pepsi colas and still make better profit margins on private-label brands than on branded colas.

Despite this compelling value proposition, few retailers were willing to sell private-label colas for fear of alienating Coca-Cola and Pepsi, whose products were a major draw of grocery store traffic. Cott's breakthrough came in 1992 when it signed a deal with Wal-Mart to supply the retailing giant with a private-label cola, called Sam's Choice (named after Wal-Mart founder Sam Walton). Wal-Mart proved to be the perfect distribution channel for Cott. The retailer was just starting to get into the grocery business, and consumers went to Wal-Mart not to buy branded merchandise but to get low prices.

As Wal-Mart's grocery business grew, so did Cott's sales. Cott soon added other flavors to its offering, such as lemon-lime soda, which would compete with Seven Up and Sprite. Moreover, pressured by Wal-Mart, other U.S. grocers had also started to introduce private-label sodas by the late 1990s, often turning to Cott to supply their needs.

By 2006, Cott had grown to become a $1.8 billion company. Its volume growth in an otherwise stagnant U.S. market for sodas has averaged around 12.5% between 2001 and 2006. Cott captured over 5% of the U.S. soda market in 2005, up from almost nothing a decade earlier, and held onto a 16% share of sodas in grocery stores, its core channel. The losers in this process have been Coca-Cola and PepsiCo, who are now facing the steady erosion of their brand loyalty and market share as consumers increasingly came to recognize the high quality and low price of private-label sodas.[a]

ABSOLUTE COST ADVANTAGES Sometimes established companies have an **absolute cost advantage** relative to potential entrants, meaning that entrants cannot expect to match the established companies' lower cost structure. Absolute cost advantages arise from three main sources: (1) superior production operations and processes due to accumulated experience, patents, or secret processes; (2) control of particular inputs required for production, such as labor, materials, equipment, or management skills, that are limited in their supply; and (3) access to cheaper funds because existing companies represent lower risks than new entrants. If established companies have an absolute cost advantage, the threat of entry as a competitive force is weaker.

CUSTOMER SWITCHING COSTS **Switching costs** arise when it costs a customer time, energy, and money to switch from the products offered by one established company to the products offered by a new entrant. When switching costs are high, customers can be locked in to the product offerings of established companies, even if new entrants offer better products.[4] A familiar example of switching costs concerns the costs associated with switching from one computer operating system to another. If a person currently uses Microsoft's Windows operating system and has a library of related software applications (for example, word-processing software, spreadsheet, games) and document files, it is expensive for that person to switch to another computer operating system. To effect the change, this person would have to buy a new set of software applications and convert all existing document files to run with the new system. Faced with such an expense of money and time, most people are unwilling to make the switch unless the competing operating system offers a substantial leap forward in performance. Thus, the higher the switching costs are, the higher is the barrier to entry for a company attempting to promote a new computer operating system.

GOVERNMENT REGULATION Historically, government regulation has constituted a major entry barrier into many industries. For example, until the mid-1990s, U.S. government regulation prohibited providers of long-distance telephone service from competing for local telephone service, and vice versa. Other potential providers of telephone service, including cable television service companies such as Time Warner and Comcast (which could, in theory, use their cables to carry telephone traffic as well as television signals), were prohibited from entering the market altogether. These regulatory barriers to entry significantly reduced the level of competition in both the local and long-distance telephone markets, enabling telephone companies to earn higher profits than might otherwise have been the case. All this changed in 1996 when the government deregulated the industry significantly. In the months that followed this announcement, local, long-distance, and cable television companies all announced their intention to enter each other's markets, and a host of new players emerged. The five forces model predicts that falling entry barriers due to government deregulation will result in significant new entry, an increase in the intensity of industry competition, and lower industry profit rates, and indeed, that is what occurred.

In summary, if established companies have built brand loyalty for their products, have an absolute cost advantage with respect to potential competitors, have significant scale economies, are the beneficiaries of high switching costs, or enjoy regulatory protection, the risk of entry by potential competitors is greatly diminished; it is a weak competitive force. Consequently, established companies can charge higher prices, and industry profits are higher. Evidence from academic research suggests that the height of barriers to entry is one of the most important determinants of profit rates in an industry.[5] Clearly, it is in the interest of established companies to pursue strategies consistent with raising entry barriers to secure these profits. By the same token, potential new entrants have to find strategies that allow them to circumvent barriers to entry.

LIMITS OF ENTRY BARRIERS   Even when entry barriers are very high, new firms may still enter an industry if they perceive that the benefits outweigh the substantial costs of entry. This is what appears to have occurred in the telecommunications industry following deregulation in 1996. Deregulation led to a flood of new entrants such as Level 3 Communications, 360networks, and Global Crossing, who built fiber-optic networks to serve what they perceived as explosive growth in the amount of Internet traffic. These entrants had to undertake billions of dollars in capital expenditure to build their networks and match the scale advantages of established companies such as WorldCom. However, the new entrants were able to raise the capital to do so from investors who shared management's euphoric vision of future demand in the industry (Level 3 alone raised $13 billion). As it turned out, the euphoric vision of demand growth was based on the erroneous assumption that Internet traffic was growing at 1,000 percent a year when in fact it was growing at only 100 percent a year. When the euphoric vision proved to be false, many of the new entrants went bankrupt, but not before their investments had created excess capacity in the industry and sparked intense price competition that depressed the returns for all players, new entrants and established companies alike.

● **Rivalry Among Established Companies**

The second of Porter's five competitive forces is the intensity of rivalry among established companies within an industry. Rivalry refers to the competitive struggle between companies in an industry to gain market share from each other. The competitive struggle can be fought using price, product design, advertising and promotion spending, direct selling efforts, and after-sales service and support. More intense rivalry implies lower prices or more spending on non-price-competitive weapons, or both. Because intense rivalry lowers prices and raises costs, it squeezes profits out of an industry. Thus, intense rivalry among established companies constitutes a strong threat to profitability. Alternatively, if rivalry is less intense, companies may have the opportunity to raise prices or reduce spending on non-price-competitive weapons, which leads to a higher level of industry profits. The intensity of rivalry among established companies within an industry is largely a function of four factors: (1) industry competitive structure, (2) demand conditions, (3) cost conditions, and (4) the height of exit barriers in the industry.

INDUSTRY COMPETITIVE STRUCTURE   The competitive structure of an industry refers to the number and size distribution of companies in it, something that strategic managers determine at the beginning of an industry analysis. Industry structures vary, and different structures have different implications for the intensity of rivalry. A fragmented industry consists of a large number of small or medium-sized companies, none of which is in a position to determine industry price. A consolidated industry is dominated by a small number of large companies (an oligopoly) or, in extreme cases, by just one company (a monopoly), and companies often are in a position to determine industry prices. Examples of fragmented industries are agriculture, dry cleaning, video rental, health clubs, real estate brokerage, and sun tanning parlors. Consolidated industries include the aerospace, soft drink, automobile, pharmaceutical, stockbrokerage and beer industries. In the beer industry, for example, the top three firms account for 80% of industry sales (see the Opening Case).

Many fragmented industries are characterized by low entry barriers and commodity-type products that are hard to differentiate. The combination of these traits tends to result in boom-and-bust cycles as industry profits rise and fall. Low entry barriers imply that whenever demand is strong and profits are high, new entrants will flood the market, hoping to profit from the boom. The explosion in the number of video stores, health clubs, and sun tanning parlors during the 1980s and 1990s exemplifies this situation.

Often the flood of new entrants into a booming fragmented industry creates excess capacity, so companies start to cut prices in order to use their spare capacity. The difficulty companies face when trying to differentiate their products from those of competitors can exacerbate this tendency. The result is a price war, which depresses industry profits, forces some companies out of business, and deters potential new entrants. For example, after a decade of expansion and booming profits, many health clubs are now finding that they have to offer large discounts in order to hold on to their membership. In general, the more commodity-like an industry's product is, the more vicious will be the price war. This bust part of the cycle continues until overall industry capacity is brought into line with demand (through bankruptcies), at which point prices may stabilize again.

A fragmented industry structure, then, constitutes a threat rather than an opportunity. Most booms are relatively short-lived because of the ease of new entry and will be followed by price wars and bankruptcies. Because it is often difficult to differentiate products in these industries, the best strategy for a company is to try to minimize its costs so it will be profitable in a boom and survive any subsequent bust. Alternatively, companies might try to adopt strategies that change the underlying structure of fragmented industries and lead to a consolidated industry structure in which the level of industry profitability is increased. Exactly how companies can do this is something we shall consider in later chapters.

In consolidated industries, companies are interdependent because one company's competitive actions or moves (with regard to price, quality, and so on) directly affect the market share of its rivals and thus their profitability. When one company makes a move, this generally forces a response from its rivals, and the consequence of such competitive interdependence can be a dangerous competitive spiral. Rivalry increases as companies attempt to undercut each other's prices or offer customers more value in their products, pushing industry profits down in the process. The fare wars that have periodically created havoc in the airline industry provide a good illustration of this process.

Companies in consolidated industries sometimes seek to reduce this threat by following the prices set by the dominant company in the industry.[6] However, companies must be careful, for explicit face-to-face price-fixing agreements are illegal. (Tacit, indirect agreements, arrived at without direct or intentional communication, are legal.) Instead, companies set prices by watching, interpreting, anticipating, and responding to each other's behavior (something discussed in detail in Chapter 5 when the competitive dynamics of game theory is examined). However, tacit price-leadership agreements often break down under adverse economic conditions, as has occurred in the breakfast cereal industry, profiled in Strategy in Action 2.2.

Strategy in Action

2.2

Price Wars in the Breakfast Cereal Industry

For decades, the breakfast cereal industry was one of the most profitable in the United States. The industry has a consolidated structure dominated by Kellogg, General Mills, and Kraft Foods with its Post brand. Strong brand loyalty, coupled with control over the allocation of supermarket shelf space, helped to limit the potential for new entry. Meanwhile, steady demand growth of around 3% per annum kept industry revenues expanding. Kellogg, which accounted for over 40% of the market share, acted as the price leader in the industry. Every year, Kellogg increased cereal prices, its rivals followed, and industry profits remained high.

This favorable industry structure started to change in the early 1990s when growth in demand slowed and then stagnated as a latte and bagel or muffin replaced cereal as the morning fare for many American adults. Then came the rise of powerful discounters such as Wal-Mart, which entered the grocery industry in the early 1990s and began to promote aggressively its own brand of cereal, priced significantly below the brand-name cereals. As the decade progressed, other grocery chains such as Kroger's started to follow suit, and brand loyalty in the industry began to decline as customers realized that a $2.50 bag of wheat flakes from Wal-Mart tasted about the same as a $3.50 box of Cornflakes from Kellogg. As sales of cheaper store-brand cereals began to take off, supermarkets were no longer as dependent on brand names to bring traffic into their stores and began to demand lower prices from the branded cereal manufacturers.

For several years, the manufacturers of brand cereals tried to hold out against these adverse trends, but in the mid-1990s the dam broke. In 1996, Kraft (then owned by Philip Morris) aggressively cut prices by 20% for its Post brand in an attempt to gain market share. Kellogg soon followed with a 19% price cut on two-thirds of its brands, and General Mills quickly did the same. The decades of tacit price collusion were officially over.

If the breakfast cereal companies were hoping that the price cuts would stimulate demand, they were wrong. Instead, demand remained flat while revenues and margins followed prices down, and Kellogg's operating margins dropped from 18% in 1995 to 10.2% in 1996, a trend experienced by the other brand cereal manufacturers.

By 2000, conditions had only worsened. Private-label sales continued to make inroads, gaining over 10% of the market. Moreover, sales of breakfast cereals started to contract at 1% per annum. To cap it off, an aggressive General Mills continued to launch expensive price and promotion campaigns in an attempt to take share away from the market leader. Kellogg saw its market share slip to just over 30% in 2001, behind the 31% now held by General Mills. For the first time since 1906, Kellogg no longer led the market. Moreover, profits at all three major producers remained weak in the face of continued price discounting.

In mid-2001, General Mills finally blinked and raised prices a modest 2% in response to its own rising costs. Competitors followed, signaling perhaps that after a decade of costly price warfare, pricing discipline might once more emerge in the industry. Both Kellogg and General Mills tried to move further away from price competition by focusing on brand extensions, such as Special K containing berries and new varieties of Cheerios. Kellogg's efforts with Special K helped the company recapture market leadership from General Mills. More important, the renewed emphasis on nonprice competition halted years of damaging price warfare, at least for the time being.[b]

● **Industry Demand**   The level of industry demand is a second determinant of the intensity of rivalry among established companies. Growing demand from new customers or additional purchases by existing customers tend to moderate competition by providing greater scope for companies to compete for customers. Growing demand tends to reduce rivalry because all companies can sell more without taking market share away from other companies. High industry profits are often the result. Conversely, declining demand results in more rivalry as companies fight to maintain market share and revenues (as in the breakfast cereal industry). Demand declines when customers are leaving the marketplace or each customer is buying less. Now a company can grow only by taking market share away from other companies. Thus, declining demand constitutes a major threat because it increases the extent of rivalry between established companies.

● **Cost Conditions**   The cost structure of firms in an industry is a third determinant of rivalry. In industries where fixed costs are high, profitability tends to be highly leveraged to sales volume, and the desire to grow volume can spark intense rivalry. Fixed costs are the costs that must be borne before the firm makes a single sale. For example, before they can offer service, cable television companies have to lay cable in the ground; the cost of doing so is a fixed cost. Similarly, to offer air express service, a company like FedEx must invest in planes, package-sorting facilities, and delivery trucks—all fixed costs that require significant capital investments. In industries where the fixed costs of production are high, if sales volume is low, firms cannot cover their fixed costs and will not be profitable. Thus, they have an incentive to cut their prices and/or increase promotion spending to drive up sales volume so that they can cover their fixed costs. In situations where demand is not growing fast enough and too many companies are engaged in the same actions (cutting prices and/or raising promotion spending in an attempt to cover fixed costs), the result can be intense rivalry and lower profits. Research suggests that it is often the weakest firms in an industry that initiate such actions precisely because they are the ones struggling to cover their fixed costs.[7]

● **Exit Barriers**   Exit barriers are economic, strategic, and emotional factors that prevent companies from leaving an industry.[8] If exit barriers are high, companies become locked into an unprofitable industry where overall demand is static or declining. The result is often excess productive capacity, which leads to even more intense rivalry and price competition as companies cut prices in the attempt to obtain the customer orders needed to use their idle capacity and cover their fixed costs.[9] Common exit barriers include the following:

● Investments in assets such as specific machines, equipment, and operating facilities that are of little or no value in alternative uses or cannot be sold off. If the company wishes to leave the industry, it has to write off the book value of these assets.

● High fixed costs of exit, such as the severance pay, health benefits, and pensions that have to be paid to workers who are being made redundant when a company ceases to operate.

● Emotional attachments to an industry, as when a company's owners or employees are unwilling to exit from an industry for sentimental reasons or because of pride.

● Economic dependence on the industry because a company relies on a single industry for its revenue and profit.

● The need to maintain an expensive collection of assets at or above some minimum level in order to participate effectively in the industry.

● Bankruptcy regulations, particularly in the United States, where Chapter 11 bankruptcy provisions allow insolvent enterprises to continue operating and reorganize themselves under bankruptcy protection. These regulations can keep unprofitable assets in the industry, result in persistent excess capacity, and lengthen the time required to bring industry supply in line with demand.

As an example of the effect of exit barriers in practice, consider the express mail and parcel delivery industry. The key players in this industry, such as Federal Express and UPS, rely on the delivery business entirely for their revenues and profits. They have to be able to guarantee their customers that they will deliver packages to all major localities in the United States, and much of their investment is specific to this purpose. To meet this guarantee, they need a nationwide network of air routes and ground routes, an asset that is required in order to participate in the industry. If excess capacity develops in this industry, as it does from time to time, Federal Express cannot incrementally reduce or minimize its excess capacity by deciding not to fly to and deliver packages in, say, Miami because that proportion of its network is underused. If it did that, it would no longer be able to guarantee to its customers that it would be able to deliver packages to all major locations in the United States, and its customers would switch to some other carrier. Thus, the need to maintain a nationwide network is an exit barrier that can result in persistent excess capacity in the air express industry during periods of weak demand. Finally, both UPS and Federal Express managers and employees are emotionally tied to this industry because they both were first movers, in the ground and air segments of the industry, respectively, and because their employees are also major owners of their companies' stock and they are dependent financially on the fortunes of the delivery business.

The Bargaining Power of Buyers

The third of Porter's five competitive forces is the bargaining power of buyers. An industry's buyers may be the individual customers who ultimately consume its products (its end-users) or the companies that distribute an industry's products to end-users, such as retailers and wholesalers. For example, while soap powder made by Procter & Gamble and Unilever is consumed by end-users, the principal buyers of soap powder are supermarket chains and discount stores, which resell the product to end-users. The bargaining power of buyers refers to the ability of buyers to bargain down prices charged by companies in the industry or to raise the costs of companies in the industry by demanding better product quality and service. By lowering prices and raising costs, powerful buyers can squeeze profits out of an industry. Thus, powerful buyers should be viewed as a threat. Alternatively, when buyers are in a weak bargaining position, companies in an industry can raise prices and perhaps reduce their costs by lowering product quality and service, thus increasing the level of industry profits. Buyers are most powerful in the following circumstances:

- When the industry that is supplying a particular product or service is composed of many small companies and the buyers are large and few in number. These circumstances allow the buyers to dominate supplying companies.

- When the buyers purchase in large quantities. In such circumstances, buyers can use their purchasing power as leverage to bargain for price reductions.

- When the supply industry depends on the buyers for a large percentage of its total orders.

- When switching costs are low so that buyers can play the supplying companies against each other to force down prices.

- When it is economically feasible for buyers to purchase an input from several companies at once so that buyers can play one company in the industry against another.

- When buyers can threaten to enter the industry and produce the product themselves and thus supply their own needs, also a tactic for forcing down industry prices.

The auto component supply industry, whose buyers are large automobile manufacturers such as GM, Ford, and DaimlerChrysler, is a good example of an industry in which buyers have strong bargaining power and thus a strong competitive threat. Why? The suppliers of auto components are numerous and typically small in scale; their buyers, the auto manufacturers, are large in size and few in number. DaimlerChrysler, for example, does business with nearly two thousand different component suppliers in the United States and normally contracts with a number of different companies to supply the same part. Additionally, to keep component prices down, both Ford and GM have used the threat of manufacturing a component themselves rather than buying it from auto component suppliers. The automakers have used their powerful position to play suppliers against each other, forcing down the price they have to pay for component parts and demanding better quality. If a component supplier objects, the automakers use the threat of switching to another supplier as a bargaining tool.

Another issue is that the relative power of buyers and suppliers tends to change in response to changing industry conditions. For example, because of changes now taking place in the pharmaceutical and health care industries, major buyers of pharmaceuticals (hospitals and health maintenance organizations) are gaining power over the suppliers of pharmaceuticals and have been able to demand lower prices. Strategy in Action 2.3 discusses how Wal-Mart's buying power has changed over the years as the company has become larger.

● The Bargaining Power of Suppliers

The fourth of Porter's five competitive forces is the bargaining power of suppliers—the organizations that provide inputs into the industry, such as materials, services, and labor (which may be individuals, organizations such as labor unions, or companies that supply contract labor). The bargaining power of suppliers refers to the ability of suppliers to raise input prices or to raise the costs of the industry in other ways—for example, by providing poor-quality inputs or poor service. Powerful suppliers squeeze profits out of an industry by raising the costs of companies in the industry. Thus, powerful suppliers are a threat. Alternatively, if suppliers are weak, companies in the industry have the opportunity to force down input prices and demand higher-quality inputs (such as more productive labor). As with buyers, the ability of suppliers to make demands on a company depends on their power relative to that of the company. Suppliers are most powerful in these situations:

- The product that suppliers sell has few substitutes and is vital to the companies in an industry.

- The profitability of suppliers is not significantly affected by the purchases of companies in a particular industry, in other words, when the industry is not an important customer to the suppliers.

- Companies in an industry would experience significant switching costs if they moved to the product of a different supplier because a particular supplier's products are unique or different. In such cases, the company depends on a particular supplier and cannot play suppliers against each other to reduce price.

- Suppliers can threaten to enter their customers' industry and use their inputs to produce products that would compete directly with those of companies already in the industry.

- Companies in the industry cannot threaten to enter their suppliers' industry and make their own inputs as a tactic for lowering the price of inputs.

Strategy in Action

Wal-Mart's Bargaining Power over Suppliers

When Wal-Mart and other discount retailers began in the 1960s, they were small operations with little purchasing power. To generate store traffic, they depended in large part on stocking nationally branded merchandise from well-known companies such as Procter & Gamble and Rubbermaid. Since the discounters did not have high sales volume, the nationally branded companies set the price. This meant that the discounters had to look for other ways to cut costs, which they typically did by emphasizing self-service in stripped-down stores located in the suburbs where land was cheaper (in the 1960s, the main competitors for discounters were full-service department stores like Sears that were often located in downtown shopping areas).

Discounters such as Kmart purchased their merchandise through wholesalers, who in turn bought from manufacturers. The wholesaler would come into a store and write an order, and when the merchandise arrived, the wholesaler would come in and stock the shelves, saving the retailer labor costs. However, Wal-Mart was located in Arkansas and placed its stores in small towns. Wholesalers were not particularly interested in serving a company that built its stores in such out-of-the-way places. They would do it only if Wal-Mart paid higher prices.

Wal-Mart's Sam Walton refused to pay higher prices. Instead he took his fledgling company public and used the capital raised to build a distribution center to stock merchandise. The distribution center would serve all stores within a 300-mile radius, with trucks leaving the distribution center daily to restock the stores. Because the distribution center was serving a collection of stores and thus buying in larger volumes, Walton found that he was able to cut the wholesalers out of the equation and order directly from manufacturers. The cost savings generated by not having to pay profits to wholesalers were then passed on to consumers in the form of lower prices, which helped Wal-Mart continue growing. This growth increased its buying power and thus its ability to demand deeper discounts from manufacturers.

Today Wal-Mart has turned its buying process into an art form. Since 8% of all retail sales in the United States are made in a Wal-Mart store, the company has enormous bargaining power over its suppliers. Suppliers of nationally branded products, such as Procter & Gamble, are no longer in a position to demand high prices. Rather, Wal-Mart is now so important to Procter & Gamble that it is able to demand deep discounts on its purchases. Moreover, Wal-Mart has itself become a brand that is more powerful than the brands of manufacturers. People don't go to Wal-Mart to buy branded goods; they go to Wal-Mart for the low prices. This simple fact has enabled Wal-Mart to bargain down the prices it pays, always passing on cost savings to consumers in the form of lower prices.

Since 1991, Wal-Mart has provided suppliers with real-time information on store sales through the use of individual stock keeping units (SKUs). These have allowed suppliers to optimize their own production processes, matching output to Wal-Mart's demands and avoiding under- or overproduction and the need to store inventory. The efficiencies that manufacturers gain from such information are passed on to Wal-Mart in the form of lower prices, and Wal-Mart then passes on those cost savings to consumers.[c]

An example of an industry in which companies are dependent on a powerful supplier is the personal computer industry. Personal computer firms are heavily dependent on Intel, the world's largest supplier of microprocessors for PCs. The industry standard for personal computers runs on Intel's microprocessor chips. Intel's competitors, such as Advanced Micro Devices (AMD), must develop and supply chips that are compatible with Intel's standard. Although AMD has developed competing chips, Pentium still supplies about 85% of the chips used in PCs primarily because only Intel has the manufacturing capacity required to serve a large share of the market. It is beyond the financial resources of Intel's competitors, such as AMD, to match the scale and efficiency of Intel's manufacturing systems. Thus, while PC manufacturers can buy some microprocessors from Intel's rivals, most notably AMD, they still have to turn to Intel for the bulk of their supply. Because Intel is in a powerful bargaining position, it can charge higher prices for its microprocessors than would be the case if its competitors were more numerous and stronger (that is, if the microprocessor industry were fragmented).

● Substitute Products

The final force in Porter's model is the threat of substitute products: the products of different businesses or industries that can satisfy similar customer needs. For example, companies in the coffee industry compete indirectly with those in the tea and soft drink industries because all three serve customer needs for nonalcoholic drinks. The existence of close substitutes is a strong competitive threat because this limits the price that companies in one industry can charge for their product, and thus industry profitability. If the price of coffee rises too much relative to that of tea or soft drinks, coffee drinkers may switch to those substitutes.

If an industry's products have few close substitutes, so that substitutes are a weak competitive force, then, other things being equal, companies in the industry have the opportunity to raise prices and earn additional profits. Thus, there is no close substitute for microprocessors, which gives companies like Intel and AMD the ability to charge higher prices than would be the case if there were a substitute for microprocessors.

● A Sixth Force: Complementors

Andrew Grove, the former CEO of Intel, has argued that Porter's five forces model ignores a sixth force: the power, vigor, and competence of complementors.[10] **Complementors** are companies that sell products that add value to (complement) the products of companies in an industry because when used together, the products better satisfy customer demands. For example, the complementors to the personal computer industry are the companies that make software applications to run on those machines. The greater the supply of high-quality software applications to run on personal computers, the greater is the value of personal computers to customers, the greater the demand for PCs, and the greater the profitability of the personal computer industry.

Grove's argument has a strong foundation in economic theory, which has long argued that both substitutes and complements influence demand in an industry.[11] Moreover, recent research has emphasized the importance of complementary products in determining demand and profitability in many high-technology industries, such as the computer industry in which Grove made his mark.[12] The issue, therefore, is that when complements are an important determinant of demand for an industry's products, industry profits depend critically on there being an adequate supply of complementary products. When the number of complementors is increasing and they produce attractive complementary products, this boosts demand and profits in the industry and can open up many new opportunities for creating value. Conversely, if complementors are weak and are not producing attractive complementary products, this can be a threat that slows industry growth and limits profitability.

● **Porter's Model Summarized**

The systematic analysis of forces in the industry environment using the Porter framework is a powerful tool that helps managers to think strategically. It is important to recognize that one competitive force often affects the others, so that all forces need to be considered when performing industry analysis. Indeed, industry analysis leads managers to think systematically about how their strategic choices will be affected by the forces of industry competition and also about how their choices will affect the five forces and change conditions in the industry. For an example of industry analysis using Porter's framework, see the Running Case.

RUNNING CASE

Dell Computer and the Personal Computer Industry

The global personal computer industry is very competitive. On a global basis, Dell was the worldwide market share leader in 2005 with 18.1%, followed by Hewlett-Packard (15.6%), Lenovo (6.2%), Acer (4.7%), Fujitsu (4.1%), and Apple (2.2%). The remaining 49% of the market is accounted for by a long list of small companies, some of which focus on local markets and make unbranded so-called white box computers.

The long list of small companies reflects relatively low barriers to entry. The open architecture of the personal computer means that key components, such as an Intel compatible microprocessor, a Windows operating system, memory chips, a hard drive, and so on, can be purchased easily on the open market. Assembly is easy, requiring very little capital equipment or technical skills, and economies of scale in production are not particularly significant. Although small entrants lack the brand-name recognition of the market share leaders, they survive in the industry by pricing their machines a few hundred dollars below those of the market leaders and capturing the demand of price-sensitive consumers. This puts constant pressure on the prices that brand-name companies can charge.

Moreover, most buyers view the product offerings of different branded companies as very close substitutes for each other, so competition between them often defaults to price. Consequently, the average selling price of a PC has fallen from around $1,700 in 1999 to under $1,000 in 2006, and projections are that it may continue to fall, fueled in part by aggressive competition between Dell Computer and Hewlett-Packard.

The constant downward pressure on prices makes it hard for personal computer companies to have big gross margins, and this factor results in lower profitability. The downward pressure on prices has been exacerbated by slowing demand growth in many developed nations, including the world's largest market, the United States, where the market is now mature and demand is limited to replacement demand plus an expansion in the overall population.

To make matters worse, personal computer companies have long had to deal with two very powerful suppliers: Microsoft, which supplies the industry standard operating system, Windows, and Intel, which supplies the industry standard microprocessor. Microsoft and Intel have been able to charge high prices for their products, which has raised input costs for personal computer manufacturers and thus reduced their profitability.

In sum, the personal computer industry is not particularly attractive. The combination of low entry barriers, intense rivalry among established companies, slowing demand growth, buyers who are indifferent to the offerings of various companies and often look at price before anything else, and powerful suppliers who have raised the prices for key inputs all come together to make it difficult for established companies to earn decent profits. Against this background, the performance of Dell Computer over the last decade is nothing short of remarkable and illustrates just how strong the company's business model and competitive advantage had been.[d]

Strategic Groups Within Industries

Companies in an industry often differ significantly from each other with respect to the way they strategically position their products in the market in terms of such factors as the distribution channels they use, the market segments they serve, the quality of their products, technological leadership, customer service, pricing policy, advertising policy, and promotions. As a result of these differences, within most industries, it is possible to observe groups of companies in which each company follows a business model that is similar to that pursued by other companies in the group but is different from the business model followed by companies in other groups. These different groups of companies are known as strategic groups.[13]

Normally, the basic differences between the business models that companies in different strategic groups use can be captured by a relatively small number of strategic factors. For example, in the pharmaceutical industry, two main strategic groups stand out (see Figure 2.3).[14] One group, which includes such companies as Merck, Eli Lilly, and Pfizer, is characterized by a business model based on heavy R&D spending and a focus on developing new, proprietary, blockbuster drugs. The companies in this proprietary strategic group are pursuing a high-risk, high-return strategy. It is a high-risk strategy because basic drug research is difficult and expensive. Bringing a new drug to market can cost up to $800 million in R&D money and a decade of research and clinical trials. The risks are high because the failure rate in new drug development is very high: only one out of every five drugs entering clinical trials is ultimately approved by the U.S. Food and Drug Administration. However, the strategy is also a high-return one because a single successful drug can be patented, giving the innovator a twenty-year monopoly on its production and sale. This lets these proprietary companies charge a high price for the patented drug, allowing them to earn millions, if not billions, of dollars over the lifetime of the patent.

The second strategic group might be characterized as the generic drug strategic group. This group of companies, which includes Forest Labs, Mylan Labs, and Watson Pharmaceuticals, focuses on the manufacture of generic drugs: low-cost copies of

FIGURE 2.3

Strategic Groups in the Pharmaceutical Industry

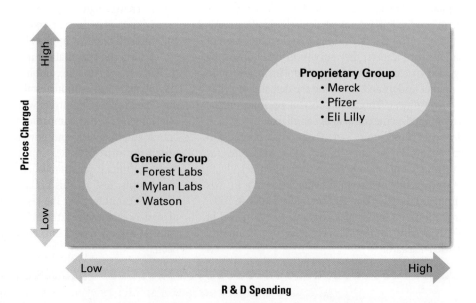

drugs that were developed by companies in the proprietary group whose patents have now expired. Low R&D spending, production efficiency, and an emphasis on low prices characterize the business models of companies in this strategic group. They are pursuing a low-risk, low-return strategy. It is low risk because they are not investing millions of dollars in R&D. It is low return because they cannot charge high prices.

● Implications of Strategic Groups

The concept of strategic groups has a number of implications for the identification of opportunities and threats within an industry. First, because all the companies in a strategic group are pursuing a similar business model, customers tend to view the products of such enterprises as direct substitutes for each other. Thus, a company's closest competitors are those in its strategic group, not those in other strategic groups in the industry. The most immediate threat to a company's profitability comes from rivals within its own strategic group. For example, a group of companies in the retail industry might be characterized as discounters. Included in this group are Wal-Mart, Kmart, Target, and Fred Meyer. These companies compete most vigorously with each other rather than with other retailers in different groups, such as Nordstrom or The Gap. Kmart, for example, was driven into bankruptcy in late 2001 not because Nordstrom or The Gap took business from it but because Wal-Mart and Target gained share in the discounting group by virtue of their superior strategic execution of the discounting business model.

A second competitive implication is that different strategic groups can have a different standing with respect to each of the competitive forces; thus, each strategic group may face a different set of opportunities and threats. The risk of new entry by potential competitors, the degree of rivalry among companies within a group, the bargaining power of buyers, the bargaining power of suppliers, and the competitive force of substitute and complementary products can each be a relatively strong or weak competitive force depending on the competitive positioning approach adopted by each strategic group in the industry. For example, in the pharmaceutical industry, companies in the proprietary group have historically been in a very powerful position in relation to buyers because their products are patented and there are no substitutes. Also, rivalry based on price competition within this group has been low because competition in the industry revolves around being the first to patent a new drug (so-called patent races), not around drug prices. Thus, companies in this group have been able to charge high prices and earn high profits. In contrast, companies in the generic group have been in a much weaker position because many companies are able to produce different versions of the same generic drug after patents expire. Thus, in this strategic group, products are close substitutes, rivalry has been high, and price competition has led to lower profits for this group compared to companies in the proprietary group.

● The Role of Mobility Barriers

It follows from the two issues discussed above that some strategic groups are more desirable than others because competitive forces open up greater opportunities and present fewer threats for those groups. Managers, after having analyzed their industry, might identify a strategic group where competitive forces are weaker and higher profits can be made. Sensing an opportunity, they might contemplate changing their business model and move to compete in that strategic group. However, taking advantage of this opportunity may be difficult because of mobility barriers between strategic groups.

Mobility barriers are within-industry factors that inhibit the movement of companies between strategic groups. They include the barriers to entry into a group and the barriers to exit from a company's existing group. For example, Forest Labs would encounter mobility barriers if it attempted to enter the proprietary group in the pharmaceutical industry because it lacks R&D skills, and building these skills would be an expensive proposition. Essentially, over time, companies in different groups develop different cost structures and skills and competencies that give them different pricing options and choices. A company contemplating entry into another strategic group must evaluate whether it has the ability to imitate, and indeed outperform, its potential competitors in that strategic group. Managers must determine if it is cost-effective to overcome mobility barriers before deciding whether the move is worthwhile.

In summary, an important task of industry analysis is to determine the sources of the similarities and differences among companies in an industry and to work out the broad themes that underlie competition in an industry. This analysis often reveals new opportunities to compete in an industry by developing new kinds of products to meet the needs of customers better. It can also reveal emerging threats that can be countered effectively by changing competitive strategy. This issue is taken up in Chapters 5, 6, and 7, which examine crafting competitive strategy in different kinds of markets to build a competitive advantage over rivals and best satisfy customer needs.

Industry Life Cycle Analysis

An important determinant of the strength of the competitive forces in an industry (and thus of the nature of opportunities and threats) is the changes that take place in it over time. The similarities and differences between companies in an industry often become more pronounced over time, and its strategic group structure frequently changes. The strength and nature of each of the competitive forces also change as an industry evolves, particularly the two forces of risk of entry by potential competitors and rivalry among existing firms.[15]

A useful tool for analyzing the effects of industry evolution on competitive forces is the **industry life cycle** model, which identifies five sequential stages in the evolution of an industry that lead to five distinct kinds of industry environment: embryonic industry, growth, shakeout, mature industry, and decline (see Figure 2.4). The task facing managers is to anticipate how the strength of competitive forces will

FIGURE 2.4

Stages in the Industry
Life Cycle

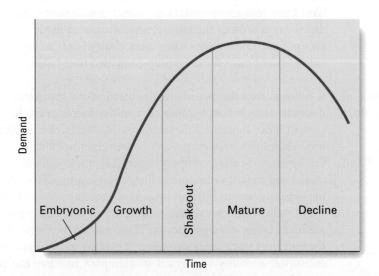

change as the industry environment evolves and to formulate strategies that take advantage of opportunities as they arise and that counter emerging threats.

● Embryonic Industries

An embryonic industry is just beginning to develop (for example, personal computers and biotechnology in the 1970s, wireless communications in the 1980s, Internet retailing in the early 1990s, and nanotechnology today). Growth at this stage is slow because of such factors as buyers' unfamiliarity with the industry's product, high prices due to the inability of companies to reap any significant scale economies, and poorly developed distribution channels. Barriers to entry tend to be based on access to key technological know-how rather than cost economies or brand loyalty. If the core know-how required to compete in the industry is complex and difficult to grasp, barriers to entry can be quite high, and established companies will be protected from potential competitors. Rivalry in embryonic industries is based not so much on price as on educating customers, opening up distribution channels, and perfecting the design of the product. Such rivalry can be intense, and the company that is the first to solve design problems often has the opportunity to develop a significant market position. An embryonic industry may also be the creation of one company's innovative efforts, as happened with microprocessors (Intel), vacuum cleaners (Hoover), photocopiers (Xerox), and small package express delivery (FedEx). In such circumstances, the company has a major opportunity to capitalize on the lack of rivalry and build a strong hold on the market.

● Growth Industries

Once demand for the industry's product begins to take off, the industry develops the characteristics of a growth industry. In a growth industry, first-time demand is expanding rapidly as many new customers enter the market. Typically, an industry grows when customers become familiar with the product, prices fall because experience and scale economies have been attained, and distribution channels develop. The U.S. wireless telephone industry was in the growth stage for most of the 1990s. In 1990, there were only 5 million cellular subscribers in the nation. By 2006, this figure had increased to around 220 million, and overall demand was still growing.

Normally, the importance of control over technological knowledge as a barrier to entry has diminished by the time an industry enters its growth stage. Because few companies have yet achieved significant scale economies or built brand loyalty, other entry barriers tend to be relatively low as well, particularly early in the growth stage. Thus, the threat from potential competitors generally is highest at this point. Paradoxically, however, high growth usually means that new entrants can be absorbed into an industry without a marked increase in the intensity of rivalry. Thus, rivalry tends to be relatively low. Rapid growth in demand enables companies to expand their revenues and profits without taking market share away from competitors. A strategically aware company takes advantage of the relatively benign environment of the growth stage to prepare itself for the intense competition of the coming industry shakeout.

● Industry Shakeout

Explosive growth cannot be maintained indefinitely. Sooner or later, the rate of growth slows, and the industry enters the shakeout stage. In the shakeout stage, demand approaches saturation levels: most of the demand is limited to replacement because there are few potential first-time buyers left.

As an industry enters the shakeout stage, rivalry between companies becomes intense. Typically, companies that have become accustomed to rapid growth continue to add capacity at rates consistent with past growth. However, demand is no longer

FIGURE 2.5

Growth in Demand
and Capacity

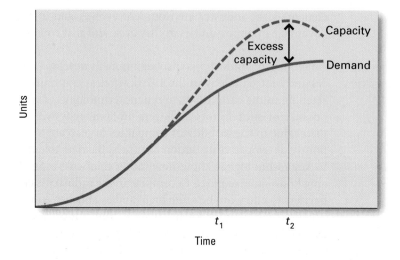

growing at historic rates, and the consequence is the emergence of excess productive capacity. This condition is illustrated in Figure 2.5, where the solid curve indicates the growth in demand over time and the broken curve indicates the growth in productive capacity over time. As you can see, past point t_1, demand growth becomes slower as the industry becomes mature. However, capacity continues to grow until time t_2. The gap between the solid and broken lines signifies excess capacity. In an attempt to use this capacity, companies often cut prices. The result can be a price war, which drives many of the most inefficient companies into bankruptcy and is enough to deter any new entry.

● **Mature Industries**   The shakeout stage ends when the industry enters its mature stage: the market is totally saturated, demand is limited to replacement demand, and growth is low or zero. What growth there is comes from population expansion that brings new customers into the market or an increase in replacement demand.

As an industry enters maturity, barriers to entry increase, and the threat of entry from potential competitors decreases. As growth slows during the shakeout, companies can no longer maintain historic growth rates merely by holding on to their market share. Competition for market share develops, driving down prices and often producing a price war, as has happened in the airline and personal computer industry. To survive the shakeout, companies begin to focus on minimizing costs and building brand loyalty. The airlines, for example, tried to cut operating costs by hiring nonunion labor and to build brand loyalty by introducing frequent-flyer programs. Personal computer companies have sought to build brand loyalty by providing excellent after-sales service and working to lower their cost structures. By the time an industry matures, the surviving companies are those that have brand loyalty and efficient low-cost operations. Because both these factors constitute a significant barrier to entry, the threat of entry by potential competitors is often greatly diminished. High entry barriers in mature industries can give companies the opportunity to increase prices and profits, although this does not always occur.

As a result of the shakeout, most industries in the maturity stage have consolidated and become oligopolies. Examples include the beer industry (see the Opening Case), breakfast cereal industry, and pharmaceutical industry. In mature industries, companies tend to recognize their interdependence and try to avoid price wars. Stable demand gives them the opportunity to enter into price-leadership agreements. The net effect is to reduce the threat of intense rivalry among established companies, thereby allowing greater profitability. Nevertheless, the stability of a mature industry is always threatened by further price wars. A general slump in economic activity can depress industry demand. As companies fight to maintain their revenues in the face of declining demand, price-leadership agreements break down, rivalry increases, and prices and profits fall. The periodic price wars that occur in the airline industry seem to follow this pattern.

● Declining Industries   Eventually, most industries enter a decline stage: growth becomes negative for a variety of reasons, including technological substitution (for example, air travel for rail travel), social changes (greater health consciousness hitting tobacco sales), demographics (the declining birthrate hurting the market for baby and child products), and international competition (low-cost foreign competition pushing the U.S. steel industry into decline). Within a declining industry, the degree of rivalry among established companies usually increases. Depending on the speed of the decline and the height of exit barriers, competitive pressures can become as fierce as in the shakeout stage.[16] The main problem in a declining industry is that falling demand leads to the emergence of excess capacity. In trying to use this capacity, companies begin to cut prices, thus sparking a price war. The U.S. steel industry experienced these problems because steel companies tried to use their excess capacity despite falling demand. The same problem occurred in the airline industry in the 1990–1992 period and again in 2001–2003, as companies cut prices to ensure that they would not be flying with half-empty planes (that is, that they would not be operating with substantial excess capacity). Exit barriers play a part in adjusting excess capacity. The greater the exit barriers, the harder it is for companies to reduce capacity and the greater is the threat of severe price competition.

● Industry Life Cycle   In summary, a third task of industry analysis is to identify the opportunities and threats that are characteristic of different kinds of industry environments in order to develop an effective business model and competitive strategy. Managers have to tailor their strategies to changing industry conditions. And they have to learn to recognize the crucial points in an industry's development so that they can forecast when the shakeout stage of an industry might begin or when an industry might be moving into decline. This is also true at the level of strategic groups because new embryonic groups may emerge as a result of shifts in customer needs and tastes, or some groups may grow rapidly because of changes in technology and others will decline as their customers defect.

Limitations of Models for Industry Analysis

The competitive forces, strategic groups, and life cycle models provide useful ways of thinking about and analyzing the nature of competition within an industry to identify opportunities and threats. However, each has its limitations, and managers need to be aware of their shortcomings.

● Life Cycle Issues   It is important to remember that the industry life cycle model is a generalization. In practice, industry life cycles do not always follow the pattern illustrated in Figure 2.4. In some cases, growth is so rapid that the embryonic stage is skipped altogether. In others, industries fail to get past the embryonic stage. Industry growth can be revitalized after long periods of decline through innovation or social change. For example, the health boom brought the bicycle industry back to life after a long period of decline.

The time span of the stages can also vary significantly from industry to industry. Some industries can stay in maturity almost indefinitely if their products become basic necessities of life, as is the case for the car industry. Other industries skip the mature stage and go straight into decline, as in the case of the vacuum tube industry. Transistors replaced vacuum tubes as a major component in electronic products even though the vacuum tube industry was still in its growth stage. Still other industries may go through several shakeouts before they enter full maturity, as appears to be happening in the telecommunications industry.

● **Innovation and Change**

Over any reasonable length of time, in many industries competition can be viewed as a process driven by innovation.[17] Indeed, innovation is frequently the major factor in industry evolution and causes the movement through the industry life cycle. Innovation is attractive because companies that pioneer new products, processes, or strategies can often earn enormous profits. Consider the explosive growth of Toys "R" Us, Dell Computer, and Wal-Mart. In a variety of different ways, all of these companies were innovators. Toys "R" Us pioneered a new way of selling toys (through large discount warehouse-type stores), Dell pioneered a whole new way of selling personal computers (directly via telephone and then the Web), and Wal-Mart pioneered the low-price discount superstore concept.

Successful innovation can transform the nature of industry competition. In recent decades, one frequent consequence of innovation has been to lower the fixed costs of production, thereby reducing barriers to entry and allowing new and smaller enterprises to compete with large established organizations. For example, two decades ago, large integrated steel companies such as US Steel, LTV, and Bethlehem Steel dominated the steel industry. The industry was a typical oligopoly, dominated by a small number of large producers, in which tacit price collusion was practiced. Then along came a series of efficient mini-mill producers such as Nucor and Chaparral Steel, which used a new technology: electric arc furnaces. Over the past twenty years, they have revolutionized the structure of the industry. What was once a consolidated industry is now much more fragmented and price competitive. The successor company to US Steel, USX, now has only a 12% market share, down from 55% in the mid-1960s, and both Bethlehem and LTV went bankrupt. In contrast, the mini-mills as a group now hold over 40% of the market, up from 5% twenty years ago.[18] Thus, the mini-mill innovation has reshaped the nature of competition in the steel industry.[19] A competitive forces model applied to the industry in 1970 would look very different from a competitive forces model applied in 2004.

Michael Porter, the originator of the competitive forces and strategic group concepts, has explicitly recognized the role of innovation in revolutionizing industry structure. Porter now talks of innovations as "unfreezing" and "reshaping" industry structure. He argues that after a period of turbulence triggered by innovation, the structure of an industry once more settles down into a fairly stable pattern, and the five forces and strategic group concepts can once more be applied.[20] This view of the evolution of industry structure is often referred to as punctuated equilibrium.[21] The punctuated equilibrium view holds that long periods of equilibrium, when an industry's structure is stable, are punctuated by periods of rapid change when industry structure is revolutionized by innovation; there is an unfreezing and refreezing process.

FIGURE 2.6

Punctuated Equilibrium
and Competitive
Structure

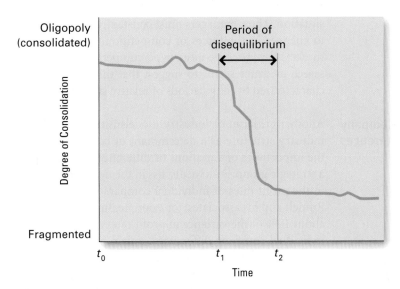

FIGURE 2.6

Punctuated Equilibrium and Competitive Structure

Figure 2.6 shows what punctuated equilibrium might look like for one key dimension of industry structure: competitive structure. From time t_0 to t_1, the competitive structure of the industry is a stable oligopoly, with a few companies sharing the market. At time t_1, a major new innovation is pioneered by either an existing company or a new entrant. The result is a period of turbulence between t_1 and t_2. After a while, the industry settles down into a new state of equilibrium, but now the competitive structure is far more fragmented. Note that the opposite could have happened: the industry could have become more consolidated, although this seems to be less common. In general, innovations seem to lower barriers to entry, allow more companies into the industry, and as a result lead to fragmentation rather than consolidation.

During a period of rapid change when industry structure is being revolutionized by innovation, value typically migrates to business models based on new positioning strategies.[22] In the stockbrokerage industry, value migrated away from the full-service broker model to the online trading model. In the steel industry, the introduction of electric arc technology led to a migration of value away from large, integrated enterprises and toward small mini-mills. In the book-selling industry, value has migrated away from small boutique bricks-and-mortar booksellers toward large bookstore chains like Barnes & Noble and online bookstores such as Amazon.com.

Because the competitive forces and strategic group models are static, they cannot adequately capture what occurs during periods of rapid change in the industry environment when value is migrating. Similarly, a simple view of the industry life cycle does not allow for an industry to repeat a stage or even jump stages that technological upheavals can lead to. Nevertheless, they are useful tools for analyzing industry structure during periods of stability.

Some scholars question the validity of the punctuated equilibrium approach. Richard D'Avani has argued that many industries are hypercompetitive, meaning that they are characterized by permanent and ongoing innovation and competitive change (the computer industry is often cited as an example of a hypercompetitive industry).[23] The structure of such industries is constantly being revolutionized by innovation, so there are no periods of equilibrium or stability. When this is the case, some might argue that the competitive forces and strategic group models are of limited value because they represent no more than snapshots of a constantly changing situation. Thus, managers must constantly repeat industry analysis and pay attention to changes in the forces of competition. Moreover, D'Avani and others claim that markets have become more hypercompetitive in the modern era, although recent research evidence seems to suggest that this is not the case, and many industries are characterized by long periods of relative stability.[24]

● **Company Differences**

Another criticism of industry models is that they overemphasize the importance of industry structure as a determinant of company performance and underemphasize the importance of variations or differences among companies within an industry or a strategic group.[25] As we discuss in the next chapter, there can be enormous variance in the profit rates of individual companies within an industry. Research by Richard Rumelt and his associates, for example, suggests that industry structure explains only about 10% of the variance in profit rates across companies.[26] The implication is that individual company differences explain much of the remainder. Other studies have put the explained variance closer to 20%, which is still not a large figure.[27] Similarly, a growing number of studies have found only weak evidence of a link between strategic group membership and company profit rates, despite the fact that the strategic group model predicts a strong link.[28] Collectively, these studies suggest that the individual resources and capabilities of a company are far more important determinants of its profitability than is the industry or strategic group of which the company is a member. Put differently, there are strong companies in tough industries where average profitability is low (for example, Anheuser-Busch in the beer industry and Dell in the personal computer industry), and weak companies in industries where average profitability is high.

Although these findings do not invalidate the five forces and strategic group models, they do imply that the models are only imperfect predictors of enterprise profitability. A company will not be profitable just because it is based in an attractive industry or strategic group. As we discuss in Chapters 3 and 4, more is required.

The Macroenvironment

Just as the decisions and actions of strategic managers can often change an industry's competitive structure, so too can changing conditions or forces in the wider macroenvironment, that is, the broader economic, global, technological, demographic, social, and political context in which companies and industries are embedded (see Figure 2.7). Changes in the forces in the macroenvironment can have a direct impact on any or all of the forces in Porter's model, thereby altering the relative strength of these forces and, with it, the attractiveness of an industry.

● **Macroeconomic Forces**

Macroeconomic forces affect the general health and well-being of a nation or the regional economy of an organization, which in turn affect companies' and industries' ability to earn an adequate rate of return. The four most important macroeconomic forces are the growth rate of the economy, interest rates, currency exchange rates, and inflation (or deflation) rates. Economic growth, because it leads to an expansion in customer expenditures, tends to produce a general easing of competitive pressures within an industry. This gives companies the opportunity to expand their operations and earn higher profits. Because economic decline (a recession) leads to a reduction in customer expenditures, it increases competitive pressures. Economic decline frequently causes price wars in mature industries.

FIGURE 2.7

The Role of the
Macroenvironment

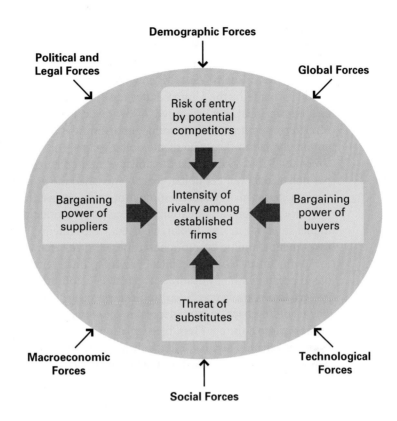

The level of interest rates can determine the demand for a company's products. Interest rates are important whenever customers routinely borrow money to finance their purchase of these products. The most obvious example is the housing market, where mortgage rates directly affect demand. Interest rates also have an impact on the sale of autos, appliances, and capital equipment, to give just a few examples. For companies in such industries, rising interest rates are a threat and falling rates an opportunity.

Interest rates are also important insofar as they influence a company's cost of capital and therefore its ability to raise funds and invest in new assets. The lower interest rates are, the lower will be the cost of capital for companies and the more investment there will be. This is not always a good thing. In the late 1990s, the very low cost of capital allowed dot-com and telecommunications companies with questionable business plans to raise large amounts of money and invest those funds in computers and telecommunications gear (the low cost of capital lowered barriers to entry by enabling start-ups to raise the capital required to circumvent entry barriers). This was initially good for the manufacturers of telecommunications equipment and computers, but the demand signal that was being sent was not sustainable: many of the dot-com and telecommunications start-ups of the 1990s went bankrupt between 2000 and 2002. Secondhand computers and telecommunications equipment from these bankrupt companies flooded the market, depressing first-time demand for that equipment and helping to plunge the computer and telecommunications equipment businesses into a deep slowdown. (For example, in January 2002, Internet auction house eBay listed more than three thousand Cisco products that were being auctioned for much less than their initial prices.)

Currency exchange rates define the value of different national currencies in relation to each other. Movement in currency exchange rates has a direct impact on the competitiveness of a company's products in the global marketplace. For example, when the value of the dollar is low compared with the value of other currencies, products made in the United States are relatively inexpensive and products made overseas are relatively expensive. A low or declining dollar reduces the threat from foreign competitors while creating opportunities for increased sales overseas. For example, the fall in the value of the dollar against the Japanese yen that occurred between 1985 and 1995, when the dollar-to-yen exchange rate declined from 240 yen per dollar to 85 yen per dollar, sharply increased the price of imported Japanese cars, giving U.S. car manufacturers some protection against those imports.

Price inflation can destabilize the economy, producing slower economic growth, higher interest rates, and volatile currency movements. If inflation keeps increasing, investment planning becomes hazardous. The key characteristic of inflation is that it makes the future less predictable. In an inflationary environment, it may be impossible to predict with any accuracy the real value of returns that can be earned from a project five years hence. Such uncertainty makes companies less willing to invest. Their holding back in turn depresses economic activity and ultimately pushes the economy into a slump. Thus, high inflation is a threat to companies.

Price deflation also has a destabilizing effect on economic activity. If prices are deflating, the real price of fixed payments goes up. This is particularly damaging for companies and individuals with a high level of debt who must make regular fixed payments on that debt. In a deflationary environment, the increase in the real value of debt consumes more of household and corporate cash flows, leaving less for other purchases and depressing the overall level of economic activity. Although significant deflation has not been seen since the 1930s, in the 1990s it started to take hold in Japan.

● Global Forces

Enormous changes in the world economic system have occurred over the last half-century. We review these changes in some detail in Chapter 8 when we discuss global strategy. For now, the important points to note are that barriers to international trade and investment have tumbled, and more and more countries are enjoying sustained economic growth. Economic growth in places like Brazil, China, and India is creating large new markets for companies' goods and services and is giving companies an opportunity to grow their profits faster by entering these nations. Falling barriers to international trade and investment have made it much easier to enter foreign nations. For example, twenty years ago, it was almost impossible for a western company to set up operations in China. Today, western and Japanese companies are investing over $50 billion a year in China. By the same token, however, falling barriers to international trade and investment have made it easier for foreign enterprises to enter the domestic markets of many companies (by lowering barriers to entry), thereby increasing the intensity of competition and lowering profitability. Because of these changes, many formerly isolated domestic markets have now become part of a much larger, and more competitive, global marketplace, creating myriad threats and opportunities for companies. We shall return to this topic and discuss it in more detail in Chapter 8.

● Technological Forces

Since World War II, the pace of technological change has accelerated.[29] This has unleashed a process that has been called a "perennial gale of creative destruction."[30] Technological change can make established products obsolete overnight and simultaneously create a host of new product possibilities. Thus, technological change is both creative and destructive—both an opportunity and a threat.

One of the most important impacts of technological change is that it can affect the height of barriers to entry and therefore radically reshape industry structure. The Internet, because it is so pervasive, has the potential for changing the competitive structure of many industries. It often lowers barriers to entry and reduces customer switching costs, changes that tend to increase the intensity of rivalry in an industry and lower both prices and profits.[31] For example, the Internet has lowered barriers to entry into the news industry. Providers of financial news now have to compete for advertising dollars and customer attention with new Internet-based media organizations that sprang up during the 1990s, such as TheStreet.com, the Motley Fool, and Yahoo!'s financial section. The resulting increase in rivalry has given advertisers more choices, enabling them to bargain down the prices that they must pay to media companies. Similarly, in the automobile industry, the ability of customers to comparison-shop for cars online and purchase cars online from a number of distributors such as Auto Nation has increased the ability of customers to find the best value for their money. Customers' increased bargaining power enables them to put downward pressure on car prices and squeeze profits out of the automobile industry.

● **Demographic Forces**

Demographic forces are outcomes of changes in the characteristics of a population, such as age, gender, ethnic origin, race, sexual orientation, and social class. Like the other forces in the general environment, demographic forces present managers with opportunities and threats and can have major implications for organizations. Over the past thirty years, for example, women have entered the work force in increasing numbers. Between 1973 and 2006, the percentage of women in the work force increased from 44 to 60% in the United States (with similar increases in many other developed nations).[32] This dramatic increase has brought issues such as equal pay for equal work and sexual harassment at work to the forefront of issues that managers must address if they are to attract and make full use of the talents of female workers.

Changes in the age distribution of a population are another example of a demographic force that affects managers and organizations. Currently, most industrialized nations are experiencing the aging of their populations as a consequence of falling birth- and deathrates and the aging of the babyboom generation. In Germany, for example, the percentage of the population over age 65 is expected to rise from 15.4% in 1990 to 20.7% in 2010. Comparable figures for Canada are 11.4 and 14.4%; for Japan, 11.7 and 19.5%; and for the United States, 12.6 and 13.5%.[33]

The aging of the population is increasing opportunities for organizations that cater to older people; the home health care and recreation industries, for example, are seeing an upswing in demand for their services. As the babyboom generation from the late 1950s to the early 1960s has aged, it has created a host of opportunities and threats. During the 1980s, many baby boomers were getting married and creating an upsurge in demand for the customer appliances normally bought by couples marrying for the first time. Companies such as Whirlpool Corporation and General Electric capitalized on the resulting upsurge in demand for washing machines, dishwashers, dryers, and the like. In the 1990s, many of these same baby boomers were starting to save for retirement, creating an inflow of money into mutual funds and creating a boom in the mutual fund industry. In the next twenty years, many of these same baby boomers will retire, creating a boom in retirement communities.

● **Social Forces**

Social forces refer to the way in which changing social mores and values affect an industry. Like the other macroenvironmental forces discussed here, social change creates opportunities and threats. One of the major social movements of recent decades has been the trend toward greater health consciousness. Its impact has been immense, and companies that recognized the opportunities early have often reaped significant gains. Philip Morris, for example, capitalized on the growing health consciousness trend when it acquired Miller Brewing Company and then redefined competition in the beer industry with its introduction of low-calorie beer (Miller Lite). Similarly, PepsiCo was able to gain market share from its rival, Coca-Cola, by being the first to introduce diet colas and fruit-based soft drinks. At the same time, the health trend has created a threat for many industries. The tobacco industry, for example, is in decline as a direct result of greater customer awareness of the health implications of smoking.

● **Political and Legal Forces**

Political and legal forces are outcomes of changes in laws and regulations. They result from political and legal developments within society and significantly affect managers and companies.

Political processes shape a society's laws, which constrain the operations of organizations and managers and thus create both opportunities and threats.[34] For example, throughout much of the industrialized world, there has been a strong trend toward deregulation of industries previously controlled by the state and privatization of organizations once owned by the state. In the United States, deregulation of the airline industry in 1979 allowed twenty-nine new airlines to enter the industry between 1979 and 1993. The increase in passenger-carrying capacity after deregulation led to excess capacity on many routes, intense competition, and fare wars. To respond to this more competitive task environment, airlines have had to look for ways to reduce operating costs. The development of hub-and-spoke systems, the rise of nonunion airlines, and the introduction of no-frills discount service are all responses to increased competition in the airlines' task environment. Despite these innovations, the airline industry still experiences intense fare wars, which have lowered profits and caused numerous airline company bankruptcies. The global telecommunications service industry is now experiencing the same kind of turmoil following the deregulation of that industry in the United States and elsewhere.

In most countries, the interplay between political and legal forces, on the one hand, and industry competitive structure, on the other, is a two-way process in which the government sets regulations that influence competitive structure, and firms in an industry often seek to influence the regulations that governments enact by a number of means. First, when permitted, they may provide financial support to politicians or political parties that espouse views favorable to the industry and lobby government legislators directly to shape government regulations. For example, during the 1990s and early 2000s, the now-bankrupt energy trading company Enron lobbied government legislators to persuade them to deregulate energy markets in the United States, an action that Enron would benefit from. Second, companies and industries may lobby the government through industry associations. In 2002, the United States Steel Industry Association was a prime mover in persuading President Bush to enact a 30% tariff on imports of foreign steel into the United States. The purpose of the tariff was to protect American steel makers from foreign competitors, thereby reducing the intensity of rivalry in the United States steel markets.

Summary of Chapter

1. An industry can be defined as a group of companies offering products or services that are close substitutes for each other. Close substitutes are products or services that satisfy the same basic customer needs.

2. The main technique used to analyze competition in the industry environment is the five forces model. The five forces are (1) the risk of new entry by potential competitors, (2) the extent of rivalry among established firms, (3) the bargaining power of buyers, (4) the bargaining power of suppliers, and (5) the threat of substitute products. The stronger each force is, the more competitive the industry and the lower the rate of return that can be earned.

3. The risk of entry by potential competitors is a function of the height of barriers to entry. The higher the barriers to entry are, the lower is the risk of entry and the greater are the profits that can be earned in the industry.

4. The extent of rivalry among established companies is a function of an industry's competitive structure, demand conditions, cost conditions, and barriers to exit. Strong demand conditions moderate the competition among established companies and create opportunities for expansion. When demand is weak, intensive competition can develop, particularly in consolidated industries with high exit barriers.

5. Buyers are most powerful when a company depends on them for business but they themselves are not dependent on the company. In such circumstances, buyers are a threat.

6. Suppliers are most powerful when a company depends on them for business but they themselves are not dependent on the company. In such circumstances, suppliers are a threat.

7. Substitute products are the products of companies serving customer needs similar to the needs served by the industry being analyzed. The more similar the substitute products are to each other, the lower is the price that companies can charge without losing customers to the substitutes.

8. Some argue for a sixth competitive force of some significance: the power, vigor, and competence of complementors. Powerful and vigorous complementors may have a strong positive impact on demand in an industry.

9. Most industries are composed of strategic groups: groups of companies pursuing the same or a similar strategy. Companies in different strategic groups pursue different strategies.

10. The members of a company's strategic group constitute its immediate competitors. Because different strategic groups are characterized by different opportunities and threats, it may pay for a company to switch strategic groups. The feasibility of doing so is a function of the height of mobility barriers.

11. Industries go through a well-defined life cycle: from an embryonic stage, through growth, shakeout, and maturity, and eventually decline. Each stage has different implications for the competitive structure of the industry, and each gives rise to its own set of opportunities and threats.

12. The five forces, strategic group, and industry life cycles models all have limitations. The five forces and strategic group models present a static picture of competition that de-emphasizes the role of innovation. Yet innovation can revolutionize industry structure and completely change the strength of different competitive forces. The five forces and strategic group models have been criticized for de-emphasizing the importance of individual company differences. A company will not be profitable just because it is based in an attractive industry or strategic group; much more is required. The industry life cycle model is a generalization that is not always followed, particularly when innovations revolutionize an industry.

13. The macroenvironment affects the intensity of rivalry within an industry. Included in the macroenvironment are the global environment, the technological environment, the demographic and social environment, and the political and legal environment.

Discussion Questions

1. Under what environmental conditions are price wars most likely to occur in an industry? What are the implications of price wars for a company? How should a company try to deal with the threat of a price war?

2. Discuss Porter's five forces model with reference to what you know about the U.S. beer industry (see the Opening Case). What does the model tell you about the level of competition in this industry?

3. Identify a growth industry, a mature industry, and a declining industry. For each industry, identify the following: (a) the number and size distribution of companies, (b) the nature of barriers to entry, (c) the height of

barriers to entry, and (d) the extent of product differentiation. What do these factors tell you about the nature of competition in each industry? What are the implications for the company in terms of opportunities and threats?

4. Assess the impact of macroenvironmental factors on the likely level of enrollment at your university over the next decade. What are the implications of these factors for the job security and salary level of your professors?

Practicing Strategic Management

SMALL-GROUP EXERCISE
Competing with Microsoft

Break up into groups of three to five and discuss the following scenario. Appoint one group member as a spokesperson who will communicate the groups findings to the class.

You are a group of managers and software engineers at a small start-up. You have developed a revolutionary new operating system for personal computers that offers distinct advantages over Microsoft's Windows operating system: it takes up less memory space on the hard drive of a personal computer; it takes full advantage of the power of the personal computer's microprocessor, and in theory it can run software applications much faster than Windows; it is much easier to install and use than Windows; and it responds to voice instructions with an accuracy of 99.9%, in addition to input from a keyboard or mouse. The operating system is the only product offering that your company has produced.

Complete the following exercises:

1. Analyze the competitive structure of the market for personal computer operating systems. On the basis of this analysis, identify what factors might inhibit adoption of your operating system by customers.
2. Can you think of a strategy that your company might pursue, either alone or in conjunction with other enterprises, in order to beat Microsoft? What will it take to execute that strategy successfully?

ARTICLE FILE 2

Find an example of an industry that has become more competitive in recent years. Identify the reasons for the increase in competitive pressure.

STRATEGIC MANAGEMENT PROJECT
Module 2

This module requires you to analyze the industry environment in which your company is based using the information you have already gathered:

1. Apply the five forces model to the industry in which your company is based. What does this model tell you about the nature of competition in the industry?
2. Are any changes taking place in the macroenvironment that might have an impact, positive or negative, on the industry in which your company is based? If so, what are these changes, and how might they affect the industry?
3. Identify any strategic groups that might exist in the industry. How does the intensity of competition differ across these strategic groups?
4. How dynamic is the industry in which your company is based? Is there any evidence that innovation is reshaping competition or has done so in the recent past?
5. In what stage of its life cycle is the industry in which your company is based? What are the implications of this for the intensity of competition both now and in the future?
6. Is your company based in an industry that is becoming more global? If so, what are the implications of this change for competitive intensity?
7. Analyze the impact of national context as it pertains to the industry in which your company is based. Does national context help or hinder your company in achieving a competitive advantage in the global marketplace?

ETHICS EXERCISE

In the summer of 2006, word began to spread about a new type of beer soon to hit the market—a beer that answered the low-carb, aftertaste, and calorie concerns of today's beer drinkers all at once. Although a number of beers focusing on one issue, such as low-carb concerns, had recently been released, a beer addressing all three concerns at once could blow the market wide open. Chris, a long-time employee of the company behind the new beer, began to formulate a plan.

Over the next week, Chris spent much of his time chatting with a mid-level secretary named Clare. "Listen, Clare, we've both worked here a long time, and what have they shown us in the way of appreciation? Have you been promoted at all? I haven't had a raise since 2001! This is our chance, Clare! Our chance to really make some money and stick it to the higher-ups at the same time!" By Friday afternoon, Chris could see that Clare was on board. She agreed to come in over the weekend and, using an executive assistant's set of keys, find and copy the new beer formula.

Chris and Clare's plan seemed perfect. Clare had copied the necessary documents, and Chris, through a friend working at a rival brewery, had set up a meeting with one of the company's many executives. At the meeting a few days later, the executive expressed great interest in buying the formula at significant profit to its sellers, and Chris and Clare began to get excited. Much to their surprise, on Thursday morning, security met Chris and Clare as they entered the building in which they worked. The executive at the rival brewery had notified their superiors and the game was up!

1. Discuss the ethical dilemma presented in this case.
2. Why do you think the rival brewery notified the brewery at which Chris and Clare worked rather than taking the formula and using it to its own advantage?
3. What do you think the brewery at which Chris and Clare worked might do to ensure that it is protected against actions such as that taken by Chris and Clare?

CLOSING CASE

The Pharmaceutical Industry

Historically, the pharmaceutical industry has been a profitable one. Between 2002 and 2006, the average rate of return on invested capital (ROIC) for firms in the industry was 16.45%. Put differently, for every dollar of capital invested in the industry, the average pharmaceutical firm generated 16.45 cents of profit. This compares with an average return on invested capital of 12.76% for firms in the computer hardware industry, 8.54% for grocers, and 3.88% for firms in the electronics industry. However, the average level of profitability in the pharmaceutical industry has been declining of late. In 2002, the average ROIC in the industry was 21.6%; by 2006, it had fallen to 14.5%.

The profitability of the pharmaceutical industry can be best understood by looking at several aspects of its underlying economic structure. First, demand for pharmaceuticals has been strong and has grown for decades. Between 1990 and 2003, there was a 12.5% annual increase in spending on prescription drugs in the United States. This growth was driven by favorable demographics. As people grow older, they tend to need and consume more prescription medicines, and the population in most advanced nations has been growing older as the post–World War II baby-boom generation ages. Looking forward, projections suggest that spending on prescription drugs will increase between 10 and 11% annually through 2013.

Second, successful new prescription drugs can be extraordinarily profitable. Lipitor, the cholesterol-lowering drug sold by Pfizer, was introduced in 1997, and by 2005, this drug had generated a staggering $12.2 billion in annual sales for Pfizer. The costs of manufacturing, packing, and distributing Lipitor amounted to only about 10% of revenues. Pfizer spent close to $500 million on promoting Lipitor and perhaps as much again on maintaining a sales force to sell the product. That still left Pfizer with a gross profit of perhaps $10 billion. Since the drug is protected from direct competition by a twenty-year patent, Pfizer has a temporary monopoly and can charge a high price. Once the patent expires, which is scheduled to occur in 2010, other firms will be able to produce generic versions of Lipitor and the price will fall—typically by 80% within a year.

Competing firms can produce drugs that are similar (but not identical) to a patent-protected drug. Drug firms patent a specific molecule, and competing firms can patent similar, but not identical, molecules that have a similar pharmacological effect. Thus, Lipitor does have competitors in the market for cholesterol-lowering drugs, such as Zocor sold by Merck and Crestor sold by AstraZeneca. But these competing drugs are also patent-protected. Moreover, the high costs and risks associated with developing a new drug and bringing it to market limit new competition. Out of every five thousand compounds tested in the laboratory by a drug company, only five enter clinical trials, and only one of these will ultimately make it to the market. On average, estimates suggest that it costs some $800 million and takes anywhere from ten to fifteen years to bring a new drug to market. Once on the market, only three out of ten drugs ever recoup their R&D and marketing costs and turn a profit. Thus, the high profitability of the pharmaceutical industry rests on a handful of blockbuster drugs. At Pfizer, the world's largest pharmaceutical company, 55% of revenues were generated from just eight drugs.

To produce a blockbuster, a drug company must spend large amounts of money on research, most of which fails to produce a product. Only very large companies can shoulder the costs and risks of doing so, making it difficult for new companies to enter the industry. Pfizer, for example, spent some $7.44 billion on R&D in 2005 alone, equivalent to 14.5% of its total revenues. In a testament to just how difficult it is to get into the industry, although a large number of companies have been started in the last twenty years in the hope that they might develop new pharmaceuticals, only two of these companies, Amgen and Genentech, were ranked among the top twenty in the industry in terms of sales in 2005. Most have failed to bring a product to market.

In addition to R&D spending, the incumbent firms in the pharmaceutical industry spend large amounts of money on advertising and sales promotion. While the $500 million a year that Pfizer spends promoting Lipitor is small relative to the drug's revenues, it is a large amount for a new competitor to match, making market entry difficult unless the competitor has a significantly better product.

There are also some big opportunities on the horizon for firms in the industry. New scientific breakthroughs in genomics are holding out the promise that within the next decade, pharmaceutical firms might be able to bring new drugs to market that treat some of the most intractable medical conditions, including Alzheimer's, Parkinson's disease, cancer, heart disease, stroke, and AIDS.

However, there are some threats to the long-term dominance and profitability of industry giants like Pfizer. First, as spending on health care rises, politicians are looking for ways to limit health care costs, and one possibility is some form of price control on prescription drugs. Price controls are already in effect in most developed nations, and although they have not yet been introduced in the United States, they could be.

Second, between 2006 and 2009, twelve of the top thirty-five selling drugs in the industry will loose their patent protection. By one estimate, some 28% of the global drug industry's sales of $307 billion will be exposed to generic challenge in America alone, due to drugs going off patent between 2006 and 2012. It is not clear to many industry observers whether the established drug companies have enough new drug prospects in their pipelines to replace revenues from drugs going off patent. Moreover, generic drug companies have been aggressive in challenging the patents of proprietary drug companies and in pricing their generic offerings. As a result, their share of industry sales has been growing. In 2005, they accounted for more than half of all drugs prescribed by volume in the United States, up from one-third in 1990.

Third, the industry has come under renewed scrutiny following studies showing that some FDA-approved prescription drugs, known as COX-2 inhibitors, were associated with a greater risk of heart attacks. Two of these drugs, Vioxx and Bextra, were pulled from the market in 2004.[35]

Case Discussion Questions

1. Drawing on the five forces model, explain why the pharmaceutical industry has historically been a very profitable industry.

2. After 2002, the profitability of the industry, measured by ROIC, started to decline. Why do you think this occurred?

3. What are the prospects for the industry in the future? What are the opportunities? What are the threats? What must pharmaceutical firms do to exploit the opportunities and counter the threats?

Internal Analysis: Distinctive Competencies, Competitive Advantage, and Profitability

OPENING CASE

Southwest Airlines

Southwest Airlines has long been one of the standout performers in the U.S. airline industry. It is famous for its low fares, which are often about 30% beneath those of its major rivals. These are balanced by an even lower cost structure, which has enabled it to record superior profitability even in bad years such as 2002, when the industry faced slumping demand in the wake of the September 11 terrorist attacks. Indeed, during 2001 to 2005, quite possibly the worst four years in the history of the airline industry, when every other major airline lost money, Southwest made money every year and earned a return on invested capital of 5.8%.

What is the source of Southwest's competitive advantage? Many people immediately point to the company's business model and low cost structure. With regard to their business model, while operators like American Airlines and United route passengers through congested hubs, Southwest Airlines flies point-to-point, often through smaller airports. By competing in a way that other airlines do not, Southwest has found that it can capture enough demand to keep its planes full. Moreover, because it avoids many hubs, Southwest has experienced fewer delays. In the first eight months of 2006, Southwest planes arrived on schedule 80% of the time, compared to 76% at United and 74% at Continental.

As for Southwest's low cost structure, this has a number of sources. Unlike most airlines, Southwest flies only one type of plane, the Boeing 737. This reduces training costs, maintenance costs, and inventory costs while increasing efficiency in crew and flight scheduling. The operation is nearly ticketless and there is no seat assignment, which reduces cost and back-office accounting functions. There are no meals or movies in flight, and the airline will not transfer baggage to other airlines, reducing the need for baggage handlers.

The most important source of the company's low cost structure, however, seems to be very high employee productivity. One way airlines measure employee productivity is by the ratio of employees to passengers carried. According to figures from company 10-K statements, in 2005, Southwest had an employee-to-passenger ratio of 1 to 2,400, the best in the industry. By comparison, the ratio at United Airlines during 2005 was 1 to 1,175 and at Continental, it was 1 to

1,125. These figures suggest that holding size constant, Southwest runs its operation with far fewer people than competitors. How does it do this?

First, Southwest devotes enormous attention to the people it hires. On average, the company hires only 3% of those interviewed in a year. When hiring, it emphasizes teamwork and a positive attitude. Southwest rationalizes that skills can be taught but a positive attitude and a willingness to pitch in cannot. Southwest also creates incentives for its employees to work hard. All employees are covered by a profit-sharing plan, and at least 25% of an employee's share of the profit-sharing plan has to be invested in Southwest Airlines stock. This gives rise to a simple formula: the harder employees work, the more profitable Southwest becomes, and the richer the employees get. The results are clear. At other airlines, one would never see a

pilot helping to check passengers onto the plane. At Southwest, pilots and flight attendants have been known to help clean the aircraft and check in passengers at the gate. They do this to turn around an aircraft as quickly as possible and get it into the air again because an aircraft doesn't make money when it is sitting on the ground. This flexible and motivated work force leads to higher productivity and reduces the company's need for more employees.

Second, because Southwest because flies point-to-point rather than through congested airport hubs, there is no need for dozens of gates and thousands of employees to handle banks of flights that come in and then disperse within a two-hour window, leaving the hub empty until the next flights a few hours later. The result: Southwest can operate with far fewer employees than airlines that fly through hubs.[1]

OVERVIEW

Why, within a particular industry or market, do some companies outperform others? What is the basis of their (sustained) competitive advantage? The Opening Case provides some clues. The competitive advantage of Southwest Airlines comes from efficiency, customer responsiveness, and reliability. Southwest's efficiency is primarily due to high labor productivity, which translates into lower operating costs. Southwest is responsive to customers because it flies point-to-point, and does not force passengers to fly through congested hubs that might lengthen their journey. Southwest is more reliable because a greater proportion of its flights arrive on time, in part because the company tries to avoid congested hubs, and partly because the company's flexible work force can turn around a plane at the gate in fifteen minutes, making sure that planes that arrive late leave closer to their scheduled departure time. As you will see in this chapter, efficiency, customer responsiveness, and reliability, which is an aspect of product quality, are three of the four main building blocks of competitive advantage. The other building block is innovation.

This chapter focuses on internal analysis, which is concerned with identifying the strengths and weaknesses of the company. Together with an analysis of the company's external environment, internal analysis gives managers the information they need to choose the business model and strategies that will enable their company to attain a sustained competitive advantage. Internal analysis is a three-step process. First, managers must understand the process by which companies create value for customers and profit for themselves, and they need to understand the role of resources, capabilities, and distinctive competencies in this process. Second, they need to understand how important superior efficiency, innovation, quality, and customer responsiveness are in creating value and generating high profitability. Third, they must be able to analyze the sources of their company's competitive advantage to identify what is driving the profitability of their enterprise and where opportunities for improvement might lie. In other words, they must be able to identify how the strengths of the enterprise boost its profitability and how any weaknesses lead to lower profitability.

Three more critical issues in internal analysis are addressed in this chapter. First, what factors influence the durability of competitive advantage? Second, why do successful companies often lose their competitive advantage? Third, how can companies avoid competitive failure and sustain their competitive advantage over time?

After reading this chapter, you will understand the nature of competitive advantage and why managers need to perform internal analysis, just as they must conduct industry analysis, to achieve superior performance and profitability.

The Roots of Competitive Advantage

A company has a *competitive advantage* over its rivals when its profitability is greater than the average profitability of all companies in its industry. It has a *sustained competitive advantage* when it is able to maintain above-average profitability over a number of years, as Dell has done in the personal computer industry and Southwest Airlines has done in the airline industry. The primary objective of strategy is to achieve a sustained competitive advantage, which in turn will result in superior profitability and profit growth. What are the sources of competitive advantage, and what is the link among strategy, competitive advantage, and profitability?

● **Distinctive Competencies**

Competitive advantage is based on distinctive competencies. **Distinctive competencies** are firm-specific strengths that allow a company to differentiate its products from those offered by rivals, and/or achieve substantially lower costs than its rivals. Southwest Airlines, for example, has a distinctive competence in managing its work force, which leads to higher employee productivity and lower costs (see the Opening Case). Similarly, it can be argued that Toyota, which is the standard outperformer in the automobile industry, has distinctive competencies in the development and operation of manufacturing processes. Toyota pioneered a whole range of manufacturing techniques, such as just-in-time inventory systems, self-managing teams, and reduced setup times for complex equipment. These competencies, collectively known as the Toyota lean production system, helped it attain superior efficiency and product quality, which are the basis of its competitive advantage in the global automobile industry.[2] Distinctive competencies arise from two complementary sources: resources and capabilities.[3]

RESOURCES **Resources** refer to the assets of a company. A company's resources can be divided into two types: tangible and intangible. **Tangible resources** are physical entities, such as land, buildings, plant, equipment, inventory, and money. **Intangible resources** are nonphysical entities that are created by managers and other employees, such as brand names; the reputation of the company; the knowledge that employees have gained through experience; and the intellectual property of the company, including intellectual property protected through patents, copyrights, and trademarks.

Resources are particularly valuable when they enable a company to create strong demand for its products and/or to lower its costs. Toyota's valuable tangible resources include the equipment associated with its lean production system, much of which has been engineered specifically by Toyota for exclusive use in its factories. These valuable tangible resources allow Toyota to lower its costs relative to competitors. Similarly, Microsoft has a number of valuable intangible resources, including its brand name and the software code that underlies its Windows operating system. These valuable resources allow Microsoft to sell more of its products, relative to competitors.

Valuable resources are more likely to lead to a sustainable competitive advantage if they are rare, in the sense that competitors do not possess them, and difficult for rivals to imitate; that is, if there are *barriers to imitation* (we will discuss the source of barriers to imitation in more detail later in this chapter). For example, the software code underlying Windows is rare because only Microsoft has full access to it. The code is also difficult to imitate. A rival cannot simply copy the software code underlying Windows and sell its own version of Windows because the code is protected by copyright law, and copying it is illegal. Similarly, Toyota's specialized production equipment is rare (only Toyota has it), and it is difficult for competitors to imitate because Toyota does not allow competitors to examine the details of that equipment.

CAPABILITIES   **Capabilities** refer to a company's skills at coordinating its resources and putting them to productive use. These skills reside in an organization's rules, routines, and procedures, that is, the style or manner through which it makes decisions and manages its internal processes to achieve organizational objectives.[4] More generally, a company's capabilities are the product of its organizational structure, processes, control systems and hiring systems. They specify how and where decisions are made within a company, the kind of behaviors the company rewards, and the company's cultural norms and values. (We discuss how organizational structure and control systems help a company obtain capabilities in Chapters 12 and 13.) Capabilities are intangible. They reside not so much in individuals as in the way individuals interact, cooperate, and make decisions within the context of an organization.[5]

Like resources, capabilities are particularly valuable if they enable a company to create strong demand for its products and/or to lower its costs. The competitive advantage of Southwest Airlines is based in large part on its capability to select, motivate, and manage its work force in such a way that leads to high employee productivity and lower costs (see the Opening Case). As with resources, valuable capabilities are also more likely to lead to a sustainable competitive advantage if they are both rare and protected from copying by barriers to imitation.

RESOURCES, CAPABILITIES, AND COMPETENCIES   The distinction between resources and capabilities is critical to understanding what generates a distinctive competency. A company may have firm-specific and valuable resources, but unless it has the capability to use those resources effectively, it may not be able to create a distinctive competency. It is also important to recognize that a company may not need firm-specific and valuable resources to establish a distinctive competency so long as it does have capabilities that no competitor possesses. For example, the steel mini-mill operator Nucor is widely acknowledged to be the most cost-efficient steel maker in the United States. Its distinctive competency in low-cost steel making does not come from any firm-specific and valuable resources. Nucor has the same resources (plant, equipment, skilled employees, know-how) as many other mini-mill operators. What distinguishes Nucor is its unique capability to manage its resources in a highly productive way. Specifically, Nucor's structure, control systems, and culture promote efficiency at all levels within the company.

In sum, for a company to have a distinctive competency, it must, at a minimum, have either (1) a firm-specific and valuable resource and the capabilities (skills) necessary to take advantage of that resource or (2) a firm-specific capability to manage resources (as exemplified by Nucor). A company's distinctive competency is strongest

FIGURE 3.1

Strategy, Resources, Capabilities, and Competencies

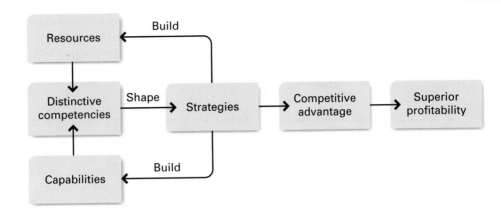

when it possesses both firm-specific and valuable resources and firm-specific capabilities to manage those resources.

THE ROLE OF STRATEGY Figure 3.1 illustrates the relationship of a company's strategies, distinctive competencies, and competitive advantage. Distinctive competencies shape the strategies that the company pursues, which lead to competitive advantage and superior profitability. However, it is also very important to realize that the strategies a company adopts can build new resources and capabilities or strengthen the existing resources and capabilities of the company, thereby enhancing the distinctive competencies of the enterprise. Thus, the relationship between distinctive competencies and strategies is not a linear one; rather, it is a reciprocal one in which distinctive competencies shape strategies, and strategies help to build and create distinctive competencies.[6]

The history of The Walt Disney Company since the 1980s illustrates the way this process works. In the early 1980s, Disney suffered a string of poor financial years that culminated in a 1984 management shakeup when Michael Eisner was appointed CEO. Four years later, Disney's sales had increased from $1.66 billion to $3.75 billion, its net profits had increased from $98 million to $570 million, and its stock market valuation had increased from $1.8 billion to $10.3 billion. What brought about this transformation was the company's deliberate attempt to use its resources and capabilities more aggressively: Disney's enormous film library, its brand name, and its filmmaking skills, particularly in animation. Under Eisner, many old Disney classics were re-released, first in movie theaters and then on video, earning the company millions in the process. Then Eisner reintroduced the product that had originally made Disney famous: the full-length animated feature. Putting together its brand name and in-house animation capabilities, Disney produced a stream of major box office hits, including *The Little Mermaid, Beauty and the Beast, Aladdin, Pocahontas,* and *The Lion King.* Disney also started a cable television channel, the Disney Channel, to use this library and capitalize on the company's brand name. In other words, Disney's existing resources and capabilities shaped its strategies.

Through his choice of strategies, Eisner also developed new competencies in different parts of the business. In the filmmaking arm of Disney, for example, Eisner created a new low-cost film division under the Touchstone label, and the company had a string of low-budget box office hits. It entered into a long-term agreement with the computer animation company Pixar to develop a competency in computer-generated animated films. This strategic collaboration produced several hits, including *Toy Story* and *Monsters Incorporated* (in 2004, Disney acquired Pixar). In sum, Disney's transformation was based not only on strategies that took advantage of the company's existing resources and capabilities but also on strategies that built new resources and capabilities, such as those that underlie the company's competency in computer-generated animated films.

● **Competitive Advantage, Value Creation, and Profitability**

Competitive advantage leads to superior profitability. At the most basic level, how profitable a company becomes depends on three factors: (1) the value customers place on the company's products, (2) the price that a company charges for its products, and (3) the costs of creating those products. The value customers place on a product reflects the utility they get from a product, the happiness or satisfaction gained from consuming or owning the product. Utility must be distinguished from price. Utility is something that customers get from a product. It is a function of the attributes of the product, such as its performance, design, quality, and point-of-sale and after-sale service. For example, most customers would place a much higher utility value on a top-end Lexus car from Toyota than on a low-end basic economy car from General Motors (they would value it more) precisely because they perceive the Lexus to have better performance and superior design, quality, and service. A company that strengthens the utility (or value) of its products in the eyes of customers has more pricing options: it can raise prices to reflect that utility (value) or hold prices lower to induce more customers to purchase its products, thereby expanding unit sales volume.

Whatever pricing option a company chooses, however, the price a company charges for a good or service is typically less than the utility value placed on that good or service by the customer because the customer captures some of that utility in the form of what economists call a consumer surplus.[7] The customer is able to do this because the company is competing with other companies for the customer's business, so the company must charge a lower price than it could were it a monopoly supplier. Moreover, it is normally impossible to segment the market to such a degree that the company can charge each customer a price that reflects that individual's unique assessment of the utility of a product—what economists refer to as a customer's reservation price. For these reasons, the price that gets charged tends to be less than the utility value placed on the product by many customers. Nevertheless, remember the basic principle here: the more utility that consumers get from a company's products or services, the more pricing options the company has.

These concepts are illustrated in Figure 3.2: *U* is the average utility value per unit of a product to a customer, *P* is the average price per unit that the company decides

FIGURE 3.2

Value Creation per Unit

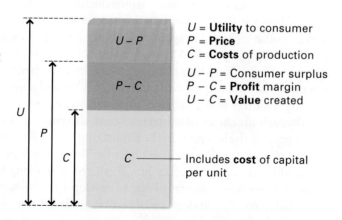

U = **Utility** to consumer
P = **Price**
C = **Costs** of production

$U - P$ = Consumer surplus
$P - C$ = **Profit** margin
$U - C$ = **Value** created

C ——— Includes **cost** of capital per unit

to charge for that product, and C is the average unit cost of producing that product (including actual production costs and the cost of capital investments in production systems). The company's average profit per unit is equal to $P - C$, and the consumer surplus is equal to $U - P$. In other words, $U - P$ is a measure of the value the consumer captures, and $P - C$ is a measure of the value the company captures. The company makes a profit so long as P is more than C, and its profitability will be greater the lower C is relative to P. Bear in mind that the difference between U and P is in part determined by the intensity of competitive pressure in the marketplace; the lower the intensity of competitive pressure, the higher the price that can be charged relative to U, but the difference between U and P is also determined by the company's pricing choice.[8] As we shall see, a company may choose to keep prices low relative to volume because lower prices enable the company to sell more products, attain scale economies, and boost its profit margin by lowering C relative to P.

Note also that the value created by a company is measured by the difference between the utility a consumer gets from the product (U) and the costs of production (C), that is, $U - C$. A company creates value by converting factors of production that cost C into a product from which customers get a utility of U. A company can create more value for its customers by lowering C or making the product more attractive through superior design, performance, quality, service, and the like. When customers assign a greater utility to the product (U increases), they are willing to pay a higher price (P increases). This discussion suggests that a company has a competitive advantage and high profitability when it creates more value for its customers than its rivals do.[9]

The company's pricing options are captured in Figure 3.3. Suppose a company's current pricing option is the one pictured in the middle column of Figure 3.3. Imagine that the company decides to pursue strategies to increase the utility of its product offering from U to U^* in order to boost its profitability. Increasing utility initially raises production costs because the company has to spend money to increase product performance, quality, service, and other factors. Now there are two different pricing options that the company can pursue. Option 1 is to raise prices to reflect the higher utility: the company raises prices more than its costs increase, and profit per unit ($P - C$) increases. Option 2 involves a very different set of choices: the company lowers

FIGURE 3.3

Value Creation and
Pricing Options

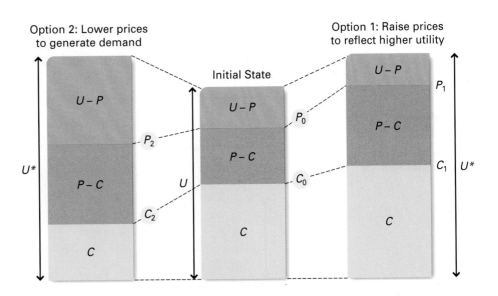

prices in order to expand unit volume. Basically, what is happening is that customers recognize that they are getting a great bargain because price is now much lower than utility (the consumer surplus has increased), so they rush out to buy more (demand has increased). As unit volume expands due to increased demand, the company is able to realize scale economies and reduce its average unit costs. Although creating the extra utility initially costs more and prices are now lowered, profit margins widen because the average unit costs of production fall as volume increases and scale economies are attained.

Managers need to understand the dynamic relationships among utility, pricing, demand, and costs and make decisions on the basis of that understanding to maximize competitive advantage and profitability. Option 2 in Figure 3.3, for example, might not be a viable strategy if demand did not increase rapidly with lower prices or if there are few economies of scale to be had by increasing volume. Managers must understand how value creation and pricing decisions affect demand and also how unit costs change with increases in volume. In other words, they must have a good grasp of the demand for the company's product and its cost structure at different levels of output if they are to make decisions that maximize profitability.

Consider the automobile industry. According to a 2006 study by Harbour & Associates, in 2005, Toyota made $1,200 in profit on every vehicle it manufactured in North America. General Motors, in contrast, lost $2,496 on every vehicle it made.[10] What accounts for the difference? First, Toyota has the best reputation for quality in the industry. According to annual surveys issued by J. D. Power and Associates, Toyota consistently tops the list in terms of quality, while GM cars are at best in the middle of the pack. The higher quality translates into a higher utility and allows Toyota to charge 5 to 10% higher prices than General Motors for equivalent cars. Second, Toyota has a lower cost per vehicle than General Motors in part because of its superior labor productivity. For example, in Toyota's North American plants, it took an average of 29.40 employee hours to build a car, compared to 33.19 at GM plants in North America. That 3.49 hour productivity advantage translates into much lower labor costs for Toyota and, hence, a lower overall cost structure. Therefore, as summarized in Figure 3.4, Toyota's advantage over GM derives from greater utility (U), which has allowed the company to charge a higher price (P) for its cars, and from a lower cost structure (C), which taken together implies significantly greater profitability per vehicle (P − C).

Toyota's decisions with regard to pricing are guided by its managers' understanding of the relationship of utility, prices, demand, and costs. Given its ability to build more utility into its products, Toyota could have charged even higher prices

FIGURE 3.4

Comparing Toyota and General Motors

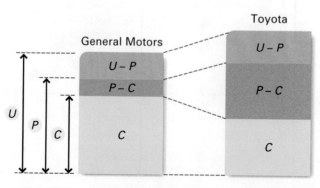

than illustrated in Figure 3.4, but that might have led to lower sales volume, fewer scale economies, higher unit costs, and lower profit margins. Toyota's managers have sought to find the pricing option that enables the company to maximize its profits given their assessment of demand for its products and its cost function. Thus, to create superior value, a company does not have to have the lowest cost structure in an industry or create the product with the highest utility in the eyes of customers. All that is necessary is that the gap between perceived utility (U) and costs of production (C) is greater than the gap attained by competitors.

Note that Toyota has differentiated itself from General Motors by its superior quality, which allows it to charge higher prices, and its superior productivity translates into a lower cost structure. Thus, its competitive advantage over General Motors is the result of strategies that have led to distinctive competencies, resulting in greater differentiation and a lower cost structure.

Indeed, at the heart of any company's business model is the combination of congruent strategies aimed at creating distinctive competencies that (1) differentiate its products in some way so that its consumers derive more utility from them, which gives the company more pricing options, and (2) result in a lower cost structure, which also gives it a broader range of pricing choices.[11] Achieving a sustained competitive advantage and superior profitability requires the right choices with regard to utility through differentiation and pricing given the demand conditions in the company's market and the company's cost structure at different levels of output. This issue is addressed in detail in the following chapters.

The Value Chain

All of the functions of a company—such as production, marketing, product development, service, information systems, materials management, and human resources-have a role in lowering the cost structure and increasing the perceived utility (value) of the products through differentiation. As the first step in examining this concept, consider the value chain, which is illustrated in Figure 3.5.[12] The term **value chain** refers to the idea that a company is a chain of activities for transforming inputs into outputs that customers value. The transformation process involves a number of primary activities and support activities that add value to the product.

● **Primary Activities**   **Primary activities** have to do with the design, creation, and delivery of the product; its marketing; and its support and after-sales service. In the value chain illustrated in

FIGURE 3.5

The Value Chain

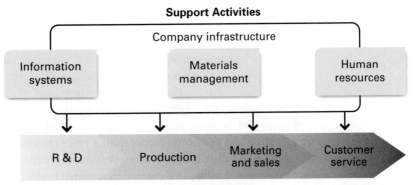

Figure 3.5, the primary activities are broken down into four functions: research and development (R&D), production, marketing and sales, and customer service.

RESEARCH AND DEVELOPMENT   **Research and development** is concerned with the design of products and production processes. Although we think of R&D as being associated with the design of physical products and production processes in manufacturing enterprises, many service companies also undertake R&D. For example, banks compete with each other by developing new financial products and new ways of delivering those products to customers. Online banking and smart debit cards are two recent examples of the fruits of new-product development in the banking industry. Earlier examples of innovation in the banking industry were ATM machines, credit cards, and debit cards.

By creating superior product design, R&D can increase the functionality of products, which makes them more attractive to customers, thereby adding value. Alternatively, the work of R&D may result in more efficient production processes, thereby lowering production costs. Either way, the R&D function can help to lower costs or raise the utility of a product and permit a company to charge higher prices. At Intel, for example, R&D creates value by developing ever more powerful microprocessors and helping to pioneer ever more efficient manufacturing processes (in conjunction with equipment suppliers).

It is important to emphasize that R&D is not just about enhancing the features and functions of a product; it is also about the elegance of a product's design, which can create an impression of superior value in the minds of consumers. For example, part of the success of Apple Computer's iPod player has been based on the elegance and appeal of the iPod design, which has turned this piece of electronic equipment into a fashion accessory. For another example of how design elegance can create value, see Strategy in Action 3.1, which discusses value creation at the fashion house, Burberry.

PRODUCTION   **Production** is concerned with the creation of a good or service. For physical products, when we talk about production, we generally mean manufacturing. For services such as banking or retail operations, production typically takes place when the service is delivered to the customer, as when a bank makes a loan to a customer. By performing its activities efficiently, the production function of a company helps to lower its cost structure. For example, the efficient production operations of Honda and Toyota help those automobile companies achieve higher profitability relative to competitors such as General Motors. The production function can also perform its activities in a way that is consistent with high product quality, which leads to differentiation (and higher value) and lower costs.

MARKETING AND SALES   There are several ways in which the marketing and sales functions of a company can help to create value. Through brand positioning and advertising, the marketing function can increase the value that customers perceive to be contained in a company's product (and thus the utility they attribute to the product). Insofar as these help to create a favorable impression of the company's product in the minds of customers, they increase utility. For example, in the 1980s, the French company Perrier persuaded U.S. customers that slightly carbonated bottled water was worth $1.50 per bottle rather than a price closer to the $0.50 that it cost to collect, bottle, and distribute the water. Perrier's marketing function essentially increased the perception of utility that customers ascribed to the product. Similarly, by helping to rebrand the company and its product offering, the marketing department at Burberry

Strategy in Action   3.1

Value Creation at Burberry

When Rose Marie Bravo, the highly regarded president of Saks Fifth Avenue, announced in 1997 that she was leaving to become CEO of ailing British fashion house Burberry, people thought she was crazy. Burberry, best known as a designer of raincoats with their trademark tartan linings, had been described as an outdated, stuffy business with a fashion cachet of almost zero. When she stepped down in 2006, Bravo was heralded in Britain and the United States as one of the world's best managers. In her tenure at Burberry, she had engineered a remarkable turnaround, leading a transformation of Burberry into what one commentator called an "achingly hip" high-end fashion brand whose famous tartan bedecks everything from raincoats to bikinis, and handbags to luggage in a riot of color from pink to blue to purple. In less than a decade, Burberry had become one of the most valuable luxury fashion brands in the world.

When asked how she achieved the transformation, Bravo explains that there was hidden value in the brand that was unleashed by constant creativity and innovation. Bravo hired world-class designers to redesign Burberry's tired fashion line and bought in Christopher Bailey, one of the very best, to lead the design team. The marketing department worked closely with advertisers to develop hip ads that would appeal to a younger well-heeled audience. The ads featured supermodel Kate Moss promoting the line, and Burberry hired a top fashion photographer to shoot Moss in Burberry. Burberry exercised tight control over distribution, pulling its products from stores whose image was not consistent with the Burberry brand, and expanding its own chain of Burberry stores.

Bravo also noted that "creativity doesn't just come from designers . . . ideas can come from the sales floor, the marketing department, even from accountants, believe it or not. People at whatever level they are working have a point of view and have something to say that is worth listening to." Bravo emphasized the importance of teamwork. "One of the things I think people overlook is the quality of the team. It isn't one person, and it isn't two people. It is a whole group of people—a team that works cohesively towards a goal—that makes something happen or not." She notes that her job is to build the team and then motivate them, "keeping them on track, making sure that they are following the vision."[a]

helped to create value (see Strategy in Action 3.1). Marketing and sales can also create value by discovering customer needs and communicating them back to the R&D function of the company, which can then design products that better match those needs.

CUSTOMER SERVICE. The role of the service function of an enterprise is to provide after-sales service and support. This function can create superior utility by solving customer problems and supporting customers after they have purchased the product. For example, Caterpillar, the U.S.-based manufacturer of heavy earthmoving equipment, can get spare parts to any point in the world within twenty-four hours, thereby minimizing the amount of downtime its customers have to face if their Caterpillar equipment malfunctions. This is an extremely valuable support capability in an industry where downtime is very expensive. It has helped to increase the utility that customers associate with Caterpillar products, and thus the price that Caterpillar can charge for its products.

● Support Activities   The **support activities** of the value chain provide inputs that allow the primary activities to take place. These activities are broken down into four functions: materials management (or logistics), human resources, information systems, and company infrastructure (see Figure 3.5).

MATERIALS MANAGEMENT (LOGISTICS) The materials-management (or logistics) function controls the transmission of physical materials through the value chain, from procurement through production and into distribution. The efficiency with which this is carried out can significantly lower cost, thereby creating more value. Dell Computer has a very efficient materials-management process. By tightly controlling the flow of component parts from its suppliers to its assembly plants, and into the hands of consumers, Dell has dramatically reduced its inventory holding costs. Lower inventories mean lower costs, and hence greater value creation. Another company that has benefited from very efficient materials management, the Spanish fashion company Zara, is discussed in Strategy in Action 3.2.

HUMAN RESOURCES The human resources function can help an enterprise to create more value in several ways. This function ensures that the company has the right mix of skilled people to perform its value creation activities effectively. It is also the job of the human resources function to ensure that people are adequately trained, motivated, and compensated to perform their value creation tasks. If the human resources

Strategy in Action   3.2

Competitive Advantage at Zara

The fashion retailer Zara is one of Spain's fastest growing and most successful companies, with sales of about $8.5 billion and a network of 2,800 stores in sixty-four countries. Zara's competitive advantage centers around one thing—speed. While it takes most fashion houses six to nine months to go from design to having merchandise delivered to a store, Zara can pull off the entire process in just five weeks. This rapid response time enables Zara to quickly respond to changing fashions.

Zara achieves this by breaking many of the rules of operation in the fashion business. While most fashion houses outsource production, Zara has its own factories and keeps about half of its production in-house. Zara also has its own designers and stores. Its designers are in constant contact with the stores, not only tracking what is selling on a real-time basis through information systems but also talking to store managers once a week to get their subjective impressions of what is hot. This information supplements data gathered from other sources, such as fashion shows.

Drawing on this information, Zara's designers create approximately 40,000 new designs a year, from which 10,000 are selected for production. Zara then purchases basic textiles from global suppliers but performs capital-intensive production activities in its own factories. These factories use computer-controlled machinery to cut pieces for garments. Zara does not produce in large volumes to attain economies of scale; instead it produces in small lots. Labor-intensive activities, such as sewing, are performed by subcontractors located close to Zara's factories. Zara makes a practice of having more production capacity than necessary so that if it spots an emerging fashion trend, it can quickly respond by designing garments and ramping up production.

Once a garment has been made, it is delivered to one of Zara's own warehouses and then shipped to its own stores once a week. Zara deliberately underproduces products, supplying small batches of products in hot demand before quickly shifting to the next fashion trend. Often its merchandise sells out quickly. The empty shelves in Zara stores create a scarcity value, which helps to generate demand. Customers quickly snap up products they like because they known they may soon be out of stock and not produced again.

As a result of this strategy, which is supported by competencies in design, information systems, and logistics management, Zara carries fewer inventories than competitors (Zara's inventory amounts to about 10% of sales, compared to 15% at rival stores like The Gap and Benetton). This means fewer price reductions to move products that haven't sold and higher profit margins.[b]

function operates well, employee productivity rises (which lowers costs) and customer service improves (which raises utility), thereby enabling the company to create more value. As we saw in the Opening Case, much of the competitive advantage of Southwest Airlines lies in its human resources practices, which have created a highly productive work force.

INFORMATION SYSTEMS Information systems are the largely electronic systems for managing inventory, tracking sales, pricing products, selling products, dealing with customer service inquiries, and so on. Information systems, when coupled with the communications features of the Internet, are holding out the promise of being able to improve the efficiency and effectiveness with which a company manages its other value creation activities. Again, Dell uses Web-based information systems to efficiently manage its global logistics network and increase inventory turnover. World-class information systems are also an aspect of Zara's competitive advantage (see Strategy in Action 3.2).

COMPANY INFRASTRUCTURE Company infrastructure is the companywide context within which all the other value creation activities take place: the organizational structure, control systems, and company culture. Because top management can exert considerable influence in shaping these aspects of a company, top management should also be viewed as part of the infrastructure of a company. Indeed, through strong leadership, top management can shape the infrastructure of a company and, through that, the performance of all other value creation activities that take place within it. A good example of this process is given in Strategy in Action 3.1, which looks at how Rose Marie Bravo helped to engineer a turnaround at Burberry.

The Building Blocks of Competitive Advantage

Four factors help a company to build and sustain competitive advantage—superior efficiency, quality, innovation, and customer responsiveness. Each of these factors is the product of a company's distinctive competencies. Indeed, in a very real sense, they are "generic" distinctive competencies. These generic competencies allow a company to (1) differentiate its product offering, and hence offer more utility to its customers, and (2) lower its cost structure (see Figure 3.6). These factors can be considered generic distinctive competencies because any company, regardless of its industry or the products or services it produces, can pursue them. Although they are discussed sequentially below, they are highly interrelated, and the important ways they affect each other should be noted. For example, superior quality can lead to superior efficiency, and innovation can enhance efficiency, quality, and responsiveness to customers.

● **Efficiency**

In one sense, a business is simply a device for transforming inputs into outputs. Inputs are basic factors of production such as labor, land, capital, management, and technological know-how. Outputs are the goods and services that the business produces. The simplest measure of efficiency is the quantity of inputs that it takes to produce a given output, that is, Efficiency = outputs/inputs. The more efficient a company is, the fewer the inputs required to produce a given output.

The two most important components of efficiency for many companies are employee productivity and capital productivity. **Employee productivity** refers to the

FIGURE 3.6

Building Blocks of
Competitive
Advantage

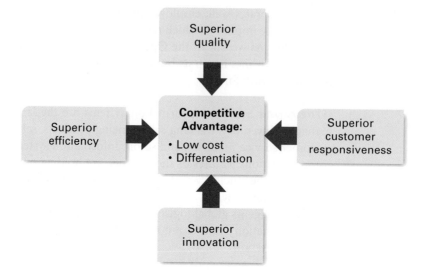

output produced per employee. For example, if it takes General Motors thirty hours of employee time to assemble a car and it takes Ford twenty-five hours, we can say that Ford has higher employee productivity than GM and is thus more efficient. As long as other things are equal, such as wage rates, we can assume from this information that Ford will have a lower cost structure than GM. Thus, employee productivity helps a company attain a competitive advantage through a lower cost structure. You will recall from the Opening Case that Southwest Airline's low cost structure was due in large part to higher labor productivity.

Capital productivity refers to the sales produced per dollar of capital invested in a business. An analysis of financial statements suggests that in 2005, Dell Computer generated $12.07 of sales for every dollar of capital it invested in its business, whereas its competitor Hewlett-Packard generated $2.14 of sales for every dollar of capital it invested in its business. Dell was far more efficient than Hewlett-Packard in the way it used its capital to generates sales revenues. Other things being equal, this will lead to lower costs and higher profitability (for a full comparison of Dell and Hewlett-Packard, see the Running Case in this chapter).

The concept of productivity is not limited to employee and capital productivity. Pharmaceutical companies, for example, often talk about the productivity of their R&D spending, by which they mean how many new drugs they develop from their investment in R&D. Other companies talk about their sales force productivity, which means how many sales they generate from every sales call, and so on. The important point to remember is that high productivity leads to greater efficiency and lower costs.

● **Quality as Excellence and Reliability**

A product can be thought of as a bundle of attributes.[13] The attributes of many physical products include their form, features, performance, durability, reliability, style, and design.[14] A product is said to have *superior quality* when customers perceive that its attributes provide them with higher utility than the attributes of products sold by rivals. For example, a Rolex watch has attributes-such as design, styling, performance, and reliability—that customers perceive as being superior to the same attributes in many other watches. Thus, we can refer to a Rolex as a high-quality product: Rolex has differentiated its watches by these attributes.

When customers evaluate the quality of a product, they commonly measure it against two kinds of attributes: those related to *quality as excellence* and those related to *quality as reliability*. From a quality-as-excellence perspective, the important attributes are things such as a product's design and styling, its aesthetic appeal, its features and functions, the level of service associated with the delivery of the product, and so on. For example, customers can purchase a pair of imitation leather boots for $20 from Wal-Mart, or they can buy a handmade pair of butter-soft leather boots from Nordstrom for $500. The boots from Nordstrom will have far superior styling, feel more comfortable, and look much better than those from Wal-Mart. The utility consumers will get from the Nordstrom boots will in all probability be much greater than the utility derived from the Wal-Mart boots but, of course, they will have to pay far more for them. That is the point: when excellence is built into a product offering, consumers have to pay more to own or consume it.

With regard to quality as reliability, a product can be said to be reliable when it consistently does the job it was designed for; does it well; and rarely, if ever, breaks down. As with excellence, reliability increases the utility a consumer gets from a product and thus the price the company can charge for that product. Toyota's cars, for example, have the highest reliability ratings in the automobile industry, and therefore consumers are prepared to pay more for them than for cars that are very similar in other attributes. As we shall see, increasing product reliability has been the central goal of an influential management philosophy that came out of Japan in the 1980s and is commonly referred to as **total quality management**.

The position of a product against two dimensions, reliability and other attributes, can be plotted on a figure similar to Figure 3.7. For example, a Lexus has attributes—such as design, styling, performance, and safety features—that customers perceive as demonstrating excellence in quality and that are viewed as being superior to those of most other cars. Lexus is also a very reliable car. Thus, the overall level of quality of the Lexus is very high, which means that the car offers consumers significant utility, and that gives Toyota the option of charging a premium price for the Lexus. Toyota also produces another very reliable vehicle, the Toyota Corolla, but this is aimed at less wealthy customers and it lacks many of the superior attributes of the Lexus.

FIGURE 3.7

A Quality Map for
Automobiles

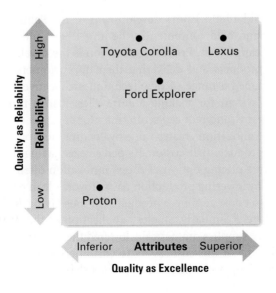

Thus, although the Corolla is also a high-quality car in the sense of being reliable, it is not as high quality as a Lexus in the sense of being an excellent product. At the other end of the spectrum, we can find poor-quality products that have both low reliability and inferior attributes, such as poor design, performance, and styling. An example is the Proton, which is built by the Malaysian car firm of the same name. The design of the car is over a decade old and has a dismal reputation for styling and safety. Moreover, Proton's reliability record is one of the worst of any car, according to J. D. Power.[15]

The concept of quality applies whether we are talking about Toyota automobiles, clothes designed and sold by The Gap, the customer service department of Citibank, or the ability of airlines to arrive on time. Quality is just as relevant to services as it is to goods.[16] The impact of high product quality on competitive advantage is twofold.[17] First, providing high-quality products increases the utility those products provide to customers, which gives the company the option of charging a higher price for them. In the automobile industry, for example, Toyota can charge a higher price for its cars because of the higher quality of its products.

The second impact of high quality on competitive advantage comes from the greater efficiency and the lower unit costs associated with reliable products. When products are reliable, less employee time is wasted making defective products or providing substandard services and less time has to be spent fixing mistakes, which translates into higher employee productivity and lower unit costs. Thus, high product quality not only enables a company to differentiate its product from that of rivals, but if the product is reliable, it also lowers costs.

The importance of reliability in building competitive advantage has increased dramatically over the past decade. Indeed, so crucial is the emphasis placed on reliability by many companies that achieving high product reliability can no longer be viewed as just one way of gaining a competitive advantage. In many industries, it has become an absolute imperative for survival.

● **Innovation**   Innovation refers to the act of creating new products or processes. There are two main types of innovation: product innovation and process innovation. **Product innovation** is the development of products that are new to the world or have superior attributes to existing products. Examples are Intel's invention of the microprocessor in the early 1970s; Cisco's development of the router for routing data over the Internet in the mid 1980s; Palm's development of the PalmPilot, the first commercially successful hand-held computer, in the mid 1990s; and Apple's development of the iPod in the early 2000s. **Process innovation** is the development of a new process for producing products and delivering them to customers. Examples include Toyota, which developed a range of new techniques collectively known as the Toyota lean production system for making automobiles: just-in-time inventory systems, self-managing teams, and reduced setup times for complex equipment.

Product innovation creates value by creating new products or enhanced versions of existing products that customers perceive as having more utility, thus increasing the company's pricing options. Process innovation often allows a company to create more value by lowering production costs. Toyota's lean production system, for example, helped to boost employee productivity, thus giving Toyota a cost-based competitive advantage.[18] Similarly, Staples's application of the supermarket business model to retail office supplies dramatically lowered the cost of selling office supplies. Staples passed on some of this cost saving to customers in the form of lower prices, which enabled the company to increase its market share rapidly.

In the long run, innovation of products and processes is perhaps the most important building block of competitive advantage.[19] Competition can be viewed as a process driven by innovations. Although not all innovations succeed, those that do can be a major source of competitive advantage because, by definition, they give a company something unique—something its competitors lack (at least until they imitate the innovation). Uniqueness can allow a company to differentiate itself from its rivals and charge a premium price for its product or, in the case of many process innovations, reduce its unit costs far below those of competitors.

● Customer Responsiveness

To achieve superior responsiveness to customers, a company must be able to do a better job than competitors of identifying and satisfying its customers' needs. Customers will then attribute more utility to its products, creating a differentiation based on competitive advantage. Improving the quality of a company's product offering is consistent with achieving responsiveness, as is developing new products with features that existing products lack. In other words, achieving superior quality and innovation is integral to achieving superior responsiveness to customers.

Another factor that stands out in any discussion of responsiveness to customers is the need to customize goods and services to the unique demands of individual customers or customer groups. For example, the proliferation of soft drinks and beers can be viewed partly as a response to this trend. Automobile companies have become more adept at customizing cars to the demands of individual customers. For instance, following the lead of Toyota, the Saturn division of General Motors builds cars to order for individual customers, letting them choose from a wide range of colors and options.

An aspect of responsiveness to customers that has drawn increasing attention is **customer response time**: the time that it takes for a good to be delivered or a service to be performed.[20] For a manufacturer of machinery, response time is the time it takes to fill customer orders. For a bank, it is the time it takes to process a loan or that a customer must stand in line to wait for a free teller. For a supermarket, it is the time that customers must stand in checkout lines. For a fashion retailer, it is the time required to take a new product through from design to a retail store (see Strategy in Action 3.2 for a discussion of how the Spanish fashion retailer Zara minimizes response time). Customer survey after customer survey has shown slow response time to be a major source of customer dissatisfaction.[21]

Other sources of enhanced responsiveness to customers are superior design, superior service, and superior after-sales service and support. All of these factors enhance responsiveness to customers and allow a company to differentiate itself from its less responsive competitors. In turn, differentiation enables a company to build brand loyalty and charge a premium price for its products. Consider how much more people are prepared to pay for next-day delivery of Express Mail as opposed to delivery in three to four days. In 2006, a two-page letter sent by overnight Express Mail within the United States cost about $12, compared with 39 cents for regular mail. Thus, the price premium for express delivery (reduced response time) was $11.61, or a premium of 3,079% over the regular price.

● Business Models, the Value Chain, and Generic Distinctive Competencies

As noted in Chapter 1, a business model is managers' conception, or gestalt, of how the various strategies that a firm pursues fit together into a congruent whole, thus enabling the firm to achieve a competitive advantage. More precisely, a business model represents the way in which managers configure the value chain of the firm through strategy, as well as the investments they make to support that configuration,

FIGURE 3.8

Competitive Advantage and the Value Creation Cycle

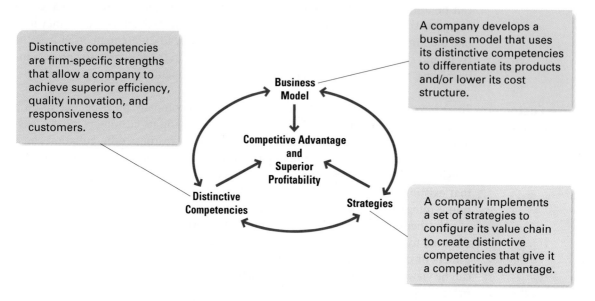

so that they can build the distinctive competencies necessary to attain the efficiency, quality, innovation, and customer responsiveness required to support the firm's low-cost or differentiated position, thereby achieving a competitive advantage and generating superior profitability (see Figure 3.8).

For example, the main strategic goal of Wal-Mart is to be the lowest-cost operator offering a wide display of general merchandise in the retail industry. Wal-Mart's business model involves offering general merchandise in a self-service supermarket type of setting. Wal-Mart's strategies flesh out this business model and help the company to attain its strategic goal. For example, to reduce costs, Wal-Mart limits investments in the fittings and fixtures of its stores. One of the keys to generating sales and lowering costs in this setting is rapid inventory turnover, which is achieved through strategic investments in logistics and information systems. Wal-Mart in fact makes major investments in process innovation to improve the effectiveness of its information and logistics systems, which enables the company to respond to customer demands for low-priced goods when they walk in the door and to do so in a very efficient manner.

Wal-Mart's business model is very different from that found at a retailer such as Nordstrom. Nordstrom's business model is to offer high quality, and high-priced apparel, in a full-service and sophisticated setting. This implies differences in the way the value chain is configured. Nordstrom devotes far more attention to in-store customer service than Wal-Mart does, which implies significant investments in its salespeople. Moreover, Nordstrom invests far more in the furnishings and fittings for its stores, as opposed to Wal-Mart, whose stores have a basic warehouse feel to them. Nordstrom recaptures the costs of this investment by charging higher prices for higher-quality merchandise. Thus, even though Wal-Mart and Nordstrom both sell apparel (Wal-Mart is in fact the biggest seller of apparel in the United States), their business models imply a very different positioning in the marketplace and a very different configuration of value chain activities and investments.

Analyzing Competitive Advantage and Profitability

If a company's managers are to perform a good internal analysis, they need to be able to analyze the financial performance of their company, identifying how its strategies contribute (or not) to profitability. To identify strengths and weaknesses effectively, they need to be able to compare, or benchmark, the performance of their company against that of competitors and the historic performance of the company itself. This will help them determine whether they are more or less profitable than competitors and whether the performance of the company has been improving or deteriorating through time, whether their company strategies are maximizing the value being created, whether their cost structure is out of line with those of competitors, and whether they are using the resources of the company to the greatest effect.

As we noted in Chapter 1, the key measure of a company's financial performance is its profitability, which captures the return that a company is generating on its investments. Although several different measures of profitability exist, such as return on assets and return on equity, many authorities on the measurement of profitability argue that return on invested capital (ROIC) is the best measure because "it focuses on the true operating performance of the company."[22] (However, return on assets is very similar in formulation to return on invested capital.)

ROIC is defined as net profit over invested capital, or ROIC = net profit/invested capital. Net profit is calculated by subtracting the total costs of operating the company away from its total revenues (total revenues – total costs). *Net profit* is what is left over after the government takes its share in taxes. *Invested capital* is the amount that is invested in the operations of a company: property, plant, equipment, inventories, and other assets. Invested capital comes from two main sources: interest-bearing debt and shareholders' equity. Interest-bearing debt is money the company borrows from banks and those who purchase its bonds. Shareholders' equity is the money raised from selling shares to the public, plus earnings that the company has retained in prior years and can use to fund current investments. ROIC measures the effectiveness with which a company is using the capital funds that it has available for investment. As such, it is recognized to be an excellent measure of the value a company is creating.[23]

A company's ROIC can be algebraically decomposed into two major components: return on sales and capital turnover.[24] Specifically:

$$\text{ROIC} = \text{net profits/invested capital}$$

$$= \text{net profits/revenues} \times \text{revenues/invested capital}$$

where net profits/revenues is the return on sales, and revenues/invested capital is capital turnover. Return on sales measures how effectively the company converts revenues into profits. Capital turnover measures how effectively the company employs its invested capital to generate revenues. These two ratios can be further decomposed into some basic accounting ratios, as shown in Figure 3.9 (the terms in these ratios are defined in Table 3.1).[25]

The decomposition of ROIC shown in Figure 3.9 was first developed by managers at the DuPont Company in the early 1900s as a methodology for identifying the drivers of profitability, and the decomposition formula is sometimes referred to as "the DuPont Formula." Figure 3.9 says that a company's managers can increase ROIC by pursuing strategies that increase the company's return on sales. To increase the

FIGURE 3.9

Drivers of Profitability
(ROIC)

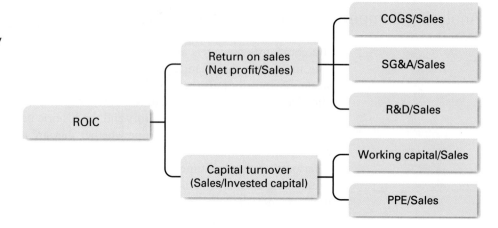

company's return on sales, they can pursue strategies that reduce the cost of goods sold (COGS) for a given level of sales revenues (COGS/sales); reduce the level of spending on sales force, marketing, general, and administrative expenses (SG&A) for a given level of sales revenues (SG&A/sales); and reduce R&D spending for a given level of sales revenues (R&D/sales). Alternatively, they can increase return on sales by pursuing strategies that increase sales revenues more than they increase the costs of the business, as measured by COGS, SG&A, and R&D expenses. That is, they

TABLE 3.1

Definitions of Basic Accounting Terms

Term	Definition	Source
Cost of goods sold (COGS)	Total costs of producing products.	Income statement
Sales, general, and administrative expenses (SG&A)	Costs associated with selling products and administering the company.	Income statement
R&D expenses (R&D)	Research and development expenditure.	Income statement
Working capital	The amount of money the company has to work with in the short term: Current assets — current liabilities.	Balance sheet
Property, plant, and equipment (PPE)	The value of investments in the property, plant, and equipment that the company uses to manufacture and sell its products. Also know as *fixed capital.*	Balance sheet
Return on sales (ROS)	Net profit expressed as a percentage of sales. Measures how effectively the company converts revenues into profits.	Ratio
Capital turnover	Revenues divided by invested capital. Measures how effectively the company uses its capital to generate revenues.	Ratio
Return on invested capital (ROIC)	Net profit divided by invested capital.	Ratio
Net profit	Total revenues minus total costs before tax.	Income statement
Invested capital	Interest-bearing debt plus shareholders equity.	Balance sheet

can increase the return on sales by pursuing strategies that lower costs or increase value through differentiation, and thus allow the company to increase its prices more than its costs.

Figure 3.9 also tells us that a company's managers can boost the profitability of their company by getting greater sales revenues from their invested capital, thereby increasing capital turnover. They do this by pursuing strategies that reduce the amount of working capital, such as the amount of capital invested in inventories, needed to generate a given level of sales (working capital/sales) and then pursuing strategies that reduce the amount of fixed capital that they have to invest in plant, property, and equipment (PPE) to generate a given level of sales (PPE/sales). That is, they pursue strategies that reduce the amount of capital that they need to generate every dollar of sales, and thus their cost of capital. Now recall that cost of capital is part of the cost structure of a company (see Figure 3.2), so strategies designed to increase capital turnover also lower the cost structure.

To see how these basic drivers of profitability help us to understand what is going on in a company and to identify its strengths and weaknesses, read the Running Case, which compares the financial performance of Dell Computer against its major rival, Hewlett-Packard.

RUNNING CASE

Comparing Dell to Hewlett-Packard

Figure 3.10 compares the financial performance of Dell Computer to that of its rival, Hewlett-Packard, for 2005. Note first that Dell was much more profitable than HP, measured by ROIC. Indeed, Dell's ROIC of 77.1% was astoundingly high. HP earned a mediocre ROIC of 5.91%, which may have been less than its cost of capital.

To explain this performance difference, first look at the difference in return on sales. Dell's ROS, at 6.39%, was more than double that of HP's at 2.77%. Why? It certainly is not because Dell is charging customers a high markup over its cost of goods sold. Indeed, Dell's COGS/sales ratio is higher than HP's, suggesting that Dell is pricing its products aggressively. However, Dell spends far less on SG&A expenses and on R&D than its rival. This lower level of spending reflects important strategic choices. Because Dell sells direct, it does not have a big sales forces; hence its SG&A expenses are much lower than HP's. In addition, Dell has decided not to spend heavily on R&D primarily because it sees itself as being in a commodity business. In Dell's view, R&D is something

that its suppliers, such as Intel and Microsoft, undertake. HP is moving toward this view, but its higher level of R&D reflects the company's traditional strategic posture that it tries to compete in part through product innovation. Dell does not.

Now look at the difference in capital turnover. Here, the difference is striking. Dell generates $12.07 of sales for every dollar of capital invested in the business, HP just $2.14 of sales for every dollar. This difference drives most of the difference in ROIC. Why is Dell so much more efficient that HP in its use of capital? There are two reasons. First, Dell undertakes only final assembly, with everything else being outsourced to suppliers. Consequently, it has to invest less in property, plant, and equipment (PPE) than does HP.

Second, Dell is very efficient at managing its inventory, which is why its working capital to sales ratio is so much lower than HP's. Because Dell sells direct, it can build to order—it does not have to fill a retail channel with inventory. Moreover, it takes order information received over its website, and through telephone sales, and transmits

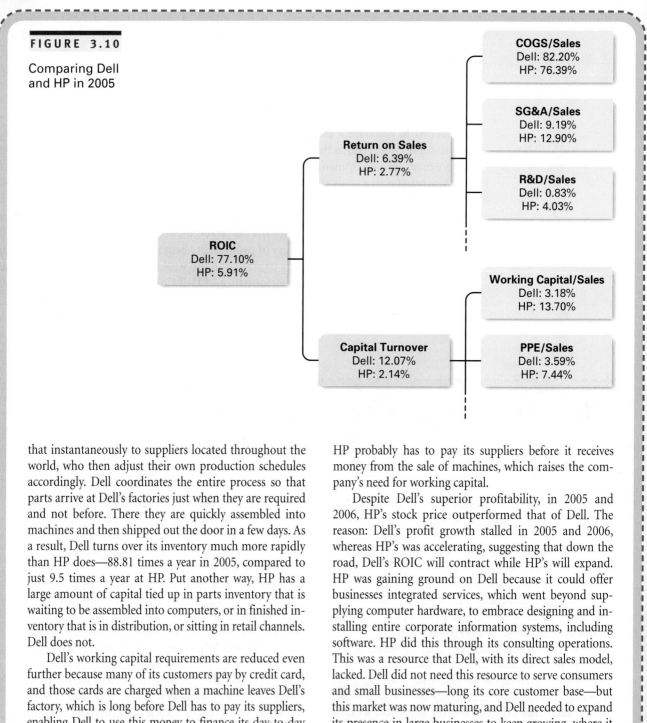

FIGURE 3.10

Comparing Dell and HP in 2005

COGS/Sales
Dell: 82.20%
HP: 76.39%

SG&A/Sales
Dell: 9.19%
HP: 12.90%

R&D/Sales
Dell: 0.83%
HP: 4.03%

Return on Sales
Dell: 6.39%
HP: 2.77%

ROIC
Dell: 77.10%
HP: 5.91%

Working Capital/Sales
Dell: 3.18%
HP: 13.70%

PPE/Sales
Dell: 3.59%
HP: 7.44%

Capital Turnover
Dell: 12.07%
HP: 2.14%

that instantaneously to suppliers located throughout the world, who then adjust their own production schedules accordingly. Dell coordinates the entire process so that parts arrive at Dell's factories just when they are required and not before. There they are quickly assembled into machines and then shipped out the door in a few days. As a result, Dell turns over its inventory much more rapidly than HP does—88.81 times a year in 2005, compared to just 9.5 times a year at HP. Put another way, HP has a large amount of capital tied up in parts inventory that is waiting to be assembled into computers, or in finished inventory that is in distribution, or sitting in retail channels. Dell does not.

Dell's working capital requirements are reduced even further because many of its customers pay by credit card, and those cards are charged when a machine leaves Dell's factory, which is long before Dell has to pay its suppliers, enabling Dell to use this money to finance its day-to-day operations. In contrast, due to its lower inventory turnover,

HP probably has to pay its suppliers before it receives money from the sale of machines, which raises the company's need for working capital.

Despite Dell's superior profitability, in 2005 and 2006, HP's stock price outperformed that of Dell. The reason: Dell's profit growth stalled in 2005 and 2006, whereas HP's was accelerating, suggesting that down the road, Dell's ROIC will contract while HP's will expand. HP was gaining ground on Dell because it could offer businesses integrated services, which went beyond supplying computer hardware, to embrace designing and installing entire corporate information systems, including software. HP did this through its consulting operations. This was a resource that Dell, with its direct sales model, lacked. Dell did not need this resource to serve consumers and small businesses—long its core customer base—but this market was now maturing, and Dell needed to expand its presence in large businesses to keep growing, where it was at a disadvantage versus HP.[c]

The Durability of Competitive Advantage

The next question we must address is: How long will a competitive advantage last once it has been created? In other words, what is the durability of competitive advantage given that other companies are also seeking to develop distinctive competencies that will give them a competitive advantage? The answer depends on three factors: barriers to imitation, the capability of competitors, and the general dynamism of the industry environment.

● Barriers to Imitation

A company with a competitive advantage will earn higher-than-average profits. These profits send a signal to rivals that the company has some valuable distinctive competency that allows it to create superior value. Naturally, its competitors will try to identify and imitate that competency and, insofar as they are successful, ultimately their increased success may whittle away the company's superior profits.[26]

How quickly rivals will imitate a company's distinctive competencies is an important issue because the speed of imitation has a bearing on the durability of a company's competitive advantage. Other things being equal, the more rapidly competitors imitate a company's distinctive competencies, the less durable its competitive advantage will be, and the more important it is that the company endeavor to improve its competencies to stay one step ahead of the imitators. It is important to stress at the outset that ultimately almost any distinctive competency can be imitated by a competitor. The critical issue is time: the longer it takes competitors to imitate a distinctive competency, the greater the opportunity the company has to build a strong market position and reputation with customers, which are then more difficult for competitors to attack. Moreover, the longer it takes to achieve an imitation, the greater is the opportunity for the imitated company to improve on its competency or build other competencies, thereby staying one step ahead of the competition.

Barriers to imitation are a primary determinant of the speed of imitation. Barriers to imitation are factors that make it difficult for a competitor to copy a company's distinctive competencies; the greater the barriers to imitation, the more sustainable is a company's competitive advantage.[27] Barriers to imitation differ depending on whether a competitor is trying to imitate resources or capabilities.

IMITATING RESOURCES In general, the easiest distinctive competencies for prospective rivals to imitate tend to be those based on possession of firm-specific and valuable tangible resources, such as buildings, plant, and equipment. Such resources are visible to competitors and can often be purchased on the open market. For example, if a company's competitive advantage is based on sole possession of efficient-scale manufacturing facilities, competitors may move fairly quickly to establish similar facilities. Although Ford gained a competitive advantage over General Motors in the 1920s by being the first to adopt an assembly line manufacturing technology to produce automobiles, General Motors quickly imitated that innovation, competing away Ford's distinctive competency in the process. A similar process is occurring in the auto industry now as companies try to imitate Toyota's famous production system. However, Toyota has slowed down the rate of imitation by not allowing competitors access to its latest equipment.

Intangible resources can be more difficult to imitate. This is particularly true of brand names, which are important because they symbolize a company's reputation. In the heavy earthmoving equipment industry, for example, the Caterpillar brand name is synonymous with high quality and superior after-sales service and support. Similarly, the St. Michael's brand name used by Marks & Spencer, Britain's largest clothing retailer, symbolizes high-quality but reasonably priced clothing. Customers often display a preference for the products of such companies because the brand name is an important guarantee of high quality. Although competitors might like to imitate well-established brand names, the law prohibits them from doing so.

Marketing and technological know-how are also important intangible resources and can be relatively easy to imitate. The movement of skilled marketing personnel between companies may facilitate the general dissemination of marketing know-how. For example, in the 1970s, Ford was acknowledged as the best marketer among the big three U.S. auto companies. In 1979, it lost a lot of its marketing know-how to Chrysler when its most successful marketer, Lee Iacocca, joined Chrysler and subsequently hired many of Ford's top marketing people to work with him at Chrysler. More generally, successful marketing strategies are relatively easy to imitate because they are so visible to competitors. Thus, Coca-Cola quickly imitated PepsiCo's Diet Pepsi brand with the introduction of its own brand, Diet Coke.

With regard to technological know-how, the patent system in theory should make technological know-how relatively immune to imitation. Patents give the inventor of a new product a twenty-year exclusive production agreement. For example, the biotechnology company Immunex discovered and patented Enbrel, which is capable of halting the disease-causing mechanism that leads to rheumatoid arthritis. All prior treatments simply provided patients with some relief from the symptoms of rheumatoid arthritis. Approved by the Food and Drug Administration in 1998, Enbrel racked up sales of over $400 million in its first year on the market and may ultimately generate annual revenues of $4 billion. (In 2002, Immunex was acquired by Amgen.) Despite the large market, Immunex's patent stops potential competitors from introducing their own version of Enbrel. Whereas it is relatively easy to use the patent system to protect a biological product from imitation, this is not true of many other inventions. In electrical and computer engineering, for example, it is often possible to invent around patents: that is, produce a product that is functionally equivalent but does not rely on the patented technology. One study found that 60% of patented innovations were successfully invented around in four years.[28] This suggests that, in general, distinctive competencies based on technological know-how can be relatively short-lived.

IMITATING CAPABILITIES Imitating a company's capabilities tends to be more difficult than imitating its tangible and intangible resources chiefly because capabilities are based on the way in which decisions are made and processes managed deep within a company. It is hard for outsiders to discern them.

On its own, the invisible nature of capabilities would not be enough to halt imitation; competitors could still gain insights into how a company operates by hiring people away from that company. However, a company's capabilities rarely reside in a single individual. Rather, they are the product of how numerous individuals interact within a unique organizational setting.[29] It is possible that no one individual within a company may be familiar with the totality of a company's internal operating routines and procedures. In such cases, hiring people away from a successful company in order to imitate its key capabilities may not be helpful.

Capability of Competitors

According to work by Pankaj Ghemawat, a major determinant of the capability of competitors to imitate a company's competitive advantage rapidly is the nature of the competitors' prior strategic commitments.[30] By strategic commitment, Ghemawat means a company's commitment to a particular way of doing business—that is, to developing a particular set of resources and capabilities. Ghemawat's point is that once a company has made a strategic commitment, it will have difficulty responding to new competition if doing so requires a break with this commitment. Therefore, when competitors have long-established commitments to a particular way of doing business, they may be slow to imitate an innovating company's competitive advantage. Its competitive advantage will thus be relatively durable.

The U.S. automobile industry again offers an example. From 1945 to 1975, the industry was dominated by the stable oligopoly of General Motors, Ford, and Chrysler, all of which geared their operations to the production of the large cars that American customers demanded at the time. When the market shifted from large cars to small, fuel-efficient ones during the late 1970s, U.S. companies lacked the resources and capabilities required to produce these cars. Their prior commitments had built the wrong kind of skills for this new environment. As a result, foreign producers, and particularly the Japanese, stepped into the market breach by providing compact, fuel-efficient, high-quality, and low-cost cars. The failure of U.S. auto manufacturers to react quickly to the distinctive competency of Japanese auto companies gave the latter time to build a strong market position and brand loyalty, which subsequently have proved difficult to attack.

Another determinant of the ability of competitors to respond to a company's competitive advantage is the absorptive capacity of competitors.[31] **Absorptive capacity** refers to the ability of an enterprise to identify, value, assimilate, and use new knowledge. For example, in the 1960s and 1970s, Toyota developed a competitive advantage based on its innovation of lean production systems. Competitors such as General Motors were slow to imitate this innovation primarily because they lacked the necessary absorptive capacity. General Motors was such a bureaucratic and inward-looking organization that it was very difficult for the company to identify, value, assimilate, and use the knowledge that underlay lean production systems. Indeed, long after General Motors had identified and understood the importance of lean production systems, it was still struggling to assimilate and use that new knowledge. Put differently, internal inertial forces can make it difficult for established competitors to respond to a rival whose competitive advantage is based on new products or internal processes—that is, on innovation.

Taken together, factors such as existing strategic commitments and low absorptive capacity limit the ability of established competitors to imitate the competitive advantage of a rival, particularly when that competitive advantage is based on innovative products or processes. This is why when innovations reshape the rules of competition in an industry, value often migrates away from established competitors and toward new enterprises that are operating with new business models.

Industry Dynamism

A dynamic industry environment is one that is changing rapidly. We examined the factors that determine the dynamism and intensity of competition in an industry in Chapter 2 when we discussed the external environment. The most dynamic industries tend to be those with a very high rate of product innovation—for instance, the customer electronics industry and the personal computer industry. In dynamic industries, the rapid rate of innovation means that product life cycles are shortening and that competitive advantage can be fleeting. A company that has a competitive advantage today may find its market position outflanked tomorrow by a rival's innovation.

In the personal computer industry, the rapid increase in computing power during the past two decades has contributed to a high degree of innovation and a turbulent environment. Reflecting the persistence of innovation, Apple Computer in the late 1970s and early 1980s had an industrywide competitive advantage due to its innovation. In 1981, IBM seized the advantage by introducing its first personal computer. By the mid 1980s, IBM had lost its competitive advantage to high-power clone manufacturers such as Compaq that had beaten IBM in the race to introduce a computer based on Intel's 386 chip. In turn, in the 1990s, Compaq subsequently lost its competitive advantage to Dell, which pioneered new low-cost ways of delivering computers to customers using the Internet as a direct-selling device.

● **Summarizing Durability of Competitive Advantage**

The durability of a company's competitive advantage depends on the height of barriers to imitation, the capability of competitors to imitate its innovation, and the general level of dynamism in the industry environment. When barriers to imitation are low, capable competitors abound, and the environment is dynamic, with innovations being developed all the time, then competitive advantage is likely to be transitory. But even within such industries, companies can build a more enduring competitive advantage if they are able to make investments that build barriers to imitation.

During the 1980s, Apple Computer built a competitive advantage based on the combination of a proprietary disk operating system and an intangible product image. The resulting brand loyalty enabled Apple to carve out a fairly secure niche in an industry where competitive advantage has otherwise proven to be very fleeting. However, by the mid-1990s, its strategy had been imitated primarily because of the introduction of Microsoft's Windows operating system, which imitated most of the features that had enabled Apple to build brand loyalty. By 1996, Apple was in financial trouble, providing yet another example that no competitive advantage lasts forever. Ultimately, anything can be imitated. However, Apple has shown remarkable resilience; in the late 1990s, it clawed its way back from the brink of bankruptcy to establish a viable position within its niche once again, a position it still held on to by the mid 2000s.

Avoiding Failure and Sustaining Competitive Advantage

How can a company avoid failure and escape the traps that have snared so many once successful companies? How can managers build a sustainable competitive advantage? Much of the remainder of this book deals with these issues. Here, we make a number of key points that set the scene for the coming discussion.

● **Why Companies Fail**

When a company loses its competitive advantage, its profitability falls. The company does not necessarily fail; it may just have average or below-average profitability and can remain in this mode for a considerable time, although its resource and capital base is shrinking. Failure implies something more drastic. A failing company is one whose profitability is now substantially lower than the average profitability of its competitors; it has lost the ability to attract and generate resources so that its profit margins and invested capital are shrinking rapidly.

Why does a company lose its competitive advantage and fail? The question is particularly pertinent because some of the most successful companies of the last half-century have seen their competitive position deteriorate at one time or another. IBM, General Motors, American Express, Digital Equipment, and Sears, among many others, at one time were held up as examples of managerial excellence but then have gone through periods where their financial performance was poor and they clearly lacked any competitive advantage. We explore three related reasons for failure: inertia, prior strategic commitments, and the Icarus paradox.

INERTIA The inertia argument says that companies find it difficult to change their strategies and structures in order to adapt to changing competitive conditions.[32] IBM is a classic example of this problem. For thirty years, it was viewed as the world's most successful computer company. Then in the space of a few years, its success turned into a disaster: it lost $5 billion in 1992, leading to layoffs of more than 100,000 employees. IBM's troubles were caused by a dramatic decline in the cost of computing power as a result of innovations in microprocessors. With the advent of powerful low-cost microprocessors, the locus of the computer market shifted from mainframes to small, low-priced personal computers, leaving IBM's huge mainframe operations with a diminished market. Although IBM had, and still has, a significant presence in the personal computer market, it had failed to shift the focus of its efforts away from mainframes and toward personal computers. This failure meant deep trouble for one of the most successful companies of the twentieth century (IBM has now executed a successful turnaround with a repositioning as a provider of e-commerce infrastructure and solutions).

One reason that companies find it so difficult to adapt to new environmental conditions seems to be the role of capabilities in causing inertia. Organizational capabilities—the way a company makes decisions and manages its processes—can be a source of competitive advantage, but they are difficult to change. IBM always emphasized close coordination among operating units and favored decision processes that stressed consensus among interdependent operating units as a prerequisite for a decision to go forward.[33] This capability was a source of advantage for IBM during the 1970s, when coordination among its worldwide operating units was necessary to develop, manufacture, and sell complex mainframes. But the slow-moving bureaucracy that it had spawned was a source of failure in the 1990s, when organizations had to adapt readily to rapid environmental change.

Capabilities are difficult to change because a certain distribution of power and influence is embedded within the established decision-making and management processes of an organization. Those who play key roles in a decision-making process clearly have more power. It follows that changing the established capabilities of an organization means changing its existing distribution of power and influence, and those whose power and influence would diminish resist such change. Proposals for change trigger turf battles. This power struggle and the political resistance associated with trying to alter the way in which an organization makes decisions and manages its process—that is, trying to change its capabilities—bring on inertia. This is not to say that companies cannot change. However, because change is so often resisted by those who feel threatened by it, change in most cases has to be induced by a crisis. By then, the company may already be failing, as happened at IBM.

Prior Strategic Commitments A company's prior strategic commitments not only limit its ability to imitate rivals but may also cause competitive disadvantage.[34] IBM, for instance, had major investments in the mainframe computer business, so when the market shifted, it was stuck with significant resources specialized for that particular business: its manufacturing facilities were geared to the production of mainframes, its research organization was similarly specialized, and so was its sales force. Because these resources were not well suited to the newly emerging personal computer business, IBM's difficulties in the early 1990s were in a sense inevitable. Its prior strategic commitments locked it into a business that was shrinking. Shedding these resources was bound to cause hardship for all organization stakeholders.

The Icarus Paradox Danny Miller has postulated that the roots of competitive failure can be found in what he termed the Icarus paradox.[35] Icarus is a figure in Greek mythology who used a pair of wings, made for him by his father, to escape from an island where he was being held prisoner. He flew so well that he went higher and higher, ever closer to the sun, until the heat of the sun melted the wax that held his wings together and he plunged to his death in the Aegean Sea. The paradox is that his greatest asset, his ability to fly, caused his demise. Miller argues that the same paradox applies to many once successful companies. According to Miller, many companies become so dazzled by their early success that they believe more of the same type of effort is the way to future success. As a result, they can become so specialized and inner-directed that they lose sight of market realities and the fundamental requirements for achieving a competitive advantage. Sooner or later, this leads to failure.

Miller identifies four major categories among the rising and falling companies, which he labels craftsmen, builders, pioneers, and salesmen. The craftsmen, such as Texas Instruments and Digital Equipment Corporation (DEC), achieved early success through engineering excellence. But then they became so obsessed with engineering details that they lost sight of market realities. (The story of DEC's demise is summarized in Strategy in Action 3.3.) Among the builders are Gulf & Western and ITT. Having built successful, moderately diversified companies, they then became so enchanted with diversification for its own sake that they continued to diversify far beyond the point at which it was profitable to do so. Miller's third group are the pioneers like Wang Labs. Enamored of their own originally brilliant innovations, managers here continued to search for additional brilliant innovations and ended up producing novel but completely useless products. The final category comprises the salesmen, exemplified by Procter & Gamble and Chrysler. They became so convinced of their ability to sell anything that they paid scant attention to product development and manufacturing excellence and, as a result, spawned a proliferation of bland, inferior products.

● **Steps to Avoid Failure**

Given that so many traps wait for companies, an important question arises: How can strategic managers use internal analysis to find them and escape them? We now look at several tactics that managers can use.

Focus on the Building Blocks of Competitive Advantage Maintaining a competitive advantage requires a company to continue focusing on all four generic building blocks of competitive advantage—efficiency, quality, innovation, and responsiveness to customers—and to develop distinctive competencies that contribute to superior performance

Strategy in Action   3.3

The Road to Ruin at DEC

Digital Equipment Corporation (DEC) was one of the premier computer companies of the 1970s and 1980s. DEC's original success was founded on the minicomputer, a cheaper, more flexible version of its mainframe cousins that Ken Olson and his brilliant team of engineers invented in the 1960s. They then improved on their original minicomputers until they could not be beat for quality and reliability. In the 1970s, their VAX series of minicomputers was widely regarded as the most reliable series of computers ever produced, and DEC was rewarded by high profit rates and rapid growth. By 1990, it was number 27 on the *Fortune 500* list of the largest corporations in America.

Buoyed by its success, DEC turned into an engineering monoculture: its engineers became idols; its marketing and accounting staff, however, were barely tolerated. Component specs and design standards were all that senior managers understood. Technological fine-tuning became such an obsession that the needs of customers for smaller, more economical, user-friendly computers were ignored. DEC's personal computers, for example, bombed because they were out of touch with the needs of customers, and the company failed to respond to the threat to its core market presented by the rise of computer workstations and client-server architecture. Indeed, Ken Olson was known for dismissing such new products. He once said, "We always say that customers are right, but they are not always right." Perhaps. But DEC, blinded by its early success, failed to remain responsive to its customers and changing market conditions. In another famous statement, when asked about personal computers in the early 1980s, Olson said, "I can see of no reason why anybody would ever want a computer on their desk."

By the early 1990s, DEC was in deep trouble. Olson was forced out in July 1992, and the company lost billions of dollars between 1992 and 1995. It returned to profitability in 1996 primarily because of the success of a turnaround strategy aimed at reorienting the company to serve precisely those areas that Olson had dismissed. In 1998, the company was acquired by Compaq Computer Corporation (which was subsequently purchased by Hewlett-Packard) and disappeared from the business landscape as an independent entity.[d]

in these areas. One of the messages of Miller's Icarus paradox is that many successful companies become unbalanced in their pursuit of distinctive competencies. DEC, for example, focused on engineering quality at the expense of almost everything else, including, most important, responsiveness to customers. Other companies forget to focus on any distinctive competency at all.

INSTITUTE CONTINUOUS IMPROVEMENT AND LEARNING The only constant in the world is change. Today's source of competitive advantage may soon be rapidly imitated by capable competitors or made obsolete by the innovations of a rival. In such a dynamic and fast-paced environment, the only way that a company can maintain a competitive advantage over time is to continually improve its efficiency, quality, innovation, and responsiveness to customers. The way to do this is to recognize the importance of learning within the organization.[36] The most successful companies do not stand still, resting on their laurels; they are always seeking out ways of improving their operations and in the process are constantly upgrading the value of their distinctive competencies or creating new competencies. Companies such as General Electric and Toyota have a reputation for being learning organizations. This means that they are continually analyzing the processes that underlie their efficiency, quality, innovation, and responsiveness to customers. Their objective is to learn from prior mistakes and to seek out ways to improve their processes over time. This has enabled Toyota, for example, to continually upgrade its employee productivity and product quality, and thus stay ahead of imitators.

TRACK BEST INDUSTRIAL PRACTICE AND USE BENCHMARKING   One of the best ways to develop distinctive competencies that contribute to superior efficiency, quality, innovation, and responsiveness to customers is to identify and adopt best industrial practice. Only in this way will a company be able to build and maintain the resources and capabilities that underpin excellence in efficiency, quality, innovation, and responsiveness to customers. (We discuss what constitutes best industrial practice in some depth in Chapter 4.) It requires tracking the practice of other companies, and perhaps the best way to do so is through benchmarking: measuring the company against the products, practices, and services of some of its most efficient global competitors. For example, when Xerox was in trouble in the early 1980s, it decided to institute a policy of benchmarking to identify ways to improve the efficiency of its operations. Xerox benchmarked L. L. Bean for distribution procedures, Deere & Company for central computer operations, Procter & Gamble for marketing, and Florida Power & Light for total quality management processes. By the early 1990s, Xerox was benchmarking 240 functions against comparable areas in other companies. This process has been credited with helping it dramatically improve the efficiency of its operations.[37]

OVERCOME INERTIA   Overcoming the internal forces that are a barrier to change within an organization is one of the key requirements for maintaining a competitive advantage. Suffice it to say here that identifying barriers to change is an important first step. Once this step has been taken, implementing change requires good leadership, the judicious use of power, and appropriate changes in organizational structure and control systems.

● The Role of Luck

A number of scholars have argued that luck plays a critical role in determining competitive success and failure.[38] In its most extreme version, the luck argument devalues the importance of strategy altogether. Instead, it states that, in the face of uncertainty, some companies just happen to pick the correct strategy.

Although luck may be the reason for a company's success in particular cases, it is an unconvincing explanation for the persistent success of a company. Recall our argument that the generic building blocks of competitive advantage are superior efficiency, quality, innovation, and responsiveness to customers. Keep in mind also that competition is a process in which companies are continually trying to outdo each other in their ability to achieve high efficiency, superior quality, outstanding innovation, and quick responsiveness to customers. It is possible to imagine a company getting lucky and coming into possession of resources that allow it to achieve excellence on one or more of these dimensions. However, it is difficult to imagine how sustained excellence on any of these four dimensions could be produced by anything other than conscious effort, that is, by strategy. Luck may indeed play a role in success, and managers must always exploit a lucky break. (Strategy in Action 3.4 discusses the role of luck in the early history of Microsoft and how Bill Gates exploited that luck.) However, to argue that success is entirely a matter of luck is to strain credibility. As the golfing great Gary Player once said, "The harder I work, the luckier I seem to get." Managers who strive to formulate and implement strategies that lead to a competitive advantage are more likely to be lucky.

Strategy in Action   3.4

Bill Gates's Lucky Break

The product that launched Microsoft into its leadership position in the software industry was MS-DOS, the operating system for IBM and IBM-compatible PCs. The original DOS program, however, was developed not by Microsoft but by Seattle Computer, where it was known as Q-DOS (which stood for "quick and dirty operating system"). When IBM was looking for an operating system to run its original PC, it talked to a number of software companies, including Microsoft, about developing such a system. Seattle Computer was not one of those companies. Bill Gates knew that Seattle Computer had developed a disk operating system and took action: he borrowed $50,000 from his father, a senior partner in a prominent Seattle law firm, and then went to see the CEO of Seattle Computer and offered to purchase the rights to the company's Q-DOS system. He did not, of course, reveal that IBM was looking for a disk operating system. Seattle Computer, short of cash, quickly agreed. Gates then renamed the system MS-DOS, upgraded it, and licensed it to IBM. The rest, as they say, is history.

So was Gates lucky? Of course he was. It was lucky that Seattle Computer had not heard about IBM's request. It was lucky that IBM approached Microsoft. It was lucky that Gates knew about Seattle Computer's operating system. And it was lucky that Gates had a father wealthy enough to lend him $50,000 on short notice. On the other hand, Gates's luck was hardly random. Microsoft was already a player in the embryonic personal computer software industry, and its first software program, Microsoft Basic, had been a bestseller. IBM came to Microsoft because the company had already earned respect in the industry. Moreover, to attribute all of Microsoft's subsequent success to luck would be wrong. Although MS-DOS gave Microsoft a tremendous head start in the industry, it did not guarantee that Microsoft would continue to enjoy the kind of worldwide success that it has. To do that, Microsoft had to build the appropriate set of resources and capabilities required to produce a continual stream of innovative software, which is precisely what the company did with the cash generated from MS-DOS.[e]

Summary of Chapter

1. Distinctive competencies are the firm-specific strengths of a company. Valuable distinctive competencies enable a company to earn a profit rate that is above the industry average.

2. The distinctive competencies of an organization arise from its resources (its financial, physical, human, technological, and organizational assets) and capabilities (its skills at coordinating resources and putting them to productive use).

3. In order to achieve a competitive advantage, a company needs to pursue strategies that build on its existing resources and capabilities and formulate strategies that build additional resources and capabilities (develop new competencies).

4. The source of a competitive advantage is superior value creation.

5. To create superior value, a company must lower its costs or differentiate its product so that it creates more value and can charge a higher price, or do both simultaneously.

6. Managers must understand how value creation and pricing decisions affect demand and how costs change with increases in volume. They must have a good grasp of the demand conditions in the company's market and the cost structure of the company at different levels of output if they are to make decisions that maximize the profitability of their enterprise.

7. The four building blocks of competitive advantage are efficiency, quality, innovation, and responsiveness to customers. These are generic distinctive competencies. Superior efficiency enables a company to lower its costs, superior quality allows it to charge a higher price and lower its costs, and superior customer

service lets it charge a higher price. Superior innovation can lead to higher prices, particularly in the case of product innovations, or lower unit costs, particularly in the case of process innovations.

8. If a company's managers are to perform a good internal analysis, they need to be able to analyze the financial performance of their company, identifying how the strategies of the company relate to its profitability as measured by the return on invested capital.

9. The durability of a company's competitive advantage depends on the height of barriers to imitation, the capability of competitors, and environmental dynamism.

10. Failing companies typically earn low or negative profits. Three factors seem to contribute to failure: organizational inertia in the face of environmental change, the nature of a company's prior strategic commitments, and the Icarus paradox.

11. Avoiding failure requires a constant focus on the basic building blocks of competitive advantage, continuous improvement, identification and adoption of best industrial practice, and victory over inertia.

Discussion Questions

1. What are the main implications of the material discussed in this chapter for strategy formulation?
2. When is a company's competitive advantage most likely to endure over time?
3. It is possible for a company to be the lowest-cost producer in its industry and simultaneously have an output that is the most valued by customers. Discuss this statement.
4. Why is it important to understand the drivers of profitability as measured by the return on invested capital?
5. Which is more important in explaining the success and failure of companies: strategizing or luck?

Practicing Strategic Management

SMALL-GROUP EXERCISE
Analyzing Competitive Advantage

Break up into groups of three to five. Drawing on the concepts introduced in this chapter, analyze the competitive position of your business school in the market for business education. Then answer the following questions:

1. Does your business school have a competitive advantage?
2. If so, on what is this advantage based, and is this advantage sustainable?
3. If your school does not have a competitive advantage in the market for business education, identify the inhibiting factors that are holding it back.
4. How might the Internet change the way in which business education is delivered?
5. Does the Internet pose a threat to the competitive position of your school in the market for business education, or is it an opportunity for your school to enhance its competitive position? (Note that it can be both.)

ARTICLE FILE 3

Find a company that has sustained its competitive advantage for more than ten years. Identify the source of the competitive advantage, and explain why it has lasted so long.

STRATEGIC MANAGEMENT PROJECT
Module 3

This module deals with the competitive position of your company. With the information you have at your disposal, perform the tasks and answer the following questions:

1. Identify whether your company has a competitive advantage or disadvantage in its primary industry. Its primary industry is the one in which it has the most sales.
2. Evaluate your company against the four generic building blocks of competitive advantage: efficiency, quality, innovation, and responsiveness to customers. How

does this exercise help you understand the performance of your company relative to its competitors?

3. What are the distinctive competencies of your company?

4. What role have prior strategies played in shaping the distinctive competencies of your company? What has been the role of luck?

5. Do the strategies your company is pursuing now build on its distinctive competencies? Are they an attempt to build new competencies?

6. What are the barriers to imitating the distinctive competencies of your company?

7. Is there any evidence that your company finds it difficult to adapt to changing industry conditions? If so, why do you think this is the case?

ETHICS EXERCISE

John, an official at a national beverage chain, had been working to convince a national sandwich restaurant chain to carry his company's newest beverage, Slushy Soda. Originally, John hoped that the sandwich chain would simply agree to carry the frozen soda drink, but the sandwich chain was hesitant. Together, John and the sandwich chain agreed to do a test run on the new beverage in Atlanta, where the hot weather might assist in the soda's promotion. With each purchase, the sandwich chain would offer a coupon for a free Slushy Soda. If enough coupons were redeemed, the company would consider adding the beverage to its lineup.

John and his company had a lot of money invested in this new beverage; in fact, John's job was on the line. If he could not convince the sandwich chain to pick up the beverage, he could lose his job. After a week of the test run, the numbers were less than promising. In a moment of desperation, John sent several of his employees to Atlanta, ordering them to redeem as many of the beverage coupons as possible. They were also instructed to pass out coupons and cash to customers outside the sandwich shops in the hope that they would then redeem the coupons.

It didn't take long for the sandwich chain to figure out what was going on. John's employees were called home. John became responsible not only for his own termination but for those of his employees as well. And Slushy Soda never made it out of the starting gate.

1. Define the ethical dilemma presented in this case

2. Should John and his employees have been fired for attempting to manipulate the test run?

3. What does it say about John's company that he felt he needed to behave unethically to retain his job?

CLOSING CASE

Starbucks

In 2006, Starbucks, the ubiquitous coffee retailer, closed a decade of astounding financial performance. Sales had increased from $697 million to $7.8 billion, and net profits, from $36 million to $540 million. In 2006, Starbucks was earning a return on invested capital of 25.5%, which was impressive by any measure, and the company was forecasted to continue growing earnings and maintain high profits through the end of the decade. How did this come about?

Thirty years ago, Starbucks was a single store in Seattle's Pike Place Market selling premium roasted coffee. Today, it is a global roaster and retailer of coffee with more than 12,000 retail stores, some 3,000 of which are to be found in forty countries outside the United States. Starbucks Corporation set out on its current course in the 1980s when the company's director of marketing, Howard Schultz, came back from a trip to Italy enchanted with the Italian coffeehouse experience. Schultz, who later became CEO, persuaded the company's owners to experiment with the coffeehouse format—and the Starbucks experience was born.

Schultz's basic insight was that people lacked a "third place" between home and work where they could have their own personal time-out, meet with friends, relax, and have a sense of gathering. The business model that evolved out of this was to sell the company's own premium roasted coffee, along with freshly brewed espresso-style coffee beverages, a variety of pastries, coffee accessories, teas, and other products, in a coffeehouse setting. The company devoted, and continues to devote, considerable attention to the design of its stores to create a relaxed, informal, and comfortable atmosphere. Underlying this approach was a belief that Starbucks was selling far more than coffee—it was selling an experience. The premium price that Starbucks charged for its coffee reflected this fact.

From the outset, Schultz also focused on providing superior customer service in stores. Reasoning that motivated employees provide the best customer service, Starbucks executives developed employee hiring and training programs that were the best in the restaurant industry. Today, all Starbucks employees are required to attend training classes that teach them not only how to make a good cup of coffee but also the service-oriented values of the company. Beyond this, Starbucks provides progressive compensation policies that gave even part-time employees stock option grants and medical benefits—a very innovative approach in an industry where most employees are part-time, earn minimum wage, and have no benefits.

Unlike many restaurant chains, which expanded very rapidly through franchising arrangements once they established a basic formula that appears to work, Schultz believed that Starbucks needed to own its stores. Although it has experimented with franchising arrangements in some countries and in some situations in the United States such as at airports, the company still prefers to own its own stores whenever possible.

This formula met with spectacular success in the United States, where Starbucks went from obscurity to one of the best-known brands in the country in a decade. As it grew, Starbucks found that it was generating an enormous volume of repeat business. Today, the average customer comes into a Starbucks store around twenty times a month. The customers themselves are a fairly well-heeled group—their average income is about $80,000.

As the company grew, it started to develop a very sophisticated location strategy. Detailed demographic analysis was used to identify the best locations for Starbucks stores. The company expanded rapidly to capture as many premium locations as possible before its imitators could. Astounding many observers, Starbucks would even sometimes locate stores on opposite corners of the same busy street—so that it could capture traffic going in different directions down the street.

By 1995, with almost 700 stores across the United States, Starbucks began exploring foreign opportunities. The first stop was Japan, where Starbucks proved that the basic value proposition could be applied to a different cultural setting (there are now 600 stores in Japan). Next, Starbucks embarked on a rapid development strategy in Asia and Europe. By 2001, the magazine *Brandchannel* named Starbucks one of the ten most influential global brands, a position it has held ever since. But this is only the beginning. In October 2006, with 12,000 stores in operation, the company announced that its long term goal was to have 40,000 stores worldwide. Looking forward, it expects 50% of all new store openings to be outside the United States.[39]

Case Discussion Questions

1. Identify the resources, capabilities, and distinctive competencies of Starbucks.
2. How do Starbucks's resources, capabilities, and distinctive competencies translate into superior financial performance?
3. How secure is Starbucks's competitive advantage? What are the barriers to imitation?

Building Competitive Advantage Through Functional-Level Strategy

OPENING CASE

Boosting Efficiency at Matsushita

When Kunio Nakamura became CEO at the venerable Japanese electronics giant, Matsushita, in 2000, it was a company in deep trouble. Earnings had been going south for years and the company's market capitalization had shrunk to less than half of that of long-time rival Sony. Employees were frustrated and morale was poor. By the time he retired in June 2006, Matsushita was delivering its best financial performance in more than a decade. After losing $3.7 billion in 2002, in the year ending March 2006 the company registered profits of $1.37 billion. Moreover, earnings were projected to grow 20%, to $1.7 billion, in the year ending March 2007.

Nakamura achieved this transformation by relentlessly focusing on efficiency improvements. Early in his tenure, he put an end to the internal rivalries that had led different divisions to develop identical products. The resulting duplication wasted precious research and development (R&D) money and limited the ability of the company to realize economies of scale. He reduced the number of layers in the management hierarchy and slashed the domestic workforce by 19%—a tough thing to do at Matsushita, where life time employment had been the norm—and closed thirty factories. Then he pushed factory managers to do everything possible to raise productivity.

Matsushita's factory in Saga, Japan, exemplifies the obsession with productivity improvements. By 2004, employees at the factory, which makes cordless phones, faxes, and security cameras, had already doubled productivity since 2000 by introducing robots into the assembly line, but factory managers were not happy. An analysis of flow in the production system showed that bottlenecks on the assembly line meant that robots sat idle for longer than they were working. So the plant's managers ripped out the assembly line conveyer belts and replaced them with clusters of robots grouped into cells. The cells allowed them to double up on slower robots to make the entire manufacturing process run more smoothly. Then they developed software to synchronize production so that each robot jumped into action as soon as the previous step was completed. If one robot broke down, the work flow could be shifted to another to do the same job.

The results were impressive. The time that it took to build products was drastically reduced. It used to take two and a half days in a production run before the first finished products came off the assembly line; now it takes as little as forty minutes. Phones, for example, can now be assembled in one-third of the time, doubling weekly output from the same plant with the same number of employees. Shorter cycle times enabled the factory to slash inventories. Work-in-progress, such as partly finished products, along with components such as chipsets, keypads, and circuit boards, now spent far less time in the factory.

The Saga factory is known as a mother plant within Matsushita. Once process improvements have been refined at a mother plant, they have to be transferred to other plants within the group as quickly as possible. There are six other plants in the Saga group: in China, Malaysia, Mexico, and Britain. Most were able to quickly copy what was done at Saga and saw similar cuts in inventory and boosts in productivity.

Despite the faster pace of work, the factory employees paid close attention to product quality. The short cycle times helped employees to identify the source of defective products and quickly fix any errors that led to quality problems. Consequently, at less than 1% of output, by 2006, defect rates were at an all-time low in every factory. The reduction in waste further boosted productivity and helped the company to strengthen its reputation for producing high-quality merchandise.[1]

OVERVIEW

In this chapter, we take a close look at **functional-level strategies**: those aimed at improving the effectiveness of a company's operations and thus its ability to attain superior efficiency, quality, innovation, and customer responsiveness.

It is important to keep in mind the relationships among functional strategies, distinctive competencies, differentiation, low cost, value creation, and profitability (see Figure 4.1). Note that distinctive competencies shape the functional-level strategies

FIGURE 4.1

The Roots of Competitive Advantage

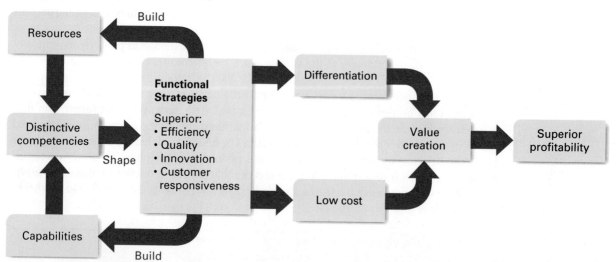

that a company can pursue and that managers, through their choices with regard to functional-level strategies, can build resources and capabilities that enhance a company's distinctive competencies. Note also that the ability of a company to attain superior efficiency, quality, innovation, and customer responsiveness will determine if its product offering is differentiated from that of rivals and if it has a low-cost structure. Recall that companies that increase the utility consumers get from their products through differentiation, while simultaneously lowering their cost structure, create more value than their rivals, and this leads to a competitive advantage and superior profitability and profit growth.

The Opening Case illustrates some of these relationships. Managers at Matsushita's Saga factory in Japan pursued functional-level strategies that raised productivity, thus increasing the efficiency of their production process while also reducing defect rates and boosting the reliability of their final product offering. The superior efficiency enabled the factory (and others like it around the world) to lower costs, while superior reliability enhanced product quality, helped to differentiate the product offering, and boosted sales volume. The result: Matsushita created more value, and its profitability increased.

Consistent with the Matsushita example, much of this chapter is devoted to looking at the basic strategies that can be adopted at the operating level to improve competitive position. By the end of this chapter, you will understand how functional-level strategies can be used to build a sustainable competitive advantage.

Achieving Superior Efficiency

A company is a device for transforming inputs (labor, land, capital, management, and technological know-how) into outputs (the goods and services produced). The simplest measure of efficiency is the quantity of inputs that it takes to produce a given output; that is, Efficiency = outputs/inputs. The more efficient a company is, the fewer the inputs required to produce a given output and therefore the lower its cost structure will be. Put another way, an efficient company has higher productivity, and therefore lower costs, than its rivals. Here we review the steps that companies can take at the functional level to increase their efficiency and thereby lower their cost structure.

● **Efficiency and Economies of Scale**

Economies of scale are unit cost reductions associated with a large scale of output. Recall from the last chapter that it is very important for managers to understand how the cost structure of their enterprise varies with output because this understanding should help to drive strategy. For example, if unit costs fall significantly as output is expanded—that is, if there are significant economies of scale—a company may benefit by keeping prices down and increasing volume.

One source of economies of scale is the ability to spread fixed costs over a large production volume. **Fixed costs** are costs that must be incurred to produce a product whatever the level of output; examples are the costs of purchasing machinery, setting up machinery for individual production runs, building facilities, advertising, and R&D. For example, Microsoft spent approximately $5 billion to develop the latest version of its Windows operating system, Windows Vista. It can realize substantial scale economies by spreading the fixed costs associated with developing the new operating system over the enormous unit sales volume it expects for this system

(95% of the world's 250 million personal computers use a Microsoft operating system). These scale economies are significant because of the trivial incremental (or marginal) cost of producing additional copies of Windows Vista: once the master copy has been produced, additional CDs containing the operating system can be produced for a few cents. The key to Microsoft's efficiency and profitability (and that of other companies with high fixed costs and trivial incremental or marginal costs) is to increase sales rapidly enough that fixed costs can be spread out over a large unit volume and substantial scale economies can be realized.

Another source of scale economies is the ability of companies producing in large volumes to achieve a greater division of labor and specialization. Specialization is said to have a favorable impact on productivity mainly because it enables employees to become very skilled at performing a particular task. The classic example of such economies is Ford's Model T car. The world's first mass-produced car, the Model T Ford was introduced in 1923. Until then, Ford had made cars using an expensive hand-built craft production method. By introducing mass-production techniques, the company achieved greater division of labor (it split assembly into small, repeatable tasks) and specialization, which boosted employee productivity. Ford was also able to spread the fixed costs of developing a car and setting up production machinery over a large volume of output. As a result of these economies, the cost of manufacturing a car at Ford fell from $3,000 to less than $900 (in 1958 dollars).

These examples illustrate that economies of scale can boost profitability, as measured by return on invested capital (ROIC), in a number of ways. Economies of scale exist in production, sales and marketing, and R&D, and the overall effect of realizing scale economies is to reduce spending as a percentage of revenues on cost of goods sold (COGS), sales, general, and administrative expenses (SG&A), and R&D expenses, thereby boosting return on sales and, by extension, ROIC (see Figure 3.9). Moreover, by making more intensive use of existing capacity, a company can increase the amount of sales generated from its property, plant, and equipment (PPE), thereby reducing the amount of capital it needs to generate a dollar of sales, and thus increasing its capital turnover and its ROIC.

The concept of scale economies is illustrated in Figure 4.2, which shows that as a company increases its output, unit costs fall. This process comes to an end at an output of Q1, where all scale economies are exhausted. Indeed, at outputs of greater

FIGURE 4.2

Economies and
Diseconomies of
Scale

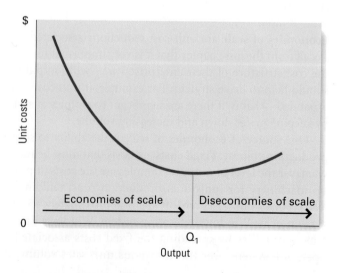

than Q1, the company may encounter **diseconomies of scale,** which are the unit cost increases associated with a large scale of output. Diseconomies of scale occur primarily because of the increasing bureaucracy associated with large-scale enterprises and the managerial inefficiencies that can result.[2] Larger enterprises have a tendency to develop extensive managerial hierarchies in which dysfunctional political behavior is commonplace, information about operating matters is accidentally and deliberately distorted by the number of managerial layers through which it has to travel to reach top decisionmakers, and poor decisions are the result. Past some point (such as Q1 in Figure 4.2), the inefficiencies that result from such developments outweigh any additional gains from economies of scale, and unit costs start to rise as output expands. This was what had occurred at Matsushita. When Kunio Nakamura became CEO in 2000, he reduced the number of layers in the management hierarchy in an attempt to eliminate diseconomies of scale (see the Opening Case).

Managers must know not only the extent of economies of scale but also where diseconomies of scale begin to occur. At Nucor Steel, for example, the realization that diseconomies of scale exist has led to a decision not to build plants that employ more than 300 individuals. The belief is that it is more efficient to build two plants, each employing 300 people, than one plant employing 600 people. Although the larger plant might theoretically be able to reap greater scale economies, Nucor's management believes that these would be swamped by the diseconomies of scale that come with larger organizational units.

● **Efficiency and Learning Effects**

Learning effects are cost savings that come from learning by doing. Labor, for example, learns by repetition how best to carry out a task. Therefore, labor productivity increases over time, and unit costs fall as individuals learn the most efficient way to perform a particular task. Equally important, management in new manufacturing facilities typically learns over time how best to run the new operation. Hence, production costs decline because of increasing labor productivity and management efficiency. Japanese companies like Toyota are noted for making learning a central part of their operating philosophy.

Learning effects tend to be more significant when a technologically complex task is repeated because there is more to learn. Thus, learning effects will be more significant in an assembly process that has 1,000 complex steps than in one with 100 simple steps. Although learning effects are normally associated with the manufacturing process, there is every reason to believe that they are just as important in service industries. For example, one famous study of learning in the context of the health care industry found that more experienced medical providers posted significantly lower mortality rates for a number of common surgical procedures, suggesting that learning effects are at work in surgery.[3] The authors of this study used the evidence to argue for establishing regional referral centers for the provision of highly specialized medical care. These centers would perform many specific surgical procedures (such as heart surgery), replacing local facilities with lower volumes and presumably higher mortality rates. Another recent study found strong evidence of learning effects in a financial institution. The study looked at a newly established document-processing unit with 100 staff members and found that, over time, documents were processed much more rapidly as the staff learned the process. Overall, the study concluded that unit costs fell every time the cumulative number of documents processed doubled.[4] Strategy in Action 4.1 looks at the determinants of differences in learning effects across a sample of hospitals performing cardiac surgery.

Strategy in Action   4.1

Learning Effects in Cardiac Surgery

A study carried out by researchers at the Harvard Business School tried to estimate the importance of learning effects in the case of a specific new technology for minimally invasive heart surgery that was approved by federal regulators in 1996. The researchers looked at sixteen hospitals and obtained data on the operations for 660 patients. They examined how the time required to undertake the procedure varied with cumulative experience. Across the sixteen hospitals, they found that average time fell from 280 minutes for the first procedure with the new technology to 220 minutes by the time a hospital had performed fifty procedures (note that not all of the hospitals performed fifty procedures, and the estimates represent an extrapolation based on the data).

Next they looked at differences across hospitals. Here they found evidence of very large differences in learning effects. One hospital, in particular, stood out. This hospital, which they called Hospital M, reduced its net procedure time from 500 minutes on case 1 to 132 minutes by case 50. Hospital M's eighty-eight-minute procedure time advantage over the average hospital at case 50 translated into a cost saving of approximately $2,250 per case, and allowed surgeons at the hospital to do one more revenue-generating procedure per day.

The researchers tried to find out why Hospital M was so superior. They noted that all hospitals had similar state-of-the-art operating rooms and used the same set of FDA-approved devices, that all adopting surgeons went through the same training courses, and that all surgeons came from highly respected training hospitals. Follow-up interviews suggested, however, that Hospital M differed in how it implemented the new procedure. The team was handpicked by the adopting surgeon to perform the surgery. It had significant prior experience working together (indeed, that was apparently a key criterion for team members). The team trained together to perform the new surgery. Before undertaking a single procedure, they met with the operating room nurses and anesthesiologists to discuss the procedure. Moreover, the adopting surgeon mandated that the surgical team and surgical procedure were stable in the early cases. The initial team went through fifteen procedures before new members were added or substituted and twenty cases before the procedures were modified. The adopting surgeon also insisted that the team meet prior to each of the first ten cases, and they also meet after the first twenty cases to debrief.

The picture that emerges is one of a core team that was selected and managed to maximize the gains from learning. Unlike other hospitals where there was less stability of team members and procedures, and where there was not the same attention to briefing, debriefing, and learning, surgeons at Hospital M both learned much faster and ultimately achieved higher productivity than their peers in other institutions. Clearly, differences in the implementation of the new procedure were very important.[a]

In terms of the unit cost curve of a company, although economies of scale imply a movement along the curve (say, from A to B in Figure 4.3), the realization of learning effects implies a downward shift of the entire curve (B to C in Figure 4.3) as both labor and management become more efficient over time at performing their tasks at every level of output. In accounting terms, learning effects in a production setting will reduce the cost of goods sold as a percentage of revenues, enabling the company to earn a higher return on sales and return on invested capital.

No matter how complex the task is, however, learning effects typically die out after a limited period of time. Indeed, it has been suggested that they are really important only during the start-up period of a new process and then cease after two or three years.[5] When changes occur to a company's production system—as a result of merger or the use of new information technology, for example—the learning process has to begin again.

FIGURE 4.3

The Impact of
Learning and Scale
Economies on
Unit Costs

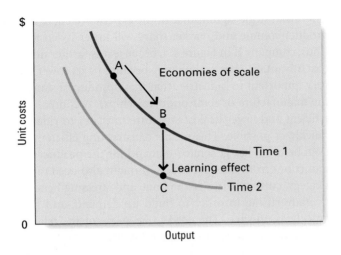

Efficiency and the Experience Curve

The **experience curve** refers to the systematic lowering of the cost structure, and consequent unit cost reductions, that have been observed to occur over the life of a product.[6] According to the experience-curve concept, unit manufacturing costs for a product typically decline by some characteristic amount each time accumulated output of the product is doubled (accumulated output is the total output of a product since its introduction). This relationship was first observed in the aircraft industry, where it was found that each time accumulated output of airframes was doubled, unit costs declined to 80 percent of their previous level.[7] Thus, the fourth airframe typically cost only 80 percent of the second airframe to produce, the eighth airframe only 80 percent of the fourth, the sixteenth only 80 percent of the eighth, and so on. The outcome of this process is a relationship between unit manufacturing costs and accumulated output similar to that illustrated in Figure 4.4. Economies of scale and learning effects underlie the experience-curve phenomenon. Put simply, as a company increases the accumulated volume of its output over time, it is able to realize both economies of scale (as volume increases) and learning effects. Consequently, unit costs and cost structure fall with increases in accumulated output.

FIGURE 4.4

The Experience Curve

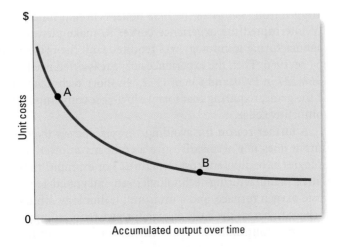

The strategic significance of the experience curve is clear: increasing a company's product volume and market share will lower its cost structure relative to its rivals. Thus, company B in Figure 4.4, because it is farther down the experience curve, has a cost advantage over company A because of its lower cost structure. The concept is very important in industries that mass-produce a standardized output (for example, the manufacture of semiconductor chips). A company that wishes to become more efficient and lower its cost structure must try to ride down the experience curve as quickly as possible. This means constructing efficient scale manufacturing facilities even before it has generated demand for the product and aggressively pursuing cost reductions from learning effects. It might also need to adopt an aggressive marketing strategy, cutting prices to the bone and stressing heavy sales promotions and extensive advertising in order to build up demand, and hence accumulated volume, as quickly as possible. The need to be aware of the relationship of demand, price options, and costs noted in Chapter 3 is clear.

Once down the experience curve because of its superior efficiency, the company is likely to have a significant cost advantage over its competitors. For example, it has been argued that Intel uses such tactics to ride down the experience curve and gain a competitive advantage over its rivals in the market for microprocessors. Similarly, one reason Matsushita came to dominate the global market for VHS videotape recorders is that it based its strategy on the experience curve.[8]

However, there are three reasons why managers should not become complacent about efficiency-based cost advantages derived from experience effects. First, since neither learning effects nor economies of scale go on forever, the experience curve is likely to bottom out at some point; indeed, it must do so by definition. When this occurs, further unit cost reductions from learning effects and economies of scale will be hard to come by. Thus, in time, other companies can lower their cost structures and match the cost leader. Once this happens, a number of low-cost companies can have cost parity with each other. In such circumstances, a sustainable competitive advantage must rely on strategic factors besides the minimization of production costs by using existing technologies—factors such as better responsiveness to customers, product quality, or innovation.

Second, as noted in Chapter 2, changes that are always taking place in the external environment disrupt a company's business model, so cost advantages gained from experience effects can be made obsolete by the development of new technologies. The price of television picture tubes followed the experience-curve pattern from the introduction of the television in the late 1940s until 1963. The average unit price dropped from $34 to $8 (in 1958 dollars) in that time. However, the advent of color TV interrupted the experience curve. To make picture tubes for color TVs, a new manufacturing technology was required, and the price of color TV tubes shot up to $51 by 1966. Then the experience curve reasserted itself. The price dropped to $48 in 1968, $37 in 1970, and $36 in 1972.[9] In short, technological change can alter the rules of the game, requiring that former low-cost companies take steps to reestablish their competitive edge.

A further reason for avoiding complacency is that producing a high volume of output does not necessarily give a company a lower cost structure. Different technologies have different cost structures. For example, the steel industry has two alternative manufacturing technologies: an integrated technology, which relies on the basic oxygen furnace, and a mini-mill technology, which depends on the electric arc furnace. Whereas the basic oxygen furnace requires high volumes to attain maximum efficiency, mini-mills are cost efficient at relatively low volumes. Moreover, even when both technologies are producing at their most efficient output levels, steel companies with basic oxygen furnaces do not have a cost advantage over mini-mills. Consequently, the pursuit of experience economies by an integrated company using basic oxygen technology may not bring the kind of cost advantages that a naive reading of the experience-curve phenomenon would lead the company to expect. Indeed, there have been significant periods of time when integrated companies have not been able to get enough orders to run at optimum capacity. Hence, their production costs have been considerably higher than those of mini-mills.[10] As we discuss next, in many industries new flexible manufacturing technologies hold out the promise of allowing small manufacturers to produce at unit costs comparable to those of large assembly line operations.

● **Efficiency, Flexible Production Systems, and Mass Customization**

Central to the concept of economies of scale is the idea that the best way to achieve high efficiency and a lower cost structure is through the mass production of a standardized output. The tradeoff implicit in this idea is between unit costs and product variety. Producing greater product variety from a factory implies shorter production runs, which implies an inability to realize economies of scale and higher costs. That is, a wide product variety makes it difficult for a company to increase its production efficiency and thus reduce its unit costs. According to this logic, the way to increase efficiency and achieve a lower cost structure is to limit product variety and produce a standardized product in large volumes (see Figure 4.5a).

This view of production efficiency has been challenged by the rise of flexible production technologies. The term **flexible production technology**—or lean production, as it is sometimes called—covers a range of technologies designed to reduce setup times for complex equipment, increase the use of individual machines through better scheduling, and improve quality control at all stages of the manufacturing

FIGURE 4.5

Tradeoff Between Costs and Product Variety

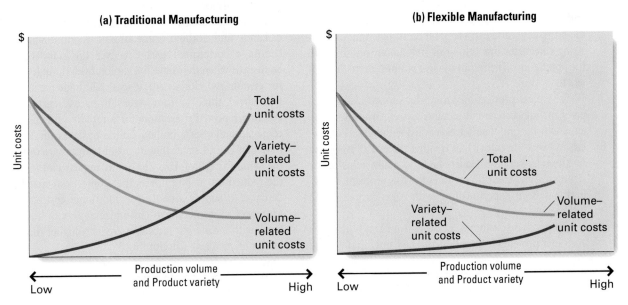

process.[11] Flexible production technologies allow the company to produce a wider variety of end-products at a unit cost that at one time could be achieved only through the mass production of a standardized output (see Figure 4.5b). Indeed, research suggests that the adoption of flexible production technologies may increase efficiency and lower unit costs relative to what can be achieved by the mass production of a standardized output, while at the same time enabling the company to customize its product offering to a much greater extent than was once thought possible. The term **mass customization** has been coined to describe the ability of companies to use flexible manufacturing technology to reconcile two goals that were once thought to be incompatible: low cost and differentiation through product customization.[12] For an extended example of the benefits of mass customization, see Strategy in Action 4.2, which looks at mass customization at Lands' End.

Strategy in Action 4.2

Mass Customization at Lands' End

Years ago, almost all clothing was made to individual order by a tailor (a job shop production method). Then along came the twentieth century and techniques for mass production, mass marketing, and mass selling. Production in the industry shifted toward larger volume and less variety based on standardized sizes. The benefits in terms of production cost reductions were enormous, but the customer did not always win. Offset against lower prices was the difficulty of finding clothes that fit as well as tailored clothes once did. Look around you and you will see that people come in a bewildering variety of shapes and sizes; then go into a store to purchase a shirt, and you get to choose between just four sizes: small, medium, large, and extra large! It is estimated the current sizing categories in clothing fit only about one-third of the population. The rest of us wear clothes where the fit is less than ideal.

The mass-production system has drawbacks for apparel manufacturers and retailers as well. Year after year, apparel firms find themselves saddled with billions of dollars in excess inventory that is either thrown away, or put on fire sale, because retailers had too many items of the wrong size and color. To try and solve this problem, Lands' End has been experimenting with mass-customization techniques.

To purchase customized clothes from Lands' End, the customer provides information on the Lands' End website by answering a series of fifteen questions (for pants) or twenty-five questions (for shirts), covering about everything from waist to inseam. The process takes about twenty minutes the first time through, but once the information is saved by Lands' End, it can be quickly accessed for repeat purchases. The customer information is then analyzed by an algorithm that pinpoints a person's body dimensions by taking these data points and running them against a huge database of typical sizes to create a unique, customized pattern. The analysis is done automatically by a computer, which then transmits the order to one of five contract manufacturer plants in the United States and elsewhere, which cut and sew the finished garment, and ship the finished product directly to the customer.

Today, customization is available for most categories of Lands' End clothing. Some 40% of its online shoppers choose a customized garment over the standard-size equivalent when they have the choice. Even though prices for customized clothes are at least $20 higher and they take about three to four weeks to arrive, customized clothing reportedly accounts for a rapidly growing percentage of the $500 million online business for Lands' End. Land's End states that its profit margins are roughly the same for customized clothes as regular clothes, but the reductions in inventories that come from matching demand to supply account for additional cost savings. Moreover, customers who customize appear to be more loyal, with reordering rates that are 34% higher than for buyers of standard-size clothing.[b]

Flexible machine cells are a common flexible production technology. Flexible machine cell is a grouping of various types of machinery, a common materials handler, and a centralized cell controller (a computer). Each cell normally contains four to six machines capable of performing a variety of operations but dedicated to producing a family of parts or products. The settings on the machines are computer-controlled, which allows each cell to switch quickly between the production of different parts or products.

Improved capacity utilization and reductions in work-in-progress (that is, stockpiles of partly finished products) and waste are major efficiency benefits of flexible machine cells. Improved capacity utilization arises from the reduction in setup times and from the computer-controlled coordination of production flow between machines, which eliminates bottlenecks. The tight coordination between machines also reduces work-in-progress. Reductions in waste are due to the ability of computer-controlled machinery to identify ways to transform inputs into outputs while producing a minimum of unusable waste material. Freestanding machines might be in use 50% of the time; the same machines, when grouped into a cell, can be used more than 80% of the time and produce the same end-product with half the waste, thereby increasing efficiency and resulting in lower costs.

The effects of installing flexible production technology on a company's cost structure can be dramatic. The Opening Case tells how Matsushita doubled its productivity by putting flexible machine cells in its factories. Ford Motor Company is currently introducing flexible production technologies into its automotive plants around the world. These new technologies should allow Ford to produce multiple models from the same line and to switch production from one model to another much more quickly than in the past. In total, Ford hopes to take $2 billion out of its cost structure by 2010.[13]

More generally, in terms of the profitability framework developed in Chapter 3, flexible production technology should boost profitability (measured by ROIC) by reducing the cost of goods sold as a percentage of revenues, reducing the working capital needed to finance work-in-progress (because there is less of it), and reducing the amount of capital that needs to be invested in property, plant, and equipment to generate a dollar of sales (because less space is needed to store inventory).

● Marketing and Efficiency

The marketing strategy that a company adopts can have a major impact on efficiency and cost structure. **Marketing strategy** refers to the position that a company takes with regard to pricing, promotion, advertising, product design, and distribution. Some of the steps leading to greater efficiency are fairly obvious. For example, riding down the experience curve to achieve a lower cost structure can be facilitated by aggressive pricing, promotions, and advertising, all of which are the task of the marketing function. Other aspects of marketing strategy have a less obvious but no less important impact on efficiency. One important aspect is the relationship of customer defection rates, cost structure and unit costs.[14]

Customer defection rates (or churn rates) are the percentage of a company's customers who defect every year to competitors. Defection rates are determined by customer loyalty, which in turn is a function of the ability of a company to satisfy its customers. Because acquiring a new customer entails certain one-time fixed costs for advertising, promotions, and the like, there is a direct relationship between defection rates and costs. The longer a company holds on to a customer, the greater is the volume of customer-generated unit sales that can be set against these fixed costs, and

FIGURE 4.6

The Relationship
Between Customer
Loyalty and Profit
per Customer

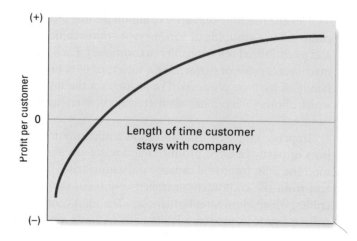

the lower the average unit cost of each sale. Thus, lowering customer defection rates allows a company to achieve a lower cost structure.

One consequence of the defection-cost relationship depicted is illustrated in Figure 4.6. Because of the relatively high fixed costs of acquiring new customers, serving customers who stay with the company only for a short time before switching to competitors often leads to a loss on the investment made to acquire those customers. The longer a customer stays with the company, the more the fixed costs of acquiring that customer can be spread out over repeat purchases, boosting the profit per customer. Thus, there is a positive relationship between the length of time that a customer stays with a company and profit per customer. If a company can reduce customer defection rates, it can make a much better return on its investment in acquiring customers and thereby boost its profitability. In terms of the profitability framework developed in Chapter 3, reduced customer defection rates mean that the company needs to spend less on sales, general, and administrative expenses to generate a dollar of sales revenue, which increases both return on sales and return on invested capital.

For an example, consider the credit card business.[15] Most credit card companies spend an average of $50 to recruit a customer and set up a new account. These costs come from the advertising required to attract new customers, the credit checks required for each customer, and the mechanics of setting up an account and issuing a card. These one-time fixed costs can be recouped only if a customer stays with the company for at least two years. Moreover, when customers stay a second year, they tend to increase their use of the credit card, which raises the volume of revenues generated by each customer over time. As a result, although the credit card business loses $50 per customer in year 1, it makes a profit of $44 in year 3 and $55 in year 6.

Another economic benefit of long-time customer loyalty is the free advertising that customers provide for a company. Loyal customers can dramatically increase the volume of business through referrals. A striking example is Britain's largest retailer, the clothing and food company Marks & Spencer, whose success is built on a well-earned reputation for providing its customers with high-quality goods at reasonable prices. The company has generated such customer loyalty that it does not need to advertise in Britain, a major source of cost saving.

The key message, then, is that reducing customer defection rates and building customer loyalty can be major sources of a lower cost structure. One study has estimated that a 5% reduction in customer defection rates leads to the following increases in profits per customer over average customer life: 75% in the credit card business, 50% in the insurance brokerage industry, 45% in the industrial laundry business, and 35% in the computer software industry.[16]

A central component of developing a strategy to reduce defection rates is to identify customers who have defected, find out why they defected, and act on that information so that other customers do not defect for similar reasons in the future. To take these measures, the marketing function must have information systems capable of tracking customer defections.

● **Materials Management, Just-in-Time, and Efficiency**

The contribution of materials management (logistics) to boosting the efficiency of a company can be just as dramatic as the contribution of production and marketing. Materials management encompasses the activities necessary to get inputs and components to a production facility (including the costs of purchasing inputs), through the production process, and out through a distribution system to the end-user.[17] Because there are so many sources of cost in this process, the potential for reducing costs through more efficient materials-management strategies is enormous. For a typical manufacturing company, materials and transportation costs account for 50 to 70% of its revenues, so even a small reduction in these costs can have a substantial impact on profitability. According to one estimate, for a company with revenues of $1 million, a return on invested capital of 5%, and materials-management costs that amount to 50% of sales revenues (including purchasing costs), increasing total profits by $15,000 would require either a 30% increase in sales revenues or a 3% reduction in materials costs.[18] In a typical competitive market, reducing materials costs by 3% is usually much easier than increasing sales revenues by 30%.

Improving the efficiency of the materials-management function typically requires the adoption of a **just-in-time (JIT)** inventory system, which is designed to economize on inventory holding costs by having components arrive at a manufacturing plant just in time to enter the production process or to have goods arrive at a retail store only when stock is almost depleted. The major cost saving comes from increasing inventory turnover, which reduces inventory holding costs, such as warehousing and storage costs, and the company's need for working capital. For example, through efficient logistics, Wal-Mart can replenish the stock in its stores at least twice a week; many stores receive daily deliveries if they are needed. The typical competitor replenishes its stock every two weeks, so it has to carry a much higher inventory and needs more working capital per dollar of sales. Compared to its competitors, Wal-Mart can maintain the same service levels with a lower investment in inventory, a major source of its lower cost structure. Thus, faster inventory turnover has helped Wal-Mart achieve an efficiency-based competitive advantage in the retailing industry.[19]

More generally, in terms of the profitability model developed in Chapter 3, JIT inventory systems reduce the need for working capital (since there is less inventory to finance) and the need for fixed capital to finance storage space (since there is less to store), which reduces capital needs; increases capital turnover; and, by extension, boosts the return on invested capital.

The drawback of JIT systems is that they leave a company without a buffer stock of inventory. Although buffer stocks are expensive to store, they can help tide a company over shortages on inputs brought about by disruption among suppliers (for instance, a labor dispute at a key supplier) and can help a company respond quickly to increases in demand. However, there are ways around these limitations. For example, to reduce the risks linked to dependence on just one supplier for an important input, a company might decide to source inputs from multiple suppliers.

Recently, the efficient management of materials and inventory has been recast in terms of **supply-chain management**: the task of managing the flow of inputs and components from suppliers into the company's production processes to minimize inventory holding and maximize inventory turnover. One of the exemplary companies in terms of supply-chain management is Dell, whose goal is to streamline its supply chain to such an extent that it *replaces inventory with information*.

● **R&D Strategy and Efficiency**

The role of superior research and development (R&D) in helping a company achieve a greater efficiency and a lower cost structure is twofold. First, the R&D function can boost efficiency by designing products that are easy to manufacture. By cutting down on the number of parts that make up a product, R&D can dramatically decrease the required assembly time, which translates into higher employee productivity, lower costs, and higher profitability. For example, after Texas Instruments redesigned an infrared sighting mechanism that it supplies to the Pentagon, it found that it had reduced the number of parts from forty-seven to twelve, the number of assembly steps from fifty-six to thirteen, the time spent fabricating metal from 757 minutes per unit to 219 minutes per unit, and unit assembly time from 129 minutes to twenty minutes. The result was a substantial decline in production costs. Design for manufacturing requires close coordination between the production and R&D functions of the company, of course. Cross-functional teams with production and R&D personnel who work jointly on the problem best achieve this objective.

The second way in which the R&D function can help a company achieve a lower cost structure is by pioneering process innovations. A process innovation is an innovation in the way production processes operate that improves their efficiency. Process innovations have often been a major source of competitive advantage. Toyota's competitive advantage is based partly on the company's invention of new flexible manufacturing processes that dramatically reduced setup times. This process innovation enabled it to obtain efficiency gains associated with flexible manufacturing systems years ahead of its competitors.

● **Human Resources Strategy and Efficiency**

Employee productivity is one of the key determinants of an enterprise's efficiency, cost structure, and profitability.[20] Productive manufacturing employees can lower the cost of goods sold as a percentage of revenues, a productive sales force can increase sales revenues for a given level of expenses, and productive employees in the company's R&D function can boost the percentage of revenues generated from new products for a given level of R&D expenses. Thus, productive employees lower the costs of generating revenues; increase the return on sales; and, by extension, boost the company's return on invested capital. The challenge for a company's human resources function is to devise ways to increase employee productivity. Among the choices it has are using certain hiring strategies, training employees, organizing the work force into self-managing teams, and linking pay to performance.

HIRING STRATEGY Many companies that are well-known for their productive employees devote considerable attention to hiring. Southwest Airlines hires people who have a positive attitude and work well in teams because it believes that people who have a positive attitude will work hard and interact well with customers, therefore helping to create customer loyalty. Nucor hires people who are self-reliant and goal-oriented because its employees work in self-managing teams where they have to be self-reliant and goal-oriented to perform well. As these examples suggest, it is important to make sure that the hiring strategy of the company is consistent with its own internal organization, culture, and strategic priorities. The people a company hires should have attributes that match the strategic objectives of the company.

EMPLOYEE TRAINING Employees are a major input into the production process. Those who are highly skilled can perform tasks faster and more accurately and are more likely to learn the complex tasks associated with many modern production methods than individuals with lesser skills. Training upgrades employee skill levels, bringing the company productivity-related efficiency gains from learning and experimentation.[21]

SELF-MANAGING TEAMS The use of **self-managing teams,** whose members coordinate their own activities and make their own hiring, training, work, and reward decisions, has been spreading rapidly. The typical team comprises five to fifteen employees who produce an entire product or undertake an entire task. Team members learn all team tasks and rotate from job to job. Because a more flexible work force is one result, team members can fill in for absent coworkers and take over managerial duties such as scheduling work and vacation, ordering materials, and hiring new members. The greater responsibility thrust on team members and the empowerment it implies are seen as motivators. (Empowerment is the process of giving lower-level employees decision-making power.) People often respond well to being given greater autonomy and responsibility. Performance bonuses linked to team production and quality targets work as an additional motivator.

The effect of introducing self-managing teams is reportedly an increase in productivity of 30% or more and a substantial increase in product quality. Further cost savings arise from eliminating supervisors and creating a flatter organizational hierarchy, which also lowers the cost structure of the company. In manufacturing companies, perhaps the most potent way to lower the cost structure is to combine self-managing teams with flexible manufacturing cells. For example, after the introduction of flexible manufacturing technology and work practices based on self-managing teams, a General Electric plant in Salisbury, North Carolina, increased productivity by 250% compared with GE plants that produced the same products four years earlier.[22]

Still, teams are no panacea; in manufacturing companies, self-managing teams may fail to live up to their potential unless they are integrated with flexible manufacturing technology. Also, teams put a lot of management responsibilities on team members, and helping team members to cope with these responsibilities often requires substantial training—a fact that many companies often forget in their rush to drive down costs, with the result that the teams don't work out as well as planned.[23]

PAY FOR PERFORMANCE It is hardly surprising that linking pay to performance can help increase employee productivity, but the issue is not quite so simple as just introducing incentive pay systems. It is also important to define what kind of job performance is to be rewarded and how. Some of the most efficient companies in the world, mindful that cooperation among employees is necessary to realize productivity gains, link pay to group or team (rather than individual) performance. Nucor divides its work force into teams of thirty or so, with bonus pay, which can amount to 30 percent of base pay, linked to the ability of the team to meet productivity and quality goals. This link creates a strong incentive for individuals to cooperate with each other in pursuit of team goals; that is, it facilitates teamwork.

Information Systems and Efficiency

With the rapid spread of computers, the explosive growth of the Internet and corporate intranets (internal corporate computer networks based on Internet standards), and the spread of high-bandwidth fiber optics and digital wireless technology, the information systems function is moving to center stage in the quest for operating efficiencies and a lower cost structure.[24] The impact of information systems on productivity is wide-ranging and potentially affects all other activities of a company. For example, Cisco Systems has been able to realize significant cost savings by moving its ordering and customer service functions online. The company has just 300 service agents handling all of its customer accounts, compared to the 900 it would need if sales were not handled online. The difference represents an annual saving of $20 million a year. Moreover, without automated customer service functions, Cisco calculates that it would need at least 1,000 additional service engineers, which would cost around $75 million.[25] Dell Computer also makes extensive use of the Internet both to lower its cost structure and to differentiate itself from rivals (see the Running Case in this chapter).

Like Cisco and Dell, many companies are using web-based information systems to reduce the costs of coordination between the company and its customers and the company and its suppliers. By using web-based programs to automate customer and supplier interactions, they can substantially reduce the number of people required to manage these interfaces, thereby reducing costs. This trend extends beyond high-tech companies. Banks and financial service companies are finding that they can substantially reduce costs by moving customer accounts and support functions online. Such a move reduces the need for customer service representatives, bank tellers, stockbrokers, insurance agents, and others. For example, it costs an average of about $1.07 to execute a transaction at a bank, such as shifting money from one account to another; executing the same transaction over the Internet costs $0.01.[26]

Similarly, the theory behind Internet-based retailers such as Amazon.com is that by replacing physical stores and their supporting personnel with an online virtual store and automated ordering and checkout processes, a company can take significant costs out of the retailing system. Cost savings can also be realized by using web-based information systems to automate many internal company activities, from managing expense reimbursements to benefits planning and hiring processes, thereby reducing the need for internal support personnel.

Infrastructure and Efficiency

A company's infrastructure—that is, its structure, culture, style of strategic leadership, and control system—determines the context within which all other value creation activities take place. It follows that improving infrastructure can help a company increase efficiency and lower its cost structure. Above all, an appropriate infrastructure can help foster a companywide commitment to efficiency and promote cooperation among different functions in pursuit of efficiency goals. These issues are addressed at length in later chapters.

For now, it is important to note that strategic leadership is especially important in building a companywide commitment to efficiency. The leadership task is to articulate a vision that recognizes the need for all functions of a company to focus on improving efficiency (this is what happen at Matsushita when Kunio Nakamura became CEO in 2000—see the Opening Case). It is not enough to improve the efficiency of production or of marketing or of R&D in a piecemeal fashion. Achieving superior efficiency requires a companywide commitment to this goal that must be articulated by general and functional managers. A further leadership task is to facilitate the cross-functional cooperation needed to achieve superior efficiency. For example, designing products that are easy to manufacture requires that production and R&D

RUNNING CASE

Dell's Utilization of the Internet

Dell Computer is famous for being the first company to implement online selling in the PC industry. Launched in June 1994, today more than 85% of Dell's computers are sold online. According to Michael Dell, "As I saw it, the Internet offered a logical extension of the direct [selling] model, creating even stronger relationships with our customers. The Internet would augment conventional telephone, fax, and face-to-face encounters, and give our customers the information they wanted faster, cheaper, and more efficiently." Dell's website allows customers to customize their orders to a degree that would have been unthinkable before the Web. Customers can mix and match product features such as microprocessors, memory, monitors, internal hard drives, CD and DVD drives, keyboard and mouse format, and so on, in order to get the system that best suits their particular requirements. By allowing customers to configure their order, Dell increases its customer responsiveness, thereby differentiating itself from rivals. Dell has also put much of its customer service functions online, reducing the need for telephone calls to customer service representatives and saving costs in the process. Each week some 200,000 people access Dell's troubleshooting tips online. Each of these visits to Dell's website saves the company a potential $15, which is the average cost of a technical support call. If just 10% of these online visitors were to call Dell by telephone instead, it would cost the company $15.6 million per year.

Dell also uses the Internet to manage its supply chain, feeding real-time information about order flow to its suppliers. Dell's suppliers use this information to better schedule their own production on a real-time basis, providing components to Dell on a just-in-time basis, thereby taking inventory out of the system and reducing Dell's need for working capital and space to store the inventory. Dell's ultimate goal is to drive all inventories out of the supply chain, apart from that in transit between suppliers and Dell, effectively replacing inventory with information. By doing so, Dell can drive significant costs out of its system.

Internet-based customer ordering and procurement systems have also allowed the company to synchronize demand and supply to an extent that few other companies can. For example, if Dell sees that it is running out of a particular component, say, seventeen-inch monitors from Sony, it can manipulate demand by offering a nineteen-inch model at a lower price until Sony delivers more seventeen-inch monitors. By taking such steps to fine-tune the balance between demand and supply, Dell can meet customers' expectations and maintain its differential advantage. Moreover, balancing supply and demand allows the company to minimize excess and obsolete inventory. Dell writes off between 0.05% and 0.1% of total materials costs in excess or obsolete inventory. Its competitors write off between 2 and 3%, which again gives Dell a significant cost advantage.[c]

personnel communicate, integrating JIT systems with production scheduling requires close communication between materials management and production, designing self-managing teams to perform production tasks requires close cooperation between human resources and production, and so on.

● Summary: Achieving Efficiency

Table 4.1 summarizes the primary roles that various functions must take to achieve superior efficiency. Bear in mind that achieving superior efficiency is not something that can be tackled on a function-by-function basis. It requires an organizationwide commitment and an ability to ensure close cooperation among functions. Top management, by exercising leadership and influencing the infrastructure, plays a major role in this process.

TABLE 4.1

Primary Roles of Value Creation Functions in Achieving Superior Efficiency

Value Creation Function	Primary Roles
Infrastructure (leadership)	1. Provide companywide commitment to efficiency 2. Facilitate cooperation among functions
Production	1. Where appropriate, pursue economies of scale and learning economics 2. Implement flexible manufacturing systems
Marketing	1. Where appropriate, adopt aggressive marketing to ride down the experience curve 2. Limit customer defection rates by building brand loyalty
Materials management	1. Implement JIT systems 2. Implement supply-chain coordination
R&D	1. Design products for ease of manufacture 2. Seek process innovations
Information systems	1. Use information systems to automate processes 2. Use information systems to reduce costs of coordination
Human resources	1. Institute training programs to build skills 2. Implement self-managing teams 3. Implement pay for performance

Achieving Superior Quality

In Chapter 3, we noted that quality can be thought of in terms of two dimensions: *quality as reliability* and *quality as excellence.* High-quality products are reliable in the sense that they do the job they were designed for and do it well, and are also perceived by consumers to have superior attributes. We also noted that superior quality gives a company two advantages. First, a strong reputation for quality allows a company to differentiate its products from those offered by rivals, thereby creating more utility in the eyes of customers, which gives the company the option of charging a premium price for its products. Second, eliminating defects or errors from the production process reduces waste, increases efficiency, and lowers the cost structure of the company and increases its profitability. For example, reducing the number of defects in a company's manufacturing process lowers the cost of goods sold as a percentage of revenues, thereby raising the company's return on sales and return on invested capital. In this section, we look in more depth at what managers can do to enhance the reliability and other attributes of the company's product offering.

● **Attaining Superior Reliability**

The principal tool that most managers now use to increase the reliability of their product offering is the Six Sigma quality improvement methodology. The Six Sigma methodology is a direct descendant of the total quality management (TQM) philosophy that was widely adopted, first by Japanese companies and then by American companies, during the 1980s and early 1990s.[27] The TQM concept was developed by a number of American management consultants, including W. Edwards Deming, Joseph Juran, and A. V. Feigenbaum.[28]

Originally, these consultants won few converts in the United States. However, managers in Japan embraced their ideas enthusiastically and even named their premier annual prize for manufacturing excellence after Deming. The philosophy underlying TQM, as articulated by Deming, is based on the following five-step chain reaction:

1. Improved quality means that costs decrease because of less rework, fewer mistakes, fewer delays, and better use of time and materials.

2. As a result, productivity improves.

3. Better quality leads to higher market share and allows the company to raise prices.

4. This increases the company's profitability and allows it to stay in business.

5. Thus the company creates more jobs.[29]

Deming identified a number of steps that should be part of any quality improvement program:

- A company should have a clear business model to specify where it is going and how it is going to get there.

- Management should embrace the philosophy that mistakes, defects, and poor-quality materials are not acceptable and should be eliminated.

- Quality of supervision should be improved by allowing more time for supervisors to work with employees and giving them appropriate skills for the job.

- Management should create an environment in which employees will not fear reporting problems or recommending improvements.

- Work standards should not only be defined as numbers or quotas but should also include some notion of quality to promote the production of defect-free output.

- Management is responsible for training employees in new skills to keep pace with changes in the workplace.

- Achieving better quality requires the commitment of everyone in the company.

It took the rise of Japan to the top rank of economic powers in the 1980s to alert western business to the importance of the TQM concept. Since then, quality improvement programs have spread rapidly throughout western industry. Strategy in Action 4.3 describes one of the most successful implementations of a quality improvement process, General Electric's Six Sigma program.

Despite such instances of spectacular success, quality improvement practices are not universally accepted. A study by the American Quality Foundation found that only 20% of U.S. companies regularly review the consequences of quality performance, compared with 70% of Japanese companies.[30] Another study, this one by Arthur D. Little, of 500 American companies using TQM found that only 36% believed that TQM was increasing their competitiveness.[31] A prime reason for this, according to the study, was that many companies had not fully understood or embraced the TQM concept. They were looking for a quick fix, whereas implementing a quality improvement program is a long-term commitment.

Strategy in Action 4.3

General Electric's Six Sigma Quality Improvement Process

Six Sigma, a quality and efficiency program adopted by several major corporations, including Motorola, General Electric, and Allied Signal, aims to reduce defects, boost productivity, eliminate waste, and cut costs throughout a company. "Sigma" comes from the Greek letter that statisticians use to represent a standard deviation from a mean: the higher the number of sigmas, the smaller the number of errors. At 6 sigma, a production process would be 99.99966 percent accurate, creating just 3.4 defects per million units. Although it is almost impossible for a company to achieve such perfection, several companies strive toward that goal.

General Electric is perhaps the most fervent adopter of Six Sigma programs. Under the direction of long-serving CEO Jack Welch, GE spent nearly $1 billion between 1994 and 1998 to convert all of its divisions to the Six Sigma faith. Welch credits the program with raising GE's operating profit margins to 16.6% in 1998, up from 14.4% three years earlier.

One of the first products designed from start to finish using Six Sigma processes was a $1.25 million diagnostic computer tomography (CT) scanner, the Lightspeed, which produces rapid three-dimensional images of the human body. The new scanner captures multiple images simultaneously, requiring only twenty seconds to do full-body scans that once took three minutes—an important time reduction because patients must remain perfectly still during the scan. GE spent $50 million to run 250 separate Six Sigma analyses designed to improve the reliability and lower the manufacturing cost of the new scanner. Its efforts were rewarded when the Lightspeed's first customers soon noticed that it ran without downtime from the start, a testament to the reliability of the product.

Achieving that reliability took a lot of work. GE's engineers deconstructed the scanner into its basic components and tried to improve the reliability of each component through a detailed step-by-step analysis. For example, the most important parts of CT scanners are vacuum tubes that focus x-ray waves. The tubes that GE used in previous scanners, which cost $60,000 each, suffered from low reliability. Hospitals and clinics wanted the tubes to operate for twelve hours a day for at least six months, but typically they lasted only half that long. Moreover, GE was scrapping some $20 million in tubes each year because they failed preshipping performance tests, and a disturbing number of faulty tubes were slipping past inspection, only to be pronounced unusable on arrival.

To try to solve the reliability problem, the Six Sigma team took the tubes apart. They knew that one problem was a petroleum-based oil used in the tube to prevent short circuits by isolating the anode, which has a positive charge, from the negatively charged cathode. The oil often deteriorated after a few months, leading to short circuits, but the team did not know why. By using statistical what-if scenarios on all parts of the tube, the researchers learned that the lead-based paint on the inside of the tube was adulterating the oil. Acting on this information, the team developed a paint that would preserve the tube and protect the oil.

By pursuing this and other improvements, the Six Sigma team was able to extend the average life of a vacuum tube in the CT scanner from three months to over a year. Although the improvements increased the cost of the tube from $60,000 to $85,000, the increased cost was outweighed by the reduction in replacement costs, making it an attractive proposition for customers.[d]

● **Implementing Reliability Improvement Methodologies**

Among companies that have successfully adopted quality improvement methodologies, certain imperatives stand out. These are discussed below in the order in which they are usually tackled in companies implementing quality improvement programs. What needs to be stressed first, however, is that improvement in product reliability is a cross-functional process. Its implementation requires close cooperation among all functions in the pursuit of the common goal of improving quality; it is a process that cuts across functions. The roles played by the different functions in implementing reliability improvement methodologies is summarized in Table 4.2.

TABLE 4.2

Roles Played by Different Functions in Implementing Reliability Improvement Methodologies

Infrastructure (leadership)	1. Provide leadership and commitment to quality
	2. Find ways to measure quality
	3. Set goals and create incentives
	4. Solicit input from employees
	5. Encourage cooperation among functions
Production	1. Shorten production runs
	2. Trace defects back to source
Marketing	1. Focus on the customer
	2. Provide customers' feedback on quality
Materials management	1. Rationalize suppliers
	2. Help suppliers implement quality improvement methodologies
	3. Trace defects back to suppliers
R&D	1. Design products that are easy to manufacture
Information systems	1. Use information systems to monitor defect rates
Human resources	1. Institute quality improvement training programs
	2. Identify and train "black belts"
	3. Organize employees into quality teams

BUILD ORGANIZATIONAL COMMITMENT TO QUALITY There is evidence that quality improvement programs will do little to improve the performance of a company unless everyone in the organization embraces it.[32] When Xerox launched its quality program, its first step was to educate the entire work force, from top management down, in the importance and operation of the program. It did so by forming groups, beginning with a group at the top of the organization that included the CEO. The top group was the first to receive basic TQM training. Each member of this group was then given the task of training a group at the next level in the hierarchy, and so on down throughout the organization, until all 100,000 employees had received basic TQM training. Both top management and the human resources function of the company can play a major role in this process. Top management has the responsibility of exercising the leadership required to make a commitment to quality an organizationwide goal. The human resources function must take on responsibility for companywide training in TQM techniques.

CREATE QUALITY LEADERS If a quality improvement program is to be successful, individuals must be identified to lead the program. Under the Six Sigma methodology, exceptional employees are identified and put through a "black belt" training course on the Six Sigma methodology. The black belts are taken out of their normal job roles and assigned to work solely on Six Sigma projects for the next two years. In effect, they become internal consultants and project leaders. Because they are dedicated to Six Sigma programs, they are not distracted from the task at hand by day-to-day operating responsibilities. To make a black belt assignment attractive, many companies now use it as a step in a career path. Successful black belts do not return to their prior job after two years but instead are promoted and given more responsibility.

FOCUS ON THE CUSTOMER Quality improvement practitioners see a focus on the customer as the starting point, and indeed, the raison d'être, of the whole quality philosophy.[33] The marketing function, because it provides the primary point of contact with the customer, should play a major role here. It needs to identify what customers want from the good or service that the company provides, what the company actually provides to customers, and the gap between what customers want and what they get, which could be called the quality gap. Then, together with the other functions of the company, it needs to formulate a plan for closing the quality gap.

IDENTIFY PROCESSES AND THE SOURCE OF DEFECTS One of the hallmarks of the Six Sigma quality improvement methodology is identifying discrete repetitive processes that can be improved. This is normally done by using flowchart methodology to break an operation into its constituent parts. Thus, as noted in Strategy in Action 4.3, to improve its Lightspeed CT scanner, GE's engineers deconstructed the scanner into its basic components and tried to improve the reliability of each component through a detailed step-by-step analysis.

Quality improvement methodologies preach the need to identify defects that arise from processes, trace them to their source, find out what caused them, and make corrections so that they do not recur. Production and materials management typically have primary responsibility for this task.

To uncover defects, Deming advocated the use of statistical procedures to pinpoint variations in the quality of goods or services. Deming viewed variation as the enemy of quality.[34] The Six Sigma methodology also relies heavily on statistical analysis of variation. Once variations have been identified, they must be traced to their source and eliminated. One technique that helps greatly in tracing defects to their source is reducing lot sizes for manufactured products. With short production runs, defects show up immediately. Consequently, they can be quickly traced to the source, and the problem can be addressed. Reducing lot sizes also means that, when defective products are produced, their number will not be large, thus decreasing waste. Flexible manufacturing techniques, discussed earlier, can be used to reduce lot sizes without raising costs. Consequently, adopting flexible manufacturing techniques is an important aspect of a TQM program.

JIT inventory systems also play a part. Under a JIT system, defective parts enter the manufacturing process immediately; they are not warehoused for several months before use. Hence, defective inputs can be quickly spotted. The problem can then be traced to the supply source and corrected before more defective parts are produced. Under a more traditional system, the practice of warehousing parts for months before they are used may mean that many defects are produced by a supplier before they enter the production process.

FIND WAYS TO MEASURE QUALITY Another imperative of any quality improvement program is to create a metric that can be used to measure quality. This is relatively easy in manufacturing companies, where quality can be measured by criteria such as defects per million parts. It tends to be more difficult in service companies, but with a little creativity, suitable metrics can be devised. For example, one of the metrics Florida Power & Light uses to measure quality is meter-reading errors per month. Another is the frequency and duration of power outages. L. L. Bean, the Freeport, Maine, mail-order retailer of outdoor gear, uses the percentage of orders that are correctly filled as one of its quality measures. For some banks, the key measures are the number of customer defections per year and the number of statement errors per thousand customers. The common theme that runs through all these examples is identifying what quality means from a customer's perspective and devising a method to gauge this.

SET GOALS AND CREATE INCENTIVES   Once a metric has been devised, the next step is to set a challenging quality goal and create incentives for reaching it. Xerox again provides an example. When it introduced its TQM program, its initial goal was to reduce defective parts from 25,000 per million to 1,000 per million. Under Six Sigma programs, the goal is 3.4 defects per million units. One way of creating incentives to attain such a goal is to link rewards, like bonus pay and promotional opportunities, to the goal. Thus, within many companies that have adopted self-managing teams, the bonus pay of team members is determined in part by their ability to attain quality goals. Setting goals and creating incentives are key tasks of top management.

SOLICIT INPUT FROM EMPLOYEES   Employees can be a vital source of information regarding the sources of poor quality. Therefore, a framework must be established for soliciting employee suggestions for improvements. Quality circles, which are meetings of groups of employees, have often been used to achieve this goal. Other companies have used self-managing teams as forums for discussing quality improvement ideas. Whatever forum is used, soliciting input from employees requires that management be open to receiving, and acting on, bad news and criticism from employees. According to Deming, one problem with U.S. management is that it has grown used to "killing the bearer of bad tidings." But, he argues, managers who are committed to the quality concept must recognize that bad news is a gold mine of information.[35]

BUILD LONG-TERM RELATIONSHIPS WITH SUPPLIERS   A major source of poor-quality finished goods is poor-quality component parts. To decrease product defects, a company has to work with its suppliers to improve the quality of the parts they supply. The primary responsibility in this area falls on the materials-management function, which interacts with suppliers.

To implement JIT systems with suppliers and to get suppliers to adopt their own quality improvement programs, two steps are necessary. First, the number of suppliers has to be reduced to manageable proportions. Second, the company must commit to building a cooperative long-term relationship with the suppliers that remain. Asking suppliers to invest in JIT and quality improvement programs is asking them to make major investments that tie them to the company. For example, in order to implement a JIT system fully, the company may ask a supplier to relocate its manufacturing plant so that it is next-door to the company's assembly plant. Suppliers are likely to be hesitant about making such investments unless they feel that the company is committed to an enduring, long-term relationship with them.

DESIGN FOR EASE OF MANUFACTURE   The more assembly steps a product requires, the more opportunities there are for making mistakes. Designing products with fewer parts should make assembly easier and result in fewer defects. Both R&D and manufacturing need to be involved in designing products that are easy to manufacture.

BREAK DOWN BARRIERS AMONG FUNCTIONS   Implementing quality improvement methodologies requires organizationwide commitment and substantial cooperation among functions. R&D has to cooperate with production to design products that are easy to manufacture, marketing has to cooperate with production and R&D so that customer problems identified by marketing can be acted on, human resources management has to cooperate with all the other functions of the company in order to devise suitable quality-training programs, and so on. The issue of achieving cooperation among subunits within a company is explored in Chapter 12. What needs stressing at this point is that ultimately it is the responsibility of top management to ensure that such cooperation occurs. Strategy in Action 4.4 describes the efforts of a service company to put quality improvement programs into practice and the benefits it has gained as a result.

● **Improving Quality as Excellence**

As we stated in Chapter 3, a product is a bundle of different attributes, and reliability is just one of them, albeit an important one. Products can also be *differentiated* by attributes that collectively define product excellence. These attributes include the form, features, performance, durability, and styling of a product. In addition, a company can create quality as excellence by emphasizing attributes of the service associated with the product, such as ordering ease, prompt delivery, easy installation, the availability of customer training and consulting, and maintenance services. Dell Computer, for example, differentiates itself on ease of ordering (via the Web), prompt delivery, easy installation, and the ready availability of customer support and maintenance services. Differentiation can also be based on the attributes of the people in the company

Strategy in Action   4.4

Six Sigma at Mount Carmel Health

Following the lead of General Electric, a number of health care organizations have adopted the Six Sigma approach or similar quality improvement tools as a way of trying to improve the quality of their service offerings. One of the first was Mount Carmel Health, a three hospital 9,000 employee health care provider in Ohio. Mount Carmel Health implemented a Six Sigma program after suffering from poor financial performance in 2000. It was initiated in late 2000, and by early 2001, forty-four employees had been trained in Six Sigma principles. These "black belts" were pulled out of their original positions and were not replaced. By the second half of 2001, they were leading some sixty projects in different phases of implementation.

One of the first projects focused on a simple and common problem among health care providers: timely and accurate reimbursement of costs. Mount Carmel discovered that it was writing off large amounts of potential revenues from the government-run Medicare programs as uncollectible because the charges were denied by Medicare administrators. Mount Carmel had low expectations for this business anyway, so it had never analyzed why the write-offs were so high. After conducting a careful

analysis as part of a Six Sigma project, it discovered that a significant portion of the denials were due to the incorrect coding of reports submitted to Medicare. If the reports were coded correctly—that is, if fewer errors were made in the production of forms—the Six Sigma team estimated that annual income would be some $300,000 higher, so they devised improved processes for coding the forms to reduce the error rate. The result was that net income rose by over $800,000. It appeared that improving the coding process for this one parameter improved the reporting of many other parameters and led to a reimbursement rate much higher than anticipated.

In another example, by examining a process flow-chart, employees at Mount Carmel were able to improve patient throughput through CT scanners from 1.8 to 2.7 patients per hour, which resulted in an annual net revenue improvement of $2.4 million per scanner. A three-week patient wait-time for CT scanners was also reduced to one or two days, greatly increasing customer responsiveness.

By 2005, Mount Carmel had over 550 Six Sigma quality improvement projects either completed or ongoing. The organization estimates that since it launched the process in July 2000, it has reduced costs by some $63 million.[e]

TABLE 4.3

Attributes Associated with a Product Offering

Product Attributes	Service Attributes	Associated Personnel Attributes
Form	Ordering ease	Competence
Features	Delivery	Courtesy
Performance	Installation	Credibility
Durability	Customer training	Reliability
Reliability	Customer consulting	Responsiveness
Style	Maintenance and repair	Communication

whom customers interact with when making a product purchase, such as their competence, courtesy, credibility, responsiveness, and communication. Singapore Airlines, for example, enjoys an excellent reputation for quality service largely because passengers perceive their flight attendants as competent, courteous, and responsive to their needs. Thus, we can talk about the product attributes, service attributes, and personnel attributes associated with a company's product offering (see Table 4.3).

For a product to be regarded as high in the excellence dimension, a company's product offering must be seen as superior to that of rivals. Achieving a perception of high quality on any of these attributes requires specific actions by managers. First, it is important for managers to collect marketing intelligence indicating which of these attributes are most important to customers. For example, consumers of personal computers may place a low weight on durability because they expect their PC to be made obsolete by technological advances within three years, but they may place a high weight on features and performance. Similarly, ease of ordering and timely delivery may be very important attributes for customers of online booksellers (as they are indeed for customers of Amazon.com), whereas customer training and consulting may be very important attributes for customers who purchase complex business-to-business software to manage their relationships with suppliers.

Second, once the company has identified the attributes that are important to customers, it needs to design its products, and the associated services, so that those attributes are embodied in the product, and it needs to make sure that personnel in the company are appropriately trained so that the correct attributes are emphasized. This requires close coordination between marketing and product development (the topic of the next section) and the involvement of the human resources management function in employee selection and training.

Third, the company must decide which of the significant attributes to promote and how best to position them in the minds of consumers, that is, how to tailor the marketing message so that it creates a consistent image in the minds of customers.[36] At this point, it is important to recognize that although a product might be differentiated on the basis of six attributes, covering all of those attributes in the company's communication messages may lead to an unfocused message. Many marketing experts advocate promoting only one or two central attributes to customers. For example, Volvo consistently emphasizes the safety and durability of its vehicles in all marketing messages, creating the perception in the minds of consumers (backed by product design) that Volvo cars are safe and durable. Volvo cars are also very reliable and have high performance, but the company does not emphasize these attributes in its marketing messages. In contrast, Porsche emphasizes performance and styling in all of its marketing messages; thus, a Porsche is positioned differently in the minds of consumers than a Volvo is. Both are regarded as high-quality products because both have superior attributes, but the attributes that the two companies have chosen to emphasize are very different. They are differentiated from the average car in different ways.

Finally, it must be recognized that competition does not stand still but instead produces continual improvement in product attributes and often the development of new-product attributes. This is obvious in fast-moving high-tech industries where product features that were considered leading edge just a few years ago are now obsolete, but the same process is also at work in more stable industries. For example, the rapid diffusion of microwave ovens during the 1980s required food companies to build new attributes into their frozen food products: They had to maintain their texture and consistency while being microwaved. A product could not be considered high quality unless it could do that. This speaks to the importance of having a strong R&D function in the company that can work with marketing and manufacturing to continually upgrade the quality of the attributes that are designed into the company's product offerings. Exactly how to achieve this goal is covered in the next section.

Achieving Superior Innovation

In many ways, building distinctive competencies that result in innovation is the most important source of competitive advantage because innovation can result in new products that better satisfy customer needs, can improve the quality (attributes) of existing products, or can reduce the costs of making products that customers want. Thus, the ability to develop innovative new products or processes gives a company a major competitive advantage that allows it to (1) differentiate its products and charge a premium price and/or (2) lower its cost structure below that of its rivals. Competitors, however, attempt to imitate successful innovations and often succeed. Therefore, maintaining a competitive advantage requires a continuing commitment to innovation.

Robert Cooper found that successful new-product launches are major drivers of superior profitability. Cooper looked at more than 200 new-product introductions and found that of those classified as successes, some 50% achieve a return on investment in excess of 33%, half have a payback period of two years or less, and half achieve a market share in excess of 35%.[37] Many companies have established a track record for successful innovation. Among them are DuPont, which has produced a steady stream of successful innovations, such as cellophane, Nylon, Freon, and Teflon; Sony, whose successes include the Walkman, the compact disc, and the PlayStation; Nokia, which has been a leader in the development of wireless phones; Pfizer, a drug company that produced eight blockbuster new drugs during the 1990s and early 2000s; 3M, which has applied its core competency in tapes and adhesives to developing a wide range of new products; Intel, which has consistently managed to lead in the development of innovative new microprocessors to run personal computers; and Cisco Systems, whose innovations helped to pave the way for the rapid growth of the Internet.

● **The High Failure Rate of Innovation** Although promoting innovation can be a source of competitive advantage, the failure rate of innovative new products is high. One study of product development in the chemical, drug, petroleum, and electronics industries suggested that only about 20% of major R&D projects ultimately result in a commercially successful product or process.[38] An in-depth case study of product development in three companies (one in chemicals and two in drugs) reported that about 60% of R&D projects reached technical completion, 30% were commercialized, and only 12% earned a profit that exceeded the company's cost of capital.[39] Another study concluded that one in nine major R&D projects, or about 11%, produced commercially successful products.[40] In sum, the evidence suggests that only 10 to 20% of major R&D projects give rise to a commercially successful product. Well-publicized product failures include Apple Computer's Newton, a personal digital assistant; Sony's Betamax format in the video player and recorder market; and Sega's Dreamcast videogame console. While many reasons have been advanced to explain why so many new products fail to generate an economic return, five explanations for failure appear on most lists: uncertainty, poor commercialization, poor positioning strategy, technological myopia, and being slow to market.[41]

UNCERTAINTY   New-product development is an inherently risky process. It requires testing a hypothesis whose answer is impossible to know prior to market introduction: Have we tapped an unmet customer need? Is there sufficient market demand for this new technology? Although good market research can reduce the uncertainty about likely future demand for a new technology, uncertainty cannot be eradicated, so a certain failure rate is to be expected.

The failure rate is higher for quantum product innovations than for incremental innovations. A **quantum innovation** represents a radical departure from existing technology—the introduction of something that is new to the world. The development of the World Wide Web can be considered a quantum innovation in communications technology. Other quantum innovations include the development of the first photocopier by Xerox, the first contact lenses by Bausch and Lomb, and the first microprocessor by Intel in 1971. **Incremental innovation** refers to an extension of existing technology. For example, Intel's Pentium Pro microprocessor is an incremental product innovation because it builds on the existing microprocessor architecture of Intel's X86 series. The uncertainty of future demand for a new product is much greater if that product represents a quantum innovation that is new to the world than if it is an incremental innovation designed to replace an established product whose demand profile is already well known. Consequently, the failure rate tends to be higher for quantum innovations.

POOR COMMERCIALIZATION   A second reason frequently cited to explain the high failure rate of new-product introductions is **poor commercialization**—something that occurs when there is definite customer demand for a new product, but the product is not well adapted to customer needs because of factors such as poor design and poor quality. For instance, many of the early personal computers failed to sell because customers needed to understand computer programming to use them. Steve Jobs at Apple Computer understood that if the technology could be made user friendly (if it could be commercialized), there would be an enormous market for it. Hence, the original personal computers that Apple marketed incorporated little in the way of radically new technology, but they made existing technology accessible to the average person. Paradoxically, the failure of Apple Computer to establish a market for the Newton, the hand-held personal digital system that Apple introduced in the summer of 1993, can be traced to poor commercialization of a potentially attractive technology. Apple predicted a $1 billion market for the Newton, but sales failed to materialize when it became clear that the Newton's handwriting software, an attribute that Apple chose to emphasize in its marketing promotions, could not adequately recognize messages written on the Newton's message pad.

POOR POSITIONING STRATEGY   Poor positioning strategy arises when a company introduces a potentially attractive new product, but sales fail to materialize because it is poorly positioned in the marketplace. **Positioning strategy** is the specific set of options a company adopts for a product on four main dimensions of marketing: price, distribution, promotion and advertising, and product features. Apart from poor product quality, another reason for the failure of the Apple Newton was poor positioning strategy. The Newton was introduced at such a high initial price (close to $1,000) that there would probably have been few buyers even if the technology had been adequately commercialized.

TECHNOLOGICAL MYOPIA   Another reason that many new-product introductions fail is that companies often make the mistake of marketing a technology for which there is not enough customer demand. **Technological myopia** occurs when a company gets blinded by the wizardry of a new technology and fails to examine whether there is customer demand for the product. This problem may have been a factor in the failure of the desktop computer introduced by NeXT in the late 1980s (NeXT was founded by Steve Jobs, the founder of Apple Computer). Technologically, the NeXT machines were clearly ahead of their time, with advanced software and hardware features that would not be incorporated into most PCs for another decade. However, customer acceptance was very slow primarily because of the complete lack of applications software such as spreadsheet and word-processing programs to run on the machines. Management at NeXT was so enthused by the technology incorporated in their new computer that they ignored this basic market reality. After several years of slow sales, NeXT eventually withdrew the machines from the marketplace. Ironically, the company itself was ultimately acquired by Apple Computer, and in 2001 a new version of the NeXT operating system, known as OS X, became the operating system for Apple's computers.

BEING SLOW TO MARKET   Finally, companies fail when they are slow to get their products to market. The more time that elapses between initial development and final marketing—that is, the slower the cycle time—the more likely it is that someone else will beat the company to market and gain a first-mover advantage.[42] By and large, slow innovators update their products less frequently than fast innovators do. Consequently, they can be perceived as technical laggards relative to the fast innovators. In the car industry, General Motors has suffered from being a slow innovator. Its product development cycle has been about five years, compared with two to three years at Honda, Toyota, and Mazda and three to four years at Ford. Because they are based on five-year-old technology and design concepts, GM cars are already out of date when they reach the market.

● **Building Competencies in Innovation**   Companies can take a number of steps to build a competency in innovation and avoid failure. Six of the most important steps are (1) building skills in basic and applied scientific research, (2) developing a good process for project selection and project management, (3) achieving cross-functional integration, (4) using product development teams, (5) using partly parallel development processes, and (6) learning from experience.[43]

SKILLS IN BASIC AND APPLIED RESEARCH   Building skills in basic and applied research requires the employment of research scientists and engineers and the establishment of a work environment that fosters creativity. To the extent that firms can do this, it increases their *absorptive capacity*, which we noted in Chapter 3 is the ability of an enterprise to identify, value, assimilate, and use new knowledge. A number of top companies try to achieve this by setting up university-style research facilities, where scientists and engineers are given time to work on their own research projects, in addition to projects that are linked directly to ongoing company research. At Hewlett-Packard, for example, company labs are open to engineers around the clock. Hewlett-Packard even encourages its corporate researchers to devote 10% of company time to exploring their own ideas and does not penalize them if they fail. 3M allows researchers to spend 15% of the workweek researching any topic that intrigues them, as long as there is the potential of a payoff for the company. The most famous outcome of this policy is the ubiquitous Post-it Notes. The idea for them evolved from a researcher's desire to find a way to keep the bookmark from falling out of his hymnal. Post-it Notes are now a major 3M business, with annual revenues of around $300 million. Google has copied this philosophy, and allows its engineers to spend 20% of their time working on projects of their own choosing that are not part of their core task. Among the products that have come out of this process are Google News and Google Earth.

PROJECT SELECTION AND MANAGEMENT   Project management is the overall management of the innovation process, from generation of the original concept through development, and into final production and shipping. Project management requires three important skills: the ability to generate as many good ideas as possible, the ability to select among competing projects at an early stage of development so that the most promising receive funding and potential costly failures are killed off, and the ability to minimize time to market. The concept of the development funnel, divided into three phases, summarizes what is required to build these skills (see Figure 4.7).[44]

The objective in phase I is to widen the mouth of the funnel to encourage as much idea generation as possible. To this end, a company should solicit input from all its functions, as well as from customers, competitors, and suppliers. At gate 1, the funnel narrows. Here ideas are reviewed by a cross-functional team of managers who did not participate in the original concept development. Concepts that are ready to

FIGURE 4.7

The Development
Funnel

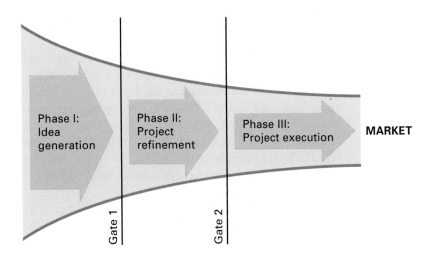

proceed then move to phase II, where the details of the project proposal are worked out. Note that gate 1 is not a go/no-go evaluation point. At this screen, ideas may be sent back for further concept development and then resubmitted for evaluation.

During phase II, which typically lasts only one or two months, the data and information from phase I are put into a form that will enable senior management to evaluate proposed projects against competing projects. Normally, this requires the development of a careful project plan, complete with details of the proposed target market, attainable market share, likely revenues, development costs, production costs, key milestones, and the like. The next big selection point, gate 2, is a go/no-go evaluation point. Senior managers review the projects under consideration and select those that seem likely winners and make the most sense from a strategic perspective, given the long-term goals of the company. The overriding objective is to select projects whose successful completion will help to maintain or build a competitive advantage for the company. A related objective is to ensure that the company does not spread its scarce capital and human resources too thinly over too many projects and instead concentrates resources on projects where the probability of success and potential returns is most attractive. Any project selected to go forward at this stage will be funded and staffed, the expectation being that it will be carried through to market introduction. In phase III, the project development proposal is executed by a cross-functional product development team.

CROSS-FUNCTIONAL INTEGRATION Tight cross-functional integration among R&D, production, and marketing can help a company to ensure that:

1. Product development projects are driven by customer needs.

2. New products are designed for ease of manufacture.

3. Development costs are kept in check.

4. Time to market is minimized.

5. Close integration between R&D and marketing is achieved to ensure that product development projects are driven by the needs of customers.

A company's customers can be one of its primary sources of new-product ideas. The identification of customer needs, and particularly unmet needs, can set the context within which successful product innovation takes place. As the point of contact with customers, the marketing function can provide valuable information. Moreover, integrating R&D and marketing is crucial if a new product is to be properly commercialized. Otherwise, a company runs the risk of developing products for which there is little or no demand.

The case of Techsonic Industries illustrates the benefits of integrating R&D and marketing. This company manufactures depth finders—electronic devices that fishing enthusiasts use to measure the depth of water beneath a boat and to track their prey. Techsonic had weathered nine new-product failures in a row when the company decided to interview sportspeople across the country to identify what it was they needed. They discovered an unmet need for a depth finder with a gauge that could be read in bright sunlight, so that is what Techsonic developed. In the year after the $250 depth finder hit the market, Techsonic's sales tripled to $80 million, and its market share surged to 40 percent.[45]

Integration between R&D and production can help a company to ensure that products are designed with manufacturing requirements in mind. Design for manufacturing lowers manufacturing costs and leaves less room for mistakes and thus can lower costs and increase product quality. Integrating R&D and production can help lower development costs and speed products to market. If a new product is not designed with manufacturing capabilities in mind, it may prove too difficult to build, given existing manufacturing technology. In that case, the product will have to be redesigned, and both overall development costs and time to market may increase significantly. For example, making design changes during product planning could increase overall development costs by 50% and add 25% to the time it takes to bring the product to market.[46] Moreover, many quantum product innovations require new processes to manufacture them, which makes it all the more important to achieve close integration between R&D and production because minimizing time to market and development costs may require the simultaneous development of new products and new processes.[47]

PRODUCT DEVELOPMENT TEAMS One of the best ways to achieve cross-functional integration is to establish cross-functional product development teams composed of representatives from R&D, marketing, and production. The objective of a team should be to take a product development project from the initial concept development to market introduction. A number of attributes seem to be important in order for a product development team to function effectively and meet all its development milestones.[48]

First, a **heavyweight project manager**—one who has high status within the organization and the power and authority required to get the financial and human resources that the team needs to succeed—should lead the team and be dedicated primarily, if not entirely, to the project. The leader should believe in the project (a champion) and be skilled at integrating the perspectives of different functions and helping personnel from different functions work together for a common goal. The leader should also be able to act as an advocate of the team in dealings with senior management.

Second, the team should be composed of at least one member from each key function. The team members should have a number of attributes, including an ability to contribute functional expertise, high standing within their function, a willingness to share responsibility for team results, and an ability to put functional advocacy aside. It is generally preferable if core team members are 100% dedicated to the project for its duration. Such dedication ensures that their focus is on the project, not on the ongoing work of their function.

Third, the team members should be located in the same physical area to create a sense of camaraderie and facilitate communication. Fourth, the team should have a clear plan and clear goals, particularly with regard to critical development milestones and development budgets. The team should have incentives to attain those goals, such as pay bonuses when major development milestones are hit. Fifth, each team needs to develop its own processes for communication and conflict resolution. For example, one product development team at Quantum Corporation, a California-based manufacturer of disk drives for personal computers, instituted a rule that all major decisions would be made and conflicts resolved at meetings that were held every Monday afternoon. This simple rule helped the team to meet its development goals.[49]

Finally, there is always a danger that a new product development team can develop shared cognitive biases that leads to a lack of objectivity and emotional commitment to a project (see Chapter 1 for a discussion of cognitive biases).[50] To guard against this possibility, it is a good idea to have well-regarded outsiders periodically evaluate the product and decide whether to proceed or not.

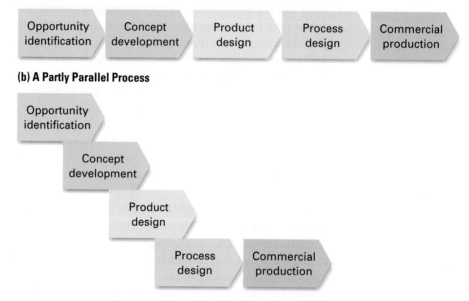

(a) A Sequential Process

Opportunity identification → Concept development → Product design → Process design → Commercial production

(b) A Partly Parallel Process

Opportunity identification
Concept development
Product design
Process design
Commercial production

PARTLY PARALLEL DEVELOPMENT PROCESSES One way in which a product development team can compress the time it takes to develop a product and bring it to market is to use a partly parallel development process. Traditionally, product development processes have been organized on a sequential basis, as illustrated in Figure 4.8a. A problem with this kind of process is that product development proceeds without manufacturing issues in mind. Most significantly, because the basic design of a product is completed prior to the design of a manufacturing process and full-scale commercial production, there is no early warning system to indicate manufacturability. As a consequence, the company may find that it cannot manufacture the product cost-efficiently and may have to send it back to the design stage for redesign. The cycle time lengthens as the product bounces back and forth between stages.

To solve this problem, companies typically use a process similar to that illustrated in Figure 4.8b. In the partly parallel development process, development stages overlap so that, for example, work starts on the development of the production process before the product design is finalized. By reducing the need for expensive and time-consuming product redesigns, such a process can significantly reduce the time it takes to develop a new product and bring it to market.

For an example, consider what occurred after Intel Corporation introduced its 386 microprocessor in 1986. A number of companies, including IBM and Compaq, were racing to be the first to introduce a 386-based personal computer. Compaq beat IBM by six months and gained a major share of the high-power market mainly because it used a cross-functional team and a partly parallel process to develop the product. The team included engineers (R&D) and marketing, production, and finance people. Each function worked in parallel rather than sequentially. While engineers were designing the product, production people were setting up the manufacturing facilities, marketing people were working on distribution and planning marketing campaigns, and finance people were working on project funding.

LEARNING FROM EXPERIENCE Evidence strongly suggests that developing competencies in innovation requires managers to take proactive steps to learn from their experience with product development, and to incorporate the lessons from past successes and failures in future new product development processes.[51] This is easier said than done. To learn, managers need to undertake an objective postmortem of a product development project, identify key success factors and the root causes of failures, and allocate resources toward fixing failures. Leaders also need to admit their own failures if they are to encourage others to step up to the plate and identify what they did wrong. Strategy in Action 4.5 looks at how Corning learned from a prior mistake to develop a potentially promising new product.

The primary role that the various functions play in achieving superior innovation is summarized in Table 4.4. The table makes two matters clear. First, top management must bear primary responsibility for overseeing the whole development process. This entails both managing the development funnel and facilitating cooperation among the functions. Second, the effectiveness of R&D in developing new products and processes depends on its ability to cooperate with marketing and production.

Strategy in Action   4.5

Corning: Learning from Innovation Failures

In 1998, Corning, then the world's largest supplier of fiber-optic cable, decided to diversify into the development and manufacture of DNA microarrays (DNA chips). DNA chips are used to analyze the function of genes and are an important research tool in the drug development process. Corning tried to develop a DNA chip that could print all 28,000 human genes onto a set of slides. By 2000, Corning had invested over $100 million in the project and its first chips were on the market, but the project was a failure and in 2001 it was pulled.

What went wrong? Corning was late to market—a critical mistake. The market was dominated by Affymetrix, which had been in the businesses since the early 1990s. By 2000, Affymetrix's DNA chips were the dominant design—researchers were familiar with them, they performed well, and few people were willing to switch to chips from unproven competitors. Corning was late because it adhered to its long-established innovation processes, which were not entirely appropriate in the biological sciences. In particular, Corning's own in-house experts in the physical sciences insisted on sticking to rigorous quality standards that customers and life scientists felt were higher than necessary. These quality standards proved to be very difficult to achieve and, as a result, the product launch was

delayed, giving Affymetrix time to consolidate its hold on the market. Moreover, Corning failed to give prototypes of its chips to potential customers, and consequently it missed incorporating some crucial features that customers wanted.

After reviewing this failure, Corning decided that it needed to bring customers into the development process earlier. And it needed to hire more outside experts if it was diversifying into an area where it lacked competencies, and to give those experts a larger say in the development process.

The project was not a total failure, however, for through it Corning discovered a vibrant and growing market—the market for drug discovery. By combining what it had learned about drug discovery with another failed businesses, photonics, which manipulates data using light waves, Corning created a new product called Epic. Epic is a revolutionary technology for drug testing that uses light waves instead of fluorescent dyes (the standard industry practice). Epic promises to accelerate the process of testing potential drugs and saving pharmaceutical companies valuable R&D money. Unlike its DNA microarray project, Corning had eighteen pharmaceutical companies test Epic before development was finalized. Corning used this feedback to refine Epic. The company believes that ultimately Epic could generate $500 million annually.[f]

TABLE 4.4

Functional Roles for Achieving Superior Innovation

Value Creation Function	Primary Roles
Infrastructure (leadership)	1. Manage overall project (i.e., manage the development function)
	2. Facilitate cross-functional cooperation
Production	1. Cooperate with R&D on designing products that are easy to manufacture
	2. Work with R&D to develop process innovations
Marketing	1. Provide market information to R&D
	2. Work with R&D to develop new products
Materials management	No primary responsibility
R&D	1. Develop new products and processes
	2. Cooperate with other functions, particularly marketing and manufacturing, in the development process
Information systems	1. Use information systems to coordinate cross-functional and cross-company product development work
Human resources	1. Hire talented scientists and engineers

Achieving Superior Responsiveness to Customers

To achieve superior responsiveness to customers, a company must give customers what they want, when they want it, and at a price they are willing to pay—so long as the company's long-term profitability is not compromised in the process. Customer responsiveness is an important differentiating attribute that can help to build brand loyalty. Strong product differentiation and brand loyalty give a company more pricing options; it can charge a premium price for its products or keep prices low to sell more goods and services to customers. Either way, the company that is more responsive to its customers' needs than are rivals will have a competitive advantage, all else being equal.

Achieving superior responsiveness to customers means giving customers value for money, and steps taken to improve the efficiency of a company's production process and the quality of its products should be consistent with this aim. In addition, giving customers what they want may require the development of new products with new features. In other words, achieving superior efficiency, quality, and innovation are all part of achieving superior responsiveness to customers. There are two other prerequisites for attaining this goal. First, a company has to develop a competency in listening to and focusing on its customers and in investigating and identifying their needs. Second, it constantly needs to seek better ways to satisfy those needs.

● **Focusing on the Customer**   A company cannot be responsive to its customers' needs unless it knows what those needs are. Thus, the first step to building superior responsiveness to customers is to motivate the whole company to focus on the customer. The means to this end are demonstrating leadership, shaping employee attitudes, and using mechanisms for bringing customers into the company.

DEMONSTRATING LEADERSHIP   Customer focus must start at the top of the organization. A commitment to superior responsiveness to customers brings attitudinal changes throughout a company that ultimately can be built only through strong leadership. A mission statement that puts customers first is one way to send a clear message to employees about the desired focus. Another avenue is top management's own actions. For example, Tom Monaghan, the founder of Domino's Pizza, stayed close to the customer by visiting as many stores as possible every week, running some deliveries himself, insisting that other top managers do the same, and eating Domino's pizza regularly.[52]

SHAPING EMPLOYEE ATTITUDES Leadership alone is not enough to attain a superior customer focus. All employees must see the customer as the focus of their activity and be trained to focus on the customer, whether their function is marketing, manufacturing, R&D, or accounting. The objective should be to make employees think of themselves as customers—to put themselves in customers' shoes. At that point, employees will be better able to identify ways to improve the quality of a customer's experience with the company.

To reinforce this mindset, incentive systems within the company should reward employees for satisfying customers. For example, senior managers at the Four Seasons hotel chain, who pride themselves on their customer focus, like to tell the story of Roy Dyment, a door attendant in Toronto who neglected to load a departing guest's briefcase into his taxi. The door attendant called the guest, a lawyer, in Washington, D.C., and found that he desperately needed the briefcase for a morning meeting. Dyment hopped on a plane to Washington and returned it—without first securing approval from his boss. Far from punishing Dyment for making a mistake and for not checking with management before going to Washington, the Four Seasons responded by naming Dyment Employee of the Year.[53] This action sent a powerful message to Four Seasons employees about the importance of satisfying customer needs.

BRINGING CUSTOMERS INTO THE COMPANY "Know thy customer" is one of the keys to achieving superior responsiveness to customers. Knowing the customer not only requires that employees think like customers themselves; it also demands that they listen to what their customers have to say and, as much as possible, bring them into the company. Although this may not involve physically bringing customers into the company, it does mean bringing in customers' opinions by soliciting feedback from customers on the company's goods and services and by building information systems that communicate the feedback to the relevant people.

For an example, consider direct-selling clothing retailer Lands' End. Through its catalog, the Internet, and customer service telephone operators, Lands' End actively solicits comments from its customers about the quality of its clothing and the kind of merchandise they want it to supply. Indeed, it was customers' insistence that initially prompted the company to move into the clothing segment. Lands' End used to supply equipment for sailboats through mail-order catalogs. However, it received so many requests from customers to include outdoor clothing in its offering that it responded by expanding the catalog to fill this need. Soon clothing became the main business, and Lands' End dropped the sailboat equipment. Today, the company still pays close attention to customer requests. Every month, a computer printout of customer requests and comments is given to managers. This feedback helps the company to fine-tune the merchandise it sells. Indeed, new lines of merchandise are frequently introduced in response to customer requests.[54]

● **Satisfying Customer Needs**   Once a focus on the customer is an integral part of the company, the next requirement is to satisfy the customer needs that have been identified. As already noted, efficiency, quality, and innovation are crucial competencies that help a company satisfy customer needs. Beyond that, companies can provide a higher level of satisfaction if they differentiate their products by (1) customizing them, where possible, to the requirements of individual customers and (2) reducing the time it takes to respond to or satisfy customer needs.

CUSTOMIZATION Customization is varying the features of a good or service to tailor it to the unique needs or tastes of groups of customers or, in the extreme case, individual customers. Although extensive customization can raise costs, the development of flexible manufacturing technologies has made it possible to customize products to a much greater extent than was feasible ten to fifteen years ago without experiencing a prohibitive rise in cost structure (particularly when flexible manufacturing technologies are linked with web-based information systems). For example, online retailers such as Amazon.com have used web-based technologies to develop a homepage customized for each user. When a customer accesses amazon.com, he or she is offered a list of recommendations for books or music to purchase based on an analysis of prior buying history, a powerful competency that gives Amazon.com a competitive advantage.

The trend toward customization has fragmented many markets, particularly customer markets, into ever smaller niches. An example of this fragmentation occurred in Japan in the early 1980s when Honda dominated the motorcycle market there. Second-place Yamaha decided to go after Honda's lead. It announced the opening of a new factory that, when operating at full capacity, would make Yamaha the world's largest manufacturer of motorcycles. Honda responded by proliferating its product line and stepping up its rate of new-product introduction. At the start of what became known as the motorcycle wars, Honda had sixty motorcycles in its product line. Over the next eighteen months, it rapidly increased its range to 113 models, customizing them to ever smaller niches. Honda was able to accomplish this without bearing a prohibitive cost penalty because it has a competency in flexible manufacturing. The flood of Honda's customized models pushed Yamaha out of much of the market, effectively stalling its bid to overtake Honda.[55]

RESPONSE TIME Giving customers what they want, when they want it, requires speed of response to customer demands. To gain a competitive advantage, a company must often respond to customer demands very quickly, whether the transaction is a furniture manufacturer's delivery of a product once it has been ordered, a bank's processing of a loan application, an automobile manufacturer's delivery of a spare part for a car that broke down, or the wait in a supermarket checkout line. We live in a fast-paced society, where time is a valuable commodity. Companies that can satisfy customer demands for rapid response build brand loyalty, differentiate their products, and can charge higher prices for them.

Increased speed often lets a company choose a premium pricing option, as the mail delivery industry illustrates. The air express niche of the mail delivery industry is based on the notion that customers are often willing to pay considerably more for overnight Express Mail as opposed to regular mail. Another example of the value of rapid response is Caterpillar, the manufacturer of heavy earthmoving equipment, which can get a spare part to any point in the world within twenty-four hours. Downtime for heavy construction equipment is very costly, so Caterpillar's ability to respond quickly in the event of equipment malfunction is of prime importance to its customers. As a result, many of them have remained loyal to Caterpillar despite the aggressive low-price competition from Komatsu of Japan.

TABLE 4.5

Primary Roles of Different Functions in Achieving Superior Responsiveness to Customers

Value Creation Function	Primary Roles
Infrastructure (leadership)	1. Through leadership by example, build a companywide commitment to responsiveness to customers
Production	1. Achieve customization through implementation of flexible manufacturing 2. Achieve rapid response through flexible manufacturing
Marketing	1. Know the customer 2. Communicate customer feedback to appropriate functions
Materials management	1. Develop logistics systems capable of responding quickly to unanticipated customer demands (JIT)
R&D	1. Bring customers into the product development process
Information systems	1. Use web-based information systems to increase responsiveness to customers
Human resources	1. Develop training programs that get employees to think like customers themselves

In general, reducing response time requires (1) a marketing function that can quickly communicate customer requests to production, (2) production and materials-management functions that can quickly adjust production schedules in response to unanticipated customer demands, and (3) information systems that can help production and marketing in this process.

Table 4.5 summarizes the steps different functions must take if a company is to achieve superior responsiveness to customers. Although marketing plays the critical role in helping a company attain this goal, primarily because it represents the point of contact with the customer, Table 4.5 shows that the other functions also have major roles. Moreover, like achieving superior efficiency, quality, and innovation, achieving superior responsiveness to customers requires top management to lead in building a customer orientation within the company.

Summary of Chapter

1. A company can increase efficiency through a number of steps: exploiting economies of scale and learning effects, adopting flexible manufacturing technologies, reducing customer defection rates, implementing just-in-time systems, getting the R&D function to design products that are easy to manufacture, upgrading the skills of employees through training, introducing self-managing teams, linking pay to performance, building a companywide commitment to efficiency through strong leadership, and designing structures that facilitate cooperation among different functions in pursuit of efficiency goals.

2. Superior quality can help a company lower its costs, differentiate its product, and charge a premium price.

3. Achieving superior quality demands an organization-wide commitment to quality and a clear focus on the customer. It also requires metrics to measure quality goals and incentives that emphasize quality, input from employees regarding ways in which quality can be improved, a methodology for tracing defects to their source and correcting the problems that produce them, a rationalization of the company's supply base, cooperation with the suppliers that remain to implement total quality management programs, products

that are designed for ease of manufacturing, and substantial cooperation among functions.

4. The failure rate of new-product introductions is high because of factors such as uncertainty, poor commercialization, poor positioning strategy, slow cycle time, and technological myopia.

5. To achieve superior innovation, a company must build skills in basic and applied research, design good processes for managing development projects, and achieve close integration among the different functions of the company primarily through the adoption of cross-functional product development teams and partly parallel development processes.

6. To achieve superior responsiveness to customers often requires that the company achieve superior efficiency, quality, and innovation.

7. To achieve superior responsiveness to customers, a company needs to give customers what they want, when they want it. It must ensure a strong customer focus, which can be attained by emphasizing customer focus through leadership, training employees to think like customers, bringing customers into the company through superior market research, customizing products to the unique needs of individual customers or customer groups, and responding quickly to customer demands.

Discussion Questions

1. How are the four generic building blocks of competitive advantage related to each other?
2. What role can top management play in helping a company achieve superior efficiency, quality, innovation, and responsiveness to customers?
3. In the long run, will adoption of Six Sigma quality improvement processes give a company a competitive advantage, or will it be required just to achieve parity with competitors?
4. In what sense might innovation be called the single most important building block of competitive advantage?

Practicing Strategic Management

SMALL-GROUP EXERCISE
Identifying Excellence
Break up into groups of three to five. Appoint one group member as a spokesperson who will communicate your findings to the class.

You are the management team of a start-up company that will produce hard disk drives for the personal computer industry. You will sell your product to manufacturers of personal computers (original equipment manufacturers). The disk drive market is characterized by rapid technological change, product life cycles of only six to nine months, intense price competition, high fixed costs for manufacturing equipment, and substantial manufacturing economies of scale. Your customers, the

original equipment manufacturers, issue very demanding technological specifications that your product has to comply with. They also pressure you to deliver your product on time so that it fits in with their own product introduction schedule.

1. In this industry, what functional competencies are the most important for you to build?
2. How will you design your internal processes to ensure that those competencies are built within the company?

ARTICLE FILE 4

Choose a company that is widely regarded as excellent. Identify the source of its excellence, and relate it to the material discussed in this chapter. Pay particular attention to the role played by the various functions in building excellence.

STRATEGIC MANAGEMENT PROJECT
Module 4

This module deals with the ability of your company to achieve superior efficiency, quality, innovation, and responsiveness to customers. With the information you have at your disposal, answer the questions and perform the tasks listed:

1. Is your company pursuing any of the efficiency-enhancing practices discussed in this chapter?
2. Is your company pursuing any of the quality-enhancing practices discussed in this chapter?
3. Is your company pursuing any of the practices designed to enhance innovation discussed in this chapter?
4. Is your company pursuing any of the practices designed to increase responsiveness to customers discussed in this chapter?
5. Evaluate the competitive position of your company in the light of your answers to questions 1–4. Explain what, if anything, the company needs to do to improve its competitive position.

ETHICS EXERCISE

A group of men and women from the beverage company ColaSmart were sitting around a large conference table suggesting marketing ideas for their new green-tea soft drink. The group was getting nowhere. Suddenly, Frank, the group's leader, called out, "Okay, what will get consumers fired up? What's one of the main concerns of adults in today's society? Fat loss, right? So what about referring to our drink as 'the fat burner?'"

A couple of people perked up. "Yeah, people will certainly buy it if they think it will help them burn fat and lose weight!"

One man, sitting at the end of the table, raised his hand. "What's up, Mike?" Frank called out.

"What if," Mike began, "people buy our drink, thinking it will burn fat, and it doesn't? If we're going to make a claim like that, shouldn't we do some tests first—make sure our claim will stand up under scrutiny?"

"Nah!" Frank scoffed. "We're selling to suckers, people who will want to believe it and who will blame themselves if it doesn't work. They'll keep trying it again and again because they'll want to believe that fat loss can be as easy as consuming a drink."

Most of the people in the room, eager for the profits the drink could provide, piped up in favor of the fat-burning claim. Only Mike and another woman from the group were against the idea.

1. Describe the ethical dilemmas presented in this case.
2. Should Mike voice his concerns to the company before the marketing campaign is solidified?
3. Do you think making an unsubstantiated claim is a breach of ethics?

CLOSING CASE

Verizon Wireless

In the wireless telecommunications industry, one metric above all others determines a company's profitability: customer churn, or the number of subscribers who leave a service within a given time period. Churn is important because it costs between $300 and $400 to acquire a customer. With monthly bills in the United States averaging $50, it can take six to eight months just to recoup the fixed costs of a customer acquisition. If churn rates are higher, profitability is eaten up by the costs of acquiring customers who do not stay long enough to provide a profit to the service provider.

The risk of churn increased significantly in the United States after November 2003, when the Federal Communications Commission allowed wireless subscribers to take their numbers with them when they switched to a new service provider. Over the next few years, a clear winner emerged in the battle to limit customer defections: Verizon Wireless. By mid-2006,

Verizon's churn rate was 0.87% a month, implying that 12% of the company's customers were leaving the service each year. While this might sound high, it was considerably lower than the churn rate at its competitors. The monthly churn rate at Cingular Wireless was 1.5%, at Sprint Nextel it was 2.1%, and at T-Mobile it was 2.2%.

Verizon's low churn rate has enabled the company to grow its subscriber base faster than rivals, which allows the company to better achieve economies of scale by spreading the fixed costs of building a wireless network over a larger customer base. In the quarter ending June 30, 2006, Verizon added 1.8 million customers, bringing its total up to 54 million. These customer additions easily outpaced those of its rivals Cingular, which added 1.5 million subscribers to bring its base up to 57 million, and Sprint, which added 0.7 million subscribers to bring its base up to 52 million.

There are several reasons for Verizon's success. First, in its early years, the company invested heavily in building a high-quality nationwide wireless network. It has the largest coverage area of any wireless provider and has successfully differentiated itself on the quality of its service. Customers report clearer connections and fewer dropped calls on the Verizon network than on any other network.

A technological choice has also played into this advantage. Verizon is one of two U.S. wireless companies that took a chance and bet on a new wireless technology know as CDMA (the other was Sprint). CDMA is less costly to install than a competing wireless technology, known as GSM, and is well suited to providing broadband services, such as wireless connections to the Internet. When Verizon chose to build a nationwide CDMA network, the technology was unproven and critics questioned its reliability and cost. But the critics were wrong, and Verizon now has an advantage over most of its competitors, who opted for the more established GSM technology. Utilizing the broadband capabilities of its CDMA network, in 2005, Verizon was the first wireless provider to offer a nationwide broadband service that allows subscribers to connect to the Internet in major metropolitan areas via a laptop or cell phone. This may well prove to be another source of differential advantage.

Verizon has communicated its coverage and quality advantage to customers with its "Test Man" advertisements. In these ads, a Verizon Test Man wearing horn-rimmed glasses and a Verizon uniform wanders around remote spots in the nation asking on his Verizon cell phone, "Can you hear me now?" Verizon says that the Test Man is actually the personification of a crew of fifty Verizon employees who each drive some 100,000 miles annually in specially outfitted vehicles to test the reliability of Verizon's network.

To further reduce customer churn, Verizon has invested heavily in its customer care function. Almost as soon as new customers receive their first monthly bill, Verizon Wireless representatives are on the phone, asking how they like the service. In that same call, a Verizon representative will ask what parts of the service a customer isn't using. If someone isn't yet using voice mail, for example, the representative will offer to set it up and get it working.

In addition, Verizon's automated software programs analyze the call habits of individual customers. Using that information, Verizon representatives will contact customers and suggest alternative calling plans that might better suit their needs. For example, Verizon might contact a customer and say, "We see that because of your heavy use on weekends, an alternative calling plan might make more sense for you and help reduce your monthly bills." The goal is to anticipate customer needs and proactively satisfy them, rather than have the customer take the initiative and possibly switch to another service provider.[56]

Case Discussion Questions

1. Do Verizon have a distinctive competency? If so, what is the source of that competency?

2. How do Verizon's customer service capabilities and coverage affect the quality of its service offering? How do you think they affect Verizon's cost structure? What are the implications for Verizon's long-run profitability and profit growth?

3. How would you characterize Verizon's business-level strategy (note, we discuss business-level strategy in detail in the next chapter)? How do the company's functional strategies enable it to implement its business-level strategy?

4. Do you think that Verizon has a sustainable competitive advantage in the wireless business?

Building Competitive Advantage Through Business-Level Strategy

OPENING CASE

E*Trade's Changing Business Strategies

In many industries, new entrants have taken advantage of the opportunities opened up by the Internet to overcome barriers to entry and compete successfully against market leaders. Consider the situation of E*Trade, the online brokerage company. For many years, large, established bricks-and-mortar brokerages like Merrill Lynch and Shearson Lehman had dominated the industry and used their protected positions to charge high brokerage fees, often over $100 per stock trade. Then in the 1990s, online entrepreneurs began to develop software that would allow them to offer online brokerage service, and one of the first online brokers was E*Trade, whose Internet software trading platform allowed customers to make their own trades online and to do so at a price that originally was set at $19.95—many times lower than before.

The low-cost competition story in the online brokerage industry did not stop there. In the last decade, E*Trade has repeatedly come under pressure from a succession of new online brokerage houses such as Schwab, TD Ameritrade, and Scottrade, which offered stock trades for fees that range from $9.95 to $4.95, undercutting E*Trade's prices by 100% or more. How could E*Trade, which had made its reputation by being the low-cost leader in the industry, compete against companies that now boasted that they were the new cost leaders?

E*Trade was forced to reduce its fee to $9.95 per trade, but to avoid further decreases, it decided to pursue a business model based on enhancing its differentiated appeal to customers by offering them a higher quality of service and a broader product line. E*Trade introduced new improved software that made it even easier for customers to use the Internet to research and trade shares, and it began offering them personalized financial advice. In addition, E*Trade's new package offered customers more financial research tools, such as streaming stock quotes that provide information on changes in stock prices in real time so that customers could take advantage of second-to-second changes in stock prices. It also provided them with investment reports that gave them access to more information about specific companies to improve their investment decisions. Finally, E*Trade decided to merge with an online bank, TeleBank, so that it could offer its customers a broad range of online banking services, such as online bill paying, CDs, and check-writing services, and thus become a one-stop online shopping site for all of a customer's financial needs. It also took over a variety of other financial service companies to offer its customers a broad financial service product line, such as auto and mortgage loans.

The realization that it could not just be a low-cost company but also had to create a differentiation advantage in the quickly evolving online financial services industry paid off for E*Trade. All these strategies helped to increase its customers' switching costs and keep them loyal; they did not move to the lowest-cost online broker because they perceived that they were receiving extra value in terms of service and reliability for the $9.95 price, and E*Trade's customer accounts increased steadily over time—as did its stock price.

In December 2006, it faced a new challenge, however, when Bank of America moved aggressively into the on-line brokerage business by offering customers *free* online brokerage service, with up to 30 free trades per month, provided they agreed to open an account with the bank and keep at least $25,000 in the account. This was a major challenge to E*Trade, (and all the other discount brokers) from a well-known brand name, and its stock price fell sharply as investors questioned if its competitive advantage is sustainable. In January 2007, the jury was still out, E*Trade announced it would not match Bank of America's offer of free online brokerage service, and the latter was beginning to aggressively roll out its free service nationally.[1]

OVERVIEW

As the Opening Case suggests, this chapter examines how a company selects and pursues a business model that will allow it to compete effectively in an industry and grow its profits and profitability. A successful business model results from business-level strategies that create a competitive advantage over rivals and achieve superior performance in an industry.

In Chapter 2, we examined how the competitive forces at work inside an industry affect its profitability. As industry forces change, so they change the profitability of an industry, and thus the profitability of any particular business model. Industry analysis is vital in formulating a successful business model because it determines (1) how existing companies will decide to change their business-level strategies to improve the performance of their business model over time, (2) whether or not established companies outside an industry may decide to create a business model to enter it, and (3) whether entrepreneurs can devise a business model that will allow them to compete successfully against existing companies in an industry.

In Chapter 3, we examined how competitive advantage depends on a company developing a business model that allows it to achieve superior efficiency, quality, innovation, and customer responsiveness, the building blocks of competitive advantage. And in Chapter 4, we discussed how every function must develop the distinctive competencies that allow a company to implement a business model that will lead to superior performance and competitive advantage in an industry.

In this chapter, we examine the competitive decisions involved in creating a business model that will attract and retain customers, and continue to do so over time, so that a company enjoys growing profits and profitability. To create a successful business model, strategic managers must (1) formulate business-level strategies that will allow a company to attract customers away from other companies in the industry (its competitors), and (2) implement those business-level strategies, which also involves the use of functional-level strategies to increase responsiveness to customers, efficiency, innovation, and quality.

By the end of this chapter, you will be able to distinguish between the principal generic business models and business-level strategies that a company uses to obtain a competitive advantage over its rivals. You will also understand why, and under what circumstances, strategic leaders of companies like E*Trade and Bank of America change their companies' strategies over time to pursue different kinds of business models to try to increase their competitive advantage over industry rivals.

Competitive Positioning and the Business Model

To create a successful business model, managers must choose a set of business-level strategies that work together to give a company a competitive advantage over its rivals; that is, they must optimize **competitive positioning**. As we noted in Chapter 1, to craft a successful business model, a company must first define its business, which entails decisions about (1) customers' needs, or what is to be satisfied; (2) customer groups, or who is to be satisfied; and (3) distinctive competencies, or how customer needs are to be satisfied.[2] The decisions managers make about these three issues determine which set of strategies they formulate and implement to put a company's business model into action and create value for customers. Consequently, we need to examine the principal choices facing managers as they make these three decisions.

● **Formulating the Business Model: Customer Needs and Product Differentiation**

Customer needs are desires, wants, or cravings that can be satisfied by means of the attributes or characteristics of a product—a good or service. For example, a person's craving for something sweet can be satisfied by a box of Godiva chocolates, a carton of Ben & Jerry's ice cream, a Snickers bar, or a spoonful of sugar. Two factors determine which product a customer chooses to satisfy these needs: (1) the way a product is differentiated from other products of its type so that it appeals to customers, and (2) the price of the product. All companies must differentiate their products to a certain degree to attract customers. Some companies, however, decide to offer customers a low-priced product and do not engage in much product differentiation. Companies that seek to create something unique about their product differentiate their products to a much greater degree than others so that they satisfy customers' needs in ways other products cannot.

Product differentiation is the process of designing products to satisfy customers' needs. A company obtains a competitive advantage when it creates, makes, and sells a product in a way that better satisfies customer needs than its rivals do. Here, the four building blocks of competitive advantage come into play because a company's decision to pursue one or more of these building blocks determines its approach to product differentiation. If managers devise strategies to differentiate a product by innovation, excellent quality, or responsiveness to customers, they are choosing a business model based on offering customers *differentiated products*. On the other hand, if managers base their business model on finding ways to increase efficiency and reliability to reduce costs, they are choosing a business model based on offering customers *low-priced products*.

Creating unique or distinctive products can be achieved in countless different ways, which explains why there are usually many different companies competing in an industry. Distinctiveness obtained from the physical characteristics of a product commonly results from pursuing innovation or quality, such as when a company focuses on developing state-of-the-art car safety systems or on engineering an SUV to give it sports-car-like handling, something Porsche and BMW strive to achieve.

Similarly, companies might try to design their cars with features such as butter-soft, hand-sewn leather interiors; fine wood fittings; and sleek, exciting body styling to appeal to customers' psychological needs, such as a personal need for prestige, status, or to declare a particular lifestyle, something Mercedes-Benz and Lexus strive for.[3]

Differentiation has another important aspect. Companies that invest their resources to create something distinct or different about their products can often charge a *higher,* or *premium, price* for their product. For example, superb design or technical sophistication allows companies to charge more for their products because customers are willing to pay these higher prices. Porsche and Mercedes-Benz buyers pay a high premium price to enjoy their sophisticated vehicles, as do customers of Godiva chocolates, which retail for about $26 a pound—much more than, say, a box of Whitman's candies or Hershey chocolates.

Consider the high-price segment of the car market, where customers are willing to pay more than $35,000 to satisfy their needs for a personal luxury vehicle. In this segment, Cadillac, Mercedes-Benz, Infiniti, BMW, Jaguar, Lexus, Lincoln, Audi, Volvo, Acura, and others are engaged in a continuing battle to design the perfect luxury vehicle—the one that best meets the needs of those who want such a vehicle. Over time, the companies that attract the most luxury car buyers—because they have designed the cars that possess the innovative features or excellent quality and reliability these customers desire the most—are the ones that achieve a sustained competitive advantage over rivals. For example, some customers value a sporty ride and performance handling; Mercedes-Benz and BMW, because of their cutting-edge technical design, can offer this driving experience better than any other automaker. Toyota's Lexus division is well known for the smoothness and quietness of its cars and their exceptional reliability. Lexus cars consistently outrank all other cars in published reliability rankings, and this excellence appeals to a large group of customers who appreciate these qualities. Volvo has a reputation for producing safe cars, and Rolls-Royce has a reputation for prestige cars. Other luxury carmakers have not fared so well. Cadillac, Lincoln, Audi, Acura, and Infiniti have found it more difficult to differentiate their cars, which sometimes compare unfavorably to their rivals in terms of ride, comfort, safety, or reliability. Although these less successful companies still sell many cars, customers often find their needs better satisfied by the attributes and qualities of their rivals' cars, and it is the latter that make above-average industry profits.

Even in the luxury car segment, however, carmakers must be concerned with efficiency because price affects a buying decision, even for highly differentiated products. Luxury carmakers compete to offer customers the car with the ride, performance, and features that provide them with the most value (satisfies their needs best) given the price of the car. Thus, Lexus cars are always several thousand dollars less than comparable cars, and Toyota can price these cars lower because of its low cost structure. For example, the Lexus LS430, introduced in 2006 at around $56,000, is about $20,000 less than the BMW 7 Series and Mercedes S Class, its nearest rivals. Most customers are discriminating and match price to differentiation even in the luxury car segment of the market, so BMW and Mercedes have to offer customers something that justifies their vehicles' higher prices.

At every price range in the car market—under $15,000, from $15,000 to $25,000, $25,000 to $35,000, and the luxury segment above $35,000—many models of cars compete to attract customers. For each price range, a carmaker has to decide how best to differentiate a particular car model to suit the needs of customers in that price range. Typically, the more differentiated a product is, the more it will cost to design and produce, and so differentiation leads to a higher cost structure. Thus, if a carmaker is to

stay within the $15,000 to $25,000 price range and yet design and produce a differentiated car that will give it a competitive advantage and allow it to outperform its rivals in the same price range, its strategic managers have to make crucial and difficult
decisions. They have to forecast what features customers will most value; for example, they may decide to trade off styling, safety, and performance so that the car will
not cost too much to produce, enabling them to make a profit and to still sell the car
for less than $25,000.

In sum, in devising a business model, strategic managers are always constrained
by the need to differentiate their products against the need to keep their cost structure under control so that they can offer the product at a competitive price—a price
that offers customers as much or more value than the products of its rivals. Companies that have built a competitive advantage through innovation, quality, and reliability can differentiate their products more successfully than their rivals can. In turn,
because customers perceive there is more value in their products, these companies
can charge a premium price.

● Formulating the Business Model: Customer Groups and Market Segmentation

The second main choice involved in formulating a successful business model is to decide
which kind of product(s) to offer to which customer group(s). Customer groups are the
sets of people who share a similar need for a particular product. Because a particular
product usually satisfies several different kinds of desires and needs, many different
customer groups normally exist in a market. In the car market, for example, some customers want basic transportation, some want top-of-the-line luxury, and others want the
thrill of driving a sports car: these are three of the customer groups in the car market.

In the athletic shoe market, the two main customer groups are those people who
use them for sporting purposes and those who like to wear them because they are casual and comfortable. Each customer group often includes subgroups composed of
people who have an even more specific need for a product. Inside the group of people who buy athletic shoes for sporting purposes, for example, are subgroups of people who buy shoes suited to a specific kind of activity, such as running, aerobics,
walking, and soccer (see Figure 5.1).

A company searching for a successful business model has to group customers according to the similarities or differences in their needs to discover what kinds of

FIGURE 5.1

Identifying Customer
Groups and Market
Segments

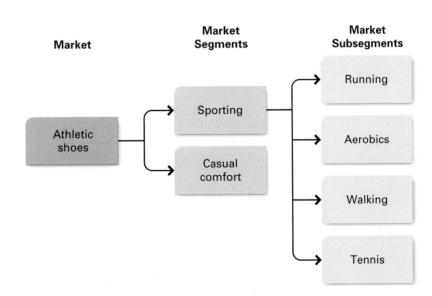

products to develop for different kinds of customers. The marketing function performs research to discover a group of customers' primary needs for a product, how they will use it, and their income or buying power (to determine the balance between differentiation and price). Other important attributes of a customer group are then identified that more narrowly target their specific needs. Once a group of customers who share a similar or specific need for a product has been identified, this group is treated as a market segment. Companies then decide whether to make and sell a product designed to satisfy the specific needs of this customer segment.

THREE APPROACHES TO MARKET SEGMENTATION Market segmentation is the way a company decides to group customers, based on important differences in their needs or preferences, in order to gain a competitive advantage.[4] First, the company must segment the market according to how much customers are able and willing to pay for a particular product—such as the different price ranges for cars mentioned above. Once price has been taken into consideration, customers can be segmented according to the specific needs that are being satisfied by a particular product, such as the economy, luxury, or speed of the cars mentioned above.

In crafting a business model, managers have to think strategically about which segments they are going to compete in and how they will differentiate their products for each segment. In other words, once market segments have been identified, a company has to decide how *responsive it should be to the needs of customers in the different segments.* This decision determines a particular company's product range. There are three main approaches toward market segmentation in devising a business model (see Figure 5.2):

- First, a company might choose not to recognize that different market segments exist and make a product targeted at the average or typical customer. In this case, customer responsiveness is at a *minimum*, and the focus is on price, not differentiation.

- Second, a company can choose to recognize the differences between customer groups and make a product targeted toward most or all of the different market segments. In this case, customer responsiveness is *high* and products are being *customized* to meet the specific needs of customers in each group, so the emphasis is on differentiation, not price.

- Third, a company might choose to target just *one or two market segments* and devote its resources to developing products for customers in just these segments. In this case, it may be highly responsive to the needs of customers in only these segments, or it may offer a bare-bones product to undercut the prices charged by companies who do focus on differentiation.

FIGURE 5.2

Three Approaches to
Market Segmentation

**No Market
Segmentation**
A product is targeted at
the "average customer."

**High Market
Segmentation**
A different product is offered
to each market segment.

**Focused Market
Segmentation**
A product is offered to one
or a few market segments.

Since a company's cost structure and operating costs increase when it makes a different product for each market segment rather than just one product for the whole market, why would a company devise a business model based on serving customers in multiple market segments? The answer is that, although operating costs increase, the decision to produce a range of products that are closely aligned with the needs of customers in different market segments attracts many more customers (because responsiveness to customers increases), and therefore sales revenues and profits increase. A car company that offers a wide range of cars customized to the needs of customers in different market segments increases the number of cars it can sell. As long as a company's revenues increase faster than its operating costs as its product range expands, profitability increases.

This does *not* mean that all companies should decide to produce a wide range of products aimed at each market segment to increase their profitability. It depends on how much customer needs for a product differ in a particular market or industry. In some industries, like cars, customer needs differ widely. There are considerable differences in buyers' primary needs for a car: income levels, lifestyles, ages, and so on. For this reason, major global carmakers broaden their product range and make vehicles to serve most market segments. A company that produces just one car model, compared to a company that produces twenty-five models, may find itself at a serious competitive disadvantage.

On the other hand, in some markets, customers have similar needs for a product and so the relative price of competing products drives their buying choices. In this situation, a company that chooses to use its resources to make and sell a single product as inexpensively as possible might gain a major competitive advantage. The average customer buys the product because it's a good value for the money. This is the business model followed by companies that specialize in making a low-cost product, such as BIC, which makes low-cost razors and ballpoint pens, and Arm & Hammer, which makes baking soda. These are products that most people use in the same way. This is also the business model followed by companies like Wal-Mart, with its mission to buy products from suppliers as cheaply as possible and then sell them to customers at the lowest possible prices. BIC and Wal-Mart do not segment the market; they decide to serve the needs of customers who want to buy products as inexpensively as possible. Wal-Mart promises everyday low prices and price rollbacks; BIC promises the lowest-priced razor blades that work acceptably.

The third approach to market segmentation is to target a product just at one or two market segments. To pursue this approach, a company must develop something very special or distinctive about its product to attract a large share of customers in those particular market segments. In the car market, for example, Rolls-Royce and Porsche target their products at specific market segments. Porsche, for example, targets its well-known sports cars at buyers in the high-priced sports car segment. In a similar way, specialty retailers compete for customers in a particular market segment, such as the segment composed of affluent people who can afford to buy expensive handmade clothing, or people who enjoy wearing trendy shoes such as Nike's Converse brand. A retailer might also specialize in a particular style of clothing, such as western wear, beachwear, or accessories. In many markets, these are enormous opportunities for small companies to specialize in satisfying the needs of a specific market segment. Often, these companies can better satisfy their customers' needs because they are so close to them and understand how their needs are changing over time.

Market segmentation is an evolving, ongoing process that presents considerable opportunities for strategic managers to improve their company's business model. For example, in the car industry, savvy strategists often identify a new customer group whose specific needs have not been met and who have had to "satisfice" and buy a model that does not meet their needs exactly but is a reasonable compromise. Now a car company can decide to treat this group as a market segment and create a product designed to meet group members' specific needs; if it makes the right choice, it has a blockbuster product. This was the origin of the minivan, sports utility vehicle, and all the recently introduced hybrid vehicles like the Honda Pilot, Toyota Prius, or Dodge Magnum. In the case of SUVs, many car buyers wanted a more rugged and powerful vehicle capable of holding many people or towing heavy loads. They liked the comfort of a car but also the qualities of a pickup; by combining the characteristics of both, carmakers created the SUV market segment. If managers make mistakes, however, and design a product for a market segment that is much smaller than they expected, the opposite can occur. In 2005, for example, Ford announced that it was ending production of its expensive luxury Lincoln truck and Excursion SUV because sales had been only in the hundreds a year, not the thousands a year it had projected.

● **Implementing the Business Model: Building Distinctive Competencies**

To develop a successful business model, strategic managers have to devise a set of strategies that determine (1) how to differentiate and price their product and (2) how much to segment a market and how wide a range of products to develop. Whether these strategies will result in a profitable business model now depends on strategic managers' ability to implement their business model, that is, to choose strategies that will create products that provide customers with the most value, while keeping their cost structure viable (because of the need to be price competitive).

In practice, this involves deciding how to invest a company's capital to build and shape distinctive competencies that result in a competitive advantage based on superior efficiency, quality, innovation, and/or responsiveness to customers. Hence, implementing a company's business model sets in motion *the specific set of functional-level strategies needed to create a successful differentiation and low-cost business strategy.* We discussed how functional strategies can build competitive advantage in Chapter 4. The better the fit between a company's business strategy and its functional-level strategies, the more value and profit a company creates.

Figure 5.3 illustrates Wal-Mart's business model. Sam Walton, the company's founder, devised a business model based on the strategy of keeping operating costs to a minimum so that he could offer customers everyday low prices and continuous price rollbacks. To this end, Walton chose business-level strategies to increase efficiency, such as having low product differentiation (Wal-Mart chooses minimal advertising and low responsiveness to customers) and targeting the mass market. His discount retail business model was based on the idea that lower costs mean lower prices.

Having devised a way to compete for customers, Walton's task was now to implement the business model in ways that would create a low-cost structure to allow him to charge lower prices. One business-level strategy he implemented was to locate his stores outside large cities, in small towns where there were no low-cost competitors; a second was to find ways to manage the value chain to reduce the costs of getting products from manufacturers to customers; and a third was to design and staff store operations to increase efficiency. The task of all functional managers in logistics, materials management, sales and customer service, store management, and so on, was to implement specific functional-level strategies that supported the low-cost/low-price business model. Figure 5.3 illustrates some of the thousands of specific choices that Wal-Mart has made to allow it to implement its business model successfully.

Wal-Mart's Business Model

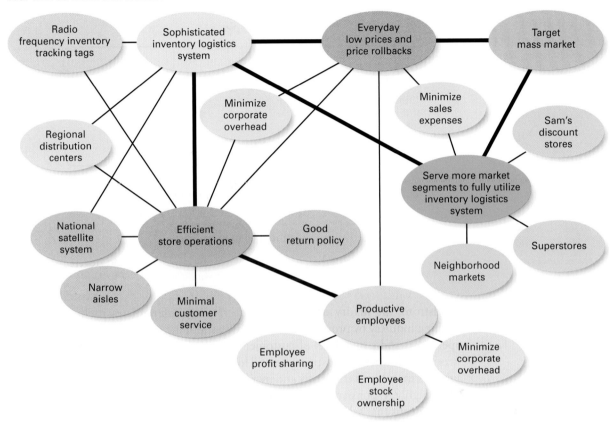

Competitive Positioning and Business-Level Strategy

Figure 5.4 presents a way of thinking about the competitive positioning decisions that strategic managers make to create a successful business model.[5] The decision to differentiate a product increases its perceived value to the customer so that market demand for the product increases. Differentiation is expensive, however; for example, additional expenditures on resources are needed to improve product quality or support a higher level of service. Therefore, the decision to increase product differentiation also raises a company's cost structure and results in a higher unit cost. In some cases, however, if increased demand for the product allows a company to make large volumes of the product and achieve economies of scale, these economies can offset some of these extra costs; this effect is showed by the dotted line in Figure 5.4.[6]

To maximize profitability, managers must choose a premium pricing option that compensates for the extra costs of product differentiation but is not so high that it chokes off the increase in expected demand (to prevent customers from deciding that the extra differentiation is not worth the higher price). Once again, to increase profitability, managers must also search for other ways to reduce the cost structure, but not in ways that will harm the differentiated appeal of their products. There are many specific functional strategies a company can adopt to achieve this. For example,

FIGURE 5.4

Competitive
Positioning at the
Business Level

Source: Copyright © C. W. L.
Hill and G. R. Jones, "The
Dynamics of Business-Level
Strategy" (unpublished
manuscript, 2005).

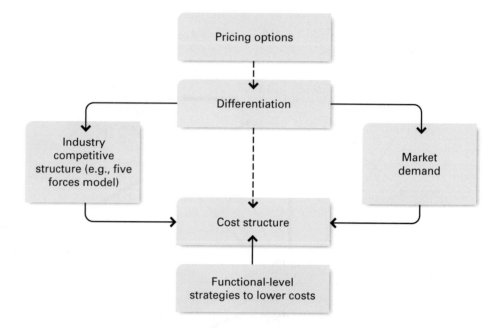

Nordstrom, the luxury department store retailer, differentiates itself in the retail clothing industry by providing a high-quality shopping experience with elegant store operations and a high level of customer service, all of which raise Nordstrom's cost structure. However, Nordstrom can still lower its cost structure by, for example, managing its inventories efficiently and increasing inventory turnover. Also, its strategy of being highly responsive to customers results in more customers and higher demand, which means that sales per square foot increase, and this revenue enables it to make more intensive use of its facilities and salespeople, which in turn leads to scale economies and lower costs. Thus, no matter what level of differentiation a company chooses to pursue in its business model, it always has to recognize the way its cost structure will vary as a result of its choice of differentiation and the other specific strategies it adopts to lower its cost structure; in other words, *differentiation and cost structure decisions affect one another.*

The last main dynamic shown in Figure 5.4 concerns the impact of the industry's competitive structure on a company's differentiation, cost structure, and pricing choices. Recall that strategic decision making takes place in an environment where watchful and agile competitors exist; therefore, one company's choice of competitive positioning is always made *with reference to those of its competitors.* If, for example, competitors start to offer products with new or improved features, a company may be forced to increase its level of differentiation to remain competitive, even if this reduces its profitability. Similarly, if competitors decide to develop products for new market segments, the company will have to follow suit or lose its competitive edge. Thus, because differentiation increases costs, increasing industry competition can drive up a company's cost structure. When that happens, a company's ability to charge a premium price to cover these high costs depends on whether its profitability increases or decreases.

In sum, maximizing the profitability of a company's business model is about making the right choices with regard to value creation through differentiation, costs, and pricing given both the demand conditions in the company's market and the competitive conditions in the company's industry. Because *all the different variables in Figure 5.4 change as the others change,* managers can never accurately predict the outcome of their decisions. This is why devising and managing a successful business model is such a difficult thing to do—and why effective strategic leadership is vital.

Competitive Positioning: Generic Business-Level Strategies

As we discussed above, a successful business model is the result of the way a company formulates and implements a set of business-level strategies to achieve a fit among its differentiation, cost, and pricing options. While no diagram can ever model all the complexities involved in business-level strategy decisions, Figure 5.5 represents a way to bring together the three issues involved in developing a successful business model. In the figure, the vertical and horizontal axes represent, respectively, the decisions of strategic managers to position a company's products in relation to the tradeoff between differentiating products (higher costs/higher prices) and achieving the lowest cost structure or cost leadership (lower costs/lower prices). In Figure 5.5, the curve connecting the axes represents the value creation frontier: the maximum amount of value that the products of different companies in an industry can provide at any one time with different business models. In other words, companies on the value frontier are those that have the most successful and profitable business models in a particular industry.

As Figure 5.5 illustrates, the value creation frontier is reached by pursuing one or more of the four building blocks of competitive advantage (quality has been split

FIGURE 5.5

Competitive Positioning and the Value Creation Frontier

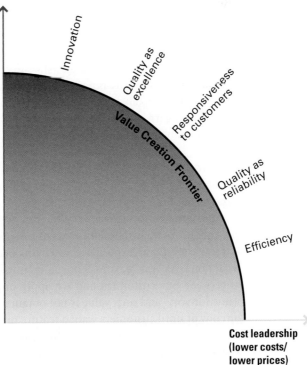

into two), which have been listed from top to bottom according to how much they can contribute to the creation of a differentiation or cost-leadership advantage. Thus innovation, a costly process that results in unique products, is closest to the differentiation axis, followed by quality as excellence, customer responsiveness, and quality as reliability; efficiency is closest to the cost-leadership axis.

To reach the value creation frontier and thus achieve above-average profitability, a company must formulate and implement a business model using one or a combination of three generic business-level strategies: cost leadership, differentiation, and focused differentiation. A **generic business-level strategy** gives a company a specific form of competitive position and advantage vis-à-vis its rivals that results in above-average profitability.[7] *Generic* means that all companies can potentially pursue these strategies regardless of whether they are manufacturing, service, or nonprofit enterprises; they are also generic because they can be pursued across different kinds of industries.

● Cost Leadership

A company pursuing a cost-leadership business model chooses strategies that do everything possible to lower its cost structure so it can make and sell goods or services at a lower cost than its competitors. These strategies include both functional strategies designed to improve its operating performance and competitive strategies intended to influence industry competition in its favor. In essence, a company seeks to achieve a competitive advantage and above-average profitability by developing a cost-leadership business model that positions it on the value creation frontier as close as possible to the lower costs/lower prices axis.

Two advantages accrue from pursuing cost leadership. First, if a company's closest rivals, such as those that compete in the same price range or for the same customer group, charge similar prices for their products, the cost leader will be more profitable than its competitors because of its lower costs. Second, the cost leader gains a competitive advantage by being able to charge a lower price than its competitors because of its lower cost structure. As discussed earlier, offering customers the same kind of value from a product but at a lower price attracts many more customers, so that even though the company has chosen a lower price option, the increased volume of sales will cause profits to surge. If its competitors try to get lost customers back by reducing their prices and all companies start to compete on price, the cost leader will still be able to withstand competition better than the other companies because of its lower costs. It is likely to win any competitive struggle. For these reasons, cost leaders are likely to earn above-average profits. A company becomes a cost leader when its strategic managers pursue the business-level strategic choices discussed below.

STRATEGIC CHOICES The cost leader chooses a low to moderate level of product differentiation relative to its competitors. Differentiation is expensive; the more a company expends resources to make its products distinct, the more its costs rise.[8] The cost leader aims for a level of differentiation obtainable at low cost.[9] Wal-Mart, for example, does not spend hundreds of millions of dollars on store design to create an attractive shopping experience, as chains like Macy's, Dillard's, or Saks Fifth Avenue have done. As Wal-Mart explains in its mission statement, "We think of ourselves as buyers for our customers and we apply our considerable strengths to get the best value for you," and such value is not obtained by building lavish stores.[10] Cost leaders often wait until customers want a feature or service before providing it. For example, a cost leader like Dell is never the first to offer high-quality graphics or video in a PC; instead, it adds such graphic or video capabilities only when it is obvious that customers demand it.

The cost leader also ignores the many different market segments in an industry. It positions its products to appeal to the average customer to reduce the costs of developing and selling many different products tailored to the needs of different market segments. In targeting the average customer, strategic managers try to produce or provide the least or smallest number of products that will be desired by the highest number of customers—which is at the heart of Dell's approach to building its computers or Wal-Mart's approach to stocking its stores. Thus, although customers may not get exactly the products they want, they are attracted by the lower prices.

To implement cost leadership, the overriding goal of the cost leader must be to choose strategies to increase its efficiency and lower its cost structure compared with its rivals. The development of distinctive competencies in manufacturing, materials management, and information technology is central to achieving this goal. For example, manufacturing companies pursuing a cost-leadership strategy concentrate on doing all they can to continually ride down the experience curve so that their cost structure keeps getting lower and lower. Achieving a cost-leadership position requires that a company develop skills in flexible manufacturing, adopt efficient materials-management techniques, and do all it can to increase inventory turnover and reduce the cost of goods sold. (Table 4.1 outlined the ways in which a company's functions can be used to increase efficiency.)

Consequently, for companies that make products, the manufacturing and materials-management functions are the center of attention, and the other functions shape their distinctive competencies to meet the needs of manufacturing and materials management.[11] The sales function, for example, may develop the competency of capturing large, stable sets of customers' orders. In turn, this allows manufacturing to make longer production runs and so achieve economies of scale and reduce costs. At Dell, for example, online customers are provided with a limited set of choices so that Dell can customize PCs to a customer's needs at low cost. Finding ways to customize products at low cost is an important task for managers pursuing a cost-leadership strategy. The human resources function may focus on instituting training programs and compensation systems that lower costs by improving employees' productivity, and the research and development function may specialize in process improvements to lower the manufacturing costs.

By contrast, companies supplying services, such as retail stores like Wal-Mart, must develop distinctive competencies in whatever functions contribute most to their cost structure. For Wal-Mart, this is the cost of purchasing products, so the logistics or materials-management function becomes of central importance. Wal-Mart has taken advantage of advances in information technology to lower the costs associated with getting goods from manufacturers to customers, just as Dell, the cost leader in the PC industry, uses the Internet to lower the cost of selling its computers. Another major source of cost savings in pursuing cost leadership is to choose an organizational structure and culture to implement this strategy in the most cost-efficient way. Thus, a low-cost strategy implies minimizing the number of managers in the hierarchy and the rigorous use of budgets to control production and selling costs. An interesting example of the way a company can craft a business model to become the cost leader in an industry is Ryanair, discussed in Strategy in Action 5.1.

COMPETITIVE ADVANTAGES AND DISADVANTAGES Porter's five forces model, introduced in Chapter 2, explains why each of the business models allows a company to pursue competitive strategies that help it reach the value creation frontier shown in Figure 5.5.[12] The five forces are threats from competitors, powerful suppliers, powerful

Strategy in Action

Ryanair Takes Control over the Sky in Europe

Ryanair, based in Dublin, Ireland, imitated and improved on the cost-leadership business model pioneered by Southwest Airlines in the United States and used it to become a leading player in the European air travel market. Ryanair's CEO, the flamboyant Michael O'Leary, saw the specific strategies Southwest had developed to cut costs and used the same strategies to position Ryanair as the lowest-cost, lowest-priced European airline. Today, the average cost of a Ryanair ticket within Europe is $48, compared to $330 on British Airways and $277 on Lufthansa, which have long dominated the European air travel market. The result is that Ryanair now flies more passengers inside Britain than British Airways, and its share of the European market is growing as fast as it can gain access to new landing spots and buy the new planes needed to service its expanding route structure.

O'Leary has managed to improve on Southwest's low-cost business model. Ryanair imitated the main elements of Southwest's model, such as using only one plane, the 737, to reduce maintenance costs, selling tickets directly to customers, and eliminating seat assignments and free in-flight meals. It also avoids high-cost airports like Heathrow and chooses smaller ones outside big cities, such as Luton, its London hub, just as Wal-Mart chose to move into smaller towns. However, to reduce cleanup costs, O'Leary also eliminated the seat-back pockets that often contain trash left by previous passengers, as well as blankets, pillows, free sodas and snacks, and even sick bags—anything at all a passenger might expect to receive on a more differentiated airline. "You get what you pay for" is Ryanair's philosophy. To implement his cost-leadership strategy, O'Leary and all employees are expected to find ways to wipe out or reduce the small, incremental expenses that arise in performing the tens of thousands of specific operations needed to run an airline. His goal is to eliminate all the differentiated qualities of an airline that can raise costs. Through all these tactics, Ryanair has lowered its cost structure so far that no other European airline can come close to offering its low-cost fares and break even, let alone make a profit.

The other side of Ryanair's business model is to add to its revenues by getting its customers to spend as much as possible while they are on its flights. To this end, Ryanair offers snacks, meals, and a variety of drinks to encourage customers to open their wallets. In addition, to cut costs his planes have no seatback LCD screens for viewing movies and playing games; passengers can rent a digital hand-held device for $6 a flight to watch movies and sitcoms or play games or music. Fourteen percent of its revenues come from these sources; they are so important that the airline gives away millions of its unsold seats free to customers so that it can at least get some revenue from passengers sitting in what would otherwise be empty seats.

How have competitors reacted to Ryanair's cost-leadership strategy? Some airlines have started a low-price subsidiary, just as United's TED division was created to compete with Southwest in the United States. However, this often results in cannibalization as their passengers move from the high-price to the low-price service. Some airlines that pursue the differentiation strategy, like British Airways, are not suffering because they are solidly profitable in the business segment of the market. However, other airlines, such as Air France and Alitalia, Italy's flagship airline, are close to bankruptcy, and Irish carrier Aer Lingus had to cut costs by 50% just to survive. The power of Ryanair was evident in 2006 when O'Leary announced he wanted to buy Aer Lingus, something the Irish government prevented. But it has become clear throughout the world that the cost-leadership business model is the only one that will fare well in the future, and all large national and U.S. airlines are rushing to adopt strategies that will allow them to pursue it.[a]

buyers, substitute products, and new entrants. The cost leader is protected from industry competitors by its cost advantage. Its lower costs also mean that it will be less affected than its competitors by increases in the price of inputs if there are powerful suppliers, and less affected by a fall in the prices it can charge if there are powerful buyers. Moreover, since cost leadership usually requires a large market share, the cost leader purchases in relatively large quantities, increasing its bargaining power over suppliers. If substitute products begin to come onto the market, the cost leader can reduce its price to compete with them and retain its market share. Finally, the leader's cost advantage constitutes a barrier to entry because other companies are unable to enter the industry and match the leader's costs or prices. The cost leader is therefore relatively safe as long as it can maintain its low-cost advantage.

The principal dangers of the cost-leadership approach lurk in competitors' ability to pursue new strategies that lower their cost structures and beat the cost leader at its own game—which is what happened to E*Trade in the Opening Case. For instance, if technological change makes experience-curve economies obsolete, new companies may apply lower-cost technologies that give them a cost advantage. The steel mini-mills discussed in Chapter 4 pursued this strategy to obtain a competitive advantage. Competitors may also draw a cost advantage from labor-cost savings. Global competitors located in countries overseas often have very low labor costs; wage costs in the United States are roughly 600% more than they are in Malaysia, China, or Mexico. Most U.S. companies now assemble their products abroad as part of their low-cost strategy; many are forced to do so simply to compete and stay in business.

Competitors' ability to imitate the cost leader's methods easily is another threat to the cost-leadership strategy. For example, companies in China routinely take apart the electronic products of Japanese companies like Sony and Panasonic to see how they are designed and assembled. Then, using Chinese-made components and a huge pool of inexpensive domestic labor, they manufacture clones of these products and flood the U.S. market with inexpensive tape players, radios, phones, and DVD players.

Finally, the pursuit of cost leadership carries a risk that strategic managers, in their single-minded desire to reduce costs, might make decisions that decrease costs but then drastically reduce demand for the product. This happened to Gateway in the early 2000s when, to reduce the costs of customer service, customer support people were instructed not to help customers who were experiencing problems with their new Gateway computers if they had installed their own new software on the machines. New buyers, most of whom install their own software, began to complain vociferously, and Gateway's sales began to fall as word spread. Within six months, managers had reversed their decision, and once again Gateway began offering full customer support.

● **Focused Cost Leadership**   A cost leader is not always a large, national company that targets the average customer. Sometimes a company can pursue a **focused cost leadership** business model based on combining the cost leadership and focused business-level strategies to compete for customers in just one or a few market segments. Focused cost leaders concentrate on a narrow market segment, which can be defined geographically, by type of customer, or by segment of the product line.[13] In Figure 5.6, focused cost leaders are represented by the smaller circles next to the cost leader's circle. For example, since a geographic niche can be defined by region or even by locality, a cement-making company, a carpet-cleaning business, or a pizza chain can pursue a cost-leadership strategy in one or more cities in a region. Figure 5.7 compares a focused cost-leadership business model with a pure cost-leadership model.

If a company uses a focused cost-leadership approach, it competes against the cost leader in the market segments where it can operate at no cost disadvantage. For example, in local lumber, cement, bookkeeping, or pizza delivery markets, the focuser may have lower materials or transportation costs than the national cost leader. The focuser may also have a cost advantage because it is producing complex or custom-built products that do not lend themselves easily to economies of scale in production and

FIGURE 5.6

Generic Business Models and the Value Creation Frontier

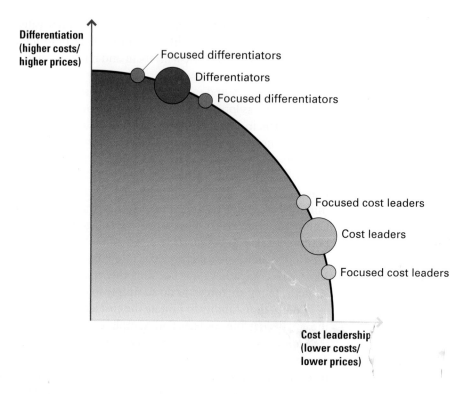

FIGURE 5.6

Generic Business Models and the Value Creation Frontier

therefore offer few cost-saving possibilities. The focused cost leader concentrates on small-volume custom products, for which it has a cost advantage, and leaves the large-volume standardized market to the national cost leader—for example, low-priced Mexican food specials versus Big Macs.

Because it has no cost disadvantage in its market segments, a focused cost leader also operates on the value creation frontier and so earns above-average profits. Such a company has a great opportunity to develop its own niche and compete against companies pursuing cost-leadership or differentiated strategies. Ryanair, for example, began as a focus company because at first it operated flights only between Dublin and London. Since there was no cost leader in the European market, it was able to quickly expand its operations; today, it is the European cost leader and its future goal seems to be to become the global cost leader! Similarly, Southwest began as a focused cost leader within the Texas market, but now it is a national air carrier and competes against new companies that pursue focused cost leadership, such as JetBlue and Song.[14]

FIGURE 5.7

Why Focus Strategies Are Different

	Offers products to only one group of customers	Offers products to many kinds of customers
Offers low-priced products to customers	Focused cost-leadership strategy	Cost-leadership strategy
Offers unique or distinctive products to customers	Focused differentiation strategy	Differentiation strategy

Because a focused company makes and sells only a relatively small quantity of a product, its cost structure will often be higher than that of the cost leader. In some industries, like cars, this can make it very difficult or impossible to compete with the cost leader. Sometimes, however, by targeting some new market segment or by implementing a business model in a superior way—such as by adopting a more advanced technology—focused companies can be a threat to large cost leaders. For example, flexible manufacturing systems have opened up many new opportunities for focused companies because small production runs become possible at a lower cost. The steel mini-mills discussed in Chapter 4 provide another good example of how a focused company, in this case Nucor, can grow so efficient by specializing in one market that it becomes *the* cost leader. Similarly, the growth of the Internet has opened up many new opportunities for focused companies to develop business models based on being the cost leader compared to bricks-and-mortar companies. Amazon.com shows how effectively a company can craft a business model to become the cost leader.

IMPLICATIONS AND CONCLUSIONS To pursue cost leadership, strategic managers need to devote enormous efforts to incorporate all the latest information, materials management, and manufacturing technology into their operations to find new ways to reduce costs. Often, as we saw in Chapter 4, using new technology will also raise quality and increase responsiveness to customers. A low-cost approach requires ongoing strategic thinking to make sure the business model is aligned with changing environmental opportunities and threats.

Strategic managers in companies throughout the industry are watching the cost leader and will move quickly to imitate its innovations because they also want to reduce their costs. Today, a differentiator cannot let a cost leader obtain too great a cost advantage because the leader might then be able to use its high profits to invest more in product differentiation and beat the differentiator at its own competitive game. For example, Toyota and Honda began as cost leaders by manufacturing simple low-priced cars. Their cars sold well, and they then invested their profits to design and make new models of cars that became increasingly differentiated based on features and quality. Today, Toyota and Honda, with cars in every market segment, pursue a differentiation strategy, although Toyota also has the lowest cost structure of any global car company.

A cost leader must also respond to the strategic moves of its differentiated competitors and increase the quality and features of its products if it is to prosper in the long run. Even low-priced products, such as Timex watches and BIC razors, cannot be too inferior to the more expensive Seiko watches or Gillette razors if the lower-costs/lower-prices policy is to succeed. Companies in an industry watch the strategies their rivals are pursuing and the changes they make to those strategies. If Seiko or Swatch introduces a novel kind of LCD watch dial or Gillette introduces a three- or four-blade razor, managers at Timex and BIC will respond within months by incorporating these innovations into their low-priced products if required. This situation is also very common in the high-priced women's fashion industry. As soon as the famous designers like Gucci and Dior have shown their spring and fall collections, their designs are copied and the plans transmitted to factories in Malaysia, where workers are ready to manufacture low-priced imitations that, within months, will reach low-price clothing retail stores around the world.

A business model like cost leadership should be thought of as a specific set of strategic choices that helps a company stay focused on how to compete most effectively over time. It is all too easy for strategic managers, flush with the success of pursuing cost leadership, to become less vigilant and lose sight of changes in the five forces of competition and in the macroenvironment that change the rules of the competitive game. McDonald's, long the cost leader in the fast-food industry, was surprised when rivals like Taco Bell began to offer 99-cent daily specials. McDonald's had to learn how to make fast food more cheaply to compete, and its managers have adopted new cooking techniques and food management practices that have ratcheted it down the experience curve, so that today 99-cent meals are a permanent fixture on the McDonald's menu.

● **Differentiation**

A **differentiation** business model is based on pursuing a business-level strategy that allows a company to achieve a competitive advantage by creating a product that customers perceive as different or distinct in some important way. A differentiator (that is, a differentiated company) has the ability to satisfy customers' needs in a way that its competitors cannot. This means that it can charge a premium price (one higher than that charged by its closest rivals). The ability to increase revenues by charging premium prices (rather than by reducing costs, as the cost leader does) allows the differentiator to reach the value frontier, outperform its competitors, and achieve superior profitability, as shown in Figure 5.6. As noted earlier, customers pay a premium price when they believe the product's differentiated qualities are worth the extra money. Consequently, differentiated products are often priced on the basis of what the market will bear.[15]

Mercedes-Benz cars are more expensive than the cars of its closest rivals because customers believe they offer more features and confer more status on their owners. Similarly, a BMW is not much more expensive to produce than a Honda, but its high price is determined by customers who want its distinctive sporty ride and the prestige of owning a BMW. (In fact, in Japan, BMW prices its entry cars quite modestly to attract young, well-heeled Japanese customers away from Honda.) Similarly, Rolex watches do not cost much to produce, their design has not changed very much for years, and their gold content represents only a small fraction of the price. Customers buy a Rolex, however, because of the distinct qualities they perceive in it: its beautiful design, and its ability to hold its value as well as to confer status on its wearer.

STRATEGIC CHOICES A differentiator invests its resources to gain a competitive advantage from superior innovation, excellent quality, and responsiveness to customer needs—the three principal routes to high product differentiation. For example, Procter & Gamble claims that its product quality is high and that its Ivory soap is 99.44% pure. Maytag stresses reliability and the best repair record of any other washer on the market. IBM promotes the quality service provided by its well-trained sales force. Innovation is commonly the source of differentiation for technologically complex products, and many people pay a premium price for new and innovative products, such as a state-of-the-art gaming PC, HD-DVD player, or car.

When differentiation is based on responsiveness to customers, a company offers comprehensive after-sales service and product repair. This is an especially important consideration for complex products such as cars and domestic appliances, which are likely to break down periodically. Maytag, Dell, and BMW all excel in responsiveness to customers. In service organizations, quality-of-service attributes are also very important. Neiman Marcus, Nordstrom, and FedEx can charge premium prices because they offer an exceptionally high level of service. Firms of lawyers, accountants, and consultants stress the service aspects—their knowledge, professionalism, and reputation—of their operations to clients.

Finally, a product's appeal to customers' psychological desires is a source of differentiation. The appeal can be prestige or status, as it is with BMWs and Rolex watches; safety of home and family, as with Aetna or Prudential Insurance; or simply providing a superior shopping experience, as with Target and Macy's. Differentiation can also be tailored to age groups and socioeconomic groups. Indeed, the bases of differentiation are endless.

A company pursuing a business model based on differentiation frequently strives to differentiate itself along as many dimensions as possible. The less it resembles its rivals, the more it is protected from competition and the wider is its market appeal. Thus, BMWs offer more than prestige; they also offer technological sophistication, luxury, reliability, and good (albeit very expensive) repair service. All these bases of differentiation help increase sales.

Generally, a differentiator chooses to divide its market into many segments and niches and to offer different products in each segment, just as Toyota and Dell do. Strategic managers recognize how much revenue can be increased when each of a company's products, targeted at different market segments, can attract more customers. A differentiator only targets the market segments in which customers are willing to pay a premium price, however. For example, Sony produces many TV models, but it targets only the niches from mid-priced to high-priced sets, and its lowest-priced model is always a few hundred dollars above that of its competitors, thus bringing into play the premium-price factor. Customers have to pay extra for a Sony.

Finally, in choosing how to implement its business model, a differentiated company concentrates on developing distinctive competencies in the functions that provide the source of its competitive advantage. Differentiation on the basis of innovation and technological competency depends on the R&D function, as discussed in Chapter 4. Efforts to improve service to customers depend on the quality of the sales and customer service function.

Pursuing a business model based on differentiation is expensive, so a differentiator has a cost structure that is higher than that of a cost leader. Building new competencies in the functions necessary to sustain a company's differentiated appeal does not mean neglecting the cost structure, however. Even differentiators benchmark how cost leaders operate to find ways to imitate their cost-saving innovations while preserving the source of their competitive advantage. A differentiator must control its cost structure to ensure that the price of its products does not exceed the price that customers are willing to pay for them, as noted in Nordstrom's case. Also, superior profitability is a function of a company's cost structure, so it is important to keep costs under control but not to reduce them so far that a company loses the source of its differentiated appeal.[16] The owners of the famous Savoy Hotel in London, England, face just this problem. The Savoy's reputation has always been based on the incredibly high level of service it offers its customers. Three hotel employees serve the needs of each guest, and in every room, a guest can summon a waiter, maid, or valet by pressing a button at bedside. The cost of offering this level of service has been so high that the hotel used to make less than 1% net profit every year; to increase profit, a room today costs at least $500 a night![17] Its owners try to find ways to reduce costs to increase profits, but if they reduce the number of hotel staff (the main source of the Savoy's high costs), they may destroy the main source of its differentiated appeal.

COMPETITIVE ADVANTAGES AND DISADVANTAGES   The advantages of the differentiation strategy can also be discussed in the context of the five forces model. Differentiation safeguards a company against competitors to the degree that customers develop brand loyalty for its products, a valuable asset that protects the company on all fronts. Powerful suppliers are less of a problem because the differentiated company's strategy is geared more toward the price it can charge than toward costs. Also, differentiators can often pass on price increases to customers because they are willing to pay the premium price. Thus, a differentiator can tolerate moderate increases in input prices better than the cost leader can. Differentiators are unlikely to experience problems with powerful buyers because they offer a distinct product; only they can supply the product and it commands brand loyalty. Differentiation and brand loyalty also create a barrier for other companies seeking to enter the industry. A new company has to find a way to make its own product distinctive to be able to compete, which involves an expensive investment in building some kind of distinctive competence.

Finally, substitute products are a threat only if a competitor can develop a product that satisfies a customer need like the differentiator's product does and so customers switch to the lower-priced product. Wired phone companies have suffered as lower-cost alternative ways of making phone calls, through digital fiber-optic cable, satellite, and the Internet, are becoming increasingly available. The issue is how much of a premium price a company can charge for distinctness before customers switch products. In the phone industry, the answer is: Not much. The large carriers have reduced prices drastically; 2.5 cents a minute is a common rate, down from 37 cents just a decade ago.

The main problems with a differentiation strategy center on how well strategic managers can maintain a product's perceived difference or distinctness in the eyes of customers. In the 2000s, it has become clear that it is easier than ever for agile competitors to imitate and copy successful differentiators. This has happened across many industries, such as retailing, computers, cars, home electronics, telecommunications, and pharmaceuticals. Patents and first-mover advantages (the advantages of being the first to market a product or service) last only so long, and as the overall quality of competing products increases, brand loyalty declines. The problems L. L. Bean has had in maintaining its competitive advantage, described in Strategy in Action 5.2, highlight many of the threats that face a differentiator.

IMPLICATIONS AND CONCLUSIONS A business model based on differentiation requires a company to make strategic choices that reinforce each other and together increase the value of a good or service in the eyes of customers. When a product is distinctive in customers' eyes, differentiators can charge a premium price. The disadvantages of pursuing differentiation are the ease with which competitors can imitate a differentiator's product and the difficulty of maintaining a premium price. When differentiation stems from the design or physical features of the product, differentiators are at great risk because imitation is easy. An increasing risk is that over time products such as HD-DVD players or LCD televisions become commodity-like products, for which the importance of differentiation diminishes as customers become more price sensitive. However, when differentiation stems from functional-level strategies that lead to superior service or reliability, or from any intangible source, such as FedEx's guarantee or the prestige of a Rolex, a company is much more secure. It is difficult to imitate intangible products, and a differentiator can often reap the benefits of this for a long time. Nevertheless, all differentiators must watch for imitators and be careful that they do not charge a price higher than the market will bear.

● **Focused Differentiation** As in the case of the focused cost leader, a company that pursues a business model based on **focused differentiation** chooses to combine the differentiation and focused generic business-level strategies and specializes in making distinctive products for one or two market segments. All the means of differentiation that are open to the differentiator are available to the focused differentiator. The point is that the focused company develops a business model that allows it to successfully position itself to

Strategy in Action   5.2

L. L. Bean's New Business Model

In 1911, Leon Leonwood Bean, a hunter who grew weary of walking miles to hunt game as his feet became wetter and wetter, decided he would create a waterproof boot. The one he invented had leather uppers attached to a large, rounded rubber base and sole. Soon he began selling his shoes through mail order. Word spread about their reliability. Backed by his policy of being responsive to customers who complained (often replacing their boots years after a sale), his company's reputation spread even faster. As the years went by, L. L. Bean expanded its now well-known product line to include products such as its canvas tote bags and, of course, its flannel dog bed. By 2000, the company's mail-order revenues exceeded $1 billion a year, and L. L. Bean became known for offering one of the broadest and highest-quality product lines of sporting clothes and accessories.

To display its product line, the company built a 160,000-square-foot signature store in Freeport, Maine, that stocks hundreds of versions of its backpacks, fleece vests, shirts, moccasins, tents, and other items, and over 3 million visitors a year shop its store. L. L. Bean established this store partly to give customers hands-on access to its products so that they would have a better understanding of the high quality they were being offered. Of course, L. L. Bean expects to command a premium price for offering such a wide variety of high-quality products, and historically it has enjoyed high profit margins. Customers buy its products for their personal use but also as gifts for friends and relatives.

Bean's business model began to suffer in the mid-1990s, however, when there was an explosion in the number of companies touting high-quality, high-priced products to customers, and Bean's catalog lost its unique appeal. Furthermore, the growth of the Internet through the 1990s gave customers access to many more companies that offered quality products, often at much lower prices, such as Lands' End, which also began to feature fleece vests, dog beds, and so on in its product lineup. The problem facing any differentiator is how to protect the distinctiveness of its products from imitators who are always searching for ways to steal away its customers by offering them similar kinds of products at reduced prices.

Finding ways to protect Bean's business model proved to be a major challenge. Its catalog sales were stagnant for several years as customers switched loyalty to low-priced companies. Bean's current CEO, Chris McCormick, has crafted new strategies to help the company rebuild its competitive advantage. One is to build a chain of L. L. Bean stores in major urban locations to allow more potential customers to examine the quality of its products and so attract them—either to buy them in the stores or to use its website.

So far, this approach has not proved to be easy because physical retail stores have a high cost structure, and Bean has had to search for the right way to implement its strategy. It has also had to lower the price of its sporting clothes and accessories in these stores; the days of premium prices are gone. Another strategy has been to launch an aggressive advertising campaign aimed at younger customers who may not know the Bean story. With physical stores, the Internet, and its catalog, it may have a better chance of getting their business.

The jury is still out, however. Not only are other differentiated sporting goods chains expanding, such as Dick's Sporting Goods and Gander Mountain, but sites like Amazon.com and Landsend.com, now owned by Sears, are offering lower-priced products. Whether McCormick will be able to successfully change L. L. Bean's business model to allow it to reach the value creation frontier remains to be seen.[b]

compete with the differentiator in just one or a few segments. For example, Porsche, a focused differentiator, competes against Toyota and GM in the sports car and luxury SUV segments of the car market.

For the focused differentiator, selecting a niche often means focusing on one type of customer, such as serving only the very rich, the very young, or the very adventurous, or focusing on only a segment of the product line, such as only on organic or vegetarian foods or very fast cars, designer clothes, or designer sunglasses. Focused differentiators are able to reach the value frontier when they are able to develop a distinctive product that better meets the needs of customers in a particular segment than the differentiator can (Figure 5.6). This may happen, for example, when a focused differentiator gains better knowledge of the needs of a small customer set (such as sports car buyers), knowledge of a region, or expertise in a particular field (such as corporate law, management consulting, or website management for retail customers or restaurants). Alternatively, it might develop superior skills in responsiveness to customers based on its ability to serve the particular needs of regional or industry customers in ways that a national differentiator would find very expensive. Similarly, concentration on a narrow range of products sometimes allows a focuser to develop innovations more quickly than a large differentiator can.

The focuser does not attempt to serve all market segments because that would bring it into direct competition with the differentiator. Instead, it concentrates on building market share in one market segment; if it is successful, it may begin to serve more and more market segments and chip away at the differentiator's competitive advantage. However, if it is too successful at what it does, or if it does try to compete with the differentiator, it may run into trouble because the differentiator has the resources to imitate the focused company's business model. For example, when Ben & Jerry's created a luxury ice cream, their huge success led other companies like Häagen-Dazs and Godiva to produce their own competing products. A good example of the way competition is changing even between focused differentiators that make a similar luxury product, in this case, designer clothing, is profiled in Strategy in Action 5.3.

In summary, a focused differentiator can protect its competitive advantage and niche to the extent that it can provide a product or service that its rivals cannot, for example, by being close to its customers and responding to their changing needs. However, if the focuser's niche disappears over time because of technological change or changes in customers' tastes, it cannot move easily to new niches, and this can be a major challenge. For example, clothing store chain Brooks Brothers, whose focus was on providing formal business attire, ran into great difficulty in the 1990s when business casual became the clothing norm at most companies. It found it hard to adapt to the changing market and was bought out in 2001. Similarly, corner diners have become almost a thing of the past because they are unable to compete with the low prices and speed of fast-food chains like McDonald's and the upscale atmosphere of Starbucks. The disappearance of niches is one reason that so many small companies fail.

The Dynamics of Competitive Positioning

Companies that successfully pursue one of the business models just discussed are able to outperform their rivals and reach the value creation frontier. They have developed business-level strategies that result in competitive advantage and above-average profitability; they are usually the most successful and well-known companies in their industry. While some companies are able to develop the business model and strategies that allow them to reach the value creation frontier, many others cannot and so only achieve average or below-average profitability. As Figure 5.8 illustrates, the most successful companies in the retail industry, such as Neiman Marcus, Macy's, Target, Wal-Mart, and Costco, have reached the value frontier, but their competitors, such as Nordstrom, Sack's, Dillard's, JCPenney's, and Sears/Kmart, have not.

Why are some companies in an industry able to reach this frontier while others fail, even *when they appear to be using the same business model, for example, differentiation or focus differentiation?* Moreover, few companies are able to continually outperform

Strategy in Action   5.3

Zara Uses IT to Change the World of Fashion

Well-known fashion houses like Chanel, Dior, Gucci, and Armani charge thousands of dollars for the fashionable suits and dresses that they introduce twice yearly in the fall and spring. Since only the very rich can afford such differentiated and expensive clothing, most luxury designers produce less expensive lines of clothing and accessories that are sold in upscale fashion retailers such as Neiman Marcus, Nordstrom, and Saks Fifth Avenue. In the 2000s, however, these luxury designers, which all pursue focus differentiation, have come under increasing pressure from small, agile fashion designers, such as England's Jaeger and Laura Ashley and Spain's Zara, which have developed capabilities in using IT (information technology) that allow them to pursue a focused differentiation strategy but at a much lower cost than the luxury fashion houses. This has allowed them to circumvent barriers to entry into the high-fashion segment and develop well-received brand names that still command a premium price.

Zara, in particular, has achieved significant success. Its sales have soared because it has created innovative information systems that lower costs and speed time to market so that it can produce fashionable clothes at lower prices and sell them in its own chain of clothing stores. Zara uses IT to manage the interface between its design and manufacturing operations efficiently. Major fashion houses like Dior and Gucci can take six or more months to design their collections and then three to six months more before their moderately-priced lines become available in upscale retailers. Zara's designers closely watch the trends in the high-fashion industry and the kinds of innovations that the major houses are introducing. Then, using its IT that is linked to its suppliers and the low-cost manufacturers abroad that make its clothing, Zara's designers can create a new collection in only five weeks. These clothes can then be made in a week and delivered to stores soon after. This short time to market gives Zara great flexibility and has allowed it to compete effectively in the rapidly changing fashion market, where customer tastes evolve quickly.

IT also gives Zara instant feedback on which of its clothes are selling well and in which countries. This information enables Zara to engage in continual product development and remain at the cutting edge of fashion, a major source of differentiation advantage. For example, Zara can manufacture more of a particular kind of dress or suit to meet high customer demand, and it can keep up with fashion by constantly changing its mix of clothes in its rapidly expanding global network of stores. Moreover, since it is following a focused strategy, it can do this at relatively small output levels. Its IT has allowed Zara to minimize the inventory it has to carry, which is the major cost of goods sold for a clothing maker/retailer. Because of the quick manufacturing-to-sales cycle and just-in-time fashion, Zara has been able to offer its collections at comparatively low prices and still make profits that are the envy of the fashion clothing industry. When Zara went public in 2001, its stock price soared because of its high ROIC, and investors believe this will continue as Zara continues to open its stores in most major cities around the world.[c]

their rivals and remain on the value creation frontier; companies such as Toyota, Dell, and Wal-Mart are rare. Why is it so hard for companies to sustain their competitive advantage over time and remain on the frontier? To understand why some companies perform better than others and why the performance of one company can change over time, it is necessary to understand the dynamics involved in positioning a company's business model so that it can compete successfully over time. In this section, we first explore another business model that helps explain why some companies are able to sustain and increase their competitive advantage over time. Second, we examine how the business model a company pursues puts it into a strategic group of competitors that affect its performance. Finally, we examine why differences in performance among companies in an industry are to be expected and why some companies run into major competitive problems that affect their very survival.

FIGURE 5.8

The Dynamics of
Competitive
Positioning

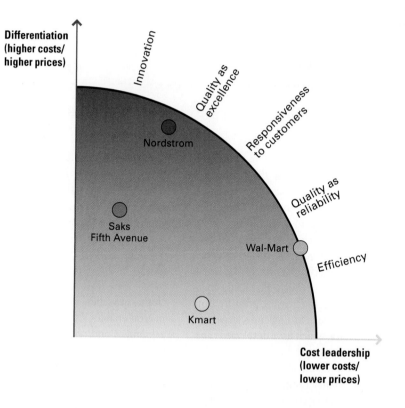

Competitive Positioning for Superior Performance: Broad Differentiation

Companies that pursue cost leadership pursue a different business model and strategies than companies that choose differentiation, yet each business model is a path to superior performance and profitability. As we have emphasized throughout this chapter, however, no matter what business model a company pursues, it cannot afford to ignore its cost structure. Managers must always try to find ways to reduce costs in this era of intense global competition in which new (focused) companies might appear with some kind of differentiation or cost advantage and use it to become a dominant competitor, as Toyota and Wal-Mart did. At the same time, all companies need to differentiate their products to some degree to attract customers, increase their market share, and grow their profits over time. Thus, a company that can combine the strategies necessary to pursue both cost leadership and differentiation successfully will develop the most profitable business model in its industry.

Today, many of the most successful companies in an industry have found ways to achieve this. These companies are well known because they can offer customers excellent-quality products at very reasonable prices; that is, they can offer customers a superior "value proposition" compared to all their rivals. The middle of the value creation frontier is occupied by **broad differentiators,** the companies that have developed business-level strategies to improve their differentiation and cost structure simultaneously. Broad differentiators operate on the value creation frontier because they have chosen a level of differentiation that gives them a competitive advantage in the market segments they have targeted, but they have achieved this *in a way that has allowed them to lower their cost structure over time* (see Figure 5.9). Thus, although they may have higher costs than cost leaders, and although they may offer a less-differentiated product than differentiators do, they have found a competitive position that offers their customers as much and normally more value than industry rivals. Broad differentiators continually use their distinctive competencies to increase the range of their products, and they are constantly seeking to enter new market segments

FIGURE 5.9

The Broad
Differentiation
Business Model

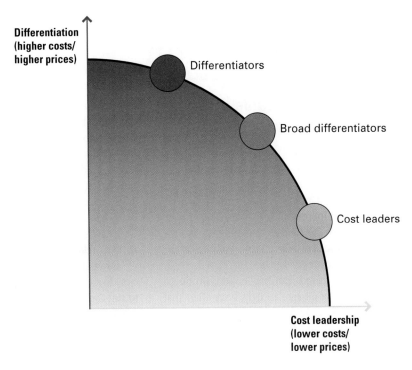

to increase their market share to grow their profits. At the same time, they also work continuously to find ways to lower their cost structure and increase their ROIC.

The companies that have formulated and implemented the business-level strategies that enable them to get to this middle, or broadly differentiated, position become an increasing threat to both differentiators and cost leaders over time. These companies make a differentiated product that allows them to charge a premium price for their product compared to a cost leader. However, because of their low cost structure, they can choose to price their product with just *some "small" premium* over the price charged by cost leaders—and, of course, a much lower price than a differentiator has to charge to cover its higher cost structure. As a result, customers often perceive the value offered by the broad differentiator's products to be well worth the premium price (superior value proposition) and so are attracted away from the cost leader's product. At the same time, those customers who are reluctant to pay the high premium price that differentiators command may decide that the qualities of the broad differentiator's product (and its price) more than make up for the loss of the extra differentiated features of the luxury premium-priced products—and choose a Mazda MX5 over a Porsche Boxter, or a box of See's chocolates over Godiva chocolates, and halve the cost of their purchase in the process.

As a result, if strategic managers have the skills to pursue this business model successfully, their companies, as broad differentiators, can steadily increase their market share and profitability over time. This provides them with more capital to reinvest in their business, and so they can continually improve their business model. For example, over time their growing profits allow broad differentiators to invest in new technology that both increases their differentiation advantage and lowers their cost structure; this weakens the competitive position of their rivals. As they build their competitive advantage and become able to offer customers a better value proposition, they push the value creation frontier to the right and knock their competitors off the frontier so they become less profitable. Toyota, profiled in Strategy in Action 5.4, is a good example of a company that used a broad differentiation business model that has increasingly put its rivals at a competitive disadvantage. The result today is that it has replaced Ford as

Strategy in Action

Toyota's Goal? A High-Value Vehicle to Match Every Customer Need

The car industry has always been one of the most competitive in the world because of the huge revenues and profits that are at stake: in 2005, annual global car sales were over $350 billion. It is small wonder, then, that industry rivalry has been increasing as carmakers have been fighting to develop new car models that better satisfy the needs of particular groups of buyers. One company at the forefront of these endeavors is Toyota.

Toyota, which pioneered lean production, produced its first car over thirty years ago: an ugly, boxy affair that was, however, inexpensive. As the quality of its car became apparent, sales increased, and Toyota, which was then a focused cost leader, plowed its profits back into improving the styling of its vehicles and into efforts to continually reduce production costs. Over time, it used its low cost structure, including its efficient design processes, to produce an ever increasing range of reasonably priced vehicles tailored to different segments of the car market. By the 1980s, its ability to go from the initial design stage to the production stage in two to three years allowed it to bring out new models faster than its competitors and to capitalize on the development of new market segments. Low costs and fast time to market have also allowed it to correct mistakes quickly if it designs a car that proves to have little market appeal—and Toyota has made mistakes.

In 1999, for example, Toyota brought out the Echo, a subcompact car that featured state-of-the-art engineering to deliver exceptional fuel economy: around fifty to sixty miles per gallon. The Echo was designed to be inexpensive to run and buy, and Toyota targeted this vehicle at buyers in their twenties, expecting them to appreciate these qualities. Its designers were disappointed when this age group displayed little enthusiasm for the car; its styling did not appeal to them even if its performance did fit their budget. The Echo's buyers turned out to be individuals in their forties who appreciated its economy and found it a useful second car to get around in.

Recognizing that they failed to position their product to hit the important market segment of young adults, the main car buyers of the future, Toyota's designers went back to the drawing board. Analyzing changing market trends and demographics, they sought to find the styling and

features for a car that was good-looking and fun to drive for this market segment and that could be sold for $16,000 to $18,000. Toyota (and several other carmakers) realized that perhaps the time was ripe for the return to the hatchback, but an updated version of it. Hatchbacks had been very popular in the early 1980s; however, the cars then were small and often had an ungainly appearance. Sales of hatchbacks had dropped off quickly when carmakers began to offer new sports utility vehicles and updated small sedans. By 1995, relatively few hatchbacks were available.

Drawing on its design and manufacturing competencies, Toyota's engineers updated and shaped the hatchback to suit the needs of young adults in their twenties: the result was the Toyota Matrix, introduced in 2002 at a price starting at $17,000. The Matrix features revolutionary body styling reflective of much more expensive, sporty cars. It is spacious inside and geared to the needs of its intended young buyers; for example, seats fold back to allow for carrying a large cargo volume, and many storage bins and two-prong plugs for power outlets allow for the use of VCRs, MP3 players, and other devices. The message is that the Matrix is designed to be functional, fun, and a sporty ride. Then, in 2003, Toyota introduced a new car, the Scion, once again a car designed to appeal to young people.

Toyota has also been a leader in positioning its whole range of vehicles to take advantage of emerging market segments. In the sports utility segment, its first offering was the expensive Toyota Land Cruiser, priced at over $35,000. Realizing the need for sports utility vehicles in other price ranges, it next introduced the 4Runner, priced at $20,000 and designed for the average sports utility customer; the RAV4, a small sports utility vehicle in the low $20,000 range, followed; then came the Sequoia, a bigger, more powerful version of the 4Runner in the upper $20,000 range. Finally, taking the technology from its Lexus R3000 vehicle, it introduced the luxury Highlander sports utility vehicle in the low $30,000 range. It now offers six models of sports utility vehicles, each offering a particular combination of price, size, performance, styling, and luxury to appeal to a particular customer group within the sports utility segment of the car market. Toyota also positions its sedans to appeal to different sets of buyers. For example, the Camry, one of the best-selling cars in the United States, is targeted toward the middle of the market, to customers who can afford to pay about $25,000 and want a balance of luxury, performance, safety, and reliability. The Camry also has a small premium price relative to similar cars of its U.S. competitors, such as the Ford 500 and the GM Impala.

Toyota's broad differentiation business model is based, on the demand side, on making a range of vehicles that optimizes the amount of value it can create for different groups of customers. On the supply side, the number of models it makes is constrained by the need to maintain a low cost structure and to choose the car-pricing options that will generate maximum sales revenues and profits. The decision about how many kinds of vehicles to produce is also affected by the strategies of its rivals because they are also trying to determine the opti-

mum range of cars to produce. Toyota was not alone in its decision to produce a hatchback in 2002: other noticeable competitors included BMW, which introduced the redesigned Mini Cooper; Honda's new Civic hatchbacks; the already well-received PT Cruiser from Daimler-Chrysler; and Ford's Fusion. In fact, the number of hatchback models doubled in the 2000s, as did the expected number of sales (up to 750,000 vehicles). Competition in this market segment is now intense. Each car company needs to anticipate the actions of its rivals, and each hopes, like Toyota, that it has made the right choices to obtain a large share of customers in this important market segment.[d]

the second largest global carmaker by sales after GM, but it is many times as profitable as GM, Ford, and most other carmakers.

Why has Toyota been so successful in pursuing a business model based on broad differentiation? Toyota is a leader in continuously improving manufacturing techniques to lower its cost structure. Recall that changes in technology, such as the constantly improving flexible manufacturing technologies we discussed in Chapter 4, as well as new digital, electronic, and information technologies (which we examine in detail in Chapter 7), have made it possible for all companies to reduce their cost structure if they can implement it in the right way. New technologies also provide many opportunities to increase product differentiation while maintaining a low cost structure. Technological developments often provide many ways for a company that has traditionally pursued a pure differentiation strategy to do so at a significantly lower cost so that it can choose a lower pricing option and build demand.

Companies like Toyota are continuously experimenting with new ways to reduce costs and segment their markets. The use of robots and flexible manufacturing cells reduces the costs of retooling the production line, and the costs associated with small production runs make it much easier to produce a wide variety of vehicle models and maintain an efficient cost structure. Today, flexible manufacturing enables a company pursuing differentiation to manufacture a range of products at a cost comparable to that of the cost leader. BMW, for example, has taken advantage of flexible manufacturing technologies to reduce its costs, and it has also chosen to charge only a modest premium price to boost its sales revenues. This new strategy has worked: its market share and profitability have increased in recent years.

Indeed, the ability of flexible manufacturing to substantially reduce the costs of differentiating products has promoted the trend toward market fragmentation and niche marketing in many consumer goods industries, such as mobile phones, computers, and appliances. Another way that a differentiated producer may be able to realize significant economies of scale is by standardizing many of the component parts used in its end products. Toyota's various models of sports utility vehicles are built on only three different car platforms. As a result, Toyota is able to realize significant economies of scale in the manufacture and bulk purchase of standardized component parts, despite its high level of market segmentation.

FIGURE 5.10

Using a Business
Model to Push
out the Value
Creation Frontier

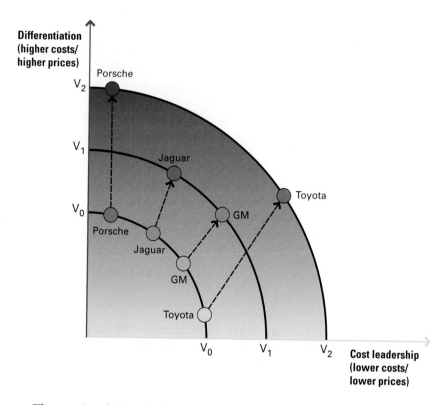

The way in which a business model based on broad differentiation can disrupt industry competition and change the rules of the competitive game is illustrated in Figure 5.10, which contrasts the car industry as it was in the days of mass production with the industry in the days of lean production. The value frontier (V_0) represents the most value that could be produced using mass-production technology, and at that time, GM was the broad differentiator, with its five divisions producing cars that gave it an 80% share of the U.S. car market. Toyota is shown as the focused cost leader on the value creation frontier because it was learning the skills involved in lean production. On the other hand, Porsche and Jaguar are shown as the differentiators on the value creation frontier: their pricey cars sold because of their innovative features, exceptional styling, and European origin.

On the V_0 frontier, GM was the dominant company, but as Toyota grew, its continuous ability to make high-quality cars efficiently and then to expand into more and more market segments changed the rules of the competitive game. Today, in an era of lean production, Toyota is the successful broad differentiator and has pushed out the value frontier to V_2, meaning that customers now receive substantially more performance, safety, and luxury from their cars than they did ten or twenty years ago; in essence, they get more value for their money. Where is GM today? To survive, GM has had to develop skills in lean manufacturing, and this has allowed it to move up to the V_1 frontier. However, GM cannot match Toyota's low cost structure, and it has also had to dramatically cut the number of models it offers to customers because it cannot sell its cars at profitable prices. By 2004, its market share had fallen to 26%, and today it is creating far less value than Toyota, something reflected in its ROIC and stock price.

Jaguar, now owned by Ford, is also in a desperate position. Ford has tried to reduce Jaguar's cost structure and strengthen its styling and image, which has always been the key to its cars' differentiated appeal. By 2004, it was clear its strategies had not worked: demand for Jaguars had been falling, while demand for BMWs, Mercedes, and Lexus cars had been soaring. As for Porsche, it also had to learn lean production skills; however, its task is a little easier because it only produces a few sports car models. In addition, its engineers have kept their performance and handling at the leading edge of technological developments, so that today Porsche enjoys record sales and profits. Toyota and Porsche are on the value frontier at V_2; although GM and Jaguar have moved forward to V_1, their enormous losses in the last twenty years because of their failure to reach the value creation frontier have led to major falls in their market share and profits. Intense competition from ever advancing technology and from countries like China that have low-cost labor has been transforming competition in many industries, including the car industry. Carmakers have been trying to find ways to compete with Toyota and reach the new value frontier—however, Toyota is continually pushing the frontier out to the right.

One set of business-level strategies that a broad differentiator commonly uses to maintain a low cost structure is to make a vehicle targeted at one segment of the global market and then allow only limited customization of that vehicle. For example, carmakers throughout the world are offering customers a mid-priced sedan with an economy, luxury, or sports package to appeal to this principal market segment. Package offerings substantially lower manufacturing costs because long production runs of the various packages are possible. Once again, the company sees gains from both differentiation and low cost. Just-in-time inventory systems can also help reduce costs and improve the quality and reliability of a company's products. Toyota's cost of goods sold is the lowest of any carmaker, and although Ford and Chrysler have spent billions to lower their costs, Toyota continues to push the value frontier out to the right, as already mentioned. In 2004, for example, its hybrid car, the Prius, which is powered by both a gasoline engine and a battery, became popular because of rising gas prices. Toyota has licensed the rights to use its hybrid technology to Ford and GM, and more and more companies are planning to bring out a range of hybrid vehicles.

Finally, many companies, such as Dell and Amazon.com, have been using the Internet and e-commerce as a way of becoming a broad differentiator. Both companies have been rapidly expanding the range of products they offer to customers and taking advantage of their highly efficient materials-management systems to drive down costs compared to bricks-and-mortar retailers. The Internet is a highly cost-effective way to inform millions of potential customers about the nature and quality of a company's products. Also, when customers do their own work on the Internet, such as by managing their own finances, stock trades, bill paying, travel booking, and purchasing, a company has shifted these costs to the customer and is no longer bearing them. Direct selling to the customer also avoids the need to use wholesalers and other intermediaries, which results in great cost savings. It has been estimated that 40% of the profit in a new car goes to the dealership that sells the car and covers costs such as those associated with marketing the car.

● **Competitive Positioning and Strategic Groups**

As this whole discussion suggests, competition in an industry is dynamic. New developments such as (1) technological innovations that permit increased product differentiation, (2) the identification of new customer groups and market segments, and (3) the continual discovery of better ways to implement a business model to lower the cost structure continually change the competitive forces at work in an industry. In such a dynamic situation, the competitive position of companies can change rapidly. Higher-performing companies are able to gain from positioning themselves competitively to pursue broad differentiation. On the other hand, poorer-performing companies are often slow to recognize how their competitive position is changing because of the actions of their rivals, so they often find their competitive advantage disappearing. Strategic group analysis, which we discussed in Chapter 2, is a useful tool to help companies in an industry better understand the dynamics of competitive positioning so they can change their business models to position themselves to achieve superior performance.

A company's business model determines how it will compete for customers in a particular market segment, market, or industry, and typically several companies are competing for the same set of customers. This means that the business-level strategies pursued by one company affect the strategies pursued by the others, and over time companies competing for the same customers become rivals locked in a competitive struggle. The goal is to be the company that reaches or pushes out the value creation frontier to obtain a competitive advantage and achieve above-average profitability.

Within most industries, strategic groups emerge, with all companies within each group pursuing a similar business model.[18] All companies in an industry competing to be the cost leader form one strategic group, all those seeking some form of differentiation advantage form another, and companies that have developed a broad differentiation strategy constitute another strategic group. Companies pursuing focused differentiation or focused cost leadership form yet other strategic groups.

The concept of strategic groups has a number of implications for competitive positioning. First, strategic managers must map their competitors according to their choice of business model. They can then identify the sets of strategies their rivals have decided to pursue, such as what customer needs to satisfy, which customer groups to serve, and which distinctive competencies to develop. They can then use this knowledge to position themselves closer to customer and differentiate themselves from their competitors. In other words, careful strategic-group analysis allows managers to uncover the most important bases of competition in an industry and to identify products and market segments where they can compete most successfully for customers. Such analysis also helps to reveal what competencies are likely to be most valuable in the future so that companies can make the right investment decision. For example, the need to develop new models of cars that can be sold across the world and can be assembled reliably by low-cost labor has dominated competitive positioning in the global car industry. U.S. car companies have bought or formed alliances with almost every foreign car manufacturer to obtain marketing, design, or manufacturing knowledge.

Second, once a company has mapped its competitors, it can better understand how changes taking place in the industry are affecting its relative standing vis-à-vis differentiation and cost structure, as well as identify opportunities and threats. Often a company's nearest competitors are those companies in its strategic group that are pursuing a similar business model. Customers tend to view the products of such companies as direct substitutes for each other. Thus, a major threat to a company's profitability can arise from within its own strategic group when one or more companies find ways to either improve product differentiation and get closer to customers or lower their cost structure. This is why companies today benchmark their closest competitors on major performance dimensions to determine if they are falling behind in some important respect. For example, UPS and FedEx are constantly examining each other's performance.

Because strategic-group analysis also forces managers to focus on the activities of companies in other strategic groups, it helps them to identify emerging threats from companies outside their strategic group, such as when a focused company has devised a business model that will bring sweeping changes to the industry. It also helps them understand opportunities that might be arising because of changes in the environment; in response to these changes, they might purchase a focused company and implement its business model across the entire company to absorb the threat.

Recall from Chapter 2 that different strategic groups can have a different standing with respect to each of Porter's five competitive forces because these forces affect companies in different ways. In other words, the risk of new entry by potential competitors, the degree of rivalry among companies within a group, the bargaining power of buyers, the bargaining power of suppliers, and the competitive force of substitute products can all vary in intensity among different strategic groups within the same industry. In the global car industry, for example, the smaller focused differentiators and cost leaders ran into trouble in the 1990s. Their input costs were rising, and they could not afford billions of dollars to design new models and build the new flexible manufacturing plants needed to produce them. Indeed, some European, Korean, and even Japanese companies started to lose billions of dollars. Large U.S. and European carmakers, which were also suffering from the emergence of Toyota and Honda as broad differentiators, realized that they had to reduce their cost structure to survive. The need to compete with Toyota and Honda led to a huge wave of global merger activity that has left just a handful of global giants to compete in the 2000s. For example, Daimler Benz took over Chrysler Suzuki, GM took control of Isuzu and Saab, Ford merged with Mazda and took over Jaguar and Volvo, and Renault took a controlling stake in Nissan to learn lean production techniques. Thus, the strategic-group map in the global car industry changed dramatically. Today, only a handful of focused companies like BMW and Porsche remain, and even they have forged alliances with other carmakers. If they make a mistake in managing their business models, they will also become a target for one of the large global companies seeking to increase product differentiation.

In sum, strategic-group analysis involves identifying and charting the business models and business-level strategies that industry rivals are pursuing. Managers can then determine which strategies are successful and unsuccessful and why a certain business model is working or not. They can also analyze how the relative competitive position of industry rivals, both those pursuing the same business model and those pursuing different business models, is changing over time. This knowledge allows them to either fine-tune or radically alter their business models and strategies to improve their own competitive position.

● Failures in Competitive Positioning

Successful competitive positioning requires that a company achieve a fit between its strategies and its business model. Thus, a cost leader cannot strive for a high level of market segmentation, as a differentiator does, and provide a wide range of products because those choices would raise its cost structure too much and the company would lose its low-cost advantage. Similarly, a differentiator with a competency in innovation that tries to reduce its expenditures on research and development, or one with a competency in after-sales service that seeks to economize on its sales force to decrease costs, is asking for trouble because it has implemented its business model in the wrong way.

To pursue a successful business model, managers must be careful to ensure that the set of business-level strategies they have formulated and implemented are working in harmony to support each other and do not result in conflicts that ruin the competitive position the company is aiming for through its choice of business model. Many companies, through neglect, ignorance, or error—or perhaps because of the Icarus paradox discussed in Chapter 1—do not work to continually improve their business model, do not perform strategic-group analysis, and often fail to identify and respond to changing opportunities and threats in the industry environment. As a result, the company's business model starts to fail because its business-level strategies do not work together and its profitability starts to decline. Sometimes its performance can decline so quickly that the company is taken over by other companies or goes bankrupt.

These companies have lost their position on the value creation frontier either because they have lost the source of their competitive advantage or because their rivals have found ways to push out the value creation frontier and leave them behind. Sometimes these companies initially pursued a successful cost-leadership or differentiation business model but then gradually began to pursue business-level strategies that worked against them. Unfortunately, it seems that most companies lose control of their business models over time, often because they become large, complex companies that are difficult to manage or because the environment is changing faster than they can change their business model—such as by adjusting product and market choices to suit changing industry conditions. This is why it is so important that managers *think strategically*.

In Chapter 1, we defined *strategic intent* as the way managers think about where they want their organization to be in the future and what kinds of resources and capabilities they will need to achieve this vision. Strategic intent provides a company with a sense of direction and stretches managers at all levels to be more inventive or innovative and to make better use of resources. Moreover, it "implies a competitive distinct point of view about the future; it holds out to employees the promise of exploring new competitive territory."[19] The experience of Holiday Inns, described in Strategy in Action 5.5, shows how a company can lose control of its business model but also how managers can change it to suit the changing competitive landscape.

There are many factors that can cause a company to make competitive positioning errors. While some focused companies may succeed spectacularly for a time, a focuser can also make a major error when, in its rush to implement its business model, it overexpands and so loses control of its business model. Take People Express, a U.S. airline that was the first cost leader to emerge after deregulation of the U.S. airline industry. It started out as a specialized air carrier serving a narrow market niche: low-priced travel on the eastern seaboard. In pursuing focused cost leadership, it was very successful, but in its rush to expand to other geographic regions, it decided to take over other airlines. These airlines were differentiators that had never pursued cost leadership; the purchases raised the company's cost structure and it lost its competitive advantage against the other national carriers. In the end, People Express was swallowed up by Texas Air and incorporated into Continental Airlines. Herb Kelleher, the founder of Southwest Airlines, watched how People Express had failed, and he stuck to the cost-leadership business model. He took *twenty* years to build his national airline, but he never deviated from the strategies necessary to pursue cost leadership.

In 2004, Southwest announced it might do away with its strategy of no seat reservations and might make other changes to deal with its expanding route structure. This means that its top managers need to be vigilant in managing its cost structure. Another focus differentiator that ran into problems was Krispy Kreme Doughnuts, which began to expand the number of its stores rapidly in the 2000s as demand for its tasty product soared. By 2004, its cost structure was out of control. Its failure to implement its business model, combined with the fall in the demand for doughnuts because of the popularity of the Atkins diet, resulted in its first loss and its stock price has plummeted.

Differentiators can also fail in the market and end up stuck in the middle if focused competitors attack their markets with more specialized or low-cost products that blunt their competitive edge. This happened to IBM in the large-frame computer market when PCs became more powerful and able to do the job of the much more expensive mainframes. Of course, the increasing movement toward flexible manufacturing has aggravated the problems facing both cost leaders and differentiators.

Strategy in Action   5.5

Holiday Inns on Six Continents

The history of the Holiday Inns motel chain is one of the great success stories in U.S. business. Its founder, Kemmons Wilson, found motels to be small, expensive, and of unpredictable quality when he vacationed in the early 1950s. This discovery, along with the prospect of unprecedented highway travel that would come with the new interstate highway program, triggered a realization: there was an unmet customer need—a gap in the market for quality accommodations. Holiday Inns was founded to meet that need. From the beginning, Holiday Inns set the standard for offering motel features such as air conditioning and icemakers while keeping room rates reasonable. These amenities enhanced the motels' popularity, and motel franchising, Wilson's invention, made rapid expansion possible. By 1960, Holiday Inns could be found in almost every city and on every major highway. Before the 1960s ended, more than one thousand of them were in full operation, and occupancy rates averaged 80%. The concept of mass accommodation had arrived.

The service that Holiday Inns offered appealed to the average traveler, who wanted a standardized product (a room) at an average price—the middle of the hotel room market. But by the 1970s, travelers were beginning to make different demands on hotels and motels. Some wanted luxury and were willing to pay higher prices for better accommodations and service. Others sought low prices and accepted rock-bottom quality and service in exchange. As the market fragmented into different groups of customers with different needs, Holiday Inns was still offering an undifferentiated, average-cost, average-quality product.

Although Holiday Inns missed the change in the market and thus failed to respond appropriately to it, the competition did not. Companies such as Hyatt siphoned off the top end of the market, where quality and service sold rooms. Chains such as Motel 6 and Days Inns captured the basic-quality, low-price end of the market. In between were many specialty chains that appealed to business travelers, families, or self-caterers (people who want to be able to cook in their hotel rooms). Holiday Inns' position was attacked from all sides. As occupancy rates dropped drastically with increasing competition, profitability declined.

Wounded but not dead, Holiday Inns began a counterattack. The original chain was upgraded to suit quality-oriented travelers. Then, to meet the needs of different kinds of travelers, Holiday Inns created new hotel and motel chains: the luxury Crowne Plazas, the Hampton Inns serving the low-priced end of the market, and the all-suite Embassy Suites. Thus, Holiday Inns attempted to meet the demands of the many niches, or segments, of the hotel market that have emerged as customers' needs have changed over time. These moves were successful in the early 1990s, and Holiday Inns grew to become one of the largest suppliers of hotel rooms in the industry. However, by the late 1990s, falling revenues made it clear that with intense competition in the industry from other chains such as Marriott, Holiday Inns was once again losing its differentiated appeal.

In the fast-changing hotel and lodging market, positioning each hotel brand or chain to maximize customer demand is a continuing endeavor. In 2000, the pressure on all hotel chains to adapt to the challenges of global competition and become globally differentiated brands led to the takeover of Holiday Inns and its incorporation into the international Six Continents Hotels chain. Today, around the globe, more than 3,200 hotels flying the flags of Holiday Inns, Holiday Inns Express, Crowne Plaza, Staybridge Suites by Holiday Inns, and luxury Inter-Continental Hotels and Resorts are positioning themselves to offer the services, amenities, and lodging experiences that will cater to almost every travel occasion and guest need. In the 2000s, the company has undertaken a massive modernization campaign in the United States to take existing full-service Holiday Inns to their next evolution. Holiday Inns plans to have a room to meet the need of every segment of the lodging market anywhere in the world.[e]

No company is safe in the jungle of competition, and each must be constantly on the lookout to take advantage of competitive advantages as they arise.

In sum, strategic managers must employ the tools discussed in this book to continually monitor how well the business-level strategies that formulate and implement their company's business model are working. No task is more important than ensuring that their company is optimally positioned against its rivals to compete for customers. And, as we have discussed, the constant changes occurring in the external environment, as well as through the actions of competitors who work to push out the value creation frontier, make competitive positioning a complex, demanding task that requires the highest degree of strategic thinking. This is why companies pay tens of millions of dollars a year to CEOs and other top managers who have demonstrated their ability to create and sustain successful business models.

Summary of Chapter

1. To create a successful business model, managers must choose business-level strategies that give a company a competitive advantage over its rivals; that is, they must optimize competitive positioning. They must first decide on (1) customer needs, or what is to be satisfied; (2) customer groups, or who is to be satisfied; and (3) distinctive competencies, or how customer needs are to be satisfied. These decisions determine which strategies they formulate and implement to put a company's business model into action.

2. Customer needs are desires, wants, or cravings that can be satisfied through the attributes or characteristics of a product. Customers choose a product based on (1) the way a product is differentiated from other products of its type and (2) the price of the product. Product differentiation is the process of designing products to satisfy customers' needs in ways that competing products cannot. Companies that create something distinct or different can often charge a higher, or premium, price for their product.

3. If managers devise strategies to differentiate a product by innovation, excellent quality, or responsiveness to customers, they are choosing a business model based on offering customers differentiated products. If managers base their business model on finding ways to reduce costs, they are choosing a business model based on offering customers low-priced products.

4. The second main choice in formulating a successful business model is to decide which kind of product(s) to offer to which customer group(s). Market segmentation is the way a company decides to group customers, based on important differences in their needs or preferences, in order to gain a competitive advantage.

5. There are three main approaches toward market segmentation. First, a company might choose to ignore differences and make a product targeted at the average or typical customer. Second, a company can choose to recognize the differences between customer groups and make a product targeted toward most or all of the different market segments. Third, a company might choose to target just one or two market segments.

6. To develop a successful business model, strategic managers have to devise a set of strategies that determine (1) how to differentiate and price their product, and (2) how much to segment a market and how wide a range of products to develop. Whether these strategies will result in a profitable business model now depends on strategic managers' ability to provide customers with the most value while keeping their cost structure viable.

7. The value creation frontier represents the maximum amount of value that the products of different companies inside an industry can give customers at any one time by using different business models. Companies on the value creation frontier are those that have the most successful business models in a particular industry.

8. The value creation frontier can be reached by choosing among four *generic competitive strategies:* cost leadership, focused cost leadership, differentiation, and focused differentiation.

9. A cost-leadership business model is based on lowering the company's cost structure so it can make and sell goods or services at a lower cost than its rivals. A cost leader is often a large, national company that targets the average customer. Focused cost leadership is developing the right strategies to serve just one or two market segments.

10. A differentiation business model is based on creating a product that customers perceive as different or distinct in some important way. Focused differentiation is providing a differentiated product for just one or two market segments.

11. The middle of the value creation frontier is occupied by broad differentiators; they have pursued their differentiation strategy in a way that has also allowed them to lower their cost structure over time.

12. Strategic-group analysis helps companies in an industry better understand the dynamics of competitive positioning. In strategic-group analysis, managers identify and chart the business models and business-level strategies their industry rivals are pursuing. Then they can determine which strategies are successful and

unsuccessful and why a certain business model is working or not. In turn, this allows them to either fine-tune or radically alter their business models and strategies to improve their competitive position.

13. Many companies, through neglect, ignorance, or error, do not work to continually improve their business model, do not perform strategic-group analysis, and often fail to identify and respond to changing opportunities and threats. As a result, their business-level strategies do not work together, their business model starts to fail, and their profitability starts to decline. There is no more important task than ensuring that one's company is optimally positioned against its rivals to compete for customers.

Discussion Questions

1. Why does each generic business model require a different set of business-level strategies? Give examples of pairs of companies in (a) the computer industry, (b) the electronics industry, and (c) the fast-food industry that pursue different types of business models.

2. How do changes in the environment affect the success of a company's business model?

3. What is the value creation frontier? How does each of the four generic business models allow a company to reach this frontier?

4. How can companies pursuing cost leadership and differentiation lose their place on the value frontier? In what ways can they regain their competitive advantage?

5. How can a focused company push the value creation frontier to the right? How does this affect other industry competitors? On the other hand, how can changes in the value creation frontier threaten focused companies?

6. Why is strategic-group analysis important for superior competitive positioning?

7. What are some of the reasons companies lose control over their business models, and thus their competitive advantage, over time?

Practicing Strategic Management

SMALL-GROUP EXERCISE
Finding a Strategy for a Restaurant

Break up into groups of three to five and discuss the following scenario. You are a group of partners contemplating opening a new restaurant in your city. You are trying to decide how to position your restaurant to give it the best competitive advantage.

1. Create a strategic-group map of the restaurants in your city by analyzing their generic business models and strategies. What are the similarities or differences between these groups?

2. Identify which restaurants you think are the most profitable and why.

3. On the basis of this analysis, decide what kind of restaurant you want to open and why.

ARTICLE FILE 5

Find an example (or several examples) of a company pursuing one of the generic business models. What set of business-level strategies does the company use to formulate and implement its business model? How successful has the company been?

STRATEGIC MANAGEMENT PROJECT
Module 5

This part of the project focuses on the nature of your company's business model and business-level strategies. If your company operates in more than one business, concentrate on either its core, or most central, business or on its most important businesses. Using all the information you have collected on your company so far, answer the following questions:

1. How differentiated are the products or services of your company? What is the basis of its differentiated appeal?

2. What is your company's strategy toward market segmentation? If it segments its market, on what basis does it do so?

3. What distinctive competencies does your company have? (Use the information on functional-level strategy in the last chapter to answer this question.) Is efficiency, quality, innovation, responsiveness to customers, or a combination of these factors the main driving force in your company?

4. What generic business model is your company pursuing? How has it formulated and implemented a set of business-level strategies to pursue this business model?

5. What are the advantages and disadvantages associated with your company's choice of business model and strategies?

6. Is your company a member of a strategic group in an industry? If so, which one?

7. How could you improve your company's business model and strategies to strengthen its competitive advantage?

ETHICS EXERCISE

George Vargus had just been hired as a salesperson for a large construction company in town. His assignment was to go out and land large contracts for the company. For the first few months, George would be shadowing the company's other salesperson, Bill Carle. During George's first week, Bill, with George in tow, attended at least one meeting per day. Most of these meetings occurred during lunch or dinner and lasted for hours. George enjoyed the easy pace of the job, along with the good food and abundant drink that seemed to be an integral part of the process. Compared to his last job working as a salesperson for a home renovation store, this job was heaven.

During his second week on the job, George began to have second thoughts. He and Bill continued to attend long, enjoyable lunches and dinners, but George was beginning to wonder if this was the way that he wanted to conduct business. Extraordinary amounts of money were being spent wining and dining potential clients and it almost felt like bribery. He asked Bill about it, wondering if they should be taking clients down to sites currently under construction and showing them recent buildings, among other things, but Bill simply said, "Hey, this is sanctioned by the higher ups—I'm certainly not going to turn down the chance to do business like a king."

Finally it was George's last week shadowing Bill. As usual, they took a group of people looking to build a high-end condominium complex downtown to a five-star restaurant. As the evening began to wind down, one of the group members asked Bill, "Can you hook us up with the nightlife, if you know what I mean?" When Bill agreed, George knew that this just wasn't the job for him. The next day, he resigned.

1. Define the ethical issue presented in this case.

2. Do you think George should have quit his job?

3. What would you have done in George's position?

4. Do you think Bill's method of conducting business was ethically inappropriate? Why or why not.

CLOSING CASE

Samsung Changes Its Business Model Again and Again

In the 2000s, Samsung, based in Seoul, Korea, has risen to become the most profitable consumer electronics company in the world. Since 1999, its revenues have doubled, and it has become the second most profitable global technology company after Microsoft.[20] The story of how Samsung's business model has changed over time explains how the company has reached its enviable position.

In the 1980s, Samsung watched as Japanese companies like Sony and Matsushita (the maker of Panasonic and JVC products) turned out thousands of innovative new consumer electronics such as the Walkman, home video recorders, high-quality televisions, and compact disk players. Samsung's strategy was to see which of these products and which of their specific features, such

as a TV with a hard disk that can store movies, customers liked the best. Then Samsung's engineers would find ways to imitate this technology, just as Japanese companies had imitated U.S. electronics companies in the 1950s when they were the world's leading electronics makers. Samsung would make a low-cost copy of these products and sell them at lower prices than Japanese companies. While this strategy was profitable, however, Samsung was not in the league of Japanese companies like Sony, which could charge premium prices for their electronics and then continually plow their enormous profits back into research to make ever more advanced state-of-the-art electronics—and thus increase their profitability.

Samsung continued to pursue its low-cost strategy until the mid-1990s, when its chair, Lee Kun Hee, made a major decision. Sensing the emerging threat posed by China and other Asian countries whose cheap labor would rob Samsung of its low-cost advantage, Lee realized that Samsung needed to find a way to enter the big leagues and compete directly against the Japanese giants. The question was: How could Samsung do this, given that companies like Sony, Panasonic, and Hitachi were leaders in electronics research and development?

Lee began his new strategy by closing down thirty-two unprofitable product divisions and laying off 40% of Samsung's work force. Having lowered its cost structure, Samsung could now invest much more of its capital in product research. Lee decided to concentrate Samsung's research budget on new-product opportunities in areas like microprocessors, LCD screens, and other new kinds of digital components that he sensed would be in demand in the coming digital revolution. Today, Samsung is a major supplier of chips and LCD screens to all global electronics makers, and it can produce these components at a much lower cost than electronics makers can because it is farther down the experience curve.

The focus of Lee's new strategy, however, was on developing research and engineering skills that would allow the company to quickly capitalize on the technology being innovated by Sony, Matsushita, Phillips, and Nokia. His engineers would take this technology and rapidly develop and improve it to create new and improved products that were more advanced than those offered by Japanese competitors. Samsung would produce a wider variety of products than competitors but only in relatively small quantities. Then, as its new products were sold in stores, newer electronic models that were still more advanced would replace them. One advantage of speeding products to market is that inventory does not sit in Samsung's warehouses or stores, nor does Samsung need to stock large quantities of components because it needs only enough to make its budgeted output of a particular product. So by making speed the center of its differentiation strategy, Samsung was able to make more efficient use of its capital even as it introduced large numbers of new products to the market.

At the same time, Samsung's ability to innovate a large number of advanced products attracts customers and has allowed it to build its market share. Today, for example, while Nokia can claim to be a leading cell phone innovator, Samsung was the first to realize that customers wanted a color screen for their phone to allow them to play games and a built-in camera that would allow them to send photographs to their friends. Both these incremental advances have allowed Samsung to dramatically increase its share of the cell phone market. To compete with Samsung, Nokia has had to learn how to innovate new models of cell phones rapidly. Although in the 2000s Nokia has introduced new phones more quickly, Samsung has been able to do so even faster.[21]

By making speed of new-product development the center of its business model, Samsung also was able to move ahead of its other major competitors like Sony. Because of its focus on developing new technology and because of the slow speed of decision making typical in Japanese companies, Sony was hard hit by Samsung's success, and its profitability and stock price declined sharply in the 2000s. Today, Samsung is not just imitating Sony's leading-edge technology but is also developing its own, as shown by the fact that in 2004, Sony and Samsung announced a major agreement to share the costs of basic research into improving LCDs, which run into billions of dollars.

Today, Samsung is in the first tier of electronics makers and is regarded by many as one of the most innovative companies in the world. Almost a quarter of Samsung's 80,000 employees work in one of its four research divisions—semiconductors, telecommunications, digital media, and flat-screen panels. Because many of its products require components developed by all four divisions, it brings researchers, designers, engineers, and marketers from all its divisions together in teams at its research facility outside Seoul to spur the innovation that is the major source of its success. At the same time, it can still make many electronic components at a lower cost than its competitors, which has further contributed to its high profitability. Given the rapid technological advances in China, however, it appears that Chinese companies may soon be able to make some of their components at a lower cost than Samsung, thus doing to Samsung what Samsung did to companies like Sony. Samsung is relying on the speed of its research and engineering to fight off their challenge, but all global electronics makers are now in a race to speed their products to market.

Case Discussion Questions

1. How has Samsung's business model and strategies changed over time?

2. What is the basis of Samsung's current business model? In what ways is it trying to improve its competitive advantage? (Go to the Internet and update the case.)

Business-Level Strategy and the Industry Environment

Competition Gets Ugly in the Toy Business

The rapid pace at which the world is changing is forcing strategic managers at all kinds of companies to speed up their decision making, otherwise they get left behind by agile competitors who do respond faster to changing customer fads and fashions. Nowhere is this truer than in the global toy industry, where in the doll business, worth over $10 billion a year in sales, vicious combat is raging. The largest global toy company, Mattel, has earned tens of billions of dollars from the world's best-selling doll, Barbie, since it introduced her almost fifty years ago.[1] Mothers who played with the original dolls bought them for their daughters, and then granddaughters, and Barbie became an American icon. However, Barbie's advantage as best-selling global doll led Mattel's managers to make major strategic errors in the 2000s.

Barbie and all Barbie accessories accounted for almost 50% of Mattel's toy sales in the 1990s, so protecting its star product was crucial. The Barbie doll was created in the 1960s when most women were homemakers, and her voluptuous shape was a response to a dated view of what the "ideal" woman should look like. Barbie's continuing success, however, led Bob Eckert, Mattel's CEO, and his top managers to underestimate how much the world had altered. Changing cultural views about the role of girls, women, sex, marriage, and working women in the last decades shifted the tastes of doll buyers. But Mattel's managers continued to bet on Barbie's eternal appeal and collectively bought into an "If it's not broken, don't fix it" approach. In fact, given that Barbie was the best-selling doll, they thought it might be dangerous to make major changes to her appearance; customers might not like these product development changes and might stop buying her. Mattel's top managers decided not to rock the boat, they left the brand and business model unchanged and focused their efforts on developing new digital kinds of toys.

So Mattel was unprepared when a challenge came along in the form of a new kind of doll, the Bratz doll, introduced by MGA Entertainment. Many competitors of Barbie had emerged over the years—the doll business is highly profitable—but no other doll had matched Barbie's appeal to young girls (or their mothers). The marketers and designers behind the Bratz line of dolls had spent a lot of time discovering what the new generation of girls, especially those aged seven to eleven, wanted from a doll, however. And it turned out that the Bratz dolls they designed met the desires of these girls. Bratz dolls have larger heads and oversized eyes, wear lots of makeup and short dresses, and are multicultural to give each doll "personality and attitude."[2] The dolls were designed to appeal to a new generation of girls brought up in a fast-changing fashion, music, and television market/age. The Bratz dolls met the untapped needs of "tween" girls and the new line took off. MGA quickly licensed the rights to make and sell the doll to toy companies overseas, and Bratz quickly became a serious competitor of Barbie.

Now Mattel was in trouble. Its strategic managers had to change its business model and strategies and bring Barbie up to date. Mattel's designers must have been wishing they had been adventurous and made more radical changes earlier when they did not need to change. However, they decided to change Barbie's "extreme" vital statistics; they killed off her old-time boyfriend Ken and replaced him with Blaine, an Aussie surfer, and so on.[3] They also recognized they had waited much too long to introduce their own new lines of dolls to meet the changing needs of tween and other girls in the 2000s. So in 2002, they rushed out the My Scene line of dolls, which were obvious imitations of Bratz dolls. This new line has

not matched the popularity of Bratz dolls. Mattel also introduced a new line called Flava in 2003 to appeal to even younger girls, but this line flopped completely. At the same time, the decisions that they made to change Barbie and her figure, looks, clothing, and boyfriends came too late, and sales of Barbie dolls continued to fall.

By 2006, sales of the Barbie collection had dropped 30%, a serious matter because Mattel's profits and stock price hinge on Barbie's success, and so they both plunged. Analysts argue that Mattel had not paid enough attention to its customers' changing needs and to introducing the new and improved products necessary to keep a company on top of its market. Mattel brought back Ken in 2006. Then, in a sign of its mounting problems, in November 2006 Mattel's lawyers filed suit against MGA Entertainment arguing that the Bratz dolls' copyright rightfully belonged to them. Mattel complained that the head designer of Bratz was a Mattel employee when he made the initial drawings for the dolls and that they had applied for copyright protection on a number of early Bratz drawings. In addition, they claimed that MGA hired key Mattel employees away from the firm and that these employees stole sensitive sales information and transferred it to MGA. Clearly, competition in the doll business is getting ugly.

OVERVIEW

As Mattel's problems with its Barbie doll suggests, a company's business model cannot just be created and left to take care of itself. If strategic managers do create a successful business model, they still face another challenge: the need to continually formulate and implement business-level strategies to sustain their competitive advantage over time in different kinds of industry environments. Different industry environments present particular kinds of opportunities and threats for companies, and a company's business model and strategies have to adapt and change to meet the changing environment.

This chapter first examines how companies in fragmented industries can develop new kinds of business-level strategies to strengthen their business models. It then considers the challenges of developing and sustaining a competitive advantage in embryonic, growth, mature, and declining industries. By the end of this chapter, you will understand how forces in the changing industry environment require managers to pursue new kinds of business-level strategies to strengthen their company's business model and keep it at the value creation frontier.

Strategies in Fragmented Industries

A *fragmented industry* is one composed of a large number of small and medium-sized companies—for example, the dry cleaning, restaurant, health club, and legal services industries. There are several reasons that an industry may consist of many small companies rather than a few large ones.[4]

First, fragmented industries are characterized by low barriers to entry because of the lack of economies of scale. Many homebuyers, for example, prefer dealing with local real estate agents, whom they perceive as having better local knowledge than national chains. Second, in some industries, there may even be diseconomies of scale. In the restaurant business, for example, customers often prefer the unique food and style of a popular local restaurant rather than the standardized offerings of some national chain. Third, low entry barriers that permit constant entry by new companies also serve to keep an industry fragmented. The restaurant industry exemplifies this situation. The costs of opening a restaurant are moderate and can be borne by a single entrepreneur. High transportation costs, too, can keep an industry fragmented, and local or regional production may be the only efficient way to satisfy customers' needs, as in the cement business. Finally, an industry may be fragmented because customers' needs are so specialized that only small job lots of products are required, and thus there is no room for a large mass-production operation to satisfy the market.

For some fragmented industries, these factors dictate that the focus business model will be the most profitable to pursue. Companies may specialize by customer group, customer need, or geographic region, so that many small specialty companies operate in local or regional markets. All kinds of custom-made products—furniture, clothing, hats, boots, and so on—fall into this category, as do all small service operations that cater to particular customers' needs, such as laundries, restaurants, health clubs, and furniture rental stores. Indeed, service companies make up a large proportion of the enterprises in fragmented industries because they provide personalized service to clients and therefore need to be responsive to customers' needs.

However, strategic managers are eager to gain the cost advantages of pursuing cost leadership or the sales/revenue-enhancing advantages of differentiation by circumventing the competitive conditions that have allowed focus companies to dominate an industry. Essentially, companies have searched for new business-level strategies that will allow them to consolidate a fragmented industry in order to enjoy the much higher potential returns possible in a consolidated industry. These companies include large retailers such as Wal-Mart and Target; fast-food chains such as McDonald's and Burger King; movie rental chains such as Blockbuster and Hollywood Video; chains of health clubs such as Bally's, and President and First Lady; repair shops like Midas Muffler; and even lawyers, consultants, and tax preparers.

To grow, consolidate their industries, and become the industry leaders, these companies have developed strategies such as chaining, franchising, creating horizontal mergers, and also using the Internet and information technology (IT) in order to realize the advantages of a cost-leadership or differentiation business model. In doing so, these companies have pushed out the value creation frontier to the right, with the result that many focus companies have lost their competitive advantage and have disappeared.

Many of the new leaders pioneered a new business model in an industry that lowers costs or confers a differentiation advantage (or both). They do this by competing in a very different way from established rivals. Managers in a fragmented industry must seek out cost or differentiation advantages that others have not recognized.

● **Chaining** Companies such as Wal-Mart and Midas International pursue a **chaining** strategy to obtain the advantages of cost leadership. They establish networks of linked merchandising outlets that are so interconnected by advanced IT that they function as one large business entity. The consolidated buying power that these companies possess through their nationwide store chains allows them to negotiate large price reductions with their suppliers, which promotes their competitive advantage. They overcome the barrier of high transportation costs by establishing sophisticated regional distribution centers, which can economize on inventory costs and maximize responsiveness to the needs of stores and customers. They also realize economies of scale from sharing managerial skills across the chain and from using nationwide, rather than local, advertising.

The U.S. food retail business during the 1950s, when supermarkets revolutionized the business model behind the selling of food products, is a good example of the advantages of chaining. Prior to the development of supermarkets, the food retail industry was fragmented, with many small mom-and-pop retailers selling a limited range of products and providing full service to customers, including home delivery. The first supermarkets were usually regionally based, with fewer than 100 stores, and they differentiated themselves by offering a much larger selection of items in a big store layout. At the same time, they lowered their costs by moving from a full-service to a self-service strategy (they needed far fewer employees to run a store), and they passed on those cost savings to customers in the form of lower prices. In other words, the supermarkets competed in a very different way from established food retailers: they adopted a new business model.

As the supermarkets started to grow, opening hundreds of more stores, they were able to capture scale economies that were not available to smaller retailers. For example, by clustering their stores around central distribution warehouses in different cities and eventually regions, they were able to gain distribution efficiencies and reduce the amount of inventory they had to hold in a store. Also, by buying from vendors in large quantities, they were able to demand deep price discounts that they passed on to customers in the form of lower prices, enabling the supermarkets to gain even more market share from smaller retailers. In the 1970s and 1980s, the supermarkets were also the first to introduce information systems based on point-of-sale terminals that tracked the sale of individual items. The information provided by the point-of-sale terminals enabled the supermarkets to optimize their stocking of items, quickly cutting back on items that were not selling and devoting more shelf space to items that were selling faster. Reducing the need to hold inventory took even more costs out of the systems and ensured a good match between customer demands and items in the supermarket, which further differentiated the supermarkets from smaller retailers. Although these information systems were expensive to implement, the supermarkets could spread the costs over a large volume of sales. The small mom-and-pop retailers could not afford such systems because their sales base was too small. As a consequence of these developments, the food retail industry was becoming consolidated by the 1980s, a trend that is accelerating today. The small mom-and-pop food retailer is now almost extinct.

The new supermarket business model that provided cost and differentiation advantages over the old established mom-and-pop model has been applied to a wide range of retail industries, consolidating one after the other. Barnes & Noble and Borders applied the supermarket business model to book retailing; Staples applied it to office supplies; Best Buy, to electronics retailing; Home Depot, to building supplies; and so on. In each case, the companies that pursued a business model based on cost leadership or differentiation changed the competitive structure of the industry to its advantage, consolidating the industry and weakening the five forces of competition in the process.

● **Franchising**

Like chaining, franchising is a business-level strategy that allows companies, particularly service companies such as McDonald's or Century 21 Real Estate, to enjoy the competitive advantages that result from cost leadership or differentiation. In franchising, the franchiser (parent) grants to its franchisees the right to use the parent's name, reputation, and business model in a particular location or area in return for a sizable franchise fee and often a percentage of the profits.[5]

One particular advantage of this strategy is that, because franchisees essentially own their businesses, they are strongly motivated to make the companywide business model work effectively and make sure that quality and standards are consistently high so that customers' needs are always satisfied. Such motivation is particularly critical for a differentiator that must continually work to maintain its unique or distinctive appeal. In addition, franchising lessens the financial burden of swift expansion and so permits rapid growth of the company. Finally, a nationwide franchised company can reap the advantages of large-scale advertising, as well as economies in purchasing, management, and distribution, as McDonald's does very efficiently in pursuing its cost-leadership model.

● **Horizontal Merger**

Companies such as Anheuser-Busch, Dillard's, and Blockbuster chose a strategy of *horizontal merger* to consolidate their respective industries. For example, Dillard's arranged the merger of regional store chains in order to form a national company. By pursuing horizontal merger, companies are able to obtain economies of scale or secure a national market for their product. As a result, they are able to pursue a cost-leadership or a differentiation business model (although Dillard's has been struggling to pursue its differentiation model effectively). The many important strategic implications of horizontal mergers are discussed in detail in Chapter 9.

● **Using Information Technology and the Internet**

The arrival of new technology often gives a company the opportunity to develop new business strategies to consolidate a fragmented industry. Amazon.com and eBay, for example, used the Internet, and the associated strategies e-commerce makes possible, to pursue a cost-leadership model and consolidate the fragmented auction and bookselling industries. Before eBay, the auction business was extremely fragmented, with local auctions in cities being the principal way in which people could dispose of their antiques and collectibles. By harnessing the Internet, eBay can now assure sellers that they are getting wide visibility for their collectibles and are likely to receive a higher price for their product. Similarly, Amazon.com's success in the book market has accelerated the consolidation of the book retail industry, and many small bookstores have closed because they cannot compete by price or selection. Clear Channel Communications, profiled in Strategy in Action 6.1, used many of the strategies discussed above to become the biggest radio broadcaster in the United States.

The challenge in a fragmented industry is to figure out the best set of strategies to overcome a fragmented market so that the competitive advantages associated with pursuing one of the different business models can be realized. It is difficult to think of any major service activities—from consulting and accounting firms to businesses satisfying the smallest customer need, such as beauty parlors and car repair shops—that have not been consolidated by companies seeking to pursue a more profitable business model.

Strategy in Action   6.1

Clear Channel Creates a National Chain of Local Radio Stations

Clear Channel Communications started out with only one radio station in San Antonio in 1995, following a pattern that was then typical of the radio broadcasting industry. Historically, the industry was fragmented because a federal law prevented any company from owning more than forty stations nationwide; as a result, a large proportion of the local radio stations were independently owned and operated. Clear Channel took advantage of the repeal of this law in 1996 to start buying radio stations and, most importantly, to develop a business model (which today is one of *broad differentiation*) that would allow it to obtain the gains from consolidating this fragmented industry. By 2005, it operated over 1,200 U.S. radio stations.

Clear Channel's strategic managers recognized from the beginning that the major way to increase the profitability of city and small town radio stations was to obtain economies of scale from operating and marketing on a national level. The issue was to find ways to raise the quality of its programming to increase its value to listeners, increase the number of listeners, and thus increase advertising revenues (because advertising rates are based on the number of listeners). At the same time, it needed to find ways to reduce each station's high operating costs, that is, lower its cost structure. How to do both simultaneously was the challenge.

On the value side of the equation, an important issue was how to achieve economies of scale from having a national reach while maintaining local ties to the community. Many listeners like to feel they are listening to a local station that understands who they are and what their needs are. Yet if all programming and service are handled on a local level, how can economies of scale from a national base be achieved? Most cost savings come from standardizing service across stations, from broadcasting uniform content. In addition, local listeners often become used to the glitzy, slick productions put on by national cable television broadcasting companies such as MTV and the main television networks. Because they are national, these companies can afford to pay large sums to stars and celebrities and invest heavily in developing quality products. Such large expenditures are beyond most radio stations' budgets and simply increase the cost of goods sold too much. Moreover, advertising rates had to be kept at a level that both large national companies

and small local ones would find acceptable; they could not simply be raised to cover higher costs.

Clear Channel's managers began to experiment with information technology and the Internet and took advantage of emerging digital technology that allowed for the easy and rapid manipulation and transfer of large volumes of data. By the late 1990s, music and programming could easily be recorded, stored in digital format, and edited. Its managers hit on a strategy called voice tracking. To obtain economies of scale, Clear Channel employed popular regional or national DJs to record its daily programs, and these same DJs customized their productions to suit the needs of local markets. For example, one technology allows DJs to isolate and listen to the end of one track and the beginning of the next; then they can insert whatever talk, news, or information is appropriate between tracks as and when they like. The local stations supply this local information; after they have customized their program, the DJs send it over the Internet, where the local operators handle it. This practice has enormous advantages. On the cost side, the programming costs of a limited number of popular DJs are much lower than the cost of employing an army of local DJs. On the differentiation side, the quality of programming is much higher because Clear Channel can invest more in its programming and because the appeal of some DJs is much higher than others. Over time, higher-quality programming increases the number of listeners, and this attracts more national advertisers, whose digital advertisements can be easily inserted in the programming by local operators.

In addition, Clear Channel developed its own proprietary brand name, KISS, across its radio stations so that when people travel, they will be attracted to its local stations wherever they are. It hoped that the resulting increased customer demand would drive up advertising revenues, thereby lowering its cost structure and increasing its future profitability. Clear Channel received a major shock in the 2000s when the growing popularity of MP3 players like the iPod, web surfing, and online videos began to sharply reduce the size of its listening audience, hurting its advertising revenues. It has been forced to experiment with new ways of tailoring radio advertising to listeners, experimenting with short sound bites, and is also allying with Google to find ways to better tailor advertising to the particular needs of the local market. Once again, nothing stays the same for long in any competitive industry environment.[a]

Strategies in Embryonic and Growth Industries

As we discussed in Chapter 2, an embryonic industry is one that is just beginning to develop, and a growth industry is one in which first-time demand is expanding rapidly as many new customers enter the market. In choosing the strategies needed to pursue a business model, embryonic and growth industries pose special challenges because the *attributes of customers change* as market demand expands and *new groups of customers* who have different and evolving needs emerge. Also, other factors affect the rate at which a market grows and expands. Strategic managers have to be aware of the way competitive forces in embryonic and growth industries change over time because they commonly have to build and develop new kinds of competencies and refine their business models to compete effectively in the long term.

Most embryonic industries emerge when a technological innovation creates new product or market opportunities. For example, a century ago, the car industry was born following the development of a new technology, the internal combustion engine, which gave rise to many new products, including the motorcar and motorbus. In 1975, the PC industry was born after new microprocessor technology was developed to build the world's first commercially available PC, the Altair 8800, sold by MITS. Shortly afterward, the PC software industry was born when a Harvard dropout, Bill Gates, and his old school friend, Paul Allen, wrote a version of a popular computer language, BASIC, that would run on the Altair 8800.[6] In 1986, the Internet protocol (IP) network equipment industry was born following the development of the router, an IP switch, by an obscure California start-up, Cisco Systems.

Customer demand for the products of an embryonic industry is frequently limited at first, for a variety of reasons. Moreover, strategic managers who understand how markets develop are in a much better position to pursue a business model and strategies that will lead to a sustained competitive advantage. Reasons for slow growth in market demand include (1) the limited performance and poor quality of the first products, (2) customer unfamiliarity with what the new product can do for them, (3) poorly developed distribution channels to get the product to customers, (4) a lack of complementary products to increase the value of the product for customers, and (5) high production costs because of small volumes of production.

Customer demand for the first cars, for example, was limited by their poor performance (they were no faster than a horse, far noisier, and frequently broke down); a lack of important complementary products, such as a network of paved roads and gas stations; and high production costs, which made them a luxury item. Similarly, demand for the first PCs was limited because buyers had to be able to program a computer to use it, and there were no software application programs that could be purchased to run on the PCs. Because of such problems, early demand for the products of embryonic industries comes from a small set of technologically sophisticated customers who are willing to put up with, and may even enjoy, imperfections in the product. Computer hobbyists, who got great joy out of tinkering with their imperfect machines and finding ways to make them work, bought the first PCs.

An industry moves from an embryonic to a growth stage when a *mass market* starts to develop for the industry's product (a mass market is one in which large numbers of customers enter the market). Mass markets typically start to develop when three things occur: (1) ongoing technological progress makes a product easier to use and increases the value of the product to the average customer; (2) key complementary products are developed that do the same; and (3) companies in the industry strive to find ways to reduce production costs so they can lower their cost structure and choose a low price option, and this stimulates high demand.[7] For example, a mass market for cars emerged when (1) technological progress increased the performance of cars; (2) a network of paved roads and gas stations was established, which meant a car could go more places and thus had more value; and (3) Henry Ford began to mass-produce cars, which dramatically lowered production costs and allowed him to reduce prices, causing the demand for cars to surge. Similarly, the mass market for PCs started to emerge when technological advances made them easier to use, a supply of complementary software such as spreadsheets and word processing programs was developed that increased the value of owning a PC, and companies in the industry started to use mass production to build PCs at low cost.

Strategic managers who understand how the demand for a product is affected by changing customer needs and groups can focus their energies on developing new strategies to protect and strengthen their business models, such as building competencies in low-cost manufacturing or speedy product development. One strategy, for example, would be to share information about new products under development with the companies that supply complementary products so that customers will be convinced the new product is worth buying. Another strategy would be to involve customers in the product development process to gain their input and their acceptance of a new product.

● The Changing Nature of Market Demand

The development of most markets follows an S-shaped growth curve similar to that illustrated in Figure 6.1. As the stage of market development moves from embryonic to mature, customer demand first accelerates and then decelerates as a market approaches saturation. As we noted in Chapter 2, in a saturated market, most customers have already bought the product, and demand is limited to replacement demand; the market is mature. Figure 6.1 shows that different groups of customers who have different needs enter the market over time—and this has major implications for a company's product differentiation and market segmentation decisions.

The first group of customers to enter the market are referred to as the *innovators.* Innovators are technocrats who get great delight from being the first to purchase and experiment with products based on a new technology, even though that technology

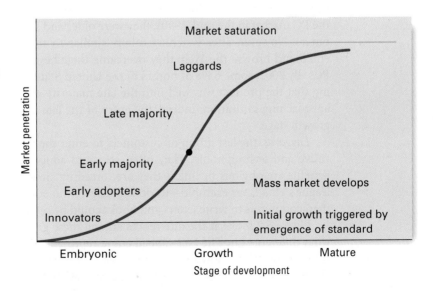

FIGURE 6.1

Market Development and Customer Groups

is imperfect and expensive. They often have an engineering mindset and want to own the technology for its own sake. In the PC industry, the first customers were software engineers and computer hobbyists who wanted to write computer code at home.[8]

The *early adopters* are the second group of customers to enter the market. Early adopters understand that the technology might have important future applications and are willing to experiment with it to see if they can pioneer uses for it, often by finding new ways to satisfy customer needs. Early adopters are often visionaries who appreciate how the technology may be used in the future and try to be the first to profit from its use. Jeff Bezos, the founder of Amazon.com, was an early adopter of the Internet and web-based technology, who saw in 1994 that the Internet could be used in innovative ways to sell books. He saw this possibility before anyone else and was one of the first dot-com pioneers to purchase web servers and related software and use them to sell products over the Internet. Amazon.com was thus an early adopter.

Both innovators and early adopters enter the market while the industry is in its embryonic stage. The next group of customers, the *early majority*, represents the leading wave or edge of the mass market; their entry signifies the beginning of the growth stage. Customers in the early majority are comfortable with the new technology and products. However, they are pragmatists: they weigh the benefits of adopting new products against their costs and wait to enter the market until they are confident that products will offer them tangible benefits. Once they start to enter the market, however, they do so in large numbers. This is what happened in the PC market after IBM's introduction of the PC in 1981. For the early majority, IBM's entry into the market legitimized the technology and signaled that the benefits of adoption would be worth the costs of purchasing and learning to use the product. The growth of the PC market was then given further impetus by the development of important applications that added value to it, such as new spreadsheet and word processing programs. These applications transformed the PC from a hobbyist's toy into a business productivity tool.

Once the mass market attains a critical mass, with something like 30% of the potential market penetrated, the next wave of customers enters the market. This wave is characterized as the *late majority*: the customers who purchase a new technology or product only when it is clear it will be around for a long time. Examples of the members of a typical late majority customer group are the customers who started to enter the PC market in the mid-1990s; they were older and somewhat intimidated by computers. However, after watching others similar to themselves buying PCs to send email and browse the Web, they overcame their hesitancy and started to purchase PCs. By 2002, some 65% of homes in the United States had at least one PC, suggesting that the product was well into the late majority group and that the market was approaching saturation. Indeed, the entry of the late majority signals the end of the growth stage.

Laggards, the last group of customers to enter the market, are inherently conservative and technophobic. They often refuse to adopt a new technology even if its benefits are obvious or unless they are forced by circumstances—to reply to a colleague's email, for example—to do so. People who stick to using typewriters rather than computers to write letters and books could be considered laggards today.

Figure 6.2 looks at the differences among these groups of consumers in a somewhat different way. The bell-shaped curve represents the total market, and the divisions in the curve show the percentage of customers who, on average, fall into each customer group. The early adopters are a very small percentage of the total customers

FIGURE 6.2

Market Share of
Different Customer
Segments

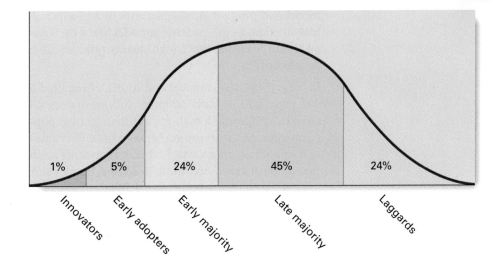

who will ultimately buy the product. Thus, the figure illustrates a vital competitive fact: *Most market demand and industry profits arise when members of the early and late majority enter the market.* And research has found that, although many of the early pioneering companies do well in attracting innovators and early adopters, many of these companies often *fail* to attract a significant share of early and late majority customers and ultimately go out of business.

● **Strategic**
Implications:
Crossing
the Chasm

Why are pioneering companies often unable to create a business model that allows them to be successful over time and remain the market leaders? *Innovators and early adopters have very different customer needs from the early majority.* In an influential book, Geoffrey Moore argues that because of the differences in customer needs between these groups, the business-level strategies required for companies to succeed in the emerging mass market are quite different from those required to succeed in the embryonic market.[9] Pioneering companies that do not change the strategies they use to pursue their business model will therefore lose their competitive advantage to those companies that implement new strategies that push the value creation frontier out to the right. Different strategies are often required to support and strengthen a company's business model as a market develops over time, for the following reasons:

● Innovators and early adopters are technologically sophisticated individuals who are willing to tolerate engineering imperfections in the product. The early majority, however, values ease of use and reliability. Companies competing in an embryonic market typically pay more attention to increasing the performance of a product than to its ease of use and reliability. Those competing in a mass market need to make sure that the product is reliable and easy to use. Thus, the product development strategies required for success are different as a market develops over time.

● Innovators and early adopters are typically reached through specialized distribution channels, and products are often sold by word of mouth. Reaching the early majority requires mass-market distribution channels and mass-media advertising campaigns that require a different set of marketing and sales strategies.

● Because innovators and the early majority are relatively few in number and are not particularly price sensitive, companies serving them typically pursue a focus model and produce small quantities of a product. To serve the rapidly growing mass market, a cost-leadership model based on large-scale mass production may be critical to ensure that a high-quality product can be produced reliably at a low price point.

In sum, the business model and strategies required to compete in an embryonic market populated by early adopters and innovators are very different from those required to compete in a high-growth mass market populated by the early majority. As a consequence, the transition between the embryonic market and the mass market is not a smooth, seamless one. Rather, it represents a *competitive chasm,* or gulf, that companies must cross. According to Moore, many companies do not or cannot develop the right business model; they fall into the chasm and go out of business. This insight is consistent with the observation that, although embryonic markets are frequently populated by large numbers of small companies, once the mass market begins to develop, the number of companies in the marketplace drops off sharply.[10]

Figure 6.3, which compares the strategies of AOL Time Warner and Prodigy, illustrates Moore's thesis by showing that a wide chasm exists between innovators and the early majority, that is, between the embryonic market and the rapidly growing mass market. Note also that other smaller chasms exist between other sets of customers, and that these too represent important, although less dramatic, breaks in the nature of the market that require changes in business-level strategy (for example, a different approach to market segmentation). The implication of Moore's thesis is that a company must often formulate and implement new strategies, and build new competencies, if it is to create a business model that can successfully cross the chasm. Strategy in Action 6.2 describes how the early leader in online services, Prodigy, fell into the chasm, while AOL successfully built a business model to cross it.

To cross this chasm successfully, managers must correctly identify the customer needs of the first wave of early majority users—the leading edge of the mass market. Once companies have identified these customers' needs, they must alter their business model by developing new strategies to redesign products and create distribution channels and marketing campaigns to reach the early majority. In this way, they will have ready a suitable product, at a reasonable price, that they can sell to the members of the early majority as they start to enter the market in large numbers. In sum, industry pioneers must abandon their old focused business model that was directed solely toward the needs of their early or initial customers because this focus may lead

FIGURE 6.3

The Chasm Between Innovators and the Early Majority: AOL and Prodigy

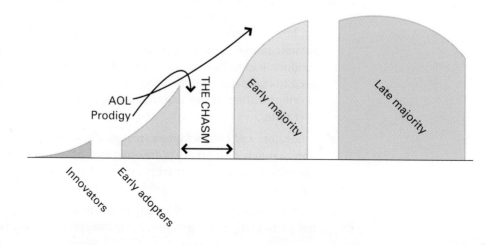

milk, the investment as much as it can. For example, a company reduces to a minimum the assets it employs in the business and forgoes investment to reduce its cost structure.[15] Then the company harvests all the sales revenues it can profitably obtain before it liquidates all its assets and exits the industry. Companies that have lost their cost-leadership position to more efficient companies are more likely to pursue a harvest strategy because a smaller market share means higher costs and they are unable to move to a focus strategy. Differentiators, in contrast, have a competitive advantage in this stage if they can move to a focus model.

● **Maturity Strategies**   By the maturity stage, companies want to reap the rewards of their previous investments in developing the business models that have made them dominant industry competitors. Until now, profits have been reinvested in the business, and dividends have been small. Investors in leading companies have obtained their rewards through the appreciation of the value of their stock because the company has reinvested most of its capital to maintain and increase market share. As market growth slows in the maturity stage, a company's investment strategy depends on the level of competition in the industry and the source of the company's competitive advantage.

In environments in which competition is high because of technological change or low barriers to entry, companies need to defend their competitive position. Strategic managers need to continue to invest heavily in maintaining the company's competitive advantage. Both cost leaders and differentiators adopt a **hold-and-maintain strategy** to defend their business models and to ward off threats from focused companies who might be appearing. They expend resources to develop their distinctive competency and thus remain the market leaders. For example, differentiated companies may invest in improved after-sales service, and low-cost companies may invest in the latest production technologies.

At this point, too many companies realize the benefits that can be obtained by investing resources to become broad differentiators to protect themselves from aggressive competitors (both at home and abroad) that are watching for any opportunity or perceived weakness to take the lead in the industry. Differentiators enter new market segments to increase their market share; they also take advantage of their growing profits to develop flexible manufacturing systems to reduce their production costs. Cost leaders also begin to enter more market segments and increase product differentiation to expand their market share. For example, Gallo moved from the bulk wine segment and began marketing premium wines and wine coolers to take advantage of its low production costs. Soon Gallo's new premium brands, like Falling Leaf chardonnay, became the best-selling wines in the United States. As time goes on, the competitive positions of the leading differentiators and cost leaders become closer, and the pattern of industry competition changes yet again, as we discuss in the next section.

Strategy in Mature Industries

As a result of fierce competition in the shakeout stage, an industry becomes consolidated, and so a mature industry is commonly dominated by a small number of large companies. Although it may also contain many medium-sized companies and a host of small, specialized ones, the large companies determine the nature of competition in the industry because they can influence the five competitive forces. Indeed, these large companies owe their leading positions to the fact that they have developed the most successful business models and strategies in the industry.

By the end of the shakeout stage, companies have learned how important it is to analyze each other's business model and strategies. They also know that if they change their strategies, their actions are likely to stimulate a competitive response from industry rivals. For example, a differentiator that starts to lower its prices because it has adopted a more cost-efficient technology not only threatens other differentiators but may also threaten cost leaders that see their competitive advantage being eroded. Hence, by the mature stage of the life cycle, companies have learned the meaning of competitive independence.

As a result, in mature industries, business-level strategy revolves around understanding how established companies *collectively* try to reduce the strength of industry competition to preserve both company and industry profitability. Interdependent companies can help protect their competitive advantage and profitability by adopting strategies and tactics, first, to deter entry into an industry and, second, to reduce the level of rivalry within an industry.

● Strategies to Deter Entry: Product Proliferation, Price Cutting, and Maintaining Excess Capacity

Companies can use three main methods to deter entry by potential rivals and hence maintain and increase industry profitability: product proliferation, price cutting, and maintaining excess capacity (see Figure 6.5). Of course, *potential entrants* will try to circumvent such entry-deterring strategies by incumbent companies. Competition is rarely a one-way street.

PRODUCT PROLIFERATION As we noted above, in the maturity stage, most companies move to increase their market share by producing a wide range of products targeted at different market segments. Sometimes, however, to reduce the threat of entry, existing companies ensure that they are offering a product targeted at every segment in the market. This creates a barrier to entry because potential competitors find it hard to break into an industry and establish themselves when there is no obvious group of customers whose needs are not being met by existing companies.[16] This strategy of "filling the niches," or catering to the needs of customers in all market segments to deter entry, is known as **product proliferation**.

Because the large U.S. carmakers were so slow to fill the small-car niches (they did *not* pursue a product proliferation strategy), they were vulnerable to the entry of the Japanese into these market segments in the United States in the 1980s. Ford and GM really had no excuse for this situation because, in their European operations, they had a long history of small-car manufacturing. Managers should have seen the opening and filled it ten years earlier, but the (mistaken) view was that "small cars mean small profits." Better small profits than no profits! In the soap and detergent industry,

FIGURE 6.5

Strategies for Deterring Entry of Rivals

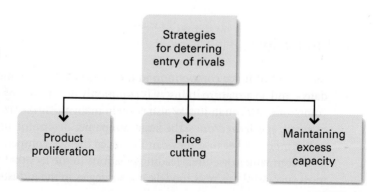

FIGURE 6.6

Product Proliferation
in the Restaurant
Industry

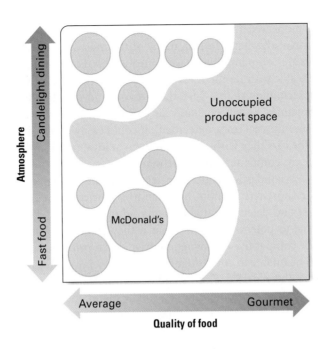

on the other hand, competition is based on the production of new kinds of soaps and detergents to satisfy or create new desires by customers. Thus, the number of soaps and detergents, and especially the way they are packaged (powder, liquid, or tablets), proliferates, making it very difficult for prospective entrants to attack a new market segment.

Figure 6.6 indicates how product proliferation can deter entry. It depicts product space in the restaurant industry along two dimensions: atmosphere, which ranges from fast food to candlelight dining, and quality of food, which ranges from average to gourmet. The circles represent product spaces filled by restaurants located along the two dimensions. Thus, McDonald's is situated in the average-quality/fast-food area. A gap in the product space gives a potential entrant or an existing rival an opportunity to enter the market and make inroads. The shaded, unoccupied product space represents areas where new restaurants can enter the market. When all the product spaces are filled, this barrier to entry makes it much more difficult for a new company to gain a foothold in the market and differentiate itself.

PRICE CUTTING In some situations, pricing strategies can be used to deter entry by other companies, thus protecting the profit margins of companies already in an industry. One entry-deterring strategy is to cut prices every time a new company enters the industry or, even better, every time a potential entrant is *contemplating* entry, and then raise prices once the new or potential entrant has withdrawn. The goal here is to send a signal to potential entrants that new entry will be met with price cuts. If incumbent companies in an industry consistently pursue such a strategy, potential entrants will come to understand that their entry will spark off a price war, the threat of new entry will be reduced, average prices will be higher, and industry profitability will increase.

However, a price-cutting strategy will not keep out an entrant that plans to adopt a new technology that will give it a cost advantage over established companies or that has pioneered a new business model that its managers expect will also give it a competitive advantage. In fact, many of the most successful entrants into mature industries are companies that have done just this. For example, the Japanese car companies were able to enter the U.S. market because they had pioneered new lean manufacturing technologies that gave them a cost and quality advantage over established U.S. companies. Today, Japanese car companies' share of the U.S. market is limited only by an informal trade agreement; it could easily double if they were allowed to import all the cars they wished and sell them at lower prices, which might drive one or more U.S. car companies out of the market.

A second price-cutting strategy is to charge a high price initially for a product and seize short-term profits, but then to cut prices aggressively in order to build market share and deter potential entrants simultaneously.[17] The incumbent companies thus signal to potential entrants that if they enter the industry, the incumbents will use their competitive advantage to drive down prices to a level at which new companies will be unable to cover their costs. This pricing strategy also allows a company to ride down the experience curve and obtain substantial economies of scale. Since costs fall with prices, profit margins can still be maintained.

Still, this strategy is unlikely to deter a strong potential competitor—an established company that is trying to find profitable investment opportunities in other industries. It is difficult, for example, to imagine 3M's being afraid to enter an industry because companies there threaten to drive down prices. A company such as 3M has the resources to withstand any short-term losses. Dell also had few worries about entering the highly competitive electronics industry and starting to sell televisions, digital cameras, and so on, because of its powerful set of distinctive competencies. Hence, when faced with such a scenario, it may be in the interests of incumbent companies to accept new entry gracefully, giving up market share gradually to the new entrants to prevent price wars from developing and thus saving their profits, if this is feasible. As Strategy in Action 6.3 details, Toys "R" Us has been forced to give up market share in the toy market, and it has lost much of its prominence as a result.

MAINTAINING EXCESS CAPACITY A third competitive technique that allows companies to deter entry involves maintaining excess capacity, that is, maintaining the physical capability to produce more of a product than customers currently demand. Existing industry companies may deliberately develop some limited amount of excess capacity to warn potential entrants that if they enter the industry, existing firms can retaliate by increasing output and forcing down prices until entry would become unprofitable. However, the threat to increase output has to be *credible*; that is, companies in an industry must collectively be able to raise the level of production quickly if entry appears likely.

● Strategies to Manage Rivalry

Beyond seeking to deter entry, companies also wish to develop strategies to manage their competitive interdependence and decrease price rivalry. Unrestricted competition over prices reduces both company and industry profitability. Several strategies are available to companies to manage industry rivalry. The most important are price signaling, price leadership, nonprice competition, and capacity control (Figure 6.7).

PRICE SIGNALING A company's ability to choose the price option that leads to superior performance is a function of several factors, including the strength of demand for a product and the intensity of competition among rivals. Price signaling is the first means by which companies attempt to control rivalry among competitors to allow the *industry* to choose the most favorable pricing option.[18] **Price signaling** is

Strategy in Action 6.3

New Competitors for Toys "R" Us

Toys "R" Us, based in Paramus, New Jersey, grew at an astonishing 25% annual rate to become the market leader in the retail toy market in 1990, with a 20% share. To reach its dominant position, the company consolidated the fragmented toy market by developing a nationwide chain of retail outlets so that it could pursue a cost-leadership strategy. To lower its cost structure, Toys "R" Us developed efficient materials-management techniques for ordering and distributing toys to its stores, and it provided a low level of customer service compared to traditional small toy shops. This business model allowed it to achieve a low expense-to-sales ratio of 17%, and it then used this favorable cost structure to promote a philosophy of everyday low pricing. The company deliberately set out to undercut the prices of its rivals, and it succeeded: two of its largest competitors, Child World and Lionel, went bankrupt.

With its dominant position in the industry established, Toys "R" Us continued to build its chain of toy stores, and it began stocking an ever larger and more complex array of products. This would raise its costs; nevertheless, its managers reasoned that they could afford to do so because they were in the driver's seat, and customers would find more value in a wider toy selection. Moreover, raising prices of the toys could offset any cost increases, or perhaps the company could negotiate higher price discounts from toymakers like Mattel or Parker Bros.

The company received a shock in 1995 when its commanding position was threatened by the entry of a new set of rivals. Recognizing the high profits that Toys "R" Us was earning, rapidly expanding companies such as Wal-Mart, Kmart, and Target began to make toy selling a major part of their business model. What could Toys "R" Us do to stop them? Not much. Because of its failure to control costs, Toys "R" Us could not stop their entry into its business by reducing its prices; in other words, by failing to pursue its cost-leadership strategy faithfully, it had lost its ability to play pricing games as it had done with its earlier rivals. The entry of these other companies also reduced its power over its suppliers, the toymakers, because they now had important new customers. Finally, some of the new entrants, Wal-Mart in particular, were now the cost leaders in the retail industry, and their size gave them the resources to withstand any problems if Toys "R" Us attempted to start a price war. In fact, Wal-Mart simply imitated the earlier approach of Toys "R" Us and began selling toys at prices that were below those of Toys "R" Us! By 2000, Wal-Mart became the leading price-setter in the toy market.

To survive, Toys "R" Us has tried to lower its cost structure in its core toy business. It installed new IT to increase the efficiency of its purchasing and distribution operations. It reduced the number of items its stores carry by over 30% to slash its cost structure. At the same time, recognizing that it will never be able to match Wal-Mart's low costs, it changed its business model to try to create customer value by developing other kinds of stores for related market segments, such as Kids "R" Us and Babies "R" Us. It also went online and attempted to develop a major Web presence. However, faced with the high costs of online selling today, it partnered with Amazon.com; toys bought in its shop on Amazon's website can be picked up at any Toys "R" Us store.

By 2004, it was clear that these moves had not halted the decline in the company's market share and profitability. In fact, in 2004, it made the surprise announcement that it was thinking of getting out of the toy business and would henceforth focus on its specialty Kids "R" Us and Babies "R" Us stores, which were making money. However, in November 2004, it still had not found a buyer for its toy stores, and in 2005, it finally announced that it was selling the entire company to a group of investors led by the KKR venture capitalist group; their goal is to reorganize the now private company to rebuild the profitability of its business model.[c]

the process by which companies increase or decrease product prices to convey their intentions to other companies and so influence the way they price their products.[19] Companies use price signaling to improve industry profitability.

Companies may use price signaling to announce that they will respond vigorously to hostile competitive moves that threaten them. For example, they may signal that if one company starts to cut prices aggressively, they will respond in kind. A

FIGURE 6.7

Strategies for
Managing Industry
Rivalry

tit-for-tat strategy** is a well-known price signaling strategy in which a company does exactly what its rivals do: if its rivals cut prices, the company follows; if its rivals raise prices, the company follows. By pursuing this strategy consistently over time, a company sends a clear signal to its rivals that it will match any pricing moves they make, the idea being that, sooner or later, rivals will learn that the company will always pursue a tit-for-tat strategy. Because rivals now know that the company will match any price reductions and that cutting prices will only reduce profits, price cutting becomes less common in the industry. A tit-for-tat strategy also signals to rivals that price increases will be imitated, increasing the probability that rivals will initiate price increases to raise profits. Thus, a tit-for-tat strategy can be a useful way of shaping pricing behavior in an industry.[20]

The airline industry is a good example of the power of price signaling, when prices typically rise and fall depending on the current state of customer demand. If one carrier signals the intention to lower prices, a price war frequently ensues as other carriers copy each other's signals. If one carrier feels demand is strong, it tests the waters by signaling an intention to increase prices, and price signaling becomes a strategy to obtain uniform price increases. Nonrefundable tickets, another strategy adopted to obtain a more favorable pricing option, originated as a market signal by one company that was quickly copied by all other companies in the industry. Carriers recognized that they could stabilize their revenues and earn interest on customers' money if they collectively acted to force customers to assume the risk of buying airline tickets in advance. In essence, price signaling allows companies to give one another information that enables them to understand each other's competitive product or market strategy and make coordinated, price-competitive moves.

PRICE LEADERSHIP **Price leadership**—in which one company assumes the responsibility for choosing the most favorable industry pricing option—is a second tactic used to reduce price rivalry and thus enhance the profitability of companies in a mature industry.[21] Formal price leadership, or price setting by companies jointly, is illegal under antitrust laws, so the process of price leadership is often very subtle. In the car industry, for example, prices are set by imitation. The price set by the weakest company—that is, the one with the highest cost structure—is often used as the basis for competitors' pricing. Thus, U.S. carmakers set their prices, and Japanese carmakers then set theirs with reference to the U.S. prices. The Japanese are happy to do this because they have lower costs than U.S. companies, so they make higher profits than U.S. carmakers without competing with them on price. Pricing is done by market segment. The prices of different auto models in the model range indicate the customer segments that the companies are aiming for and the price range they believe the market segment can tolerate. Each manufacturer prices a model in the segment with reference to the prices charged by its competitors, not by reference to competitors' costs. Price leadership also allows differentiators to charge a premium price.

Although price leadership can stabilize industry relationships by preventing head-to-head competition and thus raise the level of profitability within an industry, it has its dangers. It helps companies with high cost structures, allowing them to survive without having to implement strategies to become more productive and efficient. In the long term, such behavior makes them vulnerable to new entrants that have lower costs because they have developed new low-cost production techniques. That is what happened in the U.S. car industry after the Japanese entered the market. After years of tacit price fixing, with GM as the price leader, the carmakers were subjected to growing low-cost Japanese competition, to which they were unable to respond. Indeed, most U.S. carmakers survived only because the Japanese carmakers were foreign firms. Had the foreign firms been new U.S. entrants, the government would probably not have taken steps to protect Chrysler, Ford, or GM.

NONPRICE COMPETITION   A third very important aspect of product and market strategy in mature industries is the use of **nonprice competition** to manage rivalry within an industry. The use of strategies to try to prevent costly price cutting and price wars does not preclude competition by product differentiation. Indeed, in many industries, product differentiation strategies are the principal tool companies use to deter potential entrants and manage rivalry within their industry.

Product differentiation allows industry rivals to compete for market share by offering products with different or superior features, such as the features of the Bratz dolls, or by applying different marketing techniques. In Figure 6.8, product and market segment dimensions are used to identify four nonprice competitive strategies based on product differentiation: market penetration, product development, market development, and product proliferation. (Notice that this model applies to new market segments, not new markets.)[22]

Market penetration.   When a company concentrates on expanding market share in its existing product markets, it is engaging in a strategy of market penetration.[23] **Market penetration** involves heavy advertising to promote and build product differentiation, which Mattel has actively pursued through its aggressive marketing campaign for Barbie, for example. In a mature industry, advertising aims to influence customers' brand choice and create a brand-name reputation for the company and its products. In this way, a company can increase its market share by attracting the

FIGURE 6.8

Four Nonprice
Competitive
Strategies

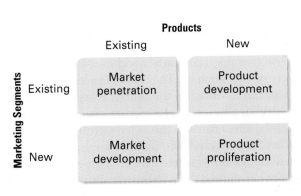

customers of its rivals. Because brand-name products often command premium prices, building market share in this situation is very profitable, which is why Mattel is trying to meet the challenge from MG Entertainment's Bratz doll.

In some mature industries—for example, soap and detergent, disposable diapers, and beer brewing—a market-penetration strategy becomes a way of life.[24] In these industries, all companies engage in intensive advertising and battle for market share. Each company fears that if it does not advertise, it will lose market share to rivals who do. Consequently, in the soap and detergent industry, Procter & Gamble spends more than 20% of sales revenues on advertising, with the aim of maintaining and perhaps building market share. These huge advertising outlays constitute a barrier to entry for prospective entrants.

Product development. **Product development** is the creation of new or improved products to replace existing ones.[25] The wet-shaving industry depends on product replacement to create successive waves of customer demand, which then create new sources of revenue for companies in the industry. Gillette, for example, periodically comes out with a new and improved razor, such as its new vibrating razor that competes with Schick's four-bladed razor, to try to boost its market share. In the car industry, each major car company replaces its models every three to five years to encourage customers to trade in their old models and buy the new one.

Product development is crucial for maintaining product differentiation and building market share. For instance, the laundry detergent Tide has gone through more than fifty changes in formulation during the past forty years to improve its performance. The product is always advertised as Tide, but it is a different product each year. Refining and improving products is a crucial strategy that companies use to fine-tune and improve their business models in a mature industry, but this kind of competition can be as vicious as a price war because it is very expensive and can dramatically increase a company's cost structure. One of Mattel's central strategies is product development, and in the 2000s, its cost structure soared as it spent tens of millions of dollars to develop successful new kinds of dolls and toys to compete in a changing environment.

Market development. **Market development** finds new market segments for a company's products. A company pursuing this strategy wants to capitalize on the brand name it has developed in one market segment by locating new market segments in which to compete—just as Mattel and Nike do by entering many different segments of the toy and shoe markets, respectively. In this way, companies can leverage the product differentiation advantages of their brand name. The Japanese auto manufacturers provide an interesting example of the use of market development. When they entered the market, each Japanese manufacturer offered a car model aimed at the economy segment of the auto market, such as the Toyota Corolla and the Honda Accord. Then they upgraded each model over time, and now each is directed at a more expensive market segment. The Accord is a leading contender in the midsize car segment, and the Corolla fills the small-car segment that used to be occupied by the Celica, which is now aimed at a sportier market segment. By redefining their product offerings, Japanese manufacturers have profitably developed their market segments and successfully attacked their industry rivals, wresting market share from these companies. Although the Japanese used to compete primarily as cost leaders, market development has allowed them to become differentiators as well. In fact, as we noted in

FIGURE 6.9

Toyota's Product
Lineup

Price	Sports Utility Vehicles	Passenger/ Sports Sedans	Passenger Vans	Personal Luxury Vehicles	Sporty Cars	Pickup Trucks
$11–20K	RAV4, Scion xB	Echo, Matrix, Corolla, Prism, Scion xA			Celica GT	Tacoma
$21–30K	4-Runner, Highlander	Camry, Avalon	Sienna	Avalon	MR2, Spyder	Tundra
$31–45K	Sequoia, RX330	GS 300, IS 300		ES 330	Camry, Solara	Tundra Double Cab
$46–75K	Land Cruiser, GX, LX	GS 430		LS 430	SC 430	

the last chapter, Toyota has used market development to become a broad differentiator. Figure 6.9 illustrates how, over time, Toyota has used market development to develop a vehicle for almost every main segment of the car market.

Product proliferation. **Product proliferation** can be used to manage rivalry within an industry and to deter entry. The strategy of product proliferation generally means that large companies in an industry all have a product in each market segment or niche and compete head-to-head for customers. If a new niche develops, such as sports utility vehicles, designer sunglasses, or Internet websites, then the leader gets a first-mover advantage, but soon all the other companies catch up. Once again, competition is stabilized, and rivalry within the industry is reduced. Product proliferation thus allows the development of stable industry competition based on product differentiation, not price—that is, nonprice competition based on the development of new products. The competitive battle is over a product's perceived uniqueness, quality, features, and performance and not over its price, something that is becoming increasingly important in the PC business, as the Running Case discusses.

CAPACITY CONTROL Although nonprice competition helps mature industries avoid the cutthroat price cutting that reduces company and industry levels of profitability, price competition does periodically break out when excess capacity exists in an industry. Excess capacity arises when companies collectively produce too much output and, to dispose of it, they cut prices. When one company cuts prices, the others quickly follow (a game theory prediction: see the discussion in a later section of this chapter) because they fear that the price cutter will be able to sell its entire inventory while they will be left with unwanted goods. The result is that a price war develops.

Excess capacity may be caused by a shortfall in demand, as when a recession lowers the demand for cars and causes car companies to give customers price incentives to purchase a new car. In this situation, companies can do nothing except wait for better times. By and large, however, excess capacity results from companies within an industry simultaneously responding to favorable conditions: they all invest in new plants to be able to take advantage of the predicted upsurge in demand. Paradoxically, each individual company's effort to outperform the others means that, collectively, the companies create industry overcapacity, which hurts them all.

RUNNING CASE

Dell Has to Rethink Its Business-Level Strategies

As we have discussed in our story of Dell so far, the company achieved its position as the cost leader on the value creation frontier because of its ability to manage its supply chain and thus make and sell a PC at a lower price than its competitors. In the 1990s, its low-cost advantage resulted in many of its competitors, such as IBM, being driven from the market, and others, like HP and Gateway, struggled to reduce their cost structures to remain profitable. By the early 2000s, however, things had changed. Dell found that its main rival HP had learned how to manage its supply chain and could now build a PC at a price competitive with Dell's, one important reason being that it used powerful low-cost chips made by AMD. Dell also found that Apple computer's new sleek designs were attracting more and more customers, especially because in 2006, Apple began to use Intel's chips, which made its machines Windows-compatible. Dell was now feeling the heat on all sides. Analysts started to criticize the pedestrian look of its computers, which were almost always plain black boxes, and make unfavorable comparisons with HP's and Apple's redesigned computers.

So, starting in 2006, Dell decided to improve the look and design of its PCs and invest resources to make them more differentiated—even though this would increase costs. It hired 500 new design engineers to beef up its internal team of industrial designers, recruiting specialists from carmakers and consumer products companies to make them more attractive and functional. And it also bought the PC focus differentiator Alienware Corp., which made high-powered/high-priced gaming PCs whose sleek futuristic machines, modeled after the beast from the movie Alien, were regarded by many as the best looking PCs on the market. One result was that in 2006, Dell introduced the $3,500 XPS M2010, a cross between a desktop and laptop targeted at entertainment enthusiasts, which features a detachable wireless keyboard and a monitor with adjustable height. And with its black, leatherlike exterior, it resembles a luxury briefcase when closed. Dell then began to introduce innovative lower-priced models such as the new $1,990 XPS 700 desktop,

also aimed at hard-core video gamers. Its new designs allowed Dell to charge a premium price for its top-of-the-line machines, which represent only about 1% of Dell's total 2005 sales of $55.9 billion.

Dell's eventual goal, however, is for all these design innovations to trickle down into its principle lines of PCs so that it can charge higher prices for them and so increase its overall profit margins. By focusing more on product development and differentiation, Dell hopes not only to increase its profits, but also to fight back the challenge from HP and Apple so that it will occupy the middle of the value creation frontier and thus strengthen its competitive advantage. With its mass-market PCs, Dell's goal is also to make them easier and more comfortable to use; for example, Dell set out to make the controls for laptop touchpads, PC keyboards, and LCD monitors more functional and easier to use. Another battle Dell has had to fight to stay on the value creation frontier is to increase the level of its customer service after it outsourced most of this function to companies in India. Long the leader in customer service, Dell lost its lead to HP and Gateway in 2005 as customer complaints about poor quality service increased. Even though its goal is to squeeze out every cent of costs, in 2006, Dell pumped back over $250 million into improved customer service and brought the corporate customer service department back to the United States to protect its dominating position in the important business server and PC market segment.

Only time will tell if Dell's new business-level strategies will work. Its stock price plummeted in 2006 as its profit margins shrank and those of HP and Apple increased. But by the fall, there were increasing signs that its new lines of PCs were attracting customers back. It also began to use AMD's chips, breaking its long alliance with Intel, to keep the cost of its new machines low and competitive. Product and market development, as well as product proliferation, is a never-ending process, especially when technology changes quickly, as it does in the computer industry.

Although demand is rising, the consequence of each company's decision to increase capacity is a surge in industry capacity, which drives down prices. To prevent the accumulation of costly excess capacity, companies must devise strategies that let them control—or at least benefit from—capacity expansion programs. Before we examine these strategies, however, we need to consider in greater detail the factors that cause excess capacity.[26]

Factors causing excess capacity. The problem of excess capacity often derives from technological developments. Sometimes new low-cost technology is the culprit because all companies invest in it simultaneously to prevent being left behind. Excess capacity occurs because the new technology can produce more than the old. In addition, new technology is often introduced in large increments, which generates overcapacity. For instance, an airline that needs more seats on a route must add another plane, thereby adding hundreds of seats even if only fifty are needed. To take another example, a new chemical process may operate efficiently only at the rate of 1,000 gallons a day, whereas the previous process was efficient at 500 gallons a day. If all companies within an industry change technologies, industry capacity may double, and enormous problems can result.

Overcapacity may also be caused by competitive factors within an industry. Entry into an industry is one such factor. The entry of South Korean companies into the global semiconductor industry in the 1990s caused massive overcapacity and price declines. Similarly, the entry of steel producers from the former Soviet Union countries into the global steel market produced excess capacity and plunging prices in the world steel market in the late 1990s and early 2000s. Sometimes the age of a company's plant is the source of the problem. For example, in the hotel industry, given the rapidity with which the quality of hotel furnishings declines, customers are always attracted to new hotels. When new hotel chains are built alongside the old chains, excess capacity can result. Often companies are simply making simultaneous competitive moves based on industry trends, but those moves eventually lead to head-to-head competition. Most fast food chains, for instance, establish new outlets whenever demographic data show population increases. However, the companies seem to forget that all other chains use the same data (they are not fully anticipating their rivals' actions). Thus, a locality that has no fast-food outlets may suddenly see several being built at the same time. Whether they can all survive depends on the growth rate of demand relative to the growth rate of the chains.

Choosing a capacity-control strategy. Given the various ways in which capacity can expand, companies clearly need to find some means of controlling it. If they are always plagued by price cutting and price wars, they will be unable to recoup the investments in their generic strategies. Low profitability within an industry caused by overcapacity forces not just the weakest companies but also sometimes the major players to exit the industry. In general, companies have two strategic choices: (1) each company individually must try to preempt its rivals and seize the initiative, or (2) the companies collectively must find indirect means of coordinating with each other so that they are all aware of the mutual effects of their actions.

To *preempt* rivals, a company must forecast a large increase in demand in the product market and then move rapidly to establish large-scale operations that will be able to satisfy the predicted demand. By achieving a first-mover advantage, the company may deter other firms from entering the market because the preemptor will usually be able to move down the experience curve, reduce its costs (and thus its prices, too), and threaten a price war if necessary.

This strategy, however, is extremely risky because it involves investing resources before the extent and profitability of the future market are clear. Wal-Mart preempted Sears and Kmart, with its strategy of locating in small rural towns to tap an underexploited market for discount goods. Wal-Mart has been able to engage in market penetration and market expansion because of the secure base it established in its rural strongholds.

A preemptive strategy is also risky if it does not deter competitors and they decide to enter the market. If the competitors have a stronger generic strategy or more resources, such as Microsoft or Intel, they can make the preemptor suffer. Thus, for the strategy to succeed, the preemptor must generally be a credible company with enough resources to withstand a possible price war.

To *coordinate* with rivals as a capacity-control strategy, caution must be exercised because collusion on the timing of new investments is illegal under antitrust law. However, tacit coordination is practiced in many industries as companies attempt to understand and forecast one another's competitive moves. Generally, companies use market signaling to secure coordination. They make announcements about their future investment decisions in trade journals and newspapers. In addition, they share information about their production levels and their forecasts of demand within an industry to bring supply and demand into equilibrium. Thus, a coordination strategy reduces the risks associated with investment in the industry. This is very common in the chemical refining and oil business, where new capacity investments frequently cost hundreds of millions of dollars.

● **Game Theory**

As we have discussed, companies are in a constant competitive struggle with rivals in their industry to gain more business from customers. A useful way of viewing this struggle is as a competitive game between companies, in which companies are continually using competitive moves and tactics to compete effectively in an industry. Companies that understand the competitive nature of the game they are playing can often improve their competitive positioning and increase the profitability of their business models. For example, managers can implement better strategies to pursue cost leadership or differentiation.

A branch of work in the social sciences known as *game theory* can be used to model competition between a company and its rivals and help managers improve their business models and strategies.[27] From a game theory perspective, companies in an industry can be viewed as players that are all simultaneously making choices about which business models and strategies to pursue to maximize their profitability. The problem strategic managers face is that the potential profitability of each business model is not some fixed amount; it varies depending on the strategies one company selects and also the strategies that its rivals select. There are two basic types of game: sequential move games and simultaneous move games. In a *sequential move game*, such as chess, players move in turn, and one player can select a strategy to pursue after considering its rival's choice of strategies. In a *simultaneous move game*, the players act at the same time, in ignorance of their rival's current actions. The classic game of rock-paper-scissors is a simultaneous move game.

In the business world, both sequential and simultaneous move games are commonplace as strategic managers jockey for competitive position in the industry. Indeed, game theory is particularly useful in analyzing situations in which a company is competing against a limited number of rivals and a considerable level of interdependence exists in the industry, as occurs in a mature industry. Several of the basic principles that underlie game theory are examined below; these principles can be useful in determining which business model and strategies managers should pursue.

LOOK FORWARD AND REASON BACK One of the most basic messages of game theory is that managers need to think strategically in two related ways: (1) look forward, think ahead, and anticipate how rivals will respond to whatever strategic moves they make; and (2) reason backward to determine which strategic moves to pursue today given their assessment of how the company's rivals will respond to various future strategic moves. Managers who take both of these approaches should be able to discover the specific competitive strategy that will lead to the greatest potential returns. This cardinal principle of game theory is known as *look forward and reason back*. To understand its importance, consider the following scenario.

Two large companies, UPS and FedEx, which specialize in next-day delivery of packages, dominate the U.S. air express industry. They have a very high fixed cost structure because they need to invest in a capital-intensive nationwide network of aircraft, trucks, and package-sorting facilities. The key to their profitability is to increase volume sufficiently so that these fixed costs can be spread out over a large number of packages, reducing the unit cost of transporting each package.

Imagine that a bright young manager at UPS calculates that if UPS cuts prices for next-day delivery service by 15%, the volume of packages the company ships will grow by over 30%, and so will UPS's total revenues and profitability. Is this a smart move? The answer depends on whether the bright young manager has remembered to look forward and reason back, and think through how FedEx would respond to UPS's price cuts.

Because UPS and FedEx are competing directly against each other, their strategies are interdependent. If UPS cuts prices, FedEx will lose market share, its volume of shipments will decline, and its profitability will suffer. FedEx is unlikely to accept this result: if UPS cuts prices by 15%, FedEx is likely to follow and cut its prices by 15% to hold on to market share. The net result is that the average level of prices in the industry will fall by 15%, as will revenues, and both players will see their profitability decline—a lose-lose situation. By looking forward and reasoning back, the new manager discovers that the strategy of cutting prices is not a good one.

Decision trees can be used to help in the process of looking forward and reasoning back. Figure 6.10 maps out the decision tree for the simple game analyzed above from the perspective of UPS. (Note that this is a sequential move game.) UPS moves first, and then FedEx must decide how to respond. Here, you see that UPS has to choose between two strategies: cutting prices by 15% or leaving them unchanged. If it leaves prices unchanged, it will continue to earn its current level of profitability, which is $100 million. If it cuts prices by 15%, one of two things can happen: FedEx matches the price cut, or FedEx leaves its prices unchanged. If FedEx matches UPS's price cut (FedEx decides to fight a price war), profits are lost in the price competition, and UPS's profit will be $0. If FedEx does not respond and leaves its prices unaltered, UPS will gain market share and its profits will rise to $180 million. So the best pricing strategy for UPS to pursue depends on its assessment of FedEx's likely response.

Figure 6.10 assigns probabilities to the different responses from FedEx: specifically, there is a 70% chance that FedEx will match UPS's price cut and a 30% chance that it will do nothing. These probabilities come from an assessment of how UPS's price cut will affect FedEx's sales volume and profitability. The bigger the negative impact of UPS's price cut is on FedEx's sales volume and profitability, the more likely it is that FedEx will match UPS's price cuts. This is another example of the principle

FIGURE 6.10

A Decision Tree for
UPS's Pricing Strategy

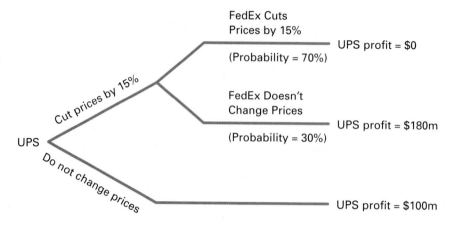

of looking forward and reasoning back. Assigning a 70% probability to the top branch in Figure 6.10 assumes that the price cut from UPS will have a significant negative impact on FedEx's business and will force the company to respond with a price cut of its own. The probabilities can also come from looking at the history of FedEx's responses to UPS's price moves. If FedEx has a long history of matching UPS's price cuts, the probability that it will do so this time is high. If FedEx does not have a history of matching UPS's price cuts, the probability will be lower.

Now let us revisit the question of what strategy UPS should pursue. If UPS does not cut prices, its profits are $100 million. If it cuts prices, its expected profits are $(.70) \times \$0 + (.30) \times \$180 = \$60$ million. Since $60 million is less than $100 million, UPS should not pursue the price-cutting strategy. If it did, FedEx would probably respond, and the net effect would be to depress UPS's profitability. Another way of looking at this scenario is to ask: Under what assumptions about the probability of FedEx's responding would it be worthwhile for UPS to cut prices by 15%? For UPS to move forward with its price cuts, the expected profits from doing so must be greater than $100 million, which is the profit from doing nothing. The way to work this out is to find the probability for which UPS is indifferent between leaving prices unaltered or changing them. We use p to signify probability: $\$100m = p \times \$180m$. Solving for p, we get $p = \$100m/\$180m = 0.556$. In other words, for UPS to go ahead with the proposed price cut, the probability that FedEx will do nothing must be greater than 55.6%.

KNOW THY RIVAL At this juncture, the question of whether this example is rather contrived might arise. After all, could UPS managers *really* anticipate how FedEx's profits could be affected if UPS cut its prices by 15%? And could UPS really assign a probability to FedEx's likely response? The answer is that, although UPS's managers cannot calculate exactly what the profit impact and probabilities would be, they can make an informed decision by collecting competitive information and thinking strategically. For example, they could estimate FedEx's cost structure by looking at FedEx's published financial accounts. And because they are in the same business as FedEx, they can assess the effect of falling demand on FedEx's cost structure and bottom line. Moreover, by looking at the history of FedEx's competitive behavior, they can assess how FedEx will respond to a price cut.

This illustrates a second basic principle of game theory: know thy rivals. In other words, in thinking strategically, managers must put themselves in the position of a rival to answer the question of how that rival is likely to act in a particular situation. If a company's managers are to be effective at looking forward and reasoning back, they must have a good understanding of what their rival is likely to do under different scenarios, and they need to be able to extrapolate their rival's future behavior based on this understanding.

FIND THE DOMINANT STRATEGY   A **dominant strategy** is one that makes you better off than you would be if you played any other strategy, *no matter what strategy your opponent uses.* To grasp this concept, consider a simultaneous move game based on a situation that developed in the U.S. car industry in the early 1990s and has been going on ever since (so far we have been considering a sequential move game). Two car companies, Ford and GM (both differentiators), have to decide whether to introduce cash-back rebate programs in November to move unsold inventory that is building up on the lots of car dealers nationwide. Each company can make one of two moves: offer cash rebates or do not offer cash rebates. Because the advanced planning associated with launching such a strategy is fairly extensive, both companies must make a decision about what to do by mid-October, which is before each has had a chance to see what its rival is doing.

In each of the previous four years, both companies have introduced just such programs on November 1 and kept them in place until December 31. Customers have become conditioned to expect these programs and increasingly have held back their new car purchases in anticipation of the cash-rebate programs beginning in November. This learned behavior by customers has increased the strategic importance of the rebate programs and made such programs increasingly expensive for the automobile companies—hence the billions of dollars GM and Ford have lost in the 2000s. Figure 6.11 lays out a payoff matrix associated with each strategy.

The four cells in this matrix represent the four possible outcomes of pursuing or not pursuing a cash-rebate strategy. The numbers in parentheses in the center of each cell represent the profit that General Motors and Ford, respectively, will get in each case (in millions of dollars). If both General Motors and Ford decide not to introduce cash rebates (cell 1), each will get $800 million in profit for the November 1–December 31 period. If GM introduces a cash-rebate program but Ford doesn't, GM will gain market share at Ford's expense, and GM will get $1,000 million in profit, while Ford gets just $200 million (cell 2). The converse holds if Ford introduces a rebate program but GM doesn't (cell 3). If both companies introduce rebate programs, both get $400 million (see cell 4; remember, the rebates are expensive and essentially represent deep price discounting to move unsold inventory). Finally, the

FIGURE 6.11

A Payoff Matrix for a Cash-Rebate Program for GM and Ford

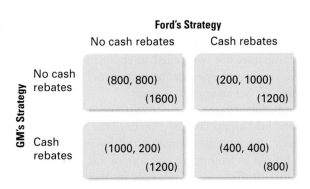

figures in parentheses in the lower right-hand corner of each cell represent the joint profit associated with each outcome.

You can see in this payoff matrix that GM's dominant strategy is to offer cash rebates because whatever strategy Ford pursues, GM does better if it offers cash rebates than if it doesn't. If Ford's strategy is to offer no cash rebates, GM's best strategy is to offer rebates and capture a profit of $1,000 million. If Ford's strategy is to offer cash rebates, GM's best strategy is again to offer cash rebates and get a profit of $400 million. So whatever Ford does, GM's best strategy is to offer cash rebates.

An interesting aspect of this game is that Ford also goes through the same reasoning process. Indeed, the payoff matrix shows that Ford's dominant strategy is also to offer cash rebates. The net result is that while both players get $400 million profit, the combined payoff of $800 million is the lowest of any combination! Clearly, both automakers could have done better if they had cooperated and jointly decided not to offer cash rebates. Why didn't they cooperate about this decision? There are two reasons. First, cooperation to set prices is illegal under U.S. antitrust law. Second, even though neither party will gain from offering rebates, *it cannot trust the other party not to offer a cash rebate because then it would be even worse off.* As the payoff matrix shows, if Ford does not offer cash rebates, GM has a very big incentive to do so, and vice versa. So both companies assume that the other will offer rebates, both end up doing so, and customers receive the value and are the winners!

The payoff structure in this game is famous. It is known as the *prisoner's dilemma game* because it was first explained using an example of two suspects, or prisoners, who are being interrogated for possible involvement in a crime. In the original exposition, the prisoners can confess to the crime and also implicate their partner in the crime to get a reduced sentence, or not confess or implicate the other. If the other prisoner also doesn't either confess or implicate the other, they both go free. The problem is that neither prisoner can trust the other not to implicate the partner to get a reduced sentence. So to reduce their losses (length of jail time), both end up confessing and implicating the other, and both go to jail.

The prisoner's dilemma is thought to capture the essence of many situations where two or more companies are competing against each other and their dominant strategy is to fight a price war, even if they would collectively be better off by *not* doing so. In other words, the prisoner's dilemma can be used to explain the mutually destructive price competition that breaks out in many industries from time to time. It also raises the question of whether companies can do anything to extricate themselves from such a situation. This brings us to the final principle of game theory, which is explored in the following section.

STRATEGY SHAPES THE PAYOFF STRUCTURE OF THE GAME An important lesson of game theory is that, through its choice of strategy, a company can alter the payoff structure of the competitive game being played in the industry. To understand this concept, consider once more the cash-rebate game played by Ford and GM, in which both companies are compelled to choose a dominant strategy that depresses total payoffs. How can they extricate themselves from this predicament? They can do it by changing the behavior of customers.

Recall that rebates were necessary only because customers had come to expect them and held off purchasing a car until the rebates were introduced. In a self-fulfilling prophecy, this depresses demand and forces the companies to introduce rebates to move unsold inventory on the lots of car dealers. If these expectations could be changed, customers would not hold off their purchases in anticipation of the rebates being introduced in November of each year, and companies would no longer have to introduce rebates to move unsold inventory on the lots of car dealers. A company can change customer behavior through its choice of strategy.

This is what GM actually did. After several years of rebate wars, GM decided to issue a new credit card that allowed cardholders to apply 5% of their charges toward buying or leasing a new GM car, up to $500 a year with a maximum of $3,500. The credit card launch was one of the most successful in history: within two years, there were 9 million GM credit card holders, and the card had replaced the other incentives that GM offered, principally the end-of-year cash rebates. Because of the card, price-sensitive customers who typically waited for the rebates could purchase a reduced-price car any time of the year. Moreover, once they had the card, they were much more likely to buy from GM than Ford. This strategy changed customer behavior. Customers no longer waited for rebates at the end of the year before buying, an inventory of unsold cars did not build up on the lots of dealers, and GM was not forced into fighting a rebate war to clear inventory.

If this strategy was so successful, what was to stop Ford from imitating it? Nothing! Ford began to offer its own credit card soon after GM did. In this case, however, imitation of the strategy led to increased profitability because both GM and Ford had found a clever way to differentiate themselves from each other: by issuing credit cards that created stronger brand loyalty. With the new cards, a GM cardholder was more likely to buy a GM car and a Ford cardholder was more likely to buy a Ford car. By reducing the tendency of customers to play GM and Ford dealers against each other, the card also had the effect of enabling both GM and Ford to raise their prices. Figure 6.12 illustrates how strategy can change the payoff matrix.

By issuing credit cards and strengthening the differentiation component of their strategy, both Ford and GM reduced the value of cash rebates and made it less likely that customers would switch to the company that offers rebates. The payoff structure of the game changed, and so did the dominant strategy. Now that GM's dominant strategy is not to offer cash rebates, whatever Ford does, GM is better off not offering rebates. The same is true for Ford. In other words, by their choice of strategy, General Motors and Ford have changed their dominant strategy in a way that boosts their profitability.

More generally, this example suggests that the way out of mutually destructive price competition associated with a prisoner's dilemma type of game is for the players to change their business models and differentiate their product offerings in the minds of customers, thereby reducing their sensitivity to price competition. In other words, by their choice of strategy and business model (one principally based on differentiation),

FIGURE 6.12

Altered Payoff Matrix
for GM and Ford

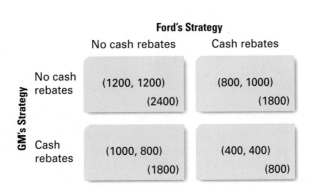

companies can alter the payoff structure associated with the game, alter their dominant strategy, and move away from a prisoner's dilemma type of game structure.

This insight also points to the need for companies to think through how their choice of business strategy might change the structure of the competitive game they are playing. Although we have looked at how strategy can transform the payoff structure of the game in a way that is more favorable, the opposite can and does occur. Companies often unintentionally change their business models and pursue strategies that change the payoff structure of the game in a way that is much less favorable to them and comes to resemble a prisoner's dilemma, as the competitive dynamics between Coca-Cola and PepsiCo in the soft drink industry did; see Strategy in Action 6.4.

The Pepsi challenge changed the long-established competitive rules in the industry. As the basis of competition shifted from differentiation by abstract lifestyle advertising to direct product comparisons, then to price competition, the payoff structure associated with their game changed and became more of a prisoner's dilemma type of structure. Had Pepsi's managers looked ahead and reasoned back, they might have realized that price competition would be the outcome of its new aggressive strategy and they might not have launched the Pepsi challenge, especially because the company was gaining market share from Coke, albeit slowly. However, because Pepsi's strategy changed the nature of differentiation in the industry, it led to a lose-lose situation.

Strategy in Action 6.4

Coca-Cola and PepsiCo Go Head-to-Head

For thirty years, until the late 1970s, the cola segment of the soft drink industry went through a golden age in which the main players, Coca-Cola and PepsiCo, were very profitable. These two companies competed against each other by advertising their respective products, Coke and Pepsi, based on abstract lifestyle product attributes. PepsiCo would introduce advertisements showing that it was cool to drink Pepsi, and Coca-Cola would produce advertisements with catchy jingles such as "things go better with Coke." Neither company competed on price. Coke led the market throughout the period, although by the mid-1970s, Pepsi was closing in.

At this point, Pepsi launched a new and innovative strategy: the Pepsi challenge. The Pepsi challenge was a taste test in which customers were blindfolded and asked which drink they preferred, Pepsi or Coke. In the test, about 55% of customers consistently said they preferred Pepsi, a significant result given that Pepsi trailed Coke in market share. Pepsi test-marketed the Pepsi challenge in Dallas, and it was so successful that in the late 1970s, Pepsi rolled out the challenge nationally, a situation that presented a real dilemma for Coke. It could not respond with its own blind taste test because in the tests, the majority of people preferred Pepsi. Moreover, the Pepsi challenge had changed the nature of competition in the industry. After thirty years of competition through product differentiation based on lifestyle product attributes with no direct (and aggressive) product comparisons, Pepsi had shifted to a direct product comparison based on a real attribute of the product: taste.

PepsiCo had altered its business model and changed how it chose to differentiate its product from Coke. As Pepsi was now gaining market share, Coca-Cola's managers decided to make an aggressive response: deep price discounts for Coke in local markets where they controlled the Coke bottler and the local Pepsi bottler was weak. This was a successful move; in markets where price discounting was used, Coke started to gain its share back. PepsiCo then decided to respond in kind and cut prices too. Before long, price discounting was widespread in the industry. Customers were coming to expect price discounting, brand loyalty had been eroded, and the value associated with differentiation had been reduced. Both Coke and Pepsi experienced declining profitability.[d]

So how did the soft drink manufacturers try to extricate themselves from this situation? Over the course of a few years, they once more shifted the way in which they differentiated their products. They introduced new products, such as Diet Coke and Cherry Coke, to rebuild brand loyalty, and they reemphasized abstract advertising by using celebrities to help create a brand image for their soda, thus differentiating it from their competitors' offerings and reducing customer price sensitivity. They are still doing this today—Pepsi, for example, uses the dancing and music of Britney Spears as a device for building a brand image that differentiates its offering from Coke. However, it took several years for Pepsi and Coke to do this, and in the interim they had to grapple with a payoff structure that reduced profitability in the industry. Moreover, price discounting is still common today.

Strategies in Declining Industries

Sooner or later, many industries enter into a decline stage, in which the size of the total market starts to shrink. Examples are the railroad industry, the tobacco industry, and the steel industry. Industries start declining for a number of reasons, including technological change, social trends, and demographic shifts. The railroad and steel industries began to decline when technological changes brought viable substitutes for their products. The advent of the internal combustion engine drove the railroad industry into decline, and the steel industry fell into decline with the rise of plastics and composite materials. As for the tobacco industry, changing social attitudes toward smoking, which are themselves a product of growing concerns about the health effects of smoking, have caused a decline in tobacco usage.

● **The Severity of Decline**   When the size of the total market is shrinking, competition tends to intensify in a declining industry and profit rates tend to fall. The intensity of competition in a declining industry depends on four critical factors, which are indicated in Figure 6.13. First, the intensity of competition is greater in industries in which decline is rapid as opposed to industries, such as tobacco, in which decline is slow and gradual.

Second, the intensity of competition is greater in declining industries in which exit barriers are high. As we noted in Chapter 2, high exit barriers keep companies locked into an industry even when demand is falling. The result is the emergence of excess productive capacity and, hence, an increased probability of fierce price competition.

Third, and related to the previous point, the intensity of competition is greater in declining industries in which fixed costs are high (as in the steel industry). The reason

FIGURE 6.13

Factors That Determine the Intensity of Competition in Declining Industries

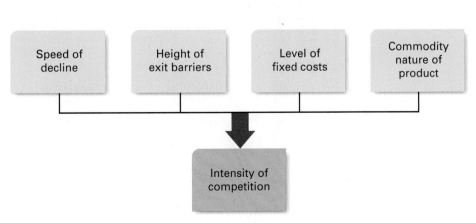

is that the need to cover fixed costs, such as the costs of maintaining productive capacity, can make companies try to use any excess capacity they have by slashing prices, which can trigger a price war.

Finally, the intensity of competition is greater in declining industries in which the product is perceived as a commodity (as it is in the steel industry) in contrast to industries in which differentiation gives rise to significant brand loyalty, as was true until very recently of the declining tobacco industry.

Not all segments of an industry typically decline at the same rate. In some segments, demand may remain reasonably strong despite decline elsewhere. The steel industry illustrates this situation. Although bulk steel products, such as sheet steel, have suffered a general decline, demand has actually risen for specialty steels, such as those used in high-speed machine tools. Vacuum tubes provide another example. Although demand for them collapsed when transistors replaced them as a key component in many electronics products, vacuum tubes still had some limited applications in radar equipment for years afterward. Consequently, demand in this vacuum tube segment remained strong despite the general decline in the demand for vacuum tubes. The point, then, is that there may be pockets of demand in an industry in which demand is declining more slowly than in the industry as a whole or is not declining at all. Price competition thus may be far less intense among the companies serving such pockets of demand than within the industry as a whole.

● **Choosing a Strategy**

There are four main strategies that companies can adopt to deal with decline: (1) a **leadership strategy**, by which a company seeks to become the dominant player in a declining industry; (2) a **niche strategy**, which focuses on pockets of demand that are declining more slowly than the industry as a whole; (3) a **harvest strategy**, which optimizes cash flow; and (4) a **divestment strategy**, by which a company sells off the business to others. Figure 6.14 provides a simple framework for guiding strategic choice. Note that the intensity of competition in the declining industry is measured

FIGURE 6.14

Strategy Selection in a Declining Industry

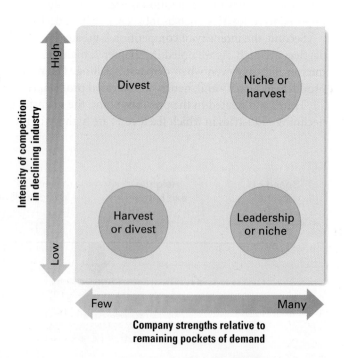

on the vertical axis and that a company's strengths relative to remaining pockets of demand are measured on the horizontal axis.

LEADERSHIP STRATEGY A leadership strategy aims at growing in a declining industry by picking up the market share of companies that are leaving the industry. A leadership strategy makes most sense (1) when the company has distinctive strengths that allow it to capture market share in a declining industry and (2) the speed of decline and the intensity of competition in the declining industry are moderate. Philip Morris has pursued such a strategy in the tobacco industry. Through aggressive marketing, Philip Morris has increased its market share in a declining industry and earned enormous profits in the process.

The tactical steps companies might use to achieve a leadership position include using aggressive pricing and marketing to build market share, acquiring established competitors to consolidate the industry, and raising the stakes for other competitors—for example, by making new investments in productive capacity. Such competitive tactics signal to other competitors that the company is willing and able to stay and compete in the declining industry. These signals may persuade other companies to exit the industry, which would further enhance the competitive position of the industry leader. Strategy in Action 6.5 offers an example of a company, Richardson Electronics, that has prospered by taking a leadership position in a declining industry. It is one of the last companies in the vacuum tube business.

Strategy in Action   6.5

How to Make Money in the Vacuum Tube Business

At its peak in the early 1950s, the vacuum tube business was a major industry in which companies such as Westinghouse, General Electric, RCA, and Western Electric had a large stake. Then along came the transistor, making most vacuum tubes obsolete, and one by one all the big companies exited the industry. One company, however, Richardson Electronics, not only stayed in the business but also demonstrated that high returns are possible in a declining industry. Primarily a distributor (although it does have some manufacturing capabilities), Richardson bought the remains of a dozen companies in the United States and Europe as they exited the vacuum tube industry, and it now has a warehouse that stocks more than 10,000 different types of vacuum tubes. The company is the world's only supplier of many of them, which helps explain why its gross margin is in the 35 to 40% range.

Richardson survives and prospers because vacuum tubes are vital parts of some older electronics equipment that would be costly to replace with solid-state equipment. In addition, vacuum tubes still outperform semiconductors in some limited applications, including radar and welding machines. The U.S. government and GM are big customers of Richardson.

Speed is the essence of Richardson's business. The company's Illinois warehouse offers overnight delivery to some 40,000 customers, and it processes 650 orders a day at an average price of $550. Customers such as GM do not really care whether a vacuum tube costs $250 or $350; what they care about is the $40,000 to $50,000 downtime loss that they face when a key piece of welding equipment isn't working. By responding quickly to the demands of such customers and being the only major supplier of many types of vacuum tubes, Richardson has placed itself in a monopoly position that many companies in growing industries would envy. However, a new company, Westrex Corp., was formed to take advantage of the growing popularity of vacuum tubes in high-end stereo systems, and today it is competing head-to-head with Richardson in some market segments. Clearly, good profits can be made even in a declining industry.[e]

NICHE STRATEGY A niche strategy focuses on pockets of demand in the industry in which demand is stable or declining less rapidly than in the industry as a whole. The strategy makes sense when the company has some unique strengths relative to those niches where demand remains relatively strong. As an example, consider Naval, a company that manufactures whaling harpoons and small guns to fire them and makes money doing so. This might be considered rather odd because the world community has outlawed whaling. However, Naval survived the terminal decline of the harpoon industry by focusing on the one group of people who are still allowed to hunt whales, although only in very limited numbers: North American Eskimos. Eskimos are permitted to hunt bowhead whales, provided that they do so only for food and not for commercial purposes. Naval is the sole supplier of small harpoon whaling guns to Eskimo communities, and its monopoly position allows it to earn a healthy return in this small market.

HARVEST STRATEGY As we noted earlier, a harvest strategy is the best choice when a company wishes to get out of a declining industry and optimize cash flow in the process. This strategy makes the most sense when the company foresees a steep decline and intense future competition or lacks strengths relative to remaining pockets of demand in the industry. A harvest strategy requires the company to cut all new investments in capital equipment, advertising, R&D, and the like. The inevitable result is that it will lose market share, but because it is no longer investing in this business, initially its positive cash flow will increase. Essentially, the company is taking cash flow in exchange for market share. Ultimately, cash flows will start to decline, and at this stage it makes sense for the company to liquidate the business. Although this strategy is very appealing in theory, it can be somewhat difficult to put into practice. Employee morale in a business that is being run down may suffer. Furthermore, if customers catch on to what the company is doing, they may defect rapidly. Then market share may decline much faster than the company expected.

DIVESTMENT STRATEGY A divestment strategy rests on the idea that a company can recover most of its investment in an underperforming business by selling it early, before the industry has entered into a steep decline. This strategy is appropriate when the company has few strengths relative to whatever pockets of demand are likely to remain in the industry and when the competition in the declining industry is likely to be intense. The best option may be to sell out to a company that is pursuing a leadership strategy in the industry. The drawback of the divestment strategy is that it depends for its success on the ability of the company to spot its industry's decline before it becomes serious and to sell out while the company's assets are still valued by others.

Summary of Chapter

1. In fragmented industries composed of a large number of small and medium-sized companies, the principal forms of competitive strategy are chaining, franchising, and horizontal merger, as well as using the Internet.

2. In embryonic and growth industries, strategy is determined partly by market demand. The innovators and early adopters have different needs from those in the early and the late majority, and a company must be prepared to cross the chasm between the two. Similarly, managers must understand the factors that affect a market's growth rate so they can tailor their business model to a changing industry environment.

3. Companies need to navigate the difficult road from growth to maturity by choosing an investment strategy that supports their business model. In choosing this strategy, managers must consider the company's competitive position in the industry and the stage of the industry's life cycle. Some main types of investment strategy are share building, growth, market concentration, share increasing, harvest, and hold-and-maintain.

4. Mature industries are composed of a few large companies whose actions are so highly interdependent that the success of one company's strategy depends on the responses of its rivals.

5. The principal strategies used by companies in mature industries to deter entry are product proliferation, price cutting, and maintaining excess capacity.

6. The principal strategies used by companies in mature industries to manage rivalry are price signaling, price leadership, nonprice competition, and capacity control.

7. Game theory suggests several management principles: look forward and reason back, know thy rival, pursue your dominant strategy, remember that strategy can alter the payoff structure of the game, and use strategy to change the payoff structure in a way that increases the profitability of your dominant strategy.

8. In declining industries, in which market demand has leveled off or is falling, companies must tailor their price and nonprice strategies to the new competitive environment. They also need to manage industry capacity to prevent the emergence of capacity expansion problems.

9. There are four main strategies a company can pursue when demand is falling: leadership, niche, harvest, and divestment. The choice is determined by the severity of industry decline and the company's strengths relative to the remaining pockets of demand.

Discussion Questions

1. Why are industries fragmented? What are the main ways in which companies can turn a fragmented industry into a consolidated one?

2. What are the key problems in maintaining a competitive advantage in embryonic and growth industry environments? What are the dangers associated with being the leader?

3. In managing their growth through the life cycle, what investment strategies should be made by (a) differentiators in a strong competitive position and (b) differentiators in a weak competitive position?

4. Discuss how companies can use (a) product differentiation and (b) capacity control to manage rivalry and increase an industry's profitability.

5. What insights would game theory offer (a) a small pizza restaurant operating in a crowded college market and (b) a detergent manufacturer seeking to bring out new products in established markets?

Practicing Strategic Management

SMALL-GROUP EXERCISE
How to Keep the Salsa Hot

Break up into groups of three to five, appoint one group member to be the spokesperson who will communicate your findings to the class, and discuss the following scenario. You are the managers of a company that has pioneered a new kind of salsa for chicken that has taken the market by storm. The salsa's differentiated appeal has been based on a unique combination of spices and packaging that has allowed you to charge a premium price. Over the past three years, your salsa has achieved a national reputation, and now major food companies such as Kraft and Nabisco, seeing the potential of this market segment, are beginning to introduce new salsas of their own, imitating your product.

1. Describe your business model and the strategies you are pursuing.

2. Describe the industry environment in which you are competing.

3. What kinds of competitive strategies can you adopt to strengthen your business model in this kind of environment?

ARTICLE FILE 6

Choose a company or group of companies in a particular industry environment, and explain how it has adopted a competitive strategy to protect or enhance its business-level strategy.

STRATEGIC MANAGEMENT PROJECT
Module 6

This part of the project considers how conditions in the industry environment affect the success of your company's business model and strategies. With the information you have at your disposal, perform the tasks and answer the questions listed:

1. In what kind of industry environment (for example, embryonic, mature) does your company operate? Use the information from Strategic Management Project: Module 2 to answer this question.

2. Discuss how your company has attempted to develop strategies to protect and strengthen its business model. For example, if your company is operating in an embryonic industry, how has it attempted to increase its competitive advantage over time? If it operates in a mature industry, discuss how it has tried to manage industry competition.

3. What new strategies would you advise your company to pursue and thus increase its competitive advantage? For example, how should it attempt to differentiate its products in the future or lower its cost structure?

4. On the basis of this analysis, do you think your company will be able to maintain its competitive advantage in the future? Why or why not?

ETHICS EXERCISE

Beverly answered her office phone to find an executive from Grey Industries on the line. "Ms. Jones," he began after pleasantries has been exchanged, "we would be honored if you would consider joining our corporate board." After gathering information, Beverly agreed. As the president of the Natural History Museum, a nonprofit organization in Denver, Colorado, she was used to receiving these requests. In fact, she currently served on two other boards.

A month later, Grey Industries donated half a million dollars to the museum. Beverly, on behalf of the museum, had received large donations from the other companies on whose boards she served. Although she knew it was good for the museum, she wondered if the companies were simply being generous or had ulterior motives. Beverly had managed to remain impartial and serve objectively despite such donations, but she knew other presidents and directors of nonprofit organizations had not and had made decisions based on donation promises. Beverly knew that the Nasdaq Stock Market was encouraging companies to put limits on their donations to nonprofit organizations if presidents and directors of those organizations served on their boards, but firm rules had yet to be put into place. Beverly thought this move would be a smart one on the part of corporations and helpful to board members.

To further complicate matters, Beverly had some serious reservations about the ways in which Grey Industries conducted business. The company's business model hadn't been updated in years, and the competition was beginning to take over. Despite obvious issues, Grey Industries was holding on to its top-level managers—individuals who had been with the company since the beginning. These very same managers seemed incapable of implementing the changes necessary to keep Grey Industries in the running. Having accepted the company's donation, Beverly had to make a difficult decision. Should she resign from the board? Or should she follow her gut instinct and insist that Grey Industries replace these managers immediately or lose to the competition?

1. Define the ethical dilemmas presented in this case.

2. Do you think presidents and directors of nonprofit organizations can remain objective despite promises of large donations?

3. What are the pros and cons of corporations offering donations to nonprofit organizations?

4. How do you think Beverly should approach the situation? Why?

CLOSING CASE

Nike's Winning Ways

Nike, headquartered in Beaverton, Oregon, was founded over thirty years ago by Bill Bowerman, a former University of Oregon track coach, and Phil Knight, an entrepreneur in search of a profitable business opportunity. Bowerman's goal was to dream up a new kind of sneaker tread that would enhance a runner's traction and speed, and he came up with the idea for Nike's waffle tread after studying the waffle iron in his home. Bowerman and Knight made their shoe and began selling it out of the trunks of their car at track meets. From this small beginning, Nike has grown into a company that sold over $12 billion worth of shoes in the $35 billion athletic footwear and apparel industries in 2004.[28]

Nike's amazing growth came from its business model, which has always been based on two original functional strategies: to create state-of-the-art athletic shoes and then to publicize the qualities of its shoes through dramatic guerrilla-style marketing. Nike's marketing is designed to persuade customers that its shoes are not only superior but also a high fashion statement and a necessary part of a lifestyle based on sporting or athletic interests. A turning point came in 1987 when Nike increased its marketing budget from $8 million to $48 million to persuade customers its shoes were the best. A large part of this advertising budget soon went to pay celebrities like Michael Jordan millions of dollars to wear and champion its products. The company has consistently pursued this strategy: in 2003 it signed basketball star LeBron James to a $90 million endorsement contract, and many other sports stars, such as Tiger Woods and Serena Williams, are already part of its charmed circle.

Nike's strategy to emphasize the uniqueness of its product has obviously paid off; its market share soared and its revenues hit $9.6 billion in 1998. However, 1998 was also a turning point because in that year, sales began to fall. Nike's $200 Air Jordans no longer sold like they used to, and inventory built up in stores and warehouses. Suddenly it seemed much harder to design new shoes that customers perceived to be significantly better. Nike's stunning growth in sales was actually reducing its profitability; somehow it had lost control of its business model. Phil Knight, who had resigned his management position, was forced to resume the helm and lead the company out of its troubles. He recruited a team of talented top managers from leading consumer products companies to help him improve Nike's business model. As a result, Nike has changed its business model in some fundamental ways.

In the past, Nike shunned sports like golf, soccer, rollerblading, and so on, and it focused most of its efforts on making shoes for the track and basketball markets to build its market share in these areas. However, when its sales started to fall, it realized that using marketing to increase sales in a particular market segment can grow sales and profits only so far; it needed to start selling more types of shoes to more segments of the athletic shoe market. So Nike took its design and marketing competencies and began to craft new lines of shoes for new market segments. For example, it launched a line of soccer shoes and perfected their design over time, and by 2004, it had won the biggest share of the soccer market from its arch-rival Adidas.[29] Also in 2004, it launched its Total 90 III shoes, which are aimed at the millions of casual soccer players throughout the world who want a shoe they can just "play" in. Once more, Nike's dramatic marketing campaigns aim to make their shoes part of the soccer lifestyle, to persuade customers that traditional sneakers do not work because soccer shoes are sleeker and fit the foot more snugly.[30]

To take advantage of its competencies in design and marketing, Nike then decided to enter new market segments by purchasing other footwear companies offering shoes that extended or complemented its product lines. For example, it bought Converse, the maker of retro-style sneakers; Hurley International, which makes skateboards and Bauer in-line and hockey skates; and Official Starter, a licensor of athletic shoes and apparel whose brands include the low-priced Shaq brand. Allowing Converse to take advantage of Nike's in-house competencies has resulted in dramatic increases in the sales of its sneakers, and Converse has made an important contribution to Nike's profitability.[31]

Nike had also entered another market segment when it bought Cole Haan, the dress shoemaker, in the 1980s. Now it is searching for other possible acquisitions. It decided to enter the athletic apparel market to use its skills there, and by 2004, sales were over $1 billion. In making all these changes to its business model, Nike was finding ways to invest its capital in new products where it could increase its market share and profitability. Its new focus on developing new and improved products for new market segments is working. Nike's ROIC has soared from 14% in 2000 to 24% in 2006, and it makes over $1 billion profit.

Case Discussion Questions

1. What business model and strategies is Nike pursuing?

2. How has Nike's business model changed the nature of industry competition?

3. What new strategies have emerged in the shoe industry as a result?

Strategy and Technology

Format War—Blu-Ray Versus HD-DVD

A format war is developing in the consumer electronics industry between two different versions of next-generation high-definition DVD players and discs. In one camp is Sony with its Blu-ray format; in the other is Toshiba, which is championing the rival HD-DVD format. Both high-definition formats offer a dramatic improvement in picture and sound quality over established DVD technology and are designed to work with high-definition televisions. Although each new format will play old DVDs, the two standards are incompatible with each other. Blu-ray players will not accept DVDs formatted for HD-DVD, and vice versa.

Format wars like this have occurred many times in the past. VHS versus Betamax in the videocassette market and Windows versus Macintosh in personal computer operating systems are classic examples. If history is any guide, format wars tend to be "winner-takes-all" contests, with the loser being vanquished to a niche (as in the case of Apple's Macintosh operating system), or exiting the market altogether (as in the case of Sony's Betamax format). Format wars are a high-stakes game.

Both Sony and Toshiba have been working hard to ensure that their format gains an early lead in sales. In turn, so the thinking goes, this will increase the supply of preformatted discs designed to play on one format or the other, which should lead to a further increase in sales of the format that has the largest share of the market, and thus to its eventual dominance. A key strategy of both companies has been to line up film studios and get them to commit to issuing discs based on their format.

Initially it looked as if Sony had the early advantage. Prior to the technology being launched in the market, Columbia Pictures and MGM (both owned by Sony), along with Disney and Fox Studios, all committed exclusively to Blu-ray. By late 2005, several other studios that had initially committed exclusively to HD-DVD, including Warner Brothers and Paramount, also indicated that they would support Blu-ray as well. Warner and Paramount cited Blu-ray's momentum among other studios and its strong copyright protection mechanisms. This left just Universal Studios committed exclusively to HD-DVD.

To further strengthen its hand, Sony announced that it would incorporate Blu-ray technology in its next-generation P3 videogame console and its Vaio line of personal computers. Hewlett-Packard and Dell Computer also indicated that they would support the Blu-ray format. Sony even licensed the Blu-ray format to several other consumer electronics firms, including Samsung, in a bid to increase the supply of Blu-ray players in stores.

Then things began to go wrong for Sony. The company had to delay delivery of its P3 videogame console by a year due to engineering problems, which sapped some of the momentum from Blu-ray. Microsoft took advantage of this misstep, announcing that it would market an HD-DVD player that would work with its own videogame console, Xbox 360. In mid-2006, the first Blu-ray and HD-DVD players hit the market—the Blu-ray

players were more expensive, as much as twice the price of entry-level HD-DVD players. According to Toshiba, HD-DVD players and discs are cheaper to manufacture, although Sony disputes this. To complicate matters, one of the first Blu-ray players, made by Sony licensee Samsung, was shipped with a bad chip that marred its image quality.

By late 2006, some firms were beginning to hedge their bets. Hewlett-Packard reversed its earlier position and said that it would support both standards. So who will win this war? At this stage, it is too early to say. One possibility, however, is that neither format will win. Faced with two incompatible formats, consumers may do what they have in the past: wait. And without consumer dollars to drive adoption of one format over the other, the market may fail to gain traction.[1]

OVERVIEW

The format war now unfolding in the consumer electronics industry between two competing and incompatible versions of next-generation high-definition DVDs is typical of the nature of competition in high-technology industries (see the Opening Case). In this chapter, we will take a close look at the nature of competition and strategy in high-technology industries. **Technology** refers to the body of scientific knowledge used in the production of goods or services. **High-technology (high-tech) industries** are those in which the underlying scientific knowledge that companies in the industry use is advancing rapidly, and by implication, so are the attributes of the products and services that result from its application. The computer industry is often thought of as the quintessential example of a high-technology industry. Other industries often considered high-tech are telecommunications, where new technologies based on wireless and the Internet have proliferated in recent years; consumer electronics, where the digital technology underlying products from high-definition DVD players to videogame terminals and digital cameras is advancing rapidly; pharmaceuticals, where new technologies based on cell biology, recombinant DNA, and genomics are revolutionizing the process of drug discovery; power generation, where new technologies based on fuel cells and cogeneration may change the economics of the industry; and aerospace, where the combination of new composite materials, electronics, and more efficient jet engines are giving birth to a new era of superefficient commercial jet aircraft such as Boeing's 787.

This chapter focuses on high-technology industries for a number of reasons. First, technology is accounting for an ever larger share of economic activity. Estimates suggest that 12 to 15% of total economic activity in the United States is accounted for by information technology industries.[2] This figure actually underestimates the true impact of technology on the economy because it ignores the other high-technology areas we just mentioned. Moreover, as technology advances, many low-technology industries are becoming more high-tech. For example, the development of biotechnology and genetic engineering transformed the production of seed corn, long considered a low-technology business, into a high-technology business. Retailing used to be considered a low-technology business, but the shift to online retailing, led by companies like Amazon, has changed this. Moreover, high-technology products are making their way into a wide range of businesses; today a Ford Explorer contains more computing power than the multimillion-dollar mainframe computers used in the Apollo space program, and the competitive advantage of physical stores, such as Wal-Mart, is based on their use of information technology. The circle of high-technology industries is both large and expanding, and even in industries not thought of as high-tech, technology is revolutionizing aspects of the product or production system.

Although high-tech industries may produce very different products, when it comes to developing a business model and strategies that will lead to a competitive advantage and superior profitability and profit growth, they often face a similar situation. For example, winner-take-all format wars are common in many high-technology industries, such as the consumer electronics and computer industries (see the Opening Case for an example of an ongoing format war). This chapter examines the competitive features found in many high-tech industries and the kinds of strategies that companies must adopt to build business models that will allow them to achieve superior profitability and profit growth.

When you have completed this chapter, you will have an understanding of the nature of competition in high-tech industries and the strategies that companies can pursue to succeed in those industries.

Technical Standards and Format Wars

Especially in high-tech industries, ownership of **technical standards**—a set of technical specifications that producers adhere to when making the product or a component of it—can be an important source of competitive advantage.[3] Indeed, in many cases, the source of product differentiation is based on the technical standard. As in the high-definition DVD market, often only one standard will come to dominate a market, so many battles in high-tech industries revolve around companies competing to be the one that sets the standard.

Battles to set and control technical standards in a market are referred to as **format wars**; they are essentially battles to control the source of differentiation and thus the value that such differentiation can create for the customer. Because differentiated products often command premium prices and are often expensive to develop, the competitive stakes are enormous. The profitability and very survival of a company may depend on the outcome of the battle. For example, the outcome of the battle now being waged over the establishment and ownership of the standard for high-definition DVDs will help determine which companies will be leaders for the next decade in that marketplace (see the Opening Case).

● **Examples of Standards**   A familiar example of a standard is the layout of a computer keyboard. No matter what keyboard you buy, the letters are all in the same pattern.[4] The reason is quite obvious. Imagine if each computer maker changed the ways the keys were laid out—if some started with QWERTY on the top row of letters (which is indeed the format used and is known as the QWERTY format), some with YUHGFD, and some with ACFRDS. If you learned to type on one layout, it would be irritating and time-consuming to have to relearn on a YUHGFD layout. The standard format (QWERTY) makes it easy for people to move from computer to computer because the input medium, the keyboard, is set out in a standard way.

Another example of a technical standard concerns the dimensions of containers used to ship goods on trucks, railcars, and ships: all have the same basic dimensions—the same height, length, and width—and all make use of the same locking mechanisms to hold them onto a surface or to bolt against each other. Having a standard ensures that containers can be moved easily from one mode of transportation to another—from trucks to railcars, to ships, and back to railcars. If containers lacked standard dimensions and locking mechanisms, it would suddenly become much more difficult to ship containers around the world. Shippers would have to make sure that they had the right kind of container to go on the ships, trucks, and railcars scheduled to carry a particular container around the world—very complicated indeed.

Consider, finally, the personal computer. Most share a common set of features: an Intel or Intel-compatible microprocessor, random access memory (RAM), a Microsoft operating system, an internal hard drive, a floppy disk drive, a CD drive, a keyboard, a monitor, a mouse, a modem, and so on. We call this set of features the dominant design for personal computers (a **dominant design** refers to a common set of features or design characteristics). Embedded in this design are several technical standards (see Figure 7.1). For example, the Wintel technical standard is based on an Intel microprocessor and a Microsoft operating system. Microsoft and Intel "own" that standard, which is central to the personal computer. Developers of software applications, component parts, and peripherals such as printers adhere to this standard when developing their own products because this guarantees that their products will work well with a personal computer based on the Wintel standard. Another technical standard for connecting peripherals to the PC is the Universal Serial Bus (USB), established by an industry standards-setting board. No one owns it; the standard is in the public domain. A third technical standard is for communication between a PC and the Internet via a modem. Known as TCP/IP, this standard was also set by an industry association and is in the public domain. Thus, as with many other products, the PC is actually based on several technical standards. It is also important to note that when a company owns a standard, as Microsoft and Intel do with the Wintel standard, it may be a source of competitive advantage and high profitability.

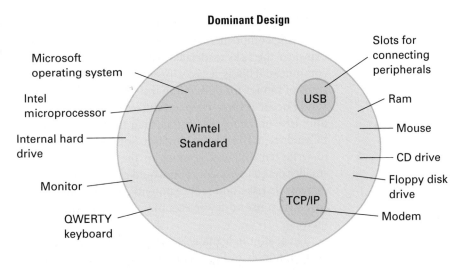

FIGURE 7.1

Technical Standards for Personal Computers

● Benefits of Standards

Standards emerge because there are economic benefits associated with them. First, having a technical standard helps to guarantee compatibility between products and their complements—other products used with them. For example, containers are used with railcars, trucks, and ships, and PCs are used with software applications. Compatibility has the tangible economic benefit of reducing the costs associated with making sure that products work well with each other.

Second, having a standard can help to reduce confusion in the minds of consumers. A few years ago, several consumer electronics companies were vying with each other to produce and market the first generation of DVD players, and they were championing different variants of the basic DVD technology—different standards—that were incompatible with each other; a DVD disk designed to run on a DVD player made by Toshiba would not run on a player made by Sony, and vice versa. The companies feared that selling these incompatible versions of the same technology would produce confusion in the minds of consumers, who would not know which version to purchase and might decide to wait and see which technology ultimately dominated the marketplace. With lack of demand, the technology might fail to gain traction in the marketplace and would not be successful. To avoid this possibility, the developers of DVD equipment established a standard-setting body for the industry, the DVD Forum, which established a common technical standard for DVD players and disks that all companies adhered to. The result was that when DVDs were introduced, they adhered to a common standard, which avoided confusion in consumers' minds. This helped to boost demand for DVD players, making them one of the fastest-selling technologies of the late 1990s and early 2000s. However, the DVD Forum has not been able to agree on a common standard for high-definition DVDs (see the Opening Case).

Third, the emergence of a standard can help to reduce production costs. Once a standard emerges, products based on that standard design can be mass-produced, enabling the manufacturers to realize substantial economies of scale and lower their cost structures. The fact that there is a central standard for PCs (the Wintel standard) means that the component parts for a PC can be mass-produced. A manufacturer of internal hard drives, for example, can mass-produce drives for Wintel PCs and thus can realize substantial scale economies. If there were several competing and incompatible standards, each of which required a unique type of hard drive, production runs for hard drives would be shorter, unit costs would be higher, and the cost of PCs would go up.

Fourth, the emergence of standards can help to reduce the risks associated with supplying complementary products and thus increase the supply for those products. Consider the risks associated with writing software applications to run on personal computers. This is a risky proposition, requiring the investment of considerable sums of money for developing the software before a single unit is sold. Imagine what would occur if there were ten different operating systems in use for PCs, each with only 10% of the market, rather than the current situation, where 95% of the world's PCs adhere to the Wintel standard. Software developers would be faced with the need to write ten different versions of the same software application, each for a much smaller market segment. This would change the economics of software development, increase its risks, and reduce potential profitability. Moreover, because of their higher cost structure and fewer economies of scale, the price of software programs would increase.

Thus, although many people complain about the consequences of Microsoft's near monopoly of PC operating systems, that monopoly does have at least one good effect: it substantially reduces the risks facing the makers of complementary products and the costs of those products. In fact, standards lead to both low-cost and differentiation advantages for individual companies and can help raise the level of industry profitability.

● **Establishment of Standards**

Standards emerge in an industry in three main ways. First, recognizing the benefits of establishing a standard, companies in an industry might lobby the government to mandate an industry standard. In the United States, for example, the Federal Communications Commission (FCC), after detailed discussions with broadcasters and consumer electronics companies, has mandated a single technical standard for digital television broadcasts (DTV) and required broadcasters to have capabilities in place for broadcasting digital signals based on this standard by 2006. The FCC took this step because it believed that without government action to set the standard, the rollout of DTV would be very slow. With a standard set by the government, consumer electronics companies can have greater confidence that a market will emerge, and this should encourage them to develop DTV products.

Second, technical standards are often set by cooperation among businesses, without government help, often through the medium of an industry forum, such as the DVD Forum. Companies cooperate in this way when they decide that competition among them to create a standard might be harmful because of the uncertainty that it would create in the minds of consumers.

When standards are set by the government or an industry association, they fall into the **public domain**, meaning that any company can freely incorporate into its products the knowledge and technology on which the standard is based. For example, no one owns the QWERTY format, and therefore no one company can profit from it directly. Similarly, the language that underlies the presentation of text and graphics on the Web, hypertext markup language (HTML), is in the public domain; it is free for all to use. The same is true for TCP/IP, the communications standard used for transmitting data on the Internet.

Often, however, the industry standard is selected competitively by the purchasing patterns of customers in the marketplace—that is, by market demand. In this case, the strategy and business model a company has developed for promoting its technological standard are of critical importance because ownership of an industry standard that is protected from imitation by patents and copyrights is a valuable asset—a source of sustained competitive advantage and superior profitability. Microsoft and Intel, for example, both owe their competitive advantage to format wars, which exist between two or more companies competing against each other to get their designs adopted as the industry standard. Format wars are common in high-tech industries because of the high stakes. The Wintel standard became the dominant standard for PCs only after Microsoft and Intel won format wars against Apple Computer's proprietary system and later against IBM's OS/2 operating system. Microsoft and Real Networks are currently competing head-to-head in a format war to establish rival technologies—Windows Media Player and RealPlayer—as the standard for streaming video and audio technology on the Web. The Opening Case tells how Sony and Toshiba are currently engaged in a format war as they try to get their respective technologies established as the standard for high-definition DVDs.

● **Network Effects, Positive Feedback, and Lockout**

It is increasingly apparent that when standards are set by competition between companies promoting different formats, network effects are a primary determinant of how standards are established.[5] **Network effects** arise in industries where the size of the network of complementary products is a primary determinant of demand for an industry's product. For example, the demand for automobiles early in the twentieth century was an increasing function of the network of paved roads and gas stations. Similarly, the demand for telephones is an increasing function of the number of other numbers that can be called with that phone, that is, of the size of the telephone network (the telephone network is the complementary product). When the first telephone service was introduced in New York City, only a hundred numbers could be called. The network was very small because of the limited number of wires and telephone switches, which made the telephone a relatively useless piece of equipment. As more and more people got telephones and as the network of wires and switches expanded, the value of a telephone connection increased. This led to an increase in demand for telephone lines, which further increased the value of owning a telephone, setting up a positive feedback loop.

To understand why network effects are important in the establishment of standards, consider the classic example of a format war: the battle between Sony and Matsushita to establish their respective technology for videocassette recorders (VCRs) as the standard in the marketplace. Sony was first to market with its Betamax technology, followed by Matsushita with its VHS technology. Both companies sold VCR recorder-players, and movie studios issued films prerecorded on VCR tapes for rental to consumers. Initially, all tapes were issued in Betamax format to play on Sony's machine. Sony did not license its Betamax technology, preferring to make all of the player-recorders itself. When Matsushita entered the market, it realized that it would have to encourage movie studios to issue movies for rental on VHS tapes to make its VHS format players valuable to consumers. The only way to do that, Matsushita's managers reasoned, was to increase the installed base of VHS players as rapidly as possible. They believed that the greater the installed base of VHS players, the greater the incentive would be for movie studios to issue movies for rental on VHS format tapes. The more prerecorded VHS tapes available for rental, the greater the value of a VHS player to consumers, and therefore, the greater the demand would be for VHS players (see Figure 7.2). Matsushita wanted to exploit a positive feedback loop.

To do this, Matsushita chose a licensing strategy under which any consumer electronics company was allowed to manufacture VHS format players under license. The strategy worked. A large number of companies agreed to manufacture VHS players,

FIGURE 7.2

Positive Feedback in the Market for VCRs

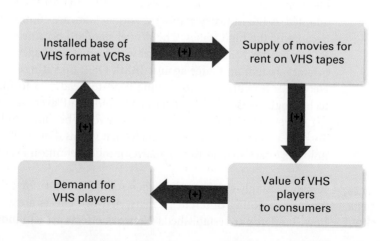

and soon far more VHS players were available for purchase in stores than Betamax players. As sales of VHS players started to grow, movie studios issued more films for rental in VHS format, and this stoked demand. Before long, it was clear to anyone who walked into a video rental store that there were more and more VHS tapes available for rent and fewer and fewer Betamax tapes. This served to reinforce the positive feedback loop, and ultimately Sony's Betamax technology was shut out of the market. The pivotal difference between the two companies was strategy: Matsushita chose a licensing strategy, and Sony did not. As a result, Matsushita's VHS technology became the de facto standard for VCRs, while Sony's Betamax technology was locked out.

The general principle that emerges from this example is that when two or more companies are competing with each other to get their technology adopted as a standard in an industry, and when network effects and positive feedback loops are important, the company that wins the format war will be the one whose strategy best exploits positive feedback loops. It turns out that this is a very important strategic principle in many high-technology industries, particularly computer hardware, software, telecommunications, and consumer electronics. Microsoft is where it is today because it exploited a positive feedback loop. So did Dolby (see Strategy in Action 7.1).

An important implication of the positive feedback process is that as the market settles on a standard, companies promoting alternative standards can become locked out of the market when consumers are unwilling to bear the switching costs required for them to abandon the established standard and adopt the new standard. In this context, switching costs are the costs that consumers must bear to switch from a product based on one technological standard to a product based on another.

To illustrate, imagine that a company developed an operating system for personal computers that was both faster and more stable (crashed less) than the current standard in the marketplace, Microsoft Windows. Would this company be able to gain significant market share from Microsoft? Only with great difficulty. Consumers buy personal computers not for their operating system but for the applications that run on that system. A new operating system would initially have a very small installed base, so few developers would be willing to take the risks in writing word-processing programs, spreadsheets, games, and other applications for that operating system. Because there would be very few applications available, consumers who did make the switch would have to bear the switching costs associated with giving up some of their applications—something that they might not be willing to do. Moreover, even if applications were available for the new operating system, consumers would have to bear the costs of purchasing those applications, another source of switching costs. In addition, they would have to bear the costs associated with learning to use the new operating system, yet another source of switching costs. Thus, many consumers would be unwilling to switch even if the new operating system performed better than Windows, and the company promoting the new operating system would thus be locked out of the market.

Consumers will bear switching costs if the benefits of adopting the new technology outweigh the costs of switching. For example, in the late 1980s and early 1990s, millions of people switched from analog record players to digital CD players even though the switching costs were significant: they had to purchase the new player technology, and many people purchased duplicate copies of their favorite music recordings. They nevertheless made the switch because for many people, the perceived benefit—the incredibly better sound quality associated with CDs—outweighed the costs of switching.

Strategy in Action

How Dolby Became the Standard in Sound Technology

Inventor Ray Dolby's name has become synonymous with superior sound in homes, movie theaters, and recording studios. The technology produced by his company, Dolby Laboratories, is part of nearly every music cassette and cassette recorder; prerecorded videotape; and, most recently, DVD movie disk and player. Since 1976, close to 1.5 billion audio products that use Dolby's technology have been sold worldwide. More than 44,000 movie theaters now show films in Dolby Digital Surround Sound, and some 50 million Dolby Digital home theater receivers have been sold since 1999. Dolby technology has become the de facto industry standard for high-quality sound in the music and film industry. How did Dolby build this technology franchise?

The story goes back to 1965, when Dolby Laboratories was founded in London by Ray Dolby (the company's headquarters moved to San Francisco in 1976). Dolby, who had a Ph.D. in physics from Cambridge University in England, had invented a technology for reducing the background hiss in professional tape recording without compromising the quality of the material being recorded. In 1968, Dolby reached an agreement to license his noise-reduction technology to KLH, a highly regarded American producer of audio equipment (record players and tape decks) for the consumer market. Soon other manufacturers of consumer equipment started to approach Dolby to license the technology. Dolby briefly considered manufacturing record players and tape decks for the consumer market, but as he later commented, "I knew that if we entered that market and tried to make something like a cassette deck, we would be in competition with any licensee that we took on. . . . So we had to stay out of manufacturing in that area in order to license in that area."

Dolby adopted a licensing business model and then had to determine what licensing fee to charge. He decided to charge a modest fee to reduce the incentive that manufacturers would have to develop their own technology. Then there was the question of which companies to license to. Dolby wanted the Dolby name associated with superior sound, so he needed to make sure that licensees adhered to quality standards. Therefore, the company set up a formal quality control program for its licensees' products. Licensees have to agree to have their products tested by Dolby, and the licensing agreement states that they cannot sell products that do not pass Dolby's quality tests. By preventing products with substandard performance from reaching the market, Dolby has maintained the quality image of products featuring Dolby technology and trademarks. Today, Dolby Laboratories tests samples of hundreds of licensed products every year under this program. By making sure that the Dolby name is associated with superior sound quality, Dolby's quality assurance strategy has increased the power of the Dolby brand, making it very valuable to license.

Another key aspect of Dolby's strategy was born in 1970 when Dolby began to promote the idea of releasing prerecorded cassettes encoded with Dolby noise-reduction technology so that they would have low noise when played on players equipped with Dolby noise-reduction technology. Dolby decided to license the technology on prerecorded tapes for free, instead collecting licensing fees just from the sales of tape players that used Dolby technology. This strategy was hugely successful and set up a positive feedback loop that helped to make Dolby technology ubiquitous. Growing sales of prerecorded tapes encoded with Dolby technology created a demand for players that contained Dolby technology, and as the installed base of players with Dolby technology grew, the proportion of prerecorded tapes that were encoded with Dolby technology surged, further boosting demand for players incorporating Dolby technology. By the mid-1970s, almost all prerecorded tapes were encoded with Dolby noise-reduction technology. This strategy remains in effect today for all media recorded with Dolby technology and encompasses not only videocassettes but also videogames and DVD releases encoded with Dolby Surround or Dolby Digital.

As a result of its licensing and quality assurance strategies, Dolby has become the standard for high-quality sound in the music and film industries. Although the company is small—its revenues were $327 million in 2005—its influence is large. It continues to push the boundaries of sound-reduction technology (it has been a leader in digital sound since the mid-1980s) and has successfully extended its noise-reduction franchise, first into films, then into DVD and videogame technology, and finally onto the Web, where it has licensed its digital technology to a wide range of media companies for digital music delivery and digital audio players, such as those built into personal computers and hand-held music players. Dolby has also licensed its technology for use in next-generation DVD players—high-definition DVDs.[a]

As this process started to get under way, a positive feedback loop started to develop, with the growing installed base of CD players leading to an increase in the number of music recordings issued on CDs, as opposed to or in addition to vinyl records. Past some point, the installed base of CD players got so big that music companies started to issue recordings only on CDs. Once this happened, even those who did not want to switch to the new technology were required to if they wished to purchase new music recordings. The industry standard had shifted: the new technology had locked in as the standard, and the old technology was locked out. It follows that despite its dominance, the Wintel standard for personal computers could one day be superseded if a competitor finds a way of providing sufficient benefits that enough consumers are willing to bear the switching costs associated with moving to a new operating system.

Strategies for Winning a Format War

From the perspective of a company pioneering a new technological standard in a marketplace where network effects and positive feedback loops operate, the key question becomes, "What strategy should we pursue to establish our format as the dominant one?" The various strategies that companies should adopt to win format wars revolve around *finding ways to make network effects work in their favor and against their competitors*. Winning a format war requires a company to build the installed base for its standard as rapidly as possible, thereby leveraging the positive feedback loop, inducing consumers to bear switching costs, and ultimately locking the market into its technology. It requires the company to jump-start and then accelerate demand for its technological standard or format so that it becomes established as quickly as possible as the industry standard, thereby locking out competing formats. Several key strategies and tactics can be adopted to try to achieve this.[6]

● **Ensure a Supply of Complements**

It is important for the company to make sure that, in addition to the product itself, there is an adequate supply of complements. For example, no one will buy the Sony PlayStation 3 unless there is an adequate supply of games to run on that machine. And no one will purchase a Palm hand-held computer unless there are enough software applications to run on it. Companies normally take two steps to ensure an adequate supply of complements.

First, they may diversify into the production of complements and seed the market with sufficient supply to help jump-start demand for their format. Before Sony produced the original PlayStation in the early 1990s, it established its own in-house unit to produce videogames for the PlayStation. When it launched the PlayStation, Sony also simultaneously issued sixteen games to run on the machine, giving consumers a reason to purchase the format. Second, companies may create incentives or make it easy for independent companies to produce complements. Sony also licensed the right to produce games to a number of independent game developers, charged the developers a lower royalty rate than they had to pay to competitors such as Nintendo and Sega, and provided them with software tools that made it easier for them to develop the games. Thus, the launch of the Sony PlayStation was accompanied by the simultaneous launch of thirty or so games, which quickly helped to stimulate demand for the machine.

● **Leverage Killer Applications**

Killer applications are applications or uses of a new technology or product that are so compelling that they persuade customers to adopt the new format or technology in droves, thereby "killing" demand for competing formats. Killer applications often help to jump-start demand for the new standard. For example, in the late 1990s, hand-held computers based on the Palm operating system became the dominant format in the market for personal digital assistants (PDAs). The killer applications that drove adoption of the Palm format were the personal information management functions and a pen-based input medium (based on Graffiti) that Palm bundled with its original PalmPilot, which it introduced in 1996. There had been PDAs before the PalmPilot, including Apple Computer's ill-fated Newton, but the applications and ease of use of the PalmPilot persuaded many consumers to enter this market. Within eighteen months of its initial launch, more than 1 million PalmPilots had been sold, making for a faster demand ramp-up than occurred for the first cell phones and pagers. Similarly, the killer applications that induced consumers to sign up for online services such as AOL were email, chatrooms, and the ability to browse the Web.

Ideally, the company promoting a technological standard will want to develop the killer applications itself—that is, develop the appropriate complementary products, as Palm did with the PalmPilot. However, it may also be able to leverage the applications that others develop. For example, the early sales of the IBM PC following its 1981 introduction were driven primarily by IBM's decision to license two important software programs for the PC, VisiCalc (a spreadsheet program) and Easy Writer (a word-processing program), both developed by independent companies. IBM saw that they were driving rapid adoption of rival personal computers, such as the Apple II, so it quickly licensed them, produced versions that would run on the IBM PC, and sold them as complements to the IBM PC, a strategy that was to prove very successful.

Aggressively Price and Market

A common tactic to jump-start demand is to adopt a **razor and blade strategy**: pricing the product (razor) low in order to stimulate demand and increase the installed base, and then trying to make high profits on the sale of complements (razor blades), which are priced relatively high. This strategy owes its name to the fact that it was pioneered by Gillette to sell its razors and razor blades. Many other companies have followed this strategy—for example, Hewlett-Packard typically sells its printers at cost but makes significant profits on the subsequent sale of its replacement cartridges. In this case, the printer is the "razor," and it is priced low to stimulate demand and induce consumers to switch from their existing printer; the cartridges are the "blades," which are priced high to make profits. The inkjet printer represents a proprietary technological format because only Hewlett-Packard cartridges can be used with the printers, and not cartridges designed for competing inkjet printers, such as those sold by Canon. A similar strategy is used in the videogame industry: manufacturers price videogame consoles at cost to induce consumers to adopt their technology, while making profits on the royalties they receive from the sales of games that run on their system.

Aggressive marketing is also a key factor in jump-starting demand to get an early lead in an installed base. Substantial upfront marketing and point-of-sales promotion techniques are often used to try to get potential early adopters to bear the switching costs associated with adopting the format. If these efforts are successful, they can be the start of a positive feedback loop. Again, the Sony PlayStation provides a good example. Sony linked the introduction of the PlayStation with nationwide television advertising aimed at its primary demographic (eighteen- to thirty-four-year-olds) and in-store displays that allowed potential buyers to play games on the machine before making a purchase.

Cooperate with Competitors

Companies have been close to simultaneously introducing competing and incompatible technological standards a number of times. A good example is the compact disk. Initially four companies—Sony, Philips, JVC, and Telefunken—were developing CD players using different variations of the underlying laser technology. If this situation had persisted, they might have ultimately introduced incompatible technologies into the marketplace, so a CD made for a Philips CD player would not play on a Sony CD player. Understanding that the nearly simultaneous introduction of such incompatible technologies can create significant confusion among consumers and often leads them to delay their purchases, Sony and Philips decided to join forces with each other and cooperate on developing the technology. Sony contributed its error-correction technology, and Philips contributed its laser technology. The result of this cooperation was that momentum among other players in the industry shifted toward the Sony-Philips alliances; JVC and Telefunken were left with little support. Most importantly, recording labels announced that they would support the Sony-Philips format but not the Telefunken or JVC format. Telefunken and JVC subsequently decided to abandon their efforts to develop CD technology. The cooperation between Sony and Philips was important because it reduced confusion in the industry and allowed a single format to come to the fore, which speeded up adoption of the technology. The cooperation was a win-win situation for both Philips and Sony, which eliminated the competitors and allowed them to share in the success of the format.

● **License the Format**   Another strategy often adopted is to license the format to other enterprises so that they can produce products based on it. The company that pioneered the format gains from the licensing fees and from the enlarged supply of the product, which can stimulate demand and help accelerate market adoption. This was the strategy that Matsushita adopted with its VHS format for the videocassette recorder. In addition to producing VCRs at its own factory in Osaka, Matsushita let a number of other companies produce VHS format players under license (Sony decided not to license its competing Betamax format and produced all Betamax format players itself), and so VHS players were more widely available. More people purchased VHS players, which created an incentive for film companies to issue more films on VHS tapes (as opposed to Betamax tapes), which further increased demand for VHS players, and hence helped Matsushita to lock in VHS as the dominant format in the marketplace. Sony, ironically the first to market, saw its position marginalized by the reduced supply of the critical complement, prerecorded films, and ultimately withdrew Betamax players from the consumer marketplace.

As we saw in Strategy in Action 7.1, Dolby adopted a similar licensing strategy to get its noise-reduction technology adopted as the technological standard in the music and film industries. By charging a modest licensing fee for use of the technology in recording equipment and forgoing licensing fees on media recorded using Dolby technology, Dolby deliberately sought to reduce the financial incentive that potential competitors might have to develop their own, possibly superior, technology. Dolby calculated that its long-run profitability would be maximized by adopting a licensing strategy that limited the incentive of competitors to enter the market.

The correct strategy to pursue in a particular scenario requires that the company consider all of these different strategies and tactics and pursue those that seem most appropriate given the competitive circumstances prevailing in the industry and the likely strategy of rivals. Although no mix of strategies and tactics can be called the best, the company must keep the goal of rapidly increasing the installed base of products based on its standard as the primary goal. By helping to jump-start demand for its format, a company can induce consumers to bear the switching costs associated with adopting its technology and leverage any positive feedback process that might exist. Also important is not pursuing strategies that have the opposite effect. For example, pricing high to capture profits from early adopters, who tend not to be as price sensitive as later adopters, can have the unfortunate effect of slowing demand growth and letting a more aggressive competitor pick up market share and establish its format as the industry standard.

Costs in High-Technology Industries

In many high-tech industries, the fixed costs of developing the product are very high, but the costs of producing one extra unit of the product are very low. This is most obvious in the case of software. For example, it reportedly cost Microsoft $5 billion to develop Windows Vista, the latest version of its Windows operating system, but the cost of producing one more copy of Windows Vista is virtually zero. Once Windows Vista was completed, Microsoft produced master disks that it sent out to PC manufacturers, such as Dell Computer, which then loaded a copy of Windows Vista onto every PC it sold. The cost to Microsoft was effectively zero, and yet it receives a significant licensing fee for each copy of Windows Vista installed on a PC.[7] For Microsoft, the marginal cost of making one more copy of Windows Vista is close to zero, although the fixed costs of developing the product are $5 billion.

Many other high-technology products have similar cost economics: very high fixed costs and very low marginal costs. Most software products share these features, although if the software is sold through stores, the costs of packaging and distribution will raise the marginal costs, and if it is sold by a sales force direct to end-users, this too will raise the marginal costs. Many consumer electronics products have the same basic economics. The fixed costs of developing a DVD player or a videogame console can be very expensive, but the costs of producing an incremental unit are very low. The costs of developing a new drug, such as Viagra, can run to over $800 million, but the marginal cost of producing each additional pill is at most a few cents.

● **Comparative Cost Economics**

To grasp why this cost structure is strategically important, a company must understand that, in many industries, marginal costs rise as a company tries to expand output (economists call this the *law of diminishing returns*). To produce more of a good, a company has to hire more labor and invest in more plant and machinery. At the margin, the additional resources used are not as productive, so this leads to increasing marginal costs. However, the law of diminishing returns often does not apply in many high-tech settings, such as the production of software or sending one more bit of data down a digital telecommunications network.

Consider two companies, α and β (see Figure 7.3). Company α is a conventional producer and faces diminishing returns, so as it tries to expand output, its marginal costs rise. Company β is a high-tech producer, and its marginal costs do not rise at all as output is increased. Note that in Figure 7.3, company β's marginal cost curve is drawn as a straight line near the horizontal axis, implying that marginal costs are close to zero and do not vary with output, whereas company α's marginal costs rise as output is expanded, illustrating diminishing returns. Company β's flat and low marginal cost curve means that its average cost curve will fall continuously over all ranges of output as it spreads its fixed costs out over greater volume. In contrast, the rising marginal costs encountered by company α mean that its average cost curve is the U-shaped curve familiar from basic economics texts. For simplicity, assume that both companies sell their product at the same price, Pm, and both sell exactly the same quantity of output, 0 (Q1). You can see from Figure 7.3 that at an output of Q1, company β has much lower average costs than company α and as a consequence is making far more profit (profit is the shaded area in Figure 7.3).

FIGURE 7.3

Cost Structures in High-Technology Industries

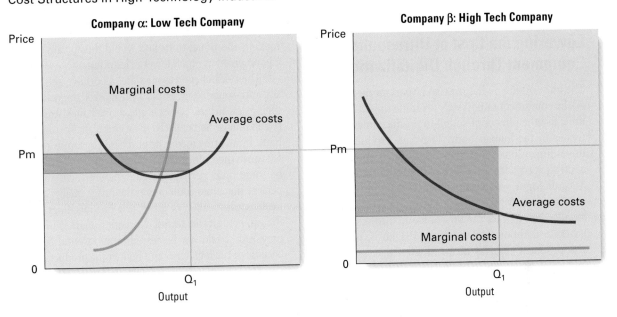

Strategic Significance

If a company can shift from a cost structure where it encounters increasing marginal costs to one where fixed costs may be high but marginal costs are much lower, its profitability may increase. In the consumer electronics industry, such a shift has been playing out for two decades. Music recordings used to be based on analog technology, where marginal costs rose as output expanded due to diminishing returns (as in the case of company α in Figure 7.3). Since the 1980s, digital systems such as CD players have replaced analog systems. Digital systems are software based, and this implies much lower marginal costs of producing one more copy of a recording. As a result, the music labels have been able to lower prices, expand demand, and see their profitability increase (their production system has more in common with company β in Figure 7.3).

This process is still unfolding. The latest technology for making copies of music recordings is based on distribution over the Internet (for example, by downloading onto an iPod). Here, the marginal costs of making one more copy of a recording are lower still. In fact, they are close to zero and do not increase with output. The only problem is that the low costs of copying and distributing music recordings have created a copyright problem that the major music labels have yet to solve (we discuss this in more detail shortly when we consider intellectual property rights). The same shift is now beginning to affect other industries. Some companies are building their strategies around trying to exploit and profit from this shift. For an example, see Strategy in Action 7.2, which looks at SonoSite.

When a high-tech company faces high fixed costs and low marginal costs, its strategy should emphasize the low-cost option: deliberately drive prices down to drive volume up. Look again at Figure 7.3 and you will see that the high-tech company's average costs fall rapidly as output expands. This implies that prices can be reduced to stimulate demand, and as long as prices fall less rapidly than average costs, per-unit profit margins will expand as prices fall. This is a consequence of the fact

Strategy in Action

Lowering the Cost of Ultrasound Equipment Through Digitalization

The ultrasound unit has been an important piece of diagnostic equipment in hospitals for some time. Ultrasound units use the physics of sound to produce images of soft tissues in the human body. They can produce detailed three-dimensional color images of organs and, by using contrast agents, track the flow of fluids through an organ. A cardiologist, for example, can use an ultrasound in combination with contrast agents injected into the bloodstream to track the flow of blood through a beating heart. In additional to the visual diagnosis, ultrasound also produces an array of quantitative diagnostic information of great value to physicians.

Modern ultrasound units are sophisticated instruments that cost around $250,000 to $300,000 each for a top-line model. They are fairly bulky instruments, weighing some 300 pounds, and are wheeled around hospitals on carts.

A few years back, a group of researchers at ATL, one of the leading ultrasound companies, came up with an idea for reducing the size and cost of a basic unit. They theorized that it might be possible to replace up to 80% of the solid circuits in an ultrasound unit with software, in the process significantly shrinking the size and reducing the weight of machines and thereby producing portable ultrasound units. Moreover, by digitalizing much of the ultrasound (replacing hardware with software), they could considerably drive down the marginal costs of

making additional units and would thus be able to make a good profit at much lower price points.

The researchers reasoned that a portable and inexpensive ultrasound unit would find market opportunities in totally new niches. For example, a small, inexpensive ultrasound unit could be placed in an ambulance or carried into battle by an army medic, or purchased by family physicians for use in their offices. Although they realized that it would be some time, perhaps decades, before such small, inexpensive machines could attain the image quality and diagnostic sophistication of top-of-the-line machines, they saw the opportunity in terms of creating market niches that previously could not be served by ultrasound companies because of the high costs and bulk of the product.

The researchers ultimately became a project team within ATL and were then spun out of ATL as an entirely new company, SonoSite. In late 1999, they introduced their first portable product, weighing just six pounds and costing around $25,000. SonoSite targeted niches that full-sized ultrasound products could not reach: ambulatory care and foreign markets that could not afford the more expensive equipment. In 2005, the company sold $150 million worth of its product.

In the long run, SonoSite plans to build more features and greater image quality into the small hand-held machines, primarily by improving the software. This could allow the units to penetrate U.S. hospital markets that currently purchase the established technology, much as client-server systems based on PC technology came to replace mainframes for some functions in business corporations.[b]

that the firm's marginal costs are low and do not rise with output. This strategy of pricing low to drive volume up and reap wider profit margins is central to the business model of some very successful high-technology companies, including Microsoft.

Managing Intellectual Property Rights

Ownership of a technology can be a source of sustained competitive advantage and superior profitability, particularly when the company owns a technology that is the standard in an industry, such as Microsoft and Intel's Wintel standard for personal computers and Dolby's ownership of the standard for noise-reduction technology in the music and film recording industries. Even if a technology is not standard but is valued by a sufficient number of consumers, ownership of that technology can still be very profitable. Apple's current personal computer technology is by no means the standard in the marketplace, much as Apple would like it to be. In fact, the company's iMac technology accounted for only about 5% of the personal computers sold in 2006. But that small slice of a very large market is still a valuable niche for Apple.

● Intellectual Property Rights

Because new technology is the product of intellectual and creative effort, we call it intellectual property. The term **intellectual property** refers to the product of any intellectual and creative effort and includes not only new technology but also a wide range of intellectual creations, including music, films, books, and graphic art. As a society, we value the products of intellectual and creative activity. Intellectual property is seen as a very important driver of economic progress and social wealth.[8] But it is also often expensive, risky, and time-consuming to create intellectual property.

For example, a new drug to treat a dangerous medical condition such as cancer can take twelve to sixteen years to develop and cost as much as $800 million. Moreover, only 20% of new drugs that are tested in humans actually make it to the market.[9] The remainder of these drugs fail because they are found to be unsafe or ineffective. Given the costs, risks, and time involved in this activity, few companies would be willing to develop a new drug and bring it to market unless they could be reasonably sure that if they were successful in developing the drug, their investment would be profitable. If the minute they introduced a successful cancer drug, their competitors produced imitations of that drug, no company would even consider making the initial investment.

To make sure that this does not happen, we grant the creators of intellectual property certain rights over their creation. These rights, which stop competitors from copying or imitating the creation for a number of years, take the legal forms of patents, copyrights, and trademarks, which all serve the same basic objective: to give individuals and companies an incentive to engage in the expensive and risky business of creating new intellectual property.

The creation of intellectual property is a central endeavor in high-technology industries, and the management of intellectual property rights has moved to center stage in many of these companies. Developing strategies to protect and enforce intellectual property rights can be an important aspect of competitive advantage. For many companies, this amounts to making sure that their patents and copyrights are respected. It is not uncommon, therefore, to see high-technology companies bringing lawsuits against their competitors for patent infringement. In general, companies often use such lawsuits not only to sanction those they suspect of violating the company's intellectual property rights, but also to signal to potential violators that the company will aggressively defend its property. Legal action alone suffices to protect intellectual property in many industries, but in others, such as software, the low costs of illegally copying and distributing intellectual property call for more creative strategies to manage intellectual property rights.

● Digitalization and Piracy Rates

Protecting intellectual property has become more complicated in the past few decades because of **digitalization**, that is, the rendering of creative output in digital form. This can be done for music recordings, films, books, newspapers, magazines, and computer software. Digitalization has dramatically lowered the cost of copying and distributing digitalized intellectual property or digital media. As we have seen, the marginal cost of making one more copy of a software program is very low, and the same is true for any other intellectual property rendered in digital form. Moreover, digital media can be distributed at a very low cost (again, almost zero), for example, by distributing over the Internet. Reflecting on this, one commentator has described the

Internet as a "giant out-of-control copying machine."[10] The low marginal costs of copying and distributing digital media have made it very easy to sell illegal copies of such property. In turn, this has helped to produce a high level of piracy (in this context, piracy refers to the theft of intellectual property).

The International Federation of the Phonographic Industry claims that about one-third of all recorded music products sold worldwide in 2005 were pirated (illegal) copies, suggesting that piracy costs the industry over $4.5 billion annually.[11] The computer software industry also suffers from lax enforcement of intellectual property rights. Estimates suggest that violations of intellectual property rights cost personal computer software firms revenues equal to $35 billion in 2005.[12] According to the Business Software Alliance, a software industry association, in 2005, some 35% of all software applications used in the world were pirated. The worst region was Latin America, where the piracy rate was 68% (see Figure 2.2). One of the worst countries was China, where the piracy rate in 2005 ran at 86% and cost the industry more than $3.9 billion in lost sales, up from $444 million in 1995. Although at 21% the piracy rate was much lower in the United States, the value of sales lost was more significant because of the size of the market, reaching an estimated $6.9 billion in 2005.[13]

The scale of this problem is so large that simply resorting to legal tactics to enforce intellectual property rights has amounted to nothing more than a partial solution to the piracy problem. Many companies now build sophisticated encryption software into their digital products, which can make it more difficult for pirates to copy digital media and thereby can raise the costs of stealing. But the pirates too are sophisticated and often seem to be able to find their way around encryption software. This raises the question of whether there are additional strategies that can be adopted to manage digital rights and thereby limit piracy.

● **Strategies for Managing Digital Rights**

One strategy is simply to recognize that while the low costs of copying and distributing digital media make some piracy inevitable, the same attributes can be used to the company's advantage.[14] The basic strategy here represents yet another variation of the basic razor and blades principle: give something away for free to boost the sales of a complementary product. A familiar example concerns Adobe Acrobat Reader, the software program for reading documents formatted by Adobe Acrobat (that is, PDF-formatted documents). Adobe developed Adobe Acrobat to allow people to format documents in a manner that resembled a high-quality printed page and to display and distribute these documents over the Web. Moreover, Adobe documents are formatted in a read-only format, meaning that they cannot be altered by individuals, nor can parts of those documents be copied and pasted to other documents. Its strategy has been to give away Adobe Acrobat Reader for free and then make money by selling its Acrobat software for formatting documents. The strategy has worked extremely well. Anyone can download a copy of Acrobat Reader from Adobe's website. Because the marginal costs of copying and distributing this software over the Web are extremely low, the process is almost free for both Adobe and its customers. The result is that the Acrobat Reader has diffused very rapidly and is now the dominant format for viewing high-quality documents distributed and downloaded over the Web. As the installed base of Acrobat Readers has grown, sales of Adobe Acrobat software have soared as more and more organizations and individuals realize that formatting their digital documents in Acrobat makes sense.

Another strategy is to take advantage of the low costs of copying and distributing digital media to drive down the costs of purchasing those media, thereby reducing the incentive that consumers have to steal. When coupled with encryption software that makes piracy more difficult and vigorous legal actions to enforce intellectual property regulations, this can slow the piracy rate and generate incremental revenues that cost little to produce. A third strategy might be to alter the firm's business model in a way that makes piracy more difficult. As discussed in Strategy in Action 7.3, the videogame industry has seen a shift from selling games outright, to renting them online.

Strategy in Action   7.3

Battling Piracy in the Videogame Industry

Over the past decade, the videogame industry has grown into a global colossus worth more than $25 billion a year in revenues. For the three biggest players in the industry, Sony with its PlayStation, Microsoft with Xbox, and Nintendo, this potentially represents a huge growth engine, but the engine is threatened by a rise in piracy, which cost the videogame industry an estimated $4 billion in 2005.

The piracy problem is particularly serious in East Asia (except for Japan), where videogame consoles are routinely "chipped"—sold with modified chips, called mod chips, that override the console's security system, allowing it to play illegally copied games and CDs. Importers or resellers, who charge a small markup for making the modification, illegally install the mod chips. In some areas, such as Hong Kong, it is almost impossible to find a console that hasn't been modified.

Because they allow users to play illegally copied games, consoles with mod chips offer a gaping gateway for software pirates, and they directly threaten the profitability of console and game makers. The big three in the industry all follow a razor and blades business model, where the console (razor) is sold at a loss, and profit is made on the sale of the game (razor blades). In the case of Microsoft's Xbox, estimates suggest the company loses as much as $200 on each Xbox it sells. To make profits, Microsoft collects royalties on the sale of games developed under license, in addition to producing and selling some games itself. Games typically retail for about $50, and Microsoft must sell six to twelve games to each Xbox user to recoup the $200 loss on the initial sale and start making a profit. If those users are purchasing pirated games and playing them on "chipped" Xbox consoles, Microsoft collects nothing in royalties and may never reach the breakeven point. Sony and Nintendo face similar problems. In East Asia, some 70% of game software sold in the region may be pirated thanks to the popularity of "chipped" consoles and the low price of pirated games, which may sell for one-third the price of the legal game.

Historically, all the big videogame companies tried to deal with the piracy problem in East Asia by ignoring the market. Sony launched its PlayStation II in East Asia two years after its Japanese launch, and Microsoft delayed its East Asian launch for a year after it launched elsewhere in the world. But this tactic is increasingly questionable in a region where there may soon be more gamers than in the United States. Industry estimates suggest that Asian gamers spent more on videogame software in 2005 than U.S. gamers did, much of it on low-priced pirated games.

Another tactic that both Sony and Microsoft are now using is to regularly alter the hardware specifications of its consoles, rendering the existing mod chips useless. But the companies have found this is just a temporary solution: within a few weeks, mod chips made to override the new specifications are available on the market.

A third tactic is to push local authorities to legally enforce existing intellectual property rights law that in theory outlaws the mod chip practice. For example, Microsoft, Sony, and Nintendo joined forces to sue the Hong Kong company, Lik Sang, which sells mod chips through its website and is one of the world's largest distributors of the chips. Some observers question the value of this tactic, however; they argue that if Lik Sang is shut down, many others in Hong Kong may be willing to take its place. What is needed, they argue, is concerted government action to stop the pirates, and so far East Asian governments have not been quick to act.

A final way of dealing with piracy is to change the business model. All three main players in the industry are now starting to push online games, where customers pay a subscription fee to play online, as opposed to a one-time fee to purchase a game. This business model makes piracy much less of an issue and it may drive growth forward in places like China, where piracy is endemic. Indeed, current estimates suggest that there are already 29 million gamers in China, most of whom play pirated games, and that this figure will increase to 55 million by 2009. If a good percentage switch to online gaming, the revenues could be significant.[c]

Capturing First-Mover Advantages

In high-technology industries, companies often compete by striving to be the first to develop revolutionary new products, that is, to be a **first mover**. By definition, the first mover, with regard to a revolutionary product, is in a monopoly position. If the new product satisfies unmet consumer needs and demand is high, the first mover can capture significant revenues and profits. Such revenues and profits signal to potential rivals that there is money to be made by imitating the first mover. As illustrated in Figure 7.4, in the absence of strong barriers to imitation, this implies that imitators will rush into the market created by the first mover, competing for the first mover's monopoly profits and leaving all participants in the market with a much lower level of returns.

Despite imitation, some first movers have the ability to capitalize on and reap substantial first-mover advantages—the advantages of pioneering new technologies and products that lead to an enduring competitive advantage. Intel introduced the world's first microprocessor in 1971 and today still dominates the microprocessor segment of the semiconductor industry. Xerox introduced the world's first photocopier and for a long time enjoyed a leading position in the industry. Cisco introduced the first Internet protocol network router in 1986 and still dominates the market for that equipment today. Some first movers can reap substantial advantages from their pioneering activities that lead to an enduring competitive advantage. They can, in other words, limit or slow the rate of imitation.

But there are plenty of counterexamples suggesting that first-mover advantages might not be easy to capture and, in fact, that there might be **first-mover disadvantages**—the competitive disadvantages associated with being first. For example, Apple Computer was the first company to introduce a hand-held computer, the Apple Newton, but the product failed; a second mover, Palm, succeeded where Apple had failed. In the market for commercial jet aircraft, DeHavilland was first to market with the Comet, but the second mover, Boeing, with its 707 jetliner, went on to dominate the market.

Clearly, being a first mover does not by itself guarantee success. As we shall see, the difference between innovating companies that capture first-mover advantages and those that fall victim to first-mover disadvantages in part turns on the strategy that the first mover pursues. Before considering the strategy issue, however, we need to take a closer look at the nature of first-mover advantages and disadvantages.[15]

FIGURE 7.4

The Impact of Imitation on the Profits of a First Mover

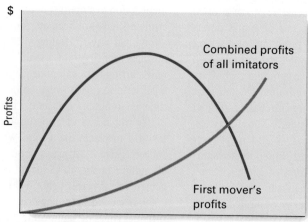

● **First-Mover
Advantages**

There are five main sources of first-mover advantages.[16] First, the first mover has an opportunity to exploit network effects and positive feedback loops, locking consumers into its technology. In the VCR industry, Sony could have exploited network effects by licensing its technology, but instead the company ceded its first-mover advantage to the second mover, Matsushita.

Second, the first mover may be able to establish significant brand loyalty, which is expensive for later entrants to break down. Indeed, if the company is successful in this endeavor, its name may become closely associated with the entire class of products, including those produced by rivals. People still talk of "Xeroxing" when they are going to make a photocopy or "FedExing" when they are going to send a package by overnight delivery.

Third, the first mover may be able to ramp up sales volume ahead of rivals and thus reap cost advantages associated with the realization of scale economies and learning effects (see Chapter 4). Once the first mover has these cost advantages, it can respond to new entrants by cutting prices to hold on to its market share and still earn significant profits.

Fourth, the first mover may be able to create switching costs for its customers that subsequently make it difficult for rivals to enter the market and take customers away from the first mover. Wireless service providers, for example, will give new customers a "free" wireless phone, but customers must sign a contract agreeing to pay for the phone if they terminate the service contract within a specified time period, such as a year. Because the real cost of a wireless phone may run from $100 to $200, this represents a significant switching cost that later entrants have to overcome.

Finally, the first mover may be able to accumulate valuable knowledge related to customer needs, distribution channels, product technology, process technology, and so on. This accumulated knowledge gives it a knowledge advantage that later entrants might find difficult or expensive to match. Sharp, for example, was the first mover in the commercial manufacture of active matrix liquid crystal displays used in laptop computers. The process for manufacturing these displays is very difficult, with a high reject rate for flawed displays. Sharp has accumulated such an advantage with regard to production processes that it has been very difficult for later entrants to match it on product quality, and thus costs.

● **First-Mover
Disadvantages**

Balanced against these first-mover advantages are a number of disadvantages.[17] First, the first mover has to bear significant pioneering costs that later entrants do not. The first mover has to pioneer the technology, develop distribution channels, and educate customers about the nature of the product. All of this can be expensive and time-consuming. Later entrants, by way of contrast, might be able to free-ride on the first mover's investments in pioneering the market and customer education.

Related to this, first movers are more prone to make mistakes because there are so many uncertainties in a new market. Later entrants may be able to learn from the mistakes made by first movers, improve on the product or the way in which it is sold, and come to market with a superior offering that captures significant market share from the first mover. For example, one of the reasons that the Apple Newton failed was that the handwriting software in the hand-held computer failed to recognize human handwriting. The second mover in this market, Palm, learned from Apple's error. When it introduced the PalmPilot, it used software that recognized letters written in a particular way, Graffiti, and then persuaded customers to learn this method of inputting data into the hand-held computer.

Third, first movers run the risk of building the wrong resources and capabilities because they are focusing on a customer set that is not going to be characteristic of the mass market. This is the crossing-the-chasm problem that we discussed in the previous chapter. Recall that the customers in the early market—those we categorized as innovators and early adopters—have different characteristics from the first wave of the mass market, the early majority. The first mover runs the risk of gearing its resources and capabilities to the needs of innovators and early adopters and not being able to switch when members of the early majority enter the market. As a result, first movers run a greater risk of plunging into the chasm that separates the early market from the mass market.

Finally, the first mover may invest in inferior or obsolete technology. This can happen when its product innovation is based on underlying technology that is advancing rapidly. By basing its product on an early version of the technology, it may lock itself into something that rapidly becomes obsolete. In contrast, later entrants may be able to leapfrog the first mover and introduce products that are based on later versions of the underlying technology. This happened in France during the 1980s when, at the urging of the government, France Telecom introduced the world's first consumer online service, Minitel. France Telecom distributed crude terminals to consumers for free, which they could hook up to their phone line and use to browse phone directories. Other simple services were soon added, and before long the French could conduct online shopping, banking, travel, weather, and news—all years before the Web was invented. The problem was that by the standards of the Web, Minitel was very crude and inflexible, and France Telecom, as the first mover, suffered. The French were very slow to adopt personal computers and then the Internet primarily because Minitel had such a presence. As late as 1998, only one-fifth of French households had a computer, compared with two-fifths in the United States, and only 2% of households were connected to the Internet, compared to over 30% in the United States. As the result of a government decision, France Telecom, and indeed an entire nation, was slow to adopt a revolutionary new online medium, the Web, because they were the first to invest in a more primitive version of the technology.[18]

Strategies for Exploiting First-Mover Advantages

The task facing a first mover is how to exploit its lead to capitalize on first-mover advantages and build a sustainable long-term competitive advantage while simultaneously reducing the risks associated with first-mover disadvantages. There are three basic strategies available: (1) develop and market the innovation itself, (2) develop and market the innovation jointly with other companies through a strategic alliance or joint venture, and (3) license the innovation to others and let them develop the market.

The optimal choice of strategy depends on the answers to three questions:

1. Does the innovating company have the complementary assets to exploit its innovation and capture first-mover advantages?

2. How difficult is it for imitators to copy the company's innovation? In other words, what is the height of the barriers to imitation?

3. Are there capable competitors that could rapidly imitate the innovation?

COMPLEMENTARY ASSETS Complementary assets are the assets required to exploit a new innovation and gain a competitive advantage.[19] Among the most important complementary assets are competitive manufacturing facilities capable of handling rapid growth in customer demand while maintaining high product quality. State-of-the-art manufacturing facilities enable the first mover to move quickly down the experience curve without encountering production bottlenecks or problems with the quality of the product. The inability to satisfy demand because of these problems, however, creates the opportunity for imitators to enter the marketplace. For example, in 1998, Immunex was the first company to introduce a revolutionary new biological treatment for rheumatoid arthritis. Sales for this product, Enbrel, ramped up very rapidly, hitting $750 million in 2001. However, Immunex had not invested in sufficient manufacturing capacity. In mid-2000, it announced that it lacked the capacity to satisfy demand and that creating additional capacity would take at least two years. This manufacturing bottleneck gave the second mover in the market, Johnson & Johnson, the opportunity to expand demand for its product rapidly, which was outselling Enbrel by early 2002. Immunex's first-mover advantage had been partly eroded because it lacked an important complementary asset, the manufacturing capability required to satisfy demand.

Complementary assets also include marketing know-how, an adequate sales force, access to distribution systems, and an after-sales service and support network. All of these assets can help an innovator build brand loyalty and achieve market penetration more rapidly.[20] In turn, the resulting increases in volume facilitate more rapid movement down the experience curve and the attainment of a sustainable cost-based advantage due to scale economies and learning effects. One of the reasons that EMI, the first mover in the market for CT scanners, ultimately lost out to established medical equipment companies, such as GE Medical Systems, was that it lacked the marketing know-how, sales force, and distribution systems required to compete effectively in the world's largest market for medical equipment, the United States.

Developing complementary assets can be very expensive, and companies often need large infusions of capital for this purpose. That is why first movers often lose out to late movers that are large, successful companies in other industries with the resources to develop a presence in the new industry quickly. Microsoft and 3M exemplify companies that can move quickly to capitalize on the opportunities when other companies open up new product markets, such as compact disks or floppy disks. For example, although Netscape pioneered the market for Internet browsers with the Netscape Navigator, Microsoft's Internet Explorer ultimately dominated the market for Internet browsers.

HEIGHT OF BARRIERS TO IMITATION   Recall from Chapter 3 that barriers to imitation are factors that prevent rivals from imitating a company's distinctive competencies and innovations. Although ultimately any innovation can be copied, the higher the barriers are, the longer it takes for rivals to imitate, and the more time the first mover has to build an enduring competitive advantage.

Barriers to imitation give an innovator time to establish a competitive advantage and build more enduring barriers to entry in the newly created market. Patents, for example, are among the most widely used barriers to imitation. By protecting its photocopier technology with a thicket of patents, Xerox was able to delay any significant imitation of its product for seventeen years. However, patents are often easy to "invent around." For example, one study found that this happened to 60% of patented innovations within four years.[21] If patent protection is weak, a company might try to slow imitation by developing new products and processes in secret. The most famous example of this approach is Coca-Cola, which has kept the formula for Coke a secret for generations. But Coca-Cola's success in this regard is an exception. A study of 100 companies has estimated that proprietary information about a company's decision to develop a major new product or process is known to its rivals within about twelve to eighteen months of the original development decision.[22]

CAPABLE COMPETITORS **Capable competitors** are companies that can move quickly to imitate the pioneering company. Competitors' capability to imitate a pioneer's innovation depends primarily on two factors: (1) research and development (R&D) skills and (2) access to complementary assets. In general, the greater the number of capable competitors with access to the R&D skills and complementary assets needed to imitate an innovation, the more rapid imitation is likely to be.

In this context, R&D skills refer to the ability of rivals to reverse-engineer an innovation to find out how it works and quickly develop a comparable product. As an example, consider the CT scanner. GE bought one of the first CT scanners produced by EMI, and its technical experts reverse-engineered it. Despite the product's technological complexity, GE developed its own version, which allowed it to imitate EMI quickly and ultimately to replace EMI as the major supplier of CT scanners.

With regard to complementary assets, the access that rivals have to marketing, sales know-how, or manufacturing capabilities is one of the key determinants of the rate of imitation. If would-be imitators lack critical complementary assets, not only do they have to imitate the innovation, but they may also have to imitate the innovator's complementary assets. This is expensive, as AT&T discovered when it tried to enter the personal computer business in 1984. AT&T lacked the marketing assets (sales force and distribution systems) necessary to support personal computer products. The lack of these assets and the time it takes to build them partly explain why, four years after it entered the market, AT&T had lost $2.5 billion and still had not emerged as a viable contender. It subsequently pulled out of this business.

THREE INNOVATION STRATEGIES The way in which these three factors—complementary assets, height of barriers to imitation, and the capability of competitors—influence the choice of innovation strategy is summarized in Table 7.1. The competitive strategy of developing and marketing the innovation alone makes most sense when (1) the innovator has the complementary assets necessary to develop the innovation, (2) the barriers to imitating a new innovation are high, and (3) the number of capable competitors is limited. Complementary assets allow rapid development and promotion of the innovation. High barriers to imitation buy the innovator time to establish a competitive advantage and build enduring barriers to entry through brand loyalty or experience-based cost advantages. The fewer the capable competitors, the less likely it is that any one of them will succeed in circumventing barriers to imitation and quickly imitating the innovation.

TABLE 7.1

Strategies for Profiting from Innovation

Strategy	Does the Innovator Have the Required Complementary Assets?	What Is the Likely Height of Barriers to Imitation?	How Many Capable Competitors Exist in the Industry?
Going it alone	Yes	High	Very few
Entering into an alliance	No	High	Moderate number
Licensing the innovation	No	Low	Many

The competitive strategy of developing and marketing the innovation jointly with other companies through a strategic alliance or joint venture makes most sense when (1) the innovator lacks complementary assets, (2) barriers to imitation are high, and (3) there are several capable competitors. In such circumstances, it makes sense to enter into an alliance with a company that already has the complementary assets—in other words, with a capable competitor. Theoretically, such an alliance should prove to be mutually beneficial, and each partner can share in high profits that neither could earn on its own. Moreover, such a strategy has the benefit of co-opting a potential rival. For example, had EMI teamed up with a capable competitor to develop the market for CT scanners, such as GE Medical Systems, instead of going it alone, the company might not only have been able to build a more enduring competitive advantage, but it would also have co-opted a potentially powerful rival into its camp.

The third strategy, licensing, makes most sense when (1) the innovating company lacks the complementary assets, (2) barriers to imitation are low, and (3) there are many capable competitors. The combination of low barriers to imitation and many capable competitors makes rapid imitation almost certain. The innovator's lack of complementary assets further suggests that an imitator will soon capture the innovator's competitive advantage. Given these factors, and because rapid diffusion of the innovator's technology through imitation is inevitable, the innovator can at least share in some of the benefits of this diffusion by licensing its technology.[23] Moreover, by setting a relatively modest licensing fee, the innovator may be able to reduce the incentive that potential rivals have to develop their own competing, and possibly superior, technology. This seems to have been the strategy Dolby adopted to get its technology established as the standard for noise reduction in the music and film businesses (see Strategy in Action 7.1).

Technological Paradigm Shifts

Technological paradigm shifts occur when new technologies come along that revolutionize the structure of the industry, dramatically alter the nature of competition, and require companies to adopt new strategies to survive. A good example of a paradigm shift that is currently unfolding is the shift from chemical to digital photography (another example of digitalization). For over half a century, the large incumbent enterprises in the photographic industry such as Kodak and Fuji film have generated most of their revenues from selling and processing film using traditional silver halide technology. The rise of digital photography is a huge threat to their business models. Digital cameras do not use film, the mainstay of Kodak's and Fuji's business. Moreover, these cameras are more like specialized computers than conventional cameras and are thus based on scientific knowledge that Kodak and Fuji have little knowledge of. Although both Kodak and Fuji are investing heavily in the development of digital cameras, they are facing intense competition from companies such as Sony, Canon, and Hewlett-Packard, which have developed their own digital cameras; from software developers such as Adobe and Microsoft, which make the software for manipulating digital images; and from printer companies such as Hewlett-Packard and Canon, which are making the printers that consumers can use to print out their own high-quality pictures at home. As digital substitution gathers speed in the photography industry, it is not clear that the traditional incumbents will be able to survive this shift; the new competitors might well rise to dominance in the new market.

If Kodak and Fuji do decline, they will not be the first large incumbents to be felled by a technological paradigm shift in their industry. In the early 1980s, the computer industry was revolutionized by the arrival of personal computer technology, which gave rise to client-server networks that replaced traditional mainframe and minicomputers for many business uses. Many incumbent companies in the mainframe era, such as Wang, Control Data, and DEC, ultimately did not survive, and even IBM went through a decade of wrenching changes and large losses before it reinvented itself as a provider of ebusiness solutions. In their place, new entrants such as Microsoft, Intel, Dell, and Compaq rose to dominance in this new computer industry.

Examples such as these raise four questions:

1. When do paradigm shifts occur, and how do they unfold?

2. Why do so many incumbents go into decline following a paradigm shift?

3. What strategies can incumbents adopt to increase the probability that they will survive a paradigm shift as profitable enterprises and emerge on the other side of the market abyss created by the arrival of new technology?

4. What strategies can new entrants into a market adopt to profit from a paradigm shift?

We shall answer each of these questions in the remainder of this chapter.

● Paradigm Shifts and the Decline of Established Companies

Paradigm shifts appear to be more likely to occur in an industry when one or both of the following conditions are in place: First, the established technology in the industry is mature and approaching or at its "natural limit," and second, a new "disruptive technology" has entered the marketplace and is taking root in niches that are poorly served by incumbent companies using the established technology.[24]

THE NATURAL LIMITS TO TECHNOLOGY Richard Foster has formalized the relationship between the performance of a technology and time in terms of what he calls the technology S-curve (see Figure 7.5).[25] This curve shows the relationship over time of cumulative investments in R&D and the performance (or functionality) of a given technology. Early in the evolution of a new technology, R&D investments in a new technology tend to yield rapid improvements in performance as basic engineering problems are solved. After a time, diminishing returns to cumulative R&D begin to set in, the rate of improvement in performance slows, and the technology starts to approach its natural limit, where further advances are not possible. For example, one can argue that there was more improvement in the first fifty years of the commercial

FIGURE 7.5

The Technology S-Curve

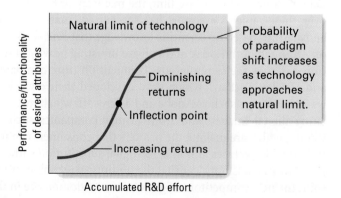

aerospace business following the pioneering flight by the Wright Brothers than there has been in the second fifty years. Indeed, the world's largest commercial jet aircraft, the Boeing 747, is based on a 1960s design, as is the world's fastest commercial jet aircraft, the Concorde. In commercial aerospace, therefore, we are now in the region of diminishing returns and may be approaching the natural limit to improvements in the technology of commercial aerospace.

Similarly, it can be argued that we are approaching the natural limit to technology in the performance of silicon-based semiconductor chips. Over the past two decades, the performance of semiconductor chips has been increased dramatically by packing ever more transistors onto a single small silicon chip. This process has helped to increase the power of computers, lower their cost, and shrink their size. But we are starting to approach limits to the ability to shrink the width of lines on a chip and therefore pack ever more transistors onto a single chip. The limit is imposed by the natural laws of physics. Light waves are used to help etch lines onto a chip, and one cannot etch a line that is smaller than the wavelength of light being used. Semiconductor companies are already using light with very small wavelengths, such as extreme ultraviolet, to etch lines onto a chip, but there are limits to how far this technology can be pushed, and many believe that we will reach those limits within the decade. Does this mean that our ability to make smaller, faster, cheaper computers is coming to an end? Probably not. It is more likely that we will find another technology to replace silicon-based computing and enable us to continue building smaller, faster, cheaper computers. In fact, several exotic competing technologies are already being developed that may replace silicon-based computing. These include self-organizing molecular computers, three-dimensional microprocessor technology, quantum computing technology, and the use of DNA to perform computations.[26]

What does all of this have to do with paradigm shifts? According to Foster, when a technology approaches its natural limit, research attention turns to possible alternative technologies, and sooner or later one of those alternatives might be commercialized and replace the established technology. That is, the probability that a paradigm shift will occur increases. Thus, sometime in the next decade or two, another paradigm shift might shake the very foundations of the computer industry as exotic computing technology replaces silicon-based computing. If and when this happens, and if history is any guide, many of the incumbents in today's computer industry will go into decline, and new enterprises will rise to dominance.

Foster pushes this point a little further, noting that, initially, the contenders for the replacement technology are not as effective as the established technology in producing the attributes and features that consumers demand in a product. For example, in the early years of the twentieth century, automobiles were just starting to be produced. They were valued for their ability to move people from place to place, but so were the horse and cart (the established technology). When automobiles originally appeared, the horse and cart were still quite a bit better than the automobile at moving people from place to place (see Figure 7.6). After all, the first cars were slow, noisy, and likely to break down. Moreover, they needed a network of paved roads and gas stations to be really useful, and that network didn't exist, so for most applications, the horse and cart were still the preferred mode of transportation—to say nothing of the fact that they were cheaper.

However, this comparison ignored the fact that in the early twentieth century, automobile technology was at the very start of its S-curve and was about to experience dramatic improvements in performance as major engineering problems were solved (and those paved roads and gas stations were built). In contrast, after 3,000 years of

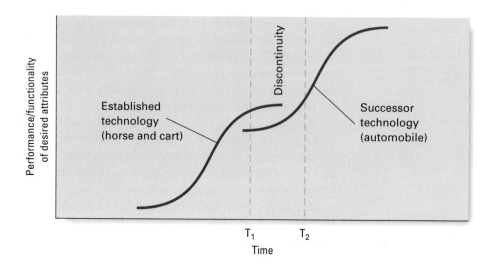

FIGURE 7.6

Established and Successor Technologies

continuous improvement and refinement, the horse and cart were almost definitely at the end of their technological S-curve. The result was that the rapidly improving automobile soon replaced the horse and cart as the preferred mode of transportation. At time T1 in Figure 7.6, the horse and cart were still superior to the automobile. By time T2, the automobile had surpassed the horse and cart.

Foster notes that because the successor technology is initially less efficient than the established technology, established companies and their customers often make the mistake of dismissing it, only to be taken off-guard by its rapid performance improvement. A final point is that more than one potential successor technology appears, usually a swarm of potential successor technologies, only one of which might ultimately come to the fore (see Figure 7.7). When this is the case, established companies are put at a disadvantage. Even if they recognize that a paradigm shift is imminent, they may not have the resources to invest in all the potential replacement technologies. If they invest in the wrong one (something that is easy to do given the uncertainty that surrounds the entire process), they may be locked out of subsequent development.

DISRUPTIVE TECHNOLOGY Clayton Christensen has built on Foster's insights and his own research to develop a theory of disruptive technology that has become very

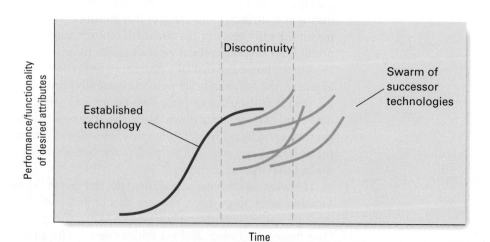

FIGURE 7.7

Swarm of Successor Technologies

influential in high-technology circles.[27] Christensen uses the term *disruptive technology* to refer to a new technology that gets its start away from the mainstream of a market and then, as its functionality improves over time, invades the main market. Such technologies are disruptive because they revolutionize industry structure and competition, often causing the decline of established companies. They cause a technological paradigm shift.

Christensen's greatest insight is that established companies are often aware of the new technology but do not invest in it because they listen to their customers, and their customers do not want it. Of course, this arises because the new technology is early in its development, and thus only at the beginning of the S-curve for that technology. Once the performance of the new technology improves, customers do want it, but by this time, new entrants, as opposed to established companies, have accumulated the knowledge required to bring the new technology into the mass market. Christensen supports his view with several detailed historical case studies, one of which is summarized in Strategy in Action 7.4.

Strategy in Action   7.4

Disruptive Technology in Mechanical Excavators

Excavators are used to dig foundations for large buildings, trenches to lay large pipes for sewers and the like, and foundations and trenches for residential construction and farm work. Prior to the 1940s, the dominant technology used to manipulate the bucket on a mechanical excavator was based on a system of cables and pulleys. Although these mechanical systems could lift large buckets of earth, the excavators themselves were quite large, cumbersome, and expensive. Thus, they were rarely used to dig small trenches for house foundations, irrigation ditches for farmers, and the like. In most cases, these small trenches were dug by hand.

In the 1940s, a new technology made its appearance: hydraulics. In theory, hydraulic systems had certain advantages over the established cable and pulley systems. Most important, their energy efficiency was higher: for a given bucket size, a smaller engine would be required for a hydraulic system. However, the initial hydraulic systems also had drawbacks. The seals on hydraulic cylinders were prone to leaking under high pressure, effectively limiting the size of the bucket that could be lifted using hydraulics. Notwithstanding this drawback, when hydraulics first appeared, many of the incumbent firms in the mechanical excavation industry took the technology seriously enough to ask their primary customers whether they would be interested in products based on hydraulics. Because the primary customers of incumbents needed excavators with large buckets to dig out the foundations for buildings and large trenches, their reply was no. For this customer set, the hydraulic systems of the 1940s were not reliable or powerful enough. Consequently, after consulting with their customers, the established companies in the industry made the strategic decision not to invest in hydraulics. Instead, they continued to produce excavation equipment based on the dominant cable and pulley technology.

It was left to a number of new entrants, which included J. I. Case, John Deere, J. C. Bamford, and Caterpillar, to pioneer hydraulic excavation equipment. Because of the limits on bucket size imposed by the seal problem, these companies initially focused on a poorly served niche in the market that could make use of small buckets: residential contractors and farmers. Over time, these new entrants were able to solve the engineering problems associated with weak hydraulic seals, and as they did so, they manufactured excavators with larger buckets. Ultimately, they invaded the market niches served by the old-line companies: general contractors that dug the foundations for large buildings, sewers, and so on. At this point, Case, Deere, Caterpillar, and their kin rose to dominance in the industry, while the majority of established companies from the prior era lost share. Of the thirty or so manufacturers of cable-actuated equipment in the United States in the late 1930s, only four survived to the 1950s.[d]

In addition to listening too closely to their customers, Christensen also identifies a number of other factors that make it very difficult for established companies to adopt a new disruptive technology. He notes that many established companies declined to invest in new disruptive technologies because initially they served such small market niches that it seemed unlikely that they would have an impact on the company's revenues and profits. As the new technology started to improve in functionality and invade the main market, their investment was often hindered by the fact that exploiting the new technology required a new business model totally different from the company's established model, and thus was very difficult to implement.

Both of these points can be illustrated by referring to one more example: the rise of online discount stockbrokers, such as Ameritrade and E*Trade, which made use of a new technology, the Internet, during the 1990s to allow individual investors to trade stocks for a very low commission fee. In contrast, full-service stockbrokers, such as Merrill Lynch, where orders had to be placed through a stockbroker who earned a commission for performing the transaction, did not.

Christensen also notes that a new network of suppliers and distributors typically grows up around the new entrants. Not only do established companies initially ignore disruptive technology, but so do their suppliers and distributors. This creates an opportunity for new suppliers and distributors to enter the market to serve the new entrants. As the new entrants grow, so does the associated network. Ultimately, Christensen suggests, the new entrants and their network may replace not only established enterprises, but also the entire network of suppliers and distributors associated with established companies. Taken to its logical extreme, this view suggests that disruptive technologies may result in the demise of the entire network of enterprises associated with established companies in an industry.

The established companies in an industry that is being rocked by a technological paradigm shift often have to cope with internal inertia forces that limit their ability to adapt, but the new entrants do not and thereby have an advantage. They do not have to deal with an established and conservative customer set and an obsolete business model. Instead, they can focus on optimizing the new technology, improving its performance, and riding the wave of disruptive technology into new market segments until they invade the main market and challenge the established companies, by which time they may be well equipped to beat them.

● Strategic Implications for Established Companies

Although Christensen has uncovered an important tendency, it is by no means written in stone that all established companies are doomed to fail when faced with disruptive technologies, as we have seen with IBM and Merrill Lynch. Established companies must meet the challenges created by the emergence of disruptive technologies.[28]

First, having access to the knowledge about how disruptive technologies can revolutionize markets is itself a valuable strategic asset. Many of the established companies that Christensen examined failed because they took a myopic view of the new technology and asked their customers the wrong question. Instead of asking, "Are you interested in this new technology?" they should have recognized that the new technology was likely to improve rapidly over time and instead asked, "Would you be interested in this new technology if it improves its functionality over time?" If they had done so, they may have made very different strategic decisions.

Second, it is clearly important for established enterprises to invest in newly emerging technologies that may ultimately become disruptive technologies. Companies have to hedge their bets about new technology. As we have noted, at any time, there may be a swarm of emerging technologies, any one of which might ultimately become a disruptive technology. Large, established companies that are generating significant cash flows can and often should establish and fund central R&D operations to invest in and develop such technologies. In addition, they may wish to acquire newly emerging companies that are pioneering potentially disruptive technologies or enter into alliances with them to develop the technology jointly. The strategy of acquiring companies that are developing potentially disruptive technology is one that Cisco Systems, a dominant provider of Internet network equipment, is famous for pursuing. At the heart of this strategy must be recognition on the part of the incumbent enterprise that it is better for the company to develop disruptive technology and then cannibalize its established sales base than to have that sales base taken away by new entrants.

However, Christensen makes the very important point that even when established companies do undertake R&D investments in potentially disruptive technologies, they often fail to commercialize those technologies because of internal forces that suppress change. For example, managers in the parts of the business that are currently generating the most cash may claim that they need the greatest R&D investment to maintain their market position and may lobby top management to delay investment in a new technology. Early in the S-curve, when it is very unclear what the long-term prospects of a new technology may be, this can be a powerful argument. The consequence, however, may be that the company fails to build a competence in the new technology and will suffer accordingly.

In addition, Christensen argues that the commercialization of new disruptive technology often requires a radically different value chain with a completely different cost structure—a new business model. For example, it may require a different manufacturing system, a different distribution system, and different pricing options and involve very different gross margins and operating margins. Christensen argues that it is almost impossible for two distinct business models to coexist within the same organization. When they try to do that, almost inevitably the established business model will suffocate the business model associated with the disruptive technology.

The solution to this problem is to separate the disruptive technology and place it in its own autonomous operating division. For example, during the early 1980s, Hewlett-Packard (HP) built a very successful laser printer business. Then along came inkjet technology. Some in the company believed that inkjet printers would cannibalize sales of laser printers and consequently argued that HP should not produce inkjet printers. Fortunately for HP, senior management at the time saw inkjet technology for what it was: a potential disruptive technology. Instead, they allocated significant R&D funds toward its commercialization. Furthermore, when the technology was ready for market introduction, they established an autonomous inkjet division at a different geographic location with its own manufacturing, marketing, and distribution activities. They accepted that the inkjet division might take sales away from the laser printer division and decided that it was better to have an HP division cannibalize the sales of another HP division than have those sales cannibalized by another company. Luckily for HP, it turns out that inkjet printers cannibalize sales of laser printers only on the margin and that both have profitable market niches. This outcome, however, does not detract from the message of the story: if your company is developing a potentially disruptive technology, the chances of success will be enhanced if it is placed in a stand-alone product division and given its own mandate.

● **Strategic Implications for New Entrants**

This work just discussed also holds implications for new entrants. The new entrants, or attackers, have several advantages over established enterprises. Pressures to continue the existing out-of-date business model do not hamstring new entrants, which do not have to worry about product cannibalization issues. They do not have to worry about their established customer base or relationships with established suppliers and distributors. Instead, they can focus all their energies on the opportunities offered by the new disruptive technology, ride the S-curve of technology improvement, and grow rapidly with the market for that technology. This does not mean that the new entrants have no problems to solve. They may be constrained by a lack of capital or have to manage the organizational problems associated with rapid growth; most importantly, they may need to find a way to take their technology from a small out-of-the-way niche into the mass market.

Perhaps one of the most important issues facing new entrants is the choice of whether to partner with an established company or go it alone in their attempt to develop and profit from a new disruptive technology. Although a new entrant may enjoy all of the advantages of the attacker, it may lack the resources required to exploit them fully. In such a case, it might want to consider forming a strategic alliance with a larger, established company to gain access to those resources. The main issues here are the same as those that we discussed earlier when examining the three strategies that companies can pursue to capture first-mover advantages: go it alone, enter into a strategic alliance, or license the technology.

Summary of Chapter

1. Technical standards are important in many high-tech industries: they guarantee compatibility, reduce confusion in the minds of customers, allow for mass production and lower costs, and reduce the risks associated with supplying complementary products.
2. Network effects and positive feedback loops often determine which standard comes to dominate a market.
3. Owning a standard can be a source of sustained competitive advantage.
4. Establishing a proprietary standard as the industry standard may require the company to win a format war against a competing and incompatible standard. Strategies for doing this include producing complementary products, leveraging killer applications, using aggressive pricing and marketing, licensing the technology, and cooperating with competitors.
5. Many high-tech products are characterized by high fixed costs of development but very low or zero marginal costs of producing one extra unit of output. These cost economics create a presumption in favor of strategies that emphasize aggressive pricing to increase volume and drive down average total costs.
6. Many digital products suffer from very high piracy rates because of the low marginal costs of copying and distributing such products. Piracy can be reduced by

the appropriate combination of strategy, encryption software, and vigorous defense of intellectual property rights.
7. It is very important for a first mover to develop a strategy to capitalize on first-mover advantages. A company can choose from three strategies: develop and market the technology itself, do so jointly with another company, or license the technology to existing companies. The choice depends on the complementary assets required to capture a first-mover advantage, the height of barriers to imitation, and the capability of competitors.
8. Technological paradigm shifts occur when new technologies come along that revolutionize the structure of the industry, dramatically alter the nature of competition, and require companies to adopt new strategies to survive.
9. Technological paradigm shifts are more likely to occur when progress in improving the established technology is slowing because it is giving diminishing returns and a new disruptive technology is taking root in a market niche.
10. Established companies can deal with paradigm shifts by hedging their bets with regard to technology or setting up a stand-alone division to exploit the technology.

Discussion Questions

1. What is different about high-tech industries? Were all industries once high tech?
2. Why are standards so important in many high-tech industries? What are the competitive implications of this?
3. You work for a small company that has the leading position in an embryonic market. Your boss believes that the company's future is ensured because it has a 60% share of the market, the lowest cost structure in the industry, and the most reliable and highest-valued product. Write a memo to him outlining why his assumptions might be incorrect.
4. You are working for a small company that has developed an operating system for PCs that is faster and

more stable than Microsoft's Windows operating system. What strategies might the company pursue to unseat Windows and establish its new operating system as the dominant technical standard in the industry?
5. You are a manager for a major music record label. Last year, music sales declined by 10%, primarily because of very high piracy rates for CDs. Your boss has asked you to develop a strategy for reducing piracy rates. What would you suggest that the company do?
6. Reread the Opening Case on the emerging format war for high-definition DVD players. On the basis of the information contained in this case, who do you think is most likely to win this format war, Sony or Toshiba? Why?

Practicing Strategic Management

SMALL-GROUP EXERCISE
Digital Books

Break up into groups of three to five, appoint one group member to be the spokesperson who will communicate your findings to the class, and discuss the following scenario. You are a group of managers and software engineers at a small start-up that has developed software that enables customers to easily download and view digital books on a variety of digital devices, from PCs to iPods and e-book readers. The same software also allows customers to share digital books using peer-to-peer technology (the same technology that allows people to share music files on the Web), and to burn digital books onto DVDs.

1. How do you think the market for this software is likely to develop? What factors might inhibit adoption of this software?
2. Can you think of a strategy that your company might pursue in combination with book publishers that will enable your company to increase revenues and with film companies to reduce piracy rates?

ARTICLE FILE 7

Find an example of an industry that has undergone a technological paradigm shift in recent years. What happened to the established companies as that paradigm shift unfolded?

STRATEGIC MANAGEMENT PROJECT
Module 7

This module requires you to analyze the industry environment in which your company is based and determine if it is vulnerable to a technological paradigm shift. With the information you have at your disposal, answer the following questions:

1. What is the dominant product technology used in the industry in which your company is based?
2. Are technical standards important in your industry? If so, what are they?
3. What are the attributes of the majority of customers purchasing the product of your company (for example, are they early adopters, early majority members, late majority members)? What does this tell you about the strategic issues that the company is likely to face in the future?
4. Did the dominant technology in your industry diffuse rapidly or slowly? What drove the speed of diffusion?
5. Where is the dominant technology in your industry on its S-curve? Are alternative competing technologies being developed that might give rise to a paradigm shift in your industry?
6. Are intellectual property rights important for your company? If so, what strategies is it adopting to protect those rights? Is it doing enough?

ETHICS EXERCISE

Sue had been hoping to get into investing for some time, but she simply didn't know how to get started. Her nephew had recommended that she visit his financial planner, and today she had her first appointment. She arrived fifteen minutes early and was shown into a spacious and classy waiting area. The receptionist offered her a choice of beverages and soon returned with a steaming cup of tea. Although initially nervous about turning over her investment decisions to a stranger, Sue was feeling more confident by the minute.

After a short wait, a tailored, middle-aged woman arrived to show Sue into an office bright with sunshine. Coming from behind the desk was a young man who promptly introduced himself as Dave. Sue was taken aback by his youth and casual attitude, but she had heard great things about this man from her nephew. As they settled themselves, Dave asked Sue about her investment wishes. He listened intently and immediately began to recommend a number of mutual funds and other investment opportunities. He also suggested that she conduct the majority of her investment activity online at his

direction. Dave was friendly and attentive, and Sue found herself being swept up by his presentation. He seemed so confident about the earning potential of these investments that Sue agreed readily to his suggestions.

Some weeks later, after seeing some initial returns on her investments, Sue began to lose money. Not knowing what to think, she called her nephew to get his opinion. He was experiencing the same run of bad luck. After digging for information from his friends in the financial industry, Sue's nephew discovered that Dave was known for recommending mutual funds for which he received extra payments from the fund firms themselves, regardless of the viability of the funds. Fortunately, Sue and her nephew were able to retrieve some of their money, and both considered that they had learned a valuable lesson.

1. Define the ethical issue presented in this case.
2. Should promoting funds to receive extra payments be legal?
3. How might an investor protect him- or herself from what happened to Sue and her nephew?

CLOSING CASE

The Failure of Friendster

In 2002, Jonathan Abrams thought that he was in the right place at the right time. With seed money raised from a wealthy Silicon Valley investor, the thirty-something engineer was developing a social networking site. The site, which debuted in March 2003, was called Friendster. It enabled people to post their profiles online, to link up with friends online, and introduce their friends to each other. Abrams's motivation for starting Friendster was that he wanted to meet girls, and he thought that a social networking site would be a pretty cool way to do it.

The site soon became one of the hot Internet properties of 2003. By the fall of 2003, Friendster had signed up over 3 million users. Publications including *Time, Esquire, Vanity Fair,* and *U.S. Weekly* were writing about Friendster before anybody had ever heard of MySpace. By November 2003, Friendster had attracted significant

investment from a clutch of high-profile venture capitalists (VCs), including the legendary John Dorr, perhaps the most successful venture capitalist in the history of Silicon Valley, who took a seat on Friendster's board. Dorr was joined by several other high-profile board members.

The buzz around Friendster led to a bid from another fast-growing VC-funded Silicon Valley start-up, Google, which wanted to buy the company for $30 million. The board, populated by venture capitalists like Dorr who were all looking for the next big thing, urged Abrams not to sell. It wasn't hard; Abrams thought Friendster would be worth much more in a short time, and he said no to Google. Three short years later, Abrams probably regrets that decision. Had he taken the Google offer, which was in stock, he would be worth about $1.5 billion today. Instead,

Abrams is no longer at Friendster, and the pioneering social networking site has been totally eclipsed by rivals like My-Space, Facebook, and Flickr. In September 2006, Friendster had just 1 million registered users; MySpace, which went live a year after Friendster, had 55.9 million!

One of Friendster's problems was that the site was soon overwhelmed by rapid growth. With 3 million users, it could take as long as forty seconds for pages to download. Another was the lack of new features on Friendster: while MySpace was rapidly introducing new features like blogs and tools that people could use to jazz up their profiles, Friendster stood still. Part of the problem was that new tools and features would only slow down Friendster even more. As for why Friendster was so slow, in part that was due to Friendster's closed system. Users at Friendster could only view the profiles of those on a relatively short chain of acquaintances. In contrast, MySpace uses an open system where anybody can look at anybody else's profile—which is much simpler to execute.

In addition, MySpace, which organized users around favorite bands, tapped into a much more energetic demographic: those in their teens and early twenties. Friendster's users, meanwhile, were somewhat older.

Other observers wonder about management problems at Friendster. The high-powered board was apparently preoccupied with big strategic issues and spent little time talking about the mundane technological problems that stymied the company's growth. There was also a revolving door for CEOs. The board felt Abrams was out of his depth, and quickly replaced him in March 2004 with one of their own, Tim Koogle, the former CEO of Yahoo. Koogle, always a caretaker CEO, stepped down after three months to be replaced by Scott Sassa, a former TV executive, who lasted just a year before being replaced by Taek Kwan, who lasted all of six months. By 2006, Friendster was on its fifth CEO, Kent Lindstrom.

The board considered shutting Friendster down, but in early 2006, they decided to keep the company afloat and injected $3.1 million into the enterprise. This was followed by an additional $10 million of venture capital funding in August 2006. Partly fueling this new investment is a feeling that while Friendster may be down, it is not yet out. Early on, Friendster filed about a dozen patent applications covering various aspects of social networking. By mid-2006, the U.S. Patent Office was starting to grant some of these patents, and Lindstrom was clearly wondering whether they could be used to extract royalties from rivals. The first patent to be granted covers "a method and apparatus for calculating and displaying and acting upon relationships in a social network." As for Friendster's service, it has been repositioned as a service for twenty-five to forty–year-olds who cannot spend hours every day online.[29]

Case Discussion Questions

1. Friendster was the first mover in the social networking space. Could it have become the dominant enterprise? In retrospect, what might the company have done differently?

2. What first-mover disadvantages did Friendster fall victim to?

3. Why did second-mover MySpace grow so much more rapidly than Friendster?

4. How might the revolving door of CEOs have hurt the young company?

5. What is the outlook for Friendster now? Do you think it is possible for the company to regain momentum? How?

Strategy in the Global Environment

MTV—A Global Brand Goes Local

MTV Networks has become a symbol of globalization. Established in 1981, the U.S.-based music TV network has been expanding outside its North American base since 1987, when it opened MTV Europe. Now owned by media conglomerate Viacom, MTV Networks, which includes siblings Nickelodeon and VH1, the music station for the aging baby boomers, generates more than $2 billion in revenues outside the United States. Since 1987, MTV has become the most ubiquitous cable programmer in the world. By 2006, the network reached a combined total of 443 million households, some 289 million of which were in 140 other countries.

While the United States still leads in number of households, the most rapid growth is elsewhere, particularly in Asia, where nearly two-thirds of the region's 3 billion people are under age thirty-five, the middle class is expanding quickly, and TV ownership is spreading rapidly. MTV Networks figures that every second of every day, over 2 million people are watching MTV around the world, the majority outside the United States.

Despite its international success, MTV's global expansion got off to a weak start. In 1987, it piped a single feed across Europe composed almost entirely of American programming with English-speaking veejays. Naïvely, the network's U.S. managers thought Europeans would flock to the American programming. But while viewers in Europe shared a common interest in a handful of global superstars, who at the time included Madonna and Michael Jackson, their tastes turned out to be surprisingly local. What was popular in Germany might not be popular in Great Britain. Many staples of the American music scene left Europeans cold. MTV suffered as a result. Soon local copycat stations were springing up in Europe that focused on the music scene in individual countries. They took viewers and advertisers away from MTV. As explained by Tom Freston, the former chair of MTV Networks, "We were going for the most shallow layer of what united viewers and brought them together. It didn't go over too well."

In 1995, MTV changed its strategy and broke Europe into regional feeds, of which there are around twenty-five, including feeds for the United Kingdom and Ireland; another for Germany, Austria, and Switzerland; one for Italy; one for France; one for Spain; one for Holland; and one for Russia. The network adopted the same localization strategy elsewhere in the world. For example, in Asia, it has ten feeds—an English-Hindi channel for India, separate Mandarin feeds for China and Taiwan, a Korean feed for South Korea, a Bahasa-language feed for Indonesia, a Japanese feed for Japan, and so on. Digital and satellite technology have made the localization of programming cheaper and easier. MTV Networks can now beam half a dozen feeds off one satellite transponder.

While MTV Networks exercises creative control over these different feeds, and while all the channels have the same familiar frenetic look and feel of MTV in the United States, a significant share of the programming and content is now local. When MTV opens a local station now, it begins with expatriates from elsewhere in the world to do a "gene transfer" of company culture and operating principles. Once these are established, however, the network switches to local employees and the expatriates move on. The idea is to discover the tastes of the local population and produce programming that matches those tastes.

Although many of the programming ideas still originate in the United States, with staples such as *The Real*

World having equivalents in different countries, an increasing share of programming is local in conception. In Italy, *MTV Kitchen* combines cooking with a music countdown. *Erotica* airs in Brazil and features a panel of youngsters discussing sex. The Indian channel produces twenty-one homegrown shows hosted by local veejays who speak Hinglish, a city-bred breed of Hindi and English. Hit shows include *MTV Cricket in Control*, appropriate for a land where cricket is a national obsession; *MTV Housefull*, which hones in on Hindi film stars (India has the biggest film industry outside Hollywood), and *MTV Bakra*, which is modeled after *Candid Camera*.

This localization push reaped big benefits for MTV, allowing the network to capture viewers back from local imitators. In India, for example, ratings increased by more than 700% between 1996, when the localization push began, and 2000. In turn, localization helps MTV to capture more of those all-important advertising revenues, even from other multinationals such as Coca-Cola, whose own advertising budgets are often locally determined.[1]

OVERVIEW

This chapter begins with a discussion of ongoing changes in the global competitive environment and discusses models that managers can use for analyzing competition in different national markets. Next, the chapter discusses the various ways in which international expansion can increase a company's profitability and profit growth. It also looks at the advantages and disadvantages of different strategies that companies can pursue to gain a competitive advantage in the global marketplace. This is followed by a discussion of two related strategic issues: (1) how managers decide which foreign markets to enter, when to enter them, and on what scale, and (2) what kind of vehicle or means a company should use to expand globally and enter a foreign country. Once a company has entered a foreign market, it becomes a **multinational company**, that is, a company that does business in two or more national markets. The vehicles that companies can employ to enter foreign markets and become multinationals include exporting, licensing, setting up a joint venture with a foreign company, and setting up a wholly owned subsidiary. The chapter closes with a discussion of the benefits and costs of entering into strategic alliances with other global companies. By the time you have completed this chapter, you will have a good understanding of the various strategic issues that companies face when they decide to expand their operations abroad to achieve competitive advantage and superior profitability.

MTV Networks, profiled in the Opening Case, previews many of the issues that we will explore in this chapter. Like many other companies, MTV moved into other countries because it saw huge growth opportunities there, and it thought it could create value by transferring its business model and American style of music programming to foreign markets. MTV initially treated foreign markets much like the United States, right down to airing the same music videos worldwide, but it soon found that this was not the correct approach. Many American music stars drew big yawns in Europe and Asia, where most of the stars were local. These national differences in customer tastes and preferences required MTV to change its approach to programming. It moved away from its one-size-fits-all strategy of global standardization and became more local in its orientation, adapting its programming to different markets, with different music videos and programs being aired in different markets. As one MTV manager has stated, "[D]espite being a global brand, we are local in our approach. We reflect the tastes and demands of our viewers and this differs in each market. Thus the need to create specific channels [in each country] that meet the need of our target audience."[2] At the same time, MTV's foreign affiliates still have the same look, feel, and overall programming philosophy of the U.S. parent. Striking the right balance between global standardization and local responsiveness let MTV reap big dividends, enabling the network to gain viewers and advertisers at the expense of competitors. As we shall see, many other enterprises have sought to do the same.

The Global and National Environments

Fifty years ago, most national markets were isolated from each other by significant barriers to international trade and investment. In those days, managers could focus on analyzing just those national markets in which their company competed. They did not need to pay much attention to entry by global competitors because there were few and entry was difficult. Nor did they need to pay much attention to entering foreign markets because that was often prohibitively expensive. All of this has now changed. Barriers to international trade and investment have tumbled, huge global markets for goods and services have been created, and companies from different nations are entering each other's home markets on a hitherto unprecedented scale, increasing the intensity of competition. Rivalry can no longer be understood merely in terms of what happens within the boundaries of a nation; managers now need to consider how globalization is affecting the environment in which their company competes and what strategies their company should adopt to exploit the unfolding opportunities and counter competitive threats. In this section, we look at the changes ushered in by falling barriers to international trade and investment, and we discuss a model for analyzing the competitive situation in different nations.

● **The Globalization of Production and Markets**

The past half-century has seen a dramatic lowering of barriers to international trade and investment. For example, the average tariff rate on manufactured goods traded between advanced nations has fallen from around 40% to under 4%. Similarly, in nation after nation, regulations prohibiting foreign companies from entering domestic markets and establishing production facilities, or acquiring domestic companies, have been removed. As a result of these two developments, there has been a surge in both the volume of international trade and the value of foreign direct investment. The volume of world merchandise trade has grown faster than the world economy since 1950.[3] From 1970 to 2005, the volume of world merchandise trade expanded twenty-sevenfold, outstripping the expansion of world production, which grew about 7.5 times in real terms. Moreover, between 1992 and 2005, the total flow of foreign direct investment from all countries increased over 500%, while world trade by value grew by some 140% and world output by around 40%.[4] These two trends have led to the globalization of production and the globalization of markets.[5]

The globalization of production has been increasing as companies take advantage of lower barriers to international trade and investment to disperse important parts of their production processes around the globe. Doing so enables them to take advantage of national differences in the cost and quality of factors of production such as labor, energy, land, and capital, which allows them to lower their cost structures and boost profits. For example, some 30% of the Boeing Company's commercial jet aircraft, the 777, is built by foreign companies. For its next jet airliner, the 787, Boeing is pushing this trend even further, with some 65% of the total value of the aircraft scheduled to be outsourced to foreign companies, 35% of which will go to three major Japanese companies, and another 20% going to companies located in Italy, Singapore, and the United Kingdom.[6] Part of Boeing's rationale for outsourcing so much production to foreign suppliers is that these suppliers are the best in the world at performing their particular activity. Therefore, the result of having foreign suppliers build specific parts is a better final product and higher profitability for Boeing.

As for the globalization of markets, it has been argued that the world's economic system is moving from one in which national markets are distinct entities, isolated from each other by trade barriers and barriers of distance, time, and culture, toward a system in which national markets are merging into one huge global marketplace. Increasingly, customers around the world demand and use the same basic product offerings. Consequently, in many industries, it is no longer meaningful to talk about the German market, the U.S. market, or the Japanese market; there is only the global market. The global acceptance of Coca-Cola, Citigroup credit cards, blue jeans, Starbucks, McDonald's hamburgers, the Nokia wireless phone, and Microsoft's Windows operating system are examples of this trend.[7]

The trend toward the globalization of production and markets has several important implications for competition within an industry. First, industry boundaries do not stop at national borders. Because many industries are becoming global in scope, actual and potential competitors exist not only in a company's home market but also in other national markets. Managers who analyze only their home market can be caught unprepared by the entry of efficient foreign competitors. The globalization of markets and production implies that companies around the globe are finding their home markets under attack from foreign competitors. For example, in Japan, Merrill Lynch and Citicorp are making inroads against Japanese financial service institutions. In the United States, Finland's Nokia has taken market share from Motorola in the market for wireless phone handsets (see Strategy in Action 8.1). In the European Union, the once-dominant Dutch company Philips has seen its market share in the customer electronics industry taken by Japan's JVC, Matsushita, and Sony.

Second, the shift from national to global markets has intensified competitive rivalry in industry after industry. National markets that once were consolidated oligopolies, dominated by three or four companies and subjected to relatively little foreign competition, have been transformed into segments of fragmented global industries in which a large number of companies battle each other for market share in country after country. This rivalry has threatened to drive down profitability and made it all the more critical for companies to maximize their efficiency, quality, customer responsiveness, and innovative ability. The painful restructuring and downsizing that has been going on at companies such as Kodak and Xerox is as much a response to the increased intensity of global competition as it is to anything else. However, not all global industries are fragmented. Many remain consolidated oligopolies, except that now they are consolidated global, rather than national, oligopolies. In the videogame industry,

Strategy in Action   8.1

Finland's Nokia

The wireless phone market is one of the great growth stories of the last decade. Starting from a very low base in 1990, annual global sales of wireless phones surged to reach 825 million units in 2005. By the end of 2005, there were over 1.7 billion wireless subscribers worldwide, up from less than 10 million in 1990. Nokia is one of the dominant players in the world market for mobile phones. Nokia's roots are in Finland, not normally a country that comes to mind when one talks about leading-edge technology companies. In the 1980s, Nokia was a rambling Finnish conglomerate with activities that embraced tire manufacturing, paper production, consumer electronics, and telecommunications equipment. By 2006, it had transformed itself into a focused telecommunications equipment manufacturer with a global reach, sales of over $40 billion, earnings of more than $5 billion, and a 34% share of the global market for wireless phones. How has this former conglomerate emerged to take a global leadership position in wireless telecommunications equipment? Much of the answer lies in the history, geography, and political economy of Finland and its Nordic neighbors.

In 1981, the Nordic nations cooperated to create the world's first international wireless telephone network. They had good reason to become pioneers: it cost far too much to lay down a traditional wire line telephone service in those sparsely populated and inhospitably cold countries. The same features made telecommunications all the more valuable: people driving through the Arctic winter and owners of remote northern houses needed a telephone to summon help if something went wrong. As a result, Sweden, Norway, and Finland became the first nations in the world to take wireless telecommunications seriously. They found, for example, that although it cost up to $800 per subscriber to bring a traditional wire line service to remote locations, the same locations could be linked by wireless cellular for only $500 per person. As a consequence, 12% of the people in Scandinavia owned cellular phones by 1994, compared with less than 6% in the United States, the world's second most developed market. This lead continued over the next decade. By the end of 2005, 90% of the population in Finland owned a wireless phone, compared with 70% in the United States.

Nokia, a long-time telecommunications equipment supplier, was well positioned to take advantage of this development from the start, but there were other forces at work that helped Nokia develop its competitive edge. Unlike almost every other developed nation, Finland has never had a national telephone monopoly. Instead, the country's telephone services have long been provided by about fifty or so autonomous local telephone companies whose elected boards set prices by referendum (which naturally means low prices). This army of independent and cost-conscious telephone service providers prevented Nokia from taking anything for granted in its home country. With typical Finnish pragmatism, its customers were willing to buy from the lowest-cost supplier, whether that was Nokia, Ericsson, Motorola, or some other company. This situation contrasted sharply with that prevailing in most developed nations until the late 1980s and early 1990s, where domestic telephone monopolies typically purchased equipment from a dominant local supplier or made it themselves. Nokia responded to this competitive pressure by doing everything possible to drive down its manufacturing costs while staying at the leading edge of wireless technology.

The consequences of these forces are clear. Nokia is now a leader in digital wireless technology. Many now regard Finland as the lead market for wireless telephone services. If you want to see the future of wireless, you don't go to New York or San Francisco; you go to Helsinki, where Finns use their wireless handsets not just to talk to each other but also to browse the Web, execute e-commerce transactions, control household heating and lighting systems, or purchase Coke from a wireless-enabled vending machine. Nokia has gained this lead because Scandinavia started switching to digital technology five years before the rest of the world.[a]

for example, three companies are battling for global dominance: Microsoft from the United States and Nintendo and Sony from Japan. In the market for wireless handsets, Nokia of Finland does global battle against Motorola of the United States, Samsung and LG from South Korea, and Sony-Ericsson, a joint venture between Sony of Japan and Ericsson of Sweden.

Finally, although globalization has increased both the threat of entry and the intensity of rivalry within many formerly protected national markets, it has also created enormous opportunities for companies based in those markets. The steady decline in barriers to cross-border trade and investment has opened up many once-protected markets to companies based outside them. Thus, for example, in recent years, western European, Japanese, and U.S. companies have accelerated their investments in the nations of Eastern Europe, Latin America, and Southeast Asia as they try to take advantage of growth opportunities in those areas.

● National Competitive Advantage

Despite the globalization of production and markets, many of the most successful companies in certain industries are still clustered in a small number of countries. For example, many of the world's most successful biotechnology and computer companies are based in the United States, and many of the most successful customer electronics companies are based in Japan and South Korea. Germany is the base for many successful chemical and engineering companies. These facts suggest that the nation-state within which a company is based may have an important bearing on the competitive position of that company in the global marketplace.

In a study of national competitive advantage, Michael Porter identified four attributes of a national or country-specific environment that have an important impact on the global competitiveness of companies located within that nation:[8]

- *Factor endowments*: A nation's position in factors of production such as skilled labor or the infrastructure necessary to compete in a given industry

- *Local demand conditions*: The nature of home demand for the industry's product or service

- *Related and supporting industries*: The presence or absence in a nation of supplier industries and related industries that are internationally competitive

- *Firm strategy, structure, and rivalry*: The conditions in the nation that govern how companies are created, organized, and managed and the nature of domestic rivalry

Porter speaks of these four attributes as constituting the diamond, arguing that companies from a given nation are most likely to succeed in industries or strategic groups in which the four attributes are favorable (see Figure 8.1). He also argues that the diamond's attributes form a mutually reinforcing system in which the effect of one attribute is dependent on the state of the others.

FACTOR ENDOWMENTS Factor endowments—the cost and quality of factors of production—are prime determinants of the competitive advantage that certain countries might have in certain industries. Factors of production include basic factors, such as land, labor, capital, and raw materials, and advanced factors, such as technological know-how, managerial sophistication, and physical infrastructure (roads, railways, and ports). The competitive advantage that the United States enjoys in biotechnology might be explained by the presence of certain advanced factors of production—for example, technological know-how—in combination with some basic factors, which might be a pool of relatively low-cost venture capital that can be used to fund risky start-ups in industries such as biotechnology.

LOCAL DEMAND CONDITIONS Home demand plays an important role in providing the impetus for upgrading competitive advantage. Companies are typically most sensitive to the needs of their closest customers. Thus, the characteristics of home demand are particularly important in shaping the attributes of domestically made products

FIGURE 8.1

National Competitive
Advantage

Source: Adapted from
M. E. Porter, "The Competitive
Advantage of Nations,"
Harvard Business Review
(March–April 1990): 77.

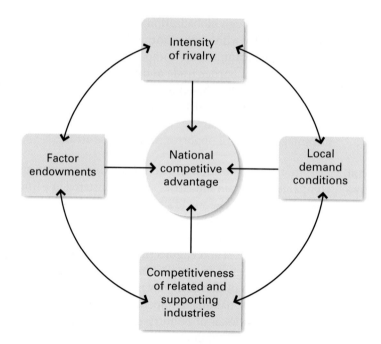

and creating pressures for innovation and quality. A nation's companies gain competitive advantage if their domestic customers are sophisticated and demanding and pressure local companies to meet high standards of product quality and produce innovative products. Japan's sophisticated and knowledgeable buyers of cameras helped stimulate the Japanese camera industry to improve product quality and introduce innovative models. A similar example can be found in the cellular phone equipment industry, where sophisticated and demanding local customers in Scandinavia helped push Nokia of Finland and Ericsson of Sweden to invest in cellular phone technology long before demand for cellular phones took off in other developed nations. As a result, Nokia and Ericsson, together with Motorola, are significant players in the global cellular telephone equipment industry. (The case of Nokia was reviewed in more depth in Strategy in Action 8.1.)

COMPETITIVENESS OF RELATED AND SUPPORTING INDUSTRIES The third broad attribute of national advantage in an industry is the presence of internationally competitive suppliers or related industries. The benefits of investments in advanced factors of production by related and supporting industries can spill over into an industry, thereby helping it achieve a strong competitive position internationally. Swedish strength in fabricated steel products (such as ball bearings and cutting tools) has drawn on strengths in Sweden's specialty steel industry. Switzerland's success in pharmaceuticals is closely related to its previous international success in the technologically related dye industry. One consequence of this process is that successful industries within a country tend to be grouped into clusters of related industries. Indeed, this was one of the most pervasive findings of Porter's study. One such cluster is the German textile and apparel sector, which includes high-quality cotton, wool, synthetic fibers, sewing machine needles, and a wide range of textile machinery.

INTENSITY OF RIVALRY The fourth broad attribute of national competitive advantage in Porter's model is the intensity of rivalry of firms within a nation. Porter makes two important points here. First, different nations are characterized by different management ideologies, which either help them or do not help them to build national competitive advantage. For example, Porter noted the predominance of engineers in top management at German and Japanese firms. He attributed this to these firms' emphasis on improving manufacturing processes and product design. In contrast, Porter noted a predominance of people with finance backgrounds leading many U.S. firms. He linked this to U.S. firms' lack of attention to improving manufacturing processes and product design. He argued that the dominance of finance led to an overemphasis on maximizing short-term financial returns. According to Porter, one consequence of these different management ideologies was a relative loss of U.S. competitiveness in those engineering-based industries where manufacturing processes and product design issues are all-important (such as the automobile industry).

Porter's second point is that there is a strong association between vigorous domestic rivalry and the creation and persistence of competitive advantage in an industry. Rivalry induces companies to look for ways to improve efficiency, which makes them better international competitors. Domestic rivalry creates pressures to innovate, improve quality, reduce costs, and invest in upgrading advanced factors. All this helps to create world-class competitors. The stimulating effects of strong domestic competition are clear in the story of the rise of Nokia of Finland in the market for wireless handsets and telephone equipment (see Strategy in Action 8.1).

● **Using the Framework**
The framework just described can help managers to identify where their most significant global competitors are likely to come from. For example, there is an emerging cluster of computer service and software companies in Bangalore, India, that includes two of the fastest-growing information technology companies in the world, Infosys and Wipro. These companies are emerging as aggressive competitors on the global stage. Indeed, there are signs that this is already happening, because both companies have recently opened offices in the European Union and United States so they can better compete against the likes of IBM and EDS.

The framework can also be used to help managers decide where they might want to locate certain productive activities. Seeking to take advantage of U.S. expertise in biotechnology, many foreign companies have set up research facilities in San Diego, Boston, and Seattle, where U.S. biotechnology companies tend to be clustered. Similarly, in an attempt to take advantage of Japanese success in customer electronics, many U.S. electronics companies have set up research and production facilities in Japan, often in conjunction with Japanese partners.

Finally, the framework can help a company assess how tough it might be to enter certain national markets. If a nation has a competitive advantage in certain industries, it might be challenging for foreigners to enter those industries. For example, the highly competitive retailing industry in the United States has proved to be a very difficult one for foreign companies to enter. Successful foreign retailers such as Britain's Marks & Spencer and IKEA from Sweden have found it tough going in the United States, precisely because the U.S. retailing industry is the most competitive in the world.

Increasing Profitability and Profit Growth Through Global Expansion

Here we look at a number of ways in which expanding globally can enable companies to increase their profitability and grow their profits more rapidly. At the most basic level, global expansion increases the size of the market that a company is addressing, thereby boosting profit growth. As we shall see, global expansion also offers opportunities for reducing the cost structure of the enterprise or adding value through differentiation, thereby potentially boosting profitability.

Expanding the Market: Leveraging Products

A company can increase its growth rate by taking goods or services developed at home and selling them internationally. Indeed, almost all multinationals started out doing just this. Procter & Gamble, for example, developed most of its best-selling products at home and then sold them around the world (Pampers and Ivory Soap being cases in point; see Strategy in Action 8.2). Similarly, from its earliest days, Microsoft has always focused on selling its software around the world. Automobile companies like Ford, Volkswagen, and Toyota also grew by developing products at home and then selling them in international markets. The returns from such a strategy are likely to be greater if indigenous competitors in the nations a company enters lack comparable products. Thus, Toyota has grown its profits by entering the large automobile markets of North America and Europe and by offering products that are differentiated from those offered by local rivals (Ford and GM) by their superior quality and reliability.

It is important to note that the success of many multinational companies is based not just on the goods or services that they sell in foreign nations, but also on the distinctive competencies (unique skills) that underlie the production and marketing of those goods or services. Thus, Toyota's success is based on its distinctive competency in manufacturing automobiles, and expanding internationally can be seen as a way of generating greater returns from this competency. Similarly, Procter & Gamble's global success was based on more than its portfolio of consumer products; it was also based on the company's skills in mass-marketing consumer goods. P&G grew rapidly in international markets between 1950 and 1990 because it was one of the most skilled mass-marketing enterprises in the world and could "outmarket" indigenous competitors in the nations it entered. Global expansion was thus a way of generating higher returns from its competency in marketing.

Pushing this further, one could say that because distinctive competencies are in essence the most valuable aspects of a company's business model, the successful global expansion by manufacturing companies like Toyota and P&G was based on their ability to transfer aspects of their business model and apply it to foreign markets. The same can be said of companies engaged in the service sectors of an economy, such as financial institutions, retailers, restaurant chains, and hotels. Expanding the market for their services often means replicating their business model in foreign nations (albeit with some changes to account for local differences, which we will discuss in more detail shortly). Starbucks, for example, is expanding rapidly outside the United States by taking the basic business model it developed at home and using it as a blueprint for establishing international operations. Similarly, McDonald's is famous for its international expansion strategy, which has taken the company into more than 120 nations that collectively generate over half of the company's revenues.

Realizing Cost Economies from Global Volume

In addition to growing profits more rapidly, expanding its sales volume through international expansion can help a company realize cost savings from economies of scale, thereby boosting profitability. Such scale economies come from several sources. First, by spreading the fixed costs associated with developing a product and setting up production facilities over its global sales volume, a company can lower its average unit cost. Thus, Microsoft can garner significant scale economies by spreading the $5 billion it cost to develop Windows Vista over global demand.

Second, by serving a global market, a company can potentially utilize its production facilities more intensively, which leads to higher productivity, lower costs, and greater profitability. For example, if Intel sold microprocessors only in the United States, it might be able to keep its factories open for only one shift, five days a week. But by serving a global market from the same factories, it might be able to utilize those assets for two shifts, seven days a week. In other words, the capital invested in those factories is used more intensively if Intel sells to a global as opposed to a national market, which translates into higher capital productivity and a higher return on invested capital.

Third, as global sales increase the size of the enterprise, so its bargaining power with suppliers increases, which may allow it to bargain down the cost of key inputs and boost profitability. Wal-Mart has been able to use its enormous sales volume as a lever to bargain down the price it pays suppliers for merchandise sold through its stores.

In addition to the cost savings that come from economies of scale, companies that sell to a global as opposed to a local marketplace may be able to realize further cost savings from learning effects. We first discussed learning effects in Chapter 4, where we noted that employee productivity increases with cumulative increases in output over time (for example, it costs considerably less to build the one-hundredth aircraft on a Boeing assembly line than the tenth because employees learn how to perform their tasks more efficiently over time). By selling to a global market, a company may be able to increase its sales volume more rapidly, and thus the cumulative output from its plants, which in turn should result in quicker learning, higher employee productivity, and a cost advantage over competitors that are growing more slowly because they lack international markets.

Realizing Location Economies

Earlier in this chapter, we discussed how countries differ from each other along a number of dimensions, including differences in the cost and quality of factors of production. These differences imply that some locations are more suited than others to producing certain goods and services.[9] **Location economies** are the economic benefits that arise from performing a value creation activity in the optimal location for that activity, wherever in the world that might be (transportation costs and trade barriers permitting). Locating a value creation activity in the optimal location for that activity can have one of two effects: (1) it can lower the costs of value creation, thus helping the company to achieve a low-cost position, or (2) it can enable a company to differentiate its product offering, which gives it the option of charging a premium price or keeping the price low and using differentiation as a means of increasing sales volume. Thus, efforts to realize location economies are consistent with the business-level strategies of low cost and differentiation. In theory, a company that realizes location economies by dispersing each of its value creation activities to the optimal location for that activity should have a competitive advantage over a company that bases all of its value creation activities at a single location. It should be able to differentiate its product offering better and lower its cost structure more than its single-location competitor. In a world where competitive pressures are increasing, such a strategy may well become an imperative for survival.

For an example of how this works in an international business, consider Clear Vision, a manufacturer and distributor of eyewear. Started in the 1970s by David Glassman, the firm now generates annual gross revenues of more than $100 million. Not exactly small, but no corporate giant either, Clear Vision is a multinational firm with production facilities on three continents and customers around the world. Clear Vision began its move toward becoming a multinational in the early 1980s. The strong dollar at that time made U.S.-based manufacturing very expensive. Low-priced imports were taking an ever larger share of the U.S. eyewear market, and Clear Vision realized it could not survive unless it also began to import. Initially the firm bought from independent overseas manufacturers, primarily in Hong Kong. However, it became dissatisfied with these suppliers' product quality and delivery. As Clear Vision's volume of imports increased, Glassman decided that the best way to guarantee quality and delivery was to set up Clear Vision's own manufacturing operation overseas. Accordingly, Clear Vision found a Chinese partner, and together they opened a manufacturing facility in Hong Kong, with Clear Vision being the majority shareholder.

The choice of the Hong Kong location was influenced by its combination of low labor costs, a skilled work force, and tax breaks given by the Hong Kong government. The firm's objective at this point was to lower production costs by locating value creation activities at an appropriate location. After a few years, however, the increasing industrialization of Hong Kong and a growing labor shortage had pushed up wage rates to the extent that it was no longer a low-cost location. In response, Glassman and his Chinese partner moved part of their manufacturing to a plant in mainland China to take advantage of the lower wage rates there. Again, the goal was to lower production costs. The parts for eyewear frames manufactured at this plant are shipped to the Hong Kong factory for final assembly and then distributed to markets in North and South America. The Hong Kong factory now employs eighty people, and the China plant, between 300 and 400.

At the same time, Clear Vision was looking for opportunities to invest in foreign eyewear firms with reputations for fashionable design and high quality. Its objective was not to reduce production costs but to launch a line of high-quality, differentiated, designer eyewear. Clear Vision did not have the design capability in-house to support such a line, but Glassman knew that certain foreign manufacturers did. As a result, Clear Vision invested in factories in Japan, France, and Italy, holding a minority shareholding in each case. These factories now supply eyewear for Clear Vision's Status Eye division, which markets high-priced designer eyewear.[10]

SOME CAVEATS Introducing transportation costs and trade barriers complicates this picture somewhat. New Zealand might have a comparative advantage for low-cost car assembly operations, but high transportation costs make it an uneconomical location from which to serve global markets. Factoring transportation costs and trade barriers into the cost equation helps explain why many U.S. companies have been shifting their production from Asia to Mexico. Mexico has three distinct advantages over many Asian countries as a location for value creation activities: low labor costs; Mexico's proximity to the large U.S. market, which reduces transportation costs; and the North American Free Trade Agreement (NAFTA), which has removed many trade barriers among Mexico, the United States, and Canada, increasing Mexico's attractiveness as a production site for the North American market. Thus, although the relative costs of value creation are important, transportation costs and trade barriers also must be considered in location decisions.

Another caveat concerns the importance of assessing political and economic risks when making location decisions. Even if a country looks very attractive as a production location when measured against cost or differentiation criteria, if its government is unstable or totalitarian, companies are usually well advised not to base production there. Similarly, if a particular national government appears to be pursuing inappropriate social or economic policies, this might be another reason for not basing production in that location, even if other factors look favorable.

● Leveraging the Skills of Global Subsidiaries

Initially, many multinational companies develop the valuable competencies and skills that underpin their business model in their home nation and then expand internationally, primarily by selling products and services based on those competencies.

However, for more mature multinational enterprises that have already established a network of subsidiary operations in foreign markets, the development of valuable skills can just as well occur in foreign subsidiaries.[11] Skills can be created anywhere within a multinational's global network of operations, wherever people have the opportunity and incentive to try new ways of doing things. The creation of skills that help to lower the costs of production, or to enhance perceived value and support higher product pricing, is not the monopoly of the corporate center.

Leveraging the skills created within subsidiaries and applying them to other operations within the firm's global network may create value. For example, McDonald's is finding more and more often that its foreign franchisees are a source of valuable new ideas. Faced with slow growth in France, its local franchisees have begun to experiment not only with the menu but also with the layout and theme of restaurants. Gone are the ubiquitous Golden Arches; gone too are many of the utilitarian chairs and tables and other plastic features of the fast-food giant. Many McDonald's restaurants in France now have hardwood floors, exposed brick walls, and even armchairs. Half of the 930 or so outlets in France have been upgraded to a level that would make them unrecognizable to an American. The menu, too, has been changed to include premier sandwiches, such as chicken on focaccia bread, priced some 30% higher than the average hamburger. In France at least, the strategy seems to be working. Following the changes, increases in same-store sales rose from 1% annually to 3.4%. Impressed with the impact, McDonald's executives are now considering adopting similar changes at other McDonald's restaurants in markets where same-store sales growth is sluggish, including the United States.[12]

For the managers of a multinational enterprise, this phenomenon creates important new challenges. First, they must have the humility to recognize that valuable skills can arise anywhere within the firm's global network, not just at the corporate center. Second, they must establish an incentive system that encourages local employees to acquire new competencies. This is not as easy as it sounds. Creating new competencies involves a degree of risk. Not all new skills add value. For every valuable idea created by a McDonald's subsidiary in a foreign country, there may be several failures. The management of the multinational must install incentives that encourage employees to take the necessary risks, and the company must reward people for successes and not sanction them unnecessarily for taking risks that did not pan out. Third, managers must have a process for identifying when valuable new skills have been created in a subsidiary, and finally, they need to act as facilitators, helping to transfer valuable skills within the firm.

Cost Pressures and Pressures for Local Responsiveness

Companies that compete in the global marketplace typically face two types of competitive pressures: *pressures for cost reductions* and *pressures to be locally responsive* (see Figure 8.2).[13] These competitive pressures place conflicting demands on a company. Responding to pressures for cost reductions requires that a company try to minimize its unit costs. To attain this goal, it may have to base its productive activities at the most favorable low-cost location, wherever in the world that might be. It may also have to offer a standardized product to the global marketplace in order to realize the cost savings that come from economies of scale and learning effects. On the other hand, responding to pressures to be locally responsive requires that a company differentiate its product offering and marketing strategy from country to country in an effort to accommodate the diverse demands arising from national differences in consumer

FIGURE 8.2

Pressures for Cost
Reductions and Local
Responsiveness

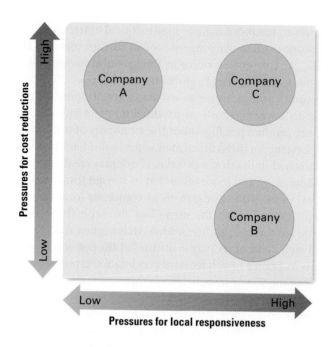

tastes and preferences, business practices, distribution channels, competitive conditions, and government policies. Because differentiation across countries can involve significant duplication and a lack of product standardization, it may raise costs.

Some companies, such as Company A in Figure 8.2, face high pressures for cost reductions and low pressures for local responsiveness, and others, such as Company B, face low pressures for cost reductions and high pressures for local responsiveness. But many companies are in the position of Company C: they face high pressures for both cost reductions and local responsiveness. Dealing with these conflicting and contradictory pressures is a difficult strategic challenge, primarily because being locally responsive tends to raise costs.

● **Pressures for Cost Reductions**

In competitive global markets, international businesses often face pressures for cost reductions. To respond to these pressures, a firm must try to lower the costs of value creation. A manufacturer, for example, might mass-produce a standardized product at the optimal location in the world, wherever that might be, to realize economies of scale and location economies. Alternatively, it might outsource certain functions to low-cost foreign suppliers in an attempt to reduce costs. Thus, many computer companies have outsourced their telephone-based customer service functions to India, where qualified technicians who speak English can be hired at a lower wage rate than in the United States. In the same vein, a retailer like Wal-Mart might push its suppliers (who are manufacturers) to also lower their prices. (In fact, the pressure that Wal-Mart has placed on its suppliers to reduce prices has been cited as a major cause of the trend among North American manufacturers to shift production to China.)[14] A service business, such as a bank, might move some back-office functions, like information processing, to developing nations where wage rates are lower.

Cost reduction pressures can be particularly intense in industries producing commodity-type products where meaningful differentiation on nonprice factors is difficult and price is the main competitive weapon. This tends to be the case for products that serve universal needs. Universal needs exist when the tastes and preferences of consumers in different nations are similar if not identical, such as for bulk chemicals, petroleum, steel, sugar, and the like. They also exist for many industrial and consumer products: for example, hand-held calculators, semiconductor chips, personal computers, and liquid crystal display screens. Pressures for cost reductions are also intense in industries where major competitors are based in low-cost locations, where there is persistent excess capacity, and where consumers are powerful and face low switching costs. Many commentators have argued that the liberalization of the world trade and investment environment in recent decades, by facilitating greater international competition, has generally increased cost pressures.[15]

● **Pressures for Local Responsiveness**

Pressures for local responsiveness arise from differences in consumer tastes and preferences, infrastructure and traditional practices, distribution channels, and host government demands. Responding to pressures to be locally responsive requires that a company differentiate its products and marketing strategy from country to country to accommodate these factors, all of which tends to raise a company's cost structure.

DIFFERENCES IN CUSTOMER TASTES AND PREFERENCES Strong pressures for local responsiveness emerge when customer tastes and preferences differ significantly between countries, as they may for historic or cultural reasons. In such cases, a multinational company's products and marketing message have to be customized to appeal to the tastes and preferences of local customers. The company is then typically pressured to delegate production and marketing responsibilities and functions to a company's overseas subsidiaries.

For example, the automobile industry in the 1980s and early 1990s moved toward the creation of so-called world cars. The idea was that global companies such as General Motors, Ford, and Toyota would be able to sell the same basic vehicle the world over, sourcing it from centralized production locations. If successful, the strategy would have enabled automobile companies to reap significant gains from global scale economies. However, this strategy frequently ran aground upon the hard rocks of consumer reality. Consumers in different automobile markets seem to have different tastes and preferences, and these require different types of vehicles. North American consumers show a strong demand for pickup trucks. This is particularly true in the South and West, where many families have a pickup truck as a second or third car. But in European countries, pickup trucks are seen purely as utility vehicles and are purchased primarily by firms rather than individuals. As a consequence, the product mix and marketing message need to be tailored to account for the different nature of demand in North America and Europe. Another example of the need to respond to national differences in tastes and preferences is given in Strategy in Action 8.2, which looks at the experience of Swedish retailer IKEA in foreign markets.

Notwithstanding the experiences of companies such as MTV and IKEA, some commentators have argued that customer demands for local customization are on the decline worldwide.[16] According to this argument, modern communications and transport technologies have created the conditions for a convergence of the tastes and preferences of customers from different nations. The result is the emergence of enormous global markets for standardized consumer products. The worldwide acceptance of McDonald's hamburgers, Coca-Cola, Gap clothes, Nokia cell phones, and Sony televisions, all of which are sold globally as standardized products, are often cited as evidence of the increasing homogeneity of the global marketplace. Others, however, consider this argument to be extreme. For example, Christopher Bartlett and Sumantra Ghoshal have observed that in the consumer electronics industry, buyers reacted to an overdose of standardized global products by showing a renewed preference for products that are differentiated according to local conditions.[17]

Strategy in Action

Localization at IKEA

IKEA may be the world's most successful global retailer. Established by Ingvar Kamprad in Sweden in 1943 when he was just seventeen years old, the home-furnishing superstore has grown into a global cult brand, with 230 stores in thirty-three countries that host 410 million shoppers a year and generated sales of €14.8 billion ($17.7 billion) in 2005. Kamprad himself, who still owns the private company, is rumored to be the world's richest man.

IKEA's target market is the global middle class who are looking for low-priced but attractively designed furniture and household items. The company applies the same basic formula worldwide: open, large warehouse stores, festooned in the blue and yellow colors of the Swedish flag, that offer 8,000 to 10,000 items, from kitchen cabinets to candlesticks. Use wacky promotions to drive traffic into the stores. Configure the interior of the stores so that customers have to pass through each department to get to the checkout. Add restaurants and child-care facilities so that shoppers stay as long as possible. Price the items as low as possible. Make sure that product design reflects the simple clean Swedish lines that have become IKEA's trademark. And then watch the results: customers who enter the store planning to buy a $40 coffee table and end up spending $500 on everything from storage units to kitchen ware.

IKEA aims to reduce the price of its offerings by 2 to 3% per year, which requires relentless attention to cost cutting. With a network of 1,300 suppliers in fifty-three countries, IKEA devotes considerable attention to finding the right manufacturer for each item. Consider the company's best-selling Klippan love seat. Designed in 1980, the Klippan, with its clean lines, bright colors, simple legs, and compact size, has sold some 1.5 million units since its introduction. Originally manufactured in Sweden, IKEA soon transferred production to lower-cost suppliers in Poland. As demand for the Klippan grew, IKEA then decided that it made more sense to work with suppliers in each of the company's big markets to avoid the costs associated with shipping the product all over the world. Today, there are five suppliers of the frames in Europe, plus three in the United States and two in China. To reduce the cost of the cotton slipcovers, production has been concentrated in four core suppliers in China and Europe. The resulting efficiencies from these global sourcing decisions enabled IKEA to reduce the price of the Klippan by some 40% between 1999 and 2005.

Despite its standard formula, however, IKEA has found that global success requires that it adapt its offerings to the tastes and preferences of consumers in different nations. IKEA first discovered this in the early 1990s, when it entered the United States. The company soon found that its European style offerings didn't always resonate with American consumers. Beds were measured in centimeters, not the king, queen, and twin sizes that Americans are familiar with. Sofas weren't big enough, wardrobe drawers were not deep enough, glasses were too small, curtains were too short, and kitchens didn't fit U.S. size appliances. Since then, IKEA has redesigned its offerings in the United States to appeal to American consumers, and it has been rewarded with stronger store sales. The same process is now unfolding in China, where the company plans to have ten stores by 2010. The store layout in China reflects the layout of many Chinese apartments, and since many Chinese apartments have balconies, IKEA's Chinese stores include a balcony section. IKEA has had to adapt its locations to China, where car ownership is still not widespread. In the West, IKEA stores are generally located in suburban areas and have lots of parking space, but in China they are located near public transportation, and IKEA offers delivery services so that Chinese customers can get their purchases home.[b]

DIFFERENCES IN INFRASTRUCTURE AND TRADITIONAL PRACTICES Pressures for local responsiveness also arise from differences in infrastructure or traditional practices among countries, creating a need to customize products accordingly. To meet this need, companies may have to delegate manufacturing and production functions to foreign subsidiaries. For example, in North America, consumer electrical systems are based on 110 volts, whereas in some European countries, 240-volt systems are standard. Thus, domestic electrical appliances have to be customized to take this difference in infrastructure into account. Traditional practices also often vary across nations. For example, in Britain, people drive on the left-hand side of the road, creating a demand for right-hand-drive cars, whereas in France (and the rest of Europe), people drive on the right-hand side of the road and therefore want left-hand-drive cars. Obviously, automobiles have to be customized to take this difference in traditional practices into account.

Although many of the country differences in infrastructure are rooted in history, some are quite recent. For example, in the wireless telecommunications industry, different technical standards are found in different parts of the world. A technical standard known as GSM is common in Europe, and an alternative standard, CDMA, is more common in the United States and parts of Asia. The significance of these different standards is that equipment designed for GSM will not work on a CDMA network, and vice versa. Thus, companies such as Nokia, Motorola, and Ericsson, which manufacture wireless handsets and infrastructure such as switches, need to customize their product offerings according to the technical standard prevailing in a given country.

DIFFERENCES IN DISTRIBUTION CHANNELS A company's marketing strategies may have to be responsive to differences in distribution channels among countries, which may necessitate delegating marketing functions to national subsidiaries. In the pharmaceutical industry, for example, the British and Japanese distribution system is radically different from the U.S. system. British and Japanese doctors will not accept or respond favorably to a U.S.-style high-pressure sales force. Thus, pharmaceutical companies have to adopt different marketing practices in Britain and Japan compared with the United States—soft sell versus hard sell.

Similarly, Poland, Brazil, and Russia all have similar per-capita income on a purchasing power parity basis, but there are big differences in distribution systems across the three countries. In Brazil, supermarkets account for 36% of food retailing; in Poland, for 18%; and in Russia, for less than 1%.[18] These differences in channels require that companies adapt their own distribution and sales strategy.

HOST GOVERNMENT DEMANDS Finally, economic and political demands imposed by host country governments may require local responsiveness. For example, pharmaceutical companies are subject to local clinical testing, registration procedures, and pricing restrictions, all of which make it necessary that the manufacturing and marketing of a drug meet local requirements. Moreover, because governments and government agencies control a significant proportion of the health care budget in most countries, they are in a powerful position to demand a high level of local responsiveness.

More generally, threats of protectionism, economic nationalism, and local content rules (which require that a certain percentage of a product be manufactured locally) dictate that international businesses manufacture locally. As an example, consider Bombardier, the Canadian-based manufacturer of railcars, aircraft, jet boats, and snowmobiles. Bombardier has twelve railcar factories across Europe. Critics of the company argue that the resulting duplication of manufacturing facilities leads to high costs and helps explain why Bombardier makes lower profit margins on its railcar operations than on its other business lines. In reply, managers at Bombardier argue that in Europe, informal rules with regard to local content favor employers who hire local workers. To sell railcars in Germany, they claim, you must manufacture in Germany. The same goes for Belgium, Austria, and France. To try to address its cost structure in Europe, Bombardier has centralized its engineering and purchasing functions, but it has no plans to centralize manufacturing.[19]

Choosing a Global Strategy

Pressures for local responsiveness imply that it may not be possible for a firm to realize the full benefits from economies of scale and location economies. It may not be possible to serve the global marketplace from a single low-cost location, producing a globally standardized product, and marketing it worldwide to achieve economies of scale. In practice, the need to customize the product offering to local conditions may work against the implementation of such a strategy. For example, automobile firms have found that Japanese, American, and European consumers demand different kinds of cars, and this necessitates producing products that are customized for local markets. In response, firms like Honda, Ford, and Toyota are pursuing a strategy of establishing top-to-bottom design and production facilities in each of these regions so that they can better serve local demands. Although such customization brings benefits, it also limits the ability of a firm to realize significant scale economies and location economies.

In addition, pressures for local responsiveness imply that it may not be possible to leverage skills and products associated with a firm's distinctive competencies wholesale from one nation to another. Concessions often have to be made to local conditions. Even McDonald's, despite being depicted as a leader for the proliferation of standardized global products, has found that it has to customize its product offerings (its menu) in order to account for national differences in tastes and preferences.

Given the need to balance the cost and differentiation (value) sides of a company's business model, how do differences in the strength of pressures for cost reductions versus those for local responsiveness affect the choice of a company's strategy? Companies typically choose among four main strategic postures when competing internationally: a global standardization strategy, a localization strategy, a transnational strategy, and an international strategy.[20] The appropriateness of each strategy varies with the extent of pressures for cost reductions and local responsiveness. Figure 8.3 illustrates the conditions under which each of these strategies is most appropriate.

FIGURE 8.3

Four Basic Strategies

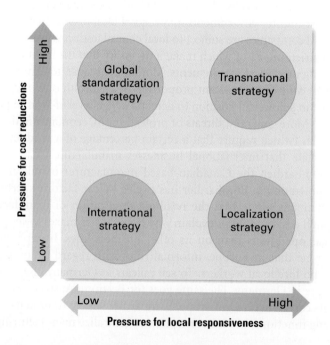

● **Global Standardization Strategy**

Companies that pursue a **global standardization strategy** focus on increasing profitability by reaping the cost reductions that come from economies of scale and location economies; that is, their business model is based on pursuing a low-cost strategy on a global scale. The production, marketing, and research and development (R&D) activities of companies pursuing a global strategy are concentrated in a few favorable locations. These companies try not to customize their product offering and marketing strategy to local conditions because customization, which involves shorter production runs and the duplication of functions, can raise costs. Instead, they prefer to market a standardized product worldwide so that they can reap the maximum benefits from economies of scale. They also tend to use their cost advantage to support aggressive pricing in world markets. Dell Computer is a good example of a company that pursues such a strategy (see the Running Case).

RUNNING CASE

Dell's Global Business Strategy

Dell has been expanding its presence outside the United States since the early 1990s. In fiscal 2006, 41% of Dell's $56 billion in revenue was generated outside the United States. Dell's strategic goal is to be the low-cost player in the global industry. It does not alter its business model from country to country; instead, it uses the same direct-selling and supply chain model that worked so well in the United States. Dell is thus pursuing a global standardization strategy.

Dell's basic approach to overseas expansion has been to serve foreign markets from a handful of regional manufacturing facilities, each established as a wholly owned subsidiary. To support its global business, it operates three final assembly facilities in the United States, one in Brazil (serving South America), two in Ireland (serving Europe), one in Malaysia (serving Southeast Asia), and two in China (serving China). Each of these plants is large enough to attain significant economies of scale. When demand in a region gets large enough, Dell considers opening a second plant; thus, it has three plants in the United States to serve North America, and two in Ireland to serve Europe. With sales growing rapidly in India, the company will bring an Indian plant online in 2007.

Each plant uses exactly the same supply chain management processes that have made Dell famous. Taking advantage of its supply chain management software, Dell schedules production of every line in every factory around the world every two hours. Every factory is run with no more than a few hours of inventory on hand, including work in progress. To serve Dell's global factories, many of Dell's largest suppliers have also located their facilities close to Dell's manufacturing plants so that they can better meet the company's demands for just-in-time inventory.

Dell has set up customer service centers in each region to handle phone and online orders and to provide technical assistance. In general, each center serves an entire region, which Dell has found to be more efficient than locating a customer service center in each country where the company does business. Beginning in 2001, Dell started to experiment with outsourcing some of its customer service functions for English-language customers to call centers in India. Although the move helped the company to lower costs, it also led to dissatisfaction from customers, particularly in the United States, who could not always follow the directions given over the phone from someone with an Indian accent. Subsequently, Dell moved its call centers for English-language businesses back to the United States and the United Kingdom. Dell continues to invest in Indian call centers for its retail customers, however, and in 2006, it announced that it was opening a fourth Indian call center.[c]

This strategy makes the most sense when there are strong pressures for cost reductions and demand for local responsiveness is minimal. Increasingly, these conditions prevail in many industrial goods industries, whose products often serve universal needs. In the semiconductor industry, for example, global standards have emerged, creating enormous demands for standardized global products. Accordingly, companies such as Intel, Texas Instruments, and Motorola all pursue a global strategy.

As both MTV and IKEA have discovered, however, in many consumer goods markets, demand for local responsiveness remains high. In these markets, the global standardization strategy is inappropriate.

● Localization Strategy

A **localization strategy** focuses on increasing profitability by customizing the company's goods or services so that they provide a good match to the tastes and preferences in different national markets. Localization is most appropriate when there are substantial differences across nations with regard to consumer tastes and preferences and where cost pressures are not too intense. By customizing the product offering to local demands, the company increases the value of that product in the local market. On the downside, because it involves some duplication of functions and smaller production runs, customization limits the ability of the company to capture the cost reductions associated with mass-producing a standardized product for global consumption. The strategy may make sense, however, if the added value associated with local customization supports higher pricing, which would enable the company to recoup its higher costs, or if it leads to substantially greater local demand, enabling the company to reduce costs through the attainment of some scale economies in the local market.

MTV is a good example of a company that has had to pursue a localization strategy (see the Opening Case). If MTV had not localized its programming to match the demands of viewers in different nations, it would have lost market share to local competitors, its advertising revenues would have fallen, and its profitability would have declined. Thus, even though it raised costs, localization became a strategic imperative at MTV.

At the same time, it is important to realize that companies like MTV still have to keep a close eye on costs. Companies pursuing a localization strategy still need to be efficient and, whenever possible, capture some scale economies from their global reach. As noted earlier, many automobile companies have found that they have to customize some of their product offerings to local market demands—for example, by producing large pickup trucks for U.S. consumers and small, fuel-efficient cars for Europeans and the Japanese. At the same time, these companies try to get some scale economies from their global volume by using common vehicle platforms and components across many different models and by manufacturing those platforms and components at efficiently scaled factories that are optimally located. By designing their products in this way, these companies have been able to localize their product offering, yet simultaneously capture some scale economies.

● Transnational Strategy

We have argued that a global standardization strategy makes the most sense when cost pressures are intense and demands for local responsiveness are limited. Conversely, a localization strategy makes the most sense when demands for local responsiveness are high but cost pressures are moderate or low. What happens, however, when the company simultaneously faces both strong cost pressures and strong pressures for local responsiveness? How can managers balance such competing and inconsistent demands? According to some researchers, the answer is by pursuing what has been called a transnational strategy.

Two of these researchers, Christopher Bartlett and Sumantra Ghoshal, argue that in today's global environment, competitive conditions are so intense that, to survive, companies must do all they can to respond to pressures for both cost reductions and local responsiveness. They must try to realize location economies and economies of scale from global volume, transfer distinctive competencies and skills within the company, and simultaneously pay attention to pressures for local responsiveness.[21]

Bartlett and Ghoshal also note that, in the modern multinational enterprise, distinctive competencies and skills do not reside just in the home country but can develop in any of the company's worldwide operations. Thus, they maintain that the flow of skills and product offerings should not be all one way, from home company to foreign subsidiary. Rather, the flow should also be from foreign subsidiary to home country, and from foreign subsidiary to foreign subsidiary. Transnational companies, in other words, must also focus on leveraging subsidiary skills.

In essence, companies that pursue a **transnational strategy** are trying to develop a business model that simultaneously achieves low costs, differentiates the product offering across geographic markets, and fosters a flow of skills between different subsidiaries in the company's global network of operations. As attractive as this may sound, the strategy is not an easy one to pursue because it places conflicting demands on the company. Differentiating the product to respond to local demands in different geographic markets raises costs, which runs counter to the goal of reducing costs. Companies like Ford and ABB (one of the world's largest engineering conglomerates) have tried to embrace a transnational strategy and have found it difficult to implement in practice.

Indeed, how best to implement a transnational strategy is one of the most complex questions that large global companies are grappling with today. It may be that few if any companies have perfected this strategic posture. But some clues to the right approach can be gleaned from a number of companies. Consider, for example, the case of Caterpillar. The need to compete with low-cost competitors such as Komatsu of Japan forced Caterpillar to look for greater cost economies. However, variations in construction practices and government regulations across countries meant that Caterpillar also had to be responsive to local demands. Therefore, Caterpillar confronted significant pressures for cost reductions and for local responsiveness. To deal with cost pressures, Caterpillar redesigned its products to use many identical components and invested in a few large-scale component-manufacturing facilities, sited at favorable locations, to fill global demand and realize scale economies. At the same time, the company augments the centralized manufacturing of components with assembly plants in each of its major global markets. At these plants, Caterpillar adds local product features, tailoring the finished product to local needs. Thus, Caterpillar is able to realize many of the benefits of global manufacturing while reacting to pressures for local responsiveness by differentiating its product among national markets.[22] Caterpillar started to pursue this strategy in 1979, and over the next twenty years, it succeeded in doubling output per employee, significantly reducing its overall cost structure in the process. Meanwhile, Komatsu and Hitachi, which are still wedded to a Japan-centric global strategy, have seen their cost advantages evaporate and have been steadily losing market share to Caterpillar.

However, building an organization capable of supporting a transnational strategy is a complex and challenging task. Indeed, some would say it is too complex because the strategy implementation problems of creating a viable organizational structure and the control systems to manage this strategy are immense. We shall return to this issue in Chapter 13.

● International Strategy

Sometimes it is possible to identify multinational companies that find themselves in the fortunate position of being confronted with low-cost pressures and low pressures for local responsiveness. Typically these enterprises are selling a product that serves universal needs, but because they do not face significant competitors, they are not confronted with pressures to reduce their cost structure. Xerox found itself in this position in the 1960s after its invention and commercialization of the photocopier. The technology underlying the photocopier was protected by strong patents, so for several years, Xerox did not face competitors—it had a monopoly. Because the product was highly valued in most developed nations, Xerox was able to sell the same basic product the world over and charge a relatively high price for it. At the same time, because it did not face direct competitors, the company did not have to deal with strong pressures to minimize its costs.

Historically, companies like Xerox have followed a similar developmental pattern as they build their international operations. They tend to centralize product development functions such as R&D at home. However, they also tend to establish manufacturing and marketing functions in each major country or geographic region in which they do business. Although they may undertake some local customization of product offering and marketing strategy, this tends to be rather limited in scope. Ultimately, in most international companies, the head office retains tight control over marketing and product strategy.

Other companies that have pursued this strategy include Procter & Gamble, which historically always developed innovative new products in Cincinnati and then transferred them wholesale to local markets. Another company that has followed a similar strategy is Microsoft. The bulk of Microsoft's product development work takes place in Redmond, Washington, where the company is headquartered. Although some localization work is undertaken elsewhere, this is limited to producing foreign-language versions of popular Microsoft programs such as Office.

● Changes in Strategy over Time

The Achilles heel of the international strategy is that, over time, competitors inevitably emerge, and if managers do not take proactive steps to reduce their cost structure, their company may be rapidly outflanked by efficient global competitors. This is exactly what happened to Xerox. Japanese companies such as Canon ultimately invented their way around Xerox's patents, produced their own photocopiers in very efficient manufacturing plants, priced them below Xerox's products, and rapidly took global market share from Xerox. Xerox's demise was not due to the emergence of competitors, because ultimately that was bound to occur, but rather to its failure to proactively reduce its cost structure in advance of the emergence of efficient global competitors. The message in this story is that an international strategy may not be viable in the long term, and to survive, companies that are able to pursue it need to shift toward a global standardization strategy, or perhaps a transnational strategy, in advance of competitors (see Figure 8.4).

The same can be said about a localization strategy. Localization may give a company a competitive edge, but if it is simultaneously facing aggressive competitors, the company will also have to reduce its cost structure, and the only way to do that may be to adopt more of a transnational strategy. Thus, as competition intensifies, international and localization strategies tend to become less viable, and managers need to orientate their companies toward either a global standardization strategy or a transnational strategy.

FIGURE 8.4

Changes over Time

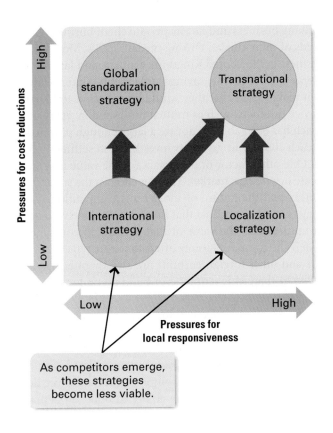

As competitors emerge, these strategies become less viable.

Basic Entry Decisions

A company contemplating foreign expansion must make three basic decisions: which overseas markets to enter, when to enter those markets, and on what scale.

● **Which Overseas Markets to Enter**

There are over 200 nation-states in the world, and they do not all hold out the same profit potential for a company contemplating foreign expansion. The choice of foreign markets must be based on an assessment of their long-run profit potential. The attractiveness of a country as a potential market for international business depends on balancing the benefits, costs, and risks associated with doing business in that country. The long-run economic benefits of doing business in a country are a function of factors such as the size of a market (in terms of demographics), the existing wealth (purchasing power) of consumers in that market, and the likely future wealth of consumers. Some markets are very large when measured by numbers of consumers (such as China and India), but low living standards may imply limited purchasing power and therefore a relatively small market when measured in economic terms. The costs and risks associated with doing business in a foreign country are typically lower in economically advanced and politically stable democratic nations and greater in less developed and politically unstable nations.

By performing benefit-cost-risk calculations, a company can come up with a ranking of countries in terms of their attractiveness and long-run profit potential.[23] Obviously, preference is given to entering markets that rank highly. For an example, consider the case of the American financial services company Merrill Lynch. Although Merrill Lynch has long had international operations, these were in its investment banking business and not its private client business (which deals with the investment needs of individuals). During the late 1990s, Merrill Lynch entered the private-client business in the United Kingdom, Canada, and Japan. All three of these countries have a large pool of private savings and exhibit relatively low political and economic risks, so it makes sense that they would be attractive to Merrill Lynch. By offering financial service products, such as mutual funds and investment advice, to individuals, Merrill Lynch has been able to capture a large enough proportion of the private savings pool in each country to justify its investment in setting up business there.

One other factor of importance is the value that a company's business model can create in a foreign market. This depends on the suitability of its business model to that market and the nature of indigenous competition.[24] Most importantly, if the company can offer a product that has not been widely available in that market and satisfies an unmet need, the value of that product to consumers is likely to be much greater than if the company simply offers the same type of product that indigenous competitors and other foreign entrants are already offering. Greater value translates into an ability to charge higher prices or build up unit sales volume more rapidly (or both).

● **Timing of Entry** Once a set of attractive national markets has been identified, it is important to consider the timing of entry: early (before other overseas companies) or late (after other international businesses have already established themselves in the market). Several first-mover advantages are frequently associated with entering a market early.[25] One advantage is the ability to preempt rivals and capture demand by establishing a strong brand name. A second is the ability to build up demand, sales revenue, and market share in that country and ride down the experience curve ahead of future rivals. Both factors give the early entrant a cost advantage over later entrants, which may enable it to respond to later entry by cutting prices below those of later entrants and drive them out of the market. A third advantage is the ability of early entrants to create switching costs that tie customers into their products or services. Such switching costs make it difficult for later entrants to win business.

The case of Merrill Lynch illustrates these ideas. Merrill Lynch was one of the first western firms to set up a private-client business in Japan. Merrill entered by acquiring fifty branch offices and 2,000 employees from the bankrupt Japanese investment firm, Yamaichi Securities. By entering the private-client market in Japan before competitors, Merrill hoped to establish a brand name that later entrants would find difficult to match. Moreover, by entering early with a valuable product offering, Merrill hoped to build up its sales volume rapidly, which would enable it to realize scale economies from establishing a network of Japanese branches. Finally, Merrill's business model is based on establishing close relationships between its financial advisers (that is, stockbrokers) and private clients. Merrill's financial advisers are taught to get to know the needs of their clients and help manage their finances more effectively. Once these relationships are established, people rarely change. In other words, because of *switching costs*, they are unlikely to shift their business to later entrants. This effect is likely to be particularly strong in a country like Japan, where long-term relationships have traditionally been very important in business and social settings. For all of these reasons, Merrill Lynch hoped to capture first-mover advantages relative to its western competitors that would enable it to enjoy a strong competitive position in Japan for years to come.

There can also be first-mover disadvantages associated with entering a foreign market before other global companies.[26] These disadvantages are associated with pioneering costs, which an early entrant has to bear and which a later entrant can avoid. **Pioneering costs** arise when the business system in a foreign country is so different from that in a company's home market that a company has to devote considerable effort, time, and expense to learning the rules of the game. Pioneering costs also include the costs of business failure if the company, because of its ignorance of the overseas environment, makes major strategic mistakes. Thus, a global company that is one of the first to enter a national market has a certain liability.[27] Research evidence suggests that the probability of survival increases if an international business enters a national market after several other overseas companies have already done so.[28] The late entrant, it would appear, benefits by observing and learning from the mistakes made by early entrants.

Pioneering costs also include the costs of promoting and establishing a product offering, including the costs of educating customers. These can be significant when the product being promoted is unfamiliar to local consumers. In contrast, later entrants may be able to ride on an early entrant's investments in learning and customer education by watching how the early entrant proceeded in the market, by avoiding costly mistakes made by the early entrant, and by exploiting the market potential created by the early entrant's investments in customer education. For example, KFC introduced the Chinese to American-style fast food, but a later entrant, McDonald's, has capitalized on the market in China.

● **Scale of Entry and Strategic Commitments**

The final issue that a company needs to consider when contemplating market entry is the scale of entry. Entering a market on a large scale involves the commitment of significant resources to that venture. Not all companies have the resources necessary to enter on a large scale, and even some large companies prefer to enter overseas markets on a small scale and then build their presence slowly over time as they become more familiar with the market.

The consequences of entering on a significant scale are associated with the value of the resulting strategic commitments.[29] A strategic commitment is a decision that has a long-term impact and is difficult to reverse. Deciding to enter a foreign market on a significant scale is a major strategic commitment. Strategic commitments, such as large-scale market entry, can have an important influence on the nature of competition in a market. For example, by entering Japan's private client business on a significant scale with fifty offices and 2,000 employees, Merrill signaled its commitment to the market. Merrill hoped this would have several effects. On the positive side, it would make it easier for Merrill to attract clients. The scale of entry gives potential clients reason for believing that Merrill will remain in the market for the long run. It may also give other overseas institutions considering entry into Japan's market pause for thought because now they will have to compete not only against Japan's indigenous institutions but also against an aggressive and successful U.S. institution. On the negative side, the move may wake up Japan's financial institutions and elicit a vigorous competitive response from them (which has occurred). Moreover, by committing itself heavily to Japan, Merrill may have fewer resources available to support expansion in other desirable markets. In other words, Merrill's commitment to Japan limits its strategic flexibility.

As this example suggests, significant strategic commitments are neither unambiguously good nor bad. Rather, they tend to change the competitive playing field and unleash a number of changes, some of which may be desirable and some of which may not. Therefore, it is important for a company to think through the implications of large-scale entry into a market and act accordingly. Of particular relevance is trying to identify how actual and potential competitors might react to large-scale entry into a market. It is also important to bear in mind a connection between large-scale entry and first-mover advantages. Specifically, the large-scale entrant is more likely than the small-scale entrant to be able to capture first-mover advantages associated with demand preemption, scale economies, and switching costs.

Balanced against the value and risks of the commitments associated with large-scale entry are the benefits of entering on a small scale. Small-scale entry has the advantage of allowing a company to learn about a foreign market while simultaneously limiting the company's exposure to that market. In this sense, small-scale entry can be seen as a way of gathering more information about a foreign market before deciding whether to enter on a significant scale and how best to enter that market. In other words, by giving the company time to collect information, small-scale entry reduces the risks associated with a subsequent large-scale entry. On the other hand, the lack of commitment associated with small-scale entry may make it more difficult for the small-scale entrant to build market share and capture first-mover or early-mover advantages. The risk-averse company that enters a foreign market on a small scale may limit its potential losses, but it may also lose the chance to capture first-mover advantages.

The Choice of Entry Mode

The issue of when and how to enter a new national market raises the question of how to determine the best mode or vehicle for such entry. There are five main choices of entry mode: exporting, licensing, franchising, entering into a joint venture with a host country company, and setting up a wholly owned subsidiary in the host country. Each mode has its advantages and disadvantages, and managers must weigh these carefully when deciding which mode to use.[30]

● **Exporting**   Most manufacturing companies begin their global expansion as exporters and only later switch to one of the other modes for serving a foreign market. Exporting has two distinct advantages: it avoids the costs of establishing manufacturing operations in the host country, which are often substantial, and it may be consistent with scale economies and location economies. By manufacturing the product in a centralized location and then exporting it to other national markets, the company may be able to realize substantial scale economies from its global sales volume. That is how Sony came to dominate the global television market, how many Japanese auto companies originally made inroads into the U.S. auto market, and how Samsung gained share in the market for computer memory chips.

There are also a number of drawbacks to exporting. First, exporting from the company's home base may not be appropriate if there are lower-cost locations for manufacturing the product abroad (that is, if the company can realize location economies by moving production elsewhere). Thus, particularly in the case of a company pursuing a global standardization or transnational strategy, it may pay to manufacture in a location where conditions are most favorable from a value creation perspective and then export from that location to the rest of the globe. This is not so much an argument against exporting as an argument against exporting from the company's home country. For example, many U.S. electronics companies have moved some of their manufacturing to Asia because low-cost but highly skilled labor is available there. They export from that location to the rest of the globe, including the United States.

Another drawback is that high transport costs can make exporting uneconomical, particularly in the case of bulk products. One way of getting around this problem is to manufacture bulk products on a regional basis, thereby realizing some economies from large-scale production while limiting transport costs. Many multinational chemical companies manufacture their products on a regional basis, serving several countries in a region from one facility.

Tariff barriers, too, can make exporting uneconomical, and a government's threat to impose tariff barriers can make the strategy very risky. Indeed, the implicit threat from the U.S. Congress to impose tariffs on Japanese cars imported into the United States led directly to the decision by many Japanese auto companies to set up manufacturing plants in the United States.

Finally, a common practice among companies that are just beginning to export also poses risks. A company may delegate marketing activities in each country in which it does business to a local agent, but there is no guarantee that the agent will act in the company's best interest. Often foreign agents also carry the products of competing companies and thus have divided loyalties. Consequently, they may not do as good a job as the company would if it managed marketing itself. One way to solve this problem is to set up a wholly owned subsidiary in the host country to handle local marketing. In this way, the company can reap the cost advantages that arise from manufacturing the product in a single location and exercise tight control over marketing strategy in the host country.

Licensing

International licensing is an arrangement whereby a foreign licensee buys the rights to produce a company's product in the licensee's country for a negotiated fee (normally, royalty payments on the number of units sold). The licensee then puts up most of the capital necessary to get the overseas operation going.[31] The advantage of licensing is that the company does not have to bear the development costs and risks associated with opening up a foreign market. Licensing therefore can be a very attractive option for companies that lack the capital to develop operations overseas. It can also be an attractive option for companies that are unwilling to commit substantial financial resources to an unfamiliar or politically volatile foreign market where political risks are particularly high.

Licensing has three serious drawbacks, however. First, it does not give a company the tight control over manufacturing, marketing, and strategic functions in foreign countries that it needs to have in order to realize scale economies and location economies—as companies pursuing both global standardization and transnational strategies try to do. Typically, each licensee sets up its own manufacturing operations. Hence, the company stands little chance of realizing scale economies and location economies by manufacturing its product in a centralized location. When these economies are likely to be important, licensing may not be the best way of expanding overseas.

Second, competing in a global marketplace may make it necessary for a company to coordinate strategic moves across countries so that the profits earned in one country can be used to support competitive attacks in another. Licensing, by its very nature, severely limits a company's ability to coordinate strategy in this way. A licensee is unlikely to let a multinational company take its profits (beyond those due in the form of royalty payments) and use them to support an entirely different licensee operating in another country.

A third problem with licensing is the risk associated with licensing technological know-how to foreign companies. For many multinational companies, technological know-how forms the basis of their competitive advantage, and they would want to maintain control over the use to which it is put. By licensing its technology, a company can quickly lose control over it. RCA, for instance, once licensed its color television technology to a number of Japanese companies. The Japanese companies quickly assimilated RCA's technology and then used it to enter the U.S. market. Now the Japanese have a bigger share of the U.S. market than the RCA brand does.

There are ways of reducing this risk. One way is by entering into a cross-licensing agreement with a foreign firm. Under a cross-licensing agreement, a firm might license some valuable intangible property to a foreign partner and, in addition to a royalty payment, also request that the foreign partner license some of its valuable know-how to the firm. Such agreements are believed to reduce the risks associated with licensing technological know-how because the licensee realizes that if it violates the spirit of a licensing contract (by using the knowledge obtained to compete directly with the licensor), the licensor can do the same to it. Put differently, cross-licensing agreements enable firms to hold each other hostage, thereby reducing the probability that they will behave opportunistically toward each other.[32] Such cross-licensing agreements are increasingly common in high-technology industries. For example, the U.S. biotechnology firm Amgen has licensed one of its key drugs, Nuprogene, to Kirin, the Japanese pharmaceutical company. The license gives Kirin the right to sell Nuprogene in Japan. In return, Amgen receives a royalty payment and, through a licensing agreement, it gains the right to sell certain of Kirin's products in the United States.

● Franchising

In many respects, franchising is similar to licensing, although franchising tends to involve longer-term commitments than licensing does. Franchising is basically a specialized form of licensing in which the franchiser not only sells intangible property to the franchisee (normally a trademark), but also insists that the franchisee agree to abide by strict rules about how it does business. The franchiser will also often assist the franchisee to run the business on an ongoing basis. As with licensing, the franchiser typically receives a royalty payment, which amounts to some percentage of the franchisee's revenues.

Whereas licensing is a strategy pursued primarily by manufacturing companies, franchising, which resembles it in some respects, is a strategy employed chiefly by service companies. McDonald's provides a good example of a firm that has grown by using a franchising strategy. McDonald's has set down strict rules about how franchisees should operate a restaurant. These rules extend to control over the menu, cooking methods, staffing policies, and restaurant design and location. McDonald's also organizes the supply chain for its franchisees and provides management training and financial assistance.[33]

The advantages of franchising are similar to those of licensing. Specifically, the franchiser does not have to bear the development costs and risks of opening up a foreign market on its own because the franchisee typically assumes those costs and risks. Thus, using a franchising strategy, a service company can build up a global presence quickly and at a low cost.

The disadvantages are less pronounced than in the case of licensing. Since franchising is often used by service companies, there is no reason to consider the need for coordination of manufacturing to achieve experience curve and location economies. But franchising may inhibit the firm's ability to take profits out of one country to support competitive attacks in another. A more significant disadvantage of franchising is quality control. The foundation of franchising arrangements is that the firm's brand name conveys a message to consumers about the quality of the firm's product. Thus, a business traveler checking in at a Four Seasons hotel in Hong Kong can reasonably expect the same quality of room, food, and service that she would receive in New York. The Four Seasons name is supposed to guarantee consistent product quality. This presents a problem because foreign franchisees may not be as concerned about quality as they are supposed to be, and the result of poor quality can extend beyond lost sales in a particular foreign market to a decline in the firm's worldwide reputation. For example, if the business traveler has a bad experience at the Four Seasons in Hong Kong, she may never go to another Four Seasons hotel and may urge her colleagues to do likewise. The geographical distance of the firm from its foreign franchisees can make poor quality difficult to detect. In addition, the sheer numbers of franchisees—in the case of McDonald's, tens of thousands—can make quality control difficult. Due to these factors, quality problems may persist.

To reduce the extent of quality problems, a company can set up a subsidiary in each country or region in which it is expanding. The subsidiary, which might be wholly owned by the company or a joint venture with a foreign company, then assumes the rights and obligations to establish franchisees throughout that particular country or region. The combination of proximity and the limited number of independent franchisees that have to be monitored reduces the quality control problem. Besides, because the subsidiary is at least partly owned by the company, the company can place its own managers in the subsidiary to ensure the kind of quality monitoring it wants. This organizational arrangement has proved very popular in practice. It has been used by McDonald's, KFC, and Hilton Hotels Corp. to expand their international operations, to name just three examples.

● **Joint Ventures**   Establishing a joint venture with a foreign company has long been a favored mode for entering a new market. One of the most famous long-term joint ventures is the Fuji Xerox joint venture to produce photocopiers for the Japanese market. The most typical form of joint venture is a 50/50 joint venture, in which each party takes a 50% ownership stake and operating control is shared by a team of managers from both parent companies. Some companies have sought joint ventures in which they have a majority shareholding (for example, a 51% to 49% ownership split), which permits tighter control by the dominant partner.[34]

Joint ventures have a number of advantages. First, a company may feel that it can benefit from a local partner's knowledge of a host country's competitive conditions, culture, language, political systems, and business systems. Second, when the development costs and risks of opening a foreign market are high, a company might gain by sharing these costs and risks with a local partner. Third, in some countries, political considerations make joint ventures the only feasible entry mode. For example, historically many U.S. companies found it much easier to get permission to set up operations in Japan if they went in with a Japanese partner than if they tried to enter on their own. This is why Xerox originally teamed up with Fuji to sell photocopiers in Japan.

Despite these advantages, there are major disadvantages with joint ventures. First, as with licensing, a firm that enters into a joint venture risks giving control of its technology to its partner. Thus, a proposed joint venture in 2002 between Boeing and Mitsubishi Heavy Industries to build a new wide-body jet raised fears that Boeing might unwittingly give away its commercial airline technology to the Japanese. However, joint-venture agreements can be constructed to minimize this risk. One option is to hold majority ownership in the venture. This allows the dominant partner to exercise greater control over its technology. But it can be difficult to find a foreign partner who is willing to settle for minority ownership. Another option is to keep secret from a partner the technology that is central to the core competence of the firm while sharing other technology.

A second disadvantage is that a joint venture does not give a firm the tight control over subsidiaries that it might need to realize experience-curve or location economies. Nor does it give a firm the tight control over a foreign subsidiary that it might need for engaging in coordinated global attacks against its rivals. Consider the entry of Texas Instruments (TI) into the Japanese semiconductor market. When TI established semiconductor facilities in Japan, it did so for the dual purpose of checking Japanese manufacturers' market share and limiting their cash available for invading TI's global market. In other words, TI was engaging in global strategic coordination. To implement this strategy, TI's subsidiary in Japan had to be prepared to take instructions from corporate headquarters regarding competitive strategy. The strategy also required the Japanese subsidiary to run at a loss if necessary. Few if any potential joint-venture partners would have been willing to accept such conditions because it would have necessitated a willingness to accept a negative return on investment. Indeed, many joint ventures establish a degree of autonomy that would make such direct control over strategic decisions all but impossible to establish.[35] Thus, to implement this strategy, TI set up a wholly owned subsidiary in Japan.

● Wholly Owned Subsidiaries

A wholly owned subsidiary is one in which the parent company owns 100% of the subsidiary's stock. To establish a wholly owned subsidiary in a foreign market, a company can either set up a completely new operation in that country or acquire an established host country company and use it to promote its products in the host market.

Setting up a wholly owned subsidiary offers three advantages. First, when a company's competitive advantage is based on its control of a technological competency, a wholly owned subsidiary will normally be the preferred entry mode because it reduces the company's risk of losing this control. Consequently, many high-tech companies prefer wholly owned subsidiaries to joint ventures or licensing arrangements. Wholly owned subsidiaries tend to be the favored entry mode in the semiconductor, computer, electronics, and pharmaceutical industries.

Second, a wholly owned subsidiary gives a company the kind of tight control over operations in different countries that it needs if it is going to engage in global strategic coordination—taking profits from one country to support competitive attacks in another.

Third, a wholly owned subsidiary may be the best choice if a company wants to realize location economies and the scale economies that flow from producing a standardized output from a single or limited number of manufacturing plants. When pressures on costs are intense, it may be more beneficial for a company to configure its value chain so that value added at each stage is maximized. Thus, a national subsidiary may specialize in manufacturing only part of the product line or certain components of the end product, and then exchanging parts and products with other subsidiaries in the company's global system. Establishing such a global production system requires a high degree of control over the operations of national affiliates. Different national operations have to be prepared to accept centrally determined decisions about how they should produce, how much they should produce, and how their output should be priced for transfer between operations. A wholly owned subsidiary would have to comply with these mandates, whereas licensees or joint-venture partners would most likely shun such a subservient role.

On the other hand, establishing a wholly owned subsidiary is generally the most costly method of serving a foreign market. The parent company must bear all the costs and risks of setting up overseas operations—in contrast to joint ventures, where the costs and risks are shared, or licensing, where the licensee bears most of the costs and risks. But the risks of learning to do business in a new culture diminish if the company acquires an established host country enterprise. Acquisitions, though, raise a whole set of additional problems, such as trying to marry divergent corporate cultures, and these problems may more than offset the benefits. (The problems associated with acquisitions are discussed in Chapter 10.)

Choosing an Entry Strategy

The advantages and disadvantages of the various entry modes are summarized in Table 8.1. Tradeoffs are inevitable in choosing one entry mode over another. For example, when considering entry into an unfamiliar country with a track record of nationalizing foreign-owned enterprises, a company might favor a joint venture with a local enterprise. Its rationale might be that the local partner will help it establish operations in an unfamiliar environment and speak out against nationalization should the possibility arise. But if the company's distinctive competency is based on proprietary technology, entering into a joint venture might mean risking loss of control over that technology to the joint-venture partner, which would make this strategy

TABLE 8.1

The Advantages and Disadvantages of Different Entry Modes

Entry Mode	Advantages	Disadvantages
Exporting	Ability to realize location- and scale-based economies	High transport costs Trade barriers Problems with local marketing agents
Licensing	Low development costs and risks	Inability to realize location- and scale-based economies Inability to engage in global strategic coordination Lack of control over technology
Franchising	Low development costs and risks	Inability to engage in global strategic coordination Lack of control over quality
Joint ventures	Access to local partner's knowledge Shared development costs and risks Political dependency	Inability to engage in global strategic coordination Inability to realize location- and scale-based economies Lack of control over technology
Wholly owned subsidiaries	Protection of technology Ability to engage in global strategic coordination Ability to realize location- and scale-based economies	High costs and risks

unattractive. Despite such hazards, some generalizations can be offered about the optimal choice of entry mode.

DISTINCTIVE COMPETENCIES AND ENTRY MODE When companies expand internationally to earn greater returns from their differentiated product offerings, entering markets where indigenous competitors lack comparable products, the companies are pursuing an international strategy. The optimal entry mode for such companies depends to some degree on the nature of their distinctive competency. In particular, we need to distinguish between companies with a distinctive competency in technological know-how and those with a distinctive competency in management know-how.

If a company's competitive advantage—its distinctive competency—derives from its control of proprietary technological know-how, licensing and joint-venture arrangements should be avoided if possible to minimize the risk of losing control of that technology. Thus, if a high-tech company is considering setting up operations in a foreign country to profit from a distinctive competency in technological know-how, it should probably do so through a wholly owned subsidiary.

However, this rule should not be viewed as a hard and fast one. For instance, a licensing or joint-venture arrangement might be structured so that it reduces the risks that a company's technological know-how will be expropriated by licensees or joint-venture partners. We consider this kind of arrangement in more detail later in the chapter when we discuss the issue of structuring strategic alliances. To take another exception to the rule, a company may perceive its technological advantage as being only transitory and expect rapid imitation of its core technology by competitors. In this situation, the company might want to license its technology as quickly as possible to foreign companies to gain global acceptance of its technology before imitation occurs.[36] Such a strategy has some advantages. By licensing its technology to competitors, the company may deter them from developing their own, possibly superior, technology. It also may be able to establish its technology as the dominant design in the industry (as Matsushita did with its VHS format for VCRs), thus ensuring a steady stream of royalty payments. Except for these situations, however, the attractions of licensing are probably outweighed by the risks of losing control of technology, and therefore licensing should be avoided.

The competitive advantage of many service companies, such as McDonald's or Hilton Hotels, is based on management know-how. For such companies, the risk of losing control of their management skills to franchisees or joint-venture partners is not that great. The reason is that the valuable asset of such companies is their brand name, and brand names are generally well protected by international laws pertaining to trademarks. Given this fact, many of the issues that arise in the case of technological know-how do not arise in the case of management know-how. As a result, many service companies favor a combination of franchising and subsidiaries to control franchisees within a particular country or region. The subsidiary may be wholly owned or a joint venture. In most cases, however, service companies have found that entering into a joint venture with a local partner to set up a controlling subsidiary in a country or region works best because a joint venture is often politically more acceptable and brings a degree of local knowledge to the subsidiary.

PRESSURES FOR COST REDUCTION AND ENTRY MODE The greater the pressures for cost reductions, the more likely it is that a company will want to pursue some combination of exporting and wholly owned subsidiaries. By manufacturing in the locations where factor conditions are optimal and then exporting to the rest of the world, a company may be able to realize substantial location economies and substantial scale economies. The company might then want to export the finished product to marketing subsidiaries based in various countries. Typically, these subsidiaries would be wholly owned and have the responsibility for overseeing distribution in a particular country. Setting up wholly owned marketing subsidiaries is preferable to a joint-venture arrangement or using a foreign marketing agent because it gives the company the tight control over marketing that might be required to coordinate a globally dispersed value chain. In addition, tight control over a local operation enables the company to use the profits generated in one market to improve its competitive position in another market. Hence, companies pursuing global or transnational strategies prefer to establish wholly owned subsidiaries.

Global Strategic Alliances

Global strategic alliances are cooperative agreements between companies from different countries that are actual or potential competitors. Strategic alliances run the gamut from formal joint ventures, in which two or more companies have an equity stake, to short-term contractual agreements, in which two companies may agree to cooperate on a particular problem (such as developing a new product).

● **Advantages of Strategic Alliances**

Companies enter into strategic alliances with competitors to achieve a number of strategic objectives.[37] First, strategic alliances may facilitate entry into a foreign market. For example, many firms feel that if they are to successfully enter the Chinese market, they need a local partner who understands business conditions and who has good connections (or *guanxi*—see Chapter 3). Thus, in 2004, Warner Brothers entered into a joint venture with two Chinese partners to produce and distribute films in China. As a foreign film company, Warner found that if it wanted to produce films on its own for the Chinese market, it had to go through a complex approval process for every film, and it had to farm out distribution to a local company, both of which made doing business in China very difficult. Due to the participation of Chinese firms, however, the joint-venture films will go through a streamlined approval process, and the venture will be able to distribute any films it produces. Moreover, the joint venture will be able to produce films for Chinese television, something that foreign firms are not allowed to do.[38]

Second, strategic alliances allow firms to share the fixed costs (and associated risks) of developing new products or processes. An alliance between Boeing and a number of Japanese companies to build Boeing's latest commercial jetliner, the 787, was motivated by Boeing's desire to share the estimated $8 billion investment required to develop the aircraft. For another example of cost sharing, see Strategy in Action 8.3, which discusses the strategic alliances between Cisco and Fujitsu.

Third, an alliance is a way to bring together complementary skills and assets that neither company could easily develop on its own.[39] In 2003, for example, Microsoft and Toshiba established an alliance aimed at developing embedded microprocessors (essentially tiny computers) that can perform a variety of entertainment functions in an automobile (e.g., run a back-seat DVD player or a wireless Internet connection). The processors will run a version of Microsoft's Windows CE operating system. Microsoft brings its software engineering skills to the alliance and Toshiba brings its skills in developing microprocessors.[40] The alliance between Cisco and Fujitsu was also formed to share know-how (see Strategy in Action 8.3).

Strategy in Action

Cisco and Fujitsu

In late 2004, Cisco Systems, the world's largest manufacturer of Internet routers, entered into an alliance with the Japanese computer, electronics, and telecommunications equipment firm, Fujitsu. The stated purpose of the alliance was to jointly develop next-generation high-end routers for sale in Japan. Routers are the digital switches that sit at the heart of the Internet and direct traffic—they are, in effect, the traffic cops of the Internet. Although Cisco has long held the leading share in the market for routers (indeed, it pioneered the original router technology), it faces increasing competition from other firms such as Juniper Technologies and China's fast growing Huawei Technologies. At the same time, demand in the market is shifting as more and more telecommunications companies adopt Internet-based telecommunications services. While Cisco has long had a strong global presence, management also felt that the company needed to have a better presence in Japan, which is shifting rapidly to second-generation high-speed Internet-based telecommunications networks.

By entering into an alliance with Fujitsu, Cisco feels it can achieve a number of goals. First, both firms can pool their R&D efforts, which will enable them to share complementary technology and develop products quicker, thereby gaining an advantage over competitors. Second,

by combining Cisco's proprietary leading-edge router technology with Fujitsu's production expertise, the companies believe that they can produce products that are more reliable than those currently offered. Third, Fujitsu will give Cisco a stronger sales presence in Japan. Fujitsu has good links with Japan's telecommunications companies and a well-earned reputation for reliability. It will leverage these assets to sell the routers produced by the alliance, which will be co-branded as Fujitsu-Cisco products. Fourth, sales may be further enhanced by bundling the co-branded routers together with other telecommunications equipment that Fujitsu sells and marketing an entire solution to customers. Fujitsu sells many telecommunications products, but it lacks a strong presence in routers. Cisco is strong in routers but lacks strong offerings elsewhere. The combination of the two company's products will enable Fujitsu to offer Japan's telecommunications companies end-to-end communications solutions. Since many companies prefer to purchase their equipment from a single provider, this should drive sales.

The alliance introduced its first products in May 2006. If it is successful, both firms should benefit. Development costs will be lower than if they did not cooperate. Cisco will grow its sales in Japan, and Fujitsu can use the co-branded routers to fill out its product line and sell more bundles of products to Japan's telecommunications companies.[d]

Fourth, it can make sense to form an alliance that will help the firm establish technological standards for the industry that will benefit the firm. For example, in 1999, Palm Computer, the leading maker of personal digital assistants (PDAs), entered into an alliance with Sony under which Sony agreed to license and use Palm's operating system in Sony PDAs. The motivation for the alliance was in part to help establish Palm's operating system as the industry standard for PDAs, as opposed to a rival Windows-based operating system from Microsoft.[41]

● **Disadvantages of Strategic Alliances**

The advantages we have discussed can be very significant. Despite this, some commentators have criticized strategic alliances on the grounds that they give competitors a low-cost route to new technology and markets.[42] For example, a few years ago, some commentators argued that many strategic alliances between U.S. and Japanese firms were part of an implicit Japanese strategy to keep high-paying, high-value-added jobs in Japan while gaining the project engineering and production process skills that underlie the competitive success of many U.S. companies.[43] They argued that Japanese success in the machine tool and semiconductor industries was built on U.S. technology acquired through strategic alliances. And they argued that U.S. managers were aiding the Japanese by entering alliances that channel new inventions to Japan and provide a U.S. sales and distribution network for the resulting products. Although such deals may generate short-term profits, so the argument goes, in the long run, the result is to "hollow out" U.S. firms, leaving them with no competitive advantage in the global marketplace.

These critics have a point; alliances have risks. Unless a firm is careful, it can give away more than it receives. But there are so many examples of apparently successful alliances between firms—including alliances between U.S. and Japanese firms—that their position seems extreme. It is difficult to see how the Microsoft–Toshiba alliance, the Boeing–Mitsubishi alliance for the 787, or the Fuji–Xerox alliance fit the critics' thesis. In these cases, both partners seem to have gained from the alliance. Why do some alliances benefit both firms while others benefit one firm and hurt the other? The next section provides an answer to this question.

● Making Strategic Alliances Work

The failure rate for international strategic alliances is quite high. For example, one study of forty-nine international strategic alliances found that two-thirds run into serious managerial and financial troubles within two years of their formation, and although many of these problems are ultimately solved, 33% are ultimately rated as failures by the parties involved.[44] The success of an alliance seems to be a function of three main factors: partner selection, alliance structure, and the manner in which the alliance is managed.

PARTNER SELECTION One of the keys to making a strategic alliance work is to select the right kind of partner. A good partner has three principal characteristics. First, a good partner helps the company achieve strategic goals such as gaining market access, sharing the costs and risks of new-product development, or gaining access to critical core competencies. In other words, the partner must have capabilities that the company lacks and that it values.

Second, a good partner shares the firm's vision for the purpose of the alliance. If two companies approach an alliance with radically different agendas, the chances are great that the relationship will not be harmonious and will end.

Third, a good partner is unlikely to try to exploit the alliance opportunistically for its own ends—that is, to expropriate the company's technological know-how while giving away little in return. In this respect, firms who have reputations for fair play—and want to maintain them—probably make the best partners. For example, IBM is involved in so many strategic alliances that it would not pay for the company to trample over individual alliance partners (in 2003, IBM reportedly had more than 150 major strategic alliances).[45] This would tarnish IBM's reputation of being a good ally and would make it more difficult for IBM to attract alliance partners. Because IBM attaches great importance to its alliances, it is unlikely to engage in the kind of opportunistic behavior that critics highlight. Similarly, their reputations make it less likely (but by no means impossible) that Japanese firms such as Sony, Toshiba, and Fuji, which have histories of alliances with non-Japanese firms, would opportunistically exploit an alliance partner.

To select a partner with these three characteristics, a company needs to conduct some comprehensive research on potential alliance candidates. To increase the probability of selecting a good partner, the company should collect as much pertinent, publicly available information about potential allies as possible; collect data from informed third parties, including companies that have had alliances with the potential

FIGURE 8.5

Structuring Alliances to Reduce Opportunism

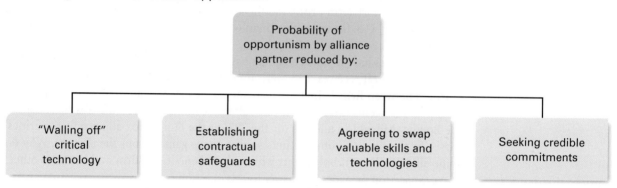

partners, investment bankers who have had dealings with them, and some of their former employees; and get to know potential partners as well as possible before committing to an alliance. This last step should include face-to-face meetings between senior managers (and perhaps middle-level managers) to ensure that the chemistry is right.

ALLIANCE STRUCTURE   Having selected a partner, the alliance should be structured so that the company's risk of giving too much away to the partner is reduced to an acceptable level. Figure 8.5 depicts the four safeguards against opportunism by alliance partners that we discuss here. (**Opportunism**, which is often defined as self-interest seeking with guile, includes the expropriation of technology or markets.) First, alliances can be designed to make it difficult (if not impossible) to transfer technology not meant to be transferred. Specifically, the design, development, manufacture, and service of a product manufactured by an alliance can be structured to protect sensitive technologies to prevent their leakage to the other participant. In the alliance between General Electric and Snecma to build commercial aircraft engines, for example, GE reduced the risk of excess transfer by walling off certain sections of the production process. The modularization effectively cut off the transfer of what GE regarded as key competitive technology while permitting Snecma access to final assembly. Similarly, in the alliance between Boeing and the Japanese to build the 767, Boeing walled off research, design, and marketing functions considered central to its competitive position, while allowing the Japanese to share in production technology. Boeing also walled off new technologies not required for 767 production.[46]

Second, contractual safeguards can be written into an alliance agreement to guard against the risk of opportunism by a partner. For example, TRW has three strategic alliances with large Japanese auto component suppliers to produce seat belts, engine valves, and steering gears for sale to Japanese-owned auto assembly plants in the United States. TRW has clauses in each of its alliance contracts that bar the Japanese firms from competing with TRW to supply U.S.-owned auto companies with component parts. By doing this, TRW protects itself against the possibility that the Japanese companies are entering into the alliances merely as a way to gain access to the North American market to compete with TRW in its home market.

Third, both parties to an alliance can agree in advance to swap skills and technologies that the other covets, thereby ensuring a chance for equitable gain. Cross-licensing agreements are one way to achieve this goal.

Fourth, the risk of opportunism by an alliance partner can be reduced if the firm extracts a significant credible commitment from its partner in advance. The long-term alliance between Xerox and Fuji to build photocopiers for the Asian market perhaps best illustrates this. Rather than enter into an informal agreement or a licensing arrangement (which Fuji Photo initially wanted), Xerox insisted that Fuji invest in a 50/50 joint venture to serve Japan and East Asia. This venture constituted such a significant investment in people, equipment, and facilities that Fuji Photo was committed from the outset to making the alliance work in order to earn a return on its investment. By agreeing to the joint venture, Fuji essentially made a credible commitment to the alliance. Given this commitment, Xerox felt secure in transferring its photocopier technology to Fuji.

MANAGING THE ALLIANCE Once a partner has been selected and an appropriate alliance structure agreed on, the task facing the company is to maximize the benefits from the alliance. One important ingredient of success appears to be sensitivity to cultural differences. Many differences in management style are attributable to cultural differences, and managers need to make allowances for these differences in dealing with their partner. Beyond this, maximizing the benefits from an alliance seems to involve building trust between partners and learning from partners.[47]

Managing an alliance successfully requires building interpersonal relationships between the firms' managers, or what is sometimes referred to as relational capital.[48] This is one lesson that can be drawn from a successful strategic alliance between Ford and Mazda. Ford and Mazda set up a framework of meetings within which their managers not only discuss matters pertaining to the alliance but also have time to get to know each other better. The belief is that the resulting friendships help build trust and facilitate harmonious relations between the two firms. Personal relationships also foster an informal management network between the firms. This network can then be used to help solve problems arising in more formal contexts (such as in joint committee meetings between personnel from the two firms).

Academics have argued that a major determinant of how much knowledge a company gains from an alliance is based on its ability to learn from its alliance partner.[49] For example, in a five-year study of fifteen strategic alliances between major multinationals, Gary Hamel, Yves Doz, and C. K. Prahalad focused on a number of alliances between Japanese companies and western (European or American) partners.[50] In every case in which a Japanese company emerged from an alliance stronger than its western partner, the Japanese company had made a greater effort to learn. Few western companies in the study seemed to want to learn from their Japanese partners. They tended to regard the alliance purely as a cost-sharing or risk-sharing device rather than as an opportunity to learn how a potential competitor does business.

For an example of an alliance in which there was a clear learning asymmetry, consider the agreement between General Motors and Toyota Motor Corp. to build the Chevrolet Nova. This alliance was structured as a formal joint venture, New United Motor Manufacturing, in which both parties had a 50% equity stake. The venture owned an auto plant in Fremont, California. According to one of the Japanese managers, Toyota achieved most of its objectives from the alliance: "We learned about U.S. supply and transportation. And we got the confidence to manage U.S. workers." All that knowledge was then quickly transferred to Georgetown, Kentucky, where Toyota opened a plant of its own in 1988. By contrast, although General Motors got a new product, the Chevrolet Nova, some GM managers complained that their new knowledge was never put to good use inside GM. They say that they should have been kept together as a team to educate GM's engineers and workers about the Japanese system. Instead, they were dispersed to different GM subsidiaries.[51]

When entering into an alliance, a company must take some measures to ensure that it learns from its alliance partner and then puts that knowledge to good use within its own organization. One suggested approach is to educate all operating employees about the partner's strengths and weaknesses and make clear to them how acquiring particular skills will bolster their company's competitive position. For such learning to be of value, the knowledge acquired from an alliance has to be diffused throughout the organization—which did not happen at GM. To spread this knowledge, the managers involved in an alliance should be used as a resource in familiarizing others within the company about the skills of an alliance partner.

Summary of Chapter

1. For some companies, international expansion represents a way of earning greater returns by transferring the skills and product offerings derived from their distinctive competencies to markets where indigenous competitors lack those skills. As barriers to international trade have fallen, industries have expanded beyond national boundaries, and industry competition and opportunities have increased.

2. Because of national differences, it pays a company to base each value creation activity it performs at the location where factor conditions are most conducive to the performance of that activity. This strategy is known as focusing on the attainment of location economies.

3. By building sales volume more rapidly, international expansion can help a company gain a cost advantage through the realization of scale economies and learning effects.

4. The best strategy for a company to pursue may depend on the kind of pressures it must cope with: pressures for cost reductions or for local responsiveness. Pressures for cost reductions are greatest in industries producing commodity-type products, where price is the main competitive weapon. Pressures for local responsiveness arise from differences in consumer tastes and preferences, as well as from national infrastructure and traditional practices, distribution channels, and host government demands.

5. Companies pursuing an international strategy transfer the skills and products derived from distinctive competencies to foreign markets while undertaking some limited local customization.

6. Companies pursuing a localization strategy customize their product offering, marketing strategy, and business strategy to national conditions.

7. Companies pursuing a global standardization strategy focus on reaping the cost reductions that come from scale economies and location economies.

8. Many industries are now so competitive that companies must adopt a transnational strategy. This involves a simultaneous focus on reducing costs, transferring skills and products, and being locally responsive. Implementing such a strategy may not be easy.

9. The most attractive foreign markets tend to be found in politically stable developed and developing nations that have free market systems.

10. Several advantages are associated with entering a national market early, before other international businesses have established themselves. These advantages must be balanced against the pioneering costs that early entrants often have to bear, including the greater risk of business failure.

11. Large-scale entry into a national market constitutes a major strategic commitment that is likely to change the nature of competition in that market and limit the entrant's future strategic flexibility. The firm needs to think through the implications of such commitments before embarking on a large-scale entry. Although making major strategic commitments can yield many benefits, there are also risks associated with such a strategy.

12. There are five different ways of entering a foreign market: exporting, licensing, franchising, entering into a joint venture, and setting up a wholly owned subsidiary. The optimal choice of entry mode depends on the company's strategy.

13. Strategic alliances are cooperative agreements between actual or potential competitors. The advantages of alliances are that they facilitate entry into foreign markets,

enable partners to share the fixed costs and risks associated with new products and processes, facilitate the transfer of complementary skills between companies, and help companies establish technical standards.

14. The drawbacks of a strategic alliance are that the company risks giving away technological know-how and market access to its alliance partner while getting very little in return.

15. The disadvantages associated with alliances can be reduced if the company selects partners carefully, paying close attention to reputation, and structures the alliance to avoid unintended transfers of know-how.

Discussion Questions

1. Plot the position of the following companies on Figure 8.3: Microsoft, Google, Coca-Cola, Dow Chemicals, Pfizer, and McDonald's. In each case, justify your answer.

2. Identify whether the following are global standardization industries, or industries where localization is more important: bulk chemicals, pharmaceuticals, branded food products, moviemaking, television manufacture, personal computers, airline travel, and fashion retailing.

3. Discuss how the need for control over foreign operations varies with the strategy and distinctive competencies of a company. What are the implications of this relationship for the choice of entry mode?

4. Licensing proprietary technology to foreign competitors is the best way to give up a company's competitive advantage. Discuss this statement.

5. What kind of companies stand to gain the most from entering into strategic alliances with potential competitors? Why?

Practicing Strategic Management

SMALL-GROUP EXERCISE
Developing a Global Strategy

Break into groups of three to five, appoint one group member to be the spokesperson who will communicate your findings to the class, and discuss the following scenario. You work for a company in the soft drink industry that has developed a line of carbonated, fruit-based drinks. You have already established a significant presence in your home market, and now you are planning the global strategy development of the company in the soft drink industry. You need to decide the following:

1. The overall strategy to pursue: a global standardization strategy, a localization strategy, an international strategy, or a transnational strategy.

2. Which markets to enter first.

3. The entry strategy to pursue, for example, franchising, joint venture, wholly owned subsidiary.

4. What information do you need to make these decisions? On the basis of what you do know, what strategy would you recommend?

ARTICLE FILE 8

Find an example of a multinational company that in recent years has switched from a localization, international, or global standardization strategy to a transnational strategy. Identify why the company made the switch and any problems that the company may be encountering while it tries to change its strategic orientation.

STRATEGIC MANAGEMENT PROJECT
Module 8

This module requires you to identify how your company might profit from global expansion, the global strategy that your company should pursue, and the entry mode that it might favor. With the information you have at your disposal, answer the questions regarding the following two situations:

Your company is already doing business in other countries.

1. Is your company creating value or lowering the costs of value creation by realizing location

economies, transferring distinctive competencies abroad, or realizing cost economies from the economies of scale? If it is not creating value or lowering the costs of value creation, does it have the potential to do so?

2. How responsive is your company to differences among nations? Does it vary its product and marketing message from country to country? Should it?

3. What are the cost pressures and pressures for local responsiveness in the industry in which your company is based?

4. What strategy is your company pursuing to compete globally? In your opinion, is this the correct strategy, given cost pressures and pressures for local responsiveness?

5. What major foreign market does your company serve, and what mode has it used to enter this market? Why is your company active in these markets and not others? What are the advantages and disadvantages of using this mode? Might another mode be preferable?

Your company is not yet doing business in other countries.

1. What potential does your company have to add value to its products or lower the costs of value creation by expanding internationally?

2. On the international level, what are the cost pressures and pressures for local responsiveness in the industry in which your company is based? What implications do these pressures have for the strategy that your company might pursue if it chose to expand globally?

3. What foreign market might your company enter, and what entry mode should it use to enter this market? Justify your answer.

ETHICS EXERCISE

Bob was nearing retirement. Although he had enjoyed his job, he was growing bored and restless. In charge of so many people and projects, he was beginning to care less and less each day, and he knew that it was time to get out. Just the other day, he had accidentally allowed one of his managers to fire one of the company's best workers for reasons more personal than professional. Once done, the action could not be reversed. Now Bob was afraid of making more mistakes.

For years now, Bob had been in charge of his company's China office. He liked living in China and working with the Chinese people. In fact, he was thinking of staying on after retirement, although he was looking forward to moving out of the hustle and bustle of Beijing. "Only one more month to go," he thought, "and I'll be free! Can I keep it together until then?"

Suddenly, a day later, Bob had a desperate phone call from company headquarters in the United States. It had just been discovered that one of Bob's managers had been embezzling funds from the company. Bob's superiors were asking him to put off his retirement and to stay for at least six extra months to help clean up the problem caused by this manager.

Bob felt conflicted. On the one hand, he felt that he could no longer perform his job well, nor did he want to anymore. On the other hand, he owed his company a great deal. Should he focus on himself and leave his company in the lurch? Or should he pull it together and help the company that had given him so much?

1. Identify the ethical dilemma at stake in this case.

2. What would you do if you were in Bob's position?

3. Do you think Bob should keep his position in his current state?

CLOSING CASE

The Evolution of Strategy at Procter & Gamble

Founded in 1837, Cincinnati-based Procter & Gamble has long been one of the world's most international companies. Today, P&G is a global colossus in the consumer products business, with annual sales in excess of $68 billion, some 56% of which are generated outside the United States. P&G sells more than 300 brands—including Ivory soap, Tide, Pampers, IAMS pet food, Crisco, Gillette, and Folgers—to consumers in 180 countries. It has production operations in eighty countries and employs close to 138,000 people globally.

P&G established its first foreign factory in 1915 when it opened a plant in Canada to produce Ivory soap and Crisco. This was followed in 1930 by the establishment of the company's first foreign subsidiary in Britain. The pace of international expansion quickened in the 1950s and 1960s as P&G expanded rapidly in western Europe, and then again in the 1970s when the company entered Japan and other Asian nations. Sometimes P&G entered a nation by acquiring an established competitor and its brands, as occurred in the case of Great Britain and Japan, but more typically the company set up operations from the ground floor.

By the late 1970s, the strategy at P&G was well established. The company developed new products in Cincinnati and then relied on semiautonomous foreign subsidiaries to manufacture, market, and distribute those products in different nations. In many cases, foreign subsidiaries had their own production facilities and tailored the packaging, brand name, and marketing message to local tastes and preferences. For years, this strategy delivered a steady stream of new products and reliable growth in sales and profits. By the 1990s, however, profit growth at P&G was slowing.

The essence of the problem was simple; P&G's costs were too high because of extensive duplication of manufacturing, marketing, and administrative facilities in different national subsidiaries. The duplication of assets made sense in the world of the 1960s, when national markets were segmented from each other by barriers to cross-border trade. Products produced in Great Britain, for example, could not be sold economically in Germany due to high tariff duties levied on imports into Germany. By the 1980s, however, barriers to cross-border trade were falling rapidly worldwide and fragmented national markets were merging into larger regional or global markets. Also, the retailers through which P&G distributed its products, such as Wal-Mart, Tesco in the United Kingdom, and Carrefour in France, were growing larger and more global. These emerging global retailers were demanding price discounts from P&G.

In 1993, P&G embarked on a major reorganization in an attempt to control its cost structure and recognize the new reality of emerging global markets. The company shut down some thirty manufacturing plants around the globe, laid off 13,000 employees, and concentrated production in fewer plants that could better realize economies of scale and serve regional markets. These actions cut some $600 million a year out of P&G's cost structure. It wasn't enough! Profit growth remained sluggish.

In 1998, P&G launched its second reorganization of the decade. Named Organization 2005, its goal was to transform P&G into a truly global company. The company tore up its old organization, which was based on countries and regions, and replaced it with one based on seven self-contained global business units, ranging from baby care to food products. Each business unit was given complete responsibility for generating profits from its products, and for manufacturing, marketing, and product development. Each business unit was told to rationalize production, concentrating it in fewer, larger facilities; to build global brands wherever possible, thereby eliminating marketing differences among countries; and to accelerate the development and launch of new products. In 1999, P&G announced that, as a result of this initiative, it would close another ten factories and lay off 15,000 employees, mostly in Europe where there was still extensive duplication of assets. The annual cost savings were estimated to be about $800 million. P&G planned to use the savings to cut prices and increase marketing spending in an effort to gain market share and thus further lower costs through the attainment of scale economies. This time, the strategy seemed to be working. Between 2003 and 2006, P&G reported strong growth in both sales and profits. Significantly, P&G's global competitors, such as Unilever, Kimberly-Clark, and Colgate-Palmolive, were struggling in 2003 to 2006.[52]

Case Discussion Questions

1. What strategy was Procter & Gamble pursuing until the late 1990s?

2. Why did this strategy succeed for so many years? Why was it no longer working by the 1990s?

3. What strategy did P&G adopt in the late 1990s and early 2000s? Does this strategy make more sense? Why?

Corporate-Level Strategy: Horizontal Integration, Vertical Integration, and Strategic Outsourcing

---

OPENING CASE

Oracle Strives to Become the Biggest and the Best

Oracle Corp., based in Redwood City, California, is the world's largest maker of database software and the third largest global software company in terms of sales after Microsoft and IBM. This commanding position is not enough for Oracle, however, which has set its sights on becoming the global leader in the corporate applications software market. Here, Germany's SAP, which has 45% of the market, is the acknowledged leader and Oracle, with only 19%, is a distant second.[1] Corporate applications is a fast growing and highly profitable market, however, and Oracle has been snapping up leading companies in this segment at a fast pace. Its goal is to quickly build the distinctive competencies it needs to expand the range of products that it can offer to its existing customers and to attract new customers to compete with SAP. Beginning in 2005, Oracle's CEO Larry Ellison spent $19 billion to acquire fourteen leading suppliers of corporate software, including two of the top five companies: PeopleSoft, a leading human resources management (HRM) software supplier it bought for $10 billion, and Siebel Systems, a leader in customer relationship management (CRM) software, which cost Oracle $5.8 billion.

Oracle expects several competitive advantages to result from its use of acquisitions to pursue the corporate strategy of horizontal integration. First, it is now able to meld or bundle the best software applications of these acquired companies—with Oracle's own first-class set of corporate and database software programs—to create a new integrated suite of software that will allow corporations to manage all their functional activities such as accounting, marketing, sales, HRM, CRM, and supply-chain management. Second, through these acquisitions, Oracle obtained access to thousands of new customers—all the companies that currently use the software of the companies it acquired. All these companies now become potential new customers for all of Oracle's other database and corporate software offerings. Third, beyond increasing the range of its products and the number of its customers, Oracle's acquisitions have consolidated the corporate software industry. By taking over some of its largest rivals, Oracle has become the second largest supplier of corporate software, and so it is better positioned to compete with the leader SAP.

Achieving the advantages of its new strategy may not be easy, however. The person in charge of assembling Oracle's new unified software package and selling it to customers is John

Wookey, Oracle's senior vice president in charge of applications, who jokingly says that his "head is the one on the chopping block if this doesn't work." CEO Ellison has been quick to fire executives who haven't performed well in the past, and he expects a lot from his top executives. To grow Oracle's market share and profits, Wookey must draw on the best of the technology Oracle obtained from each of the companies it acquired to build its new suite of state-of-the-art corporate software applications. He also has to persuade customers not to switch software vendors—for example, not to jump ship to SAP—while Oracle builds its package and then to gradually adopt more and more of Oracle's software offerings to run their functional activities.

Wookey is well placed to implement Oracle's new strategy, however: he is known as a consensus builder and product champion both inside and outside the company, and when interacting with Oracle's customers. He spends his working day sharing information with the top managers of Oracle's various businesses, and meeting with his team of fourteen senior staff members, to work out how the whole package should be put together and what it should include. He also regularly visits major customers, especially those that came with its acquisitions, to gain their input into how and what kind of software package Oracle should build. Wookey even formed an advisory council of leading customers to help make sure the final package meets their needs. One of Wookey's notable achievements was retaining the top-rate software engineers who Oracle obtained from its acquired rivals. These employees could have easily found high-paying jobs elsewhere, but most of the top engineers Oracle wanted stayed to help it achieve its new goals.

Nevertheless, by the end of 2006, there were signs that all was not going well with Oracle's new strategy. SAP is a powerful competitor; its popular software is fast becoming the industry standard, so unseating SAP in the $23.4 billion corporate software market will not be easy. SAP is still the leader in more advanced functional applications incorporating the latest technologies, and its proprietary technology is all homegrown, so it doesn't face the huge implementation issue of bringing together the applications from many different acquisitions. Preventing customers from switching to SAP may not be easy now that their loyalty to their old software supplier has been broken if it was acquired by Oracle.

Analysts also say that Oracle runs the risk of stretching itself too thin if it continues to purchase too many companies too quickly, because high-tech acquisitions are the most difficult to pull off in terms of management and execution. So, in December 2006, while Oracle announced that its second-quarter profit rose 21%, and sales rose to $4.16 billion from $3.29 billion in the previous year, it also announced that sales of corporate applications software slowed to 28% from 80%.[2] Larry Ellison is still under pressure to accelerate sales growth and surpass investors' expectations, and only if Oracle can put out corporate application software sales numbers that beat expectations will analysts regard its strategy as a success. Still, Oracle's stock gained 47% in 2006 compared to SAP's 15%, so investors clearly believe he and Wookey have a sporting chance.

OVERVIEW

Over the last few years, Oracle has acquired many companies in order to create a software empire. The overriding goal of Larry Ellison and his top managers is to maximize the value of the company for its shareholders, and Ellison embarked on his quest because he believes that by combining all these different businesses into one entity, Oracle, he will be able to increase its profitability. Clearly, the scale of Ellison's mission and vision for Oracle takes the issue of strategy formulation to a new level of complexity.

The Oracle story illustrates the use of corporate-level strategy to identify (1) which businesses and industries a company should compete in, (2) which value creation activities it should perform in those businesses, and (3) how it should enter or leave businesses or industries to maximize its long-run profitability. In formulating corporate-level strategy, managers must adopt a long-term perspective and consider how changes taking place in an industry and in its products, technology, customers, and competitors will affect their company's current business model and its future strategies. They then decide how to implement specific corporate-level strategies to redefine their company's business model so that it can achieve a competitive position in the changing industry environment by taking advantage of the opportunities and countering the threats. Thus, the principal goal of corporate-level strategy is to enable a company to sustain or promote its competitive advantage and profitability in its present business and in any new businesses or industries that it enters.

This chapter is the first of two that deals with the role of corporate-level strategy in repositioning and redefining a company's business model. We discuss three corporate-level strategies—horizontal integration, vertical integration, and strategic outsourcing—that are primarily directed toward improving a company's competitive advantage and profitability in its present business or product market. Diversification, which entails entry into new kinds of markets or industries, is examined in the next chapter, along with guidelines for choosing the most profitable way to enter new markets or industries or to exit others. By the end of this and the next chapter, you will understand how the different levels of strategy contribute to the creation of a successful and profitable business or multibusiness model. You will also be able to differentiate among the types of corporate strategies managers use to maximize long-term company profitability.

Corporate-Level Strategy and the Multibusiness Model

The formulation of corporate-level strategies is the final part of the strategy formulation process. These strategies drive a company's business model over time and determine the kinds of business- and functional-level strategies that will maximize long-run profitability. The relationship between business-level strategy and functional-level strategy was discussed in Chapter 5. Strategic managers develop a business model and strategies that use their company's distinctive competencies to strive for a cost-leadership position and/or to differentiate its products. Chapter 8 described how global strategy is also an extension of these basic principles. Throughout this chapter and the next, we repeatedly stress that to increase profitability, a corporate-level strategy should enable a company or one or more of its business divisions or units to perform value-chain functional activities (1) at a lower cost and/or (2) in a way that allows for differentiation. A company can then choose the pricing option (lowest, average, or premium) that allows it to maximize revenues and profitability. In addition, corporate-level strategy will boost profitability if it helps a company reduce industry rivalry and lowers the threat of damaging price competition. Thus, a company's corporate-level strategies should be chosen to promote the success of a company's business model and to allow it to achieve a sustainable competitive advantage at the business level. Competitive advantage leads to higher profitability.

At the corporate level, some companies like Oracle choose to compete only in one industry (the software industry in Oracle's case), but then they develop strategies to increase the profitability of their business model by entering new market segments and providing a wider range of goods and services. Oracle, for example, expanded its activities into the corporate applications software market segment to better satisfy the needs of existing customers and attract new customers.

Other companies, however, often choose to expand their business activities beyond one market or industry and enter others. When a company decides to expand into new industries, it must construct its business model at two levels. First, it must develop a business model and strategies for each business unit or division in every industry in which it competes. Second, it must also develop a higher-level *multibusiness model* that justifies its entry into different businesses and industries. This model should explain how and why entering the new industry will allow the company to use its existing functional competencies and business strategies to increase its return on investment. A multibusiness model should also explain any other ways in which a company's involvement in more than one business or industry can increase its profitability. Dell, for example, might argue that its entry into computer consulting and into the computer printer market will enable it to offer its customers a complete line of computer products and services, which will allow it to better compete with HP or IBM. This chapter first focuses on the advantages of staying in one industry by pursuing horizontal integration. It then looks at why companies use vertical integration and expand into new industries. In the next chapter, we will examine another important corporate strategy that companies employ to enter new industries to increase their profitability: diversification.

Horizontal Integration: Single-Industry Strategy

Managers use corporate-level strategy to identify which industries their company should compete in to maximize its long-run profitability. For many companies, profitable growth and expansion often entail finding ways to compete successfully within a single market or industry over time. In other words, a company confines its value creation activities to just one business or industry. Examples of such single-business companies include McDonald's, with its focus on the global fast-food restaurant business, and Wal-Mart, with its focus on global discount retailing.

Staying in one industry allows a company to focus its total managerial, financial, technological, and functional resources and capabilities on competing successfully in one area. This is important in fast-growing and changing industries, where demands on a company's resources and capabilities are likely to be substantial, but where the long-term profits from establishing a competitive advantage are also likely to be significant.

A second advantage of staying in a single industry is that a company "sticks to the knitting," meaning that it stays focused on what it knows and does best. It does not make the mistake of entering new industries where its existing resources and capabilities create little value and/or where a whole new set of competitive industry forces—new competitors, suppliers, and customers—present unanticipated threats. Both Coca-Cola and Sears, like many other companies, have committed this strategic error. Coca-Cola once decided to expand into the movie business and acquired Columbia Pictures, and it also acquired a large wine-producing business. Sears, the clothing seller, once decided to become a one-stop shopping place and bought Allstate Insurance, Coldwell Banker (a real estate company), and Dean Witter (a financial services enterprise). Both companies found that they not only lacked the competencies to compete successfully in their new industries, but also that they had not foreseen the different kinds of competitive forces that existed in these industries. They concluded that entry into these new industries dissipated rather than created value and lowered their profitability, and they ultimately sold off their new businesses at a loss.

Even when a company stays in one industry, sustaining a successful business model and strategies over time can be difficult because of changing conditions in the environment, such as advances in technology that allow new competitors into the market and blur the boundaries between different products or markets. A decade ago, the strategic issue facing telecommunications companies was how to shape their line of wired phone service products to best meet customer needs in the local and long-distance phone service market. However, a new kind of product, wireless phone service, was emerging. At first, it was so expensive that only business customers who really needed it could afford it. Within five years, however, wireless phone companies had developed a business model to lower the cost and price of wireless phone service and many customers switched to the new product, a trend that has accelerated.

At the same time, more and more people began to surf the Internet. At first, the Internet was not regarded as a substitute for wired or wireless phone service, but today millions of people are using VOIP technology to make phone calls over the Internet. And companies that want to attract customers must now include services like digital messaging and wireless email in their product line. Many of the leading phone companies did not predict how these changes in technology would affect industry competition and were late in changing their business models to add these new products and services. As a result, many have been swallowed up and acquired by companies like AT&T, WorldCom, and Verizon, which did predict the emerging threats.

Thus, even in one industry, it is all too easy for strategic managers to fail to see the "forest" (changing nature of the industry that results in new product/market opportunities) for the "trees" (focus on positioning current products). A focus on corporate-level strategy can help managers forecast future trends and position their company so it can compete successfully in a changing environment. Strategic managers must avoid becoming so immersed in positioning their company's *existing* product lines that they fail to consider new opportunities and threats. The task for corporate-level managers is to analyze how new emerging technologies might affect their business models, how and why these might change customer needs and customer groups in the future, and what kinds of new distinctive competencies will be needed to respond to these changes.

One corporate-level strategy that has been widely used to help managers better position their companies is horizontal integration. **Horizontal integration** is the process of acquiring or merging with industry competitors in an effort to achieve the competitive advantages that come with large scale and scope. An **acquisition** occurs when one company uses its capital resources, such as stock, debt, or cash, to purchase another company, and a **merger** is an agreement between equals to pool their operations and create a new entity. The Opening Case discusses how Larry Ellison made a series of major corporate software acquisitions so that Oracle could build up its competencies in all segments of the software industry, attract thousands of new customers, and compete better against SAP.

Mergers and acquisitions have occurred in many industries. In the car industry, Chrysler merged with Daimler-Benz to create DaimlerChrysler; in the aerospace industry, Boeing merged with McDonnell Douglas to create the world's largest aerospace company; in the pharmaceutical industry, Pfizer acquired Warner-Lambert to become the largest pharmaceutical firm; and in the computer hardware industry, Compaq acquired Digital Equipment Corporation and then itself was acquired by HP. In the 2000s, the rate of mergers and acquisitions has been increasing as companies jockey for global competitive advantage. Many of the largest mergers and acquisitions have been cross-border affairs as companies race to acquire overseas companies in the same industry. In 2000, companies from all nations spent around $1.1 trillion on 7,900 cross-border mergers and acquisitions, over 70% of them horizontal mergers and acquisitions; the rate has been accelerating ever since.[3]

The net result of this wave of mergers and acquisitions has been to increase the level of concentration in a wide range of industries. Consolidated oligopolies have been replacing more fragmented industry structures.[4] For example, twenty years ago, cable television was dominated by a patchwork of thousands of small, family-owned businesses, but by 2005, three companies controlled over two-thirds of the market. In 1990, the three big publishers of college textbooks accounted for 35% of the market; by 2005, they accounted for over 65%. In the manufacture of basic DRAM semiconductor chips, the four largest firms accounted for 85% of the global market by 2005 because of mergers and acquisitions, up from 45% in 1995. Why is this happening? An answer can be found by looking at the way horizontal integration can improve the competitive advantage and profitability of companies who choose to stay in one industry.

● Benefits of Horizontal Integration   In pursuing horizontal integration, managers have decided to invest their company's capital to purchase the assets of industry competitors as a way to increase the profitability of its single-business model. Profits and profitability increase when horizontal integration (1) lowers the cost structure, (2) increases product differentiation, (3) replicates the business model, (4) reduces rivalry within the industry, and (5) increases bargaining power over suppliers and buyers.

LOWER COST STRUCTURE   Horizontal integration can lower a company's cost structure because it creates increasing *economies of scale*. Suppose there are five major competitors, each operating a manufacturing plant in some region of the United States, and none of these plants is operating at full capacity. If one competitor buys up another and shuts down that plant, it can operate its own plant at full capacity and so reduce its manufacturing costs. Achieving economies of scale is very important in industries that have a high fixed-cost structure. In such industries, large-scale production allows companies to spread their fixed costs over a large volume and in this way drive down average unit costs. In the telecommunications industry, for example, the fixed costs of building a fiber-optic or wireless network are very high, and to make such an investment pay off, a company needs a large volume of customers. Thus, companies like AT&T and Verizon acquired other telecommunications companies to gain access to their customers. These new customers increased its utilization rate and thus reduced the costs of serving each customer. Similar considerations were involved in Oracle's acquisitions and in the pharmaceutical industry, where mergers have resulted from the need to realize scale economies in sales and marketing. The fixed costs of building a nationwide pharmaceutical sales force are very high, and pharmaceutical companies need a good portfolio of products to effectively use that sales force. Pfizer acquired Warner-Lambert because its salespeople would then have more products to sell when they visited physicians and their productivity would therefore increase.

A company can also lower its cost structure when horizontal integration allows it to *reduce the duplication of resources* between two companies, such as by eliminating the need for two sets of corporate head offices, two separate sales forces, and so on. Thus, one way HP justified its strategy to acquire rival computer maker Compaq was that the acquisition would save the combined company $2.5 billion in annual expenses by eliminating redundant functions, as discussed in the Running Case.

RUNNING CASE

Beating Dell: Why HP Acquired Compaq

In 2001, Hewlett-Packard (now HP) shocked the business world when its former CEO, Carly Fiorina, announced that rival computer maker Compaq had agreed to be acquired by HP. The announcement came at the end of a year in which slumping demand and strong competition from Dell had buffeted both companies. The merged company would have annual revenues of about $87.4 billion, putting it in the same league as IBM, and would be able to provide customers with a full range of computer products and services. With the exception of printers, where HP is the market leader, there was significant product overlap between HP and Compaq.

To justify the acquisition, Fiorina claimed that it would yield a number of benefits. First, there would be significant cost savings. Some $2.5 billion a year would be taken out of annual expenses by eliminating redundant administrative functions and cutting 15,000 employees. In addition, combining the PC businesses of HP and Compaq would enable HP to capture significant scale economies and compete more efficiently with Dell. The same would be true in the computer server and storage businesses, areas where Dell was gaining share. Critics, however, were quick to point out that Dell's competitive advantage was based on its cost-leadership business model, which was based on the efficient management of its supply chain—an area where both HP and Compaq lagged behind Dell. Although achieving economies of scale is desirable, would the merger allow the new HP to reduce its cost structure, such as by increasing its supply-chain efficiency? If the new HP could not change its PC business model to match Dell's low costs, then the merger would not provide any real benefit.

In addition to the cost advantages of the merger, Fiorina argued that the acquisition would give HP a critical mass in the computer service and consultancy business, where it lagged behind leader IBM significantly. By being able to offer customers a total solution to their information technology needs, both hardware *and* services, Fiorina argued that HP could gain new market share among corporate customers, who would now buy its PCs as part of the total "computer package"; moreover, HP would be entering the higher-margin service business. Here, too, however, critics were quick to perceive flaws. They argued that HP would still be a minnow in the service and consultancy area, with under 3% of market share.

In 2004, HP announced that it had achieved its cost savings target and that it was continuing to find ways to reduce the duplication of resources in the merged company. However, it also announced that Dell's entry into the printer business had hurt its profit margins and that the profit margins on the sales of its PCs were still well below those obtained by Dell. HP's stock price plunged, and its board of directors reacted by firing Fiorina and bringing in a new CEO, Mark Hurd, a person with proven skills in managing a company's cost structure. Hurd initiated another round of cost reductions by pruning HP's product line and work force. In the spring of 2006, the company astounded analysts when it announced much higher profit margins on its sales of PCs and higher profits across the company. Many of Fiorina's strategies had begun to pay off. HP's PCs were much more attractive to customers, and Dell's foray into printers had not proved highly successful against market leader HP. Neither had Dell's entry into other electronics industries, such as MP3 players, televisions, and so on.

The result was that competitive advantage in the PC industry seemed to be moving away from Dell toward HP. As we discussed in the Running Case in the last chapter, in response, Dell has been forced to find ways to increase its level of differentiation to increase the attractiveness of its machines and so defend its position against HP and Apple. Dell engaged in horizontal differentiation when it bought the upscale PC maker Alienware in one move to increase product differentiation; it also entered into physical retailing when it began to open Dell PC stores in major shopping malls in 2006, imitating Apple's strategy. To find even more cost savings, Dell also began to use AMD's cheaper chips and broke its long-term exclusive tie to Intel. Analysts worry that its move to increase product differentiation may hurt Dell's cost leadership position; despite its attempt to lower costs, they worry Dell might become stuck in the middle. However, Dell is still a strong competitor, and only time will tell how the battle for market share in the PC industry will play out as Dell, HP, and Apple work to find new ways to lower costs and differentiate their products to grow their sales, profits, and ROIC.[a]

Another example of using horizontal integration to reduce operating costs occurred in 2004 when Kmart and Sears announced that they were merging their companies to better position themselves to compete against Wal-Mart. One goal was to share common purchasing and distribution facilities and combine their HRM functions to reduce costs. Another goal was to increase differentiation, and by 2006, some Kmart stores began to carry some of Sears's well-known product lines, such as its appliances and Craftsman tools, while Sears's stores may soon begin to stock some of Kmart's designer lines, such as Martha Stewart.

INCREASED PRODUCT DIFFERENTIATION As the Sears/Kmart merger suggests, horizontal integration may also increase profitability when it increases product differentiation, for example, by allowing a company to combine the product lines of merged companies so that it can offer customers a wider range of products that can be bundled together. **Product bundling** involves offering customers the opportunity to buy a complete range of products at a single combined price. This increases the value of a company's product line because customers often obtain a price discount from buying a set of products and also become used to dealing with just one company and its representatives. A company may obtain a competitive advantage from increased product differentiation. A famous example of the value of product bundling is Microsoft Office, which is a bundle of different software programs, including a word processor, spreadsheet, and presentation program. In the early 1990s, Microsoft was number 2 or 3 in each of these product categories, behind companies such as WordPerfect (which led in the word-processing category), Lotus (which had the best-selling spreadsheet), and Harvard Graphics (which had the best-selling presentation software). By offering all three programs in a single-price package, Microsoft presented consumers with a superior value proposition, and its product bundle quickly gained market share, ultimately accounting for more than 90% of all sales of word processors, spreadsheets, and presentation software.

Another way to increase product differentiation is through **cross-selling**, which involves a company taking advantage of, or leveraging, its established relationship with customers by acquiring additional product lines or categories that it can sell to them. In this way, a company increases differentiation because it can provide a total solution and satisfy all customers' specific needs. Cross-selling and becoming a total-solution provider is an important rationale for horizontal integration in the computer sector, where information technology (IT) companies have tried to increase the value of their offerings by providing all of the hardware and service needs of corporate customers. Providing a total solution saves customers time and money because they do not have to deal with several suppliers, and a single sales team can ensure that all the different components of a customer's IT work seamlessly together. When horizontal integration increases the differentiated appeal and value of the company's products, the total-solution provider gains market share. This was the business model IBM pursued when it acquired many IT companies and is one of the main reasons for its current success in the computer sector.

REPLICATING THE BUSINESS MODEL Given the many ways in which horizontal integration can lead to both product differentiation and low-cost advantages, it can be very profitable to use this strategy to replicate a company's successful business model in *new market segments* within its industry. In the retail industry, for example, Wal-Mart took its low-cost/low-price discount retail business model to enter into the even lower-priced warehouse segment. It has also expanded the range of products it offers customers by entering the supermarket business and establishing a nationwide chain of Wal-Mart superstores that sell groceries and produce. It has replicated this business model globally by acquiring supermarket chains in several countries, such as the United Kingdom, Mexico, and most recently Japan, where it can use its efficient global materials-management processes to pursue its cost-leadership strategy. In the United States, it is currently experimenting with new small-size supermarkets it calls neighborhood markets to expand its presence in the supermarket segment.

REDUCED INDUSTRY RIVALRY Horizontal integration can help to reduce industry rivalry in two ways. First, acquiring or merging with a competitor helps to *eliminate excess capacity* in an industry, which often triggers price wars, as we discussed in Chapter 6. By taking excess capacity out of an industry, horizontal integration creates a more benign environment in which prices might stabilize or even increase.

Second, by reducing the number of competitors in an industry, horizontal integration often makes it easier to implement *tacit price coordination* among rivals, that is, coordination reached without communication (explicit communication to fix prices is illegal). In general, the larger the number of competitors in an industry, the more difficult it is to establish informal pricing agreements, such as price leadership by the dominant company, which reduces the possibility that a price war will erupt. By increasing industry concentration and creating an oligopoly, horizontal integration can make it easier to establish tacit coordination among rivals.

Both of these motives also seem to have been behind HP's acquisition of Compaq. The PC industry was suffering from significant excess capacity and a serious price war, triggered by Dell's desire to gain market share. By acquiring Compaq, HP hoped to be able to remove excess capacity in the industry and eventually impose some pricing discipline that would lead to higher prices. In fact, by 2004, the average price of PCs started to increase, and the major competitors began to look for ways to differentiate their products to compete better and to avoid new price wars breaking out.

INCREASED BARGAINING POWER Finally, some companies use horizontal integration because it allows them to obtain bargaining power over suppliers or buyers and so increase their profitability at the expense of suppliers or buyers. By consolidating the industry through horizontal integration, a company becomes a much larger buyer of suppliers' products and uses this as leverage to bargain down the price it pays for its inputs, thereby lowering its cost structure. Similarly, by acquiring its competitors, a company gains control over a greater percentage of an industry's product or output. Other things being equal, it then has more power to raise prices and profits because customers have less choice of supplier and are more dependent on the company for their products.

When a company has greater ability to raise prices to buyers or bargain down the prices paid for inputs, it has increased market power. For an example of how the process of consolidation through horizontal integration can play out, see Strategy in Action 9.1, which looks at the way in which health care providers in eastern Massachusetts have pursued horizontal integration to gain bargaining power, and hence market power, over insurance providers.

● **Problems with Horizontal Integration**

Although horizontal integration can clearly strengthen a company's business model in several ways, problems, limitations, and dangers are associated with this strategy. We discuss many of these dangers in detail in Chapter 10, but the important point to note here is that a wealth of data suggests that the majority of mergers and acquisitions do *not* create value and many actually *reduce* value.[5] For example, a well-known study by KPMG, a large accounting and management consulting company, looked at 700 large

Strategy in Action   9.1

Horizontal Integration in Health Care

In the United States, health maintenance organizations (HMOs) have become a powerful force in the health care sector. HMOs are health insurance companies that provide people with health care coverage, and often companies contract with HMOs on behalf of their employees for health insurance coverage. The HMOs then "supply" patients to health care providers. Thus, HMOs can be viewed as the suppliers of the critical input—patients—to health care providers. In turn, the revenues of health care providers are dependent on the number of patients who pass through their system. Clearly, it is in the interests of HMOs to bargain down the price they must pay health care providers for coverage, and to gain bargaining power, HMOs have used horizontal integration to merge with each other until, today, they control a large volume of patients. To fight back, however, health care providers have also resorted to horizontal integration, and the battle is raging.

As an example of how this process plays out, consider how the relationship between HMOs and hospitals evolved in eastern Massachusetts. In the early 1990s, three big HMOs controlled 75% of the market for health insurance in eastern Massachusetts. In contrast, there were thirty-four separate hospital networks in the region. Thus, the insurance providers were consolidated, while the health care providers were fragmented, giving the insurance providers considerable bargaining power. The HMOs used their bargaining power to demand deep discounts from health care providers. If a hospital wouldn't offer discounts to an HMO, the HMO would threaten to remove it from its list of providers. Because losing all of those potential patients would severely damage the revenues that a hospital could earn, the hospitals had little choice but to comply with the request.

This situation changed when two of the most prestigious hospitals in the region, Massachusetts General and Brigham & Women's Hospital, merged with each other to form Partners HealthCare System. Since then, Partners has continued to pursue the strategy of acquiring other hospitals to gain power over HMOs. By 2002, it had seven hospitals and some 5,000 doctors in its system. Other regional hospitals pursued a similar strategy, and the number of independent hospital networks in the region fell from thirty-four in 1994 to twelve by 2002.

In the 2000s, Partners has increasingly exercised its strengthened bargaining power by demanding that HMOs accept a fee increase for services offered by Partners hospitals. One of the biggest HMOs, Tufts, refused to accept the increase and informed nearly 200,000 of its 900,000 subscribers that they would no longer be able to use Partners hospitals or physicians affiliated with Partners. There was an enormous uproar from subscribers. Many employers threatened to pull out of the HMO and switch to another if the policy was not changed. Tufts quickly realized it had little choice but to accept the fee increase. Tufts went back to Partners and agreed to a 30% fee increase over three years. Thus, bargaining power in the system had shifted from the HMOs toward the hospital networks. However, the Massachusetts attorney general received so many complaints from employers about rising health care premiums that an investigation into market power and anticompetitive behavior among health care providers in eastern Massachusetts was started. Clearly, the battle is not over yet.[b]

acquisitions and found that while 30% of these did increase the profitability of the acquiring company, 31% reduced profitability, and the remainder had little impact on it.[6] The implication is that implementing a horizontal integration strategy is not an easy task for managers.

As we discuss in Chapter 10, mergers and acquisitions often fail to produce the anticipated gains for a number of reasons: problems associated with merging very different company cultures, high management turnover in the acquired company when the acquisition was a hostile one, and a tendency of managers to overestimate the benefits to be gained from a merger or acquisition and to underestimate the problems involved in merging their operation.

Another problem with horizontal integration is that, when a company uses it to become a dominant industry competitor, an attempt to keep using the strategy to grow even larger brings a company into conflict with the Federal Trade Commission, the government agency responsible for enforcing antitrust law. Antitrust authorities are concerned about the potential for abuse of market power; they believe that more competition is generally better for consumers than is less competition. They worry that large companies that dominate their industry may be in a position to abuse their market power and raise prices to consumers above the level that would exist in more competitive situations. They also believe that dominant companies can use their market power to crush potential competitors by, for example, cutting prices whenever new competitors enter a market and so force them out of business, and then raising prices again once the threat has been eliminated. Because of these concerns, any merger or acquisition that is perceived by the antitrust authorities as creating too much consolidation and the *potential* for future abuse of market power may be blocked. The proposed merger between AT&T and Bell South was held up for one year, until December 2006, because of concerns this problem would arise.

Vertical Integration: Entering New Industries to Strengthen the Core Business Model

Many companies that use horizontal integration to strengthen their business model and improve their competitive position also use the corporate-level strategy of vertical integration for the same purpose. In pursuing vertical integration, however, a company is entering new industries to support the business model of its core industry, the one that is the primary source of its competitive advantage and profitability. At this point, therefore, a company has to formulate a multibusiness model that explains how entry into a new industry will enhance its long-term profitability. The multibusiness model justifying vertical integration is based on a company entering industries that *add value* to its core products because this increases product differentiation and/or lowers its cost structure.

A company pursuing a strategy of **vertical integration** expands its operations either backward into an industry that produces inputs for the company's products (*backward vertical integration*) or forward into an industry that uses, distributes, or sells the company's products (*forward vertical integration*). To enter an industry, it may establish its own operations and build the value chain needed to compete effectively in that industry, or it may acquire or merge with a company that is already in the industry. A steel company that supplies its iron ore needs from company-owned iron ore mines exemplifies backward integration. A PC maker that sells its PCs through company-owned retail outlets illustrates forward integration. For example, in 2001, Apple Computer entered the retail industry when it decided to set up a chain of Apple Stores to sell its computers and iPods, something Dell has now imitated. IBM is a highly vertically integrated company; for example, it integrated backward into the chip and disk drive industry to produce the chips and drives that go into its computers, and it integrated forward into the computer software and consulting services industries.

Figure 9.1 illustrates four main stages in a typical raw-materials-to-customer value-added chain. For a company based in the final assembly stage, backward integration means moving into component parts manufacturing and raw materials production. Forward integration means moving into distribution and sales (retail). At each stage in the chain, *value is added* to the product, meaning that a company at that stage

FIGURE 9.1

Stages in the Raw-Materials-to-Customer Value-Added Chain

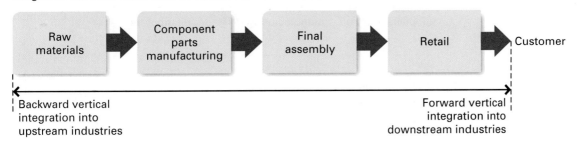

takes the product produced in the previous stage and transforms it in some way so that it is worth more to a company at the next stage in the chain and, ultimately, to the customer. It is important to note that each stage of the value-added chain is a separate industry or industries in which many different companies may be competing. Moreover, within each industry, every company has a value chain composed of the value creation activities we discussed in Chapter 3: research and development (R&D), production, marketing, customer service, and so on. In other words, we can think of a value chain that runs *across* industries, and embedded within that are the value chains of companies *within* each industry.

As an example of the value-added concept, consider how companies in each industry involved in the production of a PC contribute to the final product (Figure 9.2). At the first stage in the chain are the raw materials companies that make specialty ceramics, chemicals, and metal, such as Kyocera of Japan, which manufactures the ceramic substrate for semiconductors. These companies sell their products to the makers of PC component products, such as Intel and Micron Technology, which transform the ceramics, chemicals, and metals they purchase into PC components such as microprocessors, disk drives, and memory chips. In the process, they *add value* to the raw materials they purchase. At the third stage, these components are then sold to companies that assemble PCs, such as Gateway, Apple, Dell, and HP, and that take these components and transform them into PCs—that is, *add value* to the components they purchase. At the fourth stage, the finished PCs are then either sold directly to the final customer over the Internet or sold to retailers such as Best Buy and OfficeMax, which distribute and sell them to the final customer. Companies that distribute and sell PCs also *add value* to the product because they make it accessible to customers and provide customer service and support.

FIGURE 9.2

The Raw-Materials-to-Customer Value-Added Chain in the Personal Computer Industry

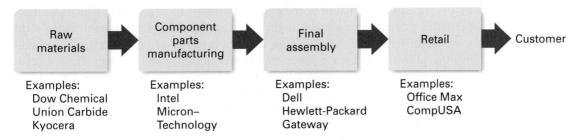

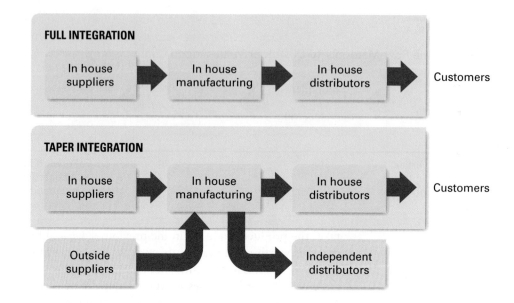

FIGURE 9.3

Full and Taper
Integration

Thus, companies in different industries add value at each stage in the raw-materials-to-customer chain. Viewed in this way, vertical integration presents companies with a choice about which industries in the raw-materials-to-customer chain to operate and compete in. This choice is determined by how much establishing operations at a stage in the value chain will increase product differentiation or lower costs, as we discuss below.

Finally, it is also important to distinguish between full integration and taper integration (see Figure 9.3).[7] A company achieves **full integration** when it produces *all* of a particular input needed for its processes or disposes of *all* of its completed products through its own operations. In **taper integration**, a company buys from independent suppliers in addition to company-owned suppliers or disposes of its completed products through independent outlets in addition to company-owned outlets. The advantages of taper integration over full integration are discussed later in the chapter.

● Increasing Profitability Through Vertical Integration

As noted earlier, a company pursues vertical integration to strengthen the business model of its original or core business and to improve its competitive position.[8] Vertical integration increases product differentiation, lowers costs, or reduces industry competition when it (1) facilitates investments in efficiency-enhancing specialized assets, (2) protects product quality, and (3) results in improved scheduling.

FACILITATING INVESTMENTS IN SPECIALIZED ASSETS A specialized asset is one that is designed to perform a specific task and whose value is significantly reduced in its next-best use.[9] The asset may be a piece of equipment that has a firm-specific use or the know-how or skills that a company or employees have acquired through training and experience. Companies invest in specialized assets because these assets allow them to lower their cost structure or to better differentiate their products, which facilitates premium pricing. A company might invest in specialized equipment to lower its manufacturing costs, for example, or it might invest in a highly specialized technology that allows it to develop better-quality products than its rivals can. Thus, specialized assets can help a company achieve a competitive advantage at the business level.

Just as a company invests in specialized assets in its own industry to build competitive advantage, it is often necessary that suppliers invest in specialized assets to produce the inputs that a specific company needs. By investing in these assets, a supplier can make higher-quality inputs that give its customer a differentiation advantage, or it can now make inputs at a lower cost so it can charge its customer a lower price to keep its business. However, it is often difficult to persuade companies in adjacent stages of the raw-materials-to-customer value-added chain to undertake investments in specialized assets. Often, to realize the benefits associated with such investments, a company has to vertically integrate and enter into adjacent industries and make the investments itself. Why does this happen?

Imagine that Ford has developed a unique high-performance fuel-injection system that will dramatically increase fuel efficiency and differentiate Ford's cars from those of its rivals, giving it a major competitive advantage. Ford has to decide whether to make the system in-house (vertical integration) or contract with an independent supplier to make the system. Manufacturing these new systems requires a substantial investment in specialized equipment that can be used only for this purpose. In other words, because of its unique design, the equipment cannot be used to manufacture any other type of fuel-injection system for Ford or any other automaker. Thus, it is an investment in specialized assets.

Consider this situation from the perspective of an independent supplier deciding whether to make this investment. The supplier might reason that once it has made the investment, it will become dependent on Ford for business because *Ford is the only possible customer for the fuel-injection system made by this specialized equipment.* The supplier realizes that this puts Ford in a strong bargaining position and that Ford might use its power to demand lower prices for the fuel-injection systems. Given the risks involved, the supplier declines to make the investment in specialized equipment.

Now consider Ford's position. Ford might reason that if it contracts production of these systems to an independent supplier, it might become too dependent on that supplier for a vital input. Because specialized equipment is required to produce the fuel-injection systems, Ford cannot switch its order to other suppliers. Ford realizes that this increases the bargaining power of the independent supplier and that the supplier might use its power to demand higher prices.

The situation of *mutual dependence* that would be created by the investment in specialized assets makes Ford hesitant to allow efficient suppliers to make the product, and makes suppliers hesitant to undertake such a risky investment. The problem is a lack of trust—neither Ford nor the supplier can trust the other to play fair in this situation. The lack of trust arises from the risk of **holdup,** that is, being taken advantage of by a trading partner after the investment in specialized assets has been made.[10] Because of this risk, Ford reasons that the only safe way to get the new fuel-injection systems is to manufacture them itself.

To generalize from this example, if achieving a competitive advantage requires one company to make investments in specialized assets so it can trade with another, the risk of holdup may serve as a deterrent and the investment may not take place. Consequently, the potential for higher profitability from specialization will be lost. To prevent such loss, companies vertically integrate into adjacent stages in the value chain. Historically, the problems surrounding specific assets have driven automobile companies to vertically integrate backward into the production of component parts, steel companies to vertically integrate backward into the production of iron, computer companies to vertically integrate backward into chip production, and aluminum companies to vertically integrate backward into bauxite mining. The way specific asset issues have led to vertical integration in the aluminum industry is discussed in Strategy in Action 9.2.

Strategy in Action
9.2

Specialized Assets and Vertical Integration in the Aluminum Industry

The metal content and chemical composition of bauxite ore, used to produce aluminum, vary from deposit to deposit, so each type of ore requires a specialized refinery—that is, the refinery must be designed for a particular type of ore. Running one type of bauxite through a refinery designed for another type reportedly increases production costs by 20% to 100%. Thus, the value of an investment in a specialized aluminum refinery and the cost of the output produced by that refinery depend on receiving the right kind of bauxite ore.

Imagine that an aluminum company has to decide whether to invest in an aluminum refinery designed to refine a certain type of ore. Also assume that this ore is extracted by a company that owns a single bauxite mine. Using a different type of ore would raise production costs by 50%. Therefore, the value of the aluminum company's investment is dependent on the price it must pay the bauxite company for this bauxite. Recognizing this, once the aluminum company has made the investment in a new refinery, what is to stop the bauxite company from raising bauxite prices? Nothing. Once it has made the investment, the aluminum company is locked into its relationship with its bauxite supplier. The bauxite supplier can increase prices because it knows that as long as the increase in the total production costs of the aluminum company is less than 50%, the aluminum company will continue to buy its ore. Thus, once the aluminum company has made the investment, the bauxite supplier can *hold up* the aluminum company.

How can the aluminum company reduce the risk of holdup? The answer is by purchasing the bauxite supplier. If the aluminum company can purchase the bauxite supplier's mine, it need no longer fear that bauxite prices will be increased after the investment in an aluminum refinery has been made. In other words, vertical integration, by eliminating the risk of holdup, makes the specialized investment worthwhile. In practice, it has been argued that these kinds of considerations have driven aluminum companies to pursue vertical integration to such a degree that, according to one study, 91% of the total volume of bauxite is transferred within vertically integrated aluminum companies.[c]

ENHANCING PRODUCT QUALITY By entering industries at other stages of the value-added chain, a company can often enhance the quality of the products in its core business and so strengthen its differentiation advantage. For example, the ability to control the reliability and performance of components such as fuel-injection systems may increase a company's competitive advantage in the luxury sedan market and enable it to charge a premium price. Conditions in the banana industry also illustrate the importance of vertical integration in maintaining product quality. Historically, a problem facing food companies that import bananas has been the variable quality of delivered bananas, which often arrive on the shelves of U.S. supermarkets too ripe or not ripe enough. To correct this problem, major U.S. food companies such as General Foods have integrated backward and now own banana plantations so they have control over the supply of bananas. As a result, they can now distribute and sell bananas of a standard quality at the optimal time to better satisfy customers. Knowing that they can rely on the quality of these brands, customers are willing to pay more for them. Thus, by vertically integrating backward into plantation ownership, banana companies have built customer confidence, which in turn has enabled them to charge a premium price for their product.

The same considerations can promote forward vertical integration. Ownership of retail outlets may be necessary if the required standards of after-sales service for complex products are to be maintained. For example, in the 1920s, Kodak owned retail outlets for distributing photographic equipment. The company felt that few established retail outlets had the skills necessary to sell and service its photographic equipment. By the 1930s, Kodak decided that it no longer needed to own its retail outlets because other retailers had begun to provide satisfactory distribution and service for Kodak products. It then withdrew from retailing.

IMPROVED SCHEDULING Sometimes important strategic advantages can be obtained when vertical integration makes it quicker, easier, and more cost effective to plan, coordinate, and schedule the transfer of a product, such as raw materials or component parts, between adjacent stages of the value-added chain.[11] Such advantages can be crucial when a company wants to realize the benefits of just-in-time inventory systems. For example, in the 1920s, Ford profited from the tight coordination and scheduling that are possible with backward vertical integration. Ford integrated backward into steel foundries, iron ore shipping, and iron ore mining. Deliveries at Ford were coordinated to such an extent that iron ore unloaded at Ford's steel foundries on the Great Lakes was turned into engine blocks within twenty-four hours, which helped to lower Ford's cost structure.

Very often, the improved scheduling that vertical integration makes possible also enables a company to respond better to sudden changes in demand. For example, if demand drops, a company can quickly cut production of components, or when demand increases, a company can quickly increase production capacity to get its products into the marketplace faster.[12]

● Problems with Vertical Integration

Vertical integration can often be used to strengthen a company's business model and increase profitability. However, the opposite can occur when vertical integration results in (1) an increasing cost structure, (2) disadvantages that arise when technology is changing fast, and (3) disadvantages that arise when demand is unpredictable. Sometimes these disadvantages are so great that vertical integration may reduce profitability rather than increase it—in which case, companies vertically disintegrate and exit industries adjacent to the industry value chain. For example, Ford, which was highly vertically integrated, sold all its companies involved in mining iron ore and making steel when more efficient and specialized steel producers emerged that were able to supply lower-priced steel.

INCREASING COST STRUCTURE Although vertical integration is often undertaken to lower a company's cost structure, it can raise costs if, over time, a company makes mistakes, such as continuing to purchase inputs from company-owned suppliers when low-cost independent suppliers can supply the same inputs. During the early 1990s, for example, General Motors's company-owned suppliers made 68% of the component parts for its vehicles; this figure was higher than for any other major carmaker and made General Motors (GM) the highest-cost global carmaker. In 1992, it was paying $34.60 an hour in United Auto Workers wages and benefits to its employees at company-owned suppliers for work that rivals could get from independent nonunionized suppliers at half that rate.[13] Thus, vertical integration can be a disadvantage when company-owned suppliers develop a higher cost structure than those of independent suppliers. Why would a company-owned supplier develop such a high cost structure?

One explanation is that company-owned or in-house suppliers know that they can always sell their components to the carmaking divisions of their company—they have a captive customer. When company-owned suppliers do not have to compete with independent suppliers for orders, they have much *less incentive* to look for new ways to reduce operating costs or increase quality. Indeed, in-house suppliers may simply pass on any cost increases to the carmaking divisions in the form of higher **transfer prices**, the prices one division of a company charges other divisions for its products. Unlike independent suppliers, which constantly have to increase their efficiency to protect their competitive advantage, in-house suppliers face no such competition, and the resulting rising cost structure reduces a company's profitability.

The term *bureaucratic costs* refers to the costs of solving the transaction difficulties that arise from managerial inefficiencies and the need to manage the handoffs or exchanges between business units to promote increased differentiation or to lower a company's cost structure. Bureaucratic costs become a significant component of a company's cost structure because considerable managerial time and effort must be spent to reduce or eliminate managerial inefficiencies—such as those that result when company-owned suppliers lose their incentive to increase efficiency or innovation.

This problem can be partially solved when a company pursues *taper*, rather than *full*, integration because now in-house suppliers do have to compete with independent suppliers. In essence, independent suppliers provide a benchmark against which a company can measure the relative efficiency of its in-house suppliers, providing an incentive for company-owned suppliers (or functions) to find ways to lower their cost structure.

TECHNOLOGICAL CHANGE When technology is changing fast, vertical integration may lock a company into an old, inefficient technology and prevent it from changing to a new one that would strengthen its business model.[14] Consider a radio manufacturer that, in the 1950s, integrated backward and acquired a manufacturer of vacuum tubes to reduce costs. When transistors replaced vacuum tubes as a major component in radios in the 1960s, this company found itself locked into a technologically outdated business. However, if it had switched to transistors, the company would have had to write off its investment in vacuum tubes, and so managers were reluctant to adopt the new technology. Instead, they continued to use vacuum tubes in their radios, while competitors that were not in the vacuum tube industry rapidly switched to the new technology. As a result, the company lost its competitive advantage, and its failing business model led to a rapid loss in market share. Thus, vertical integration can pose a serious disadvantage when it prevents a company from adopting new technology or changing its suppliers or distribution systems to match the requirements of changing technology.

DEMAND UNPREDICTABILITY Suppose the demand for a company's core product, such as cars or washing machines, is predictable and a company knows how many units it needs to make each month or year. Under these conditions, vertical integration, by allowing the company to schedule and coordinate the flow of products along the value-added chain, may result in major cost savings. However, suppose the demand for cars or washing machines fluctuates wildly and is unpredictable. Now, if demand for cars suddenly plummets, the carmaker may find itself burdened with warehouses full of component parts it no longer needs, and this is a major drain on profitability. Thus, vertical integration can be risky when demand is unpredictable because it is hard to manage the volume or flow of products along the value-added chain.

For example, an auto manufacturer might vertically integrate backward to acquire a supplier of fuel-injection systems that can make exactly the number of systems the carmaker needs each month. However, if demand for cars falls because gas prices soar, the carmaker finds itself locked into a business that is now inefficient because it is not producing at full capacity. Its cost structure then starts to rise. When demand is unpredictable, taper integration might be less risky than full integration because a company can keep its in-house suppliers running at full capacity and increase or reduce its orders from independent suppliers to match changing demand conditions.

The Limits of Vertical Integration

Although vertical integration can strengthen a company's business model in many ways, it may weaken it when (1) bureaucratic costs increase because company-owned suppliers lack the incentive to reduce operating costs and (2) changing technology or uncertain demand reduces a company's ability to change its business model to protect its competitive advantage. It is clear that strategic managers have to carefully assess the advantages and disadvantages of expanding the boundaries of their company by entering adjacent industries, either backward (upstream) or forward (downstream), in the value-added chain. While the decision to enter a new industry to make crucial component parts might have been profitable in the past, it might make no economic sense today, when many low-cost global component parts suppliers can compete for a company's business. The risks and returns on investing in vertical integration have to be continually evaluated, and companies should be as willing to vertically disintegrate as vertically integrate to strengthen their core business model. Finally, it is worth noting that taper vertical integration rather than full vertical integration may decrease bureaucratic costs because it creates an incentive for in-house suppliers to reduce operating costs. There are other ways of achieving this, however, as we discuss next.

Alternatives to Vertical Integration: Cooperative Relationships

Is it possible to obtain the differentiation and cost-savings advantages associated with vertical integration without having to bear the problems and costs associated with this strategy? In other words, is there another corporate-level strategy that managers can use to obtain the advantages of vertical integration while allowing other companies to perform upstream and downstream activities? Today, many companies have found that they can realize many of the benefits associated with vertical integration by entering into long-term cooperative relationships with companies in industries along the value-added chain. **Strategic alliances**, discussed in Chapter 8, are long-term agreements between two or more companies to jointly develop new products that benefit all companies concerned. The advantages of strategic alliances can be clarified by contrasting them with the benefits obtained if a company decides to enter into short-term contracts with other companies.

● **Short-Term Contracts and Competitive Bidding**

Many companies use short-term contracts, which last for a year or less, to establish the prices and conditions under which they will purchase raw materials or components from suppliers or sell their final products to distributors. A classic example is the carmaker that uses a *competitive bidding strategy* in which independent component suppliers compete to be the company that will be chosen to supply a particular part, made to agreed-upon specifications, at the lowest price. For example, GM typically solicits bids from global suppliers to produce a particular component and awards a one-year contract to the supplier submitting the lowest bid. At the end of the year, the contract is put out for competitive bid again. There is no guarantee that the company that wins the contract one year will hold on to it the next.

The advantage of this strategy for GM is that it forces suppliers to compete over price, which drives the cost of its inputs down. However, GM has no long-term commitment to individual suppliers, and it drives a hard bargain. For this reason, prospective suppliers will likely be unwilling to make the expensive investment in specialized assets that are needed to produce higher-quality or better-designed component parts. In addition, they will be reluctant to agree to tight scheduling because that would allow GM to obtain the benefits from a just-in-time inventory system but would increase the suppliers' operating costs and so reduce their profitability. With no guarantee it will retain GM's business, the supplier may refuse to invest in specialized assets; thus, to realize differentiation and cost gains, GM will have to vertically integrate backward.

In other words, the strategy of short-term contracting and competitive bidding, *because it signals a company's lack of long-term commitment to its suppliers,* will make it difficult or impossible for that company to realize the gains associated with vertical integration. Of course, this is not a problem when there is minimal need for close cooperation and no need to invest in specialized assets to improve scheduling or product quality. In such cases, competitive bidding may be optimal. However, when this need is significant, a competitive bidding strategy can be a serious drawback.

In the past, GM did place itself at a competitive disadvantage when it used a competitive bidding approach to negotiate with its suppliers. In 1992, the company instructed its parts suppliers to cut their prices by 10%, regardless of prior pricing agreements. In effect, GM tore up existing contracts and threatened to stop doing business with suppliers that did not agree to the price reduction. Although its action gave it a short-term benefit from lower costs, in the longer term, the loss of trust and the hostility created between the company and its suppliers resulted in problems for GM. According to press reports, several suppliers claimed that they reduced the R&D spending necessary to design GM parts in the future, a form of specialized investment. They also indicated that they would first impart their new design knowledge to Chrysler (now DaimlerChrysler) and Ford, which both focused on forging cooperative long-term relationships with their suppliers.[15]

Strategic Alliances and Long-Term Contracting

As opposed to short-term contracts, strategic alliances are long-term cooperative relationships between two or more companies who agree to commit resources to develop new products. Typically, one company agrees to supply the other, and the other company agrees to continue purchasing from that supplier; both make a commitment to jointly seek ways to lower costs or increase input quality. A strategic alliance, by creating a stable long-term relationship, becomes a *substitute* for vertical integration; it allows both companies to share in the same kinds of benefits that result from vertical integration but avoids the problems linked with having to manage a company located in an adjacent industry in the value-added chain, such as lack of incentives or changing technology.

Consider the cooperative relationships, which often go back decades, that many Japanese carmakers have with their components suppliers (the *keiretsu* system), which exemplifies successful long-term contracting. Together, carmakers and suppliers work out ways to increase the value added—for example, by implementing just-in-time inventory systems or cooperating on component-parts designs to improve quality and lower assembly costs. As part of this process, the suppliers make substantial investments in specialized assets to better serve the needs of a particular carmaker. Any cost savings that result are shared by carmakers and suppliers. Thus, Japanese carmakers have been able to capture many of the benefits of vertical integration without having to enter and own companies in new industries. Similarly, the component suppliers also benefit because their business and profitability grow as the companies they supply grow.[16]

In contrast to their Japanese counterparts, U.S. carmakers have historically pursued vertical integration.[17] According to several studies, the result is that the ever increasing cost of managing scores or even hundreds of companies in different industries has put GM and Ford at a significant cost disadvantage relative to their Japanese competitors.[18] Moreover, even when U.S. auto companies decided not to integrate vertically, they tended to use their powerful position to pursue an aggressive competitive bidding strategy, playing off component suppliers against each other.[19] This mindset now seems to be changing. For details on how DaimlerChrysler has attempted to build long-term cooperative relationships with suppliers, see Strategy in Action 9.3.

Strategy in Action

9.3

DaimlerChrysler's U.S. *Keiretsu*

For most of its history, Chrysler (now DaimlerChrysler) managed suppliers through a competitive bidding process: suppliers were selected on the basis of their ability to supply components at the lowest possible cost to Chrysler. A supplier's track record on performance and quality was relatively unimportant in this process. Contracts were renegotiated every two years, with little or no commitment from Chrysler to continuing to do business with a particular supplier. As a result, the typical relationship between Chrysler and its suppliers was characterized by mutual distrust, suspicion, and reluctance on the part of suppliers to invest too much in their relationship with Chrysler.

Since the early 1990s, Chrysler has systematically reorganized its dealings with suppliers in an attempt to build stable long-term relationships. The aim of this new approach has been to try to get suppliers to help Chrysler develop new products and improve its production processes. To encourage suppliers to cooperate and make investments specific to Chrysler's needs, the company has moved away from its old adversarial approach. The average contract with suppliers has been lengthened from two years to over four and a half years. Furthermore, Chrysler has given 90% of its suppliers commitments that business will be extended for at least the life of a model, if not beyond. The company has also committed itself to sharing with suppliers the benefits of any process improvements they might suggest. The basic thinking behind offering suppliers such credible commitments is to align incentives between Chrysler and its suppliers to create a sense of shared destiny and to encourage mutual cooperation to increase the size of the financial pie that they will share in the future.

By 1996, the fruits of this new approach were beginning to appear. By involving suppliers early in product development and giving them greater responsibility for design and manufacturing, DaimlerChrysler was able to compress its product development cycle and substantially reduce the costs of the product development effort. DaimlerChrysler's U.S. division reduced the time it took to develop a new vehicle from 234 weeks during the mid-1980s to about 160 weeks by 1996. The total cost of developing a new vehicle also dropped by 20 to 40%, depending on the model. With development costs in the automobile industry running at between $1 and $2 billion, that translates into a huge financial savings. Many of these savings were the direct result of engineering improvements suggested by suppliers or improved coordination between the company and suppliers in the design process. To facilitate this process, the number of resident engineers from suppliers who work side by side with DaimlerChrysler engineers in cross-company design teams increased from thirty in 1989 to more than 300 by 1996.

In 1990, Chrysler began implementing a program known internally as the supplier cost reduction effort (SCORE), which focuses on cooperation between DaimlerChrysler and suppliers to identify opportunities for process improvements. In its first two years of operation, SCORE generated 875 ideas from suppliers that were worth $170.8 million in annual savings to suppliers. In 1994, suppliers submitted 3,786 ideas that produced $504 million in annual savings. By December 1995, Chrysler had implemented 5,300 ideas that have generated more than $1.7 billion in annual savings. One supplier alone, Magna International, submitted 214 proposals; Chrysler adopted 129 of them for a total cost savings of $75.5 million. Many of the ideas themselves have a relatively small financial impact; for example, a Magna suggestion to change the type of decorative wood grain used on minivans saved $0.5 million per year. But the cumulative impact of thousands of such ideas has had a significant impact on DaimlerChrysler's bottom line.

DaimlerChrysler has continued to pursue this approach aggressively, so much so that in 2004, it announced that its long-term goal was for its suppliers to take over a much higher percentage of actual car production—which includes making the car body and assembling most of its major components. Chrysler believes that this will give suppliers greater motivation than its own car divisions to control quality and reduce costs. Thus, it has a radical long-term business model: it wants to be a car designer and not a carmaker. The cars that come off the assembly line may have Chrysler's name on them, but it will have only designed them, not built them.[d]

Building Long-Term Cooperative Relationships

The interesting question raised by the preceding discussion is: How does a company create a stable long-term strategic alliance with another company given the fear of holdup and the possibility of being cheated, which arise when one company makes an investment in specialized assets to trade with another? How have companies like Toyota managed to develop such enduring relationships with their suppliers?

Companies can take several steps to ensure the success of a long-term cooperative relationship and to lessen the chance that one company will renege on its agreement and try to cheat the other. One of those steps is for the company that makes the investment in specialized assets to demand a *hostage* from its partner. Another is to establish a *credible commitment* on both sides to build a trusting long-term relationship.[20]

HOSTAGE TAKING   Hostage taking is essentially a means of guaranteeing that a partner will keep its side of the bargain. The cooperative relationship between Boeing and Northrop illustrates this type of situation. Northrop is a major subcontractor for Boeing's commercial airline division, providing many components for the 747 and 767 aircraft. To serve Boeing's special needs, Northrop has had to make substantial investments in specialized assets. In theory, because of the sunk costs associated with such investments, Northrop is dependent on Boeing, and Boeing is in a position to renege on previous agreements and use the threat to switch orders to other suppliers as a way of driving down prices. In practice, however, Boeing is highly unlikely to do this because it is a major supplier to Northrop's defense division and provides many parts for the Stealth bomber. Boeing also has had to make substantial investments in specialized assets to serve Northrop's needs. Thus, the companies are *mutually dependent*. Boeing is unlikely to renege on any pricing agreements with Northrop because it knows that Northrop could respond in kind. Each company holds a hostage—the specialized investment the other has made—as insurance against any attempt by the other company to renege on its prior pricing agreements.

CREDIBLE COMMITMENTS   A credible commitment is a believable promise or pledge to support the development of a long-term relationship between companies. To understand the concept of credibility in this context, consider the following relationship between General Electric and IBM. GE is one of the major suppliers of advanced semiconductor chips to IBM, and many of the chips are customized to IBM's requirements. To meet IBM's specific needs, GE has had to make substantial investments in specialized assets that have little other value. As a consequence, GE is dependent on IBM and faces a risk that IBM will take advantage of this dependence to demand lower prices. In theory, IBM could back up its demand by threatening to switch its business to another supplier. However, GE reduced this risk by having IBM enter into a contractual agreement that committed IBM to purchase chips from GE for a ten-year period. In addition, IBM agreed to share the costs of the specialized assets needed to develop the customized chips, thereby reducing GE's investment. Thus, by publicly committing itself to a long-term contract and putting some money into the chip development process, IBM essentially made a *credible commitment* to continue purchasing those chips from GE.

MAINTAINING MARKET DISCIPLINE   Just as a company pursuing vertical integration faces the problem that its in-house suppliers might become lazy and inefficient, so a company that forms a strategic alliance with another to make its components runs the risk that the other company's costs will rise as it becomes progressively more lax or inefficient over time. This happens because the supplier knows it does not have to compete with other suppliers for the company's business. Consequently, a company seeking to form a long-term strategic alliance needs to possess some kind of power that it can use to discipline its partner should the need arise.

The company holds two strong cards over its supplier. First, even long-term contracts are periodically renegotiated, generally every four to five years, so the supplier knows that if it fails to live up to its commitments, the company may refuse to renew the contract. Second, some companies engaged in long-term relationships with suppliers use a **parallel sourcing policy**—that is, they enter into a long-term contract with *two* suppliers for the same part (as is the practice at Toyota, for example).[21] This arrangement gives the company a hedge against an uncooperative supplier because it knows that if it fails to comply with the agreement, the company can switch all its business to the other supplier. This threat rarely needs to be actualized because the mere fact that the company and its suppliers know that parallel sourcing is being used and that a supplier can be replaced at short notice injects an element of market discipline into their relationship.

The growing importance of just-in-time inventory systems as a way to reduce costs and enhance quality—and thus differentiation—is increasing the pressure on companies to form strategic alliances in a wide range of industries. The number of strategic alliances, especially global strategic alliances, formed each year is increasing, and the popularity of vertical integration may be falling because so many low-cost global suppliers now exist in countries like Malaysia, Korea, and China.

Strategic Outsourcing

Vertical integration and strategic alliances are alternative ways of managing the value chain *across industries* to strengthen a company's core business model. However, just as low-cost suppliers of component parts exist, so today many *specialized companies* exist that can perform one of a company's *own value-chain activities* in a way that contributes to a company's differentiation advantage or that lowers its cost structure.

Strategic outsourcing is the decision to allow one or more of a company's value-chain activities or functions to be performed by independent specialist companies that focus all their skills and knowledge on just one kind of activity. The activity to be outsourced may encompass an entire function, such as the manufacturing function, or it may be just one kind of activity that a function performs. For example, many companies outsource the management of their pension systems while keeping other HRM activities within the company. When a company chooses to outsource a value-chain activity, it is choosing to focus on *fewer* value creation activities to strengthen its business model.

Many companies have started to outsource activities that managers regard as noncore or nonstrategic, meaning they are not a source of a company's distinctive competencies and competitive advantage.[22] One survey found that some 54% of the companies polled had outsourced manufacturing processes or services in the past three years.[23] Another survey estimates that some 56% of all global product manufacturing is outsourced to manufacturing specialists.[24] Companies that outsource include Nike, which does not make its athletic shoes, and The Gap, which does not make its jeans and clothing; these products are made under contract at low-cost global locations. Similarly, many high-technology companies outsource much of their manufacturing activity to contract manufacturers that specialize in low-cost assembly. Cisco, the leader in the Internet router and switch business, does not actually manufacture routers and switches; rather, they are made by contract manufacturers such as Flextronics and Jabil Circuit.

While manufacturing is probably the most popular form of strategic outsourcing, as we noted earlier, many other kinds of noncore activities are also outsourced. Microsoft has long outsourced its entire customer technical support operation to an independent company, as does Dell. Both companies have extensive customer support operations in India that are staffed by skilled operatives who are paid a fraction of what their U.S. counterparts earn. BP Amoco outsourced almost all of its human resources function to Exult, a San Antonio company, in a five-year deal worth $600 million, and a few years later, Exult won a ten-year $1.1 billion contract to handle HRM activities for all Bank of America's 150,000 employees. Similarly, American Express outsourced its entire IT function to IBM in a seven-year deal worth $4 billion in 2002. The IT outsourcing market in North America was worth over $200 billion by 2006.[25] In 2006, IBM announced that it was outsourcing its purchasing function to an Indian company to save $2 billion a year.[26]

Companies engage in strategic outsourcing to strengthen their business models and increase their profitability. The process of strategic outsourcing typically begins with strategic managers identifying the value-chain activities that form the basis of a company's competitive advantage; these are obviously kept within the company to protect them from competitors. Managers then systematically review the noncore functions to assess whether they can be performed more effectively and efficiently by independent companies that specialize in those activities. Because these companies specialize in a particular activity, they can perform it in ways that lower costs or improve differentiation. If managers decide there are differentiation or cost advantages, these activities are outsourced to those specialists.

One possible outcome of this process is illustrated in Figure 9.4, which shows the primary value-chain activities and boundaries of a company before and after it has pursued strategic outsourcing. In this example, the company decided to outsource its production and customer service functions to specialist companies, leaving just R&D

FIGURE 9.4

Strategic Outsourcing of Primary Value Creation Functions

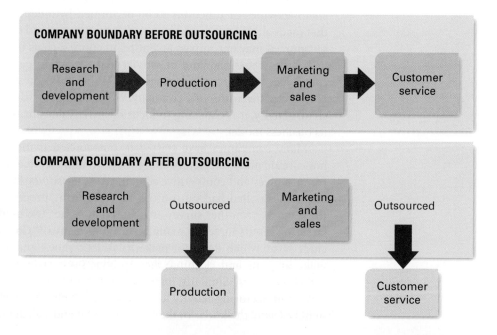

and marketing and sales within the company. Once outsourcing has been executed, the relationships between the company and its specialists are then often structured as long-term contractual relationships, with rich information sharing between the company and the specialist organization to which it has contracted the activity. The term **virtual corporation** has been coined to describe companies that have pursued extensive strategic outsourcing.[27]

● **Benefits of Outsourcing**

Strategic outsourcing has several advantages. It can help a company to (1) lower its cost structure, (2) increase product differentiation,[28] and (3) focus on the distinctive competencies that are vital to its long-term competitive advantage and profitability.

LOWER COST STRUCTURE Outsourcing reduces costs when the price that must be paid to a specialist company to perform a particular value-chain activity is less than what it would cost the company to perform that activity itself, that is, internally. Specialists are often able to perform an activity at a lower cost than the company can because they are able to realize scale economies or other efficiencies not available to the company. For example, performing HRM activities, such as managing a pay and benefits system, requires a significant investment in sophisticated HRM IT, and purchasing this IT represents a considerable fixed cost for one company. But by aggregating the HRM IT needs of many individual companies, a company that specializes in HRM, such as Exult or Paycheck, can obtain huge economies of scale in IT that any single company could not hope to achieve. Some of these cost savings are then passed on to client companies in the form of lower prices, which reduces their cost structure. A similar dynamic is at work in the contract manufacturing business. Once again, manufacturing specialists like Solectron, Flextronics, and Jabil Circuit make large capital investments to build efficient-scale manufacturing facilities, but then they are able to spread those capital costs over a huge volume of output and drive down unit costs so that they can make a specific product—an Apple iPod or Motorola Krazr, for example, at a lower cost than the company can.

Specialists are also likely to obtain the cost savings associated with learning effects much more rapidly than a company that performs an activity just for itself (see Chapter 4 for a review of learning effects). For example, because a company like Flextronics is manufacturing similar products for several different companies, it is able to build up *cumulative* volume more rapidly, and it learns how to manage and operate the manufacturing process more efficiently than any of its clients could. This drives down the specialists' cost structure and also allows them to charge client companies a lower price for a product than if the client companies made it in-house.

Specialists are also often able to perform an activity at a lower cost than a specific company because they are based in low-cost global locations. Nike, for example, outsources the manufacture of its running shoes to companies based in China because of the much lower wage rates in China. The Chinese-based specialist can now assemble shoes, which is a very labor-intensive activity, at a much lower cost than if Nike assembled its shoes in the United States. Although Nike could establish its own operations in China to manufacture running shoes, this would require a major capital investment and limit its ability to switch production to an even lower-cost location later, say, Vietnam. So for Nike and most other consumer goods companies, outsourcing manufacturing activity to both lower costs and obtain the flexibility to switch to a more favorable location should labor costs change is the most efficient way to handle production.

ENHANCED DIFFERENTIATION A company may also be able to differentiate its final products better by outsourcing certain noncore activities to specialists. For this to occur, the *quality* of the activity performed by specialists must be greater than if that same activity were performed by the company. On the reliability dimension of quality, for example, a specialist may be able to achieve a lower error rate in performing an activity precisely because it focuses solely on that activity and has developed a strong distinctive competency in it. Again, this is one advantage claimed for contract manufacturers. Companies like Flextronics have adopted Six Sigma methodologies (see Chapter 4) and driven down the defect rate associated with manufacturing a product. Thus, they can provide more reliable products to their clients, which can now differentiate their products on the basis of their superior quality.

A company can also improve product differentiation by outsourcing to specialists when they stand out on the excellence dimension of quality. For example, the excellence of Dell's U.S. customer service is a differentiating factor, and Dell outsources its PC repair and maintenance function to specialist companies. A customer who has a problem with a product purchased from Dell can get excellent help over the phone, and if it turns out that there is a defective part in the computer, a maintenance person will be dispatched to replace the part within a few days. The excellence of this service differentiates Dell and helps to guarantee repeat purchases, which is why HP has worked hard to match Dell's level of service quality. In a similar way, carmakers often outsource specific kinds of vehicle component design activities, such as microchips or headlights, to specialists that have earned a reputation for design excellence in this particular activity.

FOCUS ON THE CORE BUSINESS A final advantage of strategic outsourcing is that it allows managers to focus their energies and their company's resources on performing those core activities that have the most potential to create value and competitive advantage. In other words, companies can enhance their core competencies and thus are able to push out the value creation frontier and create more value for their customers. For example, Cisco remains the dominant competitor in the Internet router industry because it has focused on building its competencies in product design, marketing and sales, and supply-chain management. Companies that focus on the core activities essential for competitive advantage in their industry are better able to drive down the costs of performing those activities and thus better differentiate their final products.

● **Risks of Outsourcing**

Although outsourcing noncore activities has many benefits, there are also risks associated with it, risks such as holdup and the possible loss of important information. Managers must assess these risks before they decide to outsource a particular activity. As we discuss below, however, these risks can be reduced when the appropriate steps are taken.

HOLDUP In the context of outsourcing, holdup refers to the risk that a company will become too dependent on the specialist provider of an outsourced activity and that the specialist will use this fact to raise prices beyond some previously agreed-on rate. As with strategic alliances, the risk of holdup can be reduced by outsourcing to several suppliers and pursuing a parallel sourcing policy, as DaimlerChrysler and Cisco do. Moreover, when an activity can be performed well by any one of several different providers, the threat that a contract will not be renewed in the future is normally sufficient to keep the chosen provider from exercising bargaining power over the company.

For example, although IBM enters into long-term contracts to provide IT services to a wide range of companies, it would be highly unlikely to try to raise prices after the contract has been signed because it knows full well that such an action would reduce its chance of getting the contract renewed in the future. Moreover, the fact that IBM has many strong competitors in the IT services business, such as EDS, Accenture, and HP, gives it a very strong incentive to deliver significant value to its client and not to practice holdup.

LOSS OF INFORMATION A company that is not careful can lose important competitive information when it outsources an activity. For example, many computer hardware and software companies have outsourced their customer technical support function to specialists. Although this makes good sense from a cost and differentiation perspective, it may also mean that a critical point of contact with the customer, and a source of important feedback, is lost. Customer complaints can be useful pieces of information and valuable input into future product design, but if those complaints are not clearly communicated to the company by the specialists performing the technical support activity, the company can lose that information. Again, this is not an argument against outsourcing. Rather, it is an argument for making sure that there is good communication flow between the outsourcing specialist and the company. At Dell, for example, a great deal of attention is paid to making sure that the specialist responsible for providing technical support and onsite maintenance collects and communicates all relevant data regarding product failures and other problems to Dell, so that Dell can design better products.

Summary of Chapter

1. A corporate strategy should enable a company, or one or more of its business units, to perform one or more of the value creation functions at a lower cost or in a way that allows for differentiation and a premium price.

2. Horizontal integration can be understood as a way of trying to increase the profitability of a company by (a) reducing costs, (b) increasing the value of the company's products through differentiation, (c) replicating the business model, (d) managing rivalry within the industry to reduce the risk of price warfare, and (e) increasing bargaining power over suppliers and buyers.

3. There are two drawbacks associated with horizontal integration: the numerous pitfalls associated with mergers and acquisitions, and the fact that the strategy can bring a company into direct conflict with antitrust authorities.

4. Vertical integration can enable a company to achieve a competitive advantage by helping build barriers to entry, facilitating investments in specialized assets, protecting product quality, and helping to improve scheduling between adjacent stages in the value chain.

5. The disadvantages of vertical integration include increasing bureaucratic costs if a company's internal or in-house supplier becomes inefficient, and a lack of flexibility when technology is changing fast or demand is uncertain.

6. Entering into a long-term contract can enable a company to realize many of the benefits associated with vertical integration without having to bear the same level of bureaucratic costs. However, to avoid the risks associated with becoming too dependent on its partner, it needs to seek a credible commitment from its partner or establish a mutual hostage-taking situation.

7. The strategic outsourcing of noncore value creation activities may allow a company to lower its costs, better differentiate its products, and make better use of scarce resources, while also enabling it to respond rapidly to changing market conditions. However, strategic outsourcing may have a detrimental effect if the company outsources important value creation activities or becomes too dependent on the key suppliers of those activities.

Discussion Questions

1. Why was it profitable for GM and Ford to integrate backward into component-parts manufacturing in the past, and why are both companies now trying to buy more of their parts from outside suppliers?

2. Under what conditions might horizontal integration be inconsistent with the goal of maximizing profitability?

3. What value creation activities should a company outsource to independent suppliers? What are the risks involved in outsourcing these activities?

4. What steps would you recommend that a company take to build long-term cooperative relationships with its suppliers that are mutually beneficial?

Practicing Strategic Management

SMALL-GROUP EXERCISE
Comparing Vertical Integration Strategies

Break up into small groups of three to five people, appoint one group member as a spokesperson who will communicate your findings to the class, then read the following description of the activities of Seagate Technologies and Quantum Corporation, both of which manufacture computer disk drives. On the basis of this description, outline the pros and cons of a vertical integration strategy. Which strategy do you think makes most sense in the context of the computer disk drive industry?

Quantum Corporation and Seagate Technologies are major producers of disk drives for personal computers and workstations. The disk drive industry is characterized by sharp fluctuations in the level of demand, intense price competition, rapid technological change, and product life cycles of no more than twelve to eighteen months. In recent years, Quantum and Seagate have pursued very different vertical integration strategies.

Seagate is a vertically integrated manufacturer of disk drives, both designing and manufacturing the bulk of its own disk drives. Quantum specializes in design and outsources most of its manufacturing to a number of independent suppliers, including, most important, Matsushita Kotobuki Electronics (MKE) of Japan. Quantum makes only its newest and most expensive products in-house. Once a new drive is perfected and ready for large-scale manufacturing, Quantum turns over manufacturing to MKE. MKE and Quantum have cemented their partnership over eight years. At each stage in designing a new product, Quantum's engineers send the newest drawings to a production team at MKE. MKE examines the drawings and is constantly proposing changes that make new

disk drives easier to manufacture. When the product is ready for manufacture, eight to ten Quantum engineers travel to MKE's plant in Japan to spend at least a month to work on production ramp-up.

ARTICLE FILE 9

Find an example of a company whose horizontal or vertical integration strategy appears to have dissipated rather than created value. Identify why this has been the case and what the company should do to rectify the situation.

STRATEGIC MANAGEMENT PROJECT
Module 9

This module requires you to assess the horizontal and vertical integration strategies pursued by your company. With the information you have at your disposal, answer the questions and perform the tasks listed:

1. Has your company ever pursued a horizontal integration strategy? What was the strategic reason for pursuing this strategy?

2. How vertically integrated is your company? If your company does have vertically integrated operations, is it pursuing a strategy of taper or full vertical integration?

3. Assess the potential for your company to create value through vertical integration. In reaching your assessment, also consider the bureaucratic costs of managing vertical integration.

4. On the basis of your assessment in question 3, do you think your company should (a) outsource some operations that are currently performed in-house or (b) bring some operations in-house that are currently outsourced? Justify your recommendations.

5. Is your company involved in any long-term cooperative relationships with suppliers or buyers? If so, how are these relationships structured? Do you think that these relationships add value to the company? Why?

6. Is there any potential for your company to enter into (additional) long-term cooperative relationships with suppliers or buyers? If so, how might these relationships be structured?

ETHICS EXERCISE

Kelli had been out of college for five months and was desperately in need of a well paying job. She had always abhorred sales, but her mother's friend owned an insurance company and offered to train her as a medical insurance salesperson. Kelli knew the earning potential for a job like this one was good, and she needed the cash. After talking with friends and family, she decided to accept the job.

During her first week of training, Kelli began to see things that disturbed her. On Tuesday, she shadowed Bob, a salesperson with the company for ten years, as he reviewed and sold a policy to a young couple. During the discussion with the couple, Bob assured them that the policy covered severe injuries, various cancers, and other serious illnesses. Reading over the policy later, Kelli noticed that the policy did not cover many common illnesses—something Bob had neglected to mention to the couple. On Wednesday, Kelli shadowed another seasoned salesperson, Greta. In this case, Greta sold a policy to an elderly man without mentioning that it was not compatible with Medicare.

By Friday, Kelli was worried. She asked John, another salesperson almost as new as she was, about Bob and Greta's behavior and was told that this was simply how things were done. "You'll learn it soon enough, Kelli. The name of the game here is sell, sell, sell."

Kelli didn't know what to do. Was her mom's friend, who had been kind enough to give her a job despite inexperience, supportive of these business methods? If not, how could she tell her what was going on behind her back? If so, how could Kelli quit without making everyone angry?

1. Define the ethical issues presented in this case.
2. What do you think Kelli should do?
3. Do you think what Bob and Greta did was unethical? Why or why not?

CLOSING CASE

Read All About It News Corp.

Way before television and the Internet, "Read all about it" was the cry of street vendors eager to persuade news-hungry customers to buy the most recent version of their newspaper. Now, TV channels like CNN and Web portals like Yahoo! and Google provide almost instantaneous news from around the world. "Read the latest" might also describe the growth of News Corporation Limited, or News Corp., the company headed by controversial CEO Rupert Murdoch, who every year for the last several decades has engineered some kind of acquisition or divestiture that has created one of the four largest and most powerful entertainment media companies in the world. What is the news about News Corp.? What kinds of strategies did Murdoch use to create his media empire?

Rupert Murdoch was born into a newspaper family; his father owned and ran the *Adelaide News,* an Australian regional newspaper, and when his father died in 1952, Murdoch gained control of the paper. He quickly enlarged his customer base by acquiring more Australian newspapers. One of these had connections to a major British pulp newspaper, the *Mirror,* a paper similar to the *National Enquirer,* and Murdoch recognized that he had an opportunity to copy the *Mirror*'s business model but make his paper even more sensational. His business model worked, and Murdoch established the *Sun* as a leading British tabloid.

Murdoch's growing reputation as an entrepreneur showed that he could create a much higher return from the assets he controlled (ROIC) than his competitors and enabled him to borrow increasing amounts of money from investors. With this money, he bought well-known newspapers such as the *British Sunday Telegraph* and then his first U.S. newspaper, the *San Antonio Express*. Pursuing his sensational business model further, he launched the *National Star*. His growing profits and reputation allowed him to continue to borrow money, and in 1977, he bought the *New York Post*. Four years later, in 1981, he engineered a new coup when he bought the *Times* and *Sunday Times*, Britain's leading conservative publications—a far cry from the *Sun* tabloid.

Murdoch's strategy of horizontal integration through merger allowed him to create one of the world's biggest newspaper empires. However, he also realized that industries in the entertainment and media sector can be divided into those that provide media content, or "software" (books, movies, and television programs), and those that provide the media channels, or "hardware," necessary to bring software to customers (movie theaters, television channels, television cable, and satellite broadcasting). Murdoch decided that he could create the most profit by becoming involved in both the media software *and* hardware industries—that is, the entire value chain of the entertainment and media sector. This strategy of vertical integration gave him control over all the different industries, joined together like links in a chain that converted inputs such as stories into finished products like newspapers or books.

In the 1980s, Murdoch began purchasing global media companies in both the software and hardware stages of the entertainment sector. He also launched new ventures of his own. For example, sensing the potential of satellite broadcasting, he launched Sky in 1983, the first satellite television channel in the United Kingdom. He also began a new strategy of horizontal integration by purchasing companies that owned television stations. He paid $1.5 billion for Metromedia, which owned seven stations that reached over 20% of U.S. households. He scored another major coup in 1985 when he bought Twentieth Century Fox Movie Studios, a premium content provider. Now he had Fox's huge film library and its creative talents to make new films and television programming.

In 1986, Murdoch decided to create the FOX Broadcasting Company and buy or create his own U.S. network of FOX affiliates that would show programming developed by his own FOX movie studios. After a slow start, the FOX network gained popularity with sensational shows like *The Simpsons*, which became FOX's first blockbuster program. Then in 1994, FOX purchased the sole rights to broadcast all NFL games for over $1 billion, thereby shutting out NBC and becoming the fourth network. The FOX network has never looked back and, with Murdoch's sensational business model, was one of the first to create the reality programming that has proved so popular in the 2000s.

Realizing that he could create even more value by transmitting his growing media content over new channels, Murdoch also began to increase his company's presence in satellite broadcasting. In 1990, Murdoch merged his Sky satellite channel with British Satellite Broadcasting to form BSkyB, which has since become the leading satellite provider in the United Kingdom. Then, in 2003, News Corp. announced it would buy DIRECTV, one of the two largest satellite TV providers, for $6.6 billion. At the same time, News Corp. was also acquiring many other companies in both stages of the entertainment value chain to strengthen its competitive position in those industries.

By 2004, Murdoch's business model, based on strategies of horizontal and vertical integration, had created a global media empire. The company's profitability has ebbed and flowed because of the massive debt needed to fund Murdoch's acquisitions, debt that has frequently brought his company near financial ruin. However, banks that understand the value of his assets, such as Citibank, have provided the money needed to service those debts. Meanwhile, News Corp.'s ROIC has been steadily increasing through the 2000s and it has become the leading global media empire..

Case Discussion Questions

1. What kind of corporate-level strategies did News Corp. pursue to build its multibusiness model?

2. What are the advantages and disadvantages associated with these strategies?

Corporate-Level Strategy: Formulating and Implementing Related and Unrelated Diversification

Tyco's Rough Ride

Tyco International has experienced success and failure under different CEOs. Its multibusiness model was implemented differently by its former CEO Dennis Kozlowski, who took over in 1992. Tyco's sales expanded from $3.1 billion in 1992 to $38 billion in 2001, when it earned over $5 billion in profit. Much of this growth was driven by acquisitions that Kozlowski orchestrated to take Tyco into a diverse range of businesses, including medical supplies, security equipment, electronic components, plastics, financial services, and telecommunications.

Kozlowski's early success has been attributed to the way he applied a business model based on several consistent strategies. First, through its acquisitions, Tyco seeks to attain a critical mass in the industries in which it competes. Despite the fact that the company is diversified, Tyco became one of the largest providers of security systems, basic medical supplies, and electronic components in the United States. Indeed, Kozlowski used acquisitions to consolidate fragmented industries and attain economies of scale that give Tyco a cost-based advantage over smaller rivals.[1]

Second, Tyco sought out companies making basic products that have a strong market share, but the companies have been underperforming compared to their competitors—which indicates there is substantial room for improvement. Once Tyco identified a potential target, Kozlowski approached the company's managers to see if they supported the idea of being acquired. After its auditors had carefully examined the target's books and decided the company had potential, Tyco made a formal bid. When the acquisition had been completed, Tyco worked to find ways to improve the performance of the acquired unit. Corporate overhead and the company's work force were slashed, and the old top management team was removed. Unprofitable product lines were sold off or closed down, and factories and sales forces were merged with Tyco's existing operations to reduce costs and obtain scale economies. For example, within months of acquiring AMP (the world's largest manufacturer of electronic components) for $12 billion in 1999, Tyco had identified close to $1 billion in cost savings that could be implemented by closing unprofitable plants and reducing its work force by 8,000. Once costs were slashed, the new management team was then set tough goals and given strong incentives to boost profitability.

Throughout most of the 1990s, this business model worked well and Tyco's stock soared, but then in the late 1990s, things changed. Tyco's most recent acquisitions did not seem to be contributing much to profitability; the company was growing, but somehow its performance seemed to be flagging. Then, beginning in 1999, analysts began to criticize the company's top managers for using inappropriate accounting methods to disguise the fact that Tyco's business model was failing. Critics argued that Kozlowski and Tyco's chief financial officer Mark Swartz had started to systematically find ways to inflate the profitability of its operating units and new acquisitions to make Tyco's performance look better than it actually was. They were forced to resign in 2003, and in 2005, these accusations were borne out when both men were sentenced to prison for grand larceny, securities fraud, falsifying business records, and conspiring to defraud Tyco of hundreds of millions of dollars to fund lavish lifestyles.

Tyco was a ship adrift in the early 2000s; it seemed that there was no longer a rationale for keeping its empire together, its business model was a failure, and its stock price plummeted. The company's stock traded with a so-called diversification discount because investors found it impossible to evaluate the profitability of its individual business units. So, its new CEO, Edward Breen, decided that the best way to increase value to shareholders was to reverse the business model that been developed by Kozlowski.[2]

In 2006, Breen announced that he had decided to pursue a new, nondiversified business model. The company's four business units would be split into three separate companies, each of which would be headed by its own independent top management team. Tyco's electronics and health care units would be spun off in tax-free transactions, and Breen would continue to run its remaining operations, including its well-known ADT home alarm systems and security equipment, fire protection, and pump-and-valve businesses. Breen believes that the managers of each independent company will be better positioned to develop the most successful business model for their industry, and that the returns they will eventually generate will exceed those provided by Tyco's old multibusiness model, which by the end of Kozlowski's reign had simply resulted in growth without increased profitability. The spinoff is expected to take place in 2007.[3]

OVERVIEW

Tyco's current CEO Edward Breen has decided that the different businesses Tyco owns will be able to create more value if they are split into three separate companies, each of which will be managed by its own top management team. Breen believes that each of the new companies will then be better positioned in their respective industries to maintain and grow market share and improve their profit margins. Breen has developed a *multibusiness model* that will allow each company to pursue its own, industry-specific business model and thus allow it to gain a better position vis-à-vis industry competitors. As we discuss later, Breen has decided to abandon Tyco's corporate-level strategy of unrelated diversification and "de-diversify" to increase the profitability of each company and thus increase returns to shareholders.

In this chapter, we continue our discussion of how companies can utilize their distinctive competencies, and the business models that are based on them, by formulating and implementing new corporate-level strategies to grow their profits and free cash flow. Companies cannot stand still; they must continually search for ways to use their capital more efficiently and effectively. In a competitive environment, resources such as capital move to their most highly valued use, which means investors place their capital in the companies that are expected to be the most profitable in the future. If a company's managers do not strive continuously to build its distinctive competencies and competitive advantage, they will ultimately lose out to those companies that have found new ways to pursue their business models successfully over time.

This chapter discusses the corporate-level strategy of diversification, which is a company's decision to enter one or more new industries to take advantage of its existing distinctive competencies and business model. We discuss two different types of diversification, related diversification and unrelated diversification, and we examine the different kinds of distinctive competencies and multibusiness models on which they are based. Then we look at three different methods or strategies that companies can use to implement a diversification strategy: internal new ventures, acquisitions, and joint ventures. By the end of this chapter, you will understand the pros and cons associated with the decision to diversify and enter new markets and industries and the different methods companies can choose from to implement a diversification strategy.

Expanding Beyond a Single Industry

The role of managers in corporate-level strategy is to identify which markets or industries a company should compete in to maximize its long-run profitability. As we discussed in Chapter 9, for many companies, profitable growth and expansion often entail concentrating on a single market or industry. For example, McDonald's focuses on the global fast-food restaurant business and Wal-Mart focuses on global discount retailing. Companies that stay in one industry pursue horizontal integration and strategic outsourcing to strengthen their business models, expand their business, and increase their profitability. Even though vertical integration leads a company to enter industries at adjacent stages of the value chain, the intent is still to strengthen its core business model.

As a result of these strategies, a company's fortunes are tied closely to the profitability of its *original industry*—and this can be dangerous if that industry goes into decline. Moreover, as an industry matures, the opportunities to grow profits often fall. So companies that concentrate on just one industry may miss opportunities to increase their profitability by leveraging their distinctive competencies to make and sell products in *new industries*. There is compelling evidence to suggest that companies that rest on their laurels, do not engage in constant learning, and do not force themselves to stretch can lose out to agile new competitors that come along with superior business models.[4] For these reasons, many argue that companies must *leverage*, that is, find new ways to take advantage of their distinctive competencies and core business model in new markets and industries.

● **A Company as a Portfolio of Distinctive Competencies**

Gary Hamel and C. K. Prahalad have developed a model that can help managers assess how and when they should expand beyond their current market or industry. According to these authors, a fruitful approach to identifying new product market opportunities is to think of a company not as a portfolio of products but as a *portfolio of distinctive competencies*, and then consider how those competencies might be leveraged, that is, used to create more value and profit in new industries.[5]

Recall from Chapter 3 that a distinctive competency is a company-specific resource or capability that gives a company a competitive advantage. Hamel and Prahalad argue that when managers want to identify a profitable opportunity for diversification, they must first define and classify the company's *current* set of distinctive competencies. Then they can use a matrix like the one illustrated in Figure 10.1 to establish an agenda for entering new markets or industries. This matrix distinguishes between existing competencies and new ones that would have to be developed to allow a company to compete in a new industry. It also distinguishes between the existing industries

FIGURE 10.1

Matrix for Establishing a Competency Agenda

Source: Reprinted by permission of Harvard Business School Publishing. From *Competing for the Future: Breakthrough Strategies for Seizing Control of Your Industry and Creating the Markets of Tomorrow* by Gary Hamel and C. K. Prahalad, Boston, MA. Copyright (c) 1994 by Gary Hamel and C. K. Prahalad. All rights reserved.

Industry

	Existing	New
New (Competence)	**Premier plus 10** What new competencies will we need to build to protect and extend our franchise in current industries?	**Mega-opportunities** What new competencies will we need to build to participate in the most exciting industries of the future?
Existing (Competence)	**Fill in the blanks** What is the opportunity to improve our position in existing industries and better leverage our existing competencies?	**White spaces** What new products or services could we create by creatively redeploying or recombining our current competencies?

in which a company operates and the new industries in which it might operate in the future. Each quadrant in the matrix has different strategic implications.

FILL IN THE BLANKS The lower left quadrant of Figure 10.1 represents the company's existing portfolio of competencies and products. The term *fill in the blanks* refers to the opportunity to improve a company's competitive position in its existing industries by sharing its current competencies between divisions. In the 1980s, for example, Canon had distinctive competencies in precision mechanics and fine optics and used them to produce mechanical cameras. Then, it used its competencies in precision mechanics and fine optics, plus an additional competency it had developed in microelectronics, to enter the photocopier industry, so it now competed in two industries: cameras and photocopiers. In the 1990s, Canon realized it could also strengthen its camera business by giving it the microelectronics skills it had developed in its copier business. Thus, Cannon was able to make advanced cameras with electronic features such as autofocusing.

PREMIER PLUS 10 The upper left quadrant in Figure 10.1 is referred to as *premier plus 10.* The term is used to suggest another important question: What *new* distinctive competencies must be developed now to ensure that a company remains a *premier* provider of its existing products in *ten* years' time? To strengthen the business model of its copier business, Canon decided that it needed to build a new competency in digital electronic imaging (the ability to capture and store images in a digital format as opposed to the more traditional chemical-based photographic processes). By developing this new competency, Canon was able to protect its competitive advantage and make advanced products like laser copiers, color copiers, and digital cameras.

WHITE SPACES The lower right quadrant of Figure 10.1 is referred to as *white spaces* because the issue that managers must address is how the company can fill "white spaces," that is, opportunities to creatively redeploy or recombine its current distinctive competencies to produce new products in new industries. Canon was able to recombine its established competencies in precision mechanics and fine optics and its recently acquired competency in digital imaging to produce fax machines and laser printers, thereby entering the fax and printer industries. In other words, it leveraged its distinctive competencies to take advantage of opportunities in other industries and create valuable new products.

MEGA-OPPORTUNITIES Opportunities represented by the upper right quadrant of Figure 10.1 do not overlap with the company's current industries or its current competencies. Rather, they imply entry into new industries where the company currently has none of the competencies required to succeed. Nevertheless, a company may choose to pursue such opportunities if they are particularly attractive, significant, or relevant to its existing product market activities. For example, in 1979, Monsanto was primarily a manufacturer of chemicals, including fertilizers. However, the company saw enormous opportunities in the emerging biotechnology industry, and the company embarked on a massive investment program to build a world-class competence in biotechnology. This investment, funded by cash flows generated from Monsanto's operations in the chemical industry, paid off in the 1990s, when Monsanto introduced a series of genetically engineered crop seeds that were resistant to many common pests. Roundup®, a Monsanto herbicide that can be used to kill weeds but that will not kill its genetically engineered plants, became the industry leader.[6]

A focus on using or recombining existing competencies or building new competencies to enter new industries helps managers think strategically about how industry boundaries might change over time and how this will affect their current business models. By helping managers think about how to transfer and leverage competencies across industries, Prahalad and Hamel's model can help managers avoid the strategic mistake of entering new markets where their business model will fail to give them a competitive advantage, which has happened to many companies, such as Coca-Cola and Sears, discussed in the last chapter.

Increasing Profitability Through Diversification

Diversification is the process of entering new industries, distinct from a company's core or original industry, to make new kinds of products that can be sold profitably to customers in these new markets. A multibusiness model based on diversification focuses on finding ways to use the company's distinctive competencies to make products that are highly valued by customers in the new industries it has entered. A **diversified company** is one that makes and sells products in two or more industries. In each industry a company enters, it establishes an operating division or business unit, which is essentially a self-contained company that makes and sells products for its particular market. As with the other corporate strategies, to increase profitability, a diversification strategy should enable the company or its individual business units to perform one or more of the value chain functions (1) at a lower cost, (2) in a way that allows for differentiation and gives the company pricing options, or (3) in a way that helps the company to manage industry rivalry better.

The managers of most companies first consider diversification when they are generating **free cash flow**, that is, cash *in excess* of that required to fund investments in the company's existing industry and to meet any debt commitments.[7] In other words, free cash flow is cash in excess of that which can be profitably reinvested in an existing business (*cash* is simply *capital* by another name). When a company is generating free cash flow, managers must decide whether to return that capital to shareholders in the form of higher dividend payouts or invest it in diversification. Technically, any free cash flow belongs to the company's owners—its shareholders. For diversification to make sense, the return on investing free cash flow to pursue diversification opportunities, that is, the return on invested capital (ROIC), *must* exceed the return that stockholders can get by investing that capital in a diversified portfolio of stocks and bonds. If this were not the case, it would be in the best interests of shareholders for the company to return any excess cash to them through higher dividends rather than pursue a diversification strategy. Thus, a diversification strategy is *not* consistent with maximizing returns to shareholders unless the multibusiness model that managers use to justify entry into a new industry will significantly increase the value that a company can create.

Six main justifications for pursuing a multibusiness model based on diversification can be identified. Diversification can increase company profitability when managers (1) transfer competencies between business units in different industries, (2) leverage competencies to create business units in new industries, (3) share resources between business units to realize economies of scope, (4) use product bundling, (5) use diversification to reduce rivalry in one or more industries, and (6) utilize *general* organizational competencies that increase the performance of all the company's business units.

● Transferring Competencies Across Industries

Transferring competencies involves taking a distinctive competency developed by a business unit in one industry and implanting it in a business unit operating in another industry. The second business unit is often one the company has acquired. Companies that base their diversification strategy on transferring competencies believe that they can use one or more of their distinctive competencies in a value chain activity—for example, manufacturing, marketing, materials management, and research and development (R&D)—to significantly strengthen the business model of the acquired business unit or company. For example, over time, Philip Morris developed distinctive competencies in product development, consumer marketing, and brand positioning that had made it a leader in the tobacco industry. Sensing a profitable opportunity, it acquired Miller Brewing, which at the time was a relatively small player in the brewing industry. Then, to create valuable new products in Miller, Philip Morris transferred some of its best marketing experts to Miller, where they applied the skills acquired at Philip Morris to turn around Miller's lackluster brewing business (see Figure 10.2). The result was the creation of Miller Light, the first light beer, and a marketing campaign that helped to push Miller from the number 6 to the number 2 company in the brewing industry in terms of market share.

Companies that base their diversification strategy on transferring competencies tend to acquire new businesses related to their existing business activities because of commonalities between one or more of their value chain functions. A *commonality* is some kind of attribute that, when it is shared or used by two or more business units, will allow them to operate more effectively and efficiently and create more value.

FIGURE 10.2

Transfer of Competencies at Philip Morris

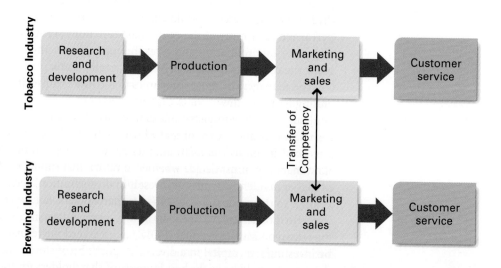

For example, Miller Brewing was related to Philip Morris's tobacco business because it was possible to create important marketing commonalities; both beer and tobacco are mass-market consumer goods where brand positioning, advertising, and product development skills are crucial to a new product's success. In general, such competency transfers can increase profitability when they either (1) lower the cost structure of one or more of a diversified company's business units or (2) enable one or more of its business units to better differentiate their products. Both also give that business unit pricing options.

For such a strategy to work, the competencies being transferred must involve value chain activities that will become the source of a specific business unit's competitive advantage in the future. In other words, the distinctive competency being transferred must have real strategic value. All too often, however, companies assume that *any* commonality between their value chains is sufficient for creating value. When they attempt to transfer competencies, they find that the anticipated benefits are not forthcoming because the different business units did not share some important attribute in common. General Motors' acquisition of Hughes Aircraft, made simply because cars and carmaking were "going electronic" and Hughes was an electronics company, demonstrates the folly of overestimating the commonalities among businesses. The acquisition failed to realize any of the anticipated gains for GM, whose competitive position did not improve, and GM subsequently sold Hughes Aircraft.

● **Leveraging Competencies**
Leveraging competencies involves taking a distinctive competency developed by a business unit in one industry and using it to create a new business unit in a different industry. Once again, the multibusiness model is based on the premise that the set of distinctive competencies that are the source of competitive advantage in one industry might be applied to create a differentiation- or cost-based competitive advantage for a new business unit in a different industry. For example, Canon used its distinctive competencies in precision mechanics, fine optics, and electronic imaging to produce laser printers, which was a new business in a new industry for Canon. Its competitive advantage in laser printers came from the fact that its competencies enabled it to produce high-quality (differentiated) printers that could be manufactured at a low cost.

The difference between leveraging competencies and transferring competencies is that, in the case of leveraging competencies, an entirely *new* business unit is being created, whereas transferring competencies involves a transfer between *existing* business units. This difference is important because each is based on a different multibusiness model. Companies that leverage competencies to establish new businesses tend to be *technology-based* companies that use their R&D competencies to create new business opportunities and units in diverse industries. In contrast, companies that transfer competencies are often industry leaders that enter new industries by acquiring established businesses. They then transfer their strong set of competencies to the acquired businesses to increase their competitive advantage and profitability, as Philip Morris did with Miller Brewing.

A number of companies have based their diversification strategy on leveraging competencies and using them to create new business units in different industries. Microsoft leveraged its skills in software development and marketing to create two business units in new industries: its online network MSN and its Xbox videogame units. Microsoft's managers believed this diversification strategy was in the best interests of shareholders because the company's competencies would enable it to attain a competitive advantage in the online and videogame industries. In fact, the results of this strategy have been mixed. In 2003, when Microsoft first broke its profits down by business unit, it turned out that the software business was generating almost all the profit and most other business units were generating a loss. However, things have improved somewhat because its new Xbox 360 has captured more market share from Sony and its MSN network is breaking even. Nevertheless, realizing that entry into new industries is not a way it can easily increase returns to shareholders, Microsoft decided to give back over $30 billion, or half its $60 billion cash hoard, to shareholders in the form of a dividend in 2004 and has declared more dividends since.

A company that is famous for its ability to leverage competencies to create new businesses in diverse industries is 3M; it leveraged its skills in adhesives to create many new products in new industries (see Strategy in Action 10.1). From a humble

Strategy in Action 10.1

Diversification at 3M: Leveraging Technology

3M is a 100-year-old industrial colossus that in 2005, generated over $21 billion in revenues and $3 billion in net income from a portfolio of more than 50,000 individual products, ranging from sandpaper and sticky tape to medical devices, office supplies, and electronic components. The company has consistently created new businesses by leveraging its scientific knowledge to find new applications for its proprietary technology. Today, the company is composed of fifty-six different business units grouped into six major sectors: Consumer and Office; Display and Graphics; Electro and Communications; Health Care; Industrial and Transportation; and Safety, Security and Protection Services. The company has consistently generated 30% of sales from products introduced within the prior five years and currently operates with the goal to produce 40% of revenues from products introduced within the previous four years.

The process of leveraging technology to create new businesses at 3M can be illustrated by the following quotation from William Coyne, head of R&D at 3M: "It began with sandpaper: mineral and glue on a substrate. After years as an abrasives company, it created a tape business. A researcher left off the mineral, and adapted the glue and substrate to create the first sticky tape. After creating many varieties of sticky tape—consumer, electrical, medical— researchers created the world's first audio and videotapes. In their search to create better tape backings, other researchers happened on multilayer films that, surprise, have remarkable light management qualities. This multiplayer film technology is being used in brightness enhancement films, which are incorporated in the displays of virtually all laptops and palm computers."

How does 3M do it? First, the company is a science-based enterprise with a strong tradition of innovation and risk taking. Risk taking is encouraged, and failure is not punished but seen as a natural part of the process of creating new products and business. Second, 3M's management is relentlessly focused on the company's customers and the problems they face. Many of 3M's products have come from helping customers solve difficult problems. Third, managers set *stretch goals* that require the company to create new products and businesses at a rapid pace (such as the current goal that 40% of sales should come from products introduced within the last four years). Fourth, employees are given considerable autonomy to pursue their own ideas. An employee can spend 15% of his or her time working on a project of his or her own choosing without management approval. Many products have resulted from this autonomy, including the ubiquitous Post-it Notes. Fifth, while products belong to business units and the business units are responsible for generating profits, the technologies belong to every unit within the company. Anyone at 3M is free to try to develop new applications for a technology developed by its business units. Sixth, 3M has implemented information technology (IT) that promotes the sharing of technological knowledge between business units so that new opportunities can be identified. Also, it hosts many in-house conferences where researchers from different business units are brought together to share the results of their work. Finally, 3M uses numerous mechanisms to recognize and reward those who develop new technologies, products, and businesses, including peer-nominated award programs; a corporate hall of fame; and, of course, monetary rewards.[a]

beginning as a manufacturer of sandpaper, 3M has become one of the most diversified U.S. companies.

● **Sharing Resources: Economies of Scope**

When two or more business units in different industries share resources and capabilities, they may also be able to realize economies of scope.[8] **Economies of scope** arise when one or more of a diversified company's business units are able to realize cost-saving or differentiation advantages because they can more effectively pool, share, and utilize expensive resources or capabilities, such as skilled people, equipment, manufacturing facilities, distribution channels, advertising campaigns, and R&D laboratories. If business units in different industries can share a common resource or function, they can collectively lower their cost structure.[9] For example, the costs of GE's consumer products advertising, sales, and service activities are spread over a wide range of products, such as small and large appliances, air conditioning, and furnaces, thus reducing unit costs. There are two major sources of these cost reductions.

First, companies that can share resources across business units have to invest proportionately less in the shared resource than companies that cannot share. For example, Procter & Gamble (P&G) makes both disposable diapers and paper towels, paper-based products valued for their ability to absorb liquid without disintegrating. Because both products need the same attribute—absorbency—P&G can share the R&D costs associated with producing an absorbent paper-based product across the two businesses. Similarly, because both products are sold to the same customer group (supermarkets), P&G can use the same sales force to sell both products (see Figure 10.3). In contrast, competitors that make just paper towels or just disposable diapers cannot achieve the same economies and have to invest proportionately more in R&D and in maintaining a sales force. The net result is that, other things being equal, P&G will have lower expenses and can earn a higher ROIC than companies that lack the ability to share resources.

Diversification to attain economies of scope is possible only when there are significant commonalities between one or more of the value chain functions of a company's existing and new business units. Moreover, managers need to be aware that the costs of coordination necessary to achieve economies of scope within a company often outweigh the value that can be created by such a strategy.[10] Consequently, the strategy should be pursued only when sharing is likely to create a

FIGURE 10.3

Sharing Resources at Procter & Gamble

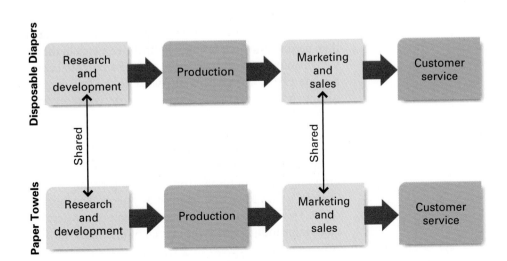

significant competitive advantage in one or more of a company's new or existing business units.

● Using Product Bundling

In their search for new ways to differentiate their products, more and more companies are entering into related industries to expand and widen their product lines to be able to satisfy customers' needs for a complete package of related products. This is currently happening in telecommunications, where customers are increasingly seeking a package price for wired phone service, wireless phone service, high-speed access to the Internet, VOIP phone service, television programming, online gaming, video on demand, or any combination of these services. To meet this need, large phone companies have been acquiring other companies that provide one or more of these services, while cable companies such as Comcast Corporation have acquired or formed strategic alliances with companies that allow them to offer their customers phone service, and so on. In 2004, Microsoft announced an alliance with SBC whereby SBC would use its new software to allow it to provide television service and video on demand over DSL phone connections, as well as its other services. Similarly, EchoStar, the satellite broadcaster, formed an alliance with Verizon to offer its television service with Verizon's phone service.

Just as manufacturing companies strive to reduce the number of their component suppliers to reduce costs and increase quality, so the final customer wants to obtain the convenience and reduced price of bundled products. Another example of product bundling comes from the medical equipment industry, where the companies that used to produce different kinds of products, such as operating room equipment, ultrasound devices, magnetic imaging, and x-ray equipment, have been merging to be able to offer hospitals a complete range of medical equipment. This development has been driven by hospitals because they want the convenience of dealing with a single supplier. In addition, because of the increased value of their orders, they also have increased bargaining power with the supplier.

● Managing Rivalry: Multipoint Competition

Sometimes a company benefits by diversifying into an industry in order to hold a competitor in check that has either entered its industry or has the potential to do so. For example, if an aggressive company based in another industry enters a company's market and tries to gain market share by cutting prices, the company could respond in kind and diversify into the aggressor's home industry and also cut prices. In this way, the company sends a signal: "If you attack me, I'll respond in kind and make things tough for you." (This is an example of the strategy of tit-for-tat discussed in Chapter 6.) The hope is that such a move will cause the aggressor to pull back from its attack, thus reducing rivalry in the company's home industry and permitting higher prices and profits. Of course, for the tit-for-tat strategy to have its desired effect, the company would then need to pull back from its competitive attack in the aggressor's home market.

An example of diversification to keep a potential competitor in check occurred in the late 1990s, when Microsoft awoke to the fact that Sony might emerge as a rival. Although Sony was in a different industry (consumer electronics as opposed to software), Microsoft realized that the Sony Playstation was in essence nothing more than a specialized computer and, moreover, one that did not use a Microsoft operating system. Microsoft's fear was that Sony might use the Playstation 2, which came equipped with web-browsing potential, as a Trojan horse to gain control of Web browsing and computing from the living room, ultimately taking customers away from PCs with Microsoft operating systems. The desire to keep Sony's ambitions in check was another part of the rationale for Microsoft's diversification into the videogame industry with the launch of the Xbox.

Many diversified companies compete against each other in several different industries. Canon and Kodak compete against each other in photocopiers and digital cameras, for example. Similarly, Unilever and P&G compete against each other in laundry detergents, personal care products, and packaged foods. When companies compete against each other in different industries, we refer to it as **multipoint competition.** Companies that are engaged in multipoint competition might be better able to manage rivalry by signaling that competitive attacks in one industry will be met by retaliatory attacks in another industry. If successful, such signaling might lead to mutual forbearance and thus less intense rivalry and higher profit in each industry in which a company competes. It follows that the desire to manage rivalry better through multipoint competition might be a motive for diversification that increases profitability.

● **Utilizing General Organizational Competencies**

General organizational competencies transcend individual functions or business units and are found at the top or corporate level of the multibusiness company. Typically, these general competencies are the skills of a company's top managers and functional experts, such as those of Tyco's top management team. When these general competencies are present—and many times they are not—they help each business unit within a company perform at a higher level than it could if it operated as an independent company, thus increasing the profitability of the whole corporation.[11] We discuss three kinds of general organizational competencies that can result in superior performance: (1) entrepreneurial capabilities, (2) organizational design capabilities, and (3) strategic capabilities. These managerial skills are often not present because they are rare and difficult to develop and put into action.

ENTREPRENEURIAL CAPABILITIES The example of 3M, profiled in Strategy in Action 10.1, provides many clues as to why entrepreneurial capabilities are important if the process of diversification is to increase profitability. A company may generate considerable excess cash flow, but to take advantage of it, managers must identify new opportunities and act on them to create a stream of new and improved products in both existing and new industries. It appears that some companies are better able to stimulate their managers to act entrepreneurially than are others; examples are 3M, HP, IBM, Toyota, Canon, and Matsushita.[12]

These companies are able to promote entrepreneurship because they have an organizational culture that stimulates managers to act entrepreneurially. Thus, these companies are able to create profitable new business units at a much higher rate than most other companies, which helps promote their diversification. We will highlight some of the systems required to generate profitable new businesses later in this chapter when we discuss internal new ventures. For now, note that the management systems of an entrepreneurial company must (1) encourage managers to take risks, (2) give them the time and resources to pursue novel ideas, (3) not punish managers when a new idea fails, but also (4) make sure the company does not waste resources pursuing too many risky ventures that have a low probability of generating a decent return on investment. Obviously, a difficult organizational balancing act is required here because the company has to simultaneously encourage risk taking while limiting the amount of risk being undertaken.

Companies with entrepreneurial capabilities are able to achieve this balancing act. 3M's corporate goal of generating 40% of revenues from products introduced within the past four years focuses the organization on developing new products and businesses. The company's famous 15% rule, which has been copied by many companies, gives employees the time to pursue novel ideas. Its long-standing commitment to helping customers solve problems helps ensure that ideas for new businesses are customer-focused. The company's celebration of employees who have created successful new businesses helps to reinforce the norm of entrepreneurship and risk taking. Similarly, there is a norm that failure should not be punished but should be viewed as a learning experience.

CAPABILITIES IN ORGANIZATIONAL DESIGN One of the main sources of entrepreneurial capabilities, as well as an important determinant of whether a company can obtain competencies at the functional level, is organizational design: a company's ability to create a structure, culture, and control systems that motivate and coordinate employees. The degree of autonomy that the structure of an organization provides its managers, the kinds of norms and values present in the organization's culture, and even the design of the buildings of its headquarters to encourage the free flow of ideas are important determinants of a diversified company's ability to reap the gains from its multibusiness model. Effective organizational structure and controls create incentives that encourage business unit (divisional) managers to maximize the efficiency and effectiveness of their units. Moreover, a good organizational design helps prevent the inertia that afflicts so many organizations, when employees become so absorbed in protecting their company's competitive position in existing markets that they lose sight of new or improved ways to do business or changing industry boundaries.

The last three chapters of this book take an in-depth look at these issues. To succeed in diversification, a company must have the structure and culture that enable it to rapidly change the way it motivates and coordinates its resources and capabilities. Companies that seem to be successful at managing their structures and cultures to further the diversification process share a number of features.[13] First, their different business units tend to be placed into self-contained divisions. Second, these business units tend to be managed by senior executives in a decentralized fashion. Rather than get involved in day-to-day operations, they set challenging financial goals for each unit, probe the managers of each unit about their strategies for attaining these goals, monitor their performance, and hold them accountable for that performance. Third, these internal monitoring and control mechanisms are linked with incentive pay systems that reward business unit managers who attain or surpass performance goals. Achieving these three goals, and aligning a company's structure with its strategy, is a complex, never-ending task and only top managers with superior organizational design skills can do it.

SUPERIOR STRATEGIC CAPABILITIES For diversification to increase profitability, a company's top or corporate managers must have superior strategic capabilities. Specifically, they must have certain intangible governance skills to manage different business units in a way that enables those units to perform better than they would if they were independent companies.[14] Simply put, the business of corporate managers in the diversified company is to manage the managers of its business units or divisions. This is not an easy thing to do well; governance skills are a rare and valuable capability. However, certain senior executives seem to have developed a skill for managing businesses and pushing the heads of business units to achieve superior performance. Examples include Jeffery Immelt at GE, Steve Ballmer at Microsoft, Steve Jobs at Apple, and Larry Ellison at Oracle.

A flair for entrepreneurship and recognizing new business opportunities is often found in top managers who have developed superior strategic capabilities or governance skills. Just as important is a top manager's ability to find ways to enhance the performance of individual managers, functions, and whole business units. Jack Welch, for example, was a master at improving the skills of his managers across the board at GE. He created organizationwide management development programs focusing on change management and created procedures to make middle managers question top management actions. At the functional and business levels, he instituted many of the techniques discussed in Chapter 4 to promote superior efficiency and quality, such as the Six Sigma quality improvement methodology, and he pushed hard to make sure that business unit managers used these techniques to improve the efficiency of their operations. Jeffrey Immelt, GE's current CEO, was one of Welch's protégés.

An especially important governance skill in the diversified company is the ability to diagnose the underlying source of the problems in a poorly performing business unit and understand how to take the appropriate steps to fix those problems, whether by recommending new strategies to the top managers of the unit or by replacing them with a new management team better able to fix the problems. Top managers who have such governance skills tend to be very good at probing business unit managers for information and helping them think through strategic problems.

Related to this skill is the ability of the top managers of a diversified company to identify inefficient and poorly managed companies, and then acquire and restructure them to improve their performance—and thus the profitability of the total corporation. The acquired company does not have to be in the same industry as the acquiring company for the strategy to work; thus, the strategy often leads to diversification. Improvements in the performance of the acquired company can come from a number of sources. First, the acquiring company usually replaces the top managers of the acquired company with a more aggressive management team. Second, the new managers of the acquired business are encouraged to sell off any unproductive assets, such as executive jets and elaborate corporate headquarters, and to reduce staffing levels. Third, the new management team is encouraged to intervene in the operations of the acquired business to discover ways to improve the unit's efficiency, quality, innovation, and customer responsiveness. Fourth, to motivate the new management team and other employees of the acquired unit to undertake such actions, increases in their pay are typically linked to increases in the performance of the acquired unit. Fifth, the acquiring company often establishes performance goals for the acquired company that cannot be met without significant improvements in operating efficiency. It also makes the new top managers aware that failure to achieve performance improvements consistent with these goals within a given amount of time will probably result in their being replaced.

Thus, the system of rewards and sanctions established by the top managers of the acquiring company gives the new managers of the acquired unit strong incentives to look for ways to improve the performance of the unit under their charge. Tyco pursued the strategy of acquiring and restructuring underperforming companies with considerable success in the past; as we discussed earlier, however, its new CEO no longer believes this is the appropriate strategy for the company in the future. We discuss why later in the chapter.

Two Types of Diversification

In the last section, we discussed six principal ways in which companies can use diversification to implant their business models and strategies in other industries to increase their long-run profitability. It is possible to differentiate between two types of diversification based on the ability to realize these benefits: related diversification and unrelated diversification.[15]

● Related Diversification

Related diversification is the strategy of establishing a business unit in a new industry that is related to a company's existing business units by some form of linkage or commonality between the value chain functions of the new and existing business units. The goal of this strategy is to obtain the benefits from transferring and leveraging distinctive competencies, sharing resources, and bundling products. The multibusiness model behind related diversification is based on taking advantage of strong technological, manufacturing, marketing, and sales commonalities between new and existing business units that can be successfully tweaked to increase the competitive advantage of one or more business units. Figure 10.4 provides some examples of the different kinds of linkages; the greater the number of linkages that can be formed, the greater the potential for increasing competitive advantage and profitability.

One more potential advantage of related diversification is that it can allow a company to apply any general organizational competencies it possesses to increase overall business unit performance, such as by creating a culture that encourages entrepreneurship across units. 3M, for example, has a set of core technologies that are then shared among different kinds of business units. However, 3M also has a general organizational competency in promoting cross-unit learning. Another example of related diversification is given in Strategy in Action 10.2, which looks at Intel's recent diversification into the communications chip business and the problems surrounding it.

● Unrelated Diversification

The multibusiness model underlying **unrelated diversification** aims to enhance profits by implanting general organizational competencies in new business units and perhaps to capture the benefits of multipoint competition. Companies pursuing a strategy of unrelated diversification have *no* intention of transferring or leveraging competencies between business units. Their focus is purely on using general managerial competencies to strengthen the business model of each individual business unit or division. Tyco, which was discussed in the Opening Case, provides a good example

FIGURE 10.4

Commonalities Between the Value Chains of Three Business Units

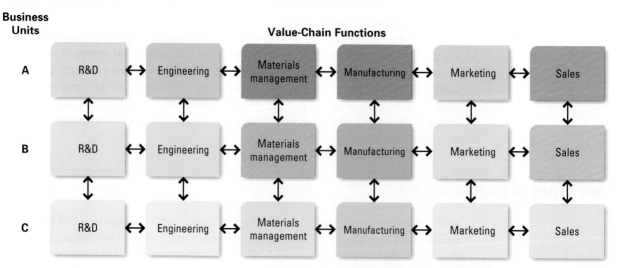

Strategy in Action

10.2

Related Diversification at Intel

Although Intel has had a small presence in the communications chip business since the 1980s, the company focused most of its attention and resources on the booming business of making microprocessors for personal computers. According to managers at Intel, "feeding the processor monster" was a way to boost profitability, and the company invested all its substantial free cash flows into designing new generations of ever more powerful microprocessors and building the large-scale, and expensive, fabrication facilities necessary to manufacture them efficiently. The decision seemed logical: Intel had the dominant position in the microprocessor market, its primary customers (PC makers like Dell) were growing by leaps and bounds, and demand for its microprocessors was soaring.

This strategy of staying in a single business changed at a contentious strategy meeting of Intel's top executives in 1996. Intel's executives came away from that meeting with two important insights. First, the PC industry would approach market saturation in the early 2000s, which meant that the growth in demand for Intel's microprocessors would slow down. To maintain its profit growth, Intel needed to find a new "growth driver." Second, its executives decided that because of the growing use of the Internet, "communications was going to be the driver for everything in the future, that all computing was connected computing, and that connectivity had as important and strategic a role to play as the microprocessor did." Moreover, it was clear that demand for products of the communications industry such as communications network gear, which needed advanced communications chips, was accelerating rapidly.

Intel's executives decided that they could boost the company's ROIC by diverting some cash flow from new PC chip development and using Intel's competencies to build a new business model in the rapidly growing communications chip industry. This was a different industry: the production technology was different, the customers were different, and the competitors were different. Intel believed, however, that because the communications chip industry was related to the microprocessor industry, it could obtain a competitive advantage by transferring its leading-edge PC microprocessor technology, as well as its manufacturing and marketing capabilities, to the communications chip industry.

Once the decision was made to enter the communications chip industry on a significant scale, Intel had to decide how best to execute the strategy. The company's managers decided that the only way they could get big enough fast enough to gain scale economies and establish a sustainable competitive advantage in this booming market was for the company to buy the required technology, fabrication facilities, and sales force. It could then improve the performance of the acquired businesses by transferring its competencies to them. So Intel went on an acquisitions binge. Between January 1997 and June 2001, it made eighteen major acquisitions of companies in the communications chip industry, for a combined total of $8 billion. As a result of these acquisitions, Intel became the fourth largest global company in the communications chip industry by mid-2001, behind only Lucent, Motorola, and Texas Instruments. Unfortunately, Intel and all these other companies were hard hit by the slump in global demand for telecommunications equipment in the early 2000s.

Then, to make matters worse, Intel's push into communications chips had launched it on the road to designing chips that were faster and faster because speed was seen as the most vital ingredient in communication. By 2003, however, it was clear that what customers wanted was chips that could support high bandwidth and could process vast amounts of information simultaneously. Both these capabilities are needed for high-quality music, movie viewing, and other multimedia applications such as videoconferencing. Intel lacked such a chip, but in the meantime Advanced Micro Devices (AMD), its major competitor, had perceived the need to develop it. Suddenly Intel found itself at a competitive disadvantage. In 2004, it announced plans to abandon its high-speed communications chips to focus on those that could support the bandwidth needed for sophisticated multimedia applications. Intel had made the mistake of not focusing on what PC users and digital content providers needed in next-generation chips. It was so concerned with the need to increase speed that it entered a new industry assuming there was a commonality based on speed, but there was none. Intel should have focused on customer needs, not its own distinctive competencies. It has since refocused its strategy and in 2006, it introduced its new dual-core and quad-core chips that once again have given it the competitive edge.[b]

of a company that pursued a strategy of unrelated diversification successfully in the past, which created a lot of value for its shareholders.

Disadvantages and Limits of Diversification

As we have discussed, many companies, such as 3M, Intel, and GE, have reaped enormous advantages from pursuing a strategy of diversification and have consistently increased their profitability over time. Nevertheless, many companies that have pursued diversification have enjoyed far less success, and for some companies, diversification has actually dissipated or reduced their profitability. As a result, over the last few decades, many companies, such as Tyco, have de-diversified and split apart or sold off their individual business units; each business unit headed by its own top management team then pursues some kind of single-business strategy. Clearly, important disadvantages may result from diversification that can make it an unprofitable strategy to pursue over time. Three main conditions can make diversification disadvantageous: changing industry- and firm-specific conditions, diversification for the wrong reasons, and the increasing bureaucratic costs of extensive diversification.

● **Changing Industry- and Firm-Specific Conditions**

Diversification is a complex strategy to pursue, and top managers must have the entrepreneurial ability to sense profitable new opportunities and the ability to implement the strategies needed to make diversification pay off. Over time, however, a company's top management team changes: sometimes its most able executives leave to join other companies and become their CEOs, and sometimes successful CEOs decide to retire or step down. When they leave, these managers often take their vision with them, and their successors may lack the skills or commitment needed to manage and implement diversification successfully over time. Thus, the multibusiness model loses its ability to create value, and as we discuss below, the cost structure of the diversified company often starts to increase, swallowing up the gains that the strategy produces.

Over time, the environment can also change rapidly and in unpredictable ways. We discussed earlier how blurring industry boundaries can destroy the source of a company's competitive advantage. If this happens in its core business, then clearly benefits from transferring or leveraging distinctive competencies will disappear and a company will now be saddled with a collection of businesses that have all become poor performers in their respective industries. When the computer industry changed, for example, and PCs and servers became the dominant product, IBM was left with unprofitable operations in the mainframe hardware and software industries that almost led to its bankruptcy. Thus, one major problem with diversification is that the future success of this strategy is hard to predict; therefore, if a company is to profit from it over time, managers should be as willing to divest businesses as they are to acquire them. Unfortunately, research suggests that managers do not behave in this way.

● **Diversification for the Wrong Reasons**

As we have discussed, if a company pursues diversification, its managers must have a clear vision of how their entry into new industries will allow them to create more value. Over time, however, as the profitability of their diversification strategy falls for reasons like those just noted, managers, rather than divesting their businesses, often use false or mistaken justifications for keeping their collection of businesses together—or even growing those businesses. There are many famous historical examples of this faulty behavior.

For example, one widely used justification for diversification used to be that diversification could be used to obtain the benefits of risk pooling or risk reduction.

Many CEOs argued that diversification, particularly unrelated diversification into industries that have different business cycles so that their revenues rise and fall in different cycles, would allow them to create a more stable companywide income stream over time—one that avoids the sharp swings up and down that can make the value of a company's stock volatile and unpredictable. An example of risk pooling might be the diversification by U.S. Steel into the oil and gas industry in an attempt to offset the adverse effects of cyclical downturns in the steel industry. According to advocates of risk pooling, a more stable income stream reduces the risk of bankruptcy and is in the best interests of the company's stockholders.

This simple argument ignores two facts. First, stockholders can easily eliminate the risks inherent in holding an individual stock by diversifying their own portfolios, and they can do so at a much lower cost than the company can. Thus, far from being in the best interests of stockholders, attempts to pool risks through diversification represent an unproductive use of resources; instead, profits should be returned to shareholders in the form of increased dividends. Second, research on this topic suggests that corporate diversification is not an effective way to pool risks because the business cycles of different industries are *inherently difficult to predict*, and a diversified company might just find that a general economic downturn hits all its industries simultaneously. If this happens, the company's profitability will plunge.[16]

When the core business is in trouble, another mistaken justification for diversification is that the new industries will rescue it. An example of a company that made this mistake is Kodak. In the 1980s, increased competition from low-cost Japanese competitors like Fuji, combined with the beginnings of the digital revolution, led Kodak's revenues and profits first to plateau and then to fall. Its managers should have done all they could to reduce its cost structure; instead, they took its still huge free cash flow and spent tens of billions of dollars to enter new industries such as health care, biotechnology, and computer hardware in a desperate and mistaken attempt to find ways to increase profitability.

This approach was a disaster because every industry Kodak entered was populated by strong companies such as 3M, Canon, and Xerox, and Kodak's corporate managers lacked any general competencies to give their new business units a competitive advantage. And the more industries they entered, the greater the range of threats they encountered and the more time they had to spend dealing with these threats. As a result, they could spend much less time improving the performance of their core film business, which continued to decline. In reality, Kodak's diversification was just for growth itself, but *growth does not create value*; growth is simply the byproduct, not the objective, of a diversification strategy. However, in desperation, companies diversify for reasons of growth alone rather than to gain any well-thought-out strategic advantage.

A large number of academic studies suggest that extensive diversification tends to reduce rather than improve company profitability.[17] For example, in a study that looked at the diversification of thirty-three major U.S. corporations over thirty-five years, Michael Porter observed that the track record of corporate diversification has been poor.[18] Porter found that most of the companies had divested many more diversified acquisitions than they had kept. He and others have concluded that the corporate diversification strategies pursued by most companies can dissipate value instead of create it.[19]

● The Bureaucratic Costs of Diversification

A company diversifies to boost its profitability from higher product differentiation or a lower cost structure, but to achieve this, it has to invest valuable resources. One reason that diversification often fails to boost profitability is that all too often, the bureaucratic costs of diversification exceed the value created by the strategy. As we mentioned in the last chapter, **bureaucratic costs** are the costs associated with solving the transaction difficulties that arise between a company's business units, and between business units and corporate headquarters, as the company attempts to obtain the benefits from transferring, sharing, and leveraging competencies. They also include the costs of using general organizational competencies to solve managerial and functional inefficiencies. The level of bureaucratic costs in a diversified organization is a function of two factors: (1) the number of business units in a company's portfolio and (2) the extent to which coordination is required among these different business units to realize the benefits of diversification.

NUMBER OF BUSINESSES The greater the number of business units in a company's portfolio, the more difficult it is for corporate managers to remain informed about the complexities of each business. Managers simply do not have the time to assess the business model of each unit. This problem began to occur at GE in the 1970s when its growth-hungry CEO Reg Jones acquired many new businesses. As Jones commented,

> I tried to review each plan [of each business unit] in great detail. This effort took untold hours and placed a tremendous burden on the corporate executive office. After a while I began to realize that no matter how hard we would work, we could not achieve the necessary in-depth understanding of the 40-odd business unit plans.[20]

The inability of top managers in extensively diversified companies to maintain a superior multibusiness model over time may lead them to base important resource allocation decisions on only the most superficial analysis of each business unit's competitive position. For example, a promising business unit may be starved of investment funds, while other business units receive far more cash than they can profitably reinvest in their operations. Furthermore, because they are distant from the day-to-day operations of the business units, corporate managers may find that business unit managers try to hide information on poor performance to save their own jobs. For example, business unit managers might blame poor performance on difficult competitive conditions, even when it is the result of their inability to craft a successful business model. But when inefficiencies such as the suboptimal allocation of capital within the company and a failure by corporate executives to successfully encourage and reward aggressive profit-seeking behavior by business unit managers become extensive, the time and effort top managers must devote to solve such problems cancel the value created by diversification.

COORDINATION AMONG BUSINESSES The coordination required to realize value from a diversification strategy based on transferring, sharing, or leveraging competencies is a major source of bureaucratic costs. The bureaucratic mechanisms needed to oversee and manage coordination and handoffs between units, such as cross-business-unit teams and management committees, are one source of these costs. A second source is the costs associated with accurately measuring the performance, and therefore the unique profit contribution, of a business unit that is transferring or sharing resources with another. Consider a company that has two business units, one making household products (such as liquid soap and laundry detergent) and another making packaged food products. The products of both units are sold through supermarkets. To lower the costs of value creation, the parent company decides to pool the marketing and sales functions of each business unit using an organizational structure similar to that illustrated in Figure 10.5. The company is organized into three divisions: a household products division, a food products division, and a marketing division.

FIGURE 10.5

Coordination Among
Related Business
Units

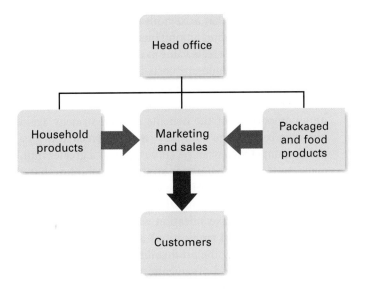

Although such an arrangement may result in substantial cost savings, it can also give rise to substantial control problems and hence bureaucratic costs. For example, if the performance of the household products business begins to slip, identifying who is to be held accountable—managers in the household products division or managers in the marketing division—may prove difficult. Indeed, each may blame the other for poor performance. Although these kinds of problems can be resolved if corporate management performs an in-depth audit of both divisions, the bureaucratic costs (managers' time and effort) involved in doing so may once again cancel any value achieved from diversification.

In sum, diversification is the most complex and difficult strategy that a company can pursue. Changing conditions both in the external environment and inside a company can reduce the value creation advantages from pursuing this strategy either because they rob business units of their competitive advantage or because they increase the bureaucratic costs associated with pursuing this strategy, which then also cancel its advantages. Thus, the existence of bureaucratic costs places a limit on the amount of diversification that can profitably be pursued. It makes sense for a company to diversify only as long as the value created by such a strategy exceeds the bureaucratic costs associated with expanding the boundaries of the organization to incorporate additional business activities.

Choosing a Strategy

● **Related Versus
Unrelated
Diversification**

Because related diversification involves more sharing of competencies, one might think it can boost profitability in more ways than unrelated diversification and so is the better diversification strategy. However, some companies can create as much or more value from pursuing unrelated diversification, so that approach must also have some substantial benefits. An unrelated company does *not* have to achieve coordination among business units, and so it has to cope only with the bureaucratic costs that arise from the number of businesses in its portfolio. In contrast, a related company has to achieve coordination among business units if it is to realize the gains that come from utilizing its distinctive competencies. Consequently, it has to cope with the bureaucratic costs that arise both from the number of business units in its portfolio *and* from coordination among business units. Although it is true that related diversified companies can create value in more ways than unrelated companies, they also have to bear higher bureaucratic costs to do so. These higher costs may cancel the higher benefits, making the strategy no more profitable than one of unrelated diversification.

How then does a company choose between these strategies? The choice depends on a comparison of the benefits of each strategy against the bureaucratic costs of pursuing it. It pays a company to pursue related diversification when (1) the company's competencies can be applied across a greater number of industries and (2) the company does have superior strategic capabilities that allow it to keep bureaucratic costs under close control—perhaps by encouraging entrepreneurship or by developing a value-creating organizational culture. Using the same logic, it pays a company to pursue unrelated diversification when (1) each business unit's functional competencies have few useful applications across industries, but the company's top managers are skilled at raising the profitability of poorly run businesses, and (2) the company's managers have good organizational design skills to build distinctive competencies and keep bureaucratic costs in control and even to reduce them.

The Web of Corporate-Level Strategy

Finally, it is important to note that while some companies may choose to pursue a strategy of related or unrelated diversification, there is nothing that stops them from pursuing both strategies at the same time—*as well as all the other corporate-level strategies we have discussed.* The purpose of corporate-level strategy is to increase long-term profitability. A company should pursue any and all strategies as long as strategic managers have weighed the advantages and disadvantages of those strategies and arrived at a multibusiness model that justifies them. Figure 10.6 shows how Sony has entered into industries that have led it to pursue various strategies.

First, Sony's core business is its electronic consumer products business, which is well known for its generic distinctive competencies of innovation and marketing

FIGURE 10.6

Sony's Web of Corporate-Level Strategy

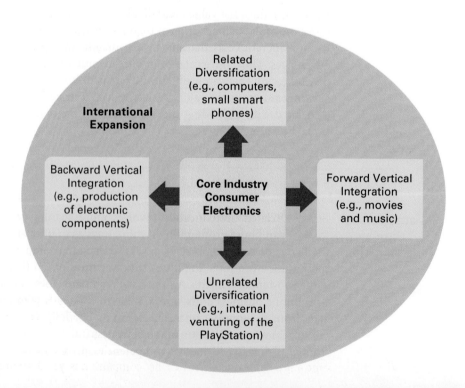

(it has one of the best-known brand names in the world). To protect the quality of its electronic products, Sony manufactures a high percentage of the component parts for its televisions, DVD players, and so on, and in this sense, it has pursued a strategy of backward vertical integration. Sony also engages in forward vertical integration: after having acquired Columbia Pictures and MGM in 2004, it now operates in the movie industry and has opened a chain of Sony stores in exclusive shopping malls. Sony also shared and leveraged its distinctive competencies by developing its own business units that operate in the computer and smart phone industries, a strategy of related diversification. Finally, in deciding to enter the home videogame industry and developing its Playstation to compete with Nintendo, it is also pursuing a strategy of unrelated diversification. Today, this division contributes more to Sony's total profits than its core electronics business.

While Sony has had enormous success pursuing all these strategies in the past, its profitability has fallen in the 2000s. Analysts claim that its multibusiness model, which led it to diversify extensively and focus on innovating high-quality products, led it to neglect its cost structure. They also claim that its strategy of giving each business unit great autonomy has led each unit to pursue its own goals at the expense of the company's multibusiness model. Sony's escalating bureaucratic costs have been draining its profitability and slowing innovation, which has allowed competitors like Samsung to catch up and even overtake it in areas like cell phones and flat-screen LCDs. Sony has been responding to these problems: it has taken major steps to reduce bureaucratic costs, speed innovation, and lower its cost structure, including exiting industries like PDAs and videocassette recorders. The next few years will show whether the company has been able to better implement its corporate strategies to improve its profitability.

Entering New Industries: Internal New Ventures

Having discussed all the corporate-level strategies that managers use to formulate the multibusiness model, we now examine the three main vehicles used to enter new industries: internal new ventures, acquisitions, and joint ventures. In this section, we look at the pros and cons of using internal new ventures. In the following sections, we look at acquisitions and joint ventures.

● **The Attractions of Internal New Venturing**

Internal new venturing is typically used to implement corporate-level strategies when a company possesses one or more generic distinctive competencies in its core business model that can be leveraged or recombined to enter a new industry. **Internal new venturing** is the process of transferring resources to and creating a new business unit or division in a new industry. As a rule, companies whose business model is based on using their technology to innovate new kinds of products for related markets or industries tend to favor internal new venturing as a way to enter a new market or industry. Thus, technology-based companies that pursue related diversification, like DuPont, which has created new markets with products such as cellophane, nylon, Freon, and Teflon, tend to use internal new venturing. 3M has a near-legendary knack for creating new or improved products from internally generated ideas and then establishing a new business unit to create the business model that enables it to dominate a new market (see Strategy in Action 10.1). Similarly, HP moved into computers and peripherals through internal new venturing.

A company may also use internal venturing to enter a newly emerging or embryonic industry—one in which no company has yet developed the competencies or business model that give it a dominant position in that industry. This was Monsanto's situation in 1979 when it contemplated entering the biotechnology field to produce herbicides and pest-resistant crop seeds. The biotechnology field was young at that time, and there were no incumbent companies focused on applying biotechnology to agricultural products. Monsanto internally ventured a new division to develop the required competencies necessary to enter and establish a strong competitive position in this newly emerging industry.

● Pitfalls of New Ventures

Despite the popularity of internal new venturing, there is a high risk of failure. Research suggests that somewhere between 33% and 60% of all new products that reach the marketplace do not generate an adequate economic return,[21] and most of these products were the result of internal new ventures. Three reasons are often put forward to explain the relatively high failure rate of internal new ventures: (1) market entry on too small a scale, (2) poor commercialization of the new-venture product, and (3) poor corporate management of the new-venture division.[22]

SCALE OF ENTRY   Research suggests that large-scale entry into a new industry is often a critical precondition for the success of a new venture. This means that in the short run, large-scale entry requires a substantial capital investment to develop the product—and thus the prospect of substantial losses. But in the long run, which can be as long as five to twelve years depending on the industry, such a large investment results in far greater returns than if a company enters on a small scale and limits its investment to reduce its potential losses.[23] Large-scale entrants can more rapidly realize scale economies, build brand loyalty, and gain access to distribution channels, all of which increase the probability of a new venture's success. In contrast, small-scale entrants may find themselves handicapped by high costs due to a lack of scale economies and a lack of market presence that limits their ability to build brand loyalty and gain access to distribution channels. These scale effects are particularly significant when a company is entering an established industry where incumbent companies do possess scale economies, brand loyalty, and access to distribution channels. Now, the new entrant has to make a major investment to succeed.

Figure 10.7 plots the relationship between scale of entry and profitability over time for successful small-scale and large-scale ventures. The figure shows that successful small-scale entry is associated with lower initial losses but that, in the long

FIGURE 10.7

Scale of Entry Versus Profitability for Small-Scale and Large-Scale Ventures

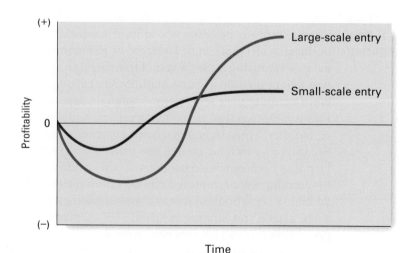

Time

run, large-scale entry generates greater returns. However, because of the costs of large-scale entry and the huge potential losses if the venture fails, many companies make the mistake of choosing a small-scale entry strategy, which often means they fail to build the market share necessary for long-term success.

COMMERCIALIZATION Many internal new ventures are driven by the use of new or high technology to make better products. But to be commercially successful, the products must be developed with customer requirements in mind. Many internal new ventures fail when a company ignores the needs of customers in a market and instead becomes blinded by the technological possibilities of a new product.[24] Thus, a new venture may fail because it is marketing a product based on a technology for which there is no demand or because the company fails to commercialize or position the product correctly in the market.

For example, consider the desktop computer marketed by NeXT, the company started by the founder of Apple, Steven Jobs. The NeXT system failed to gain market share because the computer incorporated an array of expensive technologies that consumers simply did not want, such as optical disk drives and hi-fidelity sound. The optical disk drives, in particular, turned off customers because they made it tough to switch work from a PC with a floppy drive to a NeXT machine with an optical drive. In other words, NeXT failed because its founder was so dazzled by leading-edge technology that he ignored customer needs. However, Jobs redeemed himself when he successfully commercialized Apple's iPod, which dominates the MP3 player market today.

POOR IMPLEMENTATION Managing the new-venture process and division raises difficult organizational issues.[25] For example, one common mistake some companies make is to try to increase their chance of making a successful product by establishing many different internal new-venture divisions at the same time. This shotgun approach of spreading the risks among divisions places great demands on a company's cash flow and can result in the best ventures being starved of the cash they need to succeed.[26] Another common mistake is the failure of corporate managers to carefully develop upfront all the aspects of the business model that will be needed for the new venture to succeed—and to include scientists in the model-building process. Taking a team of research scientists and giving them the resources they need to do research in their favorite field may produce novel results, but these results may have little strategic or commercial value. Managers must clarify how and why the project will lead to a product that has a competitive advantage and establish strategic objectives and a timetable to manage the venture until the product reaches the market. Failure to anticipate the time and costs involved in the new-venture process constitutes a further mistake. Many companies have unrealistic expectations regarding the time frame, expecting profits to flow in quickly. Research suggests that some companies operate with a philosophy of killing new businesses if they do not turn a profit by the end of the third year, which is clearly an unrealistic view given that it can take five to twelve years before a venture generates substantial profits.

● Guidelines for Successful Internal New Venturing

To avoid the pitfalls discussed above, a company should adopt a well-thought-out, structured approach to manage internal new venturing. New venturing begins with R&D, *exploratory research* (the "R" in R&D) to advance basic science and technology and *development research* (the "D" in R&D) to find and refine the commercial applications for a technology. Companies with a strong track record of internal new venturing excel at both kinds of R&D: they help to advance basic science and then they find commercial applications for it.[27] To advance basic science, it is important for companies to (1) have strong links with universities, where much of the scientific knowledge that underlies new technologies is discovered, and (2) to make sure that significant research funds are under the control of researchers who can pursue blue-sky projects that might ultimately yield unexpected and commercially valuable technologies and products. For example, 3M has close links with several universities, including the University of Minnesota in its hometown, and funds basic research at those universities. As already mentioned, 3M's researchers spend 15% of their time on projects of their own choosing, many of which are basic research projects.

However, if the pursuit of basic research is all that a company does well, it will probably generate few successful commercial ventures. To translate good science into good products, it is critical that a major proportion of R&D funding be directed toward commercial ventures. Companies can take a number of steps to ensure that this happens. First, many companies place much of the funding for research in the hands of business unit managers who are responsible for narrowing down and then selecting the small number of research projects they believe have the best chance of a significant commercial payoff. Second, to make effective use of its R&D skills, a company's top managers must continually spell out the strategic objectives in its business model and communicate them clearly to scientists and engineers. Research must be in the pursuit of strategic goals.[28] For example, one of the biggest research projects at Microsoft has been language recognition software because a central objective of the company is to make computers easy to use. Researchers reason that if computers can understand spoken language, commands can be input by voice rather than through a keyboard, thus making computers easier to use and strengthening the Windows platform.

A company must also foster close links between R&D and marketing to increase the probability of a new product's commercial success, because this is the best way to ensure that research projects address the needs of the market. Also, a company should foster close links between R&D and manufacturing to ensure that it has the ability to make a proposed new product. Many companies successfully integrate the activities of different functions by creating cross-functional project teams to oversee the development of new products, from their inception to their market introduction. This approach can significantly reduce the time this process takes. For example, while R&D is working on the design, manufacturing is setting up facilities and marketing is developing a campaign to show customers how much the new product will benefit them.

Finally, because large-scale entry often leads to greater long-term profits, a company can promote the success of internal new venturing by thinking big. Well in advance, a company should construct efficient-scale manufacturing facilities and establish a large marketing program to develop a campaign for building a market presence and brand loyalty quickly. Corporate managers should not panic; they should accept that there will be initial losses and realize that, as long as market share is expanding, the product will eventually succeed.

Entering New Industries: Acquisitions

In Chapter 9, we explained that acquisitions are the main vehicle that companies use to implement a horizontal integration strategy. They are also a principal way companies enter new industries to pursue vertical integration and diversification. In the

Opening Case, we saw how Tyco acquired many new businesses to pursue unrelated diversification; now, however, it is de-diversifying, so it is necessary to understand both the benefits and risks associated with using acquisitions to implement a corporate-level strategy.

● **The Attractions of Acquisitions**

Acquisitions are used to pursue vertical integration or diversification when a company lacks the distinctive competencies to compete in a new industry and therefore uses its capital to purchase an established company that has those competencies. A company is particularly likely to use acquisitions when it needs to move fast to establish a presence in an industry. Entering a new industry through internal venturing is a relatively slow process; acquisition is a much quicker way for a company to establish a significant market presence. A company can purchase a leading company with a strong competitive position in months rather than spend years building up a market leadership position through internal venturing. Thus, when speed is important, acquisition is the favored entry mode. Intel, for example, used acquisitions to build its communications chip business because it sensed that the market was developing very quickly and it would take too long to develop the required competencies internally (see Strategy in Action 10.2).

In addition, acquisitions are often perceived as somewhat less risky than internal new ventures primarily because they involve less commercial uncertainty. Because of the risks associated with an internal new venture, it is difficult to predict its future profitability and cash flows. In contrast, when a company makes an acquisition, it is acquiring a company with a reputation whose market share and profitability can be easily evaluated.

Finally, acquisitions are an attractive way to enter an industry that is protected by high barriers to entry. Recall from Chapter 2 that barriers to entry arise from factors associated with product differentiation (brand loyalty), absolute cost advantages, and economies of scale. When these barriers are substantial, a company may find it very difficult to enter an industry through internal new venturing because it will have to construct large-scale manufacturing facilities and invest in a massive advertising campaign to establish brand loyalty—difficult goals that require large capital expenditures. In contrast, if a company acquires an established company in the industry, it can circumvent most entry barriers because it has acquired a market leader that already has substantial scale economies and brand loyalty. In general, the greater the barriers to entry, the more likely it is that acquisitions will be the favored entry mode.

● **Acquisition Pitfalls**

For these reasons, acquisitions have long been a popular vehicle for executing corporate-level strategies. As we mentioned earlier, however, despite this popularity, there is ample evidence that many acquisitions fail to add value for the acquiring company and, indeed, often end up dissipating value. For example, a study by KPMG, an accounting and management consulting company, looked at 700 large acquisitions and found that, although some 30% of these actually created value for the acquiring company, 31% destroyed value, and the remainder had little impact.[29] A wealth of evidence from academic research suggests that many acquisitions fail to realize their anticipated benefits.[30] In a major study of the postacquisition performance of acquired companies, David Ravenscraft and Mike Scherer concluded that the profitability and market shares of acquired companies often declined after acquisition.[31] This evidence suggests that many acquisitions destroy rather than create value.

Acquisitions may fail to create value for four reasons: (1) companies often experience difficulties when trying to integrate different organizational structures and cultures,

(2) companies overestimate the potential economic benefits from an acquisition, (3) acquisitions tend to be very expensive, and (4) companies often do not adequately screen their acquisition targets.

INTEGRATING THE ACQUIRED COMPANY Once an acquisition has been made, the acquiring company has to integrate the acquired company and combine it with its own organizational structure and culture. Integration involves the adoption of common management and financial control systems, the joining together of operations from the acquired and the acquiring company, the establishment of bureaucratic mechanisms to share information and personnel, and the need to create a common culture. Experience has shown that many problems can occur as companies attempt to integrate their activities.

After an acquisition, many acquired companies experience high management turnover because their employees do not like the acquiring company's way of operating—its structure and culture.[32] Research suggests that the loss of management talent and expertise, to say nothing of the damage from constant tension between the businesses, can materially harm the performance of the acquired unit.[33] Strategy in Action 10.3 describes what happened at Boston Co. after it was acquired by Mellon Bank.

OVERESTIMATING ECONOMIC BENEFITS Even when companies find it easy to integrate their activities, they often overestimate the potential for creating value by joining together different businesses. They overestimate the competitive advantages that can be derived from the acquisition and so pay more for the target company than it is worth. Richard Roll has attributed this tendency to hubris on the part of top management. According to Roll, top managers typically overestimate their ability to create value from an acquisition primarily because rising to the top of a corporation has given them an exaggerated sense of their own capabilities.[34] Coca-Cola's acquisition of a number of medium-sized winemaking companies illustrates this situation. Reasoning that a beverage is a beverage, Coca-Cola thought it would be able to use its distinctive competence in marketing to dominate the U.S. wine industry. But after buying three wine companies and enduring seven years of marginal profits, Coca-Cola finally conceded that wine and soft drinks are very different products, with different kinds of appeal, pricing systems, and distribution networks. It subsequently sold the wine operations to Joseph E. Seagram & Sons at a substantial loss when adjusted for inflation.[35]

THE EXPENSE OF ACQUISITIONS Perhaps the most important reason for the failure of acquisitions is that the acquisition of companies whose stock is publicly traded tends to be very expensive—and the expense of the acquisition cancels the prospective value-creating gains from the acquisition described earlier. One reason is that the management of the target company is not likely to agree to an acquisition unless there is a substantial premium over its current market value. Another reason is that the stockholders of the acquired company are unlikely to sell their stock unless they are paid a significant premium over its current market value—and premiums tend to run 25% to 50% over a company's stock price prior to a takeover bid. Therefore, the acquiring company must be able to increase the value of the acquired company after it has been integrated by at least the same amount to make the acquisition pay: a tall order. This is a major reason why acquisitions are frequently unprofitable for the acquiring company.

Strategy in Action   10.3

Postacquisition Problems at Mellon Bank

In the search for a profitable way to expand his company's business, Frank Cahouet, the CEO of Philadelphia-based Mellon Bank, decided to reduce the large swings in Mellon's earnings (caused by changes in interest rates) by diversifying into financial services to gain access to a steady flow of fee-based income from money management operations. As part of this strategy, he acquired Boston Co. for $1.45 billion. Boston Co. is a high-profile money management company that manages investments for major institutional clients, such as state and corporate pension funds. Mellon followed up its Boston Co. acquisition with the acquisition of mutual fund provider Dreyfus Corp. for $1.7 billion. As a result, almost half of Mellon's income was now generated from fee-based financial services.

Problems at Boston Co. began to surface soon after the Mellon acquisition. From the beginning, corporate cultures clashed. At Mellon, many managers arrived at their mundane offices by 7 A.M. and put in twelve-hour days for modest pay by banking industry standards. They were also accustomed to Frank Cahouet's management style, which emphasized cost containment and frugality. Boston Co. managers also put in twelve-hour days, but they expected considerable autonomy, flexible work schedules, high pay, ample perks, and large performance bonuses. In most years, the top twenty executives at Boston Co. earned between $750,000 and $1 million each. Mellon executives who visited the Boston Co. unit were dumbstruck by its country club atmosphere and opulence. In its move to streamline Boston Co., Mellon insisted that Boston Co. cut expenses and introduced new regulations for restricting travel, entertainment, and perks.

Things started to go wrong when the Wisconsin state pension fund complained to Mellon of lower returns on a portfolio run by Boston Co. Mellon was forced to liquidate the portfolio and take a $130 million charge against earnings; it also fired the responsible portfolio manager, claiming that this manager was making "unauthorized trades." At Boston Co., however, many managers saw Mellon's action as violating the guarantees of operating autonomy that it had given Boston Co. at the time of the acquisition. They blamed Mellon for prematurely liquidating a portfolio whose strategy, they claimed, Mellon executives had approved and that, moreover, could still prove a winner if interest rates fell (which they subsequently did).

Infuriated by Mellon's interference, seven of Boston Co.'s asset unit managers, including the unit's CEO, Desmond Heathwood, proposed a management buyout to Mellon. This unit was one of the gems in Boston Co.'s crown, with over $26 billion in assets under management. Heathwood had been openly disdainful of Mellon's bankers, believing that they were out of their league in the investment business. Mellon rejected the buyout proposal, and Heathwood promptly left to start his own investment management company. A few days later, Mellon asked employees at Boston Co. to sign employment contracts that limited their ability to leave and work for Heathwood's competing business. Thirteen senior employees refused to sign and then quit to join Heathwood's new money management operation.

The defection of Heathwood and his colleagues was followed by a series of high-profile client defections. The Arizona State Retirement System, for example, pulled $1 billion out of Mellon and transferred it to Heathwood's firm, and the Fresno County Retirement System transferred $400 million in assets over to Heathwood. As one client stated, "We have a relationship with the Boston Co. that goes back over 30 years, and the people who worked on the account are the people who left—so we left too."

Reflecting on the episode, Frank Cahouet noted, "We've clearly been hurt. . . . But this episode is very manageable. We are not going to lose our momentum." Others were not so sure. In this incident, they saw yet another example of how difficult it can be to merge two divergent corporate cultures and how the management turnover that results from trying such a merger can deal a serious blow to any attempt to create value out of an acquisition. In 2006, Mellon merged with the Bank of New York to create a new financial powerhouse. Only time will tell if this merger results in yet another round of the kind of problems just discussed.[c]

The problem for the acquiring company is that the stock price of the acquisition target gets bid up enormously during the acquisition process. This frequently occurs in the case of a bidding contest where two or more companies simultaneously bid to acquire the target company. In addition, when many acquisitions are happening in a particular sector or industry, the price of *potential* target companies are bid up by investors who speculate that a bid for these companies will be made at some future point, which further increases the cost of making acquisitions. This happened in the telecommunications sector when, to make sure they could meet the needs of customers who were demanding leading-edge equipment, many large companies went on acquisition binges. Cisco Systems, Nortel, Corning, and Lucent all raced each other to buy smaller companies that were developing new telecommunications equipment. The result was that stock prices for these companies got bid up by investors. When the telecommunications boom turned to bust, the acquiring companies found that they had vastly overpaid for their acquisitions and had to take enormous accounting losses.

INADEQUATE PREACQUISITION SCREENING As the problems of these companies suggest, top managers often do a poor job of preacquisition screening, that is, evaluating the value-creating potential of potential acquisitions. After researching acquisitions made by twenty different companies, a study by Philippe Haspeslagh and David Jemison concluded that one reason for acquisition failure is managers' decision to acquire other firms without thoroughly analyzing the potential benefits and costs.[36] Indeed, in many cases after an acquisition has been completed, many acquiring companies discover that instead of buying a well-run business, they have purchased a troubled organization. Moreover, companies often have to take on an enormous amount of debt to fund these acquisitions, and they frequently are unable to pay it once the weaknesses of the acquired company's business model become clear.

● **Guidelines for Successful Acquisition**

To avoid pitfalls and make successful acquisitions, companies need to take a structured approach to purchasing companies based on four components: (1) target identification and preacquisition screening, (2) bidding strategy, (3) integration, and (4) learning from experience.[37]

IDENTIFICATION AND SCREENING Thorough preacquisition screening increases a company's knowledge about a potential takeover target and lessens the risk of purchasing a potential problem business—one with a weak business model. It also leads to a more realistic assessment of the problems involved in executing a particular acquisition so that a company can plan how to integrate the new business and blend the organizational structures and cultures. The screening process should begin with a detailed assessment of the strategic rationale for making the acquisition, an identification of the kind of company that would make an ideal acquisition candidate, and a thorough analysis of the strengths and weaknesses of its business model by comparing it to other possible acquisition targets.

Indeed, an acquiring company should scan potential acquisition candidates and evaluate each according to a detailed set of criteria, focusing on (1) its financial position, (2) its distinctive competencies and competitive advantage, (3) the changing industry boundaries, (4) its management capabilities, and (5) its corporate culture. Such an evaluation will help the company identify the strengths and weaknesses of each candidate and the potential economies of scale and scope between the acquiring and the acquired companies. It will also help it to recognize potential integration problems and the problems that might exist when it is necessary to integrate the corporate cultures of the acquiring and the acquired companies. In 2004, for example, Microsoft and SAP, the world's leading provider of enterprise resource planning software, sat down together to discuss a possible acquisition by Microsoft. Both companies decided that even though there was a strong strategic rationale for a merger—together they would dominate the global computing market for most large global companies—the problems of creating an organizational structure that could successfully integrate their hundreds of thousands of employees throughout the world and blend two very different corporate cultures were insurmountable.

Once a company has reduced the list of potential acquisition candidates to the most favored one or two, it needs to contact expert third parties, such as investment bankers like Goldman Sachs and Merrill Lynch, that may be able to provide valuable insights about the attractiveness of the potential acquisition and that will also handle the many issues surrounding the acquisition, such as the process of establishing the bidding strategy for acquiring the company's stock.

BIDDING STRATEGY The objective of the bidding strategy is to reduce the price that a company must pay for the target company. The most effective way that a company can acquire another is to make a friendly takeover bid, which means the two companies work out an amicable way to merge the two companies that satisfies the needs of stockholders and top managers. A friendly takeover helps prevent speculators from bidding up stock prices. By contrast, in a hostile bid, such as the one between Oracle and PeopleSoft, the price of the target company is often bid up by speculators who expect that the offer price will be raised by the acquirer or that another company, sometimes called a white knight, might come in with a counteroffer more favorable to the management of the target company.

Another essential element of a good bidding strategy is timing. For example, Hanson PLC, one of the most successful companies to pursue unrelated diversification, searched for essentially sound companies suffering from short-term problems due to cyclical industry factors or one underperforming division. Such companies are typically undervalued by the stock market and so can be acquired without the standard 25% to 50% stock premium. With good timing, a company can make a bargain purchase. Tyco also followed this practice; it bought essentially sound companies that were underperforming their peers because of short-term problems and then helped them establish a competitive business model.

INTEGRATION Despite good screening and bidding, an acquisition will fail unless the acquiring company possesses the essential organizational design skills needed to integrate the acquired company into its operations and so quickly develop a viable multibusiness model. Integration should center on the source of the potential strategic advantages of the acquisition—for instance, opportunities to share marketing, manufacturing, logistics, R&D, financial, or management resources. Integration should also involve steps to eliminate any duplication of facilities or functions. In addition, any unwanted business units of the acquired company should be divested.

LEARNING FROM EXPERIENCE Research suggests that, although many acquisitions do fail to create value for the acquiring company, companies that acquire many companies over time become expert in this process and so can generate significant value from their acquisitions.[38] One reason may be that they learn from their experience and develop a system of how to execute an acquisition most efficiently and effectively. Tyco, profiled in the Opening Case, did not make hostile acquisitions; it audited the accounts of the target company in detail, acquired companies to help it achieve a critical mass in an industry, moved quickly to realize cost savings after an acquisition, promoted managers one or two layers down to lead the newly acquired entity, and introduced profit-based incentive pay systems in the acquired unit.[39]

Entering New Industries: Joint Ventures

Joint ventures are most commonly used to enter a new industry that is an embryonic or growth industry. Suppose a company is contemplating creating a new venture division in an embryonic industry. Such a move involves substantial risks and costs because the company must establish from scratch the set of value chain activities needed to operate in that new market. On the other hand, an acquisition can be a dangerous proposition because there is no established leader in the emerging industry, and if there is a leading company, it will be extremely expensive to purchase.

In this situation, a joint venture often becomes the most appropriate vehicle because it allows a company to share the risks and costs associated with establishing a new business unit with another company. This is especially true when the companies share complementary skills or distinctive competencies. Now a joint venture with another company may increase the probability of success. Consider the 50/50 equity joint venture formed between UTC and Dow Chemical to build plastic-based composite parts for the aerospace industry. UTC was already involved in the aerospace industry (it builds Sikorsky helicopters), and Dow Chemical had skills in the development and manufacture of plastic-based composites. The alliance called for UTC to contribute its advanced aerospace skills and Dow to contribute its skills in developing and manufacturing plastic-based composites. Through the joint venture, both companies would become involved in new activities and would be able to realize the benefits associated with related diversification without having to merge their activities into one company or bear the costs and risks of developing new products on their own. Thus, both companies would enjoy the value-creating benefits of entering a new market without having to bear the increased bureaucratic costs.

Although in some situations joint ventures can benefit both partner companies, they have three main drawbacks. First, while a joint venture allows companies to share the risks and costs of developing a new business, it also requires that they share in the profits if it succeeds. So, if it turns out later that one partner's skills are more important than the other's, that partner will have to give away profits to the other party because of the 50/50 agreement. This can create conflict and sour the working relationship as time goes on. Second, the joint venture partners may have different business philosophies, time horizons, or investment preferences, and so once again substantial problems can arise. Conflicts over how to run the joint venture can tear it apart and result in business failure.

Third, a company that enters into a joint venture always runs the risk of giving critical know-how away to its partner, which might then take that know-how and use it to compete with the other partner in the future. For example, having gained access to Dow's expertise in plastic-based composites, UTC might have dissolved the alliance and produced these materials on its own. As we discussed in the last chapter, such a risk can be minimized if Dow gets a credible commitment from UTC, which is what it did. UTC had to make an expensive asset-specific investment to make the products that the joint venture was formed to create.

Restructuring

Many companies expand into new markets and industries to increase profitability; however, sometimes they also need to exit markets and industries to achieve the same goal or even split up their existing businesses into separate companies, like Tyco did. **Restructuring** is the process of reorganizing and divesting business units and exiting markets and industries to refocus on core distinctive competencies.[40] Why are so many companies restructuring and how do they do it?

● **Why Restructure?**   One main reason that diversified companies have restructured in recent years is that the stock market has valued their stock at a **diversification discount,** meaning that the stock of highly diversified companies is valued lower, relative to their earnings, than the stock of less diversified enterprises.[41] Investors see highly diversified companies as less attractive investments for four reasons. First, as we discussed earlier, investors often feel these companies, like Tyco, no longer have a multibusiness model that justifies their participation in many different industries. Second, the complexity of the consolidated financial statements of highly diversified enterprises disguises the performance of its individual business units and thus whether the multibusiness model is succeeding. As a result, investors perceive the company as being riskier than companies that operate in one industry and whose competitive advantage and financial statements are more easily understood. Given this situation, restructuring can be seen as an attempt to boost the returns to shareholders by splitting up a multibusiness company like Tyco into separate and independent parts.

The third reason for the diversification discount is that many investors have learned from experience that managers often have a tendency to pursue too much diversification or do it for the wrong reasons; they do not diversify to increase profitability.[42] Some top managers pursue growth for its own sake. They are empire builders who expand the scope of their company to the point where bureaucratic costs exceed the additional value such diversification creates. Restructuring thus becomes a response to declining financial performance brought about by overdiversification.

A final factor leading to restructuring is that innovations in strategic management have diminished the advantages of vertical integration or diversification. For example, a few decades ago, there was little understanding of how long-term cooperative relationships, or strategic alliances, between a company and its suppliers could be a viable alternative to vertical integration. Most companies considered only two alternatives for managing the supply chain: vertical integration or competitive bidding. As we discussed in Chapter 9, in many situations, long-term cooperative relationships can create the most value, especially because they avoid the need to incur bureaucratic costs or dispense with market discipline. As this strategic innovation has spread throughout the business world, the relative advantages of vertical integration have declined.

Summary of Chapter

1. Managers often first consider diversification when their company is generating free cash flow, which are financial resources in excess of those necessary to maintain a competitive advantage in the company's original, or core, business.

2. A diversified company can create value by (a) transferring competencies among existing businesses, (b) leveraging competencies to create new businesses, (c) sharing resources to realize economies of scope, (d) using product bundling, (e) using diversification as a means of managing rivalry in one or more industries, and (f) exploiting general organizational competencies that enhance the performance of all business units within a diversified company. The bureaucratic costs of diversification are a function of the number of independent business units within the company and the extent of the coordination needed among those business units.

3. Diversification motivated by a desire to pool risks or achieve greater growth is often associated with the dissipation of value.

4. Companies use three vehicles to enter new industries: internal new venturing, acquisition, and joint ventures.

5. Internal new venturing is typically used to enter a new industry when a company has a set of valuable competencies in its existing businesses that can be leveraged or recombined to enter the new business or industry.

6. Many internal ventures fail because of entry on too small a scale, poor commercialization, and poor corporate management of the internal venture process. Guarding against failure involves a structured approach toward project selection and management, integration of R&D and marketing to improve commercialization of a venture idea, and entry on a significant scale.

7. Acquisitions are often the best way to enter a new industry when the company lacks the important competencies (resources and capabilities) required to compete in a new market, and it can purchase a company that does have has those competencies at a reasonable price. Acquisitions also tend to be favored when the barriers to entry into the target industry are high and the company is unwilling to accept the time frame, development costs, and risks of internal new venturing.

8. Many acquisitions fail because of poor postacquisition integration, overestimation of the value that can be created from an acquisition, the high cost of acquisition, and poor preacquisition screening. Guarding against acquisition failure requires structured screening, good bidding strategies, positive attempts to integrate the acquired company into the organization of the acquiring one, and learning from experience.

9. Joint ventures are used most often to enter a new industry when (a) the risks and costs associated with setting up a new business unit are more than the company is willing to assume on its own and (b) the company can increase the probability of successfully establishing a new business by teaming up with another company that has skills and assets complementing its own.

10. Restructuring is often a response to (a) an inadequate multibusiness model, (b) the complexity of consolidated financial statements, (c) excessive diversification due to top managers' empire building, and (d) innovations in the strategic management process that have reduced the advantages of vertical integration and diversification.

Discussion Questions

1. When is a company likely to choose related diversification and when is it likely to choose unrelated diversification? Discuss with reference to an electronics manufacturer and an ocean shipping company.

2. Under what circumstances might it be best to enter a new market or industry through acquisition, and under what circumstances might internal new venturing be the preferred entry mode?

3. Imagine that IBM has decided to diversify into the cellular telecommunications provider business. What entry vehicle would you recommend that the company pursue? Why?

4. Look at Honeywell's portfolio of businesses (described in Honeywell's 10-K statements, which can be accessed on the Web at www.honeywell.com). How many different industries is Honeywell involved in? Would you describe Honeywell as a related or unrelated diversification company? How do you think that Honeywell's diversification strategy increases profitability?

Practicing Strategic Management

SMALL-GROUP EXERCISE
Dun & Bradstreet

Break into small groups of three to five, appoint one group member as a spokesperson who will communicate your findings to the class, and then read the following news release from Dun & Bradstreet. On the basis of this information, identify the strategic rationale for the split and evaluate how the split might affect the performance of the three successor companies. If you were a stockholder in the old Dun & Bradstreet Corporation, would you approve of this split? Why?

Dun & Bradstreet CEO Robert E. Weissman today announced a sweeping strategy that will transform the 155-year-old business information giant into three publicly traded, global corporations. "This important action is designed to increase shareholder value by unlocking D&B's substantial underlying franchise strengths," said Weissman.

Building on preeminent Dun & Bradstreet businesses, the reorganization establishes three independent companies focused on high-growth information markets; financial information services; and consumer-product market research.

"Since the 1800s, D&B has grown by effectively managing a portfolio of businesses and gaining economies of scale," stated Weissman. "But the velocity of change in information markets has dramatically altered the rules of business survival. Today, market focus and speed are the primary drivers of competitive advantage. This plan is our blueprint for success in the 21st century," said Weissman.

The plan, approved today at a special meeting of D&B's board of directors, calls for D&B to create three separate companies by spinning off two of its businesses to shareholders. "D&B is the leader in business information," said Weissman. "By freeing our companies to tightly focus on our core vertical markets, we can more rapidly leverage this leadership position into emerging growth areas." The three new companies are:

- Cognizant Corporation, a new high-growth company, including IMS International, the leading global supplier of marketing information to the pharmaceutical and healthcare industries; Nielsen Media Research, the leader in audience measurement for electronic media; and Gartner Group, the premier provider of advisory services to high-tech users, vendors and suppliers, in which Cognizant will hold a majority interest.

- The Dun & Bradstreet Corporation, consisting of Dun & Bradstreet Information Services, the world's largest source of business-to-business marketing and commercial-credit information; Moody's Investors Service, a global leader in rating debt; and Reuben H. Donnelley, a premier provider of Yellow Pages marketing and publishing.

- A. C. Nielsen, the global leader in marketing information for the fast-moving consumer packaged goods industry.

"These three separate companies will tailor their strategies to the unique demands of their markets, determining investments, capital structures and policies that will strengthen their respective global capabilities. This plan also clarifies D&B from an investor's perspective by grouping the businesses into three logical investment categories, each with distinct risk/reward profiles," said Weissman.

The Dun & Bradstreet Corporation is the world's largest marketer of information, software and services for business decision-making, with worldwide revenue of $4.9 billion in 1994.

ARTICLE FILE 10

Find an example of a diversified company that made an acquisition that apparently failed to create any value. Identify and critically evaluate the rationale that top management used to justify the acquisition when it was made. Explain why the acquisition subsequently failed.

STRATEGIC MANAGEMENT PROJECT
Module 10

This module requires you to assess your company's use of acquisitions, internal new ventures, and joint ventures as strategies for entering a new business area or as attempts to restructure its portfolio of businesses.

A. **Your company has entered a new industry during the past decade.**
   1. Pick one new industry that your company has entered during the past ten years.
   2. Identify its rationale for entering this industry.
   3. Identify your company's strategy for entering this industry.
   4. Evaluate the rationale for using this particular entry strategy. Do you think that this was the best entry strategy to use? Justify your answer.

5. Do you think that the addition of this business unit to the company has added or dissipated value? Again, justify your answer.

B. **Your company has restructured its corporate portfolio during the past decade.**

1. Identify your company's rationale for pursuing a restructuring strategy.
2. Pick one industry that your company has exited during the past ten years.
3. Identify your company's strategy for exiting this particular industry. Do you think that this was the best exit strategy to use? Justify your answer.
4. In general, do you think that exiting from this industry has been in the company's best interest?

ETHICS EXERCISE

For the past few years, YCN (Your Communication Network) Inc. had been on a massive buying spree, acquiring companies one after another. To outsiders, YCN looked successful, but those inside the company were beginning to wonder if the company's situation was actually a dangerous one. Scott, who worked in accounting, had just discovered what he thought was a major accounting error. It seemed the company might have illegally recorded $2 billion in capital expenditures, thereby increasing cash flow and profit.

If Scott was correct, YCN had reported the erroneous $2 billion to cover up the company's true net losses. As he understood it, capital expenditures could be deducted over a long period of time, while expenses would be immediately subtracted from revenue. Because of the way the books had been handled, investors had been buying up the company's stock, causing stock prices to rise. If Scott had truly uncovered accounting fraud, many people would be in for a shock.

Scott knew that something had to be done, but it was obvious that this fraud had been perpetrated from within. Because it was an internal matter, Scott didn't know where to turn. What should he do?

1. Define the ethical issue presented in this case.
2. What would you do if you were in Scott's position?
3. If Scott is correct, what can the company do to correct the issue?

CLOSING CASE

United Technologies Has an "ACE in Its Pocket"

United Technologies Corporation (UTC), based in Hartford, Connecticut, is a *conglomerate*, a company that owns a wide variety of other companies that operate in different businesses and industries. Some of the companies in UTC's portfolio are more well known than UTC itself, such as Sikorsky Aircraft Corporation; Pratt & Whitney, the aircraft engine and component maker; Otis Elevator Company; Carrier air conditioning; and Chubb, the security and lock maker that UTC acquired in 2003. Today, investors frown upon companies like UTC that own and operate companies in widely different industries. There is a growing perception that managers can better manage a company's business model when the company operates as an independent or stand-alone entity. How can UTC justify holding all these companies together in a conglomerate? Why would this lead to a greater increase in their long-term profitability than if they operated as separate companies? In the last decade, the boards of directors and CEOs of many conglomerates, such as Greyhound-Dial, ITT Industries, and Textron, have realized that by holding diverse companies together, they were reducing, not increasing, the profitability of their companies. As a result, many conglomerates have been broken up and their companies spun off to allow them to operate as separate, independent entities.

UTC's CEO George David claims that he has created a unique and sophisticated multibusiness model that adds value across UTC's diverse businesses. David joined Otis Elevator as an assistant to its CEO in 1975, but within one year Otis was acquired by UTC, during a decade when "bigger is better" ruled corporate America and mergers and acquisitions, of whatever kind, were seen as the best way to grow profits. UTC sent David to manage its South American operations and later gave him responsibility for its Japanese operations. Otis had formed an alliance with Matsushita to develop an elevator for the Japanese market, and the resulting Elevonic 401, after being installed widely in Japanese buildings, proved to be a disaster. It broke down much more often than elevators made by other Japanese companies, and customers were concerned about its reliability and safety.

Matsushita was extremely embarrassed about the elevator's failure and assigned one of its leading total quality management (TQM) experts, Yuzuru Ito, to head a team of Otis engineers to find out why it performed so poorly. Under Ito's direction, all the employees—managers, designers, and production workers—who had produced the elevator analyzed why the elevators were malfunctioning. This intensive study led to a total redesign of the elevator, and when their new and improved elevator was launched worldwide, it met with great success. Otis's share of the global elevator market increased dramatically, and one result was that David was named president of UTC in 1992. He was given the responsibility to cut costs across the entire corporation, including its important Pratt & Whitney division, and his success in reducing UTC's cost structure and increasing its ROIC led to his appointment as CEO in 1994.

Now responsible for all of UTC's diverse companies, David decided that the best way to increase UTC's profitability, which had been falling, was to find ways to improve efficiency and quality in all its constituent companies. He convinced Ito to move to Hartford and take responsibility for championing the kinds of improvements that had by now transformed the Otis division, and Ito began to develop UTC's TQM system, which is known as Achieving Competitive Excellence (ACE).

ACE is a set of tasks and procedures that are used by employees from the shop floor to top management to analyze all aspects of the way a product is made. The goal is to find ways to improve quality and reliability, to lower the costs of making the product, and especially to find ways to make the next generation of a particular product perform better—in other words, to encourage technological innovation. David makes every employee in every function and at every level take responsibility for achieving the incremental, step-by-step gains that can result in innovative

and efficient products that enable a company to dominate its industry—to push back the value creation frontier.

David calls these techniques process disciplines, and he has used them to increase the performance of all UTC companies. Through these techniques, he has created the extra value for UTC that justifies it owning and operating such a diverse set of businesses. David's success can be seen in the performance that his company has achieved in the decade since he took control: he has quadrupled UTC's earnings per share, and in the first six months of 1994, profit grew by 25% to $1.4 billion, while sales increased by 26% to $18.3 billion. UTC has been in the top three performers of the companies that make up the Dow Jones industrial average for the last three years, and the company has consistently outperformed GE, another huge conglomerate, in its returns to investors.

David and his managers believe that the gains that can be achieved from UTC's process disciplines are never-ending because its own R&D—in which it invests over $2.5 billion a year—is constantly producing product innovations that can help all its businesses. Indeed, recognizing that its skills in creating process improvements are specific to manufacturing companies, UTC's strategy is to acquire only those companies that make products that can benefit from the use of its ACE program—hence, its Chubb acquisition. At the same time, David only invests in companies that have the potential to remain leading companies in their industries and so can charge above-average prices. His acquisitions strengthen the competencies of UTC's existing businesses. For example, he acquired a company called Sunderstrand, a leading aerospace and industrial systems company, and combined it with UTC's Hamilton aerospace division to create Hamilton Sunderstrand, which is now a major supplier to Boeing and makes products that command premium prices.

Case Discussion Questions

1. What kind of corporate-level strategy is UTC pursuing? What is UTC's multibusiness model, and in what ways does it create value?

2. What are the dangers and disadvantages of this business model?

3. Collect some recent information on UTC from sources like Yahoo! Finance. How successful has it been in pursuing its strategy?

Corporate Performance, Governance and Business Ethics

The Rise and Fall of Dennis Kozlowski

Under the leadership of Dennis Kozlowski, who became CEO of Tyco in 1990, the company's revenues expanded from $3.1 billion to almost $40 billion. Most of this growth was due to a series of acquisitions that took Tyco into a diverse range of unrelated businesses. Tyco financed the acquisitions by taking on significant debt commitments, which exceeded $23 billion by 2002. As Tyco expanded, some questioned the company's ability to service its debt commitments and claimed that management was engaging in "accounting tricks" to pad its books and make the company appear more profitable than it actually was. These criticisms, which were ignored for several years, were finally shown to have some validity in 2002 when Kozlowski was forced out by the board and subsequently charged with tax evasion by federal authorities.

Among other charges, authorities claimed that Kozlowski treated Tyco as his personal treasury, drawing on company funds to purchase an expensive Manhattan apartment and a world-class art collection that he obviously thought were befitting of the CEO of a major corporation. Kozlowski even used company funds to help pay for an expensive birthday party for his wife—which included toga-clad women, gladiators, a naked-woman-with-exploding-breasts birthday cake, and a version of Michelangelo's David that peed vodka. Kozlowski was replaced by a company outsider, Edward Breen. In 2003, Tyco took a $1.5 billion charge against earnings for accounting errors made during the Kozlowski era (i.e., Tyco's profits had been overstated by $1.5 billion during Kozlowski's tenure). Breen also set about dismantling parts of the empire that Kozlowski had built and divested several businesses.

After a lengthy criminal trial, in June 2005, Dennis Kozlowski and Mark Swartz, the former chief financial officer of Tyco, were convicted of twenty-three counts of grand larceny, conspiracy, securities fraud, and falsifying business records in connection with what prosecutors described as the systematic looting of millions of dollars from the conglomerate (Kozlowski was found guilty of looting $90 million from Tyco). Both were sentenced to jail for a minimum of eight years. As for Tyco, CEO Ed Breen announced in 2006 that the company would be broken up into three parts, a testament to the strategic incoherence of the conglomerate that Kozlowski built.[1]

OVERVIEW

The Tyco story detailed in the Opening Case is an important one because it illustrates that not all managers adhere to what should be a cardinal principle of business: that the quest to maximize profitability should be constrained by both the law and ethical obligations. In Chapter 1, we noted that the goal of managers should be to pursue strategies that maximize long-run shareholder value, but we also note that managers must behave in a legal, ethical and socially responsible manner when pursuing this goal. Kozlowski's behavior was both unethical and illegal, and he paid a heavy price for his behavior.

In this chapter, we take a close look at the governance mechanisms that shareholders put in place to make sure that managers are acting in their interests and pursuing strategies that maximize shareholder value. We also discuss how managers need to pay attention to other stakeholders, such as employees, suppliers, and customers. Balancing the needs of different stakeholder groups is in the long-run interests of the company's owners, its shareholders. Good governance mechanisms recognize this truth. In addition, we will spend some time reviewing the ethical implications of strategic decisions, and we will discuss how managers can make sure that their strategic decisions are founded on strong ethical principles.

Stakeholders and Corporate Performance

A company's **stakeholders** are individuals or groups with an interest, claim, or stake in the company, in what it does, and in how well it performs.[2] They include stockholders, creditors, employees, customers, the communities in which the company does business, and the general public. Stakeholders can be divided into internal stakeholders and external stakeholders (see Figure 11.1). **Internal stakeholders** are stockholders and employees, including executive officers, other managers, and board members. **External stakeholders** are all other individuals and groups that have some claim on the company. Typically, this group is comprised of customers, suppliers, creditors (including banks and bondholders), governments, unions, local communities, and the general public.

All stakeholders are in an exchange relationship with the company. Each of the stakeholder groups listed in Figure 11.1 supplies the organization with important resources (or contributions), and in exchange, each expects its interests to be satisfied (by inducements).[3] Stockholders provide the enterprise with risk capital and in exchange expect management to try to maximize the return on their investment. Creditors, and particularly bondholders, also provide the company with capital in the form of debt, and they expect to be repaid on time and with interest. Employees provide labor and skills and in exchange expect commensurate income, job satisfaction, job security, and good working conditions. Customers provide a company with its revenues and in

FIGURE 11.1

Stakeholders and the Enterprise

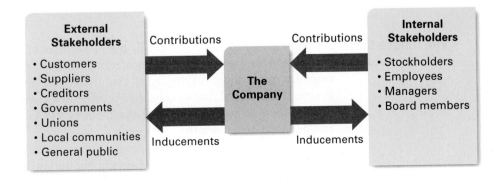

exchange want high-quality reliable products that represent value for money. Suppliers provide a company with inputs and in exchange seek revenues and dependable buyers. Governments provide a company with rules and regulations that govern business practice and maintain fair competition. In exchange, they want companies to adhere to these rules. Unions help to provide a company with productive employees, and in exchange they want benefits for their members in proportion to their contributions to the company. Local communities provide companies with local infrastructure and in exchange want companies that are responsible citizens. The general public provides companies with national infrastructure and in exchange seeks some assurance that the quality of life will be improved as a result of the company's existence.

A company must take these claims into account when formulating its strategies or stakeholders may withdraw their support. For example, stockholders may sell their shares, bondholders may demand higher interest payments on new bonds, employees may leave their jobs, and customers may buy elsewhere. Suppliers may seek more dependable buyers. Unions may engage in disruptive labor disputes. Governments may take civil or criminal action against the company and its top officers, imposing fines and in some cases jail terms. Communities may oppose the company's attempts to locate its facilities in their area, and the general public may form pressure groups, demanding action against companies that impair the quality of life. Any of these reactions can have a damaging impact on an enterprise.

Stakeholder Impact Analysis

A company cannot always satisfy the claims of all stakeholders. The goals of different groups may conflict, and in practice few organizations have the resources to manage all stakeholders.[4] For example, union claims for higher wages can conflict with consumer demands for reasonable prices and stockholder demands for acceptable returns. Often the company must make choices. To do so, it must identify the most important stakeholders and give highest priority to pursuing strategies that satisfy their needs. Stakeholder impact analysis can provide such identification. Typically, stakeholder impact analysis follows these steps:

1. Identify stakeholders.

2. Identify stakeholders' interests and concerns.

3. As a result, identify what claims stakeholders are likely to make on the organization.

4. Identify the stakeholders who are most important from the organization's perspective.

5. Identify the resulting strategic challenges.[5]

Such an analysis enables a company to identify the stakeholders most critical to its survival and to make sure that the satisfaction of their needs is paramount. Most companies that have gone through this process quickly come to the conclusion that three stakeholder groups must be satisfied above all others if a company is to survive and prosper: customers, employees, and stockholders.

The Unique Role of Stockholders

A company's stockholders are usually put in a different class from other stakeholder groups, and for good reason. Stockholders are legal owners and the providers of **risk capital**, a major source of the capital resources that allow a company to operate its business. The capital that stockholders provide to a company is seen as risk capital because there is no guarantee that stockholders will ever recoup their investment and/or earn a decent return.

Recent history demonstrates all too clearly the nature of risk capital. Many investors who bought shares in companies that went public during the late 1990s and early 2000s through an initial public offering (IPO) subsequently saw the value of their holdings decline to zero, or something close to it. For example, in early 2000, Oniva.com, a provider of an online business-to-business marketplace aimed at small businesses, went public. On the first day of trading, the shares hit $25. They fell steadily afterward, and two years later, having lost 99% of their value, they were trading at $0.25, effectively wiping out the investment many made in the company. Of course, there are also some spectacular successes: investors who purchased shares of Dell, Microsoft, or Intel at their IPO have done extraordinarily well. But this is the nature of risk capital: the variance of returns is very high. To reward stockholders for providing the company with risk capital, management is obligated to pursue strategies that maximize the returns that stockholders receive from their investment in the company's stock.

Over the past decade, maximizing returns to stockholders has taken on added importance because more and more employees have themselves become stockholders in the company for which they work through an employee stock ownership plan (ESOP). At Wal-Mart, for example, all employees who have served for more than one year are eligible for the company's ESOP. Under an ESOP, employees are given the opportunity to purchase stock in their company, sometimes at a discount compared to the market value of the stock. The company may also contribute a certain proportion of the purchase price. By making employees stockholders, ESOPs tend to increase the already strong emphasis on maximizing returns to stockholders because they now help to satisfy two key stakeholder groups: stockholders and employees.

● Profitability, Profit Growth, and Stakeholder Claims

Because of the unique position assigned to stockholders, managers normally seek to pursue strategies that maximize the returns that stockholders receive from holding shares in the company. As we noted in Chapter 1, stockholders receive a return on their investment in a company's stock in two ways: from dividend payments and from capital appreciation in the market value of a share (that is, by increases in stock market prices). The best way for managers to generate the funds for future dividend payments and to keep the stock price appreciating is for them to pursue strategies that maximize the company's long-run profitability (as measured by the return on invested capital or ROIC) and grow the profits of the company over time.[6]

As we saw in Chapter 3, ROIC is an excellent measure of the profitability of a company. It tells managers how efficiently they are using the capital resources of the company (including the risk capital provided by stockholders) to generate profits. A company that is generating a positive ROIC is covering all of its ongoing expenses and has money left over, which is then added to shareholders' equity, thereby increasing the value of a company and thus the value of a share of stock in the company. The value of each share will increase further if a company can grow its profits over time because then the profit that is attributable to every share (that is, the company's earning per share) will also grow. As we have seen in this book, to grow their profits, companies must be doing one or more of the following: (a) participating in a market that is growing; (b) taking market share from competitors; (c) consolidating the industry through horizontal integration; and (d) developing new markets through international expansion, vertical integration, or diversification.

While managers should strive for profit growth if they are trying to maximize shareholder value, the relationship between profitability and profit growth is a complex one because attaining future profit growth may require investments that reduce the current rate of profitability. The task of managers is to find the right balance between profitability and profit growth.[7] Too much emphasis on current profitability at the expense of future profitability and profit growth can make an enterprise less attractive to shareholders. Too much emphasis on profit growth can reduce the profitability of the enterprise and have the same effect. In an uncertain world where the future is unknowable, finding the right balance between profitability and profit growth is certainly as much art as it is science, but it is something that managers must try to do.

In addition to maximizing returns to stockholders, boosting a company's profitability and profit growth rate is also consistent with satisfying the claims of several other key stakeholder groups. When a company is profitable and its profits are growing, it can pay higher salaries to productive employees and can also afford benefits such as health insurance coverage, all of which help to satisfy employees. In addition, companies with a high level of profitability and profit growth have no problem meeting their debt commitments, which provides creditors, including bondholders, with a measure of security. More profitable companies are also better able to undertake philanthropic investments, which can help to satisfy some of the claims that local communities and the general public place on a company. Pursuing strategies that maximize the long-run profitability and profit growth of the company is therefore generally consistent with satisfying the claims of various stakeholder groups.

There is an important cause-and-effect relationship here. Pursuing strategies to maximize profitability and profit growth helps a company to better satisfy the demands that several stakeholder groups place on it, not the other way around. The company that overpays its employees in the current period, for example, may have very happy employees for a short while, but such action will raise the company's cost structure and limit its ability to attain a competitive advantage in the marketplace, thereby depressing its long-run profitability and hurting its ability to award future pay increases. As far as employees are concerned, the way many companies deal with this situation is to make future pay increases contingent on improvements in labor productivity. If labor productivity goes up, labor costs as a percentage of revenues will fall, profitability will rise, and the company can afford to pay its employees more and offer greater benefits.

Of course, not all stakeholder groups want the company to maximize its long-run profitability and profit growth. Suppliers are more comfortable about selling goods and services to profitable companies because they can be assured that the company will have the funds to pay for those products. Similarly, customers may be more willing to purchase from profitable companies because they can be assured that those companies will be around in the long run to provide after-sales services and support. But neither suppliers nor customers want the company to maximize its profitability at their expense. Rather, they would like to capture some of these profits from the company in the form of higher prices for their goods and services (in the case of suppliers) or lower prices for the products they purchase from the company (in the case of customers). Thus, the company is in a bargaining relationship with some of its stakeholders, which was a phenomenon we discussed in Chapter 2.

Despite the argument that maximizing long-run profitability and profit growth is the best way to satisfy the claims of several key stakeholder groups, it should be noted that a company must do so within the limits set by the law and in a manner consistent with societal expectations. The unfettered pursuit of profit can lead to behaviors that are outlawed by government regulations, are opposed by important public constituencies, or are simply unethical. Governments have enacted a wide range of regulations to govern business behavior, including antitrust laws, environmental laws, and laws pertaining to health and safety in the workplace. It is incumbent on managers to make sure that the company is in compliance with these laws when pursuing strategies.

Unfortunately, there is plenty of evidence that managers can be tempted to cross the line between the legal and illegal in their pursuit of greater profitability and profit growth. For example, in mid-2003, the Air Force stripped Boeing of $1 billion in contracts to launch satellites when it was discovered that Boeing had obtained thousand of pages of proprietary information from rival Lockheed Martin. Boeing had used that information to prepare its winning bid for the satellite contract. This was followed by the revelation that Boeing's CFO, Mike Sears, had offered a government official, Darleen Druyun, a lucrative job at Boeing while Druyun was still involved in evaluating whether Boeing should be awarded a $17 billion contract to build tankers for the Air Force. Boeing won the contract against strong competition from Airbus, and Druyun was hired by Boeing. It was clear that the job offer may have had an impact on the Air Force decision. Boeing fired the CFO and Druyun, and shortly afterward, Boeing CEO Phil Condit resigned in a tacit acknowledgment that he bore responsibility for the ethics violations that had occurred at Boeing during his tenure as leader.[8] In another case, the chief executive of Archer Daniels Midland, one of the world's largest producers of agricultural products, was sent to jail after an FBI investigation revealed that the company had systematically tried to fix the price for lysine by colluding with other manufacturers in the global marketplace. In another example of price fixing, the seventy-six-year-old chair of Sotheby's auction house was sentenced to a jail term and the former CEO to house arrest for fixing prices with rival auction house Christie's over a six-year period (see Strategy in Action 11.1).

Strategy in Action 11.1

Price Fixing at Sotheby's and Christie's

Sotheby's and Christie's are the two largest fine art auction houses in the world. In the mid-1990s, the two companies controlled 90% of the fine art auction market, which at the time was worth some $4 billion a year. Traditionally, auction houses make their profit by the commission they charge on auction sales. In good times, these commissions can range as high as 10% on some items, but in the early 1990s, the auction business was in a slump, with the supply of art for auction drying up. With Sotheby's and Christie's desperate for works of art, sellers played the two houses against each other, driving commissions down to 2% or even lower.

To try to control this situation, Sotheby's CEO, Dede Brooks, met with her counterpart at Christie's, Christopher Davidge, in a series of clandestine meetings held in car parking lots that began in 1993. Brooks claims that she was acting on behalf of her boss, Alfred Taubman, the chair and controlling shareholder of Sotheby's. According to Brooks, Taubman had agreed with the chair of Christie's, Anthony Tennant, to work together in the weak auction market and limit price competition. In their meetings, Brooks and Davidge agreed to a fixed and nonnegotiable commission structure. Based on a sliding scale, the commission structure would range from 10% on a $100,000 item to 2% on a $5 million item. In effect, Brooks and Davidge were agreeing to eliminate price competition between them, thereby guaranteeing both auction houses higher profits. The price-fixing agreement started in 1993 and continued unabated for six years until federal investigators uncovered the arrangement and brought charges against Sotheby's and Christie's.

With the deal out in the open, lawyers filed several class-action lawsuits on behalf of sellers who had been defrauded by Sotheby's and Christie's. Ultimately, some 100,000 sellers joined the class-action lawsuits, which the auction houses settled with a $512 million payment. The auction houses also pleaded guilty to price fixing and paid $45 million in fines to U.S. antitrust authorities. As for the key players, the chair of Christie's, as a British subject, was able to avoid prosecution in the United States (price fixing is not an offense for which someone can be extradited). Christie's CEO, Davidge, struck a deal with prosecutors and in return for amnesty handed over incriminating documents to the authorities. Brooks also cooperated with federal prosecutors and avoided jail (in April 2002, she was sentenced to three years' probation, six months' home detention, 1,000 hours of community service, and a $350,000 fine). Taubman, ultimately isolated by all his former co-conspirators, was sentenced to a year in jail and fined $7.5 million.[a]

Examples such as these beg the question: Why would managers engage in such risky behavior? A body of academic work collectively known as agency theory provides an explanation for why managers might engage in behavior that is either illegal or, at the very least, not in the interests of the company's shareholders.

Agency Theory

Agency theory looks at the problems that can arise in a business relationship when one person delegates decision-making authority to another. It offers a way of understanding why managers do not always act in the best interests of stakeholders and why they might sometimes behave unethically and perhaps also illegally.[9] Although agency theory was originally formulated to capture the relationship between management and stockholders, the basic principles have also been extended to cover the relationship with other key stakeholders, such as employees, as well as relationships between different layers of management within a corporation.[10] While the focus of attention in this section is on the relationship between senior management and stockholders, some of the same language can be applied to the relationship between other stakeholders and top managers and between top management and lower levels of management.

● **Principal-Agent Relationships**

The basic propositions of agency theory are relatively straightforward. First, an agency relationship arises whenever one party delegates decision-making authority or control over resources to another. The principal is the person delegating authority, and the agent is the person to whom authority is delegated. The relationship between stockholders and senior managers is the classic example of an agency relationship. Stockholders, who are the principals, provide the company with risk capital, but they delegate control over that capital to senior managers, and particularly the CEO, who as their agent is expected to use that capital in a manner that is consistent with the best interests of the stockholders. As we have seen, this means using that capital to maximize the company's long-run profitability and profit growth rate.

The agency relationship continues down within the company. For example, in the large, complex, multibusiness company, top managers cannot possibly make all important decisions, so they delegate some decision-making authority and control over capital resources to business unit (divisional) managers. Thus, just as senior managers such as the CEO are the agents of stockholders, business unit managers are the agents of the CEO (and in this context, the CEO is the principal). The CEO trusts business unit managers to use the resources over which they have control in the most effective manner so that they maximize the performance of their units, which helps the CEO to make sure that he or she maximizes the performance of the entire company, thereby discharging agency obligations to stockholders. More generally, whenever managers delegate authority to managers below them in the hierarchy and give them the right to control resources, an agency relation is established.

● **The Agency Problem**

While agency relationships often work well, problems may arise if agents and principals have different goals and if agents take actions that are not in the best interests of their principals. Agents may be able to do this because there is an **information asymmetry** between the principal and the agent: agents almost always have more information about the resources they are managing than the principal does. Unscrupulous agents can take advantage of any information asymmetry to mislead principals and maximize their own interests at the expense of principals.

In the case of stockholders, information asymmetry arises because they delegate decision-making authority to the CEO, their agent, who by virtue of his or her position inside the company is likely to know far more than stockholders do about the company's operations. Indeed, there may be certain information about the company that the CEO is unwilling to share with stockholders because it would also help competitors. In such a case, withholding some information from stockholders may be in their best interests. More generally, the CEO, who is involved in the day-to-day running of the company, is bound to have an information advantage over stockholders, just as the CEO's subordinates may well have an information advantage over the CEO with regard to the resources under their control.

The information asymmetry between principals and agents is not necessarily a bad thing, but it can make it difficult for principals to measure how well an agent is performing and thus hold the agent accountable for how well he or she is using the entrusted resources. There is a certain amount of performance ambiguity inherent in the relationship between a principal and agent: principals cannot know for sure if the agent is acting in his or her best interests. They cannot know for sure if the agent is using the resources to which he or she has been entrusted as effectively and efficiently as possible. To an extent, principals have to trust the agent to do the right thing.

Of course, this trust is not blind: principals do put mechanisms in place whose purpose is to monitor agents, evaluate their performance, and take corrective action if necessary. As we shall see shortly, the board of directors is one such mechanism because in part the board exists to monitor and evaluate senior managers on behalf of stockholders. Other mechanisms serve a similar purpose. In the United States, publicly owned companies must regularly file detailed financial statements with the Securities and Exchange Commission (SEC) that are in accordance with generally accepted accounting principles (GAAP). This requirement exists to give stockholders consistent and detailed information about how well management is using the capital with which it has been entrusted. Similarly, internal control systems within a company help the CEO make sure that subordinates are using the resources with which they have been entrusted as efficiently and effectively as possible.

Despite the existence of governance mechanisms and comprehensive measurement and control systems, a degree of information asymmetry will always remain between principals and agents, and there is always an element of trust involved in the relationship. Unfortunately, not all agents are worthy of this trust. A minority will deliberately mislead principals for personal gain, sometimes behaving unethically or breaking laws in the process. The interests of principals and agents are not always the same; they diverge, and some agents may take advantage of information asymmetries to maximize their own interests at the expense of principals and to engage in behaviors that the principals would never condone.

For example, some authors have argued that, like many other people, senior managers are motivated by desires for status, power, job security, and income.[11] By virtue of their position within the company, certain managers, such as the CEO, can use their authority and control over corporate funds to satisfy these desires at the cost of returns to stockholders. CEOs might use their position to invest corporate funds in various perks that enhance their status—executive jets, lavish offices, and expense-paid trips to exotic locations—rather than investing those funds in ways that increase stockholder returns. Economists have termed such behavior **on-the-job consumption**.[12] Dennis Kozlowski is an example of a CEO who appeared to engage in excessive on-the-job consumption (see the Opening Case).

Besides engaging in on-the-job consumption, CEOs, along with other senior managers, might satisfy their desires for greater income by using their influence or control over the board of directors to get the compensation committee of the board to grant pay increases. Critics of U.S. industry claim that extraordinary pay has now become an endemic problem and that senior managers are enriching themselves at the expense of stockholders and other employees. They point out that CEO pay has been increasing far more rapidly than the pay of average workers primarily because of very liberal stock option grants that enable a CEO to earn huge pay bonuses in a rising stock market, even if the company underperforms in the market and compared to competitors.[13] In 1950, when *Business Week* started its annual survey of CEO pay, the highest-paid executive was General Motors CEO Charles Wilson, whose $652,156 pay packet translated into $4.7 million in inflation-adjusted dollars in 2005. In contrast, the highest-paid executive in 2005, Lee Raymond of Exxon, earned $405 million[14] In 1980, the average CEO in *Business Week*'s survey of CEOs of the largest 500 American companies earned forty-two times what the average blue-collar worker earned. By 1990, this figure had increased to eighty-five times. Today, the average CEO in the survey earns more than three hundred and fifty times the pay of the average blue-collar worker.[15]

What rankles critics is the size of some CEO pay packages and their apparent lack of relationship to company performance.[16] For example, in May 2006, shareholders of Home Depot complained bitterly about the compensation package for CEO Bob Nardelli at the company's annual meeting. Nardelli, who was appointed in 2000, had received $124 million in compensation, despite mediocre financial performance at Home Depot and a 12% decline in the company's stock price since he joined. When unexercised stock options were included, his compensation exceeded $250 million.[17] Another target of complaints was Pfizer CEO, Hank McKinnell, who garnered an $83 million lump sum pension, and $16 million in compensation in 2005, despite a 40-plus percentage point decline in Pfizer's stock price since he took over as CEO.[18] Critics feel that the size of pay awards such as these is out of all proportion to the achievement of the CEOs. If so, this represents a clear example of the agency problem.

A further concern is that in trying to satisfy a desire for status, security, power, and income, a CEO might engage in empire building, or buying many new businesses in an attempt to increase the size of the company through diversification.[19] Although such growth may depress the company's long-run profitability and thus stockholder returns, it increases the size of the empire under the CEO's control and, by extension, the CEO's status, power, security, and income (there is a strong relationship between company size and CEO pay). Instead of trying to maximize stockholder returns by seeking the right balance between profitability and profit growth, some senior managers may trade long-run profitability for greater company growth by buying new businesses. Figure 11.2 graphs long-run profitability against the rate of growth in company revenues. A company that does not grow is probably missing some profitable opportunities.[20] A moderate revenue growth rate of G* allows a company to maximize long-run profitability, generating a return of Π^*. Thus, a growth rate of G1 in Figure 11.2 is not consistent with maximizing profitability ($\Pi 1 < \Pi^*$). By the same token, however, attaining growth in excess of G2 requires diversification into areas that the company knows little about. Consequently, it can

FIGURE 11.2

The Tradeoff
Between Profitability
and Revenue
Growth Rates

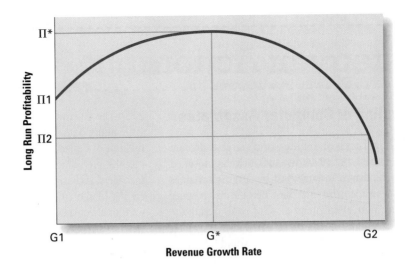

be achieved only by sacrificing profitability; that is, past G*, the investment required to finance further growth does not produce an adequate return and the company's profitability declines. Yet G2 may be the growth rate favored by an empire-building CEO because it will increase his or her power, status, and income. At this growth rate, profitability is equal only to $\Pi2$. Because $\Pi^* > \Pi2$, a company growing at this rate is clearly not maximizing its long-run profitability or the wealth of its stockholders.

For an example of this kind of excessive growth, consider again the case of Tyco International, profiled in the Opening Case. Tyco's growth through acquisitions under Dennis Kozlowski enabled him to build a corporate empire, which clearly satisfied Kozlowski's ego and financial needs, although it was financially shaky.

Just how serious agency problems can be was emphasized in the early 2000s when a series of scandals swept through the corporate world, many of which could be attributed to self-interest-seeking by senior executives and a failure of corporate governance mechanisms to hold the excess of those executives in check. Between 2001 and 2004, accounting scandals unfolded at a number of major corporations, including Enron, WorldCom, Tyco, Computer Associates, HealthSouth, Adelphia Communications, Dynegy, Royal Dutch Shell, and the major Italian food company, Parmalat. At Enron, some $27 billion in debt was hidden from shareholders, employees, and regulators in special partnerships that were kept off the balance sheet. At Parmalat, managers apparently "invented" some $8 to $12 billion in assets to shore up the company's balance sheet, assets that never existed. In the case of Royal Dutch Shell, senior managers knowingly inflated the value of the company's oil reserves by one-fifth, which amounted to 4 billion barrels of oil that never existed, making the company appear much more valuable than it actually was. At the other companies, earnings were systematically overstated, often by hundreds of millions of dollars, or even billions of dollars in the case of Tyco (see the Opening Case) and WorldCom, which understated its expenses by $3 billion in 2001. Strategy in Action 11.2 discusses accounting fraud at Computer Associates. In all of these cases, the prime motivation seems to have been an effort to present a more favorable view of corporate affairs to shareholders than was actually the case, thereby securing senior executives significantly higher pay packets.[21]

Strategy in Action

Self-Dealing at Computer Associates

Computer Associates is one of the world's largest software companies. During the 1990s, its stock price appreciated at a rapid rate, driven in large part by surging revenues and a commensurate rise in profits. Because its revenues were growing more rapidly than those of rivals during the late 1990s, investors assumed that the company was gaining market share and that high profitability would follow, so they bid up the price of the company's stock. The senior managers of Computer Associates were major beneficiaries of this process. Under a generous incentive program given to the company's three top managers—Charles Wang, then CEO and chair of the board; Sanjay Kumar, the chief operating officer; and Russell Artzt, the chief technology officer—by the board of directors, they would receive a special incentive stock award amounting to some 20 million shares if the stock price stayed above $53.13 for sixty days. In May 1998, Kumar announced that Computer Associates had "record" revenues and earnings for the quarter. The stock price surged over the $53.13 trigger and stayed there long enough for all three to receive the special incentive stock award, then valued at $1.1 billion.

In late July 1998, after all three had received the award, Kumar announced that the effect of Asian economic turmoil and the year 2000 bug "leads us to believe that our revenue and earnings growth will slow over the next few quarters." The stock price promptly fell from over $55.00 to under $40.00 a share. What followed was a series of class-action lawsuits, undertaken on behalf of stockholders, that claimed that management had misled stockholders to enrich themselves. As a result of the lawsuits, the three top managers were compelled to give back some of their gains, and the size of the award was reduced to 4.5 million shares. Wang stepped down as CEO, although he retained his position as chair of the board, and Kumar became the CEO.

This was not the end of matters, however, because Computer Associates had attracted the attention of both the Justice Department and the SEC, which launched a joint investigation into the company's accounting practices. By 2002, they were reportedly focusing on a little-noticed action the company had taken in May 2000 to reduce its revenues by 10%, or $1.76 billion, below what it had previously reported for the three fiscal years that ended March 2000. The downward revisions, detailed in the company's 10-K filings with the SEC, retroactively took hundreds of millions of dollars away from the top line in the fourteen months preceding the May 1998 stock award to senior managers, including some $513 million for the fiscal year ending March 1998. According to the company, earnings were unaffected by the revision because the lost revenue was offset by a commensurate downward revision of expenses. The downward revision reportedly came at the urging of auditor KPMG, which replaced Ernst & Young as the company's accountant in June 1999.

The implication that some observers were drawing was that Computer Associates deliberately overstated its revenues in the period prior to May 1998 to enrich the three top managers. The losers in this process were stockholders who purchased shares at the inflated price and longer-term shareholders who saw the value of their holdings diluted by the stock awarded to Wang, Kumar, and Artzt. In a statement issued after a report of the ongoing investigation was published in the *Wall Street Journal*, Computer Associates stated that it changed how it classified revenue and expenses at the advice of its auditors. "We continue to believe CA has acted appropriately," the company said. "This change in presentation had no impact on reported earnings, earnings per share, or cash flows."

By 2004, it was clear that Computer Associates had been acting anything but appropriately. According to the SEC investigation, between 1998 and 2000, the company adopted a policy of backdating contracts to boost revenues. For example, in January 2000, Computer Associates negotiated a $300 million contract with a customer but backdated the contract so that the revenues appeared in 1999. Although initially this may have been done to help secure the $1.1 billion special stock award, by 2000, the practice represented an increasingly desperate attempt to meet financial projections that the company was routinely missing. Under increasing pressure, Charles Wang stepped down in 2002 as chair, and in 2004, Kumar was forced to resign as CEO by the board of Computer Associates, which had belatedly come to recognize that the company's financial statements were fraudulent. In late 2004, in a deal with federal regulators, the company admitted to $2.2 billion in fraud. As part of the deal, Kumar was indicted by federal prosecutors on charges of obstruction of justice and securities fraud. In November 2006, Kumar was sentenced to twelve years in jail for his part in the fraud.[b]

It is important to remember that the agency problem is not confined to the relationship between senior managers and stockholders. It can also bedevil the relationship between the CEO and subordinates, and between them and their subordinates. Subordinates might use control over information to distort the true performance of their unit to enhance their pay, increase their job security, or make sure their unit gets more than its fair share of company resources.

Confronted with agency problems, the challenge for principals is to (1) shape the behavior of agents so that they act in accordance with the goals set by principals, (2) reduce the information asymmetry between agents and principals, and (3) develop mechanisms for removing agents who do not act in accordance with the goals of principals and mislead them. Principals try to deal with these challenges through a series of governance mechanisms.

Governance Mechanisms

Governance mechanisms are mechanisms that principals put in place to align incentives between principals and agents and to monitor and control agents. The purpose of governance mechanisms is to reduce the scope and frequency of the agency problem: to help ensure that agents act in a manner that is consistent with the best interests of their principals. In this section, the primary focus is on the governance mechanisms that align the interests of senior managers (as agents) with their principals, stockholders. It should not be forgotten, however, that governance mechanisms also exist to align the interests of business unit managers with those of their superiors, and so on down within the organization.

Here we look at four main types of governance mechanisms for aligning stockholder and management interests: the board of directors, stock-based compensation, financial statements, and the takeover constraint. The section closes with a discussion of governance mechanisms within a company to align the interest of senior and lower-level managers.

● The Board of Directors The board of directors is the centerpiece of the corporate governance system in the United States and the United Kingdom. Board members are directly elected by stockholders, and under corporate law, they represent the stockholders' interests in the company. Hence, the board can be held legally accountable for the company's actions. Its position at the apex of decision making within the company allows it to monitor corporate strategy decisions and ensure that they are consistent with stockholder interests. If the board's sense is that corporate strategies are not in the best interests of stockholders, it can apply sanctions, such as voting against management nominations to the board of directors or submitting its own nominees. In addition, the board has the legal authority to hire, fire, and compensate corporate employees, including, most importantly, the CEO.[22] The board is also responsible for making sure that audited financial statements of the company present a true picture of its financial situation. Thus, the board exists to reduce the information asymmetry between stockholders and managers and to monitor and control management actions on behalf of stockholders.

The typical board of directors is composed of a mix of inside and outside directors. **Inside directors** are senior employees of the company, such as the CEO. They are required on the board because they have valuable information about the company's activities. Without such information, the board cannot adequately perform its monitoring function. But because insiders are full-time employees of the company, their interests tend to be aligned with those of management. Hence, outside directors are needed to bring objectivity to the monitoring and evaluation processes. **Outside directors** are not full-time employees of the company. Many of them are full-time professional directors who hold positions on the boards of several companies. The need to maintain a reputation as competent outside directors gives them an incentive to perform their tasks as objectively and effectively as possible.[23]

There is little doubt that many boards perform their assigned functions admirably. For example, when the board of Sotheby's discovered that the company had been engaged in price fixing with Christie's, board members moved quickly to oust both the CEO and the chair of the company (see Strategy in Action 11.1). But not all boards perform as well as they should. The board of now-bankrupt energy company Enron signed off on that company's audited financial statements, which were later shown to be grossly misleading.

Critics of the existing governance system charge that inside directors often dominate the outsiders on the board. Insiders can use their position within the management hierarchy to exercise control over what kind of company-specific information the board receives. Consequently, they can present information in a way that puts them in a favorable light. In addition, because insiders have intimate knowledge of the company's operations and because superior knowledge and control over information are sources of power, they may be better positioned than outsiders to influence boardroom decision making. The board may become the captive of insiders and merely rubber-stamp management decisions instead of guarding stockholder interests.

Some observers contend that many boards are dominated by the company CEO, particularly when the CEO is also the chair of the board.[24] To support this view, they point out that both inside and outside directors are often the personal nominees of the CEO. The typical inside director is subordinate to the CEO in the company's hierarchy and therefore unlikely to criticize the boss. Because outside directors are frequently the CEO's nominees as well, they can hardly be expected to evaluate the CEO objectively. Thus, the loyalty of the board may be biased toward the CEO, not the stockholders. Moreover, a CEO who is also chair of the board may be able to control the agenda of board discussions to deflect any criticisms of his or her leadership.

In the aftermath of a wave of scandals that hit the corporate world in the early 2000s, there are clear signs that many corporate boards are moving away from merely rubber-stamping top management decisions and are beginning to play a much more active role in corporate governance. In part, they have been prompted by new legislation, such as the 2002 Sarbanes-Oxley Act in the United States, which tightened rules governing corporate reporting and corporate governance. Also important has been a growing trend on the part of the courts to hold directors liable for corporate misstatements. Powerful institutional investors such as pension funds have also been more aggressive in exerting their power, often pushing for more outside representation on the board of directors and for a separation between the roles of chair and CEO, with the chair role going to an outsider. Partly as a result, over 50% of big companies had outside directors in the chair's role by the mid-2000s, up from less than half that amount in 1990. Separating the role of chair and CEO limits the ability of corporate insiders, and particularly of the CEO, to exercise control over the board. Still, when all is said and done, it must be recognized that boards of directors do not work as well as they should in theory, and other mechanisms are need to align the interests of stockholders and managers.

● Stock-Based Compensation

According to agency theory, one of the best ways to reduce the scope of the agency problem is for principals to establish incentives for agents to behave in their best interests through pay-for-performance systems. In the case of stockholders and top managers, stockholders can encourage top managers to pursue strategies that maximize a company's long-run profitability and profit growth, and thus the gains from holding its stock, by linking the pay of those managers to the performance of the stock price.

The most common pay-for-performance system has been to give managers **stock options**: the right to buy the company's shares at a predetermined (strike) price at some point in the future, usually within ten years of the grant date. Typically, the strike price is the price that the stock was trading at when the option was originally granted. The idea behind stock options is to motivate managers to adopt strategies that increase the share price of the company because in doing so, they will also increase the value of their own stock options. Another stock-based pay-for-performance system is to grant managers stock if they attain predetermined performance targets.

Several academic studies suggest that stock-based compensation schemes for executives, such as stock options and stock grants, can align management and stockholder interests. For instance, one study found that managers were more likely to consider the effects of their acquisition decisions on stockholder returns if they themselves were significant shareholders.[25] According to another study, managers who were significant stockholders were less likely to pursue strategies that would maximize the size of the company rather than its profitability.[26] More generally, it is difficult to argue with the proposition that the chance to get rich from exercising stock options is the primary reason for the fourteen-hour days and six-day workweeks that many employees of fast-growing companies put in.

However, the practice of granting stock options has become increasingly controversial. Many top managers often earn huge bonuses from exercising stock options that were granted several years previously. While not denying that these options do motivate managers to improve company performance, critics claim that they are often too generous. A particular cause for concern is that stock options are often granted at such low strike prices that the CEO can hardly fail to make a significant amount of money by exercising them, even if the company underperforms in the stock market by a significant margin. Indeed, a serious example of the agency problem emerged in 2005 and 2006 when the Securities and Exchange Commission started to investigate a number of companies where stock options granted to senior executives had apparently been backdated to a time when the stock price was lower, enabling the executive to earn more money than if those options had simply been dated on the day that they were granted.[27] By late 2006, the SEC was investigating some 130 companies for possible fraud relating to stock option dating. Included in the list were some major corporations, including Apple Computer, Jabil Circuit, United Health, and Home Depot.[28]

Other critics of stock options, including the famous investor Warren Buffett, complain that huge stock option grants increase the outstanding number of shares in a company and therefore dilute the equity of stockholders; accordingly, they should be shown in company accounts as an expense against profits. Under accounting regulations that were in force until 2005, stock options, unlike wages and salaries, were not expensed. However, this has now changed and, as a result, many companies are starting to reduce their use of stock options. At Microsoft, for example, which had long given generous stock option grants to high-performing employees, stock options were replaced with stock grants in 2005.

Financial Statements and Auditors

Publicly traded companies in the United States are required to file quarterly and annual reports with the SEC that are prepared according to generally accepted accounting principals (GAAP). The purpose of this requirement is to give consistent, detailed, and accurate information about how efficiently and effectively the agents of stockholders—the company's managers—are running the company. To make sure that managers do not misrepresent this financial information, the SEC also requires that the accounts be audited by an independent and accredited accounting firm. Similar regulations exist in most other developed nations. If the system works as intended, stockholders can have a lot of faith that the information contained in financial statements accurately reflects the state of affairs at a company. Among other things, such information can enable a stockholder to calculate the profitability (ROIC) of a company in which he or she invests and to compare its ROIC against that of competitors.

Unfortunately, in the United States at least, this system has not always worked as intended. Although the vast majority of companies do file accurate information in their financial statements and although most auditors do a good job of reviewing that information, there is substantial evidence that a minority of companies have abused the system, aided in part by the compliance of auditors. This was clearly an issue at bankrupt energy trader Enron, where the CFO and others misrepresented the true financial state of the company to investors by creating off-balance-sheet partnerships that hid the true state of Enron's indebtedness from public view. Enron's auditor, Arthur Andersen, also apparently went along with this deception, in direct violation of its fiduciary duty. Arthur Anderson also had lucrative consulting contracts with Enron that it did not want to jeopardize by questioning the accuracy of the company's financial statements. The losers in this mutual deception were shareholders, who had to rely on inaccurate information to make their investment decisions.

There have been numerous examples in recent years of managers' manipulating financial statements to present a distorted picture of their company's finances to investors. The typical motive has been to inflate the earnings or revenues of a company, thereby generating investor enthusiasm and propelling the stock price higher, which gives managers an opportunity to cash in stock option grants for huge personal gain, obviously at the expense of stockholders who have been misled by the reports (see Strategy in Action 11.2 for an example).

The gaming of financial statements by companies such as Enron and Computer Associates raises serious questions about the accuracy of the information contained in audited financial statements. In response, in 2002, the United States passed the Sarbanes-Oxley Act into law; it represents the biggest overhaul of accounting rules and corporate governance procedures since the 1930s. Among other things, Sarbanes-Oxley set up a new oversight board for accounting firms, required CEOs and CFOs to endorse their company's financial statements, and barred companies from hiring the same accounting firm for auditing and consulting services.

The Takeover Constraint

Given the imperfections in corporate governance mechanisms, it is clear that the agency problem may still exist at some companies. However, stockholders still have some residual power because they can always sell their shares. If they start doing so in large numbers, the price of the company's shares will decline. If the share price falls far enough, the company might be worth less on the stock market than the book value of its assets. At this point, it may become an attractive acquisition target and run the risk of being purchased by another enterprise, against the wishes of the target company's management.

The risk of being acquired by another company is known as the **takeover constraint**. The takeover constraint limits the extent to which managers can pursue strategies and take actions that put their own interests above those of stockholders. If they ignore stockholder interests and the company is acquired, senior managers typically lose their independence and probably their jobs as well. So the threat of takeover can constrain management action and limit the worst excesses of the agency problem.

During the 1980s and early 1990s, the threat of takeover was often enforced by corporate raiders: individuals or corporations that buy up large blocks of shares in companies that they think are pursuing strategies inconsistent with maximizing stockholder wealth. Corporate raiders argue that if these underperforming companies pursued different strategies, they could create more wealth for stockholders. Raiders buy stock in a company either to take over the business and run it more efficiently or to precipitate a change in the top management, replacing the existing team with one more likely to maximize stockholder returns. Raiders are motivated not by altruism but by gain. If they succeed in their takeover bid, they can institute strategies that create value for stockholders, including themselves. Even if a takeover bid fails, raiders can still earn millions because their stockholdings will typically be bought out by the defending company for a hefty premium. Called **greenmail**, this source of gain stirred much controversy and debate about its benefits. While some claim that the threat posed by raiders has had a salutary effect on enterprise performance by pushing corporate management to run their companies better, others claim there is little evidence of this.[29]

Although the incidence of hostile takeover bids has fallen off significantly since the early 1990s, this should not be taken as evidence that the takeover constraint is no longer operating. Unique circumstances exist in the early 2000s that have made it more difficult to execute hostile takeovers. The boom years of the 1990s left many corporations with excessive debt: corporate America entered the new century with record levels of debt on its balance sheets. These debt levels limit the ability of companies to finance acquisitions, especially hostile acquisitions, which are often particularly expensive. In addition, the market valuations of many companies got so out of line with underlying fundamentals during the stock market bubble of the 1990s that even after a substantial fall in certain segments of the stock market, such as the technology sector, valuations are still high relative to historic norms, making the hostile acquisition of even poorly run and unprofitable companies expensive. However, takeovers tend to go in cycles, and it seems likely that once excesses are worked out of the stock market and worked off corporate balance sheets, the takeover constraint will begin to reassert itself. It should be remembered that the takeover constraint is the governance mechanism of last resort and is often invoked only when other governance mechanisms have failed.

Governance Mechanisms Inside a Company

So far, this section has focused on the governance mechanisms designed to reduce the agency problem that potentially exists between stockholders and managers. Agency relationships also exist within a company, and the agency problem can thus arise between levels of management. In this section, we explore how the agency problem can be reduced within a company by using two complementary governance mechanisms to align the incentives and behavior of employees with those of upper-level management: strategic control systems and incentive systems.

STRATEGIC CONTROL SYSTEMS Strategic control systems are the primary governance mechanisms established within a company to reduce the scope of the agency problem between levels of management. These systems are the formal target setting, measurement, and feedback systems that allow managers to evaluate whether a company is executing the strategies necessary to maximize its long-run profitability and, in particular, whether the company is achieving superior efficiency, quality, innovation, and customer responsiveness. They are discussed in more detail in subsequent chapters.

The purpose of strategic control systems is to (1) establish standards and targets against which performance can be measured, (2) create systems for measuring and monitoring performance on a regular basis, (3) compare actual performance against the established targets, and (4) evaluate results and take corrective action if necessary. In governance terms, the purpose of strategic control systems is to make sure that lower-level managers, as the agents of top managers, are acting in a way that is consistent with top managers' goals, which should be to maximize the wealth of stockholders, subject to legal and ethical constraints.

One increasingly influential model that guides managers through the process of creating the right kind of strategic control systems to enhance organizational performance is the balanced scorecard model.[30] According to the balanced scorecard model, managers have primarily used financial measures of performance, such as return on invested capital, to measure and evaluate organizational performance. Financial information is extremely important, but it is not enough by itself. If managers are to obtain a true picture of organizational performance, financial information must be supplemented with performance measures that indicate how well an organization has been achieving the four building blocks of competitive advantage: efficiency, quality, innovation, and responsiveness to customers. Financial results simply inform strategic managers about the results of decisions they have already taken; the other measures balance this picture of performance by informing managers about how accurately the organization has in place the building blocks that drive future performance.[31]

One version of the way the balanced scorecard operates is presented in Figure 11.3. Strategic managers develop a set of strategies, based on an organization's mission and goals, to build competitive advantage to achieve these goals. They then establish an organizational structure to use resources to obtain a competitive advantage.[32] To evaluate how well the strategy and structure are working, managers develop specific performance measures that assess how well the four building blocks of competitive advantage are being achieved:

- *Efficiency* can be measured by the level of production costs, the productivity of labor (such as the employee hours needed to make a product), the productivity of capital (such as revenues per dollar invested in property, plant, and equipment), and the cost of raw materials.

- *Quality* can be measured by the number of rejects, the number of defective products returned from customers, and the level of product reliability over time.

- *Innovation* can be measured by the number of new products introduced, the percentage of revenues generated from new products in a defined period, the time taken to develop the next generation of new products versus the competition, and the productivity of R&D (how much R&D spending is required to produce a successful product).

FIGURE 11.3

A Balanced Scorecard
Approach

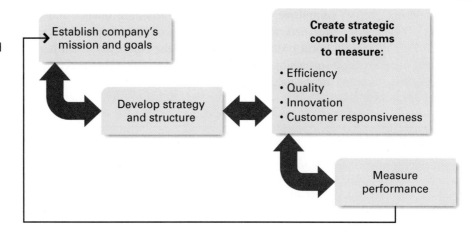

- *Responsiveness to customers* can be measured by the number of repeat customers, customer defection rates, level of on-time delivery to customers, and level of customer service.

As Kaplan and Norton, the developers of this approach, suggest, "Think of the balanced scorecard as the dials and indicators in an airplane cockpit. For the complex task of navigating and flying an airplane, pilots need detailed information about many aspects of the flight. They need information on fuel, air speed, altitude, learning, destination, and other indicators that summarize the current and predicted environment. Reliance on one instrument can be fatal. Similarly, the complexity of managing an organization today requires that managers be able to view performance in several areas simultaneously."[33]

The way in which managers' ability to build a competitive advantage translates into organizational performance is then measured using financial measures such as the return on invested capital, the return on sales, and the capital turnover ratio (see Chapter 3). Based on an evaluation of the complete set of measures in the balanced scorecard, strategic managers are in a good position to reevaluate the company's mission and goals and take corrective action to rectify problems, limit the agency problem, or exploit new opportunities by changing the organization's strategy and structure—which is the purpose of strategic control.

EMPLOYEE INCENTIVES Control systems alone may not be sufficient to align incentives among stockholders, senior management, and the rest of the organization. To help do this, positive incentive systems are often put into place to motivate employees to work toward goals that are central to maximizing long-run profitability. As already noted, employee stock ownership plans (ESOPs) are one form of positive incentive, as are stock option grants. In the 1990s, ESOPs and stock ownership grants were pushed down deep within many organizations. The logic behind such systems is straightforward: recognizing that the stock price, and therefore their own wealth, is dependent on the profitability of the company, employees will work toward maximizing profitability.

In addition to stock-based compensation systems, employee compensation can also be tied to goals that are linked to the attainment of superior efficiency, quality, innovation, and customer responsiveness. For example, the bonus pay of a manufacturing employee might depend on attaining quality and productivity targets, which, if reached, will lower the costs of the company, increase customer satisfaction, and boost profitability. Similarly, the bonus pay of a salesperson might be dependent on surpassing sales targets, and of an R&D employee, on the success of new products he or she helped develop.

Ethics and Strategy

The term **ethics** refers to accepted principles of right or wrong that govern the conduct of a person, the members of a profession, or the actions of an organization. **Business ethics** are the accepted principles of right or wrong governing the conduct of businesspeople. Ethical decisions are in accordance with those accepted principles, whereas unethical decisions violate accepted principles. This is not as straightforward as it sounds. Managers may be confronted with **ethical dilemmas**, which are situations where there is no agreement over the accepted principles of right and wrong, or where none of the available alternatives seems ethically acceptable.

In our society, many accepted principles of right and wrong are not only universally recognized but also codified into law. In the business arena, there are laws governing product liability (tort laws), contracts and breaches of contract (contract law), the protection of intellectual property (intellectual property law), competitive behavior (antitrust law), and the selling of securities (securities law). Not only is it unethical to break these laws, it is illegal.

In this book, we argue that the preeminent goal of managers in a business should be to pursue strategies that maximize the long-run profitability and profit growth of the enterprise, thereby boosting returns to stockholders. Strategies, of course, must be consistent with the laws that govern business behavior: managers must act legally while seeking to maximize the long-run profitability of the enterprise. As we have already seen in this chapter, there are examples of managers breaking the law. Moreover, managers may take advantage of ambiguities and gray areas in the law, of which there are many in our common law system, to pursue actions that are at best legally suspect and, in any event, clearly unethical. It is important to realize, however, that behaving ethically goes beyond staying within the bounds of the law. For example, see Strategy in Action 11.3, which discusses Nike's use of sweatshop labor in developing nations to make sneakers for consumers in the developed world. While Nike was not breaking any laws by using inexpensive labor (employees who worked long hours for poor pay in poor working conditions), neither were its subcontractors; however, many considered it unethical to use subcontractors who, by western standards, clearly exploited their work force. In this section, we take a closer look at the ethical issues that managers may confront when developing strategy and at the steps managers can take to ensure that strategic decisions are not only legal, but also ethical.

● **Ethical Issues in Strategy**

The ethical issues that strategic managers confront cover a wide range of topics, but most are due to a potential conflict between the goals of the enterprise, or the goals of individual managers, and the fundamental rights of important stakeholders, including stockholders, customers, employees, suppliers, competitors, communities, and the general public. Stakeholders have basic rights that should be respected, and it is unethical to violate those rights.

Strategy in Action

11.3

Nike and the Sweatshop Debate

In many ways, Nike is the quintessential global corporation. Established in 1972 by former University of Oregon track star Phil Knight, Nike is now one of the leading marketers of athletic shoes and apparel in the world. By 2004, the company had more than $12 billion in annual revenues, had a return on invested capital of 17.5%, and sold its products in some 140 countries. Nike does not do any manufacturing. Rather, it designs and markets its products and contracts for their manufacture from a global network of 600 factories owned by subcontractors scattered around the globe that together employ some 550,000 people. This huge corporation has made founder Phil Knight into one of the richest people in America. Nike's marketing phrase, "Just Do It!" has become as recognizable in popular culture as its "swoosh" logo or the faces of its celebrity sponsors, such as Tiger Woods.

For all of its successes, the company has been dogged by repeated and persistent accusations that its products are made in sweatshops where workers, many of them children, slave away in hazardous conditions for wages that are below subsistence levels. Nike's wealth, its detractors claim, has been built on the backs of the world's poor. Many see Nike as a symbol of the evils of globalization: a rich western corporation exploiting the world's poor to provide expensive shoes and apparel to the pampered consumers of the developed world. Nike's Niketown stores have become standard targets for antiglobalization protestors. Several nongovernmental organizations, such as San Francisco–based Global Exchange, a human rights organization dedicated to promoting environmental, political, and social justice around the world, have targeted Nike for repeated criticism and protests. News organizations such as CBS's *48 Hours*, hosted by Dan Rather, have run exposés on working conditions in foreign factories that supply Nike. And students on the campuses of several major U.S. universities with which Nike has lucrative sponsorship deals have protested against those deals, citing Nike's use of sweatshop labor.

Typical of the allegations were those detailed in the CBS news program *48 Hours* in 1996. The report painted a picture of young women at a Vietnamese subcontractor who worked six days a week, in poor working conditions with toxic materials, for only 20 cents an hour. The report also stated that a living wage in Vietnam was at least $3 a day, an income that could not be achieved without working substantial overtime. Nike and its subcontractors were not breaking any laws, but this report and others like it raised questions about the ethics of using sweatshop labor to make what were essentially fashion accessories. It may have been legal, it may have helped the company to increase its profitability, but was it ethical to use subcontractors who, by western standards, clearly exploited their work force? Nike's critics thought not, and the company found itself the focus of a wave of demonstrations and consumer boycotts.

Adding fuel to the fire, in November 1997, Global Exchange obtained and leaked a confidential report by Ernst & Young of an audit that Nike had commissioned of a Vietnam factory owned by a Nike subcontractor. The factory had 9,200 workers and made 400,000 pairs of shoes a month. The Ernst & Young report painted a dismal picture of thousands of young women, most under age twenty-five, laboring ten and a half hours a day, six days a week, in excessive heat and noise and foul air, for slightly more than $10 a week. The report also found that workers with skin or breathing problems had not been transferred to departments free of chemicals. More than half the workers who dealt with dangerous chemicals did not wear protective masks or gloves. The report stated that, in parts of the plant, workers were exposed to carcinogens that exceeded local legal standards by 177 times and that 77% of the employees suffered from respiratory problems.

These exposés surrounding Nike's use of subcontractors forced the company to reexamine its policies. Realizing that its subcontracting policies were perceived as unethical, Nike's management took a number of steps, including establishing a code of conduct for Nike subcontractors and setting up a scheme whereby all subcontractors would be monitored annually by independent auditors. Nike's code of conduct required that all employees at footwear factories be at least eighteen years old and that exposure to potentially toxic materials would not exceed the permissible exposure limits established by the U.S. Occupational Safety and Health Administration (OSHA) for workers in the United States. In short, Nike concluded that behaving ethically required going beyond the requirements of the law. It required the establishment and enforcement of rules that adhere to accepted moral principles of right and wrong.[c]

Stockholders have the right to timely and accurate information about their investment (in accounting statements), and it is unethical to violate that right. Customers have the right to be fully informed about the products and services they purchase, including the right to information about how those products might cause harm to them or others, and it is unethical to restrict their access to such information. Employees have the right to safe working conditions, fair compensation for the work they perform, and just treatment by managers. Suppliers have the right to expect contracts to be respected, and the firm should not take advantage of a power disparity between itself and a supplier to opportunistically rewrite a contract. Competitors have the right to expect that the firm will abide by the rules of competition and not violate the basic principles of antitrust laws. Communities and the general public, including their political representatives in government, have the right to expect that a firm will respect the basic expectations that society places on enterprises: for example, by not dumping toxic pollutants into the environment or not overcharging for work performed on government contracts.

Those who take the stakeholder view of business ethics often argue that it is in the enlightened self-interest of managers to behave in an ethical manner that recognizes and respects the fundamental rights of stakeholders because doing so will ensure the support of stakeholders and thus ultimately benefit the firm and its managers. Others go beyond this instrumental approach to ethics to argue that, in many cases, acting ethically is simply the right thing to do. They argue that businesses need to recognize their *noblesse oblige* and give something back to the society that made their success possible. *Noblesse oblige* is a French term that refers to honorable and benevolent behavior that is considered the responsibility of people of high (noble) birth. In a business setting, it is taken to mean benevolent behavior that is the moral responsibility of successful enterprises.

Unethical behavior often arises in a corporate setting when managers decide to put the attainment of their own personal goals, or the goals of the enterprise, above the fundamental rights of one or more stakeholder groups (in other words, unethical behavior may arise from agency problems). The most common examples of such behavior involve self-dealing, information manipulation, anticompetitive behavior, opportunistic exploitation of other players in the value chain in which the firm is embedded (including suppliers, complement providers, and distributors), the maintenance of substandard working conditions, environmental degradation, and corruption.

Self-dealing occurs when managers find a way to feather their own nests with corporate monies, and we have already discussed several examples in this chapter (such as Tyco and Computer Associates). **Information manipulation** occurs when managers use their control over corporate data to distort or hide information in order to enhance their own financial situation or the competitive position of the firm. As we have seen, many of the recent accounting scandals involved the deliberate manipulation of financial information. Information manipulation can also occur with regard to nonfinancial data. This occurred when managers at the tobacco companies suppressed internal research that linked smoking to health problems, violating the rights of consumers to accurate information about the dangers of smoking. When evidence of this came to light, lawyers brought class-action suits against the tobacco companies, claiming that they had intentionally caused harm to smokers: they had broken tort law by promoting a product that they knew did serious harm to consumers. In 1999, the tobacco companies settled a lawsuit brought by the states who sought to recover health care costs associated with tobacco-related illnesses; the total payout to the states was $260 billion.

Anticompetitive behavior covers a range of actions aimed at harming actual or potential competitors, most often by using monopoly power, and thereby enhancing the long-run prospects of the firm. For example, in the 1990s, the Justice Department claimed that Microsoft used its monopoly in operating systems to force PC makers to bundle Microsoft's Web browser, Internet Explorer, with Windows and to display Internet Explorer prominently on the computer desktop (the screen you see when you start a personal computer). Microsoft reportedly told PC makers that it would not supply them with Windows unless they did this. Since the PC makers had to have Windows to sell their machines, this was a powerful threat. The alleged goal of the action, which is an example of tie-in sales and is illegal under antitrust laws, was to drive a competing browser maker, Netscape, out of business. The courts ruled that Microsoft was indeed abusing its monopoly power in this case, and under a 2001 consent decree, the company agreed to stop the practice.

Putting the legal issues aside, action such as that allegedly undertaken by managers at Microsoft is unethical on at least three counts. First, it violates the rights of end-users by unfairly limiting their choice. Second, it violates the rights of downstream participants in the industry value chain, in this case PC makers, by forcing them to incorporate a particular product in their design, Third, it violates the rights of competitors to free and fair competition.

Opportunistic exploitation of other players in the value chain in which the firm is embedded is another example of unethical behavior. Exploitation of this kind typically occurs when the managers of a firm seek to unilaterally rewrite the terms of a contract with suppliers, buyers, or complement providers in a way that is more favorable to the firm, often using their power to force the revision through. For example, in the late 1990s, Boeing entered into a $2 billion contract with Titanium Metals Corporation to buy certain amounts of titanium annually for ten years. In 2000, after Titanium Metals had already spent $100 million to expand its production capacity to fulfill the contract, Boeing demanded that the contract be renegotiated, asking for lower prices and an end to minimum purchase agreements. As a major purchaser of titanium, managers at Boeing probably thought they had the power to push this contract revision through, and the investment by Titanium meant that they would be unlikely to walk away from the deal. Titanium promptly sued Boeing for breach of contract. The dispute was settled out of court, and under a revised agreement, Boeing agreed to pay monetary damages (reported to be in the $60 million range) to Titanium Metals and entered into an amended contract to purchase titanium.[34] Regardless of the legality of this action, it was arguably unethical because it violated the rights of suppliers to deal with buyers who negotiate with them in a fair and open way.

Substandard working conditions arise when managers underinvest in working conditions or pay employees below-market rates in order to reduce their costs of production. The most extreme examples of such behavior occur when a firm establishes operations in countries that lack the workplace regulations found in developed nations such as the United States. The example of Nike, which was given earlier in Strategy in Action 11.3, falls into this category. In another recent example, the Ohio Art Company ran into an ethical storm when newspaper reports alleged that it had moved production of its popular Etch A Sketch toy from Ohio to a supplier in Shenzhen Province, China, where employees, mostly teenagers, work long hours for 24 cents per hour, below the legal minimum wage of 33 cents an hour in Shenzhen Province. Moreover, production reportedly started at 7:30 A.M. and continued until 10 P.M., with breaks only for lunch and dinner. Saturdays and Sundays are treated as normal workdays. This translates into a workweek of seven twelve-hour days, or eighty-four hours a week, well above the standard forty-hour week set by authorities in Shenzhen. Such working conditions clearly violate the rights of employees in China, as specified by local regulations (which are poorly enforced). Is it ethical for the Ohio Art Company to use such a supplier? Many would say not.[35]

Environmental degradation occurs when the firm takes actions that directly or indirectly result in pollution or other forms of environmental harm. Environmental degradation can violate the rights of local communities and the general public for things such as clean air and water, land that is free from pollution by toxic chemicals, and properly managed forests (because forests absorb rainfall, improper deforestation results in land erosion and floods).

Finally, **corruption** can arise in a business context when managers pay bribes to gain access to lucrative business contracts. For example, it was alleged that Halliburton was part of a consortium that paid some $180 million in bribes to win a lucrative contract to build a natural gas plant in Nigeria.[36] Corruption is clearly unethical because it violates a bundle of rights, including the right of competitors to a level playing field when bidding for contracts and, when government officials are involved, the right of citizens to expect that government officials act in the best interests of the local community or nation and not in response to corrupt payments that feather their own nests.

● The Roots of Unethical Behavior

Why do some managers behave unethically? What motivates them to engage in actions that violate accepted principals of right and wrong, trample on the rights of one or more stakeholder groups, or simply break the law? While there is no simple answer to this question, a few generalizations can be made.[37] First, it is important to recognize that business ethics are not divorced from **personal ethics**, which are the generally accepted principles of right and wrong governing the conduct of individuals. As individuals, we are taught that it is wrong to lie and cheat and that it is right to behave with integrity and honor and to stand up for what we believe to be right and true. The personal ethical code that guides our behavior comes from a number of sources, including our parents, our schools, our religion, and the media. Our personal ethical code exerts a profound influence on the way we behave as businesspeople. An individual with a strong sense of personal ethics is less likely to behave in an unethical manner in a business setting; in particular, he or she is less likely to engage in self-dealing and more likely to behave with integrity.

Second, many studies of unethical behavior in a business setting have come to the conclusion that businesspeople sometimes do not realize that they are behaving unethically, primarily because they simply fail to ask the relevant question: Is this decision or action ethical? Instead, they apply a straightforward business calculus to what they perceive to be a business decision, forgetting that the decision may also have an important ethical dimension.[38] The fault here lies in processes that do not incorporate ethical considerations into business decision making. This may have been the case at Nike when managers originally made subcontracting decisions (see Strategy in Action 11.3). Those decisions were probably made on the basis of good economic logic. Subcontractors were probably chosen on the basis of business variables such as cost, delivery, and product quality, and key managers simply failed to ask, "How does this subcontractor treat its work force?" If they thought about the question at all, they probably reasoned that it was the subcontractor's concern, not theirs.

Unfortunately, the climate in some businesses does not encourage people to think through the ethical consequences of business decisions. This brings us to the third cause of unethical behavior in businesses: an organizational culture that de-emphasizes business ethics and considers all decisions to be purely economic ones. A related fourth cause of unethical behavior may be pressure from top management to meet performance goals that are unrealistic and can be attained only by cutting corners or acting in an unethical manner.

An organizational culture can "legitimize" behavior that society would judge as unethical, particularly when this is mixed with a focus on unrealistic performance goals, such as maximizing short-term economic performance regardless of the costs. In such circumstances, there is a greater-than-average probability that managers will violate their own personal ethics and engage in behavior that is unethical. By the same token, an organizational culture can do just the opposite and reinforce the need for ethical behavior. At Hewlett-Packard, for example, Bill Hewlett and David Packard, the company's founders, propagated a set of values known as "The HP Way." These values, which shape the way business is conducted both within and by the corporation, have an important ethical component. Among other things, they stress the need for confidence in and respect for people, open communication, and concern for the individual employee.

This brings us to a fifth root cause of unethical behavior: *unethical leadership*. Leaders help to establish the culture of an organization, and they set the example that others follow. Other employees in a business often take their cues from business leaders, and if those leaders do not behave in an ethical manner, employees might not either. It is not what leaders say that matters, but what they do. A good example is Ken Lay, the former CEO of the failed energy company Enron. While constantly referring to Enron's code of ethics in public statements, Lay simultaneously engaged in behavior that was ethically suspect. Among other things, he failed to discipline subordinates who had inflated earnings by engaging in corrupt energy trading schemes. Such behavior sent a very clear message to Enron's employees: unethical behavior would be tolerated if it boosted earnings.

● **Philosophical Approaches to Ethics**

In this section, we look at the philosophical underpinnings of business ethics because ultimately it is a philosophy that can provide managers with a moral compass that will help them to navigate their way through difficult ethical issues. We will start with the approach suggested by the Nobel Prize–winning economist Milton Friedman.

THE FRIEDMAN DOCTRINE In 1970, Milton Friedman wrote an article that has since become a classic case that business ethics scholars outline only to then tear down. Friedman's basic position is that the only social responsibility of business is to increase profits, as long as the company stays within the rules of law. He explicitly rejects the idea that businesses should undertake social expenditures beyond those mandated by the law and required for the efficient running of a business. For example, his arguments suggest that improving working conditions beyond the level required by the law and necessary to maximize employee productivity will reduce profits and is therefore not appropriate. His belief is that a firm should maximize its profits because that is the way to maximize the returns that accrue to the owners of the firm, its stockholders. If stockholders then wish to use the proceeds to make social investments, that is their right, according to Friedman, but managers of the firm should not make that decision for them.

Although Friedman is talking about social responsibility rather than business ethics per se, most business ethics scholars equate social responsibility with ethical behavior and thus believe Friedman is also arguing against business ethics. However, the assumption that Friedman is arguing against ethics is not quite true because Friedman does state the following:

> There is one and only one social responsibility of business—to use its resources and engage in activities designed to increase its profits so long as it stays within the rules of the game, which is to say that it engages in open and free competition without deception or fraud.

In other words, Friedman does state that businesses should behave in an ethical manner and not engage in deception and fraud.

Nevertheless, Friedman's arguments break down under closer examination. This is particularly true where the "rules of the game" are not well established, are ambiguous and open to different interpretations, or differ substantially from country to county. Consider again the case of sweatshop labor: using child labor may not be against the law in a developing nation, but it is still immoral to employ children because the practice conflicts with widely held views about what is the right thing to do. Similarly, there may be no rules against pollution in a developed nation, and spending money on pollution control may reduce the profit rate of the firm, but generalized notions of morality hold that it is still unethical to dump toxic pollutants into rivers or foul the air with gas releases. In addition to the local consequences of such pollution, which may have serious health effects for the surrounding population, there is also a global consequence because pollutants degrade those two global environments that we all have a stake in: the atmosphere and the oceans.

UTILITARIAN AND KANTIAN ETHICS Utilitarian and Kantian approaches to business ethics were developed in the eighteenth and nineteenth centuries. Utilitarian approaches to ethics hold that the moral worth of actions or practices is determined by their consequences.[39] An action is judged to be desirable if it leads to the best possible balance of good consequences over bad consequences. **Utilitarianism** is committed to the maximization of good and the minimization of harm. It recognizes that actions have multiple consequences, some of which are good in a social sense and some of which are harmful. As a philosophy for business ethics, it focuses attention on the need to carefully weigh all of the social benefits and costs of a business action and to pursue only those actions where the benefits outweigh the costs. The best decisions, from a utilitarian perspective, are those that produce the greatest good for the greatest number of people.

Many businesses have adopted specific tools, such as cost-benefit analysis and risk assessment, that are firmly rooted in a utilitarian philosophy. Managers often weigh the benefits and costs of a course of action before deciding whether to pursue it. An oil company considering drilling in the Alaskan wildlife preserve must weigh the economic benefits of increased oil production and the creation of jobs against the costs of environmental degradation in a fragile ecosystem.

For all of its appeal, however, the utilitarian philosophy has some serious drawbacks. One problem is measuring the benefits, costs, and risks of a course of action. In the case of an oil company considering drilling in Alaska, how does one measure the potential harm done to the fragile ecosystem of the region? In general, utilitarian philosophers recognize that benefits, costs, and risks often cannot be measured because of limited knowledge.

The second problem with utilitarianism is that the philosophy does not consider justice. The action that produces the greatest good for the greatest number of people may result in the unjustified treatment of a minority. Such action cannot be ethical precisely because it is unjust. For example, suppose that in the interests of keeping down health insurance costs, the government decides to screen people for the HIV virus and deny insurance coverage to those who are HIV positive. By reducing health costs, such action might produce significant benefits for a large number of people, but the action is unjust because it discriminates unfairly against a minority.

Kantian ethics are based on the philosophy of Immanuel Kant (1724–1804), who argued that people should be treated as ends and never purely as means to the ends of others. People are not instruments, like a machine. People have dignity and need to be respected as such. Employing people in sweatshops where they work long hours for low pay in poor work conditions is a violation of ethics according to Kantian philosophy because it treats people as mere cogs in a machine and not as conscious moral beings that have dignity. Although contemporary moral philosophers tend to view Kant's ethical philosophy as incomplete—for example, his system has no place for moral emotions or sentiments such as sympathy or caring—the notion that people should be respected and treated with dignity still resonates in the modern world.

RIGHTS THEORIES Developed in the twentieth century, rights theories recognize that human beings have fundamental rights and privileges. Rights establish a minimum level of morally acceptable behavior. One well-known definition of a fundamental right construes it as something that takes precedence over or "trumps" a collective good.[40] Thus, we might say that the right to free speech is a fundamental right that takes precedence over all but the most compelling collective goals; for example, it overrides the interest of the state in civil harmony or moral consensus. Moral theorists argue that fundamental human rights form the basis for the *moral compass* managers should navigate by when making decisions that have an ethical component. In a business setting, stakeholder theory provides a useful way for managers to frame any discussion of rights. As noted earlier, stakeholders have basic rights that should be respected, and it is unethical to violate those rights.

It is important to note that along with *rights* come *obligations*. Because we have the right to free speech, we are also obligated to make sure that we respect the free speech of others. Within the framework of a theory of rights, certain people or institutions are obligated to provide benefits or services that secure the rights of others. Such obligations also fall upon more than one class of moral agent (a moral agent is any person or institution that is capable of moral action, such as a government or corporation).

For example, in the late 1980s, to escape the high costs of toxic waste disposal in the West, several firms shipped their waste in bulk to African nations, where it was disposed of at a much lower cost. In 1987, five European ships unloaded toxic waste containing dangerous poisons in Nigeria. Workers wearing thongs and shorts unloaded the barrels for $2.50 a day and placed them in a dirt lot in a residential area. They were not told about the contents of the barrels. Who bears the obligation for protecting the safety rights of workers and residents in a case like this? According to rights theorists, the obligation rests not on the shoulders of one moral agent but on the shoulders of all moral agents whose actions might harm, or contribute to the harm of, the workers and residents. Thus, it was the obligation not just of the Nigerian government, but also of the multinational firms that shipped the toxic waste, to make sure that it did no harm to residents and workers. In this case, both the government and the multinationals obviously failed to recognize their basic obligation to protect the fundamental human rights of others.

JUSTICE THEORIES Justice theories focus on the attainment of a just distribution of economic goods and services. A **just distribution** is one that is considered fair and equitable. The most famous theory of justice is attributed to philosopher John Rawls.[41] Rawls argues that all economic goods and services should be distributed equally except when an unequal distribution would work to everyone's advantage.

According to Rawls, valid principles of justice are those with which all persons would agree if they could freely and impartially consider the situation. Impartiality is guaranteed by a conceptual device that Rawls calls the veil of ignorance. Under the veil of ignorance, everyone is imagined to be ignorant of all of his or her particular characteristics, for example, his or her race, sex, intelligence, nationality, family background, and special talents. Rawls then asks: What system would people design under a veil of ignorance? His answer is that, under these conditions, people would unanimously agree on two fundamental principles of justice.

The first principle is that each person should be permitted the maximum amount of basic liberty compatible with a similar liberty for others. Roughly speaking, Rawls takes these liberties to be political liberty (the right to vote), freedom of speech and assembly, liberty of conscience and freedom of thought, the freedom and right to hold personal property, and freedom from arbitrary arrest and seizure. The second principle is that once equal basic liberty is ensured, inequality in basic social goods—such as income, wealth, and opportunities—is to be allowed only if it benefits everyone. Rawls believes that inequalities can be just as long as the system that produces them is to the advantage of everyone. More precisely, he formulates what he calls the *difference principle*, which is that inequalities are justified if they benefit the position of the least advantaged person. So, for example, the wide variations in income and wealth that we see in the United States can be considered "just" if the market-based system that produces this unequal distribution also benefits the least advantaged members of society.

In the context of business ethics, Rawls's theory creates an interesting perspective. Managers can ask themselves whether the policies they adopt would be considered "just" under Rawls's veil of *ignorance*. Is it "just," for example, to pay foreign workers less than workers in the firm's home country? Rawls's second principle would suggest that it is, as long as the inequality benefits the least advantaged members of the global society. Alternatively, it is difficult to imagine that managers operating under a veil of ignorance would design a system where employees are paid subsistence wages to work long hours in sweatshop conditions and be exposed to toxic materials. Such working conditions are clearly unjust in Rawls's framework and therefore it is unethical to adopt them. Similarly, operating under a veil of ignorance, most people would probably design a system that imparts protection from environmental degradation, preserves a free and fair playing field for competition, and prohibits self-dealing. Thus, Rawls's veil of ignorance is a conceptual tool that helps define the moral compass managers can use to navigate through difficult ethical dilemmas.

● **Behaving Ethically**   What, then, is the best way for managers to ensure that ethical considerations are taken into account? In many cases, there is no easy answer to this question because many of the most vexing ethical problems involve very real dilemmas and suggest no obvious right course of action. Nevertheless, managers can and should do at least seven things to ensure that basic ethical principles are adhered to and that ethical issues are routinely considered when making business decisions. They can (1) favor hiring and promoting people with a well-grounded sense of personal ethics, (2) build an organizational culture that places a high value on ethical behavior, (3) make sure that leaders within the business not only articulate the rhetoric of ethical behavior but also act in a manner that is consistent with that rhetoric, (4) put decision-making processes in place that require people to consider the ethical dimension of business decisions, (5) hire ethics officers, (6) put strong governance processes in place, and (7) act with moral courage.

HIRING AND PROMOTION It seems obvious that businesses should strive to hire people who have a strong sense of personal ethics and would not engage in unethical or illegal behavior. Similarly, you would rightly expect a business not to promote people, and perhaps fire people, whose behavior does not match generally accepted ethical standards. But doing so is actually very difficult. How do you know that someone has a poor sense of personal ethics? In our society, if someone lacks personal ethics, he or she may hide this fact to retain people's trust.

Is there anything that businesses can do to make sure that they do not hire people who turn out to have poor personal ethics, particularly given that people have an incentive to hide this from public view (indeed, unethical people may well lie about their nature)? Businesses can give potential employees psychological tests to try to discern their ethical predisposition, and they can check with prior employees regarding someone's reputation, such as by asking for letters of reference and talking to people who have worked with the prospective employee. The latter approach is certainly not uncommon and does indeed influence the hiring process. As for promoting people who have displayed poor ethics, that should not occur in a company where the organizational culture values ethical behavior and where leaders act accordingly.

ORGANIZATIONAL CULTURE AND LEADERSHIP To foster ethical behavior, businesses need to build an organizational culture that places a high value on ethical behavior. Three actions are particularly important. First, businesses must explicitly articulate values that place a strong emphasis on ethical behavior. Many companies now do this by drafting a **code of ethics,** a formal statement of the ethical priorities a business adheres to. Others have incorporated ethical statements into documents that articulate the values or mission of the business. For example, the food and consumer products giant Unilever has a code of ethics that includes the following points: "We will not use any form of forced, compulsory or child labor" and "No employee may offer, give or receive any gift or payment which is, or may be construed as being, a bribe. Any demand for, or offer of, a bribe must be rejected immediately and reported to management."[42] Unilever's principles send a very clear message to managers and employees within the organization. As you can see from the Running Case, Dell also has a well established code of ethics.

Having articulated values in a code of ethics or some other document, it is important that leaders in the business give life and meaning to those words by repeatedly emphasizing their importance and then acting on them. This means using every relevant opportunity to stress the importance of business ethics and making sure that key business decisions not only make good economic sense but also are ethical. Many companies have gone a step further and hired independent firms to audit them and make sure that they are behaving in a manner consistent with their ethical code. Nike, for example, has hired independent auditors in recent years to make sure that its subcontractors are living up to Nike's code of conduct. Finally, building an organizational culture that places a high value on ethical behavior requires incentive and reward systems, including promotion systems, that reward people who engage in ethical behavior and sanction those who do not.

RUNNING CASE

Dell's Code of Ethics

Michael Dell has long put his name on a comprehensive code of ethics at Dell Computer. The code specifies with great precision what Dell requires of its employees. Dell states that the success of the company is built on "a foundation of personal and professional integrity" and that the company's employees must hold themselves to standards of ethical behavior that "go well beyond legal minimums."

At the center of the code of conduct is a set of values that Michael Dell characterizes as "the Soul of Dell." These values are as follows:

Trust—Our word is good. We keep our commitments to each other and to our stakeholders.

Integrity—We do the right thing without compromise. We avoid even the appearance of impropriety.

Honesty—What we say is true and forthcoming— not just technically correct. We are open and transparent in our communications with each other and about business performance.

Judgment—We think before we act and consider the consequences of our actions.

Respect—We treat people with dignity and value their contributions. We maintain fairness in all relationships.

Courage—We speak up for what is right. We report wrongdoing when we see it.

Responsibility—We accept the consequences of our actions. We admit our mistakes and quickly correct them. We do not retaliate against those who report violations of law or policy.

The code goes beyond these general statements, however, to detail what Dell employees cannot do. For example, with regard to bribes and gifts, the code states that "as a Dell employee you must never accept or give a bribe." The code also prohibits the receipt of any gifts with a nominal value of over $50 that may "compromise your judgment."

Dell has established a global ethics officer, a global ethics council, and regional ethics committees to make sure that the company's ethics policy is enforced. Employees can report ethics violations directly to the officer and associated committees, or via an anonymous ethics hotline.[d]

DECISION-MAKING PROCESSES In addition to establishing the right kind of ethical culture in an organization, businesspeople must be able to think through the ethical implications of decisions in a systematic way. To do this, they need a moral compass, and both rights theories and Rawls's theory of justice help to provide such a compass. Beyond these theories, some experts on ethics have proposed a straightforward practical guide, or ethical algorithm, to determine whether a decision is ethical. A decision is acceptable on ethical grounds if a businessperson can answer yes to each of these questions:

1. Does my decision fall within the accepted values or standards that typically apply in the organizational environment (as articulated in a code of ethics or some other corporate statement)?

2. Am I willing to see the decision communicated to all stakeholders affected by it— for example, by having it reported in newspapers or on television?

3. Would the people with whom I have a significant personal relationship, such as family members, friends, or even managers in other businesses, approve of the decision?

ETHICS OFFICERS To make sure that a business behaves in an ethi
ber of firms now have ethics officers. These individuals are res
sure that all employees are trained to be ethically aware, that e
enter the business decision-making process, and that the company's co
adhered to. Ethics officers may also be responsible for auditing decisions to .
sure that they are consistent with this code. In many businesses, ethics officers act as
an internal ombudsperson with responsibility for handling confidential inquiries
from employees, investigating complaints from employees or others, reporting findings, and making recommendations for change.

United Technologies, a large aerospace company with worldwide revenues of
over $28 billion, has had a formal code of ethics since 1990. There are now some 160
business practice officers (this is the company's name for ethics officers) within
United Technologies who are responsible for making sure that the code is adhered
to. United Technologies also established an ombudsperson program in 1986 that
lets employees inquire anonymously about ethics issues. The program has received
some 56,000 inquiries since 1986, and 8,000 cases have been handled by an ombudsperson.[43]

STRONG CORPORATE GOVERNANCE Strong corporate governance procedures are
needed to make sure that managers adhere to ethical norms, in particular, that senior
managers do not engage in self-dealing or information manipulation. The key to
strong corporate governance procedures is an independent board of directors that is
willing to hold top managers accountable for self-dealing and is able to question the
information provided to them by managers. If companies like Tyco, WorldCom, and
Enron had had a strong board of directors, it is unlikely that they would have been
racked by accounting scandals or that top managers would have been able to view the
funds of these corporations as their own personal treasuries.

There are five cornerstones of strong governance. The first is a board of directors
that is composed of a majority of outside directors who have no management responsibilities in the firm, are willing and able to hold top managers accountable,
and do not have business ties with important insiders. The outside directors
should be individuals of high integrity whose reputation is based on their ability to
act independently. The second cornerstone is a board where the positions of CEO
and chair are held by separate individuals and the chair is an outside director. When
the CEO is also chair of the board of directors, he or she can control the agenda,
thereby furthering his or her own personal agenda (which may include self-dealing)
or limiting criticism against current corporate policies. The third cornerstone is a
compensation committee formed by the board that is composed entirely of outside
directors. The compensation committee sets the level of pay for top managers, including stock option grants and the like. By making sure that the compensation
committee is independent of managers, one reduces the scope of self-dealing.
Fourth, the audit committee of the board, which reviews the financial statements of
the firm, should also be composed of outsiders, thereby encouraging vigorous independent questioning of the firm's financial statements. Finally, the board should use
outside auditors who are truly independent and do not have a conflict of interest.
This was not the case in many recent accounting scandals, where the outside auditors
were also consultants to the corporation and therefore less likely to ask hard questions of management for fear that doing so would jeopardize lucrative consulting
contracts.

MORAL COURAGE It is important to recognize that sometimes managers and others need significant moral courage. Moral courage enables managers to walk away from a decision that is profitable but unethical, gives employees the strength to say no to superiors who instruct them to behave unethically, and gives employees the integrity to go to the media and blow the whistle on persistent unethical behavior in a company. Moral courage does not come easily; there are well-known cases where individuals have lost their jobs because they blew the whistle on corporate behaviors.

Companies can strengthen the moral courage of employees by committing themselves to not take retribution on employees who exercise moral courage, say no to superiors, or otherwise complain about unethical actions. For example, Unilever's code of ethics includes the following:

> *Any breaches of the Code must be reported in accordance with the procedures specified by the Joint Secretaries. The Board of Unilever will not criticize management for any loss of business resulting from adherence to these principles and other mandatory policies and instructions. The Board of Unilever expects employees to bring to their attention, or to that of senior management, any breach or suspected breach of these principles. Provision has been made for employees to be able to report in confidence and no employee will suffer as a consequence of doing so.*

This statement gives permission to employees to exercise moral courage. Companies can also set up ethics hotlines that allow employees to register a complaint anonymously with a corporate ethics officer.

FINAL WORDS The steps discussed here can help to ensure that, when managers make business decisions, they are fully cognizant of the ethical implications and do not violate basic ethical prescripts. At the same time, not all ethical dilemmas have a clean and obvious solution—that is why they are dilemmas. At the end of the day, there are clearly things that a business should not do, and there are things that they should do, but there are also actions that present managers with true dilemmas. In these cases, a premium is placed on the ability of managers to make sense out of complex, messy situations and to make balanced decisions that are as just as possible.

Summary of Chapter

1. Stakeholders are individuals or groups that have an interest, claim, or stake in the company, in what it does, and in how well it performs.
2. Stakeholders are in an exchange relationship with the company. They supply the organization with important resources (or contributions) and in exchange expect their interests to be satisfied (by inducements).
3. A company cannot always satisfy the claims of all stakeholders. The goals of different groups may conflict. The company must identify the most important stakeholders and give highest priority to pursuing strategies that satisfy their needs.
4. A company's stockholders are its legal owners and the providers of risk capital, a major source of the capital resources that allow a company to operate its business. As such, they have a unique role among stakeholder groups.
5. Maximizing long-run profitability and profit growth is the route to maximizing returns to stockholders, and it is also consistent with satisfying the claims of several other key stakeholder groups.
6. When pursuing strategies that maximize profitability, a company has the obligation to do so within the limits set by the law and in a manner consistent with societal expectations.

7. An agency relationship is held to arise whenever one party delegates decision-making authority or control over resources to another.

8. The essence of the agency problem is that the interests of principals and agents are not always the same, and some agents may take advantage of information asymmetries to maximize their own interests at the expense of principals.

9. A number of governance mechanisms serve to limit the agency problem between stockholders and managers. These include the board of directors, stock-based compensation schemes, financial statements and auditors, and the threat of a takeover.

10. The term *ethics* refers to accepted principles of right or wrong that govern the conduct of a person, the members of a profession, or the actions of an organization. Business ethics are the accepted principles of right or wrong governing the conduct of businesspeople, and an ethical strategy is one that does not violate these accepted principles.

11. Unethical behavior is rooted in poor personal ethics; the inability to recognize that ethical issues are at stake, as when there are psychological and geographical distances between a foreign subsidiary and the home office; failure to incorporate ethical issues into strategic and operational decision making; a dysfunctional culture; and failure of leaders to act in an ethical manner.

12. Philosophies underlying business ethics include the Friedman doctrine, utilitarianism, Kantian ethics, rights theories, and justice theories such as that proposed by Rawls.

13. To make sure that ethical issues are considered in business decisions, managers should (a) favor hiring and promoting people with a well-grounded sense of personal ethics, (b) build an organizational culture that places a high value on ethical behavior, (c) make sure that leaders within the business not only articulate the rhetoric of ethical behavior but also act in a manner that is consistent with that rhetoric, (d) put decision-making processes in place that require people to consider the ethical dimension of business decisions, (e) hire ethics officers, (f) have strong corporate governance procedures, and (g) be morally courageous and encourage others to be the same.

Discussion Questions

1. How prevalent has the agency problem been in corporate America during the last decade? During the late 1990s, there was a boom in initial public offerings of Internet companies (dot.com companies). The boom was supported by sky-high valuations often assigned to Internet start-ups that had no revenues or earnings. The boom came to an abrupt end in 2001 when the NASDAQ stock market collapsed, losing almost 80% of its value. Who do you think benefited most from this boom: investors (stockholders) in those companies, managers, or investment bankers?

2. Why is maximizing return on invested capital consistent with maximizing returns to stockholders?

3. How might a company configure its strategy-making processes to reduce the probability that managers will pursue their own self-interest at the expense of stockholders?

4. In a public corporation, should the CEO of the company also be allowed to be the chair of the board (as allowed for by the current law)? What problems might this give rise to?

5. Under what conditions is it ethically defensible to outsource production to producers in the developing world who have much lower labor costs when such actions involve laying off long-term employees in the firm's home country?

6. Is it ethical for a firm faced with a shortage of labor to employ illegal immigrants as labor?

Practicing Strategic Management

SMALL-GROUP EXERCISE
Evaluating Stakeholder Claims

Break up into groups of three to five, appoint one group member to be a spokesperson who will communicate your findings to the class when called on by the instructor, and discuss the following:

1. Identify the key stakeholders of your educational institution. What claims do they place on the institution?
2. Strategically, how is the institution responding to those claims? Do you think the institution is pursuing the correct strategies in view of those claims? What might it do differently, if anything?
3. Prioritize the stakeholders in order of their importance for the survival and health of the institution. Do the claims of different stakeholder groups conflict with each other? If claims conflict, whose should be tackled first?

ARTICLE FILE 11

Find an example of a company that ran into trouble because it failed to take into account the rights of one of its stakeholder groups when making an important strategic decision.

STRATEGIC MANAGEMENT PROJECT
Module 11

This module deals with the relationships your company has with its major stakeholder groups. With the information you have at your disposal, perform the tasks and answer the questions that follow:

1. Identify the main stakeholder groups in your company. What claims do they place on the company? How is the company trying to satisfy those claims?
2. Evaluate the performance of the CEO of your company from the perspective of (a) stockholders, (b) employees, (c) customers, and (d) suppliers. What does this evaluation tell you about the ability of the CEO and the priorities that he or she is committed to?

3. Try to establish whether the governance mechanisms that operate in your company do a good job of aligning the interests of top managers with those of stockholders.
4. Pick a major strategic decision made by your company in recent years, and try to think through the ethical implications of that decision. In the light of your review, do you think that the company acted correctly?

ETHICS EXERCISE

Sam works for Juice International as an administrative assistant. Although unrelated, he and the CEO of the company share the same last name, and somehow a report destined for the CEO and marked both *confidential* and *urgent* had landed on Sam's desk. Normally Sam would have noticed the mistake and sent the envelope, unopened, straight to the CEO's office, but it had been a busy day and Sam hadn't noticed the error in the name until after he had opened the envelope and read the contents.

Inside the envelope were lab reports. One of Juice International's newest fruit drinks was being marketed to the public under false pretenses. The labels on the containers claimed that the juice was 100% natural, but the lab report suggested that the drink contained only the chemical equivalent of the juice. Should news of this get out, Juice International would lose customers rapidly. To make matters worse, the CEO to whom the information had been headed was known for doing anything to maintain the company's bottom line. Sam feared that by handing the lab reports over to the CEO, the information would never get out and customers would continue to purchase the juice, thinking it was 100% fruit juice. On the other hand, Sam didn't know whom he could trust with the information. He simply didn't know what to do.

1. Define the ethical issues at stake in this case.
2. What would you do if you were in Sam's position?
3. How do you think the company should handle this issue?

CLOSING CASE

Working Conditions At Wal-Mart

When Sam Walton founded Wal-Mart, now the world's largest retailer, one of his core values was that if you treated employees with respect, tied compensation to the performance of the enterprise, trusted the employees with important information and decisions, and provided ample opportunities for advancement, employees would repay the company with dedication and hard work. For years, the formula seemed to work. Employees were called associates to reflect their status within the company. Even the lowest hourly employee was eligible to participate in profit sharing schemes and could use profit sharing bonuses to purchase company stock at a discount compared to its market value. And the company made a virtue of promoting from within (two-thirds of managers at Wal-Mart started as hourly employees). At the same time, Walton and his successors always demanded loyalty and hard work from employees. Managers, for example, were expected to move to a new store on very short notice, and base pay for hourly workers was very low. Still, as long as the upside was there, little grumbling was heard from employees.

In the last ten years, however, the relationship between the company and its employees has been strained by a succession of law suits claiming that Wal-Mart pressures hourly employees to work without compensation, requires overtime without compensating them, systematically discriminates against women, and knowingly uses contractors who hire undocumented immigrant workers to clean its stores and pay them below minimum wage. For example, a class-action law suit in Washington State claims that Wal-Mart routinely (a) pressured hourly employees not to report all their time worked; (b) failed to keep true time records, sometimes shaving hours from employee logs; (c) failed to give employees full rest or meal breaks; (d) threatened to fire or demote employees who would not work off the clock; and (e) required workers to attend unpaid meetings and computer training. Moreover, the suit claims that Wal-Mart has a strict no overtime policy, punishing employees who work more than forty hours a week, but that the company also gives employees more work than can be completed in a forty-hour week. The Washington suit is one of more than thirty lawsuits that have been filed around the nation in recent years.

With regard to discrimination against women, complaints date back to 1996 when an assistant manager in a California store, Stephanie Odle, came across the W2 of a male assistant manager who worked in the same store. The W2 showed that he was paid $10,000 more than Odle. When she asked her boss to explain the disparity, she was told that her coworker had "a wife and kids to support." When Odle, who is a single mother, protested, she was asked to submit a personal household budget. She was then granted a $2,080 raise. Subsequently Odle was fired, she claims for speaking up. In 1998, she filed a discrimination suit against the company. Others began to file suits around the same time, and by 2004, the legal action had evolved into a class-action suit that covered 1.6 million current and former female employees at Wal-Mart. The suit claims that Wal-Mart did not pay female employees the same as their male counterparts, and did not provide them with equal opportunities for promotion.

In the case of both undocumented overtime and discrimination, Wal-Mart admits to no wrongdoing. The company does recognize that with some 1.6 million employees, some problems are bound to arise, but it claims that there is no systematic, companywide effort to get hourly employees to work without pay or to discriminate against women. Indeed, the company claims that this could not be the case because hiring and promotion decisions are made at the store level.

For their part, critics charge that, while the company may have no policies that promote undocumented overtime or discrimination, the hard-driving, cost-containment culture of the company had created an environment where abuses can thrive. Store managers, for example, are expected to meet challenging performance goals, and in an effort to do so, they may be tempted to pressure subordinates to work additional hours without pay. Similarly, company policy requiring managers to move to different stores on short notice unfairly discriminates against women, who lack the flexibility to uproot their families and move them to another state on short notice.

To compound matters, in the early 2000s, Wal-Mart was hit by charges from U.S. Immigration and Customs Enforcement, which claimed that the company hired hundreds of illegal immigrants at low pay to clean floors at sixty stores around the country. Wal-Mart paid an $11 million fine and promised that the practice would stop, but the successful suit was yet another embarrassment for the company.

While the pay and discrimination lawsuits are ongoing and may take years to resolve (there are some forty lawsuits in process at the time of this writing), Wal-Mart has taken steps to change its employment practices. For example, the company has created a director of diversity and a diversity compliance team, and restructured its pay scales to promote equal pay regardless of gender. In 2006, the company also created a panel that has independent outside experts on it, in addition to company insiders. The panel is charged with developing policies for extending work force diversity at Wal-Mart.[44]

Case Discussion Questions

1. What do you think are the root causes of the problems related to working conditions, discrimination, and the hiring of illegal immigrants at Wal-Mart?

2. How might these problems affect Wal-Mart in the future if they are not fixed?

3. Why do you think that problems related to poor working conditions started to emerge at Wal-Mart in the last ten years? Why didn't they arise when Wal-Mart was a smaller and faster growing enterprise?

4. Has the company done all that it can do deal with these problems? What else could it do?

Implementing Strategy in Companies That Compete in a Single Industry

OPENING CASE

Strategy Implementation at Dell Computer

Dell Computer was one of the fastest-growing companies of the 1990s, and its stock price increased at the rate of 100% a year, delighting its stockholders. Achieving this high return has been a constant challenge for Michael Dell, and one of his biggest battles has been to manage and change Dell's organizational structure, control systems, and culture as his company grows.

Dell was nineteen when, in 1984, he took $1,000 and spent it on the computer parts he assembled himself into PCs that he then sold over the phone. Increasing demand for his PCs meant that within a few weeks, he needed to hire people to help him, and soon he found himself supervising three employees who worked together around a six-foot table to assemble computers while two more employees took orders over the phone.[1]

By 1993, Dell employed 4,500 workers and was hiring over 100 new workers each week just to keep pace with the demand for the computers. When he found himself working eighteen-hour days managing the company, he realized that he could not lead the company single-handedly. The company's growth had to be managed, and he knew that he had to recruit and hire strategic managers who had experience in managing different functional areas, such as marketing, finance, and manufacturing. He recruited executives from IBM and Compaq and, with their help, created a functional structure, one in which employees are grouped by the common skills they have or tasks they perform, such as sales or manufacturing, to organize the value chain activities necessary to deliver his PCs to customers. As a part of this organizing process, Dell's structure also became taller, with more levels in the management hierarchy, to ensure that he and his managers had sufficient control over the different activities of his growing business. Dell delegated authority to control Dell's functional value chain activities to his managers, which gave him the time he needed to perform his entrepreneurial task of finding new opportunities for the company.

Dell's functional structure worked well and, under its new management team, the company's growth continued to soar. By 1993, the company had sales of over $2 billion, twice as much as in 1992. Moreover, Dell's new structure had given functional managers the control they needed to squeeze out costs, and Dell had become the lowest-cost PC maker. Analysts also reported that Dell had developed a lean organizational culture, meaning that employees had developed norms and values that emphasized the importance of working hard to help each other find innovative new ways of making products to keep costs low and increase their reliability. Indeed, with the fewest customer complaints, Dell rose to the top of the customer satisfaction rankings for PC makers; its employees became known for the excellent customer service they gave to PC buyers who were experiencing problems with setting up their computers.

However, Michael Dell realized that new and different kinds of problems were arising. Dell was now selling huge numbers of computers to different kinds of customers, for example, home, business, and educational customers and the different branches of government. Because customers now demanded computers with very different features or different amounts of computing power, the company's product line broadened rapidly. It started to become more difficult for employees to meet the needs of these different kinds of customers efficiently because each employee needed information about all product features or all of Dell's thousands of different sales offers across its product range.

In 1995, Dell moved to change his company to a market structure and created separate divisions, each geared to the needs of a different group of customers: a consumer division, a business division, and so on. In each division, teams of employees specialize in servicing the needs of one of these customer groups. This move to a more complex structure also allowed each division to develop a unique subculture that suited its tasks, and employees were able to obtain in-depth knowledge about the needs of their market that helped them to respond better to their customers' needs. So successful was this change in structure and culture that by 2000, Dell's revenues were over $35 billion and its profits were in excess of $3 billion, a staggering increase from 1984.[2]

Dell continued to alter his company's structure in the 1990s to respond to changing customer needs and to the company's increase in distinctive competencies. For example, Dell realized that he could leverage his company's strengths in materials management, manufacturing, and Internet sales over a wider range of computer hardware products. So he decided to begin assembling servers, workstations, and storage devices to compete with IBM, Sun, and Compaq. The increasing importance of the Internet led him to split the market divisions into thirty-five smaller subunits that focus on more specialized groups of customers, and they all conduct the majority of their business over the Internet. Today, for example, Dell can offer large and small companies and private buyers a complete range of computers, workstations, and storage devices that can be customized to their needs.

To help coordinate its growing activities, Dell is increasingly making use of its corporate intranet and using information technology (IT) to standardize activities across divisions and thus integrate across functions. Dell's hierarchy is shrinking as managers are increasingly delegating everyday decision making to employees who have access, through IT, to the facts they need to provide excellent customer service. To help reduce costs, Dell has also outsourced most of its customer service activities to India.[3] As a result of these moves, Dell's work force has become even more committed to sustaining its low-cost advantage, and its cost-conscious culture has become an important source of competitive advantage that is the envy of its competitors, and one that has been imitated by HP and Gateway.[4]

OVERVIEW

As the story of Dell suggests, organizational structure and culture can have a direct bearing on a company's profits. This chapter examines how managers can best implement their strategies through their organization's structure and culture to achieve a competitive advantage and superior performance. A well-thought-out business model becomes profitable only if it can be implemented successfully. In practice, however, implementing strategy through structure and culture is a difficult, challenging, and never-ending task. Managers cannot just create an organizing framework for a company's value chain activities and then assume it will keep working efficiently and effectively over time, just as they cannot select strategies and assume that these strategies will still work in the future when the competitive environment is changing.

We begin by discussing the main elements of organizational design and the way they work together to create an organizing framework that allows a company to implement its strategy. We also discuss how strategic managers can use structure, control, and culture to pursue functional-level strategies that create and build distinctive competencies. The analysis then moves to the industry level and the issues facing managers in a single industry. The next chapter takes up where this one leaves off and examines strategy implementation across industries and countries—that is, corporate and global strategy. By the end of this chapter and the next, you will understand why the fortunes of a company often rest on its managers' ability to design and manage its structure, control systems, and culture to best implement its business model.

Implementing Strategy Through Organizational Design

Strategy implementation involves the use of **organizational design,** the process of deciding how a company should create, use, and combine organizational structure, control systems, and culture to pursue a business model successfully. **Organizational structure** assigns employees to specific value creation tasks and roles, and specifies how these tasks and roles are to be linked together in a way that increases efficiency, quality, innovation, and responsiveness to customers—the distinctive competencies that build competitive advantage. The purpose of organizational structure is to coordinate and integrate the efforts of employees at all levels—corporate, business, and functional—and across a company's functions and business units so that they work together in the way that will allow it to achieve the specific set of strategies in its business model.

Organizational structure does not, by itself, provide the set of incentives through which people can be motivated to make it work. Hence, there is a need for control systems. The purpose of a **control system** is to provide managers with (1) a set of incentives to motivate employees to work toward increasing efficiency, quality, innovation, and responsiveness to customers and (2) specific feedback on how well an organization and its members are performing and building competitive advantage so that managers can constantly take action to strengthen a company's business model. Structure provides an organization with a skeleton; control gives it the muscles, sinews, nerves, and sensations that allow managers to regulate and govern its activities.

Organizational culture, the third element of organizational design, is the specific collection of values, norms, beliefs, and attitudes that are shared by people and groups in an organization and that control the way they interact with each other and with stakeholders outside the organization.[5] Organizational culture is a company's way of doing something: it describes the characteristic ways in which members of an organization get the job done, such as the way Nokia uses teams to speed innovation. As we discuss in detail below, top managers, because they can influence which kinds of beliefs and values develop in an organization, are an important determinant of how organizational members will work toward achieving organizational goals.[6]

Figure 12.1 sums up the discussion so far. Organizational structure, control, and culture are the means by which an organization motivates and coordinates its members to work toward achieving the building blocks of competitive advantage.

FIGURE 12.1

Implementing Strategy Through Organizational Design

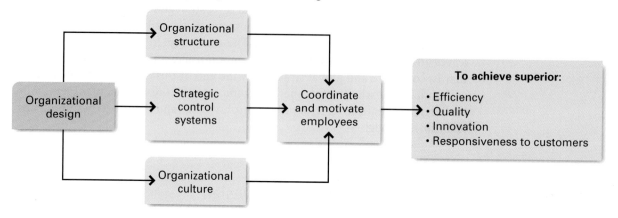

Top managers who wish to find out why it takes a long time for people to make decisions in a company, why there is a lack of cooperation between sales and manufacturing, or why product innovations are few and far between, need to understand how the design of a company's structure and control system and the values and norms in its culture affect employee motivation and behavior. *Organizational structure, control, and culture shape people's behaviors, values, and attitudes and determine how they will implement an organization's business model and strategies.*[7] On the basis of such an analysis, top managers can devise a plan to restructure or change their company's structure, control systems, and culture to improve coordination and motivation. Effective organizational design allows a company to obtain a competitive advantage and achieve above-average profitability.

Building Blocks of Organizational Structure

After formulating a company's business model and strategies, managers must make designing an organizational structure their next priority. The value creation activities of organizational members are meaningless unless some type of structure is used to assign people to tasks and connect the activities of different people and functions.[8] Managers must make three basic choices:

1. How best to group tasks into functions and to group functions into business units or divisions to create distinctive competencies and pursue a particular strategy

2. How to allocate authority and responsibility to these functions and divisions

3. How to increase the level of coordination or integration between functions and divisions as a structure evolves and becomes more complex

We first discuss basic issues and then revisit them when considering appropriate choices of structure at different levels of strategy.

● **Grouping Tasks, Functions, and Divisions**   Because an organization's tasks are, to a large degree, a function of its strategy, the dominant view is that companies choose a form of structure to match their organizational strategy. Perhaps the first person to address this issue formally was the

Harvard business historian Alfred D. Chandler.[9] After studying the organizational problems experienced in large U.S. corporations such as DuPont and GM as they grew in the early decades of the twentieth century, Chandler reached two conclusions: (1) that, in principle, organizational structure follows the range and variety of tasks that the organization chooses to pursue, and (2) that U.S. companies' structures change as their strategy changes in a predictable way over time.[10] In general, this means that most companies first group people and tasks into functions, and then functions into divisions.[11]

As we discussed earlier, a *function* is a collection of people who work together and perform the same types of tasks or hold similar positions in an organization.[12] For example, the salespeople in a car dealership belong to the sales function. Together, car sales, car repair, car parts, and accounting are the set of functions that allow a car dealership to sell and maintain cars.

As organizations grow and produce a wider range of products, the amount and complexity of the *handoffs*, that is, the work exchanges or transfers among people, functions, and subunits, increase. The communications and measurement problems and the managerial inefficiencies surrounding these transfers or handoffs are a major source of *bureaucratic costs*, which we discussed in Chapter 10. Recall that these are the costs associated with monitoring and managing the functional exchanges necessary to add value to a product as it flows along a company's value chain to the final customer.[13] We discuss why bureaucratic costs increase as companies pursue more complex strategies later in the chapter.

For now, it is important to note that managers group tasks into functions and then group functions into a business unit or division to reduce bureaucratic costs. For example, as Dell started to produce different kinds of products, it created separate divisions, each with its own marketing, sales, and accounting functions. A *division* is a way of grouping functions to allow an organization to better produce and transfer its goods and services to customers. In developing an organizational structure, managers must decide how to group an organization's activities by function and division in a way that achieves organizational goals effectively, which is what happened at Dell.[14]

Top managers can choose from among many kinds of structures to group their activities. The choice is made on the basis of the structure's ability to implement the company's business models and strategies successfully.

● Allocating Authority and Responsibility

As organizations grow and produce a wider range of goods and services, the size and number of their functions and divisions increase. The number of handoffs or transfers between employees also increases, and to economize on bureaucratic costs and effectively coordinate the activities of people, functions, and divisions, managers must develop a clear and unambiguous **hierarchy of authority,** or chain of command, that defines each manager's relative authority, from the CEO down through the middle managers and first-line managers, to the nonmanagerial employees who actually make goods or provide services.[15] Every manager, at every level of the hierarchy, supervises one or more subordinates. The term **span of control** refers to the number of subordinates who report directly to a manager. When managers know exactly what their authority and responsibility are, information distortion problems that promote managerial inefficiencies are kept to a minimum, and handoffs or transfers can be negotiated and monitored to economize on bureaucratic costs. For example, managers are less likely to risk invading another manager's turf and thus can avoid the costly fights and conflicts that inevitably result from such encroachments.

FIGURE 12.2

Tall and Flat
Structures

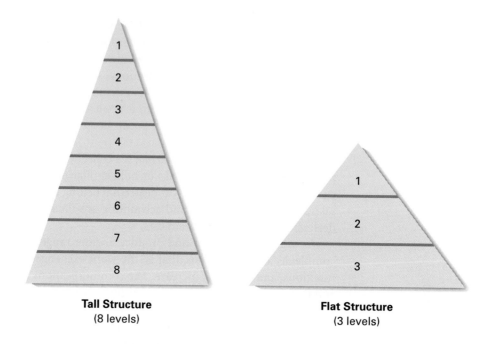

Tall Structure
(8 levels)

Flat Structure
(3 levels)

TALL AND FLAT ORGANIZATIONS Companies choose the number of hierarchical levels they need on the basis of their strategy and the functional tasks necessary to create distinctive competencies.[16] As an organization grows in size or complexity (measured by the number of its employees, functions, and divisions), its hierarchy of authority normally lengthens, making the organizational structure taller. A **tall structure** has many levels of authority relative to company size; a **flat structure** has fewer levels relative to company size (see Figure 12.2). As the hierarchy becomes taller, problems that make the organization's structure less flexible and slow managers' response to changes in the competitive environment may result. It is vital that managers understand how these problems arise so they know how to change a company's structure to respond to them.

First, communication problems may arise. When an organization has many levels in the hierarchy, it can take a long time for the decisions and orders of top managers to reach managers further down in the hierarchy, and it can take a long time for top managers to learn how well their decisions worked out. Feeling out of touch, top managers may want to verify that lower-level managers are following orders and may require written confirmation from them. Lower-level managers, who know they will be held strictly accountable for their actions, start devoting more time to the process of making decisions in order to improve their chances of being right. They might even try to avoid responsibility by making top managers decide what actions to take.

A second communication problem that can result is the distortion of commands and orders as they are transmitted up and down the hierarchy, which causes managers at different levels to interpret what is happening differently. Accidental distortion of orders and messages occurs when different managers interpret messages from their own narrow functional perspectives. Intentional distortion can occur because managers lower in the hierarchy decide to interpret information to increase their own personal advantage.

A third problem with tall hierarchies is that they usually indicate that an organization is employing too many managers, and managers are expensive. Managerial salaries, benefits, offices, and secretaries are a huge expense for organizations. Large companies such as IBM, GM, and Dell pay their managers billions of dollars a year. In the 2000s, hundreds of thousands of middle managers were laid off as dot-coms collapsed and high-tech companies like HP and Lucent attempted to reduce costs by restructuring and downsizing their work forces.

THE MINIMUM CHAIN OF COMMAND To ward off the problems that result when an organization becomes too tall and employs too many managers, top managers need to ascertain whether they are employing the right number of top, middle, and first-line managers and see whether they can redesign their hierarchies to reduce the number of managers. Top managers might well follow a basic organizing principle: the **principle of the minimum chain of command,** which states that a company should choose the hierarchy with the *fewest* levels of authority necessary to use organizational resources efficiently and effectively.

Effective managers constantly scrutinize their hierarchies to see whether the number of levels can be reduced—for example, by eliminating one level and giving the responsibilities of managers at that level to managers above and empowering employees below. This practice has become increasingly common as companies battle with low-cost overseas competitors and search for ways to reduce costs. One manager who is constantly trying to empower employees and keep the hierarchy flat is Colleen C. Barrett, the number 2 executive of Southwest Airlines.[17] Barrett, the highest-ranking woman in the airline industry, is well known for continually reaffirming Southwest's message that employees should feel free to go above and beyond their prescribed roles to provide better customer service. Her central message is that Southwest values and trusts its employees, who are empowered to take responsibility. Southwest employees are encouraged not to look to their superiors for guidance but rather to take responsibility to find ways to do the job better themselves. As a result, Southwest keeps the number of its middle managers to a minimum.

When companies become too tall and the chain of command too long, strategic managers tend to lose control over the hierarchy, which means that they lose control over their strategies. Disaster often follows because a tall organizational structure decreases, rather than promotes, motivation and coordination between employees and functions, and bureaucratic costs escalate as a result. One important way to overcome such problems, at least partially, and to lessen bureaucratic costs is to decentralize authority—that is, vest authority in the hierarchy's lower levels as well as at the top.

CENTRALIZATION OR DECENTRALIZATION? Authority is centralized when managers at the upper levels of a company's hierarchy retain the authority to make the most important decisions. When authority is decentralized, it is delegated to divisions, functions, and employees at lower levels in the company. By delegating authority in this fashion, managers can economize on bureaucratic costs and avoid communication and coordination problems because information does not have to be constantly sent to the top of the organization for decisions to be made. There are three advantages to decentralization.

First, when top managers delegate operational decision-making responsibility to middle and first-level managers, they reduce information overload and so are able to spend more time on positioning the company competitively and strengthening its business model. Second, when managers in the bottom layers of the company become responsible for implementing strategies to suit local conditions, their motivation and

Strategy in Action   12.1

Union Pacific Decentralizes to Increase Customer Responsiveness

Union Pacific, one of the biggest rail freight carriers in the United States, was experiencing a crisis in the late 1990s. The U.S. economic boom was causing a record increase in the amount of freight that the railroad had to transport, but at the same time, the railroad was experiencing record delays in moving the freight. Union Pacific's customers were irate and complaining bitterly about the problem, and the delays were costing the company millions of dollars in penalty payments—$150 million annually.

The problem stemmed from Union Pacific's very centralized management approach, devised in its attempt to cut costs. All scheduling and route planning were handled centrally at its headquarters in an attempt to promote operating efficiency. The job of regional managers was largely to ensure the smooth flow of freight through their regions. Now, recognizing that efficiency had to be balanced by the need to be responsive to customers, Union Pacific's CEO, Dick Davidson, announced a sweeping reorganization to the company's customers. Henceforth, regional managers were to be given the authority to make operational decisions at the level at which they were most important: field operations. Regional managers could now alter scheduling and routing to accommodate customer requests even if this raised costs. The goal of the organization was to "return to excellent performance by simplifying our processes and becoming easier to deal with." In making this decision, the company was following the lead of its competitors, most of which had already moved to decentralize their operations. Union Pacific has continued its decentralization approach in the 2000s. In its recent announcement that it was adding a new region, it stated that "the new four-region system will continue the effort to decentralize decision-making into the field, while fostering improved customer responsiveness, operational excellence, and personal accountability."[a]

accountability increase. The result is that decentralization promotes flexibility and reduces bureaucratic costs because lower-level managers are authorized to make on-the-spot decisions; handoffs are not needed. The third advantage is that when lower-level employees are given the right to make important decisions, fewer managers are needed to oversee their activities and tell them what to do—a company can flatten its hierarchy. Strategy in Action 12.1 shows how Union Pacific experienced some of these advantages after it decentralized its operations.

If decentralization is so effective, why don't all companies decentralize decision making and avoid the problems of tall hierarchies? The answer is that centralization has its advantages too. Centralized decision making allows for easier coordination of the organizational activities needed to pursue a company's strategy. If managers at all levels can make their own decisions, overall planning becomes extremely difficult, and the company may lose control of its decision making.

Centralization also means that decisions fit broad organization objectives. When its branch operations were getting out of hand, for example, Merrill Lynch increased centralization by installing more information systems to give corporate managers greater control over branch activities. Similarly, HP centralized research and development (R&D) responsibility at the corporate level to provide a more directed corporate strategy. Furthermore, in times of crisis, centralization of authority permits strong leadership because authority is focused on one person or group. This focus allows for speedy decision making and a concerted response by the whole organization. How to choose the right level of centralization for a particular strategy is discussed later.

● Integration and Integrating Mechanisms

Much coordination takes place among people, functions, and divisions through the hierarchy of authority. Often, however, as a structure becomes complex, this is not enough, and top managers need to use various **integrating mechanisms** to increase communication and coordination among functions and divisions. The greater the complexity of an organization's structure, the greater is the need for coordination among people, functions, and divisions to make the organizational structure work efficiently.[18] We discuss three kinds of integrating mechanisms that illustrate the kinds of issues involved.[19] Once again, these mechanisms are employed to economize on the information distortion problems that commonly arise when managing the handoffs or transfers among the ideas and activities of different people, functions, and divisions.

DIRECT CONTACT Direct contact among managers creates a context within which managers from different functions or divisions can work together to solve mutual problems. However, several problems are associated with establishing this contact. Managers from different functions may have different views about what must be done to achieve organizational goals. But if the managers have equal authority (as functional managers typically do), the only manager who can tell them what to do is the CEO. If functional managers cannot reach agreement, no mechanism exists to resolve the conflict apart from the authority of the boss. In fact, one sign of a poorly performing organizational structure is the number of problems sent up the hierarchy for top managers to solve. The need to solve everyday conflicts and solve handoff or transfer problems raises bureaucratic costs. To reduce such conflicts and solve transfer problems, top managers use more complex integrating mechanisms to increase coordination among functions and divisions.

LIAISON ROLES Managers can increase coordination among functions and divisions by establishing liaison roles. When the volume of contacts between two functions increases, one way to improve coordination is to give one manager in each function or division the responsibility for coordinating with the other. These managers may meet daily, weekly, monthly, or as needed to solve handoff issues and transfer problems. The responsibility for coordination is part of the liaison's full-time job, and usually an informal relationship forms between the people involved, greatly easing strains between functions. Furthermore, liaison roles provide a way of transmitting information across an organization, which is important in large organizations where employees may know no one outside their immediate function or division.

TEAMS When more than two functions or divisions share many common problems, direct contact and liaison roles may not provide sufficient coordination. In these cases, a more complex integrating mechanism, the **team,** may be appropriate. One manager from each relevant function or division is assigned to a team that meets to solve a specific mutual problem; team members are responsible for reporting back to their subunits on the issues addressed and the solutions recommended. Teams are increasingly being used at all organizational levels.

Strategic Control Systems

Strategic managers choose the organizational strategies and structure they hope will allow the organization to use its resources most effectively to pursue its business model and create value and profit. Then they create **strategic control systems,** tools that allow them to monitor and evaluate whether, in fact, their strategy and structure are working as intended, how they could be improved, and how they should be changed if they are not working.

Strategic control is not just about monitoring how well an organization and its members are performing currently or about how well the firm is using its existing resources. It is also about how to create the incentives to keep employees motivated and focused on the important problems that may confront an organization in the future so that they work together to find solutions that can help an organization perform better over time.[20] To understand the vital importance of strategic control, consider how it helps managers to obtain superior efficiency, quality, innovation, and responsiveness to customers, the four basic building blocks of competitive advantage:

- *Control and efficiency.* To determine how *efficiently* they are using organizational resources, managers must be able to measure accurately how many units of inputs (raw materials, human resources, and so on) are being used to produce a unit of output. They must also be able to measure the number of units of outputs (goods and services) they produce. A control system contains the measures or yardsticks that allow managers to assess how efficiently they are producing goods and services. Moreover, if managers experiment to find a more efficient way to produce goods and services, these measures tell managers how successful they have been. Without a control system in place, managers have no idea how well their organizations are performing and how they can make it perform better, something that is becoming increasingly important in today's highly competitive environment.[21]

- *Control and quality.* Today, competition often revolves around increasing the *quality* of goods and services. In the car industry, for example, within each price range, cars compete against one another in terms of their features, design, and reliability. So whether a customer buys a Ford 500, a GM Impala, a Chrysler 300, a Toyota Camry, or a Honda Accord depends significantly on the quality of each company's product. Strategic control is important in determining the quality of goods and services because it gives managers feedback on product quality. If managers consistently measure the number of customers' complaints and the number of new cars returned for repairs, they have a good indication of how much quality they have built into their product.

- *Control and innovation.* Strategic control can help to raise the level of *innovation* in an organization. Successful innovation takes place when managers create an organizational setting in which employees feel empowered to be creative and in which authority is decentralized to employees so that they feel free to experiment and take risks, such as at Nokia. Deciding on the appropriate control systems to encourage risk taking is an important management challenge and, as discussed later in the chapter, an organization's culture becomes important in this regard.

- *Control and responsiveness to customers.* Finally, strategic managers can help make their organizations more *responsive to customers* if they develop a control system that allows them to evaluate how well employees with customer contact are performing their jobs. Monitoring employees' behavior can help managers find ways to help increase employees' performance level, perhaps by revealing areas in which skills training can help employees or by finding new procedures that allow employees to perform their jobs better. When employees know their behaviors are being monitored, they may have more incentive to be helpful and consistent in the way they act toward customers.

FIGURE 12.3

Steps in Designing an Effective Strategic Control System

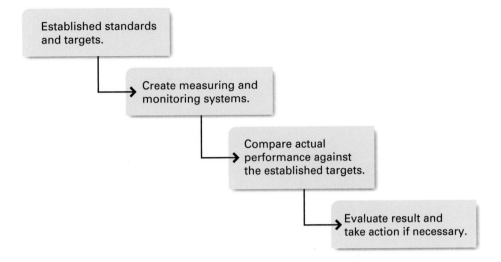

Established standards and targets.

Create measuring and monitoring systems.

Compare actual performance against the established targets.

Evaluate result and take action if necessary.

Strategic control systems are the formal target-setting, measurement, and feedback systems that allow strategic managers to evaluate whether a company is achieving superior efficiency, quality, innovation, and customer responsiveness and implementing its strategy successfully. An effective control system should have three characteristics. It should be *flexible* enough to allow managers to respond as necessary to unexpected events; it should provide *accurate information*, thus giving a true picture of organizational performance; and it should supply managers with the information in a *timely manner* because making decisions on the basis of outdated information is a recipe for failure.[22] As Figure 12.3 shows, designing an effective strategic control system requires four steps: establishing standards and targets, creating measuring and monitoring systems, comparing performance against targets, and evaluating the result.

● **Levels of Strategic Control**

Strategic control systems are developed to measure performance at four levels in a company: corporate, divisional, functional, and individual. Managers at all levels must develop the most appropriate set of measures to evaluate corporate-, business-, and functional-level performance. As the balanced scorecard approach discussed in Chapter 11 suggests, these measures should be tied as closely as possibly to the goals of developing distinctive competencies in efficiency, quality, innovativeness, and responsiveness to customers. Care must be taken, however, to ensure that the standards used at each level do not cause problems at the other levels—for example, that a division's attempts to improve its performance does not conflict with corporate performance. Furthermore, controls at each level should provide the basis on which managers at lower levels design their control systems. Figure 12.4 illustrates these links.

● **Types of Strategic Control Systems**

In Chapter 11, the balanced scorecard approach was discussed as a way to ensure that managers complement the use of ROIC with other kinds of strategic controls to ensure they are pursuing strategies that maximize long-run profitability. Here, we consider three more types of control systems: *personal control, output control,* and *behavior control.*

PERSONAL CONTROL **Personal control** is the desire to shape and influence the behavior of a person in a *face-to-face interaction* in the pursuit of a company's goals. The

FIGURE 12.4

Levels of Organizational Control

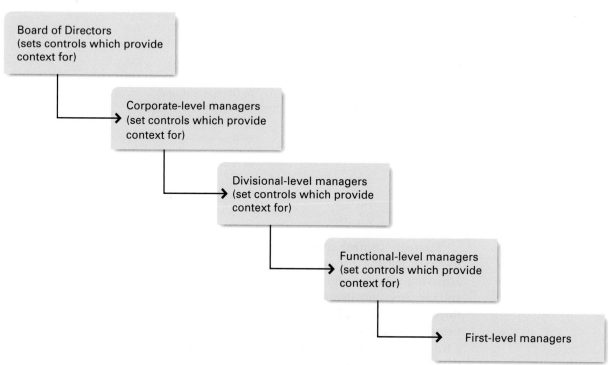

most obvious kind of personal control is direct supervision from a manager further up in the hierarchy. The personal approach is useful because managers can question and probe subordinates about problems or new issues they are facing to get a better understanding of the situation, as well as to ensure that subordinates are performing their work effectively and not hiding any information that could cause problems down the line. Personal control also can come from a group of peers, such as when people work in teams. Once again, personal control at the group level means that there is more possibility for learning to occur and competencies to develop, as well as greater opportunities to prevent free-riding or shirking.

OUTPUT CONTROL **Output control** is a system in which strategic managers estimate or forecast appropriate performance goals for each division, department, and employee and then measure actual performance relative to these goals. Often a company's reward system is linked to performance on these goals, so output control also provides an incentive structure for motivating employees at all levels in the organization. Goals keep managers informed about how well their strategies are creating a competitive advantage and building the distinctive competencies that lead to future success. Goals exist at all levels in an organization.

Divisional goals state corporate managers' expectations for each division concerning performance on dimensions such as efficiency, quality, innovation, and responsiveness to customers. Generally, corporate managers set challenging divisional goals to encourage divisional managers to create more effective strategies and structures in the future. At Dell, for example, each division is given a clear performance goal to achieve, and divisional managers are given considerable autonomy in formulating a strategy to meet this goal.

Output control at the functional and individual levels is a continuation of control at the divisional level. Divisional managers set goals for functional managers that will allow the division to achieve its goals. As at the divisional level, functional goals are established to encourage the development of the generic competencies that provide the company with a competitive advantage, and functional performance is evaluated by how well a function develops a competency. In the sales function, for example, goals related to efficiency (such as cost of sales), quality (such as number of returns), and customer responsiveness (such as the time needed to respond to customer needs) can be established for the whole function.

Finally, functional managers establish goals that individual employees are expected to achieve to allow the function to achieve its goals. Sales personnel, for example, can be given specific goals (related to functional goals) that they are required to achieve. Functions and individuals are then evaluated on the basis of achieving or not achieving their goals, and in sales, compensation is commonly pegged to achievement. The achievement of these goals is a sign that the company's strategy is working and meeting organizational objectives.

The inappropriate use of output control can promote conflict among divisions. In general, setting across-the-board output targets, such as ROIC targets, for divisions can lead to destructive results if divisions single-mindedly try to maximize divisional ROIC at the expense of corporate ROIC. Moreover, to reach output targets, divisions may start to distort the numbers and engage in strategic manipulation of the figures to make their divisions look good—which increases bureaucratic costs.[23]

BEHAVIOR CONTROL **Behavior control** is control through the establishment of a comprehensive system of rules and procedures to direct the actions or behavior of divisions, functions, and individuals.[24] The intent of behavior controls is not to specify the *goals* but to standardize the *way or means* of reaching them. Rules standardize behavior and make outcomes predictable. If employees follow the rules, then actions are performed and decisions are handled the same way time and time again. The result is predictability and accuracy, the aim of all control systems. The main kinds of behavior controls are operating budgets, standardization, and rules and procedures.

Once managers at each level have been given a goal to achieve, they establish operating budgets that regulate how managers and workers are to attain those goals. An **operating budget** is a blueprint that states how managers intend to use organizational resources to achieve organizational goals most efficiently. Most commonly, managers at one level allocate to managers at a lower level a specific amount of resources to use in the production of goods and services. Once they have been given a budget, lower-level managers must decide how they will allocate certain amounts of money for different organizational activities. They are then evaluated on the basis of their ability to stay inside the budget and make the best use of it. For example, managers at GE's washing machine division might have a budget of $50 million to develop and sell a new line of washing machines; they have to decide how much money to allocate to R&D, engineering, sales, and so on, so that the division generates the most revenue and hence makes the biggest profit. Most commonly, large companies treat each division as a stand-alone profit center, and corporate managers evaluate each division's performance by its relative contribution to corporate profitability, something discussed in detail in the next chapter.

Standardization refers to the degree to which a company specifies how decisions are to be made so that employees' behavior becomes predictable.[25] In practice, there are three things an organization can standardize: *inputs, conversion activities,* and *outputs.*

When managers standardize, they screen *inputs* according to preestablished criteria, or standards, that determine which inputs to allow into the organization. If employees are the input in question, for example, then one way of standardizing them is to specify which qualities and skills they must possess and then to select only applicants who possess them. If the inputs in question are raw materials or component parts, the same considerations apply. The Japanese are renowned for the high quality and precise tolerances they demand from component parts to minimize problems with the product at the manufacturing stage. Just-in-time inventory systems also help standardize the flow of inputs.

The aim of standardizing *conversion activities* is to program work activities so that they are done the same way time and time again. The goal is predictability. Behavior controls, such as rules and procedures, are among the chief means by which companies can standardize throughputs. Fast-food restaurants such as McDonald's and Burger King standardize all aspects of their restaurant operations; the result is consistent fast food.

The goal of standardizing *outputs* is to specify what the performance characteristics of the final product or service should be—the dimensions or tolerances the product should conform to, for example. To ensure that their products are standardized, companies apply quality control and use various criteria to measure this standardization. One criterion might be the number of goods returned from customers or the number of customers' complaints. On production lines, periodic sampling of products can indicate whether they are meeting performance characteristics.

As with other kinds of controls, the use of behavior control is accompanied by potential pitfalls that must be managed if the organization is to avoid strategic problems. Top management must be careful to monitor and evaluate the usefulness of behavior controls over time. Rules constrain people and lead to standardized, predictable behavior. However, rules are always easier to establish than to get rid of, and over time the number of rules an organization uses tends to increase. As new developments lead to additional rules, often the old rules are not discarded, and the company becomes overly bureaucratized. Consequently, the organization and the people in it become inflexible and are slow to react to changing or unusual circumstances. Such inflexibility can reduce a company's competitive advantage by lowering the pace of innovation and reducing its responsiveness to customers.

● **Using Information Technology**

Information technology is playing an increasing role in strategy implementation at all organizational levels. In fact, it is making it much easier for organizations to cost-effectively develop output and behavior controls that give strategic managers much more and much better information to monitor the many aspects of their strategies and to respond appropriately. IT, which provides a way of standardizing behavior through the use of a consistent, often cross-functional software platform, is a form of behavior control. IT is also a form of output control; when all employees or functions use the same software platform to provide up-to-date information on their activities, this codifies and standardizes organizational knowledge and makes it easier to monitor progress toward strategic objectives. IT is also a kind of integrating mechanism because it provides people at all levels in the hierarchy and across all functions with more of the information and knowledge they need to perform their

Strategy in Action   12.2

Control at Cypress Semiconductor

In the fast-moving semiconductor business, a premium is placed on organizational adaptability. At Cypress Semiconductor, CEO T. J. Rodgers was facing a problem: how to control his growing 1,500-employee organization without developing a bureaucratic management hierarchy. Rodgers believed that a tall hierarchy hinders the ability of an organization to adapt to changing conditions. He was committed to maintaining a flat and decentralized organizational structure with a minimum of management layers. At the same time, he needed to control his employees to ensure that they performed in a manner consistent with company goals. The solution that Rodgers adopted was to implement a computer-based information system through which he can manage what every employee and team is doing in the decentralized organization. Each employee maintains a list of ten to fifteen goals, such as "Meet with marketing for new product launch" or "Make sure to check with customer X." Noted next to each goal is when it was agreed on, when it is due to be finished, and whether it has been finished. All of this information is stored on a central computer. Rodgers claims that he can review the goals of all 1,500 employees in about four hours, and he does so each week. He can do this because he manages by exception, looking only for employees who are falling behind. He then calls them—not to scold but to ask whether there is anything he can do to help them get the job done. It takes only about half an hour each week for employees to review and update their lists. This system allows Rodgers to exercise control over his organization without resorting to the expensive layers of a management hierarchy.[b]

roles effectively. For example, today functional-level employees are able to access information easily from other functions using cross-functional software systems that keep them all informed about changes in product design, engineering, manufacturing schedules, and marketing plans that will have an impact on their activities. In this sense, IT overlays the structure of tasks and roles that is normally regarded as the "real" organizational structure. The many ways in which IT affects strategy implementation is discussed in different sections of this and the next chapter. Strategy in Action 12.2 illustrates one way in which IT can help managers monitor and coordinate the effectiveness with which their strategies are being put into action.

● **Strategic Reward Systems**

Organizations strive to control employees' behavior by linking reward systems to their control systems.[26] Based on the company's strategy (cost leadership or differentiation, for example), strategic managers must decide which behaviors to reward. They then create a control system to measure these behaviors and link the reward structure to them. Determining how to relate rewards to performance is a crucial strategic decision because it determines the incentive structure that affects the way managers and employees at all levels in the organization behave. As Chapter 11 pointed out, top managers can be encouraged to work in shareholders' interests by being rewarded with stock options linked to a company's long-term performance. Companies such as Kodak and GM require managers to buy company stock. When managers become shareholders, they are more motivated to pursue long-term rather than short-term goals. Similarly, in designing a pay system for salespeople, the choice is whether to motivate them through straight salary or salary plus a bonus based on how much they sell. Neiman Marcus, the luxury retailer, pays employees a straight salary because it wants to encourage high-quality service but discourage a hard-sell approach. Thus, there are no incentives based on quantity sold. On the other hand, the pay system for rewarding car salespeople encourages high-pressure selling; it typically contains a large bonus based on the number and price of cars sold.

Organizational Culture

The third element that goes into successful strategy implementation is managing *organizational culture*, the specific collection of values and norms shared by people and groups in an organization.[27] Organizational values are beliefs and ideas about what kinds of goals the members of an organization should pursue and about the appropriate kinds or standards of behavior organizational members should use to achieve these goals. Bill Gates is famous for the set of organizational values that he created for Microsoft: entrepreneurship, ownership, creativity, honesty, frankness, and open communication. By stressing entrepreneurship and ownership, he strives to get his employees to feel that Microsoft is not one big bureaucracy but a collection of smaller and very adaptive companies run by their members. Gates emphasizes giving lower-level managers autonomy and encourages them to take risks—to act like entrepreneurs, not corporate bureaucrats.[28]

From organizational values develop organizational norms, guidelines, or expectations that prescribe appropriate kinds of behavior by employees in particular situations and control the behavior of organizational members toward one another. The norms of behavior for software programmers at Microsoft include working long hours and weekends, wearing whatever clothing is comfortable (but never a suit and tie), consuming junk food, and communicating with other employees by email and the company's state-of-the-art intranet.

Organizational culture functions as a kind of control because strategic managers can influence the kind of values and norms that develop in an organization—values and norms that specify appropriate and inappropriate behaviors and that shape and influence the way its members behave.[29] Strategic managers such as Gates deliberately cultivate values that tell their subordinates how they should perform their roles; at Microsoft and Nokia, innovation and creativity are stressed. These companies establish and support norms that tell employees they should be innovative and entrepreneurial and should experiment even if there is a significant chance of failure.

Other managers might cultivate values that tell employees they should always be conservative and cautious in their dealings with others, consult with their superiors before they make important decisions, and record their actions in writing so they can be held accountable for what happens. Managers of organizations such as chemical and oil companies, financial institutions, and insurance companies—any organization in which great caution is needed—may encourage a conservative, vigilant approach to making decisions.[30] In a bank or mutual fund, for example, the risk of losing investors' money makes a cautious approach to investing highly appropriate. Thus, we might expect that managers of different kinds of organizations will deliberately try to cultivate and develop the organizational values and norms that are best suited to their strategy and structure.

Organizational socialization is the term used to describe how people learn organizational culture. Through socialization, people internalize and learn the norms and values of the culture so that they become organizational members.[31] Control through culture is so powerful that once these values have been internalized, they become part of the individual's values, and the individual follows organizational values without thinking about them.[32] Often the values and norms of an organization's culture are transmitted to its members through the stories, myths, and language that people in the organization use, as well as by other means.

Culture and Strategic Leadership

Organizational culture is created by the strategic leadership provided by an organization's founder and top managers. The organization's founder is particularly important in determining culture because the founder imprints his or her values and management style on the organization. Walt Disney's conservative influence on the company he established continued until well after his death. Managers were afraid to experiment with new forms of entertainment because they were afraid "Walt Disney wouldn't like it." It took the installation of a new management team under Michael Eisner to turn around the company's fortunes and allow it to deal with the realities of the new entertainment industry.

The leadership style established by the founder is transmitted to the company's managers, and as the company grows, it typically attracts new managers and employees who share the same values. Moreover, members of the organization typically recruit and select only those who share their values. Thus, a company's culture becomes more and more distinct as its members become more similar. The virtue of these shared values and common culture is that they *increase integration and improve coordination among organizational members.* For example, the common language that typically emerges in an organization because people share the same beliefs and values facilitates cooperation among managers. Similarly, rules and procedures and direct supervision are less important when shared norms and values control behavior and motivate employees. When organizational members buy into cultural norms and values, they feel a bond with the organization and are more committed to finding new ways to help it succeed. Strategy in Action 12.3 profiles how Ray Kroc built a strong culture at McDonald's.

Strategic leadership also affects organizational culture through the way managers design organizational structure, that is, the way they delegate authority and divide task relationships. Thus, the way an organization designs its structure affects the cultural norms and values that develop within the organization. Managers need to be aware of this fact when implementing their strategies. Michael Dell, for example, has tried to keep his company as flat as possible and has decentralized authority to lower-level managers and employees who are charged with striving to get as close to the customer as they can. As a result, he has created a cost-conscious customer service culture at Dell in which employees strive to provide high-quality customer service.

Traits of Strong and Adaptive Corporate Cultures

Few environments are stable for a prolonged period of time. If an organization is to survive, managers must take actions that enable it to adapt to environmental changes. If they do not take such action, they may find themselves faced with declining demand for their products.

Managers can try to create an **adaptive culture**, one that is innovative and that encourages and rewards middle and lower-level managers for taking the initiative.[33] Managers in organizations with adaptive cultures are able to introduce changes in the way the organization operates, including changes in its strategy and structure that allow it to adapt to changes in the external environment. Organizations with adaptive cultures are more likely to survive in a changing environment and indeed should have higher performance than organizations with inert cultures.

Strategy in Action

12.3

How Ray Kroc Established McDonald's Culture

In the restaurant business, maintaining product quality is all-important because the quality of the food and the service varies with the chefs and waiters as they come and go. If a customer gets a bad meal, poor service, or dirty silverware, that customer may not come back, and other potential customers may stay away as negative comments travel by word of mouth. This was the problem that Ray Kroc, the man who pioneered McDonald's growth, faced when McDonald's franchises began to open by the thousands throughout the United States. Kroc solved his problem by developing a sophisticated control system that specified every detail of how each McDonald's restaurant was to be operated and managed. This control system also created a distinct organizational culture.

First, Kroc developed a comprehensive system of rules and procedures for franchise owners and employees to follow in running each restaurant. The most effective way to perform tasks, from cooking burgers to cleaning tables, was worked out in advance, written down in rule books, and then taught to each McDonald's manager and employee through a formal training process. Prospective franchise owners had to attend "Hamburger University," the company's training center in Chicago, where they learned all aspects of a McDonald's operation in an intensive, month-long program. They were then expected to train their work force and make sure that employees thoroughly understood operating procedures. Kroc's goal in establishing this system of rules

and procedures was to build a common culture so that customers would always find the same level of quality in food and service. If customers always get what they expect from a restaurant, the restaurant has developed superior customer responsiveness.

Kroc also developed the McDonald's franchise system to help the company control its structure as it grew. He believed that a manager who is also a franchise owner (and thus receives a large share of the profits) is more motivated to buy into a company's culture than a manager paid on a straight salary. Thus, the McDonald's reward and incentive system allowed it to keep control over its operating structure as it expanded. Moreover, McDonald's was very selective in selling to its franchisees; they had to be people with the skills and capabilities that Kroc believed McDonald's managers should have.

Within each restaurant, franchise owners were instructed to pay particular attention to training their employees and instilling in them McDonald's concepts of efficiency, quality, and customer service. Shared norms, values, and an organizational culture also helped McDonald's standardize employees' behavior so that customers would know how they would be treated in a McDonald's restaurant. Moreover, McDonald's includes customers in its culture: it asks customers to bus their own tables, and it also shows concern for customers' needs by building playgrounds, offering Happy Meals, and organizing birthday parties for children. In creating its family-oriented culture, McDonald's ensures future customer loyalty because satisfied children are likely to become loyal adult customers.[c]

Several scholars in the field have tried to uncover the common traits that strong and adaptive corporate cultures share and to find out whether there is a particular set of values that dominates adaptive cultures that is missing from weak or inert ones. An early but still influential attempt is T. J. Peters and R. H. Waterman's account of the values and norms characteristic of successful organizations and their cultures.[34] They argue that adaptive organizations show three common value sets. First, successful companies have values promoting a *bias for action*. The emphasis is on autonomy and entrepreneurship, and employees are encouraged to take risks—for example, to create new products—even though there is no assurance that these products will be winners. Managers are closely involved in the day-to-day operations of the company and do not simply make strategic decisions isolated in some ivory tower, and employees have a hands-on, value-driven approach.

The second set of values stems from the *nature of the organization's mission.* The company must stick with what it does best and develop a business model focused on its mission. A company can easily get sidetracked into pursuing activities outside its area of expertise just because they seem to promise a quick return. Management should cultivate values so that a company sticks to its knitting, which means strengthening its business model. A company must also establish close relationships with customers as a way of improving its competitive position. After all, who knows more about a company's performance than those who use its products or services? By emphasizing customer-oriented values, organizations are able to learn customers' needs and improve their ability to develop products and services that customers desire. All of these management values are strongly represented in companies such as McDonald's, Wal-Mart, and Toyota, which are sure of their mission and continually take steps to maintain it.

The third set of values bears on *how to operate the organization.* A company should try to establish an organizational design that will motivate employees to do their best. Inherent in this set of values is the belief that productivity is obtained through people and that respect for the individual is the primary means by which a company can create the right atmosphere for productive behavior. An emphasis on entrepreneurship and respect for the employee leads to the establishment of a structure that gives employees the latitude to make decisions and motivates them to succeed. Because a simple structure and a lean staff best fit this situation, the organization should be designed with only the number of managers and hierarchical levels that are necessary to get the job done. The organization should also be sufficiently decentralized to permit employees' participation but centralized enough for management to make sure that the company pursues its strategic mission and that cultural values are followed.

In summary, these three main sets of values are at the heart of an organization's culture, and management transmits and maintains them through strategic leadership. Strategy implementation continues as managers build strategic control systems that help perpetuate a strong adaptive culture, further the development of distinctive competencies, and provide employees with the incentive to build a company's competitive advantage. Finally, organizational structure contributes to the implementation process by providing the framework of tasks and roles that reduces transaction difficulties and allows employees to think and behave in ways that enable a company to achieve superior performance.

Building Distinctive Competencies at the Functional Level

In this section, we turn to the issue of creating specific kinds of structures, control systems, and cultures to implement a company's business model. The first level of strategy to examine is the functional level because, as Chapters 3 and 4 discussed, a company's business model is implemented through the functional strategies managers adopt to develop the distinctive competencies that allow a company to pursue a particular business model.[35] What is the best kind of structure to use to group people and tasks to build competencies? The answer for most companies is to group them by function and create a functional structure.

● **Functional Structure: Grouping by Function**

In the quest to deliver a final product to the customer, two related value chain management problems increase. First, the range of value chain activities that must be performed expands, and it quickly becomes clear that a company lacks the expertise needed to perform them effectively. For example, in a new company, it quickly

FIGURE 12.5

Functional Structure

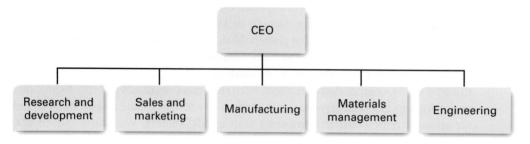

becomes apparent, as in Dell's case, that the expertise necessary to perform them effectively is lacking. It becomes apparent, perhaps, that the services of a professional accountant, a production manager, or a marketing expert are needed to take control of specialized tasks as sales increase. Second, it also becomes clear that a single person cannot successfully perform more than one value chain activity without becoming overloaded. The new company's founder, for instance, who may have been performing many value chain activities, realizes that he or she can no longer simultaneously make and sell the product. As most entrepreneurs discover, they have to decide how to group new employees to perform the various value chain activities most efficiently. Most choose the functional structure.

Functional structures group people on the basis of their common expertise and experience or because they use the same resources.[36] For example, engineers are grouped in a function because they perform the same tasks and use the same skills or equipment. Figure 12.5 shows a typical functional structure. Each of the rectangles represents a different functional specialization—R&D, sales and marketing, manufacturing, and so on—and each function concentrates on its own specialized task.[37]

Functional structures have several advantages. First, if people who perform similar tasks are grouped together, they can learn from one another and become more specialized and productive at what they do. This can create capabilities and competencies in each function. Second, they can monitor each other to make sure that all are performing their tasks effectively and not shirking their responsibilities. As a result, the work process becomes more efficient, reducing manufacturing costs and increasing operational flexibility. A third important advantage of functional structures is that they give managers greater control of organizational activities. As already noted, many difficulties arise when the number of levels in the hierarchy increases. If people are grouped into different functions, each with their own managers, then *several different hierarchies are created*, and the company can avoid becoming too tall. There will be one hierarchy in manufacturing, for example, and another in accounting and finance. Managing the business is much easier when different groups specialize in different organizational tasks and are managed separately.

● **The Role of Strategic Control**   An important element of strategic control is to design a system that sets ambitious goals and targets for all managers and employees and then develops performance measures that *stretch and encourage managers and employees* to excel in their quest to raise performance. A functional structure promotes this goal because it increases the ability of managers and employees to monitor and make constant improvements to operating procedures. The structure also encourages organizational learning because managers, working closely with subordinates, can mentor them and help develop their technical skills.

Grouping by function also makes it easier to apply output control. Measurement criteria can be developed to suit the needs of each function to encourage members to stretch themselves. Each function knows how well it is contributing to overall performance, and indeed the part it plays in reducing the cost of goods sold or the gross margin. Managers can look closely to see if they are following the principle of the minimum chain of command and whether they need several levels of middle managers. Perhaps, instead of using middle managers, they could practice **management by objectives**, a system in which employees are encouraged to help set their own goals so that managers, like Cypress's Rodgers, *manage by exception*, intervening only when they sense something is not going right. Given this increase in control, a functional structure also makes it possible to institute an effective strategic reward system in which pay can be closely linked to performance and managers can accurately assess the value of each person's contributions.

● **Developing Culture at the Functional Level**

Often functional structures offer the easiest way for managers to build a strong, cohesive culture. We discussed earlier how Ray Kroc, who first developed a functional structure to implement his cost-leadership business model, worked hard to create values and norms that were shared by the members of McDonald's different functions. To see how structure, control, and culture help create distinctive competencies, we consider how they affect the way three functions—manufacturing, R&D, and sales—operate.

MANUFACTURING In manufacturing, functional strategy usually centers on improving efficiency and quality. A company must create an organizational setting in which managers can learn how to economize on costs and lower the cost structure. Many companies today follow the lead of Japanese companies such as Toyota and Honda, which developed strong capabilities in manufacturing by operating total quality management (TQM) and flexible manufacturing systems (see Chapter 4).

With TQM, the inputs and involvement of all employees in the decision-making process are necessary to improve production efficiency and quality. Thus, it becomes necessary to decentralize authority to motivate employees to improve the production process. In TQM, work teams are created, and workers are given the responsibility and authority to discover and implement improved work procedures. Managers assume the role of coach and facilitator, and team members jointly take on the supervisory burdens. Work teams are often given the responsibility to control and discipline their own members and even to decide who should work in their team. Frequently, work teams develop strong norms and values, and work-group culture becomes an important means of control; this type of control matches the new decentralized team approach. Quality control circles are created to exchange information and suggestions about problems and work procedures. A bonus system or employee stock ownership plan (ESOP) is frequently established to motivate workers and to allow them to share in the increased value that TQM often produces.

Nevertheless, to move down the experience curve quickly, most companies still exercise tight control over work activities and create behavior and output controls that standardize the manufacturing process. For example, human inputs are standardized through the recruitment and training of skilled personnel; the work process is programmed, often by computers; and quality control is used to make sure that outputs are being produced correctly. In addition, managers use output controls such as operating budgets to continuously monitor costs and quality. The extensive use of output controls and the continuous measurement of efficiency and quality ensure that the work team's activities meet the goals set for the function by management. Efficiency and quality increase as new and improved work rules and procedures are developed to raise the level of standardization. The aim is to find the match between structure and control and a TQM approach so that manufacturing develops the distinctive competency that leads to superior efficiency and quality.

R&D The functional strategy for an R&D department is to develop distinctive competencies in innovation and quality as excellence that result in products that fit customers' needs. Consequently, the R&D department's structure, control, and culture should provide the coordination necessary for scientists and engineers to bring high-quality products quickly to market. Moreover, these systems should motivate R&D scientists to develop innovative products.

In practice, R&D departments typically have a flat, decentralized structure that gives their members the freedom and autonomy to experiment and be innovative. Scientists and engineers are also grouped into teams because their performance can typically be judged only over the long term (it may take several years for a project to be completed). Consequently, extensive supervision by managers and the use of behavior control are a waste of managerial time and effort.[38] By letting teams manage their own transfer and handoff issues rather than using managers and the hierarchy of authority to coordinate work activities, managers avoid the information distortion problems that cause bureaucratic costs. Strategic managers take advantage of scientists' ability to work jointly to solve problems and to enhance each other's performance. In small teams, too, the professional values and norms that highly trained employees bring to the situation promote coordination. A culture for innovation frequently emerges to control employees' behavior, as it did at Nokia, Intel, and Microsoft, where the race to be first energizes the R&D teams. To create an innovative culture and speed product development, Intel uses a team structure in its R&D function. Intel has many work teams that operate side by side to develop the next generation of chips. So, when it makes mistakes, as it has recently, it can act quickly to join each team's innovations together to make a state-of-the-art chip that does meet customer needs, such as for multimedia chips. At the same time, to sustain its leading-edge technology, the company creates healthy competition between teams to encourage its scientists and engineers to champion new product innovations that will allow Intel to control the technology of tomorrow.[39]

To spur teams to work effectively, the reward system should be linked to the performance of the team and company. If scientists, individually or in a team, do not share in the profits a company obtains from its new products, they may have little motivation to contribute wholeheartedly to the team. To prevent the departure of their key employees and encourage high motivation, companies such as Merck, Intel, and Microsoft give their researchers stock options, stock, and other rewards that are tied to their individual performance, their team's performance, and the company's performance.

SALES Salespeople work directly with customers, and when they are dispersed in the field, these employees are especially difficult to monitor. The cost-effective way to monitor their behavior and encourage high responsiveness to customers is usually to develop sophisticated output and behavior controls. Output controls, such as specific sales goals or goals for increasing responsiveness to customers, can be easily established and monitored by sales managers. These controls can then be linked to a bonus reward system to motivate salespeople. Behavior controls, such as detailed reports that salespeople file describing their interactions with customers, can also be used to standardize salespeople's behavior and make it easier for supervisors to review their performance.[40]

Usually, few managers are needed to monitor salespeople's activities, and a sales director and regional sales managers can oversee even large sales forces because outputs and behavior controls are employed. Frequently, however, and especially when salespeople deal with complex products such as pharmaceutical drugs or even luxury clothing, it becomes important to develop shared employee values and norms about the importance of patient safety or high-quality customer service, and managers spend considerable time training and educating employees to create such norms.

Similar considerations apply to the other functions, such as accounting, finance, engineering, and human resource management. Managers must implement functional strategy through the combination of structure, control, and culture to allow each function to create the competencies that lead to superior efficiency, quality, innovation, and responsiveness to customers. Strategic managers must also develop the incentive systems that motivate and align employees' interests with those of their companies.

● Functional Structure and Bureaucratic Costs

No matter how complex their strategies become, most companies always retain a functional orientation because of its many advantages. Whenever different functions work together, however, bureaucratic costs inevitably arise because of information distortions that lead to the communications and measurement problems discussed in Chapter 10. These problems often arise from the transfers or handoffs across different functions that are necessary to deliver the final product to the customer.[41] Indeed, the need to economize on the bureaucratic costs of solving such problems leads managers to adopt new organizational arrangements that reduce the scope of information distortions. Most commonly, companies divide their activities according to a more complex plan to match their business model and strategy in a discriminating way. These more complex structures are discussed later in the chapter. First, we review five areas in which information distortions can arise—communications, measurement, customers, location, and strategy.

COMMUNICATION PROBLEMS   As separate functional hierarchies evolve, functions can grow more remote from one another, and it becomes increasingly difficult to communicate across functions and to coordinate their activities. This communication problem stems from *differences in goal orientations*: the various functions develop distinct outlooks or understandings of the strategic issues facing a company.[42] For example, the pursuit of different competencies can often lead to different time or goal orientations. Some functions, such as manufacturing, have a short time frame and concentrate on achieving short-run goals, such as reducing manufacturing costs. Others, such as R&D, have a long-term point of view; their product development goals may have a time horizon of several years. These factors may cause each function to develop a different view of the strategic issues facing the company. Manufacturing, for example, may see the strategic issue as the need to reduce costs, sales may see it as the need to increase customer responsiveness, and R&D may see it as the need to create new products. These communication and coordination problems among functions increase bureaucratic costs.

MEASUREMENT PROBLEMS Often a company's product range widens as it develops new competencies and enters new market segments, as happened to Nokia. When this happens, a company may find it difficult to gauge or measure the contribution of a product or a group of products to its overall profitability—as we noted in Chapter 10. Consequently, the company may turn out some unprofitable products without realizing it and may also make poor decisions about resource allocation. This means that the company's measurement systems are not complex enough to serve its needs. Dell Computer's explosive growth in the early 1990s, for example, caused it to lose control of its inventory management systems; hence, it could not accurately project supply and demand for the components that go into its personal computers. Problems with its organizational structure plagued Dell, reducing efficiency and quality. As one manager commented, designing its structure to keep pace with its growth was like "building a high-performance car while going around the race track."[43] However, Dell succeeded and today it still maintains its cost advantage over competitors like Gateway and HP.

CUSTOMER PROBLEMS As the range and quality of an organization's goods and services increase, often more, and different kinds of, customers are attracted to its products. Servicing the needs of more customer groups and tailoring products to suit new kinds of customers result in increasing handoff problems among functions. It becomes increasingly difficult to coordinate the activities of value chain functions across the growing product range. Also, functions like production, marketing, and sales have little opportunity to differentiate products and increase value for customers by specializing in the needs of particular customer groups. Instead, they are responsible for servicing the complete product range. Thus, the ability to identify and satisfy customer needs may fall short in a functional structure.

LOCATION PROBLEMS Location factors may hamper coordination and control. If a growing company begins producing or selling in many different regional areas, then a functional structure may not be able to provide the flexibility needed for managers to respond to the different customer needs or preferences in the various regions. A functional structure is simply not the right way to handle regional diversity.

STRATEGIC PROBLEMS Sometimes the combined effect of all these factors is that long-term strategic considerations are ignored because managers are preoccupied with solving communication and coordination problems. As a result, a company may lose direction and fail to take advantage of new opportunities while bureaucratic costs escalate.

Experiencing one or more of these problems is a sign that bureaucratic costs are increasing and that managers must change and adapt their organization's structure, control systems, and culture to economize on bureaucratic costs, build new distinctive competencies, and strengthen the company's business model. These problems indicate that the company has outgrown its structure and that managers need to develop a more complex structure that can meet the needs of their competitive strategy. An alternative, however, is to reduce these problems by adopting the outsourcing option.

● **The Outsourcing Option**   Rather than move to a more complex, expensive structure, increasingly companies are turning to the outsourcing option (discussed in Chapter 9) and solving the organizational design problem by contracting with other companies to perform specific functional tasks. Obviously, it does not make sense to outsource activities in which a company has a distinctive competency because this would lessen its competitive advantage. But it does make sense to outsource and contract with companies to perform particular value chain activities in which they specialize and therefore have a competitive advantage.

Thus, one way of avoiding the kinds of communication and measurement problems that arise when a company's product line becomes complex is to reduce the number of functional value chain activities it performs. This allows a company to focus on those competencies that are at the heart of its competitive advantage and to economize on bureaucratic costs. Today, responsibility for activities such as a company's marketing, pension and health benefits, materials management, and information systems is being increasingly outsourced to companies that often specialize in the needs of a company in a particular industry. More outsourcing options, such as using a global network structure, are considered in Chapter 13.

Implementing Strategy in a Single Industry

Building capabilities in organizational design that allow a company to develop a competitive advantage starts at the functional level. However, to pursue its business model successfully, managers must find the right combination of structure, control, and culture that *links and combines* the competencies in a company's value chain functions so that it enhances its ability to differentiate products or lower the cost structure. Therefore, it is important to coordinate and integrate across functions and business units or divisions. In organizational design, managers must consider two important issues: one concerns the revenue side of the profit equation and the other concerns the cost side, as Figure 12.6 illustrates.

First, effective organizational design improves the way in which people and groups choose the business-level strategies that lead to increasing differentiation, more value for customers, and the opportunity to charge a premium price. For example, capabilities in

FIGURE 12.6

How Organizational Design Increases Profitability

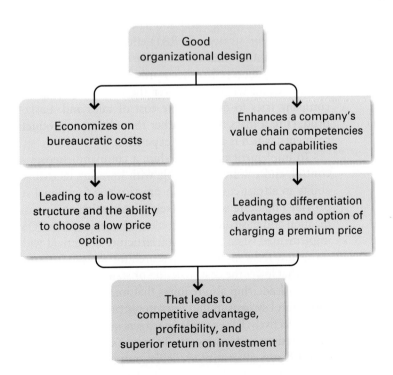

managing its structure and culture allow a company to more rapidly and effectively combine its distinctive competencies or transfer or leverage competencies across business units to create new and improved, differentiated products.

Second, effective organizational design reduces the bureaucratic costs associated with solving the measurement and communications problems that derive from factors such as transferring a product in progress between functions or a lack of cooperation between marketing and manufacturing or between business units. A poorly designed or inappropriate choice of structure or control system or a slow-moving bureaucratic culture (for example, a structure that is too centralized, an incentive system that causes functions to compete instead of cooperate, or a culture whose value and norms have little impact on employees) can cause the motivation, communication, measurement, and coordination problems that lead to high bureaucratic costs.

Effective organizational design often means moving to a more complex structure that economizes on bureaucratic costs. A more complex structure will cost more to operate because additional, experienced, and more highly paid managers will be needed; a more expensive IT system will be required; there may be a need for extra offices and buildings; and so on. However, these are simply costs of doing business, and a company will happily bear this extra expense provided its new structure leads to increased revenues from product differentiation and/or new ways to lower its *overall* cost structure by obtaining economies of scale or scope from its expanded operations.

In the following sections, we first examine the implementation and organizational design issues involved in pursuing a cost-leadership or differentiation business model. Then we describe different kinds of organizational structures that allow companies to pursue business models oriented at (1) managing a wide range of products; (2) being responsive to customers; (3) expanding nationally; (4) competing in a fast-changing, high-tech environment; and (5) focusing on a narrow product line.

Implementing Cost Leadership

The aim of a company pursuing cost leadership is to become the lowest-cost producer in the industry, and this involves reducing costs across *all* functions in the organization, including R&D and sales and marketing.[44] If a company is pursuing a cost-leadership strategy, its R&D efforts probably focus on product and process development rather than on the more expensive product innovation, which carries no guarantee of success. In other words, the company stresses competencies that improve product characteristics or lower the cost of making existing products. Similarly, a company tries to decrease the cost of sales and marketing by offering a standard product to a mass market rather than different products aimed at different market segments, which is also more expensive.[45]

To implement cost leadership, a company chooses a combination of structure, control, and culture compatible with lowering its cost structure while preserving its ability to attract customers. In practice, the functional structure is the most suitable provided that care is taken to select integrating mechanisms that will reduce communication and measurement problems. For example, a TQM program can be effectively implemented when a functional structure is overlaid with cross-functional teams because now team members can search for ways to improve operating rules and procedures that lower the cost structure or standardize and raise product quality.[46]

Cost leadership also requires that managers continuously monitor their structures and control systems to find ways to restructure or streamline them so that they operate more effectively. For example, managers need to be alert to ways of using IT to standardize operations and lower costs. To reduce costs further, cost leaders use the cheapest and easiest forms of control available: output controls. For each function, a cost leader adopts output controls that allow it to closely monitor and evaluate functional performance. In the manufacturing function, for example, the company imposes tight controls and stresses meeting budgets based on production, cost, or quality targets.[47] In R&D, the emphasis also falls on the bottom line, and to demonstrate their contribution to cost savings, R&D teams focus on improving process technology. Cost leaders are likely to reward employees through generous incentive and bonus plans to encourage high performance. Their culture is often based on values that emphasize the bottom line, such as those of Dell, Wal-Mart, and McDonald's.

● **Implementing Differentiation**

Effective strategy implementation can improve a company's ability to add value and to differentiate its products. To make its product unique in the eyes of the customer, for example, a differentiated company must design its structure, control, and culture around the *particular source* of its competitive advantage.[48] Specifically, differentiators need to design their structures around the source of their distinctive competencies, the differentiated qualities of their product, and the customer groups they serve. Commonly, in pursuing differentiation, a company starts to produce a wider range of products to serve more market segments, which means it has to customize its products for different groups of customers. These factors make it more difficult to standardize activities and usually increase the bureaucratic costs associated with managing the handoffs or transfers between functions. Integration becomes much more of a problem; communications, measurement, location, and strategic problems increasingly arise; and the demands on functional managers increase.

To respond to these problems, strategic managers develop more sophisticated control systems, increasingly make use of IT, and focus on developing cultural norms and values that overcome problems associated with differences in functional orientations and focus on cross-functional objectives. The control systems used to match the structure should be geared to a company's distinctive competencies. For successful differentiation, it is important that the various functions do not pull in different directions; indeed, cooperation among the functions is vital for cross-functional integration. However, when functions work together, output controls become much harder to use. In general, it is much more difficult to measure the performance of people in different functions when they are engaged in cooperative efforts. Consequently, a differentiator must rely more on behavior controls and shared norms and values.

That is why companies pursuing differentiation often have a markedly different kind of culture from those pursuing cost leadership. Because human resources—good scientists, designers, or marketing employees—are often the source of differentiation, these organizations have a culture based on professionalism or collegiality, one that emphasizes the distinctiveness of the human resources rather than the high pressure of the bottom line.[49] HP, Motorola, and Coca-Cola, all of which emphasize some kind of distinctive competency, exemplify companies with professional cultures.

In practice, the implementation decisions that confront managers who must simultaneously strive for differentiation and a low cost structure are dealt with together as strategic managers move to implement new, more complex kinds of organizational structure. As a company's business model and strategies evolve, strategic managers usually start to *superimpose* a more complex divisional grouping of activities on its functional structure to better coordinate value chain activities. This is especially true of companies seeking to become *broad differentiators*, the companies that have the ability to both increase differentiation and lower their cost structures. These companies are the most profitable in their industry, and they have to be especially adept at organizational design because this is a major source of a differentiation and cost advantage (see

Figure 12.6). No matter what their business model, however, more complex structures cost more to operate than a simple functional structure, but managers are willing to bear this extra cost as long as the new structure makes better use of functional competencies, increases revenues, and lowers the overall cost structure.

● **Product Structure: Implementing a Wide Product Line**

The structure that organizations most commonly adopt to solve the control problems that result from producing many different kinds of products for many different market segments is the *product structure*. The intent is to break up a company's growing product line into a number of smaller, more manageable subunits to reduce bureaucratic costs due to communication, measurement, and other problems. Nokia moved to a product structure as it grew in size; its structure is shown in Figure 12.7.

An organization that chooses a product structure first divides its overall product line into product groups or categories (see Figure 12.7). Each product group focuses on satisfying the needs of a particular customer group and is managed by its own team of managers. Second, to keep costs as low as possible, value chain support functions such as basic R&D, marketing, materials, and finance are centralized at the top of the organization, and the different product groups share their services. Each support function, in turn, is divided into product-oriented teams of functional specialists who focus on the needs of one particular product group. This arrangement allows each team to specialize and become expert in managing the needs of its product group. Because all of the R&D teams belong to the same centralized function, however, they can share knowledge and information with each other and so can build their competence over time.

Strategic control systems can now be developed to measure the performance of each product group separately from the others. Thus, the performance of each product group is easy to monitor and evaluate, and corporate managers at the center can move more quickly to intervene if necessary. Also, the strategic reward system can be linked more closely to the performance of each product group, although top managers can still decide to make rewards based on corporate performance an important part

FIGURE 12.7

Nokia's Product Structure

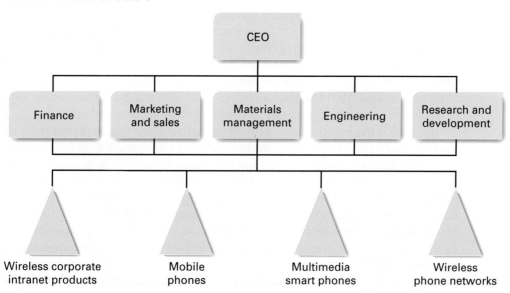

of the incentive system. Doing so will encourage the different product groups to share ideas and knowledge and promote the development of a corporate culture, as well as the product group culture that naturally develops inside each product group. A product structure is commonly used by food processors, furniture makers, personal and health products companies, and large electronics companies like Nokia.

● Market Structure: Increasing Responsiveness to Customer Groups

Suppose the source of competitive advantage in an industry depends on the ability to meet the needs of distinct and important sets of customers or different customer groups. What is the best way of implementing strategy now? Many companies develop a **market structure** that is conceptually quite similar to the product structure except that the focus is on customer groups instead of product groups.

For a company pursuing a strategy based on increasing responsiveness to customers, it is vital that the nature and needs of each different customer group be identified. Then employees and functions are grouped by customer or market segment, and a different set of managers becomes responsible for developing the products that each group of customers wants and tailoring or customizing products to the needs of each particular customer group. In other words, to promote superior responsiveness to customers, companies design a structure around their customers and a market structure is adopted. A typical market structure is shown in Figure 12.8.

A market structure brings customer group managers and employees closer to specific groups of customers. These people can then take their detailed knowledge and feed it back to the support functions, which are kept centralized to reduce costs. For example, information about changes in customers' preferences can be quickly fed back to R&D and product design so that a company can protect its competitive advantage by supplying a constant stream of improved products for its installed customer base. This is especially important when a company serves well-identified customer groups such as *Fortune 500* companies or small businesses. The Opening Case describes how Dell uses a market structure to maximize its responsiveness to important customer groups while at the same time keeping its overall cost structure as low as possible.

● Geographic Structure: Expanding Nationally

Suppose a company starts to expand nationally through internal expansion or by engaging in horizontal integration and merging with other companies to expand its geographical reach. A company pursuing this competitive approach frequently moves to a **geographic structure** in which geographic regions become the basis for the grouping of organizational activities (see Figure 12.9). A company may divide its manufacturing operations and establish manufacturing plants in different regions of

FIGURE 12.8

Market Structure

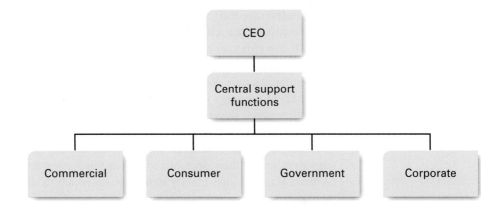

FIGURE 12.9

Geographic Structure

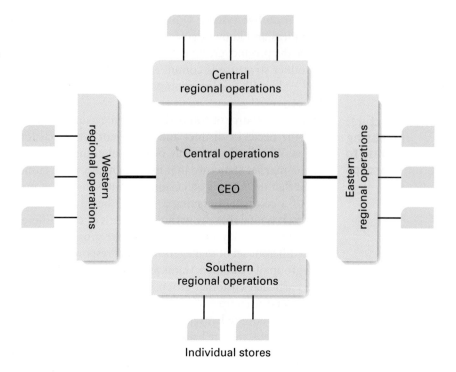

the country, for example. This allows it to be responsive to the needs of regional customers and reduces transportation costs. Similarly, as a service organization such as a store chain or bank expands beyond one geographic area, it may begin to organize sales and marketing activities on a regional level to better serve the needs of customers in different regions.

A geographic structure provides more coordination and control than a functional structure does because several regional hierarchies are created to take over the work, just as in a product structure, where several product group hierarchies are created. A company such as FedEx clearly needs to operate a geographic structure to fulfill its corporate goal: next-day delivery. Large merchandising organizations, such as Neiman Marcus, Dillard's Department Stores, and Wal-Mart, also moved to a geographic structure as they started building stores across the country. With this type of structure, different regional clothing needs (for example, sunwear in the South, down coats in the Midwest) can be handled as required. At the same time, because the information systems, purchasing, distribution, and marketing functions remain centralized, they can leverage their skills across all the regions. Thus, in using a geographic structure, a company can achieve economies of scale in buying, distributing, and selling and lower its cost structure while at the same time being more responsive (differentiated) to customer needs.

Neiman Marcus developed a geographic structure similar to the one shown in Figure 12.9 to manage its nationwide chain of stores. In each region, it established a team of regional buyers to respond to the needs of customers in each geographic area, for example, the western, central, eastern, and southern regions. The regional buyers then fed their information to the central buyers at corporate headquarters, who coordinated their demands to obtain purchasing economies and to ensure that Neiman Marcus's high-quality standards, on which its differentiation advantage depends, were maintained nationally.

● **Matrix and Product-Team Structures: Competing in Fast-Changing, High-Tech Environments**

The communication and measurement problems that lead to bureaucratic costs escalate quickly when technology is rapidly changing and industry boundaries are blurring. Frequently, competitive success depends on fast mobilization of a company's skills and resources, and managers face complex strategy implementation issues. A new grouping of people and resources becomes necessary, often one that is based on fostering a company's distinctive competencies in R&D, and managers need to make structure, control, and culture choices around the R&D function. At the same time, they need to ensure that implementation will result in new products that meet customer needs in a way that is cost-effective and will not result in high-priced products that are so expensive customers will not wish to buy them.

MATRIX STRUCTURE To address these problems, many companies choose a matrix structure.[50] In a **matrix structure,** value chain activities are grouped in two ways (see Figure 12.10). First, activities are grouped vertically by *function* so that there is a familiar differentiation of tasks into functions such as engineering, sales and marketing, and R&D. In addition, superimposed on this vertical pattern is a horizontal pattern based

FIGURE 12.3

Matrix Structure

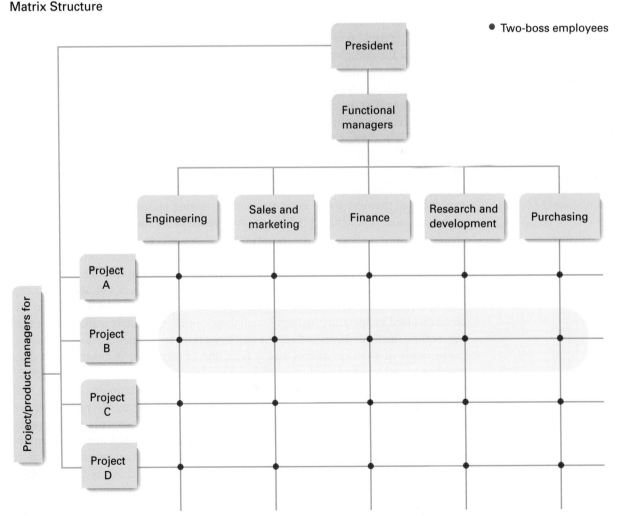

on grouping by *product or project* in which people and resources are grouped to meet ongoing product development needs. The resulting network of reporting relationships among projects and functions is designed to make R&D the focus of attention.

Matrix structures are flat and decentralized, and employees inside a matrix have two bosses: a *functional boss*, who is the head of a function, and a *product or project boss*, who is responsible for managing the individual projects. Employees work on a project team with specialists from other functions and report to the project boss on project matters and the functional boss on matters relating to functional issues. All employees who work in a project team are called **two-boss employees** and are responsible for managing coordination and communication among the functions and projects.

Implementing a matrix structure promotes innovation and speeds product development because this type of structure permits intensive cross-functional integration. Integrating mechanisms such as teams help transfer knowledge among functions and are designed around the R&D function. Sales, marketing, and production targets are geared to R&D goals, marketing devises advertising programs that focus on technological possibilities, and salespeople are evaluated on their understanding of new-product characteristics and their ability to inform potential customers about them.

Matrix structures were first developed by companies in high-technology industries such as aerospace and electronics, for example, TRW and Hughes. These companies were developing radically new products in uncertain, competitive environments, and speed of product development was the crucial consideration. They needed a structure that could respond to this need, but the functional structure was too inflexible to allow the complex role and task interactions that are necessary to meet new-product development requirements. Moreover, employees in these companies tend to be highly qualified and professional and perform best in autonomous, flexible working conditions. The matrix structure provides such conditions.

This structure requires a minimum of direct hierarchical control by supervisors. Team members control their own behavior, and participation in project teams allows them to monitor other team members and to learn from each other. Furthermore, as the project goes through its different phases, different specialists from various functions are required. For example, at the first stage, the services of R&D specialists may be called for, and then, at the next stage, engineers and marketing specialists may be needed to make cost and marketing projections. As the demand for the type of specialist changes, team members can be moved to other projects that require their services. Thus, the matrix structure can make maximum use of employees' skills as existing projects are completed and new ones come into existence. The freedom given by the matrix not only provides the autonomy to motivate employees but also leaves top management free to concentrate on strategic issues because they do not have to become involved in operating matters. On all these counts, the matrix is an excellent tool for creating the flexibility necessary for quick reactions to competitive conditions.

In terms of strategic control and culture, the development of norms and values based on innovation and product excellence is vital if a matrix structure is to work effectively.[51] The constant movement of employees around the matrix means that time and money are spent establishing new team relationships and getting the project off the ground. The two-boss employee's role, balancing as it does the interests of the project with the function, means that cooperation among employees is problematic and conflict between different functions and between functions and projects is possible and must be managed. Furthermore, the changing composition of product teams, the ambiguity arising from having two bosses, and the greater difficulty of monitoring and evaluating the work of teams increase the problems of coordinating task activities. A strong and

FIGURE 12.11

Product-Team
Structure

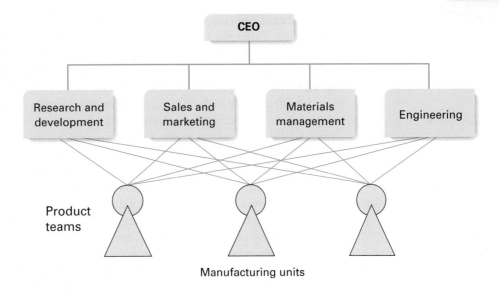

cohesive culture with unifying norms and values can mitigate these problems, as can a strategic reward system based on a group- and organizational-level reward system.

PRODUCT-TEAM STRUCTURE A major structural innovation in recent years has been the **product-team structure**. Its advantages are similar to those of a matrix structure, but it is much easier and far less costly to operate because of the way people are organized into permanent cross-functional teams, as Figure 12.11 illustrates. In the product-team structure, as in the matrix structure, tasks are divided along product or project lines. However, instead of being assigned only *temporarily* to different projects, as in the matrix structure, functional specialists become part of a *permanent* cross-functional team that focuses on the development of one particular range of products such as luxury cars or computer workstations. As a result, the problems associated with coordinating cross-functional transfers or handoffs are much lower than in a matrix structure, in which tasks and reporting relationships change rapidly. Moreover, cross-functional teams are formed at the beginning of the product development process so that any difficulties that arise can be ironed out early, before they lead to major redesign problems. When all functions have direct input from the beginning, design costs and subsequent manufacturing costs can be kept low. Moreover, the use of cross-functional teams speeds innovation and customer responsiveness because, when authority is decentralized, team decisions can be made more quickly.

A product-team structure groups tasks by product, and each product group is managed by a cross-functional product team that has all the support services necessary to bring the product to market. This is why it is different from the product structure, where support functions remain centralized. The role of the product team is to protect and enhance a company's differentiation advantage and at the same time coordinate with manufacturing to lower costs.

● **Focusing on a Narrow Product Line**

As Chapter 5 discussed, a focused company concentrates on developing a narrow range of products aimed at one or two market segments, which may be defined by type of customer or location. As a result, a focuser tends to have a higher cost structure than a cost leader or differentiator because output levels are lower, making it harder to obtain substantial scale economies. For this reason, a focused company must exercise cost control. On the other hand, some attribute of its product gives the focuser its distinctive competency—possibly its ability to provide customers with high-quality, personalized service. For both reasons, the structure and control system adopted by a focused company has to be inexpensive to operate but flexible enough to allow a distinctive competency to emerge.

A company using a focus strategy normally adopts a functional structure to meet these needs. This structure is appropriate because it is complex enough to manage the activities necessary to make and sell a narrow range of products for one or a few market segments. At the same time, the handoff problems are likely to be relatively easy to solve because a focuser remains small and specialized. Thus, a functional structure can provide all the integration necessary, provided that the focused firm has a strong, adaptive culture, which is vital to the development of some kind of distinctive competency.[52] Additionally, because such a company's competitive advantage is often based on personalized service, the flexibility of this kind of structure lets the company respond quickly to customers' needs and change its products in response to customers' requests. The way in which Lexmark reorganized itself to focus on the production of office printers, an approach examined in Strategy in Action 12.4, illustrates many of the issues in implementing a focus strategy.

Strategy in Action   12.4

Restructuring at Lexmark

Lexmark, a printer and typewriter manufacturer, was one of IBM's many divisions, but IBM sold it after years of losses brought on by high operating costs and an inability to produce new printers that could compete with those made by HP and Canon. Marvin Mann, an ex-IBM executive, was given the task of finding a way to restructure the company and turn it around. Mann realized at once that the company had to focus on producing a particular kind of printer to lower its out-of-control cost structure.

One of the biggest contributors to its high cost structure was Lexmark's structure and control system, so Mann decided to transform it. Then, he believed, he could begin to focus the company on producing a line of state-of-the-art laser and inkjet office printers. Like the rest of IBM at that time, Lexmark had developed a tall, centralized structure, and all important decision making was made by top managers. This slowed decision making and made it very difficult to communicate across functions because so many managers at different levels and in different functions had to approve new plans. Moving quickly to change this system, Mann streamlined the company's hierarchy, which meant terminating 50% of its managers. This action cut out three levels in the hierarchy. He then decentralized authority to the managers of each of the company's four product lines and told them to develop their own plans and goals. In addition, to continue the process of decentralization, product managers were instructed to develop cross-functional teams comprised of employees from all functions, with the goal of finding new and improved ways of organizing task activities to reduce costs. The teams were to use competitive benchmarking and evaluate their competitors' products in order to establish new performance standards to guide their activities. Finally, as an incentive for employees to work hard at increasing efficiency, innovation, and quality, Mann established a company stock ownership scheme to reward employees for their efforts.

Mann's strategy of restructuring Lexmark to focus on a narrow range of printers was successful. Within two years, the cost of launching new products went down by 50% and its new-product development cycle speeded up by 30%. Focusing on a narrow range of products also improved Lexmark's R&D competence. Lexmark is a technology leader in the laser and inkjet industry and makes the printers sold by Dell—showing that it is a focused cost leader in the printer market. Its stock has performed well as a result, and the company is enjoying considerable success against HP and Japanese competitors.[d]

The message of the preceding sections is clear. Strategic managers must continually monitor the performance of their organization as measured by its ability to increase differentiation, lower costs, and increase profitability. When managers sense declining performance or sense ways to increase performance, they must move quickly to change the way people and activities are organized and controlled. Organizational design, the process of combining and harmonizing structure, control, and culture, is a demanding and difficult task but one that is crucial to promoting and sustaining competitive advantage.

Restructuring and Reengineering

To improve performance, a single business company often employs restructuring and reengineering. **Restructuring** a company involves two steps: (1) streamlining the hierarchy of authority and reducing the number of levels in the hierarchy to a minimum, and then (2) reducing the number of employees to lower operating costs. When Jack Smith took over as head of GM, for example, GM had more than twenty-two levels in the hierarchy and more than 20,000 corporate managers. Describing his organization as a top-heavy bureaucracy, Smith quickly moved to slash costs and restructure the company. Today, GM has only twelve levels in the hierarchy and half as many corporate managers. In 2004, Kodak announced it would lay off 20% of its work force over a three-year period to reduce costs.

Restructuring and downsizing become necessary for many reasons.[53] Sometimes a change in the business environment occurs that could not have been foreseen; perhaps a shift in technology made the company's products obsolete, as happened to Kodak when the use of digital cameras exploded. Sometimes an organization has excess capacity because customers no longer want the goods and services it provides; maybe the goods and services are outdated or offer poor value for the money. Sometimes organizations downsize because they have grown too tall and inflexible and bureaucratic costs have become much too high—as happened to IBM. Sometimes they restructure even when they are in a strong position simply to build and improve their competitive advantage and stay on top—which Dell and Microsoft frequently do.

All too often, however, companies are forced to downsize and lay off employees because they fail to monitor and control their basic business operations and have not made the incremental changes to their strategies and structures over time that allow them to adjust to changing conditions. Advances in management, such as the development of new models for organizing work activities, or advances in information technology offer strategic managers the opportunity to implement their strategies in more effective ways.

One way of helping a company operate more effectively is to use **reengineering**, which involves the "fundamental rethinking and radical redesign of business processes to achieve dramatic improvements in critical, contemporary measures of performance such as cost, quality, service, and speed."[54] As this definition suggests, strategic managers who use reengineering must completely rethink how they organize their value chain activities. Instead of focusing on how a company's *functions* operate, strategic managers make business *processes* the focus of attention.

A **business process** is any activity that is vital to delivering goods and services to customers quickly or that promotes high quality or low costs (such as IT, materials management, or product development) and that is not the responsibility of any one function but *cuts across functions*. Because reengineering focuses on business processes and not on functions, a company that reengineers always has to adopt a different approach to organizing its activities. Companies that take up reengineering deliberately ignore the existing arrangement of tasks, roles, and work activities. They start the reengineering process with the customer (not the product or service) and ask: How can we reorganize the way we do our work, our business processes, to provide the best quality and the lowest-cost goods and services to the customer?

Frequently, when companies ask this question, they realize that there are more effective ways to organize their value chain activities. For example, a business process that encompasses members of ten different functions working sequentially to provide goods and services might be performed by one person or a few people at a fraction of the cost. Often individual jobs become increasingly complex, and people are grouped into cross-functional teams as business processes are reengineered to reduce costs and increase quality.

Hallmark Cards, for example, reengineered its card design process with great success. Before the reengineering effort, artists, writers, and editors worked separately in different functions to produce all kinds of cards. After reengineering, these same artists, writers, and editors were put in cross-functional teams, each of which now works on a specific type of card, such as birthday, Christmas, or Mother's Day. The result is that the time it takes to bring a new card to market dropped from years to months, and Hallmark's performance increased dramatically.

Reengineering and total quality management (TQM), discussed in Chapter 4, are highly interrelated and complementary. After reengineering has taken place and value chain activities have been altered to speed the product to the final customer, TQM takes over, with its focus on how to continue to improve and refine the new process and find better ways of managing task and role relationships. Successful organizations examine both issues simultaneously and continuously attempt to identify new and better processes for meeting the goals of increased efficiency, quality, and customer responsiveness. Thus, they are always seeking to improve their visions of their desired future.

Another example of reengineering is the change program that took place at IBM Credit, a wholly owned division of IBM that manages the financing and leasing of IBM computers, particularly mainframes, to IBM's customers. Before reengineering took place, a financing request arrived at the division's headquarters in Old Greenwich, Connecticut, and went through a five-step approval process that involved the activities of five different functions. First, the IBM salesperson called the credit department, which logged the request and recorded details about the potential customer. Second, this information was taken to the credit-checking department, where a credit check on the potential customer was done. Third, when the credit check was complete, the request was taken to the contracts department, which wrote the contract. Fourth, from the contracts department, it went to the pricing department, which determined the actual financial details of the loan, such as the interest rate and the term of the loan. Finally, the whole package of information was assembled by the dispatching department and delivered to the sales representative, who gave it to the customer.

This series of cross-functional activities took an average of seven days to complete, and sales representatives constantly complained that this delay resulted in a low level of customer responsiveness that reduced customer satisfaction. Also, potential customers were tempted to shop around for financing and even to look at competitors' machines. The delay in closing the deal caused uncertainty for all concerned.

The change process began when two senior IBM credit managers reviewed the finance approval process. They found that the time spent by different specialists in the different functions actually processing a loan application was only ninety minutes. The seven-day approval process was caused by the delay in transmitting information and requests between departments. The managers also learned that the activities taking place in each department were not complex; each department had its own computer system containing its own work procedures, but the work done in each department was pretty routine.

Armed with this information, IBM managers realized that the approval process could be reengineered into one overarching process handled by one person with a computer system containing all the necessary information and work procedures to perform the five loan-processing activities. If the application were complex, a team of experts stood ready to help process it, but IBM found that, after the reengineering effort, a typical application could be done in four hours rather than the previous seven days. A sales representative could go back to the customer the same day to close the deal, and all the uncertainty surrounding the transaction was removed.

As reengineering consultants Hammer and Champy note, this dramatic performance increase was brought about by a radical change to the process as a whole. Change through reengineering requires managers to go back to the basics and pull apart each step in the work process to identify a better way to coordinate and integrate the activities necessary to provide customers with goods and services. As this example makes clear, the introduction of new IT is an integral aspect of reengineering. IT also allows a company to restructure its hierarchy because it provides more and better-quality information. IT today is an integral part of the strategy implementation process.

Summary of Chapter

1. Implementing a company's business model and strategies successfully depends on organizational design, the process of selecting the right combination of organizational structure, control systems, and culture. Companies need to monitor and oversee the organizational design process to achieve superior profitability.

2. Effective organizational design can increase profitability in two ways. First, it economizes on bureaucratic costs and helps a company lower its cost structure. Second, it enhances the ability of a company's value creation functions to achieve superior efficiency, quality, innovativeness, and customer responsiveness and to obtain the advantages of differentiation.

3. The main issues in designing organizational structure are how to group tasks, functions, and divisions; how to allocate authority and responsibility (whether to have a tall or flat organization, or to have a centralized or decentralized structure); and how to use integrating mechanisms to improve coordination between functions (such as direct contacts, liaison roles, and teams).

4. Strategic control provides the monitoring and incentive systems necessary to make an organizational structure work as intended and extends corporate governance down to all levels inside the company. The main kinds of strategic control systems are personal control, output control, and behavior control. Information technology is an aid to output and behavior control, and reward systems are linked to every control system.

5. Organizational culture is the set of values, norms, beliefs, and attitudes that help to energize and motivate employees and control their behavior. Culture is a way of doing something, and a company's founder and top managers help determine which kinds of values emerge in an organization.

6. At the functional level, each function requires a different combination of structure and control system to achieve its functional objectives.

7. To successfully implement a company's business model, structure, control, and culture must be combined in ways that increase the relationships among all functions to build distinctive competencies.

8. Cost leadership and differentiation each require a structure and control system that strengthens the business model that is the source of their competitive advantage. Managers have to use organizational design in a way that balances pressures to increase differentiation against pressures to lower the cost structure.

9. Other specialized kinds of structures include the product, market, geographic, matrix, and product-team structures. Each has a specialized use and is implemented as a company's strategy warrants.

10. Restructuring and reengineering are two ways of implementing a company's business model more effectively.

Discussion Questions

1. What is the relationship among organizational structure, control, and culture? Give some examples of when and under what conditions a mismatch among these components might arise.

2. What kind of structure best describes the way your (a) business school and (b) university operate? Why is the structure appropriate? Would another structure fit better?

3. When would a company choose a matrix structure? What are the problems associated with managing this structure, and why might a product-team structure be preferable?

4. For each of the structures discussed in the chapter, outline the most suitable control systems.

5. What kind of structure, controls, and culture would you be likely to find in (a) a small manufacturing company, (b) a chain store, (c) a high-tech company, and (d) a Big Four accounting firm?

Practicing Strategic Management

SMALL-GROUP EXERCISE
Deciding on an Organizational Structure

Break up into groups of three to five people, and discuss the following scenario. You are a group of managers of a major soft drink company that is going head-to-head with Coca-Cola to increase market share. Your business model is based on increasing your product range to offer a soft drink in every segment of the market to attract customers. Currently you have a functional structure. What you are trying to work out now is how best to implement your business model in order to launch your new products. Should you move to a more complex kind of product structure and, if so, which one? Alternatively, should you establish new-venture divisions and spin off each kind of new soft drink into its own company so that it can focus its resources on its market niche? Thinking strategically, debate the pros and cons of the possible organizational structures, and decide which structure you will implement.

ARTICLE FILE 12

Find an example of a company that competes in one industry and has recently changed the way it implements its business model and strategies. What changes did it make? Why did it make these changes? What effect did these changes have on the behavior of people and functions?

STRATEGIC MANAGEMENT PROJECT
Module 12

This module asks you to identify how your company implements its business model and strategy. For this part of your project, you need to obtain information about your company's structure, control systems, and culture. This information may be hard to obtain unless you can interview managers directly. But you can make many inferences about the company's structure from the nature of its activities, and if you write to the company, it may provide you with an organizational chart and other information. Also, published information, such as compensation for top management, is available in the company's annual reports or 10-K reports. If your company is well known, magazines such as *Fortune* and *Business Week* frequently report on corporate culture or control issues. Nevertheless, you may be forced to make some bold assumptions to complete this part of the project.

1. How large is the company as measured by the number of its employees? How many levels in the hierarchy

CHAPTER 12   Implementing Strategy in Companies That Compete in a Single Industry

does it have from the top to the bottom? Based on these two measures and any other information you may have, would you say your company operates with a relatively tall or flat structure? Does your company have a centralized or decentralized approach to decision making?

2. What changes (if any) would you make to the way the company allocates authority and responsibility?

3. Draw an organizational chart showing the main way in which your company groups its activities. Based on this chart, decide what kind of structure (functional, product, or divisional) your company is using.

4. Why did your company choose this structure? In what ways is it appropriate for its business model? In what ways is it not?

5. What kind of integration or integration mechanisms does your company use?

6. What are the main kinds of control systems your company is using? What kinds of behaviors is the organization trying to (a) shape and (b) motivate through the use of these control systems?

7. What role does the top management team play in creating the culture of your organization? Can you identify the characteristic norms and values that describe the way people behave in your organization? How does the design of the organization's structure affect its culture?

8. What are the sources of your company's distinctive competencies? Which functions are most important to it? How does your company design its structure, control, and culture to enhance its (a) efficiency, (b) quality, (c) innovativeness, and (d) responsiveness to customers?

9. How does it design its structure and control systems to strengthen its business model? For example, what steps does it take to further cross-functional integration? Does it have a functional, product, or matrix structure?

10. How does your company's culture support its business model? Can you determine any ways in which its top management team influences its culture?

11. Based on this analysis, would you say your company is coordinating and motivating its people and subunits effectively? Why or why not? What changes (if any) would you make to the way your company's structure operates? What use could it make of restructuring or reengineering?

ETHICS EXERCISE

Rose checked and rechecked the petty cash log. No matter how many times she calculated the amount, the log always ended up $100 short. Only Rose, Jason, and their boss David had access to the petty cash account. A month ago, the account had been short $150, and the month before that, $75 had been missing. On both occasions, Jason figured out where the money had gone. Rose called him now. "Jason, do you know anything about a missing $100 in the petty cash account? I can't find a $100 expense anywhere in the log and we're definitely missing money." Jason told Rose he would be right down.

Jason finally arrived at Rose's desk a half an hour later. "No problem, Rose," he said. "David doesn't have the receipt anymore, but he used the money to take care of dinner with a client."

Rose paused; the same excuse had been offered on previous occasions. "Jason, we can't keep logging expenses without receipts. Accounting is going to question our records sooner or later."

Jason glanced around and said quietly, "Trust me, Rose. This is what we have to do—just do it." Then he walked away.

Rose knew something was wrong. She was worried that Jason was somehow stealing from petty cash. Finally she decided to tell David, their boss. When she arrived for her 1:00 appointment in David's office, she was surprised to see Jason already there. He wouldn't meet her eyes, and she assumed that David had already discovered his stealing. Before she could speak, David said, in a voice that Rose had never heard before, "It seems that I have to let you in on a little secret, Rose. From time to time, I need a little extra from petty cash. For a corporation this size, $100 here, $200 there is nothing. I've already had a few chats with Jason here, who needs to keep his job to help his mother. It seems to me that you need your job, too—kids at home, right? Well, if either of you mentions these little 'expenses' of mine to anyone, you'll be fired instantly. Who will they believe, you two peons, or me—with 25 years of loyal service to the company? All I have to do is tell them that you've been the ones robbing petty cash!"

1. Define the ethical dilemmas addressed in this case.

2. What should the company do to ensure that employees feel safe reporting wrongdoing?

3. What would you do if you were in Rose's situation?

CLOSING CASE

Nokia's New Product Structure

Nokia is the largest cellular or mobile phone maker in the world, with sales of over $45 billion in 2006. The company was a pioneer of cell phone technology, and throughout the 1990s, its sales surged every year; however, business has not been as good in the 2000s. Like Motorola, another cell phone pioneer, Nokia's profits have fallen because it has run into tough competition from companies like Samsung, Sony, and hand-held makers like Palm that have been rushing to offer their customers new and improved varieties of hand-held devices or smart phones. In the Opening Case to Chapter 5, we saw how Samsung was the first company to realize that customers wanted a color screen so that they could play games on their phones, and Samsung was also one of the first to realize the potential of integrating digital cameras into phones. The market is growing for game-playing phones, Internet-connected phones, and smart phones that include functions such as an MP3 player, record keeping software, and applications software for PowerPoint presentations and word processing. Also growing rapidly is the market for wireless technology that can securely link smart phones used in the field to the company's central databases and the PCs in employees' offices or homes, especially now that broadband communication is becoming the norm.

Analysts claim that Nokia was slow to sense these emerging trends partly because of its organizational structure and culture. Nokia's way of operating was to push down or decentralize decision making to lower levels, where teams of employees were responsible for developing innovative new cell phone software and hardware. Bureaucracy was kept to a minimum, and team members normally discussed product development in informal meetings. In addition, Nokia's culture was based on Finnish values and norms that emphasized democratic, shared, and informal work relationships rather than the use of formal authority.

This way of implementing strategy had led to superior innovation and a successful business model, but as Nokia grew bigger, problems emerged. While the cell phone market was changing rapidly, Nokia's team structure resulted in slow decision making. It was taking more and more time for Nokia to create new products and bring them to market. Higher-level managers had to wait longer to find out what the teams below them were doing, and then top managers from all parts of the organization had to meet in so-called company committees to decide which products should be given the most funding and the highest priority. Another problem was that Nokia's top managers, headquartered in Espoo, Finland, were remote from global customers, and its marketing and engineering managers were slow to pick up on developing wireless trends, such as customers' desire for digital cameras. In particular, they did not appreciate how fast the global market was fragmenting into customers in rich countries like Japan and the United States who wanted sophisticated, broadband-capable smart phones and were prepared to pay high prices for them, and customers in developing countries such as China, India, and those in South America who needed an inexpensive cell phone infrastructure and service, as well as inexpensive cell phones.

In the early 2000s, when the company's sales started to fall and its Japanese competitors took the lead, Nokia's managers realized they needed to change the way the company operated to quicken Nokia's response to the changing marketplace. Nokia's CEO, Jorma Ollila, announced that in 2004, Nokia would split its activities into four separate product divisions, each of which would focus on developing cell phone software and hardware for a particular market segment. Three of these were new divisions: (1) the *mobile phone* division, which would primarily design and sell low-cost, low-priced handsets mostly for voice calls; (2) the *multimedia* division, which would design and sell advanced smart phones with features such as gaming and picture taking and which would pursue differentiation and, Nokia managers hoped, premium pricing; and (3) the *networks* division, which would sell the technology necessary to build mobile phone networks and create wireless infrastructure in regions and countries around the globe. Finally, Nokia announced it would greatly expand the activities of its *enterprise solutions* division, which was responsible for developing hardware and software products for corporate customers in search of a wireless corporate intranet. Here, it was competing directly against companies like Microsoft, IBM, and HP.[55]

The plan was that each product division would be under the control of its own team of top executives and that each team would build the business model necessary to compete successfully in its market segment. By decentralizing control to each division, Nokia hoped to speed up team decision making, reasoning that managers would be in much closer contact with these teams and could intervene quickly as the need arises. Nokia hoped the new structure would allow it to innovate new models of cell phones at a faster rate and at a lower cost and thus combat the threat from Samsung. In addition, to get closer to its customers, Nokia announced that it would expand its overseas operations—for example, by outsourcing more manufacturing to Asia and establishing more local sales offices. It would also create a U.S. headquarters for its new enterprise solutions division, and it hired a former HP executive, Mary McDowell, to head the division and spearhead its push into this large and profitable corporate networking market. Only time will tell if Nokia's new structure will be successful, but the company has introduced many new products in the last few years and its sales are once again on the upward path, which has hurt competitors like Motorola and Samsung.[56]

Case Discussion Questions

1. Why and how did Nokia move to a product structure to better implement its business model?

2. What organizational design lessons could other companies learn from Nokia's example?

3. Go to the Internet and try to discover any recent changes Nokia has made to its structure.

Implementing Strategy in Companies That Compete Across Industries and Countries

OPENING CASE

Ford Has a New CEO and a New Global Structure

Designing a global business organization to operate in many countries is a critical issue for multinational companies. Ford is a good example of a company that has experienced these types of problems. Ford realized early that there was a major opportunity to increase profitability by taking its skills in carmaking to countries abroad. Over time, it established carmaking business units in different countries in Europe, Asia, and Australia. Decision-making authority was decentralized to each unit, which controlled its own activities and developed cars suited to its local market. The result was that each unit came to operate independently from the Ford parent company in the United States. Ford of Europe, for example, became the largest and most profitable carmaker in Europe.

Ford remained a highly profitable enterprise until Japanese carmakers began to flood the world with their small, reliable, low-priced cars in the 1970s and 1980s. When car buyers began buying these imports in large numbers, Ford tried to draw on the skills of its European unit to help build smaller, more fuel-efficient cars for the U.S. market. But it had never before tried to get its U.S. and European design and manufacturing units to cooperate, and this proved very difficult to achieve because of the nature of its global organizational structure. In the 1990s, Ford embarked on a massive project to create a new global matrix structure for the company that would solve the decentralized task and authority problems that were preventing it from utilizing its resources effectively. In its Ford 2000 plan, for example, it laid out a timetable of how all its global carmaking units would learn to cooperate with one set of global support functions such as design, purchasing, and so on. However, huge political problems arose with its new structure; the redesign went through one change after another; and by the mid 2000s, Ford was still operating as a collection of different "empires." Its U.S., European, and Asia/Pacific units were operating almost autonomously.

So Ford decided to restructure itself. It moved to a so-called world structure in which one set of managers was given authority over the whole of a specific global operation such as manufacturing or car design. Then it began to design cars for the global market. Its new structure never worked to quicken car design and production, even though it constantly changed global lines of authority and the locations in which it operated to increase profitability. Ford went through multiple reorganizations to try to meet the Japanese challenge but nothing worked. By 2006, it was in deep trouble. Losing billions of dollars, Ford announced in September 2006 a revamped "Way Forward" plan to turn around its U.S. and global operations, a plan that called for cutting 44,000 jobs; closing sixteen plants; and freshening 70% of the company's Ford, Mercury, and Lincoln car lineup.

But in October 2006, Ford also appointed a new president and CEO, Alan Mulally, an expert in organizational design, to help turn around its operations. Mulally, a former Boeing executive, had led that company's global reorganization effort. Now he began to work out how to change Ford's global structure to reduce costs and speed product development. In the structure Mulally inherited, Ford's Americas unit reported to the CEO, but its other global and functional operations reported to the next two most senior executives, Mark Fields, president of Ford's Americas operation, and Mark Schulz, president of international operations. Mulally decided that Ford's downsizing should be accompanied by a major reorganization of its hierarchy, and he decided to flatten Ford's structure and recentralize control. At the same time, however, he put the focus on teamwork and adopted a cross-functional approach to handling the enormous value chain challenges that still confronted the organization.

The position of president of international operations was eliminated and Mark Fields continues to report to Mulally, but so too do the heads of the other two world regions—Lewis Booth, head of Ford of Europe, and John Parker, head of Ford of Asia Pacific and Africa, and Mazda. Two levels in the hierarchy are now gone, and Mulally's new organizational design clearly defines each global executive's role in the company's hierarchy so Ford can begin acting like one company instead of separate global units, each with their own interests.[1] In addition, the heads of its global value chain functions also now

report directly to Mulally, not to Fields; these heads include Tony Brown, global head of purchasing; Nick Smither, head of information technology (IT); Richard Parry-Jones, chief technical officer; and Bennie Fowler, head of quality and advanced manufacturing engineering. Mulally's goal is to provide a centralized focus on using the company's global functional assets to better support its carmaking business units.

At the same time, Mulally also took a major restructuring step when he announced the creation of a new position, global product development chief, who is responsible for overseeing the development of Ford's entire global lines of vehicles. He appointed Derrick Kuzak, head of product development in the Americas, to head Ford's new global engineering design effort, and he also reports directly to Mulally. Kuzak oversees efforts to streamline product development and engineering systems around the world. As Mulally commented, "An integrated, global product development team supporting our automotive business units will enable us to make the best use of our global assets and capabilities and accelerate development of the new vehicles our customers prefer, and do so more efficiently."[2]

So Mulally's goal is to force a cross-functional approach on all his top managers—one that he will personally oversee—to standardize its global carmaking and allow functional units to continuously improve quality, productivity, and the speed at which new products can be introduced. But beyond streamlining and standardizing its approach, its new-product development group must also ensure that its new vehicles—vehicles that it intends to introduce at a rapid rate in the rest of the 2000s—are customized to better meet the needs of regional customers All Ford's executives understand the company's very survival is at stake; they must work together to accelerate efforts to reduce costs and catch up to more efficient competitors such as Toyota. If Mulally's new global design cannot achieve this goal, it is likely that Ford will be taken over by a competitor in the next decade.

OVERVIEW   The story of Ford's efforts to develop a competitive global business model to compete effectively in car markets around the world suggests how complex strategic thinking can become at the corporate level. Companies have to continually examine how to improve the way they implement their business and multibusiness models to increase their long-run profitability and grow their profits. This chapter takes off where the last one ends and examines how to implement strategy when a company decides to enter and compete in new industries, or in new countries when it expands globally, and when it chooses strategies such as merger or outsourcing to strengthen its business model. The strategy implementation issue remains the same: how to use organizational design and combine organizational structure, control, and culture to allow a company to pursue its business model and strategies successfully. Once a company decides to compete across industries and countries, however, it confronts a new set of problems, some of them continuations of problems discussed in Chapter 12 and some of them a direct consequence of its decision to enter and compete in overseas markets and new industries. As a result, it has to make a new series of organizational design decisions to successfully implement its new global and multibusiness model. By the end of the chapter, you will appreciate the many complex issues and choices confronting managers of multibusiness and global companies and the reasons that strategy implementation is an integral part of achieving superior performance.

Managing Corporate Strategy Through the Multidivisional Structure

As Chapter 10 discussed, corporate-level strategies such as vertical integration or diversification can be used in many ways to strengthen a company's business model to improve its competitive position. However, substantial implementation problems also arise, many of them due to the increasing bureaucratic costs associated with managing a larger collection of companies that operate in different industries. These costs are especially high when a company is seeking to gain the differentiation and low-cost advantages of transferring, sharing, or leveraging its distinctive competencies across its business units in different industries. For companies pursuing a multibusiness model, the problems and costs of managing the handoffs or transfers between value chain functions across industries to obtain these benefits rise sharply. The need to economize on these costs propels strategic managers to search for improved ways of implementing the corporate-level strategies necessary to pursue a multibusiness model.

As a company begins to enter new industries and produce completely different kinds of products such as cars, fast food, and computers, the structures described in Chapter 12, like the functional and product structures, are not up to the task. They cannot provide sufficient coordination between functions and motivation to employees that implementing a multibusiness model requires. As a result, the control problems that give rise to bureaucratic costs, such as those related to measurement, customers, location, or strategy, escalate. Experiencing these problems is a sign that the company has outgrown its structure. Strategic managers need to invest more resources to develop a more complex structure—one that can meet the needs of its multibusiness model and strategies. The answer for most large, complex companies is to move to a multidivisional structure, design a cross-industry control system, and fashion a corporate culture to reduce these problems and economize on bureaucratic costs.

The multidivisional structure possesses two main innovations over a functional or product structure, and these innovations allow a company to grow and diversify while reducing the coordination and control problems inherent in entering and competing in new industries. First, in each industry in which a company operates, strategic managers organize its business units or companies in that industry into one or more *divisions*. Sometimes each division contains a full set of all the value chain functions it needs to pursue its business model; in this case, it is called a *self-contained division*. For example, GE competes in over 150 different industries, and in each industry, all of its divisions are self-sufficient and perform all the value creation functions. Sometimes, however, divisions in *different* industries share value chain functions to obtain cost savings and to benefit from leveraging competencies across divisions, as discussed in detail below. For example, PepsiCo has two major divisions in the soft drink and snack foods industries; each has its own research and development (R&D) and manufacturing functions, but they share the marketing and distribution functions to lower operating costs and achieve the gains from differentiation.

Second, the office of *corporate headquarters staff* is created to monitor divisional activities and to exercise financial control over each of the divisions.[3] This staff contains the corporate-level managers who oversee the activities of divisional managers. Hence, the organizational hierarchy is taller in a multidivisional structure than in a product or functional structure. The role of the new level of corporate management is to develop strategic control systems that lower a company's overall cost structure, including finding ways to economize on the costs of controlling the handoffs and transfers between divisions. The extra cost of these corporate managers is more than justified if their actions can lower the cost structure of the operating divisions or increase the divisions' ability to differentiate their product—both of which boost a company's return on invested capital (ROIC).

In the multidivisional structure, the day-to-day operations of each division are the responsibility of divisional management; that is, divisional management has *operating responsibility*. The corporate headquarters, which includes top executives as well as their support staff, is responsible for overseeing the company's long-term multibusiness model and for providing guidance for interdivisional projects. These executives have *strategic responsibility*. Such a combination of self-contained divisions with a centralized corporate management provides the extra coordination and control necessary to manage entry into new industries.

Figure 13.1 illustrates a typical multidivisional structure found in a large chemical company such as DuPont. Although this company might easily have twenty different divisions, only three—the oil, pharmaceuticals, and plastics divisions—are represented here. Each division possesses some combination of the value chain functions it needs to pursue its own business model. Each is also normally treated by the corporate center as a profit center, and strategic control measures such as ROIC are used to monitor and evaluate each division's performance.[4] The use of this kind of output control makes it easier for corporate managers to identify high-performing and underperforming divisions and to take corrective action as necessary.

Because they have been separated into subunits by industry, each division is also able to develop the structure (for example, a product, matrix, or market structure) and culture that best suit its particular business model. As a result, implementing a multidivisional structure allows a multibusiness company to let each separate division adopt the structure and control systems necessary to implement its business model and strategies effectively.

Figure 13.1 shows that the oil division has a functional structure because it is pursuing cost leadership. The pharmaceuticals division has a product-team structure to encourage speedy development of new drugs, and the plastics division has a matrix structure to allow it to quickly develop new kinds of customized plastic products to suit the changing needs of its customers. These divisions are pursuing differentiation

FIGURE 13.1

Multidivisional Structure

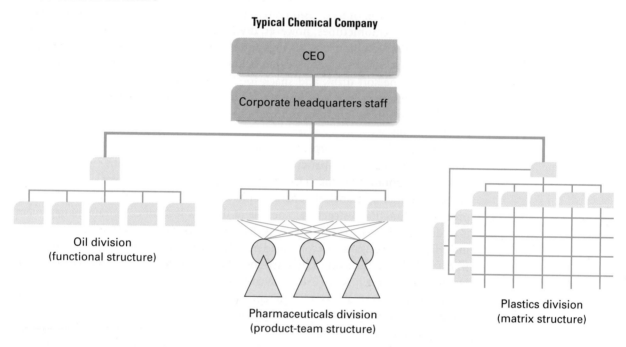

Typical Chemical Company

Oil division
(functional structure)

Pharmaceuticals division
(product-team structure)

Plastics division
(matrix structure)

based on a distinctive competence in innovation. Sometimes the size of its operations alone is enough to compel a company to use a multidivisional structure. For example, inside one industry, the car industry, Ford operates the whole corporation through a multidivisional structure, and each of its main car brands—Ford, Jaguar, Mercury, Mazda, Lincoln, and so on—is organized as a separate division. In addition, as we discussed in the Opening Case, Ford has an overseas division in each country in which it assembles cars abroad.

In fact, the executive most famous for employing the multidivisional structure in this way was also the CEO of a car company, Alfred Sloan, former CEO of GM. He implemented its multidivisional structure in 1921, noting that GM "needs to find a principle for coordination without losing the advantages of decentralization." Sloan placed each of GM's different car brands in a self-contained division with support services like sales, production, engineering, and finance. Each division became a profit center and was evaluated on its return on investment. Sloan was quite clear about the main advantage of linking decentralization to return on investment: it raised the visibility of each division's performance. And, Sloan observed, it (1) "increases the morale of the organization by placing each operation on its own foundation, . . . assuming its own responsibility and contributing its share to the final result"; (2) "develops statistics correctly reflecting . . . the true measure of efficiency"; and (3) "enables the corporation to direct the placing of additional capital where it will result in the greatest benefit to the corporation as a whole."[5]

Sloan recommended that exchanges or handoffs between divisions be set by a *transfer-pricing scheme* based on cost plus some predetermined rate of return. To avoid protecting a high-cost internal supplier, however, he also recommended a number of steps involving analysis of the operations of outside competitors to determine the fair price. Sloan established a strong, professional, centralized headquarters management staff to perform such calculations. Corporate management's primary role was to audit divisional performance and plan strategy for the total organization. Divisional managers were to be responsible for all product-related decisions.

As the Opening Case related, fierce competition from efficient Japanese competitors has resulted in Ford CEO Mulally reorganizing the way Ford's multidivisional structure operated, both domestically and globally. The duplication of R&D and engineering between divisions at home and abroad, and the purchasing of components by each global division independently, was costing the company billions of extra dollars. Globally, Ford's goal is to streamline the number of cars in its product range and the number of different plants in which its cars are made. As Ford's experience suggests, operating a multidivisional structure is a *continuing* challenge for managers. Because the multidivisional structure is so widely used, it is necessary to look closely at its advantages and disadvantages.

● **Advantages of a Multidivisional Structure**

When managed effectively at both the corporate and the divisional levels, a multidivisional structure offers several advantages. Together, they can raise corporate profitability to a new peak because they allow a company to more effectively implement its multibusiness model and strategies at all levels.

ENHANCED CORPORATE FINANCIAL CONTROL   The profitability of different business divisions is clearly visible in the multidivisional structure.[6] Because each division is its own profit center, financial controls can be applied to each business on the basis of profitability criteria such as ROIC. Typically, these controls cover establishing targets, monitoring performance on a regular basis, and selectively intervening when problems arise. Corporate headquarters is also in a better position to allocate corporate financial resources among competing divisions. The visibility of divisional performance means that corporate headquarters can identify the divisions in which investment of funds will yield the greatest long-term ROIC. In a sense, the corporate office is in a position to act as the investor or banker in an internal capital market, channeling funds to high-yield uses.

ENHANCED STRATEGIC CONTROL   The multidivisional structure frees corporate managers from business-level responsibilities. Corporate managers have the time and scope for contemplating wider strategic issues and for developing responses to environmental changes, such as quickly changing industry boundaries. The multidivisional structure also enables corporate headquarters to obtain the proper information to perform long-run strategic and scenario planning for the entire corporation, including decisions about which businesses to expand and which to exit.

GROWTH   The multidivisional structure lets the company overcome an organizational limit to its growth. Because information overload at the center is reduced, corporate managers can consider emerging opportunities for further growth and diversification. Communication problems are reduced because the same set of standardized accounting and financial output controls can be used for all divisions. Also, from a behavior control perspective, corporate managers can implement a policy of management by exception, which means that they intervene only when problems arise.

STRONGER PURSUIT OF INTERNAL EFFICIENCY   As a company grows, it often becomes difficult for managers to accurately assess the profit contribution of each functional activity because their activities are so interdependent. This means that it is often more difficult for top managers to evaluate how well their company is performing relative to others in its industry. As a result, inside one company, considerable degrees of organizational slack—that is, the unproductive use of functional resources—can go undetected. For example, the head of the finance function might employ a larger staff than is required for efficiency to reduce work pressures inside the department and to bring the manager higher status. In a multidivisional structure, however, corporate managers can compare the performance of one division against another in terms of its cost structure or the profit it generates. The corporate office is thus in a better position to identify the managerial inefficiencies that result in bureaucratic costs, and divisional managers have no alibis for poor performance.

● Problems in Implementing a Multidivisional Structure

Although research suggests that large companies that adopt a multidivisional structure outperform those that retain the functional structure, this structure has its disadvantages as well.[7] Good management can eliminate some of them, but others are inherent in the way the structure operates and require constant managerial attention, as Ford's problems suggest.

ESTABLISHING THE DIVISIONAL-CORPORATE AUTHORITY RELATIONSHIP The authority relationship between corporate headquarters and the divisions must be correctly established. The multidivisional structure introduces a new level in the hierarchy: the corporate level. The problem lies in deciding how much authority and control to delegate to the operating divisions and how much authority to retain at corporate headquarters to increase long-run profitability. This was the problem Sloan encountered when he implemented GM's multidivisional structure.[8] Sloan found that when headquarters retained too much power and authority, the operating divisions lacked sufficient autonomy to develop the business model and strategies that best met their needs. On the other hand, when too much power was delegated to the divisions, they pursued divisional objectives, with little heed to the needs of the whole corporation. As a result, not all the potential gains from using this structure could be achieved. At Ford, Mulally has recentralized control at the global level to force carmaking and functional divisions to cooperate and improve efficiency and effectiveness.

Thus, the central issue in managing the multidivisional structure is how much authority should be *centralized* at corporate headquarters and how much should be *decentralized* to the divisions. This issue must be decided by each company in reference to the nature of its business- and corporate-level strategies. There are no easy answers, and as the environment changes or the company alters its multibusiness model strategies over time, the balance between corporate and divisional control will also change.

DISTORTION OF INFORMATION If corporate headquarters places too much emphasis on each division's individual profitability—for instance, by setting very high and stringent ROIC targets—divisional managers may choose to distort the information they supply to top management and paint a rosy picture at the expense of future profitability. Bureaucratic costs now increase as divisions may attempt to make ROIC look better by cutting product development, new investments, or marketing expenditures. Although such actions might boost short-run ROIC, they do so at the cost of cutting back on the investments and expenditures that are necessary to maintain the long-term profitability of the company. The problem stems from too tight financial control. GM suffered from this problem in recent years as declining performance prompted divisional managers to try to make their divisions look good to corporate headquarters and thus secure greater funds for future investment. Managing the corporate-divisional interface requires coping with subtle power issues.

COMPETITION FOR RESOURCES The third problem of managing a multidivisional structure is that the divisions themselves may compete for resources, and this rivalry can make it difficult or impossible to obtain the gains from transferring, sharing, or leveraging distinctive competencies across business units. For example, the amount of capital for investment that corporate managers have to distribute to the divisions is fixed. Generally, the divisions that can demonstrate the highest ROIC get the lion's share of the money. Because that large share strengthens them in the next time period, the strong divisions grow stronger. Consequently, divisions may actively compete for resources and thereby reduce interdivisional coordination. As a result, the potential gains from pursuing a multibusiness model will be lost.

TRANSFER PRICING Divisional competition may lead to battles over **transfer pricing,** that is, conflicts over establishing the fair or "competitive" price of a resource or skill developed in one division that is to be transferred and sold to other divisions that require it. As we discussed in Chapter 9, one of the origins of the problems of handoffs or transfers between divisions, and thus a major source of bureaucratic costs, is the problem of setting prices for resource transfers to obtain the benefits of the multibusiness models when pursuing a vertical integration or related diversification strategy.

Rivalry among divisions is common in the transfer pricing process because each supplying division has the incentive to set the highest price for its resources or skills to maximize its own revenues and profits. However, purchasing divisions view attempts to charge high prices as undermining their own profitability—hence the problem. Such competition can completely undermine the corporate culture and turn the company into a battleground. If such battles go unresolved, the benefits of the multibusiness model will not be achieved. Hence, there is a need for the sensitive design of incentive and control systems to make the multidivisional structure work.

SHORT-TERM R&D FOCUS If corporate headquarters sets extremely high and rigid ROIC targets, there is a danger that the divisions will cut back on R&D expenditures to improve their financial performance. Although this inflates divisional performance in the short term, it undermines a division's ability to develop new products and leads to a fall in the stream of long-term profits. Hence, corporate headquarters personnel must carefully control their interactions with the divisions to ensure that both the short- and long-term goals of the business are being achieved.

DUPLICATION OF FUNCTIONAL RESOURCES Because each division often possesses its own set of value chain functions, multidivisional structures are expensive to run and manage. R&D is an especially costly activity, and so some companies centralize such functions at the corporate level to serve all divisions. The duplication of specialist services is not a problem if the cost and differentiation gains from having separate specialist functions are substantial, however. Corporate managers decide whether duplication is financially justified and, if so, which functions to centralize or decentralize to optimize short- and long-run profitability.

In sum, the advantages of divisional structures must be balanced against the problems of implementing them, but an observant, professional management team that is aware of the issues involved can manage these problems. The increasing use of information technology is also making implementation easier. We discuss information technology after we describe the use of structure, control, and culture for different kinds of multibusiness models.

● Structure, Control, Culture, and Corporate-Level Strategy

Once strategic managers select a multidivisional structure, they must then make choices about what kind of integrating mechanisms and control systems to use to make the structure work efficiently. Such choices depend on whether a company chooses to pursue a multibusiness model based on a strategy of unrelated diversification, vertical integration, or related diversification.

As discussed in Chapter 9, many possible differentiation and cost advantages derive from vertical integration. A company can coordinate resource-scheduling decisions among divisions operating in adjacent industries to reduce manufacturing costs and improve quality, for example.[9] This might mean locating a rolling mill next to a steel furnace to save the costs of reheating steel ingots and make it easier to control the quality of the final product.

The principal benefits from related diversification also come from transferring, sharing, or leveraging functional resources or skills across divisions, such as sharing distribution and sales networks to increase differentiation or lower the overall cost structure. With both strategies, the benefits to the company come from some *exchange of distinctive competencies* among divisions. To secure these benefits, the company must coordinate activities among divisions. Consequently, structure and control must be designed to manage the handoffs or transfers among divisions.

In the case of unrelated diversification, the multibusiness model is based on using general managerial capabilities in entrepreneurship, organizational design, or strategy—for example, through top managers' ability to create a culture that supports entrepreneurial behavior that leads to rapid product development; or from restructuring an underperforming company and establishing an efficient internal capital market that allows corporate managers to make superior capital allocation decisions than would be possible using the external capital market. With this strategy, there are no exchanges among divisions, each operates separately and independently, and the exchanges that need to be coordinated take place between divisions and corporate headquarters. Structure and control must therefore be designed to allow each division to operate independently while giving corporate managers easy ability to monitor and to intervene if necessary.

The choice of structure and control mechanisms depends on the degree to which a company using a multidivisional structure needs to control the handoffs and interactions among divisions. The more interdependent the divisions—that is, the more they depend on each other for skills, resources, and competencies—the greater are the bureaucratic costs associated with obtaining the potential benefits from a particular strategy.[10] Table 13.1 indicates what forms of structure and control companies should adopt to economize on the bureaucratic costs associated with the three corporate strategies of unrelated diversification, vertical integration, and related diversification.[11] We examine these strategies in detail in the next sections.

UNRELATED DIVERSIFICATION Because there are *no exchanges or linkages* among divisions, unrelated diversification is the easiest and cheapest strategy to manage; it is associated with the lowest level of bureaucratic costs. The main advantage of the structure and control system is that it allows corporate managers to evaluate divisional performance easily and accurately. Thus, companies use a multidivisional

TABLE 13.1

Corporate Strategy and Structure and Control

Corporate Strategy	Appropriate Structure	Need for Integration	Type of Control		
			Financial Control	Behavior Control	Organizational Culture
Unrelated Diversification	Multidivisional	Low (no exchanges between divisions)	Great use (e.g., ROIC)	Some use (e.g., budgets)	Little use
Vertical Integration	Multidivisional	Medium (scheduling resource transfers)	Great use (e.g., ROIC, transfer pricing)	Great use (e.g., standardization, budgets)	Some use (e.g., shared norms and values)
Related Diversification	Multidivisional	High (achieving synergies between divisions by integrating roles)	Little use	Great use (e.g., rules, budgets)	Great use (e.g., norms, values, common language)

structure, and each division is evaluated by output controls such as return on invested capital. A company also applies sophisticated accounting controls to obtain information quickly from the divisions so that corporate managers can readily compare divisions on several dimensions. UTC, Tyco, Textron, and Dover are good examples of companies that use sophisticated computer networks and accounting controls to manage their structures, which allow them almost daily access to divisional performance.

Divisions usually have considerable autonomy *unless* they fail to reach their ROIC goals. Generally, corporate headquarters will not intervene in the operations of a division unless there are problems. If problems arise, corporate headquarters may step in to take corrective action, perhaps replacing managers or providing additional financial resources, depending on the reason for the problem. If they see no possibility of a turnaround, they may decide to divest the division. The multidivisional structure allows the unrelated company to operate its businesses as a portfolio of investments that can be bought and sold as business conditions change. Often managers in the various divisions do not know one another; they may not even know what other companies are in the corporate portfolio. Hence, the idea of a corporate culture is meaningless.

The use of financial controls to manage a company means that no integration among divisions is necessary. This is why the bureaucratic costs of managing an unrelated company are low. The biggest problem facing corporate personnel is determining capital allocations to the various divisions so that the overall profitability of the portfolio is maximized. They also have to oversee divisional managers and make sure that divisions are achieving ROIC targets.

Alco Standard, based in Valley Forge, Pennsylvania, demonstrates how to operate a successful strategy of unrelated diversification. Alco is one of the largest office supply companies in the United States, distributing office and paper supplies and materials through a nationwide network of wholly owned distribution companies. The policy of Alco's top management is that authority and control should be completely decentralized to the managers in each of the company's fifty divisions. Each division is left alone to make its own manufacturing or purchasing decisions even though some potential benefits, in the form of corporatewide purchasing or marketing, are being lost. Top management pursues this nonintervention policy because it believes that the gains from allowing its managers to act as independent entrepreneurs exceed any potential cost savings that might result from coordinating interdivisional activities. It believes that a decentralized operating system allows a big company to act in a way that is similar to a small company, avoiding the problem of growing bureaucracy and organizational inertia.

At Alco, top management interprets its role as relieving the divisions of administrative chores, such as bookkeeping and accounting, and collecting market information on competitive pricing and products, which allows divisional managers to improve their business-level strategy. Centralizing these information activities reduces each division's cost structure and provides the standardization that lets top management make better decisions about resource allocation. Alco's division heads are regarded as partners in the corporate enterprise and are rewarded through stock options linked to the performance of their divisions. So far, Alco has been very successful with its decentralized operating structure and has achieved a compound growth rate of 19% a year.

VERTICAL INTEGRATION Vertical integration is a more expensive strategy to manage than unrelated diversification because *sequential resource flows* from one division to the next must be coordinated. Once again, the multidivisional structure economizes on the bureaucratic costs associated with achieving such coordination. This structure provides the centralized control necessary for the vertically integrated company to achieve benefits from the control of resource transfers. Corporate personnel assume the responsibility for devising financial output and behavior controls that solve the problems of transferring resources from one division to the next; for example, they are involved in solving transfer pricing problems. Also, complex rules and procedures are instituted that specify how exchanges are to be made to solve potential transaction problems. As previously noted, complex resource exchanges can lead to conflict among divisions, and corporate managers must try to minimize divisional conflicts. Centralizing authority at corporate headquarters must be done with care in vertically related companies. It carries the risk of involving corporate managers in operating issues at the business level to the point that the divisions lose their autonomy and motivation. These companies must strike the right balance of centralized control at corporate headquarters and decentralized control at the divisional level if they are to implement this strategy successfully.

Because their interests are at stake, divisions need to have input into scheduling and decisions regarding resource transfer. For example, the plastics division in a chemical company has a vital interest in the activities of the oil division because the quality of the products it gets from the oil division determines the quality of its own products. Divisional integrating mechanisms can bring about direct coordination and information transfers among divisions.[12] To handle communication among divisions, a company sets up teams for that purpose; it can also use **integrating roles** whereby an experienced senior manager assumes responsibility for managing complex transfers between two or more divisions. The use of integrating roles to coordinate divisions is common in high-tech and chemical companies, for example.

Thus, a strategy of vertical integration is managed through a combination of corporate and divisional controls. As a result, the organizational structure and control systems used for managing this strategy to economize on bureaucratic costs are more complex and more difficult to implement than those used for unrelated diversification. However, as long as the benefits that derive from vertical integration are realized, the extra expense in implementing this strategy can be justified.

RELATED DIVERSIFICATION In the case of related diversification, the gains from pursuing this multibusiness model derive from the transfer, sharing, or leveraging of R&D knowledge, industry information, customer bases, and so on, across divisions. Also, with this structure, the high level of resource sharing and joint production by divisions makes it hard for corporate managers to measure the performance of each individual division.[13] Thus, bureaucratic costs are substantial. The multidivisional structure helps to economize on these costs because it provides some of the extra coordination and control that is required. However, if a related company is to obtain the potential benefits from using its competencies efficiently and effectively, it has to adopt more complicated forms of integration and control at the divisional level to make the structure work.

First, output control is difficult to use because divisions share resources, so it is not easy to measure the performance of an individual division. Therefore, a company needs to develop a corporate culture that stresses cooperation among divisions and corporate rather than purely divisional goals. Second, corporate managers must establish sophisticated integrating devices to ensure coordination among divisions. Integrating roles and even integrating teams of managers are often essential because they provide the context in which managers from different divisions can meet and develop a common vision of corporate goals. This is Mulally's intention at Ford, where he is trying to essentially create a high-level integrating team composed of its top operating and functional managers to coordinate its global strategy.

An organization with a multidivisional structure must have the right mix of incentives and rewards for cooperation if it is to achieve gains from sharing skills and resources among divisions.[14] With unrelated diversification, divisions operate autonomously, and the company can quite easily reward managers on their division's individual performance. With related diversification, however, rewarding divisions is more difficult because they are engaged in so many shared activities, and strategic managers must be sensitive and alert to achieve equity in rewards among divisions. The aim always is to design structure and control systems so that they can maximize the benefits from pursuing the strategy while economizing on bureaucratic costs.

● **The Role of Information Technology**

The expanding use of IT is increasing the advantages and reducing the problems associated with implementing a multibusiness model effectively because it facilitates output control, behavior control, and integration between divisions and between divisions and corporate headquarters.

On the advantage side, IT provides a common software platform that can make it much less problematic for divisions to share information and knowledge and to obtain the benefits from leveraging their competencies. IT also facilitates output and financial control, making it easier for corporate headquarters to monitor divisional performance and decide when to intervene selectively. It also helps corporate managers better use their strategic and implementation skills because they can react more quickly given that they possess higher-quality, more timely information from the use of a sophisticated cross-organizational IT infrastructure.

In a similar fashion, IT makes it easier to manage the problems that occur when implementing a multidivisional structure. Because it provides both corporate and divisional managers with more and better information, it makes it easier for corporate managers to decentralize control to divisional managers and yet react quickly if the need arises. IT can also make it more difficult to distort information and hide bad news because divisional managers must provide standardized information that can be compared across divisions. Finally, IT eases the transfer pricing problem because divisional managers have access to detailed up-to-date information about how much a certain resource or skill would cost to buy in the external marketplace. Thus, a fair transfer price is easier to determine. The way in which SAP's enterprise resources planning (ERP) software helps to integrate the activities of divisions in a multidivisional structure is discussed in Strategy in Action 13.1.

Strategy in Action 13.1

SAP's ERP Systems

SAP is the world's leading supplier of enterprise resources planning (ERP) software; it introduced the world's first ERP system in 1973. So great was the demand for its software that it had to train thousands of IT consultants from companies like IBM, HP, Accenture, and Cap Gemini to install and customize it to meet the needs of companies around the globe. SAP's ERP system is popular because it manages functional activities at all stages of a company's value chain, as well as resource transfers between a company's different divisions.

First, SAP's software has modules specifically designed to manage each core functional activity. Each module contains the set of best practices that SAP's IT engineers have found works in building competencies in efficiency, quality, innovation, and responsiveness to customers. Each function inputs its data into its functional module in the way specified by SAP. For example, sales inputs all the information about customer needs required by SAP's sales module, and materials management inputs information about the product specifications it requires from suppliers into SAP's materials-management module. Each SAP module functions as an *expert system* that can reason through the information that functional managers put into it. It then provides managers with real-time feedback about the current state of vital functional operations—and gives recommendations that allow managers to improve them. However, the magic of

ERP does not stop there. SAP's ERP software then connects across functions inside each division. This means that managers in all functions of a division have access to other functions' expert systems, and SAP's software is designed to alert managers when their functional operations are affected by changes taking place in another function. *Thus, SAP's ERP software allows managers throughout a division to better coordinate their activities*, which is a major source of competitive advantage.

Moreover, SAP software, running on corporate mainframe computers, takes the information from all the different expert systems in the divisions and creates a companywide ERP system that provides corporate managers with an overview of the operations of all a company's divisions. In essence, SAP's ERP system creates a sophisticated corporate-level expert system that can reason through the huge volume of information being provided by all its divisions and functions. The ERP system can then recognize and diagnose common issues and problems and recommend organizationwide solutions, such as by suggesting new ways to leverage, transfer, and share competencies and resources. Top managers, armed with the knowledge that their ERP software provides, can also use it to adjust their business model with the changing environment. The result, SAP claims, is that when a multidivisional company implements its corporatewide ERP software, it can achieve productivity gains of 30 to 50%, which amounts to billions of dollars of savings for large multinational companies like Nestlé and Exxon.[a]

Implementing Strategy Across Countries

Global strategy can play a crucial role in strengthening the business model of both single-business and multibusiness companies. Indeed, few large companies that have expanded into new industries have not already expanded globally and replicated their business model in new countries to grow their profits. Companies can use four basic strategies as they begin to market their products and establish production facilities abroad:

- A *localization strategy* is oriented toward local responsiveness, and a company decentralizes control to subsidiaries and divisions in each country in which it operates to produce and customize products to local markets.

- An *international strategy* is based on R&D and marketing being centralized at home and all the other value creation functions being decentralized to national units.

- A *global standardization strategy* is oriented toward cost reduction, with all the principal value creation functions centralized at the optimal global location.

- A *transnational strategy* is focused so that it can achieve local responsiveness and cost reduction. Some functions are centralized and others are decentralized at the global location best suited to achieving these objectives.

The need to coordinate and integrate global value chain activities increases as a company moves from a localization to an international, to a global standardization, and then to a transnational strategy. To obtain the benefits of pursuing a transnational strategy, a company must transfer its distinctive competencies to the global location where they can create the most value and establish a global network to coordinate its divisions at home and abroad. The objective of such coordination is to obtain the benefits from transferring or leveraging competencies across a company's global business units. Thus, the bureaucratic costs associated with solving the communication and measurement problems that arise in managing handoffs or transfers across countries are much higher for companies pursuing a transnational strategy than it is for those pursuing the other strategies. The localization strategy does not require coordinating activities on a global level because value creation activities are handled locally, by country or world region. The international and global standardization strategies fit between the other two strategies: although products have to be sold and marketed globally, and hence global product transfers must be managed, there is less need to coordinate skill and resource transfers when using an international strategy than there is when using a transnational strategy.

The implication is that, as companies change from a localization to an international, global standardization, or transnational strategy, they require a more complex structure, control system, and culture to coordinate the value creation activities associated with implementing that strategy. More complex structures economize on bureaucratic costs. In general, the choice of structure and control systems for managing a global business is a function of three factors:

1. The decision about how to distribute and allocate responsibility and authority between managers at home and abroad so that effective control over a company's global operations is maintained

2. The selection of the organizational structure that groups divisions both at home and abroad in a way that allows the best use of resources and serves the needs of foreign customers most effectively

3. The selection of the right kinds of integration and control mechanisms and organizational culture to make the overall global structure function effectively

TABLE 13.2

Global Strategy/Structure Relationships

	Localization Strategy	International Strategy	Global Standardization Strategy	Transnational Strategy
	Low ⟵———————— Need for Coordination ————————⟶ High			
	Low ⟵———————— Bureaucratic Costs ————————⟶ High			
Centralization of Authority	Decentralized to national unit	Core competencies centralized; others decentralized to national units	Centralized at optimal global location	Simultaneously centralized and decentralized
Horizontal Differentiation	Global-area structure	Global-division structure	Global product-group structure	Global-matrix structure, matrix-in-the-mind
Need for Complex Integrating Mechanisms	Low	Medium	High	Very high
Organizational Culture	Not important	Quite important	Important	Very important

Table 13.2 summarizes the appropriate design choices for companies pursuing each of these strategies.

● **Implementing a Localization Strategy**

When a company pursues a localization strategy, it generally operates with a global-area structure (see Figure 13.2). When using this structure, a company duplicates all value creation activities and establishes an overseas division in every country or world area in which it operates. Authority is decentralized to managers in each overseas division, who devise the appropriate strategy for responding to the needs of the local environment. Managers at global headquarters use market and output controls, such as ROIC, growth in market share, and operation costs, to evaluate the performance of overseas divisions. On the basis of such global comparisons, they can make decisions about capital allocation and orchestrate the transfer of new knowledge among divisions.

A company that makes and sells the same products in many different countries often groups its overseas divisions into world regions to simplify the coordination of

FIGURE 13.2

Global-Area Structure

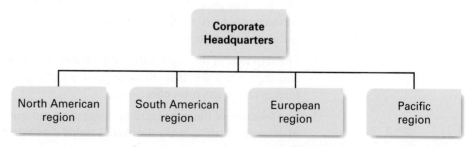

products across countries. Europe might be one region, the Pacific Rim another, and the Middle East a third. Grouping allows the same set of output and behavior controls to be applied across all divisions inside a region. Thus, global companies can reduce communications and transfer problems because information can be transmitted more easily across countries with broadly similar cultures. For example, consumers' preferences regarding product design and marketing are likely to be more similar among countries in one world region than among countries in different world regions.

Because the overseas divisions themselves have little or no contact with others in different regions, no integrating mechanisms are needed. Nor does a global organizational culture develop because there are no transfers of skills or resources or transfer of managerial personnel among the various world regions. Historically, car companies such as DaimlerChrysler, GM, and Ford used global-area structures to manage their overseas operations. Ford of Europe, for example, had little or no contact with its U.S. parent; capital was the principal resource exchanged.

One problem with a global-area structure and a localization strategy is that the duplication of specialist activities across countries raises a company's overall cost structure. Moreover, the company is not taking advantage of opportunities to transfer, share, or leverage its competencies and capabilities on a global basis; for example, it cannot apply the low-cost manufacturing expertise that it has developed in one world region to another. Thus, localization companies lose the many benefits of operating globally. As Chapter 8 discussed, the popularity of this strategic orientation has decreased.

• Implementing an International Strategy

A company pursuing an international strategy adopts a different route to global expansion. Normally, the company shifts to this strategy when it decides to sell domestically made products in markets abroad. Until the 1990s, for example, companies such as Mercedes-Benz and Jaguar made no attempt to produce in a foreign market; instead, they distributed and sold their domestically produced cars internationally. Such companies usually just add a *foreign sales organization* to their existing structure and continue to use the same control system. If a company is using a functional structure, this department has to coordinate manufacturing, sales, and R&D activities with the needs of the foreign market. Efforts at customization are minimal. In overseas countries, a company usually establishes a subsidiary to handle local sales and distribution. For example, the Mercedes-Benz overseas subsidiaries allocate dealerships; organize supplies of spare parts; and, of course, sell cars. A system of behavior controls is then established to keep the home office informed of changes in sales, spare parts requirements, and so on.

A company with many different products or businesses operating from a multidivisional structure has the challenging problem of coordinating the flow of different products across different countries. To manage these transfers, many companies create a *global division*, which they add to their existing divisional structure (see Figure 13.3).[15] Global operations are managed as a separate divisional business, with managers given the authority and responsibility for coordinating domestic product divisions with overseas markets. The global division also monitors and controls the overseas subsidiaries that market the products and decides how much authority to delegate to managers in these countries.

This arrangement of tasks and roles reduces the transaction of managing handoffs across countries and world regions. However, managers abroad are essentially under the control of managers in the global division, and if domestic and overseas managers compete for control of strategy making, conflict and lack of cooperation

FIGURE 13.3

Global Division
Structure

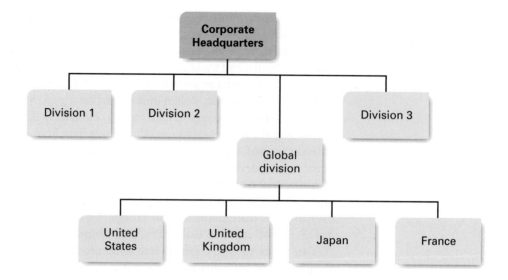

may result. Many companies such as IBM, Citibank, and DaimlerChrysler have experienced this problem. Very often, significant strategic control has been decentralized to overseas divisions. When cost pressures force corporate managers to reassess their strategy and they decide to intervene, such intervention frequently provokes resistance, much of it due to differences in culture—not just corporate but also country differences.

● **Implementing a Global Standardization Strategy**

When a company embarks on a global standardization strategy today, it locates its manufacturing and other value chain activities at the global location that will allow it to increase efficiency, quality, and innovation. In doing so, it has to solve the problems of coordinating and integrating its global value chain activities. It has to find a structure that lowers the bureaucratic costs associated with resource transfers between corporate headquarters and its overseas divisions and provides the centralized control that a global standardization strategy requires. The answer for many companies is a *global product-group structure* (see Figure 13.4).

In this structure, a product-group headquarters is created to coordinate the activities of a company's home and overseas operations. The managers at each product

FIGURE 13.4

Global Product-Group
Structure

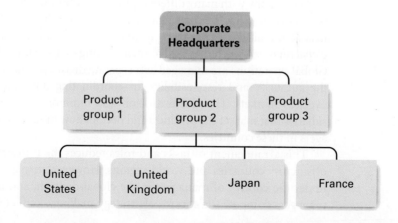

group's headquarters decide where to locate the different functions at the optimal global location for performing that activity. For example, Phillips has one product group responsible for global R&D, manufacturing, marketing, and sales of its light bulbs; another for medical equipment; and so on. The headquarters of the medical division and its R&D is located in Bothell, Washington; manufacturing is done in Taiwan; and the products are sold by sales subsidiaries in each local market.

The product-group structure allows managers to decide how best to pursue a global standardization strategy—for example, to decide which value chain activities, such as manufacturing or product design, should be performed in which country to increase efficiency. Increasingly, U.S. and Japanese companies are moving manufacturing to low-cost countries such as China but establishing product design centers in Europe or the United States to take advantage of foreign skills and capabilities and thus obtain the benefits from this strategy.

● Implementing a Transnational Strategy

The main failing of the global product-group structure is that, although it allows a company to achieve superior efficiency and quality, it is weak when it comes to responsiveness to customers because the focus is still on centralized control to reduce costs. Moreover, this structure makes it difficult for the different product divisions to trade information and knowledge and to obtain the benefits from transferring, sharing, and leveraging their competencies. Sometimes the potential gains from sharing product, marketing, or R&D knowledge among product groups are high, but so too are the bureaucratic costs associated with achieving these gains. Is there a structure that can simultaneously economize on these costs and provide the coordination necessary to obtain these benefits?

In the 1990s, many companies implemented a *global-matrix structure* to simultaneously lower their global cost structures *and* differentiate their activities through superior innovation and responsiveness to customers globally. Figure 13.5 shows such a structure that might be used by a company like Ford, HP, SAP, or Nestlé. On the vertical axis, instead of functions are the company's product *groups*. These groups provide specialist services such as R&D, product design, and marketing information

FIGURE 13.5

Global-Matrix
Structure

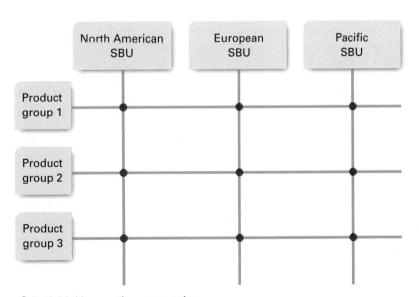

● Individual operating companies

Strategy in Action

Using IT to Make Nestlé's Global Structure Work

Nestlé, based in Vevey, Switzerland, is the world's biggest food company, with global sales in excess of $65 billion in 2004. The company has been pursuing an ambitious program of global expansion by acquiring many famous companies—for instance, Perrier, the French mineral water producer, and Rowntree, the British candy maker. In the United States, Nestlé bought the giant Carnation Company, Stouffer Foods, Contadina, Ralston Purina, and Dreyer's Grand Ice Cream.

Traditionally, Nestlé pursued a localization strategy and managed its operating companies through a global-area structure. In each country, each individual division (such as its Carnation division) was responsible for managing all aspects of its business-level strategy: in other words, companies were free to control their own product development and marketing and to manage all local operations. Nestlé's corporate executives at the Vevey headquarters made acquisitions, expansions, and corporate resource decisions such as capital investment. Because all important decisions were made centrally, the size of the corporate staff increased dramatically.

In the 1990s, Nestlé realized it had major problems. Corporate managers had become remote from the difficulties experienced by the individual operating divisions or companies, and the centralized structure slowed decision making and made it difficult for Nestlé to respond quickly to the changing environment. Moreover, the company was forfeiting all the possible benefits from sharing and leveraging its distinctive competencies in food product development and marketing, both between divisions in a product group and between product groups and world regions. Because each product group operated separately, corporate executives could not integrate product-group activities around the world. To raise corporate performance, Nestlé's managers sought to find a new way of organizing its activities.

Its CEO at the time, Helmut Maucher, started restructuring Nestlé from the top down. He stripped away the power of corporate managers by decentralizing authority to the managers of seven global product groups that he created to oversee the company's major product lines (for example, coffee, milk, and candy). Each global product group was to integrate the activities of all the operating divisions in its group to transfer and leverage distinctive competencies to create value. After the change, managers in the candy product group, for instance, began orchestrating the marketing and sale of Rowntree candy products, such as After Eight Mints and Smarties, throughout Europe and the United States, and sales climbed by 60%.

Maucher then grouped all divisions within a country or world region into one national or regional strategic business unit (SBU) and created a team of SBU managers to link, coordinate, and oversee their activities. When the different divisions started to share joint purchasing, marketing, and sales activities, major cost savings resulted. In the United States, the SBU management team reduced the number of sales officers nationwide from 115 to twenty-two and decreased the number of suppliers of packaging from forty-three to three.

Finally, Maucher decided to use a matrix structure to integrate the activities of the seven global-product groups with the operations of Nestlé's country-based SBUs. The goal of this matrix structure is to have the company pursue a transnational strategy that allows it to obtain the gains from both differentiation through global learning and cost reduction. For example, regional SBU managers now spend considerable time in Vevey with product-group executives discussing ways of exploiting and sharing the resources of the company on a global basis.

Although the new decentralized matrix structure improved Nestlé's ability to coordinate its structure, by 1998, it was clear that it still was not providing enough integration and coordination. Although more coordination was taking place between product groups *inside* a region such as the United States, little coordination was taking place across world regions. Nestlé's top managers searched for ways to improve integration on a global scale. Their conclusion was that more output and behavior control was needed so that different product groups and regional SBUs could learn from and understand what everyone else was doing—for example, what their product development plans were or how each product group handled its global supply chain.

Nestlé's solution was to sign a $300 million contract with SAP in 2002 to install and maintain a companywide ERP system to integrate across *all* its global operations.

Top managers hoped this system would give them the information they needed to exert centralized control over operations, which the matrix structure apparently did not provide. In essence, Nestlé began to use SAP's value chain management software as a *substitute* for the matrix structure. With this IT, they would no longer need to rely on divisional managers to transfer information but henceforth could obtain it from their ERP system. They would then be able to intervene at a global level as necessary.

Nestlé's Globe Project to create uniform business processes and computer systems around the world has led to major successes. Nestlé was able to shut down 15% of its global operating structure by 2005, which has saved billions of dollars and lowered its cost structure. At the same time, it has been able to leverage the competencies of its product groups around the world by creating new kinds of food and candy products. However, its ROIC is still significantly lower than that of competitors like Hershey and Cadbury Schweppes because, some analysts claim, the company's global food empire is simply too big to manage—no global structure can make it operate profitably. What Nestlé should do is sell off many of its businesses, reduce the number of its product groups, exit countries where its profits are marginal, and in this way shrink until it can increase its ROIC and profits to match those of its competitors.[b]

to its overseas divisions, which are often grouped by world region. These might be the petroleum, plastics, pharmaceuticals, or fertilizer product groups. On the horizontal axis are the company's *overseas divisions* in the various countries or world regions in which it operates. Managers at the regional or country level control local operations. Through a system of output and behavior controls, they then report to managers in product-group headquarters in the United States and ultimately to the CEO. Managers for world regions or countries are also responsible for working with U.S. product-group managers to develop the control and reward systems that will promote transfer, sharing, or leveraging of competencies.

Implementing a matrix structure thus decentralizes control to overseas managers and provides them with considerable flexibility for managing local issues, but it can still give product-group and top corporate executives in the United States the centralized control they need to coordinate company activities on a global level. The matrix structure can allow knowledge and experience to be transferred among divisions in both product groups and geographic regions because it offers many opportunities for face-to-face contact between managers at home and abroad. The matrix also facilitates the transmission of a company's norms and values and, hence, the development of a global corporate culture. This is especially important for a company with far-flung global operations for which lines of communication are longer. Club Med, for instance, uses a matrix to standardize high-quality customer service across its global vacation villages. Nestlé's experience with the global-matrix structure is profiled in Strategy in Action 13.2.

Nestlé is not the only company to find the task of integrating and controlling a global-matrix structure a difficult task. Some, like ABB and Motorola, and Ford discussed in the Opening Case, have dismantled their matrix structures and moved to a simplified global product-group approach using IT to integrate across countries. If a matrix is chosen, however, other possible ways of making it work effectively include developing a strong cross-country organizational culture to facilitate communication and coordination among managers. For example, many companies are increasingly transferring managers between their domestic and overseas operations so they can implant the domestic culture in the new location and also learn by studying how their structure and systems work in the foreign country.

Toyota has made great efforts to understand how to manage car plants in overseas locations and how to transplant its culture into those plants. When it decided to enter and make cars in the United States, it first formed a joint venture with GM, and the companies combined their expertise in this carmaking venture, which was known as NUMMI. Toyota was responsible for implanting its knowledge of lean production in this plant; all the workers were cross-trained and taught how to monitor and benchmark their own performance and how to work in quality teams to improve it. Toyota then took all its learning from this venture and transferred it to its wholly owned car plant in Georgetown, Kentucky, where it turns out cars with as good a reliability record as those produced in its Japanese plants.

Every Toyota plant is under the control of Japanese managers, however, and managers from Toyota's Japanese headquarters are constantly monitoring its plants' performance and transferring and implanting Toyota's R&D innovations into its next car models. Toyota used a similar implementation strategy when it established car component and assembly operations in south Wales to serve the European Union market. Indeed, it chose south Wales and Virginia as locations for its plants because both regions have a strong local culture based on family and tradition that closely parallels Japan's culture. Toyota's managers felt that a similar local culture would enable them to better implement Toyota's highly efficient work processes and procedures.

As the example of Toyota suggests, forming global networks of managers who can move to and work in other countries so they can turn to each other for help is an important aspect of helping a company realize the benefits from its global operations. When managers can hold a *matrix-in-the-mind*—that is, learn to think about how they could transfer competencies around the company to create value—they can work to develop an information network that lets a company capitalize globally on the skills and capabilities of its employees.[16] To foster the development of the matrix-in-the-mind concept and promote cooperation, companies are increasingly making use of IT's integrating capability by using online teleconferencing, email, and global intranets among the parts of their global operations. For example, Hitachi coordinates its nineteen Japanese laboratories by means of an online teleconferencing system. Both Microsoft and HP make extensive use of global intranets to integrate their activities, and Nestlé still hopes its Globe Project will accomplish the same goal.

Entry Mode and Implementation

As we discussed in Chapter 10, many organizations today are altering their business models and strategies and restructuring their organizations to find new ways to use their resources and capabilities to create value. This section focuses on the implementation issues that arise when companies use the three different modes of entry into new industries: internal new venturing, joint ventures, and mergers and acquisitions.

● **Internal New Venturing**

Chapter 10 discussed how companies can enter new industries by using internal new venturing and by transferring and leveraging their existing resources to create the set of value chain activities necessary to compete effectively in a new industry. How can managers create a setting in which employees are to be encouraged to act in ways that allow them to see how their functional competencies or products can be used in other industries? Specifically, how can structure, control, and culture be used to increase the success of the new-venturing process?

At the heart of the issue is that corporate managers must treat the internal new-venturing process as a form of entrepreneurship and the people who are to pioneer and lead new ventures as **intrapreneurs** (inside or internal entrepreneurs). This means that organizational structure, control, and culture must be designed to encourage creativity and give new-venture managers autonomy and freedom to develop and champion new products. At the same time, corporate managers want to make sure that the investment in new markets will be profitable and that a fit does exist between the new industry and the old one so that benefits can in fact be leveraged.[17] As we discussed in Chapter 10, 3M is one company that carefully uses structure, control, and culture to create a formal organizationwide new-venturing process that is one of the best known for promoting product innovation. 3M's goal is that at least 30% of its growth in sales each year should be attributed to new products developed within the past five years. To achieve this challenging goal, 3M has developed an implementation formula to ensure that its employees are provided with the freedom and motivation to experiment and take risks.

On the structure side, 3M recognized early the increasing importance of linking and coordinating the efforts of people in different functions to speed product development. As noted in the previous chapter, people in different functions tend to develop different subunit orientations and to focus their efforts on their own tasks to the exclusion of the needs of other functions. The danger of such tendencies is that each function will develop norms and values that suit its own needs but do little to promote organizational coordination and integration.

To avoid this problem, 3M established a system of cross-functional teams composed of members of product development, process development, marketing, manufacturing, packaging, and other functions to create organizationwide norms and values of innovation. So that all groups have a common focus, the teams work closely with customers; customers' needs become the platform on which the different functions can then apply their skills and capabilities.[18] For example, one of 3M's cross-functional teams worked closely with disposable diaper manufacturers to develop the right kind of sticky tape for their needs. To promote integration in the team and foster cooperative norms and values, each team is headed by a so-called product champion who takes responsibility for building cohesive team relationships and developing a team culture. In addition, one of 3M's senior managers becomes a management sponsor whose job is to help the team get resources and to provide support when the going gets tough. After all, product development is a highly risky process; many projects do not succeed.

3M is also careful to use integrating mechanisms such as high-level product development committees to screen new ideas. Proven entrepreneurs and experienced managers from the other divisions and from R&D, marketing, sales, and manufacturing serve on this committee to screen the new ideas. New-product champions defend their products and projects before this committee to secure the resources for developing them. (Chapter 4 described this development funnel.) On the control side, 3M copied HP and developed a companywide norm that researchers should use 15% of their time on their own projects, which helps create new products such as Post-it Notes. In addition, 3M is careful to establish career ladders for its scientists in order to gain their long-term commitment, and it rewards successful product innovators. For example, it established the Golden Step program that gives employees substantial monetary bonuses to honor and reward the launch of successful new products and to develop norms and values that support and reward the sharing of information among scientists and people in different functions.

3M's structure and control systems have created an atmosphere in which employees know it is better to take a chance and risk making a mistake than to do nothing at all. Managers understand that their job is to encourage creativity in their employees and teams and to foster a culture of innovation. However, the regular work of the organization goes on side by side with all this intrapreneurial activity.

The other main approach to internal new venturing has been championed by those who believe that the best way to encourage new-product development is to separate this effort from the rest of the organization. To provide new-venture managers with the autonomy to experiment and take risks, the company sets up a **new-venture division**, separate and independent from its other divisions, for the development of a new product. The logic behind this is that if a new-product team works from within a company's existing structure, its members will never have the freedom or autonomy to pursue radical new-product ideas. Away from the day-to-day scrutiny of top managers, new-venture managers will be able to pursue the creation of a new product and develop a new business model as though they were external entrepreneurs.

The new-venture division is controlled in a way that reinforces the entrepreneurial spirit. Thus, strict output controls are regarded as inappropriate because they can promote short-term thinking and inhibit risk taking. Instead, stock options are often used to reinforce a culture for entrepreneurship. Another issue with output controls is to keep top managers at bay. The thinking is that the upfront R&D costs of new venturing are high and its success is uncertain. After spending millions of dollars, corporate managers might become concerned about the new-venture division's performance and might try to introduce tight output controls or strong budgets to increase accountability, measures that hurt the entrepreneurial culture.[19] Corporate managers may believe it is important to institute behavior and output controls that put some limits on freedom of action; otherwise, costly mistakes may be made and resources wasted on frivolous ideas.

Recently, there have been some indications that 3M's internal approach may be superior to the use of external new-venture divisions. It appears that many new-venture divisions have failed to get successful new products to market. And even if they do, usually the new-venture division eventually begins to operate like any other division, and a company's cost structure rises because of the duplication of value chain activities.

Another issue is that scientists are often not the best people to develop successful business models because they lack formal training. Just as many medical doctors are earning MBAs today to understand the many strategic issues confronting their profession, so scientists need to be able to think strategically, and these skills may be lacking in a new-venture division.

HP illustrates many of these issues. Early in its history, HP used the new-venturing approach. As soon as a new self-supporting product was developed in one of HP's operating divisions, a new-venture division was spun off to develop and market the product. In this fashion, HP's goal was to keep its divisions small and entrepreneurial. Soon HP had over twenty-eight different divisions, each with its own value chain functions. At first, the value these divisions created exceeded their operating costs, but then problems emerged because of changing technological conditions. Because they were operated separately, the divisions could not learn from each other, and because they all had separate R&D departments, sales forces, and so on, they began to compete for resources. For example, when one HP scientist pioneered what was to become biotechnology, the managers of other divisions could not see how it related to HP's existing activities and would not fund it. HP became saddled with high operating costs and missed product opportunities. To solve the problem, it merged some divisions and brought their technologies and product lines together. It also sold off divisions to other companies to focus its activities and thus make it easier to transfer resources between its divisions.

Joint Venturing

Internal new venturing is one important way in which large, established companies can maintain their momentum and grow from within.[20] One alternative is for two companies to establish a joint venture and to collaborate on the development of a new business model to compete in a new market or industry. Often in joint venturing, two or more companies agree to pool specific resources and capabilities that they believe will create more value for both companies, and they appoint managers from both companies to oversee the new operation. In this case, no separate entity is set up. Sometimes companies do establish a separate company and agree to share ownership of the new company, often 50/50 ownership, but sometimes one company insists on having a 51% or more stake to give it the controlling interest. The companies then transfer to the new company whatever resources and capabilities they have agreed on to help it pursue the business model that will promote both companies' interests. From an implementation perspective, important issues concern the way the venture is structured and controlled and the problems that frequently emerge in managing differences between the cultures of companies in a joint venture.

Allocating authority and responsibility is the first major implementation issue companies have to decide on. Both companies need to be able to monitor the progress of the joint venture so that they can learn from its activities and benefit from their investment in it. Some companies prefer to establish a new company and obtain a 51% ownership of it because then they can solve the problem of which company will have the ultimate authority and control over the new venture. As discussed in Chapter 8, a company also risks losing control of its core technology or competence when it enters into a strategic alliance. Because the future is unknown, it is unclear which company will benefit the most from whatever innovations the new company might develop.[21] A joint venture can also be dangerous not only because the partners may take whatever they learn and then go it alone, but also because the other party might be acquired by a competitor. For example, Compaq shared its technical knowledge with a company in the computer storage industry to promote joint product development, only to watch helplessly as that company was acquired by Sun Microsystems, which consequently obtained Compaq's knowledge.

The implementation issues are strongly dependent on whether the purpose of the joint venture is to share and develop technology, jointly distribute and market products and brands, or share access to customers. Sometimes companies can simply realize the joint benefits from collaboration without having to form a new company. For example, Nestlé and Coca-Cola announced a ten-year joint venture, to be called Beverage Partners Worldwide, through which Coca-Cola will distribute and sell Nestlé's Nestea iced tea, Nescafé, and other brands throughout the globe.[22] Similarly, Starbuck's Frappuccino is distributed by Pepsi. In this kind of joint venture, both companies can gain from sharing and pooling different competencies so that both realize value that would not otherwise be possible. In these cases, issues of ownership are less important, although the issue of allocating responsibility and monitoring performance remains.

Once the ownership issue has been settled, one company appoints the CEO, who is responsible for creating a cohesive top management team from the ranks of managers who have been transferred from the parent companies. The job of the top management team is to develop a successful business model. These managers then need to choose an organizational structure, such as the functional or product team, that will make the best use of the resources and skills transferred from the parent. The need to provide a framework that combines their activities and integrates people and functions is of paramount importance. So is the need to build a new company culture that can unite the members of the hitherto different cultures. In essence, top managers need to solve all the implementation problems discussed in the previous chapter.

Because solving these issues is expensive and time-consuming, it is not surprising that, if a lot is at stake and the future possibilities are unknown, many companies decide that they would be better off by acquiring the other company and integrating it into their operations. This has been Microsoft's favored strategy in recent years as it enters new industries in the computer sector. Normally, it takes a 51% stake in an emerging company that gives it the right to buy out the company and integrate it into Microsoft should it have technology that proves vital to Microsoft's future interests. Then, Microsoft shares its resources and expertise with the new company to spur its research and development. If the stakes are less, however, and the future is easier to forecast, as in the venture between Coca-Cola and Nestlé, then it makes sense to establish a new entity that can manage the transfers of complementary resources and skills between companies.

Mergers and Acquisitions

Mergers and acquisitions are the third and most widely used vehicle that companies can use to enter new industries or countries.[23] How to implement structure, control systems, and culture to manage a new acquisition is important because many acquisitions are unsuccessful. And one of the main reasons acquisitions perform poorly is that many companies do not anticipate the difficulties associated with merging or integrating new companies into their existing operations.[24]

At the level of structure, managers of both the acquiring and acquired companies have to confront the problem of how to establish new lines of authority and responsibility that will allow them to make the best use of both companies' competencies. The massive merger between HP and Compaq illustrates the issues. Before the merger, the top management teams of both companies spent thousands of hours analyzing the range of both companies' activities and performing a value chain analysis to determine how cost and differentiation advantages might be achieved. Based on this analysis, they merged all of both company's divisions into four main product groups.

Imagine the problems deciding who would control which group and which operating division and to whom these managers would report! To counter fears that infighting would prevent the benefits of the merger from being realized, the companies' top executives were careful to announce in press releases that the process of merging divisions was going smoothly and that battles over responsibilities and control of resources were being resolved. One problem with a mishandled merger is that skilled managers who feel they have been demoted will leave the company, and if many do leave, this also may prevent the benefits of the merger from being realized.

Once the issue of lines of authority has been addressed, the merged companies must decide how to coordinate and streamline operations to reduce costs and leverage competencies. For large companies, as for HP, the answer is the multidivisional structure, but important control issues have to be resolved. In general, the more similar or related are the acquired companies' products and markets, the easier it is to integrate their operations. If the acquiring company has an efficient control system, it can be adapted to the new company to standardize the way its activities are monitored and measured. Or managers can work hard to combine the best elements of each company's control systems and cultures or introduce a new IT system.

If managers make unrelated acquisitions, however, and then try to interfere with a company's strategy in an industry they know little about or apply inappropriate structure and controls to manage the new business, then major strategy implementation problems can arise. For example, if managers try to integrate unrelated companies with related ones in the search for some elusive benefits, apply the wrong kinds of controls at the divisional level, or interfere in business-level strategy, corporate performance can suffer as bureaucratic costs skyrocket. These mistakes explain why related acquisitions are sometimes more successful than unrelated ones.[25]

Even in the case of related diversification, the business processes of each company frequently are different, and their computer systems may be incompatible, as in the Nestlé case. The issue facing the merged company is how to use output and behavior controls to standardize business processes and reduce the cost of handing off and transferring resources. While installing the SAP software, for example, managers in charge of the U.S. effort discovered that each of Nestlé's 150 different U.S. divisions was buying its own supply of vanilla from the same set of suppliers. However, the divisions were not sharing information about these purchases, and vanilla suppliers, dealing with each Nestlé division separately, tried to charge each division as much as they could, with the result that each division paid a different price for the same input![26] Each division at Nestlé used a different code for its independent purchase, and managers at U.S. headquarters did not have the information to discover this. SAP's software provides such information.

Finally, even when acquiring a company in a closely related industry, managers must realize that each company has a unique culture, or way of doing things. Such idiosyncrasies must be understood in order to manage the merged company effectively. Indeed, such idiosyncrasies are likely to be especially important when companies from different countries merge. Over time, top managers can change the culture and alter the internal workings of the company, but this is a difficult implementation task.

In sum, managers' capabilities in organizational design are vital in ensuring the success of a merger or acquisition. Their ability to integrate and connect divisions to leverage competencies ultimately determines how well the new merged company will perform.[27] The path to merger and acquisition is fraught with danger, which is why some companies claim that internal new venturing is the safest path and that it is best to grow organically from within. Yet with industry boundaries blurring and new global competitors emerging, companies often do not have the time or resources to go it alone. How to enter a new industry or country is a complex implementation issue that requires thorough strategic analysis.

Information Technology, the Internet, and Outsourcing

The many ways in which advances in information technology (IT) affect strategy implementation is an important issue today. Evidence that managerial capabilities in managing IT can be a source of competitive advantage is growing; companies that do not adopt leading-edge information systems are likely to be at a competitive disadvantage. IT includes the many different varieties of computer software platforms and databases and the computer hardware on which they run, such as mainframes and servers. IT also encompasses a broad array of communication media and devices that link people, including voice mail, email, voice conferencing, videoconferencing, the Internet, groupware and corporate intranets, cell phones, fax machines, personal digital assistants (PDAs), smart phones, and so on.[28]

● Information Technology and Strategy Implementation

At the level of organizational structure, control, and culture, IT has given strategic managers many new options in implementing their strategies. IT is instrumental in both shaping and integrating resources and capabilities—capabilities that can be difficult to imitate because they are often embedded in firm-specific IT skills. Wal-Mart, for example, legally protected what it regards as a core competency in IT by blocking the movement of some of its key programmers to dot-coms like Amazon.com. A company's ability to pursue a cost-leadership or differentiation business model depends on its possession of distinctive competencies in efficiency, quality, innovation, and customer responsiveness, and IT has a major impact on these sources of competitive advantage.[29]

Information technology enables companies to integrate knowledge and expertise across functional groups so that they can deliver new differentiated goods and services to customers. The way in which Citibank implemented an organizationwide IT system to increase responsiveness to customers is instructive. In the 2000s, Citibank set a goal to be the premier global international financial company. After studying its business model, managers found that the main customer complaint was the amount of time customers had to wait for a response to their request, so Citibank managers set out to solve this problem. Teams of managers examined the way Citibank's current IT system worked and then redesigned it to empower employees and reduce the handoffs between people and functions. Employees were then given extensive training in operating the new IT system. Citibank has been able to document significant time and cost savings, as well as an increase in the level of personalized service it is able to offer its clients, which has led to a significant increase in the number of global customers.[30]

Indeed, IT has important effects on a company's ability to innovate. It improves the base of knowledge that employees draw on when they engage in problem solving and decision making and provides a mechanism for promoting collaboration and information sharing both inside and across functions and business units. However, knowledge or information availability alone will not lead to innovation; the ability to use knowledge creatively is the key to promoting innovation and creating competitive advantage. One argument is that the absolute level of knowledge a firm possesses does not lead to competitive advantage, but the speed or velocity with which it is circulated in the firm does.[31]

IT transfers knowledge where it can add the highest value to the organization. The project-based work that is characteristic of matrix structures provides a vivid example of this process. As a project progresses, the need for particular team members waxes and wanes. Some employees will be part of a project from beginning to end, and others will be asked to participate only at key times when their expertise is required. IT provides managers with the real-time capability to monitor project progress and needs, to allocate resources accordingly, and thus to increase the value added of each employee. Traditionally, product design has involved sequential processing across functions, with handoffs as each stage of the process is completed (see Chapter 4). This linear process is being replaced by parallel, concurrent engineering made possible through the application of IT that allows employees to work simultaneously with continual interaction through electronic communication. All of this can promote innovation.

IT has major effects on other aspects of a company's structure and control systems. The increasing use of IT has been associated with a flattening of the organizational hierarchy and a move toward greater decentralization and increased integration within organizations. By providing managers with high-quality, timely, and relatively complete electronic information, IT has reduced the need for a management hierarchy to coordinate organizational activities. Email systems and the development of organizationwide corporate intranets are breaking down the barriers that have traditionally separated departments, and the result has been improved performance.[32] To facilitate the use of IT and to make organizational structure work, however, a company must create a control and incentive structure to motivate people and subunits, as Strategy in Action 13.3 suggests.

Some companies are taking full advantage of IT's ability to help them integrate their activities to respond better to customer needs. These companies make the most

Strategy in Action   13.3

Oracle's New Approach to Control

As we discussed in Chapter 9, Oracle is the second largest independent software company after Microsoft. Like Bill Gates, Microsoft's chair, Oracle's cofounder and chair, Larry Ellison, recognized in 1999 that his company had a major problem: it was not using the software it had developed to control its own activities, even though its customers were using the software to control theirs! As a result, Oracle was having a difficult time understanding its customers' needs, and internally it was not experiencing the cost savings that could result from implementing its own database and financial control software. Ellison moved quickly to change Oracle's control systems so that they were Internet-based.

One of the main advantages of Internet-based control software is that it permits the centralized management of a company's widespread operations. Corporate managers can easily compare and contrast the performance of different divisions spread throughout the globe in real time and can quickly identify problems and take corrective action. However, to his embarrassment, Ellison discovered that Oracle's financial and human resource information was located on over seventy different computing systems across the world. It took a lot of time and effort to track basic details such as the size of the company's work force and the sales of its leading products. As a result, it took a long time to take corrective action, and many opportunities were being missed.

Recognizing the irony of the situation, Ellison ordered his managers to change the way the company controlled—that is, monitored and evaluated—its activities and to implement its new Internet-based control systems as quickly as possible. His goal was to have all of Oracle's sales, cost, profit, and human resource information systems consolidated in two locations and to make this information available to managers throughout the company with one click of a mouse. In addition, he instructed managers to investigate which kinds of activities were being monitored and controlled by people and, wherever possible, to substitute Internet-based control. For example, previously Oracle had over 300 people responsible for monitoring and managing tasks such as paper-based travel planning and expense report systems. These tasks were automated into software systems and put online, and employees were made responsible for filing their own reports. These 300 people were then transferred into sales and consulting positions. The savings was over $1 billion a year.

By using Internet-based software control systems, Oracle's managers are also able to get closer to their customers. Oracle gave all its salespeople new customer relationship management software and instructed them to enter into the system detailed information about customers' purchases, future plans, Web orders, and service requests. As a result, headquarters managers can now track sales orders easily, and if they see problems such as lost sales or multiple service requests, they can quickly contact customers to solve those problems. This speed builds better customer relations.

So amazed was Ellison at the result of implementing Internet software systems that he radically rethought Oracle's control systems. He now believes that, because of the advances of modern computer information systems, Oracle's employees should be doing only one of three tasks: building its products, servicing its products, or selling its products. All other activities should be automated by developing new information control systems, and it should be the manager's job to use control only to facilitate one of these three front-line activities.[c]

cost-effective use of their employees' skills by using a virtual organizational structure. The **virtual organization** is composed of people who are linked by computers, fax machines, computer-aided design systems, and video teleconferencing and who may rarely, if ever, see one another face to face. People come and go as their services are needed, much as in a matrix structure.

Accenture, the global management consulting company, is becoming just such a virtual organization. Consultants are connected by laptops to an organization's **knowledge management system**, its company-specific information system that systematizes the knowledge of its employees and provides them with access to other employees who have the expertise to solve the problems that they encounter as they perform their jobs. The consultants pool their knowledge in a massive internal database that they can access easily through computer and the company's intranet. The company's 40,000 consultants often work from their homes, traveling to meet the company's clients throughout the world and only rarely stopping at one of Accenture's branch offices to meet their superiors and colleagues. CEO George Shaheen says that the company's headquarters are wherever he happens to be at the time. (He spends 80% of his time traveling.)[33]

● Strategic Outsourcing and Network Structure

Information technology has also affected a company's ability to pursue strategic outsourcing to strengthen its business model. As Chapter 9 discussed, the use of strategic outsourcing is increasing rapidly because organizations recognize the many opportunities it offers to promote differentiation, reduce costs, and increase flexibility. Recall that outsourcing occurs as companies use short- and long-term contracts, joint ventures, and strategic alliances to form relationships with other companies. IT increases the efficiency of such relationships. For example, it allows for the more efficient movement of raw materials and component parts between a company and its suppliers and distributors. It also promotes the transfer, sharing, and leveraging of competencies between companies, which can lead to design and engineering improvements that increase differentiation and lower costs.

As a consequence, there has been growing interest in electronic **business-to-business (B2B)** networks in which most or all of the companies in an industry (for example, carmakers) use the same software platform to link to each other and establish industry specifications and standards. Then these companies jointly list the quantity and specifications of the inputs they require and invite bids from the thousands of potential suppliers around the world. Because suppliers use the same software platform, electronic bidding, auctions, and transactions are possible between buyers and sellers around the world. The idea is that high-volume standardized transactions can help drive down costs and raise quality at the industry level. The role Li & Fung plays in managing the global supply chain for companies in Southeast Asia is instructive in this regard, as Strategy in Action 13.4 shows.

Cross-company global electronic networks reduce the costs associated with finding and monitoring competing suppliers and make global strategic alliances and joint ventures more attractive than vertical integration. In addition, companies that use electronic networks not only reduce costs because they increase the pool of potential suppliers, they also reduce the bargaining power of suppliers. Beyond using IT to link backward with suppliers, companies can also use IT to link forward in the value chain to connect its operations with those of customers, something that reduces their costs and creates a disincentive for customers to seek other suppliers.

To implement outsourcing effectively, strategic managers must decide what organizational arrangements to adopt. Increasingly, a **network structure**—the set of strategic

Strategy in Action   13.4

Li & Fung's Global Supply-Chain Management

Finding the overseas suppliers that offer the lowest-priced and highest-quality products is an important task facing the managers of global organizations. These suppliers are located in thousands of cities in many countries around the world, so finding them is difficult. Often global companies use the services of foreign intermediaries or brokers, located near these suppliers, to find the one that best meets their input requirements. Li & Fung, now run by brothers Victor and William Fung, is one of these brokers that have helped hundreds of global companies locate suitable foreign suppliers, especially suppliers in mainland China.

In the 2000s, managing global companies' supply chains became an even more complicated task because overseas suppliers were increasingly specializing in just one part of the task of producing a product in their search for ways to reduce costs. In the past, a company such as Target might have negotiated with a supplier to manufacture 1 million units of a shirt at a certain cost per unit. But with specialization, Target might find it can reduce the costs of producing the shirt even further by splitting the operations involved in producing the shirt and having different suppliers, often in different countries, perform each operation. For example, to get the lowest cost per unit, Target might first negotiate with a yarn manufacturer in Vietnam to make the yarn, then ship the yarn to a Chinese supplier to weave it into cloth, and then ship the cloth to several different factories in Malaysia and the Philippines to cut the cloth and sew the shirts. Another company might take responsibility for packaging and shipping the shirts to wherever in the world they are required. Because a company like Target has thousands of different clothing products under production and these products change all the time, the problems of managing such a supply chain to get the full cost savings from global expansion are clear.

This is the opportunity that Li & Fung has capitalized on. Realizing that many global companies do not have the time or expertise to find such specialized low-price suppliers, they moved quickly to provide such a service. Li & Fung employs 3,600 agents who travel across thirty-seven countries to find new suppliers and inspect existing suppliers to find new ways to help their clients, global companies, get lower prices or higher-quality products. Global companies are happy to outsource their supply-chain management to Li & Fung because they realize significant cost savings. And although they pay a hefty fee to Li & Fung, they avoid the costs of employing their own agents. As the complexity of supply-chain management continues to increase, more and more companies like Li & Fung will be appearing.[d]

alliances that an organization creates with suppliers, manufacturers, and distributors to produce and market a product—is becoming the structure of choice to implement outsourcing. An example of a network structure is the series of strategic alliances that Japanese carmakers such as Toyota and Honda, and now Ford and GM, have formed with their suppliers of inputs, such as car axles, gearboxes, and air conditioning systems. Members of the network work together on a long-term basis to find new ways to reduce costs and increase the quality of their products. Moreover, developing a network structure allows an organization to avoid the high bureaucratic costs of operating a complex organizational structure. Finally, a network structure allows a company to form strategic alliances with foreign suppliers, which gives managers access to low-cost foreign sources of inputs. The way Nike uses a global network structure to produce and market its sports, casual, and dress shoes is instructive.

Nike, located in Beaverton, Oregon, is the largest and most profitable sports shoe manufacturer in the world. The key to Nike's success is the network structure that Philip Knight, its founder and CEO, created to allow his company to produce and market shoes. The most successful companies today simultaneously pursue a low-cost and a differentiation strategy. Knight realized this early and created an organizational structure to allow his company to achieve this goal.

By far, the largest function at Nike's headquarters in Beaverton is the design function, which is staffed by talented designers who pioneer innovations in sports shoe design such as the air pump and Air Jordans that Nike introduced so successfully. Designers use computer-aided design (CAD) to design their shoes, and all new-product information, including manufacturing instructions, is stored electronically. When the designers have done their work, they relay the blueprints for the new products electronically to a network of suppliers and manufacturers throughout Southeast Asia with which Nike has formed strategic alliances. Instructions for the design of a new sole, for example, may be sent to a supplier in Taiwan, and instructions for the leather uppers may be sent to a supplier in Malaysia. These suppliers produce the shoe parts, which are then sent for final assembly to a manufacturer in China with which Nike has established an alliance. From China, these shoes are shipped to distributors throughout the world. Of the 99 million pairs of shoes Nike makes each year, 99% are made in Southeast Asia.

There are three main advantages to this network structure for Nike. First, Nike can lower its cost structure because wages in Southeast Asia are a fraction of what they are in the United States. Second, Nike can respond to changes in sports shoe fashion very quickly. Using its global computer system, it can, literally overnight, change the instructions it gives to each of its suppliers so that, within a few weeks, its foreign manufacturers are producing new kinds of shoes. Any alliance partners that fail to meet Nike's standards are replaced with new partners, so Nike has great control over its network structure. In fact, the company works closely with its suppliers to take advantage of any new developments in technology that can help it reduce costs and increase quality. Third, the ability to outsource all its manufacturing abroad allows Nike to keep its U.S. structure fluid and flexible. Nike uses a functional structure to organize its activities and decentralizes control of the design process to teams that are assigned to develop each of the new kinds of sports shoes for which Nike is known.

In conclusion, the implications of IT for strategy implementation are still evolving and will continue to do so as new software and hardware reshape a company's business model and its strategies. IT is changing the nature of value chain activities both inside and between organizations, affecting all four building blocks of competitive advantage. For the multibusiness company, as for the single-business company, the need to be alert to such changes to strengthen its position in its core business has become vital, and the success of companies like Dell and Wal-Mart compared to the failure of others like Gateway and Kmart can be traced, in part, to their success in developing the IT capabilities that lead to sustained competitive advantage.

Summary of Chapter

1. A company uses organizational design to combine structure, control systems, and culture in ways that allow it to implement its multibusiness model successfully.

2. As a company grows and diversifies, it adopts a multidivisional structure. Although this structure costs more to operate than a functional or product structure, it economizes on the bureaucratic costs associated with operating through a functional structure and enables a company to handle its value creation activities more effectively.

3. As companies change their corporate strategies over time, they must change their structures because different strategies are managed in different ways. In

particular, the move from unrelated diversification to vertical integration to related diversification increases the bureaucratic costs associated with managing a multibusiness model. Each requires a different combination of structure, control, and culture to economize on those costs.

4. As a company moves from a localization to an international, global standardization, and transnational strategy, it also needs to switch to a more complex structure that allows it to coordinate increasingly complex resource transfers. Similarly, it needs to adopt a more complex integration and control system that facilitates resource sharing and the leveraging of competencies around the globe. When the gains are substantial, companies frequently adopt a global-matrix structure to share knowledge and expertise or to implement their control systems and culture.

5. To encourage internal new venturing, companies must design an internal venturing process that gives new-venture managers the autonomy they need to develop new products. Corporate managers need to provide the oversight that keeps new-venture managers motivated and on track.

6. The profitability of mergers and acquisitions depends on the structure and control systems that companies adopt to manage them and the way a company integrates them into its existing businesses.

7. IT is having increasingly important effects on the way multibusiness companies implement their strategies. Not only does IT help improve the efficiency with which the multidivisional structure operates, it also allows for the better control of complex value chain activities. The growth of outsourcing has also been promoted by IT, and some companies have developed network structures to coordinate their global value chain activities.

Discussion Questions

1. When would a company decide to change from a functional to a multidivisional structure?
2. If a related company begins to buy unrelated businesses, in what ways should it change its structure or control mechanisms to manage the acquisitions?
3. What prompts a company to change from a global standardization to a transnational strategy, and

what new implementation problems arise as it does so?
4. How would you design a structure and control system to encourage entrepreneurship in a large, established corporation?
5. What are the problems associated with implementing a strategy of related diversification through acquisitions?

Practicing Strategic Management

SMALL-GROUP EXERCISE
Deciding on an Organizational Structure

This small-group exercise is a continuation of the small-group exercise in Chapter 12. Break into the same groups that you used in Chapter 12, reread the scenario in that chapter, and recall your group's debate about the appropriate organizational structure for your soft drink company. Because it is your intention to compete with Coca-Cola for market share worldwide, your strategy should also have a global dimension, and you must consider the best structure globally as well as domestically. Debate the pros and cons of the types of global structures, and decide which is most appropriate and will best fit your domestic structure.

ARTICLE FILE 13

Find an example of a company pursuing a multibusiness model that has changed its structure and control systems to manage its strategy better. What were the problems with the way it formerly implemented its strategy? What changes did it make to its structure and control systems? What effects does it expect these changes to have on performance?

STRATEGIC MANAGEMENT PROJECT
Module 13

Take the information that you collected in the strategic management project from Chapter 12 on strategy implementation and link it to the multibusiness model. You should collect information to determine if your company competes across industries or countries and also to see what role IT plays in allowing it to implement its business model. If your company *does* operate across countries or industries, answer the following questions:

1. Does your company use a multidivisional structure? Why or why not? What crucial implementation problems must your company manage to implement its strategy effectively? For example, what kind of integration mechanisms does it employ?

2. What are your company's corporate-level strategies? How do they affect the way it uses organizational structure, control, and culture?

3. What kind of international strategy does your company pursue? How does it control its global activities? What kind of structure does it use? Why?

4. Can you suggest ways of altering the company's structure or control systems to strengthen its business model? Would these changes increase or decrease bureaucratic costs?

5. Does your company have a particular entry mode that it has used to implement its strategy?

6. In what ways does your company use IT to coordinate its value chain activities?

7. Assess how well your company has implemented its multibusiness (or business) model.

ETHICS EXERCISE

Becky had been working at Cool Clothing Inc. for twelve years. Her early years with the company, then small, had been happy, stress-free ones. As the company grew and grew, however, rumors began to surface regarding practices that were less than ethical. Now, Becky was beginning to suspect that some of these rumors were in fact true.

Cool Clothing Inc. had followed the trend of using overseas workers to assemble its clothes, always maintaining that it was one of the companies adhering to strict standards regarding the treatment of its workers. The company claimed to be offering a fair wage and reasonable working hours and conditions. Regardless of its claims, rumors of mistreatment had been swirling for some time now. Some of the sources of these rumors were fairly reliable, and Becky was concerned. She had taken the matter to her supervisor, only to be dismissed. She had then requested appointments with her supervisor's boss and finally the president and CEO of the company, but her requests had been inexplicably denied.

Becky did not feel that she could continue to work for a company that would mistreat its workers, but if she quit her job, nothing would change and she would be out of a paycheck. She needed to figure out a way to stay with the company while at the same time fighting for the rights of these workers.

1. Define the ethical dilemma presented in this case.
2. What would you do if you were in Becky's position?
3. What might Becky do to verify the rumors once and for all?
4. Who could help Becky find assistance for the mistreated workers?

CLOSING CASE

GM Searches for the Right Global Structure

In the past, GM, like the other major U.S. carmakers, decentralized control of its overseas car operations to the managers who controlled its global car divisions in countries such as the United Kingdom, Germany, Australia, and Sweden. Each of GM's global car divisions was responsible for designing cars that suited local customer tastes, and each global division had its own design, component parts, manufacturing, and sales functions. Today, GM has to rethink the way its global structure operates. Although it is the world's biggest carmaker in terms of sales volume, it is one of the least profitable. GM currently makes only about 1% profit margin on the cars it sells in the United States, and it loses money on its sales overseas. The problem facing GM is finding ways to make its global structure operate more efficiently and effectively to implement its global business model.

The major reason for GM's low profit margins is its high cost structure, which is largely due to the way it has allowed its global divisions to operate autonomously in a decentralized fashion. Over time, this mode of operating led its divisions to become fiercely independent to protect their own interests, and this independence resulted in a massive duplication of functional activities. For example, when GM asked its Saab division to work on building a small car based on the Vectra platform developed by its German division as a way to share resources, Saab managers proceeded to give the car a whole new electrical system and engine mounting, expensive modifications that eroded all the potential cost savings from sharing resources.

To reduce its global cost structure, GM decided to place all authority over important car design and production decisions with top managers at its U.S. corporate headquarters. Now its top executives tell its global divisions what they must do to keep costs down, such as which global component suppliers to buy from. To show how this approach can reduce costs, GM's global divisions bought 270 different kinds of radios from global suppliers in the past. They set and achieved a goal of reducing this number to fifty by 2006, which slashed 40% off the cost of its global radio purchases.

Another goal of GM's policy of recentralizing control of decision making is to better coordinate the activities of its global engineering and design groups to speed the development of new car models. GM now tells its global divisions how they should work together and share their expertise to design cars that can be sold anywhere in the world. It currently takes GM about five years to design a new car model, whereas it takes Toyota only three—a

tremendous advantage. Now a global council in Detroit makes the key model development decisions. Although this activity involves a $7 billion yearly investment in new car design, it also prevents global car divisions from pursuing their own goals. In fact, after the Saab debacle, GM basically took away all authority from Saab's engineering department and its engineers now work according to GM's master plan. Similarly, GM's Daewoo division in Korea decided it didn't want to use an existing GM SUV platform and modify it to fit the Korean market; instead, it wanted to create a new one from scratch. GM squashed the resistance and took the steps necessary to make its Daewoo division toe the line. Although GM wants cars to be customized to the needs of each market, CEO Rich Waggoner says he wants "all these variations to be 'plug and play,'" meaning that they do not involve costly redesigns that can adds hundreds of millions of dollars to the new car design budget.

Despite its cost problems, GM, like other U.S. carmakers, has been rapidly catching up with the quality of Japanese carmakers and has closed the gap substantially. So on the differentiation side of the equation, it must facilitate communication among its global car divisions to take advantage of the enormous pool of talent that it has throughout the world. If it can use its new, more centralized global product-group structure to design cars that better satisfy customer needs more quickly, it will be able to compete effectively against companies such as Toyota and Honda in the future.

Case Discussion Questions

1. What kind of global multibusiness model is GM pursuing?

2. How has GM been changing its global structure to allow it to coordinate the production and sale of its products most effectively around the world?

Notes

Chapter 1

1. *Sources:* D. Hunter, "How Dell Keeps from Stumbling," *Business Week*, May 14, 2001, pp. 38–40; "Enter the Eco-System: From Supply Chain to Network," *Economist*, November 11, 2000; "Dell's Direct Initiative," *Country Monitor*, June 7, 2000, p. 5; D. G. Jacobs, "Anatomy of a Supply Chain," *Transportation and Distribution*, June 2003, pp. 60–61; S. Scherreik, "How Efficient Is That Company," *Business Week*, December 23, 2003, pp. 94–95; Dell Computer Corporation 10K, March 2006; A. Serwer, "Dell's Midlife Crisis," *Fortune*, November 28, 2005, pp. 147–151; L. Lee, "Dell: Facing up to Past Mistakes," *Business Week*, June 19, 2006, p. 35; K. Allison, "Can Dell Succeed in Getting Its Mojo Back?" *Financial Times*, June 29, 2006, p. 19; David Kirkpatrick, "Dell in the Penalty Box," *Fortune*, September 18, 2006, pp. 70–74.

2. There are several different ratios for measuring profitability, such as return on invested capital, return on assets, and return on equity. Although these different measures are highly correlated with each other, finance theorists argue that the return on invested capital is the most accurate measure of profitability. See Tom Copeland, Tim Koller, and Jack Murrin, *Valuation: Measuring and Managing the Value of Companies* (New York: Wiley, 1996).

3. Trying to estimate the relative importance of industry effects and firm strategy on firm profitability has been one of the most important areas of research in the strategy literature during the past decade. See Y. E. Spanos and S. Lioukas, "An Examination of the Causal Logic of Rent Generation," *Strategic Management* 22:10 (October 2001): 907–934; and R. P. Rumelt, "How Much Does Industry Matter?" *Strategic Management* 12 (1991): 167–185. See also A. J. Mauri and M. P. Michaels, "Firm and Industry Effects Within Strategic Management: An Empirical Examination," *Strategic Management* 19 (1998): 211–219.

4. This view is known as "agency theory." See M. C. Jensen and W. H. Meckling, "Theory of the Firm: Managerial Behavior, Agency Costs and Ownership Structure," *Journal of Financial Economics* 3 (1976): 305–360; and E. F. Fama, "Agency Problems and the Theory of the Firm," *Journal of Political Economy* 88 (1980): 375–390.

5. K. R. Andrews, *The Concept of Corporate Strategy* (Homewood, Ill.: Dow Jones Irwin, 1971); H. I. Ansoff, *Corporate Strategy* (New York: McGraw-Hill, 1965); C. W. Hofer and D. Schendel, *Strategy Formulation: Analytical Concepts* (St. Paul, Minn.: West, 1978). See also P. J. Brews and M. R. Hunt, "Learning to Plan and Planning to Learn," *Strategic Management* 20 (1999): 889–913; and R. W. Grant, "Planning in a Turbulent Environment," *Strategic Management* 24 (2003): 491–517.

6. www.kodak.com/US/en/corp/careers/why/valuesmission.jhtml.

7. www.ford.com/en/company/about/overview.htm.

8. These three questions were first proposed by P. F. Drucker, *Management—Tasks, Responsibilities, Practices* (New York: Harper & Row, 1974), pp. 74–94.

9. Derek F. Abell, *Defining the Business: The Starting Point of Strategic Planning* (Englewood Cliffs, N.J.: Prentice-Hall, 1980).

10. P. A. Kidwell and P. E. Ceruzzi, *Landmarks in Digital Computing* (Washington, D.C.: Smithsonian Institute, 1994).

11. J. C. Collins and J. I. Porras, "Building Your Company's Vision," *Harvard Business Review* (September–October 1996): 65–77.

12. www.nucor.com/.

13. See J. P. Kotter and J. L. Heskett, *Corporate Culture and Performance* (New York: Free Press, 1992). For similar work, see Collins and Porras, "Building Your Company's Vision."

14. E. Freeman, *Strategic Management: A Stakeholder Approach* (Boston: Pitman Press, 1984).

15. See J. P. Kotter and J. L. Heskett, *Corporate Culture and Performance* (New York: Free Press, 1992).

16. M. D. Richards, *Setting Strategic Goals and Objectives* (St. Paul, Minn.: West, 1986).

17. E. A. Locke, G. P. Latham, and M. Erez, "The Determinants of Goal Commitment," *Academy of Management Review* 13 (1988): 23–39.

18. R. E. Hoskisson, M. A. Hitt, and C. W. L. Hill, "Managerial Incentives and Investment in R&D in Large Multiproduct Firms," *Organization Science* 3 (1993): 325–341.

19. Robert H. Hayes and William J. Abernathy, "Managing Our Way to Economic Decline," *Harvard Business Review* (July–August 1980): 67–77.

20. Andrews, *Concept of Corporate Strategy*; Ansoff, *Corporate Strategy*; Hofer and Schendel, *Strategy Formulation*.

21. For details, see R. A. Burgelman, "Intraorganizational Ecology of Strategy Making and Organizational Adaptation: Theory and Field Research," *Organization Science* 2 (1991): 239–262; H. Mintzberg, "Patterns in Strategy Formulation," *Management Science* 24 (1978): 934–948; S. L. Hart, "An Integrative Framework for Strategy Making Processes," *Academy of Management Review* 17 (1992): 327–351; G. Hamel, "Strategy as Revolution," *Harvard Business Review* 74 (July–August 1996): 69–83; and R. W. Grant, "Planning in a Turbulent Environment," *Strategic Management Journal* 24 (2003): 491–517. See also G. Gavetti, D. Levinthal and J. W. Rivkin, "Strategy Making in Novel and Complex Worlds: The Power of Analogy," *Strategic Management Journal*, 26 (2005): 691–712.

22. This is the premise of those who advocate that complexity and chaos theory should be applied to strategic management. See S. Brown and K. M. Eisenhardt, "The Art of Continuous Change: Linking Complexity Theory and Time Based Evolution in Relentlessly Shifting Organizations," *Administrative Science Quarterly* 29 (1997): 1–34; and R. Stacey and D. Parker, *Chaos, Management and Economics* (London: Institute for Economic Affairs, 1994). See also H. Courtney, J. Kirkland, and P. Viguerie, "Strategy Under Uncertainty," *Harvard Business Review* 75 (November–December 1997): 66–79.

23. Hart, "Integrative Framework"; Hamel, "Strategy as Revolution."

24. See Burgelman, "Intraorganizational Ecology," and Mintzberg, "Patterns in Strategy Formulation."

25. R. A. Burgelman and A. S. Grove, "Strategic Dissonance," *California Management Review* (Winter 1996): 8–28.

26. C. W. L. Hill and F. T. Rothaermel, "The Performance of Incumbent Firms in the Face of Radical Technological Innovation," *Academy of Management Review* 28 (2003): 257–274.

27. This story was related to the author by George Rathmann, who at one time was head of 3M's research activities.

28. Richard T. Pascale, "Perspectives on Strategy: The Real Story Behind Honda's Success," *California Management Review* 26 (1984): 47–72.

29. This viewpoint is strongly emphasized by Burgelman and Grove, "Strategic Dissonance."

477

30. C. C. Miller and L. B. Cardinal, "Strategic Planning and Firm Performance: A Synthesis of More Than Two Decades of Research," *Academy of Management Journal* 37 (1994): 1649–1665. Also see P. R. Rogers, A. Miller, and W. Q. Judge, "Using Information Processing Theory to Understand Planning/Performance Relationships in the Context of Strategy," *Strategic Management* 20 (1999): 567–577.

31. P. J. Brews and M. R. Hunt, "Learning to Plan and Planning to Learn," *Strategic Management Journal* (1999) 20: 889–913.

32. P. Cornelius, A. Van de Putte, and M. Romani, "Three Decades of Scenario Planning at Shell," *California Management Review*, 48 (2005): 92–110.

33. H. Courtney, J. Kirkland, and P. Viguerie, "Strategy Under Uncertainty," *Harvard Business Review*, November–December 1997, 75, 66–79.

34. P. J. H. Schoemaker, "Multiple Scenario Development: Its Conceptual and Behavioral Foundation," *Strategic Management Journal*, 14, 1993, 193–213.

35. P. Schoemaker, P. J. H. van der Heijden, and A. J. M. Cornelius, "Integrating Scenarios into Strategic Planning at Royal Dutch Shell," *Planning Review*, 1992, 20(3), pp. 41–47; I. Wylie, "There is no alternative to . . . ." *Fast Company*, July 2002, pp. 106–111.

36. "The Next Big Surprise: Scenario Planning," *The Economist*, October 13, 2001, p. 71.

37. C. Kim and R. Mauborgne, "Procedural Justice, Strategic Decision Making, and the Knowledge Economy," *Strategic Management* 19 (1998): 323–338; W. C. Kim and R. Mauborgne, "Fair Process: Managing in the Knowledge Economy," *Harvard Business Review* 75 (July–August 1997): 65–76.

38. G. Hamel and C. K. Prahalad, *Competing for the Future* (New York: Free Press, 1994).

39. See G. Hamel and C. K. Prahalad, "Strategic Intent," *Harvard Business Review* (May–June 1989): 64.

40. See C. R. Schwenk, "Cognitive Simplification Processes in Strategic Decision Making," *Strategic Management* 5 (1984): 111–128; and K. M. Eisenhardt and M. Zbaracki, "Strategic Decision Making," *Strategic Management* 13 (Special Issue, 1992): 17–37.

41. H. Simon, *Administrative Behavior* (New York: McGraw-Hill, 1957).

42. The original statement of this phenomenon was made by A. Tversky and D. Kahneman, "Judgment Under Uncertainty: Heuristics and Biases," *Science* 185 (1974): 1124–1131. See also D. Lovallo and D. Kahneman, "Delusions of Success: How Optimism Undermines Executives' Decisions," *Harvard Business Review* 81 (July 2003): 56–67; and J. S. Hammond, R. L. Keeny, and H. Raiffa, "The Hidden Traps in Decision Making," *Harvard Business Review* 76 (September–October 1998): 25–34.

43. Schwenk, "Cognitive Simplification Processes," pp. 111–128.

44. B. M. Staw, "The Escalation of Commitment to a Course of Action," *Academy of Management Review* 6 (1981): 577–587.

45. R. Roll, "The Hubris Hypotheses of Corporate Takeovers," *Journal of Business* 59 (1986): 197–216.

46. Irvin L. Janis, *Victims of Groupthink,* 2nd ed. (Boston: Houghton Mifflin, 1982). For an alternative view, see S. R. Fuller and R. J. Aldag, "Organizational Tonypandy: Lessons from a Quarter Century of the Groupthink Phenomenon," *Organizational Behavior and Human Decision Processes* 73 (1998): 163–184.

47. See R. O. Mason, "A Dialectical Approach to Strategic Planning," *Management Science* 13 (1969): 403–414; R. A. Cosier and J. C. Aplin, "A Critical View of Dialectic Inquiry in Strategic Planning,"

Strategic Management 1 (1980): 343–356; and I. I. Mintroff and R. O. Mason, "Structuring III—Structured Policy Issues: Further Explorations in a Methodology for Messy Problems," *Strategic Management* 1 (1980): 331–342.

48. Mason, "A Dialectic Approach," pp. 403–414.

49. Lovallo and Kahneman, "Delusions of Success."

50. For a summary of research on strategic leadership, see D. C. Hambrick, "Putting Top Managers Back into the Picture," *Strategic Management* 10 (Special Issue, 1989): 5–15. See also D. Goldman, "What Makes a Leader?" *Harvard Business Review* (November–December 1998): 92–105; H. Mintzberg, "Covert Leadership," *Harvard Business Review* (November–December 1998): 140–148; and R. S. Tedlow, "What Titans Can Teach Us," *Harvard Business Review* (December 2001): 70–79.

51. N. M. Tichy and D. O. Ulrich, "The Leadership Challenge: A Call for the Transformational Leader," *Sloan Management Review* (Fall 1984): 59–68; F. Westley and H. Mintzberg, "Visionary Leadership and Strategic Management," *Strategic Management* 10 (Special Issue, 1989): 17–32.

52. Comments were made by Jim Donald at a presentation to University of Washington MBA students.

53. B. McConnell and J. Huba. *Creating Customer Evangelists* (Chicago: Dearborn Trade Publishing, 2003).

54. E. Wrapp, "Good Managers Don't Make Policy Decisions," *Harvard Business Review* (September–October 1967): 91–99.

55. J. Pfeffer, *Managing with Power* (Boston: Harvard Business School Press, 1992).

56. D. Goldman, "What Makes a Leader?" *Harvard Business Review* (November–December 1998): 92–105.

57. M. Maynard and N. Bunkley, "A Reversal of Fortune at Chrysler Too," *New York Times*, September 20, 2006, p. C1; Gail Edmondson and K. Kerwin, "Stalled: Is the Daimler Chrysler Deal a Mistake?" *Business Week*, September 29, 2003, pp. 55–56; N. Boudette and S. Power, "Gearing Down: Chrysler Turnaround Falters as Unsold Gas Guzzlers Fill Lots," *Wall Street Journal*, September 20, 2006, p. A1.

58. *Sources:* C. Y. Baldwin, *Fundamental Enterprise Valuation: Return on Invested Capital,* Harvard Business School Note 9-801-125, July 3, 2004; T. Copeland et al., *Valuation: Measuring and Managing the Value of Companies* (New York: Wiley, 2000).

Chapter 2

1. *Sources:* S. Theodore, "Brewers Take the Good with the Bad," *Beverage Industry* 97 (April 2006): 17–23. V. Tremblay, N. Iwasaki, and C. Tremblay, "The Dynamics of Industry Concentration for U.S. Micro and Macro Brewers," *Review of Industrial Organization* 26 (2005): 307–324; J. P. Nelson, "Beer Advertising and Marketing Update: Structure, Conduct and Social Costs," *Review of Industrial Organization* 26 (2005): 269–306; Beer Institute, *Brewers Almanac, 2006,* (Washington D.C.: Beer Institute, 2006).

2. M. E. Porter, *Competitive Strategy* (New York: Free Press, 1980).

3. J. E. Bain, *Barriers to New Competition* (Cambridge, Mass.: Harvard University Press, 1956). For a review of the modern literature on barriers to entry, see R. J. Gilbert, "Mobility Barriers and the Value of Incumbency," in R. Schmalensee and R. D. Willig (eds.), *Handbook of Industrial Organization*, Vol. 1 (Amsterdam: North-Holland, 1989). See also R. P. McAfee, H. M. Mialon, and M. A. Williams, "What Is a Barrier to Entry?" *American Economic Review* 94 (May 2004): 461–468.

4. A detailed discussion of switching costs and lock-in can be found in C. Shapiro and H. R. Varian, *Information Rules: A*

Strategic Guide to the Network Economy (Boston: Harvard Business School Press, 1999).

5. Most of this information on barriers to entry can be found in the industrial organization economics literature. See especially the following works: Bain, *Barriers to New Competition*; M. Mann, "Seller Concentration, Barriers to Entry and Rates of Return in 30 Industries," *Review of Economics and Statistics* 48 (1966): 296–307; W. S. Comanor and T. A. Wilson, "Advertising, Market Structure and Performance," *Review of Economics and Statistics* 49 (1967): 423–440; Gilbert, "Mobility Barriers"; and K. Cool, L. H. Roller, and B. Leleux, "The Relative Impact of Actual and Potential Rivalry on Firm Profitability in the Pharmaceutical Industry," *Strategic Management* 20 (1999): 1–14.

6. For a discussion of tacit agreements, see T. C. Schelling, *The Strategy of Conflict* (Cambridge, Mass.: Harvard University Press, 1960).

7. M. Busse, "Firm Financial Condition and Airline Price Wars," *Rand Journal of Economics* 33 (2002): 298–318.

8. For a review, see F. Karakaya, "Market Exit and Barriers to Exit: Theory and Practice," *Psychology and Marketing* 17 (2000): 651–668.

9. P. Ghemawat, *Commitment: The Dynamics of Strategy* (Boston: Harvard Business School Press, 1991).

10. A. S. Grove, *Only the Paranoid Survive* (New York: Doubleday, 1996).

11. In standard microeconomic theory, the concept used for assessing the strength of substitutes and complements is the cross elasticity of demand.

12. For details and further references, see Charles W. L. Hill, "Establishing a Standard: Competitive Strategy and Technology Standards in Winner Take All Industries," *Academy of Management Executive* 11 (1997): 7–25; and Shapiro and Varian, *Information Rules.*

13. The development of strategic group theory has been a strong theme in the strategy literature. Important contributions include the following: R. E. Caves and Michael E. Porter, "From Entry Barriers to Mobility Barriers," *Quarterly Journal of Economics* (May 1977): 241–262; K. R. Harrigan, "An Application of Clustering for Strategic Group Analysis," *Strategic Management Journal* 6 (1985): 55–73; K. J. Hatten and D. E. Schendel, "Heterogeneity Within an Industry: Firm Conduct in the U.S. Brewing Industry, 1952–71," *Journal of Industrial Economics* 26 (1977): 97–113; Michael E. Porter, "The Structure Within Industries and Companies' Performance," *Review of Economics and Statistics* 61 (1979): 214–227. See also K. Cool and D. Schendel, "Performance Differences Among Strategic Group Members," *Strategic Management* 9 (1988): 207–233; A. Nair and S. Kotha, "Does Group Membership Matter? Evidence from the Japanese Steel Industry," *Strategic Management* 20 (2001): 221–235; and G. McNamara, D. L. Deephouse, and R. A. Luce, "Competitive Positioning Within and Across a Strategic Group Structure," *Strategic Management* 24 (2003): 161–180.

14. For details on the strategic group structure in the pharmaceutical industry, see K. Cool and I. Dierickx, "Rivalry, Strategic Groups, and Firm Profitability," *Strategic Management* 14 (1993): 47–59.

15. Charles W. Hofer argued that life cycle considerations may be the most important contingency when formulating business strategy. See Hofer, "Towards a Contingency Theory of Business Strategy," *Academy of Management* 18 (1975): 784–810. There is empirical evidence to support this view. See C. R. Anderson and C. P. Zeithaml, "Stages of the Product Life Cycle, Business Strategy, and Business Performance," *Academy of Management* 27 (1984): 5–24; and D. C. Hambrick and D. Lei, "Towards an Empirical Prioritization of Contingency Variables for Business Strategy," *Academy of Management* 28 (1985): 763–788. See also G. Miles, C. C. Snow, and M. P. Sharfman, "Industry Variety and Performance," *Strategic Management* 14 (1993): 163–177; G. K. Deans, F. Kroeger, and S. Zeisel, "The Consolidation Curve," *Harvard Business Review* (December 2002): 2–3. Vol. 80(6).

16. The characteristics of declining industries have been summarized by K. R. Harrigan, "Strategy Formulation in Declining Industries," *Academy of Management Review* 5 (1980): 599–604. See also J. Anand and H. Singh, "Asset Redeployment, Acquisitions and Corporate Strategy in Declining Industries," *Strategic Management* 18 (1997): 99–118.

17. This perspective is associated with the Austrian school of economics, which goes back to Schumpeter. For a summary of this school and its implications for strategy, see R. Jacobson, "The Austrian School of Strategy," *Academy of Management Review* 17 (1992): 782–807; and C. W. L. Hill and D. Deeds, "The Importance of Industry Structure for the Determination of Industry Profitability: A Neo-Austrian Approach," *Journal of Management Studies* 33 (1996): 429–451.

18. "A Tricky Business," *Economist,* June 30, 2001, pp. 55–56.

19. D. F. Barnett and R. W. Crandall, *Up from the Ashes* (Washington, D.C.: Brookings Institution, 1986).

20. M. E. Porter, *The Competitive Advantage of Nations* (New York: Free Press, 1990).

21. The term *punctuated equilibrium* is borrowed from evolutionary biology. For a detailed explanation of the concept, see M. L. Tushman, W. H. Newman, and E. Romanelli, "Convergence and Upheaval: Managing the Unsteady Pace of Organizational Evolution," *California Management Review* 29:1 (1985): 29–44; C. J. G. Gersick, "Revolutionary Change Theories: A Multilevel Exploration of the Punctuated Equilibrium Paradigm," *Academy of Management Review* 16 (1991): 10–36; and R. Adner and D. A. Levinthal, "The Emergence of Emerging Technologies," *California Management Review* 45 (Fall 2002): 50–65.

22. A. J. Slywotzky, *Value Migration: How to Think Several Moves Ahead of the Competition* (Boston: Harvard Business School Press, 1996).

23. R. D'Avani, *Hypercompetition* (New York: Free Press, 1994).

24. G. McNamara, P. M. Vaaler, and C. Devers, "Same as It Ever Was: The Search for Evidence of Increasing Hypercompetition," *Strategic Management* 24 (2003): 261–278.

25. Hill and Deeds, "Importance of Industry Structure."

26. R. P. Rumelt, "How Much Does Industry Matter?" *Strategic Management* 12 (1991): 167–185. See also A. J. Mauri and M. P. Michaels, "Firm and Industry Effects Within Strategic Management: An Empirical Examination," *Strategic Management* 19 (1998): 211–219.

27. See R. Schmalensee, "Inter-Industry Studies of Structure and Performance," in Schmalensee and Willig (eds.), *Handbook of Industrial Organization.* Similar results were found by A. N. McGahan and M. E. Porter, "How Much Does Industry Matter, Really?" *Strategic Management* 18 (1997): 15–30.

28. For example, see K. Cool and D. Schendel, "Strategic Group Formation and Performance: The Case of the U.S. Pharmaceutical Industry, 1932–1992," *Management Science* (September 1987): 1102–1124.

29. See M. Gort and J. Klepper, "Time Paths in the Diffusion of Product Innovations," *Economic Journal* (September 1982): 630–653. Looking at the history of forty-six products, Gort and

Klepper found that the length of time before other companies entered the markets created by a few inventive companies declined from an average of 14.4 years for products introduced before 1930 to 4.9 years for those introduced after 1949.

30. The phrase was originally coined by J. Schumpeter, *Capitalism, Socialism and Democracy* (London: Macmillan, 1950), p. 68.

31. M. E. Porter, "Strategy and the Internet," *Harvard Business Review* (March 2001): 62–79.

32. U.S. Dept. of Labor, Bureau of Labor Statistics.

33. *Economist, The Economist Book of Vital World Statistics* (New York: Random House, 1990).

34. For a detailed discussion of the importance of the structure of law as a factor explaining economic change and growth, see D. C. North, *Institutions, Institutional Change, and Economic Performance* (Cambridge: Cambridge University Press, 1990).

35. *Sources:* Staff Reporter, "Pharm Exec 50," *Pharmaceutical Executive,* May 2004, pp. 61–68; J. A. DiMasi, R. W. Hansen, and H. G. Grabowski, "The Price of Innovation: New Estimates of Drug Development Costs," *Journal of Health Economics* 22 (March 2003): 151–170; "Where the Money Is: The Drug Industry," *Economist,* April 26, 2003, pp. 64–65; Value Line Investment Survey, various issues; "Heartburn: Pharmaceuticals," *Economist,* August 19, 2006, p. 57; P. B. Ginsberg et al., "Tracking Health Care Costs," *Health Affairs,* October 3, 2006, www.healthaffairs.org (accessed October 10, 2006).

Chapter 3

1. M. Brelis, "Simple Strategy Makes Southwest a Model for Success," *Boston Globe,* November 5, 2000, p. F1; M. Trottman, "At Southwest, New CEO Sits in the Hot Seat," *Wall Street Journal,* July 19, 2004, p. B1; J. Helyar, "Southwest Finds Trouble in the Air," *Fortune,* August 9, 2004, p. 38; Southwest Airlines 10-K 2005; United Airlines 10-K 2005; Bureau of Transportation Statistics at http://www.transtats.bts.gov/ (accessed March 11, 2007).

2. M. Cusumano, *The Japanese Automobile Industry* (Cambridge, Mass.: Harvard University Press, 1989); S. Spear and H. K. Bowen, "Decoding the DNA of the Toyota Production System," *Harvard Business Review* (September–October 1999): 96–108.

3. The material in this section relies on the resource-based view of the company. For summaries of this perspective, see J. B. Barney, "Company Resources and Sustained Competitive Advantage," *Journal of Management* 17 (1991): 99–120; J. T. Mahoney and J. R. Pandian, "The Resource-Based View Within the Conversation of Strategic Management," *Strategic Management* 13 (1992): 63–380; R. Amit and P. J. H. Schoemaker, "Strategic Assets and Organizational Rent," *Strategic Management* 14 (1993): 33–46; M. A. Peteraf, "The Cornerstones of Competitive Advantage: A Resource-Based View," *Strategic Management* 14 (1993): 179–191; B. Wernerfelt, "A Resource Based View of the Company," *Strategic Management* 15 (1994): 171–180; and K. M. Eisenhardt and J. A. Martin, "Dynamic Capabilities: What Are They?" *Strategic Management* 21 (2000): 1105–1121.

4. J. B. Barney, "Company Resources and Sustained Competitive Advantage," *Journal of Management* 17 (1991): 99–120.

5. For a discussion of organizational capabilities, see R. R. Nelson and S. Winter, *An Evolutionary Theory of Economic Change* (Cambridge, Mass.: Belknap Press, 1982).

6. W. Chan Kim and R. Mauborgne, "Value Innovation: The Strategic Logic of High Growth," *Harvard Business Review* (January–February 1997): 102–115.

7. The concept of consumer surplus is an important one in economics. For a more detailed exposition, see D. Besanko, D. Dranove, and M. Shanley, *Economics of Strategy* (New York: Wiley, 1996).

8. However, $P = U$ only in the special case when the company has a perfect monopoly and it can charge each customer a unique price that reflects the utility of the product to that customer (i.e., where perfect price discrimination is possible). More generally, except in the limiting case of perfect price discrimination, even a monopolist will see most customers capture some of the utility of a product in the form of a consumer surplus.

9. This point is central to the work of Michael Porter. See M. E. Porter, *Competitive Advantage* (New York: Free Press, 1985). See also P. Ghemawat, *Commitment: The Dynamic of Strategy* (New York: Free Press, 1991), chap. 4.

10. Harbour Consulting, "Productivity Gap Among North American Auto Makers Narrows in Harbour Report 2006," Harbour Consulting Press Release, July 1, 2006.

11. Porter, *Competitive Advantage.*

12. Ibid.

13. This approach goes back to the pioneering work by K. Lancaster, *Consumer Demand, a New Approach* (New York: 1971).

14. D. Garvin, "Competing on the Eight Dimensions of Quality," *Harvard Business Review* (November–December 1987): 101–119; P. Kotler, *Marketing Management* (Millennium ed.) (Upper Saddle River, N.J.: Prentice-Hall, 2000).

15. "Proton Bomb," *Economist* (May 8, 2004): p. 77.

16. C. K. Prahalad and M. S. Krishnan, "The New Meaning of Quality in the Information Age," *Harvard Business Review* (September–October 1999): 109–118.

17. See D. Garvin, "What Does Product Quality Really Mean?" *Sloan Management Review* 26 (Fall 1984): 25–44; P. B. Crosby, *Quality Is Free* (New York: Mentor, 1980); and A. Gabor, *The Man Who Discovered Quality* (New York: Times Books, 1990).

18. M. Cusumano, *The Japanese Automobile Industry* (Cambridge, Mass.: Harvard University Press, 1989); S. Spear and H. K. Bowen, "Decoding the DNA of the Toyota Production System," *Harvard Business Review* (September–October 1999): 96–108.

19. Kim and Mauborgne, "Value Innovation."

20. G. Stalk and T. M. Hout, *Competing Against Time* (New York: Free Press, 1990).

21. Ibid.

22. Tom Copeland, Tim Koller, and Jack Murrin, *Valuation: Measuring and Managing the Value of Companies* (New York: Wiley, 1996). See also S. F. Jablonsky and N. P. Barsky, *The Manager's Guide to Financial Statement Analysis* (New York: Wiley, 2001).

23. Copeland, Koller, and Murrin, *Valuation.*

24. This is done as follows: signifying net profit by π, invested capital by K, and revenues by R, then ROIC $= \pi/K$. If we multiply through by revenues, R, this becomes $R \times (\pi/K) = (\pi \times R)/(K \times R)$, which can be rearranged as $\pi/R \times R/K$. π/R is the return on sales and R/K capital turnover.

25. Note that Figure 3.9 is a simplification and ignores some other important items that enter the calculation, such as depreciation/sales (a determinant of ROS) and other assets/sales (a determinant of capital turnover).

26. This is the nature of the competitive process. For more detail, see C. W. L. Hill and D. Deeds, "The Importance of Industry Structure for the Determination of Company Profitability: A Neo-Austrian Perspective," *Journal of Management Studies* 33 (1996): 429–451.

27. As with resources and capabilities, so the concept of barriers to imitation is also grounded in the resource-based view of the

company. For details, see R. Reed and R. J. DeFillippi, "Causal Ambiguity, Barriers to Imitation, and Sustainable Competitive Advantage," *Academy of Management Review* 15 (1990): 88–102.

28. E. Mansfield, "How Economists See R&D," *Harvard Business Review* (November–December 1981): 98–106.

29. S. L. Berman, J. Down, and C. W. L. Hill, "Tacit Knowledge as a Source of Competitive Advantage in the National Basketball Association," *Academy of Management Journal* (2002): 13–33, Vol. 45.

30. P. Ghemawat, *Commitment: The Dynamic of Strategy* (New York: Free Press, 1991).

31. W. M. Cohen and D. A. Levinthal, "Absorptive Capacity: A New Perspective on Learning and Innovation," *Administrative Science Quarterly* 35 (1990): 128–152.

32. M. T. Hannah and J. Freeman, "Structural Inertia and Organizational Change," *American Sociological Review* 49 (1984): 149–164.

33. See "IBM Corporation," Harvard Business School Case #180-034.

34. Ghemawat, *Commitment.*

35. D. Miller, *The Icarus Paradox* (New York: HarperBusiness, 1990).

36. P. M. Senge, *The Fifth Discipline: The Art and Practice of the Learning Organization* (New York: Doubleday, 1990).

37. D. Kearns, "Leadership Through Quality," *Academy of Management Executive* 4 (1990): 86–89.

38. The classic statement of this position was made by A. A. Alchain, "Uncertainty, Evolution, and Economic Theory," *Journal of Political Economy* 84 (1950): 488–500.

39. *Sources:* Starbucks 10-K, various years; C. McLean, "Starbucks Set to Invade Coffee-Loving Continent," *Seattle Times*, October 4, 2000, p. E1; J. Ordonez, "Starbucks to Start Major Expansion in Overseas Market," *Wall Street Journal*, October 27, 2000, p. B10; S. Homes and D. Bennett, "Planet Starbucks," *Business Week*, September 9, 2002, pp 99–110; J. Batsell, "A Bean Counters Dream," *Seattle Times*, March 28, 2004, p. E1; "Boss Talk: It's a Grande Latte World," *Wall Street Journal*, December 15, 2003, p. B1; C. Harris, "Starbucks Beats Estimates, Outlines Expansion Plans," *Seattle Post Intelligencer*, October 5, 2006, p. C1.

Chapter 4

1. K. Hall, "No One Does Lean Like the Japanese," *Business Week* (July 10, 2006): 40–41; I. Rowley and H. Tashiro, "Lessons from Matsushita's Playbook," *Business Week* (March 21, 2005): 32; K. Hall, "Matsushita's Transformer Steps Down," *Business Week Online*, June 30, 2006.

2. G. J. Miller, *Managerial Dilemmas: The Political Economy of Hierarchy* (Cambridge: Cambridge University Press, 1992).

3. H. Luft, J. Bunker, and A. Enthoven, "Should Operations Be Regionalized?" *New England Journal of Medicine* 301 (1979): 1364–1369.

4. S. Chambers and R. Johnston, "Experience Curves in Services," *International Journal of Operations and Production Management* 20 (2000): 842–860.

5. G. Hall and S. Howell, "The Experience Curve from an Economist's Perspective," *Strategic Management Journal* 6 (1985): 197–212; M. Lieberman, "The Learning Curve and Pricing in the Chemical Processing Industries," *RAND Journal of Economics* 15 (1984): 213–228; R. A. Thornton and P. Thompson, "Learning from Experience and Learning from Others," *American Economic Review* 91 (2001): 1350–1369.

6. Boston Consulting Group, *Perspectives on Experience* (Boston: Boston Consulting Group, 1972); Hall and Howell, "The

Experience Curve," pp. 197–212; W. B. Hirschmann, "Profit from the Learning Curve," *Harvard Business Review* (January–February 1964): 125–139.

7. A. A. Alchian, "Reliability of Progress Curves in Airframe Production," *Econometrica* 31 (1963): 679–693.

8. M. Borrus, L. A. Tyson, and J. Zysman, "Creating Advantage: How Government Policies Create Trade in the Semi-Conductor Industry," in P. R. Krugman (ed.), *Strategic Trade Policy and the New International Economics* (Cambridge, Mass.: MIT Press, 1986); S. Ghoshal and C. A. Bartlett, "Matsushita Electrical Industrial (MEI) in 1987," Harvard Business School Case #388-144 (1988).

9. W. Abernathy and K. Wayne, "Limits of the Learning Curve," *Harvard Business Review* 52 (September–October 1974): 59–69.

10. D. F. Barnett and R. W. Crandall, *Up from the Ashes: The Rise of the Steel Minimill in the United States* (Washington, D.C.: Brookings Institution, 1986).

11. See P. Nemetz and L. Fry, "Flexible Manufacturing Organizations: Implications for Strategy Formulation," *Academy of Management Review* 13 (1988): 627–638; N. Greenwood, *Implementing Flexible Manufacturing Systems* (New York: Halstead Press, 1986); J. P. Womack, D. T. Jones, and D. Roos, *The Machine That Changed the World* (New York: Rawson Associates, 1990); and R. Parthasarthy and S. P. Seith, "The Impact of Flexible Automation on Business Strategy and Organizational Structure," *Academy of Management Review* 17 (1992): 86–111.

12. B. J. Pine, *Mass Customization: The New Frontier in Business Competition* (Boston: Harvard Business School Press, 1993); S. Kotha, "Mass Customization: Implementing the Emerging Paradigm for Competitive Advantage," *Strategic Management Journal* 16 (1995): 21–42; J. H. Gilmore and B. J. Pine II, "The Four Faces of Mass Customization," *Harvard Business Review* (January–February 1997): 91–101.

13. P. Waurzyniak, "Ford's Flexible Push," *Manufacturing Engineering* (September 2003): 47–50.

14. F. F. Reichheld and W. E. Sasser, "Zero Defections: Quality Comes to Service," *Harvard Business Review* (September–October 1990): 105–111.

15. The example comes from Reichheld and Sasser, op. cit.

16. Ibid.

17. R. Narasimhan and J. R. Carter, "Organization, Communication and Coordination of International Sourcing," *International Marketing Review* 7 (1990): 6–20.

18. H. F. Busch, "Integrated Materials Management," *IJDP & MM* 18 (1990): 28–39.

19. G. Stalk and T. M. Hout, *Competing Against Time* (New York: Free Press, 1990).

20. See Peter Bamberger and Ilan Meshoulam, *Human Resource Strategy: Formulation, Implementation, and Impact* (Thousand Oaks, Calif.: Sage, 2000); P. M. Wright and S. Snell, "Towards a Unifying Framework for Exploring Fit and Flexibility in Human Resource Management," *Academy of Management Review* 23 (October 1998): 756–772.

21. A. Sorge and M. Warner, "Manpower Training, Manufacturing Organization, and Work Place Relations in Great Britain and West Germany," *British Journal of Industrial Relations* 18 (1980): 318–333; R. Jaikumar, "Postindustrial Manufacturing," *Harvard Business Review* (November–December 1986): 72–83.

22. J. Hoerr, "The Payoff from Teamwork," *Business Week* (July 10, 1989): 56–62.

23. "The Trouble with Teams," *Economist* (January 14, 1995): 61.

24. T. C. Powell and A. Dent-Micallef, "Information Technology as Competitive Advantage: The Role of Human, Business, and

Technology Resource," *Strategic Management Journal* 18 (1997): 375–405; B. Gates, *Business @ the Speed of Thought* (New York: Warner Books, 1999).

25. "Cisco@speed," *Economist* (June 26, 1999): 12; S. Tully, "How Cisco Mastered the Net," *Fortune* (August 17, 1997): 207–210; C. Kano, "The Real King of the Internet," *Fortune*, (September 7, 1998): 82–93.

26. B. Gates, *Business @ the Speed of Thought* (New York: Warner Books, 1999); Anonymous, "Enter the Eco-System: From Supply Chain to Network," *The Economist* (November 11, 2000); Anonymous, "Dell's Direct Initiative," *Country Monitor* (June 7, 2000): 5; Michael Dell, *Direct from Dell: Strategies that Revolutionized an Industry* (New York: Harper Business, 1999), quote from p. 91; Staff reporter, "Survey: Shining Examples," *The Economist* (June 17, 2006): 4–5.

27. See the articles published in the special issue of the *Academy of Management Review on Total Quality Management* 19:3 (1994). The following article provides a good overview of many of the issues involved from an academic perspective: J. W. Dean and D. E. Bowen, "Management Theory and Total Quality," *Academy of Management Review* 19 (1994): 392–418. See also T. C. Powell, "Total Quality Management as Competitive Advantage," *Strategic Management Journal* 16 (1995): 15–37.

28. For general background information, see "How to Build Quality," *Economist* (September 23, 1989): 91–92; A. Gabor, *The Man Who Discovered Quality* (New York: Penguin, 1990); and P. B. Crosby, *Quality Is Free* (New York: Mentor, 1980).

29. W. E. Deming, "Improvement of Quality and Productivity Through Action by Management," *National Productivity Review* 1 (Winter 1981–1982): 12–22.

30. J. Bowles, "Is American Management Really Committed to Quality?" *Management Review* (April 1992): 42–46.

31. O. Port and G. Smith, "Quality," *Business Week* (November 30, 1992): 66–75. See also "The Straining of Quality," *Economist* (January 14, 1995): 55–56.

32. Bowles, "Is American Management Really Committed to Quality?" pp. 42–46; "The Straining of Quality," pp. 55–56.

33. Gabor, *The Man Who Discovered Quality*.

34. W. E. Deming, *Out of the Crisis* (Cambridge, Mass.: MIT Center for Advanced Engineering Study, 1986).

35. Deming, "Improvement of Quality and Productivity," pp. 12–22.

36. A. Ries and J. Trout, *Positioning: The Battle for Your Mind* (New York: Warner Books, 1982).

37. R. G. Cooper, *Product Leadership* (Reading, Mass.: Perseus Books, 1999).

38. E. Mansfield, "How Economists See R&D," *Harvard Business Review* (November–December 1981): 98–106.

39. Ibid.

40. G. A. Stevens and J. Burley, "Piloting the Rocket of Radical Innovation," *Research Technology Management* 46 (2003): 16–26.

41. Ibid.; see also S. L. Brown and K. M. Eisenhardt, "Product Development: Past Research, Present Findings, and Future Directions," *Academy of Management Review* 20 (1995): 343–378; M. B. Lieberman and D. B. Montgomery, "First Mover Advantages," *Strategic Management Journal* 9 (Special Issue, Summer 1988): 41–58; D. J. Teece, "Profiting from Technological Innovation: Implications for Integration, Collaboration, Licensing and Public Policy," *Research Policy* 15 (1987): 285–305; and G. J. Tellis and P. N. Golder, "First to Market, First to Fail?" *Sloan Management Review* (Winter 1996): 65–75.

42. Stalk and Hout, *Competing Against Time*.

43. K. B. Clark and S. C. Wheelwright, *Managing New Product and Process Development* (New York: Free Press, 1993); M. A. Schilling and C. W. L. Hill, "Managing the New Product Development Process," *Academy of Management Executive* 12:3 (August 1998): 67–81.

44. Clark and Wheelwright, *Managing New Product and Process Development*.

45. P. Sellers, "Getting Customers to Love You," *Fortune* (March 13, 1989): 38–42.

46. O. Port, "Moving Past the Assembly Line," *Business Week* (Special Issue, Reinventing America, 1992): 177–180.

47. G. P. Pisano and S. C. Wheelwright, "The New Logic of High Tech R&D," *Harvard Business Review* (September–October 1995): 93–105.

48. K. B. Clark and T. Fujimoto, "The Power of Product Integrity," *Harvard Business Review* (November–December 1990): 107–118; Clark and Wheelwright, *Managing New Product and Process Development*; Brown and Eisenhardt, "Product Development"; Stalk and Hout, *Competing Against Time*.

49. C. Christensen, "Quantum Corporation—Business and Product Teams," Harvard Business School Case #9-692-023.

50. E. Biyalogorsky, W. Boulding, and R. Starlin, "Stuck in the Past: Why Managers Persist with New Product Failures," *Journal of Marketing*, 70(2) (2006): 1–15.

51. H. Petroski, *Success through Failure: The Paradox of Design* (Princeton, NJ: Princeton University Press, 2006). See also A. C. Edmondson, "Learning from Mistakes Is Easier Said Than Done," *Journal of Applied Behavioral Science*, 40 (2004): 66–91.

52. P. Sellers, "Getting Customers to Love you", Fortune, March 13, 1989, pp. 38–45.

53. Sellers, "Getting Customers to Love You."

54. S. Caminiti, "A Mail Order Romance: Lands' End Courts Unseen Customers," *Fortune* (March 13, 1989): 43–44.

55. Stalk and Hout, *Competing Against Time*.

56. *Sources:* A. Latour and C. Nuzum, "Verizon Profit Soars Fivefold on Wireless Growth," *Wall Street Journal* (July 28, 2004): A3; S. Wooley, "Do You Fear Me Now?" *Forbes* (November 10, 2003): 78–80; A. Z. Cuneo, "Call Verizon Victorious," *Advertising Age* (March 24, 2004): 3–5; M. Alleven, "Wheels of Churn," *Wireless Week* (September 1, 2006), published online at www.wirelessweek.com.

Chapter 5

1. www.etrade.com, 2007; www.bankofamerica.com, 2006; www.etrade.com, 2006 (accessed 2007).

2. Derek F. Abell, *Defining the Business: The Starting Point of Strategic Planning* (Englewood Cliffs, N.J.: Prentice-Hall, 1980), p. 169.

3. R. Kotler, *Marketing Management*, 5th ed. (Englewood Cliffs, N.J.: Prentice-Hall, 1984); M. R. Darby and E. Karni, "Free Competition and the Optimal Amount of Fraud," *Journal of Law and Economics* 16 (1973): 67–86.

4. Abell, *Defining the Business*, p. 8.

5. Some of the theoretical underpinnings for this approach can be found in G. R. Jones and J. Butler, "Costs, Revenues, and Business Level Strategy," *Academy of Management Review* 13 (1988): 202–213; and C. W. L. Hill, "Differentiation Versus Low Cost or Differentiation and Low Cost: A Contingency Framework," *Academy of Management Review* 13 (1988): 401–412.

6. This section and the material on the business model draw heavily on C. W. L. Hill and G. R. Jones, "The Dynamics of Business-Level Strategy" (unpublished paper, 2002).

7. Many authors have discussed cost leadership and differentiation as basic competitive approaches—for example, F. Scherer, *Industrial Market Structure and Economic Performance*, 10th ed. (Boston: Houghton Mifflin, 2000). The basic cost-leadership/differentiation dimension has received substantial empirical support; see, for example, D. C. Hambrick, "High Profit Strategies in Mature Capital Goods Industries: A Contingency Approach," *Academy of Management Journal* 26 (1983): 687–707.

8. Michael E. Porter, *Competitive Advantage: Creating and Sustaining Superior Performance* (New York: Free Press, 1985), p. 37.

9. Ibid., pp. 13–14.

10. www.walmart.com (2007) (accessed January 2007).

11. D. Miller, "Configurations of Strategy and Structure: Towards a Synthesis," *Strategic Management Journal* 7 (1986): 217–231.

12. J. Guyon, "Can the Savoy Cut Costs and Be the Savoy?" Wall Street Journal, October 25, 1994, p. B1.

13. Michael E. Porter, *Competitive Strategy: Techniques for Analyzing Industries and Competitors* (New York: Free Press, 1980), p. 46.

14. Peter F. Drucker, *The Practice of Management* (New York: Harper, 1954).

15. Charles W. Hofer and D. Schendel, *Strategy Formulation: Analytical Concepts* (St. Paul, Minn.: West, 1978).

16. W. K. Hall, "Survival Strategies in a Hostile Environment," *Harvard Business Review* 58 (1980): 75–85; Hambrick, "High Profit Strategies," pp. 687–707.

17. J. Guyon, "Can the Savoy Cut Costs and Be the Savoy?" *Wall Street Journal* (October 25, 1994): B1; www.savoy.com, 2007 (accessed January 2007).

18. The development of strategic-group theory has been a strong theme in the strategy literature. Important contributions include R. E. Caves and Michael Porter, "From Entry Barriers to Mobility Barriers," *Quarterly Journal of Economics* (May 1977): 241–262; K. R. Harrigan, "An Application of Clustering for Strategic Group Analysis," *Strategic Management Journal* 6 (1985): 55–73; K. J. Hatten and D. E. Schendel, "Heterogeneity Within an Industry: Company Conduct in the U.S. Brewing Industry, 1952–1971," *Journal of Industrial Economics, (1985),* 26: 97–113; and Michael E. Porter, "The Structure Within Industries and Companies Performance," *Review of Economics and Statistics* 61 (1979): 214–227.

19. G. Hamel and C. K. Prahalad, *Competing for the Future* (Boston: Harvard Business School Press, 1994).

20. www.samsung.com (accessed 2007).

21. R. Foroohar and J. Lee, "Masters of the Digital Age," *Newsweek* (October 18, 2004): E10–E13.

Chapter 6

1. www.mattel.com. 2006.0 (accessed 2007).

2. "Doll Wars," *Business Life* (May 2005): 40–42.

3. www.mattel.com (accessed 2006).

4. M. Porter, *Competitive Strategy: Techniques for Analyzing Industries and Competitors* (New York: Free Press, 1980), pp. 191–200.

5. S. A. Shane, "Hybrid Organizational Arrangements and Their Implications for Firm Growth and Survival: A Study of New Franchisors," *Academy of Management Journal* 1 (1996): 216–234.

6. Microsoft is often accused of not being an innovator, but the fact is that Gates and Allen wrote the first commercial software program for the first commercially available personal computer. Microsoft was the first mover in their industry. See P. Freiberger and M. Swaine, *Fire in the Valley* (New York: McGraw-Hill, 2000).

7. J. M. Utterback, *Mastering the Dynamics of Innovation* (Boston: Harvard Business School Press, 1994).

8. See Freiberger and Swaine, *Fire in the Valley.*

9. G. A. Moore, *Crossing the Chasm* (New York: HarperCollins, 1991).

10. Utterback, *Mastering the Dynamics of Innovation.*

11. Everett Rogers, *Diffusion of Innovations* (New York: Free Press, 1995).

12. Charles W. Hofer and D. Schendel, *Strategy Formulation: Analytical Concepts* (St. Paul, Minn.: West, 1978).

13. Ibid.

14. Ibid.

15. Ibid.

16. J. Brander and J. Eaton, "Product Line Rivalry," *American Economic Review* 74 (1985): 323–334.

17. Ibid.

18. Porter, *Competitive Strategy*, pp. 76–86.

19. O. Heil and T. S. Robertson, "Towards a Theory of Competitive Market Signaling: A Research Agenda," *Strategic Management Journal* 12 (1991): 403–418.

20. Robert Axelrod, *The Evolution of Cooperation* (New York: Basic Books, 1984).

21. F. Scherer, *Industrial Market Structure and Economic Performance*, 10th ed. (Boston: Houghton Mifflin, 2000), chap. 8.

22. The model differs from Ansoff's model for this reason.

23. H. Igor Ansoff, *Corporate Strategy* (London: Penguin Books, 1984), pp. 97–100.

24. Robert D. Buzzell, Bradley T. Gale, and Ralph G. M. Sultan, "Market Share—A Key to Profitability," *Harvard Business Review* (January–February 1975): 97–103; Robert Jacobson and David A. Aaker, "Is Market Share All That It's Cracked Up to Be?" *Journal of Marketing* 49 (1985): 11–22.

25. Ansoff, *Corporate Strategy*, pp. 98–99.

26. The next section draws heavily on Marvin B. Lieberman, "Strategies for Capacity Expansion," *Sloan Management Review* 8 (1987): 19 27; and Porter, *Competitive Strategy*, pp. 324–338.

27. For a basic introduction to game theory, see A. K. Dixit and B. J. Nalebuff, *Thinking Strategically* (London: W.W. Norton, 1991). See also A. M. Brandenburger and B. J. Nalebuff, "The Right Game: Using Game Theory to Shape Strategy," *Harvard Business Review* (July–August 1995): 59–71; and D. M. Kreps, *Game Theory and Economic Modeling* (Oxford: Oxford University Press, 1990).

28. www.nike.com (accessed 2006).

29. www.nike.com (accessed 2004), press release; "The New Nike," yahoo.com (accessed September 12, 2004).

30. A. Wong, "Nike: Just Don't Do It," *Newsweek* (November 1, 2004): 84.

31. www.nike (accessed 2006).

Chapter 7

1. *The Economist*, "Singin the Blus; Standard Wars" (November 5, 2005): 87; Andrew Park, "HD-DVD vs Blu-ray," *Business Week* (October 30, 2006): 110; B. Dipert, "Subpar Wars: High Resolution Disc Formats Fight Each Other, Consumers Push Back," *EDN* (March 2, 2006): 40–48; B. S. Bulik, "Marketing War Looms for Dueling DVD Formats," *Advertising Age* (April 10, 2006): 20.

2. Data from Bureau of Economic Analysis, *Survey of United States Current Business, 2006.* Available online at http://www.bea.gov/ (accessed November 18, 2006).

3. J. M. Utterback, *Mastering the Dynamics of Innovation* (Boston: Harvard Business School Press, 1994); C. Shapiro and H. R. Varian,

Information Rules: A Strategic Guide to the Network Economy (Boston: Harvard Business School Press, 1999).

4. The layout is not universal, although it is widespread. The French, for example, use a different layout.

5. For details, see Charles W. L. Hill, "Establishing a Standard: Competitive Strategy and Technology Standards in Winner Take All Industries," *Academy of Management Executive* 11 (1997): 7–25; Shapiro and Varian, *Information Rules*; B. Arthur, "Increasing Returns and the New World of Business," *Harvard Business Review* (July–August 1996): 100–109; G. Gowrisankaran and J. Stavins, "Network Externalities and Technology Adoption: Lessons from Electronic Payments," *Rand Journal of Economics* 35 (2004): 260–277; and V. Shankar and B. L. Bayus, "Network Effects and Competition: An Empirical Analysis of the Home Video Game Industry," *Strategic Management Journal* 24 (2003): 375–394. R Casadesus-Masanell and P. Ghemawat, "Dynamic Mixed Duopoly: A Model Motivated by Linux vs Windows," *Management Science*, 52 (2006): 1072–1085.

6. See Shapiro and Varian, *Information Rules*; Hill, "Establishing a Standard"; and M. A. Schilling, "Technological Lockout: An Integrative Model of the Economic and Strategic Factors Driving Technology Success and Failure," *Academy of Management Review* 23:2 (1998): 267–285.

7. Microsoft does not disclose the per-unit licensing fee that it gets from original equipment manufacturers, although media reports speculate it is around $50 a copy.

8. P. M. Romer, "The Origins of Endogenous Growth," *Journal of Economic Perspectives* 8:1 (1994): 3–22.

9. Data from www.btechnews.com (accessed November 18, 2006).

10. Shapiro and Varian, *Information Rules*.

11. International Federation of the Phonographic Industry, *The Commercial Music Industry Global Piracy Report, 2005*, accessed at www.ifpi.org (accessed November 18, 2006).

12. Business Software Alliance, "Third Annual BSA and IDC Global Software Piracy Study," May 2006, www.bsa.org (accessed 2006).

13. Ibid.

14. Charles W. L. Hill, "Digital Piracy: Causes, Consequences and Strategic Responses," *Asian Pacific Journal of Management*, forthcoming 2007.

15. Much of this section is based on Charles W. L. Hill, Michael Heeley, and Jane Sakson, "Strategies for Profiting from Innovation," in *Advances in Global High Technology Management* (Greenwich, Conn.: JAI Press, 1993) 3: 79–95.

16. M. Lieberman and D. Montgomery, "First Mover Advantages," *Strategic Management Journal* 9 (Special Issue, Summer 1988): 41–58.

17. W. Boulding and M. Christen, "Sustainable Pioneering Advantage? Profit Implications of Market Entry Order," *Marketing Science* 22 (2003): 371–386; C. Markides and P. Geroski, "Teaching Elephants to Dance and Other Silly Ideas," *Business Strategy Review* 13 (2003): 49–61.

18. J. Borzo, "Aging Gracefully," *Wall Street Journal* (October 15, 2001): R22.

19. The importance of complementary assets was first noted by D. J. Teece. See D. J. Teece, "Profiting from Technological Innovation," in D. J. Teece (ed.), *The Competitive Challenge* (New York: Harper & Row, 1986), pp. 26–54.

20. M. J. Chen and D. C. Hambrick, "Speed, Stealth, and Selective Attack: How Small Firms Differ from Large Firms in Competitive Behavior," *Academy of Management Journal* 38 (1995): 453–482.

21. E. Mansfield, M. Schwartz, and S. Wagner, "Imitation Costs and Patents: An Empirical Study," *Economic Journal* 91 (1981): 907–918.

22. E. Mansfield, "How Rapidly Does New Industrial Technology Leak Out?" *Journal of Industrial Economics* 34 (1985): 217–223.

23. This argument has been made in the game theory literature. See R. Caves, H. Cookell, and P. J. Killing, "The Imperfect Market for Technology Licenses," *Oxford Bulletin of Economics and Statistics* 45 (1983): 249–267; N. T. Gallini, "Deterrence by Market Sharing: A Strategic Incentive for Licensing," *American Economic Review* 74 (1984): 931–941; and C. Shapiro, "Patent Licensing and R&D Rivalry," *American Economic Review* 75 (1985): 25–30.

24. M. Christensen, *The Innovator's Dilemma* (Boston: Harvard Business School Press, 1997); R. N. Foster, *Innovation: The Attacker's Advantage* (New York: Summit Books, 1986).

25. Foster, *Innovation*.

26. Ray Kurzweil, *The Age of the Spiritual Machines* (New York: Penguin Books, 1999).

27. See Christensen, *The Innovator's Dilemma*; and C. M. Christensen and M. Overdorf, "Meeting the Challenge of Disruptive Change," *Harvard Business Review* (March–April 2000): 66–77.

28. Charles W. L. Hill and Frank T. Rothaermel, "The Performance of Incumbent Firms in the Face of Radical Technological Innovation," *Academy of Management Review* 28 (2003): 257–274; F. T. Rothaermel and Charles W. L. Hill, "Technological Discontinuities and Complementary Assets: A Longitudinal Study of Industry and Firm Performance," *Organization Science* 16(1), (2005): 52–70.

29. *Sources*: Gary Rivlin, "Wallflower at the Web Party," *New York Times*, Business Section (October 15, 2006): 1, 9; V. Vara, "Friendster Patent on Linking Web Friends Could Hurt Rivals," *Wall Street Journal* (July 27, 2006): B1; V. Vara and R. Buckman, "Friendster Gets $10 Million Infusion for Revival Bid," *Wall Street Journal* (August 21, 2006): C4.

Chapter 8

1. *Sources*: M. Gunther, "MTV's Passage to India," *Fortune* (August 9, 2004): 117–122; B. Pulley and A. Tanzer, "Sumner's Gemstone," *Forbes* (February 21, 2000): 107–11; K. Hoffman, "Youth TV's Old Hand Prepares for the Digital Challenge," *Financial Times* (February 18, 2000): 8; presentation by Sumner M. Redstone, chair and CEO, Viacom Inc., delivered to Salomon Smith Barney 11th Annual Global Entertainment Media, Telecommunications Conference, Scottsdale, AZ, January 8, 2001, archived at www.viacom.com (accessed November 30, 2006); and Viacom 10K Statement, 2005.

2. K. Santana, "MTV Goes to Asia," Global Policy Forum, August 12, 2003, available at www.globalpolicy.org (accessed November 30, 2006).

3. World Trade Organization, *International Trade Trends and Statistics, 2005* (Geneva: WTO, 2006), and WTO press release, "World Trade for 2005: Prospects for 2006," April 11, 2006, available at www.wto.org (accessed 2006).

4. World Trade Organization, *International Trade Statistics, 2005* (Geneva: WTO, 2005), and United Nations, *World Investment Report, 2005*.

5. P. Dicken, *Global Shift* (New York: Guilford Press, 1992).

6. D. Pritchard, "Are Federal Tax Laws and State Subsidies for Boeing 7E7 Selling America Short?" *Aviation Week* (April 12, 2004): 74–75.

7. T. Levitt, "The Globalization of Markets," *Harvard Business Review* (May–June 1983): 92–102.

8. M. E. Porter, *The Competitive Advantage of Nations* (New York: Free Press, 1990). See also R. Grant, "Porter's Competitive Advantage of Nations: An Assessment," *Strategic Management Journal* 7 (1991): 535–548.

9. Porter, *Competitive Advantage of Nations.*

10. Example is disguised; it comes from interviews by Charles Hill.

11. See J. Birkinshaw and N. Hood, "Multinational Subsidiary Evolution: Capability and Charter Change in Foreign Owned Subsidiary Companies," *Academy of Management Review* 23 (October 1998): 773–795; A. K. Gupta and V. J. Govindarajan, "Knowledge Flows Within Multinational Corporations," *Strategic Management Journal* 21 (2000): 473–496; V. J. Govindarajan and A. K. Gupta, *The Quest for Global Dominance* (San Francisco: Jossey-Bass, 2001); T. S. Frost, J. M. Birkinshaw, and P. C. Ensign, "Centers of Excellence in Multinational Corporations," *Strategic Management Journal* 23 (2002): 997–1018; and U. Andersson, M. Forsgren, and U. Holm, "The Strategic Impact of External Networks," *Strategic Management Journal* 23 (2002): 979–996.

12. S. Leung, "Armchairs, TVs and Espresso: Is It McDonald's?" *Wall Street Journal* (August 30, 2002): A1, A6.

13. C. K. Prahalad and Yves L. Doz, *The Multinational Mission: Balancing Local Demands and Global Vision* (New York: Free Press, 1987). See also J. Birkinshaw, A. Morrison, and J. Hulland, "Structural and Competitive Determinants of a Global Integration Strategy," *Strategic Management Journal* 16 (1995): 637–655.

14. J. E. Garten, "Wal-Mart Gives Globalization a Bad Name," *Business Week* (March 8, 2004): 24.

15. Prahalad and Doz, *Multinational Mission.* Prahalad and Doz actually talk about local responsiveness rather than local customization.

16. Levitt, "Globalization of Markets."

17. C. A. Bartlett and S. Ghoshal, *Managing Across Borders* (Boston: Harvard Business School Press, 1989).

18. W. W. Lewis; *The Power of Productivity* (Chicago, University of Chicago Press, 2004).

19. C. J. Chipello, "Local Presence Is Key to European Deals," *Wall Street Journal* (June 30, 1998): A15.

20. Bartlett and Ghoshal, *Managing Across Borders.*

21. Ibid.

22. T. Hout, M. E. Porter, and E. Rudden, "How Global Companies Win Out," *Harvard Business Review* (September–October 1982): 98–108.

23. See Charles W. L. Hill, *International Business: Competing in the Global Marketplace* (New York: McGraw-Hill, 2000).

24. This can be reconceptualized as the resource base of the entrant, relative to indigenous competitors. For work that focuses on this issue, see W. C. Bogenr, H. Thomas, and J. McGee, "A Longitudinal Study of the Competitive Positions and Entry Paths of European Firms in the U.S. Pharmaceutical Market," *Strategic Management Journal* 17 (1996): 85–107; D. Collis, "A Resource Based Analysis of Global Competition," *Strategic Management Journal* 12 (1991): 49–68; and S. Tallman, "Strategic Management Models and Resource Based Strategies Among MNEs in a Host Market," *Strategic Management Journal* 12 (1991): 69–82.

25. For a discussion of first-mover advantages, see M. Liberman and D. Montgomery, "First Mover Advantages," *Strategic Management Journal* 9 (Special Issue, Summer 1988): 41–58.

26. J. M. Shaver, W. Mitchell, and B. Yeung, "The Effect of Own Company and Other Company Experience on Foreign Direct Investment Survival in the U.S., 1987–92," *Strategic Management Journal* 18 (1997): 811–824.

27. S. Zaheer and E. Mosakowski, "The Dynamics of the Liability of Foreignness: A Global Study of Survival in the Financial Services Industry," *Strategic Management Journal* 18 (1997): 439–464.

28. Shaver, Mitchell, and Yeung, "The Effect of Own Company and Other Company Experience."

29. P. Ghemawat, *Commitment: The Dynamics of Strategy* (New York: Free Press, 1991).

30. This section draws on numerous studies, including: C. W. L. Hill, P. Hwang, and W. C. Kim, "An Eclectic Theory of the Choice of International Entry Mode," *Strategic Management Journal* 11 (1990): 117–28; C. W. L. Hill and W. C. Kim, "Searching for a Dynamic Theory of the Multinational Enterprise: A Transaction Cost Model," *Strategic Management Journal* 9 (Special Issue on Strategy Content, 1988): pp. 93–104; E. Anderson and H. Gatignon, "Modes of Foreign Entry: A Transaction Cost Analysis and Propositions," *Journal of International Business Studies* 17 (1986): 1–26; F. R. Root, *Entry Strategies for International Markets* (Lexington, MA: D. C. Heath, 1980); A. Madhok, "Cost, Value and Foreign Market Entry: The Transaction and the Firm," *Strategic Management Journal* 18 (1997): 39–61; K. D. Brouthers and L. B. Brouthers, "Acquisition or Greenfield Start-Up?" *Strategic Management Journal* 21:1 (2000): 89–97; X. Martin and R. Salmon, "Knowledge Transfer Capacity and Its Implications for the Theory of the Multinational Enterprise," *Journal of International Business Studies* (July 2003): 356; and A. Verbeke, "The Evolutionary View of the MNE and the Future of Internalization Theory," *Journal of International Business Studies* (November 2003): 498–515.

31. F. J. Contractor, "The Role of Licensing in International Strategy," *Columbia Journal of World Business* (Winter 1982): 73–83.

32. O. E. Williamson, *The Economic Institutions of Capitalism* (New York: Free Press, 1985).

33. Andrew E. Serwer, "McDonald's Conquers the World," *Fortune* (October 17, 1994): 103–116.

34. For an excellent review of the basic theoretical literature of joint ventures, see B. Kogut, "Joint Ventures: Theoretical and Empirical Perspectives," *Strategic Management Journal* 9 (1988): 319–332. More recent studies include: T. Chi, "Option to Acquire or Divest a Joint Venture," *Strategic Management Journal* 21:6 (2000): 665–688; H. Merchant and D. Schendel, "How Do International Joint Ventures Create Shareholder Value?" *Strategic Management Journal* 21:7 (2000): 723–737; H. K. Steensma and M. A. Lyles, "Explaining IJV Survival in a Transitional Economy Through Social Exchange and Knowledge Based Perspectives," *Strategic Management Journal* 21:8 (2000): 831–851; and J. F. Hennart and M. Zeng, "Cross Cultural Differences and Joint Venture Longevity," *Journal of International Business Studies* (December 2002): 699–717.

35. J. A. Robins, S. Tallman, and K. Fladmoe-Lindquist, "Autonomy and Dependence of International Cooperative Ventures," *Strategic Management Journal* (October 2002): 881–902.

36. C. W. L. Hill, "Strategies for Exploiting Technological Innovations," *Organization Science* 3 (1992): 428–441.

37. See K. Ohmae, "The Global Logic of Strategic Alliances," *Harvard Business Review* (March–April 1989): 143–154; G. Hamel, Y. L. Doz, and C. K. Prahalad, "Collaborate with Your Competitors and Win!" *Harvard Business Review* (January–February 1989): 133–139; W. Burgers, C. W. L. Hill, and W. C. Kim, "Alliances in the Global Auto Industry," *Strategic Management Journal* 14 (1993): 419–432; and P. Kale, H. Singh, and H. Perlmutter, "Learning and Protection of Proprietary Assets in Strategic Alliances: Building Relational Capital," *Strategic Management Journal* 21 (2000): 217–237.

38. L. T. Chang, "China Eases Foreign Film Rules," *Wall Street Journal* (October 15, 2004): B2.

39. B. L. Simonin, "Transfer of Marketing Knowhow in International Strategic Alliances," *Journal of International Business Studies* (1999): 463–491: and J. W. Spencer, "Firms' Knowledge Sharing

Strategies in the Global Innovation System," *Strategic Management Journal* 24 (2003): 217–233.

40. C. Souza, "Microsoft Teams with MIPS, Toshiba," *EBN* (February 10, 2003): 4.

41. M. Frankel, "Now Sony Is Giving Palm a Hand," *BusinessWeek* (November 29, 2000): 50.

42. Kale, Singh, and Perlmutter, "Learning and Protection of Proprietary Assets."

43. R. B. Reich and E. D. Mankin, "Joint Ventures with Japan Give Away Our Future," *Harvard Business Review* (March–April 1986): 78–90.

44. J. Bleeke and D. Ernst, "The Way to Win in Cross-Border Alliances," *Harvard Business Review* (November–December 1991): 127–135.

45. E. Booker and C. Krol, "IBM Finds Strength in Alliances," *B to B* (February 10, 2003): 3, 27.

46. W. Roehl and J. F. Truitt, "Stormy Open Marriages Are Better," *Columbia Journal of World Business* (Summer 1987): 87–95.

47. See T. Khanna, R. Gulati, and N. Nohria, "The Dynamics of Learning Alliances: Competition, Cooperation, and Relative Scope," *Strategic Management Journal* 19 (1998): 193–210: P. Kale, H. Singh, H. Perlmutter, "Learning and Protection of Proprietary Assets in Strategic Alliances: Building Relational Capital," *Strategic Management Journal* 21 (2000): 217–237.

48. Kale, Singh, and Perlmutter, "Learning and Protection of Proprietary Assets."

49. Hamel, Doz, and Prahalad, "Collaborate with Competitors"; Khanna, Gulati, and Nohria, "The Dynamics of Learning Alliances: Competition, Cooperation, and Relative Scope"; and E. W. K. Tang, "Acquiring Knowledge by Foreign Partners from International Joint Ventures in a Transition Economy: Learning by Doing and Learning Myopia," *Strategic Management Journal* 23 (2002): 835–854.

50. Hamel, Doz, and Prahalad, "Collaborate with Competitors."

51. B. Wysocki, "Cross Border Alliances Become Favorite Way to Crack New Markets," *Wall Street Journal* (March 4, 1990): A1.

52. *Sources*: J. Neff, "P&G Outpacing Unilever in Five-Year Battle," *Advertising Age* (November 3, 2003): 1–3; G. Strauss, "Firm Restructuring into Truly Global Company," *USA Today* (September 10, 1999): B2; Procter & Gamble 10K Report, 2006; M. Kolbasuk McGee, "P&G Jump-Starts Corporate Change," *Information Week* (November 1, 1999): 30–34; J. Birchall, "P&G's Strong Sales Growth Beats Forecasts," *Financial Times* (August 3, 2006): 22.

Chapter 9

1. www.sap.com (2006).

2. www.oracle.com (2006).

3. United Nations, *World Investment Report 2001* (New York: United Nations, November 2001).

4. Y .J. Dreazen, G. Ip, and N. Kulish, "Why the Sudden Rise in the Urge to Merge and Create Oligopolies?" *Wall Street Journal*, February 25, 2002, p. A1.

5. For evidence on acquisitions and performance, see R. E. Caves, "Mergers, Takeovers, and Economic Efficiency," *International Journal of Industrial Organization* 7 (1989): 151–174; M. C. Jensen and R. S. Ruback, "The Market for Corporate Control: The Scientific Evidence," *Journal of Financial Economics* 11 (1983): 5–50; R. Roll, "Empirical Evidence on Takeover Activity and Shareholder Wealth," in J. C. Coffee, L. Lowenstein, and R. Sose (eds.), *Knights, Raiders and Targets* (Oxford: Oxford University Press, 1989); A. Schleifer and R. W. Vishny, "Takeovers in the 60s and 80s: Evidence and Implications," *Strategic Management Journal* 12 (Special Issue, Winter 1991): 51–60; and T. H. Brush, "Predicted Changes in Operational Synergy and Post Acquisition Performance of Acquired Businesses," *Strategic Management Journal* 17 (1996): 1–24.

6. "Few Takeovers Pay Off for Big Buyers," *Investors Business Daily* (May 25, 2001): 1.

7. K. R. Harrian, "Formulating Vertical Integration Strategies," *Academy of Management Review* 9 (1984): 638–652.

8. This is the essence of Chandler's argument. See Alfred D. Chandler, *Strategy and Structure* (Cambridge, Mass.: MIT Press, 1962). The same argument is also made by Jeffrey Pfeffer and Gerald R. Salancik, *The External Control of Organizations* (New York: Harper & Row, 1978). See also K. R. Harrigan, *Strategic Flexibility* (Lexington, Mass.: Lexington Books, 1985); K. R. Harrigan, "Vertical Integration and Corporate Strategy," *Academy of Management Journal* 28 (1985): 397–425; and F. M. Scherer, *Industrial Market Structure and Economic Performance* (Chicago: Rand McNally, 1981).

9. Oliver E. Williamson, *The Economic Institutions of Capitalism.* (New York: The Free Press, 1985). For recent empirical work that uses this framework, see L. Poppo and T. Zenger, "Testing Alternative Theories of the Firm: Transaction Cost, Knowledge Based, and Measurement Explanations for Make or Buy Decisions in Information Services," *Strategic Management Journal* 19 (1998): 853–878.

10. Williamson, *Economic Institutions of Capitalism.*

11. A. D. Chandler, *The Visible Hand* (Cambridge, Mass.: Harvard University Press, 1977).

12. Julia Pitta, "Score One for Vertical Integration," *Forbes* (January 18, 1993): 88–89.

13. Joseph White and Neal Templin, "Harsh Regimen: A Swollen GM Finds It Hard to Stick with Its Crash Diet," *Wall Street Journal* (September 9, 1992): A1.

14. Harrigan, *Strategic Flexibility*, pp. 67–87. See also Allan Afuah, "Dynamic Boundaries of the Firm: Are Firms Better Off Being Vertically Integrated in the Face of a Technological Change?" *Academy of Management Journal* 44 (2001): 1121–1228.

15. Kevin Kelly, Zachary Schiller, and James Treece, "Cut Costs or Else," *Business Week* (March 22, 1993): 28–29.

16. X. Martin, W. Mitchell, and A. Swaminathan, "Recreating and Extending Japanese Automobile Buyer-Supplier Links in North America," *Strategic Management Journal* 16 (1995): 589–619; C. W. L. Hill, "National Institutional Structures, Transaction Cost Economizing, and Competitive Advantage," *Organization Science* 6 (1995): 119–131.

17. *Standard & Poor's Industry Survey, Autos—Auto Parts,* June 24, 1993.

18. See James Womack, Daniel Jones, and Daniel Roos, *The Machine That Changed the World* (New York: Rawson Associates, 1990); and James Richardson, "Parallel Sourcing and Supplier Performance in the Japanese Automobile Industry," *Strategic Management Journal* 14 (1993): 339–350.

19. R. Mudambi and S. Helper, "The Close but Adversarial Model of Supplier Relations in the U.S. Auto Industry," *Strategic Management Journal* 19 (1998): 775–792.

20. Williamson, *Economic Institutions of Capitalism.* See also J. H. Dyer, "Effective Inter-Firm Collaboration: How Firms Minimize Transaction Costs and Maximize Transaction Value," *Strategic Management Journal* 18 (1997): 535–556.

21. Richardson, "Parallel Sourcing and Supplier Performance in the Japanese Automobile Industry."

22. W. H. Davidow and M. S. Malone, *The Virtual Corporation* (New York: Harper & Row, 1992).

23. A. M. Porter, "Outsourcing Gains Popularity," *Purchasing* (March 11, 1999): 22–24.

24. D. Garr, "Inside Outsourcing," *Fortune* 142:1 (2001): 85–92.

25. J. Krane, "American Express Hires IBM for $4 billion," *Columbian* (February 26, 2002): E2; www.ibm.com (2006).

26. www.ibm.com (2006).

27. Davidow and Malone, *The Virtual Corporation.*

28. Davidow and Malone, *The Virtual Corporation*; H. W. Chesbrough and D. J. Teece, "When Is Virtual Virtuous? Organizing for Innovation," *Harvard Business Review* (January–February 1996): 65–74; J. B. Quinn, "Strategic Outsourcing: Leveraging Knowledge Capabilities," *Sloan Management Review* (Summer 1999): 9–21.

Chapter 10

1. J. R. Laing, "Tyco's Titan," *Barron's* (April 12, 1999): 27–32; M. Maremont, "How Is Tyco Accounting for Cash Flow?"; *Wall Street Journal* (March 5, 2002): C1; J. R. Laing, "Doubting Tyco," *Barron's* (January 28, 2002): 19–20.

2. "Tyco Shares Up on Report Mulling Breakup," www.yahoo.com (accessed January 9, 2006).

3. www.tyco.com (2006), press release.

4. G. Hamel and C. K. Prahalad, *Competing for the Future* (Boston: Harvard Business School Press, 1994).

5. Ibid.

6. D. Leonard Barton and G. Pisano, "Monsanto's March into Biotechnology," Harvard Business School Case #690-009 (1990). See Monsanto's homepage for details about its genetically engineered seed products at http://www.monsanto.com.

7. This resource-based view of diversification can be traced to Edith Penrose's seminal book, *The Theory of the Growth of the Firm* (Oxford: Oxford University Press, 1959).

8. D. J. Teece, "Economies of Scope and the Scope of the Enterprise," *Journal of Economic Behavior and Organization* 3 (1980): 223–247. For recent empirical work on this topic, see C. H. St. John and J. S. Harrison, "Manufacturing Based Relatedness, Synergy and Coordination," *Strategic Management Journal* 20 (1999): 129–145.

9. Teece, "Economies of Scope." For recent empirical work on this topic, see St. John and Harrison, "Manufacturing Based Relatedness, Synergy and Coordination."

10. For a detailed discussion, see C. W. L. Hill and R. E. Hoskisson, "Strategy and Structure in the Multiproduct Firm," *Academy of Management Review* 12 (1987): 331–341.

11. See, for example, G. R. Jones and C. W. L. Hill, "A Transaction Cost Analysis of Strategy Structure Choice," *Strategic Management Journal* (1988): 159–172; and Oliver E. Williamson, *Markets and Hierarchies: Analysis and Antitrust Implications* (New York: Free Press, 1975), pp. 132–175.

12. R. Buderi, *Engines of Tomorrow* (New York: Simon & Schuster, 2000).

13. C. W. L. Hill, "The Role of Headquarters in the Multidivisional Firm," in R. Rumelt, D. J. Teece, and D. Schendel (eds.), *Fundamental Issues in Strategy Research* (Cambridge, Mass.: Harvard Business School Press, 1994), pp. 297–321.

14. See, for example, Jones and Hill, "A Transaction Cost Analysis"; Williamson, *Markets and Hierarchies*; and Hill, "The Role of Headquarters in the Multidivisional Firm."

15. The distinction goes back to R. P. Rumelt, *Strategy, Structure and Economic Performance* (Cambridge, Mass.: Harvard Business School Press, 1974).

16. For evidence, see C. W. L. Hill, "Conglomerate Performance over the Economic Cycle," *Journal of Industrial Economics* 32 (1983):

197–212; and D. T. C. Mueller, "The Effects of Conglomerate Mergers," *Journal of Banking and Finance* 1 (1977): 315–347.

17. For reviews of the evidence, see V. Ramanujam and P. Varadarajan, "Research on Corporate Diversification: A Synthesis," *Strategic Management Journal* 10 (1989): 523–551; G. Dess, J. F. Hennart, C. W. L. Hill, and A. Gupta, "Research Issues in Strategic Management," *Journal of Management* 21 (1995): 357–392; and David C. Hyland and J. David Diltz, "Why Companies Diversify: An Empirical Examination," *Financial Management* 31 (Spring 2002): 51–81.

18. M. E. Porter, "From Competitive Advantage to Corporate Strategy," *Harvard Business Review* (May–June 1987): 43–59.

19. For reviews of the evidence, see Ramanujam and Varadarajan, "Research on Corporate Diversification"; Dess, Hennart, Hill, and Gupta, "Research Issues in Strategic Management"; and Hyland and Diltz, "Why Companies Diversify."

20. C. R. Christensen et al., *Business Policy Text and Cases* (Homewood, Ill.: Irwin, 1987), p. 778.

21. See Booz, Allen, and Hamilton, "New Products Management for the 1980's" (privately published, 1982); A. L. Page, "PDMA's New Product Development Practices Survey: Performance and Best Practices" (presented at the PDMA Fifteenth Annual International Conference, Boston, October 16, 1991); and E. Mansfield, "How Economists See R&D," *Harvard Business Review* (November–December 1981): 98–106.

22. See R. Biggadike, "The Risky Business of Diversification," *Harvard Business Review* (May–June 1979): 103–111; R. A. Burgelman, "A Process Model of Internal Corporate Venturing in the Diversified Major Firm," *Administrative Science Quarterly* 28 (1983): 223–244; and Z. Block and I. C. MacMillan, *Corporate Venturing* (Boston: Harvard Business School Press, 1993).

23. Biggadike, "The Risky Business of Diversification"; Block and Macmillan, *Corporate Venturing.*

24. Buderi, *Engines of Tomorrow.*

25. I. C. MacMillan and R. George, "Corporate Venturing: Challenges for Senior Managers," *Journal of Business Strategy* 5 (1985): 34–43.

26. See R. A. Burgelman, M. M. Maidique, and S. C. Wheelwright, *Strategic Management of Technology and Innovation* (Chicago: Irwin, 1996), pp. 493–507. Also see Buderi, *Engines of Tomorrow.*

27. Buderi, *Engines of Tomorrow.*

28. Buderi, *Engines of Tomorrow.*

29. For evidence on acquisitions and performance, see R. E. Caves, "Mergers, Takeovers, and Economic Efficiency," *International Journal of Industrial Organization* 7 (1989): 151–174; M. C. Jensen and R. S. Ruback, "The Market for Corporate Control: The Scientific Evidence," *Journal of Financial Economics* 11 (1983): 5–50; R. Roll, "Empirical Evidence on Takeover Activity and Shareholder Wealth," in J. C. Coffee, L. Lowenstein, and S. Rose (eds.), *Knights, Raiders and Targets* (Oxford: Oxford University Press, 1989); A. Schleifer and R. W. Vishny, "Takeovers in the 60s and 80s: Evidence and Implications," *Strategic Management Journal* 12 (Special Issue, Winter 1991): 51–60; T. H. Brush, "Predicted Changes in Operational Synergy and Post Acquisition Performance of Acquired Businesses," *Strategic Management Journal* 17 (1996): 1–24; and T. Loughran and A. M. Vijh, "Do Long Term Shareholders Benefit from Corporate Acquisitions?" *Journal of Finance* 5 (1997): 1765–1787.

30. For evidence on acquisitions and performance, see R. E. Caves, "Mergers, Takeovers, and Economic Efficiency," *International Journal of Industrial Organization* 7 (1989): 151–174; M. C. Jensen and R. S. Ruback, "The Market for Corporate Control: The Scientific Evidence," *Journal of Financial Economics* 11 (1983): 5–50; R. Roll, "Empirical Evidence on Takeover Activity

and Shareholder Wealth," in J. C. Coffee, L. Lowenstein, and S. Rose (eds.), *Knights, Raiders and Targets* (Oxford: Oxford University Press, 1989); A. Schleifer and R. W. Vishny, "Takeovers in the 60s and 80s: Evidence and Implications," *Strategic Management Journal* 12 (Special Issue, Winter 1991): 51–60; T. H. Brush, "Predicted Changes in Operational Synergy and Post Acquisition Performance of Acquired Businesses," *Strategic Management Journal* 17 (1996): 1–24; and T. Loughran and A. M. Vijh, "Do Long Term Shareholders Benefit from Corporate Acquisitions?" *Journal of Finance* 5 (1997): 1765–1787.

31. D. J. Ravenscraft and F. M. Scherer, *Mergers, Sell-offs, and Economic Efficiency* (Washington, D.C.: Brookings Institution, 1987).

32. See J. P. Walsh, "Top Management Turnover Following Mergers and Acquisitions," *Strategic Management Journal* 9 (1988): 173–183.

33. See A. A. Cannella and D. C. Hambrick, "Executive Departure and Acquisition Performance," *Strategic Management Journal* 14 (1993): 137–152.

34. R. Roll, "The Hubris Hypothesis of Corporate Takeovers," *Journal of Business* 59 (1986): 197–216.

35. "Coca-Cola: A Sobering Lesson from Its Journey into Wine," *Business Week* (June 3, 1985): 96–98.

36. P. Haspeslagh and D. Jemison, *Managing Acquisitions* (New York: Free Press, 1991).

37. For views on this issue, see L. L. Fray, D. H. Gaylin, and J. W. Down, "Successful Acquisition Planning," *Journal of Business Strategy* 5 (1984): 46–55; C. W. L. Hill, "Profile of a Conglomerate Takeover: BTR and Thomas Tilling," *Journal of General Management* 10 (1984): 34–50; D. R. Willensky, "Making It Happen: How to Execute an Acquisition," *Business Horizons* (March–April 1985): 38–45; Haspeslagh and Jemison, *Managing Acquisitions;* and P. L. Anslinger and T. E. Copeland, "Growth Through Acquisition: A Fresh Look," *Harvard Business Review* (January–February 1996): 126–135.

38. M. L. A. Hayward, "When Do Firms Learn from Their Acquisition Experience? Evidence from 1990–1995," *Strategic Management Journal* 23 (2002): 21–39; K. G. Ahuja, "Technological Acquisitions and the Innovation Performance of Acquiring Firms: A Longitudinal Study," *Strategic Management Journal* 23 (2001): 197–220; H. G. Barkema and F. Vermeulen, "International Expansion Through Startup or Acquisition," *Academy of Management Journal* 41 (1998): 7–26.

39. Hayward, "When Do Firms Learn from Their Acquisition Experience?"

40. For a review of the evidence and some contrary empirical evidence, see D. E. Hatfield, J. P. Liebskind, and T. C. Opler, "The Effects of Corporate Restructuring on Aggregate Industry Specialization," *Strategic Management Journal* 17 (1996): 55–72.

41. A. Lamont and C. Polk, "The Diversification Discount: Cash Flows Versus Returns," *Journal of Finance* 56 (October 2001): 1693–1721; R. Raju, H. Servaes, and L. Zingales, "The Cost of Diversity: The Diversification Discount and Inefficient Investment," *Journal of Finance* 55 (February 2000): 35–80.

42. For example, see Schleifer and Vishny, "Takeovers in the 60s and 80s."

Chapter 11

1. *Sources:* "Money Well Spent: Corporate Parties," *Economist* (November 1, 2003): 79; "Tyco Pair Sentencing Expected on September 19th," *Wall Street Journal* (August 2, 2005): 1: "Off to Jail: Corporate Crime in America," *Economist,* (June 25, 2005): 81; N. Varchaver, "What's Ed Breen Thinking?" *Fortune* (March 20, 2006): 135–139.

2. E. Freeman, *Strategic Management: A Stakeholder Approach* (Boston: Pitman Press, 1984).

3. C. W. L. Hill and T. M. Jones, "Stakeholder-Agency Theory," *Journal of Management Studies* 29 (1992): 131–154; J. G. March and H. A. Simon, *Organizations* (New York: Wiley, 1958).

4. Hill and Jones, "Stakeholder-Agency Theory"; C. Eesley and M. J. Lenox, "Firm Responses to Secondary Stakeholder Action," *Strategic Management Journal* 27 (2006): 13–24.

5. I. C. Macmillan and P. E. Jones, *Strategy Formulation: Power and Politics* (St. Paul, Minn.: West, 1986).

6. Tom Copeland, Tim Koller, and Jack Murrin, *Valuation: Measuring and Managing the Value of Companies* (New York: Wiley, 1996).

7. R. S. Kaplan and D. P. Norton, *Strategy Maps* (Boston: Harvard Business School Press, 2004).

8. A. L. Velocci, D. A. Fulghum, and R. Wall, "Damage Control," *Aviation Week* (December 1, 2003): 26–27.

9. M. C. Jensen and W. H. Meckling, "Theory of the Firm: Managerial Behavior, Agency Costs and Ownership Structure," *Journal of Financial Economics* 3 (1976): 305–360; E. F. Fama, "Agency Problems and the Theory of the Firm," *Journal of Political Economy* 88 (1980): 375–390.

10. Hill and Jones, "Stakeholder-Agency Theory."

11. For example, see R. Marris, *The Economic Theory of Managerial Capitalism* (London: Macmillan, 1964); and J. K. Galbraith, *The New Industrial State* (Boston: Houghton Mifflin, 1970).

12. Fama, "Agency Problems and the Theory of the Firm."

13. A. Rappaport, "New Thinking on How to Link Executive Pay with Performance," *Harvard Business Review* (March–April 1999): 91–105.

14. R. Kirkland, "The Real CEO Pay Problem," *Fortune* (July 10, 2006): 78–82.

15. D Henry and D. Stead, "Worker vs CEO: Room to Run," *Business Week* (October 30, 2006): 13.

16. For academic studies that look at the determinants of CEO pay, see M. C. Jensen and K. J. Murphy, "Performance Pay and Top Management Incentives," *Journal of Political Economy* 98 (1990): 225–264; Charles W. L. Hill and Phillip Phan, "CEO Tenure as a Determinant of CEO Pay," *Academy of Management Journal* 34 (1991): 707–717; H. L. Tosi and L. R. Gomez-Mejia, "CEO Compensation Monitoring and Firm Performance," *Academy of Management Journal* 37 (1994): 1002–1016; and Joseph F. Porac, James B. Wade, and Timothy G. Pollock, "Industry Categories and the Politics of the Comparable Firm in CEO Compensation," *Administrative Science Quarterly* 44 (1999): 112–144.

17. Andrew Ward, "Home Depot Investors Stage a Revolt," *Financial Times* (May 26, 2006): 20.

18. R. Kirklad, "The Real CEO Pay Problem," *Fortune* (July 10, 2006): 78–82.

19. For research on this issue, see Peter J. Lane, A. A. Cannella, and M. H. Lubatkin, "Agency Problems as Antecedents to Unrelated Mergers and Diversification: Amihud and Lev Reconsidered," *Strategic Management Journal* 19 (1998): 555–578.

20. E. T. Penrose, *The Theory of the Growth of the Firm* (London: Macmillan, 1958).

21. G. Edmondson and L. Cohn, "How Parmalat Went Sour," *Business Week* (January 12, 2004): 46–50; "Another Enron? Royal Dutch Shell," *Economist* (March 13, 2004): 71.

22. O. E. Williamson, *The Economic Institutions of Capitalism* (New York: Free Press, 1985).

23. Fama, "Agency Problems and the Theory of the Firm."

24. S. Finkelstein and R. D'Aveni, "CEO Duality as a Double Edged Sword," *Academy of Management Journal* 37 (1994): 1079–1108;

B. Ram Baliga and R. C. Moyer, "CEO Duality and Firm Performance," *Strategic Management Journal* 17 (1996): 41–53; M. L. Mace, *Directors: Myth and Reality* (Cambridge, Mass.: Harvard University Press, 1971); S. C. Vance, *Corporate Leadership: Boards of Directors and Strategy* (New York: McGraw-Hill, 1983).

25. W. G. Lewellen, C. Eoderer, and A. Rosenfeld, "Merger Decisions and Executive Stock Ownership in Acquiring Firms," *Journal of Accounting and Economics* 7 (1985): 209–231.

26. C. W. L. Hill and S. A. Snell, "External Control, Corporate Strategy, and Firm Performance," *Strategic Management Journal* 9 (1988): 577–590.

27. The phenomenon of back dating stock options was uncovered by academic research and then picked up by the SEC. See Erik Lie, "On the Timing of CEO Stock Option Awards," *Management Science* 51 (2005): 802–812.

28. G. Colvin, "A Study in CEO Greed," *Fortune* (June 12, 2006): 53–55.

29. J. P. Walsh and R. D. Kosnik, "Corporate Raiders and Their Disciplinary Role in the Market for Corporate Control," *Academy of Management Journal* 36 (1993): 671–700.

30. R. S. Kaplan and D. P. Norton, "The Balanced Scorecard—Measures That Drive Performance," *Harvard Business Review* (January–February 1992): 71–79; R. S. Kaplan and D. P. Norton, *Strategy Maps* (Boston: Harvard Business School Press, 2004).

31. R. S. Kaplan and D. P. Norton, "Using the Balanced Scorecard as a Strategic Management System," *Harvard Business Review* (January–February 1996): 75–85; Kaplan and Norton, *Strategy Maps*.

32. R. S. Kaplan and D. P. Norton, "Putting the Balanced Scorecard to Work," *Harvard Business Review* (September–October 1993): 134–147; Kaplan and Norton, *Strategy Maps*.

33. Kaplan and Norton, "The Balanced Scorecard," p. 72.

34. Timet, "Boeing Settle Lawsuit," *Metal Center News* 41 (June 2001): 38–39.

35. Joseph Kahn. "Ruse in Toyland: Chinese Workers' Hidden Woe," *New York Times* (December 7, 2003): A1, A8.

36. See N. King, "Halliburton Tells the Pentagon Workers Took Iraq Deal Kickbacks," *Wall Street Journal* (January 23, 2004): A1; "Whistleblowers Say Company Routinely Overcharged," Reuters, February 12, 2004; R. Gold and J. R. Wilke; "Data Sought in Halliburton Inquiry," *Wall Street Journal* (February 5, 2004): A6.

37. Saul W. Gellerman, "Why Good Managers Make Bad Ethical Choices," *Ethics in Practice: Managing the Moral Corporation,* ed. Kenneth R. Andrews (Cambridge, Mass.: Harvard Business School Press, 1989).

38. Ibid.

39. See Tom L. Beauchamp and Norman E. Bowie, *Ethical Theory and Business,* 7th ed. (New York: Pearson, Prentice Hall, 2001), 17–23.

40. Thomas Donaldson, *The Ethics of International Business* (Oxford: Oxford University Press, 1989).

41. John Rawls, *A Theory of Justice,* rev. ed. (Cambridge, Mass.: Belknap Press, 1999, original edition 1971).

42. Can be found on Unilever's website at http://www.unilever.com/company/ourprinciples/ (accessed 2006).

43. From United Technologies website www.utc.com (accessed December 15, 2006).

44. *Sources:* S. Holt, "Wal-Mart Workers Suit Wins Class Action Status," *Seattle Times* (October 9, 2004): E1, E4; C. Daniels, "Women v Wal-Mart," *Fortune* (July 21, 2003): 79–82; C. R. Gentry, "Off the Clock," *Chain Store Age* (February 2003): 33–36; M. Grimm, "Wal-Mart Uber Alles," *American Demographic* (October 2003): 38–42; "Wal-Mart Takes Steps to Address Diversity

Criticism," *Financial Wire* (April 25, 2006): 1; Andy Serwer, "Bruised in Bentonville," *Fortune* (April 18, 2005): 84–88.

Chapter 12

1. www.dell.com (2004).

2. G. McWilliams, "Dell Looks for Ways to Rekindle the Fire It Had as an Upstart," *Wall Street Journal* (August 31, 2000): A.1, A.8; "Dell Hopes to Lead Firm out of Desert," *Houston Chronicle* (September, 3, 2000): 4D.

3. www.dell.com (2006).

4. G. Rivlin, "He Naps. He Sings. And He Isn't Michael Dell," *New York Times* (September 11, 2005): 31.

5. L. Smircich, "Concepts of Culture and Organizational Analysis," *Administrative Science Quarterly* 28 (1983): 339–358.

6. G. R. Jones and J. M. George, "The Experience and Evolution of Trust: Implications for Cooperation and Teamwork," *Academy of Management Review* 3 (1998): 531–546.

7. Ibid.

8. J. R. Galbraith, *Designing Complex Organizations* (Reading, Mass.: Addison-Wesley, 1973).

9. Alfred D. Chandler, *Strategy and Structure* (Cambridge, Mass.: MIT Press, 1962).

10. The discussion draws heavily on Chandler, *Strategy and Structure* and B. R. Scott, *Stages of Corporate Development* (Cambridge, Mass.: Intercollegiate Clearing House, Harvard Business School, 1971).

11. R. L. Daft, *Organizational Theory and Design,* 3rd ed. (St. Paul, Minn.: West, 1986), p. 215.

12. J. Child, *Organization, A Guide for Managers and Administrators* (New York: Harper & Row, 1977), pp. 52–70.

13. G. R. Jones and J. Butler, "Costs, Revenues, and Business Level Strategy," *Academy of Management Review* 13 (1988): 202–213; G. R. Jones and C. W. L. Hill, "Transaction Cost Analysis of Strategy-Structure Choice," *Strategic Management Journal* 9 (1988): 159–172.

14. G. R. Jones, *Organizational Theory, Design, and Change: Text and Cases* (Englewood Cliffs, N.J.: Prentice-Hall, 2005).

15. P. Blau, "A Formal Theory of Differentiation in Organizations," *American Sociological Review* 35 (1970): 684–695.

16. G. R. Jones, "Organization-Client Transactions and Organizational Governance Structures," *Academy of Management Journal* 30 (1987): 197–218.

17. S. McCartney, "Airline Industry's Top-Ranked Woman Keeps Southwest's Small-Fry Spirit Alive," *Wall Street Journal* (November 30, 1995): B1; www.southwest.com (2005).

18. P. R. Lawrence and J. Lorsch, *Organization and Environment* (Boston: Division of Research, Harvard Business School, 1967), pp. 50–55.

19. Galbraith, *Designing Complex Organizations,* Chapter 1; J. R. Galbraith and R. K. Kazanjian, *Strategy Implementation: Structure System and Process,* 2nd ed. (St. Paul, Minn.: West, 1986), Chapter 7.

20. R. Simmons, "Strategic Orientation and Top Management Attention to Control Systems," *Strategic Management Journal* 12 (1991): 49–62.

21. R. Simmons, "How New Top Managers Use Control Systems as Levers of Strategic Renewal," *Strategic Management Journal* 15 (1994): 169–189.

22. W. G. Ouchi, "The Transmission of Control Through Organizational Hierarchy," *Academy of Management Journal* 21 (1978): 173–192; W. H. Newman, *Constructive Control* (Englewood Cliffs, N.J.: Prentice-Hall, 1975).

23. E. Flamholtz, "Organizational Control Systems as a Managerial Tool," *California Management Review* (Winter 1979): 50–58.

24. O. E. Williamson, *Markets and Hierarchies: Analysis and Antitrust Implications* (New York: Free Press, 1975); W. G. Ouchi, "Markets, Bureaucracies, and Clans," *Administrative Science Quarterly* 25 (1980): 129–141.

25. H. Mintzberg, *The Structuring of Organizations* (Englewood Cliffs, N.J.: Prentice-Hall, 1979), pp. 5–9.

26. E. E. Lawler III, *Motivation in Work Organizations* (Monterey, Calif.: Brooks/Cole, 1973); Galbraith and Kazanjian, *Strategy Implementation*, Chapter 6.

27. Smircich, "Concepts of Culture and Organizational Analysis."

28. General Electric, Harvard Business School Case #9-385-315 (1984).

29. Ouchi, "Markets, Bureaucracies, and Clans," p. 130.

30. Jones, *Organizational Theory, Design, and Change.*

31. J. Van Maanen and E. H. Schein, "Towards a Theory of Organizational Socialization," in B. M. Staw (ed.), *Research in Organizational Behavior* (Greenwich, Conn.: JAI Press, 1979), pp. 1, 209–264.

32. G. R. Jones, "Socialization Tactics, Self-Efficacy, and Newcomers' Adjustments to Organizations," *Academy of Management Journal* 29 (1986): 262–279.

33. J. P. Kotter and J. L. Heskett, *Corporate Culture and Performance.*

34. T. J. Peters and R. H. Waterman, *In Search of Excellence: Lessons from America's Best-Run Companies* (New York: Harper & Row, 1982).

35. G. Hamel and C. K. Prahalad, "Strategic Intent," *Harvard Business Review* (May–June 1989): 64.

36. Galbraith and Kazanjian, *Strategy Implementation*; Child, *Organization*; R. Duncan, "What Is the Right Organization Structure?" *Organizational Dynamics* (Winter 1979): 59–80.

37. J. Pettet, "Wal-Mart Yesterday and Today," *Discount Merchandiser* (December 1995): 66–67; M. Reid, "Stores of Value," *Economist* (March 4, 1995): ss5–ss7; M. Troy, "The Culture Remains the Constant," *Discount Store News* (June 8, 1998): 95–98; www.walmart.com (accessed 2007).

38. W. G. Ouchi, "The Relationship Between Organizational Structure and Organizational Control," *Administrative Science Quarterly* 22 (1977): 95–113.

39. R. Bunderi, "Intel Researchers Aim to Think Big While Staying Close to Development," *Research-Technology Management* (March–April 1998): 3–4.

40. K. M. Eisenhardt, "Control: Organizational and Economic Approaches," *Management Science* 16 (1985): 134–148.

41. Williamson, *Markets and Hierarchies.*

42. P. R. Lawrence and J. W. Lorsch, *Organization and Environment.* (Boston: Graduate School of Business Administration, Harvard University, 1967).

43. K. Pope, "Dell Refocuses on Groundwork to Cope with Rocketing Sales," *Wall Street Journal* (June 18, 1987): 7–32.

44. Michael E. Porter, *Competitive Strategy: Techniques for Analyzing Industries and Competitors* (New York: Free Press, 1980); D. Miller, "Configurations of Strategy and Structure," *Strategic Management Journal* 7 (1986): 233–249.

45. D. Miller and P. H. Freisen, *Organizations: A Quantum View* (Englewood Cliffs, N.J.: Prentice-Hall, 1984).

46. J. Woodward, *Industrial Organization: Theory and Practice* (London: Oxford University Press, 1965); Lawrence and Lorsch, *Organization and Environment.*

47. R. E. White, "Generic Business Strategies, Organizational Context and Performance: An Empirical Investigation," *Strategic Management Journal* 7 (1986): 217–231.

48. Porter, *Competitive Strategy*; Miller, "Configurations of Strategy and Structure."

49. E. Deal and A. A. Kennedy, *Corporate Cultures* (Reading, Mass.: Addison-Wesley, 1985); "Corporate Culture," *Business Week* (October 27, 1980): 148–160.

50. S. M. Davis and R. R. Lawrence, *Matrix* (Reading, Mass.: Addison-Wesley, 1977); J. R. Galbraith, "Matrix Organization Designs: How to Combine Functional and Project Forms," *Business Horizons* 14 (1971): 29–40.

51. Duncan, "What Is the Right Organizational Structure?"; Davis and Lawrence, *Matrix.*

52. D. Miller, "Configurations of Strategy and Structure," in R. E. Miles and C. C. Snow (eds.), *Organizational Strategy, Structure, and Process* (New York: McGraw-Hill, 1978).

53. G. D. Bruton, J. K. Keels, and C. L. Shook, "Downsizing the Firm: Answering the Strategic Questions," *Academy of Management Executive* (May 1996): 38–45.

54. M. Hammer and J. Champy, *Reengineering the Corporation* (New York: HarperCollins, 1993).

55. A. Reinhardt, "Can Nokia Capture Mobile Workers?" *Business Week* (February 9, 2004): 80; D. Pringle, "Nokia Unveils a Major Shake-Up," *Wall Street Journal* (September 29, 2003): B6.

56. www.nokia.com (2006).

Chapter 13

1. B. Koenig, "Ford Reorganizes Executives Under New Chief Mulally," www.bloomberg.com (accessed December 14, 2006).

2. www.ford.com (2006).

3. Alfred D. Chandler, *Strategy and Structure* (Cambridge, Mass.: MIT Press, 1962); O. E. Williamson, *Markets and Hierarchies* (New York: Free Press, 1975); L. Wrigley, "Divisional Autonomy and Diversification" (Ph.D. Diss., Harvard Business School, 1970).

4. R. P. Rumelt, *Strategy, Structure, and Economic Performance* (Boston: Division of Research, Harvard Business School, 1974); B. R. Scott, *Stages of Corporate Development* (Cambridge, Mass.: Intercollegiate Clearing House, Harvard Business School, 1971); Williamson, *Markets and Hierarchies.*

5. A. P. Sloan, *My Years at General Motors* (Garden City, N.Y.: Doubleday, 1946); A. Taylor III, "Can GM Remodel Itself?" *Fortune* (January 13, 1992): 26–34; W. Hampton and J. Norman, "General Motors: What Went Wrong?" *Business Week* (March 16, 1987): 102–110; www.gm.com (2002). The quotations are on pp. 46 and 50 in Sloan, *My Years at General Motors.*

6. The discussion draws on each of the sources cited in endnotes 20–27 and on G. R. Jones and C. W. L. Hill, "Transaction Cost Analysis of Strategy-Structure Choice," *Strategic Management Journal* 9 (1988): 159–172.

7. H. O. Armour and D. J. Teece, "Organizational Structure and Economic Performance: A Test of the Multidivisional Hypothesis," *Bell Journal of Economics* 9 (1978): 106–122.

8. Sloan, *My Years at General Motors.*

9. Jones and Hill, "Transaction Cost Analysis of Strategy-Structure Choice," *Strategic Management Journal* 9 (1988): 159–172.

10. Ibid.

11. R. A. D'Aveni and D. J. Ravenscraft, "Economies of Integration Versus Bureaucracy Costs: Does Vertical Integration Improve Performance?" *Academy of Management Journal* 5 (1994): 1167–1206.

12. P. R. Lawrence and J. Lorsch, *Organization and Environment* (Boston: Division of Research, Harvard Business School, 1967); J. R. Galbraith, *Designing Complex Organizations* (Reading, Mass.:

Addison-Wesley, 1973); Michael Porter, *Competitive Advantage: Creating and Sustaining Superior Performance* (New York: Free Press, 1985).

13. P. R. Nayyar, "Performance Effects of Information Asymmetry and Economies of Scope in Diversified Service Firm," *Academy of Management Journal* 36 (1993): 28–57.

14. L. R. Gomez-Mejia, "Structure and Process of Diversification, Compensation Strategy, and Performance," *Strategic Management Journal* 13 (1992): 381–397.

15. J. Stopford and L. Wells, *Managing the Multinational Enterprise* (London: Longman, 1972).

16. C. A. Bartlett and S. Ghoshal, *Managing Across Borders: The Transnational Solution* (Cambridge, Mass.: Harvard Business School, 1991).

17. R. A. Burgelman, "Managing the New Venture Division: Research Findings and the Implications for Strategic Management," *Strategic Management Journal* 6 (1985): 39–54.

18. G. Imperato, "3M Expert Tells How to Run Meetings That Really Work," *Fast Company* (May 23, 1999): 18.

19. Burgelman, "Managing the New Venture Division."

20. R. A. Burgelman, "Corporate Entrepreneurship and Strategic Management: Insights from a Process Study," *Management Science* 29 (1983): 1349–1364.

21. G. R. Jones, "Towards a Positive Interpretation of Transaction Cost Theory: The Central Role of Entrepreneurship and Trust,"

in M. Hitt, R. E. Freeman, and J. S. Harrison (eds.), *Handbook of Strategic Management* (London: Blackwell, 2001), pp. 208–228.

22. M. Prendergast, "Is Coke Turning into a Mickey Mouse Outfit?" *Wall Street Journal* (March 5, 2001): A. 22.

23. M. S. Salter and W. A. Weinhold, *Diversification Through Acquisition* (New York: Free Press, 1979).

24. F. T. Paine and D. J. Power, "Merger Strategy: An Examination of Drucker's Five Rules for Successful Acquisitions," *Strategic Management Journal* 5 (1984): 99–110.

25. H. Singh and C. A. Montgomery, "Corporate Acquisitions and Economic Performance," unpublished manuscript, 1984.

26. B. Worthen, "Nestlé's ERP Odyssey," *CIO* (May 15, 2002): 1–5.

27. G. D. Bruton, B. M. Oviatt, and M. A. White, "Performance of Acquisitions of Distressed Firms," *Academy of Management Journal* 4 (1994): 972–989.

28. T. Dewett and G. R. Jones, "The Role of Information Technology in the Organization: A Review, Model, and Assessment," *Journal of Management* 27 (2001): 313–346.

29. M. E. Porter, *Competitive Strategy* (New York: Free Press, 1980).

30. M. Hammer and J. Champy, *Reengineering the Corporation*, (New York: Harper Collins, 1993).

31. G. Hamel and C.K. Prahalad, "*Competing for the Future* (Boston:Harvard Business Scool press, 1994).

32. Ibid.

33. "Andersen's Androids," *Economist* (May 4, 1996): 72.

Box Source Notes

Chapter 1

a. *Sources:* A. Van Duyn, "Time Inc revamp to include sale of 18 titles," *Financial Times*, September 13, 2006, page 24. M. Karnitsching, "Time Inc. Makes New Bid to be Big Web Player," *Wall Street Journal*, March 29, 2006, page B1. M. Flamm, "Time tries the web again," *Crain's New York Business*, January 16, 2006, page 3.

b. S. Gray and E. Smith. "Coffee and Music Create a Potent Mix at Starbucks," *Wall Street Journal*, July 19, 2005, p. A1.

c. John Kador, *Charles Schwab: How One Company Beat Wall Street and Reinvented the Brokerage Industry*, John Wiley & Sons, New York, 2002; Erick Schonfeld, "Schwab Puts It All Online," *Fortune*, December 7, 1998, pp. 94–99.

d. *Sources:* D. Priest and D. Linzer, "Panel Condemns Iraq Prewar Intelligence," *Washington Post*, July 10, 2004, p. A1; D. Jehl, "Senators Assail CIA Judgments of Iraq's Arms as Deeply Flawed," *New York Times*, July 10, 2004, p. A1. M. Isikoff, "The Dots Never Existed," *Newsweek*, July 19, 2004, pp. 36–40.

Chapter 2

a. *Sources:* A. Kaplan, "Cott Corporation," *Beverage World*, June 15, 2004, p. 32; J. Popp, "2004 Soft Drink Report," *Beverage Industry*, March 2004, pp. 13–18L. Sparks, "From Coca-Colinization to Copy Catting: The Cott Corporation and Retailers Brand Soft Drinks in the UK and US," *Agribusiness*, March 1997, pp. 153–127, Vol. 13, Issue 2; E. Cherney, "After Flat Sales, Cott Challenges Pepsi, Coca-Cola," *Wall Street Journal*, January 8, 2003, pp. B1, B8. Anonymous, "Cott Corporation: Company Profile," *Just Drinks*, August 2006, pp. 19–22.

b. G. Morgenson, "Denial in Battle Creek," *Forbes*, October 7, 1996, p. 44; J. Muller, "Thinking out of the Cereal Box," *Business Week*, January 15, 2001, p. 54; A. Merrill, "General Mills Increases Prices," *Star Tribune*, June 5, 2001, p. 1D; S. Reyes, "Big G, Kellogg Attempt to Berry Each Other," *Brandweek*, October 7, 2002, p. 8.

c. "How Big Can It Grow?—Wal-Mart,"*Economist*, April 17, 2004, pp. 74–76; H. Gilman, "The Most Underrated CEO Ever," *Fortune*, April 5, 2004, pp. 242–247; K. Schaffner, "Psst! Want to Sell to Wal-Mart?" *Apparel Industry Magazine*, August 1996, pp. 18–20.

d. *Standard & Poor's Industry Surveys*, Computers: Hardware, "Global Demand for PCs Accelerates," December 8, 2005; M. Dickerson, "Plain PCs Sitting Pretty," *Los Angeles Times*, December 11, 2005, p. C1; IDC Press Release, "Long Term PC Outlook Improves," September 14, 2006.

Chapter 3

a. Quotes from S. Beatty. "Bass Talk: Plotting Plaid's Future," *Wall Street Journal*, September 9, 2004, p. B1. Also see C. M. Moore and G. Birtwistle, "The Burberry Business Model," *International Journal of Retail and Distribution Management* 32 (2004), pp. 412–422. M. Dickson, "Bravo's Legacy in Transforming Burberry," *Financial Times*, October 6, 2005, p. 22.

b. "Shining Examples," *The Economist: A Survey of Logistics*, June 17, 2006, pp. 4–6; K. Capell et al., "Fashion Conquistador," *Business Week*, September 4, 2006, pp. 38–39; K. Ferdows et al., "Rapid Fire Fulfillment," *Harvard Business Review* 82 (November 2004), pp. 101–107.

c. *Source:* Data drawn from 2005 10K Reports for Hewlett-Packard and Dell Computer.

d. *Sources:* D. Miller, *The Icarus Paradox* (New York: HarperBusiness, 1990); P. D. Llosa, "We Must Know What We Are Doing," *Fortune*, November 14, 1994, p. 68.

e. Stephen Manes and Paul Andrews, *Gates* (New York: Simon & Schuster, 1993).

Chapter 4

a. G. P. Pisano, R. M. J. Bohmer, A. C. Edmondson, "Organizational Differences in Rates of Learning: Evidence from the Adoption of Minimally Invasive Cardiac Surgery," *Management Science*, 47 (2001), pp. 752–768.

b. *Sources:* J. Schlosser, "Cashing in on the New World of Me," *Fortune* (December 13, 2004): 244–249; V. S. Borland, "Global Technology in the Twenty First Century," *Textile World* (January 2003): 42–56; www.Landsend.com (accessed March 11, 2007).

c. Gates, op. cit.

d. *Sources:* C. H. Deutsch, "Six-Sigma Enlightenment," *New York Times* (December 7, 1998): 1; J. J. Barshay, "The Six-Sigma Story," *Star Tribune* (June 14, 1999): 1; D. D. Bak, "Rethinking Industrial Drives," *Electrical/Electronics Technology* (November 30, 1998): 58.

e. *Sources:* I. R. Lazarus and K. Butler, "The Promise of Six-Sigma," *Managed Healthcare Executive* (October 2001): 22–26; D. Scalise, "Six-Sigma, the Quest for Quality," *Hospitals and Health Networks* (December 2001): 41–44; S. F.Gale, "Building Frameworks for Six Sigma Success," *Workforce* (May 2003): 64–69; J. Goedert, "Crunching Data: The Key to Six Sigma Success," *Health Data Management* (April 2004): 44–48; M. Hagland, "Six Sigma: It's Real, It's Data Driven, and It's Here," *Health Care Strategic Management*, 23 (December 2005): 1–6.

f. V. Govindarajan and C. Trimble, "How Forgetting Leads to Innovation," *Chief Executive* (March 2006): 46–50; J. McGregor, "How Failure Breeds Success," *Business Week* (July 10, 2006): 42–52.

Chapter 5

a. *Sources:* D. McGinn, "Is This Any Way to Run an Airline?" *Newsweek* (October 4, 2004): E14–E19; E. Torbenson, "Budget Carriers Rule the European Skies," *Dallas Morning News* (September 22, 2004): D1; www.ryanair.com, 2006 (accessed January 2007).

b. *Sources:* www.llbean.com (accessed 2004); D. McGinn, "Swimming Upstream, *Newsweek* (October 1, 2004): E10–E12; www.llbean.com (accessed 2006).

c. *Sources:* www.zara.com (accessed 2006); C. Vitzthum, "Just-in-Time-Fashion," *Wall Street Journal* (May 18, 2001): B1, B4; www.zara.com (accessed 2007).

d. *Source:* www.toyota.com (accessed 2006).

e. *Sources:* "The Holiday Inns Trip; A Breeze for Decades, Bumpy Ride in the 1980s," *Wall Street Journal* (February 11, 1987): 1; Holiday Inns, Annual Report (1985); U.S. Bureau of Labor Statistics, U.S. Industrial Output (Washington, D.C.: U.S. Government Printing Office, 1986); Mark Gleason and Alan Salomon, "Fallon's Challenge: Make Holiday Inn More 'In,'" *Advertising Age* (September 2, 1996): 14; Julie Miller, "Amenities Range from

Snacks to Technology," *Hotel and Motel Management* (July 3, 1996): 38–40; www.sixcontinenthotels.com (accessed 2005).

Chapter 6

a. www.clearchannel.com (accessed 2006); A. W. Mathews, "From a Distance: A Giant Chain Is Perfecting the Art of Seeming Local," *Wall Street Journal* (February 25, 2002): A1, A4.

b. www.AOLTimeWarner.com (accessed 2002, 2004); Kara Swisher, *aol.com* (New York: Random House, 1998); www.aol.com (accessed 2006).

c. www.toysrus.com (accessed 2004); M. Maremont and G. Bowens, "Brawls in Toyland," *Business Week* (December 21, 1992): 36–37; S. Eads, "The Toys 'R' Us Empire Strikes Back," *Business Week* (June 7, 1999): 55–59; www.toysrus.co (accessed 2002); amazon.com (accessed 2002).

d. www.cocacola.com (accessed 2006); www.pepsico.com (accessed 2006).

e. P. Haynes, "Western Electric Redux," *Forbes* (January 26, 1998): 46–47; www.westrexcorp.com (accessed 2006).

Chapter 7

a. *Sources:* M. Snider, "Ray Dolby, Audio Inventor," *USA Today* (December 28, 2000): D3; D. Dritas, "Dealerscope Hall of Fame: Ray Dolby," *Dealerscope* (January 2002): 74–76; J. Pinkerton, "At Dolby Laboratories: A Clean Audio Pipe," *Dealerscope* (December 2000): 33–34; Company history archived at www.dolby.com (accessed November 18, 2006); L. Himelstein, "Dolby Gets Ready to Make a Big Noise," *Business Week* (February 9, 2004): 78; D. Pomerantz, "Seeing in Dolby," *Forbes* (January 30, 2006): 56.

b. *Source:* Interviews by Charles W. L. Hill.

c. *Sources:* S. Yoon, "The Mod Squad," *East Asian Economic Review* (November 7, 2002): 34–36; R. Cunningham, "Controversy as Sony Loses Mod-Chip Verdict," *Managing Intellectual Property* (September 2002): 15–18; A. Pham, "Video Game Losses Nearly $2 Billion," *Los Angeles Times* (February 18, 2002): C8; Andy Holloway, "License to Plunder," *Canadian Business* (November 10, 2003): 95; R. Grover et al., "Game Wars," *Business Week* (February 28, 2005): 60–66.

d. *Source:* Christensen, *The Innovator's Dilemma* (Boston: Harvard Business School Press, 1997).

Chapter 8

a. *Sources:* "Lessons from the Frozen North," *Economist* (October 8, 1994): 76–77; "A Finnish Fable," *Economist* (October 14, 2000); D. O'Shea and K. Fitchard, "The First 3 Billion Is Always the Hardest," *Wireless Review*, 22 (September 2005): 25–31: P. Taylor, "Big Names Dominate in Mobile Phones," *Financial Times* (September 29, 2006): 26; and Nokia website at www.nokia.com (accessed 2006).

b. *Sources:* K. Capell, A. Sains, C. Lindblad, and A. T. Palmer, "IKEA," *Business Week* (November 14, 2005): 96–101: K. Capell et al., "What a Sweetheart of a Love Seat," *Business Week* (November 14, 2005): 101: P. M. Miller, "IKEA with Chinese Characteristics," *Chinese Business Review* (July/August 2004): 36–69: C. Daniels, "Create IKEA, Make Billions, Take Bus," *Fortune* (May 3, 2004): 44.

c. *Sources:* Dell Corporation 2006 10K; Staff Reporter, "Dell Inc: Call Center in India to Expand to 2,500 Workers from 800," *Wall Street Journal* (October 6, 2006): A6.

d. *Sources:* "Fujitsu, Cisco Systems to Develop High-End Routers for Web Traffic," *Knight Ridder Tribune Business News* (December 6, 2004): 1: "Fujitsu and Cisco Introduce New High Performance Routers for IP Next Generation Networks," *JCN Newswire*, May 25, 2006 (accessed November 30, 2006).

Chapter 9

a. *Sources:* www.hp.com (2006); www.dell.com (2006); P. Burrows and A. Park, "Compaq and HP: What's an Investor to Do?" *Business Week* (March 18, 2002): 62–64; "Carly v Walter," *Economist* (January 26, 2002); "Sheltering from the Storm," *Economist* (September 8, 2001): 21–22.

b. Y. J. Dreazen, G. Ip, and N. Kulish, "Why the Sudden Rise?"; L. Kowalczyk, "A Matter of Style," *Boston Globe* (February 22, 2002): C1.

c. *Source:* J-F. Hennart, "Upstream Vertical Integration in the Aluminum and Tin Industries," *Journal of Economic Behavior and Organization* 9 (1988): 281–299.

d. *Sources:* www.chrysler.com (2004, 2006); J. H. Dyer, "How Chrysler Created an American Keiretsu," *Harvard Business Review* (July–August 1996): 42–56.

Chapter 10

a. *Sources:* www.3M.com, (2005 and 2006); W. E. Coyne, "How 3M Innovates for Long-Term Growth," *Research Technology Management* (March–April 2001): 21–24; 3M's 2004 10-K form; Ibid.

b. *Sources:* R. Arensman, "Intel's Second Try," *Electronic Business* (March 2001): 62–70; Intel 10-K Report, 2001; www.amd.com (2006); www.intel.com (2006).

c. *Sources:* M. Murray and J. Rebelled, "Mellon Bank Corp: One Big Unhappy Family," *Wall Street Journal* (April 28, 1995): B1, B4; K. Holland, "A Bank Eat Bank World—with Indigestion," *Business Week* (October 30, 1995): 130; www.mellon.com (2006).

Chapter 11

a. *Sources:* S. Tully, "A House Divided," *Fortune* (December 18, 2000): 264–275; J. Chaffin, "Sotheby's Ex CEO Spared Jail Sentence," *Financial Times* (April 30, 2002): 10; T. Thorncroft, "A Courtroom Battle of the Vanities," *Financial Times* (November 3, 2001): 3.

b. *Sources:* J. Guidera, "Probe of Computer Associates Centers on Firm's Revenues," *Wall Street Journal* (May 20, 2002): A3, A15; Ronna Abramson, "Computer Associates Probe Focus on 1998, 1999 Revenue," *The Street.Com* (accessed May 20, 2002); C. Forelle, M. Maremont, and G. Fields, "U.S. Indicts Sanjay Kumar for Fraud, Lies," *Wall Street Journal* (September 23, 2004): A1; N. Varchaver, "Long Island Confidential," *Fortune* (November 27, 2006): 172–178.

c. *Sources:* "Boycott Nike," CBS News *48 Hours,* October 17, 1996; D. Jones, "Critics Tie Sweatshop Sneakers to 'Air Jordan,'" *USA Today* (June 6, 1996): 1B; "Global Exchange Special Report: Nike Just Don't Do It," available at http://www.globalexchange.org/education/publications/newsltr6.97p2.html#nike (accessed 2003); S. Greenhouse, "Nike Shoeplant in Vietnam Is Called Unsafe for Workers," *New York Times* (November 8, 1997); V. Dobnik, "Chinese Workers Abused Making Nikes, Reeboks," *Seattle Times* (September 21, 1997): A4.

d. *Source:* Dell Computer, "Code of Conduct: Winning with Integrity," www.dell.com (accessed September 7, 2006).

Chapter 12

a. www.unionpacific.com (accessed 2007).
b. www.cypress.com, press release (1998); www.cypress.com, press release, (2006).
c. www.mcdonalds.com (2006).
d. www.lexmark.com (2006).

Chapter 13

a. www.sap.com (2005 and 2006).
b. A. Edgecliffe-Johnson, "Nestlé and Pillsbury Forge Ice Cream Alliance in U.S.," *Financial Times* (August 20, 1999): 2; B. Worthen, "Nestlé's ERP Odyssey," *CIO* (May 15, 2002): 1–5; www.nestle.com (2006).
c. M. Moeller, "Oracle: Practicing What It Preaches," *Business Week* (August 16, 1999): 1–5; www.oracle.com (2006).
d. Business Link in the Global Chain," *Economist* (June 2, 2001): 62–63; www.li&fung.com (2006).

Introduction:
Analyzing a Case Study and
Writing a Case Study Analysis

What Is Case Study Analysis?

Case study analysis is an integral part of a course in strategic management. The purpose of a case study is to provide students with experience of the strategic management problems that actual organizations face. A case study presents an account of what happened to a business or industry over a number of years. It chronicles the events that managers had to deal with, such as changes in the competitive environment, and charts the managers' response, which usually involved changing the business- or corporate-level strategy. The cases in this book cover a wide range of issues and problems that managers have had to confront. Some cases are about finding the right business-level strategy to compete in changing conditions. Some are about companies that grew by acquisition, with little concern for the rationale behind their growth, and how growth by acquisition affected their future profitability. Each case is different because each organization is different. The underlying thread in all cases, however, is the use of strategic management techniques to solve business problems.

Cases prove valuable in a strategic management course for several reasons. First, cases provide you, the student, with experience of organizational problems that you probably have not had the opportunity to experience firsthand. In a relatively short period of time, you will have the chance to appreciate and analyze the problems faced by many different companies and to understand how managers tried to deal with them.

Second, cases illustrate the theory and content of strategic management. The meaning and implications of this information are made clearer when they are applied to case studies. The theory and concepts help reveal what is going on in the companies studied and allow you to evaluate the solutions that specific companies adopted to deal with their problems. Consequently, when you analyze cases, you will be like a detective who, with a set of conceptual tools, probes what happened and what or who was responsible and then marshals the evidence that provides the solution. Top managers enjoy the thrill of testing their problem-solving abilities in the real world. It is important to remember that no one knows what the right answer is. All that managers can do is to make the best guess. In fact, managers say repeatedly that they are happy if they are right only half the time in solving strategic problems. Strategic management is an uncertain game, and using cases to see how theory can be put into practice is one way of improving your skills of diagnostic investigation.

Third, case studies provide you with the opportunity to participate in class and to gain experience in presenting your ideas to others. Instructors may sometimes call on students as a group to identify what is going on in a case, and through classroom discussion the issues in and solutions to the case problem will reveal themselves. In such a situation, you will have to organize your views and conclusions so that you can present them to the class. Your classmates may have analyzed the issues differently from you, and they will want you to argue your points before they will accept your conclusions, so be prepared for debate. This mode of discussion is an example of the dialectical approach to decision making. This is how decisions are made in the actual business world.

Instructors also may assign an individual, but more commonly a group, to analyze the case before the whole class. The individual or group probably will be responsible for a thirty- to forty-minute presentation of the case to the class. That presentation must cover the issues posed, the problems facing the company, and a series of recommendations for resolving the problems. The discussion then will be thrown open to the class, and you will have to defend your ideas. Through such discussions and presentations, you will experience how to convey your ideas effectively to others. Remember that a great deal of managers' time is spent in these kinds of situations: presenting their ideas and engaging in discussion with other managers who have their own views about what is going on. Thus, you will experience in the classroom the actual process of strategic management, and this will serve you well in your future career.

If you work in groups to analyze case studies, you also will learn about the group process involved in working as a team. When people work in groups, it is often difficult to schedule time and allocate responsibility for the case analysis. There are always group members who shirk their responsibilities and group members who are so sure of their own ideas that they try to dominate the group's analysis. Most of the strategic management takes place in groups, however, and it is best if you learn about these problems now.

Analyzing a Case Study

The purpose of the case study is to let you apply the concepts of strategic management when you analyze the issues facing a specific company. To analyze a case study, therefore, you must examine closely the issues confronting the company. Most often you will need to read the case several times—once to grasp the overall picture of what is happening to the company and then several times more to discover and grasp the specific problems.

Generally, detailed analysis of a case study should include eight areas:

1. The history, development, and growth of the company over time
2. The identification of the company's internal strengths and weaknesses
3. The nature of the external environment surrounding the company
4. A SWOT analysis
5. The kind of corporate-level strategy that the company is pursuing
6. The nature of the company's business-level strategy
7. The company's structure and control systems and how they match its strategy
8. Recommendations

To analyze a case, you need to apply the concepts taught in this course to each of these areas. To help you further, we next offer a summary of the steps you can take to analyze the case material for each of the eight points we just noted:

1. *Analyze the company's history, development, and growth.* A convenient way to investigate how a company's past strategy and structure affect it in the present

is to chart the critical incidents in its history—that is, the events that were the most unusual or the most essential for its development into the company it is today. Some of the events have to do with its founding, its initial products, how it makes new-product market decisions, and how it developed and chose functional competencies to pursue. Its entry into new businesses and shifts in its main lines of business are also important milestones to consider.

2. *Identify the company's internal strengths and weaknesses.* Once the historical profile is completed, you can begin the SWOT analysis. Use all the incidents you have charted to develop an account of the company's strengths and weaknesses as they have emerged historically. Examine each of the value creation functions of the company, and identify the functions in which the company is currently strong and currently weak. Some companies might be weak in marketing; some might be strong in research and development. Make lists of these strengths and weaknesses. The SWOT Checklist (Table 1) gives examples of what might go in these lists.

3. *Analyze the external environment.* To identify environmental opportunities and threats, apply all the concepts on industry and macroenvironments to analyze the environment the company is confronting. Of particular importance at the industry level are Porter's five forces model and the stage of the life cycle model. Which factors in the macroenvironment will appear salient depends on the specific company being analyzed. Use each factor in turn (for instance, demographic factors) to see whether it is relevant for the company in question.

   Having done this analysis, you will have generated both an analysis of the company's environment and a list of opportunities and threats. The SWOT Checklist table also lists some common environmental opportunities and threats that you may look for, but the list you generate will be specific to your company.

4. *Evaluate the SWOT analysis.* Having identified the company's external opportunities and threats as well as its internal strengths and weaknesses, consider what your findings mean. You need to balance strengths and weaknesses against opportunities and threats. Is the company in an overall strong competitive position? Can it continue to pursue its current business- or corporate-level strategy profitably? What can the company do to turn weaknesses into strengths and threats into opportunities? Can it develop new functional, business, or corporate strategies to accomplish this change? *Never merely generate the SWOT analysis and then put it aside.* Because it provides a succinct summary of the company's condition, a good SWOT analysis is the key to all the analyses that follow.

5. *Analyze corporate-level strategy.* To analyze corporate-level strategy, you first need to define the company's mission and goals. Sometimes the mission and goals are stated explicitly in the case; at other times, you will have to infer them from available information. The information you need to collect to find out the company's corporate strategy includes such factors as its lines of business and the nature of its subsidiaries and acquisitions. It is important to analyze the relationship among the company's businesses. Do they trade or exchange resources? Are there gains to be achieved from synergy? Alternatively, is the company just running a portfolio of investments? This analysis should enable you to define the corporate strategy that the company is pursuing

TABLE 1

A SWOT Checklist

Potential internal strengths	Potential internal weaknesses
Many product lines?	Obsolete, narrow product lines?
Broad market coverage?	Rising manufacturing costs?
Manufacturing competence?	Decline in R&D innovations?
Good marketing skills?	Poor marketing plan?
Good materials management systems?	Poor material management systems?
R&D skills and leadership?	Loss of customer good will?
Information system competencies?	Inadequate human resources?
Human resource competencies? .	Inadequate information systems?
Brand name reputation?	Loss of brand name capital?
Portfolio management skills?	Growth without direction?
Cost of differentiation advantage?	Bad portfolio management?
New-venture management expertise?	Loss of corporate direction?
Appropriate management style?	Infighting among divisions?
Appropriate organizational structure?	Loss of corporate control?
Appropriate control systems?	Inappropriate organizational
Ability to manage strategic change?	structure and control systems?
Well-developed corporate strategy?	High conflict and politics?
Good financial management?	Poor financial management?
Others?	Others?
Potential environmental opportunities	**Potential environmental threats**
Expand core business(es)?	Attacks on core business(es)?
Exploit new market segments?	Increases in domestic competition?
Widen product range?	Increase in foreign competition?
Extend cost or differentiation advantage?	Change in consumer tastes?
Diversify into new growth businesses?	Fall in barriers to entry?
Expand into foreign markets?	Rise in new or substitute products?
Apply R&D skills in new areas?	Increase in industry rivalry?
Enter new related businesses?	New forms of industry competition?
Vertically integrate forward?	Potential for takeover?
Vertically integrate backward?	Existence of corporate raiders?
Enlarge corporate portfolio?	Increase in regional competition?
Overcome barriers to entry?	Changes in demographic factors?
Reduce rivalry among competitors?	Changes in economic factors?
Make profitable new acquisitions?	Downturn in economy?
Apply brand name capital in new areas?	Rising labor costs?
Seek fast market growth?	Slower market growth?
Others?	Others?

(for example, related or unrelated diversification, or a combination of both) and to conclude whether the company operates in just one core business. Then, using your SWOT analysis, debate the merits of this strategy. Is it appropriate given the environment the company is in? Could a change in corporate strategy provide the company with new opportunities or transform a weakness into a strength? For example, should the company diversify from its core business into new businesses?

Other issues should be considered as well. How and why has the company's strategy changed over time? What is the claimed rationale for any changes? Often, it is a good idea to analyze the company's businesses or products to assess its situation and identify which divisions contribute the most to or detract from its competitive advantage. It is also useful to explore how the company has built its portfolio over time. Did it acquire new businesses, or did it internally venture its own? All of these factors provide clues about the company and indicate ways of improving its future performance.

6. *Analyze business-level strategy.* Once you know the company's corporate-level strategy and have done the SWOT analysis, the next step is to identify the company's business-level strategy. If the company is a single-business company, its business-level strategy is identical to its corporate-level strategy. If the company is in many businesses, each business will have its own business-level strategy. You will need to identify the company's generic competitive strategy—differentiation, low-cost, or focus—and its investment strategy, given its relative competitive position and the stage of the life cycle. The company also may market different products using different business-level strategies. For example, it may offer a low-cost product range and a line of differentiated products. Be sure to give a full account of a company's business-level strategy to show how it competes.

Identifying the functional strategies that a company pursues to build competitive advantage through superior efficiency, quality, innovation, and customer responsiveness and to achieve its business-level strategy is very important. The SWOT analysis will have provided you with information on the company's functional competencies. You should investigate its production, marketing, or research and development strategy further to gain a picture of where the company is going. For example, pursuing a low-cost or a differentiation strategy successfully requires very different sets of competencies. Has the company developed the right ones? If it has, how can it exploit them further? Can it pursue both a low-cost and a differentiation strategy simultaneously?

The SWOT analysis is especially important at this point if the industry analysis, particularly Porter's model, has revealed threats to the company from the environment. Can the company deal with these threats? How should it change its business-level strategy to counter them? To evaluate the potential of a company's business-level strategy, you must first perform a thorough SWOT analysis that captures the essence of its problems.

Once you complete this analysis, you will have a full picture of the way the company is operating and be in a position to evaluate the potential of its strategy. Thus, you will be able to make recommendations concerning the pattern of its future actions. However, first you need to consider strategy implementation, or the way the company tries to achieve its strategy.

7. *Analyze structure and control systems.* The aim of this analysis is to identify what structure and control systems the company is using to implement its strategy and to evaluate whether that structure is the appropriate one for the company. Different corporate and business strategies require different structures. You need to determine the *degree of fit between the company's strategy and structure.* For example, does the company have the right level of vertical differentiation (e.g., does it have the appropriate number of levels in the hierarchy or decentralized control?) or horizontal differentiation (does it use a functional structure when it should be using a product structure?)? Similarly, is the company using the right integration or control systems to manage its operations? Are managers being appropriately rewarded? Are the right rewards in

place for encouraging cooperation among divisions? These are all issues to consider.

In some cases, there will be little information on these issues, whereas in others there will be a lot. In analyzing each case, you should gear the analysis toward its most salient issues. For example, organizational conflict, power, and politics will be important issues for some companies. Try to analyze why problems in these areas are occurring. Do they occur because of bad strategy formulation or because of bad strategy implementation?

Organizational change is an issue in many cases because the companies are attempting to alter their strategies or structures to solve strategic problems. Thus, as part of the analysis, you might suggest an action plan that the company in question could use to achieve its goals. For example, you might list in a logical sequence the steps the company would need to follow to alter its business-level strategy from differentiation to focus.

8. *Make recommendations.* The quality of your recommendations is a direct result of the thoroughness with which you prepared the case analysis. Recommendations are directed at solving whatever strategic problem the company is facing and increasing its future profitability. Your recommendations should be in line with your analysis; that is, they should follow logically from the previous discussion. For example, your recommendation generally will center on the specific ways of changing functional, business, and corporate strategies and organizational structure and control to improve business performance. The set of recommendations will be specific to each case, and so it is difficult to discuss these recommendations here. Such recommendations might include an increase in spending on specific research and development projects, the divesting of certain businesses, a change from a strategy of unrelated to related diversification, an increase in the level of integration among divisions by using task forces and teams, or a move to a different kind of structure to implement a new business-level strategy. Make sure your recommendations are mutually consistent and written in the form of an action plan. The plan might contain a timetable that sequences the actions for changing the company's strategy and a description of how changes at the corporate level will necessitate changes at the business level and subsequently at the functional level.

After following all these stages, you will have performed a thorough analysis of the case and will be in a position to join in class discussion or present your ideas to the class, depending on the format used by your professor. Remember that you must tailor your analysis to suit the specific issue discussed in your case. In some cases, you might completely omit one of the steps in the analysis because it is not relevant to the situation you are considering. You must be sensitive to the needs of the case and not apply the framework we have discussed in this section blindly. The framework is meant only as a guide, not as an outline.

Writing a Case Study Analysis

Often, as part of your course requirements, you will need to present a written case analysis. This may be an individual or a group report. Whatever the situation, there are certain guidelines to follow in writing a case analysis that will improve the evaluation your work will receive from your instructor. Before we discuss these guidelines and before you use them, make sure that they do not conflict with any directions your instructor has given you.

The structure of your written report is critical. Generally, if you follow the steps for analysis discussed in the previous section, *you already will have a good structure for your written discussion.* All reports begin with an *introduction* to the case. In it, outline briefly what the company does, how it developed historically, what problems it is experiencing, and how you are going to approach the issues in the case write-up. Do this sequentially by writing, for example, "First, we discuss the environment of Company X. . . . Third, we discuss Company X's business-level strategy. . . . Last, we provide recommendations for turning around Company X's business."

In the second part of the case write-up, the *strategic analysis* section, do the SWOT analysis, analyze and discuss the nature and problems of the company's business-level and corporate strategies, and then analyze its structure and control systems. Make sure you use plenty of headings and subheadings to structure your analysis. For example, have separate sections on any important conceptual tool you use. Thus, you might have a section on Porter's five forces model as part of your analysis of the environment. You might offer a separate section on portfolio techniques when analyzing a company's corporate strategy. Tailor the sections and subsections to the specific issues of importance in the case.

In the third part of the case write-up, present your *solutions and recommendations.* Be comprehensive, and make sure they are in line with the previous analysis so that the recommendations fit together and move logically from one to the next. The recommendations section is very revealing because your instructor will have a good idea of how much work you put into the case from the quality of your recommendations.

Following this framework will provide a good structure for most written reports, though it must be shaped to fit the individual case being considered. Some cases are about excellent companies experiencing no problems. In such instances, it is hard to write recommendations. Instead, you can focus on analyzing why the company is doing so well, using that analysis to structure the discussion. Following are some minor suggestions that can help make a good analysis even better:

1. Do not repeat in summary form large pieces of factual information from the case. The instructor has read the case and knows what is going on. Rather, use the information in the case to illustrate your statements, defend your arguments, or make salient points. Beyond the brief introduction to the company, you must avoid being *descriptive*; instead, you must be *analytical.*

2. Make sure the sections and subsections of your discussion flow logically and smoothly from one to the next. That is, try to build on what has gone before so that the analysis of the case study moves toward a climax. This is particularly important for group analysis, because there is a tendency for people in a group to split up the work and say, "I'll do the beginning, you take the middle, and I'll do the end." The result is a choppy, stilted analysis; the parts do not flow from one to the next, and it is obvious to the instructor that no real group work has been done.

3. Avoid grammatical and spelling errors. They make your work look sloppy.

4. In some instances, cases dealing with well-known companies end in 1998 or 1999 because no later information was available when the case was written. If possible, do a search for more information on what has happened to the company in subsequent years.

Many libraries now have comprehensive web-based electronic data search facilities that offer such sources as *ABI/Inform, The Wall Street Journal Index,* the *F&S Index,* and the *Nexis-Lexis* databases. These enable you to identify any article that has been written in the business press on the company of your choice within the past few years. A number of nonelectronic data sources are also useful. For example, *F&S Predicasts* publishes an annual list of articles relating to major companies that appeared in the national and international business press. *S&P Industry Surveys* is a great source for basic industry data, and *Value Line Ratings and Reports* can contain good summaries of a firm's financial position and future prospects. You will also want to collect full financial information on the company. Again, this can be accessed from web-based electronic databases such as the *Edgar* database, which archives all forms that publicly quoted companies have to file with the Securities and Exchange Commission (SEC; e.g., 10-K filings can be accessed from the SEC's *Edgar* database). Most SEC forms for public companies can now be accessed from Internet-based financial sites, such as Yahoo's finance site (http://finance.yahoo.com/).

5. Sometimes instructors hand out questions for each case to help you in your analysis. Use these as a guide for writing the case analysis. They often illuminate the important issues that have to be covered in the discussion.

If you follow the guidelines in this section, you should be able to write a thorough and effective evaluation.

The Role of Financial Analysis in Case Study Analysis

An important aspect of analyzing a case study and writing a case study analysis is the role and use of financial information. A careful analysis of the company's financial condition immensely improves a case write-up. After all, financial data represent the concrete results of the company's strategy and structure. Although analyzing financial statements can be quite complex, a general idea of a company's financial position can be determined through the use of ratio analysis. Financial performance ratios can be calculated from the balance sheet and income statement. These ratios can be classified into five subgroups: profit ratios, liquidity ratios, activity ratios, leverage ratios, and shareholder-return ratios. These ratios should be compared with the industry average or the company's prior years of performance. It should be noted, however, that deviation from the average is not necessarily bad; it simply warrants further investigation. For example, young companies will have purchased assets at a different price and will likely have a different capital structure than older companies do. In addition to ratio analysis, a company's cash flow position is of critical importance and should be assessed. Cash flow shows how much actual cash a company possesses.

● **Profit Ratios**   Profit ratios measure the efficiency with which the company uses its resources. The more efficient the company, the greater is its profitability. It is useful to compare a company's profitability against that of its major competitors in its industry to determine whether the company is operating more or less efficiently than its rivals. In addition, the change in a company's profit ratios over time tells whether its performance is improving or declining.

A number of different profit ratios can be used, and each of them measures a different aspect of a company's performance. Here, we look at the most commonly used profit ratios.

● **Return on Invested Capital**   This ratio measures the profit earned on the capital invested in the company. It is defined as follows:

$$\text{Return on invested capital (ROIC)} = \frac{\text{Net profit}}{\text{Invested capital}}$$

Net profit is calculated by subtracting the total costs of operating the company away from its total revenues (total revenues – total costs). Total costs are the (1) costs of goods sold, (2) sales, general, and administrative expenses, (3) R&D expenses, and (4) other expenses. Net profit can be calculated before or after taxes, although many financial analysts prefer the before-tax figure. Invested capital is the amount that is invested in the operations of a company—that is, in property, plant, equipment, inventories, and other assets. Invested capital comes from two main sources: interest-bearing debt and shareholders' equity. Interest-bearing debt is money the company borrows from banks and from those who purchase its bonds. Shareholders' equity is the money raised from selling shares to the public, *plus* earnings that have been retained by the company in prior years and are available to fund current investments. ROIC measures the effectiveness with which a company is using the capital funds that it has available for investment. As such, it is recognized to be an excellent measure of the value a company is creating.[1] Remember that a company's ROIC can be decomposed into its constituent parts.

● **Return on Total Assets (ROA)**   This ratio measures the profit earned on the employment of assets. It is defined as follows:

$$\text{Return on total assests} = \frac{\text{Net profit}}{\text{Total assets}}$$

● **Return on Stockholders' Equity (ROE)**   This ratio measures the percentage of profit earned on common stockholders' investment in the company. It is defined as follows:

$$\text{Return on stockholders' equity} = \frac{\text{Net profit}}{\text{Stockholders' equity}}$$

If a company has no debt, this will be the same as ROIC.

● **Liquidity Ratios**   A company's liquidity is a measure of its ability to meet short-term obligations. An asset is deemed liquid if it can be readily converted into cash. Liquid assets are current assets such as cash, marketable securities, accounts receivable, and so on. Two liquidity ratios are commonly used.

● **Current Ratio**   The current ratio measures the extent to which the claims of short-term creditors are covered by assets that can be quickly converted into cash. Most companies should have a ratio of at least 1, because failure to meet these commitments can lead to bankruptcy. The ratio is defined as follows:

$$\text{Current ratio} = \frac{\text{Current assets}}{\text{Current liabilities}}$$

● **Quick Ratio**   The quick ratio measures a company's ability to pay off the claims of short-term creditors without relying on selling its inventories. This is a valuable

[1] Tom Copeland, Tim Koller, and Jack Murrin, *Valuation: Measuring and Managing the Value of Companies* (New York: Wiley, 1996).

measure since in practice the sale of inventories is often difficult. It is defined as follows:

$$\text{Quick ratio} = \frac{\text{Current assets} - \text{inventory}}{\text{Current liabilities}}$$

● **Activity Ratios**   Activity ratios indicate how effectively a company is managing its assets. Two ratios are particularly useful.

● **Inventory Turnover**   This measures the number of times inventory is turned over. It is useful in determining whether a firm is carrying excess stock in inventory. It is defined as follows:

$$\text{Inventory turnover} = \frac{\text{Cost of goods sold}}{\text{Inventory}}$$

Cost of goods sold is a better measure of turnover than sales because it is the cost of the inventory items. Inventory is taken at the balance sheet date. Some companies choose to compute an average inventory, beginning inventory, and ending inventory, but for simplicity, use the inventory at the balance sheet date.

● **Days Sales Outstanding (DSO) or Average Collection Period**   This ratio is the average time a company has to wait to receive its cash after making a sale. It measures how effective the company's credit, billing, and collection procedures are. It is defined as follows:

$$\text{DSO} = \frac{\text{Accounts receivable}}{\text{Total sales}/360}$$

Accounts receivable is divided by average daily sales. The use of 360 is the standard number of days for most financial analysis.

● **Leverage Ratios**   A company is said to be highly leveraged if it uses more debt than equity, including stock and retained earnings. The balance between debt and equity is called the *capital structure*. The optimal capital structure is determined by the individual company. Debt has a lower cost because creditors take less risk; they know they will get their interest and principal. However, debt can be risky to the firm because if enough profit is not made to cover the interest and principal payments, bankruptcy can result. Three leverage ratios are commonly used.

● **Debt-to-Assets Ratio**   The debt-to-assets ratio is the most direct measure of the extent to which borrowed funds have been used to finance a company's investments. It is defined as follows:

$$\text{Debt-to-assets ratio} = \frac{\text{Total debt}}{\text{Total assets}}$$

Total debt is the sum of a company's current liabilities and its long-term debt, and total assets are the sum of fixed assets and current assets.

● **Debt-to-Equity Ratio**   The debt-to-equity ratio indicates the balance between debt and equity in a company's capital structure. This is perhaps the most widely used measure of a company's leverage. It is defined as follows:

$$\text{Debt-to-equity ratio} = \frac{\text{Total debt}}{\text{Total equity}}$$

● **Times-Covered Ratio**   The times-covered ratio measures the extent to which a company's gross profit covers its annual interest payments. If this ratio declines to less than 1, the company is unable to meet its interest costs and is technically insolvent. The ratio is defined as follows:

$$\text{Times-covered ratio} = \frac{\text{Profit before interest and tax}}{\text{Total interest charges}}$$

● **Shareholder-Return Ratios**   Shareholder-return ratios measure the return that shareholders earn from holding stock in the company. Given the goal of maximizing stockholders' wealth, providing shareholders with an adequate rate of return is a primary objective of most companies. As with profit ratios, it can be helpful to compare a company's shareholder returns against those of similar companies as a yardstick for determining how well the company is satisfying the demands of this particularly important group of organizational constituents. Four ratios are commonly used.

● **Total Shareholder Returns**   Total shareholder returns measure the returns earned by time $t + 1$ on an investment in a company's stock made at time t. (Time t is the time at which the initial investment is made.) Total shareholder returns include both dividend payments and appreciation in the value of the stock (adjusted for stock splits) and are defined as follows:

$$\text{Total shareholder returns} = \frac{\begin{array}{c}\text{Stock price } (t+1) - \text{stock price } (t) \\ + \text{ sum of annual dividends per share}\end{array}}{\text{Stock price } (t)}$$

If a shareholder invests $2 at time t and at time $t + 1$ the share is worth $3, while the sum of annual dividends for the period t to $t + 1$ has amounted to $0.20, total shareholder returns are equal to $(3 - 2 + 0.2)/2 = 0.6$, which is a 60 percent return on an initial investment of $2 made at time t.

● **Price-Earnings Ratio**   The price-earnings ratio measures the amount investors are willing to pay per dollar of profit. It is defined as follows:

$$\text{Price-earnings ratio} = \frac{\text{Market price per share}}{\text{Earnings per share}}$$

● **Market-to-Book Value**   Market-to-book value measures a company's expected future growth prospects. It is defined as follows:

$$\text{Market-to-book value} = \frac{\text{Market price per share}}{\text{Earnings per share}}$$

● **Dividend Yield**   The dividend yield measures the return to shareholders received in the form of dividends. It is defined as follows:

$$\text{Dividend yield} = \frac{\text{Dividend per share}}{\text{Market price per share}}$$

Market price per share can be calculated for the first of the year, in which case the dividend yield refers to the return on an investment made at the beginning of the year. Alternatively, the average share price over the year may be used. A company must decide how much of its profits to pay to stockholders and how much to reinvest in the company. Companies with strong growth prospects should have a lower dividend payout ratio than mature companies. The rationale is that shareholders can invest the money elsewhere if the company is not growing. The optimal ratio depends on the individual firm, but the key decider is whether the company can produce better returns than the investor can earn elsewhere.

● **Cash Flow**   Cash flow position is cash received minus cash distributed. The net cash flow can be taken from a company's statement of cash flows. Cash flow is important for what it reveals about a company's financing needs. A strong positive cash flow enables a company to fund future investments without having to borrow money from bankers or investors. This is desirable because the company avoids paying out interest or dividends. A weak or negative cash flow means that a company has to turn to external sources to fund future investments. Generally, companies in strong-growth industries often find themselves in a poor cash flow position (because their investment needs are substantial), whereas successful companies based in mature industries generally find themselves in a strong cash flow position.

A company's internally generated cash flow is calculated by adding back its depreciation provision to profits after interest, taxes, and dividend payments. If this figure is insufficient to cover proposed new investments, the company has little choice but to borrow funds to make up the shortfall or to curtail investments. If this figure exceeds proposed new investments, the company can use the excess to build up its liquidity (that is, through investments in financial assets) or repay existing loans ahead of schedule.

Conclusion

When evaluating a case, it is important to be *systematic.* Analyze the case in a logical fashion, beginning with the identification of operating and financial strengths and weaknesses and environmental opportunities and threats. Move on to assess the value of a company's current strategies only when you are fully conversant with the SWOT analysis of the company. Ask yourself whether the company's current strategies make sense given its SWOT analysis. If they do not, what changes need to be made? What are your recommendations? Above all, link any strategic recommendations you may make to the SWOT analysis. State explicitly how the strategies you identify take advantage of the company's strengths to exploit environmental opportunities, how they rectify the company's weaknesses, and how they counter environmental threats. Also, do not forget to outline what needs to be done to implement your recommendations.

The Apollo Group: University of Phoenix

This case was prepared by Charles W. L. Hill, the University of Washington.

Which is the largest university system in the United States? After some thought, you might be tempted to answer that it is the giant University of California system with its eleven campuses and 208,000 students. You would be wrong. The largest provider of high education in America is the University of Phoenix, which has 293,000 students and operates around 180 campuses and learning centers in thirty-four states. The University of Phoenix is the flagship subsidiary of the Apollo Group, which also runs Western International University, the Institute for Professional Development and the College for Financial Planning. In total, the Apollo Group serves some 330,000 students in thirty-nine states.

The Apollo Group has been a very successful enterprise. Between 1996 and 2006 its revenues expanded from $214 million to $2.48 billion, and net profits increased from $21.4 million to $438 million. The University of Phoenix accounts for about 90% of the revenues of the Apollo Group. Apollo's return on invested capital, a key measure of profitability, averaged around 25% over this period, well above its cost of capital, which has been calculated to be around 10%.[1]

The Apollo Group is also a controversial enterprise. Founded by John Sperling, a former economic history professor and one-time union organizer at San Jose State University, the University of Phoenix

has been depicted by defenders of the educational establishment as a low-quality "diploma mill" that has commoditized education and is all too willing to sacrifice educational standards for the opportunity to make profits. Scott Rice, a San Jose State University English professor who has become a vocal critic of for-profit education, summarizes this view when he states that "John Sperling's vision of education is entirely mercenary. It's merely one more opportunity to turn a buck. When education becomes one more product, we obey the unspoken rule of business: to give consumers as little as they will accept in exchange for as much as they will pay. Sperling is a terrible influence on American education."[2]

Sperling, who is still chairman at eighty-five, certainly does not see things this way. In his view, the University of Phoenix serves a niche that the educational establishment long ignored: working adults who need a practical education to further their careers and who cannot afford the commitment associated with full-time education. Some high-powered academics agree. The Nobel Prize–winning economist Milton Friedman regards the triumph of the for-profit sector as inevitable because traditional universities are run "by faculty, and the faculty is interested in its own welfare."[3]

Some analysts suggest that the for-profit sector still has significant growth opportunities ahead of it. The postsecondary education market in the United States is estimated to be worth almost $300 billion, with only $17 to $18 billion of that currently captured by for-profit enterprises. Looking forward, analysts expect enrollment at for-profit schools to grow 5 to 6% per annum as they gain share from traditional higher educational institutions. Supporting this thesis are estimates that 37% of all students (more than 6 million) are older than twenty-four. A large portion of these students are likely to be working and to be attracted to the flexibility that the for-profit sector provides.[4]

On the other hand, the educational establishment is not blind to this opportunity. Many long-established public and private not-for-profit universities are now offering part-time degree programs aimed at working adults. Some believe that this emerging threat, coupled with the brand advantage enjoyed by big name universities, will limit enrollment growth going forward at the University of Phoenix.

John Sperling and the Birth of the University of Phoenix

University of Phoenix founder John Sperling was born in rural Missouri in 1921 in a cabin that already housed a family of six.[5] His mother was overbearing; his father habitually beat him. When his farther died, Sperling recalled that he could hardly contain his joy. Sperling barely graduated from high school and went off to join the merchant marine—as far away from Missouri as he could get. There he started his real education, reading through the books of his shipmates, many of whom were socialists. Sperling emerged from this experience an unabashed liberal with a penchant for challenging the status quo, something that he still delights in. (Among other things, Sperling is a regular financial contributor to ballot initiatives aimed at legalizing marijuana.)

After two years in the merchant marine, Sperling went to Reed College in Oregon. This was followed by a master's at Berkeley and a PhD in economic history at the University of Cambridge. A conventional academic career seemed the logical next step for Sperling. By the 1960s, he was a tenured professor of economic history at San Jose State University. Always the activist, he joined the American Federation of Teachers (AFT) and rose to state and national positions in the union. In his leadership role at the AFT, he persuaded professors at San Jose State to mount a walkout to support striking professors at San Francisco State University. The strike was a failure and almost resulted in the mass firing of one hundred professors. Sperling lost his credibility on campus. He was widely reviled and lost his position as head of the United Professors of California, a union that he had built almost single-handedly. But Sperling claims that the humiliating defeat taught him an important

lesson: "It didn't make a goddamn bit of difference what people thought of me. Without that psychological immunity, it would have been impossible to create and protect the University of Phoenix from hostility, legal assaults, and attempts to legislate us out of existence."[6]

By the early 1970s, Sperling's academic career was going nowhere—but that was all about to change. As part of a federal project to fight juvenile delinquency, San Jose State University arranged a series of courses for the police and schoolteachers who had to deal with the youngsters. Sperling, who had been experimenting with novel approaches to delivering education, was to run the workshops. He devised a curriculum, divided the classes into small groups, and brought in as group leaders teachers who were expert practitioners in their fields but who were not professors. He then challenged each group to complete a project that addressed the problem of juvenile delinquency.

The student feedback was very favorable. More than that, the enthusiastic participants lobbied him to create a degree program. So Sperling sketched out a curriculum for working adults in the criminal justice area and pitched the idea to the academic vice president at San Jose State. In Sperling's words, the VP was impressed and sympathetic, but utterly discouraging. He told Sperling that the university had all it could do to educate regular students and had no need to create part-time programs for working adults. Moreover, to gain approval, such a program would have to navigate its way through the academic bureaucracy at San Jose, a process that could take several years, and at the end of the day what emerged might differ significantly from Sperling's original proposal due to the input of other faculty members.

Unperturbed by the rejection, Sperling started to cast around for other schools that might want to run the program. He contacted the vice president of development at Stanford University, Frank Newman, who told Sperling that educational bureaucracies were inherently inert and innovated only when they were in financial trouble. Newman advised Sperling to find a school in financial trouble and persuade it that his program would make a profit.

The former union organizer immediately saw the value in Newman's suggestion. Left wing he might have been, but Sperling was eager to try out his ideas in the marketplace. He formed a private organization, the Institute for Professional Development (IPD), with the mission of making higher education available to the working community. Sperling approached the University of San Francisco (USF), a financially troubled Jesuit school. USF agreed to sponsor the IPD program, using its accreditation to validate the degree. The program was an immediate financial success. Before long, Sperling was contracting with other schools for similar programs. The educational establishment, however, reacted with open hostility to Sperling's for-profit venture. For the first time, but not the last, Sperling was accused of devaluing education and producing a diploma mill. Sperling's sin, in his view, was that his model cut the professors out of the educational equation, and they were not about to let that happen.

Although he had been an academic for years, Sperling had up to this point paid little attention to the process of accrediting institutions and degree programs. What he quickly discovered was legitimacy required that the sponsoring institution for a degree program be accredited by recognized accreditation agencies. In the case of USF, this was the Western Association of Schools and Colleges (WASC), which, along with the California State Department of Education, had jurisdiction over public and private schools, colleges, and universities in California. For the first time, but not for the last, Sperling discovered that these regulatory agencies had enormous power and could destroy the legitimacy of his programs by refusing to grant accreditation to the sponsoring institutions. In Sperling's own words:

> We had no idea the extent to which education is a high politicized and regulated activity, not the extent to which innovators were to be searched out and destroyed as quickly as possible by the academics who controlled the institutions and by their allies in regulatory agencies.[7]

What followed was a bitter five-year battle between Sperling, who tried to get and maintain accreditation for his programs in California, and politicians, professors, and accreditation agencies, which blocked him every step of the way. Ultimately, Sperling decided that it would be impossible to fully develop his concepts of education for working adults within the confines of an existing institution. He decided to establish a university of his own. Sperling moved to Phoenix, Arizona, where he thought regulators would be more open to his ideas. They weren't. The established state institutions were openly hostile to Sperling's venture. It took more campaigning, which

included an all-out media campaign's intensive lobbying of the state's legislature, and vitriolic debates in the committee rooms of higher education regulators, before Arizona accredited Sperling's venture in 1978, which was now named the University of Phoenix. Sperling learned the lesson well—today the Apollo Group maintains a staff of forty or so political lobbyists whose job it is to get and maintain accreditation.

University of Phoenix Business Model[8]

The University of Phoenix (UOP) is designed to cater to the needs of working adults, who make up 95% of its students. The average age is thirty-six and, until recently, the minimum age was twenty-three. The emphasis is on practical subjects such as business, information technology, teaching, criminal justice, and nursing. In addition to undergraduate degrees, UOP offers several graduate degrees, including a master's degree in business (MBA), counseling, and nursing. Today, some 51% of students at the Apollo Group are enrolled in undergraduate courses, 22% are in masters' programs, 26% are earning two-year associates' degrees, and 1.4% are doctoral students.[9]

UOP views the student as the customer, and the customer is king. Classes are offered at times that fit the busy schedules of the fully employed—often in the evening. The schedule is year round; there are no extended breaks for summer vacation. Steps are taken to make sure that it is as easy as possible for students to get to classes. One of the golden rules is that there should be plenty of parking and that students should be able to get from their cars to their classrooms in five minutes.

UOP campuses lack many of the facilities found in traditional universities, such as dormitories, student unions, athletic facilities, research laboratories, extensive networks of libraries, and the support staff required for all of these facilities. Instead, the typical campus comprises a handful of utilitarian buildings sited close to major roads.

In designing a university for working adults, Sperling introduced several key innovations. The classes are small—ten to fifteen students each—and are run as seminars. Students usually take just one class at a time. Classes generally meet once or twice a week for five to nine weeks. Faculty members act as discussion leaders and facilitators rather than lecturers. They are there to guide students through the curriculum and to provide feedback and grading. In addition to their whole-class groups, students belong to "learning teams" of three to five students, which work together on group projects and studying.

Since the mid 1990s, UOP has relied heavily on online resources to deliver much of the course content. A typical five-week undergraduate course goes something like this: Students attend class on campus for four hours the first week, giving them a chance to meet the instructor and be introduced to their learning teams and coursework. Weeks two through four are completed over the Internet, with homework assignments and participation requirements fulfilled online. Students return to campus in week five for presentations.[10]

Sperling hired as teachers working professionals who were looking for part-time employment. In 2005, only 400 of the 21,000 faculty at UOP were full time. Part-time faculty must have a master's degree or higher and five years of professional experience in an area related to the subject they teach. New faculty are subject to peer review by other faculty members, are given training in grading and instructing students, and benefit from a teaching mentorship with more experienced faculty members. There is no such thing as academic tenure at UOP or research requirements for faculty, full or part time.

UOP established "ownership" over the curriculum taught in classrooms. In traditional universities, individual faculty members develop and "own" the curriculum. This can lead to significant variation in the content offered for the same class when taught by different professors in the same university. The decentralized nature of curriculum development in traditional universities makes it very difficult for the central administration to mandate changes to the curriculum. Moreover, in traditional universities, significant curriculum change can take a large amount of time and energy, involving faculty committees and, in the case of new programs, approval from central administration. In contrast, at UOP content experts, typically the small number of full-time faculty, develop the curriculum. Part-time teachers are then expected to deliver this standardized curriculum. This centralization allows UOP to have a uniform curriculum and to rapidly include new material in a curriculum and roll it out systemwide if the need arises. When designing the curriculum, UOP solicits input from students two years after graduation and from employers who hire UOP graduates.

The centralization of curriculum has also enabled UOP to challenge the publishers of traditional textbooks. UOP contacts authors directly and contracts with them to develop course materials exactly to their specifications, cutting textbook publishers out of the loop. The goal is for all UOP programs to use customized materials that exist entirely in digital form. Today, nearly all UOP students get course materials and resources digitally through the Apollo Group's rEsource Internet portal. This eliminates the need for textbooks and is a source of added profit for UOP. The cost to undergraduate students is roughly $60 a course, while the cost to UOP is about $20.[11]

The contrast between UOP and traditional not-for-profit universities is stark. At the undergraduate level, traditional universities focus on eighteen- to twenty-five-year-olds who attend school full time. Labor costs are high due to the employment of full-time faculty, the majority of whom have doctoral degrees. Newly minted professors straight out of doctoral programs often command high starting salaries—as much as $120,000 a year plus benefits in disciplines such as business. Faculty are given low teaching loads to allow them to focus on research, which is the currency of the realm in academia. Research output is required for tenure in the "publish or perish" model of academia adopted by traditional universities.

Although the knowledge produced by research faculty can be and often is socially and economically valuable, the research culture of these knowledge factories translates into a high cost of instruction. At the University of Washington, for example, one of the nation's premier research institutions, in 2005, 3,900 full-time faculty educated 40,000 students. The average faculty salary was $76,951 for the nine months of the academic year, which translated into an instructional cost of around $300 million. In contrast, the part-time faculty at UOP are inexpensive. In 2005, the 21,000 faculty at the Apollo Group were paid $195 million, or roughly $9,200 each—and this to instruct 307,400 students. In addition, student, faculty, and research facilities dramatically increase the capital intensity of traditional universities, while their attendant staff increases the labor costs.

As a consequence of these factors, the total cost of running a traditional university are much higher than at UOP. At the University of Washington, for example, total operating expenses in 2004–2005 were $2.7 billion, compared to $1.53 billion at the Apollo Group.[12]

According to one estimate, the average *cost to the institution* of educating an undergraduate student for two semesters at a public university is around two and a half times greater than that at a for-profit institution such as UOP. At a private institution, it is more than three times greater.[13] It is the inherently low cost structure of UOP that allows the Apollo Group to make its high profits. (For financial statements, go to http://finance.yahoo.com/q?s=apol).

Naturally, such comparisons ignore the fact that the mission of many traditional universities such as the University of Washington is fundamentally different from that of the University of Phoenix. UOP produces zero new knowledge, whereas the nation's research universities have been and will continue to be major producers of the knowledge that underlies technological progress and economic growth.

On the revenue side, estimates suggest that in 2005 it cost around $22,500 to earn an associate's degree at UOP, $51,000 to earn a bachelor's degree, and $22,932 to earn a master's degree (costs vary by program).[14] Students attending UOP rely heavily on federal assistance programs to help pay for their college educations. Some 63% of undergraduate students at UOP received financial aid under Title IV programs from the U.S. Department of Education (DOE); 72% at UOP's Axia College, which awards associates' degrees, received aid. To be eligible for Title IV funding, a student has to be registered at an institution that is accredited by an agency recognized by the DOE and enrolled in a program with at least thirty weeks of instructional time and twenty-four credit hours.

In addition to Title IV financial aid programs, some 45% of UOP students received some form of tuition assistance from their employers in 2005. The Internal Revenue Code allows an employee to exclude some $5,250 a year in tuition assistance from taxable income.

Accreditation

Accreditation by a respected agency is critical for any university. Accreditation verifies that a proper college education, consistent with the institution's mission, and meeting or exceeding thresholds of approved standards of education quality, is attainable at an institution.[15] Accreditation is an important element of the brand equity of an institution, is valued by employers, allows students to transfer credits to another

institution, and is a prerequisite for Title IV financial aid. In addition, most employers offer tuition assistance only for courses from an accredited institution.

UOP is accredited by the Higher Learning Commission. Accreditation was first granted in 1978 and reaffirmed five times since. The next comprehensive review will take place in 2012. The Higher Learning Commission is one of six regional institutional accreditation agencies in the United States and is recognized by the Department of Higher Education. Regional accreditation is recognized nationally. In some states, it is sufficient authorization to operate a degree-granting institution, but in most, UOP must also get authorization from state authorities.

In addition to the Higher Learning Commission, the bachelor and master of science programs in nursing are accredited by the Commission on Collegiate Nursing Education, and the master's program in community counseling is accredited by the Council for Accreditation of Counseling and Related Educational Programs. However, the bachelor's and master's degree programs in business at UOP are not accredited by the Association to Advance Collegiate Schools of Business (AACSB). The AACSB is the largest and most influential accrediting organization for undergraduate, master's, and doctoral degree programs in business schools around the world, having granted international accreditation to more than five hundred business schools in thirty countries.

Throughout its history, UOP has found gaining accreditation an uphill battle. For example, UOP reentered California in 1980. After initially receiving a license to operate based on its accreditation by North Central, a regional accreditation agency recognized by the DOE, UOP was informed in 1981 that due to a change in California law, North Central accreditation was not sufficient to operate in California. Instead, accreditation was required from the Western Association of Schools and Colleges (WASC). The WASC was run by an old critic of Sperling, and there was zero chance that it would accredit UOP, leaving the institution with a stranded investment in California. It took another three years for UOP to resolve the issue, which it did by extensive political lobbying, ultimately getting a political ally to sponsor a bill in the California legislature that resulted in a change in the law, making WASC accreditation unnecessary for out-of-state institutions.

The hostility UOP encountered in California was repeated in many other states, and UOP was not always successful at countering it. Illinois, for example, refused to grant a license to UOP after existing institutions argued that there were already too many colleges in the state and that UOP was unnecessary since other institutions already offered similar programs.

In Sperling's view, the persistent hostility to his company reflects the cultural biases of higher education against the idea of for-profit universities. "The whole regulatory structure of higher education is designed to favor nonprofit and public colleges and universities, which it does by placing added regulatory burdens on those institutions organized for profit."[16] One of these burdens is that regulations grant Title IV eligibility to nonprofit and public institutions that have achieved candidacy for accreditation status, but grant Title IV eligibility only after the schools have achieved full accreditation.

Apollo's Growth Strategy

The company's strategy has been to grow by opening more campuses and learning centers in new states, by increasing enrollment at existing campuses and learning centers, and by offering product extensions, including online course offerings and expanded associate's degree offerings through Axia College.

UOP Expansion

The basic UOP business model has proved to be very scalable. In addition to centrally developed curriculum, UOP has developed customized computer programs that are used for student tracking, marketing, faculty recruitment and training, and academic quality management. These computer programs are intended to provide uniformity among UOP's campuses and learning centers. In turn, this enhances UOP's ability to expand rapidly into new markets.

To attract more students, UOP invests heavily in marketing and sales. In 2005, selling and promotional costs accounted for 21.5% of total revenues, much higher than at traditional universities. Of the $484 million spent on sales and promotions in 2005, $224 million went into advertising, $59 million into other promotions, and another $202 million into salaries for enrollment advisors. By way of comparison, few traditional universities spend more than $10 million on marketing.

UOP's aggressive marketing has got it into trouble with the DOE. In 2004 the department issued a report that was highly critical of how UOP compensated its enrollment advisors. According to the department, enrollment advisors at UOP soon found out that UOP based their salaries solely on the number of students they recruited, a practice that is prohibited by federal law. One recruiter who started out at $28,000 was bumped up to $85,000 after recruiting 151 students in six months. Another who started out at the same level got just a $4,000 raise after signing up 79 students. This report ultimately could have led to UOP being barred from federal loan programs, which would have been very damaging. Although an Apollo spokesperson called the report "very misleading and full of inaccuracies," the company agreed to change its compensation practices and paid a $9.8 million fine without admitting guilt.[17]

Online Education

One of the big engines of growth at UOP has been online education. UOP was an early mover in this area. In 1989, Sperling purchased a defunct distance learning company and instructed a team of technicians to come up with a viable portable electronic education system. By the time traditional universities started to discuss the idea of web-based distance education, they found that UOP was already there. Today, Apollo has more than 160,000 students enrolled in online programs and is the global leader in online education.[18]

Online classes are conducted in groups of ten to twelve students. Prior to the beginning of each class, students pay a fee to access eResource, the online delivery method for course materials. Online there is a series of eight newsgroups. The main newsgroup is designated for class discussion. There is an assignments newsgroup to which students submit their assignments, a chat newsgroup for students to discuss noncontent-related topics, a course materials newsgroup that houses the syllabus and lectures for the class, and four newsgroups that function as forums for the learning team assignments. Each week, the instructor posts a lecture to the classroom course materials newsgroup. Students log on and read the lecture or print the lecture to read at their convenience. Throughout the week, students participate in class discussions, based on the class content for that week, which is actively facilitated by the instructor. Both the instructor and students are expected to engage in content discussions five out of seven days each class week. In addition to the class participation requirement, students are also expected to complete individual assignments and to work within a small group of three to five students on a specific learning team assignment.

The online approach appeals to students who work irregular hours or who struggle to balance the demands of work, family, and school. Flexibility, not cost, is the prime selling point. The cost of an online MBA program at UOP is about $30,000, similar to online education program fees at traditional universities that are moving into this space. The cost of a getting a bachelor's degree online at UOP is about $475 per semester credit hour, which compares to an average of $398 for an online degree at a selection of state institutions, and $446 at private schools.[19]

Axia College

Another major thrust by the Apollo Group has been to expand its two-year associate's degree offerings. In the last few years, this has been done through Axia College, which initially was part of Apollo's Western International University. Today, Axia is part of UOP. The demographic strategy at Axia is very different from that at UOP. Axia targets eighteen- to twenty-four-year-old students with little or no college education. The revenue per student is lower, but this is balanced by larger class sizes (between thirty and forty), fewer dropouts, and lower student acquisition costs, which translates into slightly higher profit margins. The goal is for Axia to become a feeder for UOP, with students who gain an associate's degree at Axia transferring to UOP to gain a bachelor's, either immediately upon graduation or at some time in the future. Due to the rapid growth of Axia, most of which is online, associates' degrees have grown from about 3.9% of Apollo's student base in 2004 to about 23% in 2006. The growth of Axia has hurt Apollo's revenue per student numbers and the stock price, although many analysts see this as a good long-term strategy.[20]

The Competitive Landscape

The postsecondary education industry in the United States is estimated to be worth around $300 billion, with the for-profit sector capturing about $18 billion of that total in 2005. The industry will continue to grow, fueled by favorable demographics and tuition hikes, which historically have outpaced inflation by a wide margin. The DOE expects postsecondary enrollment to grow at 2% per annum. Analysts estimate that the for-profit sector could grow enrollments by 5 to 6% per annum as it gains share, and increase tuition at 4 to 5% per annum.[21] To back up these forecasts, analysts point to DOE figures that suggest that only 26% of Americans twenty-five and older have a bachelor's degree or higher.

Although UOP pioneered the for-profit university model and remains by far the largest institution, it is not alone in the space. Competition has increased and may continue to do so. Today, there are around 850 for-profit institutions offering degrees in the United States, up from around 600 in 1996. Most of these institutions, however, are quite small. The largest competitors to UOP are Corinthian College, with 66,000 students in 2005; ITT Educational Services, with 43,000 students; and Career Education.

Corinthian College focuses primarily on diploma or certificate courses designed for students with little or no college experience who are looking for entry-level jobs. As such, it is not a strong direct competitor to UOP. Florida Metropolitan University, the largest school operated by Corinthian College, is currently being investigated for marketing and advertising practices by the Florida attorney general. ITT Educational Services has traditionally focused on associates' degrees, but has been expanding its offerings of bachelors' degrees. ITT's niche is technical degrees, although like UOP it also offers business degrees. Career Education is the holding company for a number of for-profit establishments, including Colorado Technical University and American InterContinental University. Currently Career Education is mired in legal and accreditation issues that have constrained its ability to expand.

Analysts' estimates suggest that among for-profit universities, UOP has the premium brand but prices its offerings competitively, which constitutes a compelling value proposition for students (see Exhibit 1).

In addition to other nonprofits, UOP faces increased competition from traditional not-for-profit universities. In recent years, both private and public institutions have expanded their part-time and online offerings to adults, particularly in areas like business administration. Executive MBA programs have become major revenue generators at many state and private universities. To take one example, at the University of Washington business school, the number of students enrolled in part-time evening or executive MBA programs has expanded from around forty students ten years ago to over three hundred today. These students pay "market-based" fees, and the programs

EXHIBIT 1

Graduate Salary and Tuition for Bachelor's Degrees

School	Mean Graduate Salary	Mean Total Tuition
University of Phoenix	$52,597	$51,000
American InterContinental University	$44,363	$43,863
Florida Metropolitan University	$35,019	$50,400
ITT Technical Institute	$39,726	$69,480

Source: Data taken from Paul Bealand, "What's a Degree Worth?" Citigroup Equity Research, February 17, 2006.

are run as profit centers that contribute earnings to support the operations of the business school. The programs are structured to minimize the demands on working adults (classes are held in the evening or on weekends) and make heavy use of learning teams to facilitate the educational process.

Some traditional universities are also getting into the business of online education, although their success has been decidedly mixed so far. One of the leaders, the University of Massachusetts, had 9,200 students taking online courses in 2006. Most were working adults ages twenty-five to fifty, and 30% were from out of state. At UMass, online applicants undergo the same admission process as candidates for campus slots. Tuition is slightly higher than that for on-campus students since web-based courses are not subsidized by the state. At another state institution, Pennsylvania State University, there are some 6,000 students taking online courses, and demand is growing rapidly. The University of Maryland University College, the open enrollment arm of the state university, had 51,405 online students in 2005, up from 9,696 in 1998. Nearly 40% of these were U.S. military personnel around the world—a market that UOP also targets.[22]

On the other hand, many top schools have been reluctant to offer online courses, believing that doing so might compromise quality. Underlying this view is a belief that much of the value in education comes from face-to-face interactions with professors and other students in a classroom setting. This perspective is backed up by empirical and anecdotal evidence. In one recent survey, employers overwhelmingly preferred traditional bachelors' degrees when hiring over credentials even partially completed online. Two professors asked managers from 270 small and medium-sized companies in eight cities about their attitudes toward online credentials. The managers sought

entry-level employees or managers in engineering, business, and information technology. Ninety-six percent said they would choose traditional candidates over those with online degrees.[23]

In response to a journalist's question about the value of online degrees, a spokesperson at Texas Instruments stated: "We do not hire people with online degrees. We primarily hire engineers, and we target very well established engineering degree programs. The chance for someone with an online degree program to get in is not very likely."[24] On the other hand, several employers told the same journalist that an online degree did not limit options so long as it was from an accredited institution. These organizations included Northrop Grumman, United Parcel Service, Boeing, and Discovery Communications.

October 2006

On October 18, 2006, Apollo issued its results for its financial fourth quarter and the 2006 financial year. The results were not as strong as had been forecasted. Beginning in 2005, enrollment growth rates had started to decline. This trend worsened in mid 2006, when UOP had a decline in enrollment of 15,000, which caused a drop in profits to $93.5 million, down from $106 million in the same period of 2005. Making matters worse, Apollo had spent more on marketing and sales than in the equivalent period a year earlier as it tried to attract more students. The bright spot in the results was continued rapid enrollment growth at Axia College. However, this growth came at a cost since the revenue per student was lower at Axia than at UOP. These events had analysts wondering whether Apollo's years of rapid growth had come to an end, and if so, what the corporation's strategy should be going forward.

ENDNOTES

1. Standard & Poor's Stock Report, Apollo Group Inc, October 14, 2006.
2. Quoted in B. Breen, "The Hard Life and Restless Mind of America's Educational Billionaire," *Fast Company*, March 2003, pages 80–86.
3. Quoted in Anonymous, "Survey: Higher Ed Inc," *The Economist*, September 10, 2005, pages 19–21.
4. Paul Bealand, "What's a Degree Worth?" *Citigroup Equity Research*, February 17, 2006.
5. Sperling describes his life in his autobiography, *Rebel with a Cause*, New York: John Wiley, 2006.
6. Quoted in B. Breen, "The Hard Life and Restless Mind of America's Educational Billionaire," *Fast Company*, March 2003, pages 80–86.
7. John Sperling, *Rebel with a Cause*, New York: John Wiley, 2006, page 78.
8. Much of the material in this section is drawn from the 10K Reports of the Apollo Group filed with the Securities and Exchange Commission.
9. Apollo Group Press Release, "Apollo Group Inc Reports Fiscal 2006 Fourth Quarter and Year End Results," October 18, 2006; Paul Bealand, "What's a Degree Worth?" *Citigroup Equity Research*, February 17, 2006.
10. S. Baltes, "Phoenix Builds Presence Amid Turmoil," *Des Moines Business Record*, September 20, 2004, page 14.
11. Paul Bealand, "What's a Degree Worth?" *Citigroup Equity Research*, February 17, 2006.
12. University of Washington data is taken from the UW Fact Book, which can be accessed online at http://www.washington.edu/admin/factbook/.
13. R. S. Ruch, *Higher Ed Inc: The Rise of the For Profit University*, Baltimore, John Hopkins University Press, 2001.
14. Paul Bealand, "What's a Degree Worth?" *Citigroup Equity Research*, February 17, 2006.
15. R. S. Ruch, *Higher Ed Inc: The Rise of the For Profit University*, Baltimore, John Hopkins University Press, 2001.
16. John Sperling, *Rebel with a Cause*, New York: John Wiley, 2006, page 105.
17. W. C. Symonds, "Back to Earth for Apollo Group?" *Business Week*, January 31, 2005, page 50.
18. D. Golden, "Degrees@StateU.edu," *Wall Street Journal*, May 9, 2006, page B1.
19. Paul Bealand, "What's a Degree Worth?" *Citigroup Equity Research*, February 17, 2006.
20. K. Rowland, "Apollo Group A," *Morning Star Research Report*, October 19, 2006.
21. Paul Bealand, "What's a Degree Worth?" *Citigroup Equity Research*, February 17, 2006.
22. D. Golden, "Degrees@StateU.edu," *Wall Street Journal*, May 9, 2006, page B1.
23. A. Wellen, "Degrees of Acceptance," *Wall Street Journal*, July 30, 2006, page A26.
24. A. Wellen, "Degrees of Acceptance," *Wall Street Journal*, July 30, 2006, page A26.

Boeing Commercial Aircraft: Comeback?

This case was prepared by Charles W. L. Hill, the University of Washington.

It looked as if 2006 would be the year that Boeing could boast of a comeback in its three-decades-long duel with Airbus Industries. Long the dominant player in the commercial aerospace industry, Boeing has been steadily losing market share to Airbus from the mid-1990s onwards (represented in Exhibit 1). In 1999, for the first time in its history, Airbus garnered more orders for new commercial jet aircraft than Boeing. The European upstart repeated this achievement regularly between 2001 and 2005.

By mid-2006, however, the tide seemed to be shifting in Boeing's favor. Underlying this were strong sales of Boeing's newest jet, the super-efficient wide-bodied 787, along with surging sales of its well-established 737 and 777 jets. For the first six months of 2006, Boeing took orders for 487 aircraft; Airbus took just 117. While Boeing seemed to be leaving a decade of production problems and ethics scandals behind it, Airbus was mired in problems of its own. Its largest jet to date, the A380 super jumbo, had been delayed from entering service while the company struggled with production problems. Orders for the A380 had stalled at 159 for almost a year, and analysts were beginning to question whether the aircraft would be a commercial success. Moreover, Airbus's contender to the Boeing 787, the A350, had to be scrapped before it even left the drawing board due to negative customer feedback. The challenge facing

Boeing's management was to translate this revival in fortunes for the company into a sustainable competitive advantage. It was off to a good start, but what else needed to be done?

The Competitive Environment

By the 2000s, the market for large commercial jet aircraft was dominated by just two companies, Boeing and Airbus. A third player in the industry, McDonnell Douglas, had been significant historically but had lost share during the 1980s and 1990s. In 1997, Boeing acquired McDonnell Douglas, primarily for its strong military business. Since the mid-1990s, Airbus had been gaining orders at Boeing's expense. By the mid-2000s, the two companies were splitting the market.

Both Boeing and Airbus now have a full range of aircraft. Boeing offers five aircraft "families" that range in size from 100 to over 500 seats. They are the narrow-bodied 737 and the wide-bodied 747, 767, 777, and 787 families. Each family comes in various forms. For example, there are currently four main variants of the 737 aircraft. They vary in size from 110 to 215 seats, and in range from 2,000 to over 5,000 miles. List prices vary from $47 million for the smallest member of the 737 family, the 737-600, to $282 million for the largest Boeing aircraft, the 747-8. The newest member of the Boeing family, the 787, lists for between $138 million and $188 million, depending on the model.[1]

Similarly, Airbus offers four families: the narrow-bodied A320 family and the wide-bodied A300/310, A330/340, and A380 families. These aircraft vary in size from 100 to 550 seats. The range of list prices is similar to Boeing's. The A380 super jumbo lists for between $282 million and $302 million, while the smaller A320 lists for between $62 million and $66.5 million.[2] Both companies also offer freighter versions of their wide-bodied aircraft.

Airbus was a relatively recent entrant into the market. Airbus began its life as a consortium between a French and a Germany company in 1970. Later, a British and a Spanish company joined the consortium. Initially few people gave Airbus much chance for success, but the consortium gained ground by innovating. It was the first aircraft maker to build planes that "flew by wire," made extensive use of composites, flew with only two flight crew members (most flew with three), and used a common cockpit layout across models. It also gained sales by being the first company to offer a wide-bodied twin engine jet, the A300, that was positioned between smaller single-aisle planes like the 737 and large aircraft such as the Boeing 747.

In 2001, Airbus became a fully integrated company. The European Defense and Space Company (EADS), formed by a merger between French, German, and Spanish interests, acquired 80% of the shares in EADS, and BAE Systems, a British company, took a 20% stake.

Development and Production

The economics of development and production in the industry are characterized by a number of facts. First, the R&D and tooling costs associated with developing a new airliner are very high. Boeing spent some $5 billion to develop the 777. Its latest aircraft, the 787, is expected to cost $8 billion to develop. Development costs for Airbus's latest aircraft, the A380 super jumbo, could run as high as $15 billion.

Second, given the high upfront costs, to break even a company has to capture a significant share of projected world demand. The breakeven point for the Airbus super jumbo, for example, is estimated to be between 250 and 270 aircraft. Estimates of the total potential market for this aircraft vary widely. Boeing suggests that the total world market will be no more than 320 aircraft over the next twenty years. Airbus believes that demand for this size aircraft will be more like 1,250 jets. In any event, it may take five to ten years of production before Airbus breaks even on the A380—and that's on top of years of negative cash flow during development.[3]

Third, there are significant learning effects in aircraft production.[4] On average, unit costs fall by about 20% each time *cumulative* output of a specific model is doubled. The phenomenon occurs because managers and shop floor workers learn over time how to assemble a particular model of plane more efficiently, reducing assembly time, boosting productivity, and lowering the marginal costs of producing subsequent aircraft.

Fourth, the assembly of aircraft is an enormously complex process. Modern planes have over 1 million component parts that have to be designed to fit with each other, and then produced and brought together at the right time to assemble the engine. At several times in the history of the industry, problems with the supply of critical components have held up production schedules and resulted in losses. In 1997, Boeing took a charge of $1.6 billion against earnings when it had to halt the production of its 737 and 747 models due to a lack of component parts.

Historically, airline manufacturers tried to manage the supply process through vertical integration, making many of the component parts that went into an aircraft (engines were long the exception to this). Over the last two decades, however, there has been a trend to contract out production of components and even entire subassemblies to independent suppliers. On the 777, for example, Boeing outsourced about 65 percent of the aircraft production, by value, excluding the engines.[5] While helping to reduce costs, contracting out has placed an enormous onus on airline manufacturers to work closely with their suppliers to coordinate the entire production process.

Finally, all new aircraft are now designed digitally and assembled virtually before a single component is produced. Boeing was the first to do this with its 777 in the early 1990s and its new version of the 737 in the late 1990s.

Customers

Demand for commercial jet aircraft is very volatile and tends to reflect the financial health of the commercial airline industry, which is prone to boom and bust cycles (see Exhibits 1 and 2). After a moderate boom during the 1990s, the airline industry went through a particularly nasty downturn during 2001–2005. The downturn started in early 2001 due to a slowdown in business travel after the boom of the 1990s. It was compounded by a dramatic slump in airline travel after the terrorist attacks on the United States on September 11, 2001. Between 2001

EXHIBIT 1

Commercial Aircraft Orders, 1990–2005

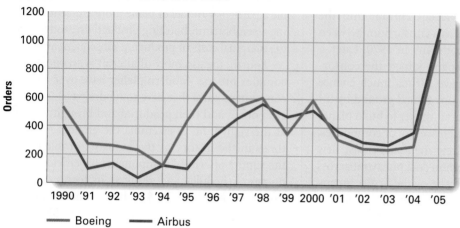

Boeing   Airbus

Sources: http://www.boeing.com/ (accessed September 2006) and http://www.airbus.com/en/ (accessed September 2006).

and 2005, the entire global airline industry lost some $40 billion, more money than it had made since its inception.[6]

For 2006, the industry is forecasted to lose $1.7 billion, which represents an incremental improvement over the $3.2 billion lost in 2005. The industry would have been profitable in both 2005 and 2006 were it not for surging jet fuel prices after January 2004 (prices for jet fuel more than doubled between 2004 and 2006—see Exhibit 3). The International Air Travel Association estimates that the fuel bill for all airlines in 2006 was around $115 billion. The bill for jet fuel represented over 25% of the industry's total operating costs in 2006, compared to less than 10% in 2001.[7]

EXHIBIT 2

World Airline Industry Revenues

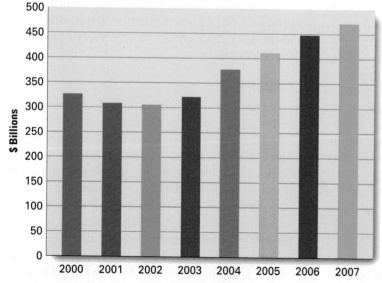

Source: IATA Data. Figures for 2006 and 2007 are forecasts. http://www.iata.org/whatwedo/economics/fuel_monitor/price_development.htm (accessed February 12, 2007).

EXHIBIT 3

Jet Fuel and Crude Oil Prices

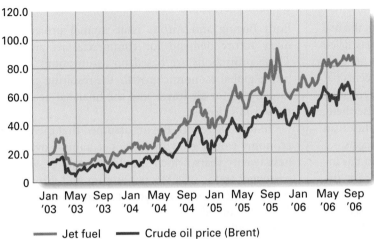

Source: IATA Data. http://www.iata.org/whatwedo/economics/fuelmonitor/
price_development.htm (accessed February 12, 2007).

Losses were particularly severe among the big six airlines in the world's largest market, the United States (American Airlines, United, Delta, Continental, US Airways, and Northwest). Three of these airlines (United, Delta, and Northwest) were forced to seek chapter 11 bankruptcy protections. Even though demand and profits plummeted at the big six airlines, some carriers continued to make profits during 2001–2005, most notably the budget airline Southwest. In addition, other newer budget airlines, including AirTran and Jet Blue (which was started in 2000), gained market share during this period. Indeed, between 2000 and 2003, the budget airlines in the United States expanded capacity by 44%, even as the majors slashed their carrying capacities and parked unused planes in the desert. In 1998, the budget airlines held a 16% share of the U.S. market; by mid-2004, their share had risen to 29%.[8]

The key to the success of the budget airlines is a strategy that gives them a 30 to 50% cost advantage over traditional airlines. The budget airlines all follow the same basic script: They purchase just one type of aircraft (some standardize on Boeing 737s, others on Airbus 320s). They hire nonunion labor and cross-train employees to perform multiple jobs (to help meet turnaround times, for example, pilots might help check tickets at the gate). As a result of flexible work rules, Southwest needs only 80 employees to support and fly an aircraft, compared to 115 at the big

six airlines. The budget airlines also favor flying "point to point" rather than through hubs, and often use less costly secondary airports rather than major ones. They focus on large markets with lots of traffic (up and down the East Coast, for example). There are no frills on the flights (passengers receive no in-flight food or complementary drinks, for example). And prices are set low to fill up the seats.

In contrast, major airlines base their operations on the network, or "hub and spoke," system. Network airlines route their flights through major hubs; one airline often dominates a single hub (United dominates Chicago's O'Hare airport, for example). This system was developed for good reason: It efficiently uses airline capacity when there isn't enough demand to fill a plane flying point to point. By using a hub and spoke system, major network airlines are able to serve some 38,000 city pairs, some of which generate fewer than fifty passengers per day. By focusing on a few hundred city pairs where there is sufficient demand to fill their planes, and flying directly between them (point to point), the budget airlines seem to have found a way around this constraint. The network carriers also suffer from a higher cost structure due to their legacy of a unionized workforce. In addition, their costs are pushed higher by their superior in-flight service. In good times, the network carriers can recoup their costs by charging higher prices than the discount airlines, particularly for business travelers, who pay more to book late and to fly business or first class. In the competitive environment of the early 2000s, however, this was no longer the case.

Due to the effect of increased competition, the real yield that U.S. airlines get from passengers has fallen from 8.70 cents per mile in 1980 to 6.37 cents per mile in 1990, 5.12 cents per mile in 2000, and 4.00 cents per mile in 2005 (these figures are expressed in constant 1978 cents).[9] Real yields are also declining elsewhere. With real yields declining, the only way that airlines can become profitable is to reduce their operating costs.

Outside of the United States, competition has intensified as deregulation has allowed low-cost airlines to enter local markets and capture share from long-established national airlines that have used the hub and spoke model. In Europe, for example, Ryanair and Easy Jet have adopted the business model of Southwest and used it to grow aggressively.

By the mid-2000s, large airlines in the United States were starting to improve their operating efficiency, helped by growing traffic volumes, higher load factors, and reductions in operating costs, particularly labor costs. Load factor refers to the percentage of a plane that is full on average, which hit a record 86% in 2006 in the United States, and 81% in international markets. Total losses for the U.S. industry were projected to be $4.5 billion in 2006, primarily due to one-time accounting charges. European airlines were projected to make profits of $1.8 billion in 2006, and Asian airlines profits of $1.7 billion. For 2007, the U.S.

airlines were projected to break even, and the global industry was projected to earn around $2 billion.[10]

Demand Projections

Both Boeing and Airbus issue annual projects of likely future demand for commercial jet aircraft. These projections are based on assumptions about future global economic growth, the resulting growth in demand for air travel, and the financial health of the world's airlines.

In its 2006 report, Boeing assumed that the world economy would grow by 3.1% per annum over the next twenty years, which should generate growth in passenger traffic of 4.8% per annum and growth in cargo traffic of 6.1% per year. On this basis, Boeing forecast demand for some 27,210 new aircraft valued at $2.6 trillion over the next twenty years (1,360 deliveries per year). Of this, some 9,580 aircraft will be replacements for aircraft retired from service, with the balance being aircraft to satisfy an expanded market. In 2025, Boeing estimates that the total global fleet of aircraft will be 35,970, up from 17,330 in 2005. Boeing believes that North America will account for 28% of all new orders, Asia Pacific for 36%, and Europe for 24%. Passenger traffic is projected to grow at 6.4% per annum in Asia versus 3.6% in North America and 3.4% in Europe.[11]

Regarding the mix of orders, Boeing believes that the majority will be for aircraft between regional jets (which have fewer than 100 seats) and the Boeing 747 (see Exhibit 4). Aircraft in the 747 range (including

EXHIBIT 4

Projected New Airplane Deliveries, 2006–2025

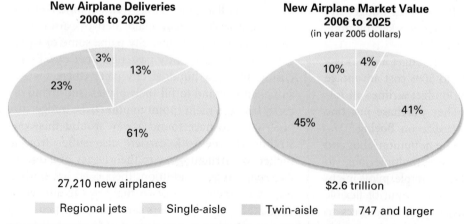

Source: Boeing, http://www.boeing.com/commercial/cmo/new.html (accessed 2007).

the Airbus A380) will account for some 3% of deliveries and 10% of value between 2006 and 2025, according to Boeing.

The latest Airbus forecast covers 2004–2023. Over that period, Airbus forecasts world passenger traffic to grow by 5.3% per annum and predicts demand for 17,328 new aircraft worth $1.9 trillion. (Note that Airbus excludes regional jets from its forecast; Boeing's forecasts include some 3,450 regional jet deliveries). Airbus believes that demand for very large aircraft will be robust, amounting to 1,648 large passenger aircraft and freighters in the 747 range and above, or 22% of the total value of aircraft delivered.[12]

The difference in the mix of orders projected by Boeing and Airbus reflect different views of how future demand will evolve. Airbus believes that hubs will continue to play an important role in airline travel, particularly international travel, and that very large jets will be required to transport people between hubs. Airbus bases this assumption partly on an analysis of data over the last twenty years, which shows that traffic between major airline hubs has grown faster than traffic between other city pairs. Airbus also assumes that urban concentrations will continue to grow, with fifteen cities having populations of more than 20 million by 2023, up from five in 2004. Airbus states that demand is simply a function of where people want to go, and most people want to travel between major urban centers. The company notes, for example, that 90% of travelers from the United States to China go to three major cities. Fifty other cities make up the remaining 10%, and Airbus believes that very few of these cities will have demand large enough to justify a nonstop service from North America or Europe. Based on this assumption, Airbus sees robust demand for very large aircraft, particularly its A380 offering.

Boeing has a different view of the future. The company theorizes that hubs will become increasingly congested and that many travelers will seek to avoid them. Boeing thinks that passengers prefer frequent nonstop service between the cities they wish to visit. Boeing also sees growth in travel between city pairs as being large enough to support an increasing number of direct long-haul flights. The company notes that continued liberalization of regulations governing airline routes around the world will allow for the establishment of more direct flights between city pairs. As in the United States, the company believes that long-haul, low-cost airlines will emerge that serve city pairs and avoid hubs.

In sum, Boeing believes that airline travelers will demand more frequent nonstop flights, not larger aircraft.[13] To support this, the company has data showing that all of the growth in airline travel since 1995 has been met by the introduction of new nonstop flights between city pairs and by an increased frequency of flights between city pairs, not by an increase in airplane size. For example, Boeing notes that following the introduction of the 767, airlines introduced more flights between city pairs in North America and Europe and more frequent departures. In 1984, 63% of all flights across the North Atlantic were in the 747. By 2004, the figure had declined to 13%, with smaller wide-bodied aircraft such as the 767 and 777 dominating traffic. Following the introduction of the 777, which can fly nonstop across the Pacific and is smaller than the 747, the same process occurred in the North Pacific. In 2006 there were seventy-two daily flights serving twenty-six city pairs in North America and Asia.

Boeing's History[14]

William Boeing established the Boeing Company in 1916 in Seattle. In the early 1950s, Boeing took an enormous gamble when it decided to build a large jet aircraft that could be sold both to the military as a tanker and to commercial airlines as a passenger plane. Known as the Dash 80, the plane had swept-back wings and four jet engines. Boeing invested $16 million to develop the Dash 80, two-thirds of the company's entire profits during the postwar years. The Dash 80 was the basis for two aircraft, the KC-135 Air Force tanker and the Boeing 707. Introduced into service in 1957, the 707 was the world's first commercially successful passenger jet aircraft. Boeing went on to sell some 856 Boeing 707s along with 820 KC-135s. The final 707, a freighter, rolled off the production line in 1994 (production of passenger planes ended in 1978). The closest rival to the 707 was the Douglas DC 8, of which some 556 were ultimately sold.

The 707 was followed by a number of other successful jet liners including the 727 (entered service in 1962), the 737 (entered service in 1967), and the 747 (entered service in 1970). The single aisle 737 went on to become the workhorse of many airlines. In the 2000s, a completely redesigned version of the 737 that could seat between 110 and 180 passengers was still selling strong. Cumulative sales of the 737 totaled 6,500 by mid-2006, making it by far the most popular commercial jet aircraft ever sold.

It was the 747 "jumbo jet," however, that probably best defined Boeing. In 1966, when Boeing's board decided to develop the 747, they were widely viewed as betting the company on the jet. The 747 was born out of the desire of Pan Am, then America's largest airline, for a 400-seat passenger aircraft that could fly 5,000 miles. Pan Am believed that the aircraft would be ideal for the growing volume of transcontinental traffic. However, beyond Pan Am, which committed to purchasing 25 aircraft, demand was very uncertain. Moreover, the estimated $400 million in development and tooling costs placed a heavy burden on Boeing's financial resources. To make a return on its investment, the company estimated it would have to sell close to 400 aircraft. To complicate matters further, Boeing's principal competitors, Lockheed and McDonnell Douglas, were each developing 250-seat jumbo jets.

Boeing's big bet turned out to be auspicious. Pan Am's competitors feared being left behind, and by the end of 1970, almost 200 orders for the aircraft had been placed. Successive models of the 747 extended the range of the aircraft. The 747-400, introduced in 1989, had a range of 8,000 miles and a maximum seating capacity of 550 (although most configurations seated around 400 passengers). By this time, both Douglas and Lockheed had exited the market, giving Boeing a lucrative monopoly in the very large commercial jet category. By 2005, the company had sold some 1,430 747s and was actively selling its latest version of the 747 family, the 747-8, which was scheduled to enter service in 2008.

By the mid-1970s, Boeing was past the breakeven point on all of its models (707, 727, 737, and 747). The positive cash flow helped to fund investment in two new aircraft, the narrow-bodied 757 and the wide-bodied 767. The 757 was designed as a replacement to the aging 727, while the 767 was a response to a similar aircraft from Airbus. These were the first Boeing aircraft to be designed with two-person cockpits, rather than three. Indeed, the cockpit layout was identical, allowing the crew to shift from one aircraft to the other. The 767 was also the first aircraft for which Boeing subcontracted a significant amount of work to a trio of Japanese manufacturers—Mitsubishi, Kawasaki, and Fuji—which supplied about 15% of the airframe. Introduced in 1981, both aircraft were successful. Some 1,049 757s were sold

during the life of the program, which ended in 2003. Over 950 767s had been sold by 2006, and the program is still going.

The next Boeing plane was the 777. A two-engine, wide-bodied aircraft with seating capacity of up to 400 and a range of almost 8,000 miles, the 777 program was initiated in 1990. The 777 was seen as a response to Airbus's successful A330 and A340 wide-bodied aircraft. Development costs were estimated at some $5 billion. The 777 was the first wide-bodied, long-haul jet to have only two engines. It was also the first to be designed entirely on computer. To develop the 777, for the first time Boeing used cross-functional teams composed of engineering and production employees. It also bought major suppliers and customers into the development process. As with the 767, a significant amount of work was outsourced to foreign manufacturers, including the Japanese trio of Mitsubishi, Kawasaki, and Fuji, which supplied 20% of the 777 airframe. In total, some 60% of parts for the 777 were outsourced. The 777 proved to be another successful venture. By mid-2006, 850 777s had been ordered, far greater than the 200 or so required to break even.

In December 1996, Boeing stunned the aerospace industry by announcing it would merge with longtime rival McDonnell Douglas in a deal estimated to be worth $13.3 billion. The merger was driven by Boeing's desire to strengthen its presence in the defense and space side of the aerospace business, where McDonnell Douglas was traditionally strong. On the commercial side of the aerospace business, Douglas had been losing market share since the 1970s. By 1996, Douglas accounted for less than 10% of production in the large commercial jet aircraft market and only 3% of new orders placed that year. The dearth of new orders meant the long-term outlook for Douglas's commercial business was increasingly murky. With or without the merger, many analysts felt that it was only a matter of time before McDonnell Douglas would be forced to exit from the commercial jet aircraft business. In their view, the merger with Boeing merely accelerated that process.

The merger transformed Boeing into a broad-based aerospace business within which commercial aerospace accounted for 40 to 60% of total revenue, depending on the stage of the commercial production cycle. In 2001, for example, the commercial aircraft group accounted for $35 billion in revenues out of a corporate total of $58 billion, or 60%. In 2005, with the delivery cycle at a low point (but the order cycle rebounding), the commercial airplane group accounted for $22.7 billion out of a total of $54.8 billion, or 41%. The balance of revenue was made up by a wide range of military aircraft, weapons and defense systems, and space systems.

In the early 2000s, in a highly symbolic act, Boeing moved its corporate headquarters from Seattle to Chicago. The move was an attempt to put some distance between top corporate officers and the commercial aerospace business, the headquarters of which remained in Seattle. The move was also intended to signal to the investment community that Boeing was far more than its commercial businesses.

To some extent, the move to Chicago may have been driven by a number of production missteps in the late 1990s that hit the company at a time when it should have been enjoying financial success. During the mid-1990s, orders had boomed as Boeing cut prices in an aggressive move to gain share from Airbus. However, delivering these aircraft meant that Boeing had to more than double its production schedule between 1996 and 1997. As it attempted to do this, the company ran into some severe production bottlenecks.[15] The company scrambled to hire and train some 41,000 workers, recruiting many from suppliers, a move it came to regret when many of the suppliers could not meet Boeing's demands and shipments of parts were delayed. In the fall of 1997, things got so bad that Boeing shut down its 747 and 737 production lines so that workers could catch up with out-of-sequence work and wait for back-ordered parts to arrive. Ultimately, the company had to take a $1.6 billion charge against earnings to account for higher costs and penalties paid to airlines for the late delivery of jets. As a result, Boeing made very little money out of its mid-1990s order boom. The head of Boeing's commercial aerospace business was fired, and the company committed itself to a major acceleration of its attempt to overhaul its production system, elements of which dated back half a century.

Boeing in the 2000s

In the 2000s, three things dominated the development of Boeing Commercial Aerospace. First, the company accelerated a decade-long project aimed at improving the company's production methods by adopting the lean production systems initially developed by Toyota and applying them to the manufacture of large jet aircraft. Second, the company considered and then rejected the idea of building a successor to the 747. Third, Boeing decided to develop a new wide-bodied, long-haul jetliner, the 787.

Lean Production at Boeing

Boeing's attempt to revolutionize the way planes are built dates back to the early 1990s. Beginning in 1990, the company started to send teams of executives to Japan to study the production systems of Japan's leading manufacturers, particularly Toyota. Toyota had pioneered a new way of assembling automobiles known as *lean production* (in contrast to conventional *mass production*).

Toyota's lean production system was developed by one of the company's engineers, Ohno Taiichi.[16] After working at Toyota for five years and visiting Ford's U.S. plants, Ohno became convinced that the mass-production philosophy for making cars was flawed. He saw numerous problems, including three major drawbacks. First, long production runs created massive inventories, which had to be stored in large warehouses. This was expensive because of the cost of warehousing and because inventories tied up capital in unproductive uses. Second, if the initial machine settings were wrong, long production runs resulted in the production of a large number of defects (that is, waste). And third, the mass-production system was unable to accommodate consumer preferences for product diversity.

In looking for ways to make shorter production runs economical, Ohno developed a number of techniques designed to reduce setup times for production equipment, a major source of fixed costs. By using a system of levers and pulleys, he was able to reduce the time required to change dies on stamping equipment from a full day in 1950 to three minutes by 1971. This advance made small production runs economical, which allowed Toyota to respond more efficiently to consumer demands for product diversity. Small production runs also eliminated the need to hold large inventories, thereby reducing warehousing costs. Furthermore, small production runs and the lack of inventory meant that defective parts were produced only in small numbers and entered the assembly process immediately. This reduced waste made it easier to trace defects to their source and fix the problem. In sum, Ohno's innovations enabled Toyota to produce a more diverse product range at a lower unit cost than was possible with conventional mass production.

Impressed with what Toyota had done, in the mid-1990s, Boeing started to experiment with applying Toyota-like lean production methods to the production of aircraft. Production at Boeing used to be all about producing parts in high volumes and then storing them in warehouses until they were ready to be used in the assembly process. After visiting Toyota, engineers realize that Boeing was drowning in inventory. A huge amount of space and capital was tied up in things that didn't add value. Moreover, expensive specialized machines often took up a lot of space and were frequently idle for long stretches of time.

Like Ohno at Toyota, company engineers started to think about how they could modify equipment and processes at Boeing to reduce waste. Boeing set aside space and time for teams of creative plant employees—design engineers, maintenance technicians, electricians, machinists, and operators—to start experimenting with machinery. They called these teams moonshiners. The term *moonshine* was coined by Japanese executives who visited the United States after World War II. They were impressed by two things in the United States—supermarkets and the stills built by people in the Appalachian hills. They noticed that people built these stills with no money. They would use salvaged parts to make small stills that produced alcohol that they sold for money. The Japanese took this philosophy back home with them and applied it to industrial machinery, which is where Boeing executives saw the concept in operation in the 1990s. With the help of Japanese consultants, they decided to apply the moonshine creative philosophy at Boeing to produce new low-cost, "right-sized" machines that could be used to increase profits.

The moonshine teams were trained in lean production techniques, given a small budget, and then set loose. Initially many of the moonshine teams focused on redesigning equipment to produce parts. Underlying this choice was a Boeing study that showed that more than 80% of the parts manufactured for aircraft were less than 12 inches long, and yet the metalworking machinery was huge, inflexible, and could economically produce parts only in large lots.[17]

Soon, empowered moonshine teams were designing their own equipment—small-scale machines that took up little space and used wheels to allow the machines to move around the plant. One team, for example, replaced a large stamping machine that cost six figures and was used to produce L-shaped metal parts in batches of 1,000 with a miniature stamping machine

powered by a small hydraulic motor that could be wheeled around the plant. With the small machine, which cost a couple of thousand dollars, parts could be produced very quickly in small lots, eliminating the need for inventory. They also made a sanding machine and a parts cleaner of equal size. Now the entire process—from stamping the raw material to the finished part—was completed in minutes (instead of hours or days) just by configuring these machines into a small cell and having them serviced by a single person. The small scale and quick turnaround now made it possible to produce these parts just in time, eliminating the need to produce and store inventory.[18]

Another example of a moonshine innovation concerned the process for loading seats onto a plane during assembly. Historically, this was a cumbersome process. After the seats would arrive at Boeing from a supplier, wheels were attached to each seat, and then the seats were delivered to the factory floor in a large container. An overhead crane lifted the container up to the level of the aircraft door. Then the seats were unloaded and rolled into the aircraft, before being installed. The process was repeated until all of the seats had been loaded. For a single-aisle plane, this could take twelve hours. For a wide-bodied jet, it would take much longer. A moonshine team adapted a hay loader to perform the same job (see Exhibit 5). It cost a lot less, delivered seats quickly through the passenger door, and took just two hours, while eliminating the need for cranes.[19]

Multiply the examples given here, and soon you have a very significant impact on production costs: A drill machine was built for 5% of the cost of a full-scale machine from Ingersoll-Rand. Portable routers were built for 0.2% of the cost of a large fixed router. One process that took 2,000 minutes for a 100-part order (20 minutes per part because of setup, machining, and transit) now takes 100 minutes (1 minute per part). Employees building 737 floor beams reduced labor hours by 74%, increased inventory turns from 2 to 18 per year, and reduced manufacturing space by 50%. Employees building the 777 tail cut lead time by 70% and reduced space and work in progress by 50%. Production of parts for landing gear support used to take 32 moves from machine to machine and required 10 months; production now takes 3 moves and 25 days.[20]

In general, Boeing found that it was able to produce smaller lots of parts economically, often from machines that it built itself, which were smaller and cost less than the machines available from outside

EXHIBIT 5

The Converted Hay Loader at Work

vendors. In turn, these innovations enabled Boeing to switch to just-in-time inventory systems and reduce waste. Boeing was also able to save on space. By eliminating large production machinery at its Auburn facility, replacing much of it with smaller, more flexible machines, Boeing was able to free up 1.3 million square feet of space, and sold seven buildings.[21]

In addition to moonshine teams, Boeing adopted other process improvement methodologies, using them when deemed appropriate. Six Sigma quality improvement processes are widely used within Boeing. The most wide-reaching process change, however, was the decision to switch from a static assembly line to a moving line. In traditional aircraft manufacture, planes are docked in angled stalls. Ramps surround each plane, and workers go in and out to find parts and install them. Moving a plane to the next workstation was a complex process. The aircraft had to be down-jacked from its workstation, a powered cart was bought in, the aircraft was towed to the next station, and then it was jacked up. This could take two shifts. A lot of time was wasted bringing parts to a stall and moving a plane from one stall to the next.

In 2001, Boeing introduced a moving assembly line into its Renton plant near Seattle, which manu-

factures the 737 (see Exhibit 6). With a moving line, each aircraft is attached to a "sled" that rides a magnetic strip embedded in the factory floor, pulling the aircraft at a rate of 2 inches per minute, moving past a series of stations where tools and parts arrive at the moment needed, allowing workers to install the proper assemblies. The setup eliminates wandering for tools and parts, as well as expensive tug pulls or crane lifts (just having tools delivered to workstations, rather than having workers fetch them, was found to save twenty to forty-five minutes on every shift). Preassembly tasks are performed on feeder lines. For example, inboard and outboard flaps are assembled on the wing before it arrives for joining to the fuselage.[22]

Like a Toyota assembly line, the moving line can be stopped if a problem arises. Lights are used to indicate the state of the line. A green light indicates a normal work flow; the first sign of a stoppage brings a yellow warning light; and, if the problem isn't solved within fifteen minutes, a purple light indicates that the line has stopped. Each work area and feeder line has its own lights, so there is no doubt where the problem is.[23]

The cumulative effects of these process innovations have been significant. By 2005, assembly time for the 737 had been cut from twenty-two days to just

EXHIBIT 6

The Moving Line

eleven days. In addition, work-in-progress inventory had been reduced by 55 percent and stored inventory by 59 percent.[24] By 2006, all of Boeing's production lines except that for the 747 had shifted from static bays to moving lines. The 747 was expected to shift to moving line when Boeing starts production of the 747-8.

The Super-Jumbo Decisions

In the early 1990s Boeing and Airbus started to contemplate new aircraft to replace Boeing's aging 747. The success of the 747 had given Boeing a monopoly in the market for very large jet aircraft, making the plane one of the most profitable in the jet age. But the basic design dated back to the 1960s, and some believed there might be sufficient demand for a super-jumbo aircraft with as many as 900 seats.

Initially the two companies considered establishing a joint venture to share the costs and risks associated with a developing a super-jumbo aircraft, but Boeing withdrew in 1995, citing costs and uncertain demand prospects. Airbus subsequently concluded that Boeing was never serious about the joint venture, and the discussions were nothing more than a ploy to keep Airbus from developing its own plane.[25]

After Boeing withdrew, Airbus started to talk about offering a competitor to the 747 in 1995. The plane, then dubbed the A3XX, was to be a super jumbo with capacity for over 500 passengers. Indeed, Airbus stated that some versions of the plane might carry as many as 900 passengers. Airbus initially estimated that there would be demand for some 1,400 planes of this size over twenty years, and that development costs would total around $9 billion (estimates ultimately increased to some $15 billion). Boeing's latest 747 offering—the 747-400—could carry around 416 passengers in three classes.

Boeing responded by drafting plans to develop new versions of the 747 family—the 747-500X and the 747-600X. The 747-600X was to have a new (larger) wing, a fuselage almost 50 feet longer than the 747-400, would carry 550 passengers in three classes and have a range of 7,700 miles. The smaller 747-500X would have carried 460 passengers in three classes and had a range of 8,700 miles.

After taking a close look at the market for a super-jumbo replacement to the 747, in early 1997 Boeing announced that it would not proceed with the program. The reasons given for this decision included the limited market and high development costs, which at the time were estimated to be $7 billion. There were also fears that the wider wing span of the new planes would mean that airports would have to redesign some of their gates to take the aircraft. Boeing, McDonnell Douglas (prior to the merger with Boeing), and the major manufacturers of jet engines all forecast demand for about 500 to 750 such aircraft over the next twenty years. Airbus alone forecast demand as high as 1,400 aircraft. Boeing stated that the fragmentation of the market due to the rise of "point-to-point" flights across oceans would limit demand for a super jumbo. Instead of focusing on the super-jumbo category, Boeing stated that it would develop new versions of the 767 and 777 aircraft that could fly up to 9,000 miles and carry as many as 400 passengers.

Airbus, however, continued to push forward with planes to develop the A3XX. In December 2000, with more than fifty orders in hand, the board of EADS, Airbus's parent company, approved development of the plane, which was now dubbed the A380. Development costs at this point were pegged at $12 billion, and the plane was forecast to enter service in 2006 with Singapore Airlines. The A380 was to have two passenger decks, more space per seat, and wider aisles. It would carry 555 passengers in great comfort, something that passengers would appreciate on long transoceanic flights. According to Airbus, the plane would carry up to 35% more passengers than the most popular 747-400 configuration, yet cost per seat would be 15 to 20% lower due to operating efficiencies. Concerns were raised about turnaround time at airport gates for such a large plane, but Airbus stated that dual-boarding bridges and wider aisles meant that turnaround times would be no more than those for the 747-400.

Airbus also stated that the A380 was designed to operate on existing runways and within existing gates. However, London's Heathrow airport found that it had to spend some $450 million to accommodate the A380, widening taxiways and building a baggage reclaim area for the plane. Similarly, eighteen U.S. airports had reportedly spent some $1 billion just to accommodate the A380.[26]

The 787

While Airbus pushed forward with the A380, in March 2001 Boeing announced the development of a radically new aircraft. Dubbed the *sonic cruiser*, the plane would carry 250 passengers 9,000 miles and fly just below the speed of sound, cutting one hour off transatlantic flights and three hours off transpacific flights. To keep down operating costs, the sonic cruiser would be built out of low-weight carbon fiber "composites." Although the announcement created considerable interest in the aviation community, in the wake of the recession that hit the airline industry after September 11, 2001, both Boeing and the airlines became considerably less enthusiastic. In March 2002, the program was cancelled. Instead, Boeing said that it would develop a more conventional aircraft using composite technology. The plane was initially known as the 7E7, with the *E* standing for *efficient* (the plane was renamed the 787 in early 2005).

In April 2004, the 7E7 program was formally launched with an order for fifty aircraft worth $6 billion from All Nippon Airlines of Japan. It was the largest launch order in Boeing's history. The 7E7 was a twin-aisle, wide-bodied, two-engine plane designed to carry 200 to 300 passengers up to 8,500 miles, making the 7E7 well suited for long-haul, point-to-point flights. The range exceeded all but the longest range plane in the 777 family, and the 7E7 could fly 750 miles more than Airbus's closest competitor, the mid-sized A330-200. With a fuselage built entirely out of composites, the aircraft was lighter and would use 20% less fuel than existing aircraft of comparable size.

The plane was also designed with passenger comfort in mind. The seats would be wider, as would the aisles, and the windows were larger than in existing aircraft. The plane would be pressurized at 6,000 feet altitude, as opposed to 8,000 feet, which is standard industry practice. Airline cabin humidity was typically kept at 10% to avoid moisture buildup and corrosion, but composites don't corrode, so humidity would be closer to 20 to 30%.[27]

Initial estimates suggested that the jet would cost some $7 to $8 billion to develop and enter service in 2008. Boeing decided to outsource more work for the 787 than on any other aircraft to date. Some 35% of the plane's fuselage and wing structure would be built by Boeing. The trio of Japanese companies that worked on the 767 and 777—Mitsubishi Heavy Industries, Kawasaki Heavy Industries, and Fuji Heavy Industries—would build another 35%, and some 26% would be built by Italian companies, particularly Alenia.[28] For the first time, Boeing asked its major suppliers to bear some of the development costs for the aircraft.

The plane was to be assembled at Boeing's wide-bodied plant in Everett, Washington. Large subassemblies were to be built by major suppliers and then shipped to Everett for final assembly. The idea was to "snap together" the parts in Everett in three days, cutting down on total assembly time. To speed up transportation, Boeing would adopt air freight as its major transportation method for many components.

Airbus's initial response was to dismiss Boeing's claims of cost savings as inconsequential. They pointed out that even if the 787 used less fuel than the A330, that was equivalent to just 4% of total operating costs.[29] However, even by Airbus's calculations, as fuel prices starting to accelerate, the magnitude of the savings rose. Moreover, Boeing quickly started to snag some significant orders for the 787. In 2004, Boeing booked 56 orders for the 787, and in 2005, some 232 orders. Another 85 orders were booked in the first nine months of 2006 for a running total of 373—well beyond breakeven point.

In December 2004, Airbus announced that it would develop a new model, the A350, to compete directly with the 787. The planes were to be long-haul, twin-aisle jets, seating 200 to 300 passengers, and constructed of composites. The order flow, however, was slow, with airlines complaining that the A350 did not match the Boeing 787 on operating efficiency, range, or passenger comfort. Airbus went back to the drawing board and, in mid-2006, announced a new version of the A350, the A350 XWB (for "extra wide body"). Airbus estimates that the A350 XWB will cost $10 billion to develop and enter service in 2012, several years behind the 787. The two-engine A350 XWB will carry between 250 and 375 passengers and fly up to 8,500 miles. The largest versions of the A350 XWB will be competing directly with the Boeing 777, not the 787. Like the 787, the A350 XWB will be built primarily of composite materials. The extra wide body is designed to enhance passenger comfort. To finance the A350 XWB, Airbus stated that it would probably seek launch aid from Germany, France, Spain, and the UK, all countries where major parts of Airbus are based.[30]

Trade Tensions

It is impossible to discuss the global aerospace industry without touching on trade issues. Over the last three decades, both Boeing and Airbus have charged that their competitor benefited unfairly from government subsidies. Until 2001 Airbus functioned as a consortium of four European aircraft manufacturers: one British (20.0% ownership stake), one French (37.9% ownership), one German (37.9% ownership), and

one Spanish (4.2% ownership). In the 1980s and early 1990s Boeing maintained that subsidies from these nations allow Airbus to set unrealistically low prices, to offer concessions and attractive financing terms to airlines, to write off development costs, and to use state-owned airlines to obtain orders. According to a study by the U.S. Department of Commerce, Airbus received more than $13.5 billion in government subsidies between 1970 and 1990 ($25.9 billion if commercial interest rates are applied). Most of these subsidies were in the form of loans at below-market interest rates and tax breaks. The subsidies financed research and development and provided attractive financing terms for Airbus's customers. Airbus responded by pointing out that Boeing had benefited for years from hidden U.S. government subsidies, particularly Pentagon R&D grants.

In 1992, the two sides appeared to reach an agreement that put to rest their long-standing trade dispute. The 1992 pact, which was negotiated by the EU on behalf of the four member states, limited direct government subsidies to 33% of the total costs of developing a new aircraft and specified that such subsidies had to be repaid with interest within seventeen years. The agreement also limited indirect subsidies, such as government-supported military research that has applications to commercial aircraft, to 3% of a country's annual total commercial aerospace revenues or 4% of commercial aircraft revenues of any single company in that country. Although Airbus officials stated that the controversy had now been resolved, Boeing officials argued that they would still be competing for years against subsidized products.

The trade dispute heated up again in 2004 when Airbus announced the first version of the A350 to compete against Boeing's 787. What raised a red flag for the U.S. government was a sign from Airbus that it would apply for $1.7 billion in launch aid to help fund the development of the A350. As far as the United States was concerned, this was too much. In late 2004, U.S. Trade Representative Robert Zoellick issued a statement formally renouncing the 1992 agreement and calling for an end to launch subsidies. According to Zoellick, "since its creation 35 years ago, some Europeans have justified subsidies to Airbus as necessary to support an infant industry. If that rationalization were ever valid, its time has long passed. Airbus now sells more large civil aircraft than Boeing." Zoellick went on to claim that Airbus has received some $3.7 billion in launch aid for the A380 plus another $2.8 billion in indirect subsidies including $1.7 billion in taxpayer-funded infrastructure improvements for a total of $6.5 billion.

Airbus shot back that Boeing too continued to enjoy lavish subsidies and that the company had received some $12 billion from NASA to develop technology, much of which had found its way into commercial jet aircraft. The Europeans also contended that Boeing would receive as much as $3.2 billion in tax breaks from Washington State, where the 787 is to be assembled, and more than $1 billion in loans from the Japanese government to three Japanese suppliers, who will build over one-third of the 787. Moreover, Airbus was quick to point out that a trade war would not benefit either side and that Airbus purchased some $6 billion a year in supplies from companies in the United States.

In January 2005, both the United States and the EU agreed to freeze direct subsidies to the two aircraft makers while talks continued. However, in May 2005 news reports suggested, and Airbus confirmed, that the jet maker had applied to four EU governments for launch aid for the A350, and that the British government would announce some $700 million in aid at the Paris Air Show in mid-2005. Simultaneously, the EU offered to cut launch aid for the A350 by 30%. Dissatisfied, the U.S. side decided that the talks were going nowhere, and on May 31 the United States formally filed a request with the World Trade Organization (WTO) for the establishment of a dispute resolution panel to resolve the issues. The EU quickly responded, filing a countersuit with the WTO claiming that U.S. aid to Boeing exceeded the terms set out in the 1992 agreement. The dispute is currently before the WTO.[31]

Although the decision to scrap the original design of the A350 took some of the heat out of the dispute, Airbus is expected to ask for launch aid for the redesigned A350 XWB.

The Next Chapter

Huge financial bets have been placed on very different visions of the future of airline travel: Airbus with the A380 and Boeing with the 787. Airbus has hedged its bets by announcing the A350 XWB, but will this be too little too late? Moreover, there are signs of production turmoil at Airbus. Orders for the A380 have stalled. In mid-2006, the company announced that deliveries for the aircraft would be delayed by six months while the company dealt with "production issues" arising from

problems installing the wiring bundles in the A380. Estimates suggest that the delay would cost Airbus some $2.6 billion over the next four years.[32] Within months, Airbus had revised the expected delay to eighteen months and stated that the number of A380s it now needed to sell to break even had increased from 250 to 420 aircraft. The company also stated that due to production problems, it would be able to deliver only 84 A380 planes by 2010, compared to an original estimate of 420.[33] In responses, several significant launch customers for the A380 were said to be reconsidering their purchase decisions. United Parcel Service, which has 10 A380 cargo planes on order, was reportedly considering switching to the Boeing 747-8, Boeing's latest offering in the venerable 747 family.

Boeing quietly launched the 747-8 program in November 2005. This plane will be a completely redesigned version of the 747 and will incorporate many of the technological advances developed for the 787, including significant use of composites. It will be offered in both a freighter and intercontinental passenger configuration that will carry 467 passengers in a three-seat configuration and have a range of 8,000 miles (the 747-400 can carry 416 passengers). The 747-8 will also use the fuel-efficient engines developed for the 787 and will have the same cockpit configuration as the 737, 777, and 787. Development costs are estimated to be around $4 billion. By October 2006, Boeing had orders for 44 787-8 freighters, but none for the passenger planes. However, some analysts speculated that with the A380 mired in delays, the 747-8 passenger configuration might begin to garner more orders.

Not all is smooth sailing at Boeing. The company experienced some problems with suppliers for the 787, who have fallen behind schedule designing some components for the project. As of late 2006, Boeing was insisting that the 787 was still on schedule. Some analysts, however, are concerned that this might be a sign of things to come and that the complexity associated with coordinating a diverse base of suppliers might lead to delays in the 787.

Complicating issues, both Airbus and Boeing have been through some changes in key management over the last few years. At Boeing, CEO Phil Condit resigned in late 2003 after it was revealed that the company's CFO, Mike Sears, had hired a key department of defense procurement officer in return for her backing of a huge order for air force tankers based on the 767. Sears was subsequently prosecuted and sent to jail. The Sears scandal was only the latest in a number that Boeing executives had become embroiled in during the early 2000s. Condit's resignation was widely taken to indicate that the board felt that a new CEO was needed to clean house. Condit was replaced by Harry Stonecipher, who was CEO of McDonnell Douglas when it was acquired by Boeing and later president of Boeing. Stonecipher resigned fifteen months later when it was revealed that he had an affair with a subordinate and communicated with her using the company's email service. Stonecipher was replaced by Jim McNerney, who moved to Boeing from the CEO position at 3M. Prior to joining 3M, McNerney had run the aircraft engine business at General Electric. McNerney was widely viewed as a skilled manager who had brought the operating discipline that GE is famous for to 3M. He was expected to do the same at Boeing, pushing the company to continue to pursue various productivity initiatives, such as lean production, Six Sigma, and global sourcing.

At Airbus, following the announcement of the delay in A380 production, there was pressure on Noel Forgeard, the CEO of EADS, Airbus's parent company, to resign. Forgeard refused, although Gustav Humbert, the CEO of Airbus, did offer to step down. After a three-week crisis, the board of EADS took matters into its own hands and fired both Forgeard and Humbert. They were replaced by Louis Gallois, a Frenchman who once ran an aerospace company that was acquired by EADS, and Christian Streiff, the former number 2 at Saint Gobain, the French glassmaker.

With new management in place at both companies, the focus is on the unfolding competitive battle. Can Airbus make money on the A380, and if it does, will it gain a monopoly that rivals Boeing's 747 dynasty? Will the 787 live up to its promise and become the right plane for a new era of global travel? Can Airbus come back at Boeing with its new version of the A350, the A350 XWB? And what of the ongoing trade dispute? How will this impact on the long-running dog fight between the two companies?

ENDNOTES

1. http://www.boeing.com/ (accessed September 2006).
2. http://www.airbus.com/en/ (accessed September 2006).
3. J. Palmer, "Big Bird," *Barron's*, December 19, 2005, pages 25–29; http://www.yeald.com/Yeald/a/33941/both_a380_and_787_have_bright_futures.html.
4. G. J. Steven, "The Learning Curve; From Aircraft to Space Craft," *Management Accounting*, May 1999, pages 64–66.
5. D. Gates, "Boeing 7E7 Watch: Familiar Suppliers Make Short List," *Seattle Times*.
6. The figures are from the International Airline Travelers Association (IATA).
7. IATA, "2006 Loss Forecast Drops to US $1.7 Billion," Press Release, August 31, 2006.
8. "Turbulent Skies: Low Cost Airlines," *The Economist*, July 10, 2004, pages 68–72; "Silver Linings, Darkening Clouds," *The Economist*, March 27, 2004, pages 90–92.
9. Data from the Air Transport Association at www.airlines.org.
10. IATA, "2006 Loss Forecast Drops to US $1.7 Billion," Press Release, August 31, 2006.
11. Boeing, Current Market Outlook, 2006. Archived on Boeing's website.
12. Airbus, http://www.airbus.com/en/myairbus/global_market_forcast.html.
13. Presentation by Randy Baseler, vice president of Boeing Commercial Airplanes, given at the Farnborough Air Show, July 2006. Archived at http://www.boeing.com/nosearch/exec_pres/CMO.pdf.
14. This material is drawn from an earlier version of the Boeing case written by Charles W. L. Hill. See C. W. L. Hill, "The Boeing Corporation: Commercial Aircraft Operations," in C. W. L. Hill and G. R. Jones, *Strategic Management*, third edition (Boston: Houghton Mifflin, 1995). Much of Boeing's history is described in R. J. Sterling, *Legend and Legacy* (St. Martin's Press, New York, 1992).
15. S. Browder, "A Fierce Downdraft at Boeing," *Business Week*, January 26, 1988, page 34.
16. M. A. Cusumano, *The Japanese Automobile Industry* (Cambridge, Mass.: Harvard University Press, 1989); Ohno Taiichi, *Toyota Production System* (Cambridge, Mass.: Productivity Press, 1990); J. P. Womack, D. T. Jones, and D. Roos, *The Machine That Changed the World* (New York: Rawson Associates, 1990).
17. J. Gillie, "Lean Manufacturing Could Save Boeing's Auburn Washington Plant," *Knight Ridder Tribune Business News*, May 6, 2002, page 1.
18. P. V. Arnold, "Boeing Knows Lean," *MRO Today*, February 2002.
19. Boeing Press Release, "Converted Farm Machine Improves Production Process," July 1, 2003.
20. P. V. Arnold, "Boeing Knows Lean," *MRO Today*, February 2002. Also "Build in Lean: Manufacturing for the Future," Boeing, http://www.boeing.com/aboutus/environment/create_build.htm; J. Gillie, "Lean Manufacturing Could Save Boeing's Auburn Washington Plant," *Knight Ridder Tribune Business News*, May 6, 2002, page 1.
21. J. Gillie, "Lean Manufacturing Could Save Boeing's Auburn Washington Plant," *Knight Ridder Tribune Business News*, May 6, 2002, page 1.
22. P. V. Arnold, "Boeing Knows Lean," *MRO Today*, February 2002.
23. M. Mecham, "The Lean, Green Line," *Aviation Week*, July 19, 2004, pages 144–148.
24. Boeing Press Release, "Boeing Reduces 737 Airplane's Final Assembly Time by 50 Percent," January 27, 2005.
25. "A Phony War," *The Economist*, May 5, 2001, pages 56–57.
26. J. D. Boyd, "Building Room for Growth," *Traffic World*, August 7, 2006, page 1.
27. W. Sweetman, "Boeing, Boeing, Gone," *Popular Science*, June 2004, page 97.
28. Anonymous, "Who Will Supply the Parts?" *Seattle Times*, June 15, 2003.
29. W. Sweetman, "Boeing, Boeing, Gone," *Popular Science*, June 2004, page 97.
30. D. Michaels and J. L. Lunsford, "Airbus Chief Reveals Plans for New Family of Jetliners," *Wall Street Journal*, July 18, 2006, page A3.
31. J. Reppert-Bismarck and W. Echikson, "EU Countersues Over U.S. Aid to Boeing," *Wall Street Journal*, June 1, 2005, page A2; United States Trade Representative Press Release, "United States Takes Next Steps in Airbus WTO litigation," May 30, 2005.
32. Anonymous, "Airbus Agonistes," *Wall Street Journal*, September 6, 2006, page A20.
33. Anonymous, "Forecast Dimmer for Profit on Airbus' A380," *Seattle Times*, October 20, 2006, Web Edition.

The Rise of Airbus, 1970–2005

This case was prepared by Dr. Isaac Cohen, San Jose State University.

For 16 consecutive months Airbus did not sell a single aircraft. As sales came to a halt in 1976, the number of "whitetails"—unsold aircraft sitting on the factory runway (their tails painted white with no airline insignia)—exceeded the consortium's total sales. Airbus was losing so much money at the time that the consortium's German partner urged Airbus management to stop production altogether. The consortium's French partner disagreed, and persuaded the German partner to keep the production line moving.

Keeping the production line moving saved the Airbus program. As sales rebounded in 1977, production shot up, the consortium gained new customers, and Airbus emerged as a global aircraft manufacturer. Over a period of 30 years and throughout the tenure of three CEOs—Bernard Lathiere (1975–1985), Jean Pierson (1985–1998), and Noel Forgeard (1998–2005)—Airbus has transformed itself from a distant competitor with an uncertain future to a leading commercial aircraft maker ahead of Boeing.

Bernard Lathiere put in place the three pillars that together made up Airbus's winning strategy. He developed families of planes with common design features—or commonalties—that ran across several related models; he introduced innovations in aircraft electronics, materials, and design which turned Airbus into a technological leader; and he devised a global sales strategy that singled out Asia as the world's fastest growing and most promising aircraft market. Jean Pierson implemented cost-cutting

This case was presented in the October 2005 meeting of the North American Case Research Association at North Falmouth, Cape Cod, Massachusetts. Dr. Cohen is grateful to the San Jose State University for its support.

measures that lowered Airbus's dependency on government subsidies, diversified Airbus's product line, and signed a landmark bilateral agreement that limited both Airbus's dependency on European governments' subsidies, and Boeing/McDonnell Douglas's dependency on indirect U.S. government funds.

As Jean Pierson retired in 1998, Noel Forgeard was selected CEO. Forgeard's most challenging task was reorganizing Airbus structurally, transforming the consortium into a stand-alone limited-liability company. Incorporated in 2001 in France, Airbus had become profitable under Forgeard, generating rates of return on sales of 7% in 2003, and nearly 10% in 2004. Under Forgeard's leadership, Airbus's total revenues jumped from $13 billion to $25 billion between 1998 and 2004. In 2003, for the first time ever, Airbus beat Boeing on total deliveries, and for the fourth time in five years, Airbus booked a larger number of aircraft orders than Boeing.[1]

Despite Airbus's remarkable achievements, Forgeard could not count on the continual prosperity of the company because Airbus faced several new challenges. Partly as a result of a steep rise in fuel prices that lowered airline profitability, and partly as a consequence of repeated threats of terrorist attacks in the skies, the worldwide demand for large commercial jets declined, and a number of major air carriers (customers of both Airbus and Boeing) cancelled previous orders. On the one side, Airbus experienced growing difficulties in selling its new 600-seat A380 "Superjumbo." On the other, Airbus faced a new threat: Boeing had just launched a brand new fuel-efficient aircraft, the 250-seat 787, in an attempt to leapfrog Airbus, yet again.

What should Forgeard do? Should Forgeard follow the strategies implemented by his predecessors in order to consolidate Airbus's competitive position relative to its arch-rival Boeing? Should he, instead, revise some of these policies? Or should he uncover whole new strategies in an attempt to weather the downturn and stay ahead of Boeing?

To assess Forgeard's strategic choices, the case looks back at Airbus's 35-year history.

The Commercial Aircraft Industry

Commercial aircraft manufacturing was an industry of enormous risks where failure was the norm, not the exception. The number of large commercial jet makers had been reduced from four in the early 1980s—Boeing, McDonnell Douglas, Airbus, and Lockheed—to two in late 1990s, turning the industry into a duopoly and pitting the two survivors—Boeing and Airbus—one against the other. One reason why aircraft manufacturers so often failed was the huge cost of product development.

Developing a new jetliner required an upfront investment of several billions of dollars, a lead time of five to six years from launch to first delivery, and the ability to sustain a negative cash flow throughout the development phase. The Boeing 747, for example, cost $1 billion to develop, the Boeing 767 cost $1.5 billion, the Airbus A320 cost $2.5 billion, the Airbus A330/A340 $3.5 billion, the Boeing 777 $5.5 billion, and the total cost of developing the Airbus A380 in the 2000s was estimated at about $15 billion.[2] Typically, to break even on an entirely new jetliner, aircraft manufacturers needed to sell a minimum of 400 planes and at least 50 planes per year.[3] Only a few commercial airplane programs had ever made money.

The price of an aircraft reflected its high development costs. New model prices were based on the average cost of producing 300 to 400 planes, not a single plane. Aircraft pricing embodied the principle of learning by doing, the so-called "learning curve":[4] workers steadily improved their skills during the assembly process, and as a result, labor cost fell as the number of planes produced rose.

The high and increasing cost of product development prompted aircraft manufacturers to utilize subcontracting as a risk-sharing strategy. For the 747, the 767, and the 777, the Boeing Company required subcontractors to share a substantial part of the airplane's development costs. Airbus did the same with its own later models, the A320, A330, A340, and A380. Risk sharing subcontractors performed detailed design

work, manufactured parts and components, and assembled subsections of the new plane, while airframe integrators (i.e., aircraft manufacturers) designed the aircraft, integrated its systems and equipment, assembled the entire plane, marketed it, and provided customer support for 20 to 30 years.[5]

Neither Airbus nor Boeing nor any other postwar commercial aircraft manufacturer produced jet engines. A risky and costly venture, engine building had become a highly specialized business. Aircraft manufacturers worked closely with engine makers—General Electric, Pratt and Whitney, and Rolls Royce—to set engine performance standards. In most cases, new airplanes were offered with a choice of engines. Over time, the technology of engine building had become so complex and demanding that it took longer to develop an engine than an aircraft. During the life of a jetliner, the price of the engines and their replacement parts was equal to the entire price of the airplane.[6]

A new model aircraft was normally designed around an engine, not the other way around. As engine performance improved, airframes were redesigned to exploit the engine's new capabilities. The most practical way to do so was to stretch the fuselage and add more seats in the cabin. Aircraft manufacturers deliberately designed flexibility into the airplane so that future engine improvements could facilitate later stretching. Hence the importance of the "family concept" in aircraft design, and hence the reason why Boeing as well as Airbus introduced families of planes made up of derivative jetliners built around a basic model, not single, standardized models.[7]

The commercial aircraft industry, additionally, gained from technological innovations in two other industries. More than any other manufacturing industry, aircraft construction benefited from advances in material applications and electronics. The development of metallic and non-metallic composite materials played a key role in improving airframe and engine performance. On the one hand, composite materials that combined light weight and great strength were utilized by aircraft manufacturers; on the other, heat-resisting alloys that could tolerate temperatures of up to 3,000 degrees were used by engine makers. Similarly, advances in electronics revolutionized avionics. The increasing use of semiconductors by aircraft manufacturers facilitated the miniaturization of cockpit instruments, and more importantly, it enhanced the use of computers for aircraft communication, navigation, instrumentation, and testing.[8] The use of computers contributed, in addition, to the design, manufacture, and assembly of new model aircraft.

Given the high cost of introducing technological innovations, commercial aircraft makers were unable to survive without government support. In the United States in the past, military contracts were extremely beneficial to commercial aircraft makers, most notably Boeing and McDonnell Douglas, especially insofar as expensive technologies like jet propulsion and swept wings were concerned. Since the mid-1960s, however, U.S. government support to commercial aircraft projects had declined, yet the Department of Defense continued funding research with potential military applications. Similarly, NASA had provided some direct funding to commercial jet makers like Boeing in recent years, but again, only for technology development, not product development. In Europe, the governments of France, Germany, Britain, and Spain furnished most of the working capital required for the development and production of Airbus's early models in the form of low-interest loans the consortium was expected to repay from future sales. Since the early 1990s, nonetheless, European governments' assistance to Airbus had declined.[9]

A final factor that influenced the dynamics of the aircraft industry was airline deregulation. Deregulation of the U.S. airlines in 1978 resulted in a substantial domestic increase in air travel, intense air-fare competition among carriers, the entry of new low-cost, low-capacity airlines into the industry, and the growing utilization of the hub-and-spoke system by the major carriers. The explosion in air travel led to a steep growth in demand for new aircraft of all kinds, yet the proliferation of low-cost, short-haul airline companies (i.e., Southwest Airlines, American West, Jet Blue), combined with the extensive use of hubs by the large carriers, brought about an increased demand for short-range, single-aisle airplanes like the Boeing 737 and the Airbus A320. Additionally, the deregulatory environment shifted the focus of airline competition from performance to cost and from service to price, as Frank Shrontz, Boeing CEO between 1988 and 1996, observed: "In the old days airlines were infatuated with technology for its own sake. Today the rationale for purchasing a new plane is cost savings and profitability."[10]

Outside the United States, international air travel experienced progressive deregulation during the 1980s and 1990s. By the early 2000s, the nations of Western Europe, Australia, and Japan had removed restrictive air travel regulations from their domestic as well as international markets. In 2001, about one-half of all worldwide air travel took place within a competitive deregulated environment, and by 2010 two-thirds of all air travel was expected to take place within a free market environment.[11] Such a trend was likely to encourage foreign (i.e., non-U.S.) air carriers to become more cost-conscious and more profit-oriented in the future. In all travel markets, in short—the U.S. domestic, international, and foreign markets—the economic deregulation of airline travel increased competition among aircraft manufacturers.

The Early History of Airbus

Airbus's early history dates back to the 1960s. Unable to develop a commercially viable passenger jet during the post-war years, French aircraft manufacturers arrived at the conclusion that the only way they could compete effectively against American jet makers was by forming an alliance with other aircraft manufacturers and their governments. Accordingly, during the Paris Air Show of June 1965, French aircraft executives initiated a series of informal meetings between representatives of the major European airline carriers and aircraft makers to discuss the possibilities of building a European short- to medium-range 250- to 300-seat wide-body jet called "airbus." Such a plane, the French officials believed, would meet the particular needs of the expanding European air travel market, and challenge America's global domination in the skies. At the time, American aircraft makers were busy launching three entirely new families of wide-body jets, the Boeing 747, the McDonnell Douglas DC-10, and the Lockheed L1011, and therefore European aircraft makers, led by the French, sought to act quickly to revive Europe's declining commercial aircraft industry before it was too late.[12]

During the next two years, representatives of the major French, British, and German aircraft companies lobbied their governments for financial assistance in support of the Airbus project. In 1967, government officials representing the three European nations signed an agreement approving "[t]he joint development and production of an airbus . . . [f]or the purpose of strengthening European cooperation in the field of aviation technology, and . . . promoting economic and technological progress in Europe." The approved Airbus model was the A300. The project was launched shortly thereafter, but not a single A300 was ordered by any air carrier during 1967, 1968, and 1969. With no orders in sight, the British government was reluctant to keep on investing in the risky venture, and in 1969 announced its decision to withdraw from the project (it rejoined ten years later). The French and German governments went ahead and formalized their partnership in 1970, creating Airbus Industrie—a cooperative partnership (or consortium) registered under French law as a "Grouping of Economic Interests" (GEI). A year later, in 1971, Spanish aircraft manufacturers associated with Construcciones Aeronauticas SA (CASA) joined Airbus Industries as a junior partner. The consortium's ownership shares were now as follows: France's aircraft maker Aerospatiale 47.9%, Germany's aircraft manufacturer Deutsche Airbus 47.9%, and Spain's CASA 4.2%.[13]

Throughout its first five years of operation, Airbus Industrie struggled as total orders fell well below the minimum number set by the partners as a precondition for launching the project. Initially, Air France, Lufthansa, and Iberia—the three national airlines representing the sponsoring governments— were reluctant to purchase the A300, yet, in the end, sustained government pressure persuaded these carriers to place orders (Iberia management, it should be noted, cancelled its early orders a few months later).[14] At the time Bernard Lathiere took the helms of Airbus—February 1975—total orders of the A300 numbered 20 units,[15] total deliveries averaged four aircraft a year,[16] and one contemporary writer concluded: "Airbus appeared to be a typical European airliner—well designed, well built, and a commercial flop."[17]

Infancy: Bernard Lathiere's Airbus, 1975–1985

Lathiere's tenure as Airbus's chief executive began with the crisis of 1975–1977. In 1975—the year referred to by Airbus executives as the consortium's "black year"—Airbus sold just one A300 aircraft while Boeing recorded a total sale of over 100 aircraft. As Airbus's sales came to a standstill, a growing criticism of the high cost of the program in the German Parliament prompted the German government to

intervene directly with Airbus management, and press Lathiere to halt production altogether. Backed by the French government and other French aircraft executives, Lathiere rejected the pressure to stop the line and decided, instead, to cut production from one aircraft to half an aircraft per month, keep the line moving, and wait a little longer for market conditions to improve.[18]

Lathiere's critical decision set Airbus on the road to recovery and success. During the three-year period, 1977–1979, Airbus sales exploded. By the end of 1979, Airbus sold over 250 planes to 32 different airlines, and held a 26% share in the global market for commercial aircraft. In 1981, as in 1979, Airbus sold a larger number of wide-body commercial planes than either Boeing or the McDonnell Douglas Corporation.[19] Airbus's sudden success prompted the British to join the consortium as full members in 1979. Under the new partnership agreement, the recently formed British Aerospace Corporation owned 20% of Airbus, Aerospatiale 37.9%, Deutsche Airbus 37.9%, and CASA 4.2%.[20]

Bringing the British back in, Lathiere moved on to consolidate the foundations under which Airbus would grow and prosper. Working closely with other Airbus executives, Lathiere devised and implemented a series of strategies that touched upon every important function of the company, including manufacturing, marketing, sales, product development, and R&D.

Technological Leadership

"You cannot compete with the dominant player if you don't offer something different," Roger Beteille, one of Airbus's co-founders, had famously said. To persuade the major airlines to switch to a new supplier, Airbus had to differentiate itself from Boeing and other aircraft manufacturers by incorporating the most advanced technologies into its planes. Airbus's technological innovations focused on three areas: materials applications, flight control systems, and aerodynamics. Under Lathiere's direction, Airbus produced the A300 model, developed and produced the A310, and designed the A320 model. On the A310, Airbus introduced a high-performance, aerodynamically efficient wing with a distinct twist at the root. To reduce total aircraft weight, Airbus increased the use of composite materials (particularly carbon fiber) in making the A310 tail surfaces and vertical fins. On the A320, Airbus introduced a computerized system of flight controls. The world's first fly-by-wire commercial aircraft, the A320 was controlled by a pilot transmitting commands to the rudder and flaps electronically, not mechanically. The fly-by-wire technology replaced pulleys, cables, and pedals with electronic signals transmitted by wire, and as such, reduced the A320's empty weight, and at the same time, improved its efficiency in cruise.[21]

Families of Planes

Boeing was the first company to use the family concept in aircraft design. Airbus took the Boeing approach several steps forward and made the concept the foundations of its manufacturing and marketing strategy.

A family of planes was made up of derivative jetliners built around a basic model. Since all derivatives of a given model shared maintenance, training, and operation procedures, as well as replacement parts and components, the use of such derivative airplanes to serve different markets enabled airline carriers to cut costs. Airbus used the family concept in two ways. First, it produced and marketed derivative jetliners with varying seat capacities and travel ranges, all belonging to a single family. Second, Airbus introduced substantial design commonalities across the entire range of its models, not just members of a single family, thus providing airline customers with additional sources of savings. Airbus's aggressive application of the family concept in aircraft design dates back to the 1970s and 1980s. Under the direction of Bernard Lathiere, Airbus introduced shared design commonalities among the A300 and A310 models, on the one hand, and among the A300/A310 and A320 families, on the other.[22]

Decentralized Production

Boeing relied heavily on subcontracting as a risk sharing strategy since at least the early 1950s. Airbus took subcontracting several steps further and made it a cornerstone of its manufacturing strategy.

Boeing built some parts of its own aircraft in the company's assembly plants and subcontracted other parts to outside suppliers. On the 747, for instance, Boeing built the wings and flight deck—as well as sections of the fuselage—and subcontracted the remaining 70% of the assembly work.[23] Airbus Industrie, by contrast, neither owned assembly plants, nor did the consortium produce any aircraft parts at all. On the contrary, the consortium subcontracted the entire assembly of any given model to its four shareholding companies, Aerospatiale, Deutsche Airbus, British Aerospace, and CASA.

During the aircraft's design and development phase, the four Airbus partner companies competed over particular work, and during the production phase, each partner performed its own share of work. Different parts of the aircraft were thus manufactured quite independently of each other, and were brought together for final assembly in Toulouse, France. Typically, on the A300, the British built the wings; the German assembled the front, rear, and (in part) center section of the fuselage; the Spanish produced the tail; and the French constructed the nose, flight deck, and control systems. The French additionally were responsible for the final assembly of the aircraft, a work performed at Aerospatiale's assembly plant in Toulouse. Stationed at Airbus headquarters in Toulouse, and spending much of his time traveling, Bernard Lathiere coordinated the entire program.[24]

Centralized Marketing

Lathiere's most important responsibility, however, was marketing and sales, not production. A former government official turned salesman, and a determined manager who often negotiated aircraft deals personally, Lathiere devised two distinctly different strategies that helped Airbus compete successfully with American aircraft manufacturers. He first targeted large segments of the emerging global markets where airline customers were willing to experiment with Airbus models. He next focused on the mature American market and offered U.S. airline customers exceedingly attractive financial incentives.

To begin with, Lathiere sought to penetrate those markets whose customers showed little loyalty to American aircraft manufacturers. Located in Asia and the Middle East, along the so-called "trans-Asian Silk Route" that ran westward from the Philippines to Europe, these markets were made up of small nationally owned airline carriers whose fleets were fast expanding. The strategic importance of dominating the Asian-Middle Eastern markets was underscored by two widely accepted industry estimates: first, a single aircraft sale was expected to generate further revenues in the form of product support for 18 to 20 years, and second, an initial aircraft sale amounted to only one-fourth to one-third of the value of the follow up orders.[25]

To persuade small neighboring airlines to purchase Airbus planes, Lathiere pointed out that the commonalities shared by Airbus models—the A300 and A310—reduced their operating cost. Such commonalities [Lathiere noted] could help Airbus's customers gain access to each other's spare parts, maintenance services, and crew training programs, and thereby benefit from substantial cost savings. Since no airline wished to become an "orphan" in its region (a carrier flying a particular type of jet not used by other carriers in the region), and since neighboring airlines often influenced each other's aircraft choice, Airbus's early success in the Far East led to subsequent successes all along the Euro-Asian Silk Road.[26]

During the three-year period 1977–1979, Airbus sold the A300/A310 to the national airlines of India, Korea, Malaysia, Indonesia, the Philippines, Singapore, Thailand, Pakistan, and Iran. Airbus sold its models both as replacements to older Boeing jets and as additional planes, practically shutting Boeing out of these markets. Following its successes in the Far East, Airbus moved on to supply the fleets of three Middle Eastern (Kuwait, Lebanon, Saudi Arabia) carriers, but this time Boeing fought back, offering these Middle Eastern airlines its newest aircraft—the wide-body B-767—as an alternative to the A300 and A310 models. "The[re] were three big battles and we won them all," Lathiere recalled.[27] By the early 1980s, the Silk Road network of Airbus customers was completed.

Airbus's successful breakthrough into the American market occurred in 1978. Eastern Airlines, a major U.S. air carrier experiencing financial difficulties, announced that it would buy 23 A300s with an option for 9 more in a deal valued a total of $778 million. Lathiere offered Eastern an unusually attractive financial deal. One element of Lathiere's offer was Airbus's "fly and try" proposal whereby Eastern could fly the aircraft for six months before buying it. Another element pertained to the deal's financial risk. To help Eastern pay for the aircraft, Airbus obtained low-interest loans from private banks and persuaded the French and German governments to guarantee these loans. As it happened, the performance of the A300/A310 in the U.S. skies—the world's busiest travel market—exceeded expectations, and Airbus had gained worldwide recognition.[28]

But Lathiere's breakthrough into the American market led to his eventual downfall. An industry downturn during 1984 left 14 "whitetail" aircraft on Airbus's tarmac at Toulouse, and Lathiere was desperate to sell them. Again, he targeted a struggling carrier—the Pan American World Airways—sending a team of 40 Airbus salespeople to negotiate the deal. Pan Am was already talking to Boeing at the time, but in the end, Airbus won the order. Although the full details of the Airbus-Pan Am $2.5 billion deal were not disclosed, one thing had become clear early on: rather than selling the planes, Airbus leased them to Pan Am, thereby undertaking the main financial risk itself. Pan Am, in turn, kept the entire transaction off the balance sheet, taking hardly any risk at all.[29]

The Pan Am deal evoked a great deal of opposition among Airbus's partner companies to Lathiere's sales strategy. When the German, British, and French partners became aware of the terms of the deal, they demanded Lathiere's resignation. Building planes without receiving orders, and selling planes with no regard to costs, let alone profits, was no longer acceptable to the consortium's partners.[30] Lathiere, consequently, stepped down in April 1985.

Growth: Jean Pierson's Airbus, 1985–1998

Replacing Lathiere in 1985, Jean Pierson led the consortium for 13 years. Pierson paved the way for the future transformation of Airbus from a government-supported partnership to a publicly owned company. An engineer by training and a gifted salesman, Pierson focused on improving Airbus's financial results, cutting costs, increasing sales, phasing out subsidies, and developing new planes. A ruthless executive with a blunt management style, Pierson turned Airbus profitable for the first time in 1995, following two decades of losses that amounted to $8 billion.[31]

Product Development

Under the leadership of Jean Pierson, Airbus embarked on two aircraft programs. First, it planned, designed, produced, and sold the A330/A340 family of planes. Second, it planned the development of the A380 program.

The Airbus A330 was designed to be powered by two engines, carry about 300 passengers in two-aisle configurations, and fly over medium- to long-range routes. A replacement for the aging A300, the A330 competed with the McDonnell Douglas's wide-body three-engine DC-10, and the Boeing's B-767. The A340 was designed to be powered by four engines and fly over "long thin" routes of up to 15,000 kilometers. Airbus's first four-engine aircraft, the A340, was intended to compete with the Boeing 747 over long-range routes where the demand for air travel was not sufficiently heavy to require the seating capacity of the B747.[32]

The design of the A330 and A340 embodied a remarkable degree of commonalities shared by other Airbus models. The A330/A340 fuselage was almost identical to that of the original A300, and the design of the A330/A340 cockpits and interiors followed closely the basic cockpit interior design of all former Airbus wide-body planes. Comparing Boeing's and Airbus's product lines in 1992, one design specialist commented: "Design development at Airbus ha[d] been more linear than at Boeing."[33]

To fill the last remaining gap in the Airbus product line, Pierson sought next to develop a model that could compete with the 747 in the lucrative market for planes carrying 400 or more passengers. Initially, in the early 1990s, Airbus collaborated with Boeing on the production of a "Very Large Commercial Transport," but in 1995, after three years of drawn out talks, the joint project collapsed and Airbus decided to go ahead with its own project. The distinctive characteristic of the A380 was its twin deck configuration, which provided for the accommodation of 600–800 passengers. Such a large aircraft was expected to compete with the 747 "from above," just as the A340 competed with the 747 "from below," squeezing the 747 from both directions in what one writer called a "pincer movement."[34]

Still, the A380 project was exceedingly risky as Hartmut Mehdorn, head of Deutsche Airbus, explained: the A380 "is outside the normal Airbus family. With the traditional step-by-step Airbus approach you have a commonality of anything between 60 to 80% between one plane and the next. But with the Superjumbo you have a commonality close to zero. Airbus has to be very careful."[35]

Sales

In his attempt to increase Airbus's sales, Pierson first focused on the North American market. Under Lathiere's leadership, Airbus's U.S. operations were tightly controlled from Toulouse, Airbus's sales force was made up of Europeans who spoke little English, and Airbus pricing decisions needed to be cleared in writing with the consortium's four partner companies before sales teams were authorized to sign deals. Under Pierson, by contrast, Airbus moved quickly to replace the Europeans with native-born Americans

and to streamline all pricing decisions. The result was a rapid increase in sales. In 1985, Airbus achieved its first sale to American Airlines, following a protracted battle with Boeing that ended up in a split order divided between the two arch rivals. A year later, Airbus sold 100 A320 to Northwest Airlines in a $3.2 billion transaction that pitted the A320 against the B-737. In both cases, Airbus charged competitive prices, selling its planes on the basis of their merit rather than giving them away in extraordinarily attractive financial deals, as had been the case formerly.[36]

Airbus's success in the U.S. was echoed elsewhere. During Pierson's first two years in office, Airbus sold more planes than it had done during Lathiere's entire ten year tenure. The A320 turned out to be Airbus's greatest sales success. In 1986, before the plane had ever gone into service, Airbus recorded nearly 250 orders, and by 1992, 35 airline carriers had ordered the plane, including two of Boeing's most loyal customers, United Airlines and All Nippon Airways. In 1992, after four years in service, the A320 achieved 700 sales, and by the late 1990s, the A320 was outselling its rival, the Boeing 737.[37] By the time Pierson entered his last year in office—Fall 1997—Airbus delivered 725 A320s, recorded a backlog of 750 additional orders,[38] and managed to capture a 33% share in the worldwide market for large commercial jets, as shown in Exhibit 1.

Subsidies

Airbus's growing success in challenging Boeing's dominant position precipitated a long-standing trade dispute between the United States and Europe. The dispute dates back to Airbus's 1978 breakthrough into the American market. The unusual financial agreement signed by Airbus and Eastern Airlines in 1978 prompted Boeing executives to seek Congressional action against Airbus, accusing the consortium of engaging in "predatory financing."[39] In subsequent years, as Pierson succeeded Lathiere, the dispute deepened. During the 1986 multilateral negotiations over the General Agreement of Tariffs and Trades (GATT), the U.S. government filed a complaint against Airbus stating that the consortium's failure to repay its government loans was in violation of the GATT accord.[40] Three years later, the U.S. Department of Commerce commissioned a consulting firm—Gellman Research Associates—to conduct an in-depth study of Airbus's financial history. Delivered to the Commerce Department in

EXHIBIT 1

Jean Pierson's Airbus: Worldwide Market Share of Shipments of Large Commercial Aircraft by Airbus, Boeing, McDonnell Douglas, and Lockheed, 1985–1997

	Airbus	Boeing	McDonnell Douglas	Lockheed
1985	13%	63%	22%	2%
1986*	8%	66%	25%	
1987*	8%	66%	25%	1%
1988	13%	60%	27%	1%
1989	21%	55%	24%	
1990	15%	62%	23%	
1991	22%	56%	2%	
1992	22%	61%	17%	
1993*	25%	60%	14%	
1994	28%	63%	9%	
1995	33%	54%	13%	
1996	32%	55%	13%	
1997	33%	67%		

* Percentages do not add up to 100 because of rounding.

Source: For Boeing, McDonnell Douglas, and Lockheed: *Aerospace Fact and Figures, 1989/1990*, p. 34, *1992/1993*, p. 34, *1997/1998*, p. 34, and the *Boeing Company 1997 Annual Report*, p. 19. For Airbus: "Airbus Orders and Deliveries 1984–2003," a document supplied by Mark Luginbill, Airbus Communication Director, January 13, 2005.

1990, the Gellman Report found that between 1970 and 1989, France, Germany, and Britain had granted Airbus loans totaling $13.5 billion, only $500 million of which had been paid back, and concluded: "No Airbus aircraft program is likely to be commercially viable."[41] Airbus, in response, rebutted the American allegations and issued its own report on federal subsidies paid to Boeing and the McDonnell Douglas Corporation. During the ten year period, 1978–1988 (the Airbus report estimated), the U.S. government granted the two American aircraft makers a total of $23 billion in subsidies, mostly in the form of indirect support delivered through defense contracts.[42]

Notwithstanding these charges and countercharges, Airbus management eventually decided to reverse course and look for ways to diffuse the conflict. To do so, Pierson invited Boeing Chairman Frank Shrontz to Toulouse to discuss the subsidies issue. As Shrontz arrived in France in September 1990, Pierson offered him a deal: Airbus was willing to accept limits on government subsidies if the U.S.

government would agree to limit its indirect subsidies to American aircraft makers. Realizing that Boeing could no longer stop Airbus, only slow it down, Shrontz accepted the blue-prints of Pierson's offer, and went ahead to lobby the U.S. government to settle the dispute. The result was the 1992 "Airbus Accord"—a bilateral agreement signed by representatives of the European Commission and the U.S. government. The accord limited all direct subsidies to 33% of the developing costs of a given aircraft model, and all indirect subsidies to 4% of the total sales of a given aircraft manufacturing company.[43]

The historic accord helped Pierson achieve two goals. First, Airbus's right to receive direct subsidies for its aircraft programs—albeit limited—was now legitimized and recognized by the U.S. government, the Boeing Company, and the McDonnell Douglas Corporation. Second, Airbus's American rivals, as well as the U.S. government, had now acknowledged that the American aircraft industry benefited from indirect subsidies and were willing to subject such subsidies to restrictions imposed by an international treaty.

Cost Cutting

The signing of the bilateral agreement of 1992 coincided with both the recession of the early 1990s and the decline in the value of the dollar (relative to European currencies and the yen). Partly as a result of the recession which intensified competition among aircraft makers, partly as a result of the weakening of the dollar which made European exports (shipped by Airbus) more expensive on the global markets, and also as a consequence of the bilateral agreement which limited the consortium's dependency on direct government subsidies, Airbus sought to reduce costs through deep cuts in jobs, the streamlining of the production process, and the speed up of deliveries. To achieve these goals, each of the consortium's partner companies implemented cost-cutting programs. In Britain, some 150 British Aerospace executives met in a conference in Spring 1993 to seek ways to gain substantial increases in productivity. Subsequent to the conference, British Aerospace cut its wing production time by 50% in two years while trimming its workforce from 15,000 to 7,000 in five years. In Germany, Daimler-Benz Airbus (formerly Deutsche Airbus, later Daimler Aerospace) reduced its fuselage production cost by 33%, fuselage production time by 50%, and workforce from 22,000 to 14,000 in six years (1992–1998). And in France, state-owned Aerospatiale (which produced cockpits and assembled aircraft models) cut its workforce by 17% between 1993 and 1996. Together, these efforts enabled Airbus to reduce its "lead time" between order and delivery from 15 to 9 months for single-aisle planes, and from 18 to 12 months for wide-body jets. Speeding up its deliveries, Airbus managed to slash costly inventories by 30%.[44]

Airbus's cost-cutting measures under Pierson stand in a stark contrast to Boeing's growing inefficiencies under Shrontz and his successor, Philip Condit. Nowhere was the contrast between the two manufacturing systems more conspicuous than on the shop floor. At Boeing's assembly plants in Seattle, a large number of workers with hand tools moved in and around the aircraft as they assembled them, one unit at a time. At Airbus's Toulouse plants, by contrast, a small number of employees worked simultaneously on four or five planes operating giant machines that fitted together cockpits, fuselages, and wings.[45] "The factory doesn't look or feel like an engineering plant," Stephen Aris, Airbus's historian observed. "There is little noise, no waste, and what few people there are on the factory floor are working mainly as machine tenders and supervisors rather than as operatives. The atmosphere is purposeful, yet surprisingly relaxed."[46]

Comparative figures bear out these differences. In 1998, Boeing used 20-30 percent more labor hours to produce a jetliner that it had done in 1994.[47] One source of Boeing's troubles was its 1997 acquisition of the McDonnell Douglas Corporation. While Airbus had already adopted a flexible, lean-production manufacturing system by the mid-1990s, the combined Boeing-McDonnell Douglas Corporation was still utilizing a standardized, mass production system that had barely changed since WWII. Hence the gap in productivity between the "new" Boeing and Airbus. In 1998, the year Pierson stepped down, Airbus employed 143 workers for every commercial aircraft produced (230 jets made by 33,000 workers), and Boeing 211 workers (560 jets manufactured by 119,000 employees)—a productivity gap of 48% in favor of Airbus.[48]

Maturity: Noel Forgeard's Airbus, 1998–2005

Despite Pierson's impressive achievements, the transformation of Airbus was far from over. In 1998, Airbus Industrie still functioned as a GEI (groupement d'interet economique), a cooperative partnership organized for the purpose of pooling resources together for a common goal. Airbus Industrie was essentially a marketing and sales organization with a few other product-related functions such as coordinating aircraft design and development, conducting test flights, obtaining aircraft certification, and advertising. All other functions, especially those related to the financing and manufacturing of the aircraft, were the responsibility of the partner companies. Registered under French law as a GEI, Airbus neither paid taxes, nor published financial accounts, nor owned any assets (apart from an office building in Toulouse). On the other hand, Airbus's partner companies were each responsible for their own cost and profit accounting. Each partner, however, did not always distinguish in its balance sheet between Airbus and non-Airbus operations, and therefore it had become exceedingly difficult to obtain an accurate picture of Airbus's overall financial results.[49]

Airbus partner companies had planned all along to turn the consortium into a "single corporate entity," but not until 1997 did the partners begin conducting serious discussions on the issue. To carry out the reorganization, Airbus's Board of Directors selected Noel Forgeard to succeed Pierson.

Replacing Pierson in early 1998, Forgeard had a clear view of his central mission: "I joined Airbus to turn it into a company." "Otherwise, I would [have] never" taken the job. "The top priority of the GEI was . . . sales and I am . . . not a salesman. I am a manager."[50]

Forgeard's leadership style stood in a marked contrast to Pierson's. An imposing man known among Airbus's employees as the "Pyrenees Bear," Pierson was a hard-line executive, combative, abrasive, and explosive. Forgeard was a consensus builder. A soft spoken executive, Forgeard worked for the French defense conglomerates the Lagardere Group for 11 years before joining Airbus in 1998. Famous for his managerial, political, as well as diplomatic skills, Forgeard specialized in building and running joint ventures between European and American defense companies. "He appears low-key, but he can be very tough, and when he has set a goal, nothing can distract him from it," a Lagardere colleague described Forgeard, adding, "He has an impressive ability to set priorities, to focus on his goals, and [to] set up a very strong team to achieve these goals."[51]

Restructuring Airbus Ownership

The key to turning Airbus Industrie into a stand-alone corporation was a cross-border merger between three of the consortium's four partner companies. In the past, the consortium partners refused to share information about their Airbus business, let alone engage in merger discussions. Using his keen political sensibilities to allocate Airbus projects, Forgeard was careful to treat all partner companies equally, diffuse nationally-based rivalries, and encourage the partners to hold serious merger talks.[52] The initial move towards merger was undertaken by Airbus's two large partners, state-owned Aerospatiale and Daimler Aerospace. To begin with, the French government privatized Aerospatiale in 1998, selling the company's largest block of private shares to the Lagardere Group. Next, Daimler Aerospace merged with Aerospatiale in July 1999 to form the European Aerospace Defense and Space Company (EADS), Europe's largest defense and space firm. Six months later, Airbus's Spanish partner, CASA, was acquired by EADS. In the meantime, British Aerospace (BAE) sought to negotiate a partnership agreement with EADS, after it had rejected an EADS' invitation to begin merger talks (wishing to maintain its ties to the American defense establishment, BAE was reluctant to jeopardize its independent status). Following another six months of difficult negotiations, in June 2000, BAE and EADS finally reached an agreement: the two companies would own together all the stocks issued by the newly formed "Airbus Integrated Company" (AIC). Under the new partnership agreement, EADS owned 80% of Airbus Integrated Company and BAE owned 20%, an arrangement which mirrored BAE's 20% share in Airbus Industrie. Following the birth of AIC, Forgeard continued running Airbus, and in addition, served as a director on EADS's board.[53]

Airbus's reorganization into a limited liability company benefited the new company in several ways. The first and most obvious advantage of reorganization was cost savings, and such savings were achieved, above all, in materials' purchasing. Consider the following example. Formerly, each of the consortium's partners—the French, German, British, and Spanish—bought its own supply of aluminum separately, and together, the four partners spent about 12 billion Euros a year on purchasing aluminum. Following reorganization, Airbus's central office bought the entire aluminum supply consumed by the firm annually at a 10% discount, saving the European aircraft maker 1.2 billion Euros a year, according to Forgeard's estimate.[54]

Another benefit of Airbus's reorganization was the speed up of the decision making process. In the past, the consortium's four partner companies needed to reach a consensus on all major decisions. Once Airbus had become an integrated company, such a consensus was no longer needed, and as a result, disagreements were settled much faster. A disagreement over the construction of the A380's wing box is a case in point. Under the GEI structure, Airbus's partners spent months discussing the question of whether the Super-jumbo's wing box should be made of metal or carbon fiber. Under the AIC structure, the issue was settled in weeks.[55]

Lastly, the restructuring of Airbus as an integrated company resulted in a leaner, more flexible organization where the lines of communication were shortened, functional units were consolidated, and redundant positions were eliminated. Airbus Industrie, for example, employed four technical directors on an on-going basis. Airbus Integrated Company, by contrast, employed only one.[56]

Diversification into Defense Products

The restructuring of Airbus offered Forgeard an opportunity. Because the commercial aircraft industry was subject to deep cyclical movements of booms and busts, and because the demand for defense products was relatively stable, military sales were likely to soften the impact of periodic slumps in commercial revenues and thus benefit Airbus and its parent company EADS. Under Forgeard's leadership, accordingly, Airbus diversified its product line to manufacture military jetliners. In May 2003, Airbus won a $23 billion contract to build military transport aircraft for the armed forces of seven European nations. The European governments considered bids from both Boeing and Airbus, and selected the Airbus A400M (a modified commercial jet) over the Boeing C-17, the standard transport jetliner used by the U.S. military. In 2004, Airbus beat Boeing again, winning a $24 billion 27-year contract to supply Britain's Royal Air Force (RAF) with fueling services, including a "filling station in the sky" anywhere in the world. The British government selected a tanker modeled on the Airbus A330 over a modified version of the Boeing B-767 because the A330 was newer than the B-767, had a larger payload, and flew over a longer range.[57]

More lucrative than these two deals was a pending contract offered by the U.S. Department of Defense. The U.S. Air Force planned to replace its giant fleet of aging tanker planes (some of which were 40 years old) beginning in 2010, and Forgeard was taking all necessary steps to prepare an Airbus bid acceptable to the Pentagon. To start, Airbus invested $90 million in redesigning its A330 passenger model according to the Pentagon's specification for tanker planes. Next, Airbus planned to use American-made parts and components for at least 50% of the content of the tanker. Additionally, Forgeard made plans to open an Airbus assembly plan in the United States either to build new A330 tanker planes or to convert old passenger aircraft to military tankers. And lastly, to improve its prospects of winning the Pentagon contract, Airbus sought a partnership agreement with a major American defense company. Under a typical agreement, Airbus would supply the aircraft, and the American partner would provide equipment such as electronics, and structural components such

as landing gears. To do so, Airbus held talks with both Lockheed and Northrop Grumman, two of the U.S.'s largest defense contractors.[58]

Airbus was likely to be awarded a share in the Pentagon contract because the U.S. Air Force could not afford relying on a single aircraft type manufactured by a single company. Such a choice was far too risky: technical problems associated with a single model could lead to the grounding of the entire fleet. Instead, to spread the risk among several different models, the U.S. government needed to divide the contract among competing manufacturers, as it had done in the past. The fleet currently in service (2005) was made up of about 500 Boeing, McDonnell Douglas, and Lockheed civilian planes. Since neither Lockheed nor McDonnell manufactured civilian planes any longer, the sole alternative to a Boeing tanker plane was an Airbus one.[59]

Furthermore, Airbus prospects of competing with Boeing improved as a result of a recent delay in the Pentagon plan to open the tanker contract to competition. Boeing planned to use the B-767 model as its proposed tanker plane, but the 767's production costs were rising. By summer 2005, commercial orders of the B-767 fell to such a low point that keeping the B-767 assembly line open was no longer economical, and Boeing needed to consider shutting down the line altogether. Announced in February 2005, the Pentagon's delay in holding competition over the contract—which could have lasted several years—thus placed Boeing in a competitive disadvantage: re-starting the assembly line in the future was bound to be expensive and add to the cost of manufacturing the B-767 tanker. Airbus, in contrast, had a substantial backlog of A330 commercial orders, and therefore did not anticipate any disruptions in the future production of the A330.[60]

Finally, EADS, Airbus's parent company, benefited from combining commercial and military sales as well. Following Airbus reorganization, EADS's revenue structure had changed to resemble that of Boeing. Just as Boeing's 1997 acquisition of the McDonnell Douglas Corporation—a major defense contractor— helped the Seattle company improve its performance during slumps in the commercial aircraft market, so did Airbus's 2001 incorporation as a subsidiary of EADS help EADS take advantage of the swings in the commercial aerospace business cycle. And just as Boeing derived 60% of its 2001 revenues from commercial aircraft sales, and 40% from the sale of defense, space and communication systems, so did EADS generate 65% of its 2002 revenues from commercial airplanes sales and 35% from the sale of defense, space, and aeronautics products and services.[61]

Globalization

The commercial [aircraft] industry "is now totally subject to the forces of globalization," an EADS executive said in 2004,[62] and indeed, by the mid-2000s, both Airbus and Boeing had become highly dependent on the global supply chain. Both aircraft makers sought to outsource the manufacture of aircraft parts, components, and subassemblies to risk sharing partners in strategic markets, a practice aimed at reducing production costs and increasing aircraft sales. Using global outsourcing as a marketing tool, Airbus focused on three strategic markets: the U.S., Japan, and China.

Under Forgeard's leadership, Airbus signed large outsourcing contracts with major U.S. suppliers, sold hundreds of jets to U.S. airline carriers, and won political friends in Washington, both among members of Congress and government officials. Between 1994 and 2004, Airbus's spending in the United States nearly doubled from $2.6 to $5 billion, as major suppliers performed extensive work on Airbus's late models. On the A380, for example, Airbus purchased engines from the General Electric Corporation, hydraulic systems from the Eaton Corporation, avionics from Honeywell, navigation equipment from Northrop Grumman, and landing gears as well as evacuation systems from the Goodrich Corporation. Altogether, the value of American-made products used in each A380 jetliner approached 45% of the plane's total cost. Airbus's heavy reliance on U.S. suppliers, Forgeard believed, was likely to help the company sell its Superjumbo in the United States as a future replacement for the Boeing 747.[63]

Similarly, Airbus signed outsourcing contracts with large Japanese suppliers in an attempt to increase its share in Japan's market for new commercial jets. In 2002, Japan's top carriers—Japan Airlines (JAL) and All Nippon Airways (ANA)—flew mostly Boeing-made jets, and Boeing held an 80% share in the market for Japanese commercial jets. Because JAL was the world's largest operator of the Boeing 747, Forgeard expected the A380 to sell well in Japan, hoping to increase Airbus's share in Japan's aircraft market from 20% to 50% in 20 years (2002–2022). To encourage JAL and ANA to purchase the Superjumbo,

Airbus contracted seven Japanese large firms—Mitsubishi Heavy Industries, Fuji Heavy Industries, Sumitomo Metal Industries, Japan Aircraft Manufacturing Corporation, and others—to supply the A380 in a deal valued at $1.5 billion in 2002.[64]

Airbus, in addition, explored outsourcing opportunities in China. In 2004, Airbus held a 25% share in the market for Chinese commercial jets—against Boeing's 72%—and in subsequent years, the European aircraft maker planned to increase its market share to 50%. Seeking to lower its labor cost as well as increase its share in China's market for commercial jets, Airbus invited two Chinese state-owned aerospace companies to participate in building its newest aircraft—the midsized long-range A350 model—awarding them in 2005 a 5% risk-sharing role in producing the new plane.[65]

Marketing and Sales

During Forgeard's seven-year tenure, Boeing continued losing ground to its European rival. While the Airbus A330/A340 series competed favorably with both the Boeing 777 and the Boeing 747, strong sales of the A320 (Exhibit 2) helped Airbus capture the industry's top spot and achieve a 53% share in the global market for large commercial jets, as shown in Exhibit 3.

Airbus's success in selling the A320 was evident among the major air carriers as well as the new discount airlines. Initially, the low-cost carriers had all followed Southwest Airlines's practice of operating an all Boeing 737 fleet, but in 2000, New York-based Jet Blue Airways had become the first budget carrier to

---

EXHIBIT 2

Total Number of Commercial Aircraft Ordered and Delivered by Airbus, 1970–Dec. 31, 2004

	Orders	Deliveries
A300/A310	851	792
A320	3,371	2,342
A330/A340	891	618
A380	139	
Total	**5,252**	**3,752**

Source: "Orders and Deliveries," Airbus.com, retrieved from Web February 1, 2005.

EXHIBIT 3

Noel Forgeard's Airbus (1998–2004): Worldwide Market Share of Shipments of Large Commercial Aircraft

	1998	1999	2000	2001	2002	2003	2004
Boeing	71%	68%	61%	62%	56%	48%	47%
Airbus	29%	32%	39%	38%	44%	52%	53%

Sources: "Commercial Airplanes: Orders and Deliveries," Boeing.com, retrieved from Web February 2, 2001, and January 15, 2005; "Airbus Orders and Deliveries 1984–December 30, 2003," a document supplied by Mark Luginbill, Airbus Communication Director, January 2005, in conjunction with Kevin Done, "The Big Gamble: Airbus Rolls Out Its New Weapon," *Financial Times*, January 17, 2005.

fly an all A320 fleet, selecting the Airbus model as its standard transport. Next, in 2002, Airbus scored a victory over Boeing when it sold 120 planes to Britain's Easy Jet, a discount carrier flying B-737s only, and in 2004, Airbus managed to persuade two other low-cost air carriers—Air Berlin, Germany's second largest airline, and AirAsia, Malaysia's principal discount carrier—to switch from the B-737 to the A320 in deals valued at $7 and $5 billion respectively.[66]

Airbus's success with a growing number of Boeing customers was rooted in its decentralized sales strategy. The European aircraft maker empowered its sales team to make pricing decisions on the spot and sign deals without having to seek approval from its corporate office at Toulouse. As such, Airbus's sales team developed, in turn, close relationships with its customer airlines. At Boeing, by contrast, the final pricing decisions were all made by a committee at the headquarters and therefore the sales process was slow and deals were more difficult to negotiate. As a result, the Chicago aircraft maker lost many of its loyal customers. The Air Berlin and AirAsia sales are two instructive examples. In each case, Boeing sales representatives on the ground had no real authority to match Airbus's lower prices, conclude the deal, and sign the contract. Speaking of the Air Berlin sale of 2004, one insider recalled: "The general sentiment [at] the [Boeing] committee was: 'They'll never switch to Airbus, so why go so far'" and accept the lower prices proposed by the sales team?[67]

Financial Performance

Airbus's sales success contributed favorably to its financial performance. As a consortium, Airbus had published no financial reports, and as a company that owned 80% of Airbus, EADS had published financial data pertaining to Airbus's operating income

(earnings before taxes and interests) only, not net income. Using several reliable sources, in conjunction with EADS's financial reports, it is nevertheless possible to arrive at a close estimate of Airbus's rates of return on sales (operating income as percentage of revenues) during the seven-year period ending December 31, 2004.

Throughout Forgeard's tenure, Airbus rate of return on sales exceeded that of Boeing for every year except 1998. "From the first day I put my foot in Airbus, I was obsessed with preparing for a downturn,"[68] Forgeard said in 2002, and as shown in Exhibit 4, nowhere was Airbus's performance more impressive than during the recession that followed the terrorist attack of September 11, 2001. Between 2001 and 2004, Airbus revenues *grew* by 37% and its annual rate of return on sales averaged nearly 8%. During the same period, Boeing's revenues (Exhibit 4) declined by 10% and its rate of return on sales averaged 4.4%. Airbus's growth in sales and profits was the result of two developments: rigorous cost-cutting measures undertaken by Forgeard, and substantial cost savings generated by Airbus's transformation from a consortium to an integrated company. Hence the contrast between Airbus's and Boeing's performance: in 2004, Boeing continued to underperform and to remain narrowly profitable while Airbus came close to achieving Forgeard's target of a 10% operating margin, as shown in Exhibit 4.[69]

Future Prospects

Forgeard was expected to leave Airbus in the summer of 2005 and assume the leadership of its parent company, the European Aerospace Defense and Space Company. As Forgeard was preparing to take charge of EADS, Airbus faced two serious challenges that

EXHIBIT 4

Noel Forgeard's Airbus (1998–2004): Highlight of Financial Data,
Airbus versus Boeing

	Airbus		Boeing	
	Sales (bil.)	Operating Income as % of Sales	Sales (bil.)	Operating Income as % of sales
1998	$13.3	——	$56.2	2.8%
1999	$16.8	5.8%	$58.0	5.5%
2000	$17.2	7.3%	$51.3	6.0%
2001	$18.2	8.1%	$58.0	6.2%
2002	$20.3	7.0%	$53.8	6.4%
2003	$23.8	7.1%	$50.3	0.8%
2004	$25.0	9.5%	$52.5	3.8%

Sources: Airbus's revenues 1998–2002 in "Airbus S.A.S.," *Hoover Handbook of World Business*, 2004, p. 30.
Airbus's revenues and operating profits 2003–2004 in EADS N.V. "Year 2003 Report," p. 7, and "Year 2004
Report," p. 7 , online, EADS.com, and in Daniel Michaels "Airbus Could Top Boeing in Sales," *Wall Street
Journal*, January 13, 2005. Airbus's operating profits for 2002 in EADS "Year 2003 Report," p. 7; for 2001, in
"EADS Delivers Solid Performance," *Business Wire*, March 10, 2003; for 2000, in Kevin Done, "EADS
Forecasts 15% Rise in Profits," *Financial Times*, March 20, 2001; for 1999, in Stephen Dunphy, "The Seattle
Times Business Newsletter Column," *Seattle Times*, June 28, 2000; and for 1998 in "Price War with Boeing
Pushed Airbus into Red Ink Last Year," *Seattle Times*, February 29, 1999. For Boeing: *The Boeing Company
2001 Annual Report*, p. 1, and *The Boeing Company 2004 Annual Report*, p. 1.

could have severely undermined its position in the industry: first, the future prospects of the A380 gamble were uncertain, and second, a new model aircraft introduced by Boeing, the B-787 "Dreamliner," threatened Airbus's competitiveness in the market for midsized jets. Related to the introduction of both the A380 and the B-787 was the U.S. government's resolve to nullify the 1992 "Airbus Accord," and launch, once again, a trade war against the European aircraft maker.

In its 2004 Global Market Forecast, Airbus predicted sales of 1,650 A380 jets over a 20-year period. Boeing disputed this forecast and predicted that over the next two decades the market for very large commercial aircraft (larger than the 747) would not exceed 400 units.[70]

Boeing's analysis was based on the changing structure of the airline industry during the last two decades of the 20th century. Deregulation fragmented the domestic (U.S.) as well as the global air travel markets [Boeing's analysis pointed out], and thereby encouraged air carriers to replace large aircraft with smaller ones. "We believe more passengers are going to fly on direct routes on mid-size airplanes instead of

to hubs on giant size airplanes," Boeing CEO Philip Condit said in 2003, and in fact, during the ten-year period 1990–2000, the number of transatlantic flights aboard Boeing 747 aircraft slightly declined while transatlantic flights aboard smaller wide-body jets like the A340 and B-777 almost tripled.[71]

A related source of concern was the plane's travel range. In the 1970s, the key to the 747's success was its giant wings and fuel tanks that gave the 747 the capability to fly farther than any commercial jet. The A380, in contrast, was not expected to fly farther than most wide-body models in service, and as a result, was likely to face stiff competition in the long-haul travel market from the B-777, B-787, A340, and A350 aircraft.[72]

Another potential risk for Airbus was the A380's cost overrun. By January 2005, the A380's development costs exceeded its projected costs by more than $4 billion, pushing the A380's breakeven point farther into the future. Initially, Airbus expected to recover the A380's development costs after selling 250 planes, but as the plane's costs climbed, the European aircraft maker acknowledged that at least 270 sales were now needed to recover its initial investment and break even. One reason why the A380 costs climbed so steeply was the decline in the value of the dollar against the Euro. In the five-year period ending January 2005, the dollar lost about 30% of its value relative to the Euro, a development that turned the A380 project far more expensive in dollar terms ($15 billion) than in Euro terms (12 billion).[73]

Still another obstacle facing Airbus was the growing difficulties the company experienced in selling the A380. By January 1, 2005, the European aircraft maker booked 139 A380 orders, yet the number of new orders recorded during the first six months of 2005—a total of 15—remained well below Airbus's expectations.[74] Moreover, neither Japan's air carriers—the world's leading users of large jets—nor any of the U.S. based airline carriers had yet ordered a single A380.

Regardless of the prospects of the A380, Boeing's introduction of the B-787 jetliner placed Airbus under increased competitive pressures. Scheduled to enter service in 2008, the Boeing 787 was a midsized 200-300 seat aircraft designed to fly over long distances of up to 9,200 nautical miles. Based on its travel market fragmentation theory, the Boeing Company expected the B-787 to compete successfully against both the A330/A340 and A380 jetliners. The first commercial aircraft built primarily of carbon fiber (composite materials that are lighter and more flexible than aluminum), the B-787 was expected to cut the costs of fuel consumption by 20%, and the costs of maintenance by up to 33%, compared to similar size jets.[75]

Boeing's decision to develop the "Dreamliner," however, was soon challenged by Airbus. Less than a year after Boeing announced the introduction of the B-787, in the summer of 2004, Airbus announced its own plans to develop a new midsized jet, the A350. Intended to compete against the B-787, the A350 was a modified version of the A330 aircraft, not a newly designed aircraft.

The B-787 had several advantages over the A350. The B-787 was more fuel efficient than the A350, was equipped with a more comfortable cabin, and flew over a longer range. The A350's basic design was 15 years old. Moreover, the new Airbus plane was not expected to enter service until 2010, two years after the introduction of the B-787. Furthermore, the A330 was still very popular among the airline carriers, and as such, was likely be "cannibalized" by the A350. Lastly, Airbus was unable to finance the A350 from its own

cash flow and needed to obtain European Government loans to support the project, as had been the case formerly with its A380 project.[76]

But the Boeing Company now vehemently opposed any government loans to Airbus. Because Airbus had already received billions of dollars in loans under the provisions of the 1992 bilateral agreement, Boeing executives contended, Airbus no longer needed any financial help, especially since it had captured the industry's top spot, passing Boeing in total deliveries in 2003, 2004, and 2005 (projected). Accordingly, the Boeing Company lobbied the U.S. government to reject the Airbus Accord of 1992 and bring charges against Airbus before the World Trade Organization.[77]

By June 2005, it had become clear that Airbus was losing its competitive edge. Sales of the A380 came to a halt with only 154 orders received, sales of the A350 did not move at all with just one customer placing ten orders, and the trade dispute with Boeing was hurting Airbus's sales, as Airbus chief commercial officer acknowledged. At Boeing, by contrast, sales of the B-787 were booming with a total number of 237 orders received from several large carriers including Northwest Airlines (Airbus's largest American customer), Korea Airlines (a major Airbus customer), Air India, and Air Canada.[78]

Suddenly, as Noel Forgeard was preparing to step up and assume EADS's leadership, Airbus faced tough strategic choices.

ENDNOTES

1. See Exhibits 3 and 4, and "The Boeing Beater," *The Economist*, January 17, 2004.
2. David C. Mowery and Nathan Rosenberg, *Technology and the Pursuit of Economic Growth* (New York: Cambridge University Press, 1989), pp. 172–173. For the A320, see Eric Vayle, "Collision Course in Commercial Aircraft: Boeing—Airbus—McDonnell Douglas, 1991 (A)," Harvard Business School, Case No. 9-391-106, October 1993, p. 3; for the A330/A340: Stanley Holmes, "Airbus Constructing Profitable Planes," *Europe*, March 1999 (online, ABI data base, Start Page 19); for the Boeing 777: Eugene Rodgers, *Flying High: The Story of Boeing* (New York: Atlantic Monthly Press, 1996), p. 431; and for the A380: J. Lynn Lunsford and Daniel Michaels, "New Friction Puts Airbus, Boeing, On Course for Fresh Trade Battle," *Wall Street Journal*, June 1, 2004, and "Taking Off In Toulouse" *The Economist*, April 30, 2005, p. 58.
3. Michael Dertouzos, Richard Lester, and Robert Solow, *Made in America: Regaining the Productive Edge* (New York: Harper Perennial, 1990), p. 203.
4. John Newhouse, *The Sporty Game* (New York: Alfred Knopf, 1982), p. 21, but see also pp. 10–20.
5. David C. Mowery and Nathan Rosenberg, "The Commercial Aircraft Industry," in Richard R. Nelson, ed., *Government and Technological Progress: A Cross Industry Analysis* (New York: Pergamon

Press, 1982), p. 116; Dertouzos et al., *Made in America*, p. 200; Paul Turk, "Aerospace: The Subsidy Question," *Europe*, May 1993 (online ABI data base, Start Page 6), and *Wall Street Journal*, June 1, 2004.

6. Dertouzos, et al., *Made in America*, p. 203.

7. Newhouse, *Sporty Game*, p. 188. Mowery and Rosenberg, "The Commercial Aircraft Industry," pp. 124–125.

8. Mowery and Rosenberg, "The Commercial Aircraft Industry," pp. 102–103, 126–128.

9. Dertouzos, et al., *Made in America*, pp. 206, 214.

10. Quoted in Janet Simpson, Lee Field, and David Garvin, "The Boeing 767: From Concept to Production," Harvard Business School, Case No. 9-688-040, April 1991, p. 6.

11. *The Boeing Company 2001 Annual Report*, p. 53.

12. "Airbus Industrie: 25 Flying Years," a *Flight International* Supplement (reprinted by Airbus Industrie, 1997, p. 7).

13. "Airbus Industrie: 25 Flying Years," pp. 8–9.

14. "Airbus 25 Years Old," *Le Figaro* magazine, October 1997 (reprinted in English translation by Airbus Industrie), p. 3; "Airbus Industrie: 25 Flying Years," p. 8.

15. Stephens Aris, *Close to the Sun: How Airbus Challenged America's Domination of the Skies* (London: Aurum Press, 2002), p. 81.

16. "Airbus 25 Years Old," p. 3.

17. Newhouse, *Sporty Game*, p. 28.

18. Ian McIntyre, *Dogfight: The Transatlantic Battle over Airbus* (Westport, Conn.: Praeger, 1992), p. 42; Aris, *Close to the Sun*, pp. 84–86.

19. Matthew Lynn, *Birds of Prey: Boeing vs. Airbus* (New York: Four Walls Eight Windows, 1995), p. 154; Newhouse, *Sporty Game*, p. 30.

20. "Airbus Industrie: 25 Flying Years," p. 11. The British decision, it should be noted, was an outcome of a protracted battle between Boeing and Airbus. While Airbus made concerted efforts to persuade British Aerospace to join the consortium, Boeing sought to establish a close alliance with British Aerospace in opposition to Airbus. Significantly, British Aerospace's decision to become a shareholder in Airbus was heavily influenced by the willingness of the British government to help subsidize the Airbus program. Aris, *Close to the Sun*, pp. 104–105.

21. "Airbus Industrie: 25 Flying Years," pp. 13, 14, 17. The quotation is on page 13. Dertouzos, et al., *Made in America*, pp. 212–213; Aris, *Close to the Sun*, p. 129; Lynn, *Birds of Prey*, p. 63.

22. Dertouzos, et al., *Made in America*, p. 212.

23. Mowery and Rosenberg, "The Commercial Aircraft Industry," p. 116; Aris, *Close to the Sun*, p. 57.

24. Aris, *Close to the Sun*, pp. 56–57.

25. Steve McGuire, *Airbus Industrie: Conflict and Cooperation in US-EC Trade Relations* (London: MacMillan, 1997), pp. 44–45; Newhouse, *Sporty Games*, p. 42.

26. Newhouse, *Sporty Games*, p. 38; McIntyre, *Dogfight*, p. 83; Lynn, *Birds of Prey*, p. 155.

27. Newhouse, *Sporty Games*, pp. 30–31, 38; but see also Lynn, *Birds of Prey*, pp. 155–156.

28. McGuire, *Airbus Industrie*, pp. 52–53; Lynn, *Birds of Prey*, pp. 120–121; Aris, *Close to the Sun*, pp. 100–102.

29. Lynn, *Birds of Prey*, pp. 165–166; Aris, *Close to the Sun*, pp. 134–135; Rodgers, *Flying High*, pp. 345, 351.

30. Aris, *Close to the Sun*, p. 136; Aris, *Close to the Sun*, p. 166.

31. According to a Lehman Brothers report cited in Gail Endmondson, "A Wake Up Call on the Continent," *Business Week*, December 30, 1996, p. 40.

32. McIntyre, *Dogfight*, p. xxi; Frank Spadars, "A Transatlantic Perspective," *Design Quarterly*, Winter 1992, pp. 22–23; McGuire, *Airbus Industrie*, pp. 115–116.

33. McGuire, *Airbus Industrie*, pp. 22–23.

34. Lynn, *Birds of Prey*, chapter 9; Aris, *Close to the Sun*, pp. 173–182.

35. Quoted in Aris, *Close to the Sun*, p. 182.

36. Lynn, *Birds of Prey*, pp. 169–170; see also Aris, *Close to the Sun*, pp. 139–140.

37. Northwest Airlines discovered early on that the A320's operating costs were lower than the B-737's, while United Airlines conducted a survey among its passengers and found that the travelling public preferred the A320 family over the B-737 family. McGuire, *Airbus Industrie*, pp. 99–100; Lynn, *Birds of Prey*, pp. 168–169; Frederic Biddle and John Helyar, "Flying Low: Behind Boeing Woes," *Wall Street Journal*, April 24, 1998.

38. *Hoover's Handbook of American Business, 1998* (Austin: Hoover's Business Press, 1998), p. 67.

39. Subsequently, a U.S. House of Representatives committee called for a subcommittee hearing on what one committee member described as "unfair trade practices" committed by Airbus, and "excessive export subsidies" received by the consortium. Airbus executives, in turn, defended the Eastern deal, pointing out that nearly a quarter of the value of the A300 was made up of parts and components manufactured in the United States. Aris, *Close to the Sun*, p. 103; McGuire, *Airbus Industrie*, p. 53.

40. Speaking for Airbus, Pierson countered that the American aircraft industry had been a long-standing recipient of indirect federal aid, and that Boeing in particular benefited from both U.S. military contracts and National Aeronautics Space Administration's R&D funding. Pierson estimated that federal spending on aerospace products and services in the Untied States exceeded $4 billion in 1984 alone. McGuire, *Airbus Industrie*, pp. 118–124.

41. Cited in Lynn, *Birds of Prey*, pp. 189–190; but see also Turk, "Aerospace: The Subsidy Question," Start Page 6.

42. Lynn, *Birds of Prey*, p. 191.

43. Aris, *Close to the Sun*, pp. 169–170; McGuire, *Airbus Industrie*, chapter 7; Lynn, *Birds of Prey*, pp. 200–201; Turk, "Aerospace: The Subsidy Question," Start Page 6.

44. Charles Goldsmith, "Re-Engineering: After Trailing Boeing for Years Airbus Aims for 50% of the Market," *Wall Street Journal*, March 16, 1998.

45. "Hubris at Airbus, Boeing Rebuilds," *The Economist*, November 28, 1998, p. 65.

46. Cited in Aris, *Close to the Sun*, p. 179.

47. According to Harry Stonecipher, Boeing President, cited in the *New York Times*, December 3, 1998.

48. *The Economist*, November 28, 1998, p. 65. My figures are slightly different than those given by the *The Economist* because I used the actual number of jets produced and the *The Economist* used projected figures.

49. McIntyre, *Dogfight*, pp. 70–71; Lynn, *Birds of Prey*, pp. 113–114; Aris, *Close to the Sun*, pp. 54–59.

50. Cited in Aris, *Close to the Sun*, pp. 196–197.

51. Cited in "Noel Forgeard, Airbus," *Business Week*, January 8, 2001, p. 76, but see also Aris, *Close to the Sun*, p. 197.

52. *Business Week*, January 8, 2001, p. 76.

53. Daniel Michaels, "Europe's Airbus Ready to Spread Wings," *Wall Street Journal*, June 23, 2000; Aris, *Close to the Sun*, chapter 13.

54. Aris, *Close to the Sun*, p. 213.

55. Aris, *Close to the Sun*, p. 213.

56. Aris, *Close to the Sun*, p. 222.

57. "Military Aircraft: Boeing Down Again," *The Economist*, January 24, 2004.

58. Leslie Wayne, "Boeing Pressed by Questions on Tunker Proposal," *New York Times*, May 8, 2004; Daniel Michaels, "Airbus Sees Military Sales Opening," *Wall Street Journal*, September 15, 2003; "Europe's Defense Industry: The Chinese Syndrome," *The Economist*, February 5, 2005, p. 59.

59. *The Economist*, February 5, 2005, p. 59.

60. Jonathan Karp, Andy Pasztor, and J. Lynn Lunsford, "Boeing Is Put at Disadvantage by Timing of U.S. Aircraft Order," *Wall Street Journal*, February 10, 2005.

61. For Boeing, see *The Boeing Company 2001 Annual Report*, p. 85; for Airbus: "EADS N.V. Year 2003 Report," p. 7, online, EADS.com. By 2004, Boeing had become far more dependent on defense sales with a 44% commercial – 54% defense breakdown of total sales. "Europe Defense Industry," *The Economist*, March 5, 2005, p. 59.

62. Cited in Daniel Michaels and J. Lynn Lunsford, "Globalization Blunts Air Trade Rivalry," *Wall Street Journal*, July 19, 2004.

63. *Wall Street Journal*, July 19, 2004; J. Lynn Lunsford and David Michaels, "New Friction Puts Airbus, Boeing on Course for Fresh Trade Battle," *Wall Street Journal*, June 1, 2004.

64. *Economist*, January 17, 2004; Todd Zaun, "Airbus Picks Japanese Parts Makers," *Wall Street Journal*, June 26, 2002.

65. Kevin Done, "The Big Gamble: Airbus Rolls Out Its New Weapon," *Financial Times*, January 17, 2005; Nisha Gopalan, "Airbus China Seeks to Challenge Boeing's Mainland Dominance," *Wall Street Journal*, October 27, 2004.

66. Pierre Sparaco, "Airbus Scores Low-Cost Market Coup," *Aviation Week and Space Technology*, October 21, 2002, pp. 50–51; Daniel Michael; J. Lynn Lunsford and Keith Johnson, "Airbus to Beat Boeing Once Again," *Wall Street Journal*, November 8, 2004.

67. Quoted in J. Lynn Lunsford, "Behind Slide in Boeing Orders," *Wall Street Journal*, December 23, 2004.

68. Quoted in Daniel Michaels, "Airbus Chief Says Company Won't Cut Jobs," *Wall Street Journal*, January 18, 2002.

69. Pierre Sparaco, "European Bounce Back: Airbus Lofty Prediction Seems to be Taking Steps," *Aviation Week and Space Technology*, June 14, 2004, pp. 34–35; Daniel Michaels, "Airbus Could Top Boeing in Sales," *Wall Street Journal*, January 13, 2005; Kevin Done, "EADS Forecasts 15% Rise in Profits," *Financial Times*, March 20, 2001.

70. Airbus, "Global Market Outlook for 2004–2023," Airbus.com; "The Super Jumbo of All Gambles," *The Economist*, January 22, 2005, pp. 55–56.

71. Carol Matlack and Stanley Holmes, "Mega Plane: Airbus Is Building the Biggest Jetliner Ever," *Business Week*, November 10, 2003, p. 55.

72. *The Economist*, January 22, 2005, p. 56.

73. Carol Matlack, "Is Airbus Caught in a Downdraft?" *Business Week*, December 27, 2004, p. 64; *The Economist*, January 22, 2005, p. 55; Robert Wall and Pierre Sparaco, "Financial Targets," *Aviation Week and Space Technology*, February 28, 2005, p 39.

74. "Taking Off in Toulouse," *The Economist*, April 30, 2005, p. 58.

75. J. Lynn Lunsford and David Michaels, "Airbus May Modify Its A330 Plane," *Wall Street Journal*, July 23, 2004; and "Northwest Nears Order of Boeing Jets," *Wall Street Journal*, April 12, 2005.

76. Mark Landler, "Airbus's Midsize Challenge to Boeing," *New York Times*, November 30, 2004; and "A Dogfight Between Jetliners," *New York Times*, April 13, 2005. See also *Wall Street Journal*, July 23, 2005.

77. *Business Week*, December 27, 2004, p. 64.

78. *The Economist*, April 30, 2005, p. 58; *New York Times*, April 13, 2005; and Bruce Stanley and John Larkin, "Boeing Wins 35-Jet Air India Order," *Wall Street Journal*, April 27, 2005.

Apple Computer

This case was prepared by Charles W. L. Hill, the University of Washington.

Back in 1997 Apple Computer was in deep trouble. The company that had pioneered the personal computer market with its easy-to-use Apple II in 1978, and had introduced the first graphical user interface with the Macintosh in 1984, was bleeding red ink. Apple's worldwide market share, which had been fluctuating between 7 and 9% since 1984, had sunk to 4%. Sales were declining. Apple was on track to lose $378 million on revenues of $7 billion, and that on top of a $740 million loss in 1996. In July 1997, the co-founder of the company, Steve Jobs, who had been fired from Apple back in 1985, returned as CEO. At an investor conference, Michael Dell, CEO of Dell Computer, was asked what Jobs should do as head of Apple. Dell quipped, "I'd shut it down and give the money back to shareholders."[1]

By 2006 the situation looked very different. Apple was on track to book record sales of over $19 billion and net profits of close to $1.9 billion. The stock price, which had traded as low as $6 a share in 2003, was in the mid-70s, and the market capitalization, at $63 billion, surpassed that of Dell Computer, which was around $48 billion. Driving the transformation were strong sales of Apple's iPod music player and music downloads from the iTunes store. In addition, strong sales of Apple's MacBook laptop computers had lifted Apple's market share in the U.S. PC business to 4.8%, up from a low of under 3% in 2004.[2]

Moreover, analysts were predicting that the halo effect of the iPod, together with Apple's recent adoption of Intel's microprocessor architecture, would drive strong sales going forward.

For the first time in twenty years, it looked as if Apple, the perennial also-ran, might be seizing the initiative. But serious questions remained. Could the company continue to build on its momentum? Would sales of Apple's computers really benefit from the iPod? Could the company break out of its niche and become a mainstream player? And how sustainable was the iPod driven sales boom? With new competitors coming along, could Apple hold onto its market leading position in the market for digital music players?

Apple 1976–1997

The Early Years

Apple's genesis is the stuff of computer industry legend.[3] On April Fools Day, 1976, two young electronics enthusiasts, Steve Jobs and Steve Wozniak, started a company to sell a primitive PC that Wozniak had designed. Steve Jobs was just twenty; Wozniak, or Woz as he was commonly called, was five years older. They had known each other for several years, having been introduced by a mutual friend who realized that they shared an interest in consumer electronics. Woz had designed the computer just for the fun of it. That's what people did in 1976. The idea that somebody would actually want to purchase his machine had not occurred to Woz, but it did to Jobs. Jobs persuaded a reluctant Woz to form a company and sell the machine. The location of the company was Steve Jobs's garage. Jobs suggested they call the company Apple and their first machine the Apple I.

EXHIBIT 1

The Apple II Computer

Source: Courtesy of Apple Inc.

They sold around two hundred of them at $666 each. The price point was picked as something of a prank.

The Apple I had several limitations—no case, keyboard, or power supply being obvious ones. It also required several hours of laborious assembly by hand. By late 1976, Woz was working on a replacement to the Apple I, the Apple II.[4] In October 1976, with the Apple II under development, Jobs and Woz were introduced to Mike Markkula. Only thirty-four, Markkula was already a retired millionaire, having made a small fortune at Fairchild and Intel. Markkula had no plans to get back into business anytime soon, but a visit to Jobs's garage changed all that. He committed to investing $92,000 for one-third of the company and promised that his ultimate investment would be $250,000. Stunned, Jobs and Woz agreed to let him join as a partner. It was a fateful decision. The combination of Woz's technical skills, Jobs's entrepreneurial zeal and vision, and Markkula's

business savvy and connections was a powerful one. Markkula told Jobs and Woz that neither of them had the experience to run a company and persuaded them to hire a president, Michael Scott, who had worked for Markkula at Fairchild.

The Apple II was introduced in 1977 at a price of $1,200. The first version was an integrated computer with a Motorola microprocessor and included a key board, power supply, monitor, and the BASIC programming software. It was Jobs who pushed Woz to design an integrated machine—he wanted something that was easy to use and not just a toy for geeks. Jobs also insisted that the Apple II look good. It had an attractive case and no visible screws or bolts. This differentiated it from most PCs at the time, which looked as if they had been assembled by hobbyists at home (as many had).

In 1978, Apple started to sell a version of the Apple II that incorporated something new—a disk drive. The disk drive turned out to be a critical innovation, for it enabled third-party developers to write software programs for the Apple II that could be loaded via floppy disks. Soon programs started to appear, among them EasyWriter, a basic word processing program, and VisiCalc, a spreadsheet. VisiCalc was an instant hit and pulled in a new customer set, business types who could use VisiCalc for financial planning and accounting. Since VisiCalc was available only for the Apple II, it helped to drive demand for the machine.

By the end of 1980, Apple had sold over 100,000 Apple IIs, making the company the leader in the embryonic PC industry. The company had successfully executed an IPO, was generating over $200 million in annual sales, and was profitable. With the Apple II series selling well, particularly in the education market, Apple introduced its next product, the Apple III, in the fall of 1980. It was a failure. The computer was filled with bugs and crashed constantly. The Apple III had been rushed to market too quickly. Apple reintroduced a reengineered Apple III in 1981, but it continued to be outsold by Apple II. Indeed, successive versions of the Apple II family, each an improvement on the proceeding version, continued to be produced by the company until 1993. In total, over 2 million Apple II computers were sold. The series became a standard in American classrooms where it was valued for its intuitive ease-of-use. Moreover, the Apple II was the mainstay of the company until the late 1980s, when an improved version of the Macintosh started to garner significant sales.

The IBM PC and Its Aftermath

Apple's success galvanized the world's largest computer company, IBM, to speed up development of its entry into the PC market. IBM had a huge and very profitable mainframe computer business, but it had so far failed to develop a PC, despite two attempts. To get to market quickly with this, its third PC project, IBM broke with its established practice of using its own proprietary technology to build the PC. Instead, IBM adopted an "open architecture," purchasing the components required to make the IBM PC from other manufacturers. These components included a 16-bit microprocessor from Intel and an operating system, MS-DOS, which was licensed from a small Washington State company, Microsoft.

Microsoft had been in the industry from its inception, writing a version of the BASIC software programming language for the MITS Atari in 1977,

the first PC ever produced. IBM's desire to license BASIC brought them to Redmond to talk with the company's CEO, Bill Gates. Gates, still in his early twenties, persuaded IBM to adopt a 16-bit processor (originally IBM had been considering a less powerful 8-bit processor). He was also instrumental is pushing IBM to adopt an open architecture, arguing that IBM would benefit from the software and peripherals that other companies could then make.

Initially IBM was intent on licensing the CP/M operating system, produced by Digital Research, for the IBM PC. However, the current version of CP/M was designed to work on an 8-bit processor, and Gates had persuaded IBM that it needed a 16-bit processor. In a series of quick moves, Gates purchased a 16-bit operating system from a local company, Seattle Computer, for $50,000. Gates then hired the designer of the operating system, Tim Paterson, renamed the system MS-DOS, and offered to license it to IBM. In what turned out to be a master stroke, Gates persuaded IBM to accept a nonexclusive license for MS-DOS (which IBM called PC-DOS).

To stoke sales, IBM offered a number of applications for the IBM PC that were sold separately, including a version of VisiCalc, a word processor called EasyWriter, and a well-known series of business programs from Peachtree Software.

Introduced in 1981, the IBM PC was an instant success. Over the next two years, IBM would sell more than 500,000 PCs, seizing market leadership from Apple. IBM had what Apple lacked, an ability to sell into corporate America. As sales of the IBM PC mounted, two things happened. First, independent software developers started to write programs to run on the IBM PC. These included two applications that drove adoptions of the IBM PC; word processing programs (Word Perfect) and a spreadsheet (Lotus 1-2-3). Second, the success of IBM gave birth to clone manufacturers who made IBM-compatible PCs that also utilized an Intel microprocessor and Microsoft's MS-DOS operating system. The first and most successful of the clone makers was Compaq, which in 1983 introduced its first PC, a 28-pound "portable" PC. In its first year, Compaq booked $111 million in sales, which at the time was a record for first-year sales of a company. Before long, a profusion of IBM clone makers entered the market, including Tandy, Zenith, Leading Edge, and Dell. The last was established in 1984 by Michael Dell, then a student at the

University of Texas, who initially ran the company out of his dorm room.

The Birth of the Macintosh

By 1980 two other important projects were underway at Apple: Lisa and the Macintosh. Lisa was originally conceived as a high-end business machine, and the Macintosh as a low-end portable machine.

The development of the Lisa and ultimately the Macintosh were influenced by two visits Steve Jobs paid to Xerox's fabled Palo Alto Research Center (PARC) in November and December 1979. Funded out of Xerox's successful copier business, PARC had been set up to do advanced research on office technology. Engineers at PARC had developed a number of technologies that were later to become central to PCs, including a graphical user interface (GUI), software programs that were made tangible through on-screen icons, a computer mouse that let a user click on and drag screen objects, and a laser printer. Jobs was astounded by what he saw at PARC and decided on the spot that these innovations had to be incorporated into Apple's machines.

Jobs initially pushed the Lisa team to implement PARC's innovations, but he was reportedly driving people on the project nuts with his demands, so President Mike Scott pulled him of the project. Jobs reacted by essentially hijacking the Macintosh project and transforming it into a skunk works that would put his vision into effect. By one account:

> He hounded the people on the Macintosh project to do their best work. He sang their praises, bullied them unmercifully, and told them "they weren't making a computer, they were making history." He promoted the Mac passionately, making people believe that he was talking about much more than a piece of office equipment.[5]

It was during this period that Bud Tribble, a software engineer on the Mac project, quipped that Jobs could create a "reality distortion field." Jobs insisted that the Mac would ship by early 1982. Tribble knew that the schedule was unattainable, and when asked why he didn't point this out to Jobs, he replied: "Steve insists that we're shipping in early 1982, and won't accept answers to the contrary. The best way to describe the situation is a term from Star Trek. Steve has a reality distortion field. . . . In his presence, reality is malleable. He can convince anyone of practically anything. It wears off when he's not around, but it makes it hard to have realistic schedules."[6]

Andy Hertzfeld, another engineer on the Macintosh project, thought Tribble was exaggerating, "until I observed Steve in action over the next few weeks. The reality distortion field was a confounding mélange of a

---

EXHIBIT 2

The Macintosh

Source: Courtesy of Apple Inc.

charismatic rhetorical style, an indomitable will, and an eagerness to bend any fact to fit the purpose at hand. If one line of argument failed to persuade, he would deftly switch to another. Sometimes, he would throw you off balance by suddenly adopting your position as his own, without acknowledging that he ever thought differently."[7]

Back at Apple, things were changing too. Mike Scott had left the company after clashes with other executives, including Markkula, who had become chairman. Jobs persuaded John Sculley to join Apple as CEO. Sculley was the former vice president of marketing at Pepsi, where he had become famous for launching the Pepsi Challenge. Jobs had reportedly asked Sculley, "Do you want to sell sugar water for the rest of your life, or do you want to change the world?" Sculley opted for changing the world. A Wharton MBA, Sculley had been hired for his marketing savvy, not his technical skills.

While the Lisa project suffered several delays, Jobs pushed the Macintosh team to finish the project and beat the Lisa team to market with a better product. Introduced in 1984, the Macintosh certainly captured attention for its stylish design and its use of a GUI, icons, and a mouse, all of which made the machine easy to use and which were not found on any other PC at the time. Jobs, ever the perfectionist, again insisted that not a single screw should be visible on the case. He reportedly fired a designer who presented a mockup that had a screw that could be seen by lifting a handle.

Early sales were strong; then they faltered. For all of its appeal, the Macintosh lacked some important features—it had no hard disk drive, only one floppy drive, and insufficient computer memory. Moreover, there were few applications available to run on the machine, and the Mac proved to be a more difficult machine to develop applications for than the IBM PC and its clones. Jobs, however, seemed oblivious to the problems and continued to talk about outsized sales projections, even when it was obvious to all around him that they were unattainable.

In early 1985, Apple posted its first loss. Aware that the drastic action necessary could not be taken while Jobs was running the Macintosh division, Sculley got backing from the board of directors to strip Jobs of his management role and oversight of the Macintosh division. In late 1985, an embittered Jobs resigned from Apple, sold all of his stock, and left to start another computer company, aptly named NeXT.

The Golden Years

With Jobs gone, Sculley shut down the Lisa line, which had done poorly in the market due to a very high price point of $10,000, and pushed developers to fix the problems with the Macintosh. In January 1986, a new version of the Macintosh, the Mac Plus, was introduced. This machine fixed the shortcomings of the original Mac, and sales started to grow again.

What also drove sales higher was Apple's domination of the desktop publishing market. Several events came together to make this happen. Researchers from Xerox PARC formed a company, Adobe, to develop and commercialize the PostScript page description language. PostScript enabled the visual display and printing of high-quality page layouts loaded with graphics such as colored charts, line drawings, and photos. Apple licensed PostScript and used it as the output for its Apple LaserWriter, which was introduced in 1985. Shortly afterwards, a Seattle company, Aldus, introduced a program called PageMaker for the Mac. PageMaker used Adobe's PostScript page description language for output. Although Aldus introduced a version of PageMaker for MS-DOS in 1986, Apple already had a lead, and with the Mac's GUI appealing to graphic artists, Apple tightened its hold on the desktop publishing segment. Apple's position in desktop publishing was further strengthened by the release of Adobe Illustrator in 1987 (a freehand drawing program) and Adobe Photoshop in 1990.

The years between 1986 and 1991 were in many ways golden ones for Apple. Since it made both hardware and software, Apple was able to control all aspects of its computers, offering a complete desktop solution that allowed customers to "plug and play." With the Apple II series still selling well in the education market, and the Mac dominating desktop publishing, Apple was able to charge a premium price for its products. Gross margins on the Mac line got as high as 55%. In 1990, Apple sales reached $5.6 billion; its global market share, which had fallen rapidly as the IBM-compatible PC market had grown, stabilized at 8%; the company had a strong balance sheet; and Apple was the most profitable PC manufacturer in the world.

During this period, executives at Apple actively debated the merits of licensing the Mac operating system to other computer manufacturers, allowing them to make Mac clones. Sculley was in favor of this move. So was Microsoft's Bill Gates, who wrote two memos to Sculley laying out the argument for licensing the Mac OS. Gates argued that the closed architecture of the Macintosh prevented independent investment in the standard by third parties and put Apple at a disadvantage next to the IBM PC standard. However, some senior executives at Apple were against the licensing strategy, arguing that once Apple licensed its intellectual property, it would be difficult to protect it. In one version of events, senior executives debated the decision at a meeting and took a vote on whether to license. Given the controversial nature of the decision, it was decided that the vote in favor had to be unanimous. It wasn't—a single executive voted against the licensing decision, and it was never pursued.[8] In another version of events, Jean-Louis Gassée, head of R&D at Apple, vigorously opposed Sculley's plans to clone, and Sculley backed down.[9] Gassée was deeply distrustful of Microsoft and Bill Gates, and believed that Gates probably had an ulterior motive given how the company benefited from the IBM standard.

Ironically, in 1985 Apple had licensed its "visual displays" to Microsoft. Reportedly Gates had strong-armed Sculley, threatening that Microsoft would stop developing crucial applications for the Mac unless Apple granted Microsoft the license. At the time, Microsoft had launched development of its own GUI. Called Windows, it mimicked the look and feel of the Mac operating system, and Microsoft didn't want to be stopped by a lawsuit from Apple. Several years later, when Apple did file a lawsuit against Microsoft, arguing that Windows 3.1 imitated the "look and feel" of the Mac, Microsoft was able to point to the 1985 license agreement to defend its right to develop Windows—a position that the judge in the case agreed with.

1990–1997

By the early 1990s, the prices of IBM-compatible PCs were declining rapidly. So long as Apple was the only company to sell machines that used a GUI, its differential appeal gave it an advantage over MS-DOS-based PCs with their clunky text-based interfaces, and the premium price could be justified. However, in 1990 Microsoft introduced Windows 3.1, its own GUI that sat on top of MS-DOS, and Apple's differential appeal began to erode. Moreover, the dramatic

growth of the PC market had turned Apple into a niche player. Faced with the choice of writing software to work with an MS-DOS/Windows operating system and an Intel microprocessor, now the dominant standard found on 90% of all PCs, or the Mac OS and a Motorola processor, developers logically opted for the dominant standard (desktop publishing remained an exception to this rule). Reflecting on this logic, Dan Eilers, then vice president of strategic planning at Apple, reportedly stated that "the company was on a glide path to history."[10]

Sculley, too, thought that the company was in trouble. Apple seemed boxed into its niche. Apple had a high cost structure. It spent significantly more on R&D as a percentage of sales than its rivals (in 1990, Apple spent 8% of sales on R&D, Compaq around 4%). Its microprocessor supplier, Motorola, lacked the scale of Intel, which translated into higher costs for Apple. Moreover, Apple's small market share made it difficult to recoup the spiraling cost of developing a new operating system, which by 1990 amounted to at least $500 million.

Sculley's game plan to deal with these problems involved a number of steps.[11] First, he appointed himself chief technology officer in addition to CEO, a move that raised some eyebrows given Sculley's marketing background. Second, he committed the company to bring out a low-cost version of the Macintosh to compete with IBM clones. The result was the Mac Classic, introduced in October 1990 and priced at $999. He also cut prices for the Macs and Apple IIs by 30%. The reward was a 60% increase in sales volume, but lower gross margins. So third, he cut costs. The workforce at Apple was reduced by 10%, the salaries of top managers (including Sculley's) were cut by as much as 15%, and Apple shifted much of its manufacturing to subcontractors (for example, the Power-Book was built in Japan, a first for Apple). Fourth, he called for the company to maintain its technological lead by bringing out hit products every six to twelve months. The results included the first Apple portable, the PowerBook notebook, which was shipped in late 1991 and garnered very favorable reviews, and the Apple Newton hand-held computer, which bombed. Fifth, Apple entered into an alliance with IBM, which realized that it had lost its hold on the PC market to companies like Intel, Microsoft, and Compaq.

The IBM alliance had several elements. One was the decision to adopt IBM's Power PC microprocessor architecture, which IBM would also use in its offerings. A second was the establishment of two joint ventures—Taligent, which had the goal of creating a new operating system, and Kaleida to develop multimedia applications. A third was a project to help IBM and Apple machines work better together.

While Sculley's game plan helped to boost the top line, the bottom line shrunk in 1993 due to a combination of low gross margins and continuing high costs. In 1994, Sculley left Apple. He was replaced by Michael Spindler, a German engineer who had gained prominence as head of Apple Europe.

It was Spindler who in 1994 finally took the step that had been long debated in the company—he decided to license the Mac OS to a handful of companies, allowing them to make Mac clones. The Mac OS would be licensed for $40 a copy. It was too little too late—the industry was now waiting for the introduction of Microsoft's Windows 95. When it came, it was clear that Apple was in serious trouble. Windows 95 was a big improvement over Windows 3.1, and it closed the gap between Windows and the Mac. While many commentators criticized Apple for not licensing the Mac OS in the 1980s, when it still had a big lead over Microsoft, ironically Bill Gates disagreed. In a 1996 interview with *Fortune*, Gates noted:

> As Apple has declined, the basic criticism seems to be that Apple's strategy of doing a unique hardware/software combination was doomed to fail. I disagree. Like all strategies, this one fails if you execute poorly. But the strategy can work, if Apple picks its markets and renews the innovation in the Macintosh.[12]

Spindler responded to Windows 95 by committing Apple to develop a next generation operating system for the Macintosh, something that raised questions about the Taligent alliance with IBM. At the end of 1995, IBM and Apple parted ways, ending Taligent, which after $500 million in investments had produced little.

By then, Spindler had other issues on his mind. The latter half of 1995 proved to be a disaster for Apple. The company seemed unable to predict demand for its products. It overestimated demand for its low-end Macintosh Performa computers and was left with excess inventory, while underestimating demand for its high-end machines. To compound matters, its new PowerBooks had to be recalled after batteries started to catch fire, and a price war in Japan cut margins in one of its best markets. As a consequence, in the last quarter of 1995, gross margins slumped to 15%, down from 29% in 1994, and Apple lost $68 million. Spindler responded in January 1996 by announcing 1,300 layoffs. He suggested that up to 4,000 might ultimately go—some 23% of the workforce.[13] That was his last significant act. He was replaced in February by Gilbert Amelio.

Amelio, who joined Apple from National Semiconductor where he had gained a reputation for his turnaround skills, lasted just seventeen months. He followed through on Spindler's plans to cut headcount and stated that Apple would return to its differentiation strategy. His hope was that the new Mac operating system would help, but work on that was in total disarray. He took the decision to scrap the project after an investment of over $500 million. Instead, Apple purchased NeXT, the computer company founded by none other than Steve Jobs, for $425 million. The NeXT machines had received strong reviews, but had gained no market traction due to a lack of supporting applications. Amelio felt that the NeXT OS could be adapted to run on the Mac. He also hired Steve Jobs as a consultant, but Jobs was rarely seen at Apple; he was too busy running Pixar, his computer animation company that was riding a wave of success after a huge hit with the animated movie *Toy Story*.[14]

Amelio's moves did nothing to stop the slide in Apple's fortunes. By mid-1997, market share had slumped to 3%, from 9% when Amelio took the helm. The company booked a loss of $742 million in 1996 and was on track to lose another $400 million in 1997. It was too much for the board. In July 1997, Amelio was fired. With market share falling, third-party developers and distributors were rethinking their commitments to Apple. Without them, the company would be dead.

The Return of Steve Jobs

Following Amelio's departure, Steve Jobs was appointed interim CEO. In April 1998, he took the position on a permanent basis, while staying on at Pixar as CEO. Jobs moved quickly to fix the bleeding. His first act was to visit Bill Gates and strike a deal with Microsoft. Microsoft agreed to invest $150 million in Apple and to continue producing Office for the Mac through until at least 2002. Then Jobs ended the licensing deals with the clone makers, spending over $100 million to acquire the assets of the leading Mac clone maker, Power Computing, including its license.

Jobs killed slow-selling products, most notably the Apple Newton hand-held computer, and reduced the number of product lines from sixty to just four. He also pushed the company into online distribution, imitating Dell Computer's direct selling model. While these fixes bought the company time and caused a favorable reaction from the stock market, they were not recipes for growth.

New Computer Offerings

Almost immediately Jobs started to think about a new product that would embody the spirit of Apple. What emerged in May 1998 was the iMac. The differentiator for the iMac was not its software, or its power, or its monitor—it was the design of the machine itself. A self-contained unit that combined the monitor and central processing unit in translucent teal and with curved lines, the iMac was a bold departure in a world dominated by putty-colored PC boxes.

To develop the iMac, Jobs gave a team of designers, headed by Jonathan Ive, an unprecedented say in the development project. Ive's team worked closely with engineers, manufacturers, marketers, and Jobs himself. To understand how to make a plastic shell look exciting rather than cheap, the designers visited a candy factory to study the finer points of making jelly beans. They spent months working with Asian partners designing a sophisticated process capable of producing millions of iMacs a year. The designers also pushed for the internal electronics to be redesigned, to make sure that they looked good through the thick shell. Apple may have spent as much as $65 a machine on the casing, compared with perhaps $20 for the average PC.[15]

Priced at $1,299, iMac sales were strong with orders placed for 100,000 units even before the machine was available. Moreover, one-third of iMac purchases were by first-time buyers, according to Apple's own research.[16] The iMac line was continually updated, with faster processors, more memory, and bigger hard drives being added. The product was also soon available in many different colors. In 1999, Apple followed up the iMac with introduction of the iBook portable. Aimed at consumers and students, the iBook had the same design theme as the iMac and was priced aggressively at $1,599.

Sales of the iMac and iBook helped push Apple back into profitability. In 1999, the company earned $420 million on sales of $6.1 billion. In 2000, it made $611 million on sales of almost $8 billion.

To keep sales growing, Apple continued to invest in development of a new operating system, based on the technology acquired from NeXT. After three years of work by nearly one thousand software engineers, and a cost of around $1 billion, the first version of Apple's new operating system was introduced in

---

EXHIBIT 3

(a) The iMac

(b) The iBook

Source: Courtesy of Apple Inc.

2001. Known as OS X, it garnered rave reviews from analysts who saw the UNIX-based program as offering superior stability and faster speed than the old Mac OS. OS X also had an enhanced ability to run multiple programs at once to support multiple users, connected easily to other devices such as digital camcorders, and was easier for developers to write applications for. In typical Apple fashion, OS X also sported a well-designed and intuitively appealing interface. Since 2001, new versions of OS X have been introduced almost once a year. The most recent version, OS X Tiger, was introduced in 2005 and retailed for $129.

To get the installed base of Mac users, who at the time numbered 25 million, to upgrade to OS X, Apple had to offer applications. The deal with Microsoft ensured that its popular Office program would be available for the OS X. Steve Jobs had assumed that the vote of confidence by Microsoft would encourage other third-party developers to write programs for OS X, but it didn't always happen. Most significantly, in 1998 Adobe Systems refused to develop a Mac version of their consumer video editing program, which was already available for Windows PCs.

Shocked, Jobs directed Apple to start working on its own applications. The first fruits of this effort were two video editing programs, Final Cut Pro for professionals, and iMovie for consumers. Next was iLife, a bundle of multimedia programs now preinstalled on every Mac, which includes iMovie, iDVD, iPhoto, Garage Band, and the iTunes digital jukebox. Apple also developed its own web browser, Safari.

Meanwhile, Apple continued to update its computer lines with eye-catching offerings. In 2001, Apple introduced its Titanium PowerBook G4 notebooks. Cased in Titanium, these ultralight and fast notebooks featured a clean postindustrial look that marked a distinct shift from the whimsical look of the iMac and iBook. As with the iMac, Jonathan Ive's design team played a central part in the product's development. A core team of designers set up a design studio in a San Francisco warehouse, far away from Apple's main campus. They worked for six weeks on the basic design and then headed to Asia to negotiate for widescreen flat-panel displays and to work with tool makers.[17]

The Titanium notebooks were followed by a redesigned desktop line that appealed to the company's graphic design customers, including the offering of elegantly designed very widescreen cinema displays. In 2004, Ive's design team came out with yet another elegant offering, the iMac G5 computer, which *PC Magazine* described as a "simple, stunning all-in-one design."[18]

EXHIBIT 4

The iMac G5

Source: Courtesy of Apple Inc.

EXHIBIT 5

World Wide Market Share and Units Sold, 2005

Company	Market Share (%)	Units Sold (millions)
Dell Computer	18.1%	37.76
Hewlett-Packard	15.6%	32.54
Lenovo	6.2%	12.93
Acer	4.7%	9.80
Fujistu-Siemens	4.1%	8.55
Apple	2.2%	4.59
Other	49.1%	102.42
Total	**100.0%**	**208.60**

Sources: Standard & Poor's Industry Surveys, Computers: Hardware, December 8, 2005.

For all of Apple's undisputed design excellence and the loyalty of its core user base—graphic artists and students—Apple's market share remained anemic, trailing far behind industry leaders Dell, Hewlett-Packard, and IBM/Lenovo (see Exhibit 5). Weak demand, combined with its low market share, translated into another loss for Apple in 2001, leading some to question the permanence of Steve Jobs's turnaround. While Apple's worldwide market share fell to as low as 1.9% in 2004, it started to pick up again in 2005 and throughout 2006. Momentum was particularly strong in the United States, where Apple shipped 1.3 million computers in the year through to July 2006, giving it a 12% year-over-year growth rate and a 4.8% share of the U.S. market. Driving growth, according to many analysts, was the surging popularity of Apple's iPod music player, which had raised Apple's profile among younger consumers and was having a spillover effect on Mac sales.[19]

Intel Inside, Windows on the Desktop

Since the company's inception, Apple had not used Intel microprocessors, which had become the industry standard for microprocessors since the introduction of the IBM PC in 1981. In June 2005, Apple announced that it would start to do so. Driving the transition was growing frustration with the performance of the PowerPC chip line made by IBM that Apple had been using for over a decade. The PowerPC had failed to keep up with the Intel chips, which were both faster and had lower power consumption—something that was very important in the portable computer market, where Apple had a respectable market share.

The transition created significant risks for Apple. Old applications and OS X had to be rewritten to run on Intel processors. By the spring of 2006 Apple had produced Intel-compatible versions of OS X and its own applications, but many other applications had not been rewritten for Intel chips. To make transition easier, Apple provided a free software program, known as Rosetta, that enabled users to run older applications on Intel-based Macs. Moreover, Apple went a step further by issuing a utility program, known as Boot Camp, which enabled Mac owners to run Windows XP on their machines. Boot Camp will be included as a part of the next version of OS X, OS X Leopard, which is due out in 2007.

Reviews of Apple's Intel-based machines were generally favorable, with many reviewers noting the speed improvement over the older PowerPC Macs—although the speed improvement tended to evaporate if the Rosetta program had to be used to run an application.[20]

In the fall of 2006, Apple reported that its transition to an Intel-based architecture was complete, some six months ahead of schedule. Although sales of Macs had been slow during late 2005 and early 2006, this seems to have been due to consumers putting off purchases while waiting for the new machines. The company's sales of the new Macs exhibited healthy growth in the second and third quarters of the year. Sales of portable MacBooks were particularly strong.

The move to Intel architecture may have helped Apple to close the price differential that had long existed between Windows-based PCs and Apple's offerings. According to one analysis, by September 2006 Apple's products were selling at a *discount* to comparable product offerings from Dell and Hewlett-Packard.[21]

Moving into Retail

In 2001 Apple made another important strategic shift—the company opened its first retail store. In an industry that had long relied on third-party retailers, or direct sales as in the case of Dell, this shift seemed risky. One concern was that Apple might encounter a backlash from Apple's long-standing retail partners. Another was that Apple would never be able to generate the sales volume required to justify expensive retail space; the product line seemed too thin. However, Apple clearly believed that it was hurt by a lack of retail presence. Many computer retailers didn't carry Apple machines, and some of those that did often buried Mac displays deep in the store.

From the start, Apple's stores exhibited the same stylish design that characterized its products with clean lines, attractive displays, and a postindustrial feel (see Exhibit 6). Steve Jobs himself was intimately involved in the design process. Indeed, he is one of the named inventors on a patent Apple secured for the design of the signature glass staircase found in many stores, and he was apparently personally involved in the design of a glass cube atop a store on New York's Fifth Avenue that opened in 2006. In an interview, Jobs noted that "we spent a lot of time designing the store, and it deserves to be built perfectly."[22]

Customers and analysts were immediately impressed by the product fluency that the employees in Apple stores exhibited. They also liked the highlight of many stores, a "genius bar" where technical experts helped customers fix problems with their Apple products. The wide-open interior space, however, did nothing to allay the fears of critics that Apple's product portfolio was just too narrow to generate the traffic required to support premium space. The critics couldn't have been more wrong. Spurred on by booming sales

of the iPod, Apple's stores did exceptionally well. By 2005, Apple had 137 stores in upscale locations that generated $2.3 billion in sales and $140 million in profits. Sales per square foot during 2005 were an almost unprecedented $4,000, making Apple the envy of other retailers.[23]

The iPod Revolution

In the late 1990s and early 2000s the music industry was grappling with the implications of two new technologies. The first was the development of inexpensive portable MP3 players that could store and play digital music files such as Diamond Media's Rio, which was introduced in 1997 and could hold two hours of music. The second was the rise of peer-to-peer computer networks such as Napster, Kazaa, Grokster, and Morpheus that enabled individuals to efficiently swap digital files over the Internet. By the early 2000s, millions of individuals were downloading music files over the Internet without the permission of the copyright holders, the music publishing companies. For the music industry, this development had been devastating. After years of steady growth, global sales of music peaked in 1999 at $38.5 billion, falling to $32 billion in 2003. Despite the fall in sales, the International Federation of the Phonographic Industry (IFPI) claimed that demand for

---

EXHIBIT 6

An Apple Store

Source: Courtesy of Apple Inc.

music was higher than ever, but that the decline in sales reflected the fact that "the commercial value of music is being widely devalued by mass copying and piracy."[24]

The music industry had tried to counter piracy over the Internet by taking legal action to shut down the peer-to-peer networks, such as Napster, and filing lawsuits against individuals who made large numbers of music files available over the Internet. Its success had been limited, in part because peer-to-peer networks offered tremendous utility to consumers. They were fast and immediate, and enabled consumers to unbundle albums, downloading just the tracks they wanted while ignoring junk filler tracks. And of course, they were free.

The music industry was desperate for a legal alternative to illegal downloading. Its own initiatives, introduced in 2002, had gained little traction. MusicNet, which offered songs from Warner Music, BMG, and EMI, had a single subscription plan—$9.85 a month for one hundred streams and one hundred downloads. After thirty days, downloads expired and couldn't be played. Pressplay, which offered music from Sony, Universal, and EMI, had four subscription plans, from $9.95 to $24.95 a month, for up to one thousand streams and one hundred downloads. The higher subscription fee service from Pressplay let users burn up to twenty songs a month onto CDs that would not expire, but no more than two songs could be burned from any one artist.[25]

Then along came the iPod and iTunes. These products were born out of an oversight—in the late 1990s when consumers were starting to burn their favorite CDs, Macs did not have CD burners or software to manage users' digital music collections. Realizing the mistake, CEO Steven Jobs ordered Apple's software developers to create the iTunes program to help Mac users manage their growing digital music collections. The first iTunes program led to the concept of the iPod. If people were going to maintain the bulk of their music collection on a computer, they needed a portable MP3 player to take music with them—a Sony Walkman for the digital age. While there were such devices on the market already, they could hold only a few dozen songs each.

To run the iPod, Apple licensed software from PortalPlayer. Apple also learned that Toshiba was building a tiny 1.8 inch hard drive that could hold over one thousand songs. Apple quickly cut a deal with Toshiba, giving it exclusive rights to the drive for eighteen months. Meanwhile, Apple focused on designing the user interface, the exterior styling, and the synchronization software to make it work with the Mac. As with so many product offerings unveiled since Jobs returned to the helm, the design team led by Jonathan Ive played a pivotal role in giving birth to the iPod. Ive's team worked in secrecy in San Francisco. The members, all paid extremely well by industry standards, worked together in a large open studio with little personal space. The team was able to figure out how to put a layer of clear plastic over the white and black core of an iPod, giving it tremendous depth of texture. The finish was superior to other MP3 players, with no visible screws or obvious joints between parts. The serial number of the iPod was not on a sticker, as with most products; it was elegantly etched onto the back of the device. This attention to detail and design elegance, although not without cost implications, was to turn the iPod into a fashion accessory.[26]

The iPod was unveiled in October 2001 to mixed reviews. The price of $399 was significantly above that of competing devices, and since the iPod worked only with Apple computers, it seemed destined to be a niche product. However, initial sales were strong. It turned out that consumers were willing to pay a premium price for the iPod's huge storage capacity. Moreover, Jobs made the call to develop a version of the iPod that would be compatible with Windows. After it was introduced in mid-2002, sales took off.

By this time, Jobs was dealing with a bigger strategic issue—how to persuade the music companies to make their music available for legal downloads. It was here that Steve Jobs's legendary selling ability came into play. With a prototype for an online iTunes store in hand, Jobs met with executives from the major labels. He persuaded them that it was in their best interest to support a legal music download business as an alternative to widespread illegal downloading of music over peer-to-peer networks, which despite its best efforts, the music industry had not been able to shut down. People would pay to download music over the Internet, he argued. Although all of the labels were setting up their own online businesses, Jobs felt that since they were limited to selling music owned by the parent companies, demand would be limited too. What was needed was a reputable independent online music retailer, and Apple fit the bill. If it was going to work, however, all of the labels needed to get on board. Under Jobs's scheme, iTunes files would be downloaded for 99 cents each. The only portable digital player that the files could be stored and played on was an iPod. Jobs's argument was that this closed world made it easier to protect copyrighted material from unauthorized distribution.

Jobs also meet with twenty of the world's top recording artists, including U2's Bono, Sheryl Crow, and Mick Jagger. His pitch to them was this—digital distribution is going to happen, and the best way to protect your interests is to support a legal online music distribution business. Wooed by Jobs, these powerful stakeholders encouraged the music recording companies to take Apple's proposal seriously.[27]

By early 2003 Jobs had all of the major labels on board. Launched in April 2003, within days it was clear that Apple had a major hit on its hands. A million songs were sold in the first week. In mid-2004, iTunes passed the 100 million download mark, and sales kept accelerating, hitting the 150 million download mark in October 2004. At that point, customers were downloading over 4 million songs per week, which represented a run rate of more than 200 million a year. While Steve Jobs admitted that Apple does not make much money from iTunes downloads—probably only 10 cents a song—it does make good margins of sales of the iPod, and sales of the iPod ballooned in 2005 (see Exhibit 7).

Helped by new models, which as always were elegantly designed, iPod sales continued to boom in the first half of Apple's fiscal 2006 (the last three months of 2005 and the first three months of 2006). In this six-month period, Apple sold 22.5 million iPods and generated $4.26 billion in sales, surpassing computer

---

EXHIBIT 7

Sales of Apple's Main Product Lines (millions)

	2003	2004	2005
Computers	$4,491	$4,923	$6,275
iPod	$345	$1,306	$4,540
iTunes	$36	$278	$899
Software	$644	$821	$1,091
Peripherals	$691	$951	$1,126

Source: Apple Computer 10K Reports, 2006.

---

sales for the first time, which stood at $3.29 billion for the six-month period. iTunes kicked in another $976 million.

As the installed base of iPods expanded, an ecosystem of companies selling iPod accessories started to emerge. The accessories include speakers, head phones, and add-on peripherals that allow iPod users to record their voices, charge their iPods on the go, play their tunes over the radio, or use their iPods wirelessly with a remote. There are also cases, neck straps, belt clips, and so on. By 2006 it was estimated that there were over one hundred companies in this system. Collectively they may have sold as much as $1 billion of merchandise during the last three months of 2005. Apple collects an unspecified royalty from companies whose products access the iPod's ports and thus benefits indirectly from the preference of buyers for the iPod over competing products that lack the same accessories.[28]

Success such as this attracts competitors, and soon there were plenty. RealNetworks, Yahoo, and Napster all set up legal downloading services to compete with iTunes. Even Wal-Mart got into the act, offering music downloads for 89 cents a track. However, iTunes continued to outsell its rivals by a wide margin. In mid-2006, iTunes was accounting for about 80% of all legal music downloads.[29] iTunes was also the fourth largest music retailer in the United States; the other three all had physical stores.

The iPod also had plenty of competition. Many of the competing devices were priced aggressively and had as much storage capacity as the iPod. Few, however, managed to gain share against the iPod, which by mid-2006 still accounted for 77% of annual sales in the U.S. market. The most successful rival to date has been SanDisk, which captured almost 10% of the market with its family of music players.

One reason for the failure of competitors to garner more market share has been hardware and software problems that arise when consumers try to download songs sold by one company onto a machine made by another. In contrast, iTunes and iPod have always worked seamlessly together.

In an effort to counter this, Microsoft announced the release of its own digital music player in 2006, Zune. Zune is designed to work with Microsoft's own online music store. Similarly, RealNetworks has announced a deal with SanDisk to make a digital music device that's specifically designed to work with RealNetworks' online music store, Rhapsody.[30] Both products are expected to debut in late 2007.

However, Apple was not standing still. New, even smaller versions of the iPod, such as the iPod Shuffle and iPod Nano, were keeping sales strong. The latest iPods, introduced in September 2006, had longer battery lives, bigger hard drives (enabling some models to store up to 15,000 songs or 150 hours of video), and brighter displays. They were priced aggressively, while still maintaining the thin, elegant look that characterized the line.

At the same time, Apple announced that the iTunes store would start to sell movie downloads. Initially, the movies were limited to offerings from Disney (where Steve Jobs had become the largest shareholder after Disney had acquired Pixar in 2005), but Apple expected to add other studios in the near future. Downloaded movies would have near DVD quality and could be played on TVs, computers, or iPods. In addition, Apple announced that it would be introducing a small "box," which would connect to a TV, cable set top box, or stereo, that would pull digital files (videos, music, and photos) wirelessly from any iTunes-enabled PC (Windows or Mac).

The Personal Computer Industry in the 2000s

While Apple dominated the music downloading and portable music player businesses with iTunes and iPod, it remained a niche player in the computer industry. After years of growth, sales of PCs had fallen for the first time ever in 2001, but the growth path had soon been resumed. According to IDC, a market research firm, total PC shipments were expected to hit 287 million units in 2008, up from 179 million units in 2004 (see Exhibit 8). The U.S. market would remain the world's largest, with 82 million units being sold in 2008, up from 58 million in 2004, representing a growth rate in the high single digits. Sales to consumers accounted for about 88.5 million of the 230 million PCs sold in 2006.[31]

The industry is characterized by a handful of players who collectively account for about half the market, and a long tail of small enterprises that produce unbranded or locally branded "white box" computers, often selling their machines at a significant discount to globally branded products (see Exhibit 5).

Among the larger players, consolidation has been a theme for several years. In 2002, Hewlett-Packard acquired Compaq Computer; Gateway and eMachines merged in 2004; and in 2005, the Chinese firm Lenovo acquired the PC business of IBM. The large PC firms compete aggressively by offering ever more powerful machines, producing them as efficiently as possible and lowering prices to sell more volume. The average selling price of a PC has fallen from around $1,700 in 1999 to under $1,000 in 2006, and projections are that it may continued to fall, fueled in part by aggressive competition between Dell Computer and Hewlett-Packard.[32]

All of these players focus on the design, assembly, and sales of PCs, while purchasing the vast majority of component parts from independent companies. In recent years, the top PC companies have reduced their R&D spending as a percentage of sales, as the industry has transitioned toward a commodity business.

The existence of the long tail of white box makers is made possible by the open architecture of the dominant PC standard, based on Intel-compatible microprocessors and a Microsoft operating system, and the low-tech nature of the assembly process. The components for these boxes, which are themselves commodities, can be purchased cheaply off the shelf. White box makers have strong positions in many developing nations. In Mexico, for example, domestic brands accounted for 60% of all sales in 2005, up from 44% in 2000. In Latin America as a whole, 70% of personal computers are produced locally. White box makers have much weaker positions in the United States, western Europe, and Japan, where consumers display a stronger preference for branded products that incorporate leading-edge technology. In contrast, in the developing world, consumers are willing to accept older components if it saves a few hundred dollars.[33]

During the 1990s and early 2000s, Dell grew rapidly to capture the market lead. Dell's success was based on the inventory management efficiencies associated with its direct selling model (Dell could build machines to order, which reduced its need to hold inventory). Dell was also helped by the problems Hewlett-Packard faced when it merged with Compaq Computer. By 2005, however, a resurgent Hewlett-Packard had lowered its costs, could price more aggressively, and was starting to gain ground against Dell. Apple Computer continued to be the odd man out in this industry and was the only major manufacturer that did not adhere to the Windows architecture.

EXHIBIT 8

Unit Shipments in the PC Industry

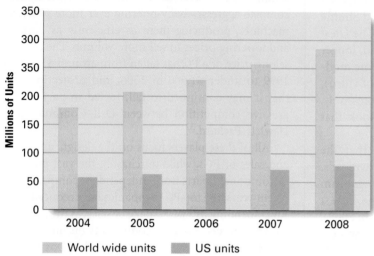

Source: Data from IDC. 2007 and 2008 are forecasts.

Strategic Issues

As 2006 drew to a close, Apple was in an enviable position. The iPod business was continuing to exhibit rapid growth, and sales of Apple computers, particularly portables, were strong. Still, there were questions surrounding the company. Apple had always been good at innovating, but never good at profiting from innovation. Would it be different this time? Forecasts called for 2006 and 2007 to be strong years for Apple, with record sales and profits, but much of this was due to the iPod boom, and there were questions about how sustainable that might be. In the PC business, Apple was still a niche player, albeit one with renewed growth prospects. The company had very limited presence in the large business market. Could this be changed? Would Apple be able to capitalize on the strong iPod business to expand its share of computer sales? And what were the implications for Apple's long-term competitive position?

ENDNOTES

1. Quoted in Pete Burrows, "Steve Jobs' Magic Kingdom," *Business Week*, February 6, 2006, pages 62–68.
2. N. Wingfield, "Apple Unveils New Computers," *Wall Street Journal*, August 8, 2006, page B3.
3. Much of this section is drawn from P. Freiberger and M. Swaine, *Fire in the Valley*, New York: McGraw-Hill, 2000.
4. For a detailed history of the development of the Apple II see Steve Weyhrich, "Apple II History," http://apple2history.org/history/ah01.html.
5. P. Freiberger and M. Swaine, *Fire in the Valley*, New York: McGraw-Hill, 2000, page 357.
6. Andy Hertzfeld, "Reality Distortion Field," http://www.folklore.org/ProjectView.py?project=Macintosh.
7. Andy Hertzfeld, "Reality Distortion Field," http://www.folklore.org/ProjectView.py?project=Macintosh.
8. This version of events was told to the author by a senior executive who was present in the room at the time.
9. Jim Carlton, "Playing Catch Up—Apple Finally Gives in and Attempts Cloning," *Wall Street Journal*, October 17, 1994, page A1.
10. D. B. Yoffie, "Apple Computer 1992," Harvard Business School Case, 792-081.
11. Andrew Kupfer, "Apple's Plan to Survive and Grow," *Fortune*, May 4, 1992, pages 68–71; B. R. Schlender, "Yet Another Strategy for Apple," *Fortune*, October 22, 1990, pages 81–85.
12. B. Schlender, "Paradise Lost: Apple's Quest for Life After Death," *Fortune*, February 1996, pp. 64–72.
13. Jim Carlton, "Apple's Losses to Stretch into 2nd Period," *Wall Street Journal*, January 18, 1996, page B7.
14. Peter Burrows, "Dangerous Limbo," *Business Week*, July 21, 1997, page 32.
15. Peter Burrows, "The Man Behind Apple's Design Magic," *Business Week*, September 2005, pages 27–34.
16. A. Reinhardt, "Can Steve Jobs Keep His Mojo Working?" *Business Week*, August 2, 1999, page 32.
17. Peter Burrows, "The Man Behind Apple's Design Magic," *Business Week*, September 2005, pages 27–34.
18. "Apple iMac G5 Review," *PC Magazine*, online at http://www.pcmag.com/article2/0,1759,1648796,00.asp.
19. Standard & Poor's Industry Surveys, Computers: Hardware, "Global Demand for PCs Accelerates," December 8, 2005; Mark Veverka, "Barron's Insight: Apple's Horizon Brightens," *Wall Street Journal*, July 23, 2006, page A4.
20. Peter Lewis, "Apple's New Core," *Fortune*, March 29, 2006, pages 182–184.
21. Citigroup Global Markets, "Apple Computer: New Products Position Apple Well for Holidays," September 13, 2006.
22. N. Wingfield, "How Apple's Store Strategy Beat the Odds," *Wall Street Journal*, May 17, 2006, page B1.

23. M. Frazier, "The Bigger Apple," *Advertising Age*, February 13, 2006, pages 4–6.

24. IFPI News Release, "Global Music Sales Down 5% in 2001," http://www.ifpi.org.

25. W. S. Mossberg, "Record Labels Launch Two Feeble Services to Replace Napster," *Wall Street Journal*, February 7, 2002, page B1.

26. Peter Burrows, "The Man Behind Apple's Design Magic," *Business Week*, September 2005, pages 27–34.

27. N. Wingfield and E. Smith. "U2's Gig: Help Apple Sell iPods," *Wall Street Journal*, October 20, 2004, page D5; Apple Computer Press Release, "iTunes Music Store Downloads Top 150 Million Songs," October 14, 2004.

28. Paul Taylor, "iPod Ecosystem Offers Rich Pickings," FT.com, January 24, 2006, page 1.

29. T. Braithwaite and K. Allison, "Crunch Time for Apple's Music Icon," *Financial Times*, June 14, 2006, page 27.

30. N. Wingfield and R. A. Guth, "iPod, They Pod: Rivals Imitate Apple's Success," *Wall Street Journal*, September 18, 2006, page B1.

31. IDC Press Release, "Long-term PC Outlook Improves," September 14, 2006.

32. Standard & Poor's Industry Surveys, Computers: Hardware, "Global Demand for PCs Accelerates," December 8, 2005.

33. M. Dickerson, "Plain PCs Sitting Pretty," *Los Angeles Times*, December 11, 2005, page C1.

The Home Videogame Industry: Pong to Xbox 360

This case was prepared by Charles W. L. Hill, the University of Washington.

An Industry is Born

In 1968, Nolan Bushnell, the twenty-four-year-old son of a Utah cement contractor, graduated from the University of Utah with a degree in engineering.[1] Bushnell then moved to California, where he worked briefly in the computer graphics division of Ampex. At home, Bushnell turned his daughter's bedroom into a laboratory. There, he created a simpler version of Space War, a computer game that had been invented in 1962 by an MIT graduate student, Steve Russell. Bushnell's version of Russell's game, which he called Computer Space, was made of integrated circuits connected to a nineteen-inch black-and-white television screen. Unlike a computer, Bushnell's invention could do nothing but play the game, which meant that, unlike a computer, it could be produced cheaply.

Bushnell envisioned videogames like his standing next to pinball machines in arcades. With hopes of having his invention put into production, Bushnell left Ampex to work for a small pinball company that manufactured 1,500 copies of his videogame. The game never sold, primarily because the player had to read a full page of directions before he or she could play the game—way too complex for an arcade game. Bushnell left the pinball company and with a friend, Ted Dabney, put up $500 to start a company that would develop a simpler videogame. They wanted to call the company Syzygy, but the name was already

taken, so they settled on *Atari*, a Japanese word that was the equivalent of "*check* in the *go.*"

In his home laboratory, Bushnell built the simplest game he could think of. People knew the rules immediately, and it could be played with one hand. The game was modeled on table tennis, and players batted a ball back and forth with paddles that could be moved up and down sides of a court by twisting knobs. He named the game "Pong" after the sonar-like sound that was emitted every time the ball connected with a paddle.

In the fall of 1972, Bushnell installed his prototype for Pong in Andy Capp's tavern in Sunnyvale, California. The only instructions were "avoid missing the ball for a high score." In the first week, 1,200 quarters were deposited in the casserole dish that served for a coin box in Bushnell's prototype. Bushnell was ecstatic; his simple game had brought in $300 in a week. The pinball machine that stood next to it averaged $35 a week.

Lacking the capital to mass-produce the game, Bushnell approached established amusement game companies, only to be repeatedly shown the door. Down but hardly out, Bushnell cut his hair, put on a suit, and talked his way into a $50,000 line of credit from a local bank. He set up a production line in an abandoned roller skating rink and hired people to assemble machines while Led Zeppelin and the Rolling Stones were played at full volume over the speaker system of the rink. Among his first batch of employees was a skinny seventeen-year-old named Steve Jobs, who would later found a few companies of his own, including Apple Computer, NeXT, and Pixar. Like others, Jobs had been attracted by a classified ad that read "Have Fun and Make Money."

In no time at all, Bushnell was selling all the machines that his small staff could make—about ten per day—but to grow, he needed additional capital. While the ambience at the rink, with its mix of rock music and marijuana fumes, put off most potential investors, Don Valentine, one of the country's most astute and credible venture capitalists, was impressed with the growth story. Armed with Valentine's money, Atari began to increase production and expand their range of games. New games included Tank and Breakout; the latter was designed by Jobs and a friend of his, Steve Wozniak, who had left Hewlett-Packard to work at Atari.

By 1974, 100,000 Pong-like games were sold worldwide. Although Atari manufactured only 10% of the games, the company still made $3.2 million that year. With the Pong clones coming on strong, Bushnell decided to make a Pong system for the home. In fact, Magnavox had been marketing a similar game for the home since 1972, although sales had been modest.[2] Bushnell's team managed to compress Atari's coin-operated Pong game down to a few inexpensive circuits that were contained in the game console. Atari's Pong had a sharper picture and more sensitive controllers than Magnavox's machine. It also cost less. Bushnell then went on a road show, demonstrating Pong to toy buyers, but he received an indifferent response and no sales. A dejected Bushnell returned to Atari with no idea of what to do next. Then the buyer for the sporting goods department at Sears came to see Bushnell, reviewed the machine, and offered to buy every home Pong game Atari could make. With Sears's backing, Bushnell boosted production. Sears ran a major television ad campaign to sell home Pong, and Atari's sales soared, hitting $450 million in 1975. The home videogame had arrived.

Boom and Bust

Nothing attracts competitors like success, and by 1976 about twenty different companies were crowding into the home videogame market, including National Semiconductor, RCA, Coleco, and Fairchild. Recognizing the limitations of existing home videogame designs, Fairchild came out in 1976 with a home videogame system capable of playing multiple games. The Fairchild system consisted of three components—a console, controllers, and cartridges. The console was a small computer optimized for graphics processing capabilities. It was designed to receive information

from the controllers, process it, and send signals to a television monitor. The controllers were hand-held devices used to direct on-screen action. The cartridges contained chips encoding the instructions for a game. The cartridges were designed to be inserted into the console.

In 1976, Bushnell sold Atari to Warner Communications for $28 million. Bushnell stayed on to run Atari. Backed by Warner's capital, in 1977 Atari developed and brought out its own cartridge-based system, the Atari 2600. The 2600 system was sold for $200, and associated cartridges retailed for $25–$30. Sales surged during the 1977 Christmas season. However, a lack of manufacturing capacity on the part of market leader Atari and a very cautious approach to inventory by Fairchild led to shortages and kept sales significantly below what they could have been. Fairchild's cautious approach was the result of prior experience in consumer electronics. A year earlier it had increased demand for its digital watches, only to accumulate a buildup of excess inventory that had caused the company to take a $24.5 million write-off.[3]

After the 1977 Christmas season, Atari claimed to have sold about 400,000 units of the 2600 VCA, about 50% of all cartridge-based systems in American homes. Atari had also earned more than $100 million in sales of game cartridges. By this point, second-place Fairchild sold around 250,000 units of its system. Cartridge sales for the year totaled about 1.2 million units, with an average selling price of around $20. Fresh from this success and fortified by market forecasts predicting sales of 33 million cartridges and an installed base of 16 million machines by 1980, Bushnell committed Atari to manufacturing 1 million units of the 2600 for the 1978 Christmas season. Atari estimated that total demand would reach 2 million units. Bushnell was also encouraged by signals from Fairchild that it would again be limiting production to around 200,000 units. At this point, Atari had a library of nine games. Fairchild had seventeen.[4]

Atari was not the only company to be excited by the growth forecasts. In 1978, a host of other companies, including Coleco, National Semiconductor, Magnavox, General Instrument, and a dozen other companies, entered the market with incompatible cartridge-based home systems. The multitude of choices did not seem to entice consumers, however, and the 1978 Christmas season brought unexpectedly low sales. Only Atari and Coleco survived an industry shakeout. Atari lost Bushnell, who was ousted by Warner executives. (Bushnell went on to start Chuck E. Cheese Pizza Time Theater, a restaurant chain that had 278 outlets by 1981.) Bushnell later stated that part of the problem was a disagreement over strategy. Bushnell wanted Atari to price the 2600 at cost and make money on sales of software; Warner wanted to continue making profits on hardware sales.[5]

Several important developments occurred in 1979. First, several game producers and programmers defected from Atari to set up their own firm, Activision, and to make games compatible with the Atari 2600. Their success encouraged others to follow suit. Second, Coleco developed an expansion module that allowed its machine to play Atari games. Atari and Mattel (which entered the market in 1979) did likewise. Third, the year 1979 saw the introduction of three new games to the home market—Space Invaders, Asteroids, and Pac Man. All three were adapted from popular arcade games and all three helped drive demand for players.

Demand recovered strongly in late 1979 and kept growing for the next three years. In 1981, U.S. sales of home videogames and cartridges hit $1 billion. In 1982, they surged to $3 billion, with Atari accounting for half of this amount. It seemed as if Atari could do no wrong; the 2600 was everywhere. About 20 million units were sold, and by late 1982, a large number of independent companies, including Activision, Imagic, and Epyx, were now producing hundreds of games for the 2600. Second-place Coleco was also doing well, partly because of a popular arcade game, Donkey Kong, which it had licensed from a Japanese company called Nintendo.

Atari was also in contact with Nintendo. In 1982, the company very nearly licensed the rights to Nintendo's Famicom, a cartridge-based videogame system machine that was a big hit in Japan. Atari's successor to the 2600, the 5200, was not selling well and the Famicom seemed like a good substitute. The negotiations broke down, however, when Atari discovered that Nintendo had extended its Donkey Kong license to Coleco. This allowed Coleco to port a version of the game to its home computer, which was a direct competitor to Atari's 800 home computer.[6]

After a strong 1982 season, the industry hoped for continued growth in 1983. Then the bottom dropped out of the market. Sales of home videogames plunged to $100 million. Atari lost $500 million in the first nine months of the year, causing the stock of parent company Warner Communications to drop by half. Part of the blame for the collapse was laid at the feet of an enormous inventory overhang of unsold games. About 15 to 20 million surplus game cartridges were left over from the 1982 Christmas season (in 1981, there were none). On top of this, around 500 new games hit the market in 1993. The average price of a cartridge plunged from $30 in 1979 to $16 in 1982, and then to $4 in 1983. As sales slowed, retailers cut back on the shelf space allocated to videogames. It proved difficult for new games to make a splash in a crowded market. Atari had to dispose of 6 million ET: The Extraterrestrial games. Meanwhile, big hits from previous years, such as Pac Man, were bundled with game players and given away free to try to encourage system sales.[7]

Surveying the rubble, commentators claimed that the videogame industry was dead. The era of dedicated game machines was over, they claimed. Personal computers were taking their place.[8] It seemed to be true. Mattel sold off its game business, Fairchild moved on to other things, Coleco folded, and Warner decided to break up Atari and sell its constituent pieces—at least, those pieces for which it could find a buyer. No one in America seemed to want to have anything to do with the home videogame business; no one, that is, except for Minoru Arakawa, the head of Nintendo's U.S. subsidiary, Nintendo of America (NOA). Picking through the rubble of the industry, Arakawa noticed that there were people who still packed video arcades, bringing in $7 billion a year, more money than the entire movie industry. Perhaps it was not a lack of interest in home videogames that had killed the industry. Perhaps it was bad business practice.

The Nintendo Monopoly

Nintendo was a century-old Japanese company that had built up a profitable business making playing cards before diversifying into the videogame business. Based in Kyoto and still run by the founding Yamauchi family, the company started to diversify into the videogame business in the late 1970s. The first step was to license videogame technology from Magnavox. In 1977, Nintendo introduced a home videogame system in Japan based on this technology that played a variation of Pong. In 1978, the company began to sell coin-operated videogames. It had its first hit with Donkey Kong, designed by Sigeru Miyamoto.

The Famicom

In the early 1980s, the company's boss, Hiroshi Yamauchi, decided that Nintendo had to develop its own videogame machine. He pushed the company's engineers to develop a machine that combined superior graphics processing capabilities and low cost. Yamauchi wanted a machine that could sell for $75, less than half the price of competing machines at the time. He dubbed the machine the Family Computer, or Famicom. The machine that his engineers designed was based on the controller, console, and plug-in cartridge format pioneered by Fairchild. It contained two custom chips—an 8-bit central processing unit and a graphics processing unit. Both chips had been scaled down to perform only essential functions. A 16-bit processor was available at the time, but to keep costs down, Yamauchi refused to use it.

Nintendo approached Ricoh, the electronics giant, which had spare semiconductor capacity. Employees at Ricoh said that the chips had to cost no more that 2,000 yen. Ricoh thought that the 2,000-yen price point was absurd. Yamauchi's response was to guarantee Ricoh a 3-million-chip order within two years. Since the leading companies in Japan were selling, at most, 30,000 videogames per year at the time, many within the company viewed this as an outrageous commitment, but Ricoh went for it.[9]

Another feature of the machine was its memory—2,000 bytes of random access memory (RAM), compared to the 256 bytes of RAM in the Atari machine. The result was a machine with superior graphics processing capabilities and faster action that could handle far more complex games than Atari games. Nintendo's engineers also built a new set of chips into the game cartridges. In addition to chips that held the game program, Nintendo developed memory map controller (MMC) chips that took over some of the graphics processing work from the chips in the console and enabled the system to handle more complex games. With the addition of the MMC chips, the potential for more sophisticated and more complex games had arrived. Over time, Nintendo's engineers developed more powerful MMC chips, enabling the basic 8-bit system to do things that originally seemed out of reach. The engineers also figured out a way to include a battery backup system in cartridges that allowed some games to store information independently—to keep track of where a player had left off or to track high scores.

The Games

Yamauchi recognized that great hardware that would not sell itself. The key to the market, he reasoned, was great games. Yamauchi had instructed the engineers, when they were developing the hardware, to make sure that "it was appreciated by software engineers." Nintendo decided that it would become a haven for game designers. "An ordinary man," Yamauchi said, "cannot develop good games no matter how hard he tries. A handful of people in this world can develop games that everyone wants. Those are the people we want at Nintendo."[10]

Yamauchi had an advantage in the person of Sigeru Miyamoto. Miyamoto had joined Nintendo at the age of twenty-four. Yamauchi had hired Miyamoto, a graduate of Kanazawa Munici College of Industrial Arts, as a favor to his father and an old friend, although he had little idea what he would do with an artist. For three years, Miyamoto worked as Nintendo's staff artist. Then in 1980, Yamauchi called Miyamoto into his office. Nintendo had started selling coin-operated videogames, but one of the new games, Radarscope, was a disaster. Could Miyamoto come up with a new game? Miyamoto was delighted. He had always spent a lot of time drawing cartoons, and as a student, he had played videogames constantly. Miyamoto believed that videogames could be used to bring cartoons to life.[11]

The game Miyamoto developed was nothing short of a revelation. At a time when most coin-operated videogames lacked characters or depth, Miyamoto created a game around a story that had both. Most games involved battles with space invaders or heroes shooting lasers at aliens; Miyamoto's game did neither. Based loosely on *Beauty and the Beast* and *King Kong*, Miyamoto's game involved a pet ape who runs off with his master's beautiful girlfriend. His master is an ordinary carpenter called Mario, who has a bulbous nose, a bushy mustache, a pair of large pathetic eyes, and a red cap (which Miyamoto added because he was not good at hairstyles). He does not carry a laser gun. The ape runs off with the girlfriend to get back at his master, who was not especially nice to the beast. The man, of course, has to get his girlfriend back by running up ramps, climbing ladders, jumping off elevators, and the like, while the ape throws objects at the hapless carpenter. Since the main character is an ape, Miyamoto called him Kong; because the main character is as stubborn as a donkey, he called the game Donkey Kong.

Released in 1981, Donkey Kong was a sensation in the world of coin-operated video arcades and a smash hit for Nintendo. In 1984, Yamauchi again summoned Miyamoto to his office. He needed more games, this time for Famicom. Miyamoto was made the head of a new research and development (R&D) group and told to come up with the most imaginative videogames ever.

Miyamoto began with Mario from Donkey Kong. A colleague had told him that Mario looked more like a plumber than a carpenter, so a plumber he became. Miyamoto gave Mario a brother, Luigi, who was as tall and thin as Mario was short and fat. They became the Super Mario Brothers. Since plumbers spend their time working on pipes, large green sewer pipes became obstacles and doorways into secret worlds. Mario and Luigi's task was to search for the captive Princess Toadstool. Mario and Luigi are endearing bumblers, unequal to their tasks yet surviving. They shoot, squash, or evade their enemies—a potpourri of inventions that include flying turtles and stinging fish, man-eating flowers and fire-breathing dragons— while they collect gold coins, blow air bubbles, and climb vines into smiling clouds.[12]

Super Mario Brothers was introduced in 1985. For Miyamoto, this was just the beginning. Between 1985 and 1991, Miyamoto produced eight Mario games. About 60 to 70 million were sold worldwide, making Miyamoto the most successful game designer in the world. After adapting Donkey Kong for Famicom, he also went on to create other top-selling games, including another classic, The Legend of Zelda. While Miyamoto drew freely from folklore, literature, and pop culture, the main source for his ideas was his own experience. The memory of being lost among a maze of sliding doors in his family's home was recreated in the labyrinths of the Zelda games. The dog that attacked him when he was a child attacks Mario in Super Mario. As a child, Miyamoto had once climbed a tree to catch a view of far-off mountains and had become stuck. Mario gets himself in a similar fix. Once Miyamoto went hiking without a map and was surprised to stumble across a lake. In the Legend of Zelda, part of the adventure is in walking into new places without a map and being confronted by surprises.

Nintendo in Japan

Nintendo introduced Famicom into the Japanese market in May 1983. Famicom was priced at $100, more than Yamauchi wanted, but significantly less than the products of competitors. When he introduced the machine, Yamauchi urged retailers to forgo profits on the hardware because it was just a tool to sell software, and that is where they would make their money. Backed by an extensive advertising campaign, 500,000 units of Famicom were sold in the first two months. Within a year, the figure stood at 1 million, and sales were still expanding rapidly. With the hardware quickly finding its way into Japanese homes, Nintendo was besieged with calls from desperate retailers frantically demanding more games.

At this point Yamauchi told Miyamoto to come up with the most imaginative games ever. However, Yamauchi also realized that Nintendo alone could not satisfy the growing thirst for new games, so he initiated a licensing program. To become a Nintendo licensee, companies had to agree to an unprecedented series of restrictions. Licensees could issue only five Nintendo games per year, and they could not write those titles for other platforms. The licensing fee was set at 20% of the wholesale price of each cartridge sold (game cartridges wholesaled for around $30). It typically cost $500,000 to develop a game and took around six months. Nintendo insisted that games not contain any excessively violent or sexually suggestive material and that they review every game before allowing it to be produced.[13]

Despite these restrictions, six companies (Bandai, Capcom, Konami, Namco, Taito, and Hudson) agreed to become Nintendo licensees, not least because millions of customers were now clamoring for games. Bandai was Japan's largest toy company. The others already made either coin-operated videogames or computer software games. Because of these licensing agreements, they saw their sales and earnings surge. For example, Konami's earnings went from $10 million in 1987 to $300 million in 1991.

After the six licensees began selling games, reports of defective games began to reach Yamauchi. The original six licensees were allowed to manufacture their own game cartridges. Realizing that he had given away the ability to control the quality of the cartridges, Yamauchi decided to change the contract for future licensees. Future licensees were required to submit all manufacturing orders for cartridges to Nintendo. Nintendo charged licensees $14 per cartridge, required that they place a minimum order for 10,000 units, (later the minimum order was raised to 30,000), and insisted on cash payment in full when the order was placed. Nintendo outsourced all manufacturing to other companies, using the volume of its orders to get rock bottom prices. The cartridges were estimated to cost Nintendo between $6 and $8 each. The licensees then picked up the cartridges from Nintendo's loading dock and were responsible for distribution. In 1985, there were seventeen licensees. By 1987, there were fifty. By this point, 90% of the home videogame systems sold in Japan were Nintendo systems.

Nintendo in America

In 1980, Nintendo established a subsidiary in America to sell its coin-operated videogames. Yamauchi's American-educated son-in-law, Minoru Arakawa, headed the subsidiary. All of the other essential employees were Americans, including Ron Judy and Al Stone. For its first two years, Nintendo of America (NOA), based originally in Seattle, struggled to sell second-rate games such as Radarscope. The subsidiary seemed on the brink of closing. NOA could not even make the rent payment on the warehouse. Then they received a large shipment from Japan: 2,000 units of a new coin-operated videogame. Opening the box, they discovered Donkey Kong. After playing the game briefly, Judy proclaimed it a disaster. Stone walked out of the building, declaring that "it's over."[14] The managers were appalled. They could not imagine a game less likely to sell in video arcades. The only promising sign was that a twenty-year employee, Howard Philips, rapidly became enthralled with the machine.

Arakawa, however, knew he had little choice but to try to sell the machine. Judy persuaded the owner of the Spot Tavern near Nintendo's office to take one of the machines on a trial basis. After one night, Judy discovered $30 in the coin box, a phenomenal amount. The next night there was $35, and $36 the night after that. NOA had a hit on its hands.

By the end of 1982, NOA had sold over 60,000 copies of Donkey Kong and had booked sales in excess of $100 million. The subsidiary had outgrown its Seattle location. They moved to a new site in Redmond, a Seattle suburb, where they located next to a small but fast-growing software company run by

an old school acquaintance of Howard Philips, Bill Gates.

By 1984, NOA was riding a wave of success in the coin-operated videogame market. Arakawa, however, was interested in the possibilities of selling Nintendo's new Famicom system in the United States. Throughout 1984, Arakawa, Judy, and Stone met with numerous toy and department store representatives to discuss the possibilities, only to be repeatedly rebuffed. Still smarting from the 1983 debacle, the representatives wanted nothing to do with the home videogame business. They also met with former managers from Atari and Caloco to gain their insights. The most common response they received was that the market collapsed because the last generation of games was awful.

Arakawa and his team decided that if they were going to sell Famicom in the United States, they would have to find a new distribution channel. The obvious choice was consumer electronics stores. Thus, Arakawa asked the R&D team in Kyoto to redesign Famicom for the U.S. market so that it looked less like a toy (Famicom was encased in red and white plastic) and more like a consumer electronics device. The redesigned machine was renamed the Nintendo Entertainment System (NES).

Arakawa's big fear was that illegal, low-quality Taiwanese games would flood the U.S. market if NES was successful. To stop counterfeit games being played on NES, Arakawa asked Nintendo's Japanese engineers to design a security system into the U.S. version of Famicom so that only Nintendo-approved games could be played on NES. The Japanese engineers responded by designing a security chip to be embedded in the game cartridges. NES would not work unless the security chips in the cartridges unlocked, or "shook hands with," a chip in NES. Since the code embedded in the security chip was proprietary, the implication of this system was that no one could manufacture games for NES without Nintendo's specific approval.

To overcome the skepticism and reluctance of retailers to stock a home videogame system, Arakawa decided in late 1985 to make an extraordinary commitment. Nintendo would stock stores and set up displays and windows. Retailers would not have to pay for anything they stocked for ninety days. After that, retailers could pay Nintendo for what they sold and return the rest. NES was bundled with Nintendo's best-selling game in Japan, Super Mario Brothers. It was essentially a risk-free proposition for retailers, but even with this, most were skeptical. Ultimately, thirty

Nintendo personnel descended on the New York area. Referred to as the Nintendo SWAT team, they persuaded some stores to stock NES after an extraordinary blitz that involved eighteen-hour days. To support the New York product launch, Nintendo also committed itself to a $5 million advertising campaign aimed at the seven- to fourteen-year-old boys who seemed to be Nintendo's likely core audience.

By December 1985, between 500 and 600 stores in the New York area were stocking Nintendo systems. Sales were moderate, about half of the 100,000 NES machines shipped from Japan were sold, but it was enough to justify going forward. The SWAT team then moved first to Los Angeles, then to Chicago, then to Dallas. As in New York, sales started at a moderate pace, but by late 1986 they started to accelerate rapidly, and Nintendo went national with NES.

In 1986, around 1 million NES units were sold in the United States. In 1987, the figure increased to 3 million. In 1988, it jumped to over 7 million. In the same year, 33 million game cartridges were sold. Nintendo mania had arrived in the United States. To expand the supply of games, Nintendo licensed the rights to produce up to five games per year to thirty-one American software companies. Nintendo continued to use a restrictive licensing agreement that gave it exclusive rights to any games, required licensees to place their orders through Nintendo, and insisted on a 30,000-unit minimum order.[15]

By 1990, the home videogame market was worth $5 billion worldwide. Nintendo dominated the industry, with a 90% share of the market for game equipment. The parent company was, by some measures, now the most profitable company in Japan. By 1992, it was netting over $1 billion in gross profit annually, or more than $1.5 million for each employee in Japan. The company's stock market value exceeded that of Sony, Japan's premier consumer electronics firm. Indeed, the company's net profit exceeded that of all the American movie studios combined. Nintendo games, it seemed, were bigger than the movies.

As of 1991, there were over 100 licensees for Nintendo, and over 450 titles were available for NES. In the United States, Nintendo products were distributed through toy stores (30% of volume), mass merchandisers (40% of volume), and department stores (10% of volume). Nintendo tightly controlled the number of game titles and games that could be sold, quickly withdrawing titles as soon as interest appeared to decline. In 1988, retailers requested 110 million cartridges from Nintendo. Market surveys suggested that perhaps 45 million could have been sold, but Nintendo allowed only 33 million to be shipped.[16] Nintendo claimed that the shortage of games was in part due to a worldwide shortage of semiconductor chips.

Several companies had tried to reverse-engineer the code embedded in Nintendo's security chip, which competitors characterized as a lockout chip. Nintendo successfully sued them. The most notable was Atari Games, one of the successors of the original Atari, which in 1987 sued NOA for anticompetitive behavior. Atari claimed that the purpose of the security chip was to monopolize the market. At the same time, Atari announced that it had found a way around Nintendo's security chip and would begin to sell unlicensed games.[17] NOA responded with a countersuit. In a March 1991 ruling, Atari was found to have obtained Nintendo's security code illegally and was ordered to stop selling NES-compatible games. However, Nintendo did not always have it all its own way. In 1990, under pressure from Congress, the Department of Justice, and several lawsuits, Nintendo rescinded its exclusivity requirements, freeing up developers to write games for other platforms. However, developers faced a real problem: what platform could they write for?

Sega's Sonic Boom

Back in 1954, David Rosen, a twenty-year-old American, left the U.S. Air Force after a tour of duty in Tokyo.[18] Rosen had noticed that Japanese people needed lots of photographs for ID cards, but that local photo studios were slow and expensive. He formed a company, Rosen Enterprises, and went into the photo-booth business, which was a big success. By 1957, Rosen had established a successful nationwide chain. At this point, the Japanese economy was booming, so Rosen decided it was time to get into another business—entertainment. As his vehicle, he chose arcade games, which were unknown in Japan at the time. He picked up used games on the cheap from America and set up arcades in the same Japanese department stores and theaters that typically housed his photo booths. Within a few years, Rosen had two hundred arcades nationwide. His only competition came from another American-owned firm, Service Games (SeGa), whose original business was jukeboxes and fruit machines.

By the early 1960s, the Japanese arcade market had caught up with the U.S. market. The problem was that game makers had run out of exciting new games to offer. Rosen decided that he would have to get into the business of designing and manufacturing games, but to do that he needed manufacturing facilities. SeGa manufactured its own games, so in 1965 Rosen approached the company and suggested a merger. The result was Sega Enterprise, a Japanese company with Rosen as its CEO.

Rosen himself designed Sega's first game, Periscope, in which the objective was to sink chain-mounted cardboard ships by firing torpedoes, represented by lines of colored lights. Periscope was a big success not only in Japan, but also in the United States and Europe, and it allowed Sega to build up a respectable export business. Over the years, the company continued to invest heavily in game development, always using the latest electronic technology.

Gulf and Western (G&W), a U.S. conglomerate, acquired Sega in 1969, with Rosen running the subsidiary. In 1975, G&W took Sega public in the United States, but left Sega Japan as a G&W subsidiary. Hayao Nakayama, a former Sega distributor, was drafted as president. In the early 1980s, Nakayama pushed G&W to invest more in Sega Japan so that the company could enter the then-booming home videogame market. When G&W refused, Nakayama suggested a management buyout. G&W agreed, and in 1984, for the price of just $38 million, Sega became a Japanese company once more. (Sega's Japanese revenues were around $700 million, but by now the company was barely profitable.)

Sega was caught off guard by the huge success of Nintendo's Famicom. Although it released its own 8-bit system in 1986, the machine never commanded more than 5% of the Japanese market. Nakayama, however, was not about to give up. From years in the arcade business, he understood that great games drove sales. Nevertheless, he also understood that more powerful technology gave game developers the tools to develop more appealing games. This philosophy underlay Nakayama's decision to develop a 16-bit game system, Genesis.

Sega took the design of its 16-bit arcade machine and adapted it for Genesis. Compared to Nintendo's 8-bit machine, the 16-bit machine featured an array of superior technological features, including high-definition graphics and animation, a full spectrum of colors, two independent scrolling backgrounds that created an impressive depth of field, and near CD quality sound. The design strategy also made it easy to port Sega's catalog of arcade hits to Genesis.

Genesis was launched in Japan in 1989 and in the United States in 1990. In the United States, the machine was priced at $199. The company hoped that sales would be boosted by the popularity of its arcade games, such as the graphically violent Altered Beast. Sega also licensed other companies to develop games for the Genesis platform. In an effort to recruit licensees, Sega asked for lower royalty rates than Nintendo, and it gave licensees the right to manufacture their own cartridges. Independent game developers were slow to climb on board, however, and the $200 price tag for the player held back sales.

One of the first independent game developers to sign up with Sega was Electronic Arts. Established by Trip Hawkins, Electronic Arts had focused on designing games for personal computers and consequently had missed the Nintendo 8-bit era. Now Hawkins was determined to get a presence in the home videogame market, and aligning his company's wagon with Sega seemed to be the best option. The Nintendo playing field was already crowded, and Sega offered a far less restrictive licensing deal than Nintendo. Electronic Arts subsequently wrote several popular games for Genesis, including John Madden football and several gory combat games.[19]

Nintendo had not been ignoring the potential of the 16-bit system. Nintendo's own 16-bit system, Super NES, was ready for market introduction in 1989—at the same time as Sega's Genesis. Nintendo introduced Super NES in Japan in 1990, where it quickly established a strong market presence and beat Sega's Genesis. In the United States, however, the company decided to hold back longer to reap the full benefits of the dominance it enjoyed with the 8-bit NES system. Yamauchi was also worried about the lack of backward compatibility between Nintendo's 8-bit and 16-bit systems. (The company had tried to make the 16-bit system so that it could play 8-bit games but concluded that the cost of doing so was prohibitive.) These concerns may have led the company to delay market introduction until the 8-bit market was saturated.

Meanwhile, in the United States, the Sega bandwagon was beginning to gain momentum. One development that gave Genesis a push was the introduction of a new Sega game, Sonic the Hedgehog. Developed by an independent team that was contracted to Sega, the game featured a cute hedgehog that impatiently tapped his paw when the player took too long to act. Impatience was Sonic's central feature—he had places to go, and quickly. He zipped along, collecting brass rings when he could find them, before rolling into a ball and flying down slides with loops and underground tunnels. Sonic was Sega's Mario.

In mid-1991, in an attempt to jump-start slow sales, Tom Kalinske, head of Sega's American subsidiary, decided to bundle Sonic the Hedgehog with the game player. He also reduced the price for the bundled unit to $150, and he relaunched the system with an aggressive advertising campaign aimed at teenagers. The campaign was built around the slogan "Genesis does what Nintendon't." The shift in strategy worked, and sales accelerated sharply.

Sega's success prompted Nintendo to launch its own 16-bit system. Nintendo's Super NES was introduced at $200. However, Sega now had a two-year head start in games. By the end of 1991, about 125 game titles were available for Genesis, compared to twenty-five for Super NES. In May 1992, Nintendo reduced the price of Super NES to $150. At this time Sega was claiming a 63% share of the 16-bit market in the United States, and Nintendo claimed a 60% share. By now, Sega was cool. It began to take more chances with mass media–defined morality. When Acclaim Entertainment released its bloody Mortal Kombat game in September 1992, the Sega version let players rip off heads and tear out hearts. Reflecting Nintendo's image of their core market, its version was sanitized. The Sega version outsold Nintendo's two to one.[20] Therefore, the momentum continued to run in Sega's favor. By January 1993, there were 320 titles available for Sega Genesis, and 130 for Super NES. In early 1994, independent estimates suggested that Sega had 60% of the U.S. market and Nintendo had 40%, figures Nintendo disputed.

3DO

Trip Hawkins, whose first big success was Electronic Arts, founded 3DO in 1991.[21] Hawkins's vision for 3DO was to shift the home videogame business away from the existing cartridge-based format and toward a CD-ROM-based platform. The original partners in 3DO were Electronic Arts, Matsushita, Time Warner, AT&T, and the venture capital firm Kleiner Perkins. Collectively they invested over $17 million in 3DO, making it the richest start-up in the history of the

home videogame industry. 3DO went public in May 1993 at $15 per share. By October of that year, the stock had risen to $48 per share, making 3DO worth $1 billion—not bad for a company that had yet to generate a single dollar in revenues.

The basis for 3DO's $1 billion market cap was patented computer system architecture and a copyrighted operating system that allowed for much richer graphics and audio capabilities. The system was built around a 32-bit RISC microprocessor and proprietary graphics processor chips. Instead of a cartridge, the 3DO system stored games on a CD-ROM that was capable of holding up to 600 megabytes of content, sharply up from the 10 megabytes of content found in the typical game cartridge of the time. The slower access time of a CD-ROM compared to a cartridge was alleviated somewhat by the use of a double-speed CD-ROM drive.[22]

The belief at 3DO—a belief apparently shared by many investors—was that the superior storage and graphics processing capabilities of the 3DO system would prove very attractive to game developers, allowing them to be far more creative. In turn, better games would attract customers away from Nintendo and Sega. Developing games that used the capabilities of a CD-ROM system altered the economics of game development. Estimates suggested that it would cost approximately $2 million to produce a game for the 3DO system and could take as long as twenty-four months to develop. However, at $2 per disc, a CD-ROM cost substantially less to produce than a cartridge.

The centerpiece of 3DO's strategy was to license its hardware technology for free. Game developers paid a royalty of $3 per disc for access to the 3DO operating code. Discs typically retailed for $40 each.

Matsushita introduced the first 3DO machine into the U.S. market in October 1993. Priced at $700, the machine was sold through electronic retailers that carried Panasonic high-end electronics products. Sega's Tom Kalinsky noted, "It's a noble effort. Some people will buy 3DO, and they'll have a wonderful experience. It's impressive, but it's a niche. We've done the research. It does not become a large market until you go below $500. At $300, it starts to get interesting. We make no money on hardware. It's a cutthroat business. I hope Matsushita understands that."[23] CD-ROM disks for the 3DO machine retailed for around $75. The machine came bundled with Crash 'n Burn, a high-speed combat racing game.

However, only 18 3DO titles were available by the crucial Christmas period, although reports suggested that 150 titles were under development. [24]

Sales of the hardware were slow, reaching only 30,000 by January 1994.[25] In the same month, AT&T and Sanyo both announced that they would begin to manufacture the 3DO machine. In March, faced with continuing sluggish sales, 3DO announced that it would give hardware manufacturers two shares of 3DO stock for every unit sold at or below a certain retail price. Matsushita dropped the price of its machine to $500. About the same time, Toshiba, LG, and Samsung all announced that they would start to produce 3DO machines.

By June 1994, cumulative sales of 3DO machines in the United States stood at 40,000 units. Matsushita announced plans to expand distribution beyond the current 3,500 outlets to include the toy and mass merchandise channels. Hawkins and his partners announced that they would invest another $37 million in 3DO. By July, there were 750 3DO software licensees, but only forty titles were available for the format. Despite these moves, sales continued at a very sluggish pace and the supply of new software titles started to dry up.[26]

In September 1996, 3DO announced that it would either sell its hardware system business or move it into a joint venture.[27] The company announced that about 150 people, one-third of the workforce, would probably lose their jobs in the restructuring. According to Trip Hawkins, 3DO would now focus on developing software for online gaming. Hawkins stated that the Internet and Internet entertainment constituted a huge opportunity for 3DO. The stock dropped $1.375 to $6.75.

Sega's Saturn

3DO was not alone in moving to a CD-ROM-based format. Both Sega and Sony also introduced CD-ROM-based systems in the mid-1990s. Sega, in fact, had beaten 3DO to the market with its November 1992 introduction of the Sega CD, a $300 CD-ROM add-on for the 16-bit Genesis. Sega sold 100,000 units in its first month alone. Sales then slowed down, however, and by December 1993 were standing at just 250,000 units. One reason for the slowdown, according to critics, was a lack of strong games. Sega was also working on a 32-bit CD-ROM system, Saturn, which was targeted for a mid-1995

introduction in the United States. In January 1994, Sega announced that Microsoft would supply the operating system for Saturn.[28]

In March 1994, Sega announced the Genesis Super 32X, a $150 add-on cartridge designed to increase the performance of Genesis cartridge and CD-ROM games. The 32X contained the 32-bit Hitachi microprocessor that was to be used in Saturn. Sega called the 32X "the poor man's 32-bit machine" because it sold for a mere $149. Introduced in the fall of 1994, the 32X never lived up to its expectations. Most users appeared willing to wait for the real thing, Sega Saturn, promised for release the following year.

In early 1995, Sega informed the press and retailers that it would release Saturn on "Sega Saturn Saturday, Sept. 2nd," but Sega released the 32-bit Saturn in May 1995. It was priced at $400 per unit and accompanied by the introduction of just ten games. Sega apparently believed that the world would be delighted by the May release of the Saturn. However, Saturn was released without the industry fanfare that normally greets a new game machine. Only four retail chains received the Saturn in May, while the rest were told they would have to wait until September. This move alienated retailers, who responded by dropping Sega products from their stores.[29] Sega appeared to have made a marketing blunder.[30]

Sony's Playstation

In the fall of 1995, Sony entered the fray with the introduction of the Sony PlayStation.[31] PlayStation used a 32 bit RISC microprocessor running at 33 MHz and using a double-speed CD-ROM drive. PlayStation cost an estimated $500 million to develop. The machine had actually been under development since 1991, when Sony decided that the home videogame industry was getting too big to ignore. Initially, Sony was in an alliance with Nintendo to develop the machine. Nintendo walked away from the alliance in 1992, however, after a disagreement over who owned the rights to any future CD-ROM games. Sony went alone.[32]

From the start, Sony felt that it could leverage its presence in the film and music business to build a strong position in the home videogame industry. A consumer electronics giant with a position in the Hollywood movie business and the music industry (Sony owned Columbia Pictures and the Columbia record label), Sony believed that it had access to significant intellectual property that could form the basis of many popular games.

In 1991, Sony established a division in New York: Sony Electronic Publishing. The division was to serve as an umbrella organization for Sony's multimedia offerings. Headed by Iceland native Olaf Olafsson, then just twenty-eight years old, this organization ultimately took the lead role in both the market launch of PlayStation and in developing game titles.[33] In 1993, as part of this effort, Sony purchased a well-respected British game developer, Psygnosis. By the fall of 1995, this unit had twenty games ready to complement PlayStation: The Haldeman Diaries, Mickey Mania (developed in collaboration with Disney), and Johnny Mnemonic, based on the William Gibson short story. To entice independent game developers such as Electronic Arts, Namco, and Acclaim Entertainment, Olafsson used the promise of low royalty rates. The standard royalty rate was set at $9 per disc, although developers that signed on early enough were given a lower royalty rate. Sony also provided approximately four thousand game development tools to licensees in an effort to help them speed games to market.[34]

To distribute PlayStation, Sony set up a retail channel separate from Sony's consumer electronics sales force. It marketed the PlayStation as a hip and powerful alternative to the outdated Nintendo and Sega cartridge-based systems. Sony worked closely with retailers before the launch to find out how it could help them sell the PlayStation. To jump-start demand, Sony set up in-store displays to allow potential consumers to try the equipment. Just before the launch, Sony had lined up an impressive 12,000 retail outlets in the United States.[35]

Sony targeted its advertising for PlayStation at males in the eighteen- to thirty-five-year-old age range. The targeting was evident in the content of many of the games. One of the big hits for PlayStation was Tomb Raider, whose central character, Lara Croft, combined sex appeal with savviness and helped to recruit an older generation to PlayStation. [36] PlayStation was initially priced at $299, and games retailed for as much as $60. Sony's Tokyo-based executives had reportedly been insisting on a $350–$400 price for PlayStation, but Olafsson pushed hard for the lower price. Because of the fallout from this internal battle, in January 1996, Olafsson resigned from Sony. By then, however, Sony was following Olafsson's script.[37]

Sony's prelaunch work was rewarded with strong early sales. By January 1996, more than 800,000 PlayStations had been sold in the United States, plus another 4 million games. In May 1996, with 1.2 million PlayStations shipped, Sony reduced the price of PlayStation to $199. Sega responded with a similar price cut for its Saturn. The prices on some of Sony's initial games were also reduced to $29.99. The weekend after the price cuts, retailers reported that PlayStation sales were up by between 350 and 1,000% over the prior week. [38] The sales surge continued through 1996. By the end of the year, sales of PlayStation and associated software amounted to $1.3 billion, out of a total for U.S. sales at $2.2 billion for all videogame hardware and software. In March 1997, Sony cut the price of PlayStation again, this time to $149. It also reduced its suggested retail price for games by $10 to $49.99. By this point, Sony had sold 3.4 million units of PlayStation in the United States, compared to Saturn's 1.6 million units.[39] Worldwide, PlayStation had outsold Saturn by 13 million to 7.8 million units, and Saturn sales were slowing.[40] The momentum was clearly running in Sony's favor, but the company now had a new challenge to deal with: Nintendo's latest generation game machine, the N64.

Nintendo Strikes Back

In July 1996, Nintendo launched Nintendo 64 (N64) in the Japanese market. This release was followed by a late fall introduction in the United States. N64 is a 64-bit machine developed in conjunction with Silicon Graphics. Originally targeted for introduction a year earlier, N64 had been under development since 1993. The machine used a plug-in cartridge format rather than a CD-ROM drive. According to Nintendo, cartridges allow for faster access time and are far more durable than CD-ROMs (an important consideration with children).[41]

The most-striking feature of the N64 machine, however, was its 3D graphics capability. N64 provides fully rounded figures that can turn on their heels and rotate through 180 degrees. Advanced ray tracing techniques borrowed from military simulators and engineering workstations added to the sense of realism by providing proper highlighting, reflections, and shadows.

N64 was targeted at children and young teenagers. It was priced at $200 and launched with just four games. Despite the lack of games, initial sales were very strong. Indeed, 1997 turned out to be a banner year for both Sony and Nintendo. The overall U.S. market was strong, with sales of hardware and software combined reaching a record $5.5 billion. Estimates suggest that PlayStation accounted for 49% of machines and games by value. N64 captured a 41% share, leaving Sega trailing badly with less than 10% of the market. During the year, the average price for game machines had fallen to $150. By year-end there were three hundred titles available for PlayStation, compared to forty for N64. Games for PlayStation retailed for $40, on average, compared to over $60 for N64. [42]

By late 1998, PlayStation was widening its lead over N64. In the crucial North American market, PlayStation was reported to be outselling N64 by a two-to-one margin, although Nintendo retained a lead in the under-twelve category. At this point, there were 115 games available for N64 versus 431 for PlayStation.[43] Worldwide, Sony had now sold close to 55 million PlayStations. The success of PlayStation had a major impact on Sony's bottom line. In fiscal 1998, PlayStation business generated revenues of $5.5 billion for Sony, 10% of its worldwide revenues, but accounted for $886 million, or 22.5%, of the company's operating income.[44]

The 128-Bit Era

When Nintendo launched its 64-bit machine in 1996, Sony and Sega didn't follow, preferring instead to focus on the development of even more powerful 128-bit machines.

Sega was the first to market a 128-bit videogame console, which it launched in Japan in late 1998 and in the United States in late 1999. The Dreamcast came equipped with a 56-kilobit modem to allow for online gaming over the Internet. By late 2000, Sega had sold around 6 million Dreamcasts worldwide, accounting for about 15% of console sales since its launch. Sega nurtured Dreamcast sales by courting outside software developers who helped develop new games, including Crazy Taxi, Resident Evil, and Quake III Arena. The company had a goal of shipping 10 million units by March 2001, a goal it never reached.[45]

Despite its position as first mover with a 128-bit machine, and despite solid technical reviews, by late 2000 the company was struggling. Sega was handicapped first by product shortages due to constraints on the supply of component parts and then by a lack of demand as consumers waited to see whether Sony's 128-bit offering, the much anticipated PlayStation 2 (PS2), would be a more attractive machine. In September 2000, Sega responded to the impending U.S. launch of Sony's PS2 by cutting the price for its console from $199 to $149. Then in late October, Sega announced that, due to this price cut, it would probably lose over $200 million for the fiscal year ending March 2001.[46]

Sony's PlayStation 2

PlayStation 2 was launched in Japan in mid-2000 and in the United States at the end of October 2000. Initially priced at $299, PS2 is a powerful machine. At its core was a 300-megahertz graphics processing chip that was jointly developed with Toshiba and consumed about $1.3 billion in R&D. Referred to as the Emotion Engine processor, the chip allows the machine to display stunning graphic images previously found only on supercomputers. The chip made the PS2 the most powerful videogame machine yet.

The machine was set up to play different CD and DVD formats, as well as proprietary game titles. As is true with the original PlayStation, PS2 could play audio CDs. The system was also compatible with the original PlayStation: any PlayStation title could be played on the PS2. To help justify the initial price tag, the unit doubled as a DVD player with picture quality as good as current players. The PS2 did not come equipped with a modem, but it did have networking capabilities and a modem could be attached using one of two USB ports.[47]

Nintendo GameCube

Nintendo had garnered a solid position in the industry with its N64 machine by focusing on its core demographic, seven- to twelve-year-olds. In 1999, Nintendo took 33% of the hardware market and 28% of the game market. Nintendo's next-generation videogame machine, GameCube, packed a modem and a powerful 400-megahertz, 128-bit processor made by IBM into a compact cube. GameCube marked a shift away from Nintendo's traditional approach of using proprietary cartridges to hold game software. Instead, software for the new player came on 8-centimeter compact disks, which are smaller than music compact disks. The disks held 1.5 gigabytes of data each, far greater storage capacity than the old game cartridges. Players could control Game-Cube using wireless controllers.[48]

Nintendo tried to make the GameCube easy for developers to work with rather than focusing on raw peak performance. While developers no doubt appreciated this, by the time GameCube hit store shelves in late 2001, PS2 had been on the market for eighteen months and boasted a solid library of games. Despite its strong brand and instantly recognized intellectual property, which included Donkey Kong, Super Mario Brothers, and the Pokemon characters, Nintendo was playing catch-up to Sony. Moreover, another new entrant into the industry launched its 128-bit offering at around the same time: Microsoft.

Microsoft's Xbox

Microsoft was first rumored to be developing a videogame console in late 1999. In March 2000, Bill Gates made it official when he announced that Microsoft would enter the home videogame market in fall 2001 with a console code named Xbox. In terms of sheer computing power, the 128-bit Xbox had the edge over competitors. Xbox had a 733-megahertz Pentium III processor, a high-powered graphics chip from Nvidia Corp, a built-in broadband cable modem to allow for online game playing and high-speed Internet browsing, 64 megabytes of memory, CD and DVD drives, and an internal hard disk drive. The operating system was a stripped-down version of its popular Windows system optimized for graphics processing capabilities. Microsoft claimed that because the Xbox was based on familiar PC technology, it would be much easier for software developers to write games for, and it would be relatively easy to convert games from the PC to run on the Xbox.[49]

Although Microsoft was a new entrant to the videogame industry, it was no stranger to games. Microsoft had long participated in the PC gaming industry and was one of the largest publishers of PC games, with hits such as Microsoft Flight Simulator and Age of Empires I and II to its credit. Sales of Microsoft's PC games have increased 50% annually between 1998 and 2001, and the company controlled about 10% of the PC game market in 2001. Microsoft had also offered online gaming for some time, including its popular MSN Gaming Zone site. Started in 1996, by 2001 the website had become the largest online PC gaming hub on the Internet with nearly 12 million subscribers paying $9.95 a month to play premium games such as Asheron's Call or Fighter Ace.

Nor is Microsoft new to hardware; its joysticks and game pads outsell all other brands, and it has an important mouse business.

To build the Xbox, Microsoft chose Flextronics, a contract manufacturer that already made computer mice for Microsoft. Realizing that it would probably have to cut Xbox prices over time, Microsoft guaranteed Flextronics a profit margin, effectively agreeing to subsidize Flextronics if selling prices fell below a specified amount. By 2003, Microsoft was thought to be losing $100 on every Xbox sold. To make that back and turn a profit, Microsoft reportedly had to sell between six and nine videogames per Xbox.[50]

Analysts speculated that Microsoft's entry into the home videogame market was a response to a potential threat from Sony. Microsoft was worried that Internet-ready consoles like PS2 might take over many web-browsing functions from the personal computer. Some in the company described Internet-enabled videogame terminals as Trojan horses in the living room. In Microsoft's calculation, it made sense to get in the market to try and keep Sony and others in check. With annual revenues in excess of $20 billion worldwide, the home videogame market is huge and an important source of potential growth for Microsoft. Still, by moving away from its core market, Microsoft was taking a big risk, particularly given the scale of investments required to develop the Xbox, reported to run as high as $1.5 billion.

Mortal Combat: Microsoft versus Sony

The launch of Xbox and GameCube helped propel sales of videogame hardware and software to a record $9.4 billion in 2001, up from $6.58 billion in 2000. Although both Xbox and Nintendo initially racked up strong sales, the momentum started to slow significantly in 2002. Microsoft, in particular, found it very difficult to penetrate the Japanese market. By September 2002, Sony had sold 11.2 million units of PS2 in the United States, versus 2.2 million units of Xbox and 2.7 million units of Nintendo's GameCube. Unable to hold onto market share in the wake of the new competition, Sega withdrew from the console market, announcing that henceforth it would focus on developing games for other platforms.

In June 2002, Sony responded to the new entry by cutting the price for PS2 from $299 to $199. Microsoft quickly followed, cutting the price for Xbox from $299 to $199, while Nintendo cut its price from $299 to $149.[51] A year later, Sony cut prices again, this time to $179 a console. Again, Microsoft followed with a similar price cut, and in March 2004 it took the lead, cutting Xbox prices to $149. Sony followed suit two months later.[52]

Microsoft's strategy, however, involved far more than cutting prices. In November 2002 Microsoft announced that it would introduce a new service for gamers, Xbox Live. For $50 a year, Xbox Live subscribers with broadband connections would be able to play online-enabled versions of Xbox games with other online subscribers. To support Xbox Live, Microsoft invested some $500 million in its own data centers to host online game playing.

Online game playing was clearly a strategic priority from the outset. Unlike the PS2 and GameCube, Xbox came with a built-in broadband capability. The decision to make the Xbox broadband-capable was made back in 1999 when less than 5% of U.S. homes were linked to the Internet with a broadband connection. Explaining the decision to build broadband capabilities into the Xbox at a time when rivals lacked them, the head of Xbox, Jay Allard, noted that "my attitude has always been to bet on the future, not against it."[53] While Sony's PS2 can be hooked up to the Internet via a broadband connection, doing so requires purchase of a special network adapter for $40.

By mid-2003, Xbox Live had some 500,000 subscribers, versus 80,000 who had registered to play PS2 games online. By this point, there were twenty-eight online games for Xbox and eighteen for PlayStation 2. By January 2004, the comparative figures stood at fifty for Microsoft and thirty-two for Sony. By mid-2004, Xbox Live reportedly had over 1 million subscribers, with Sony claiming a similar number of online players.[54] In May 2004, Microsoft struck a deal with Electronic Arts, the world's largest videogame publisher, to bring EA games, including its best-selling Madden Football, to the Xbox Live platform. Until this point, EA had produced live games only for Sony's platform.

In spite of all these strategic moves, by late 2004 Xbox was still a distant second of PlayStation 2 in the videogame market having sold 14 million consoles against Sony's 70 million (Nintendo had sold 13 million GameCube consoles by this point). While Sony was making good money from the business, Microsoft was registering significant losses. In fiscal 2004, Microsoft's home and entertainment division, of which Xbox is the major component, registered $2.45 billion in revenues, but lost $1.135 billion. By

way of contrast, Sony's game division had $7.5 billion of sales in fiscal 2004 and generated operating profits of $640 million.

Microsoft, however, indicated that it was in the business for the long term. In late 2004, the company got a boost from the release of Halo 2, the sequel to Halo, one of its best-selling games. As first-day sales for Halo 2 were totaled up, executives at Sony had to be worried. Microsoft announced that Halo 2 had sales of $125 million in its first twenty-four hours on the market in the United States and Canada, an industry record. These figures represented sales of 2.38 million units, and put Halo 2 firmly on track to be one of the biggest videogames ever with a shot at surpassing Nintendo's Super Mario 64, which had sold $308 million in the United States since its September 1996 debut. Moreover, the company was rumored to be ahead of Sony by as much as a year to bring the next-generation videogame console to market. In late 2004, reports suggested that Xbox 2 would be on the market in time for the 2005 Christmas season, probably a full year ahead of Sony's PlayStation 3. Sony was rumored to be running into technical problems as it tried to develop PlayStation 3.[55]

Microsoft Versus Sony: Round Two

As the battle between PS2 and Xbox drew to a close, it was clear that Sony was the big winner. From 2001 through to the fall of 2006, when PlayStation 3 (PS3) hit the market, Sony had sold around 110 million PS2 consoles, versus 25 million for Microsoft's Xbox and 21 million for Nintendo's GameCube.[56] Sony's advantage of an installed base translated into a huge lead in number of games sold—some 1.08 billion for PS2 by mid-2006, versus 200 million for the Xbox.[57] With the console companies reportedly making an average royalty on third-party software of $8 per game sold, the financial implications of Sony's lead with PS2 are obvious.[58] Indeed, in 2005 Sony's games division contributed to 6.24% of the company's total revenue but 38% of operating profit. In contrast, Microsoft's home and entertainment division lost $4 billion between the launch of Xbox and mid-2006.

However, by 2006, this was all history. In November 2005, Microsoft introduced its next-generation machine, Xbox 360, beating Sony and Nintendo to the market by a solid year. The Xbox 360 represented a big technological advance over the original Xbox. To deliver improved picture quality, the Xbox 360 could execute 500 million polygons/sec—a fourfold increase over the Xbox. The main microprocessor was a 3.2 gigahertz chip, thirteen times faster than the chip in the Xbox. Xbox 360 had 512 megabytes of memory, an eightfold increase, and a 20-gigabyte hard drive, two and one-half times bigger than that found on the Xbox. Xbox 360 is, of course, enabled for a broadband connection to the Internet.

The machine itself was made by Flextronics and Wistron, two contract manufactures (a third started production after launch). Priced at $299, Xbox 360 was sold at a loss. The cost for making Xbox 360 was estimated to be as high as $500 at launch, falling to $350 by late 2006. Microsoft's goal was to ultimately break even on sales of the hardware as manufacturing efficiencies drove down unit costs.

To seed the market with games, Microsoft had taken a number of steps. Taking a page out of its Windows business, Microsoft provided game developers with tools designed to automate many of the key software programming tasks and reduce development time and costs. The company had also expanded its own in-house game studios, in part by purchasing several independent game developers including Bungie Studios, makers of Halo. This strategy enabled Microsoft to offer exclusive content for the Xbox 360, something that third-party developers were reluctant to do.

With the costs of game development increasing to over $10 million for more complex games, and development time stretching out to between twenty-four and thirty-six months, Microsoft also had to provide an inducement to get third-party developers on board. Although details of royalty terms are kept private, it is believed that Microsoft offered very low royalty rates, and perhaps even zero royalties, for a specified period of times to game developers who committed early to Xbox 360. One of those to commit early was Electronic Arts, the leading independent game development company, which reportedly budgeted as much as $200 million to develop some twenty-five versions of its best-selling games, such as its sports games, for Xbox 360. Microsoft itself budgeted a similar amount to develop its own games.[59]

In the event, some 18 games were available for the November 2005 launch of Xbox 360, and by the end of 2006, this figure had increased to around 160. Halo 3, which is expected to be one of the biggest

games for Xbox 360, is scheduled to be released in 2007. As a Microsoft game, this will be exclusive to the Xbox 360. Grand Theft Auto 4, the most popular franchise on PS2, will also be launched simultaneously for both Xbox 360 and PS3 in 2007—a major coup for Microsoft.

The initial launch of Xbox 360 was marred by shortages of key components, which limited the number of machines that Microsoft could bring to market. Had Sony been on time with its launch of PS3, this could have been a serious error, but Sony delayed its launch of PS3, first until spring of 2006, and then November 2006. By the time Sony launched PS3 in November 2006, some 6 million Xbox 360 consoles had been sold, and Microsoft was predicting sales of 10 million by the end of 2006.

As with Xbox, Microsoft is pushing Xbox Live with Xbox 360. The company invested as much as $1 billion in Live from its inception. By late 2006, Microsoft was claiming that some 60% of Xbox 360 customers had also signed on for Xbox Live and that the service now had 4 million subscribers. Xbox Live allows gamers to play against each other online and to download digital content from Xbox Live Marketplace, which registered some 10 million downloads of digital content in its first five months of operation. Looking forward, there is little doubt that Microsoft sees Xbox Live as a critical element of its strategy, enabling Xbox owners to download any digital content—games, film, music—onto their consoles, which could become the hub of a home digital entertainment system.

The business model for Xbox 360 depends on the number of games sold per console, the percentage of console owners who sign up for Xbox Live, sales of hardware accessories (for example, controllers, an HD-DVD drive, wireless networking adapter), and the console itself achieving breakeven production costs. Reports suggest that Microsoft will break even if each console owner buys six to seven games and two to three accessories, and if some 10 million sign on to Xbox Live (Microsoft splits Xbox Live revenues with game developers). By the end of 2006, it was estimated that some 33 million games had been sold for Xbox 360.[60]

Sony finally introduced PS3 in November 11 in Japan, and November 17 in the United States. The delay in the launch of PS3 was due to Sony's decision to bundle a Blu-ray drive with PS3 and problems developing the "cell" processor that sits at the core of the PS3. Blu-ray is Sony's proprietary high-definition DVD format. The company is currently locked in a format war with Toshiba, which is pushing its rival HD-DVD format (which can be purchased as an accessory for the Xbox 360). Sony has argued that the combination of its cell processor and Blu-ray DVD drive will give PS3 a substantial performance edge over Xbox 360. While this is true in a technical sense (the Blu-ray discs have five times the storage capacity of the DVD discs for Xbox 360), few reviewers have noticed much in the way of difference from a game-playing perspective—perhaps because few games were initially available that showed the true power of the PS3.

What is certain is that incorporating Blu-ray drives in the PS3 has significantly raised the costs of the PS3. Sony is selling its stand-alone Blu-ray drives for $999, which suggests that the PS3, initially priced at between $500 and $600 depending on configuration, is in a sense a subsidized Blu-ray player. Shortages of blue diodes, a critical component in high-definition DVD drives, also limited supply of the PS3 after its launch. Only 93,000 PS3 players were available for the Japanese launch. Sony estimates that it will ship 2 million PS3s by the end of 2006, and 6 million by March 2007. Analysts are skeptical of these targets, however, given continuing component shortages.

At launch, there were some twenty games available for the PS3. Sony also announced its own Live offering to compete with Xbox Live, and stated that it would be free to PS3 users.

Nintendo is also back in the fray. In November 2006, it launched its own next-generation offering, Wii. The Wii is a much more modest offering than the PS3 or Xbox 360, from a technical standpoint at least, but it has the virtue of being priced much lower—at just $250. Moreover, the Wii has an interesting feature—a wireless controller that can detect arm and hand motions and transfer them to the screen. This enables the development of interactive games, with players physically controlling the action on screen by moving their arms, whether by swinging an imaginary bat or slashing a sword through the air. Like the PS3, Wii was also launched with some twenty games. Early sales were apparently good, and Nintendo was forecasting sales of 1.5 million units by the year's end.

ENDNOTES

1. A good account of the early history of Bushnell and Atari can be found in S. Cohen, *Zap! The Rise and Fall of Atari,* New York: McGraw-Hill, 1984.
2. R. Isaacs, "Videogames Race to Catch a Changing Market," *Business Week,* December 26, 1977, p. 44B.
3. P. Pagnano, "Atari's Game Plan to Overwhelm Its Competitors," *Business Week,* May 8, 1978, p. 50F.
4. R. Isaacs, "Videogames Race to Catch a Changing Market," *Business Week,* December 26, 1977, p. 44B.
5. P. Pagnano, "Atari's Game Plan to Overwhelm Its Competitors," *Business Week,* May 8, 1978, p. 50F; and D. Sheff, *Game Over,* New York: Random House, 1993.
6. S. Cohen, *Zap! The Rise and Fall of Atari,* New York: McGraw-Hill, 1984.
7. L. Kehoe, "Atari Seeks Way out of Videogame Woes," *Financial Times,* December 14, 1983, p. 23.
8. M. Schrage, "The High Tech Dinosaurs: Videogames, Once Ascendant, Are Making Way," *Washington Post,* July 31, 1983, p. F1.
9. D. Sheff, *Game Over,* New York: Random House, 1993.
10. Quoted in D. Sheff, *Game Over,* New York: Random House, 1993, p. 38.
11. D. Sheff, *Game Over,* New York: Random House, 1993.
12. D. Golden, "In Search of Princess Toadstool," *Boston Globe,* November 20, 1988, p. 18.
13. N. Gross and G. Lewis, "Here Come the Super Mario Bros.," *Business Week,* November 9, 1987, p. 138.
14. D. Sheff, *Game Over,* New York: Random House, 1993.
15. D. Golden, "In Search of Princess Toadstool," *Boston Globe,* November 20, 1988, p. 18.
16. Staff Reporter, "Marketer of the Year," *Adweek,* November 27, 1989, p. 15.
17. C. Lazzareschi, "No Mere Child's Play," *Los Angeles Times,* December 16, 1988, p. 1.
18. For a good summary of the early history of Sega, see J. Battle and B. Johnstone, "The Next Level: Sega's Plans for World Domination," *Wired,* release 1.06, December 1993.
19. D. Sheff, *Game Over,* New York: Random House, 1993.
20. J. Battle and B. Johnstone, "The Next Level: Sega's Plans for World Domination," *Wired,* release 1.06, December 1993.
21. For background details, see J. Flower, "3DO: Hip or Hype?" *Wired,* release 1.02, May/June 1993.
22. R. Brandt, "3DO's New Game Player: Awesome or Another Betamax?" *Business Week,* January 11, 1993, p. 38.
23. J. Flower, "3DO: Hip or Hype?" *Wired,* release 1.02, May/June 1993.
24. S. Jacobs, "Third Time's a Charm (They Hope)," *Wired,* release 2.01, January 1994.
25. A. Dunkin, "Videogames: The Next Generation," *Business Week,* January 31, 1994, p. 80.
26. J. Greenstein, "No Clear Winners, Though Some Losers; the Videogame Industry in 1995," *Business Week,* December 22, 1995, p. 42.
27. Staff Reporter, "3DO Says 'I Do' on Major Shift of Its Game Strategy," *Los Angeles Times,* September 17, 1996, p. 2.
28. J. Battle and B. Johnstone, "The Next Level: Sega's Plans for World Domination," *Wired,* release 1.06, December 1993.
29. J. Greenstein, "No Clear Winners, Though Some Losers: The Videogame Industry in 1995," *Business Week,* December 22, 1995, p. 42.
30. D. P. Hamilton, "Sega Suddenly Finds Itself Embattled," *Wall Street Journal,* March 31, 1997, p. A10.
31. S. Taves, "Meet Your New Playmate," *Wired,* release 3.09, September 1995.

32. I. Kunni, "The Games Sony Plays," *Business Week,* June 15, 1998, p. 128.

33. C. Platt, "WordNerd," *Wired,* release 3.10, October 1995.

34. I. Kunni, "The Games Sony Plays," *Business Week,* June 15, 1998, p. 128.

35. J. A. Trachtenberg, "Race Quits Sony Just Before U.S. Rollout of Its PlayStation Video-Game System," *Wall Street Journal,* August 8, 1995, p. B3.

36. S. Beenstock, "Market Raider: How Sony Won the Console Game," *Marketing,* September 10, 1998, p. 26.

37. J. A. Trachtenberg, "Olafsson Calls It Quits as Chairman of Sony's Technology Strategy Group," *Wall Street Journal,* January 23, 1996, p. B6.

38. J. Greenstein, "Price Cuts Boost Saturn, PlayStation Hardware Sales," *Video Business,* May 31, 1996, p. 1.

39. J. Greenstein, "Sony Cuts Prices of PlayStation Hardware," *Video Business,* March 10, 1997, p. 1.

40. D. Hamilton, "Sega Suddenly Finds Itself Embattled," *Wall Street Journal,* March 31, 1997, p. A10.

41. Staff Reporter, "Nintendo Wakes Up," *The Economist,* August 3, 1996, pp. 55–56.

42. D. Takahashi, "Game Plan: Videogame Makers See Soaring Sales Now—And Lots of Trouble Ahead," *Wall Street Journal,* June 15, 1998, p. R10.

43. D. Takahashi, "Sony and Nintendo Battle for Kids Under 13," *Wall Street Journal,* September 24, 1998, p. B4.

44. I. Kunni, "The Games Sony Plays," *Business Week,* June 15, 1998, p. 128.

45. R. A. Guth, "Sega Cites Dreamcast Price Cuts for Loss Amid Crucial Time for Survival of Firm," *Wall Street Journal,* October 30, 2000, p. A22.

46. R. A. Guth, "Sega Cites Dreamcast Price Cuts for Loss Amid Crucial Time for Survival of Firm," *Wall Street Journal,* October 30, 2000, p. A22.

47. T. Oxford and S. Steinberg, "Ultimate Game Machine Sony's PlayStation 2 Is Due on Shelves Oct. 26. It Brims with Potential—But at This Point Sega's Dreamcast Appears a Tough Competitor," *Atlanta Journal/Atlanta Constitution,* October 1, 2000, p. P1.

48. R. A. Guth, "New Players from Nintendo Will Link to Web," *Wall Street Journal,* August 25, 2000, p. B1.

49. D. Takahashi, "Microsoft's X-Box Impresses Game Developers," *Wall Street Journal,* March 13, 2000, p. B12.

50. K. Powers, "Showdown," *Forbes,* August 11, 2003, pp. 86–87.

51. "Console Wars," *The Economist,* June 22, 2002, p. 71.

52. R. A. Guth, "Game Gambit: Microsoft to Cut Xbox Price," *Wall Street Journal,* March 19, 2004, p. B1.

53. K. Powers, "Showdown," *Forbes,* August 11, 2003, pp. 86–87.

54. E. Taub, "No Longer a Solitary Pursuit: Videogames Move Online," *New York Times,* July 5, 2004, p. C4.

55. J. Greene and C. Edwards, "Microsoft Plays Video Leapfrog," *Business Week,* May 10, 2004, pp. 44–45.

56. "Playing a Long Game," *The Economist,* November 18, 2006, pp. 63–65.

57. B. Thill, "Microsoft: Got Game? Update on Vista, Xbox and the Tender," *Citigroup Capital Markets,* August 30, 2006.

58. B. Thill, "Microsoft: Got Game? Update on Vista, Xbox and the Tender," *Citigroup Capital Markets,* August 30, 2006.

59. D. Takahashi, *The Xbox 360 Uncloaked,* Los Angeles: Spider Works, 2006.

60. B. Thill, "Microsoft: Got Game? Update on Vista, Xbox and the Tender," *Citigroup Capital Markets,* August 30, 2006.

Internet Search and the Rise of Google

This case was prepared by Charles W. L. Hill, the University of Washington.

The Google Juggernaut

In the early 2000s, many Internet users started to gravitate toward a new search engine. It was called Google, and it delivered remarkable results. Put in a keyword, and in a blink of an eye the search engine would return a list of links, with the most relevant links appearing at the top of the page. People quickly realized that Google was an amazing tool, enabling users to quickly find almost anything they wanted on the Web and to effortlessly sort through the vast sea of information contained in billions of webpages and retrieve the precise information they desired. It seemed like magic. Before long, "to Google" became a verb (in June 2006, the verb *Google* was added to the *Oxford English Dictionary*). To find out more about a person, you would "Google them." To find out more about a subject, you would "Google it." If you wanted to find a good or service, enter a keyword in Google, and a list of relevant links would be returned in an instant. For many users, Google quickly became the "go to" page every time they wanted information about anything. As a result, by mid-2006 some 45% of all U.S. Internet searches were conducted through Google, far ahead of Yahoo's search engine, which had a 28.5% share, and Microsoft's MSN network, which accounted for 12.8% of searches.[1]

What captured the attention of the business community, however, was the ability of Google to monetize its search engine. Google's core business model was the essence of simplicity. The company auctioned off the keywords used in searches to advertisers. The highest bidders would have links to their sites placed on the right-hand side of a page returning search results. The advertisers would then pay Google every time someone clicked on a link and was directed to their sites. Thus, when bidding for a keyword, advertisers would bid for the price per click. Interestingly, Google did not necessarily place the advertiser who bid the highest amount per click at the top of the page. Rather, the top spot was determined by the amount per click multiplied by Google's statistical estimate of the likelihood that someone would actually click on the advertisement. This refinement maximized the revenue that Google got from its valuable real estate.

As more users gravitated to Google's site, so more advertisers were attracted to it, and Google's revenues and profits took off. From a standing start in 2001, by 2005 revenues had grown to $6.14 billion and net income to $1.47 billion. Google had become the gorilla in the online advertising space. In 2001, Google garnered 18.4% of total U.S. search ad spending. By 2005, its share had increased to 48.5%, and, according to the research firm eMarketer, 57% of all search advertising dollars will go to Google in 2006.[2] Moreover, the future looked bright. Estimates suggest that Internet advertising spending could become a $40 billion worldwide market in 2008, up from $20.5 billion in 2005.[3] Forecasts called for Google's revenues to exceed the $12 billion range by 2008 as ever more advertisers moved from traditional media to the Web.[4]

Flushed with this success, Google introduced a wave of new products, including mapping services

(Google Maps and Google Earth), a free email service (Gmail), Google Desktop (which enables users to search files on their own computers), and free online word-processing and spreadsheet programs that had much of the look, feel, and functionality of Microsoft's Word and Excel offerings. These products fueled speculation that Google's ambitions extended outside search, and that the company was trying to position itself as a platform company that supported an ecosystem that would rival that fostered by Microsoft, long the software industry's dominate player. Google's competitors, however, had no intention of being steamrollered. Both Yahoo and Microsoft were investing significant amounts in search in an attempt to grow their shares. A number of smaller search companies, including Ask and snap.com, were looking to increase their share too. Moreover, few of Google's new products had gained share against entrenched competitors, suggesting to some that the company might be overreaching itself.

Search Engines[5]

A search engine connects the keywords that users enter (queries) to a database it has created of webpages (an index). It then produces a list of links to pages (and summaries of content) that it believes are most relevant to a query.

Search engines consist of four main components: a web crawler, an index, a runtime index, and a query processor (the interface that connects users to the index). The web crawler is a piece of software that goes from link to link on the Web, collecting the pages it finds and sending them back to the index. Once in the index, webpages are analyzed by sophisticated algorithms that look for statistical patterns. Google's page rank algorithm, for example, looks at the links on a page, the text around those links, and the popularity of the pages that link to that page to determine how relevant a page is to a particular query (in fact, Google's algorithm looks at more than one hundred factors to determine a page's relevance to a query term).

Once analyzed, pages are tagged. The tag contains information about the pages, for example, whether it is porn, or spam, written in a certain language, or updated infrequently. Tagged pages are then dumped into a runtime index, which is a database that is ready to serve users. The runtime index forms a bridge between the back end of an engine, the web crawler and index, and the front end, the query processor and user interface. The query processor takes a keyword inputted by a user, transports it to the runtime index, where an algorithm matches the keyword to pages, ranking them by relevance, and then transports the results back to the user, where they are displayed on the user interface.

The computing and data storage infrastructure required to support a search engine is significant. It must scale with the continued growth of the Web and with demands on the search engine. In 2005, Google had $949 million in information technology assets on its balance sheet, had close to 200,000 computers dedicated to the job of running its search engine, and spent around $400 million on maintaining its system.[6]

The Early Days of Search

Search did not begin with Google. The first Internet search engine was Archie. Created in 1990, before the World Wide Web had burst onto the scene, Archie connected users through queries to the machines on which documents they wanted were stored. The users then had to dig through the public files on those machines to find what they wanted. The next search engine, Veronica, improved on Archie insofar as it allowed searchers to connect directly to the document they had queried.

The Web started to take off after 1993, with the number of websites expanding from 130 to more than 600,000 by 1996. As this expansion occurred, the problem of finding the information you wanted on the Web became more difficult. The first web-based search engine was the WWW Wanderer, developed by Matthew Gray at MIT. This was soon surpassed, however, by Web Crawler, a search engine developed by Brian Pinkerton of the University of Washington. Web Crawler was the first search engine to index the full text of webpages, as opposed to just the title. Web Crawler was sold to AOL for $1 million in 1995. This marked the first time anyone had ascribed an economic value to a search engine.

In December 1995 the next search engine, AltaVista, appeared on the scene. Developed by Louis Monier, an employee at Digital Equipment (DEC), AltaVista, like Web Crawler, indexed the entire text of a webpage. Unlike Web Crawler, however, AltaVista sent out thousands of web crawlers, which enabled it to build the most complete index of the Web to date.

Avid web users soon came to value the service, but the search engine was handicapped by two things. First, it was very much a stepchild within DEC, which saw itself as a hardware-driven business and didn't really know what to do with AltaVista. Second, there was no obvious way for AltaVista to make much money, which meant that it was difficult for Monier to get the resources required for AltaVista to keep up with the rapid growth of the Web. Ultimately DEC was acquired by Compaq Computer. Compaq then sold AltaVista and related Internet properties to a high-flying Internet firm, CMGI, at the height of the Internet boom in 1999 for $2.3 billion in CMGI stock. CMGI did have plans to spin off AltaVista in an initial public offering, but it never happened. The NASDAQ stock market collapsed in 2000, taking CMGI's stock down with it, and the market had no appetite for another dot-com IPO.

Around the same time that AltaVista was gaining traffic, two other companies introduced search engines, Lycos and Excite. Both search engines represented further incremental improvement. Lycos was the first search engine to use algorithms to try and determine the relevance of a webpage for a search query. Excite utilized similar algorithms. However, neither company developed a way of making money directly from search. Instead they saw themselves as portal companies, like Yahoo, AOL, and MSN. Search was just a tool to increase the value of their portal as a destination site, enabling them to capture revenues from banner ads, e-commerce transactions, and the like. Both Lycos and Excite went public and then squandered much of the capital raised on acquiring other Internet properties, before seeing their value implode as the Internet bubble burst in 2000–2001.

Another company that tried to make sense out of the Web for users was Yahoo, but Yahoo did not use a search engine. Instead it created a hierarchical directory of webpages. This helped drive traffic to its site. Other content kept users coming back, enabling Yahoo to emerge as one of the most popular portals on the Web. In contrast to many of its smaller competitors, Yahoo's industry leading scale allowed it to make good money from advertising on its site. The company added a search engine to its offering, but until 2003 it always did so through a partner. At one time, AltaVista powered Yahoo's search function, then Inktomi, and ultimately Google. Yahoo's managers did consider developing their own search engine, but

they saw it as too capital intensive—search required a lot of computing power, storage, and bandwidth. Besides, there was no business model for monetizing search. That, however, was all about to change, and it wasn't Google that pioneered the way, it was a serial entrepreneur called Bill Gross.

GoTo.com: A Business Model Emerges[7]

Bill Gross made his first million with Knowledge Adventure, which developed software to help kids learn. After he sold Knowledge Adventure to Cendant for $100 million, Gross created IdeaLab, a business incubator that subsequently generated a number of Internet start-ups, including GoTo.com.

GoTo.com was born of Gross's concern that a growing wave of spam was detracting from the value of search engines such as AltaVista. Spam arose because publishers of websites realized that they could drive traffic to their sites by including commonly used search keywords such as "used cars" or "airfares" on their sites. Often the words were in the same color as the background of the website (for example, black words on a black background), so that they could not be seen by web users, who would suddenly wonder why their search for used cars had directed them to a porn site.

Gross also wanted a tool that would help drive good traffic to the websites of a number of Internet businesses being developed by IdeaLab. In Gross's view, much of the traffic arriving at websites was undifferentiated—people who had come to a site because of spam, bad portal real estate deals, or poor search engine results. Gross established GoTo.com to build a better search engine, one that would defeat spam, produce highly relevant results, and eliminate bad traffic.

Gross concluded that a way to limit spam was to charge for search. He realized that it was unworkable to charge the Internet user, so why not charge the advertiser? This led to his key insight—the keywords that Internet users typed into a search engine were inherently valuable to the owners of websites. They drove traffic to their sites, and many sites made money from that traffic, so why not charge for the keywords? Moreover, Gross realized that if a search engine directed higher quality traffic to a site, it would be possible to charge more for relevant keywords.

By this time, GoTo.com had decided to license search engine technology from Inktomi and focus its efforts on developing the paid search model. However, GoTo.com faced a classic chicken and egg problem—to launch a service, the company needed both audience and advertisers, but it had neither.

To attract advertisers, GoTo.com adopted two strategies.[8] First, GoTo.com would charge an advertiser only when somebody clicked on a link and was directed to its website. To Gross's way thinking, for merchants this pay-per-click model would be more efficient than advertising through traditional media or through banner ads on webpages. Second, GoTo.com initially priced keywords low—as low as 1 cent a click (although, of course, they could be bid above that).

To capture an audience, a website alone would not be enough. GoTo.com needed to tap into the traffic already visiting established websites. One approach was to pay the owners of high-traffic websites to place banner ads that would direct traffic to GoTo.com's website. A second approach, which ultimately became the core of GoTo.com's business, was to syndicate its service, allowing affiliates to place a cobranded GoTo.com search box on their sites, or to use GoTo.com's search engine and identify the results as "partner results." GoTo.com would then split the revenues from search with them. GoTo.com had to pay an upfront fee to significant affiliates, who viewed their websites as valuable real estate. For example, in late 2000 GoTo.com paid AOL $50 million to syndicate GoTo.com's listings on its sites, which included AOL, Compuserve, and Netscape.

To finance its expansion, GoTo.com raised some $53 million in venture capital funding—a relatively easy proposition in the heady days of the dot-com boom. In June 1999, GoTo.com raised another $90 million through an IPO.[9]

GoTo.com launched its service in June 1998 with just fifteen advertisers. Initially GoTo.com was paying more to acquire traffic than it was earning from click-through ad revenue. According to its initial IPO filing, in its first year of operation, GoTo.com was paying 5.5 cents a click to acquire traffic from Microsoft's MSN sites, and around 4 cents a click to acquire traffic from Netscape. The average yield from this traffic, however, was still less than the cost of acquisition, resulting in red ink, not an unusual situation for a dot-com in the 1990s.

However, the momentum was beginning to shift toward the company. As traffic volumes grew, and as advertisers began to understand the value of keywords, yields improved. By early 1999 the price of popular keywords was starting to rise. The highest bidder for the keyword "software" was 59 cents a click, "books" was 38 cents a click, "vacations" 36 cents a click, and "porn," the source of so much spam, 28 cents a click.[10]

The turning point was the AOL syndication deal signed in September 2000. Prior to signing with AOL, GoTo.com was reaching 24 million users through its affiliates. After the deal, it was reaching 60 million unique users, or some 75% of the U.S. Internet audience (AOL itself had 23 million subscribers, CompuServe 3 million, and Netscape—which was owned by AOL—another 31 million registered users).[11] With over 50,000 advertisers now in its network and a large audience pool, both keyword prices and click-through rates increased. GoTo.com turned profitable shortly after the AOL deal was put into effect. In 2001, the company earned net profits $20.2 million on revenues of $288 million. In 2002 it earned $73.1 million on revenues of $667.7 million, making it one of the few dot-com companies to break into profitability.

In 2001, GoTo.com changed its name to Overture Services. The name change reflected the results of a strategic shift. By 2001, the bulk of revenues were coming from affiliate sites, with the GoTo.com website garnering only 5% of the company's total traffic.[12] Still, the fact that GoTo.com had its own website that was in effect competing with traffic going to affiliates created potential channel conflict. Many in the company feared that channel conflict might induce key affiliates, such as AOL, to switch their allegiance. After much internal debate, the company decided to phase out the GoTo.com website, focusing all of its attention on the syndication network.

Around the same time, Bill Gross apparently talked to the founders of another fast-growing search engine, Google, about whether they would be interested in merging the two companies. At the time Google had no business model. Gross was paying attention to the fast growth of traffic going to Google's website. He saw a merger as an opportunity to join a superior search engine with Overture's advertising and syndication network (the company was still using Inktomi's search engine). The talks stalled, however, reportedly because Google's founders stated that they would never be associated with a company that mixed paid advertising with organic results.[13]

Within months, however, Google had introduced its own advertising service using a pay-for-click model that looked very similar in conception to Overture's. Overture promptly sued Google for patent infringement. To make matters worse, in 2002 AOL declined to renew its deal with Overture and instead switched to Google for search services.

By 2003 it was clear that although still growing and profitable, Overture was losing traction to Google (Overture's revenues were on track to hit $1 billion in 2003, and the company had 80,000 advertisers in its network).[14] Moreover, Overture was invisible to many of its users, who saw the service as a part of the offering of affiliates, many of whom were powerful brands in their own right, including Yahoo and MSN. Yahoo and Microsoft were also waking up to the threat posed by Google. Realizing that paid search was becoming a highly profitable market, both began to eye Overture to jump-start their own paid search services. While Microsoft apparently decided to build its own search engine and ad service from scratch, Yahoo decided to bid for Overture. In June 2003, a deal was announced, with Overture being sold to Yahoo for $1.63 billion in cash. The payday was a bitter sweet one for Bill Gross. IdeaLab had done very well out of Overture, but Gross couldn't help but feel that a bigger opportunity had slipped through his fingers and into the palms of Google's founders.

As for the patent case, this settled in 2004 when Google agreed to hand over 2.7 million shares to Yahoo. This represented about 1% of the outstanding stock, which at the time was valued at $330. Today the value of those shares is closer to $1 billion.[15]

Google Rising

Google started as a research project undertaken by Larry Page while he was a computer science PhD student at Stanford in 1996. Called BackRub, the goal of the project was to document the link structure of the Web. Page had observed that while it was easy to follow links from one page to another, it was much more difficult to discover links *back*. Put differently, just by looking at a page, it was impossible to know who was linking to that page. Page reasoned that this might be very important information. Specifically, one might be able to rank the value of a webpage by discovering which pages were linking to it, and if those pages were themselves linked to by many other pages.

To rank pages, Page knew that he would have to send out a web crawler to index pages and archive links. At this point, another PhD student, Sergey Brin, became involved in the project. Brin, a gifted mathematician, was able to develop an algorithm that ranked webpages according not only to the number of links into that site, but also the number of links into each of the linking sites. This methodology had the virtue of discounting links from pages that themselves had few, if any, links into them.

Brin and Page noticed that the search results generated by this algorithm were superior to those returned by AltaVista and Excite, both of which often returned irrelevant results, including a fair share of spam. They had stumbled onto the key ingredient for a better search engine—rank search results according to their relevance using a back-link methodology. Moreover, they realized that the bigger the Web got, the better the results would be.

With the basic details of what was now a search engine worked out, Brin and Page released it on the Stanford website in August 1996. They christened their new search engine Google after *googol*, the term for the number 1 followed by 100 zeros. Early on, Brin and Page talked to several companies about the possibility of licensing Google. Executives at Excite took a look but passed, as did executives at Infoseek and Yahoo. Many of these companies were embroiled in the portal wars—and portals were all about acquiring traffic, not about sending it away via search. Search just didn't seem central to their mission.

By late 1998, Google was serving some 10,000 queries a day and was rapidly outgrowing the computing resources available at Stanford. Brin and Page realized that to get the resources required to keep scaling Google, they needed capital, and that meant starting a company. Here Stanford's deep links into Silicon Valley came in useful. Before long they found themselves sitting together with Andy Bechtolsheim, one of the founders of another Stanford start-up, Sun Microsystems. Bechtolsheim watched a demo of Google and wrote a check on the spot for $100,000.

Google was formally incorporated on September 7, 1998, with Page as CEO and Brin as president. From this point on, things began to accelerate rapidly. Traffic was growing by nearly 50% a month, enough to attract the attention of several angle investors (including Amazon founder Jeff Bezos), who collectively put in another million.

That was not enough; search engines have a voracious appetite for computing resources. To run its search engine, Brin and Page had custom-designed a low-cost, Linux-based server architecture that was modular and could be scaled rapidly. But to keep up with the growth of the Web and return answers to search queries in a fraction of second, they needed ever more machines (by late 2005, the company was reportedly using over 250,000 Linux servers to handle more than 3,000 searches a second).[16]

To finance growth of their search engine, in early 1999 Brin and Page started to look for venture capital funding. It was the height of the dot-com boom and money was cheap. Never mind that there was no business model; Google's growth was enough to attract considerable interest. By June 1999, the company had closed its first round of venture capital financing, raising $25 million from two of the premier firms in Silicon Valley, Sequoia Capital and Kleiner Perkins Caufield & Byers. Just as importantly perhaps, the legendary John Doerr, one of Silicon Valley's most successful investors and a Kleiner Perkins partner, took a seat on Google's board.

By late 1999, Google had grown to around forty employees and was serving some 3.5 million searches a day. However, the company was burning through $500,000 a month and still had no business model. It had some licensing deals with companies that used Google as their search technology, but it was not bringing in enough money to stem the flow of red ink. At this point, Google started to experiment with ads, but they were not yet pay-per-click ads. Rather, Google began selling text-based ads to clients that were interested in certain keywords. The ads would then appear on the page returning search results, but not in the list of relevant sites. For example, if someone typed in "Toyota Corolla," an ad would appear at the top of the page, above the list of links for Toyota Corolla cars. These ads were sold on a "cost per thousand impressions" basis. In other words, the cost of an ad was determined by how many people were estimated to have viewed it, not by how many clicked on it. It didn't work very well.

The management team also started to ponder placing banner ads on Google's website as a way of generating additional revenue, but before it made that decision the dot-com boom imploded, the NASDAQ crashed, and the volume of online advertising dropped precipitously. Google clearly needed to figure out a different way to make money.

Google Gets a Business Model

Brin and Page now looked closely at the one search company that seemed to be making good money, GoTo.com. They could see the value of the pay-per-click model and of auctioning off keywords, but there were things about GoTo.com that they did not like. GoTo.com would give guarantees that websites would be included more frequently in web crawls, making sure they were updated, provided that the owners were prepared to pay more. Moreover, the purity of GoTo.com's search results was biased by the desire to make money from advertisers, with those who paid the most being ranked highest. Brin and Page were ideologically attached to the idea of serving up the best possible search results to users, uncorrupted by commercial considerations. At the same time, they needed to make money.

Although Bill Gross pitched the idea of GoTo.com teaming up with Google, Brin and Page decided to go it alone. They believed they could do as good a job as GoTo.com, so why share revenues with the company?[17]

The approach that Google ultimately settled on combined the innovations of GotTo.com with Google's superior relevance-based search engine. Brin and Page had always believed that Google's webpage should be kept as clean and elegant as possible—something that seemed to appeal to users. Moreover, they knew that users valued the fact that Google served up relevant search results that were unbiased by commercial considerations. The last thing they wanted to do was alienate their rapidly growing user base. So they decided to place text-based ads on the right-hand side of a page, clearly separated from search results by a thin line.

Like GoTo.com, they decided to adopt a pay-per-click model. Unlike GoTo.com, Brin and Page decided that in addition to the price an advertiser had paid for a keyword, ads should also be ranked according to relevance. Relevance was measured by how frequently users clicked on ads. More popular ads rose to the top of the list, less popular ones fell. In other words, Google allowed their users to rank ads. This had a nice economic advantage for Google, since an ad that is generating $1.00 a click but is being clicked on three times as much as an ad generating $1.50 a click would make significantly more money for Google. It also motivated advertisers to make sure that their ads were appealing.

The system that Google used to auction off keywords was also different in detail from that used by GoTo.com. Google used a *Vickery second price auction* methodology. Under this system, the winner pays only 1 cent more than the bidder below it. Thus if there are bids of $1, 50 cents, and 25 cents for a keyword, the winner of the top place pays just 51 cents, not $1, the winner of the second place 26 cents, and so on. The auction is nonstop, with the price for a keyword rising or falling depending on bids at each moment in time. Although the minimum bid for a keyword was set at 5 cents, most were above that, and the range was wide. One of the most expensive search terms was reputed to be "mesothelioma," a type of cancer caused by exposure to asbestos. Bids were around $30 per click! They came from lawyers vying for a chance to earn lucrative fees by representing clients in suits against asbestos producers.[18]

While developing this service, Google continued to grow like wildfire. In mid-2000, the service was dealing with 18 million search queries a day and the index surpassed 1 billion documents, making it by far the largest search engine on the Web. By late 2000, when Google introduced the first version of its new service, which it called AdWords, the company was serving up 60 million search queries a day—giving it a scale that GoTo.com never came close to achieving. In February 2002, Google introduced a new version of AdWords that included for the first time the full set of pay-per-click advertising, keyword auctions, and advertising links ranked by relevance. Sales immediately started to accelerate. Google had hit on the business model that would propel the company into the big league.

In 2003, Google introduced a second product, AdSense. AdSense allows third-party publishers large and small to access Google's massive network of advertisers on a self-service basis. Publishers can sign up for AdSense in a matter of minutes. AdSense then scans the publisher's site for content and places contextually relevant ads next to that content. As with AdWords, this is a pay-per-click service, but with AdSense Google splits the revenues with the publishers. In addition to large publishers, such as online news sites, AdSense has been particularly appealing to many small publishers, such as webloggers. Small publishers find that by adding a few lines of code to their sites, they can suddenly monetize their content.

However, many advertisers feel that AdSense is not as effective as AdWords in driving traffic to their sites. Google allowed advertisers to opt out of AdSense in 2004. Despite this, AdSense has also grown into a respectable business, accounting for 15% of Google's revenues in 2005, or close to $1 billion.

Google Grows Up

Between 2001 and 2006 Google changed in a number of ways. First, in mid-2001 the company hired a new CEO, Eric Schmidt, to replace Larry Page. Schmidt had been the chief technology officer of Sun Microsystems and then CEO of Novell. Schmidt was brought on to help manage the company's growth with the explicit blessing of Brin and Page. Both Brin and Page were still in their twenties, and the board felt it needed a "grownup" who had run a large company to help Google transition to the next stage (Google turned a profit the month after Schmidt joined). Brin and Page became the presidents of technology and products, respectively. When Schmidt was hired, Google had over two hundred employees and was handling over 100 million searches a day.

According to knowledgeable observers, Schmidt, Brin, and Page act as a triumvirate, with Brin and Page continuing to exercise a very strong influence over strategies and policies at Google. Schmidt may be CEO, but Google is still very much Brin and Page's company.[19] Working closely together, the three drive the development of a set of values and an organization that have come to define the uniquely Google way of doing things.

Vision and Values

As Google's growth started to accelerate, there was concern that rapid hiring would quickly dilute the vision, values, and principles of the founders. In mid-2001, Brin and Page gathered a core group of early employees and asked them to come up with a policy for ensuring that the company's culture did not fracture as the company added employees. From this group, and subsequent discussions, emerged a vision and list of values that have continued to shape the evolution of the company. These were not new; rather, they represented the formalization of principles that Brin and Page felt they had always adhered to.

The central vision of Google is to *organize the world's information and make it universally acceptable and useful.*[20] The team also articulated a set of ten core philosophies (values), which are now listed on its website.[21] Perhaps the most significant, and certainly the most discussed of these values, is captured by the phrase *"don't be evil."* The central message underlying this phrase was that Google should never compromise the integrity of its search results. Google would never let commercial considerations bias its rankings. *"Don't be evil,"* however, has become more than that at Google; it has become a central organizing principle of the company, albeit one that is far from easy to implement. Google got positive press from libertarians when it refused to share its search data with the U.S. government, which wanted the data to help fight child porn. However, the same constituency reacted with dismay when the company caved into the Chinese government and removed from its Chinese service offending results for search terms such as "human rights" and "democracy"! Brin justified the Chinese decision by saying that "it will be better for Chinese web users, because ultimately they will get more information, though not quite all of it."[22]

Another core value at Google is *"focus on the user, and all else will follow."* In many ways, this value captures what Brin and Page initially did. They focused on giving the user the best possible search experience—highly relevant results, delivered with lightening speed to an uncultured and elegant interface. The value also reflects a belief at Google that it is okay to deliver value to users first, and then figure out the business model for monetizing that value. This belief seems to reflect Google's own early experience.

Yet another key principle, although it is not one that is written down anywhere, is captured by the phrase *"launch early and often."* This seems to underpin Google's approach to product development. Google has introduced a rash of new products over the last few years, not all of which were initially all that compelling, but through rapid upgrades, it has subsequently improved the efficacy of those products.

Google also prides itself on being a company where decisions are *data driven*. Opinions are said to count for nothing unless they are backed up by hard data. It is not the loudest voice that wins the day in arguments over strategy, it is the data. In some meetings, people are not allowed to say "I think . . . ," but instead must say, "The data suggests . . ."[23]

Finally, Google devotes considerable resources to making sure that its employees are working in a supportive and stimulating environment. To quote from the company's website:

> Google Inc. puts employees first when it comes to daily life in our Googleplex headquarters. There is an emphasis on team achievements and pride in individual accomplishments that contribute to the company's overall success. Ideas are traded, tested and put into practice with an alacrity that can be dizzying. Meetings that would take hours elsewhere are frequently little more than a conversation in line for lunch and few walls separate those who write the code from those who write the checks. This highly communicative environment fosters a productivity and camaraderie fueled by the realization that millions of people rely on Google results. Give the proper tools to a group of people who like to make a difference, and they will.[24]

Organization

By all accounts, Google has a flat organization. In November 2005, Google had one manager for every 20 line employees. At times, the ratio has been as high as 1:40. For a while, one manager had 180 direct reports.[25] The structure is reportedly based on teams. Big projects are broken down and allocated to small tightly focused teams. Hundreds of projects may be going on at the same time. Teams often throw out new software in six weeks or less and look at how users respond hours later. Google can try a new user interface, or some other tweak, with just 0.1% of its users and get massive feedback very quickly, letting it decide a project's fate in weeks.[26]

One aspect of Google's organization that has garnered considerable attention is the company's approach toward product development. Software engineers are expected to spend 20% of their time on something that interests them, away from their main jobs. Seemingly based on 3M's famous 15% rule, Google's 20% rule is designed to encourage creativity. The company has set up forums on its internal network where anyone can post ideas and discuss them. Like 3M, Google has set up a process by which projects coming out of 20% time can be evaluated, receive feedback from peers, and ultimately garner funding. Marissa Myer, one of Google's early employees, acts as a gatekeeper, helping to decide when projects are ready to be pitched to senior management (and that typically means Brin and Page). Once in front of the founders, advocates have twenty minutes, and no more, to make their pitch.[27]

One of the early products to come out 20% time was Google News, which returns news articles ranked by relevance in response to a keyword query. Put the term "oil prices" into Google News, for example, and the search will return news dealing with changes in oil prices, with the most relevant at the top of the list. A sophisticated algorithm determines relevance on a real-time basis by looking at the quality of the news source (the *New York Times*, for instance, rates higher than local news papers), publishing date, the number of other people who click on that source, and numerous other factors. The project was initiated by Krishna Bharat, a software engineer from India, who in response to the events of September 11, 2001, had a desire to learn what was being written and said around the world. Two other employees worked with Bharat to construct a demo that was released within Google. Positive reaction soon got Bharat in front on Brin and Page, who, impressed, gave the project a green light, and Bharat started to work on it full time.[28]

Another feature of Google's organization is its hiring strategy. Like Microsoft, Google has made a virtue out of hiring people with high IQs. The hiring process is very rigorous. Each prospect has to take an "exam" to test his or her conceptual abilities. This is followed by interviews with eight or more people, each of whom rates the applicant on a 1-to-4 scale (4 being "I would hire this person"). Applicants also undergo detailed background checks to find out what they are like to work with. Reportedly, some brilliant prospects don't get hired when background checks find out that they are difficult to work with. In essence, all hiring at Google is by committee, and while this can take considerable time, the company insists that the effort yields dividends.

While accounts of Google's organization and culture tend to emphasize their positive aspects, not everyone has such a sanguine view. Brain Reid, who was recruited into senior management at Google in 2002 and fired two years later, told author John Battelle, "Google is a monarchy with two kings, Larry and Sergey. Eric is a puppet. Larry and Sergey are arbitrary, whimsical people. . . . [T]hey run the company with an iron hand. . . . Nobody at Google from what I could tell had any authority to do anything of consequence except Larry and Sergey."[29] According to Battelle, several other former employees made similar statements to him.

The IPO

As Google's growth started to accelerate, the question of if and when to undertake an IPO became more pressing. There were two obvious reasons for doing an IPO: gaining access to capital and providing liquidity for early backers and the large number of employees who had equity positions. On the other hand, from 2001 onwards the company was profitable, generating significant cash flows, and could fund its expansion internally. Moreover, management felt that the longer it could keep the details of what was turning out to be an extraordinarily successful business model private, the better. In the end, the company's hand was forced by an obscure SEC regulation that required companies that give stock options to employees to report as if they were a public company by as early as April 2004. Realizing that the cat would be out of the bag anyway, Google told its employees in early 2004 that it would go public.

True to form, Google flouted Wall Street tradition in the way it structured its IPO. The company decided to auction off shares directly to the public using an untested and modified version of a Dutch auction, which starts by asking for a high price and then lowers it until someone accepts. Two classes of shares were created, Class A and B, with Class B shares having ten times the votes of Class A shares. Only Class A shares were auctioned off. Brin, Page, and Schmidt were holders of Class B shares. Consequently, although they would own one-third of the company after the IPO, they would control 80% of the votes. Google also announced that it would not provide regular financial guidance to Wall Street financial analysts. In effect, Google had thumbed its nose at Wall Street.

The controversial nature of the IPO, however, was overshadowed by the first public glimpse of Google's financials, which were contained in the offering document. They were jaw-dropping. The company had generated revenues of $1.47 billion in 2003, an increase of 230% over 2002. Google earned net profits of $106 million in 2003, but accountants soon figured out that the number was depressed by certain one-time accounting items, and that cash flow in 2003 had been over $500 million!

Google went public on August 19, 2004, at $85 a share. The company's first quarterly report showed sales doubling over the prior year, and by November the price was $200.

In September 2005, with the stock close to $300 a share, Google undertook a secondary offering, selling 14 million shares to raise $4.18 billion. With positive cash flow adding to this, by June 2006 Google was sitting on almost $10 billion in cash and short-term investments, prompting speculation as to the company's strategic intentions.

Strategy

Since 2001, Google has endeavored to keep enhancing the efficacy of its search engine, improving the search algorithms, and investing heavily in computing resources. The company has branched out from being a text-based search engine. One strategic thrust has been to extend search to as many digital devices as possible. Google started out on personal computers, but can now be accessed through PDAs and cell phones. A second strategy has been to widen the scope of search to include different sorts of information. Google has pushed beyond text into indexing and now offers searches of images, news reports, books, maps, scholarly papers, blogs, a shopping network (Froogle), and, in 2006, videos. Google Desktop, which searches files on a user's PC, also fits in with this schema. However, not all of these new search formats have advertising attached to them (for example, images and scholarly papers do not include sponsored links, while maps and book searches do).

Not all of this has gone smoothly. Book publishers have been angered by Google's book project, which seeks to create the world's largest searchable digital library of books by systematically scanning books from the libraries of major universities (for example, Stanford). The publishers have argued that Google has no right to do this without first getting permission from the publishers, and is violating copyright by doing so. Several publishers have filed a complaint with the U.S. District Court in New York. Google has responded that users will not be able to download entire books and that, in any event, creating an easy-to-use index of books is fair use under copyright law and will increase the awareness and sales of books, directly benefiting copyright holders. On another front, the World Association of Newspaper Publishers has formed a task force to examine the exploitation of content by search engines.[30]

Over the last four years, Google has introduced a rash of product offerings that do not have a strong affinity with the company's search mission. Many of these products grew out of the company's new product development process. They include free email (Gmail) and online chat programs; a calendar; a blog site (Blogger); a social networking site (Orkut); finance site (Google Money); a service for finding, editing, and sharing photos (Picasa); and plans to offer citywide free WiFi networks.

Google has also introduced two new web-based products that seem aimed squarely at Microsoft's Office franchise. In March 2006, the company acquired a word-processing program, Writely. This was quickly followed by the introduction of a spreadsheet program, Google Spreadsheets. These products have the look and feel of Microsoft Word and Excel, respectively. Both products are designed for online collaboration. They can save files in formats used by Microsoft products, although they lack the full feature set of Microsoft's offerings.

In July 2006, Google introduced a product to compete with PayPal, a web-based payment system owned by the online auction giant, eBay. Google's product, known as Checkout, offers secure online payment functionality for both merchants and consumers. For merchants, the fee for using Checkout is being priced below PayPal's. Moreover, Checkout is being integrated into Google's AdWords product, so merchants who participate will be highlighted in Google's search results. In addition, merchants who purchase Google's search advertising will get a discount on processing fees. According to one analysis, a merchant with monthly sales of $100,000 that uses Checkout and AdWords stands to reduce its transaction costs by 28%, or $8,400 a year. If it uses just Checkout, it will reduce its transaction costs by 4%, or $1,200 a year.[31] However, with 105 million accounts in mid-2006, PayPal will be difficult to challenge.

Google's track record with new product offerings has been mixed. In mid-2006, two years after its introduction, Gmail generated 25% of the traffic of email on Yahoo and MSN. Also in mid-2006, Froogle was ranked number 8 among shopping networks; Google Talk was ranked 10 in the world, with 2% of the users of market leader MSN. After two years, Orkut had just 1% of the visitors of market leader MySpace. Google Maps and Google News, both seen as successful, were the number 2 offerings in their competitive space behind Map Quest and Yahoo

News, respectively. Google Finance had a tiny market share, way behind market leader Yahoo, although it was only three months old in mid-2006.[32]

Some analysts have questioned the logic behind Google's new product efforts. One noted that "Google has product ADD. They don't know why they are getting into all of these products. They have fantastic cash flow, but terrible discipline on products."[33] Another has accused Google of having an insular culture and argued that "neither Froogle [nor] Google's travel efforts has gained any traction, at least partly because of Google's tendency to provide insufficient support to its ecosystem partners and its habit of acting in an independent, secretive manner."[34] However, others argue that Google has been successful in upgrading the quality of its new offerings, and that several products that were once laggards, such as Google News, are now the best in breed.[35]

Google has also entered into several partnership agreements. In late 2005, Google renewed its three-year-old pact to provide search engine services to AOL. In addition, however, AOL agreed to make more AOL content available to Google users. To support the partnership, Google invested $1 billion in AOL for a 5% stake in the company. At the time, it was reported that Microsoft was also negotiating with AOL on a similar deal, but Google's offer was apparently more compelling to Time Warner management.

In mid-2006, Google inked a deal with Fox Interactive under which Google will provide advertising across Fox's online network, including Fox's market-leading social networking service, MySpace (social networking sites let users post diaries, pictures, videos, and music to share with friends online). MySpace is the dominant enterprise in the social networking field with some 100 million registered users and continues to grow rapidly. Google will be the exclusive provider of search service to Fox Interactive and will have the right of first refusal on display advertising. To get access to MySpace, Google committed itself to making minimum payments of $900 million by 2010.[36]

In another mid-2006 partnership agreement, Google announced that it had reached a deal with Dell Computer under which Dell would preload Google software onto all of its systems, including Google's desktop search product and toolbar, along with a cobranded Internet homepage. Google's search would also be set as the default on Dell machines.

On the acquisition front, until recently Google stuck to purchasing small technology firms. This changed in October 2006 when Google announced that it would purchase YouTube for $1.64 billion in stock. YouTube is a simple, fun website to which anybody can upload video clips in order to share them. By October 2006, some 65,000 video clips were being uploaded every day and 100 million were being watched. Like Google in its early days, YouTube has no business model. The thinking is that Google will find ways to sell advertising that is linked to video clips on YouTube. Google's financial resources will also help YouTube to grow, and the company's legal strengths will aid YouTube in a looming battle with copyright holders, many of whom object, not surprisingly, to their material being uploaded onto YouTube without their permission.[37]

The Search Economy in 2006

There is an old adage in advertising that half of all the money spent on advertising is wasted—advertisers just don't know which half. Estimates suggest that out of worldwide advertising spending of some $428 billion in 2006, a staggering $220 billion will be wasted ($112 billion in the United States) because the wrong message is sent to the wrong audience.[38] The problem is that traditional media advertising is indiscriminate. Consider a thirty-second ad spot on broadcast TV. Advertisers pay a rate for such a spot called CPM (costs per thousand, the M being the Roman numeral for thousand). The CPM is based on estimates of how many people are watching a show. There are numerous problems with this system. The estimates of audience numbers are only approximations at best. The owners of the TV may have left the room while the commercials are airing. They may be channel surfing during the commercial break, napping, or talking on the telephone. The viewer may not be among the intended audience—a Viagra commercial might be wasted on a teenage girl, for example. Or the household might be using a TiVo or a similar digital video recorder that skips commercials.

By contrast, new advertising models based on pay-for-click are more discriminating. Rather than sending out ads to a large audience, only a few of whom will be interested in the products being advertised, consumers select search-based ads. They do this twice—first, by entering a keyword in a search engine, and second, by scanning the search results as well as the sponsored links and clicking on a link. In effect, potential purchasers pull the ads toward them through the search process. Advertisers pay only when someone clicks on their ad. Consequently, the conversion rate for search-based ads is far higher than the conversion rate for traditional media advertising.

Moreover, traditional advertising is so wasteful that most firms only advertise 5 to 10% of their products in the mass media, hoping that other products will benefit from a halo effect. In contrast, the targeted nature of search-based advertising makes it cost effective to advertise products that sell only in small quantities. In effect, search-based Internet advertising allows producers to exploit the economics of the long tail. Pay-for-click models also make it economical for small merchants to advertise their wares on the Web.

The Growth Story

Powered by the rapid growth of search-based pay-for-click advertising, total global advertising spending on the World Wide Web was predicted to total $26.5 billion in 2006, up from $15.5 billion in 2004. By 2008, total World Wide Web ad spending could hit $40.6 billion (see Exhibit 1). In 2004, some 62% of this spending was in the United States. By 2008, the figure in the United States is still expected to account for 58% of the total.[39]

Some view the growth figures as conservative given that web advertising is still underrepresented. Estimates suggest that all web advertising in the United States accounted for about 6% of total advertising

EXHIBIT 2

Share of All U.S. Searches, June 2006

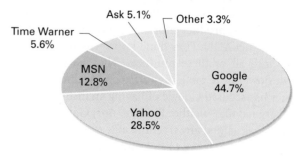

spending in 2005, even though consumers spent some 23% of their media time online.[40] Moreover, search is still growing at a rapid rate. In the second quarter of 2006, search engines dealt with 19.89 billion queries, up 30% from the same period a year earlier.[41]

Google has been the main beneficiary of this trend. In June 2006, Google was the dominant search engine in the United States with a 44.7% share of all searches. Yahoo was second with a 28.5% share, and Microsoft's MSN third with 12.8% share (see Exhibit 2).[42] Google's share of total U.S. paid search advertising was even larger, and was forecasted to hit 57.2% in 2006, up from 18.4% in 2001 (see Exhibit 3).[43] Google's lead also seemed to be accelerating. The company handled 8.75 billion queries in the second quarter of 2006, up 55% from a

EXHIBIT 1

WWW Internet Ad Spending ($ billions)

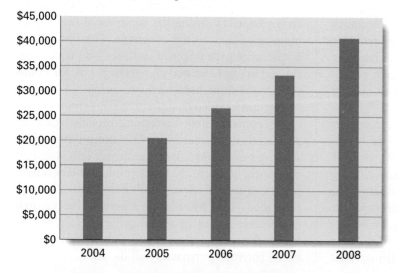

EXHIBIT 3

Google's Share of U.S. Paid Search Ad Spending Minus Traffic Acquisition Costs, 2001–2006

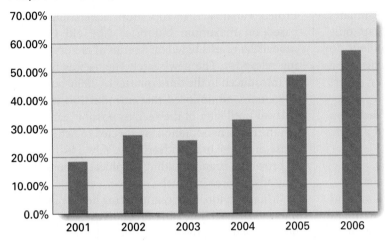

year earlier. Yahoo's search queries were up 21% over the same period, and MSN's just 8%.[44]

While search traffic volumes and online advertising revenues are growing, there are signs that the average bid price for keywords is declining, reflecting increased competition. On June 30, 2006, the average bid price was $1.27 per keyword, down from $1.43 at the end of 2005 and a high of $1.93 a word in April 2005.[45]

Google's rise is reflected in its significant share of all Internet traffic. By mid-2006, Google's websites had the fourth largest unique audience on the Web,

close behind the longer established portal sites maintained by Microsoft (MSN), Yahoo, and Time Warner (AOL), respectively (see Exhibit 4).[46]

One blemish in the growth story has been concern over click fraud. Click fraud occurs whenever a person or computer program clicks on an ad to generate a fake or improper charge per click. Perpetrators of click fraud set up bogus websites and contract with a search company like Google to place search ads on them. Then they use computer programs and anonymous proxy servers to create the illusion that visitors are clicking on the ads, resulting in charges to

EXHIBIT 4

Top 10 Websites by Parent Company, May 2006

Parent Company	Unique Audience	Time per person (hh:mm:ss)
Microsoft	114,330,000	2:06:28
Yahoo	105,504,000	3:26:55
Time Warner	102,247,000	4:40:22
Google	97,207,000	0:55:17
eBay	61,757,000	1:37:48
News Corp Online	58,423,000	1:29:12
InterActive Corp	57,717,000	0:27:51
Amazon	46,188,000	0:21:07
Walt Disney	39,406,000	0:31:41
New York Times	39,279,000	0:14:52

the advertiser, which as an affiliate site they then split with Google. The fraud perpetrators and search engine gain from this action; the advertisers lose. Early estimates suggest that click fraud was running as high as 20% of all clicks, but more recent estimates suggest that the figures are much lower, perhaps only 5%. Nevertheless, click fraud remains a problem. To deal with this, some search engines are mulling over a "cost-per-action" business model, in which an advertiser pays only when a potential customer does something that signals genuine interest, such as placing an item into an online shopping cart, filling out a form, or making a purchase.[47]

Google's Competitors

Google's most significant competitors are Yahoo and Microsoft's MSN, respectively. As paid search has grown, all three have increased their investment in search (see Exhibit 5).[48] Both Yahoo and Microsoft are playing catch-up, trying to improve their search engine technology and gain market share at the expense of Google.

Until 2004, when Yahoo purchased Overture, the company used Google's search technology. In 2005, Yahoo announced that it was making a major investment in its search engine technology to increase it monetization of search. Driving this investment were estimates that Google generated between 30% and 50% more revenue per search than Yahoo. About one-third of the higher search revenue was due to a higher price per click on Google, and two-thirds was due to higher click-through rates, as consequence of Google's superior search engine ranking model.[49] The goal of Yahoo's search engine upgrade, known as Project Panama, is to shift from advertising results based on maximum bid price (the old Overture model), to results based on a series of factors, including relevancy. The new search engine was meant to be introduced in the third quarter of 2006, but in July 2006 Yahoo announced that introduction would be delayed until later in the year, or possibly early 2007. On the other hand, Yahoo is expected to benefit from a rise in online brand advertising. Yahoo is the leader in providing brand-building graphical video and display ads, an area in which Google is weak.

Microsoft too, has been investing heavily in its online search capabilities. In May 2006, after two years in development, Microsoft introduced AdCenter, a platform that will ultimately enable advertisers to place ads everywhere, from search results and webpages to videos games, cell phones, and Internet-connected TV. Prior to AdCenter, Microsoft had been buying ad services from Yahoo. With AdCenter, Microsoft will attempt to leverage its array of platform assets, including Xbox Live, MSN, Windows Mobile, Microsoft TV, MediaCenter, Windows Live, and Microsoft Office Live. Microsoft's goal is to link users and advertisers together across all these platforms. In the middle will sit AdCenter, which is intended to work as the advertising engine. The first version of AdCenter, however, is limited to placing text ads on search result pages. Microsoft is attempting to differentiate AdCenter by providing advertisers with demographic and behavioral data that should help them to place their ads and result in a higher click-through rate.[50]

In addition to AdCenter, Microsoft is working on upgrading its own search engine capabilities. Known as Windows Live Search, which went into testing in late 2006 and will allow users to search the Web, their own desktops, and corporate databases from one interface. A goal of the service is to help users to find intelligent answers to their questions.

However, for all of its capabilities and investments, Microsoft has significant ground to make up in the search economy. Not only is it trailing Google and Yahoo by a wide margin, but recent data suggest that MSN has the lowest conversion rate of homepage use to primary searching—less than one-third of MSN homepage users also use MSN for their search needs, compared to over 40% at Yahoo and 60% at Google.[51]

EXHIBIT 5

Search Engine Research and Development Spending by Company ($ millions)

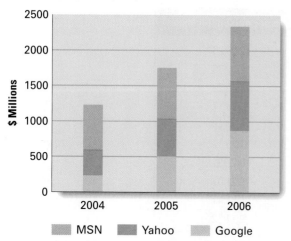

Looking Forward

With online advertising predicted to grow strongly, Google seems to be in the driver's seat. It has the largest market share in search, enjoys the greatest name recognition, and is capturing a proportionately greater share of search-based advertising than its rivals.

However, Microsoft and Yahoo cannot be dismissed. Will they be able to leverage their substantial assets and capabilities to gain ground on Google? As for Google, what is its long-term game plan? Recent strategic moves suggest that it is attempting to expand beyond search, but where will this take the company, and what does that mean for other Internet companies?

ENDNOTES

1. Nielsen/Net Ratings, "Google Accounts for Half of All U.S. Searches," May 25, 2006.
2. David Hallerman, "Search Marketing: Players and Problems," eMarketer, April 2006.
3. Citigroup Global Markets, Internet Industry Note, "Key Take-Aways from Conference Call on MSFT/GOOG Search Competition," June 4, 2006.
4. eMarketer, "Google Revenues to Exceed $10 Billion in 2007," March 20, 2006.
5. This section draws heavily on the excellent description of search given by John Battelle. See John Battelle, *The Search* (Penguin Portfolio, New York, 2005).
6. Google 10K report for 2005.
7. The basic story of GoTo.com is related in John Battelle, *The Search* (Penguin Portfolio, New York, 2005).
8. Karl Greenberg, "Pay-for-placement Search Services Offer Ad Alternatives," *Adweek*, September 25, 2000, page 60.
9. M. Gannon, "GoTo.com Inc," *Venture Capital Journal*, August 1, 1999, page 1.
10. Tim Jackson, "Cash is the Key to a True Portal," *Financial Times*, February 2, 1999, page 16.
11. Karl Greenberg, "Pay-for-placement Search Services Offer Ad Alternatives," *Adweek*, September 25, 2000, page 60.
12. Sarah Heim, "GoTo.com Changes to Overture Services, Launches Campaign," *Adweek*, September 10, 2001, page 7.
13. This little gem comes from John Battelle, *The Search* (Penguin Portfolio, New York, 2005). There is no independent confirmation of the story.
14. Anonymous, "Yahoo to Acquire Overture Services for 2.44 Times Revenues," *Weekly Corporate Growth Service*, July 21, 2003, page 8.
15. Richard Waters, "Google Settles Yahoo Case with Shares," *Financial Times*, August 19, 2004, page 29.
16. Fred Vogelstein, "Gates vs Google: Search and Destroy," *Fortune*, May 2, 2005, pages 72–82.
17. This is according to David A. Vise, *The Google Story* (Random House, New York, 2004).
18. David A. Vise, *The Google Story* (Random House, New York, 2004).
19. John Battelle, *The Search* (Penguin Portfolio, New York, 2005). There is no independent confirmation of the story.
20. http://www.google.com/corporate/index.html.
21. http://www.google.com/corporate/tenthings.html.
22. Andy Kessler, "Sellout.com," *Wall Street Journal*, January 31, 2006, page A14.
23. Quentin Hardy, "Google Thinks Small," *Fortune*, November 14, 2005, pages 198–199.
24. http://www.google.com/corporate/tenthings.html.
25. Quentin Hardy, "Google Thinks Small," *Fortune*, November 14, 2005, pages 198–199.
26. Quentin Hardy, "Google Thinks Small," *Fortune*, November 14, 2005, pages 198–199.
27. Ben Elgin, "Managing Google's Idea Factory," *Business Week*, October 3, 2005, pages 88–90.
28. David A. Vise, *The Google Story* (Random House, New York, 2004).
29. John Battelle, *The Search* (Penguin Portfolio, New York, 2005), page 233.
30. Jacqueline Doherty, "In the Drink," *Barron's*, February 13, 2006, pages 31–36.
31. Mark Mahany, "Building Out the Option Value of Google," *Citigroup Portfolio Strategist*, July 13, 2006.
32. Ben Elgin, "So Much Fanfare, So Few Hits," *Business Week*, July 10, 2006, pages 26–30.
33. Ben Elgin, "So Much Fanfare, So Few Hits," *Business Week*, July 10, 2006, page 27.
34. David Card, "Understanding Google," *Jupiter Research*, March 10, 2006.
35. Mark Mahany, "Building Out the Option Value of Google," *Citigroup Portfolio Strategist*, July 13, 2006.
36. Aline Duyn and Richard Waters, "MySpace Teams Up with Google," *Financial Times*, August 8, 2006, page 15.
37. *The Economist* "Two Kings Get Together; Google and YouTube," October 14, 2006, pages 82–83.
38. *The Economist*, "The Ultimate Marketing Machine," July 8, 2006, pages 61–64.
39. Mark Mahaney, "Key Takeaways from Conference Call on MSFT/GOOG Search Competition," *Citigroup Global Markets*, June 4, 2006.
40. *The Economist*, "The Ultimate Marketing Machine," July 8, 2006, pages 61–64.
41. comScore Press Release, "Google's U.S. Search Market Share Continues to Rise," July 18, 2006.
42. *The Economist*, "The Alliance Against Google," August 12, 2006, pages 49–50.
43. David Hallerman, "Search Marketing: Players and Problems," eMarketer, April 2006.
44. comScore Press Release, "Google's U.S. Search Market Share Continues to Rise," July 18, 2006.
45. Fathom Online Press Release, "Fathom Online Reports Q2 Decrease in Average Bid for Search Marketing Keywords," July 18, 2006.
46. Nielsen/Net Ratings Press Release, "U.S. Broadband Composition Reaches 72 Percent at Home," June 21, 2006.
47. Chris Nuttall, "Google Moves to Tackle Click Fraud," *Financial Times*, July 27, 2006, page 22.
48. David Hallerman "Search Marketing: Players and Problems," eMarketer, April 2006.
49. Mark Mahaney, "YHOO: Revisiting the Long Thesis," *Citigroup Global Market*, August 17, 2006.
50. Brian Morrissey, "Microsoft Takes Giant Steps in Advertising," *Adweek*, May 8, 2006, pages 6–8.
51. Brian Haven, "Search Loyalty is Hard to Find," *Forrester Research*, December 19, 2005.

This case was prepared by Gareth R. Jones, Texas A&M University.

Yahoo is the world's best-known interactive web portal or entryway onto the World Wide Web (WWW). It averaged over 144 million page views per day in 2006, when it earned $2 billion on revenues of $6.4 billion. Today, Yahoo employs over 11,000 people, but the portal has its origins in the website directory created as a hobby by its two founders, David Filo and Jerry Yang. Filo and Yang, who were two PhD candidates in electrical engineering at Stanford University, wanted a quick and easy way to remember and revisit the websites they had identified as the best and most useful from the hundreds of thousands of sites that were quickly appearing on the WWW in the early 1990s. They soon realized that as the list of their favorite websites grew longer and longer, the list began to lose its usefulness since they had to look through a longer and longer list of URLs, or website addresses, to find the specific site they wanted. So to reduce their search time, Filo and Yang decided to break up their list of websites into smaller and more manageable categories according to their specific content or subject matter, such as sports, business, or culture. In April 1994, they published their website directory, "Jerry's Guide to the WWW," for their friends to use. Soon hundreds, then thousands, of people were clicking on their site because it saved them time and effort to identify the most useful sites.

As they continued to develop their directory, Filo and Yang found that each of the directory's subject categories also became large and unwieldy to search, so they further divided the categories into subcategories. Now, their directory organized websites into a hierarchy, rather than a searchable index of pages, so they renamed their directory "Yahoo," supposedly short for "Yet Another Hierarchical Officious Oracle," and Yahoo's hierarchical search directory was born. However, Filo and Yang insist they selected the name because they liked the word's general meaning as originated by Jonathan Swift in *Gulliver's Travels* as someone or something that is "rude, unsophisticated, and uncouth." As their directory grew, they realized they could not possibly identify all the best sites that were appearing in the WWW, so they recruited human volunteers to help them improve, expand, and refine their directory and make it a more useful, labor-saving search device.

By 1994, hundreds of thousands of users were visiting the site every day, and it had quickly become the primary search portal of choice for people using the Internet to find the websites that provided the most useful, interesting, and entertaining content. By the fall of 1994, the website recorded its first million "hits," or Internet-user visits, per day as word of mouth spread about the utility of the Yahoo search directory. Filo and Yang's increasingly comprehensive directory had outgrown the limited hosting capacity of their Stanford University site, and they arranged to borrow server space from nearby Netscape. Yang and Filo decided to put their graduate studies on hold while they turned their attention to building Yahoo into a business.

When they first created their directory, Filo and Yang had no idea they had a potential moneymaking business on their hands. They enjoyed surfing the Internet and just wanted to make it easier for others to do so, but by 1994 it became clear that they could make money from their directory if they allowed companies to advertise their products on the site. Because the Internet was rapidly expanding, Filo and Yang realized they had to move quickly to capitalize on Yahoo's popularity. Although their directory was the first of its kind to be up and running, they knew it could be imitated by other entrepreneurs. Indeed, competitive web-crawling search sites or "search engine" companies like AltaVista that used nonhuman mathematical algorithms had already emerged to help Internet users. The virtue of Yahoo, however, was that its human-powered search engine had already done the legwork for ordinary Internet users; it listed sites handpicked for their usefulness, and at this time, these web crawlers could not match its relevant results to user queries.

As Yahoo's hits continued to increase, so did requests by companies to advertise on its web portal; and as Yahoo's advertising revenues increased, which paid for the costs of hosting their online directory, Filo and Yang realized they had a potentially hot new business on their hands. Filo and Yang's business model was based on generating revenues by renting advertising space on the pages of their fast-growing web directory. When a user clicked on an ad, this "impression," as it is known, became a charge to the advertiser's account; in general, the more impressions, the more the advertising fees. As their fledgling company grew and the number of user visits increased, Filo and Yang realized they had to find the money to pay for a sophisticated IT infrastructure to support their portal's growth. They searched for backing from venture capitalists and soon struck a deal with Sequoia Capital, a Silicon Valley firm that had supported Apple Computer and Oracle, among others. Using the $2 million seed capital to build their company's IT infrastructure, Filo and Yang's portal continued to soar in popularity. In 1996, Yahoo had its initial public offering in April when it raised $338 million by selling 2.6 million shares at $13 each.

Sequoia Capital, with its experience helping startups and new entrepreneurs, insisted that Filo and Yang, who had no business background, should hire experienced executives to take control of developing Yahoo's business model. Sequoia's partners had learned that entrepreneurs often do not make good managers when they become responsible for running a company. The skills needed to be a successful manager often diverge from those necessary to notice opportunities and start new businesses, especially if entrepreneurs have technical or scientific backgrounds and no exposure to how businesses operate. Filo and Yang hired Tim Koogle, an experienced ex-Motorola executive with an engineering background, to be their chief executive officer (CEO). Jeffrey Mallett, an ex-Novell software manager with a marketing background, was hired as chief operating officer (COO). Filo and Yang became joint co-chairmen of Yahoo and both adopted the title of "Chief Yahoo."

Developing Yahoo's Business Model

Under the control of Koogle and Mallett, who both received a significant share of the company's stock, the four executives went about building Yahoo's business model. Their first step was to strengthen Yahoo's core competences in marketing and advertising to increase revenues and fund the company's further growth. So Mallett focused on recruiting marketing experts and building the company's advertising function. At the same time, revenue growth would be driven by increasing the number of Internet users, so continuous improvement of Yahoo's web directory was vital. Filo and Yang took overall responsibility here but hired experts such as Srinija Srinivasan, or "Ontological Yahoo" as she became known in the company because of her crucial role in refining and developing the classification system that is the hallmark of Yahoo's web directory. She helped hire hundreds more IT software engineers to broaden and increase the reach and usefulness of Yahoo's directory and to manage its burgeoning IT infrastructure that was being continuously installed and upgraded to handle the millions of requests the company was receiving each day. By 1996, Yahoo listed over 200,000 individual websites in over 20,000 different categories, and hundreds of companies had signed up to advertise their products on its portal to its millions of users. This, however, was just the beginning of their efforts.

Another first step Koogle took was to take Yahoo's business model and replicate it around the world. By the end of 1996, there were eighteen Yahoo portals operating outside the United States, and Yahoo could be accessed by users in twelve languages. In each country, Yahoo's portal and web directory were customized to the tastes and needs of local users. Because there was considerable overlap between countries in terms of global news and global websites, this also allowed Yahoo to enrich its U.S. directory and help create new products to appeal to its users.

Yahoo's success with its global operations convinced Koogle to craft a new vision of Yahoo, not as an Internet website directory but as a global communication, media, and retail company whose portal could be used to enable anyone to connect with anything or anybody on the Internet. Koogle's ambition was to transform Yahoo's directory service into an intermediary that could be used not only to link people to information, but also as a retail conduit to bring together buyers and sellers, thereby facilitating e-commerce transactions over the WWW. In the vision its top executives crafted, Yahoo would not only continue to generate increasing revenues from the sale of advertising space on its web directory pages, but it would also earn significant revenues from managing e-commerce transactions by taking a small percentage of the value of each transaction executed, using its portal as its fee. In 1998, Yahoo acquired the Internet shopping portal Viaweb and the direct marketing company Yoyodyne Entertainment to create its new retail shopping platform, Yahoo Stores. This service enabled businesses to quickly create, publish, and manage secure online stores to market and sell goods and services. After launching their stores, merchants were included in searches on Yahoo Shopping, which provided customers with price comparisons of the products they were interested in.

To build brand awareness and make Yahoo the portal of choice, the company spent heavily on advertising, using radio and television ads targeted at mainstream America. To make the company's portal more useful to users, Koogle pioneered Yahoo's strategy of expanding the range of content and services it provided. Over the next decade, Yahoo continuously developed technology and made acquisitions that allowed users to access an increasing number of services such as email, instant messaging, news, stock alerts, personals, and job placement services using digital devices from conventional PCs to wireless laptops to eventually to hand-held smart phones. Yahoo also began to work with content providers and merchants to help them build and improve their online content, which in turn increased the value of Yahoo's portal to users who could access the content

and merchants through Yahoo. Yahoo also increased its value to advertisers by enabling them to better target their advertising message to specific demographic groups, for example, sports fans, teens, or investors. For example, the online broker E*Trade heavily advertised its shopping and news services on Yahoo's financial pages, in sports magazines, eBay, and Blockbuster. Such targeted advertising increased the rates at which users clicked on online ads, which translated into more online transactions and increased yields or returns of online advertising to merchants.

The results of these strategies were spectacular. By the end of 1998, the company had 50 million unique users, up from 26 million in the prior year, and 35 million of these were now registered Yahoo users; 3,800 companies were advertising on Yahoo's pages, up from 2,600 in 1997 and 700 in 1996. By 1999, 5,000 merchants were selling products on the Yahoo Shopping channel, up from 3,500 in 1998, and the company's revenues had grown from $21.5 million in 1996 to $203 million in 1998. As a result, Yahoo's stock price soared from $5 a share in 1996 to a high of $244 a share in early 1999 near the height of the dot-com boom. This valued Yahoo at an incredible $45 billion, making Yang and Filo billionaires.

More Content and More Presence

To keep Yahoo's profits growing, it was necessary to drive more and more users to its site. For this reason, Koogle's new strategies revolved around making Yahoo a "megabrand" by becoming the most useful and well-known web portal on the Internet. Not only was Yahoo focused on improving its web directory, but it also wanted to create compelling news and entertainment content by adding more and more new services and features to increase its value and appeal to web users and so encourage them to register on its website. Its goal was to lock in users and increase their switching costs of turning to a new portal. So it began to increase the degree to which users could customize Yahoo's pages and services to better meet their specific needs. For example, Yahoo's registered users could customize its popular news service to show the specific news sections or pages in which they were the most interested, such as technology, entertainment, or financial news sections. In some areas, they could do more customization; to give one example, in Yahoo Finance they could also input and track the value of their personal stock portfolio. The financial page section also provides links to message boards where individual investors could join to discuss a company's prospects. Other links connect investors to valuable content about the companies in their personal stock portfolio, including news reports and commentary, research reports, and detailed financial data. Once again, this high level of customization creates major switching costs, for having created their portfolios, personal pages, shopping lists, and so on, users are less likely to want to repeat this process at another web portal—unless it offers some other "killer application," or compelling content.

Yahoo worked hard to remain the web portal of choice by introducing new kinds of online services soon after other kinds of Internet companies showed they were popular among Internet customers. It often acquired well-known Internet companies to increase the value of its portal to users; in 1999, for example, it made three important acquisitions: First, it bought Rocketmail, an email service provider that became the basis for Yahoo email. Second was GeoCities, which provided a free web hosting service to registered users that allowed them to publish their own personal homepages containing material of their choice that they could share with friends and any other interested parties. Third, it bought Broadcast.com, an early leader in broadcasting streaming audio and video programming on the WWW. This acquisition allowed Yahoo to broadcast audio and video content on all its channels to users, in addition to ordinary text, and so made Yahoo's services even more valuable to users—and thus to advertisers as well. Then, in 2000, Yahoo acquired eGroups, a free social group/mailing list hosting service that allowed registered users to set up any kind of online group of their choosing and use it as a forum to attract any other Internet users of their choice, from school groups to national hobby societies. eGroups was used to develop and strengthen its successful Yahoo Groups service, which today has millions of registered groups of users and is a very popular mailing list service for all kinds of social networking purposes.

As Koogle had hoped, as the range of services Yahoo offered expanded, its popularity increased and it worked toward its goal of becoming a "one-stop shop" that could cater to almost every kind of service that Internet users needed—information, entertainment, and retail. Beyond the services just mentioned, Yahoo also now provided Yahoo Messenger, an instant messaging

client; online chat; a successful game-playing service, Yahoo Games; and various specialized kinds of information portals including online shopping but also an online auction service it had started up to compete with eBay's successful online auction site. Its original directory now became just one, although an important one, of the services it provided.

Most of these services were provided free to Yahoo users because the advertising revenues earned from the ads on the millions of webpages on its portal were the main source of its highly profitable business model. In addition, it earned some revenues from the fees it earned from joining sellers and buyers on its shopping and specialized retail sites. However, Yahoo also searched for opportunities to increase revenues by providing specialized, customized services to users for a monthly fee; for example, it established a personals dating service, a streaming stocks quotes service, job hunting service, and various premium email and web storage options that provided users with more kinds of value-added solutions. All this helped to increase revenues and earnings.

Indeed, the success of its strategy of bundling online services to attract ever-greater numbers of users became clear with Yahoo's explosive growth. By the end of the 1990s, 15 million people a day were visiting Yahoo; it had become the most visited portal on the WWW. Its business model—based on the idea that the more services it offered, the greater the number of Internet users it would attract, and so the greater would be the advertising fees it could charge—seemed to be working well. In 2000, Yahoo's stock price reached an astronomical height of $237.50 per share, giving the company a value of $220 billion.

Big Problems Face Yahoo

Just two years later, however, Yahoo's stock had plummeted to just $9 a share, which valued the company at less than $10 billion. Why? Because of the dot-com bust, which sent thousands of Internet companies into bankruptcy and caused the stock price of them all to fall. However, Yahoo was a dot-com powerhouse, and many analysts put some of the blame for the fall in its stock price (eBay's did not fall greatly) on managerial mistakes at the top of the company—in particular, on Yahoo's business model.

CEO Tim Koogle had staked Yahoo's continuing success on its ability to develop an increasing range of compelling web content and services to increase visits to its portal and so increase its advertising and e-commerce revenues. The problem with this business model was that it made Yahoo's profitability (and so its stock price) totally dependent on how fast advertising revenues increased—and of course how fast they fell. And the dot-com bust and the economic recession that followed in the early 2000s led to a huge decrease in the amount of money large and small companies were willing to spend on Internet advertising. As its advertising revenues plunged, Yahoo's stock price plummeted because its high stock price was based on investors' hopes of ever-increasing future growth.

Moreover, it turned out that Koogle had spent far too much money—billions too much—to pay for many of Yahoo's acquisitions such as GeoCities and eGroups, especially given that these companies' profits were also highly dependent on Internet advertising! At the same time, general advances in Internet technology lowered the value of the acquired companies' distinctive competencies and their competitive advantage in providing a specific online service—the main reason why Yahoo acquired them. Technological advances were making it easier for new upstart dot-coms to provide similar kinds of specialized Internet services as Yahoo offered, but with new twists or killer applications. Thus, in the 2000s competitors like Monster.com, MySpace, and YouTube emerged and in a few years became dominant portals in providing a particular kind of online application. These portals were major threats to Yahoo because they siphoned off its users and so reduced advertising revenues—which were based on the number of users visiting a website.

On the search engine front, too, a new threat was emerging for Yahoo—the growing popularity of Google, a small, relatively unknown search engine company in 2000. In the early 2000s, it became obvious to web watchers that Google was pioneering advances in WWW search technology that was making Yahoo's hierarchical directory classification obsolete. Yahoo, like other major web portals such as Microsoft and AOL, had not realized how the search function would increase so much in importance as the breadth and depth of the WWW increased and made it increasingly difficult for users to locate the specific information they needed. The search engine that found the information users wanted with the least number of clicks would be the one that won the search engine war, and Google's proprietary technology was attracting more and

more users by word of mouth—just as Yahoo's directory had grown in popularity. Yahoo had been providing more and more kinds of online services, but in the process had forgotten, or lost, the reason for its original success. Perhaps a professional manager at the helm was not such a good idea in the first place?

The Web Portal Industry

To appreciate the problems Yahoo is facing today, it is necessary to understand how the incredible growth in the 1990s of the Internet and WWW and quickly advancing Internet hardware and software changed the function of web portals dramatically.

Internet Service Provider Portals

The first commercial portals were entry or access portals called Internet Service Providers (ISPs) that provided people with a way to log onto the Internet; for example, companies such as CompuServe, MSN, and AOL offered customers email service and access to the WWW for time-related fees. Slow dial-up connections meant high monthly fees, and early on, ISPs charged for each email sent! Moreover, once on the WWW, users were hampered by the fact that there was no Internet web browser available to help them easily find and navigate to the thousands and then millions of webpages and websites that were emerging.

Yahoo's directory and then Netscape's Internet browser, introduced in 1994, changed all this, as did the growth in the number of search engines available to help surf the Web, including early leaders AltaVista, Inktomi, and Infoseek. Typically, a user would connect to the Web through an access portal and then go to a search engine to identify websites of interest, which could then be bookmarked as favorites using Netscape's web browser.

Product Bundling Portals Yahoo stole the lead from AltaVista with its advanced search directory, and this began the second phase of portal development, the product bundling or aggregation phase, as companies like Yahoo, AOL, MSN, and many other now defunct web portals began to compete to attract Internet users and become the portal of choice—to obtain advertising revenues. Major differences in the business models of different portals could be clearly discerned; for example, portals like Yahoo focused on offering users a wide range of free Internet services. Others, like AOL and MSN, adopted the fee-paying model in which users paid to access the Web through a dial-up connection the portal provided; then they could use the range of services they offered free or for a charge for a premium service, like personals.

Competition between these combined access/aggregation portals increased as they strived to attract the millions of new Internet users who were coming online at this time. The bigger their user base, the higher the potential fees and advertising revenues they could collect, so the price of Internet service quickly fell. By the middle 1990s, AOL made a major decision to offer its users unlimited Internet connection time for $19.95 a month. This attracted millions of new users, and AOL became the leading access and aggregation portal with over 30 million users at its height, followed by MSN, and many other smaller ISPs.

The competitive problem ISP/aggregated portals like AOL faced from the beginning was that once their users were online, they would search out the "best of breed" web portal that could provide them with the particular kinds of services they most wanted. So, millions of AOL subscribers, for example, left its entry portal and then used the myriad of services offered on Yahoo's portal—first, because they were familiar with and attracted to its search engine, and then subsequently, because they liked to use its innovative new services such as financial news, game playing, shopping site, and so on. The problem facing AOL, MSN, and others was how to improve their content to keep subscribers on their portals and so obtain the important advertising and e-commerce revenues that Yahoo was enjoying.

Also, an increasing number of new ISPs began to offer lower price Internet access service, and broadband technology started to grow in popularity by the end of the 1990s. This also worked in favor of free portals like Yahoo because fee-based portals like AOL and MSN had to find new ways to keep their revenues growing as the number of new Internet users first slowed and then dropped as they lost customers to other ISPs while their subscribers continued to desert to portals like Yahoo, eBay, and Amazon.com.

Customized Portals The next major development in web portals were those that increasingly allowed for some kind of user-customized online experience. Internet bookselling pioneer Amazon.com was one of the first portals to pioneer the development of the personalized or customized shopping experience.

Amazon.com's software focused on providing more information to users by, for example, allowing people who had bought books to provide detailed feedback to users about a particular book and, subsequently, about all kinds of products that it sold. Similarly, Amazon could track users around its site, helping them to find other similar products to the one they were interested in, and recording the products they had already considered to help users make a better buying decision. In addition, Amazon.com pioneered the 1-Click personalized checkout system that made the purchasing decision quick and easy once a buyer had registered on its site. Just as Yahoo began to provide a range of different services, so over time Amazon decided to sell an increasing range of products, but its personalized approach was the way it differentiated itself from other e-commerce portals. This became an important new development in competition between web portals of all kinds.

All the major portals began to realize the importance of offering users a customized online experience to increase their switching costs and keep them loyal and repeat users. They all began to make the "My" personal preferences choices on their portals—"MyAOL" or "MyYahoo," for instance—more important parts of their services. By offering easy online payment service, portals became more interactive with their users. This benefited Yahoo because with its wide range of offerings it was in a strong position to offer users a personalized service that locked them in to its website.

However, it was also increasingly clear that the best-of-breed web portals had developed a first-mover advantage in terms of the loyalty of their users. Amazon.com had developed a strong first place in Internet retailing. It was able to withstand the challenge from the thousands of other shopping portals that had sprung up, most of which went out of business during the dot-com bust. However, Amazon.com also beat out the shopping channels of portals such as Yahoo and AOL, which increasingly put their focus on providing a shopping advisory/comparison service that listed the prices of products of the major Internet retailers and received a fee from transactions that were completed. Similarly, Yahoo's online auction service, even though it was *free* to its registered users, could not compete with online auction leader eBay because eBay offered buyers and sellers a much larger market and therefore more selection and fairer prices.

By the early 2000s, it was clear that the two biggest sources of profit for web portals that could be gained from e-commerce would come from online advertising revenues and from the profits from retail and auction sales. So, in the early 2000s, it was rumored that Yahoo would use its strong stock price to buy eBay and that the companies would merge to capture all these sources of revenue. However, the two companies' top management could not agree on the terms of a merger, and each portal sought ways to improve its own specific competitive position—eBay by strengthening its presence in different kinds of retailing formats, including fixed price selling, for example, and Yahoo by increasing the range of its online service offerings.

The business models of these companies fared differently during the dot-com bust. While most of the dot-coms went out of business, major portals like Yahoo and Amazon survived because of their leading competitive positions. Some, like AOL and MSN, survived because of the resources of their parent organizations—Time Warner (which almost collapsed because of its mistaken acquisition of AOL) and Microsoft (which has never made a profit operating its MSN web portal). eBay was the least affected portal because its robust business model was based on the profits earned from the fees it obtained from auction sales, not the fickle revenues generated by online advertising. Indeed, eBay's stock has historically been the most resilient of any leading dot-com company.

Since the dot-com bust, some of the leading forces in the environment that have affected competition in the web portal industry have been the arrival of Google, with its unique advertising business model, and the emergence of social networking web portals that have taken personalization and customization of users' online experiences to new levels. Google, of course, not only developed advanced search capabilities that outperformed search engine competitors, including Yahoo, but it also realized that it could develop search technology that could better connect individual users to specific websites and then tailor the advertising on those sites to the specific interests of users. Thus Google invented the *website-customized advertising approach* that allowed it to offer any potential advertiser the ability to appear on a website currently being viewed by a user who is interested in the same kind of products that the potential advertiser has to offer. For example, if I

am looking for a landscaper, when I visit various landscaping websites, Google's advertising presents me with more related choices of landscaping sites to visit; the ones featured first are those who have bid more money (for example, 15 versus 10 cents a click). In addition, increasingly Google was able to personalize advertising and deliver better value to advertisers by charging them only for "impressions"—clicks on websites that actually resulted in sales—as opposed to charging advertisers for all clicks on an advertising button. This, in turn, has allowed advertisers to make better use of their advertising dollars. Also, when a particular website chose to host other Google-sponsored advertisers that offered related products, even if it did not secure a sale from a particular user, it enjoyed a small fee from being the site that provided the link that resulted in a sale. In sum, Google pioneered the concept of cross-website-tailored advertising, a huge market compared to the advertising possible on just one website such as Yahoo's. This allowed it to generate the ever-increasing advertising revenues that have led its stock price to soar.

Social Networking Portals The fourth major development in Internet portals over time has been the quick growth of social networking websites, such as MySpace and YouTube. These sites offer their registered users (1) many additional ways to personalize their personal webpages by uploading more and different kinds of content, and (2) additional avenues to find other users that share similar kinds of interests. Thus on a networking portal, users become interconnected and can often form online groups that are able to share content such as information, music, photographs, and videos, and chat with each other using webcams and so on. Although Yahoo had its Geocities service that allowed users to create personal webpages, specialist social networking websites were able to tweak and develop software that made creating personalized webpages a more exciting and enriching experience. Geocities quickly became "old hat" technology by the standards of MySpace users, especially as these networking websites were specifically targeted at young "hip" Internet users. Yahoo's expensive purchase of Geocities was increasingly looking like a major error as rapidly advancing Internet technology made newer sites more fashionable. It began to seem that fashions in the Internet industry, with the rapid growth of MySpace and

Apple's iTune, could change as quickly as fashions in the clothing industry.

A Changeover at the Top in 2001

As mentioned earlier, at the pinnacle of the Internet boom in the year 2000, it was reported that Yahoo and eBay were discussing a 50/50 merger. On January 3, 2000, Yahoo stock closed at an all-time high of $475 a share, and the company had billions of dollars it could have used to make a major acquisition such as eBay. Many analysts argued that when Yahoo's stock price was high, it should have purchased a company that was generating revenue by some other means than advertising so that it could broaden the source of its revenues. It was so heavily dependent on advertising revenues, that if they were to fall, Yahoo's profitability would also plunge and so would its stock price, but infighting among Yahoo's top managers who could not agree on the right course of action prevented the merger from occurring. And, in the next twelve months, Yahoo's stock price did plummet as the dot-com bust, coupled with a huge fall in advertising revenues caused by the economic recession that followed, showed investors how fragile the profitability of its business model was.

In fact, Yahoo's disastrous performance convinced its board of directors that new leadership was needed at the top, and both Tim Koogle and Jeff Mallett stepped down in March 2001. In April 2001, Terry Semel, an experienced Hollywood media executive who had once controlled Warner Brothers, took control as its new CEO, but Yahoo's stock was still in freefall, and in September 2001 it closed at an all-time low of $8.11! To resolve Yahoo's problems, especially as it could no longer afford to make an expensive acquisition, Semel had to redefine its business model and adopt strategies to find new ways to generate online revenues, especially as the economy recovered. Three interrelated strategies were at the center of his new business model for Yahoo.

First, there was a need to quickly develop new content and services to attract more users and so more advertising revenues. Second, Yahoo had to improve its search engine technology, a major portal attraction, to generate more users and advertising revenues. Third, as time went on and the success of Google's business model became evident, Yahoo needed to imitate Google and offer a high-quality customized advertising service (1) to companies that already had websites on Yahoo's portal, and (2) to any company that wanted to benefit from increased online sales. The result would be increased advertising revenues from Internet-wide advertising programs.

To pursue its new content-driven strategy, Yahoo both internally developed new kinds of services and acquired specialist Internet companies that could provide it with the competency it needed in an emerging new content area. In late 2001, for example, Yahoo acquired HotJobs, a leading Internet job hunting and placement company. Also starting in 2001, it began expanding its news and media services operations and started to hire experienced executives from major television networks and newspapers to build its competencies in news services. In 2002, SBC and Yahoo launched its national co-branded dial service to help build a presence in the growing broadband entry portal business, and in 2004 Yahoo made several acquisitions, such as email provider Oddpost.com, to improve its existing services.

In 2004, recognizing the growing importance of communications media for generating advertising revenues, Yahoo established a new Media Group to develop not only written but also video news content to take advantage of broadband Internet to transmit content to users as a shift away from TV took place. In 2004, Yahoo launched its video search engine, and in 2005 it launched a revamped Yahoo Music download service. In 2005 Yahoo also acquired Flickr, a leading photograph hosting and sharing site, and announced Flickr and its other social sites would become major parts of its new social networking strategy. This purchase was prompted by increasing concerns that advertising revenues were bypassing Yahoo in favor of social networking sites like MySpace and YouTube. Yahoo lost the battle to acquire YouTube to Google, which bought the company in 2006, and it was rumored to be looking at Facebook.com as a possible alternative.

Yahoo used new acquisitions and internally developed skills to give each of its hundreds of services a more customized, social network-like appeal to users. For example, it made more use of message boards and wikis to enhance the value of its travel and financial services. In 2005 Yahoo launched a personalized blogging and social networking service Yahoo 360°, revamped its MyWeb personal web hosting service, created a new PhotoMail service, and purchased online social event calendar company Upcoming.org to compete with Google's online calendar service. Continuing its push to strengthen customized and social networking services in 2005, Yahoo acquired blo.gs, a service based on RSS feed aggregation, primarily from weblogs (hence the name), which produces a simple list (and also an RSS feed) of freshly updated weblogs based on a user's specific interests. Yahoo also acquired del.icio.us, which allows registered users to create a scrapbook or notebook of information they wish to keep from the websites they visit, similar to Google's notebook service. More rumors continue to surface about Yahoo's possible acquisition intentions that may allow users to share common interests and trade information.

Thus under Semel, Yahoo has continually developed the competencies to engage its users in multiple online services, from email to financial services to job hunting. It is a leader in content categories such as finance, autos, and real estate. It can now use the thousands and millions of different web content pages it has created on its portal to sell more ads and generate more advertising revenues, and its user base has increased. Semel's other content-driven strategy has been to make Yahoo's content and services so useful and attractive to online customers that they are willing to pay for them—in the form of once-and-for-all or monthly fees for services. For example, Yahoo generates monthly fees for personal ads in its dating site or from ads to sell or rent merchandise like cars or homes; it receives fees from premium services in areas including email and storage, photo sharing, e-commerce services, message boards, and special interest topics. Yahoo also generates fees from small businesses that wish to link to its web portal and use Yahoo's specialist services to create, host, and manage their retail stores.

This user-fee strategy has worked well for Yahoo, and now over 40% of its total revenues come from the fees individuals and small business customers pay for its services. At the same time, the advertising revenues its webpages generate have also soared as the economy recovered and Yahoo kept its position as the most popular portal; its revenue more than tripled from 2003 to 2006 to over $6 billion.

Problems with a Content-Driven Strategy

In the summer of 2006, however, major questions came to be asked about how much Yahoo's content-driven strategy would continue to drive its revenues

as competition, particularly from Google and social networking portals, increased dramatically. Yahoo's stock fell 25% in 2006 as analysts became worried that these other popular websites were taking away its users and so would reduce advertising revenues and user fees in the future. Yahoo might be in trouble as Google and other specialist portals were now offering free an increasing number of the services Yahoo provided; Google had started Gmail, for example, as well as chat, storage, and word-processing services. Fewer users would also mean lower advertising revenues.

In an internal memo leaked to the media, one of Yahoo's senior managers expressed concerns that many of its new investments in content and services were too expensive, were unlikely to generate much profit, and would not allow it to keep up with agile new competitors like social networking websites. In the "peanut butter" memo, senior executive Brad Garlinghouse described Yahoo as a company in search of a successful business model and strategies: "I've heard our strategy described as spreading peanut butter across the myriad opportunities that continue to evolve in the online world. The result: a thin layer of investment spread across everything we do and thus we focus on nothing in particular. I hate peanut butter. We all should." Reasons for his concern include the fact that MySpace, YouTube, and other social networking websites had beaten Yahoo's own sites such as Yahoo360° and MySpace. And Google's new instant messaging and email service were attracting away users from Yahoo's, which had been an early leader in this area. Similarly, Yahoo had been late into Internet VOIP telephone calling, and although it had purchased Dialpad in 2005 to gain a competency in this area, eBay's Skype was the current leader in this area. Similarly, in the increasingly important online imaging and video services area, Google, MSN, and AOL had all developed imaging and video channels that offered content similar to Yahoo's, and Google drew further ahead of Yahoo after its purchase of YouTube in 2006.

Nevertheless, Yahoo still had impressive content covering sports, entertainment, and finance, in particular, and had made major advances in the mobile delivery of its services to smartphones and other hand-held devices and embarked on a major program to enhance the wireless features of all its services to better meet the needs of people on the go. By 2008, for example, mobile video is expected to be a killer application and to compete with Google. Yahoo has recently invested heavily to upgrade this service.

The Search Engine Dilemma

One of the most important factors that generates return user visits and stimulates advertising revenues is the quality of a portal's search engine service. Semel recognized that for Yahoo to achieve significant revenue and earnings growth, it also had to maximize the value of its search services to Internet users to generate the high volume of web traffic that leads to significant revenues from online advertising and facilitating e-commerce transactions. As mentioned earlier, Yahoo's original search directory was developed by its own human editors or "surfers," who identified the best websites and organized them into categories by their content. However, as the WWW grew enormously, its human surfers could not keep up, and from the early 1990s Yahoo partnered with independent "crawler-based" search engine companies to provide answers to user queries when there were no matches within its own human-powered listings directory. The independent search providers were paid by Yahoo according to the volume of queries their engines handled, and since Yahoo was the most popular search site on the Web, being Yahoo's provider could earn the search engine company significant revenues. Each year Yahoo searched for the best search engine, the one with the best search technology, and offered the company a short-term contract. OpenText was the company's first search engine partner; then AltaVista won the contract in 1996, but was dumped for Inktomi in mid-1998. This happened because Yahoo thought that AltaVista was attempting to become a competing portal while Inktomi's business model was focused on developing state-of-the-art search technology and it made no attempt to compete with access portals like Yahoo.

In 2000, however, Inktomi lost the contract to Google, which had developed a growing reputation for its high-quality search results and which, at that time, was not a competitor to Yahoo. In 2001, Yahoo paid Google $7.1 million for the volume of search queries it handled, and in 2002 it renewed Google's contract to use its search results as part of its search listings. It even introduced a new Yahoo search results page that no longer separated Yahoo's own human-powered listings from Google's crawler-based results; rather, the two were blended together. Even in 2002, some top managers at Yahoo thought that this new contract might be a mistake because as Yahoo users became increasingly aware that Google was powering their search results, they might began to move directly to Google's own website—still very "empty" of content at this time, however. Although Google handled a search volume more than double that of Yahoo's, as measured by "search hours," and had a 30% share of the U.S. search audience—very similar to Yahoo's—it was not perceived as a direct competitor because it had not developed its current content/services portal business model. In addition, Yahoo had initially partnered with Google, so its users would feel they were getting both the quality of Google and the unique view that Yahoo's human-powered results brought to the Web. Dropping Google might cause Yahoo problems if its users decided to leave for Google, even though other engines like Inktomi also provided high-quality search results.

By 2003, Google's growing popularity as the search portal of choice and its fast-developing customized advertising strategy showed Yahoo's managers they had made a major error. Recognizing the increasing threat posed by Google's customized search and advertising strategy, Semel began to look for acquisitions to strengthen and improve Yahoo's search engine. Its past relationship with search engine leader Inktomi made that company an obvious acquisition target. After buying Inktomi in 2002, Yahoo bought Overture Services in 2003, a company that specialized in identifying and ranking the popularity of websites and in helping advertisers find the best sites to advertise on; it also obtained Overture's search engine subsidiaries AltaVista and AlltheWeb. Then, in early 2004, Yahoo dropped Google's search engine service and rolled out its own, powered by Inktomi; its directory is now found in a separate category/tab on its search toolbar. Today, Yahoo and Google compete head to-head with search engines that offer remarkably similar sets of features and services; however, Google's share of the search engine market is still growing, and it now has almost double Yahoo's share of search engine users—49% compared to Yahoo's 24% in 2006. This is one more factor that led Yahoo's stock price to fall by 25% in 2006 while Google's soared.

A Push for Customized Online Search/Advertising

The third, and related part of Semel's ongoing strategy to protect and increase Yahoo's revenues has evolved over the past few years in response to the growing success of Google's customized advertising model. All the other major portals—Amazon.com, AOL, MSN, and eBay—were slow to recognize that the better able a search engine is to match ads to search queries, the more likely a user is to click through to an advertiser's website and complete an online transaction, which generates the high advertising revenues Google enjoys. In addition, the real breakthrough in Google's strategy was that it was not advertising on a particular portal that was the main source of revenue; it was the ability to create the advertising that was most closely linked to any specific webpage—the advertising that comes up when a user clicks on the search results from a particular query. Google's advertising model is to help every potential website or advertiser host customized ads that drive online transactions so that everyone would benefit—website, advertiser, and, of course, Google, which collects a small fee for each click.

Consequently, these portals have come to realize the potential threat posed by Google's Internet-wide customized advertising strategy: It has the potential to generate an enormous amount of revenue, which Google can then use to enter their businesses if it chooses and compete head to head with them. When users return to portals like Google's that offer them the quickest and most relevant search results, they are barraged by relevant ads, many useful online services, and who knows what other services they may encounter in the future as Google expands its offerings?

To meet Google's challenge, Semel combined the distinctive competencies of Inktomi and Overture with the in-house technology developed by Yahoo's search engine and advertising software engineers to develop an improved search engine that would lead to a much improved customized online advertising program, one that could compete with Google's. Yahoo began a major technology upgrade, Project Panama, to improve its search-based advertising technology with a goal of bringing the new system online in 2006. But this massive project soon fell behind schedule, and the company could not meet its revised goal of launching it in the summer of 2006, which is one more reason for the company's 38% slide in third-quarter revenues and its fourth-quarter profit warning. Nevertheless, to fight back Google's challenge, Yahoo and eBay formed a marketing/advertising alliance in 2006 that gave Yahoo the contract for creating customized advertising on eBay's webpages;

however, later in the year, eBay, which is also a major partner of Google, gave that company the contract for creating the customized advertising on all its other global websites.

Google has also improved its advertising system and seems able to maintain its first-mover advantage in customized advertising on other websites as well as improved search engine technology—hence the jump to $500 a share it reached in November 2006. Yahoo is also struggling to catch up with Google's AdSense service, which sells search-based and banner advertisements to other people's websites and blogs. Google is entering new advertising areas, offering package deals for its customers that take in radio and newspaper advertising as well as online ads. Its goal seems to be to become the leading advertiser in every communications media.

Yahoo is fighting back. In the fall of 2006, it announced a deal with seven major U.S. newspapers that allows their local papers to post jobs on Yahoo's HotJobs recruitment website in return for a revenue sharing deal, and there will be more collaborations over time in other areas of local classified and display advertising. Yahoo is the only company that could have offered the newspapers cooperation spanning online job listings, technology, content, search, and online traffic. This deal attests to the unique breadth of Yahoo's offerings and services and the many benefits it can also offer advertisers if it can get its cross-channel advertising program up to speed.

In 2005, Yahoo and Google were neck and neck with roughly 18% of Internet advertising revenues of all kinds each. However, by the start of 2006, Google's portion had grown to 23% compared to 19% for Yahoo, and Google's grew to 25% by the end of 2006. The stakes are high since Internet advertising is soaring and the $16.7 billion spent on it in 2006 is expected to grow to $29.4 billion by 2010. In November 2006, Semel told analysts he was aware of the stakes involved; moreover he said most web portals had underestimated the growth potential of Internet advertising because predictions did not include the advertising possibilities on video, social media, or mobile devices that had become so apparent in 2006. Semel believes that video will also become a major factor on the Internet and more innovative and clever ways to integrate advertising with video online will all develop quickly. To meet this challenge, Yahoo purchased AdInterax, a company that specializes in the creation and management of video and animated online ads, such as animations, dynamically expandable banners, and streaming video ads; Rich Media; and Today, an on-line advertising company that specializes in design-ing and implementing customized advertising pro-grams. Both acquisitions are intended to enhance Yahoo's new customized search advertising system by providing better support for video and rich media ads and to generate more ad volume—and compete with Google.

In December 2006, Semel decided to shake up the management structure of the company to allow it to better implement its business model and compete with its rivals, a shakeup sparked by the peanut butter memo. Yahoo's chief financial officer, Susan Decker, will replace Dan Rosensweig as the company's chief operating officer to rein in its expenditures. Yahoo an-nounced it would focus on building its most success-ful online services, stop product development just to increase its breath, and considered pruning its weak-est services. The new streamline organizational struc-ture will group Yahoo's services into three core prod-uct groups, one focused on its website's audience, one on its advertising network, and one on developing new technology. A new executive will be hired to run the group focused on satisfying Yahoo's 418 million registered users. Like Decker and Farzad Nazem, Yahoo's chief technology officer, the new executive will report to Semel, who will remain CEO.

However, Garlinghouse had proposed a more radical reorganization involving the layoff of 15 to 20% of Yahoo's 11,000 employees to reduce its cost structure. This was something that Semel had done when he took over the company in 2001; he grouped the dozens of individual Yahoo service units into larger product-focused groups. Semel hopes the reor-ganization will make Yahoo more proficient at deliver-ing online services and ads that capture the attention of online users.

Yahoo's Future

Some analysts wonder if Yahoo's problem today is that it has lost sight of its original business model and mission and that it is spreading itself too thin. It is no longer clear what the company is today and what kind of portal it aspires to be since it functions as an entry portal, a web search engine company, a re-tail portal, a media content and communications com-pany, and a social networking platform service; it also provides companies with a range of online commercial

services and customized advertising programs. On top of all this, the push to generate advertising revenues across its entire website is paramount. Others argue that it is Yahoo's unique strength that it operates in all these areas and that as long as it can catch up with Google and other specialized dot-coms, it will per-form well in the future. But can it catch up with rivals that offer Internet users a different and sometimes su-perior value proposition online?

The problem facing Yahoo is to transition so that it retains its status as the number 1 overall web portal of choice. It has to invest its resources to continually improve its wide range of content and services to meet the challenge of upstart new Internet compa-nies that are constantly appearing to offer users something new. The Internet, by its very nature, makes entry into the WWW easy, and a company survives or fails by its continuing ability to improve and refine its products to better meet the needs of Internet users. In addition, Yahoo has to meet the ad-vertising challenge of Google, which is continually expanding its own content and services, and growing its customized advertising so that over time it will be-come a direct threat to Yahoo.

In January 2007, Yahoo announced it would begin rolling out its new customized advertising system to advertisers in the spring. The company is hoping to see major improvements in advertising revenues by the summer. Revenue per search query may grow by 10% or more in the second half of the year, the com-pany forecast, and Semel said: "We believe this will deliver more relevant text ads to users, which in turn should create more high-quality leads. By the time we get to 2008 and beyond, this is a very, very, significant amount of additional profit and I'm pleased with the tangible progress we have made. I'm convinced we're on the right path." Yahoo's stock soared by over 10% as investors bet that this would be a turnaround moment in Yahoo's battle with Google. However, in February 2007, Google once again announced record advertis-ing revenues, so the battle is ongoing.

Some analysts believe the Internet will receive a greater share of global advertising spending by 2008 than outdoor outlets, such as billboards, and will overtake radio in the near future. Yahoo claims that about half a billion people around the world still reg-ularly use its portal in some way, and so it is posi-tioned to obtain a large share of these revenues. Yahoo's front page, which for so long has been the gateway of millions to the Internet, may be going out of fashion, however. Google is still winning Yahoo users over to use its web search and other services, and social networking websites siphon off millions of other users. Nevertheless, Yahoo has a lot more services to offer its users than Google or other specialized sites, and it is here particularly that Yahoo's business model under Semel has shined. Only time will tell in the fast-changing Internet world if Yahoo can maintain its premier status as the portal of choice.

SOURCES

http://www.yahoo.com, 1990–2007

Yahoo 10K reports, 1990–2007

Ask Yahoo—a question and answer column, http://ask.yahoo.com/

Blo.gs—a directory of recently updated blogs, http://blo.gs/

del.icio.us—popular social bookmarking site, http://del.icio.us/

Dialpad—a phone company, http://www.dialpad.com/

Flickr—popular photo sharing site, http://flickr.com/

GeoCities—free web hosting service, http://geocities.yahoo.com/

Kelkoo—price comparison service for ten European countries, http://www.kelkoo.co.uk/

My Yahoo—customizable portal, http://my.yahoo.com

Upcoming.org—Social event calendar driven by people, http://upcoming.org

Webjay—playlist sharing community, http://www.webjay.org/

Yahoo 360°—free blogging and social networking service, http://360.yahoo.com

Yodel Anecdotal—Yahoo's corporate blog, http://yodel.yahoo.com/

Yahoo Answers—a place where you can get your questions answered by real people in real time, http://answers.yahoo.com

Yahoo Avatars—http://avatars.yahoo.com/

Yahoo Auctions—an online auction site, http://auctions.yahoo.com/

Yahoo Autos—http://autos.yahoo.com/

Yahoo Assistant—a browser helper object for Internet Explorer

Yahoo Briefcase—free file hosting service, http://briefcase.yahoo.com/

Yahoo Broadway—http://broadway.yahoo.com/

Yahoo Buzz Log—a column that talks about what people are searching Yahoo for, http://buzz.yahoo.com/

Yahoo Developer Network—resources for software developers using Yahoo technologies and web services, http://developer.yahoo.com/

Yahoo Directory—hierarchical web directory, http://dir.yahoo.com/

Yahoo Finance—stock exchange rates and other financial information, http://finance.yahoo.com/

Yahoo Food—http://food.yahoo.com/

Yahoo Gallery—directory of applications built by third-party developers using Yahoo technology, http://gallery.yahoo.com/

Yahoo Games—playing games (online against other users), http://games.yahoo.com/

Yahoo Greetings—an e-card service with partners American Greetings, http://www.yahoo.americangreetings.com/

Yahoo Groups—electronic mailing list and Internet forum, http://groups.yahoo.com/

Yahoo HotJobs—job search engine, http://hotjobs.yahoo.com/

Yahoo Local—customized local information, http://local.yahoo.com/

Yahoo Mail—web-based email, http://mail.yahoo.com/

Yahoo Maps—mapping portal, http://maps.yahoo.com/

Yahoo Messenger—instant messaging client, http://messenger.yahoo.com/

Yahoo Mobile—Yahoo for mobile phones, http://mobile.yahoo.com/

Yahoo Movies—show times, movie trailers, movie information, gossip, http://movies.yahoo.com/

Yahoo Music—music videos and Internet radio (LAUNCHcast) plus pay service

Yahoo Music Unlimited, http://music.yahoo.com/ and Yahoo Music Engine.

Yahoo News—news updates and top stories at Yahoo News, including world, national, business, entertainment, sports, weather, technology, and weird news, http://news.yahoo.com/

Yahoo Personals—http://personals.yahoo.com/

Yahoo Photos—http://photos.yahoo.com/

Yahoo Podcasts (beta)—http://podcasts.yahoo.com/

Yahoo Publisher Network—advertising network, http://publisher.yahoo.com/

Yahoo Real Estate—http://realestate.yahoo.com/

Yahoo Research—http://research.yahoo.com/

Yahoo Search—web search engine, http://search.yahoo.com/

Yahoo Search Marketing—pay per click search engine, http://searchmarketing.yahoo.com/

Yahoo Shopping—shopping search and compare, http://shopping.yahoo.com/

Yahoo Small Business—domains, web hosting, and e-commerce services, http://smallbusiness.yahoo.com/

Yahoo Soccer Manager—online soccer game, http://uk.soccermanager.yahoo.net/

Yahoo Sports—scores, stats, and fantasy sports, http://sports.yahoo.com/

Yahoo Tech—product information and advice, http://tech.yahoo.com/

Yahoo Travel—travel guides, booking and reservation, http://travel.yahoo.com/

Yahoo TV—TV listings, scheduling recordings on TiVo box remotely, http://tv.yahoo.com/

Yahoo Video—video sharing site, http://video.yahoo.com/

Yahoo Widgets—a cross-platform desktop widget runtime environment, formerly called Konfabulator, http://widgets.yahoo.com

Yahooligans!—children's version of the web portal, http://yahooligans.yahoo.com

Amazon.com

This case was prepared by Gareth R. Jones, Texas A&M University.

In just over a decade, Amazon.com (Amazon) has grown from an online bookseller to a virtual retail supercenter selling products as diverse as books, toys, food, and electronics. Today, its mission is to be "Earth's most customer-centric company, where customers can find and discover virtually anything they might want to buy online." In many ways, the last decade has been a wild ride for Amazon as its revenues, profits, and stock price have soared and plunged as a result of the dot-com boom and then bust of the early 2000s. It has also been a wild ride for Amazon's founder, Jeff Bezos, who through it all has consistently championed his company and claimed investors have to look long term to measure the success of Amazon's business model. Indeed, he originally said he did not expect his company to become profitable for several years, and his forecast turned out to be correct.

By the early 2000s, however, Amazon had become profitable, and its business model seemed to be working. But then, around the mid-2000s, its future prospects started to look bleak again as its revenue growth seemed to stall when its new retail ventures seemed not be succeeding. In 2007, the problem facing Amazon is to find new strategies to keep its revenues growing at a fast pace and to keep its costs under control, not easy when competition is increasing in Internet commerce.

Amazon's Beginnings: The Online Bookstore Business

In 1994, Jeffrey Bezos, a computer science and electrical engineering graduate from Princeton University, was growing weary of working for a Wall Street investment bank. Seeking to take advantage of his computer science background, he saw an entrepreneurial opportunity in the fact that usage of the Internet was growing enormously as every year tens of millions of new users were becoming aware of its potential uses. Bezos decided the bookselling market offered an excellent opportunity for him to take advantage of his IT skills in the new electronic, virtual marketplace. His vision was an online bookstore that could offer millions more books to millions more customers than a typical bricks-and-mortar (B&M) bookstore. To act on his vision, he packed up his belongings and headed for the West Coast to found his new dot-com start-up. On route, he had a hunch that Seattle, the hometown of Microsoft and Starbucks, was a place where first-rate software developers could be easily found. His trip ended there, and he began to flesh out the business model for his new venture.

What was his vision for his new venture? To build an online bookstore that would be customer-friendly, be easy to navigate, provide buying advice, and offer the broadest possible selection of books at low prices. Bezos's original mission was to use the Internet to offer books "that would educate, inform and inspire." And from the beginning, Bezos realized that compared to a physical B&M bookstore, an online bookstore could offer customers a much larger and more diverse selection of books. Indeed, there are about 1.5 million books in print, but most B&M bookstores stock only around 10,000 books; the largest stores in major cities might stock 40,000 to 60,000. Moreover, online customers would be able to search easily for any book in print using computerized catalogs. There was also scope for an online company to find ways to tempt customers to browse books in different subject areas, read reviews of books, and even ask other shoppers for online recommendations—all of which would encourage people to buy more books. A popular feature of Amazon is the ability of users to submit product reviews on its website. As part of their reviews, users rate the products on a scale from one to five stars and then provide detailed information that helps other users decide whether to purchase the products. In turn, the users of these ratings can then rate the usefulness of the reviews so the best reviews are those that rise to the top and are read first in the future!

Operating from his garage in Seattle with a handful of employees, Bezos launched his online venture in 1995 with $7 million in borrowed capital. Because Amazon was one of the first major Internet or dot-com retailers, it received a huge amount of free national publicity, and the new venture quickly attracted more and more book buyers. Book sales quickly picked up as satisfied Internet customers spread the good word and Amazon became a model for other dot-com retailers to follow. Within weeks Bezos was forced to relocate to larger premises, a 2,000-square-foot warehouse, and hire new employees to receive books from book publishers and fill and mail customer orders as book sales soared. Within six months he was once again searching for additional capital to fund his growing venture; he raised another $7 million from venture capitalists, which he used to move to a 17,000-square-foot warehouse that was now required to handle increasing book sales. As book sales continued to soar month by month over the next two years, Bezos decided that the best way to raise more capital would be to take his company public and issue stock. This, of course, would reward him as the founder and the venture capitalists who had funded Amazon because they would all receive significant percentages of the company's stock. On May 1997 Amazon.com's stock began trading on the NASDAQ stock exchange.

Building Up Amazon's Value Chain

Amazon's rapid growth continued to put enormous pressure on the company's physical warehousing and distribution capabilities. The costs of operating an online website, for example, continuously developing the website's software, and maintaining and hosting the computer hardware and Internet bandwidth connections necessary to serve customers are relatively low given the hundreds of millions of visits to its website and the millions of sales that are completed. However, Bezos soon found out that the costs of developing and maintaining the physical infrastructure necessary to obtain supplies of books from book publishers and then to stock, package, and ship the books to customers were much higher than he had anticipated, as was the cost of the employees required to perform these activities.

Developing and maintaining the physical side of Amazon's value chain is the source of the greatest proportion of its operating costs, and these high costs were draining its profitability, given the low prices at which it was selling its books. And price competition was also heating up because of new competition from B&M booksellers such as Barnes & Noble and Borders that had also opened online bookstores to compete in this market segment. In fact, in 1997, as it passed the 1-million-different-customers-served point, Amazon was forced to open up a new 200,000-square-foot warehouse and distribution center and expand its old one to keep pace with demand.

On the employee front, Bezos sought ways to increase the motivation of his employees across all the company. Working to fill customer orders quickly is vital to an online company; minimizing the wait time for a product like a book to arrive is a key success factor in building customer loyalty. On the other hand, motivating Amazon's rapidly expanding army of software engineers to develop innovative software, such as its patented 1-Click (SM) Internet ordering and payment software, was also a vital issue. To ensure good responsiveness to customers, Bezos implemented a policy of decentralizing significant decision-making authority to employees and empowered them to find ways of meeting customers needs quickly. Because Amazon.com employed a relatively small number of people—about 2,500 worldwide in 2000—Bezos also empowered employees to recruit and train new employees so that they quickly get up to speed in their new jobs. And to motivate employees, Bezos decided to give all employees stock in the company. Amazon employees own over 10% of their company, a factor behind Amazon.com's rapid growth.

In fact, Jeff Bezos is a firm believer in the power of using teams of employees to spur innovation. At

Amazon, teams are given considerable autonomy to develop their ideas and experiment without interference from managers. Teams are kept deliberately small, and, according to Bezos, no team should need more than "two pizzas to feed its members"; if more pizza is needed, the team is too large. Amazon's "pizza teams," which usually have no more than about five to seven members, have come up with many innovations that have made its site so user-friendly. For example, one team developed the "Gold Box" icon that customers can click on to receive special offers that expire within an hour of opening the treasure chest; another developed "Bottom of the Page Deals," low-priced offers for products such as batteries and power bars, and one more team developed the "Search Inside the Book" feature discussed later. These teams have helped Amazon expand into many different retail storefronts and provide the wide range of IT services it does today. Indeed, Bezos and his top managers believe that Amazon is a *technology company* first and foremost, and its mission is to use and develop its technological expertise to sell more and more goods and services in ways that satisfy customers and so keep its profit growing.

Since the beginning, Bezos has personally played a very important part in energizing his employees and representing his company to customers. He is a hands-on, articulate, forward-looking executive who puts in long hours and works closely with employees to find innovative and cost-saving solutions to problems. Moreover, Bezos has consistently acted as a figurehead for his company and become well recognized in the national media as he works to further Amazon's visibility with customers. He spends a great deal of time flying around the world to publicize his company and its activities, and he has succeeded because Amazon has one of the best recognized names of any dot-com company.

An important strategy that Amazon created in 1996 to attract new customers to its website and grow sales is its Amazon Associates program. Any person or small business that operates a website can become affiliated to Amazon by putting an official Amazon hyperlink to Amazon's website on its own website. If a referral results in a sale, the Associate receives a commission from Amazon. Today about 40% of Amazon's sales come from referrals from its Associates who have received over $1 billion in sales commissions. By 2004 Amazon had signed up over 1 million

Associates, and its Associates program has been copied by many other Internet companies.

By 1998 Amazon could claim that 45% of its business was repeat business, which translated into lower marketing and sales expenses and higher profit margins. By using all his energies to act on the online bookselling opportunity, Bezos gave his company a first-mover advantage over rivals, and this has been an important contributor to its strong position in the marketplace. Nevertheless, Amazon still had to make a profit, just as Bezos had predicted.

The Bookselling Industry Environment

The book distribution and bookselling industry was changed forever in July 1995 when Jeff Bezos brought virtual bookseller Amazon.com online. His new company changed the whole nature of the environment. Previously, book publishers had sold their books indirectly to book wholesalers that supplied small bookstores, directly to large book chains like Barnes & Noble or Borders, or to book-of-the month clubs. There were so many book publishers and so many individual booksellers that the industry was relatively stable, with both large and small bookstores enjoying a comfortable, nonprice competitive niche in the market. In this stable environment, competition was relatively low, and all companies enjoyed good revenues and profits.

Amazon.com's electronic approach both to buying and selling books changed all this. First, since it was able to offer customers quick access to all of the over 1.5 million books in print and it discounted the prices of its books, a higher level of industry competition developed. Second, since it also negotiated directly with the large book publishers over price and supply because it wanted to get books quickly to its customers, the industry value chain changed: All players—book publishers, wholesalers, stores, and customers—became more closely linked. Third, as a result of these factors and continuing changes in information technology, the bookselling business began to change rapidly as the sources of competitive advantage changed, and price and service became important.

By being first into the online bookselling business, Amazon was able to capture customers' attention and establish a first-mover advantage. Its entry into the bookselling industry using its new IT posed a major threat for B&M bookstores, and Barnes &

Noble, the largest U.S. bookseller, and Borders, the second, realized that with its competitive prices, Amazon would be able to siphon off a significant percentage of industry revenues. So these B&M bookstores decided to launch their own online ventures to meet Amazon's challenge and to convince book buyers that they, not Amazon, were still the best places to shop for books. However, being first to market with a new way to deliver books to customers resulted in satisfied customers who become loyal customers. And once a customer had signed up as an Amazon customer, it was often difficult to get that person to register again at a competing website.

Amazon's early success also made it difficult for new "unknown" competitors to enter the industry because they faced the major hurdle of attracting customers to their websites rather than to Amazon.com's. Even well-known competitors such as Barnes & Noble and Borders, which imitated Amazon's online business model, faced major problems in attracting away Amazon's customer base and securing their positions. If large B&M bookstores had problems attracting customers, small specialized B&M bookstores were in desperate trouble. Their competitive advantage has been based on providing customers with hard-to-find books, a convenient location, and good customer service. Now they were faced with competition from an online bookstore that could offer customers all 1.5 million books in print at 10% lower prices, with delivery to anywhere in a few days.

Thousands of small specialized B&M bookstores closed their doors nationwide, and even the large B&M bookstores struggled to compete. Its strong competitive position, combined with Internet investors' "irrational exuberance," led Amazon's stock price to soar in the dot-com bubble of the late 1990s. By 1998, its market capitalization was $6.8 billion, almost twice that of its two biggest rivals, Barnes & Noble and Borders, whose combined sales at this time were many times that of Amazon's!

Competition increased in 1999 as large B&M bookstores began a price war with Amazon that resulted in falling book prices; this squeezed Amazon's profit margins and put more pressure on it to contain its increasing operating costs. In the spring of 1999, for example, Amazon and its largest competitors, Barnes & Noble and Borders, announced a 50% discount off the price of new best-selling books to defend their market shares; they were locked in a fierce battle to see which company would dominate the bookselling industry in the new millennium.

From Online Bookstore to Internet Retailer

While Bezos initially chose to focus on selling books, he soon realized that Amazon's IT could be used to sell other kinds of products, but he was cautious because he also now understood how high the value chain costs involved in delivering a wide range of products to customers were. However, Amazon's slow growth in the late 1990s led many of its stockholders to complain that the company was not on track to becoming profitable fast enough, so Bezos began to search for other products that could be sold profitably over the Internet. One growing online business was music CDs, and he realized CDs were a good fit with books, so in 1999 Amazon announced its intention to become the "earth's biggest book and music store." The company used its IT competences to widen its product line by selling music CDs on its retail website. The strategy of selling CDs also seemed like a good move because the leading Internet music retailers at this time, such as CD Now, were struggling because they too had discovered the high physical costs associated with delivering products bought online to customers. Amazon now had built up its skills in this area, and its online retail competencies were working to its advantage; for example, its IT now allowed it to constantly alter the mix of products it offered in its virtual store to keep up-to-date with changing customer needs.

Amazon also took many more steps to increase the usefulness of its retail sites to attract more customers and get its established customers to spend more. For example, to entice customers to send books and CDs as presents at important celebration and holiday shopping times such as birthdays, Christmas, and New Year's, Amazon opened a holiday gift store. Customers could take advantage of a gift-wrapping service as well as using a free greeting card email service to announce the arrival of the Amazon gift. Amazon began to explore other kinds of online retail ventures; for example, recognizing the growing popularity of online auctions pioneered by eBay, Bezos moved into this market by purchasing Livebid.com, the Internet's only provider of live online auctions at that time. Also in 1999, it entered into an agreement with Sotheby's, the famous auction house, to enter the high end of the online auction business.

Nevertheless, starting in 2000, Amazon's stock price fell sharply as investors came to believe that intense competition from Barnes & Noble and other retailers might keep its operating margins low into the foreseeable future. Despite his company's moves into CDs and the auction business, Bezos was being increasing criticized for being much too slow to take advantage of Amazon's brand name and core skills and to use them to sell other kinds of products online—much like a general B&M retailer sells many different kinds of products. Bezos responded that he had to make sure his company's business model would work successfully in book retailing before he could commit his company to a widespread expansion into new kinds of retail ventures. However, Amazon's plunging stock price forced him into action, and from 2000 on, it expanded its storefronts and began to sell a wider and wider range of electronic and digital products, such as cameras, DVD players, and MP3 players. To achieve a competitive advantage in these new product categories, Amazon used its IT to provide customers with more in-depth information about the nature of the products they were buying and to offer users better ways to review, rank, and comment on the products they bought on its website. Customers were increasingly seeing the utility of Amazon's service.

Bezos had pushed Amazon and its "pizza teams" to find new ways to use its core skills to expand into different kinds of retail segments, and by 2003, it had developed twenty-three different storefronts. By 2006, Amazon had thirty-five storefronts selling products as varied as books, CDs, DVDs, software, consumer electronics, kitchen items, tools, lawn and garden items, toys and games, baby products, apparel, sporting goods, gourmet food, jewelry, watches, health and personal-care items, beauty products, musical instruments, and industrial and scientific supplies. Increasingly consumers came to see Amazon as the low-price retailer for many products. Customers began to visit B&M retail stores to view the physical product, but then they would go online to buy from Amazon. One advantage Amazon has is that customers avoid paying state sales tax when they buy online, and for high-ticket items, this is an important savings, even though shipping costs must be paid for.

New Problems

As time went on, however, customers increasingly began to compare the prices charged by different online retail websites to locate the lowest priced product, and many dot-coms, desperate to survive in a highly competitive online retail environment, undercut Amazon's prices and so put more pressure on its profit margins. To strengthen Amazon's competitive position and make it the preferred online retailer, Bezos moved aggressively to find ways to attract customers, such as by offering them free shipping or "deals of the day." To make its service more convenient, Amazon also began to forge alliances with B&M companies like Toys "R" Us, Office Depot, Circuit City, Target, and many others. Now, customers could buy products online at Amazon's website, but if they wanted their purchases immediately, they could pick them up from these retailers' local B&M stores. Amazon had to share its profits with these retailers, but it also avoided high product stocking and distribution costs. These alliances also helped Bezos quickly transform his company from "online bookseller" to "leading Internet product provider." His goal was for Amazon to become the leading online retailer across many market segments and drive out the weaker online competitors in those segments and so consolidate many segments of the online retail industry.

Bezos was helped because the online retailers quickly discovered the high costs of operating the value chain functions necessary to deliver products to customers. In the bookselling market, for example, with the exception of Barnes & Noble, which still has an Internet business unit, other booksellers, such as Borders.com, Borders.co.uk, and Waldenbooks.com, could not compete with Amazon. They closed down their online operations and became Amazon Associates, directing Internet traffic from their websites to Amazon's in return for sales commissions. Amazon's competitive advantage also strengthened in 2001 when the Internet bubble burst, the stock price of dot-com companies plunged, and thousands of cut-price online retailers went out of business. Even though its own stock price plunged too, Amazon was now the strongest dot-com in the most important retail segments, and losers like CD Now, Virginmega.com, and online toy and electronics retailers also redirected traffic to Amazon's website for a fee as they shut down their operations.

Many B&M retailers that had also established virtual storefronts found they could not make their online storefronts profitable in the 2000s because of high operating costs. The ones that did succeed were those like Lands' End that already had well-developed catalog sales operations. Their failure was another opportunity for Amazon; for example, when Toys "R" Us found its virtual site too expensive to operate, it also reached an agreement to redirect customers to Amazon's Toys and Games storefront, although at first customers could still pick up their toys from Toys "R" Us's stores if they chose. Many other established B&M companies that found online retailing too complex and expensive also formed agreements with Amazon to operate their online stores. Indeed, Amazon seized this opportunity to get into the new business of using its proprietary IT to design, operate, and host other companies' online storefronts for them for a fee. It had become an IT services company as well, and this helped its revenues grow. Amazon formed agreements to operate retail websites for Target, the NBA, Sears Canada, and Bombay Company, for example.

Branching off into all these new retail market segments also allowed Amazon to more fully utilize its expensive warehouse and distribution system; faster sales across product categories increased inventory turnover and reduced costs. Moreover, its alliances with retailers allowed it to reduce the quantity of expensive merchandise it had to purchase and warehouse until sold, which helped its profit margins. In addition, by offering many different kinds of products for sale, customers could now "mix" purchases and add a book or CD to their electronic product order, and so on, which led to economies of scale for Amazon. By giving customers more and more reasons to visit its site, Amazon hoped to drive business and sales across all its product categories, using its 1-Click system to make the transactions as easy as possible for consumers. However, to keep its operating costs low from the beginning, Amazon adopted a low-key approach to providing customer service; it did not reveal a customer service telephone number anywhere on its U.S. website. However, as the complexity of its business has grown, it recognized the need to provide some level of service, and in 2006 Amazon added to its website an email link. Using this link, customers provide their phone numbers, which Amazon customer service reps then call to provide whatever help is needed, for example, with parcel tracking information. Customer service for North American customers is now handled by centers in Washington State, North Dakota, and West Virginia, as well as a number of outsourced centers.

After its failure in the online auction market, in 2001, Amazon added a new retail service that turned out to be highly profitable and important to maintaining its online leadership position in retailing. Amazon launched zShops, a fixed-price retail marketplace that became the foundation of the current and very successful Amazon Marketplace Service. This retail service allows customers to sell their used books, CDs, DVDs, and other products alongside the identical brand-new products that Amazon offers on the product pages of its retail website. This significantly added to its sales revenues. eBay bought a company called half.com to compete with Amazon Marketplace and is Amazon's main rival today as both companies compete to provide a profitable fee-based service to sellers of used products.

In the 2000s, as Amazon became the acknowledged leader in Internet retailing, it decided to offer a consulting service to other virtual retailers (it already provided this service to B&M retailers) to create for them a unique, customer-friendly storefront using Amazon's proprietary IT. Moreover, to protect the competitive advantage its proprietary IT gives it, Amazon also started lawsuits against other virtual or B&M companies that it claimed implemented checkout systems similar to 1-Click by imitating and infringing on its proprietary software that is protected by patents. This consulting service has proved to be a very profitable activity business activity, and in the process of designing storefronts for other companies, Amazon has also found opportunities to improve its own IT systems by learning from its "leading customers."

Global Expansion

Since IT is not specialized to any one country or world region, a virtual company can use the Internet and World Wide Web to sell to customers around the world—providing, of course, that the products it sells can be customized to meet the needs of overseas consumers. Bezos was quick to realize that Amazon's IT could be profitably transferred to other countries to sell books. However, the ability to enter new overseas markets was limited by one major factor: Amazon.com offered its customers the biggest selection of books written in the *English* language, so overseas customers had to be able to read English. Where to locate them?

An obvious first choice would be the United Kingdom (UK), followed by other English-speaking nations such as Australia, New Zealand, India, and

Germany (of any nation in the world, Germany has one of the highest proportion of English-as-a-second-language speakers because English is taught in all its schools). To speed entry into overseas markets, Amazon searched for overseas Internet companies that had gained a strong foothold in its local domestic market and then acquired them. In the UK, Amazon bought Bookpages.com in 1996, installed its proprietary IT, replicated its value creation functions, and renamed it Amazon.co.uk. In Germany, it acquired a new online venture, ABC Bücherdienst/Telebuch.de, and created Amazon.de in 1998. Amazon continued its path of global expansion, and by 2006, it also operated retail websites in Canada, France, China, and Japan, and shipped its English language books to customers anywhere in the world.

To facilitate the growth of its global IT and distribution systems, Amazon also has product development centers in England, Scotland, India, Germany, and France. Just as Amazon expanded the range of products it sold on its U.S. website, it also increased the range of products it sold abroad as its warehouse and distribution systems became strong enough to sustain its expansion and its local managers decided on the mix of products best suited to the needs of local customers.

New Developments

After Amazon's stock price reached a low of around $6 a share in late 2001 after the Internet bubble burst and many dot-coms went out of business, Amazon continued to persevere. When it finally turned its first profit in the fourth quarter of 2002—a meager $5 million, just 1 cent per share on revenues of over $1 billion—this was an important signal to investors. It seemed to confirm that Amazon's business model was working, it would survive, and its stock price would increase. In fact, Amazon's stock price began to soar in the early 2000s as investors now believed it would become a highly profitable online retail leader; its stock price increased to $20 by the end of 2002 and to almost $60 by the end of 2003. Amazon's net profits also increased to $35 million in 2003 and to $588 million in 2004. Revenue kept growing because of its entry into many different retail segments and global markets, from $3.9 billion in 2002, to $5.3 billion in 2003, and $6.9 billion in 2004. Amazon's future looked bright indeed as it became the largest Internet retailer and achieved a dominant position in many market segments.

New Acquisitions and Business Opportunities

To make better use of its resources and capabilities and to maintain its profit growth, Amazon began to acquire many small companies in the late 1990s. One of its goals was to acquire small IT companies that would allow it to strengthen its distinctive competencies in IT and to develop more kinds of web-based IT commercial services that it could sell to both B&M and online companies. Bezos has always preached that Amazon is first and foremost a *technology company* and that its core skills drive its retail mission. Another goal in buying small companies was to find new opportunities to increase sales of its existing retail storefronts and to allow it to establish new storefronts in new segments of the retail market. Some acquisitions have been successful and some have not.

In 1998, for example, Amazon bought Internet Movie Database (www.IMDb.com), a company that hosted a comprehensive listing of all movies in existence. Formerly a free service, Amazon transformed it into a commercial venture whose function is to help customers easily find and identify DVDs to purchase and to make related suggestions to encourage additional purchases. As with Amazon's regular site, IMDb users are allowed to review and make detailed comments on movies including starting message boards. In 1999, Amazon acquired Exchange.com, which specializes in hard-to-find book titles at its Bibliofind.com website and hard-to-find music titles and memorabilia at MusicFile.com. The acquisition also helped Amazon develop user-friendly search engines to help customers identify and buy its products, once again using its 1-Click system.

In 1998, Amazon bought PlanetAll.com, which operated a web-based address book, calendar, and reminder service that had over 1 million registered users, and Junglee.com, an XML-based data-mining start-up that had technology for searching for and tracking Internet users' website visits based on their personal interests. In 2000, after Amazon had absorbed these companies' technology, it shut them down, making their employees Amazon employees and relocating to Amazon's Seattle headquarters. For example, PlanetAll's "relationship-building" software applications were folded into Amazon's Friends and Favorites area. Within Friends and Favorites, Amazon customers were now able to set up wish lists and view those of friends, view product critiques from specific reviewers, and create and view home pages from Amazon's website. Amazon's new employees also went on to build community-focused features for Amazon's website including the unsuccessful Amazon.com Auctions, and successful Amazon.com Marketplace and Amazon.com Purchase Circles. Amazon became driven by the need to find and use the most successful new web-based techniques for attracting and keeping Internet customers as rivalry with companies like Yahoo, eBay, and then Google started to increase as these companies increasingly started to enter each other's businesses.

In pursuit of this goal, in 1999 Amazon bought Alexa Internet, which had developed software that works in conjunction with Internet Explorer to track and monitor the way people search the Internet. Amazon hoped to use this technology to help it improve its ability to track its customers as they moved around the Internet and so provide them with a personalized browsing experience, which, for example, would allow it to make product suggestions based on the specific nature of their site visits—similar to Google offering customized advertising specific to the webpage a user was visiting. In 2003, Amazon launched a separately controlled subsidiary called A9.com, Inc. to take control of all its search engine research and build innovative technologies to improve users' search experiences and so increase the utility of its e-commerce applications.

A9.com's search engine, which searches both Amazon.com and other websites, used to be powered by Google's search engine. Today it is powered by Microsoft's Live Search technology because Google emerged as the leader in this area. The differentiating feature of Amazon's A9.com search technology was meant to be that users would log into the service, and then A9 would continually record every page they searched for. By creating a personalized memory of users' visits, A9 could provide them with a highly customized search service that could take them quickly to already visited sites but that would also be able to suggest relevant new sites based on all the personal data collected by the engine. In this way, Amazon hoped it could drive more traffic to its constantly increasing storefronts.

The search engine did not prove popular with Internet users, however, because many believed the engine was highly invasive of their privacy, creating as it does a permanent record of their website visits.

Instead, in the 2000s, Google's search engine has become the search engine of choice, both because it is the technologically most advanced and because users can opt out of creating a personalized search history if they choose to disable its advanced features. Thus Google struck the right balance between usefulness and privacy and thwarted Amazon's attempts to become the leader in the crucial search engine market. In 2006, Amazon announced its A9 site would no longer ask users to log in or accumulate such personal data. Instead, it would focus on improving the usefulness of the search results users obtained on Amazon's own storefronts. For example, one of the technologies A9.com had developed was a "mini" search engine feature called "Search Inside the Book," mentioned earlier, that allows users to search within the text of books as well as searching for text on the Web. "Search Inside the Book" is a feature that makes it possible for customers to search for keywords in the full text of many of the books in its catalog to identify books that may be of interest to them. There are currently about 250,000 books in the program, and Amazon has cooperated with around 130 publishers to allow users to perform these searches. To avoid copyright violations, Amazon.com does not return computer-readable text of the book but rather a picture of the page containing the relevant text, disables printing of the pages, and puts limits on the number of pages in a book a single user can access. In 2005, A9 also developed an interactive wiki feature that allows any Amazon customer who has purchased at least one product from the company to add to or edit the relevant product descriptions or wikis, such as for books.

Thus although Amazon has used these acquisitions to steadily improve its customers' ability to search and use its own storefronts, its attempt to gain a leading position in providing generalized web-based search services to Internet users failed. Today, its A9.com generates only 0.1% of all searches compared to the leader Google, which claims over 60%. Amazon also has failed in other areas; another search technology A9.com developed was the "Find It on the Block" feature that allowed users to find not just the phone number, address, map, and directions for a business, but also to see a picture of it as well as all the businesses and shops on that same street. However, in 2006, Amazon announced it was ending this service because most users preferred the mapping services offered by Google and Yahoo. Many of Amazon's failures can be explained by the fact that established Internet companies already had a first-mover advantage in specific industries in the Internet sector. For example, Amazon.com's Auctions could not compete successfully against eBay, which with its 30 million registered sellers and buyers dominated the online auction industry; and Google's quick growth in the search engine market has prevented Amazon, and many other leading portals, from succeeding in this area.

In an effort to keep its customers loyal, Amazon began providing a range of new customer services. In January 2006, it launched Amazon Prime, a $79 per year service that allows users to get unlimited free two-day shipping and upgraded overnight shipping for $3.99 on eligible items bought from its storefronts. Also in January, Amazon established a partnership with travel meta-search company SideStep and used its service to power searches in Amazon's travel store. In March, it launched an online storage service called Amazon S3 that allows users to store an unlimited number of data objects ranging in size from 1 byte to 5 gigabytes for a storage service charge of 15 cents per gigabyte per month and data transfer fees of 20 cents per gigabyte each when users distribute their data (for example, advertisements or catalog mailing lists) using HTTP or Bit Torrent services provided by Amazon.

In July 2006, Amazon entered the grocery delivery business when its website officially launched Amazon Grocery, a new storefront that sells a wide variety of nonperishable food and household items that, once ordered, can be reordered or modified easily using Amazon's shopping-list software. To ensure competitive pricing with B&M grocery stores, customers receive free shipping on purchases of canned and packed food products over $25.

In September 2006, Amazon Business Solutions group, which serves the needs of business customers, also extended the range of its services by launching Fulfillment by Amazon and WebStore by Amazon. These services give small and medium-sized businesses access to Amazon's order fulfillment, customer service, customer shipping offers, and underlying website technology to improve the retail experience they can offer customers on their own websites. For example, Fulfillment by Amazon allows small businesses to use Amazon's own order fulfillment and after-order customer services, and gives their customers the right to receive the benefit of Amazon.com shipping offers.

Fulfillment by Amazon performs the value chain activities that free online small businesses from the time and costs required to store, pick, pack, ship, and provide customer service for the products they sell online. After paying Amazon's service fee, small businesses ship their products to an Amazon fulfillment center, which stores and sends those products to customers who order them on the small business's or Amazon's storefront. Amazon will also manage post-order customer service such as customer returns and refunds for businesses that use Fulfillment by Amazon. Amazon.com customers can also use services such as Amazon Prime and Free Super Saver Shipping when buying products that have the Fulfilled by Amazon icon. Small businesses benefit from the cost savings that result when Amazon's service fees are lower than the costs of performing the value chain service themselves.

WebStore by Amazon allows businesses to create their own privately branded e-commerce websites using Amazon technology. Businesses can choose from a variety of website layout options and can customize their sites using their own photos and branding. For example, Seattle Gift Shop now has its own WebStore at http://www.seattlesgifts.com. WebStore by Amazon users pay a commission of 7% (price includes credit card processing fees and fraud protection) for each product purchased through their site and a monthly fee of $59.95. As one business owner commented, "Not only has WebStore increased my sales dramatically, but also its easy-to-use tools give me complete control of the look and feel of my site." WebStore allows small businesses to build their brand name while using Amazon's easy-to-use flexible "back-end" technology—including Amazon's 1-Click checkout system—and allows them to refer customers through the Amazon Associates program if they choose.

Jeff Bezos and his top management team seem committed to leveraging Amazon's core competencies in whatever ways they can to find ways to realize the value of the company's assets. The range of possible services Amazon can offer seems endless. For example, Amazon established a wholly owned subsidiary, CustomFlix, Inc., to provide first a DVD and then a CD on Demand Service. The DVD and CD on Demand Services allow independent musicians, artists, labels, and other video and music content owners an inventory-free way to reach a worldwide audience and make their videos and audio CDs available to

Amazon's customers. Customers can preview a DVD or CD on the CustomFlix website and then decide whether to make a purchase, much like in the past when customers in record stores could listen to tracks before making a purchase decision. Once again, because CustomFlix can burn the DVD/CD on demand, there are no inventory costs for musicians to bear, so the service offers an easy, attractive, and low-cost way for musicians, artists, and labels to profitably connect to customers. It also expands Amazon's content offerings, making its even more unique compared to other DVD/CD retailers. If they attract a following, successful musicians and artists can then also set up their own customizable Custom-Flix E-Store so that they can personalize the products they offer to customers. CustomFlix on Demand provides high-quality DVD and CD media with full-color hub-printed faces; full-color, double-sided tray cards; and four-page, full-color inserts in over-wrapped clear jewel cases.

In another bold venture, in September 2006, Amazon launched an eagerly awaited digital download video service. Called Amazon Unbox, the new download service offered customers thousands of television shows, movies, and other video content from more than thirty studio and network partners from Hollywood and around the world. Unbox claimed to be the only video download service to offer DVD-quality picture that could be downloaded from one PC (such as an office computer) and then transferred to another PC (such as a home computer). At no additional charge, Unbox automatically included a second file optimized for playback on any Windows Media-compatible portable device. Also, Unbox used progressive download, which eliminated the need to wait for the entire video to download before watching. A broadband customer could start watching a downloaded Unbox video or movie within five minutes of ordering.

However, within weeks, this important new download service—one that Amazon investors had eagerly awaited—generated many negative comments from users. The number of movies downloaded was disappointingly few because the service's poor software caused many glitches and very slow—hours—download time. Quickly Amazon updated the movie player to fix the bugs, but many complaints remained: long download time, poor resolution, and restrictions on when and where movies could be

played. Amazon continues to improve this service and in January 2007 announced an agreement with TiVo, the set-box DVD recording company, to develop a joint program to allow TiVo's millions of customers easy access to Amazon's download service. Amazon is currently searching for more partners, but one development that may seriously impair its progress in this area is Wal-Mart's February 2007 agreement with the six major movie studios to offer movie downloads through its online store. Wal-Mart is the leading seller of DVDs with over 40% of the market, and its ability to negotiate this deal, rather than Amazon, might be a major setback.

Amazon's Future Prospects

Today, Amazon is the leading Internet retailer. It has over 12,000 employees and in 2006 earned $700 million on $10.7 billion revenues. This was a significant increase in profit from the year before, and its stock price rose significantly as investors became more optimistic about its future prospects. Nevertheless, its stock price is still lower than it was in 2004 because investors have realized many of its new ventures, such as its attempt to dominate the search engine segment, have not worked out, and because the future success of ventures such as movie downloads is not clear. Moreover, all its expenditures on developing the new IT platforms necessary to launch complex digital storefronts have been increasing its operating costs, which rose from 6.1% of revenue in 2005 to 7.8% in the second quarter of 2006. These increased operating costs have reduced its profit margins. Once again, Amazon's operating costs are rising, now not because of developing the physical infrastructure necessary to support its retail sales, but because of the investment in the IT infrastructure necessary to launch new digital products. So some analysts are concerned that in its attempts to grow profits, Amazon is losing its knack of creating the customer-friendly retail customer service technology that made it a leading dot-com company. And they are watching the growing success of Google as it enters new businesses, including retail Internet segments with its Froogle product-search service and its new online payment system that is a challenge to Amazon's 1-Click system. So investors are watching to see how operating costs will affect operating margins and net profits in the next few years and how Amazon will fend off increasing competition from companies like Wal-Mart that are building up their own online presence and are willing to charge low prices to build their market share. What new strategies can Bezos pursue to take Amazon to the next level, analysts wonder? Are any new mergers and acquisitions on the horizon?

SOURCES

Amazon.com, Annual and 10K Reports, 1997–2007. http://www.Amazon.com, 2007.

Mike Daisey. (2002). 21 Dog Years. New York: The Free Press.

A. Deutschman, "Inside the Mind of Jeff Bezos," *Fast Company,* August 2004, 50–58.

Robert Spector. (2001). Amazon.com—Get Big Fast: Inside the Revolutionary Business Model That Changed the World. New York: Harper Collins Publishers.

This case was prepared by Gareth R. Jones, Texas A&M University.

With 11,600 employees, eBay, headquartered in San Jose, California, manages and hosts an online auction and shopping website that people all around the world visit to buy and sell goods and services. eBay generated revenues of almost $6 billion in 2006, up from $4.55 billion in 2005, and generated $2 billion in earnings—an impressive figure that explains the company's stock market valuation of $46 billion in February 2007. eBay has been a stellar performer on the stock exchange under the guidance of Meg Whitman, its CEO. Its investors were extremely happy—until the last few years when its stock price fell sharply. Investors became worried its business model would not be so profitable in the future because the online auction market was becoming mature and opportunities for growth were declining. In 2006, its stock plunged in value, and it seemed like eBay's business model had run out of steam. But to understand the sources of eBay's success and the current challenges it faces, it is necessary to explore the way eBay's business model and strategies have changed over time.

eBay's Beginnings

Until the 1990s, the auction business was largely fragmented; thousands of small city-based auction houses offered a wide range of merchandise to local buyers. And a few famous global ones, such as Sotheby's and Christie's, offered carefully chosen selections of high-priced antiques and collectibles to limited numbers of dealers and wealthy collectors. However, the auction market was not very efficient, for there was often a shortage of sellers and buyers, and so it was difficult to determine the fair price of a product. Dealers were often able to influence auction prices and so obtain bargains at the expense of sellers. Typically, dealers were able to buy at low prices and then charge buyers high prices in the bricks-and-mortar (B&M) antique stores that are found in every town and city around the world, so they reaped high profits. The auction business was changed forever in 1995 when Pierre Omidyar developed innovative software that allowed buyers around the world to bid online against each other to determine the fair price for a seller's product.

Omidyar founded his online auction site in San Jose on September 4, 1995, under the name Auction-Web. A computer programmer, Omidyar had previously worked for Microsoft, but he left that company when he realized the potential opportunity to develop new software that provided an online platform to connect Internet buyers and sellers. The entrepreneurial Omidyar changed his company's name to eBay in September 1997, and the first item sold on eBay was Omidyar's broken laser pointer for $13.83. A frequently repeated story that eBay was founded to help Omidyar's fiancée trade PEZ Candy dispensers was fabricated by an eBay public relations manager in 1997 to interest the media. Apparently the story worked, for eBay's popularity grew quickly by word of mouth, and the company did not need to advertise until the early 2000s. Omidyar had tapped into a huge unmet buyer need, and people flocked to use his software.

Another major reason eBay did not advertise in its early years was that its growing global popularity had put major pressure on its internal computer information systems, both its hardware and software. In particular, the technology behind its search engine—which was not developed by Omidyar but furnished by independent specialist software companies–could not keep pace with the hundreds of millions of search requests that eBay's users generated each day. eBay was also installing powerful servers as quickly as it could to manage its fast-growing database, and it was recruiting computer programmers and IT managers to run its systems at a rapid rate.

To finance eBay's rapid growth, Omidyar turned to venture capitalists to supply the hundreds of millions of dollars his company required to build its online IT infrastructure. Seeing the success of his business model, he was quickly able to find willing investors; as part of the loan agreement, however, the venture capitalists insisted that Omidyar give control of the running of his company to an experienced top manager. They were very aware that entrepreneurs often have problems in building and implementing a successful business model over time. They recommended that Meg Whitman, an executive who had had great success as a manager of several software start-up companies, be recruited to become eBay's CEO, while Omidyar would assume the role of chairman of the company.

eBay's Evolving Business Model

From the beginning, eBay's business model and strategies were based on developing and refining Omidyar's auction software to create an easy-to-use online market platform that would allow buyers and sellers to meet and transact easily and inexpensively. eBay's software was created to make it easy for sellers to list and describe their products, and easy for buyers to search for, compare, and bid on the products they wanted to purchase. The magic of eBay's software is that the company simply provides the electronic conduit between buyers and sellers; it never takes physical possession of the products that are listed, and their shipping is the responsibility of sellers and payment the responsibility of buyers. Thus, eBay does not need to develop all the high-cost functional activities like inventory, shipping, and purchasing to deliver products to customers, unlike Amazon.com, for example, and so it operates with an extremely low cost structure given the huge volume of products it sells and sales revenues it generates—hence the $2 billion profits on $7 billion of revenues in 2007 mentioned earlier. Also, word of mouth enables eBay to avoid paying the high advertising costs, an especially important consideration early on since these are a major expense for many start-ups. And, as far as buyers are concerned, eBay is also low cost, for under current U.S. law, sellers located outside a buyer's state do not have to collect sales tax on a purchase. This allows buyers to avoid paying state taxes on expensive items such as jewelry and computers, which can save them tens or even hundreds of dollars and makes purchasing on eBay more attractive.

To make transactions between anonymous Internet buyers and sellers possible, however, Omidyar's software had to reduce the risks facing buyers and sellers. In particular, it had to convince buyers that they would receive what they paid for and that sellers would accurately describe their products online. Also, sellers had to be convinced that buyers would pay for the products they committed to purchase on eBay, although of course they were able to wait for the money to arrive in the mail, so their risk was lower; however, many buyers do not pay or pay extremely late. To minimize the ever-present possibility of fraud from sellers misrepresenting their products or from buyers unethically bidding for pleasure and then not paying, eBay's software contains a method for building and establishing trust between buyers and sellers—building a reputation over time.

After every transaction, buyers and sellers can leave online feedback about their view of the other's behavior and the value of the transaction they have completed. They can fill in an online comment form, which is then published on the Web for each seller and buyer. When sellers and buyers consistently act in an honest way in more and more transactions over time, they are able to build a stronger and stronger positive feedback score that provides them with a good reputation for honesty. More buyers are attracted to a reputable seller, so the seller obtains higher prices for their products, and sellers can also decide if they are dealing with a reputable buyer, one who pays quickly, for example. This may be more difficult because new "unknown" buyers come into the market continuously, but a seller can refuse to deal with any new or existing buyer if they wish and can remove that buyer's bid from an auction.

eBay generates the revenues that allow it to operate and profit from its electronic auction platform by charging a number of fees to sellers (buyers pay no specific fees). In the original eBay model, sellers paid a fee to list a product on eBay's site and paid a fee if the product was sold by the end of the auction. As its platform's popularity increased and the number of buyers grew, eBay has increased the fees it charges sellers. The eBay fee system is quite complex, but in the United States in 2006, eBay took between 20 cents and $80 per listing and between 2 and 8% of the final price, depending on the particular product being sold and the format in which it is sold. In addition, eBay now owns the PayPal payment system, which has fees of its own; this is discussed in detail below.

This core auction business model worked well for the first years of eBay's existence. Using this basic software platform, every day tens of millions of products such as antiques and collectibles, cars, computers, furniture, clothing, books, DVDs and a myriad of other items are listed by sellers all around the world on eBay and bought by the highest bidders. The incredible variety of items sold on eBay suggests why eBay's business model has been so successful—the same set of auction platform programs, constantly improved and refined over time from Omidyar's original programs, can be used to sell almost every kind of product, from low-priced books and magazines costing only cents, to cars and antiques costing tens or hundreds of thousands of dollars. Some of the most expensive items sold include a Frank Mulder 4Yacht Gigayacht ($85 million), a Grumman Gulfstream II jet ($4.9 million), and a 1993 San Lorenzo 80 Motoryacht (just under $2 million). One of the largest items ever sold was a World War II submarine that had been auctioned off by a small town in New England that decided it did not need the historical relic anymore.

Indeed, Meg Whitman's biggest problem was to find search engine software that could keep pace with the increasing volume of buyers' inquiries. Initially small independent suppliers provided this software; then IBM provided this service. But as search technology has advanced in the 2000s, eBay now has its own in-house search technology teams continually refining and improving its own search software. With the most pressing concerns of keeping the eBay website up and running twenty-four hours a day and meeting the needs of its growing number of buyers and sellers, CEO Whitman looked for new ways to improve eBay's business model.

First, to take advantage of the capabilities of eBay's software, the company began to expand the range and categories of the products it offered for sale to increase revenue. Second, it increased the number of retail or "selling" formats used to bring sellers and buyers together. For example, its original retail format was the seven-day auction format, where the last bidder within this time period "won" the auction, provided the bid met the seller's reserve or minimum price. Then, it introduced the "buy-it-now" format where a buyer could make an instant purchase at the seller's specified price, and later a real-time auction format in which online bidders, and bidders at a B&M auction site, compete against each other in real time to purchase the product up for bid. In this format, a live auctioneer, not the eBay auction clock, decides when to close an auction.

Beyond introducing new kinds of retail formats, over time eBay has continuously strived to improve the range and sophistication of the information services it provides its users—to make it easier for sellers to list, describe, present, and ship their products, and for buyers to make better purchasing decisions. For example, software was developed to make it easier for sellers to list their products for sale and upload photographs and add or change information to the listing. Buyers were able to take advantage of the services that are now offered in what is called My EBay; buyers can now keep a list of "watched" items so that over the life of a particular auction they can see how the price of a product has changed and how many bidders are interested in it. This is a useful service for buyers because frequently bidders for many items enter in the last few minutes to try to "snipe" an item or obtain it at the lowest possible cost. As the price of an item becomes higher, this often encourages more buyers to bid on it, so there is value to buyers (although not sellers, who want the highest prices possible) to wait or just bid a minimal amount so they can easily track the item.

By creating and then continually improving its easy-to-use retail platform for sellers and buyers, eBay revolutionized the auction market, bringing together buyers and sellers internationally in a huge, never-ending yard sale. eBay became the means of cleaning out the "closets of the world" with its user-friendly platform.

New Types of Sellers

Over time, eBay also encouraged the entry of new kinds of sellers into its electronic auction platform. Initially, it focused on individual, small-scale sellers; however, it then sought to attract larger-scale sellers using its eBay Stores selling platform, which allows sellers to list not only products up for auction but also all the items they have available for sale, perhaps in a B&M antique store or warehouse. Store sellers then pay eBay a fee for these "buy it now" sales. Hundreds of thousands of eBay stores became established in the 2000s, greatly adding to eBay's revenues.

Also by the early 2000s, not just small specialized stores but large international manufacturers and retailers such as Sears, IBM, and Dell began to open their own stores on eBay to sell their products using competitive auctions for "clearance goods" and fixed-priced buy-it-now storefronts to sell their latest products. By using eBay, these companies established a new delivery channel for their products, and they were able to bypass wholesalers such as discount stores or warehouses that take a much larger share of the profit than eBay does through its selling fees.

Software advances came faster and faster in the 2000s, in part due to eBay's new Developers Program that allows independent software developers to create new specialized applications that integrate seamlessly with eBay's electronic platform. By 2005, there were over 15,000 members in the eBay Developers Program, comprising a broad range of companies creating software applications to support specialized eBay sellers and buyers, as well as eBay Affiliates. All this progress helped speed and smooth transactions between buyers and sellers and drove up eBay's revenues and profits, something that resulted in a huge increase in the value of its stock.

Competition in the Retail Auction Industry

eBay's growing popularity and growing user or customer base made it increasingly difficult for the hundreds of other online auction houses that had also come online to compete effectively against it. Indeed, its competitive advantage was increasing because both sellers and buyers discovered they were more likely to find what they wanted and get the best prices from a bigger auction website's user base or market.

And from the beginning, eBay controlled the biggest market of buyers and sellers, and new users became increasingly loyal over time. So even when large, well-known online companies such as Yahoo and AOL attempted to enter the online auction business, and even when they offered buyers and sellers *no-fee* auction transactions, they found it was impossible to grow their user bases and establish themselves in the market. From network effects, eBay had obtained a first-mover advantage and was benefiting from this.

The first-mover advantage eBay gained from Pierre Omidyar's auction software created an unassailable business model that gave eBay effectively a monopoly position in the global online auction market. There are few online or B&M substitutes for the service that eBay provides. For example, sellers can list their items for sale on any kind of website or bulletin board, and specialist kinds of websites exist to sell highly specialized kinds of products like heavy machinery or large sailboats, but for most products, the sheer reach of eBay guarantees it a dominant position in the marketplace. There has been little new entry into the online auction business, and the fees eBay charges to sellers have steadily increased as it has grown, and so it skims off ever more of the profit in the auction value chain. Also, eBay does not have to worry about the ability of any particular buyer or seller to dictate terms to it, for it has access to millions of individual buyers and sellers. Only if sellers could band together and demand reductions in eBay's fees and charges would they be a threat to eBay.

This happened briefly in the early 2000s. Meg Whitman, desperate to keep eBay's revenues growing to protect its stock price, began to continually increase the fees charged to eBay stores to list their items on eBay. Store sellers rebelled and used the eBay community bulletin boards and chat rooms to register their complaints. eBay realized there was a limit to how much it could charge sellers. It would have to find new ways to attract more buyers to the sellers' products, and so get them better prices, if was going to be able to increase the fees it charged sellers. Or it would have to find new ways to extract profit from the auction value chain.

New Ways to Grow eBay's Value Chain

Meg Whitman has always preached to eBay's employees that to maintain and increase the value of its stock (and many employees own stock options in the company), eBay must (1) continually attract more buyers and sellers to its auction site, and (2) search for ways to generate more revenue from these buyers and sellers. To create more value from its auction business model, eBay has adopted many other kinds of strategies to grow profitability over time.

International Expansion

In the online world, buyers from any country in the world can bid on an auction, and so it became clear early on that one way to grow eBay's business would be to replicate its business model in different countries around the world. Accordingly eBay moved quickly to establish storefronts around the world customized to the needs and language of a particular country's citizens. Globally, eBay established its own online presence in countries like the United Kingdom and Australia, but in other countries, particularly non-English-speaking countries, it often acquired the national start-up online auction company that had stolen the first-mover advantage in a particular country. In 1999, for example, eBay acquired the German auction house Alando for $43 million and changed it into eBay Germany. In 2001, eBay acquired Mercado Libre, Lokau, and iBazar, Latin American auction sites, and established eBay Latin America. In 2003, eBay acquired EachNet, a leading e-commerce company in China, for $150 million to enter the Chinese market. And, in 2004, it bought Baazee.com, an Indian auction site, for $50 million and took a large stake in Korean rival Internet Auction Co. In 2006, eBay acquired Tradera.com, Sweden's leading online auction-style marketplace, for $48 million. All these global acquisitions have allowed eBay to retain firm control of the global online auction business to facilitate transactions both inside countries and between countries to build up revenue. Once eBay was up and running in a particular country, network dynamics took effect, and so it became difficult for a new auction start-up to establish a strong foothold in its domestic online auction market. Indeed, the only countries in which eBay has faced serious competition are Japan and Hong Kong, where Yahoo gained a head start over eBay and thus gained the first-mover advantage in these countries.

eBay Drop-Off Stores

A second way in which eBay has grown the revenues from its auction model is by providing more kinds of value-chain services. One service created in the early 2000s for individual sellers is eBay Drop Off. eBay licenses reputable eBay sellers who have consistently sold hundreds of items using its platform to open B&M consignment stores where any seller can "drop off" the products they want to sell. The owner of the Drop-Off Store describes, photographs, and lists the item on eBay and then handles all the payment and shipping activities involved in the auction process. The store owner receives a commission, often 15% or more of the final selling price (not including eBay's commission) for providing this service. These stores have proved highly profitable for their owners, and thousands have sprung up across the United States and the world (a search request on eBay's site allows buyers to identify the closest eBay Drop-Off Store). The advantage for eBay is that this drop-off service gives it access to the millions of people who have no experience in posting photographs online, organizing payment, or even opening an eBay account and learning how to list an item and so eBay gains from increased listing fees.

Increased Advertising

Another strategy eBay increasingly adopted in the 2000s to expand its user base was to increase its use of advertising—on television, newspapers, and on popular websites—to promote the millions of products it has for sale on its site. Its goal was to make eBay *the* preferred place to shop by demonstrating two things: first, the incredible diversity of products available for purchase on its site, and second, the frequency with which its products cost less than what buyers would pay in B&M stores or even on specialist online stores. New and used DVDs, CDs, books, designer clothing, electronic products, and computers are some of the multitude of products that can be obtained at a steep discount on eBay. Thus, while the range of the products eBay sells provides it with a differentiation advantage, the low prices that buyers can often obtain gives it a low-price advantage too—provided buyers are prepared to wait a few days to receive their newly purchased products.

PayPal Payment Service

Meg Whitman was also working to find ways to make transactions easier for eBay buyers and sellers, and one way to do this was to get involved in the other kinds of value chain activities required to complete online transactions. One of the most important functional activities is the payment system, for this poses the greatest risks to buyers that they may be taken advantage of by unscrupulous or fraudulent sellers who take their money and then fail to deliver the expected product. When eBay first started, sellers usually demanded money orders or bank cashiers' checks that are secure forms of payment from buyers, or insisted that ordinary checks had cleared through their accounts before mailing the product to customers. This increased the length of time and effort involved in a transaction for sellers and buyers and led to lost sales.

By the late 1990s, online companies like PayPal and Billpoint had emerged that offered secure online electronic payment services that greatly facilitated online commerce. To work efficiently, these services require sellers and buyers to register and enter a valid bank account number, and usually a credit card number, to authenticate the sellers' and buyers' identities and their ability to pay for the items purchased. Now payment became instantaneous; the money was taken directly from the buyer's bank account or paid for by credit card. Buyers could now purchase on credit, while sellers could immediately send off the product to the buyer. When buyers paid sellers, the online payment company collected a 3% commission, which was taken from the seller's proceeds.

Obviously, this is a very lucrative activity, and eBay realized it could increase its share of the fees involved in eBay transactions by becoming involved in online payment services. However, it was late entering this business, and it would take a long time to develop its own payment service from scratch. So, in 1999 eBay acquired the online payment service Billpoint and worked to get all eBay buyers and sellers registered with Billpoint. However, eBay found itself running up against a brick wall; just as eBay had gained the first-mover advantage in the auction business, so had PayPal gained it in the online payment business. Millions of eBay users were already signed up with PayPal. So, after failing to make Billpoint the market leader, in 2002 eBay acquired PayPal for $1.5 billion in stock—a great return for PayPal's stockholders. Then, to reduce costs, eBay switched all Billpoint customers to PayPal and shut down Billpoint. This purchase has been very profitable for eBay, for it now owns the world's leading online payment system. The PayPal acquisition has paid for itself many times over.

Indeed, eBay has since worked to make PayPal a financial powerhouse, making it a conduit through which buyers and sellers can transact internationally, something that often involves high fees for buyers and sellers. It also issues eBay credit cards. Finally, it has used PayPal as another way to reassure buyers that sellers are honest and reputable; eBay offers buyers who use PayPal free product insurance protection in the event that their purchases are either fraudulent or misrepresented. It also reassures sellers that they can trust buyers; through PayPal, eBay can police buyers and suspend their accounts if necessary.

More Retail Formats

eBay also began to make many acquisitions to facilitate its entry into new kinds of specialized retail and auction formats to increase its market reach. In 1999, it acquired the well-known auction house Butterfield & Butterfield to facilitate its entry into the auctioning of high-priced antiques and collectibles and so compete with upper-end auction houses such as Sotheby's and Christie's. However, eBay's managers discovered that a lot more involvement was needed to correctly identify, price, list, and then auction rare, high-priced antiques, and it exited the upper-end auction niche in 2002 when it sold Butterfield & Butterfield to Bonhams, an upscale auction house that wanted to develop a much bigger online presence.

To further its expansion into the highly profitable motor vehicle segment of the market, in 2003 eBay acquired CARad.com, an auction management service for car dealers, to strengthen eBay Motors. Now eBay controls the auctions in which vehicle dealers bid on cars that they then resell to individual buyers, often on eBay Motors. In another move to enter a new retail market in 2004, eBay acquired Rent.com for $415 million. This online site offers a completely free rental and roommate search service; indeed, it offers to pay users who have signed a new lease at a property found on its website $100 when they inform Rent.com. Once again, the "sellers" of the rentals on its websites are charged the fees; the online roommate search is free. Rent.com has millions of up-to-date rental listings, with thousands added every day; listings include a property's address and phone number, a detailed description, photos, floor plans, and so on, which makes it easier for prospective renters to research and select a rental.

In 2000, eBay acquired Half.com for $318 million. Half.com is an online retail platform that specializes in the sale of new and used fixed-price consumer products such as books, movies, video games, DVDs, and so on that are offered at a fixed price and sold on a first-come-first-served basis, not by auction. eBay's Buy It Now feature is similar, although sellers are allowed to set a lower start price than the buy-it-now price, and the selling process can develop into an auction if bidders start to compete for the product. In the 2000s, the popularity of fixed-price online retailing led to a significant expansion in eBay's activities in this segment of the retail market. In 2006, eBay opened its new eBay Express site, which was designed to work like a standard Internet shopping site to consumers with U.S. addresses. Select eBay items are mirrored on eBay Express, where buyers use a shopping cart to purchase products from multiple sellers. A UK version of eBay Express is also in development. The discussion of eBay Express is continued below in more detail.

In 2005, eBay acquired Shopping.com, an online price-comparison shopping site, for $635 million. With millions of products, thousands of merchants, and millions of reviews from the Epinions community, Shopping.com empowers consumers to make informed choices and, as a result, encourages more buyers to purchase products. Information provided by Shopping.com also facilitates eBay sellers' pricing knowledge about their online competitors and so helps them price their products competitively so that they can sell them more quickly. The site also allows customers to purchase products from various eBay retail formats.

In the 2000s, online local classifieds have become an increasingly popular way for people to sell their unwanted products, especially because there are usually no fees associated with them. Local classifieds are very popular for bulky products like furniture, appliances, exercise equipment, and so on, where high transportation costs represent a significant percentage of the purchase price. In 2004, to ensure its foothold in this online retail segment, eBay bought a 25% stake in the popular free online classifieds website Craigslist by buying the stock of one of Craigslist's founders.

These free local classified services have been hurting newspapers whose classified sales have decreased sharply. It remains to be seen in the future whether these classified services will remain free or whether they will also be charging fees. Clearly, eBay would like to charge a fee if it owned a controlling stake in Craigslist. Perhaps preparing for the future when money will be made from online classifieds, in 2004, eBay acquired Marktplaats, a Dutch competitor that had achieved an 80% market share in the Netherlands by focusing on small fixed-price ads, not auctions. Then, in 2005, eBay acquired Gumtree, a network of UK local city classifieds sites; the Spanish classifieds site, Loquo; and the German language classifieds site, Opus Forum.

The Skype Acquisition

Perhaps going furthest away from its core business, in 2005, eBay acquired Skype, a Voice-Over-Internet-Provider (VOIP) telephone company, for $2.6 billion. eBay's rationale for the purchase was that Skype would provide it with the ability to perform an important service for its users, specifically, to give them a quick, inexpensive way to communicate and exchange the information required to complete online transactions. Skype's software allows users to use their computers to make free calls over the Internet to anyone, anywhere in the world. Skype boasts superior call quality and the ability to allow users not just to make phone calls but also to send instant messages, transfer big files, chat with up to one hundred people at the same time, and make video conference calls. Skype also allows users to send SMS, or text, messages and to easily sort their contacts into groups like colleagues, friends, and family. It is a full-scale online communications company.

According to eBay, Skype helps eBay sellers build their online businesses. Using Skype, buyers can contact sellers anytime on their Skype phone number. Sellers can also call regular phone numbers anywhere in the world using SkypeOut at very low rates, and with a SkypeIn phone number, buyers can call a regular telephone number wherever the seller is in the world. Also, in the case of large sellers, Skype allows continuous contact between all the members of the store with SkypeIn numbers and Skype Voicemail. For buyers, Skype allows them to get all the product information they need to buy with confidence and to get answers immediately, without waiting for email. According to some analysts, it is questionable whether eBay needed to buy a VOIP company given that so many alternative methods of instant communication are now available and offered by so many online companies. However, eBay quickly started to create strategies to get sellers to integrate Skype into their storefronts and to find new ways to include it in the regular transaction process.

eBay ProStores

Another strategy eBay has used to grow its revenues is to create a new online retail consulting service called ProStores, which allows any potential seller to utilize eBay's functional competencies in online retailing to create its own online storefront using eBay's software. ProStores offers sellers a fully featured web store that can be customized specifically for each online seller and that will then be maintained and hosted by eBay. Sellers using the ProStores service might be B&M stores searching for a quick and easy way to establish an online presence, or any entrepreneur who wishes to start an online store The difference between eBay ProStores and regular eBay Stores is that ProStores sites are accessed through a URL unique to each seller and are not required to carry eBay branding. ProStores sellers are responsible for driving their own store traffic. While items on ProStores sites sell at fixed prices only, they can be simultaneously listed on the eBay marketplace in either the auction or fixed-price formats.

ProStores provides all software needed to build a storefront and then create the listing, promotion, and payment systems needed to make it work. ProStores uses templates and wizards that allow users to quickly and easily build an attractive, feature-rich store with no technical or design skills whatsoever. In return, eBay charges two basic fees to all sellers who purchase a ProStores web store: (1) a monthly subscription fee and (2) a monthly successful transaction fee calculated as a percentage of the sales price of items sold in the store. The subscription fee ranges from $6.95 to $249.95, depending on the size of the store. The successful transaction fee varies between 1.5 and 2.5%.

eBay Express

Finally, reacting to growing buyer demand for a discount, fixed-price retail format, in 2006, eBay established eBay Express, where a vast inventory of brand-new, brand-name, and hard-to-find products are offered at fixed prices by top eBay sellers. Buyers are able to obtain the products they want with no bidding and no waiting; they can fill their shopping carts from multiple eBay merchants and pay for everything, including shipping, in a single, secure payment using PayPal. eBay is touting the fact that every transaction is safe, secure, and fully covered by free buyer protection from PayPal.

New Problems for eBay

Despite all these new strategies to strengthen its business model, in the twelve months ending August 2006, eBay's stock declined 30% from its lofty height, while the stock market had risen about 8%. The problem facing eBay was that while the number of its users was increasing, it was increasing at a decreasing rate—even after all its promotional and advertising efforts and its emphasis on introducing new site features, functionality, retail formats and international expansion. Similarly, although the number of items listed on eBay's retail platforms was increasing (by 33% in 2005 and 45% in 2004), growth was also slowing. In fact, in eBay's U.S. retail segment, net transaction revenues increased only 31% in 2005 and 30% in 2004 compared to 43% in 2003, while gross merchandise volume increased 19% in 2005 and 27% in 2004 compared to 41% in 2003. eBay's revenue growth was slowing, and it seemed clear to investors that even all its new strategies and entry into online payment and communications activities would not be able to sustain its future growth—and so justify its lofty stock price.

Meg Whitman had to find new ways to increase eBay's revenues, especially since by 2006 it was clear to leading Internet companies like Yahoo, AOL, Microsoft, and eBay that they were all facing a major threat from Google, which was perfecting its incredibly lucrative online search and advertising model. Google was now the new eBay in terms of stock appreciation because of the way it was able to implant its advertising search software into its own and any other Internet website willing to share advertising revenues with Google. In fact, because eBay is one of the world's biggest buyers of web search terms, it is one of Google's largest customers. eBay manages a portfolio of 15 million keywords on different search sites, such as Google, Yahoo, and AOL. These searches are aimed at attracting bidders to one of eBay's retail formats, which is why eBay, or one of its subsidiaries, often comes up first on a search inquiry. All the large Internet companies realized they had underestimated the potential revenues to be earned from Internet advertising and were anxious to get a bigger share of the pie and copy Google's approach. eBay, which had not placed ads on its pages in the past to allow its users to focus on the products for sale, now began to have banner adds, pop-ups, and the other obtrusive and annoying ways of advertising developed by software advertising engineers. By 2007, it had placed several ads on each page in its desperate hurry to increase revenues.

In another controversial move, in the spring of 2006, eBay decided to sharply increase the fees it charged its fixed-cost storefronts to advertise on its site. By 2006, sales of fixed-price products, which carried smaller margins than auction products, had grown to over 80% of total retail sales. In charging higher fees, eBay risked alienating large fixed-cost sellers, which would be forced to pass on these increases to customers, and of alienating customers who now could choose a popular shopping comparison tool like eBay's Shopping.com or Google's Froogle to locate a lower-priced product. Analysts questioned if this strategy would backfire.

Moreover, eBay faced another threat from Google as rumors started that Google would be starting its own free online Internet auction site that would compete directly with eBay's. Since Google also had hundreds of millions of loyal users as the number 1 search engine, this could become a real threat to eBay. Also, Google had already established its own fixed-price shopping site, Froogle, that it was continually improving, so it was clearly interested in exploring the revenues that could be earned in the retail segment of the Internet. And, in 2006, Google made great progress in promoting its own online payment system that analysts thought would become a major competitor to eBay's PayPal; this was also a major threat. eBay became concerned Google would start to drain away even more of its revenues and customers, and it searched for ways to counter Google's threat. However, analysts noted that eBay could not abandon its "friendly" relationship with Google because Google is the most popular search engine on which eBay promotes its retail storefronts.

Google had also emerged as the biggest competitor to Yahoo in the growing search-based advertising market. In the spring of 2006, it was rumored that eBay and Yahoo, which was also suffering declining advertising revenues because of the popularity of Google's search engine, might form an important strategic alliance, or even merge to counter possible future threats from Google. (It was rumored these companies would merge in the 1990s, but this had

not happened.) Google was the most popular search engine and held a 43% share in the online search market in the United States compared to Yahoo's market share of 28% in early 2006.

Finally, in May 2006, Yahoo and eBay did announce a strategic alliance designed to boost their position against Google and also against Microsoft, which was also trying to increase revenues from online advertising. The alliance allowed eBay to use Yahoo search to drive buyers to eBay auctions. In return, Yahoo would be the exclusive third-party provider of all graphic ads throughout eBay's auction site. Also Yahoo agreed to promote PayPal, eBay's online payment service, as a preferred payment provider for purchases made online on the Yahoo website. PayPal would provide an array of payment options to Yahoo's users navigating the Web for shopping, auctions, and subscription services. Yahoo would also use eBay's PayPal to allow its own customers to pay for Yahoo web services.

In addition, Yahoo and eBay planned to form a cobranded toolbar that could be downloaded onto the user's web browser, which in turn would direct the users to eBay's auction site and Yahoo's search engine. On eBay's site, the toolbar would provide links to the Yahoo homepage, Yahoo Mail, and My Yahoo options on the Yahoo website. Yahoo and eBay further planned to collaborate on click-to-call functionality. Click-to-call provides a link inside an advertisement that allows buyers to directly call a seller or store to pursue a transaction. Buyers could use either eBay's Skype VOIP telephone service or Yahoo's email and messaging service. The alliance also gives Yahoo access to eBay's vast base of online shoppers, so it can hope to attract many more of them to use its services. Shares of eBay rose 8% and Yahoo's shares climbed 4% in premarket trade following the announcement.

The companies began to roll out their joint initiatives in 2007; however, talk of a merger between the two is still continuing because of slowing growth and increased competition in the Internet sector. The merged company would have the leading position in auctions, communications, payments, graphical advertising, audience reach, and geographic breadth. And the strengths of Yahoo and eBay are seen as complementary, with Yahoo in media and eBay in e-commerce. Also, Yahoo is a global leader in Asia while eBay is the leader in Europe. As Yahoo's CEO, Terry Semel, said, "The deal offers great opportunities for both companies to share great assets with each other. It's all about creating more value and a better experience for users as well as for advertisers."

A 2007 Turnaround

In February 2007, a merger seemed less likely after eBay announced some impressive financial results that provided a lift to its stock price and that once again seemed to suggest its competitive advantage was secure, even in the face of Google's challenge. Shares of eBay jumped by 8% in February 2007 when eBay reported a fourth-quarter profit that climbed 24% as sales rose more than expected, helped by a surge in its PayPal electronic payments business and higher prices for the items eBay sells online. Net income for the fourth quarter rose to $346 million, or 25 cents a share, from $279 million, or 20 cents, a year earlier. Revenue from eBay's PayPal payments business rose 37% to $417 million, or a quarter of the company's total, while sales in its online marketplace business rose 24%. These results suggested that eBay's decision to raise its charges to list items in eBay stores to some of its highest-volume sellers had paid off, the quality of the listing had improved, and more of these sellers had been encouraged to use the higher fee-paying auction method.

eBay also saw healthy revenues in its Skype Internet phone division; 170 million people were now using the service, and it had become the de facto standard for VOIP transmission. According to some estimates, about 25% of businesses are using it to phone internationally. Skype continues to expand its range of services, with such concepts as group email and instant messaging, to make it even more attractive to business users. It seems Skype may have the potential to create a great deal more new efficiencies in both the business and personal realms, and so may be a good revenue generator in the years ahead.

Finally, it was announced in February 2007 that eBay was participating in talks to supply electronic payments and auction features to the popular MySpace social network and other News Corp. online properties. Obviously, providing Skype service would be a potentially lucrative way of introducing it to a younger audience. It seems clear that eBay is now viewing Skype as a business in its own right and not just as an appendage to its auction business. Analysts started to wonder if new kinds of acquisitions were being planned and how the Internet powerhouse would morph in the future, especially if its battle with Google continues.

SOURCES

http://www.ebay.com, 1997–2007.

eBay Annual and 10K Reports, 1997–2007.

Belbin, David. (2004). *The eBay Book: Essential tips for buying and selling on eBay.co.uk*. London: Harriman House Publishing.

Cihlar, Christopher. (2006). *The Grilled Cheese Madonna and 99 Other of the Weirdest, Wackiest, Most Famous eBay Auctions Ever*. New York: Random House.

Cohen, Adam. (2002). *The Perfect Store: Inside eBay*. Boston: Little, Brown & Company.

Collier, Marsha. (2004) *eBay for Dummies*, 4th ed. New Jersey: John Wiley.

Jackson, Eric M. (2004). *The PayPal Wars: Battles with eBay, the Media, the Mafia, and the Rest of Planet Earth*. Los Angeles: World Ahead Publishing.

Nissanoff, Daniel. (2006). *FutureShop: How the New Auction Culture Will Revolutionize the Way We Buy, Sell and Get the Things We Really Want*. London: The Penguin Press.

Spencer, Christopher Matthew. (2006) *The eBay Entrepreneur*. New York: Kaplan Publishing.

SAP and the Evolving Enterprise Resource Planning Software Industry

This case was prepared by Gareth R. Jones, Texas A&M University.

In 1972, after the project they were working on for IBM's German subsidiary was abandoned, five German IBM computer analysts left the company and founded Systems Applications and Products in Data Processing, known today as SAP. These analysts had been involved in the provisional design of a software program that would allow information about cross-functional and cross-divisional financial transactions in a company's value chain to be coordinated and processed centrally—resulting in enormous savings in time and expense. They observed that other software companies were also developing software designed to integrate across value chain activities and subunits. Using borrowed money and equipment, the five analysts worked day and night to create an accounting software platform that could integrate across all the parts of an entire corporation. In 1973, SAP unveiled an instantaneous accounting transaction processing program called R/1, one of the earliest examples of what is now called an enterprise resource planning (ERP) system.

Today, ERP is an industry term for the multi-module applications software that allows a company to manage the set of activities and transactions necessary to manage the business processes for moving a product from the input stage, along the value chain, to the final customer. As such, ERP systems can recognize, monitor, measure, and evaluate all the transactions involved in business processes such as product planning, the purchasing of inputs from suppliers, the manufacturing process, inventory and order processing, and customer service itself. Essentially, a fully developed ERP system provides a company with a standardized information technology (IT) platform that gives complete information about all aspects of its business processes and cost structure across functions and divisions. This allows the business to (1) constantly search for ways to perform these processes more efficiently and lower its cost structure, and (2) improve and service its products and raise their value to customers. For example, ERP systems provide information that allows for the design of products that match customer needs and lead to superior responsiveness to customers.

To give one example, Nestlé installed SAP's newest ERP software across its more than 150 U.S. food divisions in the early 2000s. It thus discovered that each division was paying a different price for the same flavoring, vanilla. The same small set of vanilla suppliers was charging each division as much as they could get, so all divisions paid widely different prices depending on their bargaining power with the supplier. Before the SAP system was installed, managers had no idea this was happening because their IT system could not compare and measure the same transaction—purchasing vanilla—across divisions. SAP's standardized cross-company software platform revealed this problem, and hundreds of thousands of dollars in cost savings were achieved by solving this one transaction difficulty alone.

SAP focused its R/1 software on the largest multinational companies with revenues of at least $2.5 billion. Although relatively few in number, these companies, most of which were large manufacturers, stood to gain the most benefit from ERP, and they were willing to pay SAP a premium price for its product. Its focus on this influential niche of companies helped SAP develop a global base of leading companies. Its goal, as it had been from the beginning, was to create the global industry standard for ERP by providing the best business applications software infrastructure.

In its first years, SAP not only developed ERP software, but it also used its own internal consultants to install it physically on-site at its customers' corporate IT centers, manufacturing operations, and so on. Determined to increase its customer base quickly, however, SAP switched strategies in the 1980s. It decided to focus primarily on the development of its ERP software and to outsource, to external consultants, more and more of the implementation services needed to install and service its software on-site in a particular company. It formed a series of strategic alliances with major global consulting companies such as IBM, Accenture, and Cap Gemini to install its R/1 system in its growing base of global customers.

ERP installation is a long and complicated process. A company cannot simply adapt its information systems to fit SAP's software; it must use consultants to rework the way it performs its value chain activities so that its business processes, and the information systems that measure these business processes, became compatible with SAP's software. SAP's ERP system provides a company with the information needed to achieve best industry practices across its operations. The more a particular company wishes to customize the SAP platform to its particular business processes, the more difficult and expensive the implementation process and the harder it becomes to realize the potential gains from cost savings and value added to the product.

SAP's outsourcing consulting strategy allowed it to penetrate global markets quickly and eliminated the huge capital investment needed to provide this service on a global basis. For consulting companies, however, the installation of SAP's software became a major money-spinner, and SAP did not enjoy as much of the huge revenue streams associated with providing computer services, such as the design, installation, and maintenance of an ERP platform on an ongoing basis. It did earn some revenue by training consultants in the intricacies of installing and maintaining SAP's ERP system.

By focusing on ERP software development, SAP did not receive any profits from this highly profitable revenue stream and made itself dependent on consulting companies that now became the experts in the installation/customization arena. This decision had unfortunate long-term consequences because SAP began to lose firsthand knowledge of its customers' problems and an understanding of the changing needs of its customers, especially when the Internet and cross-company integration became a major competitive factor in the ERP industry. For a company whose goal was to provide a standardized platform across functions and divisions, this outsourcing strategy seemed like a strange choice to many analysts. Perhaps SAP should have expanded its own consulting operations to run parallel with those of external consultants, rather than providing a training service to these consultants to keep them informed about its constantly changing ERP software.

To some degree, its decision to focus on software development and outsource at least 80% of installation was a consequence of its German founders' "engineering" mindset. Founded by computer program engineers, SAP's culture was built on values and norms that emphasized technical innovation, and the development of leading-edge ERP software was the key success factor in the industry. SAP poured most of its money into research and development (R&D) to fund projects that would add to its platform's capabilities; consequently, it had much less desire and money to spend on consulting. Essentially, SAP was a product-focused company and believed R&D would produce the technical advances that would be the source of its competitive advantage and allow it to charge its customers a premium price for its ERP platform. By 1988, SAP was spending more than 27% of gross sales on R&D.

As SAP's top managers focused on developing its technical competency, however, its marketing and sales competency was ignored because managers believed the ERP platform would sell itself. Many of its internal consultants and training experts began to feel they were second-class citizens, despite the fact that they brought in the business and were responsible for the vital role of maintaining good relationships with SAP's growing customer base. It seemed that the classic problem of managing a growing business from the entrepreneurial to the professional management phase was emerging. SAP's top managers were not experienced business managers who understood the problems of implementing a rapidly growing company's strategy on a global basis; the need to develop a sound corporate infrastructure was being shoved aside.

In 1981, SAP introduced its second-generation ERP software, R/2. Not only did it contain many more value chain/business process software modules, but it also linked its ERP software to the databases and communication systems used on mainframe computers, thus permitting greater connectivity and ease of use of ERP throughout a company. The R/1 platform had been largely a cross-organizational accounting/financial software module; the new software modules could handle procurement, product development, and inventory and order tracking. Of course, these additional components had to be compatible with each other so that they could be seamlessly integrated together on-site, at a customer's operations. SAP did not develop its own database management software package; its system was designed to be compatible with Oracle's database management software, the global leader in this segment of the software industry. Once again, this was to have repercussions later, when Oracle began to develop its own ERP software, essentially moving from database software into ERP development.

As part of its push to make its R/2 software the industry standard, SAP had also been in the process of customizing its basic ERP platform to accommodate the needs of companies in different kinds of industries. The way value chain activities and business processes are performed differs from industry to industry because of differences in the manufacturing processes and other factors. ERP software solutions must be customized by industry to perform most effectively. Its push to become the ERP leader across industries, across all large global companies, and across all value chain business processes required a huge R&D investment. In 1988, the company went public on the Frankfurt stock exchange to raise the necessary cash. By 1990, with its well-received multilingual software, SAP had emerged as one of the leading providers of business applications software, and its market capitalization was soaring. SAP began to dominate ERP software sales in the high-tech and electronics, engineering and construction, consumer products, chemical, and retail industries. Its product was increasingly being recognized as superior to the other ERP software being developed by companies such as PeopleSoft, S. D. Edwards, and Oracle. One reason for SAP's increasing competitive advantage was that it could offer a broad, standardized, state-of-the-art solution to many companies' business process problems, one that spanned a wide variety of value chain activities spread around the globe. By contrast, its competitors, like PeopleSoft, offered more focused solutions aimed at one business process, such as human resources management.

SAP Introduces the R/3 Solution

SAP's continuing massive investment in developing new ERP software resulted in the introduction of its R/3, or third-generation, ERP solution in 1992. Essentially, the R/3 platform expanded on its previous solutions; it offered seamless, real-time integration for over 80% of a company's business processes. It had also embedded in the platform hundreds and then thousands of industry best practice solutions, or templates, that customers could use to improve their operations and processes. The R/3 system was initially composed of seven different modules corresponding to the most common business processes. Those modules are production planning, materials management, financial accounting, asset management, human resources management, project systems, and sales and distribution.

R/3 was designed to meet the diverse demands of its previous global clients. It could operate in multiple languages and convert exchange rates, and so on, on a real-time basis. SAP, recognizing the huge potential revenues to be earned from smaller business customers, ensured that R/3 could now also be configured for smaller customers and be customized to suit the needs of a broader range of industries. Furthermore, SAP designed R/3 to be "open architecturally," meaning that it could operate with whatever kind of computer hardware or software (the legacy system) that a particular company was presently using. Finally, in response to customer concerns that SAP's standardized system meant huge implementation problems in changing their business processes to match SAP's standardized solution, SAP introduced some limited customization opportunity into its software. Using specialized software from other companies, SAP claimed that up to 20% of R/3 could now be customized to work with the company's existing operating methods and thus would reduce the problems of learning and implementing the new system. However, the costs of doing this were extremely high and became a huge generator of fees for consulting companies. SAP used a variable-fee licensing system for its R/3 system; the cost to the customer was based on the number of users within a company, on the number of different R/3 modules that were installed, and on the degree to which users utilized these modules in the business planning process.

SAP's R/3 far outperformed its competitors' products in a technical sense and once again allowed it to charge a premium price for its new software. Believing that competitors would take at least two years to catch up, SAP's goal was to get its current customers to switch to its new product and then rapidly build its customer base to penetrate the growing ERP market. In doing so, it was also seeking to establish R/3 as the new ERP market standard and lock in customers before competitors could offer viable alternatives. This strategy was vital to its future success because, given the way an ERP system changes the nature of a customer's business processes once it is installed and running, there are high switching costs involved in moving to another ERP product, costs that customers want to avoid.

R/3's growing popularity led SAP to decentralize more and more control of the marketing, sale, and installation of its software on a global basis to its foreign subsidiaries. While its R&D and software development remained centralized in Germany, it began to open wholly owned subsidiaries in most major country's markets. By 1995, it had eighteen national subsidiaries; today, it has over fifty. In 1995, SAP established a U.S. subsidiary to drive sales in the huge U.S. market. Its German top managers set the subsidiary a goal of achieving $1 billion in revenues within five years. To implement this aggressive growth strategy, and given that R/3 software needs to be installed and customized to suit the needs of particular companies and industries, several different regional SAP divisions were created to manage the needs of companies and industries in different U.S. regions. Also, the regional divisions were responsible for training an army of both internal and external consultants, from companies such as Accenture, on how to install and customize the R/3 software. For every internal lead SAP consultant, there were soon about nine to ten external consultants working with SAP's customers to install and modify the software.

The problems with a policy of decentralization soon caught up with SAP, however. Because SAP was growing so fast and there was so much demand for its product, it was hard to provide the thorough training consultants needed to perform the installation of its software. Once SAP had trained an internal consultant, that consultant would sometimes leave to join the company for which he or she was performing the work or even to start an industry-specific SAP consulting practice, with the result that SAP's customers' needs were being poorly served. Since the large external consulting companies made their money based on the time it took their consultants to install a particular SAP system, some customers were complaining that consultants were deliberately taking too long to implement the new software to maximize their earnings, and were even pushing inappropriate or unnecessary R/3 modules.

The word started to circulate that SAP's software was both difficult and expensive to implement, which hurt its reputation and sales. Some companies had problems implementing the R/3 software; for example, Chevron spent over $100 million and two years installing and getting its R/3 system operating effectively. In one well-publicized case, Foxmeyer Drug blamed SAP software for the supply chain problems that led to its bankruptcy. The firm's major creditors sued SAP in court, alleging that the company had promised R/3 would do more than it could. SAP responded that the problem was not the software but the way the company had tried to implement it, but SAP's reputation was harmed nevertheless.

SAP's policy of decentralization was also somewhat paradoxical because the company's mission was to supply software that linked functions and divisions rather than separated them, and the characteristic problems of too much decentralization of authority soon became evident throughout SAP. In its U.S. subsidiary, each regional SAP division started developing its own procedures for pricing SAP software, offering discounts, dealing with customer complaints, and even rewarding its employees and consultants. There was a total lack of standardization and integration inside SAP America and indeed between SAP's many foreign subsidiaries and their headquarters in Germany. This meant that little learning was taking place between divisions or consultants, there was no monitoring or coordination mechanism in place to share SAP's *own* best practices between its consultants and divisions, and organizing by region in the United States was doing little to build core competences. For example, analysts were asking, "If R/3 has to be customized to suit the needs of a particular industry, why didn't SAP use a market structure and divide its activities by the needs of customers based in different industries?" These problems slowed down the process of implementing SAP software and prevented quick and effective responses to the needs of potential customers.

SAP's R/3 was also criticized as being too standardized because it forced all companies to adapt to what SAP had decided were best industry practices. When consultants reconfigured the software to suit a particular company's needs, this process often took a long time and sometimes the system did not perform as well as had been expected. Many companies felt that the software should be configured to suit their business processes and not the other way around, but again SAP argued that such a setup would not lead to an optimal outcome. For example, SAP's retail R/3 system could not handle Home Depot's policy of allowing each of its stores to order directly from suppliers, based upon centrally negotiated contracts between Home Depot and those suppliers. SAP's customers also found that supporting their new ERP platform was expensive and that ongoing support cost three to five times as much as the actual purchase of the software, although the benefits they received from its R/3 system usually exceeded these costs substantially.

The Changing Industry Environment

Although the United States had become SAP's biggest market, the explosive growth in demand for SAP's software had begun to slacken by 1995. Competitors such as Oracle, Baan, PeopleSoft, and Marcum were catching up technically, often because they were focusing their resources on the needs of one or a few industries or on a particular kind of ERP module (for example, PeopleSoft's focus on the human resources management module). Indeed SAP had to play catch-up in the HRM area and develop its own to offer a full suite of integrated business solutions. Oracle, the second largest software maker after Microsoft, was becoming a particular threat as it expanded its ERP offerings outward from its leading database knowledge systems and began to offer more and more of an Internet-based ERP platform. As new aggressive competitors emerged and

changed the environment, SAP found it needed to change as well.

Competitors were increasing their market share by exploiting weaknesses in SAP's software. They began to offer SAP's existing and potential customers ERP systems that could be customized more easily to their situation; systems that were less expensive than SAP's, which still were charged at a premium price; or systems that offered less expensive module options. SAP's managers were forced to reevaluate their business model, and their strategies and the ways in which they implemented them.

New Implementation Problems

To a large degree, SAP's decision to decentralize control of its marketing, sales, and installation to its subsidiaries was due to the way the company had operated from its beginnings. Its German founders had emphasized the importance of excellence in innovation as the root value of its culture, and SAP's culture was often described as "organized chaos." Its top managers had operated from the beginning by creating as flat a hierarchy as possible to create an internal environment where people could take risks and try new ideas of their own choosing. If mistakes occurred or projects didn't work out, employees were given the freedom to try a different approach. Hard work, teamwork, openness, and speed were the norms of their culture. Required meetings were rare and offices were frequently empty because most of the employees were concentrating on research and development. The pressure was on software developers to create superior products. In fact, the company was proud of the fact that it was product driven, not service oriented. It wanted to be the world's leading innovator of software, not a service company that installed it.

Increasing competition led SAP's managers to realize that they were not capitalizing on its main strength—its human resources. In 1997, it established a human resources management (HRM) department and gave it the responsibility to build a more formal organizational structure. Previously it had outsourced its own HRM. HRM managers started to develop job descriptions and job titles, and put in place a career structure that would motivate employees and keep them loyal to the company. They also put in place a reward system, which included stock options, to increase the loyalty of their technicians, who were being attracted away by competitors or were starting their own businesses because SAP did not then offer a future: a career path. For example, SAP sued Siebel Systems, a niche rival in the customer relationship software business, in 2000 for enticing twelve of its senior employees, who it said took trade secrets with them. SAP's top managers realized that they had to plan long term, and that innovation by itself was not enough to make SAP a dominant global company with a sustainable competitive advantage.

At the same time that it started to operate more formally, it also became more centralized to encourage organizational learning and to promote the sharing of its own best implementation practices across divisions and subsidiaries. Its goal was to standardize the way each subsidiary or division operated across the company, thus making it easier to transfer people and knowledge where they were needed most. Not only would this facilitate cooperation, it would also reduce overhead costs, which were spiraling because of the need to recruit trained personnel as the company grew quickly and the need to alter and adapt its software to suit changing industry conditions. For example, increasing customer demands for additional customization of its software made it imperative that different teams of engineers pool their knowledge to reduce development costs, and that consultants should not only share their best practices but also cooperate with engineers so that the latter could understand the problems facing customers in the field.

The need to adopt a more standardized and hierarchical approach was also being driven by SAP's growing recognition that it needed more of the stream of income it could get from both the training and installation sector of the software business. It began to increase the number of its consultants. By having them work with its software developers, they became the acknowledged experts and leaders when it came to specific software installations and could command a high price. SAP also developed a large global training function to provide the extensive ERP training that consultants needed and charged both individuals and consulting companies high fees for attending these courses so that they would be able to work with the SAP platform. SAP's U.S. subsidiary also moved from a regional to a more market-based focus by re-aligning its divisions, not by geography, but by their focus on a particular sector or industry, for example, chemicals, electronics, pharmaceuticals, consumer products, and engineering.

Once again, however, the lines of authority between the new industry divisions and the software development, sales, installation, and training functions were not worked out well enough and the hoped-for gains from increased coordination and cooperation were slow to be realized. Globally, too, SAP was still highly decentralized and remained a product-focused company, thus allowing its subsidiaries to form their own sales, training, and installation policies. Its subsidiaries continued to form strategic alliances with global consulting companies, allowing them to obtain the majority of revenues from servicing SAP's growing base of R/3 installations. SAP's top managers, with their engineering mindset, did not appreciate the difficulties involved in changing a company's structure and culture, either at the subsidiary or the global level. They were disappointed in the slow pace of change because their cost structure remained high, although their revenues were increasing.

New Strategic Problems

By the mid-1990s, despite its problems in implementing its strategy, SAP was the clear market leader in the ERP software industry and the fourth largest global software company because of its recognized competencies in the production of state-of-the-art ERP software. Several emerging problems posed major threats to its business model, however. First, it was becoming increasingly obvious that the development of the Internet and broadband technology would become important forces in shaping a company's business model and processes in the future. SAP's R/3 systems were specifically designed to integrate information about all of a company's value chain activities, across its functions and divisions, and to provide real-time feedback on its ongoing performance. However, ERP systems focused principally on a company's internal business processes; they were not designed to focus and provide feedback on cross-company and industry-level transactions and processes on a real-time basis. The Internet was changing the way in which companies viewed their boundaries; the emergence of global e-commerce and online cross-company transactions was changing the nature of a company's business processes both at the input and output sides.

At the input side, the Internet was changing the way a company managed its relationships with its parts and raw materials suppliers. Internet-based commerce offered the opportunity of locating new, low-cost suppliers. Developing web software was also making it much easier for a company to cooperate and work with suppliers and manufacturing companies and to outsource activities to specialists who could perform the activities at lower cost. A company that previously made its own inputs or manufactured its own products could now outsource these value chain activities, which changed the nature of the ERP systems it needed to manage such transactions. In general, the changing nature of transactions across the company's boundaries could affect its ERP system in thousands of ways. Companies like Commerce One and Ariba, which offered this supply-chain management (SCM) software, were growing rapidly and posing a major threat to SAP's "closed" ERP software.

At the output side, the emergence of the Internet also radically altered the relationship between a company and its customers. Not only did the Internet make possible new ways to sell to wholesalers, its largest customers, or directly to individual customers, it also changed the whole nature of the company–customer interface. For example, using new customer relationship management (CRM) software from software developers like Siebel Systems, a company could offer its customers access to much more information about its products so that customers could make more informed purchase decisions. A company could also understand customers' changing needs so it could develop improved or advanced products to meet those needs; and a company could offer a whole new way to manage after-sales service and help solve customers' problems with learning about, operating, and even repairing their new purchases. The CRM market was starting to boom.

In essence the Internet was changing both industry- and company-level business processes and providing companies and whole industries with many more avenues for altering their business processes at a company or industry level, so that they could lower their cost structure or increasingly differentiate their products. Clearly, the hundreds of industry best practices that SAP had embedded in its R/3 software would become outdated and redundant as e-commerce increased in scope and depth and offered improved industry solutions. SAP's R/3 system would become a dinosaur within a decade unless it could move quickly to develop or obtain competencies in the software skills needed to develop web-based software.

These developments posed a severe shock to SAP's management, who had been proud of the fact that, until now, SAP had developed all its software internally. They were not alone in their predicament. The largest software companies, Microsoft and Oracle, had been caught unaware by the quickly growing implications of web-based computing. The introduction of Netscape's web browser had led to a collapse in Microsoft's stock price because investors saw web-based computing, not PC-based computing, as the choice of the future. SAP's stock price also began to reflect the beliefs of many people that expensive, rigid, standardized ERP systems would not become the software choice as the Web developed. One source of SAP's competitive advantage was based on the high switching costs of moving from one ERP platform to another. However, if new web-based platforms allowed both internal and external integration of a company's business processes, and new platforms could be customized more easily to answer a particular company's needs, these switching costs might disappear. SAP was at a critical point in its development.

The other side of the equation was that the emergence of new web-based software technology allowed hundreds of new software industry start-ups, founded by technical experts equally as qualified as those at SAP and Microsoft, to enter the industry and compete for the wide-open web computing market. The race was on to determine which standards would apply in the new web computing arena and who would control them. The large software makers like Microsoft, Oracle, IBM, SAP, Netscape, Sun Microsystems, and Computer Associates had to decide how to compete in this totally changed industry environment. Most of their customers, companies large and small, were still watching developments before deciding how and where to commit their IT budgets. Hundreds of billions of dollars in future software sales were at stake, and it was not clear which company had the competitive advantage in this changing environment.

Rivalry among major software makers in the new web-based software market became intense. Rivalry between the major players and new players, like Netscape, Siebel Systems, Marcum, I2 Technology, and SSA, also intensified. The major software makers, each of which was a market leader in one or more segments of the software industry, such as SAP in ERP, Microsoft in PC software, and Oracle in database management software, sought to showcase their strengths to make their software compatible with web-based technology. Thus, Microsoft strove to develop its Windows NT network-based platform and its Internet Explorer web browser to compete with Netscape's Internet browser and Sun Microsystems's open-standard Java web software programming language, which was compatible with any company's proprietary software, unlike Microsoft's NT.

SAP also had to deal with competition from large and small software companies that were breaking into the new web-based ERP environment. In 1995, SAP teamed with Microsoft, Netscape, and Sun Microsystems to make its R/3 software Internet-compatible with any of their competing systems. Within one year, it introduced its R/3 Release 3.1 Internet-compatible system, which was most easily configured, however, when using Sun's Java web-programming language. SAP raised new funds on the stock market to undertake new rounds of the huge investment necessary to keep its web-based R/3 system up to date with the dramatic innovations in web software development and to broaden its product range to offer new, continually emerging web-based applications, for example, applications such as the corporate intranets, business-to-business (B2B) and business-to customer (B2C) networks, web site development and hosting, security and systems management, and streaming audio and video tele-conferencing.

Because SAP had no developed competency in web software development, its competitors started to catch up. Oracle emerged as its major competitor; it had taken its core database management software used by thousands of large companies and overlaid it with web-based operating and applications software. Oracle could now offer its huge customer base a growing suite of web software, all seamlessly integrated. The suite of software also allowed them to perform Internet-based ERP value chain business processes. While Oracle's system was nowhere near as comprehensive as SAP's R/3 system, it allowed for cross-industry networking at both the input and output sides, it was cheaper and easier to implement quickly, and it was easier to customize to the needs of a particular customer. Oracle began to take market share away from SAP.

New companies like Siebel Systems, Commerce One, Ariba, and Marcum, which began as niche players in some software applications such as SCM, CRM, intranet, or website development and hosting, also began to build and expand their product offerings so that they now possessed ERP modules that competed with some of SAP's most lucrative R/3 modules. Commerce One and Ariba, for example, emerged as the main players in the rapidly expanding B2B industry SCM market. B2B is an industry-level ERP solution that creates an organized market and thus brings together industry buyers and suppliers electronically and provides the software to write and enforce contracts for the future development and supply of an industry's inputs. Although these niche players could not provide the full range of services that SAP could provide, they became increasingly able to offer attractive alternatives to customers seeking specific aspects of an ERP system. Also, companies like Siebel, Marcum, and I2 claimed that they had the ability to customize their low-price systems, and prices for ERP systems began to fall.

In the new software environment, SAP's large customers started to purchase software on a "best of breed" basis, meaning that customers purchased the best software applications for their specific needs from different, leading-edge companies rather than purchasing all of their software products from one company as a package—such as SAP offered. Sun began to promote a free Java computer language as the industry "open architecture" standard, which meant that as long as each company used Java to craft their specific web-based software programs, they would all work seamlessly together and there would no longer be an advantage to using a single dominant platform like Microsoft's Windows or SAP's R/3. Sun was and is trying to break Microsoft's hold over the operating system industry standard, Windows. Sun wanted each company's software to succeed because it was "best of breed," not because it locked customers in and created enormous switching costs for them should they contemplate a move to a competitor's product.

All these different factors caused enormous problems for SAP's top managers. What strategies should they use to protect their competitive position? Should they forge ahead with offering their customers a broad, proprietary, web-based ERP solution and try to lock them in and continue to charge a premium price? Should they move to an open standard and make their R/3 ERP Internet-enabled modules compatible with solutions from other companies, and indeed forge alliances with those companies to ensure that their software operated seamlessly together? Since SAP's managers still believed they had the best ERP software and the capabilities to lead in the web software arena, was this the best long-run competitive solution? Should SAP focus on making its ERP software more customizable to its customers' needs and make it easier for them to buy selected modules to reduce the cost of SAP software? This alternative might also make it easier for them to develop ERP modules that could be scaled back to suit the needs of medium and small firms, which increasingly were becoming the targets of its new software competitors. Once these new firms got toeholds in the market, it would then be a matter of time before they improved their products and began to compete for SAP's installed customer base. SAP realized that it had to refocus its business model, especially because rivals were rapidly buying niche players and, at the same time, filling gaps in their product lines to be able to compete with SAP.

The mySAP.com Initiative

In 1997, SAP sought a quick fix to its problems by releasing new R/3 solutions for ERP Internet-enabled SCM and CRM solutions, which converted its internal ERP system into an externally based network platform. SCM, now know as the "back end" of the business, integrates the business processes necessary to manage the flow of goods, from the raw material stage to the finished product. SCM programs forecast future needs, and plan and manage a company's operations, especially its manufacturing operations. CRM, known as the "front-end" of the business, provides companies with solutions and support for business processes directed at improving sales, marketing, customer service, and field service operations. CRM programs are rapidly growing in popularity because they lead to better customer retention and satisfaction and higher revenues. In 1998, SAP followed with industry solution maps, business technology maps, and service maps, all of which were aimed at making its R/3 system dynamic and responsive to changes in industry conditions. In 1998, recognizing that its future rested on its ability to protect its share of the U.S. market, it listed itself on the New York Stock Exchange and began to expand the scope of its U.S. operations.

In 1999, however, the full extent of the change in SAP's business model and strategies became clear when it introduced its mySAP.com (mySAP) initiative to gain control of the web-based ERP, SCM, and CRM markets, and to extend its reach into any e-commerce or Internet-based software applications. The mySAP initiative was a comprehensive ebusiness platform designed to help companies collaborate and succeed, regardless of their industry or network environments. It demonstrated several elements of SAP's changing strategic thinking for how to succeed in the 2000s.

First, to meet its customers' needs in a new electronic environment, SAP used the mySAP platform to change itself from a vendor of ERP components to a provider of ebusiness solutions. The platform was to be the online portal through which customers could view and understand the way its Internet-enabled R/3 modules could match their evolving needs. SAP recognized that its customers were increasingly demanding access to networked environments with global connectivity, where decisions could be executed in real time through the Internet. Customers wanted to be able to leverage new ebusiness technologies to improve basic business goals like increasing profitability, improving customer satisfaction, and lowering overhead costs. In addition, customers wanted total solutions that could help them manage their relationships and supply chains.

MySAP was to offer a total solutions ERP package, including SCM and CRM applications, which would be fundamentally different from the company's traditional business application software. SAP's software would no longer force the customer to adapt to SAP's standardized architecture; mySAP software could be adapted to facilitate a company's transition into an ebusiness. In addition, the solution would create value for a company by building on its already developed core competencies; mySAP would help to leverage those core competencies, thus building a company's competitive advantage from within, rather than by creating it solely through the installation of SAP's industry best practices. SAP created a full range of front- and back-end products such as SCM and CRM software, available through its mySAP.com portal, that are specific to different industries and manufacturing technologies. These changes meant that it could compete in niche markets and make it easier to customize a particular application to an individual company's needs.

Second, mySAP provided the platform that would allow SAP's product offerings to expand and broaden over time, an especially important feature because web-based software was evolving into ever more varied applications. SAP was essentially copying other software makers, who were branching out into more segments of the software industry to capitalize on higher growth software segments and to prevent obsolescence should demand for their core software erode because of technological developments. Henceforth, SAP was not offering product-based solutions but customer-based solutions. Its mySAP ebusiness platform solutions are designed to be a scalable and flexible architecture that supports databases, applications, operating systems, and hardware platforms from almost every major vendor.

Third, SAP realized that cost was becoming a more important issue because competition from low-cost rivals demonstrated that customers could be persuaded to shift vendors if they were offered good deals. Indeed, major companies like Oracle often offered their software at discount prices or even gave it away free to well-known companies to generate interest and demand for their product. SAP focused on making mySAP more affordable by breaking up its modules and business solutions into smaller, separate products. Customers could now choose which particular solutions best met their specific needs; they no longer had to buy the whole package. At the same time, all mySAP offerings were fully compatible with the total R/3 system so that customers could easily expand their use of SAP's products. SAP was working across its whole product range to make its system easier and cheaper to use. SAP realized that repeat business is much more important than a one-time transaction, so they began to focus on seeking out and developing new, related solutions for their customers to keep them coming back and purchasing more products and upgrades.

Fourth, mySAP was aimed at a wider range of potential customers. By providing a simpler and cheaper version of its application software coupled with the introduction of the many mySAP ebusiness solution packages, SAP broadened its offerings targeted not only to large corporations but also small and medium-sized companies. MySAP allowed SAP to provide a low-cost ERP system that could be scaled down for smaller firms. For example, for small to mid-sized companies that lack the internal resources to maintain their own business applications on-site, mySAP offered hosting for data centers, networks, and applications. Small businesses could benefit greatly from the increased speed of installation and reduced cost possible through outsourcing and by paying a fee to use mySAP in lieu of having to purchase SAP's expensive software modules. SAP also focused on making its R/3 mySAP offerings easier to install and use, and reduced implementation times and consulting costs in turn reduced the costs of supporting the SAP platform for both small and large organizations.

To support its mySAP initiative, SAP had continued to build in-house training and consulting capabilities to increase its share of revenues from the services side of its business. SAP's increasing web software services efforts paid off because the company was now better able to recognize the problems experienced by customers. This result led SAP to recognize both the needs for greater responsiveness to customers and customization of its products to make their installation easier. Its growing customer awareness had also led it to redefine its mission as a developer of business solutions, the approach embedded in mySAP, rather than as a provider of software products.

To improve the cost effectiveness of mySAP installations, SAP sought a better way to manage its relationships with consulting companies. It moved to a parallel sourcing policy, in which several consulting firms competed for a customer's business, and it made sure a SAP consultant was always involved in the installation and service effort to monitor external consultants' performance. This helped keep service costs under control for its customers. Because customer needs changed so quickly in this fast-paced market and SAP continually improved its products with incremental innovations and additional capabilities, it also insisted that consultants undertake continual training to update their skills, training for which it charged high fees. In 2000, SAP adopted a stock option program to retain valuable employees after losing many key employees—programmers and consultants—to competitors.

Fifth, SAP increasingly embraced the concept of open architecture, and its mySAP offerings are compatible with the products of most other software makers. It had already ensured that its mySAP platform worked with operating systems such as Microsoft NT, Sun's Java, and UNIX, for example. Now it focused on ensuring that its products were compatible with emerging web applications software from any major software maker—by 2001 SAP claimed to have over 1,000 partners.

Indeed, strategic alliances and acquisitions became increasingly important parts of its strategy to reduce its cost structure, enhance the functionality of its products, and build its customer base. Because of the sheer size and expense of many web-based software endeavors, intense competition, and the fast-paced dynamics of this industry, SAP's top managers began to realize they could not go it alone and produce everything in-house. SAP's overhead costs had rocketed in the 1990s as it pumped money into building its mySAP initiative. Intense competition seemed to indicate that continuing massive expenditures would be necessary. SAP's stock price had decreased because higher overhead costs meant falling profits despite increasing revenues. SAP had never seemed to be able to enjoy sustained high profitability because changing technology and competition had not allowed it to capitalize on its acknowledged position as the ERP industry leader.

Given existing resource constraints and time pressures and the need to create a more profitable business model, in the 2000s SAP's managers realized that they needed to partner with companies that now dominated in various niches of the software market. By utilizing already developed best of breed software, SAP would not have to deploy the capital necessary if it were to go it alone. In addition, synergies across partner companies might allow future development to be accomplished more efficiently and enable it to bring new mySAP products to the market more quickly.

Not only did SAP form alliances with other companies, but it also used acquisitions to drive its entry into new segments of the web software market. For example, SAP acquired Top Tier Software Inc. in 2001 to gain access to its iView technology. This technology allows seamless integration between the web software of different companies and is critical for SAP because it lets customers drag-and-drop and mix information and applications from both SAP and non-SAP platform-based systems, and thus enables the open systems architecture SAP has increasingly supported. Top Tier was also an enterprise portal software maker, and in 2001 SAP teamed up with Yahoo to use these competencies to create a new U.S. subsidiary called SAP Portals, which would deliver state-of-the-art enterprise portal products that would enable people and companies to collaborate effectively and at any time. It also opened SAP hosting to provide hosting and web maintenance services.

By 2002, SAP believed that its partnerships and alliances had maneuvered it into a position of continued market dominance for the twenty-first century. Many of the major vendors of the databases, applications, operating systems, and hardware platforms that mySAP supports were once considered the competition, but the companies were now working together to create value by maximizing the range of web-based products that could be offered to customers through a common interface. MySAP adds value to its competitors' products by decreasing the exclusivity between the applications of different companies. In essence, SAP was treating these other products as complementary products, which added to the value of its own, promoted mySAP as the industry standard, and increased its dominance of the ERP web software market.

SAP's managers were shocked when it became clear that Microsoft, also recognizing the enormous potential of web software ERP sales, particularly in the small and medium business segment of the market, might be planning to compete in this market segment in 2002. Microsoft had bought two companies that competed in this segment to bolster its own web software offerings. Also, when Microsoft introduced its new XP operating system in 2001, it had not included a Java applications package to allow web software developers to write ebusiness software that would be compatible with XP, undercutting its rival Sun's attempts to bypass the Window's platform using its Java language. However, this also undercut SAP's open architecture initiatives because many of its mySAP installations were based on Java, not Microsoft's NT platform. SAP's managers saw this move as an attempt by Microsoft to wipe out the competitive advantage SAP had been gaining since the introduction of mySAP in 1999. SAP challenged Microsoft to indicate its support for the Java language. Already under scrutiny and attack by Sun and other software companies for its anticompetitive trade practices, Microsoft seemed to step back when it announced in June 2002 that its next version of XP would contain support for Java-based programming. Clearly, however, an open architecture and industry standard for web-based software are not in Microsoft's interests, especially if word processing and other important office applications become available as part of any e-commerce platform such as mySAP.

Microsoft's goal was clearly to become a formidable competitor for SAP, and with its competencies in a wide area of software products and huge resources, it could quickly and easily develop an ERP system with web-based solutions. In the past, SAP had tried to avoid this competition problem by partnering with Microsoft in a wide variety of endeavors and making sure its products were compatible with Microsoft's, thus making their interests mutual rather than divisive. In the future, however, if Microsoft believed its Windows platform was coming under increasing threat from SAP, it could now quickly move to attack SAP's and Oracle's market. The competitive battle over industry standards was far from over.

The recession that started in 2000 also increased competition in the ERP industry. SAP and Oracle, in particular, battled to protect and increase their market share. The huge drop in spending on IT by major companies and the decrease in the number of new customers hit the industry hard. The stock prices of all these companies fell dramatically, with some, like I2 Systems, also a provider of SCM solutions, fighting to survive. Competition among software companies became intense, and customers took advantage of this rivalry to demand price discounts from SAP as well as the other companies, which hurts revenues and profits. Smaller competitors like I2 and Siebel were forced to lower their prices to the point where they took a loss on a particular sale to gain market share. The weakest companies were forced to fall back on their main strengths and reduce their range of product offerings, but SAP had the resources to withstand the downturn.

SAP's number of software installations and customers increased steadily between 1998 and 2002. The number of software installations grew at a faster pace than the number of customers, a characteristic of the lock-in feature of investment in one ERP platform. In 2002, SAP was still the number 1 vendor of standard business applications software, with a worldwide market share of over 30%. Oracle was next with a 16% share of the market. SAP claimed that it had 10 million users and 50,000 SAP installations in 18,000 companies in 120 countries in 2002, and that half of the world's top 500 companies used its software.

Implementing mySAP

SAP's problems were not just in the strategy area, however. Its mySAP initiative had increased its overhead costs, and it still could not find the appropriate organizational structure to make the best use of its resources and competencies. It continued to search for the right structure for servicing the growing range of its products and the increasing breadth of the companies, in terms of size, industry, and global location, it was now serving.

Recall that in the mid-1990s, SAP had began to centralize authority and control to standardize its own business processes and manage knowledge effectively across organizational subunits. While this reorganization resulted in some benefits, it had the unfortunate result of lengthening the time it took SAP to respond to the fast-changing web software ERP environment. To respond to changing customer needs and the needs for product customization, SAP now moved to decentralize control to programmers and its sales force to manage problems where and when they arose. SAP's managers felt that in an environment where markets are saturated with ERP vendors and where customers want service and systems that are easier to use, it was important to get close to the customer. SAP had now put in place its own applications software for integrating across its operating divisions and subsidiaries, allowing them to share best practices and new developments and thus avoid problems that come with too much decentralization of authority.

To speed the software development process, SAP divided its central German software development group into three teams in 2000. One team works on the development of new products and features, the second refines and updates functions in its existing products, and the third works on making SAP products easier to install. Also, to educate its customers and speed customer acceptance and demand for mySAP, SAP changed its global marketing operations in late 2000. Following its decentralized style, each product group once had its own marketing department that operated separately to market and sell its products. This decentralization had caused major problems because customers didn't understand how the various parts of mySAP fit together. It also wasted resources and slowed the sales effort. Announcing that "SAP had to develop a laser like focus on marketing," a far cry from its previous focus on its engineering competency, SAP's top managers centralized control of marketing at its U.S. subsidiary and put control of all global marketing into the hands of one executive, who was now responsible for coordinating market efforts across all mySAP product groups and all world regions.

EXHIBIT 1

mySAP.com Product Groups

mySAP.com Solutions	mySAP.com Industry Solutions
● Industry solutions	● mySAP aerospace and defense
● Solutions for small and mid-sized businesses	● mySAP automotive
● mySAP enterprise portals	● mySAP banking
● mySAP supply chain management	● mySAP chemicals
● mySAP customer relationship management	● mySAP consumer products
● mySAP supplier relationship management	● mySAP engineering and construction
● mySAP product life cycle management	● mySAP financial service provider
● mySAP exchanges	● mySAP health care
● mySAP business intelligence	● mySAP higher education and research
● mySAP financials	● mySAP high tech
● mySAP human resources	● mySAP insurance
● mySAP mobile business	● mySAP media
● mySAP hosted solutions	● mySAP mill products
	● mySAP mining
	● mySAP oil and gas
	● mySAP pharmaceuticals
	● mySAP public sector
	● mySAP retail
	● mySAP service providers
	● mySAP telecommunications

Soon after, in 2001, once again to speed up the implementation of the mySAP initiative, SAP folded the SAPMarkets and SAP Portals subsidiaries into SAP's other operations and split the SAP product line into distinct but related mySAP product groups, each of which was to be treated as an independent profit center, with the head of each product group reporting directly to SAP's chairperson. The type of web software application or ERP industry solution being offered to the customer differentiates each product group (see Exhibit 1).

SAP also changed the way its three German engineering groups worked with the different mySAP products groups. Henceforth, a significant part of the engineering development effort would take place inside each mySAP product group so that program engineers, who write and improve the specific new mySAP software applications, were joined with the sales force for that group. Now they could integrate their activities and provide better customized solutions. The

software engineers at its German headquarters, besides conducting basic R&D, would be responsible for coordinating the efforts of the different mySAP engineering groups, sharing new software developments among groups, providing expert solutions, and ensuring all the different mySAP applications worked together seamlessly.

Each mySAP product group is now composed of a collection of cross-functional product development teams focused on their target markets. Teams are given incentives to meet their specific sales growth targets and to increase operating effectiveness, including reducing the length of installation time. The purposes of the new product group/team approach was to decentralize control, make SAP more responsive to the needs of customers and to changing technical developments, and still give SAP centralized control of development efforts. To ensure that its broadening range of software was customizable to the needs of different kinds of companies and industries,

SAP enlisted some of its key customers as "development partners" and as members of these teams. Customers from large, mid-sized, and small companies were used to test new concepts and ideas. Within every mySAP product group, cross-functional teams focused on customizing its products for specific customers or industries. SAP opened the development process to its competitors and allowed them to work with SAP teams to make their products compatible with SAP's products and with the computer platforms or legacy systems already installed in their customers' operations. Through this implementation approach, SAP was striving to pull its actual and potential customers and competitors toward the single, open standard of SAP. The company also instituted stricter training and certification methods for consultants to improve the level of quality control and protect its reputation.

At the global level, SAP grouped is national subsidiaries into three main world regions: Europe, the Americas, and Asia/Pacific. This grouping made it easier to transfer knowledge and information between countries and serve the specific demands of national markets inside each region. Also, this global structure made it easier to manage relationships with consulting companies and to coordinate regional marketing and training efforts, both under the jurisdiction of the centralized marketing and training operations.

Thus, in the 2000s SAP began to operate with a loose form of matrix structure. To increase internal flexibility and responsiveness to customers while at the same time boosting efficiency and market penetration, the world regions, the national subsidiaries, and the salespeople and consultants within them constitute one side of the matrix. The centralized engineering, marketing, and training functions and the twenty or so different mySAP product groups compose the other side. The problem facing SAP is to coordinate all these distinct subunits so they will lead to rapid acceptance of SAP's new mySAP platform across all the national markets in which it operates.

In practice, a salesperson in any particular country works directly with a client to determine what type of ERP system he or she needs. Once this system is determined, a project manager from the regional subsidiary or from one of the mySAP groups is appointed to assemble an installation team from members of the different product groups whose expertise is required to implement the new client's system.

Given SAP's broad range of evolving products, the matrix structure allows SAP to provide those products that fit the customer's needs in a fast, coordinated way. SAP's policy of decentralizing authority and placing it in the hands of its employees enables the matrix system to work. SAP prides itself on its talented and professional staff that can learn and adapt to many different situations and networks across the globe.

Developments in the 2000s

In April 2002, SAP announced that its revenues had climbed 9.2%, but its first-quarter profit fell 40% because of a larger-than-expected drop in license revenue from the sale of new software. Many customers had been reluctant to invest in the huge cost of moving to the mySAP system given the recession and continuing market uncertainty. Its rivals fared worse, however, and SAP announced it had several orders for mySAP in the works, and that the 18,000 companies around the world using its flagship R/3 software would soon move to its new software once their own customers had started to spend more money. In the meantime, SAP announced it would introduce a product called R/3 Enterprise, which would be targeted at customers not yet ready to make the leap to mySAP. R/3 Enterprise is a collection of web software that can be added easily to the R/3 platform to provide a company with the ability to network with other companies and perform many e-commerce operations. SAP hopes this new software will show its R/3 customers what mySAP can accomplish for them once it is running in their companies. SAP's managers believed these initiatives would allow the company to jump from being the third largest global software company to being the second, ahead of main competitor Oracle. They also wondered if they could use its mySAP open system architecture to overcome Microsoft's stranglehold on the software market and bypass the powerful Windows standard.

Pursuing this idea, SAP put considerable resources into developing a new business computing solution called SAP NetWeaver that is a web-based, open integration and application platform that serves as the foundation for enterprise service-oriented architecture (enterprise SOA) and allows the integration and alignment of people, information, and business processes across business and technology boundaries. Enterprise SOA utilizes open standards to enable integration with information and applications from almost any source or technology and is the technology of the future. SAP NetWeaver is now the foundation for all Enterprise SOA SAP applications and mySAP Business Suite solutions; it also powers SAP's partner solutions and a customer custom-built applications. Also NetWeaver integrates business processes across various systems, databases, and sources—from any business software supplier—and is marketed to large companies as a service-oriented application and integration platform. NetWeaver's development was a major strategic move by SAP for driving enterprises to run their business software on a single SAP platform.

Although SAP was developing and upgrading its products at a fast pace, throughout 2002 and 2003 companies worldwide continued to limit or reduce their IT expenditures, and SAP, like all other computer hardware and software companies, suffered as their revenues fell. In fact SAP's stock price plunged in 2002 from $40 to almost $10 as the stock market crashed. However, while SAP's revenues fell by 5% in 2003 because of lower ERP and consulting sales, its net income almost doubled because it had finally brought its global cost structure under control and was making better use of its resources. Strict new controls on expenses had been implemented, a hiring freeze imposed, and the company was focusing its German programmers to work on urgent problems. Consequently, its stock was back up to $35 by the end of 2003 as its future growth prospects looked good.

Outsourcing

As a part of its major push to reduce costs, SAP began to outsource its routine future programming development work overseas to low-cost countries such as India. By 2003, SAP employed 750 software programmers in India and had doubled that number by 2004. To help boost global revenues, SAP also began to use its expanding Indian research center to develop new ERP modules to serve new customers in more and more industries or vertical markets, and by 2003, it had mySAP systems designed for about twenty industry markets. At the same time, SAP used its growing army of low-cost Indian programmers to work the bugs out of its SAP modules and to increase their reliability when they were installed in a new company. This prevented embarrassing blows-ups that sometimes arose when a company implemented

SAP's ERP for the first time. Fewer bugs also made it easier to install its modules in a new company, which reduced the need for consulting and lowered costs, leading to more satisfied customers. By 2006, SAP had doubled its Indian work force again, and its Indian group was now bigger than its research group in Waldorf, Germany. Outsourcing has saved the company billions of Euros a year and has been a continuing contributor to its rising profitability in the 2000s.

The Small and Medium Enterprise Market

In 2003, SAP changed the name of its software from mySAP.com to mySAP Business Suite because more and more customers were now using a suite licensing arrangement to obtain its software rather than buying it outright. Part of the change in purchasing was because of the constant upgrades SAP was rolling out; in a licensing arrangement, its clients could expect to be continually upgraded as it improved its ERP modules. This also had the effect of locking its customers into its software platform for its raised switching costs. However, while SAP continued to attract new large business customers, the market was becoming increasingly saturated as its market share continued to grow—it already had around 50% of the global large business market by 2003. So, to promote growth and increase sales revenues, SAP began a major push to increase its share of the small and medium business enterprise (SME) market segment of the ERP industry.

The small size of these companies, and so the limited amount of money they had to spend on business software, was a major challenge for SAP, which was used to dealing with multinational companies that had huge IT budgets. Also, there were major competitors in this market segment that had specialized in meeting the needs of SMEs to avoid direct competition with SAP, and they had locked up a significant share of business in this ERP segment. By focusing primarily on large companies, SAP had left a gap in the market that large software companies like Oracle, Microsoft, and IBM took advantage of to developed their own SME ERP products and services to compete for customers and revenues in this market segment—one also worth billions of dollars in the years ahead and the main growth segment in the future ERP market. So, to reach this growing market segment as quickly as possible, SAP decided to develop two main product offerings for SMEs: SAP All-in-One and SAP Business One.

SAP All-in-One is a streamlined version of its R/3 mySAP Business Suite; it is much easier to install and maintain and much more affordable for SMEs. To develop All-in-One, SAP's software engineers took its mySAP Business Suite modules designed for large companies and scaled them down for users of small companies. All-in-One is a cut-down version of SAP's total range of products like SAP Customer Relationship Management, SAP ERP modules, SAP Product Lifecycle Management, SAP Supply Chain Management, and SAP Supplier Relationship Management. Despite its reduced size, it is still a complex business solution and one that requires a major commitment of IT resources for a SME.

So, recognizing the need to provide a much simpler and more limited and affordable ERP solution for smaller companies, SAP decided to also pursue a second SME ERP solution. To speed the development of a new suite of programs, SAP decided not to develop a new software package from scratch based on its leading R/3 product, as it did with its All-in-One solution. Rather, it took a new path and bought an Israeli software company called TopManage Financial Solutions in 2002 and rebranded its system as SAP Business One. SAP Business One is a much more limited ERP software package that integrates CRM with financial and logistic modules to meet a specific customer's basic needs. However, it still provides a powerful, flexible solution and is designed to be easy to work and affordable for SMEs. Business One software works in real time; no longer does an SME need to wait until the end of the month to do the accounts. The system manages and records the ongoing transactions involved in a business such as cost of goods received, through inventory, processing and sale, and delivery to customers, and automatically records transactions in a debit and credit account. Despite its streamlined nature, Business One contains fourteen important core modules:

- Administration Module that configures and links the activities involved in a business's value creation system
- Financials Module that controls accounting and financial activities
- Sales Opportunities Module that maintains contact with existing customers and tracks potential customers
- Sales Module that tracks when orders are entered, shipped, and invoiced

- Purchasing Module that issues purchase orders and records goods received into inventory
- Business Partners Module that maintains record and contact with customers and sellers
- Banking Module that tracks and records where cash is received and paid out
- Inventory Module that records and values inventory
- Production Module that tracks cost of materials and manufacturing
- MRP Module that increases the efficiency of input purchase and production planning
- Service Module that manages after-sales service activities and records
- Human Resources Module that records all employee information
- Reports Module that generates user-defined reports (as printouts or Excel files)
- E-commerce that allows customers to buy and sell online to consumers or other businesses

To speed the development of its new Business One solution, SAP chose its management team from engineers outside the company. Many of these managers came from TopManage, and one of these, Shai Agassi, has since risen in SAP to become its chief technology officer for all of its products and technologies. One reason is because of the growing importance of the SME segment, which became clear in 2005 when SAP began reporting revenues from the SME market segment separately from revenues for its larger customers, one way of showing its commitment to SME customers.

The Changing Competitive Environment

As mentioned above, one of the major reasons for SAP to enter and compete in the SME segment was that the large company segment was becoming increasing mature and saturated. By 2004, achieving rapid growth by increasing the number of new large business customers was becoming more and more difficult, simply because SAP's share of the global ERP market had now grown to 58%. As a result, SAP reported that it expected single digit growth in the future—growth worth billions in revenues but still growth that would not fuel a rapid rise in its stock price.

However, competition in the SME market was also increasing as its business software rivals watched

SAP develop and introduce its All-in-One and Business One solutions to dominate this segment. Now SAP's rapid growth in this segment led to increasing competition and to a wave of consolidation in the ERP industry. In 2003, PeopleSoft, the leader in the HRM software module segment, bought J. D. Edwards & Son, a leader in SCM, to enlarge its product offerings and strengthen its market share against growing competition from SAP and Oracle. However, Oracle, the dominant business software database management company, and its chairman, Larry Ellison, also realized the stakes ahead in the consolidating business software market. While SAP had never made large acquisitions to acquire new products and customers, preferring "organic growth" from the inside or small acquisitions, this was not true of Oracle. Ellison saw major acquisitions as the best way to expand Oracle's range of business modules to complement the suite of ERP modules it had been developing internally and so gain market share in the SME market segment. Through acquisitions it could quickly develop an ERP suite with the breadth of SAP's to meet the needs of SMEs. Also, it could use its new competencies and customers to attack SAP in the large company segment, which Oracle now regarded as a major growth opportunity.

So Oracle began a hostile takeover of PeopleSoft. PeopleSoft's managers battled to prevent the takeover, but Oracle offered PeopleSoft's customers special low-cost licensing deals on Oracle software and guaranteed them the changeover to its software would be smooth. It finally acquired PeopleSoft—and the resources and customers necessary to gain a large market share in the SME segment at the expense of SAP and Microsoft—in 2005. Oracle has kept up the pressure. Since January 2005, it acquired twenty-five more business software companies in a huge acquisition drive to build its distinctive competencies and market share in ERP software. PeopleSoft brought Oracle expertise in HRM, and J. D. Edwards, expertise in SCM; and, in a major acquisition of Siebel Systems, Oracle bought a leading CRM software developer. These acquisitions have allowed Oracle to dramatically increase its market share, particularly with small and medium-sized businesses. Before purchasing Seibel, for example, Oracle had a 6.8% share of this market; now it could add Seibel's 11% market share to become one of the top three CRM suppliers.

One of the latest additions to Oracle's new E-Business suite is Oracle Fusion middleware, which allows companies to leverage their existing investments in the software applications of other companies, including SAP, so that they work seamlessly with Oracle's new ERP modules. Fusion is Oracle's answer to SAP NetWeaver and is seen as a major threat to SAP, for it gives customers no incentive to move to SAP's All-in-One or Business One suite. Oracle hopes that because some of its modules, like PeopleSoft's HRM software module, have been regarded as stronger offerings than SAP's, many companies will be inclined to keep their existing PeopleSoft installations and then choose more offerings from Oracle's growing business applications suite. Also, Oracle hopes that SAP customers will now be able to keep any existing SAP application but still add on Oracle modules.

The third leading SME ERP supplier, Microsoft, is also keeping up the pressure. Using the competencies from its acquisition of Great Plains and Navision, it subsequently released a new business package called Microsoft Dynamics NAV, which is ERP software that can be fully customized to the needs of SME users, to their industries and scaled to their size. Microsoft's advantage lies in the compatibility of its ERP offerings with the Windows platform, which is still used by more than 85% of SMEs, especially as it can offer a discount when customers choose both types of software and upgrade to its new Windows Vista software in 2007 and beyond. Its offerings also work seamlessly with its Windows applications such as Word, PowerPoint, and Outlook, and with its Net framework, which is important in B2B transactions.

In 2006, many analysts were betting Oracle would emerge as the leader in the SME segment because they pointed out that SAP's reputation at the SME level was not good, and that it was perceived as a "big, scary, expensive option." SAP's managers realized the need to work hard to carefully position its All-in-One, but especially Business One, software to suit the needs of a company that might have only 30 or 300 employees rather than the 30,000 found at a large company. For example, in the U.S. and Canadian markets, it has been estimated that 90% of companies fall into the SME category, and while SAP might have the greatest product in the world, if it could not customize and market the product to suit these customers' needs, they will not adopt it. In 2004, Shai Agassi, SAP's CTO and expert in the SME software area, announced that as the $40 billion dollar a year business software industry headed for a shakeout,

SAP had to change its strategy to protect its global market share: "Training people on computer systems is stupid. We need to train the systems to work with people." SAP was finally facing up to the need to make its products easy to install, maintain, and especially use as a hoard of other competitors were now snapping at its heels.

In 2005, SAP established five new broad corporate goals: agility, high performance, simplicity, talent development, and co-innovation. Agility was becoming vital as new technological developments, particularly due to the Internet, were rapidly changing the value of its software to customers. For example, a new approach to delivering business software to customers by direct download from the Internet, along with constant upgrading from the Internet, was being pioneered by Internet start-ups such as salesforce.com, which offered its customers CRM software online at prices that undercut SAP and its competitors. High-performance meant ensuring that SAP's software worked seamlessly with its customers, was bug free, and that all the complex parts of its business suite worked totally in tandem. Simplicity meant that its software engineers should continuously work to make its modules easier to install and use by its clients.

Co-innovation was an affirmation of SAP's push through the mid-2000s to work with other software companies, including competitors, to offer products that better met the needs of some types of ERP customers. SAP had avoided making large acquisitions to grow its competencies and customer base; it relied on organic growth, that is, developing new solutions internally, from the ground up, as its growth model. Also, it sought to form strategic alliances with other software vendors to further the utility of its software and to increase the number of customers it could reach. Compare this to Oracle's aggressive and sometimes hostile acquisition strategy to grow its resources.

Co-innovation means cooperating with partners and customers to improve products and solutions, a strategy SAP had always pursued. However, SAP seemed not to realize that its rapid growth might be perceived by other large software companies as a major threat. It had used Oracle's database software for SAP applications, for example, and worked to make its modules compatible with Microsoft's software to make implementation of its own software easier for customers. It had also worked with companies like IBM to train their consultants to install its software. But Oracle and Microsoft were now major competitors and were taking advantage of their compatibility with SAP's software to lure away its customers.

Cooperation and Competition

By the mid-2000s, industry consolidation was leading to increased competition in all aspects of its business, and SAP faced the problem of having to cooperate with companies in some areas and yet be competitors in others. Indeed, after it became clear Oracle and PeopleSoft would merge, Microsoft and SAP began to talk about a possible merger. Their top managers met to discuss the issues involved and there seemed to be a natural fit, for each company would obtain access to all the customers of the other and their software was complementary. However, talks ended both because of antitrust issues and the fear that U.S. or European Union regulators would stop the merger. Talks also failed because there seemed to be major problems of merging the two different cultures: SAP's more bureaucratic German-based culture with Microsoft's more freewheeling culture. Nevertheless, the two companies realized they would gain more through cooperation than competition and formed an alliance to ensure interoperability between Microsoft's Net.platform and SAP's NetWeaver platform and create a new suite of software that will leverage each others' business applications. So they are working to cooperate, not compete, as business partners, which gives them leverage over customers and stops a movement to Oracle's suite. It also seems that Microsoft has abandoned its attempt to become the dominant player in the ERP market, sensing that it might obtain greater returns from ensuring its Windows standard remains dominant for all kinds of computing—including the increasingly important mobile computing. And, by 2006, its mobile platform, Microsoft CE, was winning the battle against other systems championed by Nokia and Sony, and SAP was working to make its software work seamlessly with Microsoft CE so, for example, managers would receive instant alerts from SAP's module when action was needed to correct some operational issue. Also, SAP seems to have reduced its support for the LINUX platform, which is a direct threat to Microsoft.

SAP also worked hard to develop strategic alliances with all kinds of software companies, and by

2007, it had formed contracts with over 1,000 independent software vendors (ISVs), who have helped it expand its offerings, and it has jointly developed 300 new ERP solutions for the 25 industries it now serves, and these applications are all powered by SAP NetWeaver3. An important alliance was announced in August 2006 when IBM announced it would invest $40 million over the next five years to develop the capabilities necessary to install SAP's new software. Also SAP will integrate NetWeaver with IBM's Blade Center and IBM Total Storage Systems, IBM's data storage solution for large companies. These moves will help boost sales, strengthen links with large companies, and offer SAP the chance to co-develop new software with IBM, which is the world's third largest global software seller. SAP and Siemens are collaborating on an IT solution to improve patient care and increase safety and efficiency and lower operating costs. In 2006, SAP and Cisco Systems entered into an agreement to jointly market governance, risk, and compliance business processes and IT control system offerings.

SAP has been making many small acquisitions to improve its position in various industries and to develop products to help companies meet the major changes in U.S. regulatory reporting requirements. For example, in the retail software industry, it acquired companies like Triversity and Khimetrics. Triversity provides point of sales, store inventory, customer relations and service solutions for retail companies, and Khimetrics helps retailers price and position products to manage demand, improve margins, and predict sales and income. It also acquired TomorrowNow, which specializes in providing maintenance and support services for PeopleSoft and J. D. Edwards & Company customers. SAP then created "safe passage programs" that are designed to help companies switch to SAP solutions, even though they now use software applications provided by Oracle. SAP plans to develop a variety of new-generation products by 2008, including new SAP industry solutions, and more applications for SMEs—so this is a direct challenge to Oracle's Fusion software.

To help companies manage complex regulations, SAP also made small acquisitions like Virsa Systems that have expertise in U.S. accounting laws and standards. Its software was then incorporated into SAP products to provide a complete approach to allowing compliance with the Sarbanes-Oxley Act, which mandates openness and conformity to strict accounting reporting requirements through their governance, Risk and Compliance (GRC) solutions. Also, SAP's modules now contain customized software that allows companies to manage trade compliance according to the regulations of different countries, for example, environmental, pharmaceutical, and banking requirements. Finally, the new Radio Frequency identification (RFID) that uses wireless ID tags to improve SCM and the tracking of shipments and inventory has required SAP incorporate software to manage this into its business applications. As all aspects of the environment change, so must SAP's software.

The Future

In 2006, software sales made up 33% of SAP's revenues, consulting 25%, maintenance 37%, and training 4%. (Maintenance provides continuous improvement, quality management, and problem solutions so clients stay up to date with the best business practices that SAP embeds into its software.) The company boasted over 2 million individual users working with SAP solutions in over 100,000 installations of SAP services in more than 36,000 companies in 25 industries ranging from aerospace and defense to wholesale distribution in 120 countries. SAP employed 38,500 people, had hired 3,500 in 2006, and was planning to hire 3,500 more in 2007. It had local offices in more than 50 countries and ran 77 training centers worldwide where people could come to learn how to install and operate its software packages.

However, major questions remain. Does SAP need to search out new ways to increase growth and generate revenues because the market is getting saturated now that most large companies have adopted best practices ERP software? Some analysts say SAP needs to generate increased revenues by increasing its involvement in service and training activities, but this would put it in direct competition with IT consulting companies such as IBM and Cap Gemini that are its allies. Or, it must continue to broaden the range of products it offers to the SME business segment, which would increase competition with Oracle, Microsoft, and new Internet companies such as salesforce.com, which are increasingly offering direct low-cost Internet download ERP services, so far mainly in CRM.

Another main issue is how big a threat is Oracle to SAP in the future? Some analysts say Oracle is not a major threat since Oracle's acquisitions in the B2B sector will not give it a permanent competitive advantage over SAP in SMEs or with large companies. What Oracle has gained is a short-term boost in market share brought about by obtaining the customers of the companies it acquired, but this will not lead to future gains. Others say Oracle is the major competitor, however, with the size, resources, and customer base to compete successfully against SAP. They point out that while over the past five years SAP's stock shot up 80%, Oracle's increased by only 25%. But also that in the last year Oracle's stock has doubled in price and increased much faster than SAP's because investors believe in the future growth potential of its acquisitions and business model.

SAP believes in its "organic growth" from the inside, however, and considers itself an innovator compared to Oracle. In a 2006 press release, SAP spokesperson Bill Wohl was quoted as saying that SAP offers a next-generation platform in business software today, while Oracle's next-generation applications exist only in "PowerPoint form" and won't be delivered until 2008 or beyond. Also that SAP had set aside $125 million to implement next-generation solutions in its current platform—so this is no idle boast. Also in 2006, SAP articulated four major priorities for the rest of the 2000s—to increase market share, especially in SME; to increase profitability by improving productivity; to better serve SAP users with new products and expand to new industries; and to help customers transition to and gain benefits from Enterprise SOA, which, using NetWeaver, allows customers to seamlessly integrate the software of different vendors into a whole and links it to the Internet, making possible real-time upgrades and improvements.

For all companies, future market growth may be limited as large companies expect to continue their efforts to tighten their IT spending budgets so the software market may grow only at a single digit rates in the next few years. However, the growth of the European Union offers SAP, much more than Oracle, many opportunities to build a worldwide ERP market as the number of countries expands and companies move their operations to low-cost locations within the EU. According to some estimates, the growth of the EU will increase the ERP market to around $13 billion by 2008, which is a 6% annual growth rate. Also, SAP is actively targeting the booming Asian, South American, and African markets.

A 2007 Surprise

SAP announced in January 2007 that its net income rose 29% in the fourth quarter from the year-earlier period to 799 million euros ($1 billion), on revenue of 3 billion euros ($3.9 billion). This was an excellent result, but its U.S. shares fell over 10% from $50 to $46, down from its December high of $56. Why the problem? SAP announced it would spend an additional 300 to 400 million euros over the next two years to attract new SME customers, and this investment will cut its operating margins by 1 to 2% and so its future profits.

The implication for investors is clear; by the end of 2006, SAP was meeting serious resistance from Oracle, it was having to work hard to build up its SME customer base, and the two companies were locked in what is likely to become a vicious battle—one that will reduce profit margins. This was a signal that profit margins were going to be lower than SAP had previously expected and that it needed to further develop tailored products, including hosted software and on-demand software delivered over the Internet, for the SME segment. SAP is facing competition in the SME market from CRM companies such as salesforce.com that specializes in on-demand software downloaded directly from the Internet. Complementing SAP's existing portfolio for midsized companies, a new solution will be introduced to leverage an "enterprise service-oriented architecture (enterprise SOA) by design" platform that will be available to customers through on-demand and hosted delivery at a significantly lower cost and that will allow them to "try-run-adapt" the software to meet their needs. This solution began initial market validation in early 2007. SAP's new CEO, Henning Kagermann, said: "We are combining the power of the new platform that SAP has developed over the last three years with a new approach in the way software is delivered and consumed to reach a broad segment of midsize companies with requirements not addressed by either traditional or on-demand solutions available today. This game-changing, 'enterprise SOA by design' addition to our product portfolio will open up an additional business that will deliver steady, continuous growth and, together with the ongoing advancement of our established business, accelerate SAP's long-term industry leadership." Also, it seems SAP may be signaling it is going to treat medium-sized customers differently from small customers. Clearly, many challenges lie ahead.

REFERENCES

Boudette, N. E., "E-Business: SAP Boosts Commerce One Stake," *Wall Street Journal,* July 2, 2001, p. B8.

Boudette, N. E., "Germany's SAP Reorganizes Its Marketing, Focuses on Web," *Wall Street Journal,* August 7, 2000, p. A8.

Boudette, N. E., "Results Show SAP Is Waiting to Benefit from Recovery," *Wall Street Journal,* April 19, 2002, p. A16.

"Burger King Corporation Selects SAP to Enable Information Technology Strategy," retrieved from http://mySAP.com (June 25, 2002).

Collett, S., "SAP: Whirlpool's Rush to Go Live Led to Shipping Snafus," Computerworld.com, November 4, 1999.

Conlin, R., "SAP Teams with Yahoo! On Portal Venture," CRMDaily.com, April 4, 2001.

Conlin, R., "SAP Upgrades CRM App, Unveils New Strategy," CRMDaily.com, April 23, 2001.

Edmondson, G., and Baker, S., "Silicon Valley on the Rhine," *Business Week,* November 7, 1997.

Hill, S., "SAP 'Opens Up,'" *Msi,* Oak Brook, August 2001.

Jacobs, F., and Whybark, D, *Why ERP? A Primer on SAP Implementation.* New York: McGraw-Hill, 2000.

Kersteller, J., "Software," *Business Week,* January 8, 2001.

Key, P. "SAP Strategy: Displace All Competing Gateways," *Philadelphia Business Journal,* September 27, 1999.

King, J., "Commerce One Deal Reflects SAP Strategy Shift," Computerworld. com, June 15, 2000.

King, S., and Ohlson, K., "Update: Commerce One Deal Reflects SAP Strategy Shift," Computerworld.com (2000).

Konicki, S., "Overwhelmed—SAP Regroups Software Business," *Information Week,* June 6, 2000.

Konicki, S., and Maselli, J., "SAP Touts Customers' Experiences," *Information Week,* June 3, 2002.

Krill, P., "SAP Takes on Its CRM Rivals," *Infoworld,* September 10, 2001.

Maselli, J., "Analysts Steer Customers Away from SAP CRM Upgrade," *Information Week,* September 10, 2001.

Meissner, G., *Inside the Secret Software Power.* New York: McGraw-Hill, 2000.

O'Brien, K., "Many Blows to SAP Strength," retrieved from http://www.it.mycareer.com.au/software/20000125/A39678-2000Jan21.html (January 25, 2000).

Pender, L., "SAP CEO: Don't Blame Us for Snafus," Zdnet.com, November 10, 1999.

SAP AG, "SAP Transforms E-Business with New mySAP Technology for Open Integration," *Business Wire,* November 6, 2001.

SAP, http://www.sap.com, 1995–2007.

SAP Annual Reports and 10K Reports, 1998–2002.

SAP 10K Reports, 2001–2007.

Scannell, E., "Accenture, SAP Jump into Bed," *Infoworld,* July 9, 2001.

Standard and Poor's Industry Overview—Software, *Industry Survey,* April 26, 2001.

Weston, R., "SAP Strategy Extends Scope," CNETNews.com, September 15, 1998.

Volantis

This case was prepared by Mike Harkey under the supervision of Professor William P. Barnett, Stanford Graduate School of Business.

Life is about timing.

—Carl Lewis, U.S. Olympian

Introduction

Matt Harris, President and CEO of the telecommunications software provider Volantis Systems, knew plenty about the importance of timing. His company's investors and founders had mis-timed its market opportunity and, by March 2006, had spent more than five years waiting for mass adoption of mobile data services.

Volantis' customers were primarily *mobile phone carriers* (e.g., 3 and Cingular) and *content providers* (e.g., eBay and lastminute.com) that needed tools to help them most efficiently deliver a wide-range of mobile phone-related services to a huge and complex market.[1] In 2005, almost two billion mobile phone subscribers worldwide were using thousands of different mobile phone handset models. Further complicating matters, mobile phone manufacturers were introducing new devices and technologies every day. Accordingly, no single operating system for mobile phones prevailed, and standards were a mess (i.e., wireless network standards differed and multimedia/audio/video standards differed).

The pace of innovation in mobile phone technology had disastrous implications for any business that wanted its mobile offering to appear as compelling to users on all phones, on all networks, in all geographies. For example, a newspaper publisher like *Financial Times* that wanted its global readership to be able enjoy its publication on any device would be hard-pressed to keep up with the ever-changing technologies. Analogously, imagine if it had to retool its printing presses every day for dozens of layouts, while preparing for an increasing number of new layouts to come.

Enter Volantis: it had built a software solution—a so-called intelligent content adapter—that could remove the complexities for any company that wanted to deliver its content to mobile devices. In fact, the process by which Volantis built its technology was yielding huge scalability benefits, so much so that the company's flexible solution was adopted by the largest list of wireless carrier customers in its market.

Indeed, with mobile data services usage increasing rapidly in many markets worldwide, Volantis was poised to fulfill its long-awaited potential. However, the company was losing over $400,000 per month, and it needed to act quickly with an updated organization plan to capitalize on its new business opportunities. One opportunity would leverage the company's core infrastructure, but would require considerable investment and resources. A second opportunity risked threatening its current operating model. In either case, Volantis was fortunate to have the luxury of such compelling prospects, after so many other wireless solutions companies had long since disappeared. As luck would have it, Volantis' timing was not ideal once again; only this time around, Harris and his team could not afford to be wrong.

Mike Harkey prepared this case under the supervision of Professor William P. Barnett, Thomas M. Siebel Professor of Business Leadership, Strategy and Organizations, as the basis for class discussion rather than to illustrate either effective or ineffective handling of an administrative situation.

Mobile Industry Landscape

Mobile Phone Use Worldwide

By the end of 2005, there were over 1.85 billion mobile phone subscribers worldwide.[2] China was by far the world's largest market, with an estimated 400 million subscribers at the end of 2005. India, with 65 million wireless subscribers, on the other hand, was one of the world's fastest growing markets. In the second half of 2005, almost 2.5 million new subscribers were signing up for cellular service every month in India, and wireless penetration remained less than seven percent. The rest of Asia—that is, Asia less China and India—accounted for 186 million subscribers in 2005.[3]

In 2005, there were 195 million wireless subscribers in the U.S., an increase of 6.9 percent over 2004. As of December 2004, Latin America had 167.2 million wireless subscribers, 41.8 percent more than in 2003. Argentina had the strongest growth rate (107.9 percent growth), more than doubling the number of its subscribers to 13.5 million.[4] The Middle East and Africa were estimated to have almost 200 million subscribers in 2005.

Europe was the world's most mature wireless market. The number of subscribers grew only two percent in 2005 to 325 million subscribers, and penetration rates were averaging over 80 percent. Germany, Italy, and the U.K. led the way in Europe, with 71.3 million, 62.8 million, and 61.1 million wireless subscribers, respectively, in 2004.

Mobile Phone Vendors

In 2005, worldwide mobile phone shipments totaled 825.5 million units, a 16.7 percent increase over the 707.3 million shipments in 2004. Asia was the world's largest market for handsets. In 2005, 197.1 million handsets were sold in Asia excluding Japan. Shipments in Japan totaled 45.4 million. One hundred sixty million mobile phones were sold in Western Europe, and 147 million were sold in the U.S.[5]

Additionally, thousands of new mobile phone handset models were flooding the market every year by hundreds of manufacturers worldwide. Finnish manufacturer Nokia held the industry's largest market share with 34.1 percent of the market in Q4 2005. (See Exhibit 1 for statistics on leading mobile phone vendors.) In early 2006, Nokia was distributing over 60 phone models in the U.S., from the 8801 model sold at an MSRP of $799 (key features included a half-megapixel camera and a 208 x 208 pixel, 256K-color screen) to the N90 model sold at an MSRP of $399 (key features included a 2 megapixel camera and personal video capabilities) to the basic 2126i model offered at an MSRP of $29.99.

Motorola, on the other hand, earned 18.2 percent share of the mobile phone market in 2005. It expanded its market share over the previous year on the success of its wildly popular Razr series phones which had an ultra-thin design and a variety of advanced features. Motorola also offered a SLVR series phone that was compatible with Apple's iTunes digital music service.

Mobile Phone Innovation

Indeed, with so many new mobile phones coming to market every year, handset vendors were forced to compete on a number of dimensions. Of course, price was important to consumers, and handset

EXHIBIT 1

Leading Mobile Phone Vendors, Worldwide Shipments and Market Share (Unit shipments are in millions.)

Rank	Vendor	4Q 2005 Shipments	4Q 2005 Market Share	4Q 2004 Shipments	4Q 2004 Market Share	Growth
1	Nokia	83.7	34.1%	66.1	32.2%	26.6%
2	Motorola	44.7	18.2%	31.8	15.5%	40.6%
3	Samsung	27.2	11.1%	21.1	10.3%	28.9%
4	LG Electronics	16.2	6.6%	13.9	6.8%	16.5%
5	Sony Ericsson	16.1	6.6%	12.6	6.1%	27.8%
	Others	57.3	23.4%	60.2	29.2%	−4.8%
	Total	**245.2**	**100.0%**	**205.7**	**100.0%**	**19.3%**

Source: Brad Smith, "Revenues Ride Growth Curve," *Wireless Week,* February 15, 2006.

vendors offered models across a wide spectrum of MSRPs, ranging from the exorbitant (e.g., Symbol Technologies MC70 Enterprise Digital Assistant with an MSRP over $2,000) to the bargain basement sub-$50 models offered by a large number of vendors. In many cases, wireless carriers subsidized the price of handsets to win subscriber business. Watson said:

> Consumers buying mobile devices are making distinctions in terms of the camera, the screen, the usability of the keyboard, the form factor (whether it's a flip or slide or whatever), what features it has, whether it interacts with a Windows machine, and so on. All of those consumer-oriented features (and there are probably around ten or fifteen attributes that matter to consumers) create an enormous number of niches in the market for phones.

Indeed, handset vendors were competing on design, form factor, and physical appearance attributes, offering phones in all sorts of colors, shapes, sizes, and ergonomic conventions. The pace of innovation in handset technology was rapid, as vendors sought to tap into the market of almost two billion mobile phone subscribers worldwide. As a result, an inventory of all of the industry's handset features would compare favorably to almost any consumer technology. By early 2006, manufacturers were turning the mobile phone into the next generation's personal computer, a catch-all for any kind of application or technology.

With screen quality greatly improving on mobile phones, vendors were merging digital imaging and video capabilities into handsets. Some phones offered multimedia options, including streaming video, digital music, FM radio, and ring tones. Even so, most phones were engineered around communications and messaging, including text messaging, instant messaging, picture messaging, conference calling, video-conferencing, paging, information alerts, fax, and email. Bluetooth and infrared features allowed some mobile users to wirelessly connect with external devices like PDAs and PCs. Additionally, many phones offered a micro-browser to allow users to surf the Internet.

Notwithstanding all of the innovation occurring in the wireless industry in early 2006, mobile phones were only as useful as the user's subscriber plan would allow. Each mobile operator was bound by the constraints of its network. As a result, service offerings varied widely from carrier to carrier, many of which operated on different technology platforms, or network standards.

Wireless Network Standards

Even though many countries had adopted a single network standard for nationwide use, the U.S. market employed several standards in early 2006. Most U.S. carriers employed so-called second-generation network platforms, including global system for mobile communications (GSM) or code division multiple access (CDMA). (See Exhibit 2 for platforms used by major U.S. carriers.)

First-generation wireless networks Introduced in the late 1970s and early 1980s, the first generation wireless systems were analog.

Second-generation (2G) 2G wireless networks supported voice and certain data services. Data transmission speeds of 14.4 kilobits per second (kbps) were common on 2G networks. CMDA was a 2G digital wireless technology that was used primarily in China, India, Japan, South Korea, and North America. (See Exhibit 3 for global CDMA subscriber statistics.) GSM was a 2G digital technology that was mostly used for voice transmissions. It had been adopted by the European Union and was the most widely used digital cellular standard worldwide. According to the trade

---

EXHIBIT 2

Technology Platforms/Standards Used by Major U.S. Carriers, 2005

Code division multiple access (CDMA)
- Alltel
- Sprint Nextel
- Verizon Wireless
- United States Cellular

Integrated dispatch enhanced network (iDEN)
- Sprint Nextel
- Nextel Partners

Global system for mobile communications (GSM)
- Cingular Wireless
- T-Mobile

Time division multiple access (TDMA)
- Cingular Wireless

Source: Kenneth Leon and Nelson Wang, "Industry Surveys, Telecommunications: Wireless," *Standard & Poor's,* November 3, 2005.

EXHIBIT 3

Global CDMA Subscriber Statistics

	Total Subscribers in September 2005 (in millions)	Percent Growth in 2004
Asia-Pacific	124.9	30%
North America	102.6	17%
Caribbean and Latin America	53.4	37%
Europe, Middle East, and Africa	4.8	34%
Total	**285.7**	**26%**

Source: CDMA Development Group.

group GSM World Association, there were 1.2 billion GSM subscribers in more than 200 countries as of mid-September 2005.[6] (See Exhibit 4 for global GSM subscriber statistics.)

Second and a half generation (2.5G) 2.5G wireless networks were a stepping stone to 3G networks because they used some of the existing 2G infrastructure in GSM and CDMA networks.

Third-generation (3G) 3G networks integrated mobile technology with high-data transmission capacity. With transmission speeds exceeding 2.0 megabits per second (Mbps) on certain 3G networks, these platforms enabled the delivery of the widest array of applications to mobile handsets. By the end of 2005,

EXHIBIT 4

Global GSM Subscriber Statistics

	Total Subscribers in September 2005 (in millions)	Percent Growth in 2004
Asia	470.8	24%
Africa	68.9	62%
Americas	53.1	121%
Eastern Europe	150.3	57%
Western Europe	352.6	7%
Middle East	63.5	34%
USA/Canada	48.0	5%
Total	**1207.2**	**29%**

Source: GSM Association.

there were three main 3G platforms: CDMA2000, wideband CDMA (WCDMA), and universal mobile telecommunications (UMTS). In 2001, Japanese carrier NTT DoCoMo began operating on the WCDMA standard. Conversely, by the end of 2005, most U.S. carriers had yet to fully upgrade to a 3G standard. ABI Research estimated that there were 42.0 million 3G subscribers worldwide, a 142 percent increase over 2004, most of which were in Japan.[7] Even though fewer than 2.3 percent of worldwide subscribers were on a 3G network, many believed that the long-anticipated platform shift was finally set to take off in 2006.

Wireless Carriers

Worldwide carrier revenues reached almost $480 billion in 2005, split between Europe/Middle East/Africa ($180 billion), Asia-Pacific ($158 billion), and the Americas ($143 billion).[8] At least eight carriers had over 50 million wireless subscriber customers. (See Exhibit 5 for leading carriers by region.) For example, China's largest carrier, China Mobile, had over 230 million subscribers and over $21 billion in wireless services revenues in 2005. In early 2006, there were hundreds of carriers worldwide, and many new entrants were coming to the market employing a different model than traditional carriers.

Mobile virtual network operators (MVNOs) did not have networks of their own, but rather resold capacity from established carriers. In 1999, Virgin Mobile launched the first MVNO in the U.K. using T-Mobile's network capacity; but by early 2006, almost 200 MVNOs were operational or had announced plans to launch. MVNOs were taking advantage of the market opportunity by employing a few different

EXHIBIT 5

Leading Carriers, by Region

		United States		
Rank	Carrier	Number of Subscribers (millions)	Market Share (%)	Service Revenues (billions)
1	Cingular Wireless	51.4	28.4%	7.7
2	Verizon Wireless	47.4	26.1%	6.9
3	Sprint PCS	26.6	14.6%	3.4
4	T-Mobile	19.2	10.6%	3.6
5	Nextel	17.8	9.8%	3.4
6	Alltel	9.1	5.0%	1.4
7	US Cellular	5.2	2.9%	0.7
8	Nextel Partners	1.8	1.0%	0.4
9	Dobson Communications	1.6	0.9%	0.2
10	Western Wireless	1.5	0.8%	0.3
	Total	**181.7**	**100.0%**	**28.0**

Source: Kenneth Leon and Nelson Wang, "Industry Surveys, Telecommunications: Wireless," *Standard & Poor's*, November 3, 2005.

Europe		
Carrier	Number of Subscribers (millions)	Service Revenues (billions)
Vodaphone	171.0	42.1
T-Mobile	83.1	17.8
Orange	70.0	14.0
Telefonica Moviles	89.0	10.1
Telecom Italia Mobile	45.6	8.0
O2	25.7	6.3

Source: Nelson Wang, "Industry Surveys, Telecommunications: Wireless Europe," *Standard & Poor's,* January 2006.

Asia		
Carrier	Number of Subscribers (millions)	Service Revenues (billions)
China Mobile	234.9	21.5
China United	124.1	8.0
NTT DoCoMo	50.1	21.6
KDDI Corp	20.9	13.3
SK Telecom	19.3	2.5
Vodaphone KK	15.0	6.7
Bharti Tele-Ventures	14.1	N/A

Source: Nelson Wang, "Industry Surveys, Telecommunications: Wireless Asia," *Standard & Poor's,* January 2006.

Latin America	
Carrier	Number of Subscribers (millions)
America Movil SA de CV	73.8
Telefonica Moviles SA	63.7
Telcel	32.3
Vivo	28.5
Telecom Italia Mobile SpA	18.3
TIM Brasil	18.0

Source: Nelson Wang, "Industry Surveys, Telecommunications: Wireless Latin America," *Standard & Poor's,* November 2005.

strategies. Well known brands like ESPN and Disney launched MVNOs with premium content and communication services to extend their brands into new areas. Targeted niche players like Boost Mobile and Amp'd Mobile were competing for the under-30 demographic with low-cost services and trendy content. Additionally, cost leaders like EasyMobile and Tesco were targeting low budget users with basic voice and data offerings. In 2005, there were 13 million MVNO subscribers in Europe (out of 325 million total wireless subscribers).

Carriers were benefiting from selling excess network capacity to MVNOs, and consumers were enjoying the incremental service offerings in the market. Naturally, the carriers were monitoring any potential cannibalization of their own business, fearful of a price war with the MVNOs. Nevertheless, prices had already begun to fall.

Most carriers charged for voice and data services either by bundling for a flat rate or priced based on usage. In 2004, the average price per minute of mobile telephone usage fell 12 percent in the U.S., following a drop of 13 percent between 2002 and 2003, continuing a downward trend. In the Scandinavian countries and the Netherlands, low-cost MVNOs had driven down the average price per minute for voice calls from $0.20 to $0.11 over a three-year period.

As of early 2006, the financial health of carriers worldwide rested on their ability to move beyond the voice-only business. Metrics like customer acquisition, customer churn rate, average minutes of use (AMOU), and average revenue per user (ARPU) would continue to be important benchmarks for any carrier. Nevertheless, one measure that would become increasingly important would be revenues from data services (e.g., music and video downloads). Data services could be highly profitable for carriers, creating higher return than the typical carriers' primary revenue generators: device sales, sale and resale of voice minutes, and extended value-added services (e.g., warranties). In addition, the mobile data services market was predicted to reach over $100 billion by 2007.

At the end of June 2005, ARPU in Asia was $18.90, compared to $13.10 in Eastern Europe, $37.40 in Western Europe, and $49.60 in the U.S. and Canada. In 2005, data services revenues accounted for 20 percent of Japan's wireless services revenues, 17 percent of those of Europe, and 10 percent of those of the U.S. As of November 2005, worldwide data services leader DoCoMo had 18.6 million subscribers to its 3G services and was earning a $63 ARPU, 25 percent of which came from data services. Data services provided carriers with not only a new potential revenue stream, but also a key vehicle for achieving differentiation in the increasingly crowded marketplace.

Challenges for Carriers

In early 2006, MVNOs and traditional carriers alike were directing resources towards the mobile content, data services opportunity. However, there was a great deal of operational complexity in creating the new business opportunity, and carriers needed to overcome a number of hurdles to get into the data services market. Specifically, they needed to consider:

- *Deployment models*: How to choose and implement a content delivery model to meet the market opportunity.

- *Technology*: How to acquire high quality solutions and efficiently integrate them, particularly when no standards existed: 1) There was no single prevailing operating system for mobile devices; 2) Network standards ranged from first generation TDMA networks to 3G networks like WCDMA; 3) There was no standard for multimedia, audio, or video files, and 4) There was no standard system for billing and user management.

- *Device management/Device diversity*: How to support the thousands of different existing and next generation handset models, each characterized by a set of different attributes.

- *Content delivery*: How to manage a catalog of content.

- *Marketing & merchandising*: How to promote services and drive revenues with cross-selling and sales promotions.

- *Charging, billing, and settlement*: How to integrate proprietary or 3rd party billing systems.

Volantis Company History (1999–2005)
Founders

The four founders of Volantis—Jennifer Bursack, Martin Gaffney, Brett Nulf, and Mark Watson—met while they were working in the U.K. for Tivoli, a subsidiary of IBM. Each came from different backgrounds—Bursack, engineering and product management; Gaffney, sales; Nulf, consulting and business development; and Watson, development, sales, and management. (See Exhibit 6 for more information about the founders' backgrounds.) But each shared a passion for start-ups.

Tivoli had a very strong entrepreneurial culture and had launched a number of spin-outs and new ventures. Indeed, Tivoli itself was founded by two former IBM employees not far from IBM's offices in Austin, TX. The company developed system management software for enterprises including performance analysis, software distribution, and workload monitoring for Unix- and Windows-based systems from multiple

EXHIBIT 6

Background Information of Selected Executives

Founders

Jennifer Bursack: co-founder and Vice President, Product Management

Prior to Volantis, Jennifer joined a pre-IPO Tivoli in the Bay Area (CA) as an early member of the Professional Services Group. She moved from the U.S. to become one of Tivoli's first employees in Europe and was initially responsible for planning and implementing projects across various industry verticals.

Jennifer moved on to join the European Product Management group responsible for Tivoli's e-commerce products. Prior to Tivoli, Jennifer was a Lead Engineer in several Bay Area start-ups focusing on CAD (computer aided design) and publishing systems. Jennifer holds a Bachelor of Science in Computer Science from Syracuse University.

Martin Gaffney: co-founder and Vice President, Strategic Sales

Prior to Volantis, Martin was the second salesman in Europe to join Tivoli. He was responsible for securing GBP30M in business over 3.5 years across a variety of retail and financial enterprises.

Previously, Martin was the longest serving worldwide Sales Executive with 100 percent record of quota achievement at Sequent Computer Systems Limited where he was also the second UK salesman. Prior to that, Martin spent 7 years at Comshare where he undertook a variety of technical and sales roles.

Brett Nulf: co-founder and Vice President, Business Development

Prior to founding Volantis, Brett managed a European Business Consultancy team at Tivoli Systems. His team was responsible for developing financial business cases and implementation planning for strategic customers.

Previously, Brett was a Strategic Sales Consultant for the telecommunications industry leading substantial sales across the European Telecommunications sector. Before Tivoli, Brett was a Lead Engineer in EDS tasked with selling, qualifying, and executing client/server, middleware, and Internet consultancy projects for Global 1000 enterprises. Brett holds a Business degree from the University of Michigan School of Business Administration.

Mark Watson: co-founder and CTO

Mark Watson co-founded Volantis Systems and is responsible for developing and implementing the company's product direction. Prior to Volantis, Mark spent 15 years at IBM in a variety of positions, including development, sales and management roles in IBM Research, IBM's Development Laboratory at Hursley in the UK, IBM Global Network Services, IBM's AIX business and finally IBM's Tivoli subsidiary. Mark's focus was on advanced networking and open systems, including a spell working on behalf of IBM as part of an open systems development consortium at the British government's National Physical Laboratory in Teddington, UK.

Mark has been Volantis' CTO since the company's inception and in that role has led Volantis' product development, definition and architecture. As a member of Volantis' board, he has also been instrumental in fundraising and wider aspects of the company's development. Mark holds an Honours degree in Politics from the University of Nottingham, England.

Additional Management Team

Matt Harris: President and Chief Executive Officer

Prior to taking the CEO position at Volantis, Matt was President and CEO of Metrowerks Corporation, a 600+ person Austin-based provider of embedded software and related tools. Matt's prior experience includes roles as President, Metrowerks EMEA, President and CEO of Lineo, Inc., various other senior management positions, and five years as a systems engineer with EDS. Matt also practiced technology law for ten years, representing a variety of clients in matters ranging from securities litigation to licensing disputes and antitrust litigation.

Matt holds a BA in Finance from the University of Washington and a JD, magna cum laude, from the University of Michigan.

John Beale: VP Marketing

John has spent nearly twenty years developing marketing programs to support business development, product marketing and corporate communications strategies. In the past ten years, he has focused on the wireless industry, initially as a consultant based in Asia, and for the past five years as head of marketing for QUALCOMM's semiconductor division.

John has a BA in Economics from the University of Victoria, British Columbia.

(*continued*)

EXHIBIT 6   (continued)

Background Information of Selected Executives

Gareth Anderson: VP Finance

As Vice President Finance, Gareth has responsibility for all aspects of Finance, HR, Legal and Facilities. Prior to Volantis, Gareth served as VP International Business Planning at Gartner, where he implemented financial processes across EMEA and AP in coordination with American business units. Previously, Gareth spent several years at Sequent in a number of financial roles, culminating in the management of Finance and Operations for EMEA. Prior to this, he held various Commercial and Finance roles in the brewing operations of Grand Met and Courage.

Gareth holds a BA in Management Science from Trinity College Dublin. Member C.I.M.A.

Chris Smith: VP Telco

Chris is responsible for the Telco line of business at Volantis, including fixed line operators, mobile operators, MVNOs, MVNEs, ASPs and ISPs. He oversees Telco product strategy, partnerships strategy, market development, business development and the Telco PnL.

Prior to joining Volantis, Chris served as Senior Vice President of Operations at iXL (UK) Ltd. where he was responsible for delivery of eBusiness consulting solutions to a number of Fortune 500 clients. Prior to iXL, Chris performed the role of Vice President and Chief Technology Officer of Indus International, an Enterprise Asset Management solutions company headquartered in San Francisco, California. Prior to Indus, Chris was a Development Director at Oracle.

Chris holds an Honours degree in Mathematics from the University of Bristol.

Vivian Vendeirinho: VP Alliances & Business Development

Vivian Vendeirinho joined Volantis Systems from Metrowerks Inc. (Austin, TX) where he was responsible for Global Software and DevTool Sales. During his four years with Metrowerks, revenue increased nearly three-fold. Prior to Metrowerks, Vivian led Freescale Semiconductor's European 8/16-bit Embedded Microcontroller marketing team.

Vivian relocated from South Africa where he completed a Bachelor of Science Engineering degree at the University of Pretoria.

John Koyle: Director of Information Services

Before John joined Volantis, he served as the IT Director for RFP Depot where he was responsible for migrating their production systems from in-house to an off-site collocation. Before working at RFP Depot, John was the IS Manager at Lineo, Inc., where he set up and managed the company's IT infrastructure worldwide.

John has over ten years of experience in the IT systems industry, including Big Planet/Nuskin Enterprises, and Caldera, Inc. John holds a BS degree in Networking and Data Communications from Utah Valley State College, USA.

Phillip Swan: VP Worldwide Sales and Services

Phillip is responsible for Sales and Professional Services, overseeing the globally deployed sales force and the international customer deployments. He joins us from Dexterra—a technology company working on Java and Windows to deliver existing IT applications to a distributed workforce—where he was COO. His responsibilities included global Sales, Marketing, Professional Services and Business Development.

Before that he was Microsoft's VP of Device Solution Sales managing the OEM relationships for Windows Mobile, Windows Embedded and dedicated Server solutions. He has also held executive sales positions with Telogy Networks (now a Texas Instrument company) and Wind River Systems, starting his career as a software engineer.

Phillip graduated with a BSc in Mathematics and Computer Sciences from the University of Glasgow in 1984.

Source: Volantis.

---

vendors. Tivoli went public in 1995 and was acquired by IBM a year later for $743 million.[9]

While still working for Tivoli in late 1999, Bursack, Gaffney, Nulf, and Watson began meeting to discuss new venture concepts. They settled upon the idea of developing a yellow pages-like directory service for mobile phones for which they could sell placements

to local businesses. InfoSpace, a U.S.-based company, had already been operating a similar business, but had not yet entered the U.K. market. Watson said:

Brett had done sales in the telecommunications sector and was the one who got us thinking about mobile devices and technologies. During one of our brainstorming sessions, he put his mobile phone in the middle of the table and said, "This is our future. This is what we should build this company around."

We all agreed with him and decided to move forward with the Infospace-like model, even if no one was particularly blown away by our copycat idea. Simply put, we believed in ourselves and thought we could make a go of it. In Europe, there is a pattern that if you ride a certain technology wave you can get away with being a few months or even a few years behind the Americans. Oftentimes you will see that when American-based start-ups become successful, they will buy into European-based start-ups for market entry. Consequently, even though a U.K. start-up may appear a little behind on an emerging trend, they may still have a shot at a decent exit opportunity, particularly in technology businesses.

Fundraising

In March 2000, the group resigned from Tivoli, drafted a business plan, and began pitching their ideas to investors. The team also came up with a name, Volantis, which comes from the Latin root *volant*, meaning quick, nimble, or capable of flying. Watson said:

> The first group of investors we met with were angel investors. Even though we had an idea for a technology that to a certain extent we thought was going to be successful in the marketplace, we were mostly pitching ourselves and our desire to start a company.

On the one hand, investors seemed eager to fund Volantis' team. In fact, the group raised a small seed round from angels and friends and family to finance the company's early days. (See Exhibit 7 for a fundraising history of the company.) On the other hand, the founders and investors alike summarily rejected Volantis' initial founding concept in short order. Watson said:

> I'm not quite sure why we killed the original idea. Perhaps, it was because the market was moving and because everybody hated it. The good news was that we had struck upon a new idea: we were going to create technologies to enable companies to build web sites for all sorts of devices—smart phones, kiosks, digital televisions, gaming consoles, and, of course, mobile phones.
>
> The technology we had in mind would have to be flexible: we wanted to be able take any company's web presence and adapt it for any device. For example, we wanted to make nike.com accessible and user-friendly for mobile phone users. In total, we believed strongly in our value proposition: our customers would be able to develop one website which could then be accessed from any device anywhere.

Investors were more enthusiastic about Volantis' *enterprise* software idea because, for one, the founders had all come from an *enterprise* software company, Tivoli. In September 2000, Volantis closed a $3.2 million series A round of financing led by Kennet Venture Partners, a venture capital firm based in London. Shortly thereafter, the team began developing its product and even assembled a small salesforce. Watson said:

> In 2000, we hired four salespeople, and we put them all out in the field. All of them were experienced enterprise sales veterans from Sequent

EXHIBIT 7

Fundraising History

Series	Common	A	B	C	D	TOTAL
Date of Closing		Sep - 2000	May - 2001	Jul - 2002	Jul - 2005	
Lead		Kennet	Softbank	Accel	Accel, Kennet	
Other			Kennet	Kennet		
Funds Raised	$306,000	$3,213,000	$9,493,933	$11,107,326	$7,527,834	$31,648,092
Pre-Money Valuation		$6,747,297	$22,743,242	$28,000,183	$35,000,000	
Post-Money Valuation		$9,960,297	$32,237,175	$39,107,509	$42,527,834	

Note: All rounds of financing except Series D are converted from United Kingdom pounds (£1.00:$1.53).

Source: Volantis.

Computer Systems. I would argue that it was a relatively large sales team for what we had—which was not a lot—given that we didn't have a product yet. Nevertheless, we directed them to pitch prospective clients; and in return, we got a lot of customer feedback, if very little in sales volume.

In May 2001, Volantis raised an additional $9.5 million in venture capital, led by Softbank UK Ventures and including a follow-on investment from Kennet. Even though the organization had grown to over 50 employees, including a 10-person sales team, the company had yet to generate substantial revenues. Watson said:

> We had salespeople running off in a number of directions trying to find a market for our products. One of our first customers, Boots, was an online pharmacist that wanted to integrate a website into a television network it had recently acquired. Another early customer was iMPOWER, with whom we were working to make government services accessible through a wide variety of devices such as digital television, mobile phones, PCs, and kiosks at government offices. We had also engineered a prototype for Ford Motor Company and a satellite company. You might say we had cobbled together a small and fairly disparate customer base with a scattered collection of implementations. Nevertheless, revenues were weak and we were losing money.

By July 2001, the company employed over 80 people, including a sales office based in the U.S. Then, after the collapse of the Internet bubble and the tragic events of September 11th, the overall market for technology start-ups appeared bleak. As a result, Volantis was forced to re-evaluate its sales outreach and, in the end, decided to scale back the size of its organization in two rounds of layoffs. By October 2001, the company employed 49 people and had closed down its U.S.-based sales office.

However, during the first half of 2002, Volantis began to recover from the market slowdown and found some success closing sales leads again. Only this time around, revenues appeared to be flowing in from a single industry, telecommunications. Volantis landed two large accounts, Telefonica (a global mobile operator) and 3 (formerly known as Hutchinson 3G, 3 was the U.K.'s leading 3G carrier). In March 2002, Volantis was chosen as the delivery platform for Telefonica's mobile portal, which was being developed to include the mobile operator's messaging and mobile internet services (e.g., magazine, alerts, email, chat, commerce, downloads, games, and third-party applications and content). In May 2002, 3 enlisted Volantis to enable the delivery of data—including digital content from 3's information and entertainment content partners—to its mobile phone service subscribers in a deal worth $3 million to Volantis.

Volantis' success closing deals with mobile carriers represented a somewhat unexpected shift in focus for the company from a multi-device service to a single device service. Watson said:

> We were still pitching Volantis as middleware. However, we were no longer saying that we were middleware for enterprises to project their Internet presence to a variety of devices. We were saying that we were middleware as an enabler for mobile phone carriers. In particular, we were riding the momentum of 3G, which everyone thought was going to be wildly successful. Indeed, not long after the 3 and Telefonica transactions, we became pretty narrowly focused on landing more and more carrier accounts.

Additional Financing

In July 2002, Volantis raised an additional $11.1 million of venture capital in a series C financing led by Accel Partners Europe. The $28.0 million pre-money valuation Volantis received reflected the enthusiasm and excitement in the venture community around the anticipated platform shift in the mobile landscape from a voice-only industry to one where high speed data transmissions were possible. As with any major structural change in an industry, the mobile industry's shift to 3G was thought to create opportunities for all types of innovators, including Volantis, which seemed poised to be a technology leader for the next generation of mobile companies.

By 2003, however, it was clear that Volantis' founders and investors had mis-timed the market, and revenues for the year-ended 2003 fell below those generated in 2002. (See Exhibit 8 for company income statement.) But they were not alone. Some 200 venture funded companies that were launched to address market opportunities related to 3G had gone out of business, and Volantis was one of only a handful that endured. In 2004, business picked up again, and in 2005, revenues reached $14.4 million.

Matt Harris

In April 2005, Matt Harris was named CEO of Volantis. His experience included leadership roles in

EXHIBIT 8

Volantis Income Statement, 2001–2005

	2005	2004	2003	2002	2001
Revenues	14,397,768	6,891,337	2,924,500	6,225,856	411,440
Cost of sales	(5,791,202)	(3,264,136)	(1,710,806)	(1,700,639)	(952,587)
Gross profit	8,606,566	3,627,201	1,213,693	4,525,217	(541,147)
Selling & administrative expenses	(13,635,903)	(8,880,793)	(8,817,900)	(7,633,190)	(7,917,039)
Operating loss	(5,029,337)	(5,253,592)	(7,604,207)	(3,107,973)	(8,458,186)
Other interest receivable and similar income	57,904	76,229	297,089	189,044	264,690
Interest payable and similar charges	(6,010)	(4,759)	(2,682)	(1,308)	(378)
Loss on ordinary activities before taxation	(4,977,443)	(5,182,122)	(7,309,800)	(2,920,238)	(8,193,874)
Taxation	547,089	464,635	1,085,130		
Loss on ordinary activities after taxation	(4,430,354)	(4,717,488)	(6,224,670)	(2,920,238)	(8,193,874)
Preferred share appropriation	(1,322,675)	(1,220,340)	(1,125,922)	(450,380)	
Retained loss for the year	(5,753,029)	(5,937,828)	(7,350,592)	(3,370,618)	
Exchange Rate (converted from U.K. pounds)	1.80	1.80	1.80	1.53	1.53

All figures in U.S. $ converted from U.K. pounds.

business and law. (See Exhibit 6 for his executive biography.) He had been President and CEO of two software companies and also had been a practicing attorney and founding partner of the Summit Law Group.

In July 2005, Volantis raised an additional $7.5 million, for a total of $31.6 million venture capital raised. Early or not, Volantis had its financing in place and was ready for mass adoption of mobile data services. Watson said:

> We learned that the infrastructure we had built initially for websites to be accessed by all types of devices was actually very useful for the mobile device environment where standards were scarce. Our business—which we call "intelligent content adaptation"—thrives in mobile because of its device diversity, network diversity, and general lack of standards.
>
> Our platform turned out to be flexible and very capable. We have five generations of phones

in our database today. Apart from getting a sense of vindication, we actually were able to adapt to the market as it moved because it was catching up with us rather than vice versa.

Volantis Company Overview (2006)

Products

In 2006, Volantis' products consisted of two principal components: its mobile content framework and its suite of mobile content applications. (See Exhibit 9 for a diagram of Volantis' products.) The mobile content framework provided the back-end (i.e., infrastructure) technology that drove the front-end (i.e., customer-facing) applications, which included (among others):

● **Volantis Mobile Content Storefront™:** an application that enabled wireless carriers and content providers to have a mobile storefront or commerce engine.

EXHIBIT 9

Diagram of Volantis' Products

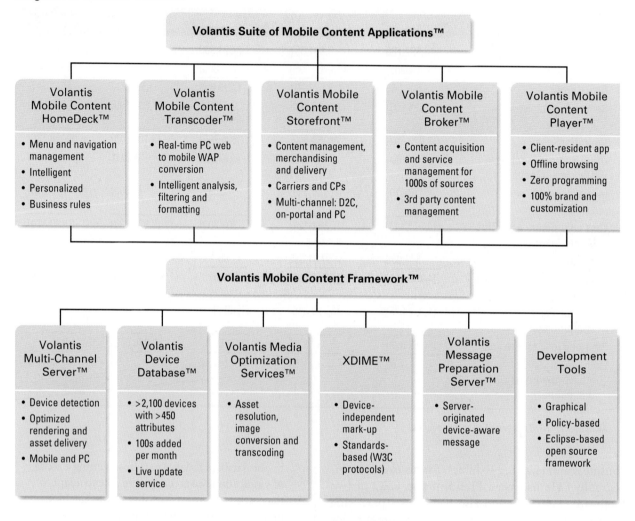

- **Volantis Mobile Content Transcoder™:** an application that converted PC websites in real-time into mobile format.

- **Volantis Mobile Content Player™:** an on-device application that provided playback of downloaded content.

Customers

In 2006, Volantis reached over 100 million consumers on over 2,100 different mobile devices, serving primarily two types of customers: wireless carriers and content providers. In 2005, its roster of 21 wireless carrier customers—which included major players like Vodaphone and T-Mobile—had accounted for over 90 percent of its revenues. (See Exhibit 10 for a list of carrier customers.) Volantis' collection of over a dozen content provider customers—which included Yahoo!, ebay.co.uk, lastminute.com, and Reuters—accounted for most of the remainder of the company's sales.

Organization Overview

In March 2006, Volantis employed over 130 people in five offices around the world. The company's corporate headquarters and U.S. regional sales office were in Seattle, WA; its European regional sales office and engineering staff were located in London; it also ran a development office in Krakow, Poland, and Asia Pacific regional sales offices in India and Hong Kong.

EXHIBIT 10

Volantis Wireless Carrier Customer List (as of March 2006)

Operator	% of Company Revenues	Revenue/Subscriber
Customer #1	24.7%	$ 0.37
Customer #2	21.6%	$ 0.06
Customer #3	8.2%	$ 0.03
Customer #4	8.0%	$ 0.06
Customer #5	5.9%	$ 0.04
Customer #6	5.5%	$ 0.02
Customer #7	5.0%	$ 0.01
Customer #8	3.8%	$ 0.02
Customer #9	3.4%	$ 0.20
Customer #10	3.3%	$ 0.37
Customer #11	3.2%	$ 0.06
Customer #12	2.9%	$ 0.08
Customer #13	1.9%	$ 0.01
Customer #14	1.2%	$ 0.06
Customer #15	0.7%	$ 0.08
Customer #16	0.7%	$ 0.13
Customer #17	0.1%	$ 0.00
Customer #18	0.0%	$ –
Customer #19	0.0%	$ –
Customer #20	0.0%	$ –
Customer #21	0.0%	$ –
Total	**100.0%**	**$ 0.04**

Volantis was organized in a matrix structure. (See Exhibit 11 for an organization chart.) Three of the four founders (Bursack, Gaffney, and Nulf) had settled into senior operating positions, and Watson had become CTO and a board member. Additionally, the company had hired (or was hiring) a number of other senior executives to cover each of the key functional areas (marketing, finance, alliances, and worldwide sales) and business units (telecommunications, content providers (open), and new markets (open)). In total, there were nine members on the company's internal executive board.

Technology Development

Watson managed the product development, product management, engineering, research and development, and managed services functions for Volantis, supporting all of the business units (carriers, content providers, and new markets). With 82 employees, the technology organization was by far the largest in the company. With the exception of the group of engineers based in Poland (a cost-saving measure), most technology employees were based in London. Watson said:

We have a layered architecture, whereby each layer has its own set of characteristics and is developed separately. Therefore, our development teams are organized by layer, one group per layer, where each one knows the principles along which that layer must work. By working in accordance with those principles, our developers know that their layer will work with the other layers in a well organized way.

Our philosophy of development builds a lot of automation into the system, where one dial controls

EXHIBIT 11

Organization Chart (as of March 2006)

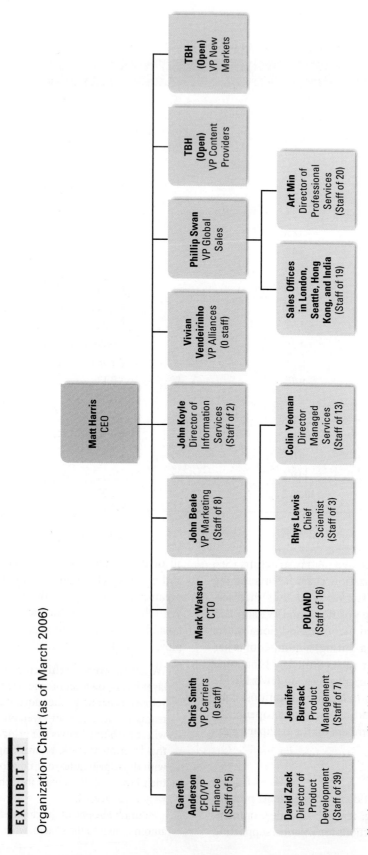

Note: In some cases, staff totals include personnel to be hired.

a bunch of other dials that controls a bunch of other dials. In other words, fine-tuning on one dial can cause a lot of different things to happen. Consequently, we have an extremely powerful system in which one person can build a site that will automatically adapt to the thousands of mobile devices and still adhere to site's design intention.

The database stored over 500 attributes on over 2,500 devices, and more were added each week. Bursack said:

> We're adding at least 30 devices a week. We do that via a combination of testing the physical devices if we have them and then researching on the Internet for additional information. If we don't have the physical device, we try to find a device that we've already tested and make a best guess decision on which attributes apply. We've got three people working full-time to add new devices to our database, and we're looking to extend that by at least two more people as soon as we can find them. As we extend our business into more service offerings and as we extend into more regions, we end up having to play catch-up to keep pace with the new device launches.
>
> We collect over 500 attributes per device and that number will grow because we are increasingly getting our information from our customers. As a result, it's actually a lot easier for us to add data than it used to be. All in all, I'd say we're fairly efficient doing our device research.

Carriers Business Unit

Chris Smith was VP/GM of carriers business unit, and he had no direct reports. He set the strategic direction for the business and was supported by each of the key functions (e.g., sales, marketing, and technology). Smith maintained an especially close relationship with the sales organization because it was responsible for sourcing and closing deals with the carriers.

In early 2006, Volantis' sales organization was run by Phillip Swan, VP of global sales, and included 39 additional personnel (when fully staffed). The company's U.S. and Latin America regional sales office based in Seattle, WA included five sales personnel and five technical support staff when fully staffed; its European regional sales office based in London included five sales personnel and six technical support staff when fully staffed; its Asia Pacific regional sales office in India included one sales account executive, and its Hong Kong office included one sales account executive and two technical support staff.

Volantis employed a traditional software sales model with most of its carrier customers like Huntington 3G: it sold licenses for the Volantis software, plus professional services for integration, plus support. In 2005, revenues were distributed as follows: 60 percent for software license fees, 25 percent for professional services, and 15 percent for support. Swan said:

> Our ability to grow as a business relies on a couple of key factors. First, we must have every sales person, every region operating efficiently, which is a function of hiring the right people. Second, we must ensure that we have a core discipline, not processes for the sake of bureaucracy. We need discipline in how we forecast our business and in how we qualify opportunities. But make no mistake, this is all about execution. The mode We're in right now is execute, execute, execute, and if we don't execute, we will fail, and somebody else will come and take the place.

Indeed, the carrier business was the revenue engine for the company, and Volantis needed to rapidly accelerate its top-line growth to achieve profitability. The biggest opportunity, and the biggest challenge, facing both Smith and Swan was the Asia Pacific market, in China, Korea, India, and Japan more specifically. Even though Volantis had two small sales offices in Asia Pacific, it had yet to secure a meaningful revenue stream out of the region.

There were several challenges Volantis would have to overcome to penetrate the Asia Pacific market. First, sales cycles with the carriers were always long, and even more so in Asia where Volantis would be a newcomer. Swan said:

> The trouble with middleware is that it is middleware. Your sales process and time to revenue is elongated by the fact that, by the time that your customers deploy your product, you're part of a larger system or implementation. For the most part, your opportunity to generate revenue is rarely in the near term. Sales cycles with telcos can be as short as like six to nine months or as long as 36 months. There's no such thing as turning a telco in 30 or 60 days to make a decision. These are large bureaucracies that are very cognizant of their brand, and with middleware, especially, they want to be able to control their brand.

Second, insofar as Volantis had been ahead of the market elsewhere, it was a laggard in Asia and had formidable competition. In addition, the infrastructure it had built out in Europe (including relationships with systems integrators and consultants) would take time to establish in Asia. Third, the size of the carrier customer had not historically correlated with the size of the revenue return to Volantis. (See Exhibit 10 for revenue per subscriber statistics.) Finally, entering the market required some additional fixed and variable investments beyond that of simply adding sales personnel on the ground. The Volantis solution would have to be modified to accommodate local requirements. Nevertheless, it was an enticing opportunity, and Smith and Swan would have to develop a market entry strategy.

Content Provider Business Unit

In early 2006, content providers of all kinds—media and entertainment companies, government and financial services companies, and online businesses—were developing strategies for adapting their content for mobile platforms. Companies were looking for solutions to ensure that their mobile experience approached the quality of their PC-based offering. In fact, Volantis had a deep backlog of leads from companies that had inquired about its services. Harris said:

> We heard from a number of content providers that they needed to get into the mobile space because they had learned from the Internet boom that everyone else was going do it eventually. Most of them told us that they didn't want to be left behind because with close to two billion people on mobile phones, everyone knows there will be opportunities in wireless.

For such customers, Volantis provided a suite of tools that enabled existing content sources such as websites, content management systems, and internal XML formats to be repurposed and optimized for delivery to mobile handsets. One such tool, the Volantis Mobile Content Transcoder, converted PC webpages into mobile format, with presentation optimized for each device. The tool was used to convert over 85 percent of Yahoo's 3,000 most commonly searched websites. In addition, Volantis' service had converted cnn.com and discoverychannel.com for easy access by mobile devices.

On the one hand, these accounts brought credibility and marketing value to Volantis. On the other hand, the larger the brand, the more competition there was for the business and the higher the cost of customer acquisition. Further, these accounts were not generating a ton of revenue because, for one, Volantis was struggling to craft a compelling business model for that segment. Harris said:

> Clearly, there is value to a start-up in doing business with some of the most well-known brands in the world that goes beyond the revenues they generate. Sure it's been a low margin business for us and there's lots of competition. But eBay, Disney, and Discovery Channel are accounts that have an emotional attachment to them. If this were a pure economic discussion, it would be a lot easier to figure out.

Volantis employed a three-part sales model with most of its content provider clients. Harris said:

> Trying to find the right business model in a concept market has probably been more painful than trying to find the right technology solution. Our fees to our content provider customers consist of three parts: 1) a managed service fee, 2) a software rental fee, and 3) a revenue share. Our model is still evolving, but at scale, it can be very profitable for us.

Meanwhile, Volantis had uncovered a new potential business opportunity.

Self-Provisioned Internet Service

As early as 2003, when content providers had begun to come out of the recession and were investigating the mobile opportunity, Volantis executives were discussing the idea of a self-provisioned Internet service. The central premise was that the company's technology for adapting websites to mobile could be directed at the billions of websites that needed a mobile presence through a self-serve model. Small businesses, content owners, and web developers could come to Volantis' website and download its application to adapt their offering for mobile. Watson said:

> We have a product that we sold to Yahoo! which is a "transcoding" product, and it basically goes to PC sites and converts them through our rendering system to work on phones, taking full advantage of our underlying technology engines. We think we have the basis of a tool that would allow any mom and pop Internet site, any blogger, any type of content owner, and—with our storefront tool—any e-commerce site, to get up and running as a mobile site within 15 minutes.

The business model for such a product is a little less clear. There is a general view that if you can kick-start the mobile Internet with sufficient content then it will become compelling, and it will start to generate its own monetization models in the same way that the Internet has. Accordingly, the default business models we're looking at are: free entry for any company to create a site and then an Internet Service Provider-type business model for additional features. For example, we might charge for additional bandwidth.

Naturally, Volantis' management was attracted to the scale of the opportunity. However, without a clear business model, Harris was concerned that Volantis would repeat its past mistakes and get trapped selling the wrong package of services. On the one hand, Volantis' investors had proven that they were patient: Kennet, for example, had invested in the series A, B, C, and D rounds. On the other hand, the company was burning cash at a rate of over $400,000 every month. Harris said:

> There is no question that the self-provisioned Internet service is a huge opportunity. I just don't know how we can support both the new business and our traditional software licensing model in the same company, or even if we should do it at all? Perhaps, we should sell the opportunity to another company? If we do build it in-house, however, I am not sure how we should organize the company because the traditional side of the business—in development and in sales—won't adapt to the self-provisioned Internet model.

Watson added:

> Once again, we have found ourselves at the immature end of an immature market. To a certain extent, we would like to be able to build a detailed go-to-market strategy, set a budget, hire the appropriate resources, and get off to the races. On the other hand, it has been my experience that you can't over-plan these things. You have to basically address it with a degree of Internet instinct. The main thing you have to plan, I think, is agility.

Allocating Resources

The widespread adoption of mobile data services would certainly be a catalyst for Volantis' business, and there was no shortage of opportunities for the company to explore. The challenge for Harris was to select which markets to pursue and how to appropriately allocate and organize his resources. In a perfect world, he would love to invest in each of Volantis' compelling business opportunities. However, the board was eager to see Harris make inroads towards profitability in 2006. Consequently, he had a number of key decisions to make.

First, he needed to decide whether or not to fill two senior management positions. His 2006 organization plan had openings for VPs to run his new markets and content provider business units. The new markets VP would be enlisted to assess the market potential of: 1) selling to enterprises (i.e., would, say, McKinsey be interested in adapting its internal web content for its consultants to access from a mobile device?); 2) adapting video content for mobile, and 3) selling to new geographies. The content provider VP would be enlisted to: 1) refine the company's business model to ensure Volantis could extract enough financial value out of its roster of big brand name accounts; 2) determine how to proceed with its backlog of leads, and 3) craft a target list of strategic leads to Swan.

Second, he needed to decide whether or not to enter the Asia Pacific market. If so, he needed to determine how he and Swan should work to reallocate resources to capitalize on the opportunity. Finally, he needed to give Watson a go or no-go decision on the self-provisioned Internet business. If his decision was "go," then Watson would need to develop a new organization plan for his technology division and a new product roadmap to support the new service offering. All in all, for Volantis and its intelligent content adaptation service, widespread adoption of mobile data services could not happen fast enough.

ENDNOTES

1. The terms "mobile" and "wireless" are used interchangeably herein and mean the same thing. Similarly, the terms "operator," "carrier," and "telco" are also used interchangeably.
2. "The 2006 Telecommunications Industry Review," *Insight Research Corporation*, January 2006.
3. Nelson Wang, "Industry Surveys, Telecommunications: Wireless Asia," *Standard & Poor's*, January 2006.
4. Nelson Wang, "Industry Surveys, Telecommunications: Wireless Latin America," *Standard & Poor's*, November 2005.
5. Nelson Wang, "Industry Surveys, Telecommunications: Wireless Asia," *Standard & Poor's*, January 2006.
6. Kenneth Leon and Nelson Wang, "Industry Surveys, Telecommunications: Wireless," *Standard & Poor's*, November 3, 2005.
7. "3G Worldwide Subscribers," *eMarketer*, February 2006.
8. Nelson Wang, "Industry Surveys, Telecommunications: Wireless Europe," *Standard & Poor's*, January 2006.
9. Jim Duffy and Michael Cooney, "IBM Drops $743M on Management Makeover," *Network World*, February 5, 1996.

Infosys Consulting in 2006: Leading the Next Generation of Business and Information Technology Consulting

---

This case was prepared by Aneesha Capur under the supervision of Professor Robert A. Burgelman, Stanford Graduate School of Business.

There is no doubt in my mind that five years from now, the Infosys Consulting model will be the standard way of doing things where technology development is done off-site. We are one of the fastest growing IT consulting firms in the world. Our major bottlenecks right now are convincing clients to break with old habits and take a chance on a new, better model and recruiting the right people—top tier talent who understand our innovative approach and fit into our unique culture.

—*Steve Pratt, CEO, Infosys Consulting*

In January 2006, the five managing partners of Infosys Consulting (ICI), also known to the leadership of ICI's parent company Infosys Technologies as "the dream team," congregated at the St. Regis resort in Orange County, California for their first team meeting of the year. CEO and managing director Steve Pratt, COO and managing director Paul Cole, managing director Romil Bahl, managing director and founder Raj Joshi, and managing director Ming Tsai (see Exhibit 1 for management bios) were all proud of how much the company had achieved since its inception in April 2004 as a wholly owned U.S. subsidiary of Infosys Technologies. The firm had more than 100 consulting engagements and had grown from its inception in April 2004 to over 200 employees in January 2006, achieving its two year recruiting target. It was also on plan for both its own revenue target and its target contribution to Infosys Technologies' revenue through the third quarter of its second year of existence. Moreover, ICI's managing partners were confident that the subsidiary had contributed to Infosys Technologies' ranking in *Wired* magazine's Top Ten Company list in May 2005

and high ratings from analysts in 2004 and 2005 (see Exhibit 2).

However, the five managing partners saw several challenges ahead for ICI. Driven by Infosys Technologies' COO Kris Gopalakrishnan's edict to "compete with the best," the team aspired to be ranked alongside IBM and Accenture, leaders in the business and information technology consulting industry (see Exhibit 3 for company rankings). They also faced internal challenges of leveraging Infosys Technologies, interfacing productively with the parent company and managing growth as they built the organization. In addition, each managing partner was committed to "changing the rules of the game within the consulting industry" in the founding partner Raj Joshi's words. By applying Infosys Technologies' approach to global delivery, the leadership team at ICI believed the firm had created a unique model in business and information technology consulting that shortened the lifecycle from business consulting to technology implementation, reduced the costs of a typical client engagement and delivered measurable benefits to clients.

Flashback to April 2004: The Inception of Infosys Consulting

The evolution of global Information Technology (IT) service companies in India began in the 1990s with the procurement of application development

EXHIBIT 1

Executive Bios of ICI Managing Partners

Steve Pratt, Chief Executive Officer and Managing Director

With over 20 years of experience in business consulting, Pratt had an established track record of growing innovative consulting practices that excelled at client service. Prior to joining Infosys Consulting, Pratt was a partner with Deloitte Consulting and co-founder of the Deloitte CRM practice.

As a founder, CEO and managing director of Infosys Consulting, Pratt fundamentally transformed the consulting industry. He created a new brand of consulting firm—one that takes innovative approaches to delivering more competitive operations, with less risk, at an overall lower cost for its clients.

Pratt was nominated as one of the Top 25 Consultants in the World in 2003 and 2005 in *Consulting Magazine* and has helped several Fortune 500 companies.

His primary areas of expertise included helping clients improve the value of their relationships with customers, and helping them become more competitive. In a survey of Siebel systems customers, clients consistently rated Pratt as #1 in Customer Satisfaction.

As co-founder (with Bo Manning, now CEO of Pivotal Software) of the Deloitte CRM practice, from 1995 to 2002, Pratt grew the practice to over 3,000 people and over $750M in revenue.

Pratt was frequently published on the topics of Customer Strategy, CRM and Web-based Sales and Service. He received Bachelors and Masters Degrees in Electrical Engineering.

Paul Cole, Chief Operating Officer and Managing Director

As a founder and managing director of Infosys Consulting, Cole was responsible for all sales and operations. With over 25 years of experience in consulting and Information Technology, Cole provided IT consulting services to some of the world's largest companies.

Cole had extensive experience in customer relationship management and was the global leader for the DRM service line at Cap Gemini Ernst & Young. He was responsible for a $1B CRM practice at Cap Gemini and is a noted industry expert in the field. He also managed the mobilization and implementation of a three year company-wide transformation effort, which accomplished significant operating performance improvements. He was also a vice president with Mercer Management Consulting.

Throughout his career in IT consulting, Cole served global Fortune 500 clients across several industries. He has managed major consulting engagements for clients such as Lloyds TSB, Hewlett-Packard, Scottish Enterprises, SBC Communications, Walt Disney World, IBM, Texas Instruments, and GTE.

Cole received a Bachelor of Science in Marketing-Management from Bentley College

Romil Bahl, Managing Director

With more than 15 years experience helping clients with business/e-business strategies, strategic technology direction and large-scale technology-enabled transformations, Bahl led the Industry Practices and Service Offering portfolio for the firm. Specifically, Bahl led the firm's Business/IT Strategy areas including Business Alignment, Next Generation IT and Portfolio Assessment using the firm's Competitive Advantage framework.

Bahl spent over eight years at A.T.Kearney/EDS, with his last role as the leader of EDS' 6,000 person Consulting Services unit. He specialized in strategic planning, new business incubation and launch.

In addition to his EDS Consulting Services experience, Bahl's previous roles included leader of A.T. Kearney's European Strategic Technology and Transformation Practice, based in London. Prior to that he worked with Deloitte Consulting and led the Southwest region's Strategic Information Systems Planning team.

Bahl received an MBA with a specialization in Information Systems Management from the University of Texas at Austin and a Bachelor of Engineering from DMET, India.

Raj Joshi, Managing Director

As a founder and managing director of Infosys Consulting, Joshi had responsibility for developing and building the Enterprise Solutions and IT Strategy practices of the company. He was also architect of the firm's Value Realization Model—a new approach that guides technology-enabled business transformation engagements while delivering measurable business value.

(*continued*)

EXHIBIT 1   (*continued*)

Executive Bios of ICI Managing Partners

Joshi had extensive experience in Information Technology consulting services and has delivered client engagements that have spanned the entire systems development life cycle. Joshi managed projects in IT strategy, business transformation, ERP implementations, custom applications development, ADM outsourcing and offshore development and maintenance.

Joshi also delivered projects that included aspects of business strategy, business process reengineering, change management and organizational design along-with IT elements.

Prior to joining Infosys Consulting, Joshi was a partner with the U.S. practice of Deloitte Consulting where he held a number of leadership positions. He founded Deloitte Offshore in India and was the CEO of this entity for more than three years. He played a key role in structuring and managing client relationships that leveraged the offshore delivery model. Some of his other roles included managing global alliances and leading the IT practice for one of Deloitte's geographical regions.

Throughout his career in IT consulting, Joshi served global Fortune 500 clients across several industries. He managed major consulting engagements for clients such as AT&T, Agilent, Alcatel, BP, DHL, Fujitsu, General Motors, Hewlett-Packard, Honeywell, NEC, Nokia, Sun, Texas Instruments and Toshiba.

Joshi received an MBA from the University of Texas at Arlington and also received Masters and Bachelors degrees in Chemical Engineering.

Ming Tsai, Managing Director

With more than 21 years of management consulting experience, Tsai had overall responsibility for a number of industry groups at Infosys, including Retail and Consumer Products, High Technology and Discrete Manufacturing and Aerospace and Automotive. He also had overall responsibility for the professional development of employees.

Tsai focused on business strategy development, business transformation and process re-engineering, customer relationship and loyalty management, and e-commerce. His clients included Wal-Mart, Target, CVS, Royal Ahold, Walgreens, Sears, Boots, Metro, PepsiCo, Kraft Foods, Miller Brewing, Coca-Cola, P&G, American Express, AT&T, McGraw-Hill, Microsoft and Xerox.

Prior to Infosys, Tsai was with IBM Business Consulting Services where he held several leadership positions, including the Global Leader of the Retail Industry, where he had overall responsibility for driving IBM's retail business. Prior to that role, Tsai was the strategy consulting leader for the Distribution Sector (CPG, Retail and Travel & Transportation), where he had cross-industry responsibility for IBM's strategy consulting practice. Tsai joined IBM when it acquired Mainspring, an e-business strategy consulting firm in June of 2001.

Prior to joining Mainspring, Tsai was a partner at Ernst & Young where he was a co-leader of the eCommerce Strategy practice in North America. Earlier, Tsai was a senior manager with The Boston Consulting Group and a senior consultant with Arthur Andersen & Co.'s Management Information Consulting Division (which later became Accenture).

Tsai received an MBA with honors from Columbia Business School where he was elected to the Beta Gamma Sigma National Honor Society and awarded the Benjamin E. Hermann prize for Marketing Excellence. He also received a Bachelor of Science in Mechanical Engineering from Yale University.

Source: Infosys Consulting.

and maintenance services by American companies. Business Process Outsourcing (BPO) work in India was largely conducted by captive units, for example, companies like General Electric would perform BPO through subsidiaries in India rather than work with third party companies like Infosys Technologies. From 1993 through 1999, as U.S. firms gained confidence in working with Indian companies and wanted to leverage the benefits of offshoring services by taking advantage of high quality services at lower price points, Indian companies like Infosys Technologies started expanding their footprint by adding service lines.

One of Infosys Technologies' main objectives was to increase revenue through repeat business with the company's client base. To that end, Infosys Technologies offered clients new opportunities to work with the company. Infosys Technologies expanded its service offering to include package implementation (e.g., SAP's enterprise resource planning software), R&D,

EXHIBIT 2

Company Ranking and Analyst Commentary

The Wired 40—

"They're masters of technology and innovation. They're global thinkers driven by strategic vision. They're nimbler than Martha Stewart's PR team. They're The Wired 40."

Wired magazine, May 2005

1. Apple Computer
2. Google
3. Samsung Electronics
4. Amazon.com
5. Yahoo!

6. Electronic Arts
7. Genentech
8. Toyota
9. **Infosys Technologies**
10. eBay

"Infosys Leads the Pack"

Forrester Research, December 2005

- Infosys is most able to compete with both the former Big Five firms for business process consulting work and the tier-one Indian vendors for follow-on technical work. Prior to the formation of Infosys Consulting, Infosys, like other tier-one vendors, had strong technical consulting capabilities managed through horizontal or vertical groups. . . . Infosys Consulting represents Infosys' renewed commitment to business process consulting capability in its effort to be taken seriously as a global consulting and IT services firm.

"India Shows the Way to Next-Generation Consulting"

AMR—Lance Travis & Dana Stiffler, April 8, 2004

- The traditional consulting model is dead. The next-generation consulting model combines global delivery that capitalizes on low-cost resources with high-quality strategic consulting.
- Business consulting linked to Infosys' existing low-cost, process-centric delivery expertise offers companies a new, high-value type of strategic consulting partner.

"Infosys Looks to Local Talent for U.S. Consulting Business"

Gartner—Fran Karamouzis, April 13, 2004

- First Take: The creation of a U.S.-based consulting company is a major step forward in Infosys' long-term strategy of presenting itself as a global service provider. Infosys' $20 million investment in this subsidiary is designed to send a clear signal to the marketplace that Infosys is differentiating itself from its Indian competitors, and intends to compete for business consulting services with the traditional consultancies.
- Gartner believes many more offshore IT service providers will follow Infosys' lead. By the end of 2004, a number of offshore firms will seek to emulate the strategy of delivering a domestic consulting offering within the U.S. enterprise market (0.7 probability).

Source: Information compiled from Infosys Consulting.

---

infrastructure management, system integration, testing as a service, and BPO. As the company's menu of services expanded, its client relationships became more complex. Infosys Technologies started working with the business side of client organizations as well as the IT side in order to manage these complex organizations. Infosys Technologies saw the opportunity to enter a client relationship earlier in the lifecycle to define problems, identify solutions and then implement a solution as a natural evolution of their service

offering. In 1999, Infosys Technologies, which then had approximately 3,700 employees and annual revenue of approximately $120 million, decided to initiate an in-house consulting business unit. However, the company's success in consulting was constrained due to its limited brand equity, investment allocation and recruiting abilities.

Raj Joshi, who drove Deloitte Consulting's recruiting in India in the late 1990s and then became the founder and CEO of Deloitte's Offshore Technology

EXHIBIT 3

Largest Computer and Internet Consulting Companies (rank based on sales; in thousands of U.S. dollars)

Rank	Company	2005 Sales (000s)	2004 Sales (000s)
1	INTERNATIONAL BUSINESS MACHINES (IBM)	$91,134,000[1]	$96,503,000
2	ELECTRONIC DATA SYSTEMS CORP (EDS)	$19,757,000[2]	$19,863,000
3	ACCENTURE	$17,094,400	$15,113,582
4	COMPUTER SCIENCES CORPORATION (CSC)	$14,058,600[3]	$14,767,600
5	CAPGEMINI	$8,305,300	$8,128,161
6	SCIENCE APPLICATIONS INTERNATIONAL CORP (SAIC)	$7,187,000	$6,720,000
7	ATOS ORIGIN SA	$6,519,790	$6,332,280
8	UNISYS CORP	$5,758,700	$5,820,700
9	AFFILIATED COMPUTER SERVICES INC	$4,351,159	$4,106,393
10	CGI GROUP INC	$3,173,600	$2,574,500
11	WIPRO LTD	$1,863,000	$1,349,800
13	**INFOSYS TECHNOLOGIES LTD**	**$1,592,000**	**$1,062,600**
NA	TATA CONSULTANCY SERVICES	NA	$1,614,000

[1] 2005 Sales from IBM's Global Services business segment were $47.4 billion.

[2] 2005 Sales from EDS' BPO services were $2.8 billion. During 2005, EDS approved a plan to sell 100 percent of its ownership interest in its A.T. Kearney management consulting business. That subsidiary, the sale of which was completed on January 20, 2006, is classified as "held for sale" in December 2005 and 2004 and its results for the years ended December 31, 2005, 2004 and 2003 are included in income (loss) from discontinued operations.

[3] 2005 Sales from CSC's IT & Professional Services business segment were $7.0 billion.

Note: Per the footnotes referenced above, with the exception of IBM and Accenture, the highest ranked companies derive sales from IT implementation services rather than Business and Information Technology consulting.

Source: Total Sales data from Plunkett Research Ltd. www.plunkettresearch.com; Segment Sales data from company annual reports.

Group in India in 2001, approached Kris Gopalakrishnan, the COO of Infosys Technologies, a few times (from 1997 to 2001) to initiate an alliance between the two firms. As Gopalakrishnan explained, a long-term partnership was not something Infosys Technologies was willing to consider:

Our belief was that if we subcontracted to somebody else then the Infosys brand would get diluted. Consulting drives downstream work and our objective was to have control of the client account, and so a partnership was really not something we were looking for. We have always believed that joint ventures have very limited life or limited validity when you start competing with one of the partners, as there is an overlap of business with one of the partners, or the long-term objectives of either one of those partners is in conflict with objectives of the joint venture. So, there could have been opportunities for partnering on a project-by-project basis, but there was no way we could see a long-term partnership opportunity with any company because Infosys wanted to be in that space ultimately, and so it would have been in conflict with the long-term objectives of the company.

Raj Joshi started working with Steve Pratt, who had grown Deloitte's Customer Relationship Management practice from scratch to $750 million, to leverage the offshore model at Deloitte Consulting in 2003. The two had often discussed the concept of a new consulting model and considered Infosys Technologies a great potential partner.

By 2004, Infosys Technologies was a billion dollar company with an employee base of 25,000 and had established stronger brand equity. The firm decided to further develop its consulting practice. As the CEO of Infosys Technologies, Nandan Nilekani, explained:

> We believed that the IT services space was going through disruptive change and saw a new way of delivery by applying our Global Delivery Model into this space. We had a vision to create the next generation IT services company by combining our great reputation for business execution with consulting services.

Infosys Technologies' options for investing in its consulting offering included making an acquisition and organically growing the business. Since Infosys Technologies wanted to establish a new model in the consulting space, the firm decided against an acquisition. The company also realized from past experience that organically growing the business would limit its ability to attract the right kind of talent for consulting. Infosys Technologies decided to create a hybrid model by setting up a U.S.-based, wholly owned subsidiary.

Both Joshi and Pratt were interested in Infosys Technologies' idea to start a U.S.-based subsidiary, and recruited a team to lead the consulting subsidiary. With the leadership team in place in April 2004,[1] the firm set out to build the consulting organization. The five partners had not been given a business plan; they were only asked what they could achieve with a new consulting business. They set themselves aggressive targets. One was to reach 500 consultants in three years. Infosys Technologies invested $20 million in the consulting subsidiary.

2006: Overview of the Information Technology (IT) Services Industry

The market for IT services was large and growing. IDC, a provider of market intelligence for the IT industry, anticipated that overall spending on worldwide IT services would grow at a 7 percent compound annual rate through 2009, reaching $803.9 billion, from $524 billion in 2003. Forrester Research Inc., a technology research firm, projected IT consulting growing 5 percent compounded annually over the next five years. Apart from the two largest players—IBM and Accenture—who still had a relatively small share of the industry, the market for business and IT consulting was fragmented.

As the concept of global delivery achieved success, firms looked to third-party vendors to provide end-to-end services from business consulting to applications development and implementation, infrastructure management and BPO, using this model. Two different approaches to leveraging global delivery emerged in the marketplace: onshore U.S.-based firms such as IBM and Accenture leveraged offshore centers for development and implementation aspects of the value chain while offshore firms in India including Tata Consultancy Services (TCS) and Wipro Technologies (Wipro)—in addition to Infosys Technologies—started offering higher-end consulting services.

TCS, Infosys Technologies and Wipro generated combined service revenues of $4.5 billion in 2004, up 47 percent from 2003.[2] Their market share, however, remained small: a combined 0.8 percent of the total worldwide services market. If growth for these players continued at 20 percent to 30 percent annually, their combined market share could increase to 1.7 percent in five years.[3]

Competition from Indian companies caused Accenture to increase the size of its work force in India from less than 5,000 in 2003 to more than 11,000 in 2004. In 2006, Accenture had 18,000 workers in India and planned to reach 34,000 in a few years. IBM also added 6,000 employees to its Indian workforce through its April 2004 acquisition of Daksh eServices, a BPO firm and call center vendor, and launched a new Global Business Solution Center in Bangalore, India, in 2006 which expanded its presence there to over 38,500 employees.

As more global IT services companies built up a presence in India, prices and wages increased. At the end of 2004, Infosys Technologies and Wipro raised the wages of their midlevel workers between 15 percent and 20 percent to combat the threat of attrition (which remained between 10 percent and 15 percent). Indian firms also introduced stock-based compensation to boost productivity in the face of increased competition.[4]

Both Indian and U.S. IT companies also focused on building a presence throughout emerging markets such as China, Malaysia, Brazil and Eastern Europe, in addition to India.

Onshore (U.S.-Based) Leading Players

IBM Business Consulting Services IBM, one of the largest and most well established IT companies, had a large global presence with significant depth and breadth of skills and services. The company's major operations comprised a Global Services segment (which included Business Consulting Services), a Systems and Technology Group, a Personal Systems Group, a Software segment, a Global Financing segment, and an Enterprises Investments segment. IBM leveraged global delivery through hub-based strategic centers: the firm had three primary offshore hubs in India, Brazil and China that offered significant scale in application services and channeled offshore work to secondary locations in Mexico, Belarus, the Philippines, Romania and Argentina that offered smaller-scale operations with critical skill sets.

IBM had a very strong global brand, a large global client base, and global presence in client and offshore markets. The firm had established a successful record of offshoring application maintenance services through its presence in China for more than 15 years. Ming Tsai, who was an early leader of Mainspring and then became a global leader in IBM's Business Consulting Services after the company acquired Mainspring, pointed to the strengths and challenges associated with a company the size of IBM:

> Along with IBM's great support network came a lot of baggage, as you can imagine. Because IBM's business was hardware, software and services, IBM had literally armies of people inside the big accounts. So you had to tread very carefully if you were trying to introduce a piece of services work because it could, in theory, put at risk the very lucrative software deal license or a perpetual hardware deal. But IBM's support network was, fortunately, everywhere also. If you had a point of view or a message or a product or an offering that you wanted to get out to lots of companies, you could do so very quickly. The marketing, the PR and the apparatus that IBM had were pervasive.

Given the scale of its global operations, IBM faced challenges with integrating its global delivery approach across all its practices and complexity in using appropriate sales channels to drive work to its global delivery in some markets. Ming Tsai believed that IBM operated more like a multinational company rather than a global company[5] and pointed to hurdles and inefficiencies he faced as a global leader at IBM when he tried to move a partner from Australia to London—a process which ended up taking over a year.

The firm also had potential conflicts with its business consulting services and custom application product offerings, especially when competing against "pure play" business consulting competitors. Ming Tsai described IBM's challenge with regard to delivering objective advice:

> At Infosys, we provide services and we don't take over and run people's data centers and we don't sell various pieces of software—in that respect it actually makes it easier to coordinate and to deliver a message that's pure. It's easier both to claim and certainly deliver an objective perspective because we're never accused of recommending something just to sell additional software or hardware. At IBM you got questioned about that all the time: were we simply telling a client to do something because it would tee up a big software sell? So I think that's a real challenge, although I think the services part of IBM is so distinct from hardware and software that the issue didn't really materialize in all practical purposes. But it exists in the client's mind. So we had to carefully manage the perception at times.

For the fiscal year ended December 31, 2005, IBM's revenues decreased 5 percent to $91.13 billion and net income from continued operations increased 7 percent to $7.99 billion. Revenues reflected the impact of the firm's divestment of its PC business. For this period, net income was impacted by an increase in gross profit margins, a decrease in research and development expense and significant increases in other income.

IBM's Business Consulting Services had 60,000 business consultants worldwide. In addition, IBM had approximately 50,000 people located in its offshore centers. The offshore resources were shared across its business units; however, the firm had started to build industry expertise in some of its offshore locations.

Accenture Accenture, a management consulting, technology services and outsourcing organization headquartered in New York, had more than 110 offices in 48 countries including service operations in India, the Philippines, Spain, China, the Czech Republic, Slovakia, Brazil and Australia. The company's business was structured around five operating groups which comprised 17 industry groups serving clients across the world. The company's offerings included discrete project services and long-term outsourcing work for ongoing maintenance and management. Accenture's business consulting services included strategy and business architecture, customer relationship management, finance and performance management, human performance, learning, procurement and supply chain management. Accenture's services spanned all phases of application services including the design, development, implementation and ongoing support of custom or packaged, new and established applications.

Accenture demonstrated world–class industry and process depth on front-end projects while maintaining low-cost destinations globally, beyond India.[6] The firm had longstanding client relationships, a strong brand, depth and breadth of expertise and capital resources. However, although Accenture achieved relative parity on offshore price points, the firm had yet to fully leverage global delivery in terms of process, methods and tools, as well as cost.[7]

For the three months ended November 30, 2005, Accenture's revenues increased 12 percent to $4.54 billion and net income rose 10 percent to $214.9 million. Revenues reflected increased income from Communications and High Tech divisions, growth in the Insurance and Banking industry groups globally and increasing outsourcing revenues in the United States. For this period, net income was affected by increased cost of services and higher sales and marketing expenses. For the fiscal year ending August 31, 2005, sales were $17.09 billion and net income was $940 million.

Accenture had more than 126,000 employees worldwide. The firm had approximately 17,000 people in its global delivery center network which was comprised of more than 40 global delivery centers worldwide that provided technology and outsourcing services.

Offshore (Indian) Leading Players

Indian IT service providers offered two distinct types of consulting services: technical consulting and business consulting. While most Indian firms extended their strong technical capabilities to offering strong technical consulting services, their business consulting strategy and capabilities varied as the skills required for this offering—identification and assessment of strategic issues, an onsite presence, an understanding of the client's local culture and market, domain expertise—were different from their core capabilities.

Unlike Infosys Technologies' approach to creating a wholly owned U.S.-based consulting subsidiary, other Indian IT service providers' consulting operations were managed through their technology businesses.

Tata Consultancy Services (TCS) TCS, headquartered in Mumbai, India and a subsidiary of the Tata Group, was the largest offshore IT service provider in India. TCS commenced operations in 1968 and had leveraged the offshore model for more than 30 years. TCS had global service delivery locations in Hungary, Brazil, Uruguay and China. TCS offered consulting services, IT services, asset-based solutions (e.g., proprietary FIG and Quartz™ software for the banking and financial services industry), IT infrastructure (e.g., complete outsourcing of IT networks), engineering and industrial services and BPO. TCS went public in 2004.

TCS had performed consulting work on an ad-hoc, opportunistic basis for many years, but only recently established a consulting strategy and created a Global Consulting business unit in 2004. In 2005, TCS brought in Per Bragee, former Skandia CIO and Ernst & Young CEO for Sweden to develop and manage a TCS Global Consulting practice.

Tata Group, made up of 90 companies ranging from steel and automobiles to IT services, had worldwide revenues of $17.8 billion for the 2005 fiscal year. The company accounted for three percent of India's GDP.

TCS had 34,000 employees and a presence in 34 countries across six continents.

Wipro Technologies (Wipro) Wipro, the third largest Indian application services provider, had a range of IT services, software solutions, IT consulting, BPO, and research and development services in the areas of hardware and software design. Wipro was part of Wipro Limited, which had three business segments: Wipro Technologies, the Global IT Services and Products business segment, which provided IT services to customers in the Americas, Europe and Japan; India and AsiaPac IT Services and Products which focused on meeting the IT products and service requirements of companies in India, Asia-Pacific and the Middle East region; and Customer Care and Lighting which offered soaps, toiletries and lighting products for the market in India. Wipro had a strong market presence in the United States and significant European representation. In addition to organic growth, Wipro made a series of strategic acquisitions such as SpectraMind in BPO, and American Management Systems' (AMS) utility practice and NerveWire in business consulting, to develop emerging market opportunities. Wipro, based in Bangalore, India, had a global service delivery operation in China.

At 225 consultants in 2005, Wipro's high-end business consulting arm, WCS, was comprised of the assets from two acquisitions: NerveWire and AMS' utility practice. Its technical consulting staff, an additional 1,000 resources, was spread throughout Wipro in different horizontal and vertical practices. The firm hired an ex-McKinsey Partner to lead the business consulting unit. Wipro's approach to consulting did not entail giving control of its consulting operations to outside experts, creating a separate sales team or investing money above and beyond what the consulting resources were able to generate.

For the fiscal year ended March 31 2005, Wipro Limited had annual sales of U.S.$1.9 billion. Wipro Technologies accounted for 75 percent of the company's revenue and 89 percent of its operating income.

Wipro had a total of 5,000 consultants spread across North America, Europe and Japan and over 10,000 itinerant employees. Wipro had a presence in 35 countries including 10 nearshore development centers.

ICI Strategy and Organization

The leadership team at ICI had a mission to lead a new generation of business consulting to help clients become more competitive and help develop their employees into great leaders. The strategy involved the delivery of high quality business consulting and disciplined technology implementation at an extremely competitive price. As explained further below, ICI could perform engagements at a blended rate of approximately $100 per hour while the rates of leading players like IBM and Accenture ranged from $175 to $225 per hour. The firm planned to extend Infosys Technologies' Global Delivery Model (GDM) to the business consulting arena and create a company structure for a unique culture which would differentiate ICI from other business consulting firms, enable the recruitment of top tier talent and deliver measurable value to clients.

Global Delivery Model (GDM)

Infosys Technologies developed a unique approach to global delivery more than 20 years ago and was considered a leader in the delivery of IT implementation projects using globally distributed teams. Projects were broken down into logical components and distributed to different locations (onsite, nearshore, or offshore) where they could then be delivered at maximum value in the most cost efficient manner (see Exhibit 4 for an application of the

---

EXHIBIT 4

Infosys Technologies' Global Delivery Model

GLOBAL DELIVERY MODEL

Client Location/PDC*

Discovery Project
- Analysis and planning
- High level design
- User interface design
- Project coordination
- Onsite testing
- Implementation

Post Implementation Support
- Rapid reaction support

Offshore Development Centers

Project
- Project management
- Detailed design
- Coding
- Testing
- Documentation

Post Implementation Support
- Bug fixes
- Warranty support
- Maintenance

Intelligent project breakdown

Leverage extended workday

Leverage cost efficiencies

*PDC = Proximity development centers

Source: Data from Infosys Consulting.

EXHIBIT 5

Value Chain of Consulting and Implementation Services ICI Extending Infosys Technologies' Global Delivery Model

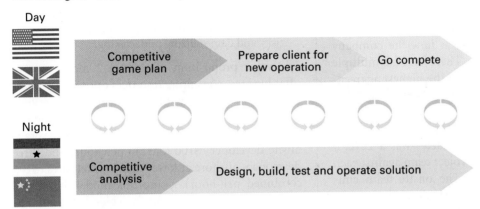

Source: Infosys Consulting company website.

global delivery value chain for Infosys Technologies). Infosys Technologies claimed that the GDM cut project costs by 30 percent and reduced time to market since the combined work of teams distributed around the world made a 24-hour project workday a reality. ICI applied this model to integrate the business consulting and technology implementation lifecycle (see Exhibit 5 for the GDM value chain including consulting services). This approach, called the "1-1-3 model," gave the client one ICI resource onsite, one Infosys Technologies resource onsite and three Infosys Technologies resources offshore (in India or other Infosys offshore centers in China, Australia, Mauritius, Czech Republic—see Appendix on Infosys, p. C193).

Ming Tsai pointed to the training and knowledge of global delivery of Infosys Technologies' onsite resources as a differentiating factor from competitors' approaches to global delivery:

> Infosys Technologies' onsite resources are more trained in, comfortable with and knowledgeable about global delivery. So it's not just that we have lots of people that are in India. It's a question of the one onsite consultant being able to understand what are the limitations of global delivery and how and when to take advantage of global delivery. Frankly, there are situations where you don't want to be offshore. You cannot send somebody offshore if you need to do an executive workshop that has to be done in New York because that is where all the bankers are. The

ability to recognize what can and can't be done to the clients' benefit offshore and onshore and how to structure a piece of work around that is, I would say, countercultural for the average IBM or Accenture consulting teams who are motivated to drive utilization up for their onshore teams.

Shortening the Lifecycle of Solution Design to Implementation

The firm had a different approach to implementing technology to enable operational improvements. For example, if a client wanted to implement SAP to improve its operations, the traditional approach to the engagement would be to analyze the firm's processes and then redesign them. The traditional approach entailed a design phase that was distinct from a development phase. Specifications would be written following the new processes or process requirements. The processes tended to be grouped by vertical functions such as sales, marketing, manufacturing, etc. SAP would then be implemented to deliver the specifications and client employees would be trained to use the technology. In the traditional cycle, the design and configuration of the specifications would be completed onsite. The data conversion and report building may have been completed offshore.

ICI's approach entailed looking at process requirements rather than functional requirements. The firm believed that inefficiencies could be identified better if horizontal processes, for example the product development process, were considered rather than vertical functional silos, such as sales and marketing. The firm also looked at process metrics. The rationale used was that every change ICI recommended needed to impact the client's performance and ultimately increase its shareholder value.

ICI applied the GDM to deploy a team onsite to work with a client and look at how the company was organized by process. There existed multiple levels of processes. Level 0 was the highest aggregation of business processes. Most companies had between five to 10 level 0 processes, for example the product development process—to develop a product from the inception of an idea—was a Level 0 process. ICI organized the project team against each identified Level 0 process. The onsite team contained process experts and SAP development experts. This team worked with the client during the day to capture the design of the process object. At night, the offshore team converted the design templates into a software configuration. The next day, the onsite team would test the software configuration with the client and undergo a second iteration of the design. At night, the offshore team would develop the second iteration.

Typically, there existed four or five iterations for each process object. Each sub-team organized against each process would take a week to design and develop the process. If there were six sub-teams, six process objects were created in one week. If a company had 200 process objects, the design and software configuration for all of them would be completed in six months, whereas using the traditional approach would take 10 to 12 months. Moreover, as the configuration was being performed on a real-time basis, the end result was intended to be exactly what the client wanted as each iteration could be tested for user acceptance during the design and configuration process.

Cost Reduction Steve Pratt pointed to several aspects of cost reduction as he described the 1-1-3 model:

> This is a killer business model because it gives, on average, a lower cost to clients and much higher margins for us to use to pay our people well, to make investors happy and to invest in our business. The main benefit to our clients is that they can take these cost savings and reinvest them into their business, and become more competitive. We've been the pioneers in creating the model of

the future. Everyone is scrambling to get to our model, so the race is whether we can scale our model fast enough. Having been on both sides of the equation, this is a lot more fun: the building and growing quickly is a lot more fun than tearing down an old model which is an expensive, risky and demoralizing undertaking.

The value proposition of the 1-1-3 model was to offer business consulting resources onsite at the market rate for premium business consulting services ($150 to $400 per hour), an onsite IT implementation resource at a rate that was lower than the average onsite developer ($100 to $150 per hour) and three developers offshore at lower than market rates ($105 combined per hour). Using this model, ICI could perform major engagements for a blended rate of approximately $100 dollars an hour.

Steve Pratt also considered the timeframe and challenges involved in replicating the cost structure of ICI's 1-1-3 model:

> Realistically, testing the replicability of our model will play out over the next three to five years, because it's at least that big of a problem for the legacy consulting firms such as IBM and Accenture to get to our model. The problem is not about scaling up offshore, but de-scaling here. If your core financial model is built on engaging your onshore employees and if the rates start collapsing, your cost structure is not sustainable. The model is not difficult to learn, but there's a structural challenge involved in replicating it. Another complicating factor for our U.S. competitors is that once we get sufficient scale, we will tip the market and collapse the price point in the consulting industry. This will hurt them in the capital markets because their margins will be squeezed. Then their utilization of people has to go up, and their ability to invest will go down.

Delivering Measurable Benefits ICI followed Infosys Technologies' philosophy of measuring everything. The parent company had raised awareness of quality standards in the software and services arena by marketing the quality of work it delivered using the Software Engineering Institute's Capability Maturity Model (CMM). CMM judged the maturity of an organization's software processes and identified key practices required to increase the maturity of these processes. Infosys Technologies was awarded a Level 5 rating, the highest quality of software development delivery, though in reality, the company exceeded the highest quality level by a factor of 20 (while the maximum allowed defects for Level 5 was 0.5, Infosys Technologies was rated at 0.026—approximately 20 times better).

ICI's focus from a broad services standpoint was to assist clients in dealing with business and technology related challenges/problems in customer operations, product operations and corporate operations. ICI determined that one clear way to deliver value was to achieve measurable improvement in business process metrics within the client's business operations as a result of its consulting engagement (see Exhibit 6 for sample metrics). Therefore, on every business transformation and operations consulting engagement, the firm made a concerted and structured effort to deliver measurable improvement in process metrics as a proxy to making a positive impact on shareholder value. For these engagements, ICI would first analyze the current operations of the client to establish a baseline of business process performance. The company would next assess process metrics that reflected the efficiency and effectiveness of each key business process and then design changes in business process structure and enable technology to deliver defined improvement in process metrics.

As an example, for a manufacturing client's order management process (quote-to-cash), process metrics such as the ones outlined below would be addressed to drive measurable improvement in process performance:

- Elapsed time between quote submission and receipt of cash from the client
- Capacity for processing orders within a specific timeframe
- Percent of orders configured with zero errors
- Percent of orders shipped on requested-ship-date
- Number of quotes with readjusted prices
- Number of days' sales outstanding per customer segment

Another example included the time-to-market metric that was critical for the high-tech industry. This metric was a key measure of success in the high-tech industry and companies recognized that the cost of coming in second with new products could be severe. So, in this case, the consulting engagement would focus on analyzing the new product introduction process with the intent of using process and technology enablers to reduce time-to-market, thereby influencing the client's success in the market by enhancing its revenue and hence impacting shareholder value.

ICI also structured engagements with clients where the fees owed to the company were contingent on project outcomes. One of ICI's clients, George Stelling, the CIO and global services leader of NVIDIA Corporation (a multi-billion leader in the graphics processor market), worked with ICI to create a "value based" case structure, where case fees were based on the success of a spend management engagement:

> We had ICI put some of their fees at risk, based on the identification of cost savings in targeted spend categories. We set clear metrics at the beginning of the engagement so there was a high degree of transparency for us and ICI. At the end of the engagement, ICI was paid their full fee. For us, we got value in terms of focusing on "quick hit" cost savings opportunities as well as long-term spend management strategies. Since the original case, we've engaged ICI in the implementation phase of our long-term strategy. These "value based" deals are great, if you can structure them. These kinds of "win-win" relationships work when you can align incentives on both sides.

George Stelling added that ICI's measurements-driven approach was the most important factor in his decision to hire the consulting firm.

ICI also developed its own set of metrics to track the quality of the work the firm performed by asking clients to rate each engagement (see Exhibit 7). The firm would elicit feedback from clients to see whether they had met the client's expectations, or even exceeded them. ICI created a rating scale of zero to 200 where 100 indicated that the firm had met client expectations. As of 2006, ICI maintained an average rating of over 130 based on more than 100 client engagements.

Company Organization

Although Infosys Technologies went to market as one company, in order to establish a successful consulting business, ICI was given the autonomy to create its

EXHIBIT 6

ICI Sample Core Process Metrics—Designed for an ERP Implementation Project for the Software Industry Sub-Vertical Within the High Tech Discrete Manufacturing Practice

| *High Tech Software Industry Segment Process Structure* | | | | |
Level	Level No.	Level (Process) Name	Objective	Metric
0	1.0	Solution Development to Sunset	Develop and manage solutions that are valued by customers and maximize profitability for the business	● Product revenues ● Market share ● Cost of sale
0	2.0	Channel Development to Agreement	Identify channels and customer segments to maximize penetration in existing markets, increase customer base and drive growth in emerging markets.	● Market share by geography ● Market share by channel ● Market share by product category ● Pipeline conversion rates ● Account growth ● Account penetration ● Customer/channel acquisition cost
0	3.0	High Tech Channel Management	Manage channel customers effectively to drive customer satisfaction, strengthen relationships and increase revenues	● Length of accounts ● Profitability of accounts ● Revenue growth of channels ● Number of new product agreements with channels ● Channel feedback scores
0	4.0	Supply Chain Management	Effectively manage the supply chain process to manage partner/vendor resources to minimize inventory and optimize fulfillment needs that usher operational transparency	● Inventory age ● Inventory turns ● Obsolete/excess inventory per month ● Ratio of company and vendor managed inventory ● Variance of estimated & actual delivery dates ● Percent available to promise satisfied
0	5.0	Quote to Cash	Provide accurate and prompt billing for all products/services to ensure revenues are fully captured	● Percentage of shipments billed ● Days sales outstanding
0	7.0	Human Resources	Hire talent to fit role definitions, devise training to motivate employees and manage PR to enhance corporate image	● Staff turnover ● Training feedback score
0	8.0	Information Technology	Maintain and manage IT infrastructure; plan & execute IT requirement to support business strategy	● System down-time ● Return on investment of IT initiatives
0	9.0	Facilities	Manage company assets that maximize return on investment, support operations and minimize risk	● Maintenance costs ● Return on investment on real estate assets

Source: Data from Infosys Consulting.

own culture, recruitment strategy, organizational structure and compensation packages.

Building a Unique Culture The leadership team of ICI decided that they needed to create a unique culture to differentiate them from other business consulting firms while maintaining the attributes required for successful consultants and adopting the essential values of the parent company. Steve Pratt described this challenge:

> What we need to do is build a company that successfully straddles the personality of a confident, assertive business advice consultant while ensuring that we have integration with the Infosys culture. Creating the culture that fits in that square is very important because if we go too far to the extreme and become an arrogant consulting firm, that will be in direct conflict with the Infosys culture and will fail. Likewise, if we go too far to the side of being too deferential, we won't be able to give good advice to our clients. A big challenge internally is to build the right culture. A related challenge is how do we take a group of people from different consulting firms and build a unique culture. We're also facing the same issue we've always had in our careers, which is how do we take people that have no consulting experience and integrate them into our culture.

The leadership team set out to build a culture based on Infosys Technologies' values of delivering high quality work, measuring every aspect of performance and maintaining a sense of humility. The team wanted to apply the rigorous analytical process of providing advice within an open and transparent culture.

Recruiting the Right People ICI management decided to follow the chairman of the parent company, Narayana Murthy's philosophy: hire first-rate employees only. In addition to MBA recruiting, the firm used a referral-based system to target the top 10 percent of talent from other consulting companies. Steve Pratt explained:

> We hired an executive search firm and it didn't work. For whatever reason, people have to emotionally buy-in to our approach. That's a different kind of recruiting—more of a "Do you want to be a pioneer?" kind of recruiting. And we've done a good job convincing the people we want—people that have come to us through referrals—to join us.

ICI also interviewed and retained approximately half of the employees from Infosys Technologies' original consulting business unit. ICI found that most of these employees were better aligned with the sales and delivery model of the parent organization and did not have relevant business development and client relationship experience for the consulting organization.

Although ICI had reached its recruiting target of 200 employees by the end of December 2005, Steve Pratt pointed to challenges that lay ahead for the firm to meet its recruitment goals:

> We're trying to hire more women. We're making good progress, but I'd like to do better there. One of the things we're doing strategically for Infosys Technologies is creating local presences. More than 80 percent of our consultants are citizens of the local country. We've started operations in the U.K. and Germany, so we want to establish a local presence in all of the markets in which we operate. It's very important for Infosys to continue to emerge as a global company. Right now, the vast majority of Infosys Technologies employees are Indian. The goal is to have more representation in local communities.

Creating a Differentiated Approach ICI decided to build an organizational structure based on meritocracy and transparency. Paul Cole, the COO, commented:

> What keeps me up at night is "Are we doing things differently?" If you take five guys from four different companies, each with 20 years of experience, God help us if we do the same old stuff we did with our predecessor companies. The big question is: how can we do things differently and better?

An example of ICI's approach to doing things differently was their staffing model where the responsibility for contributing to the firm was given to individual employees. Paul Cole explained how the model was different from the traditional consulting staffing model:

> Consulting firms use the terms *beach* and *bench* for unutilized staff. We don't have such things. Nobody's on the beach, nobody's sitting on the bench. They're learning, teaching, billing, contributing—so they're always adding useful value to the firm and we want them to take control of their careers.

EXHIBIT 7

ICI Client Feedback Form

Infosys® CONSULTING

CLIENT FEEDBACK FORM

Infosys Consulting would like to thank you for taking the time to provide feedback on the effort we have recently completed for your organization. This feedback is critical not only in improving the quality of service we will provide you and other clients in the future, but also in determining a portion of our consultants' compensation. The survey should only take about 15-30 minutes and can be kept anonymous if you prefer.

Would you like anonymity as the responder to this feedback form?   Yes _____   No _____

Client Name
Client Company
Address

Engagement Name
Project Code (if any)
Milestone
Period

I. Overall Satisfaction

Overall, we would like to understand how satisfied you were with the work delivered by Infosys Consulting on *(engagement)*, using a scale of 1–7 (where 7 is extremely satisfied, 6 is very satisfied, 5 is satisfied, 4 is neither satisfied/dissatisfied, 3 is dissatisfied, 2 is very dissatisfied, and 1 is extremely dissatisfied).

If your rating above was a 3 or lower, please share with us your key areas where we may improve. May we follow-up with you?   **Rating:** _____

For Sections 2–4, please rate each "attribute" on a scale from 1 to 7 in terms of its *importance to you* in selecting Infosys Consulting and *how well the team performed*.

II. Quality

Starting with the *quality* of what was delivered, how important was it that Infosys Consulting *(insert attribute)?* And how well did Infosys Consulting perform on *(same attribute)?*

Importance
(1 = not at all important
7 = extremely important)

Performance
(1 = poor performance
7 = excellent performance)

a. deliver significant business insights
b. deliver practical recommendations
c. demonstrate quantified financial benefits
d. provide the proper blend of fact-based and creative analysis
e. help your company to become more competitive

III. Project Management

Now, in terms of overall *project management*, how important was *(insert attribute)?* And how well did Infosys Consulting perform on *(same attribute)?*

Importance
(1 = not at all important
7 = extremely important)

Performance
(1 = poor performance
7 = excellent performance)

a. adherence to schedule
b. being on budget
c. handling ambiguity and ad hoc requirements
d. proactively identifying and managing of risks
e. timely closure of issues
f. making critical project resources available
g. transfer of knowledge to your organization
h. providing the appropriate level of change management

IV. Teamwork/Collaboration

Finally, in terms of how well Infosys Consulting collaborated with your organization, how important was *(insert attribute)?* And how well did Infosys Consulting perform *(same attribute)?*

Importance
(1 = not at all important
7 = extremely important
"N/A" = not applicable)

Performance
(1 = not at all important
7 = extremely important
"N/A" = not applicable)

a. oral communication skills
b. written communication skills
c. demonstrated industry knowledge
d. demonstrated functional knowledge
e. analytical skills
f. being confident but not arrogant
g. interacting effectively within your organization
h. being proactive
i. effectively using global resources
j. adapting to your culture

V. Infosys Consulting Core Values

One of the areas that Infosys Consulting takes very seriously in evaluating its people is living the Company's values. Please read these value statements and respond with whether our behavior lived up to each value.

a. Client Delight (Did we meet or exceed the results you expected?) Yes No
b. Leadership by Example (Did our project leaders lead by example?) Yes No
c. Integrity and Transparency (Were we truthful and open?) Yes No
d. Fairness (Were we fair?) Yes No
e. Pursuit of Excellence (Did we put in the effort to achieve excellent results?) Yes No

VI. Client Feedback

a. In general, what did you like best about working with Infosys Consulting?

b. In what ways could Infosys Consulting better serve your needs in the future? Are there services/capabilities/approaches we could add or strengthen?

c. In comparing your overall experience with Infosys Consulting vs. our competitors, how would you rate our performance?

Infosys Consulting was better than other firms
Infosys Consulting was equivalent to other firms
Infosys Consulting was worse than other firms
No experience with a competitor to make this judgement

d. Going forward, how likely would you be to recommend Infosys Consulting to someone else within your organization?

Very likely
Somewhat likely
Not at all likely

e. Are there any other comments/feedback that you would like to provide?

VII. Business Value – Summary Rating

Infosys Consulting strives to maximize the business value we deliver to our clients. We would therefore like to understand the degree to which this project's expectations were met. Please rate us on a % basis of the anticipated *business value* that the engagement delivered, where:

200% = "Infosys Consulting greatly exceeded expectations"
100% = "Infosys Consulting met expectations"
0% = "Infosys Consulting drastically under-met expectations"

Rating: _____ %

IMPORTANT NOTE: This answer will be used as a quantitative input to our consultants' compensation.

Infosys Consulting would like to thank you for your candid and constructive feedback!

Source: Infosys Consulting.

ICI implemented a staffing system where employees could input their skills into a database. A project manager could then search the database, match results against a calendar and see which employees with the requisite skills were available for an engagement. Employees could request engagements they were interested in, and had the option to opt out of being selected for certain engagements. The firm purchased an auctioning module for its staffing system so that employees could bid on projects in a reverse auction.[8] ICI also created the Personal Margin Contribution where each employee could see his or her individual margin contribution or revenue allocation on each project.

Another example of ICI's efforts to create a meritocratic and transparent organization included incorporating staff nominations for promotion. Under this system, the firm's senior employees who were being considered for promotion published the criteria on which their promotions should be based and all the employees could nominate and score each leader.

The firm recognized that by leveraging the GDM, they had created a 24-hour work cycle, given the time differential of the various teams that were deployed on a specific engagement. Although this seemed to be the next wave of productivity in a global work environment, in order to prevent employees from burning out through overextending their hours (as there was the potential to work during every hour of the day), they asked employees to block out certain times in their calendars when they would not be available to work. Mark Holmstrom, a practice leader who was the seventh employee to join ICI, described the challenge of working in a global delivery environment:

> One of the challenges for this global delivery model is that it requires a different way of thinking about work that's not the traditional eight to five, eight to six model. A lot of what we do becomes much more asynchronous. What I mean by that is it's much more email based. There are traditional times when meetings take place that are during the week. I actually block my calendar at certain times that most people wouldn't think of in a traditional company. One of the things I really enjoy doing is putting my little daughters to bed. So I block out time to say, "I'm not going to work during these hours." Everyone has got to figure out their own rhythm, their own pace and figure out what success looks like within the global delivery model.

Rewarding Employees   ICI generally compensated employees at the higher end of market rates; for example, the base compensation for MBA campus hires for 2005 was between $110,000 and $125,000. ICI's bonus structure linked back to the value ICI had created for its clients and overall client value. Steve Pratt explained: "We're the only consulting firm that actually pays people based on delivered client value. It always used to bug us that people got paid based on consulting revenue only, as we considered that to be a downstream metric while we wanted an upstream metric."

At the end of every engagement, ICI asked its clients what percentage of the business value that they had anticipated ICI would provide was actually realized. That percentage translated into a direct multiplier of employee bonuses. The firm also created a client mutual fund where the firm took the total amount of fees each client paid them and translated that amount into a purchase of each client's equity. ICI then monitored how their client fund performed against the S&P 500. That percentage differential was translated into a multiplier of employee bonuses as well.

Managing the Relationship with Infosys Technologies

The management of both Infosys Technologies and ICI recognized that building a seamless interface between the parent company and the subsidiary was essential for success. ICI was organized to mirror the parent company (both companies were organized by industry) and metrics were established in order to measure how well the two companies worked together. Steve Pratt described this process:

> First of all, getting the interface with Infosys Technologies right is very important. Get the right metrics, get the right business planning in place. Each of the Infosys Technologies business units has a specific goal related to consulting, and we have specific goals related to revenue for Infosys Technologies. So the goals are understood, and the metrics are largely correct to drive the behavior to work together. We're always redefining. There's a constant education. The more engagements we do with clients, the more we understand what Infosys Technologies really does, and they understand more what we really do.

Leveraging the Parent Company

ICI leveraged the relationships that already existed with Infosys Technologies to get client engagements.

The firm actively sought opportunities where there was a targeted need to offer existing Infosys Technologies' clients business consulting services. Ming Tsai provided a rationale for this approach:

> Out of the approximately 450 existing Infosys Technologies accounts, we have targeted ones that are the most strategic, most receptive or the most in need of skills that we provide and combined that with the account teams that are the most open minded and willing to work with us within the Infosys account teams. So they tend to be good clients of Infosys, having seen and worked with Infosys for multiple years. They tend to be clients that have particular pain points around business transformation—something in a particular business process or business area that is in need of change, or has a technical or technology aspect to it. Approximately 70 percent of our business comes from existing Infosys clients.

George Stelling explained that the rationale to hire ICI for a strategy engagement rather than first hold a competitive bidding process open to other consulting firms was because of the client relationship that Infosys Technologies had established with NVIDIA:

> In the past, we used Infosys Technologies in the IT area successfully on projects, but we had never used Infosys Consulting. There was a dialog going on with our CEO, CFO, and Infosys when I joined. It was clear that Infosys Consulting and NVIDIA shared common values around value creation. The chemistry was a key consideration. It's very important to pick consultants that you feel comfortable with and those that reflect your corporate style.

Infosys Technologies adapted its sales process to include ICI in its service offerings. The firm changed its incentive structure for its sales force to ensure that engagements awarded to ICI were rewarded as much as the engagements where the parent company had exclusive ownership. The parent company developed an internal program called "One Infy" to structure incentives and set goals to enhance collaboration among employees across the firm. The overall objectives of the initiative were to create and reinforce One Infy thinking through training programs; include One Infy behavior in the measurement systems across the organization; reward examples of collaborative business planning and create role models for the rest of the organization; and create cultural integration mechanisms such as forums for people to meet and learn from each other across the business units.

As Infosys Technologies grew in size and expanded its footprint of services, it became increasingly important that all the capabilities of the firm were in alignment with the goal of serving clients and winning in the marketplace. The program involved improving internal collaborative mechanisms so that clients saw Infosys Technologies as one company and not a collection of parts. One Infy focused on improving the training programs for employees—to improve understanding of service offerings across the organization, build collaborative skills and ensure that new employees went through cross-business training. The One Infy initiative served to focus the overall organization on the value of leveraging the broad and deep capabilities of the company across business units and subsidiaries. The initiative also focused on joint account planning and pursuit management. The intent was to create joint planning teams at the account level, with participation from the relevant business units. The account leader position was viewed as integrating efforts across different units and ensuring consistency in the value delivery processes. The firm planned to create forums where account leaders could strategize, develop opportunities and resolve delivery issues on an ongoing rather than opportunistic basis. The objective was to make the initiative self-sustaining. Infosys Technologies planned to structure goals and incentives of the individuals in line with the overall account strategies.

Initially, there were tensions in the company over which entity would lead the client relationship and pursuit of engagements. For example, the sales force was faced with client situations where an overlap between business transformational work and enterprise solutions offerings caused uncertainty whether the client pursuit and relationship would go to ICI or Infosys Technologies' Enterprise Solutions business unit. Both the parent company and ICI worked together to create a methodology, known as "The Fork in the Road," where the pursuit of the client relationship would be allocated to the area of the company that best served the client's situation. Raj Joshi and C. Kakal, the head of the Enterprise Solutions practice within Infosys Technologies, formalized an approach that had the two groups working together to collaboratively decide which opportunities were transformational in nature and better suited for ICI, versus more technology-related work which was better aligned with the Enterprise Solutions practice. This decision, representing the fork in the road, drove better collaboration and established clear ownership of the sales pursuit strategy and tactics. By clearly formulating accountability of tasks and decision-making, it enhanced the overall process of working together to pursue large complex client opportunities.

Romil Bahl described a practical approach that the company employed when dealing with client engagements that provided an overlap between Infosys Technologies' and ICI's services:

> It gets real muddy where there's a business process opportunity. Frankly, Infosys Technologies has phenomenal domain industry expertise and they have very smart people. They all want to do more anyway, so it gets real interesting in these situations and I find that often you can't talk about it and you can't conceptualize it, you have to go do engagements together. Infosys sees a better end product when a true cross-functional team of people comes together on it. There's no magical way for somebody to say, you guys will draw a line here in the middle. It just doesn't happen.

ICI also brought in new client relationships for Infosys Technologies. Ming Tsai described this second channel for ICI: "We also target old clients of ours that we've known personally in our past lives, whether at Capgemini, IBM, BCG, etc. We've brought in over a dozen marquee clients—Fortune 500 clients that Infosys had never done any work for before."

Interface Challenges

Infosys Technologies recognized that all pieces of the company needed to work together in a manner that optimized performance. A challenge facing Infosys Technologies was to ensure that ICI received enough airtime from the parent company given its relatively small size (ICI had 200 employees versus Infosys' 50,000 employees). Senior management realized that active intervention was required in order to ensure that the subsidiary received the attention it needed to be successful. Infosys Technologies set up a board led by Kris Gopalakrishnan to review the subsidiary's performance. Quarterly meetings were held where ICI's performance was monitored and issues were discussed.

Infosys Technologies also viewed their relationship with ICI as an opportunity to transform the company's culture and build the brand into a global transformation enabler. Senior management viewed the quarterly meetings as an opportunity to learn about a new space and evolve the company. The leadership of both Infosys Technologies and ICI agreed that interacting with each other regularly provided a constant education for everyone. Paul Cole described the attention to detail given by the leadership of Infosys Technologies to the operations of ICI, citing that the chairman, Narayana Murthy, regularly reviewed weekly status reports from the subsidiary. Steve Pratt described ICI's approach to interfacing with the parent company: "We're guests here and we have to be respectful of that. We're here to learn and listen more than we speak. We want to demonstrate over time, which we have already, that we're a good thing for the clients of Infosys."

In order to be viewed as a global company, Infosys Technologies recognized that it needed to incorporate different global perspectives by bringing in managers from the United States and Europe. The leadership of Infosys Technologies hoped to see migration of management from ICI to the parent company over time.

Conclusion

Steve Pratt was convinced that ICI had enabled disruptive change in the business and information technology industry through its unique approach and organization. However, in considering the firm's strategy in the future, he evaluated the ways in which the firm could "stay ahead of the game." In addition to the internal challenges of building the business, managing growth and interfacing productively with the parent company, plus the external challenge of capturing and maintaining market share in the consulting industry, CEO Steve Pratt's key concern was "to get the right people to do the right things":

> We need to make sure that we stay focused on the high priority things. Are we spending the right amount of time building the connection to Infosys Technologies? Are we spending the right amount of time selling? Are we spending the right amount of time developing our people, and who is doing what and where are they spending their time doing that? Are the MDs working together? Are we working optimally with clients, and when there are really important events with clients, where can I be helpful? I need to make sure that the right people are in the right roles.

Appendix: Infosys Technologies

Infosys Technologies Limited (NASDAQ: INFY), a global technology services company, was incorporated in 1981. The company provided end-to-end business solutions which leveraged technology for its clients, including consulting, design, development, software re-engineering, maintenance, systems integration, package evaluation and implementation, and infrastructure management services. Infosys Technologies' wholly owned subsidiaries included Infosys Technologies (Australia) Pty. Limited (Infosys Australia), Infosys Technologies (Shanghai) Co. Limited (Infosys China) and Infosys Consulting Inc. (Infosys Consulting). Through Progeon Limited (Progeon), a majority-owned subsidiary, Infosys Technologies provided business process management services, such as offsite customer relationship management, finance and accounting, and administration and sales order processing. Infosys Technologies marketed in North America, Europe and the Asia-Pacific region. The company served clients in financial services, manufacturing, telecommunications, retail, utilities, logistics and other industries. In 2006, the company had over 52,700 employees worldwide and planned to hire another 25,000 employees over the next year.

Through its Global Delivery Model, Infosys Technologies divided projects into components which were executed simultaneously at client sites and at its development centers in India and around the world. It had 25 global development centers, of which nine were located in India; 29 sales offices; one disaster recovery center and four subsidiary offices. Infosys Technologies' service offerings included custom application development, maintenance and production support, software re-engineering, package evaluation and implementation, information technology (IT) consulting and other solutions, including testing services, operations and business process consulting, engineering services, business process management, systems integration and infrastructure management services.

Infosys Technologies competitors included Accenture, BearingPoint, Capgemini, Deloitte Consulting, HP, IBM, Computer Sciences Corporation, EDS, Keane, Logica CMG, Perot Systems, Cognizant Technologies, Satyam Computer Services, Tata Consultancy Services, Wipro, Oracle and SAP.

For the three months ended March 31, 2006, Infosys Technologies' revenues increased 30.3 percent to $593 million and net income increased 19.6 percent to $152 million from the previous year. The profit margins for the company fell in the quarter ended in March, the fourth quarter of its fiscal year, to 26.3 percent from 29.4 percent in the previous quarter. The company cited a stronger rupee, higher depreciation on buildings and equipment, and accelerated hiring for the falloff. Yet, despite 15 percent wage increases in the spring, Infosys Technologies said that it expected its profit margins for the fiscal 2007 year to be about 28 percent, unchanged from the previous year. Infosys Technologies expected revenues to increase 28 percent to 30 percent in the fiscal 2007 year.

Custom Application Development

Infosys Technologies provided customized software solutions for its clients. The company created new applications and enhanced the functionality of its clients' existing software applications. Its projects involved all aspects of the software development process, including defining requirements, designing, prototyping, programming, module integration and installation of the custom application. Infosys Technologies performed system design and software coding, and ran pilots primarily at its global development centers, while transition planning, user training and deployment activities were performed at the client's site. The company's application development services spanned the entire range of mainframe, client server and Internet technologies. Infosys Technologies' application development engagements were related to emerging platforms, such as Microsoft's .NET, or open platforms, such as Java 2 enterprise edition (J2EE) and Linux.

Maintenance and Production Support

Infosys Technologies provided maintenance services for its clients' software systems that covered a range of technologies and businesses, and were typically critical to a client's business. The company focused on long-term functionality, stability and preventive maintenance to avoid problems that typically arise from incomplete or short-term solutions. While Infosys Technologies performed the maintenance work at its global development centers using secure and redundant communication links to client's systems, the company also maintained a team at the client's facility to coordinate key interface and support functions.

Software Re-engineering

The company's software re-engineering services assisted its clients in converting their existing IT systems to newer technologies and platforms developed by third-party vendors. Its re-engineering services included

Web-enabling its clients' existing legacy systems, database migration, implementing product upgrades and platform migrations, such as mainframe to client server and client server to Internet platforms. Infosys Technologies' solution provided an enterprise-wide platform for over 50 applications for 10,000 users spread across North America, Europe and Asia.

Package Evaluation and Implementation

Infosys Technologies assisted its clients in the evaluation and implementation of software packages, which were developed by third-party vendors, and provided training and support services in the course of their implementation. The company specialized in enterprise resource planning packages developed by vendors, including Oracle, PeopleSoft, Retek and SAP; supply chain management packages developed by vendors, including i2, Manugistics and Oracle; customer relationship management packages developed by vendors, including PeopleSoft (Vantive) and Siebel; business intelligence packages developed by vendors, such as Business Objects and Cognos, and enterprise application integration packages developed by vendors like IBM and TIBCO. It provided its services in a range of industries, such as automotive, beverages, financial services, food, healthcare, manufacturing, pharmaceuticals, retail, technology and telecommunications.

IT Consulting

The company provided technical advice in developing and recommending appropriate IT architecture, hardware and software specifications to deliver IT solutions designed to meet specific business and computing objectives. It offered IT consulting in migration planning, institution-wide implementation and overall project management involving multiple vendors under a common architecture. Infosys technologies also conducted IT infrastructure assessment, which included assessing its clients' IT capabilities against existing and future business requirements and appropriate technology infrastructure, and technology roadmap development, which allowed clients to evaluate emerging technologies and develop the standards and methodologies for applying those emerging technologies.

Other Solutions

Infosys Technologies offered testing services, engineering services, business process management, systems integration, infrastructure management, and operational and business process consulting. Testing services offered end-to-end validation solutions and services, including enterprise test management, performance benchmarking, test automation and product certification. Its consulting services included strategic and competitive analysis to help the clients improve their business operations. It also assisted clients in implementing operational changes to their businesses. The company offered engineering services which primarily assisted its clients in the manufacturing sector, in their new product development process and in managing the life cycles of their existing product lines.

The company's business process management offered services to banking industry, insurance and healthcare industries, and securities and brokerage industry. Systems integration developed and delivered solutions that enhanced the compatibility between various components of its clients' IT infrastructure. Infrastructure management services included data center management, technical support services, application management services and process implementation/enhancement services. Banking software products included Finacle Core Banking, Finacle eChannels, Finacle eCorporate, Finacle CRM and Finacle Treasury. The Finacle suite, a flexible, scalable and Web-enabled solution, addressed banks' core banking, treasury, wealth management, consumer and corporate e-banking, mobile banking and Web-based cash management requirements.

Source: Infosys Technologies company Web site and Reuters, Inc.

ENDNOTES

1. Ming Tsai joined formally in May but was involved from the start.
2. Standard & Poor's Industry Survey, "Computers: Commercial Services," *Standard & Poor's,* August 18, 2005, p. 5.
3. Ibid.
4. Infosys Technologies started offering ESOPs in 1994 and discontinued them in 2003.
5. "The multinational and the global corporation are not the same thing. The multinational corporation operates in a number of countries, and adjusts its products and practices in each—at high relative costs. The global corporation operates with resolute constancy—at low relative cost—as if the entire world (or major regions of it) were a single entity; it sells the same things in the same way everywhere." Theodore Leavitt, "The Globalization of Markets," *Harvard Business Review* (May-June 1983), pp. 92–93.
6. Gartner Research, "Magic Quadrant for Offshore Application Services, 2006," *Gartner, Inc.,* 16 February 2006, p. 9.
7. Ibid.
8. A reverse auction (also called "online reverse auction," "e-sourcing," "sourcing event," or "tender") is a type of auction in which the role of the buyer and seller are reversed. Unlike an ordinary auction, where buyers compete for the right to obtain a good, in a reverse auction, sellers compete for the right to provide a good. (Wikipedia, The Free Encyclopedia, http://en.wikipedia.org/wiki/Reverse_auction.)

Blockbuster's Challenges in the Video Rental Industry

This case was prepared by Gareth R. Jones, Texas A&M University.

In January 2007, John Antioco, Blockbuster Inc.'s CEO, was reflecting on the challenges facing the company in the year ahead. The pace of change was quickening as Netflix's online video rental business model was proving very robust. And there was a growing movement to directly download or stream videos using the Internet, which would bypass Blockbuster's store. With its nearly 9,000 global stores, 6,000 in the United States alone, Blockbuster had an enviable brand name and enormous marketing clout, but how could it best use its resources to keep its number 1 place in the movie-rental market and keep its revenues and profits growing? What strategies needed to be developed to strengthen Blockbuster's business model?

Blockbuster's History

David Cook, the founder of Blockbuster, formed David P. Cook & Associates, Inc., in 1978 to offer consulting and computer services to the petroleum and real estate industries. He created programs to analyze and evaluate oil and gas properties and to compute oil and gas reserves. When oil prices began to decline in 1983 due to the breakdown of the OPEC cartel, his business started to decline, and Cook began evaluating alternative businesses in which he could apply his skills. He decided to exit

his current business by selling his company and to enter the video-rental business based on a concept for a "video superstore." He opened his first superstore, called "Blockbuster Video," in October 1985 in Dallas.

Cook developed his idea for a video superstore by analyzing the trends in the video industry that were occurring at that time. During the 1980s, the number of households that owned VCRs was increasing rapidly and, consequently, so were the number of video-rental stores set up to serve their needs. In 1983, 7,000 video-rental stores were in operation, by 1985 there were 19,000, and by 1986 there were over 25,000, of which 13,000 were individually owned. These "mom-and-pop" video stores generally operated for only a limited number of hours, offered customers only a limited selection of videos, and were often located in out-of-the-way strip shopping centers. These small stores often charged a membership fee in addition to the tape rental charge, and generally, customers brought an empty box to the video-store clerk who would exchange it for a tape if it was available—a procedure that was often time-consuming, particularly at peak times such as evenings and weekends.

Cook realized that as VCRs became more widespread and the number of film titles available steadily increased, customers would begin to demand a larger and more varied selection of titles from video stores. Moreover, they would demand more convenient store locations and quicker in-store service than mom-and-pop stores could offer. He realized that the time was right for the development of the next generation of video stores, and he used this opportunity to implement his video superstore concept, which is still the center of Blockbuster's strategy.

The Video Superstore Concept

Cook's superstore concept was based on several components. First, Cook decided that in order to give his video superstores a unique identity that would appeal to customers, the stores should be highly visible stand-alone structures, rather than part of a shopping center. In addition, his superstores were to be large—between 3,800 and 10,000 square feet—well lit, and brightly colored (for example, each store has a bright blue sign with "Blockbuster Video" displayed in huge yellow letters). Each store would have ample parking and would be located in the vicinity of a large urban population to maximize potential exposure to customers.

Second, each superstore was to offer a wide variety of tapes, such as adventure, children's, instructional, and videogame titles. Believing that movie preferences differ in different locations, Cook decided to have each store offer a different selection of between 7,000 and 13,000 film titles organized alphabetically in over thirty categories. New releases were arranged alphabetically against the back wall of each store to make it easier for customers to make their selections.

Third, believing that many customers, particularly those with children, wanted to keep tapes for longer than a one-day period, he created the concept of a three-day rental period for $3. (In 1991, a two-evening rental program was implemented, making new releases only $2.50 for two evenings during the first three weeks after release; after this period, the usual $3 for three evenings would apply.) If the tape was available, it was behind the cover box. The customer would take the tape to the checkout line and hand the cassette and his or her membership card to the clerk, who would scan the bar codes on both the tape and the card. The customer was then handed the tape and told that it was due back by midnight two days later. For example, if the tape were rented Thursday afternoon, it would be due back Saturday at midnight.

Fourth, Cook's superstores targeted the largest market segments, adults in the eighteen- to forty-nine-year-old group, and children in the six- to twelve-year-old group. Cook believed that if his stores could attract children, then the rest of the family probably would follow. Blockbuster carried no X-rated movies, and its goal was to be "America's Family Video Store." New releases were carefully chosen based on reviews and box-office success to maximize their appeal to families.

Finally, believing that customers wanted to choose a movie and get out of the store quickly, Cook decided that his superstores would offer customers the convenience of long operating hours and quick service, generally from 10:00 A.M. to midnight seven days a week. Members received a plastic identification card that was read by the point-of-sale equipment that was developed by the company. This system used a laser bar-code scanner to read important information from both the rental cassette and the ID card. The rental amount was computed by the system and due at the time of rental. Movie returns were scanned by laser, and any late or rewind fees were recorded on the account and automatically recalled the next time the member rented a tape. This system reduced customer checkout time and increased convenience. In addition, it provided Blockbuster with data on customer demographics, cassette rental patterns, and the number of times each cassette has been rented, all of which resulted in a database that increased in value over time as it grew bigger.

These five elements of Blockbuster's approach were successful, and customers responded well. Wherever Blockbuster opened, the local mom-and-pop stores usually closed down, unable to compete with the number of titles and the quality of service that a Blockbuster store could provide. By 1986, Blockbuster owned eight stores and had franchised eleven more to interested investors who could see the potential of this new approach to video rental. Initially, the company opened stores in markets with a minimum population of 100,000; franchises were located in Atlanta, Chicago, Detroit, Houston, San Antonio, and Phoenix. New stores, which cost about $500,000 to $700,000 to equip, grossed an average of $70,000 to $80,000 a month.

Early Growth and Expansion

John Melk, an executive at Waste Management Corp. who had invested in a Blockbuster franchise in Chicago, was to change the history of the company. In February 1987, he contacted H. "Wayne" Huizinga, a former Waste Management colleague, to tell him of the enormous revenue and profits his franchise was making. Huizinga had experience in growing small companies in fragmented industries. In 1955, he had quit college to manage a three-truck trash-hauling operation; in 1962 he bought his own operation, Southern Sanitation. In 1968, Southern Sanitation merged with Ace Partnership, Acme Disposal, and Atlas Refuse Service to form Waste Management. In succeeding years, Huizinga borrowed against Waste Management stock to buy over 100 small companies that provided such services as auto-parts cleaning, dry cleaning, lawn care, and portable-toilet rentals. He used their cash flows to purchase yet more firms. By the time Huizinga, the vice chairman, resigned in 1984, Waste Management was a $6 billion *Fortune 500* company and Huizinga was a wealthy man.

Although Huizinga had a low opinion of video retailers, he agreed to visit a Blockbuster store. Expecting a dingy store renting X-rated films, he was pleasantly surprised to find a brightly lit family video supermarket. Detecting the opportunity to take Cook's superstore concept national, Huizinga, Melk, and Donald Flynn (another Waste Management executive) agreed to purchase 33% of Blockbuster from Cook for $18.6 million in 1986; they became directors at this time. In 1987, CEO David Cook decided to take his money and leave Blockbuster to pursue another venture at Amtech Corp. With the departure of the founder, Huizinga took over as CEO in April 1987 with the goal of making Blockbuster a national company and the industry leader in the video-rental market.

Blockbuster's Explosive Growth

Huizinga and his new top management team mapped out Blockbuster's growth strategy, the elements of which follow.

Location

Store location is a critical issue to a video-rental store, and Huizinga moved quickly with Luigi Salvaneschi, a marketing guru renowned for selecting retail locations for maximum profits, to obtain the best store locations in each geographic area that Blockbuster expanded into. They developed a "cluster strategy" whereby they targeted a particular geographic market, such as Dallas, Boston, or Los Angeles, and then opened up new stores one at a time until they had saturated the market. Thus, within a few years, the local mom-and-pop stores found themselves surrounded, and many, unable to compete with Blockbuster, closed down. Video superstores were always located near busy, well-traveled routes to establish a broad customer base. The cluster strategy eventually brought Blockbuster into 133 television markets (the geographic area that television reaches), where it reached 75 to 85% of the U.S. population.

Marketing

On the marketing side, Blockbuster's chief marketing officer, Tom Gruber, applied his knowledge of McDonald's family-oriented advertising strategy to strengthen Cook's original vision of the video retail business. In 1988, he introduced "Blockbuster Kids" to strengthen the company's position as a family video store. This promotion, aimed at the six- to twelve-year-old age group, introduced four characters and a dog to appeal to Blockbuster's young customers. To further demonstrate commitment to families, each store stocked forty titles recommended for children and a kids' clubhouse with televisions and toys so that children could amuse themselves while their parents browsed for videos. In addition, Blockbuster allowed its members to specify what rating category of tapes (such as PG or R) could be rented through their account. A policy called "Youth-Restricted Viewing" forbade R-rated tape rentals to children under seventeen. Blockbuster also implemented the free "Kidprint Program," through which a child's name, address, and height were recorded on a videotape that was given to parents and local police for identification purposes. In addition, Blockbuster started a program called "America's Most Important Videos Are Free," which offered free rental of public-service tapes about topics such as fire safety and parenting. Finally, to attract customers and to build brand recognition, Gruber initiated joint promotions between Blockbuster and companies like Domino's Pizza, McDonald's, and Pepsi-Cola, something it continues to do today.

Operations

Blockbuster also made great progress on the operations side of the business. As discussed earlier, the operation of a Blockbuster superstore is designed to provide fast checkout and effective inventory management. The company designed its point-of-sale computer system to make rental and return transactions easy; this system is available only to company-owned and franchised stores.

Rapid expansion strains a company's operating systems. To support its stores, Blockbuster opened a

25,000-square-foot distribution center in 1986 in Dallas. The distribution center had the capacity to store 200,000 cassettes tapes that were removed from the original containers and labeled with security devices affixed to the cassettes. Each videotape was then bar-coded and placed into a hard plastic rental case. The facility could process the initial inventory requirement of about 10,000 tapes for up to three superstores per day. In addition, Blockbuster supplied the equipment and fixtures needed to operate new stores, such as computer software and hardware, shelving, signs, and cash registers. In 1987, the physical facilities of the distribution center were expanded to double capacity to 400,000 videocassettes.

Blockbuster's growing buying power also gave it another operations advantage. As the then largest single purchaser of prerecorded videotapes in the U.S. market, it was able to negotiate discounts off retail price. Cassettes were bought at an average of $40 per tape and rented three nights for $3. Thus, the cash investment on "hit" videotapes was recovered in forty-five to sixty days, and the investment on non-hit titles was regained in two-and-a-half to three months. In its early days, Blockbuster was also able to use its efficient distribution system to distribute extra copies of films declining in popularity to new stores where demand was increasing. This ability to transfer tapes to where they were most demanded was very important because customers wanted new tapes on the shelves when they came out. It also allowed the company to use its inventory to the best advantage and to receive the maximum benefit from each videotape.

Management and Structure

For Blockbuster, as for any company, rapid growth posed the risk of losing control over daily operations and allowing costs to escalate. Recognizing this, Blockbuster established three operating divisions to manage the functional activities necessary to retain effective control over its operations as it grew. Blockbuster Distribution Corp. was created to handle the area licensing and franchising of new stores, and to service their start-up and operation—offering assistance with the selection, acquisition, assembling, packaging, inventorying, and distribution of videocassettes, supplies, and computer equipment. Blockbuster Management Corp. was established to assist with the training of new store management, facility location and acquisition, and

employee training. Finally, Blockbuster Computer Systems Inc. was formed to install, maintain, and support the software programs for the inventory and point-of-sale equipment. Together these three divisions provided all the support services necessary to manage store expansion.

Rapid growth also led Blockbuster to oversee store operations through a regional and district level organizational structure. In 1988, responsibility for store development and operations was decentralized to the regional level. However, corporate headquarters was kept fully informed of developments in each regional area, and even in each store, through its computerized inventory and sales system. For example, Blockbuster's corporate inventory and point-of-sale computer systems tracked sales and inventory in each store and each region. The role of regional management was to oversee the stores in their regions, providing advice and monitoring stores' performance to make sure that they kept up Blockbuster's high standards of operation as its chain of superstores grew.

New-Store Expansion

With Blockbuster's functional-level competencies in place, the next step for Huizinga was to begin a rapid program of growth and expansion. Huizinga believed that expanding rapidly to increase revenue and market share was crucial for success in the video-rental industry. Under his leadership, Blockbuster opened new stores quickly, developed a franchising program, and began to acquire competitors to increase the number of its stores.

To facilitate rapid expansion, Blockbuster began to use its skills in store location, distribution, and sales. At first Blockbuster focused on large markets, preferring to enter a market with a potential capacity for 500 stores—normally a large city. Later, Blockbuster decided to enter smaller market segments, like towns with a minimum of 20,000 people within driving distance. All stores were built and operated using the superstore concept described earlier. Using the services of its three divisions, Blockbuster steadily increased its number of new-store openings until by 1993 it owned over 2,500 video stores.

Blockbuster's rapid growth was also attributable to Huizinga's skills in making acquisitions. Beginning in 1986, the company began to acquire many smaller regional video chains to gain a significant market presence in a city or region. In 1987, for example, the twenty-nine video stores of Movies To Go were acquired to expand Blockbuster's presence in the Midwest. Blockbuster then used this acquisition as a jumping-off point for opening many more stores in the region. Similarly, in 1989, it acquired 175 video stores from Major Video Corp. and Video Library to develop a presence in southern California. In 1991, it took over 209 Erol's Inc. stores to obtain the stronghold that Erol's previously held in the Mid-Atlantic states. All acquired stores were made to conform to Blockbuster's standards, and any store that could not was closed down. Most acquisitions were financed by existing cash flow or by issuing new shares of stock rather than taking on new debt. These deals reflect Huizinga's reluctance to borrow money.

Licensing and Franchising

Recognizing the need to build market share rapidly and develop a national brand name, Huizinga also recruited top management to put in place his ambitious franchise program. Franchising, in which the franchisee is solely responsible for all financial commitments connected with opening a new store, allowed Blockbuster to expand rapidly without incurring debt. The downside of franchising was that Blockbuster had to share profits with the franchise owners. When franchising, it is important to maintain consistency in stores. Thus, the franchisees were required to operate their stores in the same way as company-owned stores and to follow the same store format for rental selection and the use of proprietary point-of-sale equipment.

Franchising facilitated the rapid expansion of Blockbuster Video. By 1992, the company had over 1,000 franchised stores as compared to 2,000 company-owned stores. However, recognizing the long-term profit advantages of owning its own stores, Blockbuster began to repurchase attractive territories from franchisees. In 1993, the company spent $248 million to buy the 400 stores of its two largest franchisees and, with a new store opening every day, by the end of 1993, it owned over 2,500 stores. However, by the end of 1992, despite its rapid growth, Blockbuster still controlled only about 15% of the market—its 27,000 smaller rivals shared the rest. Consequently, in 1993, Blockbuster announced plans for a new round of store openings and acquisitions that would give it a 25 to 30% market share within two or three years.

The Home-Video Industry

By 1990, revenues from video rentals exceeded the revenues obtained in movie theaters. For example, video-rental revenues rose to $11 billion in 1991 compared to movie theaters' $4.8 billion. The huge growth in industry revenues led to increased competition for customers, and, as noted above, 28,000 video stores operated in the United States in 1990.

Blockbuster's rapid growth had put it in a commanding position. In 1990, it had no national competitor and was the only company operating beyond a regional level. The next largest competitor, West Coast Video, had only $120 million in 1991 revenues while Blockbuster had revenues of $868 million. However, Blockbuster faced many competitors at the local and regional levels.

Mature Market

As the video-rental market matured, the level of competition in the industry changed. During the 1980s, video rentals grew rapidly due to the proliferation of VCRs. By 1990, however, 70% of households had VCRs, compared to 2% in 1980, and industry growth dropped from the previous double digits to 7%. The slow growth in VCR ownership and rentals made competition more severe. To a large degree, competition in the video-rental industry was fierce because new competitors could enter the market with relative ease; the only purchase necessary was videotapes. However, unlike small video-rental companies, Blockbuster was able to negotiate discounts with tape suppliers because it bought new releases in such huge volumes.

New Technology

One growing problem facing Blockbuster by the early 1990s was the variety of new ways in which customers could view movies and other kinds of entertainment. Blockbuster had always felt competition both from other sources of movies—such as cable TV and movie theaters—and from other forms of entertainment—such as bowling, baseball games, and outdoor activities. In the 1990s, technology began to give customers more ways to watch movies. New technological threats included pay-per-view (PPV) or video-on-demand (VOD) systems, digital compression, and direct broadcast satellites.

Pay-per-view movies became a major competitive threat to video-rental stores. With PPV systems, cable customers can call their local cable company and pay a fee to have a scheduled movie, concert, or sporting event aired on their television set. In the future, perhaps cable customers would be able to call up their local "video company" and choose any movie to be aired on their televisions for a fee; the cable company would make the movies available when customers wanted them. Increasingly, telephone companies were becoming interested in the potential for pay-for-view because the networks of fiber-optic cable they installed throughout the country in the 1990s can be used to transmit movies as well. Huizinga claimed Blockbuster was not overly concerned about PPV systems because only one-third of U.S. households have access to PPV, and fiber optics were expensive. Also, he claimed home-video rental was cheaper than PPV, and new releases are attained thirty to forty-five days before PPV.

VOD takes the PPV concept further. Bellcore, the research branch of the regional Bell companies, invented VOD. With this system (still in the development stage for many companies), a customer will use an interactive box to select a movie from a list of thousands and the choice will be transmitted to an "information warehouse" that stores thousands of tapes in digital formats. The selected video is then routed back to the customer's house through either fiber-optic cable or phone lines. This bypasses the local video-rental store because the movies are stored digitally on tape at the cable company's headquarters.

Movie companies or video stores like Blockbuster could function as the information warehouse from which the video selections are made; Blockbuster actively tried to canvass movie studios to become the warehouse so that it could control the VOD market. However, it could not put any deal together. The linking of phone companies with other entertainment companies could also become a direct threat, but Huizinga believed the local Blockbuster store would eventually become the hub of the VOD network. He felt that phone companies would prefer to deal with Blockbuster than with companies like Time Warner or Paramount, which lacked both Blockbuster's skills in video retailing and its established customer base—the 30 million customers who make 600 million trips per year to the local store.

Blockbuster's Emerging Strategies

In the 1990s, 70% of the world's VCRs were in countries outside the United States, and foreign countries accounted for half of total world video-rental revenues.

In 1991, the United States was the largest video market with revenues of $11 billion, Japan was second with $2.6 billion, followed by the UK with $1.4 billion and Canada with $1.2 billion. Blockbuster began to expand into international markets in 1989 when it saw the opportunity to exploit its marketing expertise, superstore concept, operating knowledge, financial strength, and ability to attract franchisees abroad.

Just as in the United States, Blockbuster started a program both to build new video superstores and to acquire foreign competitors abroad. Planning to be a leader in home entertainment around the world, Blockbuster's objective was to obtain a 25% share of international revenue by 1995 and to have 2,000 stores in international markets by 1996. In 1989, stores were opened in Canada and the UK. In 1990, Blockbuster opened its first store in Puerto Rico. It continued its expansion into the UK, Canada, the Virgin Islands, Venezuela, and Spain. Franchise agreements were also signed in Japan, Australia, and Mexico.

To expand in the UK in 1992, Blockbuster purchased Cityvision PLC, the UK's largest video retailer, for $81 million cash and 3.9 million shares of stock. At this time, Cityvision ran 875 stores in Britain and Austria under the name Ritz. Blockbuster transformed the Ritz outlets into Blockbuster stores and used the chain as a start for further expansion into Europe, just as it had taken over large video chains in the United States on its way to becoming the national leader. Joint ventures were also negotiated in France, Germany, and Italy. Blockbuster increased the number of franchise stores in Mexico, Chile, Venezuela, and Spain. By 1995, the company had over 2,000 stores in nine foreign countries.

Blockbuster created an international home-video division to oversee and manage its expansion into foreign markets. Besides having expertise in international operations, marketing, merchandising, product purchasing, distribution, franchising, real estate, and field support, this division is proficient at dealing with differences in entertainment, language, and business culture between different countries and is successfully implementing Blockbuster's domestic strategy in its foreign operations.

Blockbuster became a national video-rental chain because of the way it positioned itself in the market as a family-oriented store with a wide selection of videos, convenient hours and locations, and fast checkout. Blockbuster began to expand its entertainment concept into several new markets or industries such as film entertainment programming and music retailing. Also, to increase its revenue, Blockbuster made deals to broaden its range of product offerings.

To enter the entertainment programming, Blockbuster invested in Spelling Entertainment Group and Republic Pictures. Both of these companies have large film libraries—a source of inexpensive movies for Blockbuster's retail operations. Blockbuster also chose the music retail business as an area into which it could expand its entertainment concept. Blockbuster saw a fit between selling records, cassettes, and compact disks and renting or selling videos, so it decided to employ the same strategy it had used in the video-rental market: opening new stores and acquiring chains of music stores using the revenues from its video superstores. Blockbuster agreed to buy Sound Warehouse and Music Plus, two record-store chains, for $185 million. At the time, Sound Warehouse was the seventh largest music retailer and Music Plus was the twelfth largest. These two retail chains had a total of 236 stores in thirty-five states, primarily in California and the South. This acquisition made Blockbuster the seventh largest music chain.

Huizinga Sells Blockbuster to Viacom

Although Blockbuster, with its rapid growth and large positive cash flow, seemed poised to become an entertainment powerhouse, Huizinga knew there were clouds ahead. The rapid advance in digital technology including broadband Internet meant VOD was increasingly likely to become a reality. Some analysts were suggesting even that Blockbuster was a "dinosaur." At the same time, Huizinga soon found out the music retailing industry was highly competitive and had many more experienced competitors than the video-rental industry. Major competitors like Sam Goody's and Tower Records also had plans to accelerate the development of their own music megastores, and profit margins in music retailing were low. Moreover, Wal-Mart began a major push to lower the prices of CDs and then VHS tapes, and price wars were developing. Moreover, even in the video-rental business, entrepreneurs who had watched Blockbuster's rapid growth still believed there were opportunities for entry. Chains such as Hollywood Video began to expand rapidly, and increased competition seemed imminent here too.

Huizinga decided that the time was ripe to sell the Blockbuster chain, just as he had sold other chains before. His opportunity came when Sumner Redstone, chairman of Viacom, become involved in an aggressive bidding war to buy Paramount Studios, the movie company. Redstone recognized the value of Blockbuster's huge cash flow in helping to fund the debt needed to take over Paramount. Ignoring the risks involved in taking over Blockbuster, in 1994 Viacom acquired the company for $8.4 billion in stock (further details about the logic behind the acquisition are found in Case 30 on Viacom), and Huizinga cashed in his huge stockholdings.

Just the next year, in 1995, a tidal wave of problems hit the Blockbuster chain. First, a brutal price war hit the video-rental industry as new video chain start-ups fought to find a niche in major markets to get some of the lucrative industry revenues. Second, movie studios started to lower the price of tapes, realizing they could make more money by selling them directly to customers rather than letting companies like Blockbuster make the money through tape rentals. Third, as both Blockbuster's video and music operations expanded, it became obvious that the company did not have in hand the materials management and distribution systems needed to manage the complex flow of products to its stores. Overhead costs started to soar, so that together with declines in revenues, the company turned from making a profit to a loss. Blockbuster's cash flow was much less useful to Redstone now, burdened as he was by the huge debt for Paramount. Blockbuster's declining performance led to Viacom's stock price dropping sharply, and Redstone reacted by firing its top managers and searching for an experienced executive to turn the Blockbuster division around.

Blockbuster, 1996–1998

To control Blockbuster's soaring overhead costs, Redstone looked for an executive with experience in low-cost merchandising, and in 1996, he pulled off a coup by hiring William Fields, the heir apparent to David Glass, Wal-Mart's CEO, and an information systems and logistics expert. Fields began planning on a huge state-of-the-art distribution facility that would serve all Blockbuster's U.S. stores to replace its outdated facility. He also started the development of a new state-of-the-art point-of-sale merchandising information system that would give Blockbuster real-time feedback on which videos were generating the most money and when they should be transferred to stores in other regions to make the most use of Blockbuster's stock of videos—its most important physical resource. Third, Fields added more retail merchandise to Blockbuster's product mix, such as candy, comics, and audio books. The results of these efforts would take a couple of years to bear fruit, however.

Some analysts believed that by 1997, Redstone, recognizing the negative impact of Blockbuster's operations on Viacom's stock price, was trying to cut costs to boost short-term profits and "harvest" the company so that he could spin off Blockbuster—sensing that the troubled division was not going to be fixed quickly. Apparently, Fields and Redstone came into conflict over what was Blockbuster's future in the Viacom empire. And, with its performance continuing to decline in the first quarter of 1997 with a drop in profit of 20%, only thirteen months after taking over at Blockbuster, Fields resigned in April 1997. Viacom's stock fell to a three-year low. Redstone argued that this was absurd because Blockbuster generated $3 billion in revenue and $800 in cash flow for Viacom in 1996. However, the specter of video-on-demand and increased price competition in the music and video business made analysts wonder if Blockbuster was going to recover. Furthermore, Fields was the expert in distribution and logistics.

Once again, Redstone looked around for an executive who could help turn around Blockbuster, and in the news was John Antioco, the chief of PepsiCo's Taco Bell restaurants. In just eight months, Antioco, by introducing a new menu, new pricing, and new store setup, had engineered a 180-degree turnaround in Taco Bell's performance, turning a mounting loss into rising profit. Antioco seemed the perfect choice as Blockbuster's CEO.

After Antioco took the helm, he started to assess the situation. The video-rental market was still flat; sales of movie videos were soaring as their prices came down in outlets such as Wal-Mart. Fields's strategy of enlarging the entertainment product lines carried in Blockbuster stores, while it seemed like a logical move, had failed as costs continued to rise and products had short shelf lives because changing fads and fashions made the value of Blockbuster's inventory unpredictable. What should be Blockbuster's merchandising mix? And how should Antioco manage the purchase and distribution of Blockbuster's biggest ongoing expense, videotapes,

to create a value chain that would lead to increased profitability?

Antioco realized he needed to focus on how to reorganize Blockbuster's value chain to simultaneously reduce costs and generate more revenues. Blockbuster's biggest expense and asset was its inventory of videos, so this was the logical place to start. Antioco and Redstone examined the way Blockbuster obtained its movies. It was presently purchasing tapes from the big studios—MGM, Disney, and so on—at the high price of $65. Because it had to pay this high price, it could not purchase enough copies of a particular hit movie to satisfy customer demand when the movie was released. As a result, customers left unsatisfied and revenues were lost. Perhaps there was a better way of managing the process for both the movie studios and Blockbuster to raise revenues from movie tape rental.

Antioco and Redstone proposed that Blockbuster and the movie studios enter into a revenue sharing agreement, whereby the movie studios would supply Blockbuster with tapes at cost, around $8, which would allow it to purchase 800% more copies of a single title; Blockbuster would then split rental revenues with the studios 50/50. The result, they hoped, would be that they could "grow the market" for rental tapes by 20 to 30% a year; thus both Blockbuster's and the movie studios' revenues would grow. This would also counter the threat from satellite programming, which was taking away all their revenues; 6 million households were now subscribing to direct satellite services. While this deal was being negotiated in 1997, video rentals at Blockbuster dropped 4% more, and the studios that had been hesitating to enter into this radically different kind of sales agreement came on board. This came at a crucial point for Blockbuster, too, since its cash flow continued to drop as it faced higher write-off costs for outdated tapes. With the new revenue sharing agreement signed, however, the profitability of its new business model would increase dramatically. (Blockbuster's market share increased from something less than 30% to over 40% in the next five years, and after a few years, the division returned to profitability.) The move studios also benefited as their stream of income increased enormously.

Antioco's second major change in strategy was to abandon the attempt to transform Blockbuster's stores into more general entertainment outlets to refocus on its core movie-rental business. It abandoned its idea to expand its music chain, and, in October 1998, it sold its 378 Blockbuster music chains to Wherehouse Entertainment for $115 million.

Nevertheless, all these changes hurt Blockbuster's performance in the short term. In 1998, Viacom announced it would record a $437 million charge in the second quarter to write down the value of its Blockbuster tape inventory since it now had to revise the accounting method it adopted when it entered the new revenue sharing agreement for tapes from Hollywood studios. These charges wiped out Viacom's profits, and Redstone once again announced that a spinoff or initial public offering of Blockbuster was likely because the unit was punishing Viacom's stock price and threatening Viacom's future profitability.

On the plus side, however, significantly, the revenue sharing agreement resulted in a sharp increase in revenues; same-store video rentals increased by 13% in 1998. Since rental tapes would now be amortized over only a three-month period—the time of greatest rental sales—not the old six to twenty-six months, the new business model seemed poised to finally increase cash flows. One good year for Blockbuster would allow Redstone, who had been increasingly criticized for his purchase of Blockbuster, to go forward with his desire to pursue an "IPO carve out" whereby Viacom would sell between 10 and 20% of the Blockbuster stock to the public in an IPO to create a public market for the stock and make an eventual spinoff possible.

By the end of 1998, there were continuing signs of recovery. The move to a revenue sharing agreement had allowed Blockbuster's managers to develop strategies to increase responsiveness to customers that allowed them to pursue their business model in a profitable way. With the huge increase in the supply of new tapes made possible by the revenue sharing agreement, Blockbuster was now able to offer the Blockbuster Promise to its customers that their chosen title would be in stock or "next time, it's free." Also, lower prices could now be charged for older video titles to generate additional revenues without threatening profitability. It turned out that the real threat to Blockbuster in the 1990s was not from new technology like video-on-demand, but the lack of the right strategies to keep customers happy—like having the products in stock that they wanted—and a failure to understand the important dynamics behind the value chain, such as revenue sharing, that would grow the market.

Outside the United States, Blockbuster had been increasing the scope of its international operations. In 1994, it opened its first stores in Italy and New Zealand; in 1995, it entered Israel, Brazil, Peru, Colombia, and Thailand; in 1996, Ecuador, Portugal, El Salvador, Panama, and Scandinavia, where it purchased Christianshavn Video In Denmark. In 1996, in went into Taiwan and Uruguay; in 1998, it acquired Video Flick's stores in Australia; in 1999, it entered Hong Kong as a gateway to China and opened its two-hundredth store in Mexico; and in 2000, it expanded its operations in Central America to Costa Rica and Guatemala. By 2002, it operated almost 2,600 stores outside the United States. The main advantage of its global operations is that it can constantly distribute copies of tapes that are less in demand overseas to other countries where they will appear as new releases and customers will be willing to pay the highest rental prices for them. In turn, the tapes will trickle down to other countries so that even though revenues might be less, since the cost of the tape has already been amortized, operations will still be profitable. On the other hand, it can also identify foreign-made movies that might attract a large U.S. viewing audience as its customers search its shelves.

In 1998, Blockbuster finally opened its 820,000-square-foot distribution center in Kinney, Texas; now it was in a real position to reduce costs and speed delivery of tapes to locations where they were most in demand, and to move them when demand dropped. Also in 1998, Blockbuster began to offer "neighborhood favorites," a program in which each store stocked tapes customized to local tastes. In keeping with this differentiation approach, Blockbuster Rewards, its frequent renters program, was developed. It is a rewards program designed to keep its customers returning regularly to its stores and seeing the changes it has made, with a coupon for a free video every month.

Antioco Transforms Blockbuster, 1999–2002

A major turning point for Blockbuster occurred in 1999. After reestablishing Blockbuster's business model, Antioco orchestrated a successful initial public stock offering in August 1999. It turned out that 1999 was the first of four consecutive years of same-store sales increases as Antioco set about to change the entertainment mix in stores to increase revenues. Having gotten rid of music, candy, and comics, a new opportunity arose in 1999 with the introduction of DVDs, whose high quality suggested that they would soon become the next entertainment media of choice. DVDs were a natural product-line extension for Blockbuster. In 1999, Blockbuster introduced DVDs into 3,000 of its stores to assess their promise; customer reaction was favorable as sales of DVD players and other digital media were soaring.

It was here that Antioco apparently made a major error, for given the success of the video revenue sharing deal with movie studios, it seemed likely that the same kind of deal could be negotiated for DVDs. Reportedly Warner Brothers started the ball rolling by offering Blockbuster a DVD revenue sharing deal. Antioco turned down the offer, however; one reason seems to have been Antioco's belief that the high price of DVDs would deter rental customers from buying them. He believed that Blockbuster would reap more returns from buying the DVDs themselves and then renting them. Another reason was that Blockbuster was about to face a lawsuit from independent video retailers, who claimed that the company had gained an unfair competitive advantage from the sharing agreement; signing a new DVD revenue sharing agreement might therefore generate more potential lawsuits.

In any event, to test the popularity of DVD rentals, in 2000 Blockbuster increased the number of DVDs titles it carried because they had much higher profit margins than VHS tapes—DVDs rented for a couple of dollars more. The result was dramatic: revenues soared and the pace of change speeded up. In 2001, Blockbuster abandoned attempts to customize tape offerings to local markets and eliminated 25% of the company's less productive VHS tapes in order to focus on the booming market for DVD rentals. Once again, it took a charge to amortize these tapes, but then shipped them to its stores overseas to capitalize on growing global demand for its products. The result was that by the end of 2001 the company achieved record revenues, strong cash flow, and increased profitability while it lowered its debt by more then $430 million. Since 1997, Antioco had grown Blockbuster's revenues from $3.3 billion to over $5 billion and turned free cash flow from a negative position to over $250 million for 2001. Its stock rose as investors realized that the company now had a business model that generated cash.

By 2002, it became clear the future was in DVDs. Blockbuster announced it was switching even more quickly to high-margin DVDs and phasing out even more of its VHS and that DVDs would account for 40% of the chain's rental inventory. This percentage has increased sharply ever since. DVDs swept away VHS tapes much as CDs swept away vinyl records. DVD rentals increased 115%, and in the spring of 2002, Blockbuster made $66 million in net income.

Growing Videogame Market

Antioco searched for more ways to broaden Blockbuster's product line to keep revenues increasing and ward off possible future declines from rental revenues. One answer came at the end of 2001 when Microsoft introduced its Xbox videogame console to compete with the Sony PlayStation 2 and Nintendo GameCube and the robust nature of sales in the videogame market became clear—it was a $15 billion a year revenue market. Blockbuster decided to carry a full lineup of GameCube, Xbox, and PlayStation software and hardware for rental as well as deciding to rent and sell videogames in its stores. It also began to try to work exclusive deals with game makers for old gaming systems and software since there is a huge installed base of older-generation videogames. The attraction of this kind of products to customers is that they can try any game they want before they are forced to pay the high price of buying a game that they may not like. Videogames seemed to be a natural complementary product line, and in May 2002, Blockbuster announced that it wanted to become "gamers' most comprehensive rental and retail resource."

Blockbuster's new product line was a success, and it pushed to double its videogame rentals by 2003. To help achieve this goal, in the summer of 2002, Blockbuster began to offer $19.95 monthly rental service for unlimited videogame rentals. This fit well with Blockbuster's family profile since parents could come into a store to rent a DVD while their children picked up a videogame.

The company tested a new concept of a videogame store-in-store called Game Rush in 2003, and its success at attracting new customers, who also paid a monthly fee for unlimited videogame rental, led to its fast decision to roll the game program out to half its stores by 2004. However, all its new initiatives cost between $80 and $100 million marketing dollars, and this, together with the high capital costs of maintaining its stores, caused its net income to fall despite growing revenues.

A Blockbuster Performance?

In June 2003, Blockbuster went to court to confront independent video retailers who claimed that Blockbuster's VHS revenue sharing agreement that had saved the company in 1999 violated antitrust laws by discriminating against them since they did not obtain preferential price treatment. Independents argued that before the revenue sharing deals were negotiated, Blockbuster had only 24% of the market while they had 55%, but by 2003, Blockbuster's share had grown to 40%. The court ruled that the independents had had a similar opportunity to negotiate such revenue sharing agreements and dismissed the suit against Blockbuster, however. Now the case was over, and as DVD rentals soared, Antioco tried to establish a new revenue sharing agreement for DVDs with movie studios. Antioco argued that raising wholesale prices and developing a rental sharing agreement would generate the highest long-term returns for both movie studios and Blockbuster—but it was too late.

The main reason was that by 2002 the movie studios had began to sell DVDs directly to the general public, and they decided to set the wholesale price of DVDs relatively low to generate sales. However, sales took off, there was an unexpectedly strong customer demand to own DVDs and develop a home-movie library, and the movie studios were generating billions of dollars in DVD sales and they no longer saw the need for a middleman like Blockbuster to take a major share of DVD sales revenues.

This came as a major blow to Blockbuster, but Antioco tried to make the best of it by becoming a major player in the DVD retail market, hoping it could generate high DVD sales revenues, in addition to its increasing DVD rental revenues. However, he was in for a shock because the movie studios were obtaining such high revenues from DVD sales they were willing to reduce their wholesale prices for major low-cost retailers like Wal-Mart and Best Buy that could sell millions of copies in their stores. Wal-Mart, in particular, began to aggressively discount DVDs and sell at prices well below Blockbuster's; the result was that Blockbuster gained a much smaller share of the DVD retail market than expected. And, because customers were not going to its stores to buy them, it also did not enjoy any spillover from increased DVD rentals.

In fact, the boom in DVD sales starting in 2002 caused a major shift as by 2003 customers spent significantly more on purchasing movies on DVDs and tapes than on movie rentals. Thus while Blockbuster's retail sales of movies rose 19% to $12.3 billion, movie rentals slipped 3% to $9.9 billion; the result was that same-store sales at Blockbuster stores opened for one year fell by 6%—a very disappointing result. Although Blockbuster could claim record revenues and profits because of its decision in 2002 and 2003 to switch to DVD rentals, revenues also had increased because it had opened over 550 new stores in 2003—so this was growth without profitability. Moreover, things were not so rosy as they might appear because a large part of these extra profits had come from aggressive cost-cutting efforts in its stores throughout this period and by a substantial reduction in local and national advertising to reduce operating costs—once and for all, gains that could not be repeated.

Blockbuster had to find new ways to increase rental revenues and do it quickly. To reduce customers' incentive to buy DVDs and build up their own movie libraries, Blockbuster tested a new marketing strategy, a monthly fee of $24.99 for unlimited DVD rentals in some of its stores. The program was successful, and Blockbuster began to roll it out nationally in 2004 and experiment with variations in pricing and number of rentals per visit. As mentioned earlier, it already had a similar program in videogame rentals that was performing well.

In another major move, it announced the end to late fees in 2004 as it became clear this was a major motivation of customers to buy DVDs and not to rent them; also, other forms of movie delivery such as pay-per-view were becoming more common, and these had no late fees. This was a significant decision because late fees were a significant contributor to Blockbuster's revenues and profits; indeed, it was estimated that late fees accounted for over 35% of Blockbuster's profit! It hoped no late fees would translate into more rentals, but this did not happen and put a damper on revenue growth in 2004 and 2005.

The Split from Viacom

Recall that Viacom had decided to take Blockbuster public once again in August 1999 at $15 a share, but it maintained an 82% stake in the company. Blockbuster stock traded as high as $30 a share in May 2000, and although Viacom originally planned to sell the rest of Blockbuster to the public soon after the 1999 stock offering, the company decided to retain its stake—in part because of the business's steady cash flow and because Viacom became distracted by integrating CBS, which it acquired in 2001, into its operations.

Through its aggressive cost cutting, particularly in marketing, Blockbuster continued to perform well financially into 2003 when Blockbuster generated 22.5% of Viacom's $19.1 billion in revenue and 12% of its $4.4 billion in cash flow. But Blockbuster's 8% revenue growth was anemic, and with most of the cost cuts already made and the continuing high fixed costs of running its stores, it was clear that future revenue growth and stock appreciation was going to be challenging. Also, the uncertainty concerning how quickly home-video and videogame rentals might fall in the future because of the growth in broadband technology once again began to worry Viacom. So throughout 2003, Redstone tried, but failed, to find a buyer for Viacom's Blockbuster shares while they were on the rise.

In January 2004 (well before it announced the end to late fees), Blockbuster's stock hit a high of $20. Believing that the two companies' business models were now diverging too fast, Viacom announced that it would totally spin off its Blockbuster unit by allowing holders of Viacom shares to swap them for shares in Blockbuster. To sweeten the deal, shareholders would also receive a substantial once-and-for all dividend for swapping their Viacom stock for Blockbuster stock. Enough shareholders took advantage of the offer for Viacom to unload its 82% stake, and Blockbuster was now spun off as a fully independent company. Antioco now had to find a way to increase Blockbuster's revenues and free cash flow, but there were still many challenges confronting the company.

The Growing Use of Broadband

Since the 1990s, the new technology of PPV or VOD, the direct download or streaming of movies to customers over cable, satellite, phone lines, or other forms of broadband connection, had been seen as a growing threat to Blockbuster's business model. Essentially, this technology would bypass the need for a bricks-and-mortar store, and the potential threat of this new technology had depressed Blockbuster's stock for years.

In 2000, recognizing the growing importance of satellite programming in PPV delivery, Blockbuster formed an alliance with DIRECTTV to provide a co-branded PPV service on DIRECTTV. Blockbuster also became a new distribution channel for DIRECTTV; under their deal, Blockbuster received a fee for each dish sold, a share of future monthly payments, and a share of revenues from DIRECTTV customers' future orders of PPV movies that would provide a higher net profit than Blockbuster made from each in-store rental and so lessen its dependence on video rentals. Antioco hoped this alliance would boost Blockbuster's ambition to be the major player in PPV, and at the very least, add 5% to Blockbuster's revenues, enough to make a substantial impact on its bottom line.

In an attempt to maintain its dominant position in the movie-rental marketplace and gain more control of the content or "entertainment software" end of the business, in 2000 Blockbuster announced an agreement with MGM to digitally stream and download recent theatrical releases, films, and television programming from the MGM library to Blockbuster's website for PPV consumption. It started to roll out its "Blockbuster on Demand" PPV, arguing that video rentals and PPV could exist side by side. Initial testing of the program started at the end of 2000, and Blockbuster announced it would try to form similar agreements with other movie studios. It even signed a deal with TiVo, a maker of set-top digital recorders, to offer a VOD service through broadband using TiVo's recorders. TiVo agreed to put demonstration kiosks in over 4,000 Blockbusters stores to its 65 million customers. However, all these moves failed to establish Blockbuster as a major player in the PPV delivery market.

The push toward VOD steadily increased in the mid 2000s as new technologies to ensure its fast delivery to customers over broadband connections improved. In August 2005, for example, five major movie studios—Sony, Time Warner, Universal, MGM, and Paramount—announced a plan to bypass powerful middlemen like Blockbuster and HBO and offer their own PPV service directly to customers, although this service was still not up and running by 2006. In addition, Disney and Twentieth-Century Fox also were planning their own PPV services, and in 2006, Disney announced its intention of being the hub of the future PPV service and make Blockbuster redundant with its new PPV technology that it reportedly is going to roll out in 2007. Also in 2006, Amazon.com launched a form of PPV service whereby its customers could download a wide range of movie content. Its PPV ran into technology glitches including long download times, which it has since improved, but it is not clear it has made much of an impression in the industry. Also in 2006, Apple made a big push into the VOD market with its new video iPods; by 2007, Apple had formed two major agreements with large media companies Disney and Paramount to allow its customers to download both TV shows and movies. Analysts believe Apple clearly intends to try to establish itself as the primary PPV video wholesaler, just as it has become the main wholesaler in the music download business.

PPV buy rates are still relatively low and below expectations, however, because cable TV companies and phone companies or satellite operators simply do not have the Internet bandwidth necessary for fast downloads, especially at peak periods such as in the evening or on weekends. Also, VOD was conceived as a more convenient way to watch movies at home; rather than fighting traffic and risking late fees, customers could watch new video releases without leaving their couches—and without waiting. But the process of selecting and downloading a movie is still not easy. Movie studios, too, have a policy of not releasing films for PPV/VOD for at least thirty days after they are first released to protect DVD rentals at video stores; this generates billions more in revenue than home PPV services.

Nevertheless, by 2007, the threat of new easy-to-use digital technology had become an emerging reality as movie studios and distributors like Amazon and Apple fought to become the hub of choice, and it was clear by now that although Antioco's goal, just as Huizinga before him, was that Blockbuster should provide this pivotal role, it obviously had no special technological competencies in the digital PPV media arena—no more than movie studios, cable operators, satellite providers, and so on. Moreover, in the future, all movies could be licensed to any VOD on a nonexclusive basis so each studio would control the pricing and availability of its films. Now, as PCs, TVs, and even MP3 players like iPod began to converge, the potentially huge VOD market would annihilate Blockbuster's niche. By 2006, Blockbuster's stock had dropped to a low of $5.

The Netflix Battle

Although the way future broadband PPV service will unfold will have major consequences for Blockbuster's business model, in the last few years, Blockbuster has also had to deal with the growing threat from online DVD rental services, such as that offered by Netflix, which has also cut into its rental business. The emergence of Netflix in 2003, with its business model of using the combination of the Internet and regular mail service to rent and deliver DVDs to customers, was revolutionary in the movie-rental industry. The big appeal of Netflix's new plan was the promise of multiple movie rentals for a single monthly price. With Netflix's most popular plan, subscribers can rent an unlimited number of movies for $17.99 a month, keeping as many as three DVDs at a time. Once they send the movies back, by popping them into a postage-paid envelope and dropping them in a mailbox, they can immediately get more. The services don't limit the number of DVDs that can be ordered in any one month.

Obviously, using the Internet to deliver DVDs to customers is a far less expensive way of renting DVDs than owning a chain of bricks-and-mortar video stores. Apparently Blockbuster was offered the chance to buy Netflix in the early 2000s for $100 million, but Antioco refused; he did not consider that this market segment was big enough to be profitable, given that most movie rentals tend to be spur of the moment decisions. He believed few customers would sit down and work out in advance which movies to watch. Netflix, however, went to work to attract customers, and through massive online advertising and mailing campaigns, it began to attract increasing numbers of customers and became a real threat. By 2004, Netflix claimed to have over 1.4 million customers, and the proven success of its business model showed Antioco he had made a mistake.

In 2004, Blockbuster announced it would also launch an online DVD rental service, although Antioco still commented that he thought this segment would only ever reach about 3 million customers. Blockbuster claimed its new program would be better than Netflix's because customers who ordered DVDs online could then return them to Blockbusters stores if they chose. Antioco argued Blockbuster's business model was the best because it was the only company able to provide a simultaneous online *and* bricks-and-mortar service that would give customers more options and better service. For example, if Blockbuster customers returned DVDs to their local store, as part of Blockbuster's "Total Service" plan, they would then receive a coupon for a free in-store rental.

The point, of course, is that by getting customers into its stores, Blockbuster could potentially generate more rental, sales, and other kinds of revenues. Also, Blockbuster's hybrid service overcame one of the big disadvantages of Netflix for rental customers—the inability to get a movie instantly if you suddenly decide Saturday night you want to rent something. Blockbuster's program allowed for advance planning *and* spontaneous rental.

Given that Blockbuster has 48 million members, an online DVD service may prove a useful way of increasing future revenues, but in the short run, the problem for Blockbuster was that the new service required a major financial investment to set up the online infrastructure and national marketing campaign. This helped drain Blockbuster's profits, and its stock price fell from $20 a share at the beginning of 2004 to just $10 share at the beginning of 2005 as investors became concerned it could not provide the online service in a cost-effective way. Analysts also wondered if Netflix had gained the first-mover advantage and so would be hard to compete with. To make things worse, Wal-Mart, which already sold low-priced DVDs to attract customers, started a similar online rental program.

However, in 2006, Antioco announced that the company, after a shaky start, had achieved its year-end goal of 2 million subscribers to Total Access. Moreover, significant subscriber growth was achieved without any broadcast media advertising, except in a handful of test markets; in-store and online marketing had been the key to Blockbuster's success. Nevertheless, Netflix and Blockbuster were now locked in a vicious battle for subscribers, and both companies were paying heavily for online ads on major websites such as eBay and Yahoo.

Once again, Antioco argued, because customers no longer have to choose between renting online or renting in-store, they never need to be without a movie, and this would make Blockbuster.com the fastest growing online DVD rental service in 2007.

And, of course, cable TV operators, and then movie studios, started PPV services that allowed consumers to order a movie over the TV or computer to watch immediately for $3 or $4. These offerings have all the convenience of a video because movies can be paused, rewound, or fast-forwarded for as long as twenty-four hours after the initial rental and they have no late fees.

Global Problems

Blockbuster has over 3,000 stores globally, but it has faced challenging problems in recent years in managing problems that have arisen in different countries. For example, in the UK it has maintained steady expansion both into DVDs and videogame rentals, and its video store chain is profitable. But in Germany it shut down its operations in 2006 because in the German rental market, there is no profit without sex and violence, which is not part of Blockbuster's policy of stocking only family entertainment and movie classics. Similarly, it closed all twenty-four of its Hong Kong stores in 2005 because of intense competition from pirated DVDs available for sale throughout China for a dollar each! Blockbuster had planned to use Hong Kong as a gateway to the huge market in mainland China, but the availability of pirated low-cost movies for sale in China made this impossible. Nevertheless, Blockbuster continues to operate in a number of markets where video piracy is a big problem, including Taiwan, Thailand, and Mexico.

The Future

Year 2007 may be a pivotal year in Blockbuster's history as the company tries to position itself for success in the quickly changing movie DVD sales and rental business. In January 2007, Blockbuster's stock rose when it announced that it would sell its Rhino videogame chain, which has ninety-four stores, and use the capital to pay down debt and fund its expansion into online movie rental. Its stock then rose sharply a few days later when Antioco announced that Blockbuster was contemplating reducing the size of its DVD inventory in its stores to focus more of its resources on its online business to attract more customers there.

However, a few days later, Netflix, responding to criticism that it was allowing Blockbuster to catch up and take its customers, announced a major new instant movie streaming service to its users' PCs over the Internet that is being offered at no additional charge. Netflix expects to introduce the instant viewing system to about 250,000 more subscribers each week through June 2007 to ensure its computers can cope with the increased demand. The allotted viewing time will be tied to how much customers already pay for their DVD rentals. Under Netflix's most popular $17.99 monthly package, subscribers will receive eighteen hours of Internet viewing time. A major drawback of the instant viewing system is that it works only on PCs and laptops equipped with a high-speed Internet connection and Windows; movies can't be watched on cell phones, TVs, or video iPods or on Apple Inc.'s operating system.

Also, new technology has emerged that allows for DVDs obtained through the mail or downloaded online to "self-destruct" within some defined time period, preventing the threat of video piracy. This technology is also available for physical DVDs, which also self-destruct when the rental time period has expired. This is likely to be important because of the growth in the number of DVD rental kiosks that have appeared in supermarkets and fast-food restaurants that allow users to quickly rent a just-released movie. Currently, these kiosks charge expensive late fees, but with self-destruct technology, they could be seen as a convenient way to rent new movies in the future.

So what future strategies Blockbuster will take was unclear in early 2007. Will Blockbuster contemplate closing more and more of its stores if its online business model proves more profitable? And if so, what will be its mix of mail versus Internet movie delivery, and what kind of PPV technology will it adopt? Certainly a virtual business would be a more appropriate hub for a complete VOD operation with a recognized brand name, but what then would happen to its physical stores? Is the combination of bricks-and-mortar and online retailing still the ideal mix in this market for movie and videogame rentals and sales? How quickly movie and video storefronts like Apple's, Amazon.com's, and Disney's become popular is likely to determine this. Is there a potential buyer for the company on the horizon? Could Blockbuster stores become Apple stores?

Finally, a new dilemma emerged for the company in 2007 when on January 25 Netflix announced it ended the fourth quarter with about 6.31 million subscribers, compared with a total of 4.18 million at the end of 2005. The total also represents 12% growth over the third-quarter total of 5.66 million, and its revenue climbed to $277.2 million from $193 million a year earlier. Now, its stock shot up and Blockbuster's plunged. Clearly, Netflix remains a major competitor, the fight to dominate the movie-rental market and movie and TV program instant streaming video service in the future is open, and who will win remains to be seen.

SOURCES

Bruce Apar, "Ruminations on Burstyn, Bezos & Blockbuster," *Video Store*, January 14–January 20, 2001, p. 6.

Thomas K. Arnold, "Broadbuster," *Video Store*, August 6–August 12, 2000, pp. 1, 38.

Blockbuster 10Ks and Annual Reports, 1988–2001, http://www.blockbuster.com.

"Citibank Reaches Pact To Install Its ATMs In Blockbuster Stores," *Wall Street Journal*, May 28, 1998, p. A11.

Greg Clarkin, "Fast Forward," *Marketing and Media Decisions*, March 1990, pp. 57–59.

Gail DeGeorge, *Business Week*, January 22, 1990, pp. 47–48.

Gail DeGeorge, Jonathan Levine, and Robert Neff, "They Don't Call It Blockbuster for Nothing," *Business Week*, October 19, 1992, pp. 113–114.

Doug Desjardins, "Blockbuster Scores With Games, DVDs," *DSN Retailing Today*, May 6, 2002, p. 5.

Geraldine Fabrikant, "Blockbuster President Resigns: Video Chain Revamps to Adapt to New Units," *New York Times*, January 5, 1993, p. D6.

Daniel Frankel, "Blockbuster Revamps Play Areas," *Video Business*, May 27, 2002, p. 38.

John Gaudiosi, "Blockbuster Pushes PS2," *Video Store*, December 2–December 8, 2001, pp. 1, 38.

"Global Notes: Focus 1-Blockbuster Entertainment Corp. (BV)," *Research Highlights*, October 26, 1990, p. 9.

Laurie Grossman and Gabriella Stern, "Blockbuster to Buy Controlling Stake in Spelling in Swap," *Wall Street Journal*, March 9, 1993, p. B9.

Laura Heller, "Radio Shack, Blockbuster Put Synergies to the Test," *DSN Retailing Today*, June 4, 2001, p. 5.

Scott Hume, "Blockbuster Means More than Video," *Advertising Age*, June 1, 1992, p. 4.

Daniel Kadlec, "How Blockbuster Changed the Rules," *New York Times*, August 3, 1998, pp. 48–49.

Kyra Kirkwood, "Blockbuster Moves Into Used DVDs," *Video Store*, March 25, 2000, p. 1.

M. McCarthy, *Wall Street Journal*, March 22, 1991, pp. A1, A6.

Bruce Orwall, "Five Studios Join Venture for Video on Demand," *Wall Street Journal*, August 17, 2001, p. A3.

QRP Merrill Lynch Extended Company Comment, November 16, 1990.

Johnnie Roberts, "Blockbuster Officials Envision Superstores for Music Business," *Wall Street Journal*, October 28, 1992, p. B10.

Trudi M. Rosenblum, "Blockbuster to Add Audiobooks," *Publishers Weekly*, June 19, 2000, p. 14.

S. Sandomir, *New York Times*, June 19, 1991, pp. S22–S25.

Eric Savitz, "An End to Fast Forward?" *Barron's*, December 11, 1989, pp. 13, 43–46.

Eben Shapiro, "Heard on the Street: Chief Redstone Tries to Convince Wall Street There's Life Beyond Blockbuster at Viacom," *Wall Street Journal*, April 24, 1997, p. C2.

Eben Shapiro, "Movies: Blockbuster Seeks a New Deal With Hollywood," *Wall Street Journal*, March 25, 1998, p. B1.

Eben Shapiro, "Viacom Net Drops 70% as Cash Flow Slips on Weakness at Blockbuster Unit," *Wall Street Journal*, October 30, 1997, p. B8.

Eben Shapiro, "Viacom Sets Major Charge Tied to Blockbuster," *Wall Street Journal*, July 23, 1998, p. A3.

Eben Shapiro, "Viacom Trims Blockbuster's Expansion, Igniting Speculation of Eventual Spinoff," *Wall Street Journal*, March 28, 1997, p. B5.

Eben Shapiro and Nikhil Deogun, "Antioco Takes Top Job at Troubled Blockbuster," *Wall Street Journal*, June 4, 1997, p. A3.

Eben Shapiro and Susan Pulliam, "Heard on the Street: Viacom to Name Wal-Mart's Heir Apparent, William Fields, to Head Block-buster Video," *Wall Street Journal*, March 29, 1996, p. C2.

Paul Sweeting, "Big Blue Trimming Tapes," *Video Business*, September 17, 2001, p. 1.

Greg Tarr, "DirecTB Teams With Blockbuster," *Twice*, May 15, 2000, p. 1.

Richard Tedesco, "MGM, Blockbuster to Stream TV, Films," *Broadcasting & Cable*, January 24, 2000, p. 128.

"TiVo, Blockbuster Ink Cross-Promo Deal," *Twice*, January 17, 2000, p. 24.

"Video Stocks Stumbled," *Video Business*, September 3, 2001, p. 4.

Joan Villa, "Blockbuster Game Exclusive," *Video Store*, January 20–January 26, 2002, pp. 1, 40.

Audrey Warren and Martin Peers, "Video Retailers Have Day in Court—Plaintiffs Say Supply Deals Between Blockbuster Inc. and Studios Violate Laws," *Wall Street Journal*, June 13, 2002, p. B10.

The Evolution of the Small Package Express Delivery Industry, 1973–2006

This case was prepared by Charles W. L. Hill, the University of Washington.

The small package express delivery industry is that segment of the broader postal and cargo industries that specializes in rapid (normally one to three days) delivery of small packages. It is generally agreed that the modern express delivery industry in the United States began with Fred Smith's vision for Federal Express Company, which started operations in 1973. Federal Express transformed the structure of the existing air cargo industry and paved the way for rapid growth in the overnight package segment of that industry. A further impetus to the industry's development was the 1977 deregulation of the U.S. air cargo industry. This deregulation allowed Federal Express (and its emerging competitors) to buy large jets for the first time. The story of the industry during the 1980s was one of rapid growth and new entry. Between 1982 and 1989, small package express cargo shipments by air in the United States grew at an annual average rate of 31%. In contrast, shipments of air freight and air mail grew at an annual rate of only 2.7%.[1] This rapid growth attracted new entrants such as United Parcel Service (UPS) and Airborne Freight (which operated under the name Airborne Express). The entry of UPS triggered severe price cutting, which ultimately drove some of the weaker competitors out of the market and touched off a wave of consolidation in the industry.

By the mid-1990s, the industry structure had stabilized with four organizations—Federal Express,

UPS, Airborne Express, and the U.S. Postal Service—accounting for the vast majority of U.S. express shipments. During the first half of the 1990s, the small package express industry continued to grow at a healthy rate, with shipments expanding by slightly more than 16% per annum.[2] Despite this growth, the industry was hit by repeated rounds of price cutting as the three big private firms battled to capture major accounts. In addition to price cutting, the big three also competed vigorously on the basis of technology, service offerings, and the global reach of their operations. By the late 1990s and early 2000s, however, the intensity of price competition in the industry had moderated, with a degree of pricing discipline being maintained, despite the fact that the growth rate for the industry slowed down. Between 1995 and 2000, the industry grew at 9.8% per year. In 2001, however, the volume of express parcels shipped by air fell by 5.9%, partly due to an economic slowdown and partly due to the aftereffects of the September 11 terrorist attack on the United States.[3] Growth picked up again in 2002, and estimates suggest that the global market for small package express delivery should continue to grow by a little over 6% per annum between 2005 and 2025. Most of that growth, however, is forecasted to take place outside of the now mature North American market, where the annual growth rate is predicted to be 3.8%.[4]

In North America, the biggest change to take place in the early 2000s was the 2003 entry of DHL into the North American market with the acquisition of Airborne Express for $1 billion. DHL is itself owned by Deutsche Post World Net, formally the German post office, which since privatization has been rapidly transforming itself into a global express mail and logistics operation. Prior to 2003 DHL lacked a strong presence in the all-important U.S. market. The acquisition of Airborne has given DHL a foothold in the United States. Still, DHL has a very long way to go before it can match the dominance of UPS and FedEx, particularly in the important air express market (see Exhibit 1), although the scale of its parent, which in 2005 had revenues of $60 billion, suggests that it could use its deep pockets to support aggressive expansion in North America.

The Industry Before FedEx

In 1973, roughly 1.5 billion tons of freight were shipped in the United States. Most of this freight was carried by surface transport, with air freight accounting for less than 2% of the total.[5] While shipment by air freight was often quicker than shipment by surface freight, the high cost of air freight had kept down demand. The typical users of air freight at this time were suppliers of time-sensitive, high-priced goods, such as computer parts and medical instruments, which were needed at dispersed locations but which were too expensive for their customers to hold as inventory.

The main cargo carriers in 1973 were major passenger airlines, which operated several all-cargo planes and carried additional cargo in their passenger planes, along with a handful of all-cargo airlines such as Flying Tiger. From 1973 onward, the passenger airlines moved steadily away from all-cargo planes and began to concentrate cargo freight in passenger planes. This change was a response to increases in fuel costs, which made the operation of many older cargo jets uneconomical.

With regard to distribution of cargo to and from airports, in 1973 about 20% of all air freight was delivered to airports by the shipper and/or picked up by the consignee. The bulk of the remaining 80% was accounted for by three major intermediaries: (1) Air Cargo Incorporated, (2) freight forwarders, and (3) the U.S. Postal Service. Air Cargo Incorporated was a trucking service, wholly owned by twenty-six airlines, which performed pickup and delivery service for the airlines' direct customers. Freight forwarders were trucking carriers who consolidated cargo going to the airlines. They purchased cargo space from the airlines and retailed this space in small amounts. They dealt primarily with small customers, providing pickup and delivery services in most cities, either in their own trucks or through contract agents. The U.S. Postal Service used air service for transportation of long-distance letter mail and air parcel post.[6]

The Federal Express Concept

Founded by Fred Smith Jr., Federal Express was incorporated in 1971 and began operations in 1973. At that time, a significant proportion of small package air freight flew on commercial passenger flights. Smith believed that there were major differences between packages and passengers, and he was convinced that the two had to be treated differently. Most passengers moved between major cities and wanted the convenience of daytime flights. Cargo shippers preferred nighttime service to coincide with late-afternoon pickups and next-day delivery. Because small package air freight was subservient to the requirements of passengers' flight schedules, it was often difficult for the major airlines to achieve next-day delivery of air freight.

Smith's aim was to build a system that could achieve next-day delivery of small package air freight (less than seventy pounds). He set up Federal Express with his $8 million family inheritance and $90 million in venture capital (the company's name was changed to FedEx in 1998). Federal Express established a hub-and-spoke route system, the first airline to do so. The hub of the system was Memphis, chosen for its good weather conditions, central location, and the fact that it was Smith's hometown. The spokes were regular routes between Memphis and shipping facilities at public airports in the cities serviced by Federal Express.

EXHIBIT 1

U.S. Market Share Estimates for Small Package Delivery Market, 2006

Organization	Ground Market Share	Air Express Market
UPS	63%	35%
FedEx	19%	45%
U.S. Postal Service	16%	6%
DHL	NA	10%
Other	3%	5%

Source: Raw data from John Kartsonas, "United Parcel Service," *Citigroup Global Capital Markets,* November 13, 2006, B. Barnard, "Logistics Spur Deutsche Post," *Journal of Commerce,* November 8, 2006, page 1.

Every weeknight, aircraft would leave their home cities with a load of packages and fly down the spokes to Memphis (often with one or two stops on the way). At Memphis, all packages were unloaded, sorted by destination, and reloaded. The aircraft then returned back to their home cities in the early hours of the morning. Packages were ferried to and from airports by Federal Express couriers driving the company's vans and working to a tight schedule. Thus, from door to door, the package was in Federal Express's hands. This system guaranteed that a package picked up from a customer in New York at 5 p.m. would reach its final destination in Los Angeles (or any other major city) by noon the following day. It enabled Federal Express to realize economies in sorting and to utilize its air cargo capacity efficiently. Federal Express also pioneered the use of standard packaging with an upper weight limit of seventy pounds and a maximum length plus girth of 108 inches. This standard helped Federal Express to gain further efficiencies from mechanized sorting at its Memphis hub. Later entrants into the industry copied Federal Express's package standards and hub-and-spoke operating system.

To accomplish overnight delivery, Federal Express had to operate its own planes. Restrictive regulations enforced by the Civil Aeronautics Board (CAB), however, prohibited the company from buying large jet aircraft. To get around this restriction, Federal Express bought a fleet of twin-engine executive jets, which it converted to minifreighters. These planes had a cargo capacity of 6,200 pounds, which enabled Federal Express to get a license as an air taxi operator.

After 1973, Federal Express quickly built up volume. By 1976, it had an average daily volume of 19,000 packages, a fleet of 32 aircraft, 500 delivery vans, and 2,000 employees, and it had initiated service in 75 cities. After three years of posting losses, the company turned in a profit of $3.7 million on revenues of $75 million.[7] However, volume had grown so much that Federal Express desperately needed to use larger planes to maintain operating efficiencies. As a result, Smith's voice was added to those calling for Congress to deregulate the airline industry and allow greater competition.

Deregulation and Its Aftermath

In November 1977, Congress relaxed regulations controlling competition in the air cargo industry, one year before passenger services were deregulated. This involved a drastic loosening of standards for entry into the industry. The old CAB authority of naming the carriers that could operate on the various routes was changed to the relatively simple authority of deciding which among candidate carriers was fit, willing, and able to operate an all-cargo route. In addition, CAB controls over pricing were significantly reduced. The immediate effect was an increase in rates for shipments, particularly minimum- and high-weight categories, suggesting that prices had been held artificially low by regulation. As a result, the average yield (revenue per ton mile) on domestic air freight increased 10.6% in 1978 and 11.3% in 1979.[8]

Freed from the constraints of regulation, Federal Express immediately began to purchase larger jets and quickly established itself as a major carrier of small package air freight. Despite the increase in yields, however, new entry into the air cargo industry was limited, at least initially. This was mainly due to the high capital requirements involved in establishing an all-cargo carrier. Indeed, by the end of 1978, there were only four major all-cargo carriers serving the domestic market: Airlift International, Federal Express, Flying Tiger, and Seaboard World Airlines. While all of these all-cargo carriers had increased their route structure following deregulation, only Federal Express specialized in next-day delivery for small packages. Demand for a next-day delivery service continued to boom. Industry estimates suggest that the small package priority market had grown to about 82 million pieces in 1979, up from 43 million in 1974.[9]

At the same time, in response to increasing competition from the all-cargo carriers, the passenger airlines continued their retreat from the all-cargo business (originally begun in 1973 as a response to high fuel prices). Between 1973 and 1978, there was a 45% decline in the mileage of all-cargo flights by the airlines. This decrease was followed by a 14% decline between 1978 and 1979. Instead of all-cargo flights, the airlines concentrated their attentions on carrying cargo in passenger flights. This practice hurt the freight forwarders badly. The freight forwarders had long relied on the all-cargo flights of major airlines to achieve next-day delivery. Now the freight forwarders were being squeezed out of this segment by a lack of available lift capacity at the time needed to ensure next-day delivery.

This problem led to one of the major post-deregulation developments in the industry: the acquisition and operation by freight forwarders of their own fleets of aircraft. Between 1979 and 1981, five of the six largest freight forwarders became involved in this activity. The two largest were Emery Air Freight and Airborne Express. Emery operated a fleet of sixty-six aircraft at the end of 1979, the majority of which were leased from other carriers. In mid-1980, this fleet was providing service to approximately 129 cities, carrying both large-volume shipments and small package express.

Airborne Express acquired its own fleet of aircraft in April 1980 with the purchase of Midwest Charter Express, an Ohio-based all-cargo airline. In 1981, Airborne opened a new hub in Ohio, which became the center of its small package express operation. This enabled Airborne to provide next-day delivery for small packages to 125 cities in the United States.[10] Other freight forwarders that moved into the overnight mail market included Purolator Courier and Gelco, both of which offered overnight delivery by air on a limited geographic scale.

Industry Evolution, 1980–1986
New Products and Industry Growth

In 1981, Federal Express expanded its role in the overnight market with the introduction of an overnight letter service, with a limit of two ounces. This guaranteed overnight delivery service was set up in direct competition with the U.S. Postal Service's Priority Mail. The demand for such a service was illustrated by its expansion to about 17,000 letters per day within its first three months of operation.

More generally, the focus of the air express industry was changing from being predominantly a conduit for goods to being a distributor of information—particularly company documents, letters, contracts, drawings, and the like. As a result of the growth in demand for information distribution, new product offerings such as the overnight letter, and Federal Express's own marketing efforts, the air express industry enjoyed high growth during the early 1980s, averaging more than 30% per year.[11] Indeed, many observers attribute most of the growth in the overnight delivery business at this time to Federal Express's marketing efforts. According to one industry participant, "Federal Express pulled off one of the greatest marketing scams in the industry by making

people believe they absolutely, positively, had to have something right away."[12]

Increasing Price Competition

Despite rapid growth in demand, competitive intensity in the industry increased sharply in 1982 following the entry of UPS into the overnight-delivery market. UPS was already by far the largest private package transporter in the United States, with an enormous ground-oriented distribution network and revenues in excess of $4 billion per year. In addition, for a long time, UPS had offered a second-day air service for priority packages, primarily by using the planes of all-cargo and passenger airlines. In 1982, UPS acquired a fleet of twenty-four used Boeing 727-100s and added four DC-8 freighters from Flying Tiger. These purchases allowed UPS to introduce next-day air service in September 1982—at roughly half the price Federal Express was charging at the time.[13]

Federal Express countered almost immediately by announcing that it would institute 10:30 A.M. priority overnight delivery (at a cost to the company of $18 million). None of the other carriers followed suit, however, reasoning that most of their customers are usually busy or in meetings during the morning hours, so delivery before noon was not really that important. Instead, by March 1983, most of the major carriers in the market (including Federal Express) were offering their high-volume customers contract rates that matched the UPS price structure. Then three new services introduced by Purolator, Emery, and Gelco Courier pushed prices even lower. A competitive free-for-all followed, with constant price changes and volume discounts being offered by all industry participants. These developments hit the profit margins of the express carriers. Between 1983 and 1984, Federal Express saw its average revenue per package fall nearly 14%, while Emery saw a 15% decline in its yield on small shipments.[14]

Beginning around this time, customers began to group together and negotiate for lower prices. For example, Xerox set up accounts with Purolator and Emery that covered not only Xerox's express packages but also those of fifty other companies, including Mayflower Corp., the moving company, and the Chicago Board of Trade. By negotiating as a group, these companies could achieve prices as much as 60% lower than those they could get on their own.[15]

The main beneficiary of the price war was UPS, which by 1985 had gained the number 2 spot in the industry, with 15% of the market. Federal Express, meanwhile, had seen its market share slip to 37% from about 45% two years earlier. The other four major players in the industry at this time were Emery Air Freight (14% of market share), Purolator (10% of market share), Airborne Express (8% of market share), and the U.S. Postal Service (8% of market share).[16] The survival of all four of these carriers in the air express business was in question by 1986. Emery, Purolator, and the U.S. Postal Service were all reporting losses on their air express business, while Airborne had seen its profits slump 66% in the first quarter of 1986 and now had razor-thin margins.

Industry Evolution, 1987–1996

Industry Consolidation

A slowdown in the growth rate of the air express business due to increasing geographic saturation and inroads made by electronic transmission (primarily fax machines) stimulated further price discounting in 1987 and early 1988. Predictably, this discounting created problems for the weakest companies in the industry. The first to go was Purolator Courier, which had lost $65 million during 1985 and 1986. Purolator's problems stemmed from a failure to install an adequate computer system. The company was unable to track shipments, a crucial asset in this industry, and some of Purolator's best corporate customers were billed 120 days late.[17] In 1987, Purolator agreed to be acquired by Emery. Emery was unable to effect a satisfactory integration of Purolator, and it sustained large losses in 1988 and early 1989.

Consolidated Freightways was a major trucking company and parent of CF Air Freight, the third largest heavy shipment specialist in the United States. In April 1989, Consolidated Freightways acquired Emery for $478 million. However, its shipment specialist, CF Air Freight, soon found itself struggling to cope with Emery's problems. In its first eleven months with CF, Emery lost $100 million. One of the main problems was Emery's billing and tracking system, described as a "rat's nest" of conflicting tariff schedules, which caused overbilling of customers and made tracking packages en route a major chore. In addition, CF enraged corporate customers by trying to add a "fuel surcharge" of 4 to 7% to prices in early 1989. Competitors held the line on prices and picked up business from CF/Emery.[18]

As a result of the decline of the CF/Emery/Purolator combination, the other firms in the industry were able to pick up market share. By 1994, industry estimates suggested that Federal Express accounted for 35% of domestic air freight and air express industry revenues; UPS had 26%; Airborne Express was third with 9%; and Emery and the U.S. Postal Service each held onto 4% of the market. The remainder of the market was split among numerous small cargo carriers and several combination carriers, such as Evergreen International and Atlas Air. (Combination carriers specialize mostly in heavy freight but do carry some express mail.)[19]

The other major acquisition in the industry during this time was the purchase of Flying Tiger by Federal Express for $880 million in December 1988. Although Flying Tiger had some air express operations in the United States, its primary strength was as a heavy cargo carrier with a global route structure. The acquisition was part of Federal Express's goal of becoming a major player in the international air express market. However, the acquisition had its problems. Many of Flying Tiger's biggest customers, including UPS and Airborne Express, were Federal Express's competitors in the domestic market. These companies had long paid Tiger to carry packages to those countries where they had no landing rights. It seemed unlikely that these companies would continue to give international business to their biggest domestic competitor. Additional problems arose in the process of trying to integrate the two operations. These problems included the scheduling of aircraft and pilots, the servicing of Tiger's fleet, and the merging of Federal's nonunionized pilots with Tiger's unionized pilots.[20]

During the late 1980s and early 1990s, there were also hints of further consolidations. TNT Ltd., a large Australian-based air cargo operation with a global network, made an unsuccessful attempt to acquire Airborne Express in 1986. TNT's bid was frustrated by opposition from Airborne and by the difficulties inherent in getting around U.S. law, which currently limits foreign firms from having more than a 25-percent stake in U.S. airlines. In addition, DHL Airways, the U.S. subsidiary of DHL International, was reportedly attempting to enlarge its presence in the United States and was on the lookout for an acquisition.[21]

Pricing Trends

In October 1988, UPS offered new discounts to high-volume customers in domestic markets. For the first time since 1983, competitors declined to match the cuts.

Then in January 1989, UPS announced a price increase of 5% for next-day air service, its first price increase in nearly six years. Federal Express, Airborne, and Consolidated Freightways all followed suit with moderate increases. Additional rate increases of 5.9% on next-day air letters were announced by UPS in February 1990. Federal Express followed suit in April, and Airborne also implemented selective price hikes on noncontract business of 5%, or 50 cents, per package on packages up to twenty pounds.

Just as prices were stabilizing, however, the 1990–1991 recession came along. For the first time in the history of the U.S. air express industry, there was a decline in year-on-year shipments, with express freight falling from 4,455 million ton miles in 1989 to 4,403 million ton miles in 1990. This decline triggered off another round of competitive price cuts, and yields plummeted. Although demand rebounded strongly, repeated attempts to raise prices in 1992, 1993, and 1994 simply did not stick.[22]

Much of the price cutting was focused on large corporate accounts, which by this time accounted for 75% by volume of express mail shipments. For example, as a result of deep price discounting in 1994, UPS was able to lure home shopping programmer QVC and computer mail-order company Gateway 2000 away from Federal Express. At about the same time, however, Federal Express used discounting to capture retailer Williams-Sonoma away from UPS.[23] This prolonged period of price discounting depressed profit margins and contributed to losses at all three major carriers during the early 1990s. Bolstered by a strong economy, prices finally began to stabilize during late 1995, when price increases announced by UPS were followed by similar announcements at Federal Express and Airborne.[24]

Product Trends

Second-Day Delivery Having seen a slowdown in the growth rate of the next-day document delivery business during the early 1990s, the major operators in the air express business began to look for new product opportunities to sustain their growth and margins. One trend was a move into the second-day delivery market, or deferred services, as it is called in the industry. The move toward second-day delivery was started by Airborne Express in 1991, and it was soon imitated by its major competitors. Second-day delivery commands a substantially lower price point than next-

day delivery. In 1994, Federal Express made an average of $9.23 on second-day deliveries, compared to $16.37 on priority overnight service. The express mail operators see deferred services as a way to utilize excess capacity at the margin, thereby boosting revenues and profits. Since many second-day packages can be shipped on the ground, the cost of second-day delivery can more than compensate for the lower price.

In some ways, however, the service has been almost too successful. During the mid-1990s, the growth rate for deferred services was significantly higher than for priority overnight mail because many corporations came to the realization that they could live with a second-day service. At Airborne Express, for example, second-day delivery accounted for 42% of total volume in 1996, up from 37% in 1995.[25]

Premium Services Another development was a move toward a premium service. In 1994, UPS introduced its Early AM service, which guaranteed delivery of packages and letters by 8:30 a.m. in select cities. UPS tailored Early AM toward a range of businesses that needed documents or materials before the start of the business day, including hospitals, who were expected to use the service to ship critical drugs and medical devices; architects, who needed to have their blueprints sent to a construction site; and salespeople. Although demand for the service was predicted to be light, the premium price made for high profit margins. In 1994, UPS's price for a letter delivered at 10:30 a.m. was $10.75, while it charged $40 for an equivalent Early AM delivery. UPS believed that it could provide the service at little extra cost because most of its planes arrived in their destination cities by 7:30 a.m. Federal Express and Airborne initially declined to follow UPS's lead.[26]

Logistics Services Another development of some note was the move by all major operators into third-party logistics services. Since the latter half of the 1980s, more and more companies have been relying on air express operations as part of their just-in-time inventory control systems. As a result, the content of packages carried by air express operators has been moving away from letters and documents and toward high-value, low-weight products. By 1994, less than 20% of Federal Express's revenues came from documents.[27] To take advantage of this trend, all of the major operators have been moving into logistics services that are designed to assist business customers in their warehousing, distribution, and assembly operations. The emphasis of this business is on helping their customers reduce the time involved in their production cycles and gain distribution efficiencies.

In the late 1980s, Federal Express set up a Business Logistics Services (BLS) division. The new division evolved from Federal Express's Parts Bank. The Parts Bank stores critical inventory for clients, most of whom are based in the high-tech electronics and medical industries. On request, Federal Express ships this inventory to its client's customers. The service saves clients from having to invest in their own distribution systems. It also allows their clients to achieve economies of scale by making large production runs and then storing the inventory at the Parts Bank.

The BLS division has expanded this service to include some assembly operations and customs brokerage and to assist in achieving just-in-time manufacturing. Thus, for example, one U.S. computer company relies on BLS to deliver electronic subassemblies from the Far East as a key part of its just-in-time system. Federal Express brings the products to the United States on its aircraft, clears them through customs with the help of a broker, and manages truck transportation to the customer's dock.

UPS moved into the logistics business in 1993 when it established UPS Worldwide Logistics, which it positioned as a third-party provider of global supply-chain management solutions, including transportation management, warehouse operations, inventory management, documentation for import and export, network optimization, and reverse logistics. UPS's logistics business is based at its Louisville, Kentucky, hub. In 1995, the company announced that it would invest $75 million to expand the scope of this facility, bringing total employment in the facility to 2,200 by the end of 1998.[28]

Airborne Express also made a significant push into this business. Several of Airborne's corporate accounts utilize a warehousing service called Stock Exchange. As with Federal Express's Parts Bank, clients warehouse critical inventory at Airborne's hub in Wilmington, Ohio, and then ship those items on request to their customers. In addition, Airborne set up a commerce park on 1,000 acres around its Wilmington hub. The park was geared toward companies that wanted to outsource logistics to Airborne and could gain special advantages by locating at the company's hub. Not the least of these advantages is the ability to make shipping decisions as late as 2 a.m. Eastern time.

Information Systems

Since the late 1980s, the major U.S. air express carriers have devoted more and more attention to competing on the basis of information technology. The ability to track a package as it moves through an operator's delivery network has always been an important aspect of competition in an industry where reliability is so highly valued. Thus, all the major players in the industry have invested heavily in bar-code technology, scanners, and computerized tracking systems. UPS, Federal Express, and Airborne have also all invested in Internet-based technology that allows customers to schedule pickups, print shipping labels, and track deliveries online.

Globalization

Perhaps the most important development for the long-run future of the industry has been the increasing globalization of the airfreight industry. The combination of a healthy U.S. economy, strong and expanding East Asian economies, and the move toward closer economic integration in western Europe all offer opportunities for growth in the international air cargo business. The increasing globalization of companies in a whole range of industries from electronics to autos, and from fast food to clothing, is beginning to dictate that the air express operators follow suit.

Global manufacturers want to keep inventories at a minimum and deliver just in time as a way of keeping down costs and fine-tuning production, which requires speedy supply routes. Thus, some electronics companies will manufacture key components in one location, ship them by air to another for final assembly, and then deliver them by air to a third location for sale. This setup is particularly convenient for industries producing small high-value items (for example, electronics, medical equipment, and computer software) that can be economically transported by air and for whom just-in-time inventory systems are crucial for keeping down costs. It is also true in the fashion industry, where timing is crucial. For example, the clothing chain The Limited manufactures clothes in Hong Kong and then ships them by air to the United States to keep from missing out on fashion trends.[29] In addition, an increasing number of wholesalers are beginning to turn to international air express as a way of meeting delivery deadlines.

The emergence of integrated global corporations is also increasing the demand for the global shipment of contracts, confidential papers, computer printouts, and other documents that are too confidential for Internet transmission or that require real signatures. Major U.S. corporations are increasingly demanding the same kind of service that they receive from air express operators within the United States for their far-flung global operations.

As a consequence of these trends, rapid growth is predicted in the global arena. According to forecasts, the market for international air express is expected to grow at approximately 18% annually from 1996 to 2016.[30] Faced with an increasingly mature market at home, the race is on among the major air cargo operators to build global air and ground transportation networks that will enable them to deliver goods and documents between any two points on the globe within forty-eight hours.

The company with the most extensive international operations by the mid-1990s was DHL. In 1995, DHL enjoyed a 44% share of the worldwide market for international air express services (see Exhibit 2).[31] Started in California in 1969 and now based in Brussels, DHL is smaller than many of its rivals, but it has managed to capture as much as an 80% share in some markets, such as documents leaving Japan, by concentrating solely on international air express. The strength of DHL was enhanced in mid-1992 when Lufthansa, Japan Airlines, and the Japanese trading company Nisho Iwai announced that they intended to invest as much as $500 million for a 57.5% stake in DHL. Although Lufthansa and Japan Airlines are primarily known for their passenger flights, they are also among the top five airfreight haulers in the world, both because they carry cargo in the holds of their passenger flights and because they each have a fleet of all-cargo aircraft.[32]

EXHIBIT 2

International Air Express Market Shares, 1995

Company	Market Share
DHL International	44%
Federal Express	21%
UPS	12%
TNT	12%
Others	11%

Source: Standard & Poor's, "Aerospace and Air Transport," Industry Surveys, February 1996.

TNT Ltd., a $6 billion Australian conglomerate, is another big player in the international air express market, with courier services from 184 countries as well as package express and mail services. In 1995, its share of the international air express market was 12%, down from 18% in 1990.[33]

Among U.S. carriers, Federal Express was first in the race to build a global air express network. Between 1984 and 1989, Federal Express purchased seventeen other companies worldwide in an attempt to build its global distribution capabilities, culminating in the $880 million purchase of Flying Tiger. The main asset of Flying Tiger was not so much its aircraft but its landing rights overseas. The Flying Tiger acquisition gave Federal Express service to 103 countries, a combined fleet of 328 aircraft, and revenues of $5.2 billion in fiscal year 1989.[34]

However, Federal Express has had to suffer through years of losses in its international operations. Start-up costs were heavy, due in part to the enormous capital investments required to build an integrated air and ground network worldwide. Between 1985 and 1992, Federal Express spent $2.5 billion to build an international presence. Faced also with heavy competition, Federal Express found it difficult to generate the international volume required to fly its planes above the breakeven point on many international routes. Because the demand for outbound service from the United States is greater than the demand for inbound service, planes that left New York full often returned half empty.

Trade barriers have also proved very damaging to the bottom line. Customs regulations require a great deal of expensive and time-consuming labor, such as checking paperwork and rating package contents for duties. These regulations obviously inhibit the ability of international air cargo carriers to effect express delivery. Federal Express has been particularly irritated by Japanese requirements that each inbound envelope be opened and searched for pornography, a practice that seems designed to slow down the company's growth rate in the Japanese market.

Federal Express has also found it extremely difficult to get landing rights in many markets. For example, it took three years to get permission from Japan to make four flights per week from Memphis to Tokyo, a key link in the overseas system. Then, in 1988, just three days before the service was due to begin, the Japanese notified Federal Express that no packages weighing more than seventy pounds could pass through Tokyo. To make matters worse, until 1995 Japan limited Federal Express's ability to fly on from Tokyo and Osaka to other locations in Asia. The Japanese claimed, with some justification, that due to government regulations, the U.S. air traffic market is difficult for foreign carriers to enter, so they see no urgency to help Federal Express build a market presence in Japan and elsewhere in Asia.[35]

After heavy financial losses, Federal Express abruptly shifted its international strategy in 1992, selling off its expensive European ground network to local carriers to concentrate on intercontinental deliveries. Under the strategy, Federal Express relies on a network of local partners to deliver its packages. Also, Federal Express entered into an alliance with TNT to share space on Federal Express's daily trans-Atlantic flights. Under the agreement, TNT flies packages from its hub in Cologne, Germany, to Britain, where they are loaded onto Federal Express's daily New York flight.[36]

UPS has also built up an international presence. In 1988, UPS bought eight smaller European airfreight companies and Hong Kong's Asian Courier Service, and it announced air service and ground delivery in 175 countries and territories. However, it has not been all smooth sailing for UPS either. UPS had been using Flying Tiger for its Pacific shipments. The acquisition of Flying Tiger by Federal Express left UPS in the difficult situation of shipping its parcels on a competitor's plane. UPS was concerned that its shipments would be pushed to the back of the aircraft. Since there were few alternative carriers, UPS pushed for authority to run an all-cargo route to Tokyo, but approval was slow in coming. "Beyond rights" to carry cargo from Tokyo to further destinations (such as Singapore and Hong Kong) were also difficult to gain.

In March 1996, UPS sidestepped years of frustrations associated with building an Asian hub in Tokyo by announcing that it would invest $400 million in a Taiwan hub, which would henceforth be the central node in its Asian network. The decision to invest in an Asian hub followed closely on the heels of a 1995 decision by UPS to invest $1.1 billion to build a ground network in Europe. In September 1996, UPS went one step further toward building an international air express service when it announced that it would start a pan-European next-day delivery service for small packages. UPS hoped that these moves would push the international operations of the carrier into the black after eight years of losses.[37]

Industry Evolution, 1997–2006

Pricing Trends

The industry continued to grow at a solid rate through 2000, which helped to establish a stable pricing environment. In 2001, things took a turn for the worse, with recessionary conditions in the United States triggering a 7.6% decline in the number of domestic packages shipped by air. Even though the economy started to rebound in 2002, growth remained sluggish by historic comparison, averaging only 4% per annum.[38] Despite this, pricing discipline remained solid. Unlike the recession in 1990–1991, there was no price war in 2001–2002. Indeed, in early 2002, UPS pushed through a 3.5% increase in prices, which was quickly followed by the other carriers. The carriers were able to continue to raise prices, at least in line with inflation, through to 2006. They were also successful in tacking on a fuel surcharge to the cost of packages to make up for sharply higher fuel costs in 2001, and again during 2005 and 2006.[39] During 2002–2006, the average revenue per package at both UPS and FedEx increased as more customers opted for expedited shipments and as both carriers shipped high proportions of heavier packages.[40]

Continuing Growth of Logistics

During 1997–2006, all players continued to build their logistics services. During the 2000s, UPS was much more aggressive in this area than FedEx. By 2006, UPS's logistics business had revenues of over $6 billion. UPS was reportedly stealing share from FedEx in this area. FedEx reportedly decided to stay more focused on the small package delivery business (although it continues to have a logistics business). Most analysts expected logistics services to continue to be a growth area. Outside of the North American market, DHL emerged as the world's largest provider of logistics services, particularly following its 2006 acquisition of Britain's Exel, a large global logistics business.

Despite the push of DHL and UPS into the global logistics business, the market remains very fragmented. According to one estimate, DHL, now the world's largest logistics company, has a 5.5% share of the global market in contract logistics, UPS has a 3% share, and TNT has a 2.2% share.[41] The total global market for contract logistics was estimated to be worth over $200 billion in 2005. In 2006, TNT sold its logistics business to Apollo Management LP for $1.88 billion so that it could focus more on its small package delivery business.

Expanding Ground Network

In the late 1990s and early 2000s, all the main carriers began supplementing their air networks with extensive ground networks and ground hubs to ship packages overnight. With more customers moving from overnight mail to deferred services, such as second-day delivery, this shift in emphasis became a necessity. Demand for deferred services held up reasonably well during 2001, even as demand for overnight packages slumped. Prices for deferred and ground services were considerably lower than were prices for air services, but so were the costs.

UPS has been the most aggressive in building ground delivery capabilities (of course, it already had extensive ground capabilities before its move into the air). In 1999, UPS decided to integrate overnight delivery into its huge ground transportation network. The company spent about $700 million to strengthen its ground delivery network by setting up regional ground hubs. By doing so, it found it could ship packages overnight on the ground within a 500-mile radius. Because ground shipments are cheaper than air shipments, the result was a significant cost savings for UPS. The company also deferred delivery of about 123 aircraft that were on order, reasoning that they would not be needed as quickly because more of UPS's overnight business was moved to the ground.[42]

FedEx entered the ground transportation market in 1998 with its acquisition of Caliber Systems for $500 million. This was followed by further acquisitions in 2001 and 2006 of significant U.S. trucking companies, including the 2006 acquisition of Watkins Motor Lines, a provider of long-haul trucking services in the United States with sales of around $1 billion. Watkins was rebranded as FedEx National LTL. By 2002, FedEx was able to provide ground service to all U.S. homes, giving it a similar capability to UPS.

In addition, FedEx struck a deal in 2001 with the U.S. Postal Service (USPS), under which FedEx would provide airport-to-airport transportation for 250,000 pounds of USPS Express Mail packages nightly and about 3 million pounds of USPS Priority Mail packages. The Priority Mail would be moved on FedEx planes that normally sit idle during the day. The deal was reportedly worth $7 billion in additional revenues to FedEx over the seven-year term of the agreement. In addition, FedEx was expected to reap cost savings from the better utilization of its lift capacity.[43]

Bundling

Another industrywide trend has been a move toward selling various product offerings—including air delivery, ground package offerings, and logistics services—to business customers as a bundle. The basic idea behind bundling is to offer complementary products at a bundled price that is less than would have been the case if each item had been purchased separately. Yet again, UPS has been the most aggressive in offering bundled services to corporate clients. UPS is clearly aiming to set itself up as a one-stop shop offering a broad array of transportation solutions to customers. FedEx has also made moves in this area. Airborne Express started to bundle its product offerings in mid-2001.[44]

Retail Presence

In 2001, UPS purchased Mail Boxes Etc. for $185 million. Mail Boxes Etc. had 4,300 franchisees, most in the United States, who operated small retail packaging, printing, and copying stores. At the time, Mail Boxes Etc. was shipping some 40 million packages a year, around 12 million of which were via UPS. UPS stated that it would continue to allow the Mail Boxes stores to ship packages for other carriers. In 2003, the stores were rebranded as the UPS Store. While some franchisees objected to this move, the vast majority ultimately switched to the new brand.[45] In addition to the franchise stores, UPS has also begun to open wholly owned UPS stores, not just in the United States, but also internationally, and by 2006 had 5,600 outlets. In addition to the UPS Store, UPS put UPS Centers in office supplies stores, such as Office Depot, and by 2006 it had some 2,200 of these.

In 2004, FedEx followed UPS by purchasing Kinko's for $2.4 billion. Kinko's, which had 1,200 retail locations, 90% in the United States, focused on providing photocopying, printing, and other office services to individuals and small businesses. FedEx has plans to increase the network of Kinko's stores to 4,000. In addition to providing printing, photocopying, and package services, FedEx is also experimenting with using Kinko's stores as mini-warehouses to store high-value goods, such as medical equipment, for its supply-chain management division.[46]

Deutsche Post and the Entry of DHL

In the late 1990s, DHL was acquired by Deutsche Post. Deutsche Post also spent approximately $5 billion to acquire several companies in the logistics business between 1997 and 1999. In November 2000, Deutsche Post went private with an initial public offering that raised $5.5 billion and announced its intention to build an integrated global delivery and logistics network. Many believed it was only a matter of time before the company entered the United States. Thus, few were surprised when in 2003 DHL acquired Airborne. Under the terms of their agreement, Airborne Express sold its truck delivery system to DHL for $1.05 billion. Airborne's fleet of planes were spun off into an independent company called ABX Air, owned by Airborne's shareholders, and which continues to serve DHL Worldwide Express under a long-term contract. This arrangement overcame the U.S. law that prohibits foreign control of more than 25% of a domestic airline. In the meantime, DHL spun its own fleet of U.S.-based planes into a U.S.-owned company called Astar, also to escape the charge that its U.S. airline was foreign owned. Between 2003 and 2005, DHL reportedly invested some $1.2 billion to upgrade the capabilities of assets acquired from Airborne.[47]

The DHL acquisition created three major competitors in both the U.S. and global delivery markets (see Exhibit 3 for a comparison). By the fall of 2003, DHL had launched an ad campaign aimed at UPS and FedEx customers promoting the service and cost advantages that they would benefit from because of its merger with Airborne. DHL targeted specific zip code areas in its advertising promoting its claim to be the number 1 in international markets, something important to many companies given the increasing importance of global commerce. In its ads, DHL reported that "current Airborne customers will be connected to DHL's extensive international delivery system in more than 200 countries."[48]

DHL's stated goal is to become a powerhouse in the U.S. delivery market. While its share of the U.S. small package express market remains small at around 10%, DHL clearly stands to benefit from ownership by Deutsche Post and from its own extensive ex-U.S. operations. When it first acquired Airborne, Deutsche Post stated that the U.S. operation would be profitable by the end of 2006. However, the company ran into "integration problems" and suffered from reports of poor customer services and missed delivery deadlines. Now management does not see the unit turning profitable until 2009—although the express delivery service is profitable in the rest of the world. DHL lost some $500 million in the United States in 2006 and is forecasted to do the same in 2007.[49]

In 2005, Deutsche underlined its commitment to building a global logistics business when it purchased Exel of Britain for $7.2 billion. Exel was one of the

---

EXHIBIT 3

The Major Express Package Operators in 2005

	FedEx	UPS	DHL (Deutsche Post)	TNT
Revenues	$32,294 million	$42,581 million	$32,646 million[1]	$12,500 million[3]
Net Income	$1,806 million	$3,870 million	$405 million[2]	$951 million
Employees	221,000	407,000	280,000 (DHL only)	128,000
Countries Served	220	200+	220	200+
Aircraft	671	579	420	NA
Average Daily Shipment Volume	14.8 million	6 million	NA	NA

Sources: Company documents.

[1] Revenues and profits are for DHL only. DHL accounts for 57% of Deutsche Post revenues.

[2] Loss in United States reduced DHL's operating profits by $500 million in 2005.

[3] Figures for TNT include logistics business, which was sold off in 2006.

largest independent third-party logistics companies in the world with extensive operations in Europe, Asia, and North America. Combining Exel with Deutsche Post's existing businesses created a global logistics business with projected revenues of $25 billion, four times as large as the logistics business of UPS. Quickly on the heels of this acquisition, DHL won a contract worth $3 billion over ten years to manage the supply chain and deliver some 500,000 products to the 600 hospitals in Britain's National Health Service.[50]

Continued Globalization

Between 1997 and 2006, UPS and FedEx continued to build out their global infrastructure. By 2006, UPS delivered to more than 200 countries. Much of the within-country delivery is handled by local enterprises. The company has five main hubs. In addition to its main U.S. hub in Louisville, Kentucky, it has hubs in Cologne, Taipei, Miami (serving Latin American traffic), and the Philippines. In 2002, UPS launched an intra-Asian express delivery network from its Philippines hub. In 2004, it acquired Menio World Wide Forwarding, a global freight forwarder, to boost its global logistics business. In the same year, it also acquired complete ownership of its Japanese delivery operation (which was formally a joint venture with Yamato Transport Company). In 2005, UPS acquired operators of local ground networks in the UK and

Poland, and it is pushing into mainland China, which it sees as a major growth opportunity.

Like UPS, FedEx serves more than 200 countries around the world, although also like UPS, most of the local ground delivery is in the hands of local partners. FedEx has recently been focusing on building a presence in both China and India. The company has announced the development of a new Asian Pacific hub in Guangzhou, China. This will be FedEx's fourth international hub. The others are in Paris (handling intra-European express), the Philippines (handling intra-Asian express), and Alaska (handling packages flowing between Asia, North America, and Europe). In 2006, FedEx signaled its commitment to the Chinese market by buying out its joint venture partner, Tianjin Datian W. Group, for $400 million. The acquisition will give FedEx control of 90 parcel handling facilities and a 3,000 strong work force in China.[51]

While UPS and FedEx dominate the U.S. market for small package express delivery services, in Europe DHL and TNT lead with 23% and 11% respectively (TNT, formally an Australian enterprise, was acquired by the Royal Netherlands Post Office in 1996). In the intercontinental market, DHL leads with a 36% share, while in intra-Asian traffic Asia Yamato of Japan is the leader with a 20% share, followed by Sagawa with 16% (see Exhibit 4). The fragmented nature of the European and intra-Asia Pacific markets suggest that much is still at stake in this increasingly global business.

EXHIBIT 4

Market Share (%) for Small Package Express, 2005

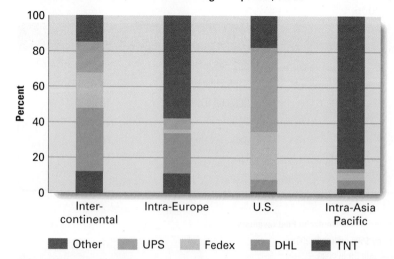

Source: Estimates from TNT posted on company website at www.tnt.com.

ENDNOTES

1. Standard & Poor's, "Aerospace and Air Transport," Industry Surveys, February 1996.
2. Ibid.
3. Standard & Poor's, "Airlines," Industry Surveys, March 2002.
4. John Kartsonas, "United Parcel Service," *Citigroup Global Capital Markets*, November 13, 2006.
5. Christopher H. Lovelock, "Federal Express (B)," Harvard Business School Case No. 579–040, 1978.
6. Standard & Poor's, "Aerospace and Air Transport," Industry Surveys, January 1981.
7. Lovelock, "Federal Express (B)."
8. Standard & Poor's, "Aerospace and Air Transport," Industry Surveys, January 1981.
9. Ibid.
10. Ibid.
11. Standard & Poor's, "Aerospace and Air Transport," Industry Surveys, January 1984.
12. Carol Hall, "High Fliers," *Marketing and Media Decisions*, August 1986, p. 138.
13. Standard & Poor's, "Aerospace and Air Transport," Industry Surveys, January 1984.
14. Standard & Poor's, "Aerospace and Air Transport," Industry Surveys, December 1984.
15. Brian Dumaine, "Turbulence Hits the Air Couriers," *Fortune*, July 21, 1986, pp. 101–106.
16. Ibid.
17. Chuck Hawkins, "Purolator: Still No Overnight Success," *Business Week*, June 16, 1986, pp. 76–78.
18. Joan O'C. Hamilton, "Emery Is One Heavy Load for Consolidated Freightways," *Business Week*, March 26, 1990, pp. 62–64.
19. Standard & Poor's, "Aerospace and Air Transport," Industry Surveys, February 1996.
20. "Hold That Tiger: FedEx Is Now World Heavyweight," *Purchasing*, September 14, 1989, pp. 41–42.
21. Standard & Poor's, "Aerospace and Air Transport," Industry Surveys, April 1988.
22. Standard & Poor's, "Aerospace and Air Transport," Industry Surveys, February 1996.
23. David Greising, "Watch Out for Flying Packages," *Business Week*, November 1994, p. 40.
24. "UPS to Raise Its Rates for Packages," *Wall Street Journal*, January 9, 1995, p. C22.
25. Marilyn Royce, "Airborne Freight," Value Line Investment Survey, September 20, 1996.
26. Robert Frank, "UPS Planning Earlier Delivery," *Wall Street Journal*, September 29, 1994, p. A4.
27. Frank, "Federal Express Grapples with Changes in U.S. Market." Wall Street Journal, March 24, 1995, p. A6.
28. Company press releases (http://www.ups.com/news/).
29. Joan M. Feldman, "The Coming of Age of International Air Freight," *Air Transport World*, June 1989, pp. 31–33.
30. Standard & Poor's, "Aerospace and Air Transport," Industry Surveys, February 1996.
31. Ibid.
32. Peter Greiff, "Lufthansa, JAL, and a Trading Firm Acquire a Majority Stake in DHL," *Wall Street Journal*, August 24, 1992, p. A5.
33. Standard & Poor's, "Aerospace and Air Transport," Industry Surveys, February 1996.
34. "Hold That Tiger: FedEx Is Now a World Heavyweight."
35. Douglas Blackmon, "FedEx Swings from Confidence Abroad to a Tightrope," *Wall Street Journal*, March 15, 1996, p. B4.
36. Daniel Pearl, "Federal Express Plans to Trim Assets in Europe," *Wall Street Journal*, March 17, 1992, p. A3.
37. Company press releases (http://www.ups.com/news/).
38. C. Haddad and M. Arndt, "Saying No Thanks to Overnight Air," *Business Week*, April 1, 2002, p. 74.
39. Salomon Smith Barney Research, "Wrap It Up—Bundling and the Air Express Sector," May 3, 2002; John Kartsonas, "United Parcel Service," *Citigroup Global Capital Markets*, November 13, 2006.
40. John Kartsonas, "FedEx Corp," *Citigroup Global Capital Markets*, November 13, 2006.
41. Data from Deutsche Post World Net, 2005 Annual Report.
42. C. Haddad and M. Arndt, "Saying No Thanks to Overnight Air," *Business Week*, April 1, 2002, p. 74.
43. E. Walsh, "Package Deal," *Logistics*, February 2001, pp. 19–20.
44. Salomon Smith Barney Research, "Wrap It Up—Bundling and the Air Express Sector," May 3, 2002.
45. R. Gibson, "Package Deal: UPS's purchase of Mail Boxes Etc. Looked Great on Paper," *Wall Street Journal*, May 8, 2006, p. R13.
46. Andrew Ward, "Kinko's Plans to Push the Envelope Further," *Financial Times*, August 7, 2006, p. 22.
47. J. D. Schultz, "DHL Crashes the Party," *Logistics*, August 2005, pp. 59–63.
48. P. Needham, "Coming to America," *Journal of Commerce*, April 22, 2002, p. 12.
49. B. Barnard, "Logistics Spurs Deutsche Post," *Journal of Commerce*, November 8, 2006, p. 1.
50. "DHL Gets $3 Billion UK Deal," *Journal of Commerce*, September 5, 2006, p. 1.
51. A. Ward, "A Dogfight for Courier Service Dominance," *Financial Times*, February 15, 2006, p. 10.

Airborne Express: The Underdog

This case was prepared by Charles W. L. Hill, the University of Washington.[1]

Airborne Inc., which operated under the name Airborne Express, was an air express transportation company providing express and second-day delivery of small packages (less than seventy pounds) and documents throughout the United States and to and from many foreign countries. The company owned and operated an airline and a fleet of ground-transportation vehicles to provide complete door-to-door service. It was also an airfreight forwarder, moving shipments of any size on a worldwide basis. In 2003, Airborne Express held third place in the U.S. air express industry, with 9% of the market for small package deliveries. Its main domestic competitors were Federal Express, which had 26% of the market, and United Parcel Service (UPS), which had 53% of the market. There were several smaller players in the market at the time, including DHL Airways, Consolidated Freightways (CF), and the U.S. Postal Service, each of which held under 5% of the market share.[2] In 2003, after years of struggling to survive in the fiercely competitive small package express delivery industry, Airborne was acquired by DHL, which was itself owned by Deutsche Post, the large German postal, express package, and logistics company.

The evolution of the air express industry and the current state of competition in the industry were discussed in a companion case to this one, "The Evolution of the Small Package Express Delivery Industry, 1973–2006." The current case focuses on the operating structure, competitive strategy, organizational structure, and cultures of Airborne Express from its inception until it was acquired by DHL in 2003.

History of Airborne Express

Airborne Express was originally known as Pacific Air Freight when it was founded in Seattle at the close of World War II by Holt W. Webster, a former Army Air Corps officer. (See Exhibit 1 for a listing of major milestones in the history of Airborne Express.) The company was merged with Airborne Freight Corp. of California in 1968, taking the name of the California company but retaining management direction by the former officers of Pacific Air Freight. Airborne was initially an exclusive airfreight forwarder. Freight forwarders such as Airborne arrange for the transportation of air cargo between any two destinations. They purchase cargo space from the airlines and retail this in small amounts. They deal primarily with small customers, providing pickup and delivery services in most cities, either in their own trucks or through contract agents.

Following the 1977 deregulation of the airline industry, Airborne entered the air express industry by leasing the airplanes and pilots of Midwest Charter, a small airline operating out of its own airport in Wilmington, Ohio. However, Airborne quickly became dissatisfied with the limited amount of control they were able to exercise over Midwest, which made it very difficult to achieve the kind of tight coordination and control of logistics that was necessary to become a successful air express operator. Instead of continuing to lease Midwest's planes and facility, in 1980 Airborne decided to buy "the entire bucket of slop; company, planes, pilots, airport and all."

EXHIBIT 1

Major Milestones at Airborne Express[3]

1946: Airborne Flower Traffic Association of California is founded to fly fresh flowers from Hawaii to the mainland.

1968: Airborne of California and Pacific Air Freight of Seattle merge to form Airborne Freight Corp. Headquarters are in Seattle, Washington.

1979–1981: Airborne Express is born. After purchasing Midwest Air Charter, Airborne buys Clinton County Air Force Base in Wilmington, Ohio, becoming the only carrier to own and operate an airport. The package sort center opens, creating the "hub" for the hub-and-spoke system.

1984–1986: Airborne is first carrier to establish a privately operated Foreign Trade Zone in an air industrial park.

1987: Airborne opens the Airborne Stock Exchange, a third-party inventory management and distribution service. In the same year, service begins to and from more than 8,000 Canadian locations.

1988: Airborne becomes the first air express carrier to provide same-day delivery, through its purchase of Sky Courier.

1990: The International Cargo Forum and Exposition names Airborne the carrier with the most outstanding integrated cargo system over the previous two years.

1991: A trio of accolades: Airborne is the first transportation company to receive Volvo-Flyg Motors' Excellent Performance Award. Computerworld ranks us the "most effective user of information systems in the U.S. transportation industry." In addition, we receive the "Spread the Word!" Electronic Data Interchange (EDI) award for having the largest number of EDI users worldwide in the air express and freight forwarding industry.

1992: Airborne introduces Flight-ReadySM, the first prepaid Express Letters and Packs.

1993: Airborne introduces Airborne Logistics Services (ALS), a new subsidiary providing outsourced warehousing and distribution services. IBM consolidates its international shipping operation with Airborne.

1994: Airborne opens its Ocean Service Division, becoming the first express carrier to introduce ocean shipping services. Airborne Logistics Services (ALS) establishes the first new film distribution program for the movie industry in 50 years. We also become the first company to provide online communication to Vietnam.

1995: Airborne Alliance Group, a consortium of transportation, logistics, third-party customer service operations and high-tech companies providing value-added services, is formed. Airborne opens a second runway at its hub, which is now the United States' largest privately owned airport. We also expand our fleet, acquiring Boeing 767-200 aircraft.

1996: Airborne Express celebrates 50 years of providing value-added distribution solutions to business.

1997: Airborne Express has its best year ever, with net earnings increasing three-and-a-half-fold over the previous year. Airborne's stock triples, leading to a two-for-one stock split in February, 1998.

1998: Airborne posts record profits and enters the Fortune 500. The first of 30 Boeing 767s is introduced to our fleet. The Business Consumer Guide rates Airborne as the Best Air Express Carrier for the 4th consecutive year.

1999: Airborne@home, a unique alliance with the United States Postal Service, is introduced. It enables e-tailers, catalog companies and similar businesses to ship quickly and economically to the residential marketplace. Optical Village is created. Part of Airborne Logistics Services, this new division brings together some of the biggest competitors in the optical industry to share many costs and a single location in their assembly, logistics, and delivery options.

2000: Airborne announces several changes in senior management, including a new President and Chief Operating Officer, Carl Donaway. Several new business initiatives are announced, most notably a ground service scheduled to begin April 1, 2001. Airborne also wins the Brand Keys Customer Loyalty Award, edging out our competition for the second consecutive year.

2001: Airborne launches Ground Delivery Service and 10:30 A.M. Service, giving Airborne a comprehensive, full-service industry competitive capability. Airborne.com launches its Small Business Center, as well as a variety of enhancements to help all business customers speed and simplify the shipping process. We also release the Corporate Exchange shipping application, simplifying desktop shipping for customers while giving them greater control. Advanced tracking features are added to airborne.com and Airborne eCourier is released, enabling customers to send confidential, signed documents electronically.

2003: Airborne's ground operations acquired by DHL for $1.1 billion.

Among other things, the Midwest acquisition put Airborne in the position of being the only industry participant to own an airport. Airborne immediately began the job of developing a hub-and-spoke system capable of supporting a nationwide distribution system. An efficient sorting facility was established at the Wilmington hub. Airborne upgraded Midwest's fleet of prop and propjet aircraft, building a modern fleet of DC-8s, DC-9s, and YS-11 aircraft. These planes left major cities every evening, flying down the spokes carrying letters and packages to the central sort facility in Wilmington, Ohio. There the letters and packages were unloaded, sorted according to their final destinations, and then reloaded and flown to their final destinations for delivery before noon the next day.

During the late 1970s and early 1980s, dramatic growth in the industry attracted many competitors. As a consequence, despite a high growth rate, price competition became intense, forcing a number of companies to the sidelines by the late 1980s. Between 1984 and 1990, average revenues per domestic shipment at Airborne fell from around $30 to under $15 (in 2003, they were just under $9). Airborne was able to survive this period by pursuing a number of strategies that increased productivity and drove costs down to the lowest levels in the industry. Airborne's operating costs per shipment fell from $28 in 1984 to around $14 by 1990, and to $9.79 by 2001. As a consequence, by the late 1980s Airborne had pulled away from a pack of struggling competitors to become one of the top three companies in the industry, a position it still held when acquired by DHL in 2003.

Air Express Operations

The Domestic Delivery Network

As of 2002, its last full year as an independent enterprise, Airborne Express had 305 ground stations within the United States. The stations were the ends of the spokes in Airborne's hub-and-spoke system, and the distribution of stations allowed Airborne to reach all major population centers in the country. In each station, there were about fifty to fifty-five or so drivers plus staff. About 80% of Airborne's 115,300 full-time and 7,200 part-time employees were found at this level. The stations were the basic units in Airborne's delivery organization. Their primary task was to ferry packages between clients and the local air terminal. Airborne utilized approximately 14,900 radio-dispatch delivery vans and trucks to transport packages, of which 6,000 were owned by the company. Independent drivers under contract with the company provided the balance of the company's pickup and delivery services.

Airborne's drivers made their last round of major clients at 5 P.M. The drivers either collected packages directly from clients or from one of the company's 15,300 plus drop boxes. The drop boxes were placed at strategic locations, such as in the lobbies of major commercial buildings. To give clients a little more time, in most major cities there were also a few central drop boxes that are not emptied until 6 P.M. If a client needed still more time, so long as the package could be delivered to the airport by 7 P.M., it would make the evening flight.

When a driver picked up a package, he or she read a bar code that is attached to the package with a hand-held scanner. This information was fed directly into Airborne's proprietary FOCUS (Freight, On-Line Control and Update System) computer system. The FOCUS system, which had global coverage, recorded shipment status at key points in the life cycle of a shipment. Thus, a customer could call Airborne on a twenty-four-hour basis to find out where in Airborne's system their package was. FOCUS also allowed a customer direct access to shipment information through the Internet. All a customer needed to do was access Airborne's website and key the code number assigned to a package, and the FOCUS system would tell the customer where in Airborne's system the package was.

When a driver completed a pickup route, she or he took the load to Airborne's loading docks at the local airport. (Airborne served all ninety-nine major metropolitan airports in the United States.) There the packages were loaded into C-containers (discussed later in this case study). C-containers were then towed by hand or by tractor to a waiting aircraft, where they were loaded onto a conveyor belt and in turn passed through the passenger door of the aircraft. Before long the aircraft was loaded and took off. It would either fly directly to the company's hub at Wilmington, or make one or two stops along the way to pick up more packages.

Sometime between midnight and 2 A.M., most of the aircraft would have landed at Wilmington. An old strategic air command base, Wilmington's location places it within a 600-mile radius (an overnight drive or one-hour flying time) of 60% of the U.S.

population. Wilmington has the advantage of a good-weather record. In all the years that Airborne operated at Wilmington, air operations were "fogged out" on only a handful of days. In 1995, Airborne opened a second runway at Wilmington. Developed at a cost of $60 million, the second runway made Wilmington the largest privately owned airport in the country. The runway expansion was part of a $120 million upgrade of the Wilmington sort facility.

After arrival at Wilmington, the plane taxied down the runway and parked alongside a group of aircraft that were already disgorging their load of C-containers. Within minutes the C-containers were unloaded from the plane down a conveyor belt and towed to the sort facility by a tractor. The sort facility had the capacity to handle 1.2 million packages per night. At the end of 2001, the facility handled an average of 1 million packages a night. The bar codes on the packages were read, and then the packages were directed through a labyrinth of conveyor belts and sorted according to final destination. The sorting was partly done by hand and partly automated. At the end of this process, packages were grouped together by final destination and loaded into a C-container. An aircraft bound for the final destination was then loaded with C-containers, and by 5 A.M. most aircraft had taken off.

Upon arrival at the final destination, the plane was unloaded and the packages sorted according to their delivery points within the surrounding area. Airborne couriers then took the packages on the final leg of their journey. Packages had a 75% probability of being delivered to clients by 10:30 A.M., and a 98% probability of being delivered by noon.

Regional Trucking Hubs

Although about 71% of packages were transported by air and passed through Wilmington, Airborne also established ten regional trucking hubs that dealt with the remaining 29% of the company's domestic volume. These hubs sorted shipments that originated and had destinations within approximately a 300-mile radius. The first one opened in Allentown, Pennsylvania, centrally located on the East Coast. This hub handled packages transported between points within the Washington, D.C., to Boston area. Instead of transporting packages by air, packages to be transported within this area were sorted by the drivers at pickup and delivered from the driver's home station by scheduled truck runs to the Allentown hub. There

they were sorted according to destination and taken to the appropriate station on another scheduled truck run for final delivery.

One advantage of ground-based transportation through trucking hubs was that operating costs were much lower than for air transportation. The average cost of a package transported by air was more than five times greater than the cost of a package transported on the ground. However, this cost differential was transparent to the customer, who assumed that all packages were flown. Thus, Airborne could charge the same price for ground-transported packages as for air-transported packages, but the former yielded a much higher return. The trucking hubs also had the advantage of taking some of the load of the Wilmington sorting facility, which was operating at about 90% capacity by 2003.

International Operations

In addition to its domestic express operations, Airborne was also an international company providing service to more than 200 countries worldwide. International operations accounted for about 11% of total revenues in 2002. Airborne offered two international products: freight products and express products. Freight products were commercial-sized, larger-unit shipments. This service provides door-to-airport service. Goods were picked up domestically from the customer and then shipped to the destination airport. A consignee or an agent of the consignee got the paperwork and cleared the shipment through customs. Express packages are small packages, documents, and letters. This was a door to door service, and all shipments were cleared through customs by Airborne. Most of Airborne's international revenues come from freight products.

Airborne did not fly any of its own aircraft overseas. Rather, it contracted for space on all-cargo airlines or in the cargo holds of passenger airlines. Airborne owned facilities overseas in Japan, Taiwan, Hong Kong, Singapore, Australia, New Zealand, and London. These functioned in a manner similar to Airborne's domestic stations. (That is, they had their own trucks and drivers and were hooked into the FOCUS tracking system.) The majority of foreign distribution, however, was carried out by foreign agents. Foreign agents were large, local, well-established surface delivery companies. Airborne entered into a number of exclusive strategic alliances with large foreign agents. It had alliances in Japan, Thailand, Malaysia, and South Africa. The rationale for entering strategic alliances, along with Airborne's approach to global expansion, is discussed in greater detail later in this case.

Another aspect of Airborne's international operations was the creation at its Wilmington hub of the only privately certified Foreign Trade Zone (FTZ) in the United States. While in an FTZ, merchandise is tax free and no customs duty is paid on it until it leaves. Thus, a foreign-based company could store critical inventory in the FTZ and have Airborne deliver it just in time to U.S. customers. This allowed the foreign company to hold inventory in the United States without having to pay customs duty on it until the need arose.

Aircraft Purchase and Maintenance

As of 2002, Airborne Express owned a fleet of 118 aircraft, including 24 DC-8s, 74 DC-9s, and 20 Boeing 767s. In addition, approximately 70 smaller aircraft were chartered nightly to connect smaller cities with company aircraft that then operated to and from the Wilmington hub. To keep down capital expenditures, Airborne preferred to purchase used planes. Airborne converted the planes to suit its specifications at a maintenance facility based at its Wilmington hub. Once it got a plane, Airborne typically gutted the interior and installed state-of-the-art electronics and avionics equipment. The company's philosophy was to get all of the upgrades that it could into an aircraft. Although this could cost a lot up front, there was a payback in terms of increased aircraft reliability and a reduction in service downtime. Airborne also standardized cockpits as much as possible. This made it easier for crews to switch from one aircraft to another if the need arose. According to the company, in the early 1990s, the total purchase and modification of a secondhand DC-9 cost about $10 million, compared with an equivalent new-plane cost of $40 million. An additional factor reducing operating costs was that Airborne's DC-9 aircraft required only two-person cockpit crews, as opposed to the three-person crews required in most Federal Express and UPS aircraft at the time.

After conversion, Airborne strove to keep aircraft maintenance costs down by carrying out virtually all of its own fleet repairs. (It was the only all-cargo carrier to do so.) The Wilmington maintenance facility could handle everything except major engine repairs and had the capability to machine critical aircraft parts if needed. The company saw this in-house facility as a major source of cost savings. It estimated that maintenance labor costs were 50 to 60% below the costs of having the same work performed outside.

In December 1995, Airborne announced a deal to purchase twelve used Boeing 767-200 aircraft between the years 1997 and 2000, and it announced plans to purchase an additional ten to fifteen used 767-200s between the years 2000 and 2004. These were the first wide-bodied aircraft in Airborne's fleet. The cost of introducing the first twelve aircraft was about $290 million, and the additional aircraft would cost $360 million. The shift to wide-bodied aircraft was promoted by an internal study, which concluded that with growing volume, wide-bodied aircraft would lead to greater operating efficiencies.

During 2001, Airborne was using about 66.6% of its lift capacity on a typical business day. This compared with 76.7% capacity utilization in 1997, and 70% utilization in 2000. In late 2001, Airborne reduced its total lift capacity by some 100,000 pounds to about 4 million pounds a day. It did this to try to reduce excess capacity of certain routes and better match supply with demand conditions.

C-Containers

C-containers are uniquely shaped 60-cubic-foot containers developed by Airborne Express in 1985 at a cost of $3.5 million. They are designed to fit through the passenger doors of DC-8 and DC-9 aircraft. They replaced the much larger A-containers widely used in the air cargo business. At six times the size of a C-container, A-containers can be loaded only through specially built cargo doors and require specialized loading equipment. The loading equipment required for C-containers is a modified belt loader, similar to that used for loading baggage onto a plane, and about 80% less expensive than the equipment needed to load A-containers. The use of C-containers meant that Airborne did not have to bear the $1 million per plane cost required to install cargo doors that would take A-containers. The C-containers are shaped to allow maximum utilization of the planes' interior loading space. Fifty of the containers fit into a converted DC-9, and about 83 fit into a DC-8-62. Moreover, a C-container filled with packages can be moved by a single person, making it easy to load and unload. Airborne Express took out a patent on the design of the C-containers.

Information Systems

Airborne utilized three information systems to help it boost productivity and improve customer service. The first of these systems was the LIBRA II system. LIBRA II equipment, which included a metering device and PC computer software, was installed in the mailroom of clients. With minimum data entry, the metering device weighed the package, calculated the shipping charges, generated the shipping labels, and provided a daily shipping report. By 2002, the system was in use at approximately 9,900 domestic customer locations. The use of LIBRA II not only benefited customers but also lowered Airborne's operating costs since LIBRA II shipment data were transferred into Airborne's FOCUS shipment tracking system automatically, thereby avoiding duplicate data entry.

FOCUS was the second of Airborne's three main information systems. As discussed earlier, the FOCUS system was a worldwide tracking system. The bar codes on each package were read at various points (for example, at pickup, at sorting in Wilmington, at arrival, and so forth) using hand-held scanners, and this information was fed into Airborne's computer system. Using FOCUS, Airborne could track the progress of a shipment through its national and international logistics system. The major benefit was in terms of customer service. Through an Internet link, Airborne's customers could track their own shipment through Airborne's system on a twenty-four-hour basis.

For its highest-volume corporate customers, Airborne developed Customer Linkage, an electronic data interchange (EDI) program and the third information system. The EDI system was designed to eliminate the flow of paperwork between Airborne and its major clients. The EDI system allowed customers to create shipping documentation at the same time they were entering orders for their goods. At the end of each day, shipping activities were transmitted electronically to Airborne's FOCUS system, where they were captured for shipment tracking and billing. Customer Linkage benefited the customer by eliminating repetitive data entry and paperwork. It also lowered the company's operating costs by eliminating manual data entry. (In essence, both LIBRA II and Customer Linkage pushed off a lot of the data-entry work into the hands of customers.) The EDI system also included electronic invoicing and payment remittance processing. Airborne also offered its customers a program known as Quicklink, which significantly reduced the programming time required by customers to take advantage of linkage benefits.

Strategy

Market Positioning

In the early 1980s, Airborne Express tried hard to compete head to head with Federal Express. This included an attempt to establish broad market coverage, including both frequent and infrequent users. Frequent users are those that generate more than $20,000 of business per month, or more than 1,000 shipments per month. Infrequent users generate less than $20,000 per month, or less than 1,000 shipments per month.

To build broad market coverage, Airborne followed Federal Express's lead of funding a television advertising campaign designed to build consumer awareness. However, by the mid-1980s, Airborne decided that this was an expensive way of building market share. The advertising campaign bought recognition but little penetration. One of the principal problems was that it was expensive to serve infrequent users. Infrequent users demanded the same level of service as frequent users, but Airborne would typically get only one shipment per pickup with an infrequent user, compared with ten or more shipments per pickup with a frequent user, so far more pickups were required to generate the same volume of business. Given the extremely competitive nature of the industry at this time, such an inefficient utilization of capacity was of great concern to Airborne.

Consequently, in the mid-1980s, Airborne decided to become a niche player in the industry and focused on serving the needs of high-volume corporate accounts. The company slashed its advertising expenditure, pulling the plug on its TV ad campaign, and invested more resources in building a direct sales force, which grew to be 460 strong. By focusing on high-volume corporate accounts, Airborne was able to establish scheduled pickup routes and use its ground capacity more efficiently. This enabled the company to achieve significant reductions in its unit cost structure. Partly due to this factor, Airborne executives reckoned that their cost structure was as much as $3 per shipment less than that of FedEx. Another estimate suggested that Airborne's strategy reduced labor costs by 20% per unit for pickup, and 10% for delivery.

Of course, there was a downside to this strategy. High-volume corporate customers have a great deal more bargaining power than infrequent users, so they can and do demand substantial discounts. For example, in March 1987, Airborne achieved a major coup when it won an exclusive three-year contract to handle all of IBM's express packages weighing less than 150 pounds. However, to win the IBM account, Airborne had to offer rates up to 84% below Federal Express's list prices! Nevertheless, the strategy does seem to have worked. As of 1995 approximately 80% of Airborne's revenues came from corporate accounts, most of them secured through competitive bidding. The concentrated volume that this business represents helped Airborne to drive down costs.

Delivery Time, Reliability, and Flexibility

Another feature of Airborne's strategy was the decision not to try to compete with Federal Express on delivery time. Federal Express and UPS have long guaranteed delivery by 10:30 A.M. Airborne guaranteed delivery by midday, although it offered a 10:30 guarantee to some very large corporate customers. Guaranteeing delivery by 10:30 A.M. would mean stretching Airborne's already tight scheduling system to the limit. To meet its 10:30 A.M. deadline, FedEx has to operate with a deadline for previous days' pickups of 6:30 P.M. Airborne could afford to be a little more flexible and can arrange pickups at 6:00 P.M. if that suited a corporate client's particular needs. Later pickups clearly benefit the shipper, who is, after all, the paying party.

In addition, Airborne executives felt that a guaranteed 10:30 A.M. delivery was unnecessary. They argued that the extra hour and a half does not make a great deal of difference to most clients, and they are willing to accept the extra time in exchange for lower prices. In addition, Airborne stressed the reliability of its delivery schedules. As one executive put it, "A package delivered consistently at 11:15 A.M. is as good as delivery at 10:30 A.M." This reliability was enhanced by Airborne's ability to provide shipment tracking through its FOCUS system.

Deferred Services

With a slowdown in the growth rate of the express mail market toward the end of the 1980s, in 1990 Airborne decided to enter the deferred-delivery business with its Select Delivery Service (SDS) product. The SDS service provides for next-afternoon or second-day delivery. Packages weighing five pounds or less are generally delivered on a next-afternoon basis, with packages of more than five pounds being delivered on a second-day basis. SDS shipment comprised approximately 42% of total domestic shipments in 1995. They were priced lower than overnight express products, reflecting the less time-sensitive nature of these deliveries. The company utilized any spare capacity on its express flights to carry SDS shipments. In addition, Airborne used other carriers, such as passenger carriers with spare cargo capacity in the bellies of their planes, to carry less urgent SDS shipments.

Early in 1996, Airborne began to phase in two new services to replace its SDS service. Next Afternoon Service was available for shipments weighing five pounds or less, and Second Day Service was offered for shipments of all weights. By 2001, deferred shipments accounted for 46% of total domestic shipments.

Ground Delivery Service

In April 2001, Airborne launched a Ground Delivery Service (GDS) in response to similar offerings from FedEx and UPS. Airborne came to the conclusion that it was very important to offer this service in order to retain parity with its principal competitors, and to be able to offer bundled services to its principal customers (that is, to offer them air, ground, and logistics services for a single bundled price). Airborne also believed that it could add the service with a relatively minor initial investment, $30 million, since it leveraged existing assets, including trucks, tracking systems, and regional ground hubs and sorting facilities.

The new service was initially introduced on a limited basis and targeted at large corporate customers. GDS was priced less than deferred services, reflecting the less time-sensitive nature of the GDS offering. GDS accounted for 1.5% of domestic shipments in 2001, and 4% in the fourth quarter of 2001.

Logistics Services

Although small package express mail remained Airborne's main business, through its Advanced Logistics Services Corp. (ALS) subsidiary the company increasingly promoted a range of third-party logistics services. These services provided customers with the ability to maintain inventories in a 1-million-square-foot "stock exchange" facility located at Airborne's Wilmington hub or at sixty smaller "stock exchange" facilities located around the country. The inventory could be managed either by the company or by the customer's personnel. Inventory stored at Wilmington could be delivered utilizing either Airborne's airline system or, if required, commercial airlines on a next-flight-out basis. ALS's central print computer program allowed information on inventories to be sent electronically to customers' computers located at Wilmington, where Airborne's personnel monitored printed output and shipped inventories according to customers' instructions.

For example, consider the case of Data Products Corp., a producer of computer printers. Data Products takes advantage of low labor costs to carry out significant assembly operations in Hong Kong. Many of the primary component parts for its printers, however, such as microprocessors, are manufactured in the United States and have to be shipped to Hong Kong. The finished product is then shipped back to the United States for sale. In setting up a global manufacturing system, Data Products had a decision to make: either consolidate the parts from its hundreds of suppliers in-house and then arrange for shipment to Hong Kong, or contract out to someone who could handle the whole logistics process. Data Products decided to contract out, picking Airborne Express to consolidate the component parts and arrange for shipments.

Airborne controlled the consolidation and movement of component parts from the component part suppliers through to the Hong Kong assembly operation in such a way as to minimize inventory-holding costs. The key feature of Airborne's service was that all of Data Products' materials were collected at Airborne's facility at Los Angeles International Airport. Data Products' Hong Kong assembly plants could then tell Airborne what parts to ship by air as they are needed. Airborne was thus able to provide inventory control for Data Products. In addition, by scheduling deliveries so that year-round traffic between Los Angeles and Hong Kong could be guaranteed, Airborne was able to negotiate a better air rate from Japan Air Lines for the transportation of component parts.

International Strategy

One of the major strategic challenges that Airborne faced (along with the other express mail carriers) was how best to establish an international service that is comparable to their domestic service. Many of Airborne's major corporate clients were becoming ever more global in their own strategic orientations. As this occurred, they were increasingly demanding a compatible express mail service. In addition, the rise of companies with globally dispersed manufacturing operations that relied on just-in-time delivery systems to keep inventory holding costs down created a demand for global air express services that could transport critical inventory between operations located in different areas of the globe (consider the example of Data Products discussed earlier in this case study).

The initial response of FedEx and UPS to this challenge was to undertake massive capital investments to establish international airlift capability and international ground operations based on the U.S. model. Their rationale was that a wholly owned global delivery network was necessary to establish the tight control, coordination, and scheduling required for a successful air express operation. In the 1990s, however, FedEx pulled out of its European ground operations, while continuing to fly its own aircraft overseas.

Airborne decided on a quite different strategy. In part born of financial necessity (Airborne lacks the capital necessary to imitate FedEx and UPS), Airborne decided to pursue what it referred to as a *variable cost strategy*. This involved two main elements: (1) the utilization of international airlift on existing air cargo operators and passenger aircraft to get packages overseas, and (2) entry into strategic alliances with foreign companies that already had established ground delivery networks. In these two ways, Airborne hoped to be able to establish global coverage without having to undertake the kind of capital investments that Federal Express and UPS have borne.

Airborne executives defend their decision to continue to purchase space on international flights rather than fly their own aircraft overseas by making a number of points. First, they pointed out that Airborne's international business was 70% outbound and 30% inbound. If Airborne were to fly its own aircraft overseas, this would mean flying them back half-empty. Second, on many routes Airborne simply didn't have the volume necessary to justify flying its own planes. Third, national air carriers were giving Airborne good prices. If Airborne began to fly directly overseas, the company would be seen as a competitor and might no longer be given price breaks. Fourth, getting international airlift space was not a problem. While space can be limited in the third and fourth quarters of the year, Airborne was such a big customer that it usually had few problems getting lift.

On the other hand, the long-term viability of this strategy was questionable given the rapid evolution in the international air express business. Flying Tiger was once one of Airborne's major providers of international lift. However, following the purchase of Flying Tiger by FedEx, Airborne has reduced its business with Flying Tiger. Airborne worried that its packages will be "pushed to the back of the plane" whenever Flying Tiger had problems of capacity overload.

With regard to strategic alliances, Airborne had joint venture operations is Japan, Thailand, Malaysia, and South Africa. The alliance with Mitsui was announced in December 1989. Mitsui is one of the world's leading trading companies. Together with Tonami Transportation Co., Mitsui owns Panther Express, one of the top five express carriers in Japan and a company with a substantial ground network. The deal called for the establishment of a joint venture between Airborne, Mitsui, and Tonami. To be known as Airborne Express Japan, the joint venture combined Airborne's existing Japanese operations with Panther Express. Airborne handled all of the shipments to and from Japan. The joint venture was 40% owned by Airborne, 40% by Mitsui, and 20% by Tonami. The agreement specified that board decisions had to be made by consensus among the three partners. A majority of two could not outvote the third. In addition, the deal called for Mitsui to invest $40 million in Airborne Express through the purchase of a new issue of nonvoting 6.9% cumulative convertible preferred stock and a commitment to Airborne from Mitsui of up to $100 million for aircraft financing. There is no doubt that Airborne executives saw the Mitsui deal as a major coup, both financially and in terms of market penetration into the Japanese market. The primary advantage claimed by Airborne executives for expanding via strategic alliances is that the company got an established ground-based delivery network overseas without having to make capital investments.

Organization

In 2001, Carl Donaway became CEO, replacing the long-time top management team of Robert Cline, the CEO, and Robert Brazier, the president and COO, both of whom had been with the company since the early 1960s. Prior to becoming CEO, Donaway was responsible for the airline operations, included managing the Wilmington hub, the package sorting facility, and all aircraft and flight maintenance operations. The philosophy at Airborne was to keep the organizational structure as flat as possible, to shorten lines of communication and allow for a free flow of ideas within the managerial hierarchy. The top managers generally felt that they were open to ideas suggested by lower-level managers. At the same time, the decision-making process was fairly centralized. The view was that interdependence between functions made centralized decision making necessary. To quote one executive, "Coordination is the essence of this business. We need centralized decision making in order to achieve this."

Control at Airborne Express was geared toward boosting productivity, lowering costs, and maintaining a reliable high-quality service. This was achieved through a combination of budgetary controls, pay-for-performance incentive systems, and a corporate culture that continually stressed key values.

For example, consider the procedure used to control stations (which contained about 80% of all employees). Station operations were reviewed on a quarterly basis using a budgetary process. Control and evaluation of station effectiveness stressed four categories. The first was service, measured by the time between pickup and delivery. The goal was to achieve 95 to 97% of all deliveries before noon. The second category was productivity, measured by total shipments per employee hour. The third category was controllable cost, and the fourth station profitability. Goals for each of these categories were determined each quarter in a bottom-up procedure that involved station managers in the goal-setting process. These goals were then linked to an incentive pay system whereby station managers could earn up to 10% of their quarterly salary just by meeting their goals with no maximum on the upside if they go over the goals.

The direct sales force also had an incentive pay system. The target pay structure for the sales organization was 70% base pay and a 30% commission. There was, however, no cap on the commissions for salespeople. So in theory, there was no limit to what a salesperson could earn. There were also contests that were designed to boost performance. For example, there was a so-called Top Gun competition for the sales force, in which the top salesperson for each quarter won a $20,000 prize.

Incentive pay systems apart, however, Airborne is not known as a high payer. The company's approach is not to be the compensation leader. Rather, the company tries to set its salary structure to position it in the middle of the labor market. Thus, according to a senior human resource executive, "We target our pay philosophy (total package—compensation plus benefits) to be right at the 50th percentile plus or minus 5 percent."

A degree of self-control was also achieved by trying to establish a corporate culture that focused employees' attention on the key values required to maintain a competitive edge in the air express industry. The values continually stressed by top managers at Airborne, and communicated throughout the organization by the company's newspaper and a quarterly video, emphasized serving customers' needs, maintaining quality, doing it right the first time around, and excellent service. There was also a companywide emphasis on productivity and cost control. One executive, when describing the company's attitude to expenditures, said, "We challenge everything. . . . We're the toughest sons of bitches on the block." Another noted that "among managers I feel that there is a universal agreement on the need to control costs. This is a very tough business, and our people are aware of that. Airborne has an underdog mentality—a desire to be a survivor."

Airborne in 2002

By 2002 Airborne Express faced a number of key strategic opportunities and threats. These included (1) the rapid globalization of the air express industry, (2) the development of logistics services based on rapid air transportation, (3) the growth potential for deferred services and ground-based delivery services, (4) lower margins associated with the new GDS offering, (5) the superior scale and scope of its two main competitors, FedEx and UPS, (6) an economic slowdown in the United States, and (7) persistently high fuel costs (oil prices rose from $18 a barrel in mid-1995 to $25 a barrel in 2002). The company's financial performance, which had always been volatile, was poor during 2001, when the company lost $12 million on revenues of $3.2 billion. In 2002, Airborne earned $58 million on revenues of $3.3 billion, even though average revenue per shipment declined to $8.46 from $8.79 a year earlier. Management attributed the improved performance to strong employee productivity, which improved 9.4% over the prior year. In their guidance for 2003, management stated that they would be able to further improve operating performance—then, in March 2003, DHL made its takeover bid for the company. Under the terms of the deal, which was finalized in 2003, DHL acquired the ground assets of Airborne Express, while the airline continued as an independent entity.

ENDNOTES

1. This case was made possible by the generous assistance of Airborne Express. The information given in this case was provided by Airborne Express. Unless otherwise indicated, Airborne Express and Securities and Exchange Commission's 10–K filings are the sources of all information contained within this case. The case is based on an earlier case, which was prepared with the assistance of Daniel Bodnar, Laurie Martinelli, Brian McMullen, Lisa Mutty, and Stephen Schmidt.
2. Standard & Poors Industry Survey, Airlines, March, 2002.
3. *Source:* http://www.airborne.com/Company/History.asp?nav= AboutAirborne/CompanyInfo/History.

This case was prepared by Dr. Isaac Cohen, San Jose State University.

Since the passage of the Airline Deregulation Act in 1978, eight major U.S. air carriers filed for bankruptcy. All were old, established carriers flying domestic as well as international routes. Three of the major carriers—Pan American Airways, Eastern Airlines, and Trans World Airways (TWA)—were eventually liquidated and their assets were sold to rival carriers. Two others—Continental Airlines and U.S. Air—filed for bankruptcy protection at least twice. And the remaining three—United, Delta, and Northwest Airlines—were operating in 2005–2006 under Chapter 11 of the Bankruptcy Code. Alone among all U.S. international majors, American Airlines (AA) had never filed for bankruptcy protection.

American's financial position was stronger than that of its competitors all through the era of deregulation. During the first two decades of the new era, Robert Crandall ran AA, first as President (1980–1985), and then as CEO (1985–1998). An executive widely regarded as the industry's most innovative strategist, Crandall introduced the frequent-flier program and the two-tier wage system, expanded American globally, formed alliances with other carriers, and established a successful regional airline affiliated with AA.

As Crandall retired in 1998, Donald Carty was selected CEO. An insider whose tenure was overshadowed by the terrorist attack of September 11, 2001, Carty was a lackluster leader, and his career ended in a public scandal that led to his replacement by Gerald Arpey in April 2003. Arpey needed to act quickly. Following the unprecedented losses incurred

This case was presented in the October 2006 meeting of the North American Case Research Association at San Diego, California. Copyright Isaac Cohen and NACRA. Dr. Cohen is grateful to the San Jose State University College of Business for its support.

by American as a result of the September 11 attack—a loss of over $5 billion dollars during 2001 and 2002, and an additional loss of over $1 billion in the first quarter of 2003—American Airlines was on the brink of bankruptcy.

What should Arpey do?

Should Arpey follow the strategies undertaken by Crandall to cut operating costs, improve AA's financial position, and turn the carrier profitable? Should Arpey, rather, reject some of the policies introduced by his predecessor? Or should he, instead, introduce brand new innovative strategies applicable to the airline industry in the 21st century?

To assess Arpey's strategic choices, this case looks back at the experience of his legendary predecessor. How precisely did Robert Crandall manage to turn American around?

The Airline Industry

The airline industry dates back to the Air Mail Service of 1918–1925. Using its own planes and pilots, the Post Office Department directly operated scheduled flights to ship mail. With the passage of the Air Mail Act (Kelly Act) of 1925, the Post Office subcontracted air mail transport to private companies and thereby laid the foundation of a national air transport system. The Post Office paid contractors substantial sums and encouraged them to extend their routes, buy larger planes, and expand their services.

The formative period of the private airline industry was the Great Depression. The five or six years following Charles Lindbergh's 1927 flight across the Atlantic were years of mergers and acquisitions in which every major carrier came into existence, mostly through the acquisition of smaller lines. American,

United, Delta, Northwest, Continental and Eastern Airlines were all formed during this period. The increase in passenger transport during the 1930s led, in turn, to growing competition, price cutting, bankruptcies, and serious safety problems. It convinced the architects of the New Deal that the entire transport system—not just the air mail—required federal regulation. The outcome was the passage of the Civil Aeronautics Act (CAA) of 1938.[1]

The CAA had two major provisions. First, it prohibited price competition among carriers, and second, it effectively closed the industry to newcomers. The Civil Aeronautics Board (CAB) required that all air carriers flying certain routes charge the same fares for the same class of passengers. Similarly, the CAB required all applicants wishing to enter the industry to show that they were "fit, willing and able" to do so and that their service was "required by the public convenience and necessity." Typically, between 1950 and 1975 the board denied all 79 applications it had received from carriers asking to enter the domestic, scheduled airline industry.[2] The number of scheduled air carriers was reduced from 16 in 1938 to just 10 in the 1970s, following mergers, consolidations, and route transfers among carriers.[3]

By the mid-1970s, the airline industry had experienced serious financial troubles. Rising fuel prices, an economic recession, and the introduction of expensive wide-body aircraft (Boeing 747s, Lockheed L-1011s, and McDonnell Douglas DC-10s) led to climbing costs, higher fares, reduced traffic, falling revenues, and a growing public demand for opening up the airline industry to competition. As a result, in 1975, a Senate subcommittee chaired by Edward Kennedy held hearings on the airlines. Working closely with Kennedy was a Harvard law professor named Stephen Breyer, who later became a U.S. Supreme Court Justice. A specialist in regulation, the author of *Regulation and Reform*, and the Staff Director of the Kennedy hearings, Breyer helped Kennedy build up a strong case against airline regulation.

Together, Breyer and Kennedy contrasted intrastate air service—which had never been regulated by the CAB—with interstate service—which had been regulated since 1938. The figures were astounding. Air fares charged by an interstate carrier flying the New York-Boston route (191 miles) were almost double the fares charged by an intrastate carrier (Southwest Airlines) flying the Houston-San Antonio route (also 191 miles), and air fares charged by an interstate airline

servicing the Chicago-Minneapolis city pair market (339 miles) were more than double those charged by an intrastate airline (Pacific Southwest Airlines) serving the Los Angeles-San Francisco market (338 miles). The experience of Southwest Airlines in Texas—like that of Pacific Southwest Airlines in California—Breyer and Kennedy concluded, demonstrated the efficiency of the free market and the urgent need for deregulation.[4] Three years later, in 1978, Congress deregulated the airline industry.

Company Background

The early history of American Airlines dates back to 1929 when dozens of small airline companies merged together to form American Airways, a subsidiary of an aircraft manufacturing/airline service conglomerate called the Aviation Corporation (AVCO). From the outset, American Airlines shipped mail along the southern sub-continental route from Los Angeles to Atlanta via Dallas. With the passage of the Air Mail Act of 1934, Congress prohibited aircraft manufacturing firms from owning airline companies, and redistributed existing airmail contracts on a new, competitive bidding basis. To bid successfully on the new contracts, American Airways changed its name to American Airlines, and reorganized itself as a stand alone company, independent of AVCO. Winning back its original government contracts, AA resumed its air mail operations, and moved aggressively to expand its nascent passenger service.[5]

For the next 35 years, 1934–1968, a single CEO—Cyrus Rowlett Smith—ran American Airlines. A Texan, C. R. Smith managed to improve AA performance in the 1930s, and led the company to sustained growth during the following three decades. He paid particular attention to two critical aspects of airline management, namely, aircraft technology, and labor relations.

Smith played a key role in the introduction of the DC-3 aircraft in 1936, a well-designed, and efficient plane with two piston engines. The first commercially viable passenger aircraft ever produced, the DC-3 dominated the world's airways until after WWII. Because AA operated the largest fleet of DC-3s in the industry, it soon became the industry leader, carrying about 30% of the domestic passenger traffic in the late 1930s.[6]

Working together with Donald Douglas on the design and development of the DC-3, C. R. Smith laid the foundations for long lasting relations between AA and the Douglas (since 1967, McDonnell Douglas) Corporation. Not until 1955 did Smith select a Boeing model over a Douglas one (AA ordered its first jet—the B-707—from Boeing),[7] but soon thereafter American Airlines resumed its customer relations with Douglas. The two companies continued cooperating for decades. In 2005, long after C.R. Smith had retired, and nearly a decade after the Boeing Company bought the McDonnell Douglas Corporation, American Airlines' fleet was made up of 327 MD-80 McDonnell Douglas planes, and 320 Boeing planes (the B-737, 757, 767, and 777 models), a 46/45% mix which reflected AA's traditional ties with the McDonnell Douglas Corporation.[8]

C. R. Smith, in addition, played a central role in shaping AA's labor relations. AA employees, like the employees of virtually all other major airlines, had become highly unionized by the late 1940s, and subsequently, the company experienced growing labor troubles. Responding to two large-scale pilot strikes that shut down American airlines in 1954 and 1958, C. R. Smith proposed the establishment of a cooperative arrangement among air carriers known as the Mutual Aid Pact (MAP). Thinking in terms of the entire industry, Smith saw the pact as a self-protecting measure designed to check the rising power of unions. Originally established in 1958 by American and five other carriers (United, TWA, Pan American, Eastern, and Capital), the pact authorized airlines benefiting from a strike that shut down one or more carriers to transfer their strike-generated revenues to the struck carrier(s), an arrangement which reduced the financial losses of the struck carrier(s) and thereby increased management bargaining power across the industry. In its several different forms, the MAP survived for twenty years, providing AA and its rival carriers with a measure of protection against lengthy strikes.[9]

Smith's last four years at American Airlines, 1964–1967, were AA's most profitable. In 1968, he retired, and was succeeded by George Spater, a corporate lawyer whose tenure at American was marred by recession and scandal. Spater not only failed to improve AA's performance during the recession of the early 1970s, but he also admitted making illegal corporate contributions to President Nixon's reelection campaign. As a result, the AA board forced Spater to resign in 1973, and invited C.R. Smith to rejoin American as a caretaker for a short transitional period. Smith served just seven months until the board recruited Albert Casey, a media executive, to head the company.[10]

Casey's early years at American coincided with the political debate over airline deregulation. On the one side, AA financial results during these years were impressive: Casey turned a loss of $34 million in 1975 to a record profit of $122 million in 1978, and raised AA's cash position from $115 million in 1974 to $537 million in 1978. But on the other, Casey opposed deregulation. Casey's management team believed that airline deregulation would promote competition with low-cost carriers and shift passenger traffic away from transcontinental and semi-transcontinental routes—AA's most profitable ones—to short and medium haul routes. "We opposed [deregulation] all the way," Casey recalled years later. "We had the wrong route structure. We had the wrong aircraft. . . . We weren't equipped right. [And w]e had very unfavorable union contracts."[11]

Notwithstanding his opposition to deregulation, Casey expected Congress to pass the deregulation act. To prepare for the passage of the act, Casey undertook two early initiatives which later contributed to AA's eventual success under deregulation. First, he established a major hub airport at Dallas/Fort Worth (D/FW) and moved the company's headquarters from New York to Dallas. Second, he promoted Robert Crandall to the presidency of American Airlines.

The Crandall Era, 1980–1998

Crandall's management style was distinctly different from that of Casey. Casey had a personable, relaxed, and jolly manner. Crandall was famous for his charismatic, intense, and combative style. Casey was diplomatic. Crandall was forthright, temperamental, and impatient. "The [airline] business is intensely, vigorously, bitterly, savagely competitive,"[12] Crandall once said, adding, "I want to crush all my competition. That is what competition is about."[13]

Crandall served as AA President for five years, and as CEO for 13 years. During the early period of 1980–1985, Casey turned over to Crandall the day-to-day operation of the company, and focused his attention on American's financial performance.[14] During the later period, Crandall assumed full responsibility for AA's financial performance, becoming one of the industry's longest serving chief executives. As both President and CEO, Crandall developed a large body of corporate level strategies which helped American gain a competitive advantage over its rivals.

Developing the Hub-and-Spoke System

The hub-and-spoke system was the product of airline deregulation. During the regulatory era, government rules restricted the entry of carriers into new travel markets. With the coming of deregulation, such restrictions were removed, and airlines were free to establish their own connecting hubs for the purpose of transferring passengers from incoming to outgoing flights. Utilizing the hub-and-spoke system, carriers were able to cut costs in at least two ways. First, centralizing aircraft maintenance in hubs reduced the fleet's maintenance costs, and second, increasing the carriers' load factor and bringing it close to capacity resulted in a more efficient operation. In addition, the hub-and-spoke system resulted in greater flight frequency for passengers—a service benefit valued especially by business travelers.[15]

Throughout the first two years of his presidency, 1981–1982, Crandall added 17 new domestic cities to AA's D/FW hub, and seven new international destinations (in Mexico as well as the Caribbean). The sheer number of daily flights AA operated in D/FW climbed from 100 to 300 in 1981 alone. Building its central hub in D/FW, American shifted passenger traffic away from other carriers serving Dallas's outlaying cities, subjecting these carriers to relentless competitive pressure. Braniff International Airways is a case in point. The leading carrier serving the D/FW airport in the 1970s, Braniff filed bankruptcy and suspended operation in 1982 largely as a result of the cutthroat competition it was subject to by American Airlines in the Dallas area.[16]

Under Crandall's direction, AA expanded its hub-and-spoke operations in the 1980s, establishing major hubs in Chicago, Miami, and San Juan, Puerto Rico, and focusing on long-haul fights, the most profitable segment of the industry. By the mid-1990s, these new hubs—together with the D/FW one—had all become major international airports serving passengers flying to destinations in Europe, South America, Central America, and the Caribbean.[17]

Introducing the Two-Tier Wage System

Dubbed "the father of the two-tier pay scale," Crandall had little to do with the origins of the two-tier plan. The idea grew out of management's endless discussions of the need to achieve low cost growth. Rejecting employee concessions as an insufficient means to attain a low cost operation, Crandall nurtured the two-tier idea and transformed it from an abstract notion into a concrete policy—practical, consistent, and effective.[18]

The two-tier wage system distinguished between two types of employees: current employees paid by an A-scale and newly-hired employees paid by a B-scale. Initially, under the system established by Crandall at American, the two scales were not intended to merge at all; in other words, the top pay received by B-scale employees was expected to be significantly lower than the top pay received by A-scale employees. To persuade AA's labor unions to accept the two-tier plan, Crandall offered employees job security, job expanding opportunities, higher wages and benefits, and profit sharing. He also threatened to shrink the carrier unless the unions accepted the two-tier deal. Believing that lay-offs were eminent, American unionized employees agreed to the new wage structure, and in 1983, AA signed the industry's first two-tier contracts with its principal unions, the Allied Pilots Association (APA, representing the pilots), the Transport Workers Union (TWU, representing the machinists and other ground workers), and the Association of Professional Flight Attendants (APFA, representing the flight attendants). AA's major competitors—United, Delta, U.S. Air, and others—negotiated similar labor agreements. Consequently, the number of two-tier union contracts signed in the airline industry jumped from 8 in 1983, to 35 in 1984, and 62 in 1985.[19]

AA's two-tier wage plan resulted in a significant pay gap between old and new employees. A newly-hired B-727 captain with a five year experience earned $68 an hour or less than half the $140 paid to his/her veteran counterpart. Such a wage gap led to substantial cost savings: between 1984 and 1989 American Airlines' labor cost fell from 37% to 34% of the carrier's total expenses.[20]

Creating a Holding Company

In 1982, Crandall oversaw the formation of the AMR Corporation—a holding company created "to provide [American] with access to sources of financing that otherwise might be unavailable."[21] AMR owned American Airlines together with several other non-airline subsidiaries, an arrangement which gave management greater flexibility in shifting assets among airline and non-airline subsidiaries, and in identifying new profit sources. Equally important was the protection AMR gave the airline from the swings of the business cycle: profits generated by AMR's non-airline units were expected to mitigate the impact of the industry's periodic downturns.

Consider the following example. During the downturn of 1990–1993, Crandall devised a "transition plan" that called for shifting assets from AMR's unprofitable airline operation to its profitable non-airline businesses. He even suggested leaving the airline business altogether. As AA's losses were mounting—and profits generated from AMR's non-airline units were increasing—Crandall threatened to sell AA and keep instead AMR's non-airline subsidiaries only.[22]

AMR's principal subsidiary—apart from AA—was the Sabre computer reservation system. Owned by AMR, Sabre (Semi Automatic Business Research Environment) had become AMR's most profitable unit during the 1990s, generating far higher returns on sales than the airline itself. In 1995, for instance, Sabre recorded total sales of $1.5 billion, or 9% of AMR revenues, and an operating profit of 19%.[23]

Building a Regional Airline

Another subsidiary of AMR was American Eagle. American Eagle was established in 1984 as AA's regional affiliate. Operating under the affiliate name, several small regional airlines were franchised by AA to supply connecting flights to American air services. From the start, American Eagle offered customers "seamless service," that is, assigned seats, boarding passes, and frequent flyer mileage. In 1987, AMR began acquiring American Eagle's franchised carriers, and in 1990, it consolidated these carriers into six airline systems that served the D/FW, Nashville, New York City, Chicago, Raleigh/Durham and San Juan regional markets. To better coordinate planning, operation, schedules, training, and marketing of commuter services, AMR sought further consolidation. Accordingly, in 1998, it merged the six regional airlines into a single entity carrier, the America Eagle Airlines, creating the world's largest regional airline system. Operating 1,450 daily flights to 125 destinations in the U.S., Canada, and the Caribbean; employing 10,000; and generating $1 billion in revenue; American Eagle was named "Airline of the Year" by *Commuter World* magazine in 1998.[24]

American Eagle's growth helped improve AMR's financial results. Originally, American Eagle operated as a regional carrier feeding passengers to American Airlines flights. But by the mid-1990s, Crandall had replaced a growing number of routes flown by AA pilots with routes flown by American Eagle pilots, a move which resulted in substantial labor cost savings, given the higher pay received by American than Eagle pilots (in 1997 AA pilots earned an average yearly pay of $120,000 and Eagle pilots $35,000).[25]

Upgrading the Computer Reservation System (CRS)

The Sabre computer reservation system was born in 1962, following a decade-long research effort carried out jointly by American Airlines engineers and IBM technicians. Initially, Sabre lagged behind comparable CRS systems used by its competitors, namely, United's Apollo, TWA's PARS, and Eastern Airlines' System One. But by the mid-1970s, with the appointment of Crandall to the position of AA's Vice President for Marketing, Sabre received a new lease of life. As marketing chief, Crandall controlled the company's budget for technology research and development. He recruited a strong team of Sabre computer engineers, and supplied the team with ample funding. At the same time, he launched a campaign to build an industry-wide CRS owned jointly by the major airlines, and used by travel agents. Confident that its own CRS was ahead of its competitors, United declined to join the industry-wide project, and instead, decided to sell its Apollo system's services directly to travel agents. Crandall reacted quickly. Implementing a carefully crafted back-up plan, he sent hundreds of sales people and technicians to travel agents all across the country, offering them a variety of Sabre services. Caught unprepared, United was unable to deliver its own computer reservation system's services until months later. The result was a swift victory of American over United in the race to wire travel agents.[26]

Sabre provided American Airlines with several information technology services. First, it calculated the yield of each American flight, setting and resetting the price of every seat sold. Second, it managed an inventory of close to one billion spare parts used by American's fleet in its maintenance facilities. Third, it directed the routing and tracking of all baggage and freight. And fourth, it supplied American with ongoing data on aircraft fuel requirements, take off weight, and flight plan.[27]

More important were Sabre's travel services. Sabre provided travel agents around the world with fares and schedules for flights offered by hundreds of carriers, not only American and American Eagle. In 1997, Sabre signed a comprehensive 25-year agreement to manage the information technology infrastructure of U.S. Air, and in addition, it renewed a five-year contract with Southwest Airlines to operate the carrier's reservation and inventory systems. Sabre and Canadian Airlines International signed a similar agreement in 1994.

Sabre's clients, it should be noted, were not limited to the airline industry. Both the London Underground and the French National Railway were Sabre's customers in the 1990s; the first contracted Sabre to manage its train and crew scheduling, the second, to design its computer reservation system. Under Crandall's leadership, furthermore, Sabre signed agreements with both Dollar Rent-a-Car and Thrifty Rent-a-Car to manage each company's reservation system.[28]

Under Crandall's leadership, Sabre had become the largest U.S. computer reservation system with a 40% share of all travel agent bookings in 1996. Nearly 30,000 travel agent offices in 70 countries subscribed to Sabre, and more than 2.5 million individual passengers subscribed to Travelocity, Sabre's Internet service. In 1995, the total value of travel-related products and services reserved through Sabre was estimated at $40 billion.[29]

Promoting Yield Management

Developing a revenue maximizing process called yield management was impossible without enhanced computer capabilities. To fill all empty seats on a given flight, American Airlines needed to obtain information pertaining to the desirable number of seats that could be sold at full versus discount fares, and the optimal mix of fares that could maximize the yield of a given flight. Obtaining such information required complex computer calculations based on the carrier's past performance. Hence the key role played by Sabre. Sabre could track any passenger on any seat traveling any distance at any time. It could find out how early business travelers booked their flights, how far in advance coach passengers did so, and how sensitive each of these two groups was to fare price changes. With Sabre's growing computer capabilities, American began offering a large variety of discounted fares, as Don Reed, author of *Bob Crandall and American Airlines*, explained:

> Instead of offering first-class, coach, and one level of discount fares, American began offering several layers of discounts. The bigger the savings off full-fare prices, the more restrictions the tickets had. The more modest the savings, the fewer restrictions. So fourteen-day and seven-day advance purchase discount fares cost more than twenty-one-day fares, but they were less restricted. Because of this sliding scale of discounts, American could juggle the percentage of seats on any airplane allocated to one fare type or another.... By the late 1980s American would be able to, and often did, juggle the mix of fares right up until the moment of departure.[30]

Sabre's yield management system gave American a clear competitive advantage over its rivals. On any given flight, AA was able to offer a variety of discounted fares using projections based on past experience. Sabre's technology permitted Crandall to match or undercut the cheaper fares offered by competitors by simply lowering American's own discount prices for some seats and/or increase the number of seats available at the lowest price category. There was no need to reduce fares on all seats. While competitors lacking American's technology were unable to match AA's price flexibility, they soon introduced their own yield management systems; nevertheless, American Airlines managed to retain its leadership position in the field for decades.

Pioneering the Frequent-Flyer Program

Just as Sabre promoted the development of AA's yield management system, so did it facilitate the introduction of American's AAdvantage frequent flyer program, an innovation that allowed regular passengers to earn free tickets on miles traveled with American. And just as the hub-and-spoke system was the outgrowth of deregulation, so was the frequent flyer program. While deregulation promoted competition, the frequent flyer program protected carriers from the competitive market forces by creating brand loyalty among travelers.

Crandall introduced the AAdvantage program—the first in the industry—in 1981, a year after he became president. Managed by Sabre, the frequent flyer innovation was an effective marketing program which lowered the advertising costs by targeting individual AAdvantage card-holders reachable through mailing and/or email distribution lists. Sabre had been gathering information on passengers early on. As Mike Gunn, AA's Vice President for Marketing under Crandall, noted: "One reason we were able to seize the competitive edge was that we already knew who many of our best customers were and how to reach them quickly. As other airlines struggled to match our initiative and identify their base of frequent-flyers, we were already placing AAdvantage cards and welcome letters in the hands of our best customers."[31]

More than one million passengers joined AAdvantage before the end of 1981, and another million joined the frequent flyer programs introduced by other airlines in 1981 in response to AAdvantage. Ten years later, 28 million travelers were card-carrying members of at least one frequent flyer program, and they held, on average, membership in 3.5 programs. American Airlines' program was the industry's largest. In 1991, American's frequent flier program had one million members more than that of its closest competitor, United, and four million more than Delta, the nation's third largest carrier.[32]

At the time Crandall left office in 1998, the frequent flyer program had become an airline industry standard feature. It impacted other industries as well, and generated both revenues and profits for the airlines. American sold miles to a variety of companies which awarded, in turn, AA miles to loyal customers as an incentive. In 1998, over 2,500 companies awarded miles to customers using the AAdvantage Incentive Miles program, most of which were retail stores and food serving establishments.[33]

Expanding Internationally

Before the passage of the airline regulation act in 1978, American Airlines had virtually no international presence. The dominant U.S. international carriers at the time were TWA and Pan America World Airways, and neither United nor Delta Airlines served any foreign destinations.[34] The Deregulation Act removed government restrictions on entry into new travel markets, promoted the development of hub-and-spoke systems, and as such, prompted the leading domestic airlines—United, American, and Delta—to begin serving a growing number of international destinations.

From the outset, AA's domestic hub system supported international expansion, helping the carrier fill empty seats on overseas flights. In the early 1980s, Crandall extended AA's route network to Mexico and the Caribbean, but not until 1990 did he launch a massive drive at global expansion, adding many more overseas destinations in Europe and Latin America.

Crandall's decision to extend AA's international route network was informed by air-traffic projections. Over the ten-year period 1990–2000, U.S. air traffic was expected to grow at a modest rate of 3%–4% a year while transatlantic air traffic, as well as traffic between the U.S. and Latin America's destinations, was projected to increase at an annual rate of 6%–7%. To take advantage of these projections, Crandall committed $11 billion, or half of AA's investment budget, to global expansion over the five-year period, 1990–1995. He also made two important acquisitions, both in 1989–1991. He first bought TWA's Chicago-London route in 1989, and six more TWA-London routes in 1991. He next acquired Eastern Airline's Latin America route system in 1990. In the Latin American market, AA used its strong Miami hub to handle traffic from 20 cities in 15 South and Central American countries. In the European market, Crandall embarked on what he called a "fragmentation strategy," namely, the break-up of the traditional route system linking one international city to another, for example, New York-London (and flying large commercial aircraft such as the 400-seat Boeing B-747), and replacing it with a route system that linked less congested cites like Chicago and Brussels or Chicago and Glasgow (and flying smaller 200-seat aircraft such as the Boeing B-767).[35]

Five years later, Crandall's plan achieved its main goals. By the mid-1990s, AA had become the dominant U.S. carrier serving Latin America, and the number two U.S. carrier serving Europe, closely behind Delta. In Latin America, AA carried 58% of all U.S. airline traffic to and from the region, served 27 nations, and opened two new U.S. gateway hubs, one in New York, the other in Dallas/Fort Worth, in addition to its principal one in Miami. In the transatlantic travel market, AA's share accounted for 23% of all airline traffic. In 1995, American derived 14%–15% of its airline revenues from the Latin America market, and 13% from the European market. As expected, both international markets were quite profitable: in 1996, AA generated an operating profit margin of 10% in Latin America, and 8% in Europe.[36]

Forming Alliances

Signing code-sharing agreements with foreign carriers was another growth strategy undertaken by Crandall.

Code-sharing allowed American to assign its two letter code—AA—to flights operated by another carrier, thereby offering passengers flights to destinations not served by American. Enhanced by shared computer reservation systems and joint frequent-flyer programs, such agreements enabled American to increase its passenger traffic without extending its own route network, hence saving the carrier the expensive and risky cost of starting new international services.

American signed its first code-sharing agreement with Canadian Airlines International (CAI) in 1995. The agreement extended AA's route network to dozens of Canadian cities served by CAI and linked CAI route system to dozens of U.S. destinations served by AA. Seeking to extend AA's route structure to Asia, Crandall signed another code-sharing agreement with CAI in 1997. The 1997 agreement offered AA passengers trans-Pacific service on flights operated by CAI between Vancouver and Taipei. To further increase its Asia-bound traffic, American formed an alliance with China Eastern Airlines in 1998—the first code-sharing agreement between a U.S. carrier and an airline based in the People's Republic of China. Under the agreement's provisions, American placed its code on flights operated by China Eastern from Los Angeles and San Francisco to both Shanghai and Beijing, thereby offering passengers from destinations as distant as Latin America full service to Mainland China. Finally, in September 1998, a few months after Crandall stepped down, American Airlines announced the formation of OneWorld Alliance, a code-sharing agreement signed by five international carriers: American Airlines, British Airways, Canadian Airlines International, Qantas Airway (Australia), and Cathy Pacific Airlines (Hong Kong).[37]

Escalating the War with the Unions, 1990–1998

AA's labor relations under Crandall may be divided into two distinctly different periods: 1980–1989, and 1990–1998. In the 1980s, relations between labor and management at American were, for the most part, cooperative and peaceful. Crandall, as discussed, managed to convince the leadership of the pilots', flight attendants', and machinists' unions to negotiate and sign two-tier labor agreements which allowed management to place newly hired employees on a lower, B-type wage scale.

In the 1990s, by contrast, labor relations at American were stormy and contentious. Contract negotiations were long and difficult to conclude, and labor disputes triggered strikes, strike threats, and repeated instances of federal intervention to avert strikes. As a consequence, labor disputes were costly, resulting in revenue and income losses.

One major cause of the 1990s labor troubles was the lingering dissatisfaction—expressed by AA employees—with the two-tier wage system. For any unionized job, B-scale employees were paid much lower wages than their veteran counterparts, and over the years, these lower paid employees had turned extremely resentful towards management. As Crandall hired a growing number of B-scale recruits in the 1980s and 1990s, the "B-scalers" had eventually become the majority of all AA's unionized employees.

Two labor disputes at American during the 1990s stand out. The first involved a strike staged by the Professional Association of Flight Attendants. In 1993, 21,000 flight attendants struck American airlines during Thanksgiving Day weekend, crippling the carrier and ruining whatever prospects management had of posting profits that year (AA ended the year with a small loss of $110 million on $15.8 billion in revenues). Union leaders pointed out that Crandall's unwillingness to bend during negotiations precipitated the strike. Industry analysts agreed, noting Crandall's compulsion to keep labor cost low. As the strike entered its fifth day, President Clinton intervened and pressured both sides to accept binding arbitration. The dispute was later settled, but the flight attendants remained disgruntled.[38]

A pilots' strike-threat underlay the second labor dispute. In November 1996, the Allied Pilots Association's board of directors approved a tentative pilots' contract, and presented it to the union membership for ratification. Persuaded by a dissident group of grassroots union activists made largely of B-scale pilots, the membership rejected the contract by a margin of almost two to one. The union leadership, in turn, hardened its position, and threatened to strike the carrier. As the strike deadline approached, President Clinton intervened, invoking a rarely used provision of the 1926 Railway Act which empowered him to appoint a three-member emergency board to help settle the dispute. In the meantime American's losses were mounting. By April 1997, AA lost at least $100 million in advanced bookings, as passengers avoided flying an airline facing impending walkout days. The contract was eventually ratified, but here again, the pilots remained embittered, and they

EXHIBIT 1

Robert Crandall's American Airlines Highlights of Financial Data, 1985–1998

	Revenues ($Mil.)	Net Income ($Mil.)	Income as % of Revenues
1985	6,131	346	5.6%
1986	6,018	279	4.6%
1987	7,198	198	2.8%
1988	8,824	477	5.4%
1989	10,480	455	4.3%
1990	11,120	(40)	—
1991	12,887	(240)	—
1992	14,396	(935)	—
1993	15,816	(110)	—
1994	16,137	228	—
1995	16,910	167	1.0%
1996	17,753	1,067	5.7%
1997	18,570	985	5.3%
1998	19,205	1,314	6.8%

Sources: "AMR Corporation," *Hoover's Handbook of American Business*, 1992, p. 110; 2002, p. 165.

continued resenting Crandall's heavy-handed management methods.[39]

Improving Financial Results, 1985–1997

AA's financial performance under Crandall needs to be analyzed in conjunction with Crandall's evolving strategy. Serving as CEO for 13 years, Crandall shaped and reshaped his strategy, paying close attention to changes in the business cycle. In the 1980s, Crandall undertook a growth strategy that resulted in a rapid expansion of American Airlines' fleet, as well as workforce. The larger AA grew, the lower were its costs, the higher its revenues, and the larger its profits. In the early 1990s, as the air travel market slid into a protracted recession, and AA experienced four years of losses, Crandall embarked on a retrenchment strategy, laying off employees, grounding old planes, exiting unprofitable markets, and outsourcing selected services. Following the recession of 1990–1993, the industry expanded once again, and Crandall introduced a second growth plan. His renewed efforts at increasing revenues and improving profits were sustained by AA's industry-leading yield management system, its formidable AAdvantage frequent flyer program, and its extensive global route network. Notwithstanding the labor troubles of 1996–1997, the carrier had become profitable again, posting a net income of over $1 billion in 1996, close to $1 billion in 1997, and $1.3 billion in 1998, as Exhibit 1 shows, and reducing its debt as a percentage of capitalization from 83% in 1994 to 66% at the end of 1996.[40]

Donald Carty and the September 11, 2001 Terrorist Attack

Donald Carty served as American Airlines CEO for five years. An AA career executive, he was hand picked by Crandall to lead the carrier, first as President, and then, following Crandall's retirement in 1998, as CEO. Carty's five-year tenure was marred by labor troubles, recession, and terrorism, and ended in a public scandal: as a result of the September 11, 2001 attack, American Airlines was losing several million dollars a day, yet in Spring 2003, at the time the carrier was inching towards bankruptcy, AA's senior executives—including Carty—received undisclosed bonuses and pension guarantees worth millions of dollars.

Carty's labor problems began early on. In 1999, he convinced the AMR board to acquire a small low-cost commuter airline called Reno Air. The proposed acquisition evoked a staunch opposition on the part of American pilots. Believing that Carty planned to replace them with low-paid Reno pilots, members of the Allied Pilots Association staged an 11-day sickout which forced American to cancel 6,700 fights, left 600,000 passengers stranded, and cost the carrier $225 million in lost earnings. Also in 1999, AA flight attendants rejected a tentative contract offer and threatened to strike the carrier. In 2001, AA's flight attendants agreed to accept a contract agreement only after exhaustive negotiations that ended hours before a strike deadline.[41]

Notwithstanding these labor differences, Carty moved to expand the airline by merger, purchasing TWA—a trunk-line carrier experiencing serious financial problems. Approved in April 2001, AA's merger with TWA created the nation's largest airline, adding 188 commercial airplanes to American's fleet (TWA's 104 McDonnell Douglas MD-80 jets fit nicely into AA's fleet), and providing American with a central hub at St. Louis. The cost of the transaction was just $742 million—a modest sum by any industry standards—and more importantly, the merger was supported by all major unions. Backed by the unionized employees of both carriers, Carty managed to integrate the two companies smoothly, earning the praise of industry analysts.[42]

Yet the TWA acquisition was untimely. The merger was approved at the time the entire airline industry was moving rapidly into a recession. Following the merger's approval in Spring 2001, business travel dropped precipitously, leisure travel fell too, and fuel prices were rising. As a result, AA lost $550 million during the first half of 2001.[43] Less than three

months later, the 9/11 terrorist attack erupted, destroying two AA passenger jets at midair, and shutting down all airline travel in the U.S. for two days.

The impact of the 9/11 attack on American's financial performance was long lasting. As shown in Exhibit 2, AA lost $1.8 billion in 2001, and a record $3.5 billion in 2002. In April 2003, following another loss of a billion dollars during the first quarter of the year, American Airlines was nearly bankrupt.

To avoid filing bankruptcy under Chapter 11, Carty asked the three unions representing the majority of AA employees to agree to major wage and benefit concessions. The leadership of each union accepted management's demand for a concessional contract and put the issue before the membership for a vote. Within two weeks, AA employees ratified a collective bargaining agreement that gave the carrier back a total of $1.8 billion, or 20% of the carrier's annual payroll.[44]

A day later the deal began to unravel. Following the contract ratification, union leaders, as well as members, learned from news reports that the AMR corporation awarded Carty and five other executives bonuses that equaled twice their annual salaries, and set aside a $41 million trust that was intended to protect the pensions of 45 executives in the event of bankruptcy. As it turned out, the carrier delayed filing a report detailing these executive compensation plans with the Security and Exchange Commission until after the contract vote was completed.[45]

The belated disclosure angered the employees and prompted two of the three unions to call for another contract vote. Carty, in turn, sent a letter to AA employees apologizing for his conduct, and announcing the cancellation of the proposed bonuses: "My mistake was failing to explicitly describe these

---

EXHIBIT 2

Donald Carty's American Airlines Highlights of Financial Data, 1998–2002

	Revenues ($Mil.)	Net Income ($Mil.)	Income as % of Revenues	Stock Prices FY Close
1998	19,205	1,314	6.8%	$26.54
1999	17,730	985	5.3%	29.95
2000	19,703	813	5.7%	39.19
2001	18,963	(1,762)	—	22.30
2002	17,299	(3,511)	—	6.60

Source: "AMR Corporation," *Hoover's Handbook of American Business,* 2005, p. 88.

retention benefits. . . . Please know that it was never my intention to mislead you."[46] The disclosure, in addition, surprised several members of the AMR board who felt misled by top management, believing that Carty had discussed the executive compensation package with the union leaderships prior to the contract vote. In response to the mounting public outcry over the disclosure, AMR board of directors sought Carty's resignation. Pressured by the board, Carty promptly stepped down, and the directors moved at once to elect a new CEO.[47]

The Future: Gerard Arpey's American Airlines, 2003–

A few board members suggested rehiring Robert Crandall. Others rejected Crandall's choice and sought instead a candidate who was likely to create a sense of management continuity in AA and act quickly to save the company from filing bankruptcy. Such a candidate, the majority of directors agreed, was American Airlines President Gerard Arpey. Elected by the board to replace Carty, Arpey had 24 hours to save the carrier. Crafting a revised labor management agreement that included the essential $1.8 billion cuts in wages and benefits, and offered the employees a number of additional non-monetary gains, Arpey managed to convince the union leaderships to approve the new labor agreement and thereby save the carrier from filing for bankruptcy protection. Passing his first test as a chief executive, Arpey outlined a key management objective he would strive to accomplish throughout his tenure as AA CEO: "There is a definite need to rebuild trust [between management and labor] within the company. I hear that loud and clear . . . and I commit myself to earning everybody's trust."[48]

Gerard Arpey spent his entire career at American Airlines, joining the company as a financial analyst in 1982. Before accepting the top job, the 46-year-old Arpey sought, and received, the approval of AA's union leaders: "He said he wouldn't take the position unless . . . he had our support," John Darrah, President of the Allied Pilots Association recalled, adding, "I have a great deal of respect for Mr. Arpey. . . . I can honestly [say] there's not a person I have more respect for or trust in."[49]

Arpey's turnaround plan was based on several elements. First, Arpey believed that in order to compete successfully in the post 9/11 world, American Airlines needed to shift its strategic focus from revenue growth to cost reduction. To achieve this goal, he introduced a cooperative labor management scheme, a continuous improvement program, and other labor cost cutting measures. Second, Arpey realized that American could take advantage of its global positioning to expand profitable international operation and curtail unprofitable domestic services. To achieve this goal, he sought to form closer alliances with foreign carriers. Altogether, Arpey embarked on four distinct strategies in his efforts to turn American around.

International Expansion

Referring to his plan to expand AA's international operation, Arpey explained:

> One of the things that we can capitalize on is the depth and breadth of our network. It's one of the ways that we can compete more effectively with low-cost carriers that operate primarily in the domestic market. . . . We have very aggressive plans internationally. . . . Our strengths include a very broad network that spans the globe . . . the [industry's] largest frequent-flyer program, Admiral airport clubs, and a great first-class product. . . . [W]e get more revenue per passenger than the low cost carrier[s and] . . . we can sustain a revenue premium.[50]

Arpey expected AA's international service to grow from over 30% of capacity in 2005 to 40% by the end of the decade. He planned to expand, above all, trans-Pacific travel service. In 2005, American introduced two non-stop services to Japan, operating flights between Chicago and Nagoya, and between Dallas and Osaka. Similarly, in 2005, AA started a non-stop service to India, flying the 7,500-mile route between Chicago and New Delhi, American's longest, in 14–15 hours. American also competed aggressively over the contested rights to serve China, planning to introduce a Chicago-Shanghai non-stop service as early as approval by the Chinese government was granted. Additionally, AA formed alliances with Aloha Airlines and Mexicana Airlines, on the one side, and consolidated its code-sharing agreement with British Airways, on the other.[51]

Labor-Management Cooperation

To improve his relations with the unions, Arpey instituted an open door policy. During his first two years in office, Arpey spent more time meeting union leaders than the time spent for this purpose by any other chief executive in the company's 75-year history. "You demonstrate commitment by where you put your time," he told a *Financial Times* reporter in 2005. "We are trying to make our unions our business partners."[52] Unlike Crandall and Carty, Arpey constantly highlighted the importance of getting AA employees involved in the business of airline management. Once elected CEO, he traveled widely, visited AA operations in one city after another, conducted town-hall meetings with AA employees, and solicited employee suggestions. "I try to spend as much time as I can [with the employees] when I travel," Arpey explained in a 2004 interview, "going to break rooms, talking to agents at the gate, talking to flight attendants on board [of] the airplane, riding jump seats, and . . . answering all the email[s I] get."[53]

Still, Arpey was unable to change AA's climate of labor-relations single-handedly. He needed external help. To improve labor management relations at American, Arpey hired an employee-relations consultancy called the Overland Resource Group in Summer 2003. Instrumental in improving labor-relations at Boeing, Ford, and the Goodyear Corporation, the Overland group instructed AA managers to follow three fundamental principles, or maxims, in their relations with AA's employees: "Involve before Deciding," "Discuss before Implementing," and "Share before Announcing." More importantly, the Overland group created a Joint Leadership Team (JLT) chaired by Arpey and the national presidents of AA's three main unions (representing the pilots, flight attendants, and mechanics and ground workers), and attended by the company CFO as well as four vice presidents, on management side, and three representatives of each union, on labor side. The team met once a month to discuss issues ranging from AA's corporate-level strategies to union demands and grievances. The team also reviewed AA's financial data on a quarterly basis, an arrangement that helped senior union officials understand the airline business.[54] To help team members communicate, two Overland consultants attended all JLT meetings, acting as the dialogue facilitators. To ensure an honest, open, and free-flowing discussion with no fear of reprisal, each JLT participant signed a non-disclosure agreement.[55]

In addition to the team headed by Arpey and the union presidents, Overland facilitated the formation of seven regional JLTs located in different airports and maintenance bases throughout AA network. A local JLT met once a month to review the region's financial performance and to evaluate employee cost-saving ideas.[56]

Overland presence at AA enhanced employee motivation and morale. The higher level of employee motivation was reflected, first and foremost, in the growing number of cost savings suggestions initiated by employees. While AA management routinely ignored employee suggestions in the past [one union leader observed], Overland consultants now encouraged the adoption of such suggestions. And while Arpey's management team was actively soliciting employee ideas, no employee whose ideas were adopted received any compensation; on the contrary, helping the company was the employee's sole motivation.[57]

As a result of implementing employee-identified cost-saving ideas, AA saved about $100 million in 2004.[58] The overall decline in labor cost was larger. Partly as a consequence of introducing cost-saving ideas, and partly as a result of implementing the landmark concessional contract of April 2003, AA unit labor cost under Arpey declined by more than 20% in two years, as shown in Exhibit 3.

Continuous Improvement

The Continuous Improvement (CI) program was implemented across all AA's maintenance facilities. During 2001–2004, United Airlines, Northwest Airlines, and U.S. Airways closed several of their maintenance

---

EXHIBIT 3

Labor Cost of U.S. Network Carriers, 4th Quarter 2002 and 4th Quarter 2004, Cents per Available Seat Mile (CASM)

Network	4Q02 CASM	4Q04 CASM
American	3.93	3.12
Continental	3.10	30.2
Delta	4.01	3.67
Northwest	3.98	3.82
United	4.51	3.25
US Airways	4.15	3.11
Network	4.01	3.34

Sources: Eclat Consulting, *Aviation Daily*, May 4, 2004, p. 7, and May 26, 2005, p. 7.

bases, and sought instead to outsource heavy maintenance to outside contractors.[59] American Airlines, by contrast, kept maintenance work in house, and launched a massive drive at efficiency, seeking productivity gains in the shop floor.

The Continuous Improvement program had three main goals: the elimination of waste in any form, the standardization of maintenance work, and the optimal utilization of "human talent." The idea—and practice—of CI was based on the assumption that workers, not managers, were the real experts, and that employee empowerment was critical for building effective work teams. The CI program addressed a variety of issues ranging from shop floor reorganization to engine-overhaul turnover time reduction. To achieve these objectives, a "5S" technique ("sort, strengthen, standardize, shine, sustain") was introduced throughout AA's maintenance facilities. At American's largest maintenance base in Tulsa, Oklahoma, for example, Continuous Improvement teams in the avionic shop used the 5S technique to free nearly 12,000 sq. ft. of floor space and thereby save the company $1.5 million in inventory cost.[60]

Employee-identified CI ideas included new ways to reduce the cost of replacing aircraft parts and components. On the McDonnell Douglas MD-80 model, for instance, the cargo door torque (spring) tube needed to be replaced once a year. To do so, the company bought new tubes at a cost of $660 per tube. The CI team investigated the issue and ascertained that repairing broken tubes at a cost of only $134 per unit saved the company a total of $250,000 a year. On the Boeing 737, similarly, AA economized by replacing passenger light bulbs and cabin windows only when needed. In the past, AA replaced all light bulbs and cabin windows at the same time regardless of whether the bulbs were burned out or the windows worn out. The selective replacement of light bulbs and cabin windows saved AA $100,000 per year.[61]

American used CI teams to reduce engine overhaul times as well. One team of engine mechanics drafted a series of diagrams showing the most efficient way to disassemble a jet engine. Another devised a "point-of-use tool box" which contained all the tools necessary for an engine's assembly and disassembly. Together, the two teams helped AA cut an engine's overhaul turnaround time from 53 days in 2003 to 40 days in 2004, an improvement of 25% in a single year.[62]

Continuous Improvement teams helped AA cut costs in still other ways. To service American Airlines fleet, company mechanics used thousands of drill bits monthly at a cost of $20 to $200 a piece. Two AA mechanics invented a drill bit-sharpening tool which refurbished bits for reuse at a cost savings of $300,000–400,000 a year. And in 2004, a CI team came up with the idea of reusing parts of obsolete DC-10 coffee makers on other AA airplanes, generating a one-time savings of $675,000.[63]

Taken together, all these improvements helped AA reduce its maintenance cost by 34% in two years (2002–2004). A comparison between American's maintenance cost reduction and that of five other U.S.-based network carriers shows that AA led the way, exceeding the industry average by 13 percentage points, and well ahead of any of its competitors (Exhibit 4).

Other Cost Cutting Measures

"Simplification and standardization drives efficiency,"[64] Arpey said in 2004, and he moved quickly to both simplify and standardize AA's fleet of aircraft. To simplify the fleet, Arpey reduced the number of aircraft types flown by American from 14 to 6, retiring many old models. The move reduced American spending on spare parts as well as crew training, especially pilots and mechanics training. In addition, Arpey standardized aircraft seating, arranging all seats on a given aircraft type in a single configuration, as

---

EXHIBIT 4

Maintenance Cost of U.S. Network Carriers, 4th Quarter 2002 and 4th Quarter 2004, Cents per Available Seat Mile (CASM)

Network	4Q02 CASM	4Q04 CASM	% CASM
American	1.65	1.09	34%
Continental	0.96	0.93	3%
Delta	0.98	0.92	6%
Northwest	1.43	1.08	24%
United	1.41	1.24	12%
U.S. Airways	1.67	1.30	22%
Network	1.36	1.08	21%

Sources: Eclat Consulting, *Aviation Daily*, May 4, 2004, p. 7, and May 26, 2005, p. 7.

the two following examples suggest. Under Carty's leadership, the MD-80 fleet had two seating configurations, one designed to serve AA's business routes, the other to serve AA's low fare routes. Under Carty likewise, the B-777 had two seating configurations, one aimed at flights over the Pacific, the other at flights over the Atlantic. In an effort to simplify both aircraft maintenance and flight schedules, Arpey standardized all seating on the MD-80 and B-777 models in a single arrangement, a reconfiguration that resulted in substantial cost savings.[65]

Arpey reversed two other Carty initiatives, first, the creation of more legroom for passengers, and second, the transformation of TWA's St. Louis hub into a major AA hub. In 2000, Carty launched the "More Room in Coach" marketing campaign in an attempt to increase revenues. AA, accordingly, removed more than 7,000 economy seats from its fleet, reducing the fleet's seating capacity by 6.4%. Carty's initiative, however, failed to generate the expected revenues, and therefore Arpey decided to undo it. In 2004, AA added two rows of seats to its fleet of 140 B-757s and 34 A-300s, and used both models to serve low-fare leisure markets. In 2005, AA added six more seats to its B-737 fleet, seven more to its fleet of MD-80s and B-767s, and nine more seats to its fleet of B-777s. The change in seating capacity was projected to generate a revenue increase of over $100 million a year.[66]

Lastly, Arpey announced early on his decision to scale back significantly AA's St. Louis operation. Expecting TWA's central hub in St. Louis to fit nicely into American route system, Carty, as noted, purchased TWA in 2001. Arpey, however, did not share Carty's vision. To improve AA's financial performance, Arpey shifted flights from routes out of the St. Louis hub to more profitable routes out of AA's Chicago and Dallas hubs. As a result, AA laid off more than 2,000 employees at the St. Louis airport in 2003 alone.[67]

Future Prospects and Concerns

One result of the successful implementation of Arpey's turnaround strategy was the deep decline in AA's operating costs. As shown in Exhibit 5, by 2005, American operating costs were lower than those of any other network carriers save Continental. American's stock prices too performed well. Following a sharp drop in AMR stock price during the post 9/11 years, AMR's stock more than doubled in value in 2005, rising

EXHIBIT 5

Operating Cost of U.S. Network Carriers, 1st Quarter 2005, Cents per Available Seat Mile (CASM)

Network	1Q05 CASM
American	9.9
Continental	9.9
United	10.4
U.S. Air	10.7
Northwest	11.2
Delta	12.2

Source: Back-Aviation Solutions in Micheline Maynard and Jeremy Peters, "Circling a Decision," *New York Times,* August 18, 2005.

101% and outperforming the share prices of all major U.S. carriers, including Southwest Airlines. AA's cash position, furthermore, was stronger than that of other network carriers. AA managed to increase its cash surplus from $3 billion in 2004 to $4.3 billion in 2005, a margin sufficiently comfortable to give the carrier a greater staying power in the industry than its rivals.[68]

Nevertheless, American Airlines still faced a number of daunting challenges. First and most important was the need to achieve profitability. During Arpey's first three years in office, AMR continued to post large losses that amounted to $1.2 billion in 2003, $0.8 billion in 2004, and $0.9 billion in 2005. While analysts were impressed by AA's cost cutting measures (as well as its collaborative labor management relations, strong cash position, rising fares, and trimmed capacity), and while AA stock doubled in value in 2005 in anticipation of profits in 2006, the continual increase in fuel costs during 2006 clouded AA's recovery prospects.[69]

Another concern pertained to labor relations. AA employees resented a stock-related bonus paid to American managers in 2006. The payout was authorized by an 18-year-old "Long Term Incentive Program" which tied executive pay to AA's stock performance. Because AA's stock prices outperformed the stock prices of its five competitors (United, Delta, Continental, U.S. Air, Northwest) in 2005, American's top 1,000 mangers were eligible to share $80 million in cash. The payout, however, was viewed by American's unionized employees as extra compensation for managers not shared by other AA employees. A letter sent by top management to members of the Allied Pilots Association congratulating the pilots on saving $80 million in fuel cost in 2005—an amount equivalent to management's bonus—angered the pilots further, and threatened to undermine the cooperative labor relations at American.[70]

A final concern stemmed from AA's pension crisis. In 2005, American's pension plans were underfunded by about $2.7 billion. To be sure, AA's funding deficit was smaller than that of Delta ($5.3 billion) and Northwest ($3.8 billion), yet unlike Delta and Northwest, American's commitment to protecting its employees' pensions was embedded in a collective bargaining agreement: a key union demand incorporated into the 2003 labor agreement that saved AA from bankruptcy was the preservation of the carrier's pension plan intact. In 2006, Delta, Northwest, United, and other network carriers were all engaged in a process of converting their pension plans from defined benefit plans (plans that paid employees lifetime retirement pensions funded by the employer) to the less expensive defined contribution plans (plans that operated like retirement saving accounts funded by both the employee and the employer). American Airlines, accordingly, experienced a growing competitive pressure to convert its pension plans too, but such a move was likely to jeopardize the long-standing industrial peace at American which Arpey had worked so hard to craft and preserve.[71]

ENDNOTES

1. Henry Ladd Smith, *Airways: The History of Commercial Aviation in the United States* (1942, reprinted, New York: Russell and Russell, 1964).

2. Stephen Breyer, *Regulation and Its Reform* (Cambridge, Mass.: Harvard University Press, 1982), p. 205.

3. Thomas K. McCraw, *Prophets of Regulations* (Cambridge, Mass.: Harvard University Press, 1984), p. 3.

4. McCraw, *Prophets of Regulations*, pp. 266–67; Breyer, *Regulation and Its Reform*, pp. 204–205.

5. Smith, *Airways*, Chapters 12, 16, 22.

6. "AMR Corporation," *Hoover's Handbook of American Business 1992* (Austin: Hoovers Business Press, 1992), p. 110; "AMR Corporation," *International Directory of Company Histories* (Detroit: St. James Press, 1999), p. 23.

7. Robert Serling, *Eagle: The Story of American Airlines* (New York: St. Martin, 1985), p. 280.

8. "Carrier Profile," *Aviation Daily*, April 5, 2005.

9. Mark Kahn, "Airlines," in Gerald Somers, ed., *Collective Bargaining: Contemporary American Experience* (Bloomingdale, Illinois: Industrial Relations Research Association Series, 1980), pp. 354–58; Serling, *Eagle*, pp. 270–273, 304–306.

10. Dan Reed, *The American Eagle: The Ascent of Bob Crandall and American Airlines* (New York: St. Martin, 1993), Chapter 2.

11. Dan Reed, *American Eagle*, pp. 100–102. The quotation is on page 101.

12. Cited in Stewart Toy and Seth Payne, "The Airline Mess," *Business Week*, July 6, 1992, p. 50.

13. Cited in, "American Airlines Loses its Pilot," *Economist*, April 18, 1998, p. 58.

14. Reed, *American Eagle*, p. 207.

15. Steven Morrison and Clifford Winston, *The Evolution of the Airline Industry* (Washington D.C.: The Brooking Institution, 1995), pp. 44–45.

16. Reed, *American Eagle*, pp. 158–164, 174–175.

17. AA, in addition, established secondary hubs in Nashville, Tennessee, Raleigh/Durham, North Carolina, and San Jose, California, but following the recession of the early 1990s, American closed these three hubs, withdrawing from unprofitable short-hall travel markets. See Suzanne Loeffelholz, "Competitive Anger," *Financial World*, January 10, 1989, p. 31; and Perry Flint and Danna Henderson, "American at Bay," *Air Transport World*, March 1997. Online. ABI database, Start Page 28.

18. Dan Reed, *American Eagle*, pp. 204–205.

19. Seth Rosen, "A Union Perspective," in Jean McKelvey, ed., *Cleared for Takeoff: Airline Labor Relations Since Deregulation* (Ithaca, New York: ILR Press, 1988), p. 22; Robert Crandall, "The Airlines: On Track or Off Course," in McKelvey, ed., *Clear for Takeoff*, p. 352; Dan Reed, *American Eagle*, pp. 202–204.

20. *Financial World*, January 10, 1989, pp. 29–30.

21. According to the company's annual report cited in "AMR Corporation," *International Directory of Company Histories*, p. 24.

22. Don Bedwell, *Silverbird: The American Airlines Story* (Sandpoint, Idaho: Airway International Inc., 1999), pp. 137, 244.

23. Perry Flint, "Sabre Unlimited," *Air Transport World*, November 1996, p. 95.

24. Bedwell, *Silverbird*, p. 132, and Chapter 20.

25. Ronald Lieber, "Bob Crandall's BOO-BOOS," *Fortune*, April 28, 1997, p. 368; Don Lee and Jennifer Oldham, "American Woos Wary Travelers," *Los Angeles Times*, February 16, 1997.

26. Reed, *American Eagle*, Chapter 5; Bedwell, *Silverbird*, pp. 130–131, 250–251.

27. Kenneth Labich, "The Computer Network that Keeps American Flying," *Fortune*, September 24, 1990, p. 46.

28. Bedwell, *Silverbird*, p. 248.

29. *Air Transport World*, November 1996, p. 95.

30. Reed, *American Eagle*, p. 184.

31. Cited in Bedwell, *Silverbird*, p. 161.

32. Reed, *American Eagle*, pp. 176–177; Morrison and Winston, *The Evolution of the Airline Industry*, p. 59.

33. Bedwell, *Silverbird*, p. 161.

34. Seth Rosen, "Corporate Restructuring," in Peter Cappelli, ed., *Airline Labor Relations in the Global Era* (Ithaca, New York: ILR Press, 1995), p. 33.

35. Kenneth Labich, "American Takes on the World," *Fortune*, September 24, 1990, pp. 41–42; Read, *American Eagle*, pp. 249, 251, 269; and "AMR Corporation," *International Directory of Company Histories*, p. 24.

36. *Air Transport World*, March 1997. Online. ABI Data Base. Start page 28.

37. Bedwell, *Silverbird*, pp. 233–236; "AMR Corporation," *International Directory of Company Histories*, p. 25.

38. Jeri Clausing, "Crandall's Hard-Ball Style Legendary," *Seattle Times*, November 25, 1993; James Peltz, "A 'Mellower' AMR Chief?" *Los Angeles Times*, February 14, 1997.

39. *Fortune*, April 28, 1997, p. 368; *Los Angeles Times*, February 14, 1997; Scott McCartney, "The Deal Breakers," *Wall Street Journal*, February 11, 1997; "American Airlines Loses its Pilot," *Economist*, April 18, 1998, p. 58.

40. *Air Transport World*, March 1997. Online. ABI Data Base. Start page 28.

41. Peter Elkind, "Flying for Fun & Profits," *Fortune*, October 25, 1999, pp. 36–37; James Peltz, "Carty Has Been Forced to Guide AMR Through Turbulent Times," *Los Angeles Times,* November 14, 2001; John Helyar, "American Airlines: A Wing and a Prayer," *Fortune*, December 10, 2001, p. 182.

42. *Los Angeles Times*, November 14, 2001; "American, TWA Deal Approved," *Aviation Daily*, April 10, 2001; and U.S. Senate, *TWA/American Airlines Workforce Integration,* Hearing before the Committee on Health, Education, and Pensions, 108th Cong., 1st Sess., June 12, 2003, p. 24.

43. *Los Angeles Times*, November 14, 2001.

44. Scott McCarthney, "At American, 48 Hours of Drama Help Airline Avert Bankruptcy, *Wall Street Journal*, April 28, 2003.

45. Brad Foss, "How It All Went Wrong," *Chicago Sun Times*, April 27, 2003.

46. Cited in *Chicago Sun Times*, April 27, 2003.

47. *Wall Street Journal*, April 28, 2003; and Edward Wong and Micheline Maynard, "A Taut, Last-minute Stretch to Save an Airline," *New York Times*, April 27, 2003.

48. Cited in the *Wall Street Journal*, April 28, 2003; but see also *New York Times*, April 27, 2003.

49. Cited in Eve Tahmincioglu, "Back from the Brink," *Workforce Management*, December 2004. Online. ABI Data Base. Start page 32. See also Sara Goo, "Key Union Accepts Cuts at American," *Washington Post*, April 26, 2003.

50. Cited in Melanie Trottman, "Boss Talk," *Wall Street Journal*, December 30, 2004.

51. David Field, "The American Way," *Airline Business*, December 2004, p. 31; "American Enters India," *Aviation Daily*, July 13, 2005.

52. Cited in Caroline Daniel, "A Top Flight Employee Strategy," *Financial Times*, April 4, 2005.

53. Cited in the *Wall Street Journal*, December 30, 2004.

54. *Financial Times*, April 4, 2005; *Workforce Management*, December 2004. Online. ABI Data Base. Start page 32.

55. *Workforce Management*, December 2004. Online. ABI Data Base. Start page 32.

56. *Financial Times*, April 4, 2005.

57. *Workforce Management*, December 2004. Online. ABI Data Base. Start page 32.

58. *Workforce Management*, December 2004. Online. ABI Data Base. Start page 32.

59. Perry Flint, "Rewired for Success: American Embraces Continuous Improvement," *Air Transport World*, August 2004, p. 39.

60. *Air Transport World*, August 2004, p. 39.

61. *Air Transport World*, August 2004, p. 39.

62. *Air Transport World*, August 2004, p. 39.

63. *Workforce Management*, December 2004. Online. ABI Data Base. Start page 32.

64. Cited in *Airline Business*, December 2004, p. 31.

65. *Wall Street Journal*, December 30, 2004; Michael Maynard, "No Longer on the Brink, American Air is Still in Peril," *New York Times,* March 18, 2004; Scott McCartney, "Low Cost Rivals Prompt American Airlines to Try Flying Like One of Them," *Wall Street Journal*, June 8, 2004; *Airline Business*, December 2004, p. 31.

66. *Airline Business*, December 2004, p. 33; Edward Wong, "American Air is Adding Seats," *New York Times*, May 22, 2003; "American Looks to Counteract $1.4 Billion Fuel Cost Increase," *Aviation Daily*, March 13, 2005.

67. *Wall Street Journal*, June 8, 2004; Edward Wong, "In a Sign of Stronger Finances, American Reports a Profit," *New York Times*, October 23, 2003.

68. Melanie Trottman, "AMR Investors Bet on Clearer Skies Ahead," *Wall Street Journal,* February 16, 2006; Caroline Daniel, "In Hard Times, Saving Dollars Makes Sense," *Financial Times*, March 15, 2005.

69. "AMR Company Records, Financials," *Hoovers*. Online. ABI Data Base. *Wall Street Journal*, February 16, 2006.

70. Scott McCartney, "Airline Discord May Hurt Travelers," *Wall Street Journal*, February 7, 2006.

71. Brad Foss, American Path Less Traveled," *Seattle Times*, June 11, 2005.

Cola Wars Continue: Coke and Pepsi in 2006

This case was prepared by David B. Yoffie and Michael Slind,
Harvard Business School.

For more than a century, Coca-Cola and Pepsi-Cola vied for "throat share" of the world's beverage market. The most intense battles in the so-called cola wars were fought over the $66 billion carbonated soft drink (CSD) industry in the United States.[1] In a "carefully waged competitive struggle" that lasted from 1975 through the mid-1990s, both Coke and Pepsi achieved average annual revenue growth of around 10%, as both U.S. and worldwide CSD consumption rose steadily year after year.[2] According to Roger Enrico, former CEO of Pepsi:

> The warfare must be perceived as a continuing battle without blood. Without Coke, Pepsi would have a tough time being an original and lively competitor. The more successful they are, the sharper we have to be. If the Coca-Cola company didn't exist, we'd pray for someone to invent them. And on the other side of the fence, I'm sure the folks at Coke would say that nothing contributes as much to the present-day success of the Coca-Cola company than . . . Pepsi.[3]

That cozy relationship began to fray in the late 1990s, however, as U.S. per-capita CSD consumption declined slightly before reaching what appeared to be a plateau. In 2004, the average American drank

a little more than 52 gallons of CSDs per year. At the same time, the two companies experienced their own distinct ups and downs, as Coke suffered several operational setbacks and as Pepsi charted a new, aggressive course in alternative beverages. Although their paths diverged, however, both companies began to modify their bottling, pricing, and brand strategies.

As the cola wars continued into the 21st century, Coke and Pepsi faced new challenges: Could they boost flagging domestic CSD sales? Would newly popular beverages provide them with new (and profitable) revenue streams? Was their era of sustained growth and profitability coming to a close, or was this slowdown just another blip in the course of the cola giants' long, enviable history?

Economics of the U.S. CSD Industry

Americans consumed 23 gallons of CSDs annually in 1970, and consumption grew by an average of 3% per year over the next three decades. (See Exhibit 1—U.S. Beverage Industry Consumption Statistics.) Fueling this growth were the increasing availability of CSDs and the introduction of diet and flavored varieties. Declining real (inflation-adjusted) prices played a large role as well.[4] There were many alternatives to CSDs, including beer, milk, coffee, bottled water, juices, tea, powdered drinks, wine, sports drinks, distilled spirits, and tap water. Yet Americans drank more soda than any other beverage. Within the CSD category, the cola segment maintained its dominance, although its market share dropped from 71% in 1990 to 60% in 2004.[5] Non-cola CSDs included lemon/lime, citrus, pepper-type, orange, root beer, and other flavors. CSDs consisted of a flavor base (called "concentrate"), a sweetener, and carbonated

Professor David B. Yoffie and Research Associate Yusi Wang prepared the original version of this case "Cola Wars Continue: Coke and Pepsi in the Twenty-First Century," HBS Case No. 702-442 which derives from earlier cases by Professor David B. Yoffie and Professor Michael E. Porter (HBS Case No. 391-179). This version was prepared by Professor David B. Yoffie and Research Associate Michael Slind from published sources. HBS cases are developed solely as the basis for class discussion. Cases are not intended to serve as endorsements, sources of primary data, or illustrations of effective or ineffective management.

EXHIBIT 1

U.S. Beverage Industry Consumption Statistics

	1970	1975	1981	1985	1990	1994	1996	1998	2000	2002	2003	2004
Historical Carbonated Soft Drink Consumption												
Cases (millions)	3,090	3,780	5,180	6,500	7,780	8,710	9,290	9,880	9,950	10,087	10,140	10,240
Gallons/capita	22.7	26.3	34.2	40.3	46.9	50.0	52.0	54.0	53.0	52.5	52.3	52.3
As share of total beverage consumption	12.4%	14.4%	18.7%	22.1%	25.7%	27.4%	28.5%	29.6%	29.0%	28.8%	28.7%	28.7%
U.S. Liquid Consumption Trends (gallons/capita)												
Carbonated soft drinks	22.7	26.3	34.2	40.3	46.9	50.0	52.0	54.0	53.0	52.5	52.3	52.3
Beer	22.8	21.8	20.6	24.0	24.0	22.4	21.8	21.8	21.8	21.8	21.7	21.6
Milk	18.5	21.6	24.3	25.0	24.2	23.0	22.7	22.0	21.3	20.7	20.4	20.1
Bottled Water[b]	—	1.2	2.7	4.5	8.1	9.6	11.0	11.8	13.2	15.4	16.6	17.7
Coffee[a]	35.7	33	27.2	26.9	26.2	23.3	20.2	18.0	16.8	16.8	16.7	16.6
Juices	6.5	6.8	6.9	8.1	8.5	9.0	9.0	9.5	9.5	8.9	8.5	8.6
Tea[a]	5.2	7.3	7.3	7.3	7.0	7.1	6.9	6.9	7.0	7.0	7.0	7.0
Sports Drinks[c]	—	—	—	—	—	1.2	1.5	1.9	2.2	2.6	3.0	3.5
Powdered drinks	—	4.8	6	6.2	5.4	4.8	4.8	3.7	3.0	2.4	2.5	2.6
Wine	1.3	1.7	2.1	2.4	2.0	1.7	1.8	1.9	1.9	2.0	2.1	2.1
Distilled spirits	1.8	2	2	1.8	1.5	1.3	1.2	1.2	1.2	1.3	1.3	1.3
Subtotal	114.5	126.5	133.3	146.5	153.8	153.3	152.2	152.7	150.9	151.4	152.1	153.4
Tap water/hybrids/all others	68.0	56.0	49.2	36.0	28.7	29.2	30.3	29.8	31.6	31.1	30.4	29.1
Total[d]	182.5	182.5	182.5	182.5	182.5	182.5	182.5	182.5	182.5	182.5	182.5	182.5

Sources: Compiled from *Beverage Digest Fact Book 2001, The Maxwell Consumer Report,* Feb. 3, 1994; *Adams Liquor Handbook,* casewriter estimates; and *Beverage Digest, Beverage Digest Fact Book 2005.* Data for 1990 and afterward comes from *Beverage Digest Fact Book 2005,* which reports that some of that data has been "restated compared to previous editions of the Fact Book."

[a] For 1985 and afterward, coffee and tea data are based on a three-year moving average.

[b] Bottled water includes all packages, single-serve as well as bulk.

[c] For pre-1992 data, sports drinks are included in "Tap water/hybrids/all others."

[d] This analysis assumes that each person consumes, on average, one half-gallon of liquid per day.

water. The production and distribution of CSDs involved four major participants: concentrate producers, bottlers, retail channels, and suppliers.[6]

Concentrate Producers

The concentrate producer blended raw material ingredients, packaged the mixture in plastic canisters, and shipped those containers to the bottler. To make concentrate for diet CSDs, concentrate makers often added artificial sweetener; with regular CSDs, bottlers added sugar or high-fructose corn syrup themselves. The concentrate manufacturing process involved little capital investment in machinery, overhead, or labor. A typical concentrate manufacturing plant cost about $25 million to $50 million to build, and one plant could serve the entire United States.[7]

A concentrate producer's most significant costs were for advertising, promotion, market research, and bottler support. Using innovative and sophisticated campaigns, they invested heavily in their trademarks over time. While concentrate producers implemented and financed marketing programs jointly with bottlers, they usually took the lead in developing those programs, particularly when it came to product development, market research, and advertising. They also took charge of negotiating "customer development agreements" (CDAs) with

nationwide retailers such as Wal-Mart. Under a CDA, Coke or Pepsi offered funds for marketing and other purposes in exchange for shelf space. With smaller regional accounts, bottlers assumed a key role in developing such relationships, and paid an agreed-upon percentage—typically 50% or more—of promotional and advertising costs. Concentrate producers employed a large staff of people who worked with bottlers by supporting sales efforts, setting standards, and suggesting operational improvements. They also negotiated directly with their bottlers' major suppliers (especially sweetener and packaging makers) to achieve reliable supply, fast delivery, and low prices.[8]

Once a fragmented business that featured hundreds of local manufacturers, the U.S. soft drink industry had changed dramatically over time. Among national concentrate producers, Coca-Cola and Pepsi-Cola (the soft drink unit of PepsiCo) claimed a combined 74.8% of the U.S. CSD market in sales volume in 2004, followed by Cadbury Schweppes and Cott Corporation. (See Exhibit 2—U.S. Soft Drink Market Share by Case Volume. See also Exhibit 3—Financial Data for Coca-Cola, Pepsi-Cola, and Their Largest Bottlers.) In addition, there were private-label manufacturers and several dozen other national and regional producers.

EXHIBIT 2

U.S. Soft Drink Market Share by Case Volume (percent)

	1966	1970	1975	1980	1985	1990	1995	2000	2004E
Coca-Cola Company									
Coke Classic	—	—	—	—	5.2	20.1	20.8	20.4	17.9
Coca-Cola	27.7	28.4	26.2	25.3	16.5	0.6	0.1	—	—
Diet Coke	—	—	—	—	6.8	9.3	8.8	8.7	9.7
Sprite and Diet Sprite	1.5	1.8	2.6	3.0	4.7	4.5	5.7	7.2	6.3
Caffeine Free Coke, Diet Coke, Tab	—	—	—	—	1.8	2.9	2.6	2.2	2.0
Fanta[a]	—	—	—	—	0.9	0.7	0.7	0.2	1.3
Barq's and Diet Barq's	—	—	—	—	—	—	0.2	1.2	1.2
Minute Maid brands	—	—	—	—	—	0.7	0.7	1.5	0.4
Tab	1.4	1.3	2.6	3.3	1.1	0.2	0.1	—	—
Others	2.8	3.2	3.9	4.3	2.5	2.1	2.6	2.6	4.3
Total	**33.4**	**34.7**	**35.3**	**35.9**	**39.5**	**41.1**	**42.3**	**44.1**	**43.1**

(continued)

EXHIBIT 2   *(continued)*

U.S. Soft Drink Market Share by Case Volume (percent)

	1966	1970	1975	1980	1985	1990	1995	2000	2004E
PepsiCo, Inc.									
Pepsi-Cola	16.1	17.0	17.4	20.4	19.3	17.6	15.0	13.6	11.5
Mountain Dew	1.4	0.9	1.3	3.3	3.1	3.9	5.7	7.2	6.3
Diet Pepsi	1.9	1.1	1.7	3.0	3.9	6.3	5.8	5.3	6.1
Sierra Mist	—	—	—	—	—	—	—	0.1	1.4
Diet Mountain Dew	—	—	—	—	—	0.5	0.7	0.9	1.3
Caffeine Free Pepsi, and Diet Pepsi	—	—	—	—	2.5	2.3	2.0	1.7	1.4
Mug Root Beer	—	—	—	—	—	0.3	0.3	0.8	0.7
Wild Cherry Pepsi (reg and diet)	—	—	—	—	—	—	0.2	0.5	0.6
Mountain Dew Code Red	—	—	—	—	—	—	—	—	0.4
Slice and Diet Slice	—	—	—	—	0.7	1.0	1.0	0.5	0.3
Others	1.0	0.8	0.7	1.1	0.8	0.5	0.2	0.8	1.7
Total	**20.4**	**19.8**	**21.1**	**27.8**	**30.3**	**32.4**	**30.9**	**31.4**	**31.7**
Cadbury Schweppes[b]									
Dr Pepper (all brands)	—	—	—	—	—	—	6.8	7.5	7.2
7UP (all brands)	—	—	—	—	—	—	3.3	2.8	1.8
A&W brands	—	—	—	—	—	—	1.7	1.5	1.4
Royal Crown brands	—	—	—	—	—	—	—	—	1.1
Sunkist	—	—	—	—	1.2	0.7	0.7	0.8	1.0
Canada Dry	—	—	—	—	1.5	1.2	1.0	0.9	0.8
Schweppes	—	—	—	—	0.5	0.6	0.5	0.4	0.4
Others	—	—	—	—	1.5	0.7	1.1	0.8	0.8
Total					**4.7**	**3.2**	**15.1**	**14.7**	**14.5**
Dr Pepper/Seven-Up Cos.[c]									
Dr Pepper brands	2.6	3.8	5.5	6.0	4.5	5.2	—	—	—
7UP brands	6.9	7.2	7.6	6.3	5.8	3.9	—	—	—
Others	—	—	—	—	—	0.5	—	—	—
Total						**9.6**	—	—	—
Cott Corporation	—	—	—	—	—	—	2.7	3.3	5.5
Royal Crown Cos.	6.9	6.0	5.4	4.7	3.1	2.6	2.0	1.1	—
Other companies	29.8	28.5	25.1	19.3	12.1	11.1	7.0	5.4	5.2
Total (million cases)	**2,927**	**3,670**	**4,155**	**5,180**	**6,385**	**7,780**	**8,970**	**9,950**	**10,240**

Sources: Compiled from *Beverage Digest Fact Book 2001*; *The Maxwell Consumer Report*, February 3, 1994; the Beverage Marketing Corporation, cited in *Beverage World*, March 1996 and March 1999; and *Beverage Digest Fact Book 2005*.

[a] For the period before 1985, Fanta sales are included under "Others."

[b] Cadbury Schweppes acquired A&W brands in 1993, Dr Pepper/Seven-Up Cos. (DPSU) brands in 1995, and Royal Crown in October, 2000.

[c] Dr Pepper/Seven-Up Companies (DPSU) was formed in 1988. Prior to 1988, Dr Pepper and 7UP brand shares refer to the shares of the respective independent companies, the Dr Pepper Company and the Seven-Up Company. DPSU was acquired by Cadbury Schweppes in 1995.

EXHIBIT 3

Financial Data for Coca-Cola, Pepsi-Cola, and Their Largest Bottlers ($ millions)

	1975	1980	1985	1990	1995	2000	2001	2002	2003	2004
Coca-Cola Company[a]										
Beverages, North America										
Sales	—	1,486	1,865	2,461	5,513	7,870	7,526	6,264	6,344	6,643
Operating profits/sales	—	11.1%	11.6%	16.5%	15.5%	17.9%	19.7%	23.9%	18.9%	24.2%
Beverages, International										
Sales	—	2,349	2,677	6,125	12,559	12,588	12,386	13,089	14,477	15,076
Operating profit/sales	—	21.0%	22.9%	29.4%	29.1%	27.1%	37.1%	35.8%	33.3%	33.6%
Consolidated										
Sales	2,773	5,475	5,879	10,236	18,127	20,458	20,092	19,564	21,044	21,962
Net profit/sales	9.0%	7.7%	12.3%	13.5%	16.5%	10.6%	19.8%	15.6%	20.7%	22.1%
Net profit/equity	21.0%	20.0%	24.0%	36.0%	55.4%	23.4%	34.9%	25.8%	30.9%	30.4%
Long-term debt/assets	3.0%	10.0%	23.0%	8.0%	7.6%	4.0%	5.4%	11.0%	9.2%	3.7%
PepsiCo, Inc.[b]										
Beverages, North America										
Sales	1,065	2,368	2,725	5,035	7,427	6,171	6,888	7,200	7,733	8,313
Operating profit/sales	10.4%	10.3%	10.4%	13.4%	16.7%	22.3%	21.3%	21.9%	21.9%	23.0%
Beverages, International										
Sales	—	—	—	1,489	3,040	1,981	2,012	2,036	—	—
Operating profit/sales	—	—	—	6.3%	3.9%	8.0%	10.5%	12.8%	—	—
Consolidated										
Sales	2,709	5,975	7,585	17,515	19,067	20,438	26,935	25,112	26,971	29,261
Net profit/sales	4.6%	4.4%	5.6%	6.2%	7.5%	10.7%	9.9%	13.2%	13.2%	14.4%
Net profit/equity	18.0%	20.0%	30.0%	22.0%	19.4%	30.1%	30.8%	35.6%	30.0%	31.0%
Long-term debt/assets	35.0%	31.0%	36.0%	33.0%	35.9%	12.8%	12.2%	9.3%	6.7%	
Coca-Cola Enterprises (CCE)										
Sales	—	—	—	3,933	6,773	14,750	15,700	16,889	17,330	18,158
Operating profit/sales	—	—	—	8.3%	6.9%	7.6%	4.3%	8.0%	8.6%	7.9%
Net profit/sales	—	—	—	2.4%	1.2%	1.6%	−2.0%	2.9%	3.9%	3.3%
Net profit/equity	—	—	—	6.0%	5.7%	8.3%	−11.5%	14.9%	15.5%	11.1%
Long-term debt/assets	—	—	—	39.0%	46.3%	46.7%	43.7%	46.1%	41.1%	39.9%
Pepsi Bottling Group (PBG)[b]										
Sales	—	—	—	—	—	7,982	8,443	9,216	10,265	10,906
Operating profit/sales	—	—	—	—	—	7.4%	8.0%	9.7%	9.3%	9.0%
Net profit/sales	—	—	—	—	—	2.9%	3.6%	4.6%	4.1%	4.2%
Net profit/equity	—	—	—	—	—	13.9%	19.1%	23.5%	22.1%	23.4%
Long-term debt/assets	—	—	—	—	—	42.3%	41.8%	45.1%	38.9%	41.6%

Sources: Company annual reports.

[a] Coca-Cola's beverage sales consisted mainly of concentrate sales. Coke's stake in CCE was accounted for by the equity method of accounting, with its share of CCE's net earnings included in its consolidated net income figure. In 1994, Coke began reporting U.S. data as part of a North American category that included Canada and Mexico.

[b] PepsiCo's sales figures included sales by company-owned bottlers. In 1998, PepsiCo began reporting U.S. data as part of a North American category that included Canada. As of 2000, data for "Beverages, North America" combined sales for what had been the Pepsi-Cola and Gatorade/Tropicana divisions. In 2003, PepsiCo ceased reporting its international beverage business separately from its international food business. PBG financial data for the pre-1999 period refer to the PepsiCo bottling operations that were combined and spun off to form PBG in 1998. From 1999, PepsiCo's share of PBG's net earnings was included in PepsiCo's consolidated net income figure.

Bottlers

Bottlers purchased concentrate, added carbonated water and high-fructose corn syrup, bottled or canned the resulting CSD product, and delivered it to customer accounts. Coke and Pepsi bottlers offered "direct store door" (DSD) delivery, an arrangement whereby route delivery salespeople managed the CSD brand in stores by securing shelf space, stacking CSD products, positioning the brand's trademarked label, and setting up point-of-purchase or end-of-aisle displays. (Smaller national brands, such as Shasta and Faygo, distributed through food store warehouses.) Cooperative merchandising agreements, in which retailers agreed to specific promotional activity and discount levels in exchange for a payment from a bottler, were another key ingredient of soft drink sales.

The bottling process was capital-intensive and involved high-speed production lines that were interchangeable only for products of similar type and packages of similar size. Bottling and canning lines cost from $4 million to $10 million each, depending on volume and package type. In 2005, Cott completed construction of a 40-million-case bottling plant in Fort Worth, Texas, at an estimated cost of $40 million.[9] But the cost of a large plant with four lines, automated warehousing, and a capacity of 40 million cases, could range as high as $75 million.[10] While a handful of such plants could theoretically provide enough capacity to serve the entire United States, Coke and Pepsi each required close to 100 plants to provide effective nationwide distribution.[11] For bottlers, packaging accounted for 40% to 45% of sales, concentrate for roughly the same amount, and sweeteners for 5% to 10%. Labor and overhead made up the remaining variable costs.[12] Bottlers also invested capital in trucks and distribution networks. Bottlers' gross profits routinely exceeded 40%, but operating margins were usually in the 7% to 9% range. (See Exhibit 4—Comparative Costs of a Typical U.S. Concentrate Producer and Bottler, 2004.)

The number of U.S. soft drink bottlers had fallen steadily, from more than 2,000 in 1970 to fewer than 300 in 2004.[13] Coke was the first concentrate producer to build a nationwide franchised bottling network, and Pepsi and Cadbury Schweppes followed suit. The typical franchised bottler owned a manufacturing and sales operation in an exclusive geographic territory, with rights granted in perpetuity by the franchiser. In the case of Coke, territorial rights did not extend to national fountain accounts, which the company handled directly. The original Coca-Cola franchise agreement, written in 1899, was a fixed-price contract that did not provide for renegotiation, even if ingredient costs changed. After considerable negotiation, often accompanied by bitter legal disputes, Coca-Cola amended the contract in 1921, 1978, and 1987. By 2003, more than 88% of Coke's

---

EXHIBIT 4

Comparative Costs of a Typical U.S. Concentrate Producer and Bottler, 2004

	Concentrate Producer		Bottler	
	Dollars per Case[a]	Percent of Sales	Dollars per Case	Percent of Sales
Net sales	$0.97	100%	$4.70	100%
Cost of sales	$0.16	17%	$2.82	60%
Gross profit	$0.81	83%	$1.88	40%
Selling and delivery	$0.02	2%	$1.18	25%
Advertising and marketing	$0.42	43%	$0.09	2%
General and administration	$0.08	8%	$0.19	4%
Pretax profit	$0.29	30%	$0.42	9%

Sources: Industry analysts and casewriter estimates. Profit and loss percentage data are adapted from Andrew Conway, "Global Soft Drink Bottling Review and Outlook: Consolidating the Way to a Strong Bottling Network," Morgan Stanley Dean Witter, August 4, 1997, p. 2, and supplemented with 2004 data supplied by Corey Horsch, of Credit Suisse First Boston.

[a] One case is equivalent to 192 oz.

EXHIBIT 5

U.S. CSD Industry Pricing and Volume Statistics, 1998–2004

	1988	1990	1992	1994	1996	1998	2000	2002	2004
Retail price per case[a]	$8.78	$8.99	$8.87	$8.63	$8.70	$8.55	$9.08	$9.38	$9.68
Change in retail price[b]	—	1.2%	−0.7%	−1.4%	0.4%	−0.9%	3.1%	1.6%	1.6%
Total Change 1988–2004: 0.6%									
Concentrate price per case	$0.79	$0.86	$0.97	$1.00	$1.07	$1.14	$1.29	1.35	1.45[c]
Change in concentrate price	—	4.3%	6.2%	1.5%	3.4%	3.2%	6.4%	2.3%	3.6%
Total Change 1988–2004: 3.9%									
Volume (cases, in billions)	4.9	5.2	5.3	5.8	6.2	6.6	6.6	6.7	6.8
Change in volume	—	3.0%	1.0%	4.6%	3.4%	3.2%	0.0%	0.8%	0.7%
Total Change 1988–2004: 2.1%									
Consumption (gallons/capita)	40.3	46.9	47.2	50.0	52.0	54.0	53.0	52.5	52.3
Change in consumption	—	7.9%	0.3%	2.9%	2.0%	1.9%	−0.9%	−0.5%	−0.2%
Total Change 1988–2004: 1.6%									
Consumer Price Index[d]	100	110	119	125	133	138	146	152	160
Change in CPI	—	5.1%	3.6%	2.8%	2.9%	1.9%	2.8%	2.0%	2.6%
Total Change 1988–2004: 3.0%									

Sources: Compiled from *Beverage Digest Fact Book 2001* and *Beverage Digest Fact Book 2005*, and using the Inflation Calculator tool, U.S. Bureau of Labor Statistics website, http://data.bls.gov/cgi-bin/cpicalc.pl, accessed November 2005.

[a] "Case" refers to a 288-oz case.
[b] All change figures are calculated using Compounded Annual Growth Rate (CAGR).
[c] Concentrate price for 2004 is based on a weighted average of concentrate prices for the top 10 CSD brands. Concentrate price data for previous years appear in aggregated form in *Beverage Digest Fact Book 2003*, p. 64.
[d] CPI data use 1988 as the index year (1988 = 100).

U.S. volume was covered by its 1987 Master Bottler Contract, which granted Coke the right to determine concentrate price and other terms of sale.[14] Under this contract, Coke had no legal obligation to assist bottlers with advertising or marketing. Nonetheless, to ensure quality and to match Pepsi, Coke made huge investments to support its bottling network.[15] In 2002, for example, Coke contributed $600 million in marketing support payments to its top bottler alone.[16]

The 1987 contract did not give complete pricing control to Coke, but rather used a formula that established a maximum price and adjusted prices quarterly according to changes in sweetener pricing. This contract differed from Pepsi's Master Bottling Agreement with its top bottler. That agreement granted the bottler perpetual rights to distribute Pepsi's CSD products but required it to purchase raw materials from Pepsi at prices, and on terms and conditions, determined by Pepsi. Pepsi negotiated concentrate

prices with its bottling association, and normally based price increases on the consumer price index (CPI).[17] From the 1980s to the early 2000s, concentrate makers regularly raised concentrate prices, even as inflation-adjusted retail prices for CSD products trended downward. (See Exhibit 5—U.S. CSD Industry Pricing and Volume Statistics, 1998–2004.)

Franchise agreements with both Coke and Pepsi allowed bottlers to handle the non-cola brands of other concentrate producers. These agreements also allowed bottlers to choose whether to market new beverages introduced by a concentrate producer. Bottlers could not carry directly competing brands, however. For example, a Coke bottler could not sell Royal Crown Cola, yet it could distribute 7UP if it chose not to carry Sprite. Franchised bottlers could decide whether to participate in test marketing efforts, local advertising campaigns and promotions, and new package introductions (although they could only use packages authorized by their franchiser). Bottlers also had the final say in decisions about retail pricing.

In 1971, the Federal Trade Commission initiated action against eight major concentrate makers, charging that the granting of exclusive territories to bottlers prevented intrabrand competition (that is, two or more bottlers competing in the same area with the same beverage). The concentrate makers argued that interbrand competition was strong enough to warrant continuation of the existing territorial agreements. In 1980, after years of litigation, Congress enacted the Soft Drink Interbrand Competition Act, which preserved the right of concentrate makers to grant exclusive territories.

Retail Channels

In 2004, the distribution of CSDs in the United States took place through supermarkets (32.9%), fountain outlets (23.4%), vending machines (14.5%), mass merchandisers (11.8%), convenience stores and gas stations (7.9%), and other outlets (9.5%). Small grocery stores and drug chains made up most of the latter category.[18] Costs and profitability in each channel varied by delivery method and frequency, drop size, advertising, and marketing. (See Exhibit 6—U.S. Refreshment Beverages: Bottling Profitability Per Channel, 2005.)

The main distribution channel for soft drinks was the supermarket, where annual CSD sales reached $12.4 billion in 2004.[19] CSDs accounted for 5.5% of "the total edible grocery universe," and were also a big traffic draw for supermarkets.[20] Bottlers fought for shelf space to ensure visibility for their products, and they looked for new ways to drive impulse purchases, such as placing coolers at checkout counters. An ever-expanding array of products and packaging types created intense competition for shelf space.

The mass merchandiser category included warehouse clubs and discount retailers, such as Wal-Mart. These companies formed an increasingly important channel. Although they sold Coke and Pepsi products, they (along with some drug chains) often had their own private-label CSD, or they sold a generic label such as President's Choice. Private-label CSDs were usually delivered to a retailer's warehouse, while branded CSDs were delivered directly to stores. With the warehouse delivery method, the retailer was responsible for storage, transportation, merchandising, and stocking the shelves, thereby incurring additional costs.

Historically, Pepsi had focused on sales through retail outlets, while Coke had dominated fountain sales. (The term "fountain," which originally referred to drug store soda fountains, covered restaurants, cafeterias, and any other outlet that served soft drinks by the glass using fountain-type dispensers.) Competition for national fountain accounts was intense, and CSD companies frequently sacrificed profitability in order to land and keep those accounts. As of 1999, for example, Burger King franchises were believed to pay about $6.20 per gallon for Coke syrup, but they received a substantial rebate on each gallon; one large Midwestern franchise owner said that his annual rebate ran $1.45 per gallon, or about 23%.[21] Local fountain accounts, which bottlers handled in

EXHIBIT 6

U.S. Refreshment Beverages: Bottling Profitability per Channel, 2005

	Super-markets	Convenience and Gas	Super-centers[a]	Mass Retailers[a]	Club Stores[a]	Drug Stores	Fountain and Vending	Total
Share of industry volume[b]								
	31%	15%	9%	4%	4%	3%	34%	100%
Index of bottling profitability[c]								
Net Price	1.00	1.54	0.95	1.08	1.07	1.19	1.48	NA
Variable Profit	1.00	1.86	0.90	1.17	0.81	1.31	1.80	NA

Sources: Compiled from estimates provided by beverage industry source, April 2006.

[a] "Supercenters" include Wal-Mart Supercenter stores and similar outlets. "Mass Retailers" include standard Wal-Marts stores, Target stores, and the like. "Club Stores" include Sam's Club, Costco, and similar membership-based retailers.

[b] Figures here and below refer to the entire refreshment beverage industry, encompassing CSD and non-carb beverage volume.

[c] Using supermarket information as a baseline, these figures indicate variance by channel of both by-volume pricing and by-volume profit. The variable profit figures take into account cost of goods sold as well as delivery costs.

most cases, were considerably more profitable than national accounts. Overall, according to a prominent industry observer, operating margins were 10 percentage points lower in fountain sales than in bottle and can sales.[22] To support the fountain channel, Coke and Pepsi invested in the development of service dispensers and other equipment, and provided fountain customers with cups, point-of-sale advertising, and other in-store promotional material.

After Pepsi entered the fast-food restaurant business by acquiring Pizza Hut (1978), Taco Bell (1986), and Kentucky Fried Chicken (1986), Coca-Cola persuaded competing chains such as Wendy's and Burger King to switch to Coke. In 1997, PepsiCo spun off its restaurant business under the name Tricon, but fountain "pouring rights" remained split along largely pre-Tricon lines.[23] In 2005, Pepsi supplied all Taco Bell and KFC restaurants and the great majority of Pizza Hut restaurants, and Coke retained exclusivity deals with Burger King and McDonald's (the largest national account in terms of sales). Competition remained vigorous: In 2004, Coke won the Subway account away from Pepsi, while Pepsi grabbed the Quiznos account from Coke. (Subway was the largest account as measured by number of outlets.) And Coke continued to dominate the channel, with a 68% share of national pouring rights, against 22% for Pepsi and 10% for Cadbury Schweppes.[24]

Coke and Cadbury Schweppes had long retained control of national fountain accounts, negotiating pouring rights contracts that in some cases (as with big restaurant chains) covered the entire United States or even the world. Local bottlers or the franchisors' fountain divisions serviced these accounts. (In such cases, bottlers received a fee for delivering syrup and maintaining machines.) Historically, PepsiCo had ceded fountain rights to local Pepsi bottlers. In the late 1990s, however, Pepsi began a successful campaign to gain from its bottlers the right to sell fountain syrup via restaurant commissary companies.[25]

In the vending channel, bottlers took charge of buying, installing, and servicing machines, and for negotiating contracts with property owners, who typically received a sales commission in exchange for accommodating those machines. But concentrate makers offered bottlers financial incentives to encourage investment in machines, and also played a large role in the development of vending technology. Coke and Pepsi were by far the largest suppliers of CSDs to this channel.

Suppliers to Concentrate Producers and Bottlers

Concentrate producers required few inputs: the concentrate for most regular colas consisted of caramel coloring, phosphoric or citric acid, natural flavors, and caffeine.[26] Bottlers purchased two major inputs: packaging (including cans, plastic bottles, and glass bottles), and sweeteners (including high-fructose corn syrup and sugar, as well as artificial sweeteners such as aspartame). The majority of U.S. CSDs were packaged in metal cans (56%), with plastic bottles (42%) and glass bottles (2%) accounting for the remainder.[27] Cans were an attractive packaging material because they were easily handled and displayed, weighed little, and were durable and recyclable. Plastic packaging, introduced in 1978, allowed for larger and more varied bottle sizes. Single-serve 20-oz PET bottles, introduced in 1993, steadily gained popularity; in 2005, they represented 36.7% of CSD volume (and 56.7% of CSD revenues) in convenience stores.[28]

The concentrate producers' strategy toward can manufacturers was typical of their supplier relationships. Coke and Pepsi negotiated on behalf of their bottling networks, and were among the metal can industry's largest customers. In the 1960s and 1970s, both companies took control of a portion of their own can production, but by 1990 they had largely exited that business. Thereafter, they sought instead to establish stable long-term relationships with suppliers. In 2005, major can producers included Ball, Rexam (through its American National Can subsidiary), and Crown Cork & Seal.[29] Metal cans were essentially a commodity, and often two or three can manufacturers competed for a single contract.

The Evolution of the U.S. Soft Drink Industry[30]

Early History

Coca-Cola was formulated in 1886 by John Pemberton, a pharmacist in Atlanta, Georgia, who sold it at drug store soda fountains as a "potion for mental and physical disorders." In 1891, Asa Candler acquired the formula, established a sales force, and began brand advertising of Coca-Cola. The formula for Coca-Cola syrup, known as "Merchandise 7X," remained a well-protected secret that the company kept under guard in an Atlanta bank vault. Candler granted Coca-Cola's first bottling franchise in 1899 for a nominal one dollar, believing that the future of the drink rested with soda fountains. The company's bottling network grew quickly, however, reaching 370 franchisees by 1910.

In its early years, imitations and counterfeit versions of Coke plagued the company, which aggressively fought trademark infringements in court. In 1916 alone, courts barred 153 imitations of Coca-Cola, including the brands Coca-Kola, Koca-Nola, and Cold-Cola. Coke introduced and patented a 6.5-oz bottle whose unique "skirt" design subsequently became an American icon.

Candler sold the company to a group of investors in 1919, and it went public that year. Four years later, Robert Woodruff began his long tenure as leader of the company. Woodruff pushed franchise bottlers to place the beverage "in arm's reach of desire," by any and all means. During the 1920s and 1930s, Coke pioneered open-top coolers for use in grocery stores and other channels, developed automatic fountain dispensers, and introduced vending machines. Woodruff also initiated "lifestyle" advertising for Coca-Cola, emphasizing the role that Coke played in a consumer's life.

Woodruff developed Coke's international business as well. During World War II, at the request of General Eisenhower, he promised that "every man in uniform gets a bottle of Coca-Cola for five cents wherever he is and whatever it costs the company." Beginning in 1942, Coke won exemptions from wartime sugar rationing for production of beverages that it sold to the military or to retailers that served soldiers. Coca-Cola bottling plants followed the movement of American troops, and during the war the U.S. government set up 64 such plants overseas—a development that contributed to Coke's dominant postwar market shares in most European and Asian countries.

Pepsi-Cola was invented in 1893 in New Bern, North Carolina, by pharmacist Caleb Bradham. Like Coke, Pepsi adopted a franchise bottling system, and by 1910 it had built a network of 270 bottlers. Pepsi struggled, however; it declared bankruptcy in 1923 and again in 1932. But business began to pick up when, during the Great Depression, Pepsi lowered the price of its 12-oz bottle to a nickel—the same price that Coke charged for a 6.5-oz bottle. In the years that followed, Pepsi built a marketing strategy around the theme of its famous radio jingle: "Twice as much for a nickel, too."

In 1938, Coke filed suit against Pepsi, claiming that the Pepsi-Cola brand was an infringement on the Coca-Cola trademark. A 1941 court ruling in Pepsi's favor ended a series of suits and countersuits between the two companies. During this period, as Pepsi sought to expand its bottling network, it had to rely on small local bottlers that competed with wealthy, established Coke franchisees.[31] Still, the company began to gain market share, surpassing Royal Crown and Dr Pepper in the 1940s to become the second-largest-selling CSD brand. In 1950, Coke's share of the U.S. market was 47% and Pepsi's was 10%; hundreds of regional CSD companies, which offered a wide assortment of flavors, made up the rest of the market.[32]

The Cola Wars Begin

In 1950, Alfred Steele, a former Coke marketing executive, became CEO of Pepsi. Steele made "Beat Coke" his motto and encouraged bottlers to focus on take-home sales through supermarkets. To target family consumption, for example, the company introduced a 26-oz bottle. Pepsi's growth began to follow the postwar growth in the number of supermarkets and convenience stores in the United States: There were about 10,000 supermarkets in 1945; 15,000 in 1955; and 32,000 in 1962, at the peak of this growth curve.

Under the leadership of CEO Donald Kendall, Pepsi in 1963 launched its "Pepsi Generation" marketing campaign, which targeted the young and "young at heart." The campaign helped Pepsi narrow Coke's lead to a 2-to-1 margin. At the same time, Pepsi worked with its bottlers to modernize plants and to improve store delivery services. By 1970, Pepsi bottlers were generally larger than their Coke counterparts. Coke's network remained fragmented, with more than 800 independent franchised bottlers (most of which served U.S. cities of 50,000 or less).[33] Throughout this period, Pepsi sold concentrate to its bottlers at a price that was about 20% lower than what Coke charged. In the early 1970s, Pepsi increased its concentrate prices to equal those of Coke. To overcome bottler opposition, Pepsi promised to spend this extra income on advertising and promotion.

Coke and Pepsi began to experiment with new cola and non-cola flavors, and with new packaging options, in the 1960s. Previously, the two companies had sold only their flagship cola brands. Coke launched Fanta (1960), Sprite (1961), and the low-calorie cola Tab (1963). Pepsi countered with Teem (1960), Mountain Dew (1964), and Diet Pepsi (1964). Both companies introduced non-returnable glass bottles and 12-oz metal cans in various configurations. They also diversified into non-CSD industries. Coke purchased Minute Maid (fruit juice), Duncan Foods (coffee, tea, hot chocolate), and Belmont Springs Water. In 1965,

Pepsi merged with snack-food giant Frito-Lay to form PepsiCo, hoping to achieve synergies based on similar customer targets, delivery systems, and marketing orientations.

In the late 1950s, Coca-Cola began to use advertising messages that implicitly recognized the existence of competitors: "American's Preferred Taste" (1955), "No Wonder Coke Refreshes Best" (1960). In meetings with Coca-Cola bottlers, however, executives discussed only the growth of their own brand and never referred to its closest competitor by name. During the 1960s, Coke focused primarily on overseas markets, apparently basing its strategy on the assumption that domestic CSD consumption was approaching a saturation point. Pepsi, meanwhile, battled Coke aggressively in the United States, and doubled its U.S. share between 1950 and 1970.

The Pepsi Challenge

In 1974, Pepsi launched the "Pepsi Challenge" in Dallas, Texas. Coke was the dominant brand in that city, and Pepsi ran a distant third behind Dr Pepper. In blind taste tests conducted by Pepsi's small local bottler, the company tried to demonstrate that consumers actually preferred Pepsi to Coke. After its sales shot up in Dallas, Pepsi rolled out the campaign nationwide.

Coke countered with rebates, retail price cuts, and a series of advertisements that questioned the tests' validity. In particular, it employed retail price discounts in markets where a company-owned Coke bottler competed against an independent Pepsi bottler. Nonetheless, the Pepsi Challenge successfully eroded Coke's market share. In 1979, Pepsi passed Coke in food store sales for the first time, opening up a 1.4 share-point lead. In a sign of the times, Coca-Cola president Brian Dyson inadvertently uttered the name Pepsi at a 1979 bottlers' conference.

During this period, Coke renegotiated its franchise bottling contract to obtain greater flexibility in pricing concentrate and syrups. Its bottlers approved a new contract in 1978, but only after Coke agreed to link concentrate price changes to the CPI, to adjust the price to reflect any cost savings associated with ingredient changes, and to supply unsweetened concentrate to bottlers that preferred to buy their own sweetener on the open market.[34] This arrangement brought Coke in line with Pepsi, which traditionally had sold unsweetened concentrate to its bottlers. Immediately after securing approval of the new agreement, Coke announced a significant concentrate price increase. Pepsi followed with a 15% price increase of its own.

Cola Wars Heat Up

In 1980, Roberto Goizueta was named CEO of Coca-Cola, and Don Keough became its president. That year, Coke switched from using sugar to using high-fructose corn syrup, a lower-priced alternative. Pepsi emulated that move three years later. Coke also intensified its marketing effort, more than doubling its advertising spending between 1981 and 1984. In response, Pepsi doubled its advertising expenditures over the same period. Meanwhile, Goizueta sold off most of the non-CSD businesses that he had inherited, including wine, coffee, tea, and industrial water treatment, while retaining Minute Maid.

Diet Coke, introduced in 1982, was the first extension of the "Coke" brand name. Many Coke managers, deeming the "Mother Coke" brand sacred, had opposed the move. So had company lawyers, who worried about copyright issues. Nonetheless, Diet Coke was a huge success. Praised as the "most successful consumer product launch of the Eighties," it became within a few years not only the most popular diet soft drink in the United States, but also the nation's third-largest-selling CSD.

In April 1985, Coke announced that it had changed the 99-year-old Coca-Cola formula. Explaining this radical break with tradition, Goizueta cited a sharp depreciation in the value of the Coca-Cola trademark. "The product and the brand," he said, "had a declining share in a shrinking segment of the market."[35] On the day of Coke's announcement, Pepsi declared a holiday for its employees, claiming that the new Coke mimicked Pepsi in taste. The reformulation prompted an outcry from Coke's most loyal customers, and bottlers joined the clamor. Three months later, the company brought back the original formula under the name Coca-Cola Classic, while retaining the new formula as its flagship brand under the name New Coke. Six months later, Coke announced that it would henceforth treat Coca-Cola Classic (the original formula) as its flagship brand.

New CSD brands proliferated in the 1980s. Coke introduced 11 new products, including Caffeine-Free Coke (1983) and Cherry Coke (1985). Pepsi introduced 13 products, including Lemon-Lime Slice (1984) and Caffeine-Free Pepsi-Cola (1987). The number of packaging types and sizes also increased dramatically, and the battle for shelf space in supermarkets and other stores became fierce. By the late 1980s, Coke and Pepsi each offered more than 10 major brands and 17 or more container types.[36] The struggle for market share intensified, and retail price discounting became the norm. Consumers grew accustomed to such discounts.

Throughout the 1980s, the growth of Coke and Pepsi put a squeeze on smaller concentrate producers. As their shelf space declined, small brands were shuffled from one owner to another. Over a five-year span, Dr Pepper was sold (all or in part) several times, Canada Dry twice, Sunkist once, Shasta once, and A&W Brands once. Philip Morris acquired Seven-Up in 1978 for a big premium, racked up huge losses in the early 1980s, and then left the CSD business in 1985. In the 1990s, through a series of strategic acquisitions, Cadbury Schweppes emerged as the third-largest concentrate producer—the main (albeit distant) competitor of the two CSD giants. It bought the Dr Pepper/Seven-Up Companies in 1995, and continued to add such well-known brands as Orangina (2001) and Nantucket Nectars (2002) to its portfolio. (See Appendix A—Cadbury Schweppes: Operations and Financial Performance.)

Bottler Consolidation and Spin-Off

Relations between Coke and its franchised bottlers had been strained since the contract renegotiation of 1978. Coke struggled to persuade bottlers to cooperate in marketing and promotion programs, to upgrade plant and equipment, and to support new product launches.[37] The cola wars had particularly weakened small, independent bottlers. Pressures to spend more on advertising, product and packaging proliferation, widespread retail price discounting—together, these factors resulted in higher capital requirements and lower profit margins. Many family-owned bottlers no longer had the resources needed to remain competitive.

At a July 1980 dinner with Coke's 15 largest domestic bottlers, Goizueta announced a plan to refranchise bottling operations. Coke began buying up poorly managed bottlers, infusing them with capital, and quickly reselling them to better-performing bottlers. Refranchising allowed Coke's larger bottlers to expand outside their traditionally exclusive geographic territories. When two of its largest bottling companies came up for sale in 1985, Coke moved swiftly to buy them for $2.4 billion, preempting outside bidders. Together with other recently purchased bottlers, these acquisitions placed one-third of Coke's volume in company-owned operations. Meanwhile, Coke began to replace its 1978 franchise agreement with what became the 1987 Master Bottler Contract.

Coke's bottler acquisitions had increased its long-term debt to approximately $1 billion. In 1986, the company created an independent bottling subsidiary, Coca-Cola Enterprises (CCE), selling 51% of its shares to the public and retaining the rest. The minority equity position enabled Coke to separate its financial statements from those of CCE. As Coke's first "anchor bottler," CCE consolidated small territories into larger regions, renegotiated contracts with suppliers and retailers, merged redundant distribution and purchasing arrangements, and cut its work force by 20%. CCE also invested in building 50-million-case production lines that involved high levels of automation. Coke continued to acquire independent franchised bottlers and to sell them to CCE.[38] "We became an investment banking firm specializing in bottler deals," said Don Keough. In 1997 alone, Coke put together more than $7 billion in such deals.[39] By 2004, CCE was Coke's largest bottler. It handled about 80% of Coke's North American bottle and can volume, and logged annual sales of more than $18 billion. Some industry observers questioned Coke's accounting practice with respect to CCE, since Coke retained substantial managerial influence in the putatively independent anchor bottler.[40]

In the late 1980s, Pepsi acquired MEI Bottling for $591 million, Grand Metropolitan's bottling operations for $705 million, and General Cinema's bottling operations for $1.8 billion. After operating the bottlers for a decade, Pepsi shifted course and adopted Coke's anchor bottler model. In April 1999, the Pepsi Bottling Group (PBG) went public, with Pepsi retaining a 35% equity stake in it. By 2004, PBG produced 57% of PepsiCo beverages in North America and about 40% worldwide, while the total number of Pepsi bottlers had fallen from more than 400 in the mid-1980s to a mere 102.[41]

Bottler consolidation made smaller concentrate producers increasingly dependent on the Pepsi and Coke bottling networks for distribution of their products. In response, Cadbury Schweppes in 1998 bought and merged two large U.S. bottling companies to form its own bottler. In 2004, Coke had the most consolidated system, with its top 10 bottlers producing 94.7% of domestic volume. Pepsi's and Cadbury Schweppes' top 10 bottlers produced 87.2% and 72.9% of the domestic volume of their respective franchisors.[42]

Adapting to the Times

Starting in the late 1990s, the soft drink industry encountered new challenges that suggested a possible long-term shift in the marketplace. Most notably, demand for its core product seemed to have leveled off. Although Americans still drank more CSDs than any other beverage, U.S. sales volume grew at a rate of 1% or less in the years 1998 to 2004. Total U.S. volume topped 10 billion cases in 2001, but had risen to only 10.2 billion cases in 2004. (A case was equivalent to 24 eight-ounce containers, or 192 ounces.) That was in contrast to annual growth rates of 3% to 7% during the 1980s and early 1990s.[43] Globally, too, demand remained flat. Worldwide volume in 2003 was 31.26 billion cases, which marked only a slight increase over the 1999 total of 31 billion cases. During that period, worldwide annual per-capita consumption declined from 125 eight-ounce servings to 119 servings.[44]

In responding to changing times, Coca-Cola struggled more than PepsiCo, in part because of its own internal difficulties and execution failures, and in part because of its greater reliance on a traditional CSD-oriented model. But, in their different ways, both companies sought to retain or recapture their historically high growth and profitability within an apparently new environment. Toward that end, they focused on addressing challenges related to performance and execution, on providing alternative beverages to increasingly health-conscious consumers, on adjusting key strategic relationships, and on cultivating international markets.

Reversal of Fortune

When Coke CEO Robert Goizueta died unexpectedly in 1997, the company that he had led was at its zenith. During Goizueta's 16-year tenure, Coke's share price rose by 3,500%, and its brand was routinely deemed the most valuable in the world.[45] Pepsi, meanwhile, lagged behind its rival in most key measures of its beverage operations, including market share and sales growth.[46] By the middle of the following decade, however, Coke appeared to stumble from one embarrassment to another, while Pepsi was flying high.

Under the brief, rocky tenure of CEO Douglas Ivester (1997–1999), Coke lost a high-profile race-discrimination suit, underwent financial shocks caused by currency crises in Asia and Russia, and conducted the largest recall in its history after a contamination scare in Belgium. In the latter episode, there was no

evidence of actual contamination; nonetheless, it was a public relations disaster.[47] Troubles continued under the next CEO, Douglas Daft (1999–2004). Layoffs of 7,000 employees from 2001 to 2004 cut Coke's work force by 20%—damaging morale and seriously weakening its executive ranks, many observers believed.[48] A contamination scare in India in 2003 hindered Coke's (as well as Pepsi's) push into a promising market, and a similar crisis in 2004 led the company to abort plans to roll out its Dasani water brand in Europe.[49] A series of legal problems burdened the company as well. In 2003, Coke agreed to pay Burger King $21 million following the revelation that it had rigged a marketing test involving the restaurant chain. That same year, the U.S. Justice Department and the Securities Exchange Commission (SEC) launched wide-ranging investigations of various Coke accounting practices, focusing on allegations of "channel stuffing." Under this practice, Coke pressured bottlers to buy excess concentrate in order to meet earnings targets. Coke in 2005 settled with the SEC on charges involving the Japanese market, but a shareholder suit alleging such practices in Europe, North America, and elsewhere remained in the courts.[50]

Coke also suffered from clumsy execution (or non-execution) of several initiatives. In 2001, it bailed out on a planned joint venture with Procter & Gamble. Around the same time, after two years of negotiation, it opted against buying the South Beach Beverage Co. (SoBe), only to watch Pepsi acquire that company. Similarly, in 2000 Coke allowed Pepsi to purchase Quaker Oats. Daft had agreed to buy Quaker for $15.75 billion, but several Coke directors halted the deal, arguing that the price was too high.[51] Coke installed a new CEO, E. Neville Isdell, in April 2004.[52] A 35-year Coke veteran, Isdell focused early in his tenure on regaining the company's lost luster as a high-performing soft drink maker. "We are not talking about radical change in strategy. We are talking about a dramatic change in execution," he said in November 2004.[53] Yet, at around the same time, he noted the need for Coke to take "corrective actions with a great urgency." During his first year as CEO, he committed to spending an additional $400 million per year on marketing and innovation, and on addressing Coke's "people deficit and skills deficit."[54]

While Coke struggled, Pepsi quietly flourished. In 2001, Steve Reinemund succeeded Roger Enrico as its CEO.[55] At a broad level, both men pursued the same simple strategy, which Reinemund couched in this way: "Grow the core and add some more."[56] Along with launching new CSDs, such as Sierra Mist (2000) and Mountain Dew Code Red (2001), Pepsi expanded into other beverage categories—an effort capped by its $14 billion acquisition of Quaker Oats, maker of Gatorade, in 2000.[57] Partly as a result, the company's North American beverage volume grew by 3% in 2004, compared with virtually flat volumes for Coke.[58] As the world's fourth-largest food and beverage company, meanwhile, Pepsi also benefited from having a more diversified portfolio of products.

Financial returns for the two companies told a stark tale. Between 1996 and 2004, Coca-Cola logged an average annual growth in net income of 4.2%—a huge drop from the 18% average growth of the years 1990–1997. PepsiCo, by contrast, saw its net income rise by an average of 17.6% per year over the 1996–2004 period.[59] In 2003, Pepsi recorded a return on invested capital of 29.3%, up from 9.5% in 1996; for the first time in decades, it surpassed Coke in that measure.[60] From 1997 to 2004, Pepsi shareholders enjoyed a return of 46%, while Coke shareholders suffered a return of -26%.[61] (Coke shares, which reached a peak price of $89 in 1998, traded at half that amount in 2005.[62])

The Quest for Alternatives

Early in 2005, Pepsi announced that it would no longer set its marketing course by its regular cola brand. "We are treating Diet Pepsi as the flagship brand," said Dave Burwick, chief marketing officer for Pepsi-Cola North America. Although the marketing budget for regular Pepsi still exceeded that of the diet brand, the balance of attention and resources would now shift within the company.[63] More importantly, the move was a bellwether of a larger shift throughout the beverage industry. After several years of little or no growth in CSD sales—especially sales of regular, sugared sodas—companies responded aggressively to consumers' increasing demand for alternative beverages.

New federal nutrition guidelines, issued in 2005, identified regular CSDs as the largest source of obesity-causing sugars in the American diet.[64] Schools in New York City, throughout California, and elsewhere banned the sale of soft drinks on their premises.[65] Late in 2005, using earlier actions against tobacco companies as a model, lawyers planned to file a suit against CSD makers for allegedly causing harm to children's health.[66] The American Beverage Association, an industry group, responded to such pressures by announcing

rules to limit CSD sales in some schools. (In another noteworthy development, the ABA had changed its name from the National Soft Drink Association in 2004.)[67] But the widespread linkage of CSDs with obesity and other health-related concerns was hard to dispel from people's minds. From 2003 to 2004, according to a Morgan Stanley survey, the proportion of Americans who said that cola was "too fattening" increased from 48% to 59%.[68]

In such a climate, diet sodas offered one path to reviving sales. In the U.S. market, their share of total CSD volume grew from 24.6% in 1997 to 29.1% in 2004, thus making up for a decline in regular-soda consumption.[69] New or renamed products, such as Coca-Cola Zero (2005) and Sierra Mist Free (2004), targeted consumers—especially younger men—who shunned the "diet" label. With products like Pepsi One (2005) and Diet Coke with Splenda (2005), CSD makers sought to expand the diet market still further.[70]

But the search for alternatives centered on non-carbonated beverages, or "non-carbs"—a category that included juices and juice drinks, sports drinks, energy drinks, and tea-based drinks—and also on bottled water. In 2004, CSD volume in the United States grew by just 1%, whereas non-carb volume increased by 7.6% and single-serve bottled-water volume leaped by 18.8%. That year, CSDs accounted for 73.1% of U.S. non-alcoholic refreshment beverage volume (down from 80.8% in 2000), with bottled water comprising 13.2% (up from 6.6% in 2000) and non-carbs comprising 13.7% (up from 12.6%) of the remainder.[71] In 2001, non-carbs and bottled water together contributed more than 100% of Coke's total volume growth and roughly three-fourths of Pepsi's volume growth.[72]

Pepsi was more aggressive than Coke in shifting to non-CSDs. "Politicians expect us to be on the defensive when we talk about health and wellness but we're not," said Pepsi CEO Reinemund. "It's a huge opportunity to build new brands and products."[73] His company launched a "Smart Spot" program that labeled all products (including diet sodas and non-carbs) that met certain "good for you" criteria; in 2004, such products reportedly grew at twice the rate of other Pepsi food and beverage items.[74] Declaring itself to be a "total beverage company," Pepsi developed a portfolio of non-CSD products that outsold Coke's rival product in each key category: In 2004 volume sales, Gatorade (80.4%) led PowerAde (18.1%) in the $5.4 billion sports drink segment, Lipton (35.2%) led

Nestea (23.9%) in the $3.2 billion tea-based drink segment, and Tropicana (26.8%) led Minute Maid (14.8%) in the $3.8 billion refrigerated juice segment. In the U.S. non-carb market overall (excluding bottled water), Pepsi had a market share of 47.3%, compared with Coke's share of 27.0%.[75]

Missed opportunities marked Coke's U.S. non-carb operations. In 2001, Coke acquired the Planet Java coffee-drink brand and the Mad River line of juices and teas; two years later, it folded both brands.[76] KMX, the company's entry in the fast-growing, $1.9 billion energy-drink segment, also foundered. Coke hoped for better luck with Full Throttle, introduced in 2005 to compete with segment leader Red Bull.[77] Observers noted Coke's continued focus on its traditional source of strength. "Regardless of what the skeptics think, I know carbonated soft drinks can grow," said Coke CEO Isdell.[78] In 2005, CSDs still accounted for 80% of Coke's worldwide beverage volume, while making up just two-thirds of Pepsi's volume.[79]

Coke fared better in the $11.4 billion bottled-water category. Both Pepsi (with Aquafina, 1998) and Coke (with Dasani, 1999) had introduced purified-water products that had surged to become leading beverage brands. (See Exhibit 7—Non-Alcoholic Refreshment Beverge Megabrands, 2004 and 2000.) Using their distribution prowess, they had outstripped competing brands, many of which sold spring water. By 2004, Aquafina (13.6%) led the segment in market

EXHIBIT 7

Non-Alcoholic Refreshment Beverage Megabrands,[a] 2004 and 2000

Brand (Owner)	Category	2004 Cases (mil)	2004 Share	2000 Cases (mil)	2000 Share	Annual Volume Change[b] 2004–04	Annual Share Change[b] 2004–04
Coke (Coke)	CSD	3,272.3	23.4%	3,192.6	25.9%	0.6%	−2.5%
Pepsi (Pepsi)	CSD	2,098.4	15.0%	2,159.9	17.5%	−0.7%	−3.8%
Mountain Dew (Pepsi)	CSD	871.1	6.2%	809.8	6.6%	1.8%	−1.5%
Dr Pepper (Cadbury)	CSD	738.3	5.3%	747.5	6.1%	−0.3%	−3.5%
Sprite (Coke)	CSD	683.2	4.9%	713.0	5.8%	−1.1%	−4.1%
Gatorade (Pepsi)	Non-Carb	546.0	3.9%	325.0	2.6%	13.9%	10.7%
Aquafina (Pepsi)	Water	251.0	1.8%	100.7	0.8%	25.7%	22.5%
Dasani (Coke)	Water	223.0	1.6%	65.1	0.5%	36.0%	33.8%
Poland Spring (Nestlé Waters)	Water	217.0	1.5%	91.8	0.7%	24.0%	21.0%
7UP (Cadbury)	CSD	186.7	1.3%	276.1	2.2%	−9.3%	−12.3%
Minute Maid (Coke)	CSD/Non-Carb	176.4	1.3%	145.0	1.2%	5.0%	2.0%
Sierra Mist (Pepsi)	CSD	166.9	1.2%	—	—	—	—
Lipton (Pepsi/Unilever)	Non-Carb	164.0	1.2%	155.2	1.3%	1.4%	−2.0%
Crystal Geyser (CG Roxanne)	Water	135.5	1.0%	50.2	0.4%	28.2%	25.7%
Arrowhead (Nestlé Waters)	Water	127.0	0.9%	46.6	0.4%	28.5%	18.9%
PowerAde (Coke)	Non-Carb	122.7	0.9%	62.6	0.5%	18.3%	15.9%
Nestlé Pure Life (Nestlé Waters)	Water	113.2	0.8%	—	—	—	—
Barq's (Coke)	CSD	112.5	0.8%	121.2	1.0%	−1.8%	−5.4%
Sunkist (Cadbury)	CSD	105.2	0.8%	80.3	0.7%	7.0%	3.4%

Sources: Compiled from *Beverage Digest Fact Book 2005*; *Beverage Digest Fact Book 2001*; and casewriter estimates.

[a] *Beverage Digest Fact Book* defines a "megabrand" as a "brand or trademark with total volume of more than 100 million 192-oz cases." A megabrand encompasses all varieties (Coke Classic, Diet Coke, Cherry Coke, and so on) of a given trademark ("Coke"). Only single-serve products are included here.

[b] All changes calculated using Compounded Annual Growth Rate (CAGR).

share, with Dasani (12.1%) trailing close behind.[80] Moreover, by arrangement with Danone, Coke handled U.S. marketing and distribution of that company's water brands, including Dannon and Evian. In 2004, Coke/Danone had an overall market share of 21.9%, behind market leader Nestlé Waters (42.1%) and ahead of Pepsi (13.6%). Coke bought out Danone's share of the venture in 2005.[81]

Evolving Structures and Strategies

Early in the 21st century, both Coke and Pepsi worked to improve "system profitability"—the arrangement whereby concentrate makers and their bottlers created and then divided overall profits from beverage sales. Bottler consolidation continued apace, and the relationship between Coke or Pepsi (on the one hand) and bottlers like CCE or PBG (on the other) became a key element of the cola wars. In the 1990s, a price war in the supermarket channel had highlighted a divergence of interest between the two camps. To compete against bargain private-label brands, bottlers had pursued a low-price strategy. Through the decade, retail CSD prices decreased or remained flat, even as the CPI inched up and as concentrate prices rose; Coke, for instance, raised its concentrate prices by 7.6% in 2000. Bottlers, already burdened by huge debts from consolidation and infrastructure investments, saw profit margins dwindle. In 1999 and 2000, they shifted course, as CCE increased its retail pricing in the supermarket channel by 6% to 7% and as PBG followed suit. Consumers balked, sales volume dipped, and concentrate makers saw their profits drop as a result.[82]

In later years, Coke struggled to adjust its relations with CCE and other bottlers—relations that one writer in 2004 called "dysfunctional."[83] In 2001, the company made an arrangement with CCE to link concentrate prices more tightly to CCE's wholesale CSD prices.[84] Starting in 2003, the two companies began negotiating a deal that would move toward "incidence pricing," an approach that Coke often used with its overseas bottlers. Under that system, concentrate prices varied according to prices charged in different channels and for different packages. As a rule, bottlers favored such arrangements in a deflationary market (which the CSD market had become) but resisted them in an inflationary market.[85] Neville Isdell, Coke's new CEO in 2004 and a former bottler himself, emphasized the need to improve bottler relations. Yet late that year, he tabled the CCE pricing initiative.[86] He also oversaw a proposed rise in concentrate prices

that led Coca-Cola FEMSA, the Coke system's largest Mexican bottler, to threaten a cut in its marketing expenditure.[87]

Pepsi, observers noted, had less difficulty than Coke in aligning its strategy with that of its bottlers. "We believe PBG's relationship with PepsiCo is strong and has been critical to its success," one analysts' report asserted in 2003. During that period, PBG consistently posted net-revenue-per-case growth that exceeded CCE's growth by several percentage points. Supported by Pepsi, PBG excelled in higher-margin channels—especially the convenience-and-gas channel, in which the bottler actually led CCE. Bottlers profited immensely in such "immediate consumption" venues, where sales of the increasingly popular 20-oz PET bottle yielded margins as high as 35%, compared with the 5% to 7% margin on cans.[88]

All CSD companies faced the challenge of achieving pricing power in the take-home, or future-consumption, channels. Supermarket retail prices did rise, modestly but steadily, in the mid-2000s.[89] Yet retailers, accustomed to using CSD sales to drive in-store traffic, still resisted price increases.[90] Rapid growth of the mass-merchandiser channel, led by Wal-Mart and various club stores, posed a new threat to profitability for Coke, Pepsi, and their bottlers. By 2004, Wal-Mart was the largest U.S. food retailer; for PepsiCo, it represented 14% of the company's total (food and beverage) net revenue.[91] Such retailers not only used their size to exert pricing pressure; they also demanded that beverage companies alter long-standing business practices. Wal-Mart, for example, insisted on negotiating chain-wide marketing and shelving arrangements directly with concentrate makers. Although bottlers continued to handle deliveries to these accounts, relations between Coke or Pepsi and their bottlers underwent a great deal of stress because of this channel shift.[92]

To counter these pressures, CSD makers focused on enticing consumers through stepped-up marketing and innovation. In 2005, Coke combined authority for all of its marketing and product development in a new position that became the company's "de facto No. 2 spot."[93] It also launched a major advertising campaign, built around a new tag line: "The Coke Side of Life."[94] (See Exhibit 8—Advertisement Spending for Selected Refreshment Beverage Brands.) Packaging innovation received special emphasis. Coke in 2001 rolled out its Fridge Pack (later imitated by Pepsi, which introduced a Fridge Mate package), a reconfiguration of the

EXHIBIT 8

Advertisement Spending for Selected Refreshment Beverage Brands
($ thousands)

	Share of market[a]		Advertisement Spending[b]		
	2004	2003	2004	2003	per 2004 share point
Coca-Cola	23.4%	24.3%	246,243	167,675	10,523
Pepsi-Cola	15.0%	15.5%	211,654	236,396	14,110
Mountain Dew	6.2%	6.4%	57,803	60,555	9,323
Dr Pepper	5.3%	5.3%	104,762	96,387	19,766
Sprite	4.9%	5.3%	45,035	31,835	9,191
Gatorade	3.9%	3.5%	141,622	130,993	36,313
Aquafina	1.8%	1.7%	22,037	24,647	12,243
Dasani	1.6%	1.5%	17,633	18,833	11,021
7UP	1.3%	1.5%	34,608	25,071	26,206
Minute Maid	1.3%	1.5%	35,797	21,097	27,228
Sierra Mist	1.2%	1.2%	60,327	64,129	50,273
PowerAde	0.9%	0.8%	11,008	10,100	12,231

Sources: Compiled from "Special Report: 100 Leading National Advertisers," *Advertising Age,* June 27, 2005, and casewriter estimates.

[a] Share of the total single-serve non-alcoholic beverage market (about 14 billion cases in 2004).

[b] Spending as measured across 17 national media channels using data compiled by TNS Media Intelligence.

standard 12-pack of cans that seemed to improve CSD sales.[95] In 2004, the company introduced a 1.5-liter bottle in select markets, aiming to replace the 2-liter version and thus to boost per-ounce pricing. While the launching of new products and packages brought clear benefits, it also increased costs for bottlers, which had to produce and manage an ever-rising number of stock-keeping units (SKUs).[96] (See Exhibit 9—Retailers' Assessment of Brand Performance, 2004.) That problem was most salient in the area of non-CSD beverages. The proliferation of such products, many of them sold in relatively low volume, led to an increasing use of "split pallets." By loading more than one product type on a pallet (the hard, wooden bed used to organize and transport merchandise), bottlers incurred higher labor costs.

In general, alternative beverages complicated CSD makers' traditional production and distribution practices. CSD manufacturing was a cold-fill process. Some non-CSD beverages (such as Lipton Brisk) were also cold-fill products, and bottlers could adapt their infrastructure to those products with little difficulty. But other beverage types (such as Gatorade and Lipton Iced Tea) required costly new equipment and major process changes. More often than not, Coke and Pepsi took direct charge of manufacturing such beverages, which they then sold to their bottlers. The bottlers, in turn, distributed these finished goods alongside their own bottled products at a percentage markup. In others cases, especially that of bottled water, Coke and Pepsi paid for half or more of the cost of building bottling plants that allowed for filtration and other necessary processes. Bottlers then either purchased concentrate-like additives from the concentrate maker (as with Dasani's mineral packet) or compensated Coke or Pepsi via per-unit royalty fees (as with Aquafina). In addition, Coke and Pepsi distributed some non-carbs (such as Gatorade) through food brokers and wholesalers, rather than through DSD delivery.[97]

These arrangements affected profitability in ways that were complex and evolving. With many non-carb beverages, especially energy drinks and sports drinks, high retail pricing and consumers' preference for immediate, single-serve consumption meant that margins were actually higher than they were for CSDs. Yet

EXHIBIT 9

Retailers' Assessment of Brand Performance, 2004

	Top 6 Brands[a]					
	P&G	**Kraft**	**Gen'l Mills**	**Pepsi-Cola**	**Coca-Cola**	**Unilever**
Brands most important to retailers	57.1%	47.3%	19.8%	15.8%	13.7%	11.8%
	Kraft	**P&G**	**Gen'l Mills**	**Nestle**	**Con-Agra**	**Pepsi-Cola**
Best combination of growth, profitability	33.3%	27.6%	26.3%	13.6%	12.5%	11.2%
	Kraft	**P&G**	**Gen'l Mills**	**Pepsi-Cola**	**Nestle**	**Frito-Lay**
Best sales force/customer teams	32.7%	31.5%	26.4%	14.1%	13.9%	8.4%
	P&G	**Kraft**	**Gen'l Mills**	**Pepsi-Cola**	**Coca-Cola**	**Unilever**
Most innovative marketing programs	30.7%	29.6%	28.9%	14.7%	13.4 %	12.7%
	P&G	**Kraft**	**Gen'l Mills**	**Nestle**	**Pepsi-Cola**	**Coca-Cola**
Most helpful customer information	50.3%	27.2%	23.1%	13.1%	9.4%	9.1%
	P&G	**Kraft**	**Gen'l Mills**	**Nestle**	**Campbell's**	**Unilever**
Best supply chain management	55.0%	36.9%	25.9%	15.9%	10.2%	8.8%

Source: Cannondale Associates, PoweRanking Survey®, 2004.

[a] Each brand measured by percentage of respondents who rank the brand first, second, or third for each category.

volume for such products, while growing fast, remained very small in comparison with CSD volume.[98] With bottled water, a different set of dynamics was in play. Here, sales volume soared (bottled water, one observer noted, was "the most frequent next stop for lapsed soft-drink users"[99]), and the cost, production, and distribution structures closely matched those of the traditional CSD industry. In the early 2000s, bottler margins on water were high; one research report estimated that a bottle of Pepsi's Aquafina garnered a profit of 22.4%, compared with a 19.0% profit for a bottle of Pepsi-Cola.[100] But as consumption shifted from single-serve to multi-pack options, pricing shifted accordingly. At some locations, at one point in 2002, a 24-bottle case of Dasani or Aquafina sold for $3.99, which was less than the cost of bottling it.[101] By 2006, according to one estimate, multi-serve products accounted for about 70% of the bottled water market, up from about 30% a decade earlier. Rising plastic costs also cut sharply into margins in this category.[102] In addition, compared with the CSD market, the water market appeared to involve low brand loyalty and high price sensitivity. A 2002 survey found that while 37% of respondents said that they chose a CSD because "it's my favorite brand," only 10% of respondents said so about a bottled water choice.[103]

Internationalizing the Cola Wars

As U.S. demand for CSDs reached an apparent plateau, Coke and Pepsi increasingly looked abroad for new growth. In 2004, the United States remained by far the largest market, accounting for about one-third of worldwide CSD volume. The next largest markets were, in order, Mexico, Brazil, Germany, China, and the United Kingdom.[104] But improved access to markets in Asia and Eastern Europe stimulated a new, intense phase of the cola wars. In many such markets, per-capita consumption levels were a small fraction of the level seen in the United States. For example, while the average American drank 837 eight-ounce cans of CSDs in 2004, the average Chinese drank just 21. Among major world regions, Coke dominated in Western Europe and much of Latin America, while Pepsi had a marked presence in the Middle East and Southeast Asia.[105] (See Exhibit 10—CSD Industry: Selected International Consumption Rates and Market Shares, 2003 and 1999.) Although the growth potential of both established and emerging markets held great attraction, those markets also posed special challenges.

Coke flourished in international markets, and also relied upon them, far more than Pepsi. As far back as the end of World War II, the company had

EXHIBIT 10

CSD Industry: Selected International Consumption Rates and Market Shares, 2003 and 1999

	Population (thousands)	Consumption (8-oz servings per capita) 2003	Consumption (8-oz servings per capita) 1999	Annual Growth[a] 1999–2003	2003 Share[b] Coke	2003 Share[b] Pepsi	2003 Share[b] Cadbury	1999 Share[b] Coke	1999 Share[b] Pepsi	1999 Share[b] Cadbury
Europe (23.4%)										
Germany	82,476	340	344	−0.3%	51	5	1	56	8	1
United Kingdom	59,251	420	370	3.2%	47	11	0	43	12	0
Spain	41,060	425	386	2.4%	65	15	5	60	16	5
Italy	57,423	216	212	0.5%	44	6	1.5	45	8	1
France	60,144	180	158	3.3%	60	6	18.6	60	8	5
Russia	143,246	70	52	7.7%	21	18	0	26	12	0
Poland	38,587	167	155	1.9%	19	15	1	28	17	1
Netherlands	16,149	335	356	−1.5%	80	14	0	45	15	1
Hungary	9,877	279	273	0.5%	49	25	4	57	29	5
Romania	22,334	145	104	8.7%	46	8	0	44	9	0
Czech Republic	10,236	410	215	17.5%	13	7	1	36	13	2
Latin America (24.3%)										
Mexico	103,457	610	590	0.9%	73	20	5.1	70	19	3
Brazil	178,470	312	276	3.1%	46	7	0	51	7	0
Argentina	38,428	400	374	1.7%	50	19	0	59	24	0
Colombia	44,222	159	181	−3.2%	51	11	0	60	8	0
Venezuela	25,699	205	290	−8.3%	49	21	0	70	30	0
Chile	15,805	402	392	0.6%	73	5	0	81	4	0
Peru	27,167	166	108	11.4%	39	9	0	50	16	0
Asia Pacific (13.6%)										
China	1,304,196	21	22	−1.2%	51	24	0	34	16	0
Philippines	79,999	187	205	−2.3%	80	16	0	70	18	0
Japan	127,654	80	92	−3.4%	64	11	0	55	11	0
Australia	19,731	490	502	−0.6%	56	10	18.5	57	10	16
Thailand	62,833	95	114	−4.5%	56	43	0	52	45	0
India	1,065,462	8	6	7.5%	45	43	0	56	44	0
South Korea	47,700	118	108	2.2%	47	17	0	54	13	0
Indonesia	219,883	14	9	11.7%	75	5	0	94	6	0
Pakistan	153,578	24	14	14.4%	26	73	0	25	71	3
Vietnam	81,377	20	15	9.3%	39	34	0	63	36	0
Africa/Middle East (7.8%)										
South Africa	45,026	218	207	1.3%	94	0	0	97	0	0
Saudi Arabia	24,217	270	229	4.2%	15	82	0	24	76	0
Egypt	71,931	61	50	5.1%	48	42	0	60	40	0
Israel	6,433	452	400	3.1%	55	11	0	70	14	0
Morocco	30,566	56	63	−2.9%	87	3	8	96	4	0
North America										
United States	290,809	837	874	−1.1%	44	31	14	44	31	15
Canada	31,510	463	489	−1.4%	38	37	9	39	35	9
Total Worldwide	6,305,252	119	125	−1.2%	51	22	6	53	21	6

Sources: Compiled from *Beverage Digest Fact Book 2005* and *Beverage Digest Fact Book 2001.*

[a] Change calculated using Compounded Annual Growth Rate (CAGR).   [b] Share of worldwide market by volume.

secured a position as the largest international producer of soft drinks. Coke steadily expanded its overseas operations in the following decades, and the name Coca-Cola became synonymous with American culture. By the early 1990s, Coke CEO Roberto Goizueta would note, "Coca-Cola used to be an American company with a large international business. Now we are a large international company with a sizable American business."[106] Roughly 9 million outlets, located in more than 200 countries, sold Coke products in 2004.[107] About 70% of Coke's sales and about 80% of its profits came from outside the United States; only about one-third of Pepsi's beverage sales took place overseas.[108] Coke enjoyed a world market share of 51.4%, compared with 21.8% for Pepsi and 6% for Cadbury Schweppes.[109]

Pepsi entered Europe soon after World War II. Later, benefiting from Arab and Soviet exclusion of Coke, it moved into the Middle East and Soviet bloc. During the 1970s and 1980s, however, Pepsi put relatively little emphasis on its overseas operations. By the early 1990s, the company once again attacked Coke in the latter's core international markets—though with relatively little success, since Coke struck back aggressively. In one high-profile skirmish, Pepsi's longtime bottler in Venezuela defected to Coke in 1996, temporarily reducing Pepsi's 80% share of the cola market there to nearly nothing.[110] Pepsi had moved away from bruising head-to-head competition with Coke by the early 2000s. Instead, it focused on emerging markets that were still up for grabs.[111] In 2004, its international division (which also covered food offerings) grew faster than any other division, and that division's operating profit was up by 25%. Its international beverage volume was up by 12% overall for the year, driven by a strong performance in its Asia Pacific (up 15%) and Europe, Middle East, and Africa (up 14%) divisions. For both CSDs and non-carbs, the company logged double-digit growth overseas, and double-digit growth also marked volume sales in China, India, and Russia.[112]

Both beverage giants encountered obstacles in their international operations, including antitrust regulation, price controls, advertising restrictions, foreign exchange controls, lack of infrastructure, cultural differences, political instability, and local competition. When Coke acquired most of Cadbury Schweppes's international CSD business in 1999, regulators in Europe, Mexico, and Australia barred the transaction from occurring in those markets.[113] In Germany, a

2003 bottle return law (later rescinded) led many retailers to stop carrying Coke and Pepsi products; for Coke, that disruption resulted in a year-over-year sales drop of 11%.[114] In Colombia, Marxist rebels in 2003 killed a local Coke executive in a bombing, while union activists accused the company of collaborating with right-wing death squads.[115] In many Latin American countries, low-cost upstarts like Peru's Kola-Real dented market share or eroded pricing power for the larger companies. In 2003, for example, these "B-brands" claimed 30% of CSD share in Brazil, up from about 3% in the early 1990s.[116]

Waging the cola wars in non-U.S. markets enabled Coke and Pepsi not only to expand revenue, but also to broaden their base of innovation. To cope with immature distribution networks, for example, they created novel systems of their own, such as Coke's network of vending machines in Japan—a high-margin channel that at one point accounted for more than half of the company's Japanese sales.[117] Japan also proved to be an impressive laboratory for new products. Teas, coffees, juices, and flavored water made up the majority of that country's 200-plus Coke items, and Coke's largest-selling product there was not soda but canned coffee. "If you're looking for a total beverage business we've got one in Japan," said Coke CEO Isdell.[118] During the same period, Coke introduced 20 new products with a health or diet emphasis into the Mexico market. New approaches to packaging abounded as well.[119] In China and India, use of small returnable glass bottles allowed Coke to reach poor, rural consumers at a very low price point, while boosting revenue-per-ounce.[120]

The End of an Era?

In the early years of the 21st century, growth in soft drink sales for both Coke and Pepsi was falling short of precedent and of investors' expectations. Was the fundamental nature of the cola wars changing? Was a new form of rivalry emerging that would entail reduced profitability and stagnant growth—both inconceivable under the old form of rivalry? Or did the changes under way represent simply another step forward in the evolution of two of the world's most successful companies? In 2000, a Coke executive noted, "the cola wars are going to be played now across a lot of different battlefields."[121] What remained unclear in 2006 was whether those wars were still about "cola," and whether anyone knew for certain where those battlefields were located.

Appendix A—Cadbury Schweppes: Operations and Financial Performance

By the late 1990s, Cadbury Schweppes had emerged as the clear, albeit distant, third-largest player in the U.S. soft drink industry. Its products accounted for 14.5% of CSDs and 9.3% of non-carbs sold in 2004. Its brands include Dr Pepper, 7UP, RC Cola, Schweppes, Canada Dry, A&W, Squirt, Sundrop, Welch's, Country Time, Clamato, Hawaiian Punch, Snapple, Mistic, and Stewart's.

The U.K.-based firm was born of the 1969 merger between Jacob Schweppes' mineral water business (founded in 1783) and John Cadbury's cocoa and chocolate business (founded in 1842). In the mid-1980s, the group decided to focus on its core international confectionery and soft drink businesses. In 1989, its beverage headquarters relocated from London, England, to Stamford, Connecticut. During the 1980s and the early 1990s, its soft drink and confectionery brand portfolio was extended through the acquisition of a number of key brands, notably Mott's (1982), Canada Dry (1986), Trebor (1989), and Bassett's (1989). Its acquisition of Dr Pepper/Seven-Up Companies in 1995 boosted its U.S. CSD market share from 4.6% in 1994 to 15.1% in 1995, and its acquisition of Triarc's Mistic and Snapple brands in 2001 more than doubled its non-carb market from 6.0% in 1999. Further acquisitions included the Orangina and Yoo-Hoo brands (bought from Pernod Ricard in 2001), Squirt (a top-selling brand in Mexico, purchased in 2002), and Nantucket Nectars (bought in 2002 and folded into the Snapple brand). In 1999, Cadbury Schweppes disposed of its soft drink brands in around 160 countries, concentrating its beverages interests on North America, Europe, and Australia.

In 2004, Cadbury Schweppes operated primarily as a licensor, selling concentrate and syrup to independently owned bottling and canning operations (some of which were affiliated with competitors). It also provided marketing support and technical manufacturing oversight to these companies. In the United States, Cadbury Schweppes had a 40% interest in the Dr Pepper/Seven Up Bottling Group (DPSUBG), which accounted for 28.7% of its CSD volume. With its non-carb products and in certain markets (particularly Mexico), it manufactured and distributed its beverages directly or through third-party bottlers.

TABLE A

Cadbury Schweppes Financial Data ($ millions)

	2004	2003	2002	2001	2000
Americas Beverages					
Sales	$3,854	$3,239	$3,190	$2,770	$1,950
Operating profits/sales	25.2%	29.3%	29.5%	29.7%	32.7%
Europe Beverages[a]					
Sales	$1,253	$1,236	$882	$560	$477
Operating profit/sales	17.9%	17.3%	19.0%	18.2%	15.4%
Consolidated[b]					
Sales	$12,927	$11,500	$8,528	$7,220	$6,161
Operating margin	13.6%	11.6%	17.4%	17.9%	18.9%
Return on assets	5.2%	3.9%	7.0%	7.6%	8.4%

Sources: Company financial reports; OneSource, Global Business Browser, http://globalbb.onesource.com/web/Reports/cia.aspx?KeyID=L5018&Process=CP, accessed November 2005.

[a] Soft drink sales in Asia Pacific; Africa, India, and Middle East; and Central and Other divisions are not reported separately from confectionery sales in those regions.

[b] Consolidated figures include worldwide confectionery sales.

ENDNOTES

1. *Beverage Digest Fact Book 2005*, p. 14.
2. See Exhibit 1 and Exhibit 3 at the end of this case.
3. Roger Enrico, *The Other Guy Blinked and Other Dispatches from the Cola Wars* (Bantam Books, 1988).
4. Robert Tollison, et al., *Competition and Concentration* (Lexington Books, 1991), p. 11.
5. *Beverage Digest Fact Book 2005*, p. 45.
6. Unless otherwise noted, information on industry participants and structures comes from Michael E. Porter (with research associate Rebecca Wayland), "Coca-Cola versus Pepsi-Cola and the Soft Drink Industry," HBS Case No. 391-179 (Harvard Business School Publishing, 1994); Andrew J. Conway, et al., "Global Soft Drink Bottling Review and Outlook: Consolidating the Way to a Stronger Bottling Network" (analysts' report), Morgan Stanley Dean Witter, August 4, 1997; and from casewriter interviews with industry executives.
7. Casewriter conversation with industry insider, April 2006.
8. Ibid.
9. "Cott Begins Shipping from New Fort Worth, Texas Plant," Cott Corporation press release, July 13, 2005; casewriter conversation with industry analyst, November 2005.
10. "Louisiana Coca-Cola Reveals Crown Jewel," *Beverage Industry*, January 1999.
11. Casewriter conversation with industry insider, April 2006.
12. Bonnie Herzog and Daniel Bloomgarden, "Coca-Cola Enterprises" (analysts' report), Salomon Smith Barney, February 19, 2003, pp. 31–32; Bonnie Herzog and Daniel Bloomgarden, "Pepsi Bottling Group" (analysts' report), Salomon Smith Barney, February 24, 2003, pp. 26–27.
13. Timothy Muris, David Scheffman, and Pablo Spiller, *Strategy, Structure, and Antitrust in the Carbonated Soft Drink Industry* (Quorum Books, 1993), p. 63; *Beverage Digest Fact Book 2005*, p. 76.
14. Coca-Cola 2003 Annual Report.
15. Bonnie Herzog, "The Coca-Cola Company" (analyst's report), Credit Suisse First Boston, September 8, 2000, p. 16.
16. Dean Foust, with Geri Smith, "Coke: The Cost of Babying Bottlers," *BusinessWeek*, December 9, 2002, p. 93.
17. Herzog, "The Coca-Cola Company," p. 16.
18. *Beverage Digest Fact Book 2005*, p. 43.
19. Ibid, p. 20.
20. Ibid.
21. Nikhil Deogun and Richard Gibson, "Coke Beats Out Pepsi for Contracts with Burger King, Domino's," *The Wall Street Journal*, April 15, 1999.
22. Casewriter conversation with industry observer, December 2005.
23. "History" section of entry for PepsiCo, Hoover's Online, http://www.hoovers.com, accessed December 2005; *Beverage Digest Fact Book 2005*, p. 62.
24. *Beverage Digest Fact Book 2005*, pp. 62–63.
25. Ibid, p. 63.
26. Casewriter examination of ingredients lists for Coke Classic and Pepsi-Cola, November 2005.
27. Casewriter conversation with industry analyst, January 2006.
28. *Beverage Digest Fact Book 2005*, p. 71.
29. Ibid, p. 74.
30. Unless otherwise attributed, all historical information in this section comes from J.C. Louis and Harvey Yazijian, *The Cola Wars* (Everest House, 1980); Mark Pendergrast, *For God, Country, and Coca-Cola* (Charles Scribner's, 1993); and David Greising, *I'd Like the World to Buy a Coke* (John Wiley & Sons, 1997).
31. Louis and Yazijian, *The Cola Wars*, p. 23.
32. David B. Yoffie, *Judo Strategy* (Harvard Business School Press, 2001), Chapter 1.
33. Pendergrast, *For God, Country, and Coca-Cola*, p. 310.

34. Ibid, p. 323.
35. Timothy K. Smith and Laura Landro, "Coke's Future: Profoundly Changed, Coca-Cola Co. Strives to Keep on Bubbling," *The Wall Street Journal*, April 24, 1986.
36. Timothy Muris, et al., *Strategy, Structure, and Antitrust in the Carbonated Soft Drink Industry*, p. 73.
37. Greising, *I'd Like the World to Buy a Coke*, p. 88.
38. Ibid, p. 292.
39. *Beverage Industry*, January 1999, p. 17.
40. Albert Meyer and Dwight Owsen, "Coca-Cola's Accounting," *Accounting Today*, September 28, 1998; Herzog and Bloomgarden, "Coca-Cola Enterprises," p. 22; Dean Foust, with Nanette Byrnes, "Gone Flat," *BusinessWeek*, December 20, 2004, p. 76.
41. *Beverage Digest Fact Book 2005*, p. 77.
42. Ibid.
43. Ibid, p. 38.
44. Ibid, pp. 90, 93; *Beverage Digest Fact Book 2001*, pp. 77, 80.
45. Foust, with Byrnes, "Gone Flat." On Coca-Cola, see also Andrew Ward, "Coke Gets Real," *Financial Times*, September 25, 2005, p. 17; Michael Santoli, "A New Formula for Coke: How to Put the Fizz Back in the World's Most Famous Brand," *Barron's*, October 4, 2004, p. 21; Betsy Morris, "The Real Story: How Did Coca-Cola's Management Go from First-Rate to Farcical in Six Short Years?" *Fortune*, May 31, 2004, p. 84; Chad Terhune and Betsy McKay, "Bottled Up: Behind Coke's Travails," *The Wall Street Journal*, May 4, 2004, p. A1; Julie Creswell and Julie Schlosser, "Has Coke Lost Its Fizz?" *Fortune*, November 10, 2003, p. 215.
46. Jeremy Grant and Andrew Ward, "A Better Model? Diversified Pepsi Steals Some of Coke's Sparkle," *Financial Times*, February 28, 2005, p. 19. On PepsiCo, see also Patricia Sellers, "The Brand King's Challenge," *Fortune*, April 5, 2004, p. 192; Bethany McLean, "Guess Who's Winning the Cola Wars," *Fortune*, April 2, 2001, p. 164; John A. Byrne, "PepsiCo's New Formula," *BusinessWeek*, April 17, 2000, p. 172.
47. Luisa Dillner, "Mass Hysteria Blamed in Coke Safety Scare," *Chicago Sun-Times*, July 7, 1999, p. 42; Bert Roughton Jr., "Food Scare Put Belgium on Edge," *Atlanta Journal-Constitution*, July 17, 1999, p. D1; "Coca-Cola Recalls Bottles of Drink Sold in Belgium," *The Wall Street Journal*, May 21, 2001, p. B11.
48. Claudia H. Deutsch, "Coca-Cola Reaches into Past for New Chief," *The New York Times*, May 5, 2004, p. 1.
49. Amy Waldman, "India Tries to Contain Tempest over Soft Drink Safety," *The New York Times*, August 23, 2003, p. 3; Terhune and McKay, "Bottled Up: Behind Coke's Travails."
50. Creswell and Schlosser, "Has Coke Lost Its Fizz?"; Betsy McKay and Chad Terhune, "Coca-Cola Settles Regulatory Probe," *The Wall Street Journal*, April 19, 2005, p. A3.
51. Foust, with Byrnes, "Gone Flat"; Morris, "The Real Story."
52. Theresa Howard, "Coke CEO Takes Open Approach to Problems," *USA Today*, September 29, 2004, p. B3.
53. Foust, with Byrnes, "Gone Flat."
54. Chad Terhune, "CEO Says Things Aren't Going Better with Coke," *The Wall Street Journal*, September 16, 2004, p. A1; Renee Pas, "The Top 100 Beverage Companies," *Beverage Industry*, June 1, 2005, p. 38
55. Barbara Murray, "PepsiCo, Inc.," Hoover's Online, http://www.hoovers.com, accessed November 2005; Nanette Byrnes, "The Power of Two at Pepsi," *BusinessWeek*, January 29, 2001, p. 102.
56. Theresa Howard, "Deal Puts Reinemund on the Fast Track," *USA Today*, December 5, 2000, p. B3.
57. Betsy McKay, "Pucker Up! Pepsi's Latest Weapon Is Lemon-Lime," *The Wall Street Journal*, October 2000, p. B1; Greg Winter, "PepsiCo Looks to a New Drink to Jolt Soda Sales," *The New York Times*, May 1, 2001, p. C1; McLean, "Guess Who's Winning the Cola Wars."
58. Grant and Ward, "A Better Model?"

59. "Historical Financials" section of entries for both Coca-Cola and PepsiCo, Hoover's Online, http://www.hoovers.com, accessed December 2005; Foust, with Byrnes, "Gone Flat"; Grant and Ward, "A Better Model?"

60. Sellers, "The Brand King's Challenge."

61. Foust, with Byrnes, "Gone Flat."

62. Caroline Wilbert, "Coke CEO Neville Isdell: Boss Confident About Strategy," *The Atlanta Journal-Constitution*, November 13, 2005, p. D1.

63. Chad Terhune, "In Switch, Pepsi Makes Diet Cola Its New Flagship," *The Wall Street Journal*, March 16, 2005, p. B1.

64. Rosie Mestel, "Soft Drink, Soda, Pop: Whatever You Call Them, These Sugar Drinks Are Getting Nutritional Heat," *The Evansville Courier*, September 26, 2005, p. D1; Scott Leith, "Obesity Weighs Heavily on Colas," *The Atlanta Journal-Constitution*, February 6, 2005, p. C1; Raja Mishra, "In Battle of Bulge, Soda Firms Defend Against Warning," *The Boston Globe*, November 28, 2004, p. A1.

65. Jeff Cioletti, "Weathering the Perfect Storm," *Beverage Aisle*, April 15, 2004, p. 23.

66. Melanie Warner, "Lines Are Drawn for Big Suit Over Sodas," *The New York Times*, December 7, 2005, p. C1.

67. Betsy McKay, "Soda Marketers Will Cut Back Sales to US Schools," *The Wall Street Journal*, August 17, 2005, p. B1.

68. Ward, "Coke Gets Real."

69. *Beverage Digest Fact Book 2005*, p. 51.

70. Stuart Elliott, "What's in a Name? Higher Sales, or That's the Hope of Some Soft Drink Makers Excising the Word 'Diet,'" *The New York Times*, December 20, 2004, p. C9; Scott Leith, "Refining Diet Drinks: Fewer Men Equate 'Low-Cal' with 'Girly,'" *The Atlanta Journal-Constitution*, February 16, 2005, p. C1.

71. *Beverage Digest Fact Book 2005*, p. 11; *Beverage Digest Fact Book 2001*, p. 11.

72. Herzog and Bloomgarden, "Coca-Cola Enterprises," pp. 36–37.

73. Grant and Ward, "A Better Model?"

74. Joanna Cosgrove, "The 2005 Soft Drink Report," *Beverage Industry*, March 2005, p. 22; Melanie Wells, "Pepsi's New Challenge," *Forbes*, January 10, 2003, p. 68; Grant and Ward, "A Better Model?"

75. *Beverage Digest Fact Book 2005*, pp. 104, 109, 184–195.

76. Scott Leith, "Coke Just So-So in Small Brands: Record Less Than Stellar in Noncarbonated Category," *The Atlanta Journal-Constitution*, June 13, 2004, p. G1.

77. Terhune and McKay, "Bottled Up: Behind Coke's Travails"; Leith, "Coke Just So-So in Small Brands"; Alan R. Elliott, "Energy Drinks Fuel Soda Field," *Investor's Business Daily*, May 23, 2005, p. A11.

78. Terhune, "CEO Says Things Aren't Going Better with Coke."

79. Grant and Ward, "A Better Model?"

80. *Beverage Digest Fact Book 2005*, pp. 116–118.

81. Ibid, p. 118; Chad Terhune, "Coke to Buy Danone's Stake in Bottled-Water Joint Venture," *The Wall Street Journal*, April 25, 2005, p. B4; Barbara Murray, "The Coca-Cola Company," Hoover's Online, http://www.hoovers.com, accessed November 2005.

82. Foust, with Byrnes, "Gone Flat"; Bonnie Herzog and Bloomgarden, "Pepsi Bottling Group," p. 23.

83. Santoli, "A New Formula for Coke."

84. Herzog and Bloomgarden, "Coca-Cola Enterprises," p. 17.

85. Casewriter conversation with industry insider, April 2006.

86. Scott Leith, "Coke, Bottler Work on Plan to Align Goals," *The Atlanta Journal-Constitution*, December 5, 2003, p. C1; Chad Terhune and Betsy McKay, "Coke Shelves Initiative of Ex-Chief," *The Wall Street Journal*, September 28, 2004, p. A3.

87. Chad Terhune, "Coke Bottler in Mexico Threatens to Cut Marketing," *The Wall Street Journal*, November 1, 2005, p. B5.

88. Herzog and Bloomgarden, "Pepsi Bottling Group," pp. 18, 20, 26.

89. *Beverage Digest Fact Book 2005*, pp. 66–68.

90. Herzog and Bloomgarden, "Pepsi Bottling Group," pp. 23–25.

91. Herzog and Bloomgarden, "Coca-Cola Enterprises," pp. 33–34; Richard Joy, "Foods and Nonalcoholic Beverages" (industry survey), Standard & Poor's, June 9, 2005, pp. 11–12.

92. Casewriter conversation with industry insider, April 2006.

93. Melanie Warner, "Making Room on Coke's Shelf Space," *The New York Times*, April 5, 2005, p. C1.

94. Chad Terhune, "Coke Readies New Ads to Boost Its Soda Sales," *The Wall Street Journal*, December 8, 2005, p. A3.

95. Scott Leith, "Designing the Next Big (or Small) Thing," *The Atlanta Journal-Constitution*, September 27, 2003, p. B1; "Fridge Packs Appear to Be Plus for Coke System," *Beverage Digest*, March 28, 2003, http://www.beverage-digest.com/editorial/030328.php, accessed December 2005.

96. "CSDs Have Most—and Proliferating—SKU's, but Number Is Small Relative to Volume," *Beverage Digest*, November 22, 2002, http://www.beverage-digest.com/editorial/021122.php, accessed December 2005; casewriter communication with industry analyst, November 2005.

97. Casewriter conversation with industry insider, April 2006.

98. Ward, "Coke Gets Real"; casewriter communication with industry analyst, November 2005.

99. Ward, "Coke Gets Real."

100. Sherri Day, "Summer May Bring a Bottled Water Price War," *The New York Times*, May 10, 2003, p. C1.

101. Betsy McKay, "Liquid Assets: In a Water Fight, Coke and Pepsi Try Opposite Tacks," *The Wall Street Journal*, April 18, 2002, p. A1.

102. Casewriter conversation with industry insider, April 2006.

103. "Water: Supermarkets Account for 50+% of Volume, Morgan Stanley Study Finds Low Brand Loyalty," *Beverage Digest*, June 7, 2002, http://www.beverage-digest.com/editorial/020607.php, accessed December 2005.

104. *Beverage Digest Fact Book 2005*, pp. 90–91.

105. Ibid, pp. 92–93.

106. John Huey, "The World's Best Brand," *Fortune*, May 31, 1993.

107. Paul Klebnikov, "Coke's Sinful World," *Forbes*, December 22, 2003, p. 86.

108. Ward, "Coke Gets Real."

109. *Beverage Digest Fact Book 2005*, p. 90.

110. Nikhil Deogun, "Burst Bubbles: Aggressive Push Abroad Dilutes Coke's Strength As Big Markets Stumble," *The Wall Street Journal*, February 8, 1999, p. A1.

111. Grant and Ward, "A Better Model?"

112. PepsiCo 2004 Annual Report, p. 60.

113. *Beverage Digest Fact Book 2005*, p. 90.

114. James Kanter, "European Court Sides with Coke Against Germany," *The Wall Street Journal*, December 15, 2004, p. 18.

115. Klebnikov, "Coke's Sinful World."

116. David Luhnow and Chad Terhune, "Latin Pop: A Low-Budget Cola Shakes Up Markets South of the Border," *The Wall Street Journal*, October 27, 2003, p. A1.

117. June Preston, "Things May Go Better for Coke amid Asia Crisis, Singapore Bottler Says," *Journal of Commerce*, June 29, 1998, p. A3.

118. Creswell and Schlosser, "Has Coke Lost Its Fizz?"; Ward, "Coke Gets Real."

119. Caroline Wilbert and Shelley Emling, "Obesity Weighs on Coke," *Atlanta Journal-Constitution*, October 27, 2005, p. A1.

120. Leslie Chang, Chad Terhune, and Betsy McKay, "As Global Growth Ebbs, Coke Makes Rural Push into China and India," *The Asian Wall Street Journal*, August 11, 2004, p. A1.

121. Betsy McKay, "Juiced Up: Pepsi Edges Past Coke, and It Has Nothing to Do with Cola," *The Wall Street Journal*, November 6, 2000, p. A1.

Staples

It was 1985, and a thirty-six-year-old retailer named Tom Stemberg was being interviewed by the CEO of the Dutch-based warehouse club, Makro, for the top job at Makro's nascent U.S. operation. Stemberg didn't think Makro's concept would work in the United States, but he was struck by one thing as he toured Makro's first U.S. store in Langhorne, Pennsylvania: Office supplies were flying off the shelves. "It was obvious that this merchandise was moving very fast," he later recalled, "That aisle (where the office supplies were located) was just devastated."[1] Stemberg began to wonder whether an office supplies supermarket would be a viable concept. He thought it might be possible that a supermarket selling just office supplies could do to the office supplies business what Toys "R" Us had done to the fragmented toy retailing industry: consolidate it and create enormous economic value in the process.

Within a year Stemberg had founded Staples, the first office supplies supermarket. Twenty years later, Staples was a leading retailer in the office supplies business with 1,800 stores in the United States and Canada, and another 250 in Europe. Its revenues for 2006 were forecast to exceeded $17.8 billion, net profit was over $950 million, the company had earned a return on invested capital of between 12.6% and 18.5% for the last six years (which is considered high for retailing), and the company generated $2 billion in free cash flow during the prior three years.[2]

The Founding of Staples

Tom Stemberg

Despite his young age, by 1985 Stemberg had assembled an impressive resume in retailing. Stemberg had been born in Los Angeles but spent much of his teens in Austria, where his parents were originally from. He moved back to the United States to enter Harvard University, ultimately graduating with an MBA from Harvard Business School in 1973. Stemberg was hired out of Harvard by the Jewel Corp., which put him to work at Star Market, the company's supermarket grocery division in the Boston area.

Henry Nasella, Stemberg's first boss at Jewel, who would later work for Stemberg at Staples, remembers meeting Stemberg on his first day at Jewel: "He came in 15 minutes late, his hair too long, his tie over his shoulder, his shirt hanging out over the back of his pants. I thought, what in the world do I have here?"[3] (Stemberg is still known for his disheveled appearance.) What he had was a man who started out on the store floor, bagging groceries, stocking the aisle, and ringing up sales at the checkout counter. Stemberg rose rapidly, however, and by the time he was twenty-eight he had been named vice president of sales and marketing at Star Market, the youngest VP in the history of the Jewel Corp.

At Jewel, Stemberg became known as an aggressive marketer, competing vigorously on price and introducing generic brands (Stemberg developed and launched the first line of "generic" foods sold in the country).[4] According to Stemberg, "It was a nutso thing we were trying to do, and the fact that it worked out well was a miracle. We opened all these big stores, and we were trying to take market share away from people who were much better financed than we were. They retaliated and lowered prices. . . . I learnt to experience the challenges of rapid growth. There was no better experience to have been through. It taught me the necessity of having infrastructure and putting it in place."[5]

One of the supermarkets that Stemberg found himself battling with was Heartland Food Warehouse, the first successful deep discount warehouse supermarket in the country. Heartland was run by Leo Kahn, one of the country's leading supermarket retailers. Kahn had started the Purity Supreme supermarket chain in the late 1940s, making him one of the founding fathers of the supermarket business. Stemberg and Kahn fought relentless marketing battles with each other. In a typical example of their tussles, at one point Kahn ran ads guaranteeing that his customers would get the best price on Thanksgiving turkeys. Stemberg responded with his own ads promising that Star would match the lowest advertised price on turkeys. Technically that made Kahn's claim incorrect, a point that Stemberg made to the Massachusetts attorney general's office, which told Kahn to pull his ad.

In 1982 Stemberg left Jewel to run the grocery division of another retailer, First National Supermarkets Inc. To build market share, he decided to take the company into the warehouse food business, imitating Leo Kahn's Heartland chain. Stemberg soon came into conflict with the CEO at First National. As he later admitted, "I probably didn't do a very good job, in a corporate political sense, of making sure he understood the risks in what we were trying to do. The situation was very stressful."[6] In January 1985, things came to a head and Stemberg was fired. It was probably the best thing that ever happened to him.

When Kahn heard that Stemberg had been fired, he quickly got in touch with him. Kahn had just sold his own business for $80 million, and he was looking for investment opportunities. He had developed a great respect for his old adversary, and wanted to back him in a new retailing venture. As Stemberg paraphrases it, Kahn said, "I want to back you in a business, kid, what have you got in mind?"[7] Kahn agreed to put up $500,000 in seed money to help Stemberg develop a new venture opportunity. He also took on the role of mentor, evaluating Stemberg's ideas.

Initially Kahn and Stemberg looked at the business they both knew best, supermarket grocery retailing. But they were put off by the intense competition now raging in the business, and the high price they would have to pay for properties. At this juncture, Bob Nakasone, then president of Toys "R" Us, stepped into the picture. Nakasone had worked at Jewel alongside Stemberg before moving to Toys "R" Us. It was Nakasone who urged Stemberg to "think outside of the food box." Nakasone told Stemberg that there were more similarities than differences across product categories, and that profit margins were much better outside of the grocery business.

While mulling over possible entrepreneurial opportunities, Stemberg continued to explore other options, including working for an established retailer. It was this parallel search that took him down to Makro for a job interview, and it was there that he suddenly realized there was a possible opportunity to be had in starting the Toys "R" Us of office supplies.

Stemberg's Insight

Hot on the heels of his trip to Makro, Stemberg started to think about his idea. The first thing was to get a handle on the nature of the market. Stemberg started by asking people if they knew how much they spent on office supplies. In his words: "There was this lawyer I knew in Hartford, which is where I lived then. If ever there was a cheap bastard in this world, he was a cheap bastard. And I said, 'Gee, how much do you spend on office supplies?' He said, "Oh, I don't know, I guess about a couple of hundred bucks a person, 40 people in the office, I bet you we spend ten grand.' I said, 'Do me a favor will you? You've got good records. Go through your records and tell me exactly how much you spend: he calls me up the next day.' 'Son of a bitch, I spend $1,000 apiece! But I'm getting a discount, I'm paying 10% of list.' I said, 'Toys "R" Us' is paying 60% of list.' He says, 'Are you kidding me? You mean I could save like half? I could save like twelve grand?' In his mind, this is the payment on his new Jaguar."[8]

Stemberg began to think that this idea had some potential. He reasoned that people want to save money, and in this case the money they could save might be substantial, but they didn't even know they were paying too much. Small businesses in particular, he thought, might be a viable target market. While working on the idea, the printer ribbon on Stemberg's printer ran out. It was a weekend. He drove down to the local office supply store in Hartford, and it was closed. He went to another, but that was also closed. He ended up going to BJ's Wholesale Club, a deep discount warehouse club. BJ's was open, they sold office supplies at low prices, but the selection was limited and they didn't carry the type of ribbon Stemberg wanted. Stemberg immediately saw the opportunity.

Around the same time, Stemberg went to see another mentor of his, Walter Salmon, who taught retailing at Harvard Business School. Over lunch they discussed the supermarket business and Stemberg's quest. Salmon asked Stemberg if he had thought of applying his retailing skills to a product category that was growing faster than the grocery business and was not well served by modern retailers. Stemberg replied that he had been thinking about office supplies. Salmon's response, "Gee, this is a really big idea."

Scoping Out the Opportunity

Stemberg ended up hiring a former teaching assistant of Salmon's for $20,000 to do some basic market research on the industry and validate the market. As he tells the story: "I never forget the night I went to her house and we went through the slide deck. I always want to jump ahead. And she puts her hand on my hand and says, 'Wait, we will walk though it.' She's teasing us! Finally she said it was a $45 billion market growing at 15% per year. And it turns out she was lying. That was actually at the manufacturer level. It was actually more than $100 billion already if you looked at retail. She confirmed that the pricing umbrellas were as big as we thought they were, and that small businesses were getting raped the way we had said they were. I was pretty damn excited during the long drive home."[9]

The market growth, it turned out, was being driven by some favorable demographic trends. The U.S. economy was recovering from the recessions of the late 1970s and early 1980s, and underlying economic growth was strong. A wave of new technology was finding its way into U.S. businesses, including personal computers, printers, faxes, and small copiers, and this was driving demand for office supplies including basic equipment along with consumables from paper and printer ink, to diskettes and copy toner.

The wave of downsizing that had swept corporate America in the early 1980s also had a beneficial side effect—unemployed people were starting their own businesses. The rate of new business formation was the highest in years. There were 11 million small businesses in the country, Stemberg's proposed target market, the vast majority of which had less than twenty employees. This sector was the engine of job growth in the economy—between 1980 and 1986 small enterprises had been responsible for a net increase of 10.5 million jobs. Many of these new jobs were in the service sector, which was a big consumer of office supplies. Each new white-collar job meant another $1,000 a year in office supplies.

Stemberg's research started to uncover an industry that was highly fragmented at the retail level, but had some huge participants. Upstream in the value chain were the manufacturers. This was a very diverse collection of companies that included paper manufacturers such as Boise Cascade; office furniture makers; manufacturers of pencils, pens, and markers such as the Bic Corp.; companies like 3M, which supplied Post-it Notes and a whole lot more besides; office equipment companies such as Xerox and Canon (manufacturers of copiers and consumables); and manufacturers of personal computers, printers, and faxes such as Apple, Compaq, and Hewlett-Packard.

Then there were the wholesalers, some of which were very large such as United Stationers and McKesson. The wholesalers bought in bulk and sold to business clients and smaller retail establishments, either directly or through a network of dealers. The dealers often visited businesses to collect orders and arranged for delivery. The dealers themselves ranged in scale from small one-person enterprises to large firms that sold through central warehouses. Some dealers also had a retail presence, while other did not. Manufacturers and wholesalers also sold directly to large business through catalogs or a direct sales presence.

The retailers fell into two main categories. There were the local office supply retailers, generally small business themselves, and there were the general merchandise discounters, such as BJ's Wholesale and Wal-Mart. The smaller retailers had an intrinsically high cost structure. They were full-service retailers who purchased in small lots and delivered in trucks or sold out of the store. The general merchandise discounters purchased from wholesalers or direct from manufacturers, and their prices were much lower, but they did not carry a wide range of product.

On the consumer side, most large businesses had dedicated personnel for purchasing office supplies. They either bought from dealers, who purchased directly from manufacturers or through wholesalers, or bought direct from the manufacturer themselves. Large firms were able to negotiate on price and received discounts that could be as large as 80% of the list price on some items. Businesses of fewer than one hundred people did not generally have someone dedicated to managing office supplies, and they tended to rely primarily on dealers. For these companies, product availability, not price, was viewed as key. In even smaller firms, it was the convenience of being able to get office supplies that seemed to matter more than anything else.

Consistent with his initial insight, Stemberg found that smaller firms were ignored by the big dealers. To verify this he called Boise Cascade, which operated as both a dealer and a manufacturer, to see what service they might offer. First he called on behalf of Ivy Satellite Network, a small company that Stemberg owned that broadcast events of Ivy League schools to alumni around the world. Boise couldn't even be bothered to send a catalog to this company. Then he called Boise back, this time representing the one-hundred-person office of a friend of his who was a food broker. This time Boise was happy to send a representative to the food broker. The representative offered the broker deep discounts. A Bic pen from Boise that cost Ivy $3.68 from the local stationary store was offered for just $0.85. More generally, Stemberg found that while an office manager in a company with more than one thousand employees could often obtain discounts averaging 50% from dealers, small businesses with fewer than twenty employees were lucky to get a 10% discount, and often had to pay full price.[10]

Stemberg also found a study produced by researchers at the Wharton School that seemed to confirm his suspicions. "Essentially they first asked dealers, 'What does the customer want?' Ninety percent of the dealers said, 'Better service' and 10% said, 'Other.' Then they asked customers, and 90% of the customers said what they really wanted was lower prices. Ha! The dealers were totally out of touch. They were making 40% to 50%, the wholesalers were making 30%, and the manufacturers were making huge margins. Everybody's rich, fat, and happy, and they're all going, 'What's wrong with this?'"[11]

Creating the Company

Stemberg know from experience that for Staples to succeed it would have to execute well, and do to that, it needed experienced management. Stemberg turned to people he knew, managers who, like him, had risen quickly through the ranks at the Jewel Corp. or other Boston area retailers. From Jewel came Myra Hart,

who was to become Staples's group vice president for growth and development; Todd Krasnow, who became vice president for marketing; Paul Korian, the Staples vice president of merchandising; and Henry Nasella, Stemberg's mentor at Star Market who subsequently became president of Staples. The CFO was Bob Leombruno, who had bought Mammoth Mart, a failed retail operation, out of bankruptcy for a group of investors. Stemberg took on the CEO role, while Kahn became chairman. Most of these people started working full time on January 1, 1986. They gave up secure jobs, high salaries, and annual bonuses for salary cuts, loss of bonuses, and fourteen-hour days.

According to Stemberg, the pitch to prospective managers was this: "I'm going to give you a big chunk of stock in this thing. This is your chance. We're all going to work our tails off. We're going to work crazy hours. But here you'll be part of a retailing revolution. If you own 2% of the company and it gets to be worth $100 million, you're going to make $2 million."[12] In the end, each member of the top management team got a 2.5% stake in the company.

By now Stemberg had a name for this nascent company, Staples. Reflecting on how it came about years later, he noted that "I'm driving between Hartford and Boston. I'm thinking about names. Pencils? Pens? 8½ by 11? Staples? Staples! Staples the Office Superstore. That was it. The bad thing about the name was that when we started out, we had to explain to everybody what it was. Office Depot basically copied Home Depot and put the 'office' in front. It was Home Depot for the office, and it lived off the Home Depot name. Office Club was a Price Club for the office. It lived off the Price Club name. In the early days ours was actually a problem. But those other names aren't a brand. Ours is a brand."[13]

With the management team in place, the next steps were to refine the concept and raise capital. The concept itself was relatively straightforward; implementing it would not be. The plan was to offer a wide selection of merchandise in a warehouse-type setting with prices deeply discounted from those found in mom-and-pop retailers. Because it was to be a supermarket, the idea was to move from full service to a self-service format. At the same time, the management team recognized the staff would need to be trained in office supplies so that they could provide advice when asked.

To make the concept viable, a number of issues had to be dealt with. They had to decide where to locate the stores. How big a population base would be needed to support a store? What kind of selection was required? How many Stock Keeping Units (SKUs) should the store offer? There was the problem of educating customers. If potential customers currently didn't know that they were paying excessive prices for office supplies and consistently underestimated how much they spent on the category, what could Staples do to change this?

To get low prices, Staples would need to cut costs to the bone and be managed very efficiently. They would have to get manufacturers or wholesalers to deliver directly to Staples. How could this be done? Wouldn't wholesalers and manufacturers create channel conflict with dealers and established retailers by delivering straight to Staples? How was this to be resolved? Staples also needed to minimize its inventory, thereby reducing its working capital needs. Management knew that if they could turn inventory over twelve times a year and delay payment to vendors for thirty days, then vendors would essentially finance Staples's inventory. Pulling that off would require state-of-the-art information systems, and the state of the art at the time in office supplies did not include bar coding on individual items. How was Staples to deal with this?

There was also the potential competition to worry about. Stemberg was sure that once Staples unveiled its concept, others would follow quickly. To preempt competitors, the plan called for rapid rollout of the concept, with sales ramping up from nothing to $42 million after three years. This would require a lot of capital. It also required that the concept be very easy to replicate so that once the first store was opened, others could be opened in quick succession. This meant that the systems that were put in place for the first store had to be the right ones and able to support rapid expansion. There wasn't much room for error here.

As the management team refined the concept, they came to the realization that the information systems were one of the keys to the entire venture. With the right information systems in place, Staples could track sales and inventory closely at the level of individual items, figure out its gross profit on each item sold, and adjust its merchandising mix accordingly. This would be a departure from existing retailers, the majority of whom lacked the ability to calculate profit on each item sold and could calculate only the average gross profit across a range of items. The right information systems could also be used to collect data on customers at the point of sales, and this would assist greatly in market research and direct marketing to customers.

On the other hand, raising capital proved to be easier than they thought. Stemberg valued Staples, which was still little more than a concept, a management team, and a business plan full of unanswered questions at $8 million. He went looking for $4 million, which he would exchange for 50% of the company. The venture capitalists were initially reluctant. They seemed to hold back, waiting to see who would commit first. They valued Staples at $6 million and wanted a 67% stake for the $4 million in first-round financing. Stemberg balked at that and instead focused his efforts on one firm that seemed more willing to break away from the pack. The firm was Bain Venture Capital, whose managing general partner, Mitt Romney, later observed that "a lot of retailing startups come by, but a lot of them are a twist on an old theme, or a better presentation. . . . Stemberg wasn't proposing just a chain of stores, but an entirely new retailing category. That really captures your attention. It slaps you in the face with the idea that this could be big."[14]

To validate the business concept, Romney's firm surveyed one hundred small businesses after being urged to do so by Stemberg. Auditing invoices from these companies for office supplies, Romney discovered what Stemberg already knew—the companies were spending about twice what they estimated. Romney then ran the numbers on his own company and found that his firm would save $117,000 a year by purchasing supplies at the discount that Stemberg promised. That was enough for Romney, and he committed to investing. Others followed, and Staples raised $4.5 million in its first round of financing, which closed on January 23, 1986. This gave the company enough capital to go ahead with the first store. In return for the financing, Staples had to give the VCs a 54% stake in the company. To get the money, however, Staples had to commit to opening its first store on May 1, 1986, and to meet a plan for rolling out additional stores as quickly as possible.

The First Store

With just four months to open their first store, the management team went into overdrive. They would meet every morning at about 7 A.M. in a session that could run from thirty minutes to two hours. Someone would rush out to get sandwiches for lunch, and they would keep working. The workday came to a close at 9:00 P.M. or 10:00 P.M. Not only was there no template for what they were doing, they knew they had to put a system in place that would allow them to quickly roll out additional stores.

One of the most difficult tasks fell on the shoulders of Leombruno, the CFO. In addition to setting up an accounting system, he was put in charge of installing the entire information system for Staples. The system had to be able to track customer purchases so that Staples could reorder products. The cash registers, which were to be connected individually to the system, had to be easy to operate so that there would be no congestion at the checkout stands. Stemberg himself was adamant that the register receipts indicate the list price of each item, as well as a much lower Staples price, and an even lower price for customers who became Staples members. He also wanted the system to collect detailed demographics on each customer.

Leombruno insisted that the system be able to do two things: first, calculate the gross profit margin Staples made on each item sold. Most retailers at the time could calculate only the average profit margin across the mix of inventory. Second, Leombruno wanted to make sure that inventory turned over at least twelve times a year, and good information systems were the key to that. With most vendors requiring payment in thirty days, an inventory turnover of greater than twelve would allow Staples to cut its working capital requirements.

As the wish list for the information systems grew, it soon became apparent that it would not be possible to do everything in the allotted time span. No existing software package did what the management team wanted, and they had to hire consultants to customize existing packages. In the end, several proposed features were dropped. However, at Stemberg's insistence, the three-way price requirements remained. To track sales and inventory levels, Staples assigned a six-digit look-up code for each item. While entering the codes was a slower process than scanning items, most manufacturers in the office supplies business were still not marking their products with bar codes, which meant scanning was not feasible.

Another problem was to get suppliers to ship products to the first Staples store. The company was asking suppliers to bypass the existing distribution system and risk alienating long-time customers in the established channel of distribution. To get suppliers on board, Staples used a number of tactics. One was a visionary pitch. The company told suppliers that it was out to revolutionize the retail end of the industry. Staples would be very big, they said, and it was in the best interests of the suppliers to back the start-up. Stemberg's punch line was simple: "I'm going to be very loyal to those who stick their necks out for us. But it's going to cost you a lot more to get in later."[15] Connections also helped to get suppliers to deliver to Staples. One of the VC backers of Staples, Bessemer Venture Partners, also owned a paper manufacturer, Ampad. Bessemer told Ampad to start selling to Staples, which it did, even though existing distributors complained bitterly about the arrangement.

Finding real estate also presented a problem. As an enterprise with no proven track record, Staples found it difficult to rent decent real estate large enough to stock and display the 5,000 SKUs that it was planning for its first store, and to do so at a decent price. Most landlords wanted sky-high rent from Staples. In the end, the best that Staples could do was a site in Brighton, Massachusetts, that was within site of a housing project and had failed as a site for several different retailers. The one redeeming feature of the site was that it was smack in the middle of a high concentration of small businesses.

Despite all of the problems, Staples was able to open its first store on May 1, 1986. The opening day was busy, but only because everybody who worked at Staples had invited everybody they knew. On the second day, just sixteen people came through the store. On the third day, it was the same number. A few weeks of this, and Staples would have to shut its doors. Desperate, Krasnow decided to bribe customers to get them into the store. The company sent $25 to each of thirty-five office managers, inviting them to shop in the store and pass along their reactions. According to Krasnow, "A week later we called them back. They had all taken the money, but none of them had come into the store. I was apoplectic."[16] In the end, nine of them finally came in, and they gave Staples rave reviews. Slowly the momentum started to build, and by August lines were starting to form at the cash registers at lunch time.

The 1990s: Growth, Competition, and Consolidation

Growth

Staples had set of target of $4 million in first year sales from its Brighton store, but within a few months the numbers were tracking up toward a $6 million annual run rate. The concept was starting to work. The number of customers coming through the door every month was growing, but it was not only customers who were coming. One day Joe Antonini, the CEO of Kmart, was spotted walking around the Staples store. Around the same time, Stemberg heard from contacts that Staples had been mentioned at a Wal-Mart board meeting. He realized that if other discount retailers were noticing Staples when it had just one store, competition could not be far behind.

Within five months of the opening of the first Staples store, a clone had appeared in the Southeast: Office Depot. Needing money fast to fund expansion and lock in Staples territory, Stemberg went back to the venture capitalists. While the initial backers were willing to value Staples at only $15 million, Stemberg held out for and got a valuation of $22 million, raising another $14 million. He pulled off this trick by finding institutional investors who were willing to invest on a valuation of $22 million. He then went back to the original VCs and told them that the deal was closing fast, which persuaded them to commit.

By May 1987, Staples had three stores open and planed to increase the number to twenty by the end of 1988 (it actually opened twenty-two). Sales were running at anywhere from $300 to $800 per square foot. In contrast, high-volume discount stores were lucky to get $300 per square foot. By mid-1989, three years after its first store opened, Staples had twenty-seven stores open in the Northeast and an annual sales run rate of $120 million, way above the original three-year target of $42 million. The stores now averaged 15,000 square feet and stocked 5,000 items.

Explaining the success, Stemberg noted: "From a value perspective, I think there is no question that we have been a friend to the entrepreneur. If you look at the average small town merchant, we've lowered the costs of his office products—where he was once paying say $4,000 to $5,000 a year, now he's paying $2,000 or $3,000. We've made him more efficient."[17]

Helping to drive sales growth was the development of a direct marketing pitch. Every time Staples opened a store, it purchased a list of small businesses within fifteen minutes' driving distance. Then a group of telemarketers would go to work, calling up the buyer of office supplies at the businesses. The telemarketers would tell them Staples was opening up a store like Toys "R" Us for office supplies, ask them how much they spent on office supplies every year (often they did not know), cite typical cost savings at small businesses, and send them a coupon for a free item such as copy paper. Slowly at first the customers would come in, but momentum would build up as customers realized the scale of the savings they were getting.

Every time a customer redeemed a coupon at a store, they were given a free Staples Card. This "membership" card entitled cardholders to even deeper discounts on select items. The card quickly became the lynchpin of Staples's direct marketing effort. From the card application, Staples gathered information about the customer—what type of business it was in, how many employees it had, where it was located. This information was entered into a customer database, and every time a card member used that card, the card number and purchases were logged into the database via the cash register. This gave Staples up-to-date information about what was being purchased and by whom. This information then allowed Staples to target promotions at certain customer groups—for example, card members who were not making purchases. The goal was to get existing customers to spend more at Staples, a goal that over time was attained.

Because Staples started to reach so many of its customers through direct marketing, (about 80% of its sales were made to cardholders) it was able to spend less on media ads—in some areas, it dropped media advertising altogether, saving on costs. This was an important source of cost savings in the Northeast where the media is expensive.

A problem that continued to bedevil Staples as it expanded was the shortage of good real estate locations that could be rented at a reasonable price, particularly in the Northeast. Finding a good site in the early days required flexibility; at various times Staples converted anything and everything, from restaurants to massage parlors, into Staples stores. As the company grew, its real estate strategy started to take a defensive aspect, with Staples bidding for prime sites in order to preempt competitors.

The high cost of real estate in the Northeast led Staples to establish its first distribution center in 1987 (today it has some thirty such centers in North America). This decision was hotly debated within the company and opposed by some of the investors who thought that the capital should be used to build more stores, but Stemberg prevailed. The distribution center was located off an interstate highway in an area of rural Connecticut where land was cheap. The facility cost $6 million to build and tied up a total of $10 million in working capital, almost $0.29 out of every dollar that the company had raised to that point. But Stemberg saw this as a necessary step. The inventory storage capacity at the distribution center enabled the company to operate with smaller stores than many of its rivals, but still offer the same variety of goods. By 1989 the average Staples store was 35% smaller than the Office Depot outlets that were then opening up all over the Southeast, saving on real estate costs. The distribution center also helped save labor costs since wages are lower in rural areas. Equally important, inventory storage at the distribution centers allowed the stores to remain fully stocked. As Stemberg noted: "In competition with the clones, it will come down to who has the lowest costs and the best in stock position."[18]

The expansion strategy at Staples was very methodical. Stores were clustered together in a region, even to the extent that they cannibalized each other on the margin, so that Staples could become the dominant supplier in that market. The early focus was on major metropolitan areas such as Boston, New York, Philadelphia, and Los Angeles. Although high real estate and labor costs in these areas were a disadvantage, strong demand from local businesses helped compensate, as did the distribution centers. In 1990, Staples opened its second distribution center in California to support expansion there.

The expansion at Staples was fueled by the proceeds from a 1989 initial public offering, which raised $61.7 million of capital—enough for Staples to accelerate its store openings. By mid-1991, Staples's store count passed over one hundred.

Competition

A rash of imitators to Staples soon appeared on the market. The first of these was Office Depot, focused on the Southeast. By the end of 1988, Office Depot had twenty-six stores, Office Club had opened fifteen, Biz Mart had established ten, and Office Max around a dozen. More than a dozen other office supplies superstores had sprung up. Some of these businesses were financed by venture capitalists looking to repeat the success with Staples; other were financed by established retailers, or even started by them. For example, Ben Franklin started Office Station in 1987, but shut it down in 1989 as it failed to gain traction.

Initially, most of the competitors focused in unique regions—Office Depot on the Southeast, Office Club on California, Office Max on the Midwest,

BizMart on the Southwest—but as the number of entrants increased, head-to-head competition started to become more frequent. Stemberg's belief had always been that competition was inevitable and that the winners in the competitive race would not necessarily be those that grew the fastest, but those that executed best. It was this philosophy that underpinned Stemberg's insistence that the company should grow by focusing on key urban areas and achieving a critical mass of stores served by a central distribution system.

Not everyone agreed with this recipe for success. Office Depot did the opposite—the company grew as fast as possible, entering towns quickly to preempt competitors. Office Depot lacked the centralized distribution systems, but made up for that by locating in less expensive areas than Staples, persuading suppliers to ship directly to stores and keeping more back-up inventory on the premises. Although this meant larger stores, the lower rental costs in Office Depot's markets offset this.

What soon became apparent was that the rash of entrants included a number of companies that simply could not execute. Very quickly a handful of competitors emerged in the forefront of the industry—Staples, Office Depot, Office Max, and Office Club. As the market leaders grew, they increasingly came into contact with each other. The result was price wars. These first broke out in California. Staples entered the market in 1990 and initially focused on pricing not against Office Club, but against Price Club. Although Price Club was a warehouse store selling food and general merchandise, it still had the largest share of the office supplies market in California. Staples positioned itself as having the same low prices as Price Club, but a wider selection of office supplies and no membership fee.

Todd Krasnow, the executive VP of marketing at Staples, describes what happened next: "What we failed to realize was that Price Club was very worried about Office Club—and was pricing against Office Club. So when we went and matched Price Club, we were matching Office Club. And Office Club was saying: 'We are not going to let anybody have the same prices as us.'"[19] Office Club lowered its prices, causing Price Club to lower prices, and Staples followed. Not willing to be beat, Office Club cut prices again, and so they continued the spiral down. The price war drove profit margins down by as much as 8%.

Ultimately, Krasnow noted, "We realized that by engaging in this price war, we were focusing on our competitors, not our customers. Our customers weren't paying attention to this spat. So we raised our prices a little. You feel like you're just doing absolutely the wrong thing, because your whole position is: We have the lowest price."[20] Be that as it may, Office Club and Price Club followed suit, and prices started to rise again. Ultimately the three companies carved out different prices niches, each unwilling to be undercut on about twenty or so top-selling items, but in general, they were not the same items.

What happened in California also occurred elsewhere. When Office Max entered the Boston market in 1992, for example, a price war broke out again. There was an unanticipated effect this time, though— the price cuts apparently broadened the market by making buying from Staples attractive to customers with between twenty-five and one hundred employees, who previously bought directly from mail-order and retail stationers.[21]

Ultimately, Kransow noted, price wars such as those that started to break out in California and Boston started to moderate. "We finally realized that it's not in any company's self-interest to have a price war because you can get lots of market share without having a price war. And having a price war among low priced competitors doesn't get you more market share. It doesn't serve any purpose."[22] Other factors that may have contributed toward more rational pricing behavior in the market were the strong economy of the 1990s and industry consolidation.

Industry Consolidation

At its peak in 1991, there were twenty-five chains in the office supply industry.[23] Industry consolidation started when some of the clones began to fall by the wayside, filing for bankruptcy. U.S. Office Supply, itself the result of a merger between two office supplies chains, filed for bankruptcy in 1991, as did Office Stop. Consolidation was also hastened by acquisitions. In 1991, Office Depot acquired Office Club, giving the primary rival of Staples more than twice the number of stores. For its part, Staples acquired HQ Office Supplies Warehouse in 1991, and in 1992, it purchased another smaller chain, Workplace.[24]

As these trends continued, by the mid-1990s it was apparent that three players were rising to dominance in the industry: Office Depot, Staples, and Office Max. By mid-1996, Office Depot led the industry with 539 stores, followed by Staples with 517, and Office Max with around 500 stores. In terms of revenues, Office Depot had a clear lead with $5.3 billion in 1996, Staples was second with $3.07 billion, and Office Max third with $2.6 billion. Staples remained concentrated in the Northeast and California, with a large number of stores in dense urban areas. Office Depot's stores were concentrated in the South, and the company continued to stay clear of congested cities. Office Max was still strongest in the Midwest.[25]

The consolidation phase peaked in September 1996 when Staples announced an agreement to purchase its larger rival, Office Depot, for $3.36 billion. The executives of the two companies had apparently been talking about merger possibilities for years, while continuing to pursue their own independent growth strategies. If the merger went through, Tom Stemberg would step into the CEO role. The two companies sold the merger to the investment community of the basis of cost savings. The combined firm would have almost 1,100 stores and revenues of $8.5 billion. The combination, Stemberg argued, would attain terrific economies of scale that would allow it to significantly lower costs, saving an estimated $4.9 billion over five years, including $2.2 billion in product cost savings.

In a move to preempt a possible investigation by the Federal Trade Commission (FTC), the companies claimed that since their stores focused on different territories, the combination would not reduce competition. They also noted that Staples still faced intense competition not only from Office Max, but also from the likes of Wal-Mart, Circuit City, and mail-order outlets. Indeed, Stemberg claimed that the combined company would still account for only 5% of the total sales of office supplies in the United States.[26]

The FTC didn't buy the arguments, quickly started an investigation, and, in May 1997, sought an injunction to block the deal. The FTC claimed that the deal would stifle competition and raise prices for office supplies, especially in those markets where the two firms competed head to head. To buttress its case, the FTC released a report of pricing data that showed that nondurable office supplies such as paper were 10% to 15% higher in markets where Staples faced no direct rivals. Staples claimed that the FTC's pricing surveys were done selectively and were biased.

In July 1997, a federal judge granted the FTC's request for an injunction to halt the merger. Staples realized that it was in a losing fight and pulled its bid for Office Depot. But the failure had a silver lining— not anticipating much interference from the FTC,

Office Depot had put most of its expansion plans on hold, opening just two stores in eight months. In comparison, Staples opened forty-three, allowing the company to close the gap between itself and its larger rival.

Staples's Evolving Strategy

Moving into Small Towns

Stemberg has described Staples initial strategy to deal with the high costs of doing business in the Northeast as follows: "Establish superstores that were smaller than most, save on rent and operating costs, cluster them in densely populated areas to justify paying for expensive advertisements, and stock the stores from a distribution center."[27] The drawback with this strategy, in retrospect, was that Staples ignored a lot of potentially lucrative markets in smaller towns. While Office Depot was barnstorming into towns with populations of just 75,000, Staples could not see how they made it pay. Surely towns of that size were just too small to support an office supplies superstore?

As it turned out, they were not. The mistake Staples made was to assume that a store would serve customers within a ten- to fifteen-minute drive. But in smaller cities, customers would drive much further to get good prices. The revelation did not hit home until Staples opened its first store in Portland, Maine. With a population of 200,000, the town was smaller than most areas focused on by Staples, but within a few months the store was doing very well. To test the hypothesis, in 1992 and 1993 Staples opened stores in a number of smaller towns. The results were surprising. Many of the stores actually generated higher sales per square foot that those located in large cities. Sales were helped by the fact that in many of these small towns the only competitors were small mom-and-pop stationers, and that many small towns also lacked supermarket electronic retailers, such as Circuit City, selling low-priced office equipment, allowing Staples to pick up a much larger share of that business. Moreover, the lower rent, labor costs, advertising costs, and shrinkage made these stores significantly more profitable.

From that point on, Staples moved into small towns and suburban locations, where the same economics apply. Stemberg has described not moving into small towns earlier as "one of the dumbest mistakes I made." In 1994, some 10% of Staples stores were in small towns; by 1998, that figure had risen to 28%, and some of the most profitable stores in the Staples network were located in small towns.[28]

Selling Direct

Established as a retailer, Staples initially turned its back on customer requests for delivery and mail- or telephone-order service. The reason for doing this was simple; Staples saw itself as a low-cost retailer, and a delivery service would probably raise costs. However, Staples's competitors started to offer mail-order and delivery service, and customers continued to ask for the service, so in 1988 Staples began to experiment with this.

Initially the experimentation was halfhearted. Store managers were not enthusiastic about supporting a delivery service that they believed decreased store sales, and Staples discouraged delivery by tacking a 5% delivery charge onto the order price. Moreover, the company questioned whether it could generate the volume of business to cover the costs of a delivery service and make a decent return on capital.

What changed this was a study undertaken for Staples by a management consulting firm. The study found that the customers who purchased via a catalog and required delivery were not always the same ones who brought directly from the store. While there was a lot of cross shopping, the mail-order customers tended to be bigger and somewhat more interested in service, whereas those buying from the store were often buying for home offices. Staples also could not help but notice that its major rivals were offering a delivery service and that business seemed to be thriving.

In 1991, Staples set up an independent business unit within the company to handle the mail/telephone order and delivery service, known as Contract and Commercial. The guts of this business unit was a division know as Staples Direct (it is now called Staples Business Delivery). The man put in charge of this business, Ronald Sargent, would ultimately replace Stemberg as CEO of Staples in 2003.

One issue that had to be dealt with was the potential conflict between Staples Direct and the stores. The stores didn't want to push business the way of Staples Direct because they would not get credit for the sale. As Sargent commented later, "We were like the bad guys inside Staples, because the feeling was that if customers got products delivered they wouldn't shop inside our stores."[29] To align incentives, Staples changed the compensation systems so that (a) the store would get credit if a delivery order was placed through the store, and (b) the annual bonus of store employees was based partly on how well they met goals for generating delivery sales.

As Staples Direct started to grow, the company discovered that the delivery infrastructure it put in place could be used to serve clients in addition to the company's established small-business customers, which typically had less than fifty employees. Increasingly, medium-sized business (with fifty to one hundred employees), and larger businesses with more than one hundred employees started to utilize Staples Direct. To support this new business, Staples started to grow by acquisition, purchasing a number of regional stationary companies with established customers and delivery systems. Typically Staples kept the owners of these businesses on as Staples employees, often because they had long-established relationships with key accounts in large organizations such as Xerox, Ford, and PepsiCo. Staples, however, established a consistent product line, brand image, and computer and accounting systems across all of the acquisitions.

Between 1991 and 1996, Staples Direct grew from a $30 million business to an almost $1 billion one. As sales volume ramped up, so Staples was able to get greater efficiencies out of its distribution network, which helped to drive down the costs of doing business through this channel. Staples used a network of regional distribution centers to hold an inventory of some 15,000 SKUs for delivery, compared to 8,000 SKUs in a typical store. In 1998, a web-based element was added to Staples Direct, Staples.com. Through the Web or catalog, Staples customers could get access to some 130,000 SKUs, many of which were shipped directly from manufacturers with Staples acting as an intermediary and consolidator.

To continue building the direct business, in 1988, Staples acquired Quill Corp. for $685 million in Staples stock. Established in 1956, Quill is a direct mail catalog business with a targeted approach to servicing the business products needs of around a million small and medium-sized businesses in the United States. Quill differentiated itself through excellent customer service. Staples decided to let Quill keep its own organization, setting it up as a separate division within the Contract and Commercial business unit, but integrated Quill's purchasing with those of the rest of Staples to gain economies on the input side. Quill now operates under two brands—Staples National Advantage, which focuses on large multiregional businesses, and Staples Business advantage, which focuses on large and medium-sized regional companies and which has the flexibility to handle smaller accounts (although these are mostly handled via Staples Direct). In justifying the acquisition of Quill, Stemberg noted that the direct business amounted to a $60 billion a year industry, but it was highly fragmented with the top eight players accounting for less than 20% of the market.[30]

By 2005, the combined delivery business had grown to become a $4.95 billion enterprise in its own right.

Going International

Staples's first foray into international markets occurred in the early 1990s when the company was approached by a Canadian retailer, Jack Bingleman, who wanted to start a Staples-type chain north of the border. Bingleman also approached Office Depot and Office Max, but preferred Staples because of the close geographic proximity. Board members at Staples initially opposed any expansion into Canada, arguing that scarce resources should be dedicated toward growth in the much larger United States, but Stemberg liked Bingleman's vision and pushed the idea. Ultimately, in 1991, Staples agreed to invest $2 million in Bingleman's start-up for a 16% equity stake.

Known as Business Depot, the Canadian venture expanded rapidly, modeling itself after Staples. Between 1991 and 1994, the number of Canadian Business Depot stores expanded to 30, and the enterprise turned profitable in 1993. In 1994, Staples announced an agreement to purchase Business Depot outright for $32 million.[31] By 2006, there were more than 260 stores in Canada.

The Canadian venture was soon followed by investments in Europe. Staples entered the UK market in 1992, partnering with Kingfisher PLC, a large UK retailer that operated home improvement and consumer electronics stores among other things. The Canadian venture had taught Staples that a local partner was extremely valuable. As one Staples executive noted later: "You absolutely cannot do it yourself. There are too many cultural impediments for you to know where the booby traps lie. In a retail startup, the most important task is to generate locations. There's no way a U.S. national can go into any country and generate the real estate it needs. That person will be chasing his tail for a long time."[32]

On the heels of entry into the UK, Staples purchased MAXI-Papier, a German company that was attempting to copy what Staples had done in the United States. This was followed by entry into the Netherlands and Portugal. By 2006, Staples had 137 stores in the UK, 55 in Germany, 44 in the Netherlands, 19 in Portugal, and 3 in Belgium. By 2006, the European operations were generating close to $2 billion in revenues. In late 2002, Staples purchased the mail-order business of a French company, Guilbert, for nearly $800 million, which boosted delivery sales in Europe from $50 million a year to $450 million a year almost overnight.[33]

Changing the Shopping Experience

By the early 2000s, Staples started to realize that its stores looked very similar to those of its two main competitors, Office Depot and Office Max. As the number of markets where all three companies competed grew, head-to-head competition increased. Management then started to look for ways to differentiate their stores from those of competitors. What emerged was a new store design, known as "Dover." The core to "Dover" was a customer-centric philosophy known as "Easy." Rolled out across the company in 2005, "Easy" is all about making the shopping experience for customers as easy as possible— through store design and layout, through a merchandising strategy that aims to ensure that items are never out of stock, and through superior in-store customer service. The idea is to help to get the customer in and out of the store as expeditiously as possible.

To execute Easy, Staples has had to redesign its store layout, invest in upgrading the knowledge level of its sales associates, and improve its supply-chain management processes.[34] Staples started a big push to improve the efficiency of its supply-chain management

process in 2003, and that is still ongoing today. Elements of this push include better use of information systems to link Staples with its suppliers and extensive use of "cross-docking" techniques at distribution centers, so that merchandise spends less time in distribution centers. As a consequence of this strategy, Staples has increased inventory turnover, reduced inventory holdings, and improved its in-stock experience for customers.

Staples in 2006

In February 2002, Tom Stemberg announced that he was stepping down as CEO and passing the baton on to Ron Sargent. Stemberg would remain on as chairman. On taking over as CEO, Sargent put the brakes on store expansion, declaring that Staples would open no more than 75 new stores a year, down from over 130 in 2000. He used the slowdown to refocus attention on internal operating efficiencies. The product line within stores was rationalized, with Staples cutting back on the stocking of low-margin items such as personal computers. He also set up a task force to look for ways to take every excess cent out of the cost structure. As a result, operating margins at Staples stores came in at 5.9% of sales in 2002, the best in the industry, and up from 4.5% in 2000. (See Exhibit 1.)

By 2003, Sargent was refocusing on attaining profitable growth for the company. Although by this point Staples or one of its competitors operated in all major markets in North America, the company's management decided that Staples was in a strong enough position to go head-to-head with major competitors. In 2005, Staples pushed into Chicago, a market previously served by just Office Depot and

EXHIBIT 1

Leaders in Office Supplies

Company	2006 Revenues	Number of Stores in North America	% of Sales from Retail
Staples	$17.8 billion	1522	56%
Office Depot	$15.0 billion	1047	46%
Office Max	$9.2 billion	874	50%

Source: Company reports.

Office Max, where the company opened twenty-five stores. The Chicago experience proved to be a pivotal one for Staples. In the words of COO, Mike Miles, "What we found in Chicago was we can come into a two-player market and make it a three-player market successfully. There was a little trepidation about that because the model in the first 10 to 15 years was that office superstores were interchangeable."[35]

As of 2006, there were still a lot of major markets in North America where Staples lacked a presence, including Houston, Miami, Denver, Las Vegas, St. Louis, and Minneapolis. Reflecting on this, Sargent is on record as stating that Staples could more than double its North American network to some 4,000 stores. (See Exhibit 2 as evidence of the growth rate.) Commenting on this, he notes that "I don't think Wal-Mart spends a lot of time worrying if K-Mart is in the market when they decide to open new stores."[36]

Outside of the retail market, Sargent has turned his attention to the business where he made his name, the direct delivery business. He points out that although the number of independent office supplies dealers is down to 6,000 from 15,000 a decade ago, the delivery market is still highly fragmented and very large. Ultimately Sargent believes that direct delivery from warehouses can be as big a business as Staples office supplies stores. He also sees huge potential for growth in Europe, which is the second largest office supplies market in the world and still years behind the United States in terms of consolidation.

At the same time, Staples continues to face strategic challenges. Clearly additional expansion by Staples in North America is likely to bring it into head-to-head contact with Office Depot or Office Max. To compound matters, in mid-2003, Boise Cascade, the large wood and paper products company that has long had its own direct delivery business, purchased Office Max for $1.2 billion. Prior to the purchase, Office Max had 2002 sales of $4.8 billion against Staples's sales of $11.6 billion and Office Depot's sales of $11.4 billion. The merger boosted the combined office supplies sales of the new company to $8.3 billion. In 2006, Boise Cascade sold off its timber and paper assets to focus on the office supplies business. The company, which changed its corporate name back to Office Max, has 874 office superstores in North America and a large delivery business. Staples also faces continued competition from Sam's Club and Costco, both of which are focusing on small businesses and continue to sell office supplies. In addition, FedEx Kinko's, which has a nationwide network of 1,000 copying and printing stores, is contemplating offering more office supplies in a new store layout.

EXHIBIT 2

Staples Stores in North America, 1996–2006

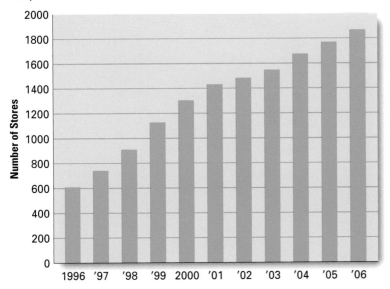

Source: Company reports.

ENDNOTES

1. Stephen D. Solomon. "Born to be Big," *Inc.*, June 1989, page 94.
2. Value Line. Value Line Investment Survey, Staples, October 13, 2006.
3. Stephen D. Solomon. "Born to be Big," *Inc.*, June 1989, page 96.
4. Tom Stemberg. *Staples for Success,* Knowledge Exchange, Santa Monica, California, 1996.
5. Michael Barrier, "Tom Stemberg Calls the Office," *Nation's Business*, July 1990, page 42.
6. Michael Barrier, "Tom Stemberg Calls the Office," *Nation's Business*, July 1990, page 44.
7. Michael Barrier, "Tom Stemberg Calls the Office," *Nation's Business*, July 1990, page 44.
8. Tom Stemberg and David Whiteford. "Putting a Stop to Mom and Pop," *Fortune Small Business*, October 2002, page 39.
9. Tom Stemberg and David Whiteford. "Putting a Stop to Mom and Pop," *Fortune Small Business*, October 2002, page 40.
10. Tom Stemberg. *Staples for Success,* Knowledge Exchange, Santa Monica, California, 1996.
11. Tom Stemberg and David Whiteford. "Putting a Stop to Mom and Pop," *Fortune Small Business*, October 2002, page 40.
12. Tom Stemberg. *Staples for Success,* Knowledge Exchange, Santa Monica, California, 1996, page 17.
13. Tom Stemberg and David Whiteford. "Putting a Stop to Mom and Pop," *Fortune Small Business*, October 2002, page 41.
14. Stephen D. Solomon. "Born to be Big," *Inc.*, June 1989, pages 94 and 95.
15. Tom Stemberg. *Staples for Success,* Knowledge Exchange, Santa Monica, California, 1996, page 24.
16. Tom Stemberg. *Staples for Success,* Knowledge Exchange, Santa Monica, California, 1996, page 27.
17. Tom Stemberg and David Whiteford. "Putting a Stop to Mom and Pop," *Fortune Small Business*, October 2002, page 40.
18. Stephen D. Solomon. "Born to be Big," *Inc.*, June 1989, page 100.
19. Tom Stemberg. *Staples for Success,* Knowledge Exchange, Santa Monica, California, 1996, page 97.
20. Tom Stemberg. *Staples for Success,* Knowledge Exchange, Santa Monica, California, 1996, page 97.
21. Norm Alster. "Penney Wise," *Forbes*, February 1, 1993, pages 48–51.
22. Tom Stemberg. *Staples for Success,* Knowledge Exchange, Santa Monica, California, 1996, page 97.
23. Renee Covion Rouland. "And Then There Were Three," *Discount Merchandiser*, December 1994, page 27.
24. Leland Montgomery. "Staples: Buy the Laggard," *Financial World*, November 9, 1993, page 22; Anonymous, "The New Plateau in Office Supplies," *Discount Merchandiser*, November 1991, pages 50–54.
25. James S. Hirsch and Eleena de Lisser. "Staples to Acquire Archrival Office Depot," *Wall Street Journal*, September 5, 1996, page A3.
26. Joseph Pereira and John Wilke. "Staples Faces FTC in Antitrust Showdown on Merger," *Wall Street Journal*, May 19, 1997, page B4.
27. Tom Stemberg. *Staples for Success,* Knowledge Exchange, Santa Monica, California, 1996, page 128.
28. William M. Bulkeley. "Office Supplies Superstores Find Bounty in the Boonies," *Wall Street Journal*, September 1, 1998, page B1.
29. William C. Symonds. "Thinking Outside the Big Box," *Business Week*, August 11, 2003, page 62.
30. William M. Bulkeley. "Staples, Moving Beyond Superstores, Will Buy Quill for $685 Million in Stock," *Wall Street Journal*, April 8, 1998, page A1.
31. Steff Gelston. "Staples Goes on Buying Spree to Acquire Business Depot, National Office Supply Company," *Boston Herald*, January 25, 1994, page 24.
32. Tom Stemberg. *Staples for Success,* Knowledge Exchange, Santa Monica, California, 1996, page 90.
33. William C. Symonds. "Thinking Outside the Big Box," *Business Week*, August 11, 2003, pages 62–64.
34. Mike Troy. "Office Supplies: Staples Positioned as the Architect of 'Easy,'" *Retailing Today*, August 7, 2006, page 30.
35. Anonymous. "Moving In on Major Markets," *DSN Retailing Today*, May 22, 2006, page 10.
36. Anonymous. "Moving In on Major Markets," *DSN Retailing Today*, May 22, 2006, page 10.

Whole Foods Market: Will There Be Enough Organic Food to Satisfy the Growing Demand?

This case was prepared by Patricia Harasta and Alan N. Hoffman, Bentley College.[a]

Reflecting back over his three decades of experience in the grocery business, John Mackey smiled to himself over his previous successes. His entrepreneurial history began with a single store which he has now grown to the nation's leading natural food chain. While proud of the past, John had concerns about the future direction the Whole Foods Market chain should head. Whole Foods Market was an early entrant into the organic food market and it has used its early mover advantage to solidify its position and continue its steady growth.

With the changing economy and a more competitive industry landscape, John Mackey is uncertain about how to meet the company's aggressive growth targets. Whole Foods Market's objective is to reach $10 billion in revenue with 300+ stores by 2010 without sacrificing quality and its current reputation. This is not an easy task and John is unsure of the best way to proceed.

Company Background

Whole Foods carries both natural and organic food offering customers a wide variety of products. "Natural" refers to food that is free of growth hormones or antibiotics, where "certified organic" food conforms to

[a] The authors would like to thank Ann Lawrence, Christopher Ferrari, Robert Marshall, Julie Giles, Jennifer Powers and Gretchen Alper for their research and contributions to this case.

the standards, as defined by the U.S. Department of Agriculture in October 2002.[1] Whole Foods Market® is the world's leading retailer of natural and organic foods, with 172 stores in North America and the United Kingdom. John Mackey, current president and cofounder of Whole Foods, opened "Safer Way" natural grocery store in 1978. The store had limited success as it was a small location allowing only for a limited selection, focusing entirely on vegetarian foods.[2] John joined forces with Craig Weller and Mark Skiles, founders of "Clarsville Natural Grocery" (founded in 1979), to create Whole Foods Market.[3] This joint venture took place in Austin, Texas, in 1980, resulting in a new company, a single natural food market with a staff of nineteen.

In addition to the supermarkets, Whole Foods owns and operates several subsidiaries. Allegro Coffee Company was formed in 1977 and purchased by Whole Foods Market in 1997, now acting as its coffee roasting and distribution center. Pigeon Cove is Whole Foods' seafood processing facility, which was founded in 1985 and known as M & S Seafood until 1990. Whole Foods purchased Pigeon Cove in 1996, located in Gloucester, Massachusetts. The company is now the only supermarket to own and operate a waterfront seafood facility.[4] The last two subsidiaries are Produce Field Inspection Office and Select Fish, which is Whole Foods' West Coast seafood processing facility acquired in 2003.[5] In addition to the above, The company has eight distribution centers, seven regional bake houses and four commissaries.[6]

"Whole Foods Market remains uniquely mission driven: The company is highly selective about what they sell, dedicated to stringent quality standards, and committed to sustainable agriculture. They believe in a virtuous circle entwining the food chain, human beings and Mother Earth: each is reliant upon the others through a beautiful and delicate symbiosis."[7] The message of preservation and sustainability are followed while providing high quality goods to customers and high profits to investors.

Whole Foods has grown over the years through mergers, acquisitions and several new store openings.[8] Today, Whole Foods Market is the largest natural food supermarket in the United States.[9] The company consists of 32,000 employees operating 172 stores in the United States, Canada, and the United Kingdom with an average store size of 32,000 square feet.[10] While the majority of Whole Foods locations are in the U.S., the company has made acquisitions expanding its presence in the UK. European expansion provides enormous potential growth due to the large population and it holds "a more sophisticated organic-foods market than the U.S. in terms of suppliers and acceptance by the public."[11] Whole Foods targets its locations specifically by an area's demographics. The company targets locations where 40% or more of the residents have a college degree as they are more likely to be aware of nutritional issues.[12]

Whole Foods Market's Philosophy

Its corporate website defines the company philosophy as follows, "Whole Foods Market's vision of a sustainable future means our children and grandchildren will be living in a world that values human creativity, diversity, and individual choice. Businesses will harness human and material resources without devaluing the integrity of the individual or the planet's ecosystems. Companies, governments, and institutions will be held accountable for their actions. People will better understand that all actions have repercussions and that planning and foresight coupled with hard work and flexibility can overcome almost any problem encountered. It will be a world that values education and a free exchange of ideas by an informed citizenry; where people are encouraged to discover, nurture, and share their life's passions."[13]

While Whole Foods recognizes it is only a supermarket, it is working toward fulfilling its vision within the context of its industry. In addition to leading by example, it strives to conduct business in a manner consistent with its mission and vision. By offering minimally processed, high quality food, engaging in ethical business practices and providing a motivational,

respectful work environment, the company believes it is on the path to a sustainable future.[14]

Whole Foods incorporates the best practices of each location back into the chain.[15] This can be seen in the company's store product expansion from dry goods to perishable produce, including meats, fish and prepared foods. The lessons learned at one location are absorbed by all, enabling the chain to maximize effectiveness and efficiency while offering a product line customers love. Whole Foods carries only natural and organic products. The best tasting and most nutritious food available is found in its purest state—unadulterated by artificial additives, sweeteners, colorings, and preservatives.[16]

Whole Foods continually improves customer offerings, catering to its specific locations. Unlike business models for traditional grocery stores, Whole Foods products differ by geographic regions and local farm specialties.

Employee and Customer Relations

Whole Foods encourages a team based environment allowing each store to make independent decisions regarding its operations. Teams consist of up to eleven employees and a team leader. The team leaders typically head up one department or another. Each store employs anywhere from 72 to 391 team members.[17] The manager is referred to as the "store team leader." The "store team leader" is compensated by an Economic Value Added (EVA) bonus and is also eligible to receive stock options.[18]

Whole Foods tries to instill a sense of purpose among its employees and has been named one of the "100 Best Companies to work for in America" by *Fortune* magazine for the past six years. In employee surveys, 90% of its team members stated that they always or frequently enjoy their job.[19]

The company strives to take care of its customers, realizing they are the "lifeblood of our business," and the two are "interdependent on each other."[20] Whole Foods' primary objective goes beyond 100% customer satisfaction with the goal to "delight" customers in every interaction.

Competitive Environment

American shoppers spent nearly $45.8 billion on natural and organic products in 2004, according to research published in the *24th Annual Market Overview* in the June issue of *The Natural Foods Merchandiser.* In 2004, natural products sales increased 6.9% across all sales channels, including supermarkets, mass marketers, direct marketers, and the Internet. Sales of organic products rose 14.6% in natural products stores. As interest in low-carb diets waned, sales of organic baked goods rose 35%. Other fast-growing organic categories included meat, poultry and seafood, up 120%; coffee and cocoa, up 64%; and cookies, up 63%.

At the time of Whole Foods' inception, there was almost no competition with less than six other natural food stores in the United States. Today, the organic foods industry is growing and Whole Foods finds itself competing hard to maintain its elite presence. As the population has become increasingly concerned about their eating habits, natural foods stores, such as Whole Foods, are flourishing. Other successful natural food grocery chains today include Trader Joe's Co. and Wild Oats Market[21] (see Exhibit 1).

Trader Joe's, originally known as Pronto Markets, was founded in 1958 in Los Angeles by Joe Coulombe. By expanding its presence and product offerings while maintaining high quality at low prices, the company has found its competitive niche.[22] The company has 215 stores, primarily on the west and east coasts of the United States. The company "offers upscale grocery fare such as health foods, prepared meals, organic produce and nutritional supplements."[23] A low cost structure allows Trader Joe's to offer competitive prices while still maintaining its margins. Trader Joe's stores have no service department and average just 10,000 square feet in store size. A privately held company, Trader Joe's enjoyed sales of $2.5 million in 2003, a 13.6% increase from 2002.[24]

Wild Oats was founded in 1987, in Boulder, Colorado. Its founders had no experience in the natural foods market, relying heavily on their employees to learn the industry. Acknowledging the increased competition within the industry, Wild Oats is committed to strengthening and streamlining its operations in an effort to continue to build the company.[25] Its product offerings range from organic foods to traditional grocery merchandise. Wild Oats, a publicly owned company on NASDAQ, is traded under the ticker symbol of OATS and "is the third largest natural foods supermarket chain in the United States in terms of sales." Although it falls behind Whole Foods and Trader Joe's, the company enjoyed $1,048,164 in sales in 2004, a 7.5% increase over 2003. Wild Oats operates 100 full service stores in 24 states and Canada.[26]

Additional competition has arisen from grocery stores, such as Stop 'N Shop and Shaw's, which now incorporate natural foods sections in their conventional stores, placing them in direct competition with Whole Foods. Because larger grocery chains have more flexibility in their product offerings, they are more likely to promote products through sales, a strategy Whole Foods rarely practices.

Despite being in a highly competitive industry, Whole Foods maintains its reputation as "the world's #1 natural foods chain."[27] As the demand for natural and organic food continues to grow, pressures on suppliers will rise. Only 3% of U.S. farmland is organic so there is limited output.[28] The increased demand for these products may further elevate prices or result in

EXHIBIT 1

Sales

Company	Sales (in millions)						
	2000	2001	% Growth	2002	% Growth	2003	% Growth
Whole Foods Market[1]	$1,838.60	$2,272.20	23.60%	$2,690.50	18.40%	$3,148.60	17.00%
Trader Joe's Company[2]	$1,670.00	$1,900.00	13.80%	$2,200.00	15.80%	$2,500.00	13.60%
Wild Oats Market[3]	$838.10	$893.20	6.60%	$919.10	2.90%	$969.20	5.50%

[1] Hoovers Online: http://www.hoovers.com/whole-foods/–ID_10952–/free-co-factsheet.xhtml: December 1, 2004.

[2] Hoovers Online: http://www.hoovers.com/trader-joe's-co/–ID_47619–/free-co-factsheet.xhtm: December 1, 2004.

[3] Hoovers Online: http://www.hoovers.com/wild-oats-markets/–ID_41717–/free-co-factsheet.xhtml: December 1, 2004.

goods being out of stock, with possible price wars looming.

The Changing Grocery Industry

Before the emergence of the supermarket, the public was largely dependent upon specialty shops or street vendors for dairy products, meats, produce, and other household items. In the 1920s, chain stores began to threaten independent retailers by offering convenience and lower prices by procuring larger quantities of products. Appel explains that the emergence of the supermarkets in the 1930s was a result of three major changes in society:

(1) The shift in population from rural to urban areas

(2) An increase in disposable income

(3) Increased mobility through ownership of automobiles.[29]

Perhaps the earliest example of the supermarket as we know it today is King Kullen, "America's first supermarket," which was founded by Michael Cullen in 1930. "The essential key to his plan was volume, and he attained this through heavy advertising of low prices on nationally advertised merchandise." As the success of Cullen's strategy became evident, others such as Safeway, A&P, and Kroger adopted it as well. By the time the United States entered World War II, 9,000 supermarkets accounted for 25% of industry sales.[30]

Low prices and convenience continue to be the dominant factors driving consumers to supermarkets today. The industry is characterized by low margins and continuous downward pressure on prices made evident by coupons, weekly specials, and rewards cards. Over the years firms have introduced subtle changes to the business model by providing additional conveniences, such as the inclusion of bakeries, banks, pharmacies, and even coffee houses co-located within the supermarket. Throughout their existence, supermarkets have also tried to cater to the changing tastes and preferences of society such as healthier diets, the Atkins diet, and low carbohydrate foods. The moderate changes to strategy within supermarkets have been imitated by competitors, which are returning the industry to a state of price competition. Supermarkets themselves now face additional competition from wholesalers such as Costco, BJ's and Sam's Club.

A Different Shopping Experience

The setup of the organic grocery store is a key component to Whole Foods' success. The store's setup and its products are carefully researched to ensure that they are meeting the demands of the local community. Locations are primarily in cities and are chosen for their large space and heavy foot traffic. According to Whole Foods' 10K, "approximately 88% of our existing stores are located in the top 50 statistical metropolitan areas."[31] The company uses a specific formula to choose its store sites that is based upon several metrics, which include but are not limited to income levels, education, and population density.

Upon entering a Whole Foods supermarket, it becomes clear that the company attempts to sell the consumer on the entire experience. Team members (employees) are well trained and the stores themselves are immaculate. There are in-store chefs to help with recipes, wine tasting and food sampling. There are "Take Action food centers"[32] where customers can access information on the issues that affect their food such as legislation and environmental factors. Some stores offer extra services such as home delivery, cooking classes, massages and valet parking.[33] Whole Foods goes out of its way to appeal to the above-average income earner.

Whole Foods uses price as a marketing tool in a few select areas, as demonstrated by the 365 Whole Foods brand name products, priced less than similar organic products that are carried within the store. However, the company does not use price to differentiate itself from competitors.[34] Rather, Whole Foods focuses on quality and service as a means of standing out from the competition.

Whole Foods only spent 0.5%[35] of its total sales from the fiscal year 2004 on advertising; it relies on other means to promote its stores. The company relies heavily on word-of-mouth advertising from its customers to help market itself in the local community. It is also promoted in several health conscious magazines, and each store budgets for in-store advertising each fiscal year.

Whole Foods also gains recognition via its charitable contributions and the awareness that its brings to the treatment of animals. The company donates 5% of its after tax profits to not-for-profit charities.[36] The company is also very active in establishing systems to make sure that the animals used in its products are treated humanely.

The Aging Baby Boomers

The aging of the Baby Boomer generation will expand the senior demographic over the next decade as their children grow up and leave the nest. Urban singles are another group that has extra disposable income due to their lack of dependents. These two groups present an opportunity for growth for Whole Foods. Americans spent 7.2% of their total expenditures on food in 2001, making it the seventh highest category on which consumers spend their money.[37] Additionally, U.S. households with income of more than $100,000 per annum represent 22% of aggregate income today compared with 18% a decade ago.[38]

This shift in demographics has created an expansion in the luxury store group, while slowing growth in the discount retail market.[39] To that end, there is a gap in supermarket retailing between consumers who can only afford to shop at low cost providers, like Wal-Mart, and the population of consumers who prefer gourmet food and are willing to pay a premium for perceived higher quality.[40] "'The Baby Boomers are driving demand for organic food in general because they're health-conscious and can afford to pay higher prices,' says Professor Steven G. Sapp, a sociologist at Iowa State University who studies consumer food behavior."[41]

The perception that imported, delicatessen, exotic and organic foods are of higher quality, therefore commanding higher prices, continues to bode well for Whole Foods Market. As John Mackey explains, "'We're changing the [grocery-shopping] experience so that people enjoy it.' . . . 'It's a richer, [more fun], more enjoyable experience. People don't shop our stores because we have low prices.'"[42] The consumer focus on a healthy diet is not limited to food. More new diet plans emerged in America in the last half of the 20th century than in any other country. This trend has also increased the demand for nutritional supplements and vitamins.[43]

In recent years, consumers have made a gradual move toward the use of fresher, healthier foods in their everyday diets. Consumption of fresh fruits and vegetables, pasta and other grain-based products has increased.[44] This is evidenced by the aggressive expansion by consumer products companies into healthy food and natural and organic products.[45] "Natural and organic products have crossed the chasm to mainstream America."[46] The growing market can be attributed to the acceptance and widespread expansion of organic product offerings, beyond milk and dairy.[47] Mainstream acceptance of the Whole Foods offering can be attributed to this shift in consumer food preferences as consumers continue to cite taste as the number one motivator for purchasing organic foods.[48]

With a growing percentage of women working out of the home, the traditional role of home cooked meals, prepared from scratch, has waned. As fewer women have the time to devote to cooking, consumers are giving way to the trend of convenience through prepared foods. Sales of ready-to-eat meals have grown significantly. "The result is that grocers are starting to specialize in quasi-restaurant food."[49] Just as women entering the work force has propelled the sale of prepared foods, it has also increased consumer awareness of the need for the one-stop shopping experience. Hypermarkets such as Wal-Mart, that offer non-food items and more mainstream product lines, allow consumers to conduct more shopping in one place rather than moving from store to store.

The growth in sales of natural foods is expected to continue at the rate of 8–10% annually, according to the National Nutritional Foods Association. The sale of organic food has largely outpaced traditional grocery products due to consumer perception that organic food is healthier.[50] The purchase of organic food is perceived to be beneficial to consumer health by 61% of consumers, according to a Food Marketing Institute (FMI)/*Prevention* magazine study. Americans believe organic food can help improve fitness and increase the longevity of life.[51] Much of this perception has grown out of fear of how non-organic foods are treated with pesticides for growth and then preserved for sale. Therefore, an opportunity exists for Whole Foods to contribute to consumer awareness by funding non-profit organizations that focus on educating the public on the benefits of organic lifestyles.

Operations

Whole Foods purchases most of its products from regional and national suppliers. This allows the company to leverage its size in order to receive deep discounts and favorable terms with its vendors. The company still permits stores to purchase from local producers to keep the stores aligned with local food trends and is seen as supporting the community. The company owns two procurement centers and handles the majority of procurement and distribution itself.

Whole Foods also owns several regional bake houses, which distribute products to its stores. The largest independent vendor is United Natural Foods which accounted for 20% of Whole Foods total purchases for fiscal year 2004.[52] Product categories at Whole Foods include, but are not limited to:

- Produce
- Seafood
- Grocery
- Meat and Poultry
- Bakery
- Prepared Foods and Catering
- Specialty (Beer, Wine and Cheese)
- Whole body (nutritional supplements, vitamins, body care and educational products such as books)
- Floral
- Pet Products
- Household Products[53]

While Whole Foods carries all the items that one would expect to find in a grocery store (and plenty that one would not), its "heavy emphasis on perishable foods is designed to appeal to both natural foods and gourmet shoppers."[54] Perishable foods accounted for 67% of its retail sales in 2004 and are the core of Whole Foods' success.[55] This is demonstrated by its own statement that, "We believe it is our strength of execution in perishables that has attracted many of our most loyal shoppers."[56]

Whole Foods also provides fully cooked frozen meal options through its private label Whole Kitchen, to satisfy the demands of working families. For example, the Whole Foods Market located in Woodland Hills, California has redesigned its prepared foods section more than three times[57] in response to a 40% growth in prepared foods sales.[58]

Whole Foods doesn't take just any product and put it on its shelves. In order to make it into the Whole Foods grocery store, products have to undergo a strict test to determine if they are "Whole Foods material." The quality standards that all potential Whole foods products must meet include:

- Food that is free of preservatives and other additives
- Food that is fresh, wholesome and safe to eat
- Promote organically grown foods
- Foods and products that promote a healthy life[59]

Meat and poultry products must adhere to a higher standard:

- No antibiotics or added growth hormones
- An affidavit from each producer that outlines the whole process of production and how the animals are treated
- An annual inspection of all producers by Whole Foods Market
- Successful completion of a third party audit to attest to these findings[60]

Also, due to the lack of available nutritional brands with a national identity, Whole Foods decided to enter into the private label product business. It currently has three private label products with a fourth program called Authentic Food Artisan, which promotes distinctive products that are certified organic. The three private label products: 1) 365 Everyday Value: A well recognized and trusted brand that meets the standards of Whole Foods and is less expensive then the regular product lines; 2) Whole Kids Organic: Healthy items that are directed at children; and 3) 365 Organic Everyday Value: All the benefits of organic food at reduced prices.[61]

When opening a new store, Whole Foods stocks it with almost $700,000 worth of initial inventory, which their vendors partially finance.[62] Like most conventional grocery stores, the majority of Whole Foods inventory is turned over fairly quickly; this is especially true of produce. Fresh organic produce is central to Whole Foods' existence and turns over on a faster basis than other products.

Financial Operations

Whole Foods Market focuses on earning a profit while providing job security to its workforce to lay the foundation for future growth. The company is determined not to let profits deter it from providing excellent service to its customers and a quality work environment for its staff. Its mission statement defines its recipe for financial success.

> Our motto—Whole Foods, Whole People, Whole Planet—emphasizes that our vision reaches far beyond just being a food retailer. Our success in fulfilling our vision is measured by customer satisfaction, Team Member excellence and happiness, return on capital investment, improvement in the state of the environment, and local and larger community support.[63]

EXHIBIT 2

Whole Foods Annual Sales

	Annual Income (values in 000's)			
	2001	**2002**	**2003**	**2004**
Sales	2,272,231	2,690,475	3,148,593	3,864,950
%	23.58%	18.04%	17.03%	22.75%
Net Income	$67,880	$84,491	$103,687	$132,657
%		24.47%	22.72%	27.94%
Increase from 2000–2003 = 87%				

Whole Foods also caps the salary of its executives at no more than fourteen times that of the average annual salary of a Whole Foods worker; this includes wages and incentive bonuses as well. The company also donates 5% of its after tax profits to non-profit organizations.[64]

Over a five-year period from 2000 through 2004, the company experienced an 87% growth in sales, with sales reaching $3.86 billion in 2004. Annual sales increases during that period were equally dramatic: 24% in 2001, 18% in 2002, 17% in 2003 and 22% in 2004.[65] (See Exhibit 2.) This growth is perhaps more impressive, given the relatively negative economic environment and recession in the United States.

Whole Foods strategy of expansion and acquisition has fueled growth in net income since the company's inception. This is particularly evident when looking at the net income growth in 2002 (24.47%), 2003 (22.72%) and 2004 (27.94%).[66]

The Ticker for Whole Foods, Inc. is WFMI. In reviewing the performance history of Whole Foods stock since its IPO reveals a mostly upward trend. The 10-year price trend shows the company increasing from under $10 per share to a high of over $100 per share, reflecting an increase of over 1,000%.[67] For the past year, the stock has been somewhat volatile, but with a mostly upward trend. The current price of $136 with 65.3 million shares outstanding gives the company a market valuation of $8.8 billion (Aug. 2005).[68]

The Code of Conduct

From its inception, the company has sought to be different from conventional grocery stores, with a heavy focus on ethics. Besides an emphasis on organic foods, the company has also established a contract of animal rights, which states the company will only do business with companies that treat their animals humanely. While it realizes that animal products are vital to its business, it opposes animal cruelty.[69]

The company has a unique fourteen-page Code of Conduct document that addresses the expected and desired behavior for its employees. The code is broken down into the following four sections:

- Potential Conflicts of Interest,

- Transactions or situations that should never occur

- Situations where you may need the authorization of the Ethics committee before proceeding and finally

- Times when certain actions must be taken by executives of the company or team leaders of individual stores.[70]

This Code of Conduct covers, in detail, the most likely scenarios a manager of a store might encounter. It includes several checklists that are to be filled out on a regular, or at least an annual, basis by team leaders and store managers. After completion, the checklists must be signed and submitted to corporate headquarters and copies retained on file in the store.[71] They ensure that the ethics of Whole Foods are being followed by everyone. The ethical efforts of Whole Foods don't go unrecognized; they were ranked number 70 out of the "100 Best Corporate Citizens."[72]

Possible Scarce Resources: Prime Locations and the Supply of Organic Foods

Prime store locations and the supply of organic foods are potential scarce resources and could be problematic for Whole Foods Market in the future.

Whole Foods likes to establish a presence in highly affluent cities, where its target market resides. The majority of Whole Foods customers are well-educated, thereby yielding high salaries enabling them to afford the company's higher prices. Whole Foods is particular when deciding on new locations, as location is extremely important for top and bottom line growth. However, there are a limited number of communities where 40% of the residents have college degrees.

Organic food is another possible scarce resource. Organic crops yield a lower quantity of output and are rarer, accounting for only 3% of U.S. farmland usage.[73] Strict government requirements must be satisfied; these are incredibly time consuming, more effort intensive, and more costly to adhere to. With increased demands from mainstream supermarkets also carrying organics, the demand for such products could outreach the limited supply. The market for organic foods grew from $2.9 billion in 2001 to $5.3 billion in 2004, an 80.5% increase in the three-year period.[74]

Whole Foods recognizes that the increased demand for organic foods may adversely affect its earnings and informs its investors as such. "Changes in the availability of quality natural and organic products could impact our business. There is no assurance that quality natural and organic products will be available to meet our future needs. If conventional supermarkets increase their natural and organic product offerings or if new laws require the reformulation of certain products to meet tougher standards, the supply of these products may be constrained. Any significant disruption in the supply of quality natural and organic products could have a material impact on our overall sales and cost of goods."[75]

ENDNOTES

1. http://www.organicconsumers.org/organic/most071904.cfm.
2. *Fortune:* September 15, 2003, Volume 148, Issue 5, page 127. "No Preservatives, No Unions, Lots of Dough"; Julia Boorstin.
3. Whole Foods: http://www.wholefoods.com/company/timeline.html (November 4, 2004).
4. *Fortune:* September 15, 2003, Volume 148, Issue 5, page 127. "No Preservatives, No Unions, Lots of Dough"; Julia Boorstin.
5. Whole Foods: http://www.wholefoods.com/company/facts.html (November 5, 2004).
6. Whole Foods: http://www.wholefoods.com/issues/org_commentsstandards0498 .html (November 5, 2004).
7. Whole Foods: http://www.wholefoods.com/company/index.html (November 5, 2004).
8. Whole Foods: http://www.wholefoods.com/company/history.html (November 5, 2004).
9. "The Natural: Whole Foods Founder John Mackey Builds an Empire on Organic Eating" Time, Inc. 2002.
10. Whole Foods: http://www.wholefoods.com/company/facts.html (November 11, 2004).
11. "Whole Foods Buying Chain of Stores Based in London: $38 Million Deal Marks U.S. Health-food Retailer's Initial Thrust into Overseas Market," Robert Elder Jr., January 17, 2004.
12. *Puget Sound Business Journal:* Seattle August 13, 2004. Volume 25, issue 15, page 1. "Whole Foods is Bagging Locations"; Jeanne Lang Jones.
13. Whole Foods: http://www.wholefoodsmarket.com/company/sustainablefuture.html (November 5, 2004).
14. Whole Foods: http://www.wholefoodsmarket.com/company/sustainablefuture.html (November 5, 2004).
15. *Fortune:* September 15, 2003, Volume 148, Issue 5, page 127. "No Preservatives, No Unions, Lots of Dough"; Julia Boorstin.
16. http://www.wholefoodsmarket.com/products/index.html (July 25, 2005).
17. Whole Foods 10K-Q 2003 (page 7). November 11, 2004, http://www.wholefoodsmarket.com/investor/10K-Q/2003_10K.pdf.
18. Whole Foods10K-Q 2003 (page 7). November 11, 2004, http://www.wholefoodsmarket.com/investor/10K-Q/2003_10K.pdf.
19. Whole Foods 10K-Q 2004 (page 10). August 15, 2005, http://www.wholefoodsmarket.com/investor/10K-Q/2004_10KA.pdf.
20. http://www.wholefoodsmarket.com/company/declaration.html (July 29, 2005).
21. Hoovers Online: http://www.hoovers.com/whole-foods/--ID_10952--/free-co-factsheet.xhtml (November 8, 2004).
22. Trader Joe's Company: www.traderjoes.com (November 8, 2004).
23. Hoovers Online: http://www.hoovers.com/trader-joe's-co/--ID-47619--/free-co-factsheet.xhtm (November 8, 2004).
24. Hoovers Online: http://www.hoovers.com/trader-joe's-co/--ID-47619--/free-co-factsheet.xhtm (November 8, 2004).
25. Wild Oats Market: www.wildoats.com (November 8, 2004).
26. Hoovers Online: http://www.hoovers.com/wild-oats-markets/--ID_41717--/free-co-factsheet.xhtml (November 8, 2004).
27. Hoovers Online: http://www.hoovers.com/whole-foods/--ID_10952--/free-co-factsheet.xhtml (November 8, 2004).
28. *Knight Ridder Tribune Business News.* Washington: September 28, 2004. page 1. "Providence, RI, Grocery Targets New Approach to Pricing"; Paul Grimaldi.
29. Appel, David. "The Supermarket: Early Development of an Institutional Innovation." *Journal of Retailing.* Volume 48, Number 1, Spring 1972. (p. 40).
30. Appel, David. "The Supermarket: Early Development of an Institutional Innovation." *Journal of Retailing.* Volume 48, Number 1, Spring 1972. (p. 40). (Appel, 47).
31. Whole Foods 10K-Q for 2003 (page 8) November 11, 2004 http://www.wholefoodsmarket.com/investor/10K-Q/2003_10K.pdf.
32. Whole Foods 10K-Q for 2003 (page 8) November 11, 2004, http://www.wholefoodsmarket.com/investor/10K-Q/2003_10K.pdf.
33. Whole Foods 10K-Q for 2003 (page 8) November 11, 2004, http://www.wholefoodsmarket.com/investor/10K-Q/2003_10K.pdf.
34. Whole Foods http://www.wholefoodsmarket.com/investor/10K-Q/2003_10K.pdf (page 10) November 12, 2004.
35. Whole Foods 10K-Q 2004 (page 10) August 15, 2005. http://www.wholefoodsmarket.com/investor/10K-Q/2004_10KA.pdf.
36. Whole Foods 10K-Q 2003 (page 9) November 11, 2004, http://www.wholefoodsmarket.com/investor/10K-Q/2003_10K.pdf.
37. Consumer Lifestyles in the United States (May 2003) 12.2 Expenditure on Food. *Euromonitor.* Solomon Smith Baker Library, Bentley College, Waltham, MA. November 1, 2004.
38. Gapper, John. "Organic Food Stores are on a Natural High." *The Financial Times,* September 2004.
39. Gapper, John. "Organic Food Stores are on a Natural High." *The Financial Times,* September 2004.
40. Gapper, John. "Organic Food Stores are on a Natural High." *The Financial Times,* September 2004.
41. Murphy McGill, Richard, "Truth or Scare." *American Demographics.* March 2004, Ithaca. Vol. 26, Issue 2, page 26.

42. Sechler, Bob, "Whole Foods Picks Up the Pace of its Expansion." *Wall Street Journal* (Eastern edition), September 29, 2004. New York, NY. Page 1.

43. Consumer Lifestyles in the United States (May 2003) 12.7 What Americans Eat. *Euromonitor.* Solomon Smith Baker Library, Bentley College, Waltham, MA. November 1, 2004.

44. Consumer Lifestyles in the United States (May 2003) 12.4 Popular Foods. *Euromonitor.* Solomon Smith Baker Library, Bentley College, Waltham, MA. November 1, 2004.

45. "Profile in B2B Strategy: Supermarket News Sidles into Natural, Organic Trend with New Quarterly." *Business CustomerWire.* Regional Business News. October 25, 2004.

46. "Profile in B2B Strategy: Supermarket News Sidles into Natural, Organic Trend with New Quarterly." *Business CustomerWire.* Regional Business News. October 25, 2004.

47. The World Market for Dairy Products (January 2004). 4.5 Organic Foods. 4.5.1 Global Market Trends in Organic Foods. *Euromonitor.* Solomon Smith Baker Library, Bentley College, Waltham, MA. November 1, 2004.

48. The World Market for Dairy Products (January 2004). 4.5 Organic Foods. 4.5.1 Global Market Trends in Organic Foods. *Euromonitor.* Solomon Smith Baker Library, Bentley College, Waltham, MA. November 1, 2004.

49. "Supermarkets' Prepared Meals Save Families Time." *KRTBN Knight-Ridder Tribune Business.* Daily News, Los Angeles. September 13, 2004.

50. Packaged Food in the United States (January 2004) 3.4 Organic Food. *Euromonitor.* Solomon Smith Baker Library, Bentley College, Waltham, MA. November 1, 2004.

51. Packaged Food in the United States (January 2004) 3.4 Organic Food. *Euromonitor.* Solomon Smith Baker Library, Bentley College, Waltham, MA. November 1, 2004.

52. Found on 10K-Q for 2004 (page 10) August 15, 2005. http://www.wholefoodsmarket.com/investor/10K-Q/2004_10KA.pdf. Found on 10K-Q for 2003 (page 8) November 11, 2004.

53. Whole Foods 10K-Q for 2003 (page 6) November 13, 2004.

54. Whole Foods 10K-Q 2003 (page 5) Whole Foods http://www.wholefoodsmarket.com/investor/10K-Q/2003_10K.pdf, November 13, 2004.

55. Whole Foods 10K Q 2004 (page 14) August 15, 2005 http://www.wholefoodsmarket.com/investor/10K-Q/2004_10KA.pdf.

56. Whole Foods 10K-Q 2003 (page 6) http://www.wholefoodsmarket.com/investor/10K-Q/2003_10K.pdf, November 13, 2004.

57. "Supermarkets' Prepared Meals Save Families Time." *KRTBN Knight-Ridder Tribune Business.* Daily News, Los Angeles. September 13, 2004.

58. "Supermarkets' Prepared Meals Save Families Time." *KRTBN Knight-Ridder Tribune Business.* Daily News, Los Angeles. September 13, 2004.

59. Whole Foods 10K-Q 2003 (page 5) http://www.wholefoodsmarket.com/investor/10K-Q/2003_10K.pdf, November 13, 2004.

60. Whole Foods 10K-Q 2003 (page 6) http://www.wholefoodsmarket.com/investor/10K-Q/2003_10K.pdf, November 13, 2004.

61. http://www.wholefoodsmarket.com/investor/10K-Q/2003_10K.pdf Found on 10K-Q for 2003 (page 7) November 11, 2004.

62. Whole Foods 10K-Q for 2003 http://www.wholefoodsmarket.com/investor/10K-Q/2003_10K.pdf (Page 8) November 7, 2004.

63. Whole Foods www.WholeFoodsmarket.com/company/declaration.html, November7, 2004.

64. Whole Foods www.WholeFoodsmarket.com/company/declaration.html, November7, 2004.

65. Whole Foods 10K-Q for 2003 www.WholeFoodsmarket.com/investor/10k-Q/2003_10k.pdf, November 7, 2004.

66. Whole Foods 10K-Q for 2003 www.WholeFoodsmarket.com/investor/10k-Q/2003_10k.pdf, November 7, 2004.

67. Nasdaq.com Market Symbol for Whole Foods is WFMI http://quotes.nasdaq.com/quote.dll?page=charting&mode=basics&intraday=off&timeframe=10y&charttype=ohlc&splits=off&earnings=off&movingaverage=None&lowerstudy=volume&comparison=off&index=&drilldown=off&symbol=WFMI&selected=WFMI, November 11, 2004.

68. Nasdaq.com Market Symbol for Whole Foods is WFMI http://quotes.nasdaq.com/Quote.dll?mode=stock&symbol=wfmi&symbol=&symbol=&symbol=&symbol=&symbol=&symbol=&symbol=&symbol=&symbol=&multi.x=31&multi.y=6, November 11, 2004.

69. Whole Foods: http://www.wholefoodsmarket.com/investor/10K-Q/2003_10K.pdf (Page 6) November 11, 2004.

70. Whole Foods Code of Conduct found at company website http://www.wholefoodsmarket.com/investor/codeofconduct.pdf, November 11, 2004.

71. Whole Foods Code of Conduct found at company website http://www.wholefoodsmarket.com/investor/codeofconduct.pdf (page 11).

72. Business Ethics 100 Best companies to work for http://www.business-ethics.com/100best.htm, November 12, 2004.

73. *Knight Ridder Tribune Business News.* Washington: September 28, 2004. page 1. "Providence, RI, Grocery Targets New Approach to Pricing"; Paul Grimaldi.

74. http://www.preparedfoods.com/PF/FILES/HTML/Mintel_Reports/Mintel_PDF/Summaries/sum-OrganicFoodBeverages-Aug2004.pdf.

75. Whole Foods 10K (Page 14) http://www.wholefoodsmarket.com/investor/10K-Q/2004_10KA.pdf.

Organizational Transformation at the BBC

This case was prepared by Vinay Kumar, under the direction of Vivek Gupta, ICFAI Center for Management Research (ICMR).

> *"My main challenge in the BBC is taking a fantastic British institution and figuring out, with everyone in the BBC, how to get it ready for this completely different world. All of my energy is going into getting the organisation to think about quite radical change. So I see myself as a bit of a gadfly in a way, saying, 'don't assume that we can carry on as we always have.'"[1]*
>
> —Mark Thompson, Director General,
> British Broadcasting Corporation, in 2006.

> *"The last 10 years at the BBC, we have seen terrible mismanagement. We had two director generals who really did not know how to run a large corporation."[2]*
>
> —Kate Adie, Former BBC Reporter,
> on the leadership of John Birt and Greg Dyke, in 2004.

Thompson Makes His Mark

On May 21, 2004, Mark Thompson (Thompson) was appointed Director General of the British Broadcasting Corporation (BBC), the world's first public broadcasting corporation. The immediate task on his hands—to reform the 82-year-old BBC, which had been severely criticized in the Hutton Report.[3] The Hutton Report, which went into a BBC report on the British Government's claims about Iraq's weapons of mass destruction, described the BBC's editorial system as defective and said that the editors had not scrutinized the script before it was aired. It also found fault with the BBC's management for having failed to act on a complaint given by the Government saying that the report by BBC correspondent Andrew Gilligan (Gilligan) was false. On January 29, 2004, following the publication of the Hutton Report, Greg Dyke (Dyke), Thompson's predecessor, who had stood by Gilligan's story, resigned.

Thompson took charge on June 21, 2004. He was quick to acknowledge the efforts of Dyke, but emphasized that the corporation would require some "real and radical changes" to sustain itself in the coming years. On his very first day, he announced the restructuring of the BBC's executive committee, the first of the many steps toward creating a simpler and more effective organization structure. The executive committee was divided into three boards—creative, journalism, and commercial—covering the principal activities of the BBC. Thompson himself headed the creative board (refer to Exhibit 1 for the Old and New Executive Committees).

Thompson also announced that the other businesses of the BBC such as production, commercial businesses, and commissioning would be reviewed with the sole aim of cutting costs and improving the efficiency of the organization as a whole. He said, "We're going to have to change the BBC more rapidly and radically over the next three to five years than at

This case was written by Vinay Kumar, under the direction of Vivek Gupta, ICFAI Center for Management Research (ICMR). It was complied from published sources, and is intended to be used as a basis for class discussion rather than to illustrate either effective or ineffective handling of a management situation.

EXHIBIT 1

BBC's Old and New Executive Committees

Previous Executive Committee

DG	Greg Dyke
Deputy DG and Dir. World Service & Global News	Mark Byford
Dir. Finance, Property & Business Affairs	John Smith
Dir. Strategy & Distribution	Carolyn Fairbairn
Dir. Policy & Legal	Caroline Thomson
Dir. BBC People	Stephen Dando
Dir. Marketing, Communications & Audiences (MC&A)	Andy Duncan
Dir. Television	Jana Bennett
Dir. Radio & Music	Jenny Abramsky
Dir. New Media & Technology	Ashley Highfield
Dir. News & Current Affairs	Richard Sambrook
Dir. Drama, Entertainment & CBBC (DEC)	Alan Yentob
Dir. Sport	Peter Salmon
Dir. Nations & Regions (N&R)	Pat Loughrey
Chief Executive, BBC Worldwide	Rupert Gavin

New Executive Board and Committees

DG	Mark Thompson
Deputy DG	Mark Byford
Chief Operating Officer	John Smith
Dir. Strategy & Distribution	Carolyn Fairbairn
Dir. BBC People	Stephen Dando
Dir. MC&A	Andy Duncan
Dir. Television	Jana Bennett
Dir. Radio & Music	Jenny Abramsky
Dir. New Media & Technology	Ashley Highfield

Creative Board

Chair	Mark Thompson
Deputy DG	Mark Byford
Creative Director and Dir. DEC	Alan Yentob
Dir. F&L	John Willis
Dir. Sport	Peter Salmon
The directors of TV, Radio, New Media, N&R, MC&A News divisional heads as appropriate	

Journalism Board

Chair	Mark Byford
Dir. News & Current Affairs	Richard Sambrook
Dir. N&R	Pat Loughrey
Dir. World Service & Global News	To be confirmed
Directors of TV, Radio, New Media, F&L as appropriate	

(continued)

EXHIBIT 1 (*continued*)

BBC's Old and New Executive Committees

Commercial Board	
Chair	John Smith
Chief Exec, BBC Worldwide	Rupert Gavin
Heads of BBC Broadcast, BBC Resources, BBC Vecta	
Dir. MC&A	Andy Duncan
Dir. Strategy & Distribution	Carolyn Fairbairn

Source: "Change and Reorganization—Signs of Things to Come as Thompson Becomes DG," www.bbc.co.uk, June 22, 2004.

any previous point in its history. It feels like the task of really changing the BBC has only begun."[4]

A number of people felt that Thompson had come in at a critical time when the BBC's integrity was under question, employee morale was down, and the impact of digital technology was looming large. They predicted that the journey further down the road would in no way be an easy one for him. However, analysts were confident about Thompson's capability to solve at least some of BBC's problems. Tessa Jowell (Jowell), Secretary of State for Culture, Media, and Sport, believed that Thompson was the right man for the post under such circumstances. Jane Root, Former Controller of the BBC-owned BBC2, said, "He thinks very strategically about the big issues in television, and that is more than anything what the BBC needs its new director general to do. There is going to be an incredible amount of turbulence in television in the next few years; Mark was always a big-range thinker who didn't just think about the here and now."[5]

Background Note

The BBC was created on October 18, 1922, as the British Broadcasting Company, by a group of wireless manufacturers including Guglielmo Marconi (Marconi), inventor of the radio. Regular broadcasting began from Marconi's London studio on November 14, 1922. The company's mission was "to inform, educate, and entertain."

In 1927, the company's name was changed to the British Broadcasting Corporation and it was granted a Royal Charter, which put it under the control of the UK government (refer to Exhibit 2 for details on Royal Charter). The Charter defined the BBC's objectives, powers, and obligations. The BBC was operated through a 12-member Board of Governors, who acted

EXHIBIT 2

BBC's Royal Charter

A Royal Charter was the only way to get incorporated in the early 20th century. A number of cities, theaters, and charity institutions were established under the Charter. For the BBC, the Charter along with an agreement gives it editorial independence (freedom to report) and sets out public obligations. It also gives the BBC the flexibility to adapt to changes. This makes the BBC answerable only to the public. The Charter is renewed every ten years and the review process takes around three years. For example, if the due date for renewing the Charter is January 2007, the review starts from January 2003 onward and ends in December 2006.

During the Charter review, the public is consulted and its opinion regarding the services rendered by the BBC is considered. The BBC, meanwhile, would have to justify the extension of the Charter and also the license fee. It has to give its own charter manifesto outlining what it wants to do during the next charter period. The government issues a Green Paper in response to the manifesto. The Green Paper outlines initial options for the BBC on how it should operate in the future, raises issues if any, and gives the BBC time to respond. After the BBC responds, the government issues a White Paper which firms up the options in the Green Paper. There will be further deliberations in Parliament before the government publishes the Royal Charter.

Adapted from various sources.

as trustees and ensured that the organization was accountable for its work to the public while maintaining its independence in reporting news. The day-to-day operations were managed by an Executive Board, which consisted of nine members and was led by a Director General. The BBC, which had no competitor at that time, gained revenues only through a license fee (10 shillings), set by the British parliament and paid for by radio owners. It was not allowed to indulge in commercial activities such as advertising. In 1932, the BBC began broadcasts (BBC Empire Service) outside Britain for the English-speaking people under the then British Empire.

After starting experimental broadcasts in 1932, the BBC officially started television services in November 1936, under the name BBC Television Service. It also issued 8.5 million radio licenses covering around 98% of Britain's population. However, during the Second World War, television broadcasts were suspended for security reasons and these recommenced only in 1946. Though television services were suspended during the War, the BBC continued with its radio broadcasts. The Corporation earned a reputation for honest and accurate news reporting and its 9 o'clock news became very popular. The BBC Empire Service, which was renamed BBC External Service in 1940, was broadcasting radio programs in 40 languages by the end of the War. The BBC acquired the reputation of being impartial and its news was regarded as authoritative. The Third Programme service, which it launched in 1946, triggered the expansion of radio services. The Third Programme broadcast cultural programs such as concerts, opera, drama, talks, and features. In the same year, the combined license fee of £2 for television and radio was introduced. The Wireless Telegraphy Act of 1949 required any person who possessed a television set to pay the license fee.

Till the early 1950s, radio dominated over television in Britain. There were around 12 million exclusive radio licenses while the combined licenses for radio and TV were only 350,000. The budget allocated for the television division was also negligible. However, this scenario changed with the coronation of Queen Elizabeth II in 1953. For the first time, television was allowed to cover a royal ceremony and it was estimated that around 20 million TV viewers worldwide watched the coronation ceremony.

In September 1955, the BBC's monopoly ended with the launch of ITV[6] (Independent Television), which was not funded through license fees and thus was the first commercial channel in the UK. ITV bought television programs from the US television channels and aired them along with its own programs. Its popularity rose very quickly and the BBC's market share fell to as low as 28% in 1957. By the end of the 1950s, innovative programs such as *Grandstand with David Coleman, Monitor with Huw Weldon, Benny Hill Show, Your Life in Their Hands,* and *Whicker's World* did help the BBC increase its viewership. However, it was never the same, post the ITV launch.

In 1964, BBC2 was launched to provide experimental and new kinds of programs to the audience. In the same year, the BBC Television Service was renamed BBC1. In 1967, BBC2 started color broadcasts and BBC1 joined in 1969. In 1971, the radio only licenses were abolished and the license fee was meant only for television. The BBC saw its popularity and income increase in the 1970s as more and more people bought televisions. It offered a variety of programs belonging to various genres such as drama and comedy, documentaries, etc.

Need for Restructuring

Until 1982, there were only four television channels in the UK—BBC1, BBC2, ITV, and Channel 4[7]—all of which used the terrestrial television broadcasting[8] method to air their programs. The early 1980s saw the rise of satellite television[9] in the UK. Launched in 1982, Satellite Television was the first of such channels. It was purchased by News Corporation[10] in 1984 and re-launched as Sky Channel, a pan European network. In February 1989, Sky Channel was again launched as a four-channel network for the UK—Sky Channel (later Sky One), Sky News, Sky Movies, and Eurosport. After a lot of delay, the British Satellite Broadcasting[11] (BSB) was launched in March 1990, to compete with Sky Channel. Both companies lost huge amounts and in December 1990, they merged to form BSkyB. BSkyB slowly rose to become a major competitor of BBC.

Meanwhile, in 1984, the UK government decided to introduce cable television, which had already gained huge popularity in the US, and it passed the Cable and Broadcasting Act the same year. Swindon Cable was given the first license in 1984. The Cable Authority was created with a view to further expanding the cable television business, and it awarded licenses to the cable operators. Aberdeen Cable (later known

EXHIBIT 3

Growth in Television Channels in the UK (1950–2002)

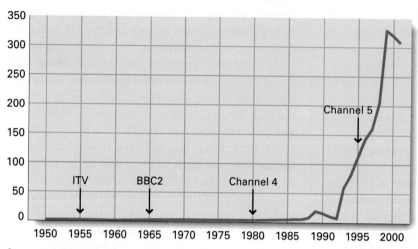

Source: www.ofcom.org.uk.

as Atlantic) was given the first license by the Cable Authority. By the end of 1990, the Cable Authority had issued about 124 licenses to independent cable operators (refer to Exhibit 3 for the growth of television channels in the UK between 1950 and 2002).

Apart from competition, the BBC also faced pressure to reduce its rising operating costs during the 1990s. In 1992, Sir John Birt (Birt) was appointed as BBC's Director General. Birt reduced the workforce by 4000, which resulted in a saving of US$ 465 million, and merged the news divisions of radio, television, and BBC World Service.[12] The BBC expanded overseas by forming a joint venture with the Public Broadcasting System in the US. In February 1997, Birt sold the home transmission division to Castle Transmission Services for £244 million. In November 1997, Birt started BBC News 24, a satellite channel that was offered without any subscription fee, and later launched four more subscription channels. It imported hit serials such as *ER*, *X-Files*, etc. from the US and sold its programs to television channels in other countries.

By the late 1990s, digital broadcast services began in the UK. The digital technology was superior to analog in terms of picture quality and the number of channels offered. Moreover, it provided other services such as accessing the Internet and other interactive services. In 1997, Birt launched BBC Online (www.bbc.co.uk), which went on to become one of the most popular websites in the UK. In the same

year, he started BBC Worldwide,[13] a commercial arm of the BBC, which was involved in global channels and television sales, content and production, etc. In September 1998,[14] BBC Choice, the first complete digital broadcast service in the UK, was started.

Some of Birt's decisions, however, came in for a lot of criticism from industry analysts and the media. In 1993, he introduced the internal market concept dubbed "Producer Choice" which gave producers the right to choose between the production resources (studios, cameras, crew, etc.) provided by the BBC and outsiders. The BBC's in-house production department had already been affected by the Broadcasting Act of 1990, which required all the television channels to source 25% of their television programs from independent producers—people who did not own more than 25% shareholding in a broadcaster or were not owned more than 25% by a broadcaster.

Under this concept, the producers favored outsiders as the BBC departments were charging high prices. Each individual item borrowed was charged and nearly 400,000 bills were issued to producers every year. In fact, the departments were asked to charge real prices for their services. For example, the BBC pronunciation department, which helped drama actors and news readers in the pronunciation of difficult words, charged £12 per word. Hence, the producers usually looked to outside people or managed themselves. Renting a CD from the BBC library was also costlier than buying a CD outside and charges were levied even if the producers wanted video and audio clips. The same was the case with the other departments such as costumes, scenic, and make-up. Ironically, the high costs charged left these resources idle most of the time. This resulted in a number of job losses with 5000 alone in very first year. "Producer Choice" was described as an "abysmal act of vandalism" by a number of media and industry observers.

In another major decision to restructure the BBC, Birt separated the production and broadcast divisions as he felt that the in-house production department was not considering the views of the audience while producing programs and the BBC was becoming a producer-controlled organization. However, this step boomeranged as the broadcast commissioners showed little faith in the in-house production department. The developers went through a long bureaucratic process to submit their programs only to find most of them being rejected. The production department, therefore, started producing programs that had been ordered by the commissioners. The commissioners, for their part, looked to market researchers and focus groups for advice on the type of programs to be made for gaining public attention. Thus, control over the nature of the program shifted to these groups which affected the quality of programs. Further, fewer dramas were produced as their cost of production was higher than that of fact-based programs and reality shows.

Birt also made the BBC bigger. The BBC internal market had 190 business units which looked after the trading between various BBC departments. He started a new department called Corporate Center to provide key strategic services to the BBC such as legal services, planning, personnel, etc. The Center employed hundreds of people and cost the BBC around £60 million pounds every year, which was more than the costs incurred in running BBC's Radio 1. He also used the services of around five management consultancies at a cost of about £22 million per year. Former BBC officials came down heavily on this step, but Birt convinced everyone of the increasing importance of management consultants.

There was no cooperation between the various departments. The Corporate Center and the drama division had differences over budget allocation. The drama department was forced to air programs on the lines of the popular programs on ITV. The radio division was left with the feeling that it was being sidelined by the television division. The BBC was not able to acquire broadcast rights for prestigious sporting events such as Formula One, the Ryder Cup, etc. and lost out to BSkyB, Channel 4, and ITV. Further, the competition from satellite and cable television affected the BBC and its audience share fell from 51% in 1981 to less than 38% in 2000. Above all, employee morale was at a real low.

A number of analysts expressed concern over the BBC's declining audience share as it directly affected the corporation's revenues. They wanted the license fee to be abandoned and advocated alternate methods such as commercial advertising, privatization through share holding, etc. to fund the BBC. Analysts said that the BBC should generate more revenues through advertising rather than through the license fee.

Greg Dyke Becomes Director General

In January 2000, Birt was replaced by Dyke, CEO of Pearson Television. Dyke, who took over as Director General on February 1, 2000, found the BBC's organizational structure extremely complex. There were far too many layers and the organization was much too bureaucratic. He immediately announced the creation of the "One BBC" program where various departments and their employees would cooperate with each other and work toward achieving common goals. Commenting on the program, Dyke said, "Our aim is to create One BBC, where people enjoy their job and are inspired and united behind the common purpose of making great programs and delivering outstanding services."[15]

Dyke announced a change in the organization structure aimed at giving the top management more power and reducing duplication. He abandoned the Corporate Center and replaced it with six Professional Service Divisions—Public Policy; Human Resources & Internal Communications; Distribution & Technology; Finance, Property & Business Affairs; Marketing & Communications; and Strategy—to support the BBC's operations. Though he retained "Producer Choice," the number of business units was reduced from 190 to 50. He removed the library charges and producers and researchers could access video clips and printed materials for free.

Dyke created a new Executive Committee with 17 directors who reported directly to him. Of the 17, nine were heads of programming and broadcasting. This move aimed at shifting the decision making on programming to the top management (refer to Exhibit 4 for BBC's Organizational Chart under Dyke). It brought

EXHIBIT 4

BBC's Organizational Chart under Dyke

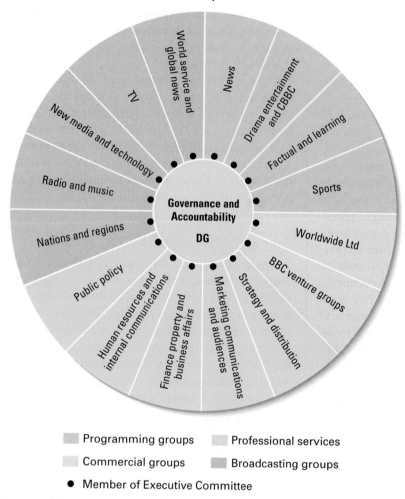

■ Programming groups   ■ Professional services
■ Commercial groups   ■ Broadcasting groups
● Member of Executive Committee

Source: www.bbc.co.uk.

Dyke closer to all the key operations of the BBC. The division heads were given full autonomy to run their own divisions, which was new to them. Dyke soon found that all the divisions were fighting for a bigger slice of the annual budget and so announced budgets for each of the divisions until the year 2006. He created a new Leadership Group by pooling 60 people from the organization. This group discussed the latest developments in the market and came up with new ideas for improving the BBC.

Dyke said that the BBC would reduce overhead costs from 24% of its total income to 15% by 2005. He laid off 900 employees and planned to reduce the amount spent on consultants. These savings were to be used for developing quality programs and another £200 million were to be spent on programming every

year. Dyke aimed to save a cumulative amount of about £1.2 billion by 2007.

Dyke invested money on developing dramas and increased the budget for this by £100 million every year. The BBC also started spending more on sports and other events such as the Queen's Jubilee celebrations, concerts in Buckingham Palace, etc. In November 2001, the BBC launched the BBC interactive television service (BBCi), which was made available on all digital television platforms—digital cable, digital satellite, and digital terrestrial television (refer to Exhibit 5 for the list of BBC's television and radio services in the UK).

In April 2002, ITV Digital[16] shut down its operations and its digital terrestrial TV (DTT) licenses went up for sale. The consortium led by the BBC and backed by Crown Castle and BSkyB won the DTT

BBC's Television and Radio Services in the UK

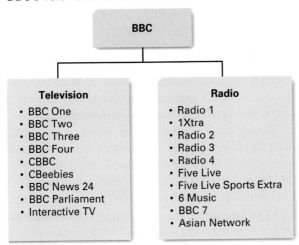

Source: www.bbc.co.uk.

license in July 2002. BBC got one license while Crown Castle got two. The BBC announced that it would offer 24 free-to-air digital channels, some channels of BSkyB, and interactive and digital radio services. To receive all the channels, consumers would have to pay £99 for a set-top box. All the channels were available after the launch of Freeview in October 2002.

In its annual report for the financial year 2002–03, the BBC said it had reduced its overheads by 13%. This was 2% more than the announced target and the corporation also increased its net income by £54 million. BBC's digital services reached 35% of people who received digital television programs as against 23% during the year 2001–02. To gain popularity among the young audience, the BBC started BBC Three and IXtra, a radio channel. There was better understanding among the BBC staff and corporate level communication too improved. However, issues such as collaboration between various departments still remained a concern.

Just when things seemed to be finally going right for the BBC, the Dr. David Kelly episode happened and the Hutton report exposed BBC's vulnerable editorial process. According to the report:

- The editorial system at the BBC was defective as the editors did not see Gilligan's script before allowing it to be broadcast.

- The BBC management did not examine the notes of Gilligan's interview with Dr. Kelly.

- The BBC management had defects in the complaints investigation process.

- The BBC governors failed to order an enquiry into the truthfulness of the Gilligan report and to accept that his notes did not support his May 29 broadcast.

Dyke, who strongly defended the BBC during the row, apologized for the unfortunate incident. Accepting responsibility, he resigned twenty hours after the BBC's Chairman Gavyn Davies stepped down. At the time of his resignation, Dyke said, "I don't want to go. But if in the end you screw up you have to go. I do not necessarily accept the findings of Lord Hutton."[17]

Many analysts and the media criticized the BBC in light of the revelations in the Hutton report. The British newspapers carried articles on the front page— *The Times'* headline read "Blizzard of blame chills BBC" and *The Guardian's* said "Crisis cuts through the BBC." Gerald Kaufman, Labour Member of Parliament, said, "The BBC is no longer relied on in the way it was claimed. It's placed itself in a situation where its word isn't accepted automatically anymore. It's gone from being an institution to just another broadcaster, and a shoddy one at that."[18]

BBC radio saw a decrease in the number of listeners after the publication of the report though the BBC itself attributed the decline to factors such as the absence of Sarah Montague, presenter of the *Today* program, who was on maternity leave. Strong doubts were raised on the BBC's ability to regain the faith of the viewers. The worst was the timing of the incident, coming as it did before the renewal of the Charter, due in December 2006. This was described as "the worst crisis in the BBC's 80-year history."

On February 18, 2004, Mark Byford (Byford), acting Director General,[19] appointed a committee led by the BBC's former Director of News and Current Affairs Ronald Neil (Neil) to examine the issues raised in the Hutton Report, to identify the lesson to be learnt from the episode, and to make recommendations on improving the editorial and complaints handling mechanism at the BBC. Neil was supported by other former and working BBC executives.[20]

Thompson Takes Charge

The committee submitted its report on June 23, 2004, a day after Thompson took charge as the Director General of the BBC. The Neil Report called for a vast improvement in the training process of the journalists. It suggested establishment of a college of journalism and a greater role for editors and lawyers in the BBC's editorial process. The committee wanted the BBC to continue to broadcast reports based on a single source but only after proper examination. It emphasized that only the most accurate information should be given to the public (refer to Exhibit 6 for a summary of the Neil Report).

Neil said, "As the largest employer of journalists in the UK, the BBC has an obligation to take the lead in strengthening training in craft skills and promoting debate about journalistic standards and ethics in broadcasting. All programs operating under the BBC's journalistic banner must work to the same values, professional disciplines, and journalistic culture."[21]

Thompson asked Byford to implement the Neil Report recommendations as soon as possible. He announced new journalism guidelines under which the rules were tightened on the use of reports prepared from conversations, anonymous sources, and a single source. These could be used only after a thorough internal review. As the Neil Report wanted the program editors to take full responsibility for whatever content their team produced, the editors were given the right to know the identity of the source (single or anonymous) from the journalist before approving the story for broadcast. It was up to the editors to exercise this right after considering the experience and track record of the journalist. It was reported that the disclosure of an anonymous source was required only if the report contained any serious allegations.

During the Neil investigation, seniors in the BBC news division expressed the fear that journalists who were not qualified were aiming to climb up the corporate ladder and take on higher responsibilities. The BBC therefore planned to establish a training college led by an academic by mid-2005 to give the minimum level of training every year to its 7000 journalists.

EXHIBIT 6

Summary of the Neil Report

- Accuracy and precision in all BBC journalism is paramount. It must be based on robust and tested evidence and reinforced by accurate note-taking.
- Accurate and reliable note-taking is a prime journalistic skill and should be part of journalist training in the BBC.
- It is a guiding principle of BBC journalism that we are fair to all—fair to those against whom allegations are being made, fair to the audience, and to contributors. Fairness to people and organizations against whom allegations are going to be made by the BBC is of great importance.
- Serious and potentially defamatory allegations must always be put in time for a considered response before transmission other than in rare cases when there are compelling countervailing reasons not to do so.
- Because of the trusted place in which BBC's journalism is held, allegations made by a third party will often be regarded by many viewers and listeners as also being made by the BBC itself.
- The BBC should not normally break stories making serious allegations in live two-ways.
- Granting anonymity to a source should never be done casually or automatically. A named on the record source is always to be preferred. However, with an anonymous source, the audience must be told why the source is anonymous and, in the BBC's view, credible. Protection of confidential sources is a fundamental principle of journalism.
- The BBC transmits hundreds of hours of news and current affairs output every day. As the custodians of the BBC's editorial values, individual editors and executive producers must take the day-to-day responsibility for them.
- Presenters are answerable to their individual editors and in all of their journalistic work must embody the BBC's core editorial values.
- At the heart of the BBC's journalism is a well-trained journalistic workforce. In a fast-changing world, life-long training at every level is vital. Competence based training should be the key to competence based promotion. We recommend that the BBC establishes an industry-wide, residential college of journalism under the leadership of an academic principal.
- The handling of complaints needs reform. All complaints should be handled in the same way regardless of who is making them. The Director-General should not be directly involved in the normal process of responding to complaints. The Head of the Editorial Complaints Unit must be empowered to act independently of those responsible for output. When mistakes are made, the BBC must develop a system and a culture that encourages fast clarification and unambiguous correction.

Source: "BBC Journalism: The Neil Report," www.bbc.co.uk, June 2004.

Changes were also brought about in the complaints procedure. These included keeping the Director General out of the process of responding to the complaints. This change came in the wake of Dyke's strong resistance to accepting the BBC's fault involving Dr. Kelly. Lawyers were put in the main newsrooms to review the complaints. The BBC said that it would start to accept and apologize for its mistakes and try to learn from them. In this connection, it started a website, NewsWatch, which dealt with complaints and feedback from the audience. All serious mistakes and their corrections were to be published across all the BBC platforms along with explanations. The BBC also commenced a similar feedback program NewsWatch on the News 24 Channel.

A few analysts criticized the BBC's actions post the Hutton Report and, in particular, the recommendations of the Neil Report. They felt that the BBC had always set very high standards and the Neil Report was absolutely unnecessary. According to Julie Kirkbride, Secretary of Shadow Culture,[22] the establishment of a training college was an additional expenditure and would require the BBC to go beyond its core activities. According to Brian MacArthur, a columnist at *The Times*, the BBC had been better than most of the British newspapers which never apologized for their mistakes. He said, "The Neil Report does not expose a single real problem with the standards of BBC journalism, because there never was a problem in the first place. In my view, if you take away the lapse by Andrew Gilligan, newspapers could learn a lot from BBC journalism. It seems to me to be of a very high standard, and always has been."[23]

Charter Manifesto

Since the early 2000s, the license fee charged by the BBC had come under severe criticism. In August 2003, the Conservative Party, the second largest political party in the UK, charged that the viewers were paying for programs that had been copied from commercial channels and demanded that the fee be cut. It said that the BBC was getting an unfair advantage by receiving £2.7 billion[24] as annual fee (refer to Exhibit 7 for how the license fee is spent by the BBC).

On June 29, 2004, the BBC announced its Charter manifesto called "Building Public Value" aimed at providing value to its customers in the wake of changing customer preferences and the competition. The Charter manifesto, which consisted of BBC's proposals

EXHIBIT 7

How the Monthly License Fee Is Spent by BBC

	2006 (Monthly Cost in £)
BBC One	3.52
BBC Two	1.52
Transmission and collection costs	1.08
Nations and English Regions television	1.04
BBC Radio 1,2,3,4 and Five Live	1.02
Digital television channels	1.00
Local and Nations' radio	0.68
Bbc.co.uk	0.36
BBC Jam	0.14
Digital radio stations	0.10
Interactive TV (BBCi)	0.08
Total	**10.54**

Source: www.bbc.co.uk.

for the coming years, would be sent to the government to peruse while reviewing the Royal Charter. The manifesto justified the continuance of the license fee and the Charter for the next ten years. In the wake of criticism over the license fee, Thompson announced sweeping measures in the nine-point manifesto. The measures were:

- **Leading the digital transformation:** The BBC reiterated its commitment to leading the UK in the digital television segment by fully shifting to digital terrestrial broadcasting by 2012. It would launch a service that would allow all its television programs to be downloaded within seven days of broadcast.

- **Original programs:** The BBC would develop original content and try to refrain from being a "copycat," a criticism that it often faced. It would produce quality programs by understanding the customers' needs, producing better dramas on its television and radio, and investing more on current affairs and comedy shows.

- **Public value test:** To assess the quality of new programs and monitor the performance of current programs, the BBC governors would put all the BBC's programs to a public value test on four criteria—reach, quality, impact, and value for money—before they were launched. The BBC also established a framework of measuring the performance of the Corporation based on the same criteria (refer to Exhibit 8 for the framework for measuring BBC's performance).

- **Scale and scope of services:** The BBC would use public value to decide on the scale and scope of its services. This would be applicable to the breadth of the BBC (multimedia and a range of other services) and depth (BBC-owned commercial divisions, etc.).

- **Fostering partnerships:** The BBC planned to enter into joint ventures with outside partners to carry out educational, cultural, and other activities. It would publish a partnership contract by the end of 2004, which would set forth the principles and standards that the BBC would bring to any partnership. It would also publish a partner guide to attract potential partners.

- **Expanding out of London:** The BBC would shed its image of being "too London-centric" and move about half of its businesses out of the capital over the next ten years. It would spend more than £1 billion every year on programs made out of London.

- **A transparent BBC:** The BBC, which had always been more of a closed organization, planned to open up to suit the views of the modern day customers. More information would be provided about the organization on its website (www.bbc .co.uk/info). Its various media would feature comments and complaints about its programs. On the whole, the BBC would put the audience at the center of all its activities.

- **Reforming license fee payment:** In the opinion poll conducted by the Market and Opinion Research International[25] (MORI) in early 2004, two-thirds of the respondents did not support the license fee and

EXHIBIT 8

Framework for Measuring Performance of BBC

Source: www.bbc.co.uk.

suggested alternate methods such as advertising, sponsorship to programs, etc. to fund the BBC. However, the BBC believed that the license fee would enable it to perform better. To reduce the burden of license fee on the public the BBC would try to reduce its overhead costs by 10% of the expenditure. It said it would modernize the license fee payment by moving from a paper-based system to online payment and make the fee affordable to the poor.

- **Improving the BBC governance:** The role and responsibilities of the governors would be clearly outlined to make them more independent of the management. It would create a new 'governance unit' to help them regulate the BBC and to do tests of public value for the approval of programs. This was in response to the criticism in the Hutton Report that the BBC governors were being controlled by the management.

Implementing Change at BBC

In the first week of December 2004, Thompson began implementing the manifesto by announcing a new vision aimed at making the BBC a more creative and efficient digital broadcaster. He announced that his vision had three aspects—"a bold new program and content strategy based above all around the idea of excellence," "a transformation of the BBC into a state-of-the art digital broadcaster," and "an irreversible shift in the culture of the BBC toward simplicity, opportunity, and creativity."

Thompson announced that 2,900 of the BBC's employees (more than one-tenth of its total workforce) would be laid off to reduce costs. Of the total job cuts, 2,500 would be in finance, marketing, legal services, and other departments that were not involved in program making and the remaining in the educational departments. According to Thompson, the job cuts were aimed at reducing costs by up to £320 million per year within the next three years. This was £165 million more than the savings announced before Thompson's appointment. Further, Thompson asked the individual departments (radio, television, news, etc.) of the BBC to reduce their costs by 15% and hinted at outsourcing some of the other jobs.

Thompson also announced that BBC's main channel BBC1 would broadcast fewer reruns and would reduce the production of formula-based and copied shows (refer to Exhibit 9 for details of BBC's television channels). He said the BBC would try and differentiate its programs from the ones being aired by competing commercial channels by developing original content. According to Thompson, the change was necessitated by the emergence of digital technology, which had raised people's expectations of the BBC. He said that it would have to make investments in developing

---

EXHIBIT 9

Details of BBC's Television Channels

BBC One: It is the oldest channel in the BBC stable and broadcasts news, sports, drama, comedy shows, film premieres, and documentaries.

BBC Two: The second oldest among the BBC channels, it initially broadcast programs catering to a niche audience and programs related to educational and community functions. However, in the recent years it has moved away to become a mainstream channel.

BBC Three: Launched in 2003, the channel focuses on young adults with new comedy, drama, entertainment, current affairs, etc.

BBC Four: Launched in March 2002, the channel is available to the digital television audience. It focuses on arts, culture, and world cinema, dramas, documentaries, and debates.

CBBC: CBBC (Children's BBC) targets children between six and twelve years.

CBeebies: Launched in February 2002, CBeebies target children below six years.

NEWS24: Started in 1997, News24 is a 24-hour news channel.

BBC Parliament: Launched in 1998, BBC Parliament broadcasts live and recorded versions of the sessions of the British House of Commons, House of Lords, etc.

BBCi: Started in 1999 as BBC Text, BBCi stands for BBC interactive television. It offers up to date information on the weather, education, entertainment, etc. to all digital television audiences.

Compiled from various sources.

programs related to big-budget drama, factual event shows, music, comedy, reality shows, children's TV and radio, and others where the BBC was strong.

Thompson also addressed the contentious issue of the percentage of BBC programs that could be made by independent producers, which was at 25%. Though he retained the existing quota, he introduced a new concept called "window of creative competition" which allowed the independent companies to compete against the in-house production department of the BBC for another 25% of its programs. Thus, the BBC was guaranteed only 50% in-house production for its programs. According to Thompson, this kind of competition would provide the best of the programs to the BBC's viewers.

In order to make the BBC represent the whole of the UK, nearly 1,800 staff of various divisions—Children's TV and radio, BBC Sport, BBC Radio 5 Live, research and development, etc. were planned to be moved to the newly created state-of-the-art center in Manchester. It was also decided that the television drama production outside London would be increased from 30% to 50% from the next charter period between 2007 and 2016.

Regarding the commercial activities of the BBC, Thompson said such activities should "exploit and/or export BBC content and its brand," and hinted that the some of the activities would be carried out in collaboration with private parties. BBC's divisions such as BBC Broadcast and BBC Resources would enter into partnerships and joint ownerships for commercial purposes.

The job cuts proposed by Thompson were met with severe opposition from the employee union Broadcasting Entertainment Cinematograph and Theatre Union (BECTU)[26] and also from a number of analysts. BECTU members said that Thompson was trying to appease the British government in its efforts to retain the license fee. Analysts charged that the BBC had always promised something or the other before every Charter review but never really gone about achieving it. The "window of creative competition" was seen more as vindicating the fact that Thompson had no faith in the efficiency of the BBC's production department. Analysts felt that Thompson was taking too many measures at one time.

Thompson defended his decision and said, "Both I, Greg Dyke, and John Birt before him have all looked at the issue of the BBC's bureaucracy, our processes, our layers. Now is the moment where we really do have to grasp some nettles there and say is there a way

we can run this organization more simply, more directly, with fewer meetings and less complexity and therefore transfer many, many millions of pounds out of that part of the BBC and into programs."[27]

In March 2005, Thompson announced that another 1,500 jobs would be cut in the news and programs division over the next three years. He also increased the savings target from £320 million to £355 million. In the same month, the Department for Culture, Media, and Sport (on behalf of the government) published the Green Paper[28] based on the feedback given by Lord Burns, the Secretary of State's independent adviser on the Charter Review, and his team. The feedback was prepared based on the views of a number of viewers consulted by the team.

According to the Green Paper, the BBC was to be granted a new Charter for the next ten years starting from January 1, 2007, and ending December 31, 2016. It was felt that the ten years would enable the BBC, and the television industry, to stabilize during the switchover to digital television. The government also saw no viable alternative to the license fee and decided to continue with it, but said it would review it to find suitable alternatives after the digital transformation took place in 2012.[29] All the BBC governors would be removed and replaced by a new entity called the BBC Trust.

The Green Paper also raised some issues. About 33% of the respondents felt that the BBC was not providing value for money. One third of the viewers felt that the quality of programs was deteriorating. They expressed concern over the BBC's lack of accountability to the viewers. To address this concern, it was proposed that the BBC governors would be replaced by the BBC Trust, which would be accountable to the viewers. All BBC services should try to accomplish a set of five purposes during the next charter period (refer to Table 1 for the five purposes).

The issues raised would be considered by a parliamentary committee and an independent enquiry would be conducted by the House of Commons Select Committee on Culture, Media, and Sport. Further, parliamentary scrutiny and consultations would take place and these would form the basis for the Royal Charter.

In May 2005, the BBC responded to the Green Paper. It welcomed the decision to grant a new Charter and to continue the license fee funding. Thompson gave the assurance that the BBC would provide original and quality content to the viewers and try to explore opportunities to serve people better. However,

TABLE 1

BBC's Five Purposes

- Sustaining citizenship and civil society,
- Promoting education and learning,
- Stimulating creativity and cultural excellence,
- Representing the UK, its nations, regions and communities,
- Bringing the UK to the world and the world to the UK.

Another purpose was to be technically ahead in adopting technology and to play an active part during the transformation to digital television.

Source: "Review of the BBC's Royal Charter," www.bbc.co.uk, March 2005.

Michael Grade, Chairman of the BBC, said that the Paper had underrated the impact of digital technologies on the relationship between audience and media and expressed opposition to the review of the license fee after the digital transformation.

The BBC Journalism College

In the last week of June 2005, the BBC launched the BBC Journalism College at an investment of £5 million to train journalists working in various divisions of the BBC such as news, the World Service, etc. As opposed to the concept of classroom training, the instructions were imparted through interactive e-learning sessions, seminars, and workshops (conducted by Neil) at various locations across the globe. The training was aimed at supporting the five editorial principles mentioned in the Neil Report—truth and accuracy; serving the public interests; independence from any external influence; accountability to audience and; impartiality in reporting. The e-learning module would reduce costs for the BBC, which planned to increase the spending on journalism training to £10 million by 2008 to develop "interactive learning modules" which could be accessed by BBC journalists from any BBC office across the world. Every journalist was to be provided a minimum of 20 hours of training every year.

The staff was given "training passports" which were stamped after they completed the training sessions. Completion of training was made one of the requirements for promotion. Further, no journalist was allowed to apply for senior posts unless he/she had completed training and acquired the necessary skills, even if he/she had the relevant work experience. For example, a senior broadcast journalist would have to finish some training sessions before becoming an editor. Training would also focus on the environment and issues in Europe, the Middle East etc. which were thought to be complicated.

Most of the courseware was developed in-house except for the material for the external training activities. The college concentrated not only on imparting core journalistic skills to the reporters, but also values and ethics at the editorial level. Commenting on this, Byford said, "This is an exciting and ambitious training initiative which will, we hope, set a gold standard for broadcast journalism training in the UK. We want to offer our staff career-long training and development to support them in their dealing with today's complex journalistic environment."[30]

Despite these efforts, the BBC believed that its training and editorial procedures did not face any major problem. It said that it produced 120 hours of news programming every day and due to the size of its operations, mistakes were bound to happen. Richard Sambrook, Director of the BBC's Global News division, said, "It's not that there was a big problem before but the environment has changed very rapidly. New technology such as digital cameras, laptops, and the Internet have brought about more 24-hour services. Competition and pressures on journalists in terms of decisions they have to take have vastly increased."[31]

In October 2005, the BBC submitted a proposal for an increase in the license fee by 2.3% above the inflation rate to meet its cumulative requirement of £5.5 billion in the next seven years in order to improve its programs and digital services. Of the total requirement, the BBC would get £3.9 billion through the ongoing cost cutting measures and the license fee increase would bridge the gap. This meant that the license fee, which was £126.50 per annum, would be increased by £3.14 every year until 2013.

In March 2006, the Department for Culture, Media, and Sport published a White Paper which outlined the way the BBC should be run. This paper was to be the basis for the renewal of BBC's Royal Charter. While the purpose set in the Green Paper and other proposals such as scrapping of the post of governors remained the same, the BBC was asked to give priority to entertainment and stop being "copycats" or "rating chasers." The Government retained its proposal to consider alternatives to the license fee such as subscriptions, etc. after 2012. Further, in April 2006, Jowell said that the license fee increase would be much lower than the BBC had proposed. There would be further deliberations in Parliament and the Royal Charter would be published during the last quarter of 2006.

In April 2006, Thompson announced "Creative Future"—a set of themes and ideas proposed to achieve the purposes laid out in the White Paper and prepare the BBC for the digital age. Thompson appointed two teams in April 2005 to study how the world might be in 2012, the tastes and preferences of

the audiences and the steps the BBC should take to meet the requirements. The "Creative Future" strategy aimed at making the BBC content appealing and easily available to the young audience.

Recommendations were made on the "eight critical areas of output"—Journalism, Sport, Drama, Music, Comedy, Entertainment, Children & Teens, and Knowledge Building. According to Thompson, "Five Big Themes" emerged out of the study—Martini Media, Serious About Entertainment, The Young, Findability, and The Active Audience (refer to Exhibit 10 for details of BBC's Creative Future Strategy). Commenting

EXHIBIT 10

BBC—Details of the Creative Future Strategy

Recommendations on Eight Critical Areas of Output

Sport: Start a broadband portal that offers live video and audio, comments, and analysis from specialists, interactive comments on sporting events. Start an exclusive news program for sports on television, appoint a BBC Sports Editor, and phase out old programs.

Music: Have a single music strategy across all platforms along with regular cross-platform events and make them available for download through broadband, mobile, and podcasting.

Kids & Teens: Consolidate children's programs across all platforms under CBeebies and CBBC brands. Launch a broadband-based teen brand targeting 12–16-year-olds.

Comedy: Invest in developing more sitcoms and comedy shows across all television and radio networks. Foster talent, start a comedy website, and increase access to the shows through new media.

Drama: Make television dramas more energetic while retaining the hit shows. Create fewer long television dramas and support single and experimental dramas.

Entertainment: Improve Saturday night's content on BBC ONE and have an effective collaboration with other genres like leisure and factual to create innovative shows.

Knowledge Building: Make available all the BBC content to audience permanently after transmission on all platforms.

Five Themes

Martini Media: Martini Media is the media that allows the content to move from one media to another across various devices and is available everywhere and at any time. This means that the BBC would have to follow an entirely new process for developing, commissioning, and production of programs. The BBC has already started working on this project called BBC Web 2.0.

Serious About Entertainment: The new generation audience doesn't want just knowledge and information from the BBC. They want the BBC to provide thorough entertainment through drama, comedy, and factual programs.

The Young: The young audience has been moving away from the BBC since the beginning of the 2000s and this trend is rising. The BBC would aim to reach the younger audience by starting exclusive websites and television programs, etc. for them without neglecting the older sections.

Findability: The BBC plans to coordinate the whole content efficiently in order to make it easy for the viewers to search and find. Powerful search tools would be launched and the content would be branded to make the search more user-friendly in fields like Sport, Music, Natural History, Leisure, and Health.

The Active Audience: In future, the viewers are expected to take part in discussions and debates, and create, communicate, etc. apart from watching programs. The BBC would encourage the audience to add their content and ideas in areas like Natural History, Leisure, Health, etc.

Adapted from "BBC Creative Future: Mark Thompson's speech in full," www.media.guardian.co.uk, April 25, 2006 & "Creative Future—BBC Addresses Creative Challenges of On-Demand," www.bbc.co.uk, April 25, 2006.

EXHIBIT 11

BBC—Pictorial Representation of the Organizational Changes (July 2006)

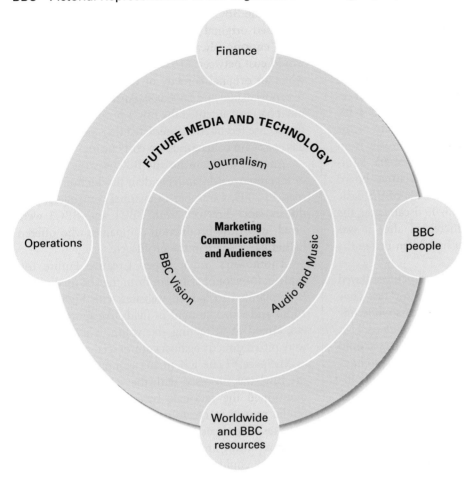

Source: www.bbc.co.uk.

on the strategy, Thompson said, "The BBC should no longer think of itself as a broadcaster of TV and radio and some new media on the side. We should aim to deliver public service content to our audiences in whatever media and on whatever device makes sense for them, whether they are at home or on the move."[32]

The BBC also started exploring various opportunities to develop its international commercial activities through BBC Worldwide. It planned video-on-demand services and to start BBC.com, a commercial website for people outside the UK, by the end of 2006.

In July 2006, the BBC announced organizational changes to facilitate the implementation of Creative Future. Future media and technology formed the core of the new change and the BBC content was organized into journalism, BBC vision, and audio and music (refer to Exhibit 11 for pictorial representation of the organizational changes under Thompson in July 2006). According to Thompson, the main aim of the reorganization, effective from April 2007, was to facilitate cross-platform commissioning and production and make the BBC a creative organization.

The Road Ahead

Though the BBC had been cutting costs, the compensation paid to the top executives remained the same, and for a few executives, it was actually rising every year. The bonuses paid to them were criticized severely by many industry analysts and BECTU as they came at a time when the television viewership was falling. For 2004-05, Thompson received a bonus of £64,000 on a £210,000 basic pay and Byford received £92,000 on his salary of £351,000. BBC's CEO John Smith (Smith) received £72,000 on £287,000 and BBC People director, Stephen Dando, received £65,000 bonus on £245,000. Byford's salary jumped 30% from the financial year 2003–04 and Smith's basic pay by 20%. However, they also assumed additional responsibilities in the BBC.

In July 2005, reacting to the criticism related to compensation, Thompson waived his performance-related incentives worth £135,000 for the year 2004–05. This cut, along with the reduction in the size of the executive board, reduced cumulative bonuses from £546,000 in 2003–04 to £320,000 in 2004–05. Similarly, the incentives for the BBC executive board members were also cut from about 30% of the basic salary to 10% starting from 2005–06 fiscal. Later, the salary of the members was increased after it was found that their compensation had fallen below the market average.

Many analysts, politicians, and competitors flayed the BBC's proposal to increase the license fee. They said that the BBC had overstated its costs while understating its savings. Charles Allen, CEO of ITV, said, "The BBC's back-of-a-fag-packet figures should come with their own health warning. They systematically underplay their estimates for savings and efficiencies and overplay their funding requirements. The government should reject the BBC's bid and send them back to the drawing board."[33]

Analysts also found fault with the newly formed BBC Trust.[34] They said that it was not too different from the earlier Board of Governors and would not last long. According to Dame Pauline Neville-Jones, Member of BBC's Board of Governors between 1997 and 2004, the governors were caught between their conflicting roles of governing and regulating. The Trust would be no different in dealing with such issues and this could affect the functioning of the whole organization. She said, "The new structures created to govern and regulate the corporation will be elaborate and complex and a great deal more expensive to run than the present set-up. Will they be more effective and will they result in better programs? This is a good deal less clear. The White Paper . . . creates in the trust, having both governance and regulatory duties, a body as likely to suffer from schizophrenia as the existing governors."[35]

The BBC faced ire of the public over its repeat telecasts. Though Thompson had promised to reduce the number of repeat telecasts, BBC1 aired 2,683 hours of repeat telecasts in 2004-05 fiscal, 88 hours more than 2003–04. On the whole, 24,000 hours of repeat telecasts were aired across all the BBC channels. However, if the BBC had reduced its repeat telecasts and increased original content, it would have increased costs enormously. For example, a repeat telecast would cost between £15,000 and £30,000 every hour while an original comedy or drama would cost between £500,000 and £600,000. Further, as the government had not accepted the BBC's proposal to increase the license fee, analysts predicted that the BBC would have to again concentrate on cost cutting.

Another problem for the BBC was the poaching of its employees by independent production companies. In 2005, a number of channel controllers, producers, and directors from BBC1 and BBC3 were lured by private production companies who offered higher pay, a share in the profits, etc.

Thompson's much hyped Creative Future too came in for a lot of criticism from the UK media. The BBC planned to launch websites with high quality audio and video content in fields like sports, music, etc. aimed at attracting the youth. These websites were pitted directly against commercial websites such as MySpace.[36] The UK media complained that that the BBC was obsessed with the youth segment and questioned the rationale behind Thompson using public money to create competition to commercial websites. The rivals complained that the government was not putting any brakes on the BBC, whose steps, they said, could prove detrimental to the Corporation. The Guardian Media Group[37] said that the BBC's plan to launch a commercial website for overseas users would hit its online and regional newspaper business. It found fault with the BBC spending £69.2 million in 2004–05 for developing the bbc.co.uk website (into the most popular website in the UK), as the license fee money was originally intended to fund only television operations.

Despite the criticism, a number of analysts commended Thompson's leadership and his vision for the BBC. They said that the BBC had never targeted young audiences earlier as it had not been funded by the advertisers who craved young audiences. In this context, they appreciated Thompson's efforts to take the BBC to the new generation audience. According to John Naughton, columnist at *The Observer*,[38] "Most broadcasters seem to be unable to see what's coming—a world where all media products will be delivered and accessed via the Internet, with all that implies in terms of active, empowered, fickle, and knowledgeable audiences. Somehow, Mark Thompson and his team have shaken off that mindset and understood what's required if the BBC is to thrive in the new environment. So they clearly understand what needs to be done. The question is: can they do it?"[39]

ENDNOTES

1. "Mark Thompson Interview," www.libdems.org.uk, March 17, 2006.
2. Claire Cozens, "BBC Review 'Doesn't Go Far Enough'," www.mediaguardian.co.uk, December 7, 2004.
3. In September 2002, the UK government produced a dossier about the weapons of mass destruction allegedly possessed by Iraq. In that, it claimed that the weapons could be deployed within 45 minutes. On May 29, 2003, Andrew Gilligan in the *Today* program on BBC Radio 4 reported that the 45-minute claim had been included intentionally and was not supported by the intelligence authorities. The UK government condemned the report while the BBC said that it had received the information from a reliable source. On July 9, 2003, the BBC revealed the name of Dr. David Kelly (a weapons expert) as the source. On July 17, 2003, Kelly was found dead. The government appointed Lord Hutton to probe into the "circumstances surrounding the death of Kelly." On January 28, 2004, the findings of Hutton were published. The report did not find the government guilty but found fault with the BBC's editorial system. It also said that Kelly had committed suicide.
4. "New BBC Boss Announces Shake-up," www.news.bbc.co.uk, June 22, 2004.
5. "Grade Gets His Man as BBC Ends Months of Turmoil," www.media.guardian.co.uk, May 22, 2004.
6. ITV was started by a network of commercial television broadcasters. For 2004, ITV's net operating revenues were £2,053 million with a net profit of £139 million.
7. Channel 4 was started in 1982 by an Act of Parliament. It was initially managed by the Independent Broadcasting Authority and the revenues were received from ITV franchises located across the UK. The advertising was taken care of by the franchises operating in a particular region and thus ITV had no direct relationship with advertisers.
8. Terrestrial broadcasting, also called over-the-air broadcasting, is a broadcasting method where television signals are sent over the air and are received using an antenna.
9. The satellite television service involves the use of satellite for broadcasting. Signals, sent from the earth using an uplink transmitter, are received by one of the transponders in the satellite which converts them to another frequency and sends them back to earth. These signals are received using a downlink antenna and a receiver.
10. News Corporation, controlled by Rupert Murdoch, is one of the largest media conglomerates in the world. Its businesses consist of production and distribution of films, television networks, newspapers and magazines, websites, book publishing, etc. For the year ended July 31, 2005, its total sales were US$ 24 billion and its net income was US$ 2 billion.
11. British Satellite Broadcasting was started in 1986 to provide direct to home satellite television service in the UK. However, due to technical problems, it started to broadcast services only in early 1990.
12. The External Service was renamed BBC World Service in 1988.
13. BBC Worldwide distributes and licenses the BBC TV programs across the world. It owns or has a stake in about 20 channels, owns nearly 40 magazines, sells books, videos, music, and DVDs. It also provides radio content, language teaching products, etc. For the year ended March 2005, its total sales were £706 million and net income was £28 million.
14. BBC Choice went off the air in February 2003 and was replaced by BBC Three.
15. "Dyke Unveils Moves to Build 'One BBC'," www.bbc.co.uk, April 3, 2000.
16. Started in 1998, ITV Digital was the first terrestrial digital broadcaster offering about 35 channels. In August 2001, it bought the broadcasting rights to the Football League for three years for £315 million and launched ITV Sport. This proved to be a costly step as sports failed to attract audience and advertisers. In October 2002, Freeview, a new digital terrestrial television service, was launched to replace ITV Digital.
17. "BBC Apologizes as Dyke Quits," www.news.bbc.co.uk, January 29, 2004.
18. Dame Anita Roddick, "Rupert vs. The BBC—The 'Foxification' of Britain," www.mediachannel.org, October 23, 2003.
19. Mark Byford was appointed as the Deputy Director General of the BBC in January 2004. After Dyke left, he became the acting Director General of the BBC until Mark Thompson was appointed. Thompson appointed Byford as the Head of Journalism in June 2004 in addition to his Deputy Director General post.
20. The other members of the group were Glenwyn Benson (Controller Factual Commissioning Television), Helen Boaden (Controller Radio 4 and BBC 7), Adrian Van Klaveren (Head of Newsgathering, BBC News), Richard Tait (Former Editor-in-Chief, ITN), and Stephen Whittle (Controller Editorial Policy, BBC).
21. "BBC Outlines Post-Hutton Reforms," www.news.bbc.co.uk, June 23, 2004.
22. A group of members from the opposition party (officially called Her Majesty's Loyal Opposition) in the House of Commons forms a cabinet called The Official Loyal Opposition Shadow Cabinet or simply The Shadow Cabinet. The Shadow Cabinet members scrutinize their counterparts in the government and suggest alternative policies.
23. "BBC Report: 'A Lot of Unnecessary Self-Laceration'," www.business.timesonline.co.uk, June 23, 2004.
24. For 2006–07, the license fee was £131.50 per year for a color television and £44 for a black and white television. The license was free if the person was more than 75 years old, and the fee was half in the case of persons registered as blind.
25. MORI combined with Ipsos UK in October 2005 to form the second largest research company in the UK. The company conducts research in five segments—Marketing, Advertising, Media, Loyalty, and Public Affairs.
26. Formed in 1991, BECTU is an independent union which comprises workers belonging to broadcasting, theater, film, leisure, entertainment, and related areas in the UK.
27. "Thompson Says BBC 'Must Keep Up'," www.news.bbc.co.uk, December 8, 2004.
28. A Green Paper contains government's policy proposals for stimulating debate and discussion, based on which a final decision can be taken.
29. The UK government planned to discontinue with analog transmissions completely and switch over to digital television by 2012. The process which would start in 2008 was expected to be completed by 2012. Shifting to digital television provides benefits such as extra channels as standard, better quality, new features, etc.
30. "BBC Journalism College Launched," www.news.bbc.co.uk, June 28, 2005.
31. "What You'll Need to Get a Passport to Promotion," www.pressgazette.co.uk, July 7, 2005.
32. "The Future Starts Here? BBC Strengthens Its Role in Digital World," www.iabuk.net, April 27, 2006.
33. "What the BBC's Critics Say," www.ft.com, May 30, 2006.

34. The BBC Trust which would replace the BBC Board of Governors would consist of twelve trustees headed by Michael Grade, Chairman of the BBC. As of May 2006, the government had announced the names of only four members.

35. Chris Tryhorn and Ben Dowell, "Dyke's 'Posh Lady' Attacks BBC Trust," www.media.guardian.co.uk, April 12, 2006.

36. MySpace, founded in 2003 and owned by News Corporation, is a US-based community website. It is one of the world's most popular community websites.

37. The Guardian Media Group (GMG) is UK-based multimedia organization whose core business is publishing and printing. Apart from publishing newspapers (regional and national), the group is also into regional radio stations, websites, television station and magazines.

38. The *Observer*, founded in 1791 and owned by Guardian Media Group, is a newspaper published on Sundays.

39. "The BBC's Digital Future—But Will It Work?" www.media.guardian.co.uk, April 30, 2006.

NBC in Trouble

This case was prepared by Vinay Kumar, under the direction of Vivek Gupta, ICFAI Center for Management Research (ICMR).

"I can tell you, it's like a weird monkey off the back in a way. Business is cyclical . . . nobody stays on top all the time."[1]

—Kevin Reilly, President, NBC Entertainment, on the declining NBC Viewership, in 2005.

"We're not as strong as we've been, maybe, but we're only one breakout hit away from being there again. Of course, breakout hits are harder to come by these days."[2]

—Jeff Zucker, then President of NBC Universal Television Group, on NBC's poor performance in 2004–05.

"NBC is still arguably the face of that division. Should NBC have another year like last year, there could be advertising fallout and the perception of NBC may change for investors"[3]

—Robert Schenosky, Analyst at Boyd Jefferies & Company[4] in 2005.

Introduction

In the television rankings for the 2005–06 season,[5] NBC Television Network (NBC) was ranked fourth for the second consecutive year in the most popular broadcast network category. The rankings were released by Nielsen Media Research[6] in May 2006. NBC trailed behind rival networks CBS Television (CBS), FOX Broadcasting Company (FOX) and American Broadcasting Company (ABC) (refer to Exhibit 1 for details of NBC's competitors). CBS had been the top network since 2002–03 season during which it dethroned NBC from the top spot. In the 2005–06 season, NBC had lost 1% of its viewers as compared to 2004–05 season (refer to Table 1 for viewership details in 2005–06). FOX emerged as the most popular network among the

This case was written by Vinay Kumar, under the direction of Vivek Gupta, ICFAI Center for Management Research (ICMR). It was complied from published sources, and is intended to be used as a basis for class discussion rather than to illustrate either effective or ineffective handling of a management situation.

18–49 year-old segment (where advertisers paid premiums) for the second consecutive time, while NBC stood fourth here too. Moreover, the Thursday night primetime[7] slot, which had earlier been dominated by NBC, was now taken over almost completely by CBS (refer to Exhibit 2).

NBC, the television network division of NBC Universal, suffered as its own hit series like *Friends*, *ER*, etc. completed their run, while at the same time, rivals moved in (refer to Exhibit 3 for logo of NBC). FOX's *American Idol* was the "most popular television show" (second consecutive time) during the 2005–06 season. CBS had a great hit in *CSI: Crime Scene Investigation* and ABC had *Desperate Housewives*. But NBC had no new shows to boast of. Its biggest hit was the game show *Deal or No Deal*, but this came in 13th in terms of viewership in the year 2005–06 (refer to Exhibit 4 for primetime rankings for 2005–06). Even the telecast of Winter Olympics (held in Turin) in February 2006, which usually drew a big audience, could not help NBC. Bill

EXHIBIT 1

Profile of Major Competitors of NBC

CBS: In 1928, William S. Paley acquired United Independent Broadcasters Inc., a network of 16 independent radio stations, and renamed it Columbia Broadcast System. In July 1931, CBS began television broadcasting. By 1944, CBS Radio Network had 144 stations, making it the largest in the US. In 1960, CBS became the first network to broadcast the Olympics. From 1967 on, CBS started broadcasting all its programs in color. In April 1971, Columbia Broadcast System officially changed its name to CBS Inc. In mid-1980s, Laurence Tisch (Tisch) acquired 25% stake in CBS. CBS suffered under his leadership. Its financial performance weakened and its shows often appealed only to older people.

Under pressure from all quarters, Tisch sold CBS to Westinghouse Electric Corporation (WEC) for US$ 5.4 billion in 1995. In 1996, WEC acquired Infinity Broadcasting Corporation (IBC) and CBS Radio Network was put under Westwood One, a subsidiary of IBC. In December 1997, WEC changed its name to CBS Corporation. In May 2000, CBS was acquired by Viacom to form Viacom Inc. In December 2005, Viacom Inc. divided its businesses into two: i) CBS Corporation, which consisted of the CBS Television Network, UPN, CBS Stations Group, CBS Paramount Television, King World, Showtime, CBS Radio, CBS Outdoor, Simon & Schuster, Paramount Parks, CBS Digital Media, CSTV and CBS Consumer Products; and ii) Viacom Inc. which consisted of BET, Famous Music, MTV Networks (MTV, VH1, Nickelodeon, Nick at Nite, Comedy Central, etc.), Paramount Pictures and Paramount Home Entertainment.

ABC: ABC was formed in 1944 when NBC sold its NBC Blue Network to Edward J. Noble, owner of Lifesavers Candy. He renamed it American Broadcasting Company in 1945. In April 1948, ABC began its television broadcasting services. In February 1953, ABC merged with United Paramount Theatres Inc., a spin-off of Paramount Pictures Corporation and owned by Leonard Goldenson. In 1954, ABC entered into an alliance with Disney for a Walt Disney TV series called *Disneyland*. This was ABC's first series to be included in Nielsen Top Ten Hits. In 1955, ABC had another successful primetime series *Cheyenne*, produced by Warner Brothers. In mid-1960s, ABC started its own production division called ABC Films.

In 1984, ABC acquired 80% stake in ESPN (the other 20% was held by Hearst Corporation). By this time, ABC found itself in trouble due to lack of innovation, high expenses and declining ratings. In 1986, Capital Cities Communication, a U.S. media company, purchased ABC for US$ 3.5 billion and formed Capital Cities/ABC Inc. Under the new management, ABC again bounced back. In 1995, Walt Disney acquired Capital Cities/ABC for US$ 19 billion. In 1999, ABC started the blockbuster show *Who Wants To Be A Millionaire*? As the show was aired 5 or 6 days a week, its popularity faded. In 2004, ABC bounced back with its blockbuster series *Desperate Housewives*. As of 2006, ABC network consisted of ABC News, ABC Family, ABC Kids, ABC Sports and ABC Radio apart from its flagship ABC.

FOX: In March 1985, the Rupert Murdoch-owned News Corporation acquired Fox Studios[a] for US$ 575 million. He brought together Fox Studios and Metromedia's independent television stations, acquired in the same year, and formed Fox Broadcasting Company in 1986. FOX's first television program was launched in October 1986. Since its launch, FOX positioned itself as a vibrant and youthful channel attracting the 18–34 market. FOX was seen as a potential competitor to CBS, ABC and NBC. In 1993, NFL awarded FOX the rights to broadcast its league till 1997. In early 2000s, FOX lost its foothold due to heavy competition. However, it bounced back with *American Idol*, launched in June 2002. The show was rated number one even in 2006. As of 2006, Fox Broadcasting Company is the third largest broadcast television network in the U.S. after CBS and ABC, with about 200 affiliate stations and 35 own broadcast outlets.

[a] FOX Studios was involved in the development, production and worldwide distribution of feature films and television programs, television broadcasting and cable network programming.

Compiled from various sources.

Caroll, Vice president and Director of Programming at Katz Television Group, remarked, "If you were optimistic about the Olympics, you'd have to be somewhat disappointed with the numbers NBC delivered."[8]

To revive its sagging ratings, NBC acquired the rights to televise the prestigious National Football League[9] (NFL) games which were to start in September 2006. NBC acquired these rights after a gap of seven years. NBC was hopeful that the NFL games along with its new shows would boost its ratings in 2006. Walter Podrazik, Chicago-based writer and communications and logistics consultant said, "Getting NFL football onto the NBC primetime lineup is a major accomplishment. If they have that as an initial lure, it's not that they're one hit away from being the No. 1 network, because they're a little too far behind. But if they can start getting clusters of shows that spill over and get people interested in other shows, then they build in something that gives them, over two or three years, the potential for a comeback."[10]

TABLE 1

Viewership of Television Networks (2005–2006)

Network	Viewer Average (in millions)	% Change from 2004–05
CBS	12.6	−2
ABC	10.8	+7
FOX	10.1	+1
NBC	**9.7**	**−1**
WB	3.1	−7
UPN	3.1	−7

Source: Andrew Wallenstein, "Primetime Wrap-up," www.hollywoodreporter.com, May 26, 2006.

EXHIBIT 2

Top Primetime Network (1994–2006)

Year	Overall	18–49 Age Group	Thursday (8:00–10:30 pm)
1994–95	ABC	ABC	**NBC**
1995–96	**NBC**	**NBC**	**NBC**
1996–97	**NBC**	**NBC**	**NBC**
1997–98	**NBC**	**NBC**	**NBC**
1998–99	CBS	**NBC**	**NBC**
1999–00	ABC	ABC	**NBC**
2000–01	ABC	**NBC**	**NBC**
2001–02	**NBC**	**NBC**	**NBC**
2002–03	CBS	**NBC**	CBS
2003–04	CBS	**NBC**	CBS
2004–05	CBS	FOX	CBS
2005–06	CBS	FOX	CBS

Adapted from various sources.

EXHIBIT 3

NBC Logo

Source: NBCU Photo Bank

EXHIBIT 4

Primetime Rankings (2005–2006)

S. No.	Series	Channel	Viewers (in millions)
1	American Idol (Tuesday)	FOX	31.2
2	American Idol (Wednesday)	FOX	30.2
3	CSI: Crime Scene Investigation	CBS	25.2
4	Desperate Housewives	ABC	22.2
5	Grey's Anatomy	ABC	19.9
6	Without a Trace	CBS	18.7
7	Dancing With the Stars (Thursday)	ABC	18.6
8	Survivor: Guatemala	CBS	18.3
9	CSI: Miami	CBS	18.1
10	House	FOX	17.3
11	Survivor: Panama-Exile Island	CBS	16.8
12	Monday Night Football	ABC	16.0
13	Deal or No Deal (Monday)	NBC	15.8
14	The Unit	CBS	15.5
15	Lost	ABC	15.5
16	NCIS	CBS	15.3

Source: Andrew Wallenstein, "Primetime Wrap-Up," www.hollywoodreporter.com, May 26, 2006.

Background Note

In 1919, Radio Corporation of America (RCA) was created to market radio receivers produced by GE, Westinghouse, AT&T and United Fruit Company. In 1926, RCA started the National Broadcasting Company (NBC) for radio broadcasting. In 1927, RCA divided NBC into NBC-Red for broadcasting entertainment and music programs, and NBC-Blue for cultural and news items. In the late 1920s, RCA also began working on television broadcasting and started putting its profits from radio into television R&D. In 1931, NBC began experimental television broadcasts from the Empire State Building in New York.

In 1932, differences among the four companies resulted in an independent RCA with NBC coming under its control. RCA continued funding NBC's television research and in 1939, NBC started regular television broadcasts. RCA slowly became a major producer and marketer of radio receivers and radio content. The NBC network also gained significant popularity and achieved a dominant position in the broadcasting business. This dominance received attention of the U.S. government which ordered the Federal Communications Commission (FCC)[11] to investigate into NBC's practices. FCC found that NBC's two stations dominated the broadcasting market and suggested the sale of one of the networks. RCA took the matter to the court but lost the case. In 1943, NBC-Blue was sold to Edward J. Noble and it was later renamed ABC Networks.

The early 1950s saw a rapid increase in the sales of television sets in the U.S. In 1952, NBC started early morning news. In 1953, it started color broadcasts. In 1964, NBC produced the first movie made for television. In the fifties and sixties, NBC started investing in other television stations, and by the mid-1960s, it owned 13 television stations and one television network in eight countries. During the same time, CBS had emerged as a strong competitor to NBC. With shows such as *The Ed Sullivan Show*, *Gunsmoke*, *The Beverly Hillbillies* and *Green Acres*, *All in the Family*, and *M*A*S*H*, CBS dominated over NBC between the mid-1950s and mid-1970s both in the primetime and daytime rankings.

The rapid boom in television sales affected NBC's radio business, and by 1975, it had nothing much to offer on radio except some hourly news. While NBC was battling with the strong CBS, ABC came up as another formidable television network and pushed NBC from second to third place in the ratings (refer to Exhibit 5 for a note on the U.S. television industry).

EXHIBIT 5

The U.S. Television Industry

The television industry picked up in the U.S. after World War II with radio companies CBS, NBC owned by RCA, and ABC starting their own television stations—CBS, NBC and ABC. DuMont Television Network, owned by DuMont Laboratories, was the fourth television network. They used, and still use, the terrestrial television broadcasting method to air their programs. The early 1950s saw a rapid increase in the sales of television sets and by 1955 nearly half of the U.S. households owned a television set, mostly black and white, though color transmissions had already started. In 1953, DuMont was in deep financial trouble and merged with ABC.

During the 1950s, television networks were allowed to only own up to five television stations across the U.S. Naturally, the networks opted for big cities[b] with huge populations and used affiliates—independent television stations with whom networks share a relationship—to reach smaller markets. Initially, the networks used to start the day with news in the morning while dramas filled the afternoon slot. In the evening, news was followed by shows. Most of the dramas and shows were modified versions of radio programs.

In the 1940s, advertising agencies conceived and produced programs on behalf of sponsors, and even decided the network and the slot to air the program. However, this model didn't work and by the 1950s, the networks controlled the scheduling and programming. The networks allotted a one-minute slot to each advertiser who communicated the uniqueness of the product. The shift to full color transmissions in the 1960s increased advertising revenues rapidly.

In late 1960s, to restrict the monopoly of the three networks, the Federal Communications Commission announced the Financial Interest and Syndication Rules (Fin-Syn) which did not permit networks to produce, distribute and syndicate (selling the program after the first broadcast to others) television programs. Instead, the rights were given to the independent production companies (Hollywood studios which were into television production). The production companies also had the right to own the profits that were generated through syndication.

THE DAWN OF CABLE TELEVISION

The three networks accounted for nearly 90% of the U.S. households during the primetime in the early 1970s. The U.S. had about 600 television stations by 1972, up from 104 stations in 1950. This was also the period that saw the rise of cable television or community antenna television—first used during 1950s to broadcast programs of networks to far-off places which couldn't catch the broadcast signal.

(continued)

EXHIBIT 5   *(continued)*

The U.S. Television Industry

In 1972, Time Life Inc. started the first cable television channel called Home Box Office (HBO), a movie channel for its local cable system in New York. By 1975, HBO became a national channel. In 1977, it started using satellite to distribute its signals to cable operators who received them using a dish. The operator was charged 10 cents a month per subscriber (basic service). This was a huge success as viewers were shown movies without commercials. Soon after this, Ted Turner (Turner), who owned WTBS station, put his station's signal on the same satellite as HBO and started broadcasting games. This meant that cable operators got WTBS programs with their existing dishes for free.

This attracted many other cable services which could be got only for money (paid service). In 1978, Viacom, which owned cable systems across the U.S., launched pay channels called Showtime which showed movies, and Spotlight, a sports channel. In 1979, Warner launched a paid movie channel—The Movie Channel. It also started Nickelodeon, a children's channel. Time started another network called Cinemax, a sibling to HBO. Other services to join the race included Bravo, Playboy and The Entertainment Channel.

During the same time, cable services that accepted advertisements were also started. ESPN was one such channel whose sports events became very popular. The others included MTV, USA, CBN, etc. In 1980, Turner started Cable News Network (CNN), which went on to become one of the most popular news channels in the world. These also came under basic service as they could be obtained for a low fee.

As the cable channels had specific target audiences such as sports fans, movie buffs, etc., much of the network audience became cable viewers. The growing popularity of cable television attracted CBS and ABC. In 1981, CBS launched CBS Cable, a cultural channel. However, it proved a disaster as the service evoked little response among subscribers and advertisers. In 1983, CBS shut down the service after losing US$ 50 million. During the same time, ABC started its own cultural channel called ARTS. It also launched Satellite News Channel (SNC), a 24-hour news channel in partnership with Westinghouse, to compete with CNN.

During the early and mid-1980s, a number of cable services were announced. However, most of them couldn't either materialize or sustain themselves. After the early 1980s, a number of changes took place in the cable television industry. Some of the paid services such as Bravo converted themselves to basic services. ARTS and The Entertainment Channel combined their programming to form Arts and Entertainment. ABC/Westinghouse's SNC was acquired by CNN. Playboy and its partner Escapade parted ways while MTV was acquired by Viacom. In 1984, ABC purchased ESPN from Texaco. Apart from these, a number of channels either changed their programming content or target audience.

THE MAKEOVER

Since mid-1980s, the US television industry has seen many changes. In March 1985, Rupert Murdoch-owned News Corporation acquired Fox Studios and formed the fourth broadcast network FOX Broadcasting Company (FOX) in 1986. In the process, he acquired 100 independent television stations (not affiliated to the big three networks) which became a part of FOX. The acquisition of FOX Studios facilitated the in-house production of its television shows.

In 1986, RCA sold NBC to GE and Capital Cities Communication, a US media company, purchased ABC and formed Capital Cities/ABC Inc. In 1986, Laurence Tisch, a businessman, bought 25% of CBS and assumed the posts of president and CEO. In 1990, Time and Warner Bros. combined to form Time Warner.

By the early 1990s, technology had improved which allowed delivery of up to 500 channels to homes. Channels that aired specific content such as news, cartoons, traveling, religion and science fiction increased. Though cable television reached 85% (according to some estimates) of the U.S. households, its average viewership was half of CBS, ABC, NBC and FOX in a given week. One of the reasons has been the increasing subscription costs for consumers.

In 1991, the networks challenged the Fin-Syn rule in the Los Angeles US Circuit Court. The court was convinced that the networks were no longer the dominant force in the television industry and ruled out the Fin-Syn rule. Judge Manuel Real wrote, "Certainly with the entry of the Fox network, the substantial rise in the number of program producers, the dramatic increase in cable television stations and the development in the sophistication of VCRs, the competitive climate today would unfairly penalize NBC, ABC and CBS in the financing and syndication of off-network programming."[c]

(continued)

EXHIBIT 5   (continued)

The U.S. Television Industry

This gave rise to a number of changes in the US media and entertainment industry. In 1995, the major studio Walt Disney acquired Capital Cities/ABC while Tisch sold CBS to Westinghouse Electric Corporation (WEC) in 1995 and the merged entity was later called CBS Corporation (CBSC). A few Hollywood studios entered the network race to create their own broadcast network or cable network. In 1995, Warner Brothers launched WB network (WB) and Paramount (owned by Viacom) launched UPN and thus increased the total number of broadcast networks to six. Warner Brothers partnered with Tribune Broadcasting while Paramount Pictures partnered with Chris-Craft's United Television. The two broadcast networks fought intense battles during their early days. In 1996, Time Warner acquired Turner Broadcasting System.

Further changes occurred with Viacom acquiring CBSC in 1999. The new entity, called Viacom, was the second largest media company (worth US$ 80 billion) behind Time Warner. Meanwhile, troubles started between Chris-Craft and Paramount. In 2000, the differences between the two UPN partners aggravated and Viacom acquired Chris-Craft's stake completely. In 2003, NBC acquired the U.S. entertainment assets of Vivendi Universal, a French media company, to form NBC Universal. The assets consisted of Universal Studios, Universal Parks, etc.

In December 2005, Viacom divided itself into Viacom Inc. and CBS (UPN was brought under CBS). In January 2006, Warner Bros. and CBS announced their intention to merge WB and UPN networks to form CW by September 2006. This was because UPN and CW failed to compete with the big four networks and usually commanded lower viewership. This resulted in five major broadcast networks which had studios—CBS (Paramount), NBC (Universal), ABC (Disney), FOX (FOX Studios), and CW (both Paramount and Warner Brothers).

[b] The networks opted for New York, Chicago, Philadelphia, Schenectady, Chicago, and Los Angeles.
[c] Cynthia Littleton, "A Tale of Two Networks," www.hollywoodreporter.com, January 11, 2005.
Compiled from various sources.

In 1981, Grant Tinker[12] (Tinker) was appointed as the Chairman and CEO of NBC. Together with the Chief Programmer Brandon Tartikoff (Tartikoff), Tinker initiated a program to revive NBC's fortunes. NBC started airing series like *St. Elsewhere*, *Family Ties* and *Cheers*—all of which received moderate ratings to begin with. Tinker and Tartikoff continued with these programs even though they were not immediate winners, as they felt that they had the potential to become hits. Meanwhile, the duo launched another series called *Hill Street Blues*.

Things changed dramatically for NBC in 1984 with its situational comedy *The Cosby Show*, which featured the popular comedian, Bill Cosby, who chose to work with NBC over CBS. The show was a blockbuster and enjoyed good viewership on Thursdays 8:00 pm until the year 1990 (refer to Exhibit 6 for top television programs between 1980 and 2005). Meanwhile, the other television series from NBC also started gaining popularity. *The Cosby Show*, *Family Ties*, *Cheers*, *Night Court* and *Hill Street Blues* established NBC as a dominant network on Thursday nights between 8 and 10 pm. The Thursday night lineup, called "Must See TV," continued its dominance until the early 2000s (refer to Exhibit 7 for programs

in Must See TV). In the year 1984–85, NBC's eight shows featured among the top 20 TV shows and the number increased to nine in the following season. Its profits jumped from US$ 48 million in 1984 to US$ 333 million in 1985.

GE Acquires NBC

In 1986, General Electric (GE) purchased RCA, mainly to acquire control of NBC, for US$ 6.3 billion. In 1986, Tinker announced his resignation. John F. Welch (Welch), then Chairman of GE, appointed Robert C. Wright, who had been serving as the President of GE Credit Corporation, as the President and CEO of NBC in August 1986.

Wright's Strategy

Wright, in a bid to focus solely on television, sold NBC's radio network operations to Westwood One[13] in 1988. In the same year, he sold RCA's music network RCA-Victor to Germany-based media company Bertelsmann AG. He felt that NBC was overstaffed and laid off 150 workers. In 1987, he sold RCA's consumer electronics operations to Thomson.

EXHIBIT 6

Top Television Programs (1980–2005)

Year	Program	Channel
1980–81	Dallas	CBS
1981–82	Dallas	CBS
1982–83	60 Minutes	CBS
1983–84	Dallas	CBS
1984–85	Dynasty	ABC
1985–86	**The Cosby Show**	**NBC**
1986–87	**The Cosby Show**	**NBC**
1987–88	**The Cosby Show**	**NBC**
1988–89	**The Cosby Show**	**NBC**
1989–1990	**The Cosby Show**	**NBC**
1990–91	**Cheers**	**NBC**
1991–92	60 Minutes	CBS
1992–93	60 Minutes	CBS
1993–94	60 Minutes	CBS
1994–95	**Seinfeld**	**NBC**
1995–96	**ER**	**NBC**
1996–97	**ER**	**NBC**
1997–98	**Seinfeld**	**NBC**
1998–99	**ER**	**NBC**
1999–2000	Who Wants To Be A Millionaire?	ABC
2000–01	Survivor	CBS
2001–02	**Friends**	**NBC**
2002–03	CSI: Crime Scene Investigation	CBS
2003–04	CSI: Crime Scene Investigation	CBS
2004–05	American Idol	FOX
2005–06	American Idol	FOX

Adapted from various sources.

During this period, the cable television market was growing rapidly. Since its introduction in the late 1970s, cable television had grown to reach 56% of U.S. homes in 1989. The cable channels were grabbing advertising revenues from television networks. Wright felt that a presence in the cable business was a must for NBC, and to this end, he launched a 24-hour financial news channel CNBC (Consumer News and Business Channel) in 1989. However, CNBC lost US$ 60 million in the first two years of its operation due to the slowdown in the U.S. stock market. In 1991, NBC bought CNBC's major rival, the Financial News Network, for more than US$ 100 million and merged it with CNBC.

In the early 1990s, the audience of NBC's TV programs was losing interest in shows like *The Golden Girls*, *The Cosby Show*, and *L.A. Law*. To regain viewership, NBC paid a whooping US$ 401 million to acquire the broadcasting rights for the 1992 Olympics in Barcelona. The next highest bid was US$ 300 million by CBS and ABC. NBC also spent about US$ 225 million for promoting and producing its Olympics coverage. To recoup the costs, NBC partnered with Cablevision to broadcast Olympics on a pay-per-view basis. For US$ 125, viewers would get commercial-free Olympics coverage on three channels (Triplecast) along with the normal over-the-air network. However, this venture proved a disaster as it could attract only 250,000 homes. NBC lost more than US$ 60 million and Cablevision lost US$ 50 million. NBC registered its first loss making year under GE in 1991. In 1992, though it reported a profit of US$ 204 million, it was far lower than US$ 603 million profit in 1989. For the 1992–93 season, NBC's only top-ten hit show was *Cheers* and all its episodes had been aired, so it would not be carrying on into the next year.

Welch had decided to sell any of GE's business divisions if they were not among top 1 or 2 worldwide, so he started looking out for potential buyers for NBC. In 1992, he came close to finalizing a deal with Paramount Communications Inc.'s Chairman Martin S. Davis, but the latter backed out at the last moment.

Between 1990 and 1993, NBC had lost nearly one-third of its viewers. A number of analysts suggested that Wright should be replaced. However, Welch persisted with him. In 1993, Wright appointed Don Ohlemeyer (Ohlemeyer), then executive producer of sports at NBC, as President of NBC West Coast. Ohlemeyer and Wright began taking steps to bring out NBC from the slump.

In February 1993, with *Cheers* (9:00 pm Thursday) nearing completion, NBC moved *Seinfeld* (a sitcom started in 1989) to Thursday nights (9:30 pm) after *Cheers*. This move clicked as *Seinfeld* quickly entered the top ten. After *Cheers* ended, *Seinfeld* was moved to 9:00 pm. By late 1993, *Seinfeld* became the most popular of all NBC's shows drawing viewers of all ages. In the same year, NBC launched another sitcom *Frasier*, touted as a spin-off of *Cheers*, and *Late Night with Conan O'Brien*, a talk show. In 1994, NBC started another sitcom, *Friends*. NBC also signed up

EXHIBIT 7

Must See Television

Season	Time	Series	Season	Time	Series
1984–85	8:00	The Cosby Show		9:30	Frasier
	8:30	Family Ties		10:00	L.A. Law
	9:00	Cheers	1994–95	8:00	Mad About You
	9:30	Night Court		8:30	Friends
	10:00	Hill Street Blues		9:00	Seinfeld
1985–86	8:00	The Cosby Show		9:30	Madman Of
	8:30	Family Ties			The People
	9:00	Cheers		10:00	ER
	9:30	Night Court	1995–96	8:00	Friends
	10:00	Hill Street Blues		8:30	The Single Guy
1986–87	8:00	The Cosby Show		9:00	Seinfeld
	8:30	Family Ties		9:30	Caroline In The City
	9:00	Cheers		10:00	ER
	9:30	Night Court	1996–97	8:00	Friends
	10:00	Hill Street Blues		8:30	The Single Guy
1987–88	8:00	The Cosby Show		9:00	Seinfeld
	8:30	A Different World		9:30	Suddenly Susan
	9:00	Cheers		10:00	ER
	9:30	Night Court	1997–98	8:00	Friends
	10:00	Hill Street Blues		8:30	Union Square
1988–89	8:00	The Cosby Show		9:00	Seinfeld
	8:30	A Different World		9:30	Veronica's Closet
	9:00	Cheers		10:00	ER
	9:30	Dear John. . .	1998–99	8:00	Friends
	10:00	L.A. Law		8:30	Jesse
1989–90	8:00	The Cosby Show		9:00	Frasier
	8:30	A Different World		9:30	Veronica's Closet
	9:00	Cheers		10:00	ER
	9:30	Dear John. . .	1999–00	8:00	Friends
	10:00	L.A. Law		8:30	Jesse
1990–91	8:00	The Cosby Show		9:00	Frasier
	8:30	A Different World		9:30	Stark Raving Mad
	9:00	Cheers		10:00	ER
	9:30	Grand	2000–01	8:00	Friends
	10:00	L.A. Law		8:30	Cursed
1991–92	8:00	The Cosby Show		9:00	Will & Grace
	8:30	A Different World		9:30	Just Shoot Me
	9:00	Cheers		10:00	ER
	9:30	Wings	2001–02	8:00	Friends
	10:00	L.A. Law		8:30	Inside Schwartz
1992–93	8:00	A Different World		9:00	Will & Grace
	8:30	Final Appeal		9:30	Just Shoot Me
	9:00	Cheers		10:00	ER
	9:30	Wings	2002–03	8:00	Friends
	10:00	L.A. Law		8:30	Scrubs
1993–94	8:00	Mad About You		9:00	Will & Grace
	8:30	Wings		9:30	Good Morning, Miami
	9:00	Seinfeld		10:00	ER

Source: "The Shows of NBC's 'Must See TV'," www.cse.psu.edu, 2003.

popular director Steven Spielberg as an executive producer of the medical drama *ER*.

All these series were primarily targeted at the youth. The tremendous success of *Seinfeld* helped in gaining a huge audience for the other primetime series like *Friends* and *ER*. *Seinfeld* led NBC's Thursday night primetime during most of its broadcasting period which ended in May 1998. *Friends* and *ER* were also popular, with *Friends* becoming one of the most popular sitcoms in the history of television in the U.S. This made NBC regain its popularity with the 18–49 year segment and it emerged as the top network in the U.S. in the early 1990s. In the meantime, the stock market picked up and CNBC gained popularity. It doubled its profits to US$ 50 million in 1995.

In October 1994, it was reported that Time Warner and GE were in talks, and there was speculation that GE was going to sell NBC to Time Warner. It was reported that Time Warner was ready to acquire a 49% stake in NBC for US$ 2.5 billion and would manage NBC's entertainment operations. Welch wanted Time Warner to take control of NBC's other operations such as news, sports, etc. also. But the deal never materialized.

In 1995, NBC launched CNBC Asia, a 24-hour business news channel for the Asian region. In the same year, NBC started NBC Digital Publishing for publishing CD-ROMs and other digital products and NBC Online Ventures to start websites for its news, sports and entertainment channels. In 1995, NBC became the first television network to launch a full-fledged website—NBC.com.

During the late 1980s and 1990s, when the media industry was witnessing consolidations, Wright too wanted to acquire other media companies. However, the finance department of GE stopped him, citing financial constraints. Wright remarked, "We would try to do things, but the financial guys would say, 'This is going to kill us'."[14] Welch also supported them saying that a big media company required huge investment which could hit GE's earnings per share. In the mid-1990s, Wright asked Welch why it was possible for News Corporation, which was smaller than GE, to create the first global entertainment and news network (by acquiring Fox Studios in 1985), while GE was unwilling to make NBC a global network (which would make and distribute programs globally).

Welch was convinced, and Wright and he started scouting around for possible acquisitions. However, acquisitions weren't easy to come by. NBC failed to persuade Ted Turner to merge his Turner Broadcasting System (TBS), which owned channels such as CNN and TNT, with NBC. If it had come through, this deal would have made NBC the largest cable network in the U.S. However, Turner differed with NBC on the issue of managing the merged entity and finally sold TBS and its assets to Time Warner in 1996. Commenting on this, John Malone, CEO of Tele-Communications Inc. said, "If NBC had joined with Ted (Turner), it would have caught Rupert Murdoch.[15] They would have married a domestic broadcast network to worldwide cable networks. It's all about trying to catch Rupert. He's the guy out in the lead. The broad strategy is to take the programming you create and to exploit it as a worldwide business by using facilities that you own. To become vertically integrated worldwide—that's the game."[16]

Welch wanted Wright to make NBC a prominent part of GE and to go global just like Fox which promoted and distributed its programs globally. His aim was to make NBC the top television network in the world. In July 1996, NBC entered into an alliance with Microsoft Corporation[17] (Microsoft) and started MSNBC, a 24-hour cable news channel, and a website, MSNBC.com. Microsoft agreed to invest US$ 220 million for a 50% share in the cable channel and to share half of the operating expenses for both television and website for an unspecified time. By the end of 1996, MSNBC had 22 million subscribers, the highest for any new cable channel. NBC also launched CNBC Europe in the same year.

Again in mid-1999, there were rumors that NBC would be sold to Time Warner. In December 1999, Welch announced publicly that NBC would not be put for sale again. This stance led some analysts to believe that Welch was aiming to take on Rupert Murdoch.

In 1999, NBC bought a 32% stake in Paxson Communications Corporation (Paxson) for US$ 415 million. Paxson owned PAX-TV which completely owned or had a financial stake in 72 television stations in the U.S., plus contracts with 52 affiliate stations.[18] Under this deal, Paxson aired NBC programs after they were aired on NBC. The deal, which was visualized as the first step towards acquiring Paxson, gave NBC the option to acquire a controlling stake in Paxson within ten years. However, this would be possible only if the FCC raised the rule which did not permit companies to own a broadcasting network that reached more than 35% of the U.S. households (refer to Table 2 for details of FCC rules).

TABLE 2

FCC Rules Before 2003

- The owners of a broadcast station were not allowed to own daily newspapers in the same market and vice versa.
- No company could own broadcast stations that reached more than 35% of US households.
- A company should not own more than eight radio stations in a single listening area. The number of stations varied depending on the population of the area.
- A company should not own more than two broadcast television stations in a particular market.
- The four major networks—NBC, CBS, FOX and ABC—were prevented from merging with each other.

Adapted from "Action Alert: FCC Ready to Roll Back Limits on Media Consolidation," www.fair.org, December 5, 2002.

In 1999, during the dot-com boom, NBC launched NBCi (NBC Internet), a publicly held Internet firm. NBCi tied up with Xoom.com, a San Francisco-based online community center and e-commerce website with 7.5 million viewers, and Snap.com, news and search website jointly owned by NBC (60%) and Cnet (40%). GE owned a 53% stake in NBCi while Xoom.com and Snap.com owned 34% and 13% respectively. NBCi was positioned as a general-interest website to attract a large audience and many advertisers by leveraging the rich content and e-commerce experience of the two sites. The site, which operated under Snap.com name, included a search facility, email, chat, NBC content, e-commerce, etc. and was seen as a competitor to Yahoo! Describing NBCi, Marty Yudkovitz, President of NBC Interactive, said, "To users, this means that they will only have to go to one place—Snap.com—on the Web to search, chat with users of like interest, email . . . and purchase products."[19]

NBC in the New Millennium

The year 2000 brought bad news for NBC. Due to the dot-com bubble bust,[20] Internet advertising fell drastically. The U.S. economy was experiencing a downturn, and a number of online companies were closed. NBCi, which had grown rapidly and employed about 800 employees, also ran into trouble. It lost US$ 662 million in 2000 and a number of employees were laid off. Apart from the fall in advertising revenues, there were other reasons for NBCi's problems. NBC did not have a clearly defined Internet strategy, according to some analysts, and it had not differentiated NBCi from other portals such as Yahoo! David Card, Analyst at Jupiter Research said, "There's nothing wrong with a general-purpose portal, especially for a media company that is already a network. But they executed horribly. They didn't take advantage of their TV network or the natural affinities of their programming. On top of that, they were late."[21]

In April 2001, NBC bought the remaining equity stake in NBCi from Xoom.com and Snap.com and integrated all its assets. Commenting on the acquisition, Wright said, "NBC has been a pioneer in new technologies, and the steps we took to create NBCi were in keeping with that tradition. However, recent changes in the portal space and the Internet advertising market have caused us to reexamine this initiative. This acquisition will enable us to build on our competitive advantage in the Internet arena while leveraging our core competencies as a network."[22]

On September 7, 2001, Jeffrey R. Immelt (Immelt), who was working as President and CEO of GE Medical Systems, replaced Welch as the Chairman and CEO of GE. Immelt was keener on media businesses than his predecessor and thus he complemented Wright's ambitions. In April 2002, NBC purchased the broadcast and cable business of Telemundo Communications Group (Telemundo), a Spanish television network, for US$ 1.98 billion in equity. The acquisition of Telemundo made NBC the only major television network to devote a full channel to the rapidly growing Spanish-speaking population in the U.S.

This deal resulted in a feud with Paxson. With the acquisition of Telemundo, NBC owned three stations each in four markets—New York, Dallas, Chicago and Miami; this could be considered a violation of the FCC rule.[23] However, since NBC had a 32% stake (less than the FCC threshold of 35%) in Paxson, the stations were not counted as "NBC-owned" by the FCC. According to Paxson, this was violating their contract, as NBC would not be able to purchase it in future. In December 2001, Paxson commenced a binding arbitration process against NBC. It also made a filing with the FCC requesting it to disallow

NBC from acquiring Telemundo. In April 2002, the FCC rejected the appeal stating that it was a private matter of NBC and Paxson.

In December 2002, NBC acquired Bravo cable network, managed by Rainbow Media Holdings LLC, a subsidiary of Cablevision Systems Corporation (Cablevision) for US$ 1.25 billion. Industry analysts felt the acquisition was a good bet as Bravo reached more than 68 million homes in the U.S. It generated close to US$ 100 million in cable licensing fees, and earned about US$ 60 million through advertising in 2002.

In June 2003, FCC revised the media rules and increased the national television ownership limit from 35% to 45%. However, this ruling was stayed by the U.S. Court of Appeals for the Third Circuit in Philadelphia, after some coalition groups such as the Media Alliance, Fairness and Accuracy in Reporting, the Center for Digital Democracy and the Consumer Federation of America appealed against the proposed changes. They alleged that the new rules would give a few media companies too much control over the industry which would nullify the public voice. This further aggravated the disagreement with Paxson.[24]

Forming NBC Universal

Wright had long been interested in acquiring companies that created content. This was something he couldn't do under Welch. However, in mid-2003 when Vivendi Universal Entertainment (Vivendi), the French media and telecommunications company, announced the sale of its U.S. entertainment business—Universal Pictures, Universal Parks, Universal Television and a number of cable channels, many U.S. media giants were interested. Metro Goldwyn Mayer (MGM), Viacom, Liberty Media and NBC competed with each other to acquire Universal's assets.

One of Vivendi's largest shareholders, Edgar Bronfman (Bronfman),[25] made an offer of €13 billion in cash to buy all of Vivendi's assets and promised to pay off some of the debts of the division. Wall Street analysts estimated that Vivendi was worth US$ 11 billion. Bronfman's high offer forced MGM and Liberty Media out of the bidding. There was speculation that Bronfman would be selected. However, Vivendi preferred NBC over Bronfman, and thus NBC had its first big acquisition under Wright. Vivendi's preference for GE (NBC) was surprising because GE wanted to be a majority stakeholder and was not interested in putting cash into

the deal. Vivendi may have not wanted to be fully taken over by Bronfman. NBC was keen to leverage on Universal's rich content in its film and television production divisions. It also intended to sell and distribute Universal's DVD titles, television programs and films in more than 200 countries.

In October 2003, Vivendi and GE signed agreements to combine Vivendi's U.S. entertainment assets with NBC. The new company was named NBC Universal and was expected to generate US$ 15 billion in revenues every year while its assets were worth around US$ 43 billion. As per the deal, GE paid US$ 3.8 billion in cash and assumed Vivendi's US$ 1.7 billion debt. GE also allowed Vivendi to acquire a 20% stake (worth US$ 8.6 billion) in NBC Universal. Wright was appointed as the CEO of the new entity. Commenting on the importance of the deal, Immelt said, "With this merger, NBC will stay in the forefront of the fundamental changes taking place in television and other media. The new NBC Universal will have the assets, the management team and the operating focus to prosper in a digital world and enhance value for GE and Vivendi Universal shareholders."[26] The merger was completed by May 2004 (refer to Exhibit 8 for businesses of NBCU).

NBC Slips in Ratings

The ratings woes for NBC started in February 2001, when CBS shifted its blockbuster reality series *Survivor* to Thursdays (between 8:00 and 9:00 pm) opposite *Friends* on NBC. To counter this, NBC increased the duration of *Friends* by 10 minutes (up to 8:40 pm) to affect the second half of *Survivor*. CBS also moved its crime series *CSI: Crime Scene Investigation* after *Survivor* to take on NBC's *Will & Grace*.

When the ratings for the first week were reported, *Survivor* beat *Friends* convincingly even in the 18–49 demographics. Though NBC was still the winner with four of its shows featuring in the Top 5, CBS exposed NBC's vulnerability on Thursday nights. *CSI* had lost to *Will & Grace*, but its popularity rose continuously. Even so, NBC had topped the overall ratings for the year 2001–02.

CBS tightened the screws starting from the 2002–03 season. Led by the increasingly popular *CSI*, CBS became the most watched network for the 2002–03 season. CSI, watched by 26.2 million viewers, comfortably overtook *Friends* which had 21.8 million viewers. Other shows of CBS's such as *Survivor* and

Everybody Loves Raymond also featured in the top ten. On the whole, CBS had four series in the top ten while NBC and Fox had three each. CBS's average viewership increased by 2% as compared to the previous season, while NBC's decreased by 2%. The CBS shows continued their dominance even during the 2003–04 season with *CSI* being the most watched show and CBS being the top network in terms of viewership.

The start of 2004 spelled more trouble for NBC. Its blockbuster sitcom *Friends* was due to end in May 2004 while *Scrubs* was receiving moderate ratings. *Friends* had been the linchpin for NBC's dominance on Thursday nights and the network had still to find another suitable show to match the blockbuster. *Frasier*, another sitcom aired on Tuesday nights, was also due to end in May.

Meanwhile, NBC started *The Apprentice* in January 2004 on Thursday at 8:30 pm. The popular one-hour show was shifted to Wednesday nights after the first two weeks. However, it could not match the popularity of FOX's *American Idol*. In the face-off, *American Idol* attracted 29 million viewers while *The Apprentice* managed only 12 million viewers. NBC shifted back the show to Thursday nights at 9:00 pm from the next week. This shuffle was also aimed at strengthening NBC's Thursday lineup after *Friends* was over. Commenting on the shuffling, Mitch Metcalf, Head of Scheduling at NBC said, "Two of the hottest shows on television right now are 'The Apprentice' and 'American Idol.' We think it's a disservice to viewers to have them squaring off against each other. We consider these moves a 'win-win' for NBC and the audience."[27]

In early 2004, NBC had about 14 new shows in development. At that time, it was reported that *Friends* would be replaced with *Father of the Pride*, which contained computer-generated animation by Dreamworks SKG.[28] However, later NBC announced that *Friends* would be replaced by another sitcom *Joey* with Matt LeBlanc (of *Friends* fame) in the lead role as an aspiring actor who wanted to make it big in Los Angeles.

There were very high expectations of *Joey* in the media and in the audience. NBC spared no efforts in promoting *Joey*. It advertised in more than 6,500 movie screens which were showing big films like *Spider-Man 2, I, Robot*, etc. Meanwhile, analysts felt that NBC would be much weaker after *Friends*. Gail Berman, President of FOX Entertainment said, "We believe that NBC will remain competitive on Thurs-

day night. But we also believe that they will be down significantly from where they were with *Friends*."[29]

Meanwhile, CBS announced that it would start the second spin-off of *CSI* called *CSI: New York* (*CSI: Miami* was the first spin-off announced in 2002). The new show was scheduled for October 2004 (Wednesday 10:00 pm) airing and would take on NBC's super hit show *Law & Order*.

The first episode of *Joey* was aired on September 9, 2004 and was watched by 18.5 million viewers. Contrary to NBC's expectations, most of them termed the show "average" and said it was no match for *Friends*. In September 2004, NBC as a whole lost 16% of its audience, with *Joey* losing 48%. Also, *CSI: New York* comfortably surpassed *Law & Order* to take the Wednesday night crown for the first time. About 18.51 million people watched the premier of *CSI: New York* which was 2 million more than *Law & Order*. This continued even after the first week. Also, NBC's Thursday night show *ER* was beaten by CBS's, *Without a Trace* (which showed an FBI's Missing Persons Squad searching for missing persons) for the first time. As a result, CBS now took over NBC's primetime viewership.

The decline of popularity for *Joey* continued as people thought it was awful and lacked humor. Other NBC shows such as *Father of the Pride*, *LAX* and *Hawaii* had also been disappointments. The failure of *Joey* resulted in NBC slipping to fourth position among the 18–49 year olds and brought down its advertising revenues significantly. The advertising commitments which were US$ 2.9 billion for 2004–05 season, slipped to US$ 1.9 billion for the 2005–06 season. Advertisers were not impressed by NBC's 2005–06 schedule and shows which included sitcom *My Name Is Earl*, drama *E-Ring*, and the reality series *Three Wishes*. On the other hand, ABC which climbed to third in rankings was expected to increase its advertising revenues by US$ 500 million.

Further, NBC's Sunday night successes like *Crossing Jordan* and *Law & Order: Criminal Intent* started facing stiff competition from ABC's *Desperate Housewives*. In fact, NBC's executives had rejected the script of *Desperate Housewives* when its writer Marc Cherry approached them before finalizing the deal with ABC. Series like *American Dreams* (aired during ABC's reality show *Extreme Makeover: Home Edition*) and *ER* (aired during CBS's *Without a Trace*) decreased viewership for NBC. On the other hand, CBS had a strong 2004–05 season with *Survivor*, *CSI: Miami* (Monday). NBC's management was very disappointed with the

EXHIBIT 8

NBCU

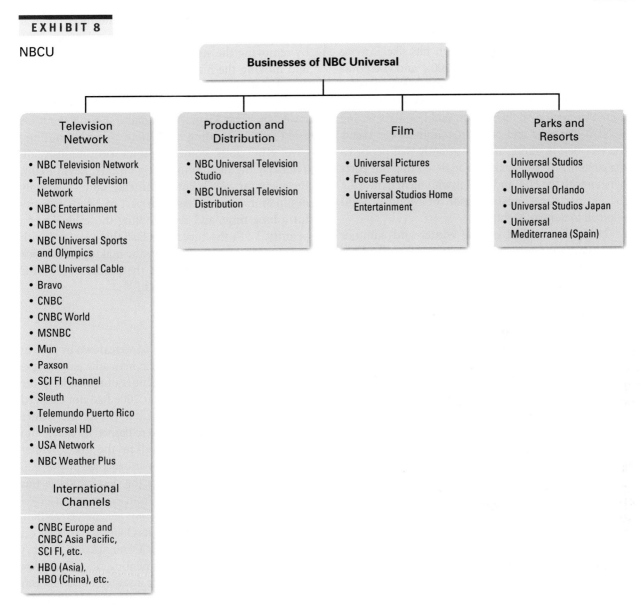

Businesses of NBC Universal

Television Network
- NBC Television Network
- Telemundo Television Network
- NBC Entertainment
- NBC News
- NBC Universal Sports and Olympics
- NBC Universal Cable
- Bravo
- CNBC
- CNBC World
- MSNBC
- Mun
- Paxson
- SCI FI Channel
- Sleuth
- Telemundo Puerto Rico
- Universal HD
- USA Network
- NBC Weather Plus

International Channels
- CNBC Europe and CNBC Asia Pacific, SCI FI, etc.
- HBO (Asia), HBO (China), etc.

Production and Distribution
- NBC Universal Television Studio
- NBC Universal Television Distribution

Film
- Universal Pictures
- Focus Features
- Universal Studios Home Entertainment

Parks and Resorts
- Universal Studios Hollywood
- Universal Orlando
- Universal Studios Japan
- Universal Mediterranea (Spain)

Source: www.nbcuni.com.

decline in ratings and felt that it would take at least two years to turn things around. Commenting on this, Jeff Zucker (Zucker), President of NBC Universal said, "There's no question we're in a downturn right now, and it doesn't turn around overnight."[30]

The Turnaround Efforts

To revive its sagging fortunes, NBC turned its focus to sports. Zucker said, "Sports is going to play a critical role in the rebuilding of NBC prime time."[31] On April 18, 2005, NBC finalized an important six-year deal with the National Football League (NFL) to bring back the NFL telecasts to the channel after having lost the rights to CBS in 1998. The deal was the result of the ABC's, decision to not renew the contract with NFL for the NFL season starting in 2006. The deal, worth approximately US$ 3.6 billion, would give NBC the right to broadcast primetime American football[32] on Sunday nights (Sunday Night Football) and the highlights of the Sunday afternoon games on its pre-game show (scheduled before the start of the Sunday night game). NBC also bagged rights to broadcast two Super Bowls in 2009 and 2012.

The deal was expected to revive NBC's fortunes. Sunday nights had usually more viewership and ABC had been dominating the slot with hits like *Extreme Makeover: Home Edition* (8:00–9:00), and *Desperate Housewives* (9:00–10:00). The NFL telecast was expected to bring advertising revenues up to US$ 6 million per hour. Elaborating on this, Wright said, "Content is king at NBC Universal and NFL programming represents the very best in strong and consistently well-performing content. We are thrilled to be re-igniting our partnership with the NFL and joining with them in moving the 36-year American institution of Monday Night Football to Sunday Nights."[33]

NBC also banked on the winter and summer Olympics, for which it had rights till 2012.[34] It hoped to gain both viewers and advertising revenues with the most watched sporting event. NBC Universal planned to sell specific events of the Olympics through its cable television, Internet and video-on-demand format to cash in on the viewer's interest for real-time highlights.

NBC also had high hopes on *The Apprentice* show with Martha Stewart[35] (Stewart) on September 21, 2005. The series, in which 16 candidates competed for an opportunity to work with Stewart, was named *The Apprentice: Martha Stewart*. The show's original host Donald Trump made way for Stewart and acted as one of the executive producers. However, the show was unable to match the popularity of the original version and was thus limited to just one series. However, NBC claimed that it always wanted to telecast only one series with Stewart.

Commenting on NBC's futile efforts, Bill Carroll, Vice-president and Director of Programming at Katz Television Group, said, "NBC is struggling and executives have to be disappointed. The one bright spot is *My Name Is Earl* but there's not much other than that. Having the Winter Olympics on the near horizon and football for the Fall will help but ultimately, it is series programming that makes the difference and NBC hasn't been able to make a turnaround in that area yet."[36]

In December 2005, NBC inked a deal with Apple Computers Inc.[37] to sell its television shows through iTunes Music Store, from where people could download and play on an Apple video iPod. Under the deal, NBC offered about 300 specific episodes from its new shows such as *Law & Order*, and *The Office*, and old shows such as *Alfred Hitchcock Presents* etc., through the iTunes Music Store.

In the same month, NBC announced that it would reshuffle its Thursday lineup in January 2006 by removing the struggling *Joey* and *The Apprentice* and moving the hit comedy *My Name Is Earl* from Tuesday to Thursday. The new lineup consisted of *Will & Grace* (which was to end in May 2006), followed by *Four Kings*, *My Name Is Earl*, *The Office*, and the long standing *ER* at 10:00 pm. The shuffling gave NBC four comedy shows continuously on Thursday nights. Commenting on this, Kevin Reilly, President of NBC Entertainment, said, "Certainly destination comedy has been part of NBC's identity for a long time, and reassembling those blocks is a priority. With the success of *Earl* this year and with *Office* finding its legs, we have the makings of a block of shows we felt perfectly fit the profile of an NBC Thursday night comedy lineup."[38]

What Next?

NBC's revenues for the year 2005 were down by 23% to US$ 5.1 billion while all other networks gained revenues (refer to Table 3 for revenues of networks in the years 2004 and 2005). The year 2006 had not changed NBC's fortunes by much. NBC's hopes for the Winter Olympics in February 2006 were dashed as viewership was down 34% as compared to the 2002 Winter Olympics. Though the poor performance of the U.S. athletes was one of the reasons, the viewership loss was primarily due to competition from *American Idol, Desperate Housewives, Grey's Anatomy, Survivor*, etc. NBC's aggressive cross promotion of its Olympics coverage on USA Network, CNBC, and NBCOlympics.com couldn't increase its viewership. Commenting on this, Jordan Breslow, Director of Broadcast Research at MediaCom

TABLE 3

Revenues of Television Networks for the Years 2004 and 2005

Network	Revenues (in million US$)		
	2004	2005	Growth
CBS	4,449	4,671	5%
ABC	3,514	3,911	11%
NBC	5,062	3,900	−23%
FOX	2,405	2,624	9%

Source: John M. Higgins, "CBS: In the Money," January 9, 2006.

said, "The Olympics rarely go up against original programming, and the other networks decided to put their best products forward. It has never gone up against *American Idol*, and I don't think anyone should be surprised that the older-skewing Olympics should not have any impact on 'Idol.' I look at the Olympics as fall-back programming. It's like, take your pick of first-run product and if there isn't anything there, then, great, tune into NBC."[39]

In March 2006, *Joey* returned on NBC and this time against *American Idol* on Tuesday. The serial attracted only 4 million viewers as against 7.28 million when it was aired on Thursdays, and was immediately pulled back. In April 2006, Katie Couric, the Co-host of the *Today* show, the most profitable news program on television generating close to US$ 500 million in advertising revenues annually for NBC, announced that she was moving to CBS, after being with NBC for 15 years. Some analysts said that it would have a major impact on NBC.

In May 2006, NBC announced its schedule for 2006–07, which included the important *Sunday Night Football* and six new dramas such as *Friday Night Lights, Studio 60 on the Sunset Strip, Kidnapped,* and four comedy series such as *Twenty Good Years and 30 Rock,* etc. Commenting on this, Reilly said, "The face of NBC is changing. We took the first step this season with Thursday hits *My Name Is Earl* and *The Office.* Next season we'll add momentum and excitement with the addition of 'Sunday Night Football' and establish a foundation of quality across the week by standing behind shows that each say something about who we are."[40]

However, NBC announced a revised lineup in the very next week, after ABC announced that it was moving its *Grey's Anatomy* to Thursday 9:00 pm slot during which NBC planned to air its big bet *Studio 60 on the Sunset Strip.* NBC also shuffled some of its other programs which were against its rival's big hits. Reilly said that NBC aimed to not to put its best bets against top programs of the rivals to allow them to gain popularity.

Analysts felt that NBC could not continue with such defensive strategies for long and advocated that it should take some measures to come back strongly. They found fault with NBC pushing *Studio 60 on the Sunset Strip* to Monday night at 10:00 pm. They felt it should have been shown early to gain a larger audience, and also to avoid clashing with ESPN's *Monday Night Football.*

Analysts felt that NBC was unable to leverage the brand image it had built through its hit shows like *Cheers, Friends,* and *Seinfeld.* It couldn't develop great new programs to fill the slots vacated by *Friends* and other hit shows. David Thomas, a Chicago-based writer and publisher of blogs—Miami Dolphins and OrangeAndTeal.com—said, "NBC could never fill that 8:30 p.m. slot between *Friends* and *Seinfeld* ever. It was poor development. That slot was like the sure sign of death for a new show. . . . If you couldn't get success there for all those years, the development everywhere else was probably not doing so well. . . . There was never an interesting drama or cult hit like *Alias.* So they had no credibility. And then they lost the folks like us who loved the network but went elsewhere like HBO for good content."[41]

Despite NBC's poor show, some analysts said that the network was finally making serious turnaround efforts. They supported NBC's rescheduling and felt that it was important for the network to shield its new big programs against the established mighty ones. As NBC acquired *Studio 60 on the Sunset* Strip by winning a bid against CBS and would pay around US$ 3 million per episode, it was important for it to be off the competition to gain advertising revenues and viewers. Analysts were optimistic about the advertising revenues that could be generated by the drama *Friday Night Lights,* and the NFL games. Satisfied with the efforts of NBC, John Rash of Campbell Mithun, a marketing communications agency, said, "I'm encouraged at the direction NBC is headed. They've definitely got some buzz going for a few new shows."[42]

ENDNOTES

1. David Bianculli, "We Got Clobbered, but We'll be Back," www.nydailynews.com, July 25, 2005.
2. "NBC: Now It's Wait-And-See TV," www.businessweek.com, May 9, 2005.
3. Paul R. La Monica, "Must-flee TV?" www.money.cnn.com, August 31, 2005.
4. Started in 1962 by Boyd Jefferies, Jefferies & Company is a global investment bank and institutional securities firm. Headquartered in New York, the company is into financial advisory services, institutional brokerage, securities research and asset management business.
5. A television season in the U.S. usually starts in mid-September and ends in May of the next year. Networks vie with each other to attract advertisers by showcasing their lineups for the Fall (September–December).
6. Headquartered in New York, Nielsen Media Research provides television audience measurement and advertising information services worldwide. It has offices around the world in more than 40 countries.
7. Thursday night primetime, between 8:00 pm and 10:00 pm, was made a most popular slot for TV viewers by NBC during the 1980s

and 1990s when it began showing blockbuster serials at this time. Since then, the television networks have been vying with each other to dominate this slot by airing their best shows and advertisers have been paying premiums to advertise during that time.

8. Paul R. La Monica, "Olympics Didn't Sweep Away ABC and FOX," www.money.cnn.com, March 2, 2006.

9. Started in 1920 as American Professional Football Association, National Football League is the largest professional American football league with thirty-two teams from all of America. The teams are divided into two groups—American Football Conference (AFC) and National Football Conference (NFC). Each Conference is further divided into East, West, North and South, each consisting of four teams. The NFL pre-season starts somewhere in August while the regular season starts on the first Sunday after the Labor Day (first Monday of September every year). Majority of the matches are played on Sundays and Mondays and a few on Thursdays. The winner is selected in the final Super Bowl, usually held in February. The season ends with a match between the stars of AFC and NFC groups called Pro Bowl.

10. David B. Wilkerson, "NBC's Bid To 'Heist' Ratings Gold," www.marketwatch.com, February 6, 2006.

11. Established in 1934, the FCC is an independent government agency which regulates interstate and international communications by radio, television, wire, satellite and cable (Source: www.fcc.gov).

12. Grant Tinker co-founded MTM Enterprises, a production company, along with his wife in 1970 to produce *The Mary Tyler Moore Show* for CBS. The show became highly popular. The company was sold to News Corporation in 1996.

13. Based in New York, Westwood One is one of the largest radio networks in the U.S. It produces and distributes radio programs in the U.S. and is managed by CBS Radio.

14. Devin Leonard, "The Unlikely Mogul Jack Welch was his Friend. But Jeff Immelt has Given NBC Chief Bob Wright What He's Always Wanted: An Empire," www.money.cnn.com, September 29, 2003.

15. Born in March 1931 in Melbourne, Australia, Rupert Murdoch is the chairman and managing director of News Corporation, one of the largest media conglomerates in the world which owns FOX Broadcasting Company.

16. "The Race for a Global Network," www.kenauletta.com, 1996.

17. Headquartered in Redmond, Washington, Microsoft Corporation is the world's largest software company. The company provides operating systems such as Windows XP, home entertainment products, owns an internet portal MSN and has presence in the television market. For the year ended June 2005, Microsoft's annual revenues were US$ 39.8 billion and profits were US$ 12.25 billion.

18. Affiliate stations are television stations owned by other companies which enter into a contractual agreement with the network stations to air programs of the network.

19. Deborah Solomon, "NBC Links up With Xoom, Snap to Form New Net Firm," www.sfgate.com, May 11, 1999.

20. Between 1995 and 2000, a number of firms that provided products and services related to or by using the Internet grew rapidly in number, as many individuals ambitiously started their own companies. The firms, known as dot-com companies, offered more or less similar products and services. The uncontrolled proliferation of such companies ended with the bubble bursting in March 2000 leading to the closure of many such companies.

21. Aparna Kumar, "Short Life, Long Death of NBCi," www.wired.com, April 12, 2001.

22. "NBC to Acquire NBC Internet Inc. (NBCi)," www.prnewswire.com, April 9, 2001.

23. In addition, the acquisition resulted in NBC owning three stations in Los Angeles–one already owned by NBC (KNBC-TV, Channel 4) and the other two (KWHY-TV Channel 22 and KVEA(TV) Channel 52) acquired from Telemundo. NBC requested FCC for one year time to divest KWHY-TV, Channel 22).

24. The dispute ended in November 2005, when NBC agreed to buy a controlling stake in Paxson. Under the deal, NBC got an 18-month's time to buy all of Bud Paxson's shares. If the federal rules didn't change within the next 18 months, NBC could transfer the right to a third party. In case the third party could not exercise the rights, NBC would have to pay US$ 105 million to Paxson's shareholders.

25. Bronfman was the biggest shareholder of VU. He was heading Seagram in 2000 when it merged with Vivendi to form Vivendi Universal.

26. Kenneth N. Gilpin, "GE and Vivendi Agree on Terms of NBC Universal Merger," www.nytimes.com, October 8, 2003.

27. "Idol Sends NBC, Apprentice Scrambling," www.zapt2it.com, January 23, 2004.

28. Dreamworks SKG was a studio started by noted film director Steven Spielberg, and David Geffen and Jeffrey Katzenberg in 1994. It was sold to Viacom in late 2005.

29. Ronald Grover, "Filling the Shoes of Missing Friends," www.businessweek.com, August 18, 2004.

30. Andrew Wallenstein, "NBC Doldrums Might Continue, Reilly Admits," www.mediaweek.com, July 25, 2005.

31. Paul J. Gough, "Zucker: NBC Expected Upfront Hit," www.mediaweek.com, June 22, 2005.

32. American football, called football in America and Canada, is different from the normal football and is played with an oval shaped ball. The game closely resembles rugby.

33. "NFL Returns to NBC," www.thefutoncritic.com, April 18, 2005.

34. NBC had acquired Olympic broadcasting rights for the U.S. for Athens (2004), Torino (2006), Beijing (2008), Vancouver (2010) and London (2012).

35. Martha Stewart, born in August 1941, is a multimedia and lifestyle entrepreneur. In October 2004, Stewart was jailed for five months at a federal prison for lying to federal investigators, in connection with her involvement in a dubious stock sale of Im-Clone Systems, a pharmaceutical company.

36. Paul R. La Monica, "ABC and CBS Clean House During Sweeps," www.money.cnn.com, November 30, 2005.

37. Based in Cupertino, California, Apple is considered the pioneer of the personal computer revolution in the late 1970s. Started by Steve Jobs and Steve Wozniack in 1976, Apple started manufacturing computers and later developed the powerful Macintosh range of computers. Apple now is more famous for its iPod, a hard-drive based music player. For the financial year ended September 2005, Apple's sales were US$ 13.93 billion and profits were US$ 1.335 billion.

38. Andrew Wallenstein, "NBC to Shuffle Primetime Lineup in January," www.hollywoodreporter.com, December 2, 2005.

39. Kevin Downey, "NBC's New Big Worry: Losing Sweeps," www.medialifemagazine.com, February 16, 2006.

40. "NBC Announces 2006–07 Primetime Schedule," www.comingsoon.net, May 15, 2006.

41. Diego Vasquez, "On Giving The Axe To NBC's Jeff Zucker," www.medialifemagazine.com, June 15, 2006.

42. Brooks Barnes, "Can 'Studio 60' Save NBC," www.online.wsj.com, May 15, 2006.

Tsingtao Brewery Co., Ltd. (A)

This case was prepared by Shengjun Liu, Richard Ivey School of Business, the University of Western Ontario.

IVEY

On July 31, 2001, Peng Zuoyi, the charismatic general manager of Tsingtao Brewery Co., Ltd. (Tsingtao Brewery), died of a sudden heart attack while swimming in the sea. This sudden event made the company, which had been running fast on the road of acquisition, lose its "driver." Since 1996, Peng had expanded Tsingtao Brewery to a giant, by merging dozens of beer enterprises. As a result, the company raised its market share from 2.2 per cent in 1998 to 11 per cent in 2001, and regained the leading position in China. Nonetheless, frequent acquisitions also led to some negative effects. Although as its major business revenue rose from RMB1.05 billion in 1993 to RMB5.28 billion in 2001, the net profit decreased from RMB225 million to RMB103 million.[1] By the end of April 2002, one-third of the company's 48 subsidiaries were making profits, another one-third were breaking even and the remaining subsidiaries were in deficit.[2] Investors doubted the value of company's acquisitions: the H-share price of Tsingtao Brewery decreased by 52.38 per cent while the Hang

Dr. Shengjun Liu prepared this case solely to provide material for class discussion. The author does not intend to illustrate either effective or ineffective handling of a managerial situation. The author may have disguised certain names and other identifying information to protect confidentiality.

Ivey Management Services is the exclusive representative of the copyright holder and prohibits any form of reproduction, storage or transmittal without its written permission. This material is not covered under authorization from CanCopy or any reproduction rights organization. To order copies or request permission to reproduce materials, contact Ivey Publishing, Ivey Management Services, c/o Richard Ivey School of Business, The University of Western Ontario, London, Ontario, Canada, N6A 3K7; phone (519) 661-3208; fax (519) 661-3882; e-mail cases@ivey.uwo.ca.

Copyright © 2005, CEIBS (China Europe International Business School) Version: (A) 2006-01-13

Seng Index increased by 45.30 per cent between 1995 and 2001.

On August 29, 2001, the board of Tsingtao Brewery appointed Jin Zhiguo, ex-president of the North China Region, as general manager.[3] Jin began his employment in the company in 1975, as a worker. Later, he worked as a workshop head, as an assistant to the factory manager and as the general manager of Xi'an subsidiary. Jin was recognized by his competitors as a person who was a tough rival and had a good knowledge of beer. In 1996, he was appointed as general manager of the Xi'an subsidiary. Within four years, he turned the company from a loss-maker into a profit-generator. The sales volume of Xi'an subsidiary rose from 30,000 tons to 180,000 tons, with the annual profit reaching more than RMB70 million, half of the total profit of all of Tsingtao Brewery's acquired subsidiaries. Although it was the third time for him to face a great challenge, Jin still felt nervous. The excessive expansion put extreme pressures on funds and personnel in the company. Approximately 50 subsidiaries needed to be restructured, and 100 brands needed to be refreshed. Jin remarked:

> In the past few years, Tsingtao Brewery was pursuing an expansion growth strategy, which was like driving a car on an expressway and even sometimes overtaking other cars. The situation is highly risky and there is danger of losing control in the integration of acquired companies.

After a careful investigation, Jin believed that the company should change its strategy from "growing large to become powerful" to "becoming powerful to grow large." The current challenge of the company was implementing the post-acquisition integration.

China's Beer Industry

General Situation

China's beer producing can be traced back to the beginning of the 20th century. By 1949, China's annual beer output was only 7,000 tons. In the period from 1980 to 2001, the output enjoyed an annual growth rate of six per cent, compared with America's one per cent. Until 2000, beer accounted for 78 per cent of the total output of alcoholic beverage drinks. In 2001, beer output reached 22.74 million tons (see Exhibit 1). After nine years of being the second largest beer market, China overtook the United States as the world's largest beer producer in 2002.

The beer brewing process consists of four basic but sophisticated procedures: making malt, boiling, fermentation and aging. The beer industry was considered both capital- and technology-intensive; therefore, entry barriers into the industry were quite high.[4] Moreover, brewing equipment needed to be in line with strict sanitation standards, and beer companies were difficult to transform into other businesses. As a result, many brewers had to struggle for survival despite continuous losses. Furthermore, more than 90 per cent of beer producers in China used glass bottles. Due to the drawbacks of glass

bottles, such as their friability and short shelf-life, producers had a small market coverage. Consequently, regional markets were largely dominated, usually with no more than three beer companies. Compared with multinational companies, whose normal production capacities were more than 10 million tons annually, most Chinese beer producers were on a smaller scale, with approximately 200,000 tons in annual output capacity.

Industry Competition Competition was extremely severe in the beer industry in China. Most companies sought to differentiate their products by packaging, because they all shared similar core technologies and techniques purchased from developed countries. Although there were more than 1,000 kinds of beers in the United States, almost all the beers in Chinese market were ales. Due to the similarities in taste, most beer brands competed by means of advertising, price-cutting and government protection. Management, marketing and production scales became key factors in determining competence.[5] Since the removal of investment constrictions in the beer industry in 1994, more than 700 beer companies had emerged. Most of them were small, poorly equipped

---

EXHIBIT 1

Beer Output and its Growth in China, 1980 to 2001 (in 000s tons)

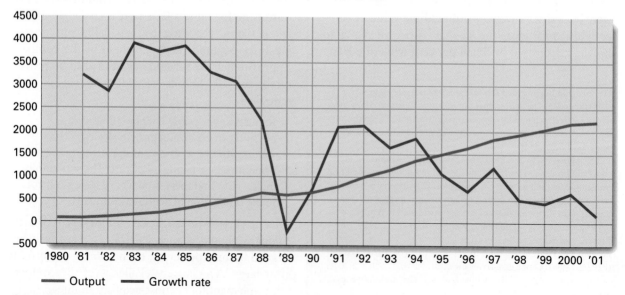

—— Output   —— Growth rate

Source: Shi Yanping, "Mergers, Acquisitions and Restructuring: An Intensified Integration in the Beer Industry," *CITIC Securities Research,* 2002, No. 9.

EXHIBIT 2

Financial Indices of the Beer Industry in China (RMB millions)

Indices	1996	1997	Y2Y Increase (%)	1998	Y2Y Increase (%)	2001
Production value	328.0	398.0	21.3	410.0	3.0	469.0
Output (10,000 tons)	1,681.9	1,888.5	12.3	1,987.7	5.3	2,274.0
Sales revenue	363.0	377.0	3.9	378.0	0.3	499.0
Earning before tax	80.0	85.3	6.6	92.8	8.8	104.8
Profit	22.0	14.3	(0.4)	16.7	16.8	18.9
Profit per ton	130.8	75.7	—	84.2	—	82.9

Source: Shi Yanping, "Mergers, Acquisitions and Restructuring: An Intensified Integration in the Beer Industry," *CITIC Securities Research*, 2002, No. 9.

and badly managed. They were owned by the state or a collective and tried to survive by means of local protection and price wars. By the end of 2001, there were more than 500 beer companies in China, an average of one beer company for every three counties. However, only 23 companies reached an output of more than 200,000 tons annually, accounting for 50.4 per cent of the total output. Seventy-nine companies had an output between 50,000 and 200,000 tons annually, accounting for 20.8 per cent of the total output. The lack of economies of scale resulted in the loss of 41.7 per cent of the companies in the industry. This industry situation encouraged Peng Zuoyi to implement his aggressive expansion plan. Peng said in a humorous tone: "In front of us are wolves, behind us are tigers and in the middle are mice. We will beat mice first and then tigers and wolves."[6]

After 1996, the beer market changed to a buyer's market, due to the slowdown of demand. The fiercer competition reduced the profitability of large companies, threw medium and small companies into corners and slackened the increase of profit and revenue in the beer industry (see Exhibit 2.[7]) The beer industry had become one of the most competitive and market-oriented industries in China. The industry's competition could be divided into three levels. The first level of competition was between domestic producers and foreign producers. In the early 1990s, more than 50 foreign brands rushed into China and seized the high-grade market. The second level was the competition among major domestic producers. Tsingtao Brewery, China Resources Beer (CR Beer)

and Yanjing Beer initiated the "big fish eating little fish" acquisitions by taking advantage of their strong brands and abundant capital. All three, who had a production capacity of more than two million tons, formed the first group. Harbin Beer, Chongqing Beer and Zhujiang Beer formed the second group of competitors with a production capacity of about one million tons each (see Exhibit 3). The third level of competitors was the alliance of middle- and small-sized enterprises. Due to their complementary brands, technology and management, they chose to respond to competition in a cooperative way, by sharing resources, markets and benefits.

EXHIBIT 3

China's Top 10 Brewers in 2001 (in 10,000 tons)

Ranking	Name	Output
1	Tsingtao Brewery	251.2
2	Yanjing Beer	170.0
3	Zhujiang Beer	75.1
4	Sichuan CR Lanjian Beer	68.4
5	Golden Star Beer	60.9
6	Harbin Beer	54.9
7	Chongqing Beer	53.2
8	Shenyang CR Snow Beer	41.3
9	Huiquan Beer	40.1
10	Jinlongquan Beer	39.8

Source: China Beer Association.

At present, global beer consumption amounted to 130 million tons. Despite having the largest population in the world, China had a per capita beer consumption of only 18 litres, much less than the global average level of 25 litres, and 83 litres, 55 litres and 30 litres in America, Japan and Hong Kong respectively. Hence, with improving living standards and growth in the rural markets, a steady growth was expected in China's beer consumption. In fact, the Chinese market could be described as a combination of regional markets, as very few companies were allowed to engage in nationwide marketing. There was a dominant beer producer in almost every major city—people from Beijing drank Yanjing beer; Tsingtao people preferred Tsingtao beer and Guangzhou people were loyal to Zhujiang beer.

The Three Beer Giants

In China, Tsingtao Brewery, Yanjing Beer and CR Beer accounted for 30 per cent of the national market, and were humorously referred to as the "Three Kingdoms."[8]

Tsingtao Brewery   Tsingtao Brewery, the former Tsingtao Company Stock of the German Beer Corporation, established by British and German businessmen in 1903, was the first beer producer in China. In 1993, Tsingtao Brewery was transformed from a state-owned enterprise (SOE) to a joint stock company and issued H-shares in the Hong Kong Stock Exchange and A-shares in the Shanghai Stock Exchange.[9] By the end of 2001, Tsingtao Brewery had established manufacturing bases in 17 provinces, with a total annual capacity of more than three million tons. Tsingtao Brewery was the largest brewery with respect to output, sales, earnings before tax, market share and export. As the most famous Chinese beer brand, Tsingtao Brewery focused on high-grade beers and successfully sold its Tsingtao Beer, made from Laoshan spring water, to developed countries, accounting for half of China's total beer export.

In spite of its famous brand, Tsingtao Brewery market dominance was once surpassed by Yanjing Beer and CR Beer, in the mid-1990s. After 1996, Tsingtao Brewery switched from its focus on a high-grade market to a mass market, to implement its strategy of "reducing cost by low-end beer and making money by high-grade beer." Meanwhile, Tsingtao Brewery tried to raise its market share through a series of acquisitions, building its existence from South China to North China with an emphasis on the Yangtze Delta and Zhujiang Delta, the most developed areas in China. In the hinterlands, its North Department, Northeast Department and Luzhong Department constituted a powerful triangle (see Exhibit 4).

Yanjing Beer   The Beijing-based Yanjing Beer (Yanjing) surprised Chinese by its quick growth. Established in 1980, Yanjing Beer's total assets amounted to RMB6.3 billion, and its output reached 1.7 million tons in 2001. Thanks to its 85 per cent market share in Beijing, Yanjing Beer was the number one producer in 1995. Yanjing also expanded by acquiring companies that had large market shares, abundant assets, sound management and mature corporate cultures. By the end of 2001, Yanjing Beer owned 14 subsidiaries. In 2000, Yanjing entered Shandong market as a counter-attack to Tsingtao Brewery's acquisition of Beijing-based Five-Star Beer. Yanjing acquired Wuming Beer and Sankong Beer, which were respectively the third- and second-largest producers in Shandong, the hometown of Tsingtao Brewery, and which together accounted for 25 per cent of Shandong market.

CR Beer   China Resources was one of China's "window companies" in Hong Kong. It successfully expanded its business from an agent to a well-diversified business in both Hong Kong and the Chinese mainland. Its principal activities covered retail, beverage, food processing and distribution, and textile and petroleum distribution. In 1993, China Resources set up CR Beer Co., Ltd. as a joint venture with South African Breweries (SAB). China Resources controlled a 51 per cent stake of CR Beer. China Resources also established Shenyang CR Snow Beer, Dalian CR Beer and Anshan CR Beer, thereby controlling the Northeast China market. In addition, CR Beer acquired Lanjian Beer, the second largest producer in Southwest China. Although most of CR Beer's management were not beer experts, SAB was one of the top four beer producers in the world,[10] and China Resources was also powerful in terms of capital availability.[11] By the end of 2001, CR Beer controlled 24 subsidiaries with a total annual capacity of more than three million tons.

Foreign Beer Producers

In the mid-1990s, nearly 60 foreign beer producers, including Budweiser, Heineken, San Miguel and Carlsberg, established joint ventures in China by focusing on high-grade markets. However, most were unsuccessful,

EXHIBIT 4

Tsingtao Brewery's Organization Chart

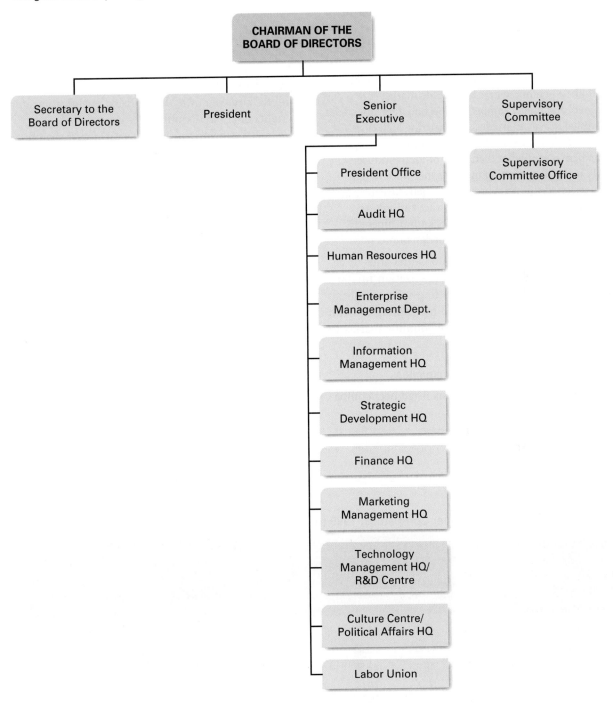

Source: www.tsingtaobeer.com.cn.

due to prices, tastes and positioning strategies incompatible with the Chinese market. Some chose to withdraw parts of their investment or retreat from the Chinese market. Li Guirong, chairman of the board of Tsingtao Brewery, made an analysis:

> There are several reasons for foreign brewers' bad experience in China. First, they focused on high-grade products while the consumption structure is like a pyramid where high-grade market is small and highly competitive. Second, they invested heavily in fixed asset, incurring high costs. Third, their personnel, operation and marketing expenses are higher than those of local producers. Fourth, the marketing methods that work well in developed countries prove to be ineffective in China due to the immature market and country difference. Finally, local brewers know Chinese consumers much better than foreign brewers.

Many foreign brands returned to China after its accession into the World Trade Organization in 2001. They changed strategies by putting more emphasis on localization and affinity and by teaming up with local brands, hoping to seize the booming market in an incremental way.

Performances of Listed Beer Companies

By the end of 2001, there were six listed beer companies in China:

- Tsingtao Brewery,
- Yanjing Beer,
- Lanzhou Yellow River Beer,
- Chongqing Beer,
- Honghe Guangming and
- Tibet Development.

The average earnings per share (EPS) of the six companies dropped from RMB0.23 in 2000 to RMB−0.03 in 2001, and the average return on equity (ROE) decreased to −2.09 per cent. Tsingtao Brewery's EPS and ROE ranked fifth, thus missing qualifications for a rights offer (see Exhibit 5).[12]

In 2001, the price of raw material for beer production rose quickly and pushed up the cost of listed companies. As a result, the average expenses increased by 68.76 per cent over the previous year. Again, the sales profitability, major business profitability and return on assets of Tsingtao Brewery ranked fifth (see Exhibit 6).

However, Tsingtao Brewery performed best in terms of growth of revenue. In 2001, Tsingtao Brewery's major business increased by 40.11 per cent, compared with the industry average of 22.57 per cent (see Exhibit 7).

Acquisitions

The Expansion Motivation Among Chinese brewers, Tsingtao Brewery was the first to enter the market but the last to become market-oriented. In 1996, its annual output was as low as 350,000 tons. In the same year, Peng Zuoyi, the newly appointed general manager, set a grand goal for Tsingtao Brewery—to have an output of five million tons by 2005, and eight million

EXHIBIT 5

Comparison Among Listed Beer Companies, 1999 to 2001

Companies	Debt/Asset (%)			Net Profit/Equity (%)			Net Profit/Number of Shares (RMB per share)		
	1999	2000	2001	1999	2000	2001	1999	2000	2001
Yanjing	4.41	10.85	12.70	12.25	7.79	7.96	0.53	0.40	0.43
Tsingtao	51.10	60.53	55.82	3.98	4.26	3.47	0.10	0.11	0.10
Chongqing	29.85	48.33	46.59	6.97	7.35	5.95	0.24	0.26	0.20
Tibet Development	39.70	33.56	40.62	20.74	8.53	9.02	0.43	0.16	0.18
Lanzhou Yellow River	49.53	44.61	54.96	6.21	0.67	(44.92)	0.33	0.03	(1.29)
Honghe Guangming	10.53	13.92	9.85	6.60	11.40	6.10	0.22	0.42	0.21
Average	30.85	35.30	36.76	9.45	6.67	(2.09)	0.31	0.23	(0.03)

Source: 2001 Annual Reports of relevant companies.

EXHIBIT 6

Comparison of Profitability of Listed Beer Companies, 1999 to 2001

Company	Gross Margins/Sales (%)			Net Profit/Major Business Revenue (%)			Net Profit/Asset (%)		
	1999	2000	2001	1999	2000	2001	1999	2000	2001
Yanjing	44.48	43.30	31.05	19.22	15.37	12.49	11.54	6.63	6.50
Tsingtao	40.14	40.38	28.74	3.66	2.53	1.95	1.73	1.36	1.25
Chongqing	49.14	46.71	35.85	13.68	13.25	6.33	4.64	3.57	1.67
Tibet Development	53.45	42.42	33.55	40.49	25.22	23.48	12.36	5.61	4.20
Lanzhou Yellow River	32.89	37.15	(33.55)	12.25	1.77	(98.52)	2.84	0.36	(19.34)
Honghe Guangming	46.89	54.37	45.74	27.75	37.33	29.10	8.29	9.81	5.44
Average	44.49	44.05	23.58	19.50	15.91	(4.20)	6.90	4.56	(0.05)

Source: 2001 Annual Reports of relevant companies.

tons by 2010. In 1993, Tsingtao Brewery got listed on the Hong Kong Stock Exchange and raised HK$890 million, and then raised HK$638 million in the Shanghai Stock Exchange in the same year. Sufficient capital reserves facilitated Tsingtao Brewery's acquisitions. Meanwhile, the resounding "CSH phenomenon" further encouraged Peng's aggressive plan.[13]

Since the 1990s, beer multinational companies (MNCs) expanded their business in China through establishing factories, acquiring factories or original equipment manufacturers (OEM), or entering such important markets as the Zhujiang River Delta and the Yangtze River Delta. Many gained exclusive sales in hotels, which seriously threatened the market for high-grade Tsingtao beers. By 1996, the consumption of high-grade beer was about one million tons, which was six per cent of total beer consumption. Foreign brands, Tsingtao Brewery and other brewers respectively accounted for 630,000, 300,000 and 100,000 tons in total volume of high-grade beer consumption. To respond to the foreign impact, Tsingtao Brewery put forward the strategy of "low-cost expansion, high jump-off point" to raise its market share.

In addition, the environment was favorable for expansion. Tsingtao Brewery was one of the 512 pillar SOEs listed by the State Council, one of the 10 beer enterprises supported by the Light Industry Institute and one of the eight key enterprises listed by Shandong municipal government. The strong position made the company qualified for many favorable policies concerning acquisitions.[14]

Expansion Strategy Peng judged that Tsingtao Brewery was facing a historic opportunity for acquisition of other companies:

First, the government encouraged large companies to take over medium- and small-sized enterprises by favorable policies; second, many foreign brewers wanted to retreat due to poor performance; third, many local government invited Tsingtao Brewery to acquire some unprofitable beer SOEs.

Thus, Tsingtao Brewery decided to realize an extraordinary growth, based on the concepts of a "big famous brand strategy," "pyramid ideology," "low-cost expansion, high jump-off point," "fresh rate management" and "regional department system." The "big famous brand strategy" was considered the core of its company strategy, implying that the Tsingtao brand facilitated growth and interactively enhanced the value of other companies that were associated with it. Before 1996, Tsingtao Brewery considered itself a "nobleman" and focused on high-grade products. Unfortunately, it was finally surpassed by Yanjing Beer, which focused on medium- and low-grade products. The "pyramid strategy" was intended to form a high-medium-low product structure for creating more market space (see Exhibit 8). The "fresh rate management" was a quality strategy to ensure that customers living in Tsingtao could drink fresh beer produced within one week, and customers in Shandong province could access the beer produced within one month.

EXHIBIT 7

Comparison of Growth Rate of Listed Beer Companies, 2000 to 2001 (RMB10,000)

	Major Business Revenue				Operation Profit				Net Profit			
Companies	2000	Growth Rate (%)	2001	Growth Rate (%)	2000	Growth Rate (%)	2001	Growth Rate (%)	2000	Growth Rate (%)	2001	Growth Rate (%)
Yanjing	174,587	15.14	228,788	29.00	28,668	(13.14)	27,092	(5.50)	26,828	(7.96)	28,569	6.49
Tsingtao	376,625	54.01	527,672	40.11	9,168	5.72	7,132	(22.21)	9,520	15.18	10,288	8.08
Chongqing	33,815	8.58	46,671	38.01	4,567	(6.22)	4,624	1.25	4,479	7.26	3,428	(23.44)
Tibet Development	11,010	(7.54)	13,452	22.17	2,276	(54.57)	3,227	41.78	2,776	(42.44)	3,158	13.75
Lanzhou Yellow River	18,591	(30.31)	15,451	(16.88)	107	(60.81)	(17,569)	—	329	(89.93)	(15,222)	—
Honghe Guangming	5,644	40.57	6,941	22.98	2,205	152.00	2,180	(1.13)	2,106	89.14	2,020	(4.13)
Average	103,379	13.41	139,829	22.57	7,831	3.83	4,448	2.84	7,673	(4.79)	5,374	0.15

Source: 2001 Annual Reports of relevant companies.

EXHIBIT 8

The Product Pyramid

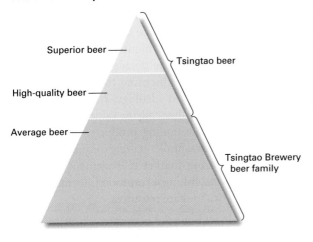

Superior beer ——
High-quality beer ——
Average beer ——

Tsingtao beer

Tsingtao Brewery
beer family

Preparation Tsingtao Brewery held that proposed acquisitions should be low cost and profit-oriented to avoid possible burdens. Tsingtao Brewery made detailed plans to guide acquisitions:

- The Development Department organized other related departments, including finance, production and quality control, to conduct a feasibility analysis. Final decisions would be made by the board.

- All acquisitions adhered to four principles: (1) reasonable market arrangement: a target should have a minimum market circle with a radius of 150 kilometres without overlap with other subsidiaries; (2) significant demand potential: the local population density, consumption level and consumption habit should be in line with beer sales; (3) qualified staff: teams were to be created with skillful workers and experienced managers and (4) a balance of short-term and long-term interests.

- Annual investment budget should be approved by the board, and each acquisition should be sanctioned by the general manager.

- Any investment of more than RMB10 million was to be evaluated by the board.

- Restrictions on the size of the deals: no more than RMB10 million for a capacity of 30,000 tons and corresponding production startup investment should be no more than RMB5 million;

no more than RMB30 million for a capacity of 50,000 to 60,000 tons and corresponding production startup investments should be no more than RMB15 million.

To facilitate the expansion plan, Tsingtao Brewery adjusted its organization structure accordingly. First, it switched to a regional department system, and set up South China Holdings, East China Holdings, North Department, Northeast Department, Huaihai Department, Luzhong Department and Southwest Department. In the new system, Tsingtao Brewery was the hub of the entire system, controlling strategic decisions, capital operations, and investment and corporate culture. Regional departments were responsible for making profits and regional management decisions, and all subsidiaries were in charge of quality control and cost control.

Tsingtao Brewery established the Development Department, which specialized in acquisition implementation, and the Investment Management Department, which specialized in after-acquisition integration.[15] The Investment Management Department generally entered the acquired subsidiary when negotiations ended. The five employees of this department were in charge of transplanting Tsingtao Brewery's management model, harmonizing the relationship between subsidiaries and headquarters, and monitoring production and operation. Upon receiving complaints from the subsidiary, the Investment Management Department made on-site investigations and handled possible problems. Each month, the department would submit two reports on the acquired subsidiaries to the board: one on production and operation and the other on sales performance. Both reports were the basis for the subsidiaries' performance appraisal.[16] The chief executives of all subsidiaries were called to headquarters to make reports every half year.

Integration Plan The transplant of the Tsingtao Brewery model was regarded as the core of integration. The so-called Tsingtao Brewery model consisted of one core, six systems and two supports. One core referred to a combination of scientific and strict management and harmonious interpersonal relationships. Six systems included quality assurance, production, human resource management, marketing, financial management, and development and innovation systems. Two supports were technologies and corporate culture. To implement the integration, Tsingtao Brewery established an integration team led by a vice general manager. The team would enter the acquired target when negotiations were completed and stayed only until the target passed its final examination. Duties of the team included the following:

1. *Inoculating Tsingtao Brewery culture*—The team focused on people, publicizing the history of Tsingtao Brewery and educating employees to share the honors and duties. Tsingtao Brewery tried to make employees more aggressive through post-competitions in acquired subsidiaries. Moreover, subsidiaries set positions paralleled to those of Tsingtao Brewery and introduced an interactive selection system in which employees elected their favorite managers, and managers selected employees. Staff training was another key element. Tsingtao assigned experienced workers to educate workers in newly acquired organizations and organized face-to-face training courses. Finally, Tsingtao Brewery emphasized internal promotion and annual salary bonuses. Managers were required to sign subcontracts with subordinates to spread out responsibilities.

2. *Building rules and systems to enforce the Tsingtao Brewery model*—Most of the targets set out by SOEs did not have effective regulations and management systems. The rules and systems of the team required that all new mergers were well-organized and systematic without repetition, and overlap was to be abided by all employees. After a thorough investigation, the team was expected to make suggestions for improvements in nine areas that included general management, material, production, statistics, equipment, computation, human resources, finance and marketing. Meanwhile, the subsidiaries were required to work out a detailed schedule and arrangement of duties under the supervision of the team. The team would re-examine and confirm the working schedule after one or two months and provide a formal appraisal and further suggestions about half a year later.

3. *Implementing the ISO 9000 system*—Tsingtao Brewery's ISO team consisted of members who were well-trained and had related certifications. When the acquired subsidiary reached basic qualifications, the ISO team would provide on-site guidance. Before formal authentication, the ISO team would conduct a pre-authentication.

4. *Sharing market networks*—Subsidiaries were expected to implement a marketing system characterized by fresh rate management, direct supply, intensive networks and market expansion. The implementation would be conducted by the marketing and sales department, as well as by the acquired subsidiary. The detailed measures of this system included segmenting the market according to the pyramid ideology, fully utilizing the Tsingtao brand, enhancing the value of local brands and carefully positioning products, strengthening market networks, implementing fresh rate management, enhancing market management and feedback, and establishing a common information and fund network to share resources.

5. *Establishing a financial management system focusing on complete budget management,*[17] *cost control and fund management*—The subsidiary needed to improve its financial structure and strengthen its financial analysis and cost control. In addition, Tsingtao Brewery sent a financial director to each subsidiary.

6. *Absorbing the Tsingtao Brewery techniques*—As soon as the acquisition was complete, a technique team would be sent to diagnose the production operation of the subsidiary, and recommend improvements to its product quality, technique design and production procedure. The headquarters would review the improvements, examine beer quality periodically and organize beer contests.

Acquisitions By April 2002, Tsingtao Brewery had acquired 47 beer companies in 17 provinces. The total output of the acquired companies reached 2.02 million tons in 2001, which was approximately 80 per cent of the total output of Tsingtao Brewery.

In 1994, Tsingtao Brewery took over Yangzhou Beer for RMB80 million, starting its expansion battle. It then acquired Xi'an Hans Beer in 1995. In 1997 and 1998, Tsingtao Brewery merged two and three small beer companies respectively in Shandong province. Most acquisitions happened in 1999 and 2000, when Tsingtao Brewery purchased a total of 30 companies. In 1999, Tsingtao Brewery took over 14 beer companies—half of them located out of Shandong province—with a total output of 1.5 million tons for a cost of more than RMB400 million. In 2000, Tsingtao Brewery acquired 16 companies with a total output of 1.2 million tons for about RMB600 million. It purchased controlling stakes of Shanghai Carlsberg, Beijing Five Star and Beijing Sanhuan Beer for RMB150 million, US$10 million and US$12.5 million respectively. In 2001, Tsingtao Brewery slowed down its expansion and acquired only nine companies with a total output of 600,000 tons for RMB260 million (see Exhibit 9). The frequent acquisitions resulted in a sharp increase in asset and production capacity (see Exhibits 10 to 13). As Peng commented, "We are in battle for 360 days a year."

In 2000, those subsidiaries that had joined Tsingtao before the end of 1999 achieved output of 927,500 tons (up 57.6 per cent year to year), revenue of RMB2.47 billion (up 123.8 per cent year to year) and profit of RMB63.4 million (up 580 per cent). Meanwhile, subsidiaries that had joined Tsingtao Brewery before the end of 1998 produced 551,600 tons in 2000 (up 60.11 per cent year to year), reaching a revenue of RMB1.74 billion (up 93.58 per cent year to year) and profit of RMB96.1 million (up 379 per cent year to year). The most significant example of growth was Xi'an subsidiary that raised its output from 25,000 tons in 1996 to 180,000 tons in 2000, turning a loss of RMB24.3 million into a profit of RMB75.4 million.

EXHIBIT 9

Geographic Distribution of Acquired Subsidiaries

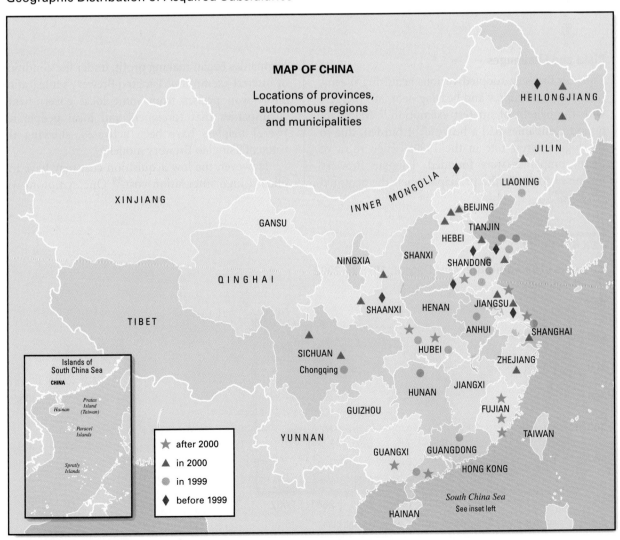

EXHIBIT 10

Asset Increase of Tsingtao Brewery, 1997 to 2001
(in RMB100 million)

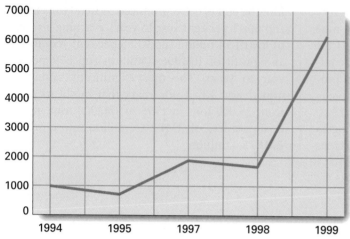

Source: Annual Reports of Tsingtao Brewery.

Risks and Challenges

Tsingtao Brewery adopted various acquiring means, including bankruptcy and bearing debt and mergers with the benefit of interest exemption.[18] Many acquired companies had a heavy debt burden, due to the high interest rate in the 1980s, when most of these companies were founded. Tsingtao Brewery promised to repay the principal when the acquired companies began making profit, under the condition of interest exemption. Tsingtao Brewery's integration effort won praises from some local governments: "Companies that foreigners and local people felt [were] helpless have been activated, showing the value of Tsingtao Brewery model."

However, the low acquisition cost may have implied a high integration cost.[19] One symptom was

EXHIBIT 11

Changes in Tsingtao Brewery Output, 1978 to 2002
(in 10,000 tons)

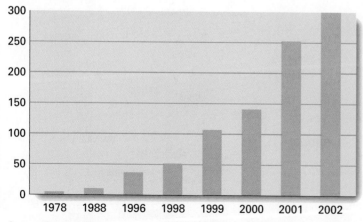

Source: "Tsingtao Brewery Strategic Expansion," www.holyhigh.com.

EXHIBIT 12

Acquired Assets and Liabilities by Year (RMB10,000)

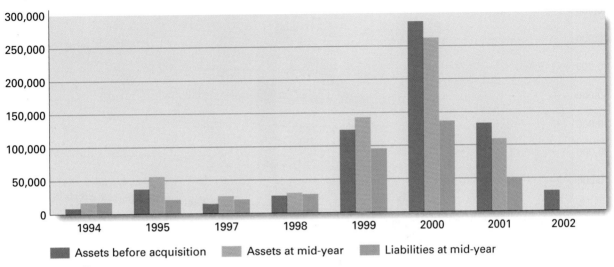

Source: Company files.

the high expenditure of technology improvement, which ranged from millions to tens of millions (see Exhibit 14). Wang Wei, a mergers and acquisitions (M&A) expert said:

> Tsingtao Brewery's acquisitions have obvious characteristics of a planned economy. Though many targets are problematic and should bankrupt,

Tsingtao Brewery spent much resources in saving them, which may negatively influence Tsingtao itself rather than achieving economies of scale.

A research fellow of an investment bank pointed out:

> Peng's aggressive plan has brought about huge fund pressure to Tsingtao Brewery. With the excuse of economies of scale, many useless companies joined

EXHIBIT 13

Change in Acquired Capacities by Year (in 10,000 tons)

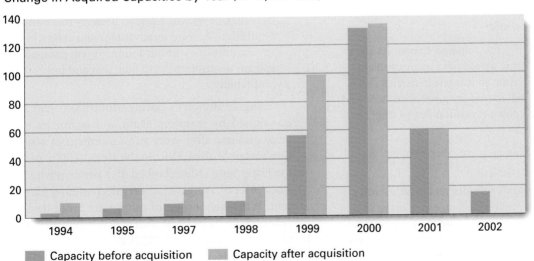

Source: Company files.

EXHIBIT 14

Investment In Technology Improvement and Policy Benefits by Year (RMB10,000)

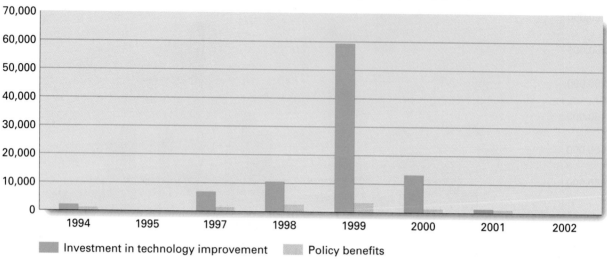

■ Investment in technology improvement   ■ Policy benefits

Source: Company files.

Tsingtao Brewery. Taking into consideration . . . possible government intervention behind the scene, these kinds of acquisitions will do harm to Tsingtao Brewery's profitability in the end.

Wu Feng of the Investment Management Department said:

> Seemingly, many acquired companies have many difficulties in product quality and market expansion. The fundamental reason for it is poor management. . . . Sometimes they prefer plots to strategies and prefer maneuvers to plots.

Zhang Ruixiang, the securities representative of Tsingtao Brewery, said:

> Frankly speaking, few acquired companies are profitable because we acquired many problem companies. Despite an increase in market share, profit decreased. Even if Peng was alive, he would have slow[ed] down expansion due to [the] current situation.

The Quality Management Department found in investigation:

> Tsingtao Brewery's subsidiaries are rather scattered and it is really a challenge to manage so many companies. Frequent price wars often lead to bad product quality or less profit despite heavy investment. Some managers ignored quality control and internal management.

In December 1994, Tsingtao Brewery took over Yangzhou Beer Factory in Jiangsu province at a cost of RMB80 million. Despite its estimated annual capacity of 50,000 tons, the factory only realized an output of 20,000 tons. After consuming a lot of money in technology improvements, the factory failed to increase its sales. As a result, it suffered a loss of RMB50 million despite doubling its output in three years. However, Tsingtao Brewery had forecasted optimistically that Jiangsu province was a high-potential beer market without any influential brewer. Peng concluded in an emotional tone:

> Hereafter, never will Tsingtao Brewery make any acquisitions beyond its advantage and ability, any acquisitions without sound growth prospect and any acquisitions with high cost and low profitability.

Tsingtao Brewery's daring acquisitions had been questioned by investors again and again. Its stock price declined after every announcement of acquisition was published. During the 1995 to 2001 period, the Hang Seng index climbed 45.3 per cent while the stock price of Tsingtao Brewery decreased by 52.4 per cent. With the increase of output, its profit declined year by year. In 1993, it reached an output of 300,000 tons with a profit of RMB225 million. In 1995, 2000 and 2001, its profit dropped to RMB170 million, RMB92 million and RMB103 million respectively.

In its 2001 annual report, Tsingtao Brewery attributed the poor performance to the heated competition, negative policy and management turnover:

> Initiated by our company, the beer industry is undergoing restructuring. Beer giants all choose [the] purchase of medium- and small-sized companies as their strategies, resulting in the changing of competition pattern. Beer giants have all penetrated some key regional markets, seizing market shares, and intensifying competition.[20] Since May 1, 2001, the consumption tax has been raised from 220 to 250 yuan per ton for beers with a price of more than 3,000 yuan per ton, reducing our profit by 10 million yuan. In the second half of 2001, beer consumption dropped greatly and the sales growth rate decreased from 4.6 per cent in the first half to −0.6 per cent in the second half. Sales decreased by 38.5 per cent in the fourth quarter over the third quarter in [the] medium and high-grade market. The sudden death of Peng Zuoyi, our former general manager, did influence the company's operation, sales, and staffs.

Nonetheless, its poor performance was considered the result of an unsuccessful integration by some analysts.[21] According to a report by Nomura International Hong Kong, half of the 46 acquired subsidiaries were running a deficit in 2001. Among 46 acquired subsidiaries, South China Department, Xi'an subsidiary and Tsingtao subsidiary made a profit of RMB150 million, RMB80 million and RMB170 million respectively. Comparatively, Tsingtao Brewery suffered a severe loss in the region of East China, North China and Northeast China, even in the two largest cities, Shanghai and Beijing (see Exhibit 15). Jin Zhiguo admitted that:[22]

> Among all the acquired subsidiaries, one-third are profitable, another one-third are losing money and the remaining subsidiaries narrowly make ends meet. Except for Tsingtao and Weifang, Tsingtao Brewery failed to gain a market share of more than 30 per cent in all neighboring markets. This high-investment-low-profit situation will definitely lead to an increase in sales expenses and consequently influence profitability.
>
> Losses may be attributed to several reasons. The first is the poor cost control, loose budget execution and high-cost marketing operation; the second is the unreasonable product structure, low price and low profitability; the third is the lack of modern marketing concepts and techniques and a scientific analysis of marketing plans.
>
> We have invested in 48 subsidiaries which requested a lot of capital and managers. We now feel that it is hard to meet these requirements. We have sent too many people from headquarters into the integration process. Some employees from headquarters considered themselves gods and looked down upon local managers, turning the integration into an individual show.

Sun Mingbo, the vice-general manager of Tsingtao Brewery and chief in M&A, said:

> Hubris did exist in the process of acquisition. Sometimes we underestimate competitors, and sometimes we are overconfident in our brand power. The lack of talented people is the primary bottleneck of integration. Tsingtao Brewery does

EXHIBIT 15

The Most Profitable and Unprofitable Subsidiaries in 2001 (RMB10,000)

Ranking	Subsidiaries	Assets	Major Business Revenue	Net Profits
1	Xi'an	50,179	66,792	6,483
2	Shenzhen Asahi	83,591	39,122	6,333
3	Shenzhen Sales	11,539	69,641	2,611
Last	Beijing Sanhuan	29,163	12,674	(3,590)
Second last	East China Sales	3,631	6,287	(3,573)
Third last	Xingkaihu	13,955	4,595	(1,716)

Source: 2001 Annual Report of Tsingtao Brewery.

EXHIBIT 16

Number of Acquired Employees by Year

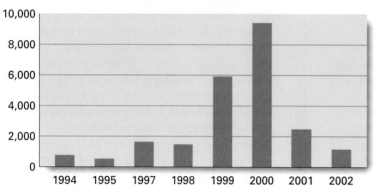

Source: Company files.

have a scientific integration method, but reality is always different from what you expected.

In China's SOEs, employment is the utmost issue and also a focus of local government. Thus it is difficult to shut down a factory without considering the local employment, so you have to act cautiously [see Exhibit 16]. Many employees had outdated concepts and reimbursed all their expenses including family expenses. It would take a long time to change their mindsets. It is a big challenge to prepare enough managers because internal training is time-consuming and external recruitment is often unsuccessful.

Zhang Ruixiang said:

> What worries us most are Shandong province and Northeast China, where there is heated competition or low consumption ability. We try to minimize our losses. In South China and coastal regions, there is a huge growth potential. With the government's favorable policies, the demand in western regions will increase gradually.

Admittedly, some integration turned out to be very successful, such as the South China Department. Led by Yan Xu, a competent professional manager recruited by Peng Zuoyi, Tsingtao Brewery's market share increased 184 per cent in South China in one year. Some subsidiaries, including Sanshui, Zhujiang and Shenzhen Asahi, made considerable profits in the same year they were acquired. Yan Xu said:

> The successful integration should be attributed to both sound conditions of these companies and strong integration ability. A favorable factor is that Southern people have a strong market

consciousness and make analysis from a pure business perspective, making it easy to establish a cooperative relationship.

According to Tsingtao Brewery's acquisition strategy, Tsingtao Brewery should send three managers—the general manager, chief engineer and financial director—to each subsidiary. It was hardly possible to prepare more than 100 managers for these subsidiaries in a short period. Jin Zhiguo admitted that what Tsingtao Brewery needed most was effective management. From the eyes of the media, Tsingtao Brewery was still in an SOE style. Executives at the general management level still had administrative titles equivalent to those of government officials, making turnover a difficult decision. In order to eliminate government intervention, Jin planned to recruit vice general managers publicly.

Brand integration was another challenge. Having acquired several companies in the same regions, Tsingtao Brewery found itself trapped in two conflicts—conflict between different local brands and conflict of local brands and the Tsingtao Beer brand. As an illustration, Tsingtao Brewery took over three factories in Weifang—Weicheng, Shouguang and Anqiu. Tsingtao Brewery made Weicheng produce Lanzai beer, a local brand owned by Shouguang. However, the two companies had been direct competitors for years and could not sit together to resolve discrepancies. As a result, Tsingtao Brewery still lost money despite its 80 per cent market share in Weifang. Although Tsingtao Brewery wanted to shut down some factories, it was committed to not reducing staff. Taking into consideration the probable resistance from local government, Tsingtao Brewery had to give up this idea.

As expressed by an expert, Tsingtao Brewery was very careful in using its core brand:

> Tsingtao Brewery didn't give everything to its subsidiaries. For example, beers with the brand "1903" could only be made [at Tsingtao headquarters]. As far as the use of brands is concerned, subsidiaries either adopted original brands plus "Produced by Tsingtao Brewery" or put "Tsingtao Brewery" before the original brand names. No acquired subsidiary could use the core brand name, avoiding the risk of destroying this valuable asset.

Tsingtao Brewery had more than 100 brands, and the output for its core brand had reached 600,000 to 700,000 tons in 2001, about one-fourth of total output. A consultant analysed:

> Tsingtao Brewery's core brand should realize an output of one million tons or one-third of the total. Moreover, it should develop several regional brands such as Hans and Five-Star as the second rundle. Other brands should go their own way to form the third rundle.

Though Tsingtao Brewery had regained the position of top seller, an article pointed out sharply:

> Companies acquired by Tsingtao Brewery each do things in their own way, continuing [the] original brand, original production line and sales region, and the only change is the beer itself. The output of 1.8 million tons in 2000 was nothing but a simple sum of all subsidiaries. The largest single-factory output of Tsingtao Brewery is 400,000 tons; much lower than the 800,000 tons of Yanjing Beer. Tsingtao Brewery is probably the only brewer that has so many small-sized subsidiaries with so many brands in the world. On average, the capacity of each subsidiary is as small as 45,000 tons.[23]

An investigation by the investment management department found:

> Since each subsidy has its own sales team, there are some overlap of sales networks and internal conflicts in the same market sometimes.

In addition, it was a real challenge to hold a meeting of chiefs of all subsidiaries due to the difficulty in time arrangements and the huge travel costs. Li Guirong was worried:

> The size expansion and increase in management levels have caused information delay and distortion and some wrong executions. If we do nothing with this, Tsingtao Brewery will definitely catch the so-called "big company disease."

Tsingtao Brewery's financial condition was not optimistic either. By mid-2001, its debt-asset ratio was 56 per cent, and its current ratio and quick ratio were on the low side. Meanwhile, its short-term loan and liquid liabilities reached RMB2.5 billion and RMB4.3 billion respectively. Without the financing cash flow, its net cash flow would have been negative for two consecutive years. After raising RMB787 million through seasoned offering in February 2001, its financial condition improved greatly, and the debt-asset ratio dropped to 40 per cent. However, Zhang Ruixiang said:

> In the beer industry, a debt-asset ratio of 60 per cent is reasonable due to the capital-intensive nature of beer industry. Since the production cycle of Tsingtao Brewery is relatively long, it should have a reasonable debt-asset ratio.

Frequent acquisitions also pushed up its operation and management expenses. In 1998, the operation and management expenses of Tsingtao Brewery were RMB402 million, about 76.3 per cent of major business profit. By 2001, the number rose to RMB1.380 million and 88.4 per cent respectively. Meanwhile, the corresponding expenses of all subsidiaries rose from the RMB85.4 million in 1998 to RMB929.4 million in 2001, increasing by 1,088 per cent. The corresponding profit increased from the RMB91.2 million in 1998 to RMB889.7 million in 2001, increasing 976 per cent.[24]

Facing the Crisis

Jin Zhiguo earned fame through the successful integration of Tsingtao Brewery Xi'an Company. After the acquisition of Xi'an Hans Beer in 1995, Jin was appointed as the new general manager in 1996. At that time, Tsingtao Brewery's market share in Xi'an was less than one per cent, and the output was as low as 20,000 tons, resulting in an annual loss of RMB24 million and a debt-asset ratio of 64 per cent. By counting beer bottles in the open market every night, Jin obtained first-hand sales information. Then he managed to smooth the sales network channel and stimulate dealers. Within four years, Tsingtao Brewery's market share jumped to more than 90 per cent with a profit of RMB70 million. A small change reflected Jin's management style: two-thirds of the general manager's office in the Tsingtao Beer Tower had been the manager's working area and one-third had been for meeting guests before Jin moved into office.

Now only one-third was used for working and two-thirds had been allocated to guests.

After taking the post, Jin suddenly stopped the unreasonable expansion of Tsingtao Brewery and conducted only two acquisitions in one year. Recognizing the importance of integration, Jin held that Tsingtao Brewery should change its strategy from "growing large to become powerful" to "growing powerful to become large." He said: "Acquisition is only a means while integration is essence!"

Jin had his own experience of integration:

Integration teams should be concerned with the emotion of their staff. It needs to be borne in minds that you should not act as a god, and rather as a missionary assisting them in transforming concepts and improving management and technology.

The after-acquisition integration is actually a Revolution, of which the most important part is concept transformation.

Jin also called on a slogan of "Speculating today on the prospect of the future":

No company alone can monopolize the beer market in China. The future market would be dominated by five to 10 regional giants. There is no need for Tsingtao Brewery to exert its force in every corner and fight for every regional market. Thus the market competition will become more rational rather than destructive.

A focus on integration doesn't necessarily mean a slowdown of growth. Jin explained:

Hereafter, Tsingtao Brewery should help each subsidiary to develop its full potential and strengthen market development. Meanwhile, Tsingtao Brewery will choose suitable targets in non-existence market or high-consumption market to perfect its market arrangement.

Jin Zhiguo, a practice-oriented person, investigated all the subsidiaries within two months after his inauguration. His final conclusion was that Tsingtao Brewery should make a strategic transformation, from "growing large to become powerful" to "growing powerful to become large," from external expansion to "system integration and mechanism innovation so as to enhance core competence." Jin said:

Tsingtao Brewery has merged 47 beer companies and set up nine regional departments or holding companies with a sales team of more than 5,000 people. Cost is rising, hierarchy is becoming more and more bureaucratic, and power-control and self-interest is moving in the wrong direction. The "big company disease" is worsening due to the concentration of operation risk.

Tsingtao Brewery is still a production and finance oriented company in that its complete budget management emphasizes control rather than market.

Jin Zhiguo had a strong sense of crisis:

Guided by the Big Famous Brand Strategy, Tsingtao Brewery has made significant achievements. However, these achievements were a result of the maladjustment of foreign brewers, the poor management of most domestic companies, the lack of dominant players in the industry, the inertia of a long-history company and the grasp of opportunities. We are still young and immature and should be aware of continuity and cruelty of competition.

God only blesses those who are well prepared. To face changes, Tsingtao Brewery should focus on developing its core resources from now on, which is beer itself including beer-related people, technology, networks, brand, and so on.

What helped Tsingtao Brewery survive over the past 100 years were results of its brand, product as well as its culture—the most important factor. The culture management of Tsingtao Brewery still needed improvement. The highest destination of beer business is making it an art and taking into consideration the cultural characteristics of beer.

If the size of a company doubled or tripled in a short time, former operation models must be updated and the company's environment, mission and core competence shall be adjusted accordingly.

A comment in *China Business* said:

The major challenge of Tsingtao Brewery is to integrate the different cultures and values of more than 40 subsidiaries. Discrepancy of value is considered the primary reason for the failure of most acquisitions in the world. Though Tsingtao Brewery has a 100-year history and rich culture, it also has a malpractice of old SOEs including the obscure property rights, poor incentive systems, and a lack of professional managers. Moreover, it acquired various kinds of enterprises including SOEs, foreign invested companies, joint ventures and collectively owned enterprises, which have different cultures and values.[25]

Overlooking the beautiful beach of Tsingtao, Jin Zhiguo fell into deep thoughts. What should he do to reorganize the jumbled system, integrate various resources and enhance the performance so that Tsingtao Brewery could "grow powerful to become large"?

ENDNOTES

1. Yuan is the basic unit of the Chinese currency, Renminbi (RMB), which literally means "the people's currency." In 2003, US$1 was equivalent to 8.28 yuan.
2. Yuan Zhaohui, "Tsingtao Brewery in Strategic Restructuring," *Securities Market Weekly*, August 12, 2002.
3. According to the board's announcement, Jin Zhiguo possessed the capability and experience of whole programming and leadership, and had strategic vision, as well as a strong innovative consciousness. He would surely endure more risky and challenging tasks.
4. It takes about RMB500 million to build a well-equipped beer factory with a capacity of 100,000 tons.
5. In the first three quarters of 2001, 41 per cent of beer companies lost money. The 90 large beer companies accounted for 55.9 per cent of the total sales and 60.2 per cent of the total profit, the 144 middle-sized companies accounted for 23.9 per cent of the total sales and 24.96 per cent of the total profit.
6. The beer industry concentration in China was relatively low. By 1999, there were only 19 companies with an annual output of 200,000 tons, accounting for 35.3 per cent of the total output. In comparison, the top 10 manufacturers controlled 94 per cent of the market in the United States, and 48.2 per cent by A-B alone. In Japan, the top four manufacturers grabbed a 80 per cent market share.
7. In 1997 and 1998, the sales per ton decreased by 7.5 per cent and 4.99 per cent respectively on a year-to-year basis.
8. "The Romance of Three Kingdoms" was one of the most popular historical novels of China. The story tells of the epic battles among the three kingdoms for the dominance of all of China, from 184–286 AD, a total of 96 years.
9. A share referred to the stock issued by a mainland company in domestic stock exchanges, and denominated and traded in RMB. H share referred to the stock issued by a mainland company in the Hong Kong Stock Exchange, denominated and traded in Hong Kong dollars.
10. SAB was a public company listed in London and South Africa, and the second largest beer producer in the world in terms of sales.
11. By the end of 2002, China Resources' assets amounted to HK$56 billion with a revenue of HK$32.2 billion. The company had 80,000 employees and five listed companies, as the largest Chinese enterprises in Hong Kong.
12. According to rules of the China Securities Regulatory Commission, a listed company required a weighted average ROE of no less than six per cent in the most recent three years to apply for a rights offer.
13. Since 1992, China Strategic Holdings Ltd. (CSH), owned by a Singapore businessman, acquired many SOEs in China. By 1994, it had invested in more than 100 joint ventures in various industries, including beer, rubber and so on, with a total investment of RMB2.5 billion. It also reorganized Beijing Beer Factory, Hangzhou Beer Factory, Yantai Beer Factory, etc. to form the China Beer Holdings registered in Bermuda, and then made an initial public offering (IPO) in Toronto. More recently, CSH sold beer assets to Asahi, a Japanese brewer.
14. Such favorable policies included interest exemption, exemption of value-added tax (VAT), consumption tax, operation tax, city maintenance and construction tax, additional education expenses, land tax and other local taxes temporarily and exemption of Fixed Asset Investment Tax Suspended.
15. These two departments were later integrated into one department: the Strategic Development Department.
16. The centre for economic responsibility appraisal was a budget management system in which development plans were made on the basis of the economic objectives of Tsingtao Brewery. Performance appraisal was a quantitative description of profit, output, sales and asset objectives.
17. A complete budget was an integration of the operation budget, the capital expenditure budget and the financial budget. Sub-budgets were well connected and coherent. A complete budget started from operation objectives, analysed and forecasted market demand, focused on the sales budget and included aspects such as production, cost and cash income and expenditure. The complete budget also analysed the influence of operation activities on financial conditions and profits and ended with a foreseeing financial report.
18. In an acquisition by bearing debt, the acquirer gained all assets and debts of the target without any payment. Thus, the acquiring company could increase its capacity quickly if only liquid funds were available.
19. It would take RMB6 billion to invest in a new company with an output of two million tons, while an equivalent output could be achieved through acquisitions for only RMB1 billion.
20. Due to the fury fight between Tsingtao Brewery and Yanjing Beer in Shandong province, the 42 beer companies there reached an output of 2.8 million tons and raised their sales by 13.2 per cent, while profit declined by 21.2 per cent. Meanwhile, profit per ton dropped from RMB112 to RMB79, RMB0.01 for each bottle of beer.
21. CR Beer and Yanjing Beer also encountered a crisis in integration. According to the Shandong Beer Association, the three acquired subsidiaries of Yanjing were far from making ends meet. Despite years of fighting, CR Beer didn't make a profit until 2001.
22. Tan Yihua, "Is Tsingtao Brewery Changed?" CEO & CIO, *Tsingtao Beer Tides*, August 2002, all issues.
23. Guo Hong, "How Strong Is Tsingtao Brewery's Integration Ability?" *China Business*, December 12, 2000.
24. Liu Lijuan, "Tsingtao Brewery: The Large Integration After Acquisitions," *Business Weekly*, June 2002.
25. Guo Hong, "How Strong is Tsingtao Brewery's Integration Ability?" *China Business*, December 12, 2000.

Tsingtao Brewery Co., Ltd. (B)

This case was prepared by Shengjun Liu, Richard Ivey School of Business, the University of Western Ontario.

IVEY

Overview

After several months of rumors about the incoming successor, the board of Tsingtao Brewery finally appointed Jin Zhiguo as the new president in August 2001. Despite his past achievements, most people continued to doubt whether he would succeed. Employees were in a state of anxiety; the company was striving hard to meet analysts' expectations, while implementing internal reform and fighting against its competitors. It was easy to change the slogan from "Getting Bigger to Be Stronger" to "Getting Stronger to Be Bigger," but turning it into reality was much more challenging. Jin was given little time to warm up for the new role. He said:

> Even I myself doubted my competence too at that time. After all, it will be unforgivable to ruin the company. Since I have worked in the company for about 27 years, people here know my merits and shortcomings well. Some of them have been my superordinates. My primary achievements were gained in Tsingtao Brewery

Xi'An, so no wonder people shed doubt on my new role, I had to demonstrate my ability through my performance.[1]

The first training organized by Jin was a mountain-climbing game. In the game, Jin acted as the guide, and other people, blindfolded, followed him hand-in-hand. After finally making it to the peak, everyone cried because of the tough journey. Jin Zhiguo understood his responsibility better through the game, and he said, "No matter how rugged the road will be, I am determined to lead them to the peak."[2]

After a long time of investigation in the company's subsidiaries, Jin had a clear picture in his mind and decided to implement an overall restructuring in organization structure, marketing, brands, capital structure, etc.

A Tough Situation

After three months of investigation, Jin was quite anxious about the situation:

> The quick expansion imposed high pressures on the company. Despite a quick increase in output, Tsingtao Brewery's profit decreased significantly. Many negative symptoms appeared. Some subsidiaries boosted their sales and profits, the headquarters had little information about subsidiaries, and debts rose to a dangerous level. Moreover, the huge difference in technology and management across subsidiaries may endanger product quality as well as the Tsingtao brand.

Jin was familiar with these challenges. In his tenure at Xi'An, he kept a close eye on the company's acquisitions and gave suggestions to top management from time to time. Jin only supported acquisitions that could bring about a synergy effect. Jin questioned the company's post-acquisition integration process:

> The previous integration model looks good but it was not effective. It lacks adaptation and functionality. In addition, introducing Tsingtao Brewery's management model without adaptation may result in "indigestion." We have to move step-by-step cautiously, and make specific solutions for each company acquired rather than a uniform plan. The integration should focus on brands, profitability and management.

Back to the Core

In order to stop the blind expansion, Jin put forward a slogan, which said "What we want is not factory but market." Accordingly, Tsingtao Brewery should put more resources into building strong marketing networks and increasing market share rather than making more acquisitions. Jin defined the core competence of the company as the following:

> Tsingtao Brewery must focus on its core resources— the beer. If we successfully build beer-related talents, technology, network and brand, then the company will have strong core competences.
>
> Core competence is more concerned with "soft" resources, such as values, management system, sales channel, upper and lower stream of the value chain, brand, network and responsiveness, than with "hard" resources, such as equipment and technologies. Especially, the company should strengthen abilities in four aspects: knowledge management, supply chain management, integration of external resources and process reengineering.
>
> Fast expansion urgently requires effective integration. A fighter cannot forget to defend while attacking. Therefore, post-acquisition integration is one of the most important tasks ahead. We will not slow down, but we will switch from expansion through acquisitions to efficient organic growth.[3]

Jin made a list of the pros and cons of the company. The positives were that the company would enhance its image, product, sales and market position; but on the other hand, it would reduce investments in or even divest non-core businesses. Jin said: "The number one challenge is to change one's mindset. It is a kind of a revolution to discard traditional ideas. This is a painful but necessary process."

An important step of divestment was to outsource logistics to a third-party logistics company. In the first season of outsourcing, its logistic costs decreased by 36 per cent. Jin said: "The outsourcing of logistics will enable Tsingtao Brewery to commit to high quality and low cost, and expand geographic coverage."

As a means to leverage its financial resources, Tsingtao Brewery only acquired 30 per cent, rather than a majority stake as it did before in its stake of Guangxi Nanning Wantai Brewery Co. According to Jin's strategy, Tsingtao Brewery should learn to cooperate with other companies to attain a win-win solution.

Personnel Reform

Jin made a radical personnel reform after taking the post. At the beginning of 2002, seven out of the eight business units and 20 out of the 46 subsidiaries changed leaders. The number of departments was reduced from more than 20 to nine, and management-level staff decreased from more than 300 to 82 people. Managers were forced to compete for each position and received two internal reviews each year. Some general managers of subsidiaries were removed from their positions and even became unemployed. In August 2002, around 80 middle-level managers lost their current positions. In addition, the company ordered some employees close to retirement age to retire ahead of time. According to Jin, the personnel reform would be a continuous process:

> For such a large company whose staff and sales increased several times in a short period, top management must review the management system, culture as well as adaptability to the new situation, and then make necessary adjustments.
>
> Actually, Tsingtao Brewery has no human resource management system. Therefore, it is an urgent task to establish this type of system.
>
> We have to break the so called "communal pot" and "iron rice bowl" through competition. Roughly speaking, about 20 per cent of the staff lost their jobs.

The new human resource management (HRM) system gave more weight to talents. According to Jin, everybody has talents, and innovative people were special resources and the source of core competences. Moreover, in the new system, compensation would be based on performance.

Process Reengineering Through ERP

In order to facilitate internal communication and ease the "big company disease," Jin Zhiguo accelerated the implementation of enterprise resource planning (ERP) introduced by his predecessor. Jin explained: "By investing in ERP, we are not chasing fashion but upgrading the inefficient management system."[4]

In order to minimize the risk of ERP implementation, Tsingtao Brewery first introduced the ERP system to its South China Business Unit and then to other business units step-by-step. After implementing ERP in all units, headquarters then merged the system at the company level.

The return of ERP investment was surprising and greatly enhanced management efficiency. In the past, all heads of the 48 subsidiaries had to fly to Tsingtao city for important meetings. Now, what they needed was just to push a button to enjoy the convenience of video conferencing. Most importantly, ERP made information sharing possible at all levels of the company with an average employee able to access all public information. Even during the nationwide Severe Acute Respiratory (SARS) Syndrome in 2003, Tsingtao Brewery still held more than 10 video conferences, thus ensuring unhindered communications. Jin said: "ERP makes it possible for headquarters to oversee and guide each subsidiary 24 hours a day."

The benefits went beyond that. Through this electronic platform, the company integrated all factories, hundreds of sales agents and thousands of retailing units, making all units market-driven and customer-oriented.

Redesigning the Incentive System

With assistance from Stern Stewart & Corporation, Tsingtao Brewery established a management-by-objective system which was based on the economic value-added (EVA) concept.[5] In the new system, performance measurements would be value added instead of profits. Wang Tianyu, the finance director, explained:

> For example, the profit of one subsidiary is RMB1.62 million, but actually it is making a loss of RMB420,000 according to the EVA method. EVA can accurately reflect the real cost of capital.[6]

Despite its famous brand, Tsingtao Brewery still had a state-owned enterprise-style incentive system, characterized by low compensation and egalitarianism. Though the company promised to give bonuses at the end of year, the promise seldom came to fruition, due to a high threshold. Now, Jin bravely threw away previous practices and significantly increased compensation for executives and managers.

Jin Zhiguo admitted that it was hardly possible for a president to take care of everything in such a large company. Therefore, he delegated each of the vice-presidents (VPs) to be in charge of a business region and receive performance-related pay. As a result, VPs had more autonomy and passion while taking more risks and duties at the same time. In the past, all top management of subsidiaries had been selected by headquarters, but now Jin only decided on the candidates for the general manager, finance director and chief engineer positions.

Organizational Restructure

Jin took measures to make the organization structure horizontal to cure the big company disease. After restructuring, headquarters was positioned as the center for investment decisions, resource allocation and strategic planning. Meanwhile, each business unit was positioned as the center for regional management as well as the profit center, and would take care of all tasks related to production, marketing, sales and finance in its own region. Zhang Ruixiang, the company's representative for securities affairs, said:

> Each business unit can control several subsidiaries, and each business unit reports to the headquarters. In this way, we reduced management levels and enhanced efficiency.[7]

With the re-positioning of headquarters, several new departments were established: the department of strategy, marketing, human resource management, management integration and information management. Meanwhile, the finance department expanded its functions to include investment and financing management, and the political department switched its focus to corporate culture.

Another problem is that most business divisions were primarily production-oriented instead of market-oriented. Therefore, Jin decided to restructure the divisions according to geographic coverage, factory distribution, production capacity, consumption demands, traffic conditions, the difficulty of management, and so on. Business divisions were cut down from 10 to seven. Moreover, all subsidiaries were reorganized into independent legal entities and the headquarters only assumed limited liabilities. After the reorganization, the number of subsidiaries was reduced from 49 to 17.

Strategic Alliances

According to Jin, Tsingtao Brewery should focus more on strategy than tactics. Jin emphasized the importance of external partners.

> We hired Johnson Stokes & Master as counselor, HSBC as financial counselor, PWC as taxation counselor, and Stern Stewart as strategy counselor. These world-class companies can provide independent opinions. . . . However, we regard their suggestions as a reference rather than ready-made plans.

On October 21, 2002, Tsingtao Brewery and Anheuser Busch (A-B) entered into a strategic partnership agreement.[8] According to the agreement, A-B would buy Tsingtao Brewery's convertible bonds of $182 million, and was entitled the rights to convert the bonds into shares within seven years. If all bonds were converted into shares, A-B's stake in Tsingtao Brewery would increase from 4.5 per cent to 27 per cent. From Tsingtao Brewery's perspective, this alliance provides a great opportunity to learn from A-B. Zhang Ruixiang said:

> A-B has developed an effective method of integration during its long history. Hopefully, Tsingtao Brewery can transplant these experiences to China and integrate its subsidiaries in a better way.[9]

As agreed by both sides, A-B will send expatriates to Tsingtao Brewery to help improve integration and management. A-B representatives would take seats in the boards of Tsingtao Brewery. Jin Zhiguo said:

> We initiated the communication of best practices immediately. The first phase includes best practices in finance, marketing, human resource management, quality management and strategy.
>
> Tsingtao Brewery will take advantage of this opportunity to improve corporate governance and form a health check and balance among the board, top management and supervisory board.[10]

According to the proposal of the A-B team, the first phase of communication would center on consistency of beer quality, standard operation procedures, beer techniques and so on. Tsingtao Brewery staff were surprised at A-B's management concept focusing on implementation, continuous improvement and details, rational decision based on data analysis, effective supervision over material quality, perfect quality control and generous investments in quality, environment protection and employee safety. After achieving quality consistency, Tsingtao Brewery would go on to improve production efficiency.

Integration of Culture and Values

Post-acquisition integration is one of the most challenging things in the business world. In the integration process, the change of mindset is especially difficult. According to Jin, the key to a successful change of mindset lay in instilling, integrating and innovating corporate culture. How does one make all the subsidiaries accept Tsingtao Brewery's culture of "strenuous enterprising and devotion to society"? To solve this problem, Tsingtao Brewery sent specialists to subsidiaries to give cultural training workshops. Meanwhile, the subsidiaries' representatives were invited to the headquarters in Tsingtao to understand the culture through first-hand experience. Some subsidiaries initiated programs that were modeled after the No. 1 and No. 2 factories of Tsingtao Brewery. In addition, the company promoted corporate values by means of newspaper articles, clubs, and so on, to stimulate the staff's interest in company culture. The company set up a beer museum to leverage its long history. In order to minimize the resistance from acquired companies, Tsingtao Brewery established a dining hall, shed and bathhouse for their employees.

Inspired by the successful experiences in the Shenzhen and Xi'An branches, Jin Zhiguo firmly believed in the value of corporate culture. Tsingtao Brewery Xi'An, located inland in Western China, was formerly a typical company with an outdated mindset and poor management. Jin was shocked to find that the salesmen only sat in their company offices comfortably waiting for orders. In order to change their mindset, Jin took the lead to visit restaurants to conduct market research. Jin explained to his underlings:

> We have to know, in a given restaurant, how much beer is consumed and what percentage our beer accounts for? Why do consumers disregard our beer? What is wrong with our product?[11]

Tsingtao Brewery also considered the integration process an opportunity for headquarters to learn from subsidiaries, as illustrated by "investment in product quality will lead to success in the market," a slogan used in Xi'An's Tsingtao Brewery. It was a quote that was put on the first page of *Quality First*, a book published inside the company and designed especially for building corporate culture.

In the process of integration, a key issue is how to balance consistency and localization. Some subsidiaries overemphasized the importance of localization, resulting in poor cultural integration. Therefore, Tsingtao Brewery required that the Tsingtao Brewery model should be implemented without any comprise, i.e., "to reform rather than to amend."

Building a Learning Organization

Jin considered that the improvement of a manager's competence was a necessary precondition for sustainable success. Thus, various workshops and programs were held to help the management team learn management skills and enhance their internal

---

EXHIBIT 1

Recent History of Tsingtao Brewery

2001	
August 29	The board appointed Jin Zhiguo as general manager.
November 14	Tsingtao Brewery acquired 30 per cent stake in Guangxi Nanning Wantai Brewery Co. Ltd. at the cost of RMB96 million.
December 31	Tsingtao Brewery invested RMB401 million to establish the Tsingtao Brewery Industrial Park with a capacity of 400,000 tons of beer.
2002	
April 15	Tsingtao Brewery and Merchants Logistics Co. signed a cooperation agreement.
May 31	Tsingtao Brewery and Tsingtao Beer Festival Office established Beer World, which is the largest recreation ground characterized by the city's beer culture in Tsingtao.
July 1	The Southeast Division of Tsingtao Brewery was founded.
July 10	Tsingtao Brewery established a joint venture in Taiwan with an investment of 1.5 billion Taiwan dollars.
July 21	The No. 1 Factory of Tsingtao Brewery initiated an advice-giving program and received 61 suggestions, thereby reducing the electricity cost by about 20 per cent.
July 30	Tsingtao Brewery and A-B signed an exclusive negotiation agreement.
August 22	Tsingtao Brewery's net profits, sales and export increased 73, 27 and 61 per cent respectively in the first half of 2002 over the same period of 2001. Meanwhile, its market share rose by two percentage points to 12.8 per cent.
September 18	In the first eight months, Tsingtao Brewery's export increased by 99 per cent. Its market share in Taiwan jumped to 7.5 per cent. Meanwhile, its share prices increased from HK$2.20 to HK$3.90.
October 21	Tsingtao Brewery signed a strategic investment agreement with A-B.
2003	
January 20	Tsingtao Brewery Xi'An announced that it would sell the assets of Baoji Brewery.
February 22	Tsingtao Brewery received 1,619 suggestions from employees and reduced cost by more than RMB3 million.
April 1	Tsingtao Brewery delivered convertible bonds of HK$116.4 million to A-B.
August 15	Tsingtao Brewery celebrated its 100th anniversary and established the first beer museum in China.
November 4	Tsingtao Brewery gained the first Hazard Analysis Critical Control Point (HACCP) certification in China's beer industry.
2004	
February 21	Guangxi Nanning Tsingtao Brewery Co., Ltd. was founded.

communications. As a good example of the so-called "study forever," Jin himself completed his EMBA studies in a business school in Shanghai. He was determined to build Tsingtao Brewery into a learning organization that could adapt to the rapidly changing business environment. Jin put an emphasis on team spirit:

> There is a perfect team but no perfect individual.
>
> We need a management team with strong learning abilities. Only passion and experience are not enough. Why a learning organization? For a long time, Tsingtao Brewery has been an arrogant company. We must have an open mind and learn from other companies. Only then can we achieve sustainable success. In the end, a strong learning ability will lead to powerful innovations.[12]

Look Into the Future

Led by Jin Zhiguo, a low-profile and practical person, Tsingtao Brewery put more emphasis on efficiency and effectiveness. As a result, its profits increased faster than revenues, and revenues increased faster than sales. Not surprisingly, its stock price had been gradually picking up (see Exhibit 1). Jin Zhiguo passionately longed for the future of Tsingtao Brewery:

> Tsingtao Brewery will transform from a production-oriented to a service-oriented company and establish strong connections between the company and the market.
>
> Looking into the future, we will spare no effort to build a "perfect team" and establish a management model characterized by modern management and harmonious interpersonal relationships. . . . Staff will develop with the growth of the company.
>
> I dream that the 100-year old Tsingtao Brewery has the soul of a small company, i.e., "the ability to act quickly and having infinite vigor and innovation ability."

Having celebrated its 100th anniversary in August 2003, Tsingtao Brewery still had a long way to go.

ENDNOTES

1. Nan Yan, "Jin Zhiguo: Changing the Taste of Tsingtao Beer," (Jin Zhi Guo Gei Qing Pi Huan Ge Kou Wei) *China Entrepreneur* (Zhong Guo Qi Ye Jia), July 2002.
2. Tian Ge, "The New Smell of Tsingtao Beer," (Qing Dao Pi Jiu De Xin Wei Dao) *Financial Weekly* (Cai Jing Zhou Kan), August 18, 2004.
3. Lei Yongjun, "The First Year of Jin Zhiguo's New Role in Tsingtao Brewery," (Qing Dao Pi Jiu Jin Zhi Guo Yong Jie Shuai Yin, Lin Wei Shou Ming Di Yi Nian) *Tank* (Zhi Nang), October 14, 2002.
4. Li Yun, "Capital Remolds Tsingtao Brewery According to Global Standard," (Yi Quan Qiu Wei Zuo Biao, Zi Ben Chong Su Qing Pi) *Southern Metropolitan Newspaper* (Nan Fang Du Shi Bao), July 25, 2002.
5. EVA is the financial performance measure that comes closer than any other to capturing the true economic profit of an enterprise. EVA = Net Operating Profit after Taxes – Capital × Cost of Capital. See www.sternstewart.com.
6. CCTV, "Reborn with Enhanced Corporate Governance, Tsingtao Brewery Advanced into Top 10 Beer Makers in the World," (Zai Zhi Li Zhong Huan Fa Xin Sheng, Bai Nian Qing Pi Ji Shen Shi Jie Shi Qiang) www.cctv.com.
7. Yuan Chaohui, "Tsingtao Brewery with a New Strategy," (Zhan Lue Chong Gou Xia De Qing Pi) *Securities Market Weekly* (Zheng Quan Shi Chang Zhou Kan), August 12, 2002.
8. Anheuser-Busch is the largest beer maker in the world, accounting for around half of the U.S. market.
9. Wang Gongbin, "Selling State-owned Assets," (Mai Mai Guo Zi) *21st Century Business Herald* (21 Shi Ji Jing Ji Bao Dao), December 30, 2002.
10. Jiang Peiyu, "Compatible with Tsingtao Brewery: The Foreign Sands in the Beer," (Jian Rong Anheuser Busch, Qing Dao Pi Jiu Zhong De Yang Sha Zi) *21st Century Business Herald* (21 Shi Ji Jing Ji Bao Dao), January 27, 2005.
11. "M&A Is Nothing but Means, While Integration Is the Essence," (Gou Bing Shi Shou Duan, Zheng He Shi Ben Zhi) *World Manager's Digest* (Shi Jie Jing Li Ren Wen Zhai), June 10, 2002.
12. Tian Ge, "The New Smell of Tsingtao Beer," (Qing Dao Pi Jiu De Xin Wei Dao) *Financial Weekly* (Cai Jing Zhou Kan), August 18, 2004.

Honda Motor Company and Hybrid Electric Vehicles

This case was prepared by Darryl Davis, Tom Davis, Sara Moodie, and Melissa A. Schilling, New York University.[a]

In 1997, Honda Motor Company introduced a two-door gas/electric hybrid vehicle called the Insight to Japan. The Insight's fuel efficiency was rated at 61 miles per gallon in the city, and 68 miles per gallon on the highway, and its battery did not need to be plugged into an electrical outlet for recharging. By 1999, Honda was selling the Insight in the United States, and winning accolades from environmental groups. In 2000 the Sierra Club gave Honda its "Award for Excellence in Environmental Engineering," and in 2002 the Environmental Protection Agency rated the Insight the most fuel-efficient vehicle sold in the U.S. for the 2003 model year. By August, 2005, Honda had sold its 100,000th hybrid to retail customers.[1]

Developing environmentally friendly automobiles was not a new strategy for Honda. In fact, Honda's work on developing cleaner transportation alternatives had begun decades earlier. Honda had achieved remarkable technological successes in its

[a] This case builds on an earlier case, "Honda Insight: Development and Launch of a Hybrid-Electric Vehicle." Special thanks go to James Johng, Yong-Joo Kang, Jane Sul, and Masayuki Takanashi who contributed to the earlier version of the case. For permission contact Melissa Schilling at mschilli@stern.nyu.edu.

development of solar cars and electric cars and was an acknowledged leader in the development of hybrid cars. Gaining mass-market acceptance of such alternatives, however, had proven more challenging. Despite apparent enthusiasm over environmentally-friendly technologies, market adoption of environmentally-friendly vehicles had been relatively slow, making it difficult for automakers to achieve the economies of scale and learning curve effects that would enable efficient mass production. Some industry participants felt that the hybrid market would never be large enough to make it worth the research and development expense; Honda and Toyota were betting otherwise, and hoping that their gamble would pay off in the form of leadership in the next generation of automobiles.

Honda's History

Honda was founded in Hamamatsu Japan by Soichiro Honda in 1946 as the Honda Technical Research Institute. The company began as a developer of engines for bicycles, but by 1949 it had produced its first motorcycle, called the "Dream." In 1959, Honda entered the U.S. automobile and motorcycle market by opening the American Honda Motor Company. A few years later, in 1963, Honda released its first sports car, the S500, in Japan. Honda Motor Co. Inc. grew rapidly to become one of the largest automobile companies in the world. Its "Glocalization" strategy of building factories around the world that would meet the needs of local customers had resulted in a total worldwide presence of more than 100 factories in 33 countries. Furthermore, while other auto manufacturers engaged in a frenzy of merger and acquisition activities in the late 1990s, Honda steadfastly maintained its independence. Honda has grown into one of the world's largest automobile manufacturers and has also evolved into one of the most respected global brands.

For the year ended March 31, 2006, the company boasted operating profits of ¥464 billion ($5.1 billion). See Exhibits 1 and 2 for summary financials, Exhibit 3 for some key events in Honda's evolution, and Tables 1 and 2, which highlight Honda's sales by major business divisions and geographic mix.

EXHIBIT 1

Honda Income Statement (millions of $US)

	Mar 06	Mar 05	Mar 04
Revenue	84,218.0	80,446.0	75,912.2
Cost of Goods Sold	59,588.0	56,155.0	52,171.2
Gross Profit	24,629.9	24,291.0	23,741.0
Gross Profit Margin	29.2%	30.2%	31.3%
SG&A Expense	15,015.3	16,323.9	16,174.6
Depreciation & Amortization	2,228.9	2,099.5	1,985.0
Operating Income	7,385.7	5,867.6	5,581.3
Operating Margin	8.8%	7.3%	7.4%
Nonoperating Income	(360.3)	1,555.8	483.4
Nonoperating Expenses	101.2	421.8	94.8
Income Before Taxes	6,924.2	6,108.3	5,969.9
Income Taxes	2,696.1	2,480.0	2,350.5
Net Income After Taxes	4,228.1	3,628.3	3,619.4
Continuing Operations	5,074.8	4,521.6	4,318.3
Discontinued Operations	—	—	—
Total Operations	5,074.8	4,521.6	4,318.3
Total Net Income	5,074.8	4,521.6	4,318.3
Net Profit Margin	6.0%	5.6%	5.7%
Diluted EPS from Total Net Income ($)	—	4.84	—
Dividends per Share	0.39	0.28	0.18
Total Current Liabilities	33,910.0	34,861.6	31,013.8
Long-Term Debt	15,971.5	14,503.3	12,969.9
Other Noncurrent Liabilities	4,908.9	6,692.4	6,741.9
Total Liabilities	54,790.4	56,057.4	50,725.6
Shareholder's Equity			
Preferred Stock Equity	—	—	—
Common Stock Equity	35,068.9	30,590.4	26,731.9
Total Equity	35,068.9	30,590.4	26,731.9
Shares Outstanding (mil.)	36.5	36.5	1,948.8

Source: Retrieved from Hoovers, January 2007.

EXHIBIT 2

Honda Balance Sheet

	Mar 06	Mar 05	Mar 04
Assets			
Current Assets			
Cash	6,352.3	7,193.9	6,737.1
Net Receivables	20,334.3	18,845.2	17,300.0
Inventories	8,808.6	8,020.0	7,118.5
Other Current Assets	3,825.0	3,222.1	2,819.6
Total Current Assets	39,320.1	37,281.3	33,975.3
Net Fixed Assets	15,429.8	14,733.5	13,350.4
Other Noncurrent Assets	35,109.4	34,633.0	30,131.8
Total Assets	89,859.3	86,647.8	77,457.5
Liabilities and Shareholder's Equity			
Current Liabilities			
Accounts Payable	18,460.9	18,530.4	16,332.3
Short-Term Debt	11,485.2	12,131.1	11,359.0
Other Current Liabilities	3,963.8	4,200.1	3,322.5

Source: Retrieved from Hoovers, January 2007.

EXHIBIT 3

Selected Key Events in Honda's History

Date	Event
1946	Soichiro Honda establishes Honda Technical Research Institute
1948	Honda Motor Co., Ltd. incorporated
1959	American Honda established
1960	Motorcycle production begins
1963	Honda's first sports car and light truck launched
1982	Honda's first American plant begins production
1989	Second car production plant begins production
1995	Honda introduces first gasoline powered vehicle to meet ultra low emission standards
1996	Human robot prototype announced
1998	Honda's 50th anniversary
1999	Honda announces its FCX-V1 and FCX-V2 fuel cell vehicles
2000	FCX-V3 announced
2001	FCX-V4 announced, Alabama plant begins operations
2002	Honda FCX fuel cell vehicle delivered in Japan and the U.S.
2004	Honda's FC stack, next generation fuel cell, developed; launches first hybrid scooter
2005	Honda delivers FCX fuel cell vehicle to world's first individual consumer; 100,000th hybrid vehicle sold in U.S.

Source: Honda fiscal 2004 20-F Securities and Exchange Commission filing and authors' calculations.

TABLE 1

Honda Sales by Business Unit, 2006

Fiscal Period 2006	% of Total Revenue
Automobile Business	80.8%
Motorcycle Business	12.4%
Financial Services	3.0%
Other	3.7%

Source: Company annual report and case writers' calculations.

TABLE 2

Honda Geographic Sales Mix

	Net Sales (millions of Yen) 2006
Japan	1,693,994
North America	5,463,359
Europe	1,009,421
Asia	1,085,451
Other	655,721

Source: Company annual report and case writers' calculations.

Hybrid Electric Vehicles

The standard combustion engine has been a part of daily human life for well over a century now, first in factories and in large forms of transportation (locomotives, ships) and then as the power source for automobiles. Hybrid automobile engines—engines that utilize *both* petrochemicals and electricity for power—were developed well over 150 years ago, but until recently, technological limitations hindered the advancement of these innovations for practical use. Electric-powered vehicles were used in the late 1800s, but they required large, heavy batteries, which limited their adoption.

In the early 1900s, American auto buyers preferred electric cars to gasoline-powered cars almost 2:1, and American automakers responded by producing along that ratio.[2] However, in 1904 Henry Ford's quieter gas engines and production process innovations (the famed assembly-line methodology) allowed gas-powered engines to be made cheaply, reliably, and quickly. Consequently, hybrid and electric engine technology took a back seat for generations. While experimentation and innovation in the hybrid and electric engine arena never died, the research on these engines became more academic. It was not until the 1970s, when oil embargoes severely reduced U.S. access to oil and petrol products, that interest in hybrid engine technology was revived. The U.S. Congress passed the "Electric and Hybrid Vehicle Research, Development, and Demonstration Act" in 1976 to spur research related to the technologies, and some of the larger automakers also established hybrid and alternative fuel vehicle R&D efforts. General Motors (GM), for example, spent $20 million in 1977-9 years on electric car development.[3]

The 1990s economic boom and the Sport Utility Vehicle (SUV) trend stifled consumer interest, and thus industry interest, in smaller more fuel-efficient cars. Bigger gas-powered engines were popular and rising consumer incomes offset the declining mileage-per-gallon (mpg) ratings in each new model year.[4] Electric cars were marketed in the late 1990s (especially by GM, Honda, and Toyota), but they failed to catch on beyond a small segment of consumers and interest in purely electric vehicles withered.[5]

In 2004, however, the combination of concerns about global warming, high gasoline prices and the costs (direct and indirect) of U.S. dependence on foreign oil brought hybrid engines back in the news. Celebrity interest and industry timing all appeared to be aligning to make hybrid vehicles a market reality. In fact, in 2004 demand for hybrid cars far outpaced supply.[6] A 2006 survey by Advertising Age indicated that 45% of Americans expected to be driving an alternative-fuel vehicle such as a hybrid within ten years.

Hybrid electric vehicles (HEVs) have several advantages over gasoline vehicles such as regenerative braking capability, reduced engine weight, lowered overall vehicle weight, and increased fuel efficiency and decreased emissions. First, the regenerative braking capability of HEVs helps to minimize energy loss and recover the energy used to slow down or stop a vehicle. Given this fact, engines can also be sized to accommodate average loads instead of peak loads, significantly reducing the engine weight of HEVs. Additionally, the special lightweight materials that are used for the manufacture of HEVs further reduce the overall vehicle weight of the vehicle. Finally, both the lowered vehicle weight and the dual power system greatly increase the HEV's fuel efficiency and reduce its emissions.

Honda's Hybrid Engine

While Toyota was the first to market hybrid cars (Prius debuted in Japan in 1997), Honda was the first to market hybrids in the U.S. The Insight was released in 1999 and quickly won accolades.[7] Though both vehicles use a combination of electricity and gasoline for power, they do not use identical hybrid designs. Honda's hybrid models are designed for fuel-efficiency, in contrast to Toyota's hybrid vehicles, which are designed for reduced emissions. These differences in design goals translate into very different hybrid engine architectures.

The Honda Insight was designed as a "parallel" hybrid system, where the electrical power system and the gasoline power system run in parallel to simultaneously turn the transmission, and the transmission then turns the wheels (see Exhibit 4).[8] The electric motor in the Insight aided the gas engine by providing extra power while accelerating or climbing, and supplemented braking power. The electric motor could also start the engine, obviating the need for a traditional starter component. The Insight's electric engine was not powerful enough alone to propel the car; therefore, the gas engine had to be running simultaneously. The Insight mileage ratings were 61 mpg in cities and 70 mpg on highways, with 0-60 miles per hour acceleration in approximately 11 seconds. At lower speeds the electrical components provided the extra horsepower to propel the car, reducing the gas engine's effort and thus saving fuel. The batteries were regenerated by capturing energy during braking or slowing and through standard electricity-generation provided by the traditional generator component in a standard car engine. Therefore, one did not have to plug in the Insight, or any of Honda's hybrids, to recharge the batteries.

In contrast to the parallel system configuration, a "series" hybrid system is designed to have a gas-powered engine turn a generator, which in turn powers an electric motor that rotates the transmission or recharges the batteries. The gas-powered engine does not directly power the vehicle.[9] The Toyota Prius was designed to reduce emissions during urban driving, and its design incorporates both parallel and series system elements (see Exhibit 5). To reduce emissions, the Prius utilizes a power-train design, in which the car runs at its most efficient speed by virtue of a "power split device" that links the gas and electric engines through the generator with a parallel system design, but allows the car to run exclusively on electrical power at lower speeds similar to a "pure" series

Parallel Hybrid System (e.g., Honda Insight)

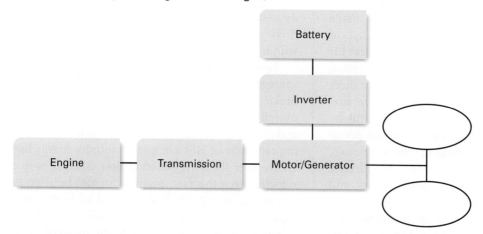

Source: Adapted from E. Kawahara & S. Ogawa, "Automobile Industry: Special Report—Hybrid Car Diffusion Offers New Players Expanding Business Opportunities," J. P. Morgan Asia Pacific Equity Research report, July 7, 2004.

EXHIBIT 5

Series-Parallel Hybrid System

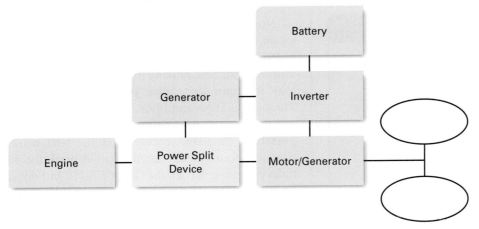

Source: Adapted from E. Kawahara & S. Ogawa, "Automobile Industry: Special Report—Hybrid Car Diffusion Offers New Players Expanding Business Opportunities," J. P. Morgan Asia Pacific Equity Research report, July 7, 2004.

system design (see Exhibit 6). Consequently no gas is burned and emissions are negligible under these conditions.[10] Thus, for low speed urban traffic, the Prius meets its engine design goal of reduced emissions, with better mileage ratings than the heavier Honda Insight. In addition, unlike the Insight, the Prius was a four-door mid-sized sedan with back seats for extra passengers, something that the original two-door Honda Insight lacked, but was later offered on hybrid Civic and Accord models.

EXHIBIT 6

Toyota's Power Split Device

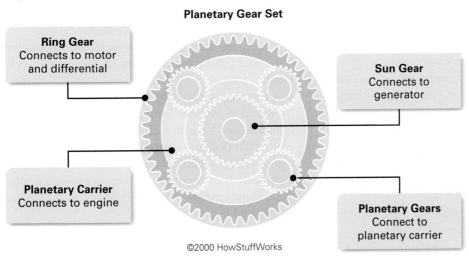

Source: K. Nice, Howthingsworks.com, "How Hybrid Cars Work," Figure 9, (http://auto.howstuffworks.com/hybrid-car.html), accessed December 2, 2004.

TABLE 3

Total Hybrid Electric Passenger Vehicle Sales
in the U.S., 2000–2006

Year	Units Sold in U.S.
2000	9,367
2001	20,287
2002	35,961
2003	47,525
2004	83,153
2005	189,916[a]
2006	232,590[b]

[a] Does not include Ford Escape/Mercury Mariner Hybrid sales of 15K+.

[b] Does not include one month of Camry Hybrid sales, three months of GS450h sales, and eight months of Escape/Mariner Hybrid sales.

Source: Electric Drive Transportation Association, www
.electricdrive.org, April 15, 2006.

Obstacles to the Adoption of Hybrids

The hybrid market had exhibited rapid growth (see Table 3). However, the numbers of hybrid vehicles sold were still very small compared to traditional automobiles. There was still considerable uncertainty about the direction engine design would go in the next few years. Would one hybrid design rise to dominate the others? By late 2006, hybrid customers were clamoring for versions of the cars that could be plugged in to increase their driving range on electric power alone. Adding to this uncertainty were questions about whether hybrids would be quickly displaced by other alternative fuel technologies such as new "green diesel" engines, fuel cells or hydrogen combustion.

Hybrid cars were also expensive to produce relative to traditional automobiles. While Honda charged a sales price for the Insight that was comparable to its non-hybrid counterparts—around $20,000 depending on options—it was estimated that Honda lost as much as $8,000 per car when the hybrids were originally launched due to insufficient volume to achieve economies of scale.[11]

Strategy at Honda

At Honda, being an environmental leader means never uttering the words, "It can't be done." That's why for more than two decades Honda has led the way in balancing what consumers want with what the

environment needs. Technologies change over time— but our commitment to the environment never will.

—Honda Corporate Website

Honda's strategy had consistently emphasized innovation, independence, and environmental friendliness. In 1972, Honda introduced the Civic, which became an immediate success, ranking first in U.S. fuel-economy tests for four consecutive years starting in 1974. Through the 1980s and 1990s, Honda made a number of advancements in environmentally-friendly transportation. In 1986, it developed the first mass-produced four-cylinder car that could break the 50 miles per gallon barrier, the Civic CRX-HF. In 1989, it became the first auto manufacturer in the U.S. to use solvent-free paint in its mass production facilities. In 1996, Honda introduced a record-breaking solar powered car (a prototype not designed for commercial production), and in 1998 it introduced a completely electric vehicle. Though the electric car was not a commercial success, developing the electric vehicle built a foundation of expertise that Honda would later employ in its development of fuel cell technology. Fuel cells were considered to offer great potential for the eventual replacement of combustion engines.

Manufacturing and Logistics

Like most of the large automakers, Honda utilizes a Japanese-style logistics and operations program for its production, both in the United States as well as abroad.[12] Just-in-time inventory ordering and storage, as well as "lean" manufacturing processes, keep production efficient, as costs remain low and productivity high. Honda's production processes are technology intensive using robots, automated manufacturing lines, and proprietary software to coordinate work. Honda's international presence and large U.S. domestic presence provide economies of scale and scope for its inbound logistics and production efforts. Outbound logistics are also aided by economies of scale, where Honda utilizes its extensive network to transport and distribute Honda products—including hybrids—to its dealers. Furthermore, by using franchised dealerships Honda avoids most direct retail-based costs for sales to end-users.

Research and Development

Honda places tremendous emphasis on research and development. Since its inception, Honda has supported and promoted a culture of innovation. This focus on innovation transcends all of Honda's businesses, from hand-pushed mowers to hybrid scooters. To achieve its leading position in hybrids, Honda spent billions of dollars and assigned a generation of engineers to research and develop the technology. Though Honda's size put it at a disadvantage in terms of R&D expenditures compared to larger automakers (Honda's R&D budget was roughly 35% smaller than most automaker R&D budgets), Honda's R&D program was highly efficient and its success at R&D was world-renowned.

Honda's management believed strongly that visionary research required independence from manufacturing operations. Honda thus created two autonomous firms called Honda R&D Co. Ltd. and Honda Engineering Co. Ltd., which operated without interference from the business units.[13] Honda R&D conducts product related research, while Honda Engineering focuses on manufacturing and process innovations. These organizations were complemented by additional research centers on each continent that could work on more market-specific projects. Each of the R&D centers were permitted great autonomy to encourage independence and long-term focus, as noted by Takeomi Mihyoshi, former executive chief

engineer at Honda's Tochigi R&D center: "Our R&D operates as a separate entity that allows for creative freedom. We are isolated from outside voices. R&D is a long-term operation."[14]

Despite their independence, all of the research entities coordinated closely through significant and constant communication to promote cross fertilization of ideas. Honda, for example, has always moved its employees around the world to observe and learn from other internal groups. Honda employees and managers also conduct quasi-brainstorming sessions called "waigayas" to generate and parse new ideas. One previous chairman said, "Although [Mr. Honda] was a genius who served as an inspiration to others, he was a man who did things his own way. So a waigaya is an avenue through which a group of non-genius people can use their collective brainpower to express their dreams and desires to produce new ideas and concepts."[15]

Marketing

Honda advertised its hybrids through television and radio advertising campaigns, and select magazine advertisements. Honda also leveraged public exposure of its hybrids by placing them with urban area car

---

TABLE 4

Brand Ranking and Advertising Spending

Rank	Brand	Market Share 2005	Market Share 2004	Ad Spending in 18 Measured Media, 2005 (millions of $US)	Ad Spending in 18 Measured Media, 2004 (millions of $US)	Ad Spending in 18 Measured Media, per 2005 Unit Sold
1	Toyota Camry	5.4%	5.5%	$65.6	$118.6	$151.9
2	Honda Accord	4.6	5.0	114.3	156.0	309.4
3	Honda Civic	3.9	4.0	112.0	116.1	363.1
4	Nissan Altima	3.2	3.0	132.1	211.1	517.2
5	Chevrolet Impala	3.1	3.8	58.5	10.6	237.3
6	Toyota Corolla	2.9	2.8	47.7	65.9	205.8
7	Chevrolet Cobalt	2.7	0.1	116.8	48.0	549.3
8	Chevrolet Malibu	2.6	2.3	27.5	140.5	135.2
9	Ford Taurus	2.5	3.2	0.1	4.0	0.5
10	Ford Focus	2.3	2.7	50.5	82.9	273.1
	Total top 10	33.2	32.4			

Source: Halliday, J. "Amid Sea Change, Goal is to Stay Afloat." Advertising Age, June 26, 2006:S17.

TABLE 5

Honda and Toyota U.S. Hybrid Sales, 2006

Honda Hybrid Models		Toyota Hybrid Models	
Honda Accord	5,598	Toyota Prius	106,971
Honda Civic	31,253	Toyota Highlander	31,485
Honda Insight	722	Lexus RX 400h	20,161

Source: Electric Drive Transportation Association, www.electricdrive.org, April 15, 2006.

rental agencies such as ZipCar. The Insight also played a "starring role" in the John Travolta movie *Be Cool*, the sequel to *Get Shorty*.[16]

Despite its smaller size, Honda spent amounts on advertising its main models comparable to Toyota, Nissan, and Chevrolet. According to data from Advertising Age, the Honda Accord and Honda Civic were the number 2 and number 3 (respectively) auto brands in the U.S., behind the Toyota Camry (see Table 4).

Collaboration Strategies . . . or Rather Lack Thereof

In Honda's research and development of its hybrid engine system, management decided to keep collaboration to a minimum, essentially "going solo" with a risky—but potentially profitable—strategy to change basic automotive power design for the first time in a century. Honda's decision to not collaborate stood in stark contrast to the licensing and joint venture strategies pursued by Toyota. Toyota had aggressively pursued collaboration agreements for its hybrid technology and had accrued over 1,000 patents on hybrid-related technology as of 2006. Toyota also promoted its hybrid technology design by licensing the technology to Ford and Nissan.[17] While some industry observers were perplexed by Honda's decision to avoid collaboration, others pointed out that Honda's independence both gave it more control over its technological direction, and ensured that the accumulated learning remained in-house. Consistent with this, Honda's management insisted that keeping development exclusively in-house compelled Honda to understand all aspects of a technology, from its strengths to its weaknesses. This in-house know-how could lead to sources of competitive advantage that were difficult for competitors to imitate.

It's better for a person to decide about his own life rather than having it decided by others.

—Hiroyuki Yoshino, 2002

By the end of 2006, Toyota's hybrids were outselling Honda's hybrids by about four-to-one (see Table 5), causing many analysts to question Honda's staunch position on pursuing a different hybrid technology from Toyota and to not collaborate or license with other auto producers. Honda's Insight was faring so poorly, in fact, that Honda decided to cease production in September of 2006.[18]

The Future of Hybrids

By the end of 2006, hybrid electric vehicles were widely believed to have the potential to allow continued growth in the automotive sector, while also reducing critical resource consumption, dependence on foreign oil, air pollution, and traffic congestion. The success of hybrids, however, was far from assured. While the technology's capabilities held great promise, the widespread penetration of hybrids hinged on the economics of producing a complex hybrid power system. The hybrid's complexity, and the fact that some of the necessary complementary technologies (such as storage and conversion systems) still had room for improvement, caused opinions to be mixed on the hybrids' ultimate impact in the marketplace. Some industry analysts believed that the success of hybrids would require convergence on a single hybrid standard that could gain economies of scale through production by multiple producers. Some skeptics, however, still felt that automakers should not bother with hybrid technology at all—it was a diversion of R&D funds away from better long-term alternatives such as fuel cells or hydrogen combustion engines.

Hydrogen Combustion, Hydrogen Fuel Cells, Natural Gas and Diesel

Hydrogen is the most abundant resource on earth and its combustion produces only water vapor as an emission. Many environmentalists and industry participants thus believed that the auto industry should focus its investment on technologies that utilized hydrogen as the fuel source. The two primary technologies under consideration were direct hydrogen combustion and hydrogen fuel cells. Hydrogen combustion worked much like traditional engines except that hydrogen would be used instead of gasoline in an internal combustion engine. Fuel cells converted fuel to electricity that was stored in a large battery. By converting chemical energy directly into electrical energy, fuel cells had been known to achieve a conversion efficiency of better than 50%—twice the efficiency of internal combustion engines. Either method resulted in only water vapor being produced as an emission. However the development and commercialization of fuel-cell powered vehicles had been significantly hindered by the state of battery technology.[19] Furthermore, widespread adoption of either alternative would first require building an almost entirely new fuel infrastructure. There was also speculation that fuel cell or hydrogen combustion vehicles would be dangerous since the hydrogen fuel (a highly combustible substance) would have to be stored under great pressure.

Honda had developed fuel cell vehicles in parallel with its hybrid development. In July 2002, Honda succeeded in manufacturing the first fuel cell vehicle to receive certification by the U.S. Environment Agency (EPA) and the California Air Resources Board (CARB) by meeting all applicable standards. This new fuel cell vehicle, called the FCX, was certified as a Zero Emission Vehicle and by the EPA as a Tier-2 Bin 1 National Low Emission Vehicle (NLEV), the lowest national emission rating. In 2005, Honda's FCX became the very first fuel cell vehicle in the world to be sold to an individual consumer (a family in southern California).

Honda had also invested in developing vehicles that burned natural gas and developing "new age" diesel engines that would burn much cleaner than traditional diesel. Honda began selling the Civic GX natural gas vehicle in 2005, and planned to expand retail distribution in 2006. Honda hoped to introduce new vehicles with clean diesel technology by 2009.

While Honda claimed that its work in hybrids helped it create internal knowledge of component design and manufacture that improved its options with respect to fuel cell technologies, some questioned whether it made sense to invest simultaneously in multiple technologies. Was simultaneously pursuing multiple technology paths spreading Honda too thin? Would it make more sense for Honda to focus solely on a single technology? Or was it important for Honda to pursue synergies (and preserve its options) by developing and promoting multiple alternatives to traditional gasoline-combustion vehicles? Honda senior researcher Akira Fujimura noted, "The ultimate technology that solves both harmful emissions and depletion of oil reserves is fuel cell technology. But hybrid technologies will be around for a very long time."[20]

ENDNOTES

1. J. Johnson, "Production of Cleaner-burning Hybrids on the Rise for All," Waste News, 11(19):12, 2006.
2. Hybridcars.com (www.hybridcars.com/history), accessed September 26, 2004.
3. Ibid.
4. J. Voorheis, "Hybrid Gasoline-Electric Cars: Driving to a Brighter Future," webpage (www.unc.edu/~voorheis/research.html), September 26, 2004.
5. Hybridcars.com (www.hybridcars.com/history), September 26, 2004.
6. R. Rayasam, "Austin Faces 2-year Wait for Prius," Austin American Statesman, June 3, 2004; M. Garriga, "Gas Costs Keep Honda, Toyota Hybrids Hot Sellers in New Haven, Conn.-Area," New Haven Register, June 9, 2004; G. Chambers Williams III, "Hybrid Demand Outpaces Supply," San Gabriel Valley Tribune, May 28, 2004.
7. Hybridcars.com (www.hybridcars.com/history), accessed September 26, 2004.
8. K. Nice, Howthingswork.com, "How Hybrid Cars Work" (http://auto.howstuffworks.com/hybrid-car.htm), accessed September 26, 2004.
9. Ibid.
10. Ibid.
11. D. Welch, "Reinventing the Hybrid Wheel," BusinessWeek Online, October 6, 2003.
12. Honda website (www.hondacorporate.com/worldwide), accessed October 23, 2004.
13. Ibid.
14. Ibid.
15. R Shook, "Honda: An American Success Story," 1988, pp. 154–155.
16. Gregory Solman, "Honda Charts Fresh Hybrid Territory," BrandWeek, October 18, 2004.
17. Reuters, "Mercedes, Porsche Eye Hybrid Cars," October 25, 2004; "Porsche Seeks Toyota Hybrid Deal," November 23, 2004.
18. "Honda's Pioneer Bites the Dust," Automotive News, 80(6203):62, May 22, 2006.
19. M. Wald, "Cheaper Part for Fuel Cells to be Announced Today," New York Times, p. C4, October 5, 2004.
20. J.B. Treece, "Hybrid Who's Who," Automotive News, 80(6208):28f, June 12, 2006.

vCustomer: Shaping the Outsourcing Industry

This case was prepared by Sandip Basu under the guidance of Professor Suresh Kotha, the University of Washington.

Sanjay Kumar sat in the conference room at his office in Kirkland, a rapidly expanding suburb of Seattle, Washington. He was getting ready for a meeting that could decide the future strategic direction of vCustomer, the company he founded in October 1999. The room had two clocks, one displaying U.S. Pacific Time and the other, Indian Standard Time. It was a warm Seattle morning in the spring of 2005. As he glanced to see what time it was in India, he reflected on the disparities between the two countries, which extended well beyond the twelve-and-a-half hour time difference. Indeed leveraging these differences had been the primary value proposition of his foray into the IT Enabled Services (ITES) and Business Process Outsourcing (BPO) space with the formation of vCustomer.

Since its founding, vCustomer had a track record of coupling aggressive growth with 100% customer retention. *Inc.* magazine ranked it as the fastest growing private company in business services in 2004. Currently, vCustomer was one of the largest private companies involved in "consumer based technical support" in the world. Its 18 clients were some of the largest diversified global leaders in the computer/networking/peripherals manufacturing space. With a total capacity of around 3,300 workstations, the company handled 3 million calls a month.[1]

This case was written by Research Associate Sandip Basu under the guidance of Professor Suresh Kotha from the University of Washington Business School, as the basis for class discussion rather than to illustrate either effective or ineffective handling of an administrative situation. The case is based on publicly available information at the time of writing. Copyright © Kotha & Basu 2005. All rights reserved.

The Offshore Outsourcing Phenomenon

From Manufacturing to Services

Outsourcing is a generic business practice in which firms decide to buy inputs or services from external sources rather than make them in-house. While over 85% of outsourcing activity is domestic, the term has come to be associated with "offshore outsourcing" or simply "off-shoring," which involves sourcing from business organizations in foreign countries. The adoption of offshore outsourcing in manufacturing activity started taking off in the late 1980s and early 1990s. As transport and communications costs fell and logistics technology improved, American manufacturers of automobiles and consumer electronics began moving production to cheaper nearby countries like Mexico. By the late 1990s, China had emerged as a major destination for outsourcing of manufacturing.[2]

When telecommunications costs fell similarly, U.S. firms started moving their business services abroad too. Countries like India, where skilled labor could be accessed at relatively lower costs, became attractive destinations for this type of work. IT services were one of the primary activities to become outsourced. Indian IT companies got their first big boost with the "Y2K crisis" at the turn of the millennium as they still had programmers who could read old computer code such as COBOL. Meanwhile, internal IT departments of corporations were struggling to cope with the growing complexity of managing their own information systems. Since different sorts of computer systems had been bought at different times, these departments were spending most of their time maintaining the tangle of legacy systems and trying to adapt these systems to changing needs. These companies also looked to outsource their IT work offshore. Standardization of network protocols now allowed easy routing of voice and data traffic through global networks. To deal with new IT concerns, globally dispersed development teams could be quickly assembled based on expertise and cost considerations.

Business Process Outsourcing

After IT offshoring gained momentum, U.S. companies recognized that other IT-related service jobs not requiring highly qualified computer programmers and engineers could also be farmed out. They began digitalizing and telecommunicating paper-based back office functions around the world. Routine telephone inquiries were bundled together into call-centers in locations outside the United States. Such operations collectively called Business Process Outsourcing included sales and marketing, human resources, finance and administration, and logistics activities (see Exhibit 1).

India's BPO industry started with foreign "captives," or subsidiary organizations that handled the respective parents' in-house work. Pioneers in BPO operations like GE, American Express, and British Airways arrived in India in the late 1990s. For instance, GE's Indian subsidiary, GECIS, handled administrative processing work for the parent firm's financial businesses. These companies were joined by some domestic call-center operations such as 24 × 7, EXL, Spectramind, Daksh, and vCustomer.[3]

Indian BPO firms also faced competition from specialist American call-center companies, which like the IT firms earlier, had been adjusting to competition from Indian companies by locating their operations in India. Among the more successful of these firms were Convergys, the world's largest call-center operator with a staff of 60,000, and the Sutherland Group, a U.S.-based company with over 6,000 employees. See Exhibit 2 for a list of major players engaged in BPO in India. However, given that the global volume of BPO activity is estimated to grow from $125 billion in 2000 to around $175 billion by 2008 (Exhibit 3), many analysts believe that there is enough room for multiple players in this space.

EXHIBIT 1

Scope of BPO Services

Function	Human Resources	Payment Services	Manufacturing, Distribution, Logistics	Finance and Administration	Sales, Marketing, Customer Care
Activities	Payroll/Benefits Processing	Loan Administration	Inventory and Warehousing	Document Management	Customer Service
	Training and Development	Credit/ Debit Card Services	Industry Management	Billings	Customer Analysis
				Claims Processing	
	Hiring/ Staffing	Check Processing	Order Fulfillment/ Procurement	Accounts Receivable	Call Centers
	Employee Benefits Management		Transportation and Distribution	Accounts Payable	Consumer Information Services
				General Ledger	
	401K			Accounting Services	
				Shareholder Services	
Share of Revenues	14%	9%	59%	11%	7%

Source: Gartner Dataquest.

EXHIBIT 2

Categories of Players in Indian BPO Market

Category	Geographic Presence	Process Competences	IT Competences	Major Players
Former captive operations	Limited but expanding	Built in captive context, limited consulting skills	Limited	Genpact, WNS Global
Major IT players	Moving aggressively	Learning as they go	Obvious strength	Cognizant, HCL, Infosys, TCS, Wipro
Voice-oriented players	Global players are well-established	Established but shallow	Limited	Indian: 24/7, ICICI OneSource, ITC Infotech, Transworks, vCustomer Global: Convergys, SITEL, Sykes, Sutherland
Niche players	Highly limited	Deep but narrow	Limited but focused	Datamatics, Outsource Partners International
Knowledge services specialists	Highly limited	Often not relevant since work undertaken is discrete	Limited	Office Tiger, EMR Technology Ventures, Evaluserve

Source: Forrester Research, March 2006.

Outsourcing's Impact on Firms and Societies

The advantages to corporations outsourcing business operations abroad were not limited to cost savings alone. First, outsourcing allowed companies to move from a fixed cost structure to a variable cost structure, resulting in greater financial and strategic agility. Second, work outsourced abroad could be carried out round-the-clock as data was ferried back and forth.

EXHIBIT 3

Global Spending on IT and BPO Offshoring

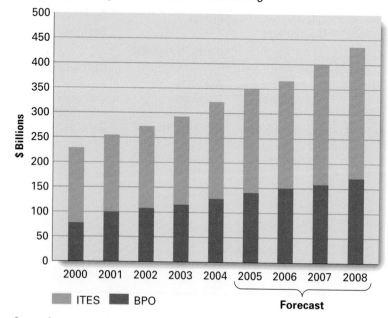

Source: Gartner, reproduced in *The Economist,* November 2004.

This enabled companies to leverage the time differences between the two nations to their advantage. Third, they could exploit local programming talent, which might have customization skills not found in the home country. Finally, by outsourcing non-critical operations, organizations could focus on core operations vital to their survival and prosperity.[4]

Outsourcing brought several benefits for destination countries, the primary one being employment. For example, forecasts indicate that more than 3.5 million people in India will be employed in the ITES and BPO industries by 2012.[5] Besides, firms in destination countries had the opportunity to develop cutting-edge capabilities in such services, which could then stimulate further innovation.

Contrary to the political rhetoric often heard in the U.S., there were also advantages for the home country that offshored work. For the U.S., the resultant savings in costs allowed businesses to stay competitive globally, thereby benefiting both shareholders and consumers. Besides, these increased earnings resulting from cost savings often made their way back into the U.S. economy. U.S. companies, in turn, often spent their increased profits on improving existing products and introducing new ones. Such investments also stimulated innovation and created new value-added jobs to replace those lost to other nations. Lastly, outsourcing firms in countries like India needing infrastructure and equipment usually bought these from large U.S. multinationals.[6] McKinsey & Co, the U.S. consulting firm, estimates that for every dollar that American firms spend on service work from India, the U.S. economy receives $1.14 in return, while India gains just $0.33 (see Exhibit 4).

EXHIBIT 4

Value Potential to the U.S. from $1 of Spending Offshored to India, 2002

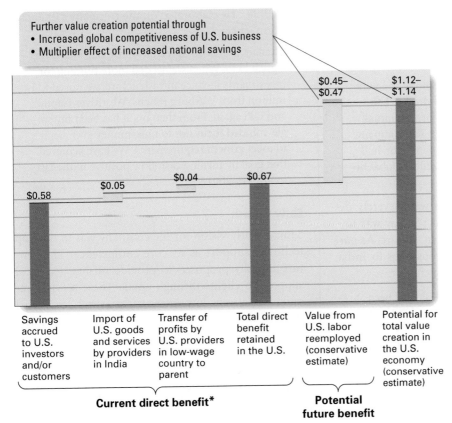

* Estimated based on historical reemployment trends from job loss through trade in the U.S. economy

Source: McKinsey Global Institute.

The Genesis of vCustomer

The Entrepreneur and Opportunity Recognition

At the age of seventeen, Sanjay Kumar left India to study at Carnegie Mellon University in the United States. Upon finishing his studies there, he moved to the University of Pennsylvania to earn a doctorate in Computer Science, which he completed in 1991. Sanjay's first visit to Seattle was for an interview with the aerospace giant, Boeing Corporation. Based on conversations with friends, he instead ended up at Microsoft.

Microsoft's recognition of the potential of the Internet led to investments in networking, broadband and telephony using the Windows platform, all of which Sanjay was a part of because of his technical computing expertise. At Microsoft, Sanjay was soon promoted to lead a group of around 200 people. Most of his subordinates benefited from Microsoft's explosive growth during that period and were already millionaires.

In the late '90s, Sanjay left Microsoft to join Teledesic Corporation, a satellite communications services start-up, which was funded by numerous prominent Seattle investors including Boeing. He still vividly remembered why he made that transition:

> Working on the broadband technology and with the Winsock Forum, a group that drove ATM support to the Windows NT platform eventually took me to Teledesic Corporation. The company, in which Bill Gates himself was an investor, had launched an amazing project to build a global hi-speed services network.

Unfortunately, Teledesic's projects were severely delayed.[7] During his stint at Teledesic, Sanjay was toying with the idea of starting his own venture. As part of his work, he had made numerous trips to India. He particularly remembered one such visit:

> While my first transition to Teledesic had been very smooth, I was now wondering what I would do once I left this organization. In 1998, it was the visit to the facility of a big customer GE in Gurgaon[8] that opened my eyes to the potential of the BPO industry in India. It took GE, a U.S.-based company, to figure out that potential in the early days.

Sanjay considered riding this wave on his own. He was confident that he could do so effectively because of his expertise in communications technology, his experiences in dealing with the FCC and other regulatory bodies at Teledesic, and his tenure at Microsoft, a company that often outsourced. Although friends and colleagues were skeptical about outsourcing as a business opportunity, Sanjay felt that the venture he was proposing was more likely to secure funding. Sanjay went on to put together an impressive team of financial backers including Scott Oki, who had built up Microsoft's international division, and the noted venture capital firm Warburg Pincus. His early investors put in about $20 million, a level of venture funding rare for a start-up intending to enter the outsourcing business. Recalls Sanjay:

> In those days, people were willing to put a lot of money behind ideas, and this business had a ready clientele. There was an unfulfilled demand for critical support that already existed. We were not banking on some kind of futuristic technology, hoping and praying that it worked and someone bought it.

Flush with funds, Sanjay launched vCustomer in June 1999.[9] He elaborated on the company's financial position since:

> The fact that Scott agreed to sit on our board was a great help. When we needed more funding for investments in voice infrastructure, we raised $11 million from Warburg Pincus, WestRiver Capital, and Oki again. From then on, it has been my single-minded focus not to raise money ever again to meet growth requirements. We have achieved that goal by turning cash flow positive in the last quarter of 2001.

Early Growth

Sanjay's early vision for the company was to develop technical support as its core competence. The venture initially proposed to provide off-line technical support to clients through email. These services required relatively low infrastructure and few social skills of the employees manning the help lines. The context was thus tailor-made for using Indian employees, and ten personnel were initially hired at a facility in Gurgaon near New Delhi. In 2000, vCustomer acquired its first client, the data storage company Iomega Corp that needed support for the FAQs on its portal.

The year 2000 proved to be a remarkable one for the young firm in terms of increasing its scope of services. During that year, the company also moved to "real-time" technical support using instant messaging. Then, later that year, Sanjay spotted another emerging opportunity, this time in telephony services, as Voice-Over-Internet-Protocol (VoIP) technology became operational and scalable. He noted the significance of that decision:

> We made a bit of a technological gamble at that point, betting the company's voice services on the yet untested VoIP rather than the traditional Time Division Multiplexing (TDM) standard, which required a large amount of equipment to be installed at the delivery side. A key reason for choosing the VoIP network was the ease of integrating business applications resulting in significant cost savings. All applications today are based on IP and it becomes easy to offer customized solutions for our clients. Since vCustomer was an IP installation from the very beginning, we felt that we would reap maximum benefits from this technology without worrying about interoperability with classic TDM based systems.

Soon, vCustomer was using a combination of communication media (voice, chat, and email) to provide hardware and software product support for PCs, peripherals, networking and storage equipment, and enterprise applications for its clients.

vCustomer's initial growth came from a focus on customer satisfaction that was largely influenced by its founder's approach. Sanjay had a "hands-on" attitude towards attending to operational problems and decisions, which kept the company tuned to customer needs. He spent nearly five or six hours a day talking to customers, a practice which he retained even when the company grew bigger. In this he was aided by technology—he had one phone number that clients could contact him at, irrespective of whether he was at home, at his Seattle office, or anywhere in India. Hence, his primarily U.S.-based customers were assured that the vendor's senior personnel were relatively close by and therefore accessible. A large portion of his remaining time was spent talking to department heads in New Delhi and trying to solve their operational problems.

At the same time, Sanjay recognized that he would have to inculcate customer quality at vCustomer through more formal mechanisms. Moreover, the company needed to provide a greater breadth of services to a client, which would also help in building switching costs and thus enable the company to retain clients.

Assembling the Management Team

As the company's customer base grew, expanding the management team became imperative. The management team at Seattle kept expanding and by 2003, comprised 15 personnel at senior levels for important functions like sales and marketing, client services, finance, and human services. Many managers were recruited either through a formal hiring process that aimed to get the best available talent in this fledgling business, or were personally persuaded by Sanjay to join the firm.

A few senior-level managers were also hired in India so that Sanjay and the U.S. team could focus on broader strategic issues and cut down on travel between Seattle and India. Additionally, the number of operating employees increased exponentially when the company started two other centers in New Delhi by 2003. There were about 3,000 employees in December 2003. The company had plans to double this base in the next few years. More employees were hired as two new centers commenced operations in Pune, Maharashtra and New Delhi again, in mid-2004 and end-2004 respectively (see Exhibit 5 for milestones in the company's growth).[10]

vCustomer's Approach to Outsourcing
The Value Proposition

The primary value proposition that vCustomer offered its clients was significant cost savings. Moreover, these savings would accompany a quality of service that was comparable to, or even better than, what the client could accomplish in-house. Clients could also increase revenues significantly without corresponding expenditure on infrastructure and scale. Describes Sanjay:

> To achieve these objectives for every client, we put together dedicated teams trained extensively in the respective businesses. These teams acted like the de-facto employees of the client, except that they were operating out of our offices. Each associate went live only after rigorous training in computer skills, accent and modulation, language, culture, listening and comprehension, tele-etiquette, not to mention industry and process-specific issues.

To upgrade skills, vCustomer frequently brought in teachers from the U.S. to impart soft skills to the employees. These procedures and systems may have

---

EXHIBIT 5

Key Milestones

- June 1999: vCustomer incorporated with funding from founders
- October 1999: First India processing center set up
- January 2000: First client signed for email support—50 startup employees
- June 2000: Second round of funding in which Warburg Pincus invests
- December 2000: Voice support enabled from vCustomer India
- June 2001: First million dollar quarter
- March 2002: Second processing center goes live in New Delhi
- June 2002: First million dollar month
- September 2002: Touches the 1000 employee mark
- January 2003: Third round of funding from WestRiver Capital
- May 2003: Touches the 2000 employee mark
- October 2003: Third processing center goes live in New Delhi, total capacity reaches 2300 workstations
- November 2003: Touches the 3000 employee mark
- April 2004: Fourth processing center in Pune goes live
- September 2004: Fifth facility goes live in New Delhi

Source: vCustomer website, accessed in September 2005.

increased the costs of servicing a contract, but contributed substantially to building quality and trust, thereby helping retain existing customers and draw new ones.

Emphasizing Quality and Security

Sanjay's faith in the superior value provided by vCustomer stemmed from the confidence that it had developed certain technology-based distinctive capabilities derived from timely investments in advanced technology infrastructure. The venture capital funding obtained provided sufficient cash reserves to execute its plans. Sanjay recalled those plans as follows:

Using the money raised, we equipped the delivery centers with cutting-edge hardware and software, self-generated power facilities, and secure back-up recovery capabilities. For communicating between the U.S. and India we used one of the world's largest Wide Area Networks that utilized four pathways between the two countries and spanned both oceans. We also formed a beneficial working relationship with Sprint in 2002 to acquire private line circuits exclusively for our client base. These investments gave us the reliability and scalability to provide real-time services.

Additionally, he also built more formal quality systems early on by instituting processes such as ISO 9001 and Six Sigma, groundbreaking steps for a company engaged in outsourcing at that time. Obtaining certification in these processes formed the foundation for creating the company's service delivery methodology. Besides, resources were invested at all levels to ensure that desired quality levels were sustained. For instance, the company had one quality supervisor for every 16 agents as compared to the industry norm of one supervisor for every 35 agents.

The company had launched new initiatives in physical and data security, believing that this would become a key issue for clients in the future. For example, vCustomer evolved into a paperless office. Agents were not allowed to carry pens and paper to work, and could not loiter around another area where the work of a different client was being handled.[11]

As the business grew, vCustomer could also afford to get selective about its future clients. The company's management was less inclined now to sign on clients like Wal-Mart or Dell who merely emphasized cost savings and negotiated deals accordingly. They believed that the "superior" value that vCustomer provided could not be offered at the prices that these firms demanded.

Creating Barriers

Through investments in technology and scale, the company was able to offer some distinctive benefits to clients vis-à-vis rivals. Sanjay described how this was possible:

> Early on, I noticed that many players in this business were building a similar set of competences. So I wanted to differentiate vCustomer from the competition. The idea was that even in an industry thought to have "zero" intellectual property, it would take a while for competitors to duplicate our approach if we focused on developing solutions through advanced technology and more rigorous process management.

His willingness to exploit emerging technologies earlier than anyone else also enabled development of important technological capabilities. This was best exemplified in the investment in yet uncertain VoIP technology, which transferred data through packets instead of circuits, leading to easy integration of the voice services with other existing services that were already using the IP network.[12] The company continued to invest heavily in R&D, especially for an IT-enabled services (ITES) company. In 2003, despite the growing need to support growth, the company committed itself to spending $2-3 million over the next 12 months toward building new solutions for its clients in ITES, workflow analyses, and other emerging applications discussed later.[13]

Sanjay's overall vision kept the company focused on its core competence of technology support even while branching out into other BPO activities. This focus paid off handsomely when billing rates charged for services plummeted due to intense competition and price wars in the BPO space. vCustomer, however, could still maintain billing rates of $10–$16 an hour for tech support.[14] At the same time, he differentiated vCustomer from Indian rivals by focusing exclusively on inbound call-center operations and shunning telemarketing altogether. Explains Sanjay:

> Typically, our contracts last between one to three years, whereas in telemarketing this can be just one to three months. There is no comparison between the two services, because if there has been no impact for a client from a telemarketing campaign, people will look back at the value of the contract and say it amounted to a zero benefit.

Exploiting the Context

Sanjay elaborated how some early decisions pertaining to location of the call-centers turned out to quite advantageous for the company in retrospect.

> vCustomer's initial call center was set up in New Delhi rather than in South India.[15] A significant reason for this decision was the lower wage levels in Northern India, which was relatively untouched by the IT boom happening in the South. There was an apparent negative aspect of this decision because English was more prevalent in the South than in the North. However, I did not view this necessarily as a deterrent to setting up the Delhi center. My thinking at that time was that it was probably easier to train people who weren't natural English speakers to listen carefully and develop a new accent, than those who already spoke English in a particular way.

Sanjay's experience in dealing with regulatory agencies allowed him to work effectively with relevant Indian governmental agencies too. For instance, to ensure uptime of the network that was critical to the voice and chat services that the company offered, he made intensive efforts early on to strike up cooperative relations with the Videsh Sanchar Nigam Ltd. (VSNL). VSNL was a government-controlled organization that regulated the direction of the country's telecommunications progress.[16] Sanjay got VSNL's managers to subscribe to his vision and subsequently make authorization decisions more quickly.

Willingness to Take Risks

The investments made in promoting quality and technology infrastructure represented Sanjay's differing approach to risk vis-à-vis his competitors. He was willing to invest up-front in building distinctive competences through process management techniques. As long as an initiative was consistent with the values of the company, it was not considered too risky (see Exhibit 6): Notes Sanjay:

> Of the 8 Indian start-up firms in 2000 with call-center operations, only two, 24 × 7 and EXL, remained owned by their original founders in 2004. Many of the others exited the market by selling out at good prices to larger corporations, probably because the founders lacked the appetite for greater risk and were quite happy with where they had gotten so far. My approach to bearing risk was to go ahead with a risky initiative

EXHIBIT 6

vCustomer Values

- **Partnership**
  Growth through shared goals
- **Quality**
  Continuous process improvement
- **Excellence**
  Recognizing and rewarding employee excellence
- **Integrity**
  Doing the right thing
- **Respect**
  Dignity at every level in the organization
- **Exceeding Customer Expectations**
  Consistently encouraging proactive behavior

Source: vCustomer website, accessed in September 2005.

provided the potential adverse impact to the core business was low and that the timeline one had for turning things around was long (say, by using equity/internal accruals for investments as against debt).

Moving Beyond IT Services

Although Sanjay initially focused his venture on IT services, he subsequently expanded into the emerging BPO business services segment. By 2002, vCustomer had signed up clients interested in back-office processing operations such as customer relationship management and business documentation management. Sanjay remembered the initial difficulties:

> The BPO end of the services, especially the more real-time ones, though requiring less technical skill from the associates, often required them to be trained extensively on cultural norms, etiquette and language idiosyncrasies of the stakeholders they would be interacting with.

The company also began to provide services to a wider range of sectors. Notes Sanjay:

> With the move to BPO came diversification into services to other sectors or "verticals" like retail, hospitality and utilities. Our moves were somewhat serendipitous as they resulted from positive reactions to casual enquiries made by prominent players in each of these sectors. The addition of a new sector required a dramatically non-linear effort from the company to execute

successfully since the complexities of the new business had to be effectively understood by the operating personnel.

Enhancing seat utilization, a key driver of business success in the industry, was the primary motivation towards moving into greater back-office work for existing and new clients. vCustomer's current seat utilization went up to around 1.2–1.3 (one workstation was being utilized for a little more than a shift of eight hours), but the objective was to push it up to 1.5 by 2005.

Challenges Confronting vCustomer

For the fiscal year 2003–04, the company recorded revenues of $33 million, nearly twice the levels of the previous year, and intended to maintain a similar growth rate in 2004.[17] Sanjay had accumulated a war chest of $25 million that could be used for acquisitions. He had built a talented pool of executives of whom nearly 50% were engineers. To strengthen his management team, he was recruiting MBAs from the top Indian business schools. vCustomer was now a mid-sized BPO company and faced a new set of challenges. Sanjay and his management team were concerned with increasing service and resource competition and possible imitation of vCustomer's competences. They also felt the need to scout for new low-cost destinations with complementary skill sets in other parts of the world.

Emerging Low-Cost Labor Destinations

The wage differential between the U.S. and India was gradually shrinking, further eroding the competitive advantage of firms operating in India. Sanjay estimated that the differential was about 5 times when he started out in 1999, but this was down to around 3 times in 2005. Increasing wage structures on account of the demand for skilled employees outstripping supply were partly responsible.[18] As wages in India grew, and as the outsourcing phenomenon spread beyond the IT industry, the Philippines was fast emerging as an alternative destination for outsourced work. It offered similar benefits in terms of workforce because basic education there was also primarily in English, and its citizens had always been customer-service oriented. Besides, it was probably culturally closer to the U.S., having been a U.S. territory for the first half of the 20th century. Additionally, China and Russia were also fast attracting a

EXHIBIT 7

Cross-Country Comparison

	U.S.A.	India	China	Philippines	Russia
Land Area (sq. km)	9,161,923	2,973,190	9,326,410	298,170	16,995,800
Population ('000)	295,734	1,080,264	1,306,314	87,857	143,420
Median age	36.27	24.66	32.26	22.27	38.15
Literacy	97%	59.5%	90.9%	92.6%	99.6%
GDP per capita	$40,100	$3,100	$5,600	$5,000	$9,800
GDP growth	4.4%	6.2%	9.1%	5.9%	6.7%
Unemployment rate	5.5%	9.2%	20%	11.7%	8.3%
Inflation rate	2.5%	4.2%	4.1%	5.5%	11.5%
Electricity consumption (billion kWh)	3,660	510.1	1,630	46.05	894.3
Oil consumption (million bbl/day)	19.65	2.13	4.956	0.338	2.31
Telephone lines in use (million)	181.599	48.917	263	3.311	35.5
Cellular phones in use ('000)	158,722	26,154.4	269,000	15,201	17,608.8
TV broadcast stations	>1,500	562	3,240	225	7,306
Internet users (million)	159	18.481	94	3.5	6
Airports	14,857	333	472	255	2,586
Highways (km)	6,393,603	2,525,989	1,765,222	202,124	537,289

Source: CIA —The World Factbook, accessed in December 2005.

healthy share of IT and R&D work. China in particular, had a large pool of employable engineering graduates, and infrastructure in that country was better than that available in India.[19] Exhibit 7 compares relevant data across these countries.

Sanjay believed that India was still very competitive geographically. Though wage levels in the bigger cities were rising rapidly, firms could move towards hiring employees from Tier II and Tier III cities where there was an abundant talent pool able and willing to work at lower wages. Additionally, vCustomer had already taken some effective steps in order to retain skilled employees by making employment

in this sector seem more socially acceptable.[20] Sanjay reflected:

> We see increased demand for skilled people but do not expect a shortfall in the supply. Recruiting people with the right mix of capabilities could become challenging, but Indian suppliers who possess highly evolved and targeted processes should not be impacted.[21]

Sanjay was bullish about the Philippines emerging as an alternative destination. Besides exploiting the larger wage differential, a base in this part of Asia might also be beneficial in enhancing revenues. Local companies with the U.S. as their key market would look to work with an outsourcing firm closer to home. Moreover, it would not be an alien context for the company as their present CFO was from the Philippines. However, the management team at vCustomer was concerned whether the company could maintain the quality of services it was proud of, from a new location. It would also take a while to understand and work within the regulatory context of a new country.

Growing Competitive Threats

The nature of the outsourcing industry was changing. Some large IT companies were entering this space and recognizing potential synergies that could be achieved with their existing businesses. In mid-2004 IBM acquired one of vCustomer's rivals, Daksh Services, in a deal worth about $170 million.[22] The acquisition sparked off speculation about similar deals in the offing from IBM's global IT competitors.[23] Besides, domestic IT firms such as Wipro and others were also consolidating to meet the challenge of multinationals entering their home turf.[24] How could vCustomer continue to hold onto its competitive advantage in the face of a direct challenge from IBM and other large rivals?

However, the BPO market in India was forecasted to grow at a compounded rate of 46% annually (see Exhibit 8). Potential new clients were looking for new services to outsource and for vendors who had a broad set of capabilities. Currently, a typical client maintained outsourcing relationships with several vendors for its diverse requirements. This pattern of behavior had emerged not only because outsourcing companies had built up core competencies in different areas over time, but also because clients sought to avoid excessive dependence on any one such vendor.[25] This was expected to change in the future.

Besides the larger incumbents and new entrants, there were nearly 4,000 firms involved in BPO in 2005, though quite a few of these were little more than fly-by-night operators. Margins were falling and contracts were becoming more short-term as clients were increasingly looking for new vendors to associate with. Therefore, it was becoming clear that the company could not maintain its rate of growth by remaining focused only on its current businesses.

Available Options

Entering the Healthcare Segment In the face of growing competition, one option that vCustomer had was to diversify into a business area that offered a great potential for growth. This move could increase vCustomer's scale of operations resulting in improved efficiencies and could potentially reduce the threat posed by new large entrants. Currently a typical business relationship fetched revenues of $50,000–$200,000 a month for vCustomer and was assigned 50–100 dedicated personnel (workstations). The managers that advocated further expansion in BPO activity recognized the importance of getting clients to sign up for transactions of higher value, say $200,000–$1,000,000 a

---

EXHIBIT 8

Growth of BPO Market in India

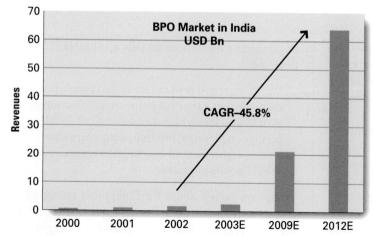

Source: vCustomer website, 2005.

month. Higher value transactions would make vCustomer more important to its clients and they would be more reluctant to switch to other vendors in the future. However, to make the transition to bigger deals, the company needed a broader base of delivery capabilities so that clients would consider it a "one-stop-shop" for all their outsourcing needs.

Specifically, Sanjay was considering the entry into the Healthcare vertical. Outsourcing of services in healthcare was slowly gaining traction as U.S. companies recognized that a variety of activities could potentially be outsourced (see Exhibit 9). Primary reasons why healthcare firms were looking to outsource, specifically to offshore destinations, included reducing operating costs, focusing on core business, avoiding necessary investments, overcoming inability to staff appropriately, and upgrading current service levels.[26]

Sanjay recognized the challenges inherent in entering this new vertical:

Moving into a new vertical such as healthcare is extremely challenging. It is almost like starting over. It is difficult to convince potential customers that they should be our first client in this new vertical. Healthcare has its own significant challenges in terms of core competencies and service platforms that we would have to create to show that we understand the business. Acquisition of capability in this vertical is probably an easier path for us to go down.

Despite these difficulties, he was of the opinion that vCustomer should try and provide greater value to their clients than basic call-center services in this new vertical. vCustomer's management had come to realize that the data generated through more basic operations

---

EXHIBIT 9

Outsourcing Trends in Healthcare Sector in 2005

Issues facing Healthcare players:
- Managing increasing medical costs and balancing customer satisfaction
- Reducing operating back-office costs
- Complying with the standards and requirements of the Health Insurance Portability and Accountability Act
- Upgrading IT infrastructure and moving to the web to provide real time connectivity
- Focusing on survival and developing strategies to differentiate products from competitors

Organizations most likely to pursue an offshore initiative:
- Health plans
- Healthcare payers
- Third party health benefit administrators
- Independent software vendors
- Application service and BPO service providers

Activities being outsourced offshore:
- Enrollment services (enrollment of new members, eligibility verification)
- Claims adjudication (claims data entry, reference to policy, managing billing and EOBs, claims re-pricing)
- Customer service (call-center handling, email/web support)
- Imaging and data digitization (mailroom services, scanning of documents, converting text into electronic data)
- Premium administration (application of money received to individual accounts, end of day balancing of suspense accounts)
- Policy administration (maturities, policy changes, beneficiaries)
- Underwriting (risk assessment, pre-existing condition evaluation)

Emerging models in Healthcare offshore BPO:
- Managed services outsourcing (outsourcing of low value and non-strategic activities that are transactional in nature, e.g., imaging and data digitization)
- Business function outsourcing (outsourcing of complete business functions and processes, e.g., claims adjudication, policy administration)
- Enterprise operations outsourcing (outsourcing of complete back-office operations in one package to specialized vendor)

Source: Report by NewHorizons Consulting, 2005.

was usually amenable to a greater degree of analysis, which made more value-add possible. However, personnel with suitable skills would have to be hired.

Acquisition of MCI's Assets vCustomer had come to learn that the telecommunications company MCI, Inc. was looking for a buyer for its call-center operations comprising eight call-centers in multiple locations across the U.S. and one call-center in the Philippines. MCI itself was on the verge of a mega-merger with its competitor Verizon, which also possessed similar call-center resources.

This acquisition could potentially be the answer to the challenges that vCustomer was confronted with. It would nearly double the company's size and bring its employee strength close to 6,000 (the Philippines center employed around 1,500 people alone). The company would acquire the capabilities to start onshore outsourcing, and even cater to regional requirements due to the diversity of locations of the U.S. call-centers. It could then better match its clients' diverse needs and provide a migration path over the lifecycle of the relationship with a specific client. It would provide a base in the Philippines, which was emerging as an attractive location. If vCustomer drove a hard bargain, they could consummate the acquisition for $45 million, a figure just around their budgeted levels.[27]

vCustomer would also diversify its businesses through the acquisition. Among the services that these call-centers were performing were Relay Service and Directory & Operator Assistance (DA). The Relay Service business had been born as a result of the U.S. government's ADA initiative to support equality of access to services for deaf and hard of hearing persons. It involved carrying out telephonic transactions on behalf of handicapped persons through dedicated call-centers. Billing was done on a per-call per-minute basis to State and Federal Governments, which fix the compensation level for these services. In contrast, DA involved services to provide round-the-clock directory information to callers with enquiries. These could range from mundane information on phone numbers or street addresses to more specific "enhanced" enquiries on weather forecasts, sports scores or stock prices. MCI was willing to let the acquirer perform these operations on its behalf for an initial 7-year period. Therefore, these new services could become a significant revenue stream for the company. The relay services could bring in $70-90 million annually, whereas the DA services would be likely to generate $10-30 million annually. Though vCustomer had now reached a size of nearly $50 million through its existing ITES and BPO businesses, the acquisition could still more than double its size.

The acquisition would change the primary business of the company from a business-to-business (b-to-b) model to a business-to-customer (b-to-c) model. Doing business directly with the end-customer diversified the risks associated with relying upon sales to large enterprises, which were characterized by long cycle-times and high degrees of variability. Moreover, with MCI's U.S. assets vCustomer could begin meeting the growing demand for "onshore" outsourcing of operations. The domestic (U.S.) market had always been the largest market for outsourcing. Additionally, many corporations had realized by now that offshore outsourcing was not a panacea for all their troubles. If improperly managed, offshoring lead to a drop in the quality of the services outsourced or cost advantages initially conceived were significantly offset by higher monitoring requirements. These corporations were looking for some critical activities primarily involving voice communication, to be outsourced to firms with U.S. operations and were willing to pay a higher price for such services.

In spite of some clear benefits, Sanjay and his management team recognized that there were risks. First, MCI was a large and mature organization and their employees possessed a different mindset than their counterparts at vCustomer. The cultural differences might also make integration of these employees into vCustomer and retaining them a tougher task than imagined. Therefore, the proposed advantages due to the skills they possessed might not accrue. Second, vCustomer didn't have any brand equity as a b-to-c services provider. The capabilities required for these emerging services would have to be developed afresh, a difficult task in an uncertain environment. While this was still synergistic with its current b-to-b operations, it could divert attention away from its core ITES and BPO businesses at a time when these segments were still growing. Going ahead with this acquisition would probably force the company to postpone plans of entering the healthcare vertical. Third, although "onshore" outsourcing was an appealing prospect for vCustomer, the cost advantages in starting onshore outsourcing, especially through an acquisition, were unclear. Further, since vCustomer had never managed a U.S. operation or operated out of the Philippines, integrating these geographically dispersed assets might prove to be challenging for a small company with limited resources.

It Was Time to Make Some Decisions

As the members of his top management began entering the conference room, Sanjay glanced at the clock showing Indian Standard Time and began to call the Head of his Indian operations, who was probably ending his workday. Given the way the industry was evolving, it was clear that the current strategy of growing the company organically was not enough to meet expected growth rates in the future. Hence, would the MCI acquisition be the right approach to take the company in new directions? Alternatively, would the company be better off by focusing its efforts on entering the healthcare vertical?

Finally, Sanjay was also grappling with a personal dilemma that not all members of his team were aware of. IBM's acquisition of Daksh had opened the floodgates for similar acquisitions by other IT corporations. vCustomer had also been approached recently as an acquisition target, by a large IT firm wanting to enter the BPO business. With the "hot" market for acquisitions, a sale at this point could generate around 12 times earnings. This would definitely be a right time for vCustomer to exit the market. On a personal level, this decision would offer Sanjay a well-deserved break from his hectic lifestyle and true financial freedom. Sanjay had to decide how to proceed, and once he was clear, he had to inform his managers about his decision.

ENDNOTES

1. "vCustomer Upbeat, in Expansion Mode." *Financial Times.* November 27, 2003.
2. "Men and Machines." *The Economist*, November 11, 2004.
3. "The Place to Be." *The Economist*, November 11, 2004.
4. "Relocating the Back Office—Offshoring." *The Economist*, December 13, 2003.
5. "The Place to Be." *The Economist*, November 11, 2004.
6. "Relocating the Back Office—Offshoring." *The Economist*, December 13, 2003.
7. In 2002, Teledesic cut back on capital expenditures required to construct and launch satellites and significantly reduced its staff as well. The venture is still in existence but the commercial launch of its proposed services is yet to happen.
8. Gurgaon is a suburb of New Delhi, the capital city of India.
9. "Sleepless in Seattle." *The Economic Times*, October 2003.
10. "vCustomer—Emerging BPO Vendor." *ComputerWire*, April 16, 2004.
11. "vCustomer Set to Double Revenue." *Rediff.com*, June 16, 2004.
12. "Managing Calls with Voice Over IP." *Networking Computing Asia*, August 2, 2004.
13. "vCustomer to Invest $18 m in Ramp-up." *Indian Express*, October 13, 2003.
14. "vCustomer to Set Up More Facilities." *Financial Times*, August 16, 2003.
15. Cities like Bangalore and Hyderabad, located in South India, are the epicenter of India's IT activity.
16. VSNL was divested in part by the Indian government to a large corporate house in 2002.
17. "vCustomer Set to Double Revenue." *Rediff.com*, June 16, 2004.
18. Many also believed that Indian companies were overstaffed to ensure comparable quality to a similar U.S. operation and hence had lower productivity and growing operating costs. Moreover, because of the rapid turnover of personnel in this business, costs spent on training employees were never fully recovered.
19. "Ensuring India's Offshoring Future." *McKinsey Quarterly*, Special edition, 2005.
20. It was portraying employment here as a long-term career rather than a short-term arrangement. Employees were encouraged to travel across centers to understand the company's culture, values, and capabilities. In case employees of proven ability wanted to get further education in business administration, the company often paid 50% of the tuition fees at select business schools it had a tie-up with.
21. "India 2005: Facing the Challenges of Labor Shortage and Rising Costs." *Outsourcing Journal*, January 2005.
22. "Can Big Blue Succeed in BPO?" *Knowledge@Wharton*, November, 2004.
23. Also GE sold a major stake in its captive unit GECIS to two U.S. investment firms. GE was thereby asking its erstwhile subsidiary to survive as a stand-alone enterprise and seek orders externally.
24. Wipro had already acquired Spectramind, India's largest call-center firm, and NerveWire, a Massachusetts-based IT consultancy. Infosys had established a BPO subsidiary called Progeon, and acquired Expert, an Australian IT firm. TCS had purchased Phoenix, a Bangalore-based subsidiary of an American insurance and asset management firm.
25. Having ensured standardization of its processes through formal quality systems like ISO and Six Sigma, vCustomer was well poised to take advantage of this trend. The company was highlighting that clients didn't need to become tied down to its services since they were compatible with other services of the same standard.
26. Report by Ravi Shah of NewHorizons Consulting.
27. "vCustomer in Deal for Onshore Center in US." *Cyber Media*, April 21, 2005.

Verizon Communications Inc.: The Telecommunications Industry

This case was prepared by Dr. Robert J. Mockler.

Introduction

As of December 2005, Verizon Communications Inc. maintained the position as the largest U.S. fixed-line and wireless services provider and earned the number one ranking in *Fortune's* list of most admired telecommunications companies. Under the leadership of chairman and chief executive officer, Ivan Seidenberg, the company achieved the enviable position of having a reputation for operational excellence and the most satisfied customers in the wireless industry [Verizon Communications Inc., 2004]. In a dynamic industry, such as telecommunications, and faced with increasing deregulation in the wireless industry, new opportunities were created for competition. The overall task for Mr. Seidenberg was to develop an effective differentiating enterprise-wide strategy if Verizon Communications Inc. was to survive and prosper against aggressive competition over the intermediate and long-term future.

The telecommunications industry was once dominated by a single, regulated monopoly, AT&T, until 1984 when changes in government regulation, which resulted in its divestiture, led to the introduction of competition which consisted of seven regional Bell operating companies (Baby Bells), including Bell Atlantic. Bell Atlantic pursued unregulated businesses such as wireless, Internet, directory publishing, and catalog sales of computer parts and office supplies. In 1999, the FCC granted Bell Atlantic permission to sell long-distance phone services in New York, making the company the first of the seven Baby Bells to be allowed to offer long-distance in its home territory.

In 2000, Bell Atlantic and Vodofone combined their U.S. wireless operations to form Verizon Wireless. Verizon Communications, Inc. was formed later that year upon approval for acquisition of the non-Bell local phone company, GTE. In 2001, the Company received permission to offer long-distance in Massachusetts, Connecticut, and Pennsylvania; in 2002, it received permission for Delaware, New Hampshire, and Rhode Island, and in 2003, it received permission for Maryland, West Virginia, and Washington, D.C.

Apart from concerns of increasing competition brought about by the deregulation of the industry, Verizon Communications Inc. was faced with a number of critical long-term decisions. Some of these strategic decisions included: Should the company undergo a drastic upgrade of the equipment used in the transmission of an increasing variety of data? What services should the company offer that were better suited to the needs of its customers? How could the company retain the customers it had and increase market share? The main question to be resolved was how to differentiate Verizon Communications Inc. from its competition and so achieve a winning edge over competitors within intensely competitive, rapidly changing immediate, intermediate, and long-term time frames.

Industry and Competitive Market Analysis: the Telecommunications Industry

The telecommunications industry in 2005 was the most dynamic industry in the United States. During the 1990s, the growth of the Internet, advances in a range of technologies, the deregulation of the telecommunications industry, and rapid increases in the demand for telecommunications services helped fuel swift growth [Bureau of Labor Statistics, 2005]. The industry was based primarily on services provided for the transmission of a variety of information using fixed-line or wireless networks, or a combination of both. Each network was made by using specific equipment housed in the facilities described below. The main consumer product was telephone handsets while other products included accessories to telephone handsets and calling cards.

Transmission was defined as any method by which a variety of information including data, graphics and video was conveyed. The method of transmission could be one of three types: fixed-line, wireless, or fixed-wireless. Information conveyed over a fixed-line network used wire, cable or fiber optic links to connect devices while wireless networks used radio signals for mobile devices allowing for convenience and portability.

The industry consisted of two types of companies: companies that provided services and companies that provided accompanying products or electronic devices. Telephone companies were companies that provided primarily voice services and data services. Some telephone companies provided services using both fixed-line and wireless networks while other telephone companies focused on providing services specific to a particular network. Companies such as AT&T Inc. and Verizon Communications Inc. provided primarily local and international voice and data services, using both fixed-line and wireless networks. MCI Inc. provided long-distance voice and data communications using traditional and broadband fixed-line networks and Sprint Nextel Corporation provided mainly wireless voice and data services. Changes in technology and regulation allowed cable and satellite television providers to compete with telephone companies. Cable companies such as Time Warner Cable provided high-speed data and digital voice services that competed directly with the fixed-line broadband services offered in the industry. Direct TV was an example of a satellite television company that provided high-speed data and digital voice services over a wireless network and competed directly with the wireless broadband services offered in the industry. Other companies that participated in this industry were product manufacturers such as Nokia, Motorola and Siemens whose main consumer product was wireless telephone handsets.

Figure 1 outlines the main sections of the telecommunications industry, which were Transmission, Facilities and Equipment, Services/Products, Customers, Customer Service, Geographic Region, Distribution/Marketing, Mergers and Acquisitions, and Competition.

The Essence of the Telecommunications Business Model

Customers were either individuals requiring telecommunications services for personal use or businesses requiring telecommunications services for operational purposes. Customers wished to exchange data or non-voice information and to have conversations with other customers within the area (locally), in other areas within the same country (long-distance) or in other countries (internationally). They could talk to each other and send and receive information such as messages, documents, pictures or graphics and video, and they were also able to perform searches for any kind of information. Transmission occurred as signals across three types of networks: fixed-line along the cables that connected telecommunications facilities and equipment; wireless as radio waves or fixed wireless, which was a combination of fixed-line and wireless networks.

Customers purchased products (handsets, computers, laptops, personal digital assistants and other electronic devices) that had all the features they desired. They also had to purchase the accompanying services offered by telecommunications services providers that allowed the products to function as communication devices. These services gave customers access to a company's network over which they could send information. Examples of services were voice services (exchange of information through conversation), data services which could be short text or picture messages and email through the use of the Internet, and information/directory publishing services where customers could access contact information for businesses and individuals alike.

Advantages of immediate response and increasing instant gratification paved the way for modern day communications. Telephones, also known as handsets, allowed for direct conversation between any two entities. Data consisted of pictures, graphics, and text documents. Information was sent using facsimile devices over fixed-line networks. With the advent of the Internet, data could be sent to and from

FIGURE 1

The Telecommunications Industry

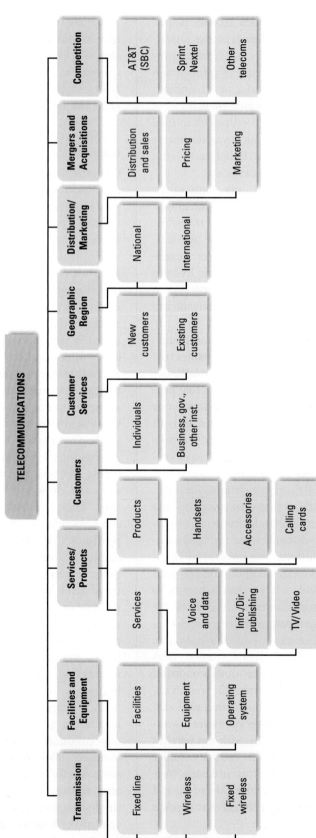

virtually anywhere in the world. Electronic mail or email made it easier, faster and cheaper to correspond when compared to the use of Postal Services. The Internet provided the ability to send short messages through instant messaging applications and recently, voice as data packets over the Internet. An example of the use of digital signals in the transmission of conversations over the Internet was known as Voice over Internet Protocol (VoIP). The Internet could be accessed through the use of a desktop computer connected to a fixed-line or a laptop computer that used wireless transmission. The increasing popularity of the Internet has also caused product manufacturers to develop innovative wireless handsets through which customers could access the Internet. The growing popularity of wireless services promoted the development of devices that provided customers with continuous accessibility to information and the added advantage of mobility. Examples of these devices were Palm Pilot and RIM Blackberry. Many of these devices provided the ability to access web content remotely, over wireless networks.

Individuals selected telecommunications services providers based on affordability, reliability, customer service, look and features of the products, and the ability of the company to satisfy all of their needs such as conversation, exchange information, entertainment, and others. Business customers focused on reliability of the network, security, and the company's ability to provide all services needed by the particular business such as video conferencing, web access, information security, remote access and e-business applications. Customers chose companies based on the ability of the company to appeal to most or all of their needs, a "one stop and shop" deal where that one company would provide services for different networks.

Customers who wished to have telecommunications services solicited information from company-owned retail stores, independent retail stores, company websites, or advertisements. It was through these channels that a customer could also purchase such services on a subscription basis. Products such as phones and accessories of product manufacturers with whom agreements were made were also sold through these channels. Companies had to have the facilities and equipment needed to provide any kind of service; they either had their own or they leased it to other companies known as telecommunications resellers. To effectively provide services for customers they were expected to have top quality transmission facilitating faster transmission rates and network reliability, and better coverage over a greater area. Customer Service played a key role in a company's performance as this would have a tremendous effect on customer retention rates, also known as churn rates in the telecommunications industry.

Given a competitive industry such as this, companies had to mass market their services through all forms of media in an effort to promote services and establish brand recognition. In addition to the services offered, it was the innovative, attractive products that gripped the customer's attention and therefore product design was important. A services provider was expected to obtain agreements with telecommunications product manufacturers gaining exclusive access to "hot" or impressive new products, particularly handsets, to maintain a competitive advantage.

Transmission

Original forms of communication included Morse code and telegrams, and mail sent through the use of postal services. In subsequent years, voice communication provided direct contact where two individuals anywhere in the world were able to converse or send information to each other. There was no longer an extended period of time lapse between correspondence and exchange. Since the 1990s, the Internet has played a major part in the ease of communication. The Internet, sometimes called simply "the Net," is a worldwide system of computer networks—a network of networks in which users can, if they have permission, send and get information. For many Internet users, electronic mail has practically replaced the Postal Service for short written transactions and was the most widely used application on the Internet. The Internet was an increasingly popular method of communication as it provided the transfer of large amounts of data which ranged from documents, pictures and graphics, video, music.

There were three types of networks used in transmission: fixed-line, wireless, and a combination of the two, known as fixed-wireless.

Fixed-Line Fixed-line networks used coaxial and fiber optic cables to connect customers' premises to central offices. The rising popularity of the Internet led to an increase in customers' use of the fixed-line network to transmit data and other electronic materials.

Increasing demands for the transmission of a wider variety of information has led to the development of new technology known as broadband, which was a high-capacity, two-way link used to transmit information. Information was sent on many different channels within the band concurrently, allowing more information to be transmitted in a given amount of time (similar to having more lanes on a highway allowing for more cars to travel on it at the same time). Broadband gave users access to the Internet and Internet-related services at significantly higher speeds. It had the potential technical capability to meet consumers' broad communication, entertainment, information, and commercial needs and preferences [FCC, 2005]. Customers were also capable of transmitting voice over the Internet (VoIP) through the use of broadband networks.

Wireless Wireless communication involved transmitting signals through air and space using radio waves. A higher radio frequency required greater bandwidth to allow for a better data carrying capacity of the wireless system. Wireless networks communicated with each other and a variety of devices allowed subscribers to send and receive data and/or video messages by using satellites. Narrowband was broadly defined by the FCC to provide wireless telephony, data, advanced paging, and other services to individuals and businesses [FCC, 2005]. Narrowband was only that portion devoted to voice and limited data transmission. Wireless broadband referred to larger band of frequencies over which a variety of data could be transmitted such as pictures and video.

Fixed Wireless Fixed wireless was essentially a combination of fixed-line and wireless networks. It was a method for providing a network segment between two set locations using wireless devices or systems. Fixed wireless referred to the operation of wireless devices or systems such as laptops and wireless printers in set locations such as homes and offices. Fixed wireless devices normally derived their electrical power from electricity outlets, as opposed to portable wireless devices that normally derived their power from batteries. The fixed-line was connected to the antenna, which created a wireless environment by converting fixed-line signals into wireless signals enabling wireless transmission. With advancing technology and increasing consolidation in the industry, many companies began offering both fixed-line and wireless services. "The wireless communications industry has been experiencing consolidation and [analysts] expect that

this trend will continue. This consolidation trend may enhance the ability of wireless service providers . . ." [Mergent Online, 2005]. It was those companies that operated multiple networks that were better able to provide any and all services that fit a wide variety of customers' needs and desires.

In addition to this, most companies were moving away from traditional fixed-line services to offering services using broadband, which offered greater bandwidth and faster transmission rates. "They seem to think that the way to expand and thrive in today's telecom world is by focusing on growth in the profitable wireless and broadband markets . . ." [Rosenbush, 2005]. The overall industry trend was to develop the wireless and the fixed-line broadband services. Companies had to have the necessary facilities and equipment to expand services. Changes in technology brought about by the introduction of broadband and wireless capability created new markets for telecommunications services providers. On-line usage grew significantly in the last few years with 70% of U.S. households now having access to the Internet and over 1/3 of those homes using broadband connections [Verizon Communications Inc., 2004].

It was more important to provide a network that was reliable, fast and efficient and these qualities depended on the equipment used.

Facilities and Equipment

The facilities, equipment and operating systems used in the telecommunications industry are discussed in more detail below.

Facilities Facilities referred to the central offices maintained by telecommunications companies that contain switching equipment which route content to its final destination or to another switching center. This was typical of fixed-line networks.

Wireless equipment was used to create cell sites. A cell was the geographical area covered by a wireless transmitter. The transmitter facility itself was called the cell site. The cell provided by a cell site could be from one mile to twenty miles in diameter, depending on terrain and transmission power. Several coordinated cell sites were called a cell system. Wireless services providers generally gave customers access to their cell system, which was essentially local. When traveling out of the range of this cell system, the cell system enabled you to be transferred to a neighboring company's cell system without one being aware of it.

In order to increase coverage, network reliability and transmission rates of wireless networks, companies had to increase the number of cell sites. The cost to build new cell sites was estimated to be anywhere from $100,000 to $1 million per cell site, depending on the difficulty associated with building it [Rulison, 2005]. An increase in cell sites facilitated price competitiveness as companies used their own facilities to provide wireless transmission.

A company had to have significant capital resources to expand and build-out any of the above networks in order to introduce new services. Companies should upgrade their networks to provide faster transmission, more bandwidth for the increasing amount of information customers wished to exchange and remain competitive. These qualities were attributed to the equipment used for each network.

The following is a discussion of the equipment housed in these facilities.

Equipment The main equipment used in the fixed-line network included switches and routers, converters, remote access servers, IP telephony equipment used to transmit data and voice communications over the same network, optical networking components, and network service and security systems. These devices were connected by copper lines, coaxial cables or fiber optic links. The main equipment used in setting up wireless connectivity included transreceivers, bridges, signal amplifiers, modems and antennas. Fixed-wireless network equipment consisted of the equipment used in setting up a fixed-line network, except for the cables used to connect the devices, and equipment used to create the wireless connection for the operation of wireless devices. The companies that owned their own equipment were able to lease it to other companies called telecommunications resellers.

Switches channeled incoming data from any of multiple input ports to the specific output port that took the data toward its intended destination in a telecommunications network.

Routers determined the next system point to which a data packet should be forwarded enroute toward its destination. Each data packet sent contained a unique address that was stored in an address look-up table. The router was connected to at least two systems and determined which way to send each data packet based on the address look-up table.

Converters were used to transfer data across different media, that is, they were used to change data signals to voice signals or vice versa. For phone conversations, fixed-line networks had to convert voice signals to data signals that were transferred across the coaxial cables or optical cables and these signals were reconverted to voice signals by other converters at the end of transmission.

A remote access server sometimes called a communications server was the computer and associated software that was set up to handle users seeking access to a network from an isolated location.

IP telephony equipment included all equipment used to exchange spoken or other telephone information over the Internet rather than through the use of traditional telephone service. A modem varied the frequency of outgoing data signals from electronic devices to voice signals for a conventional copper twisted pair telephone line and extracted information from the varied frequency of the incoming voice signal and converted it to a data signal for the electronic device.

Copper lines formed the traditional medium used to connect networks. These were either twisted or shielded twisted pair. Twisted pair was the ordinary copper wire that connected home and many business computers to the telephone company. It was made up of two insulated copper wires twisted around each other. Each connection on twisted pair required both wires. Since some telephone sets or desktop locations required multiple connections, twisted pair was sometimes installed in two or more pairs, all within a single cable. For some business locations, twisted pair was enclosed in a shield; this was known as shielded twisted pair.

Coaxial cable was the kind of copper cable used by cable TV companies between the community antenna and user homes and businesses. It was sometimes used by telephone companies from their central office to the telephone poles near users. It was also widely installed for use in business and corporation. Coaxial cables had more bandwidth than copper lines and faster transmission rates.

Fiber optic (or "optical fiber") referred to the medium and the technology associated with the transmission of information as light impulses along a glass or plastic wire or fiber. Fiber optic wire carried more information than any other type of connection and was far less subject to electromagnetic interference. It was also much cheaper to maintain.

Bandwidth referred to the transmission capacity of a telecommunications network and was a measurement of a network's transmission speed, that is, how much data a network could transfer in a given amount of time. Efficiency of the network was based on the speed of data transmission.

It was important to focus on the type of connections used create the networks. Different types of connections varied in the transmission capacity, bandwidth, and hence varied in speed. Increased bandwidth could have been used to deliver new services. Faster transmission rates led to improved customer perception of the services and increased competitiveness against cable providers.

Equipment used in setting up wireless connectivity included transreceivers, bridges, signal amplifiers, modems and antennas.

A station that transmitted and received data referred to as a transceiver was used to create an access point which connected users to other users within the network. It also served as the point of interconnection between the wireless and a fixed-line network. The number of access points a wireless network needed was determined by the number of users and the size of the network.

A wireless bridge was used to connect two or more system segments that were separated physically. A bridge worked at the data-link or physical level of a network, copying data from one network to the next network along the communications path. Signal amplifiers are electronic devices that increase the power of signals so that information carried as signals can be transmitted.

An antenna was a specialized transducer (an electronic device) that converted radio-frequency (RF) fields into alternating current (AC) or vice versa. There were two basic types: the receiving antenna, which intercepted RF energy and delivered AC to electronic equipment, and the transmitting antenna, which was fed with AC from electronic equipment and generated a RF field.

Operating Systems   Operating systems were the software platforms telecommunications equipment and devices used to transmit voice and data. Operating systems were found as part of any electronic device, especially those used every day, from computers to cell phones to wireless access points. The purpose of an operating system was to organize and control hardware and software so that the device it "lived in" behaved in a flexible but predictable way. It manages the hardware and software resources of the system. The operating systems used for fixed-line networks managed hardware, which included

such things as the processor, memory, disk space and so forth. The most common operating systems were the Windows family of operating systems developed by Microsoft, the Macintosh operating systems developed by Apple and the UNIX family of operating systems [Coustan and Franklin, 2005]. With respect to functionality, operating systems were very similar for fixed-line networks and were comparable in their ability to transmit information efficiently.

For wireless networks, different operating systems had distinct functionality. An operating system provided electrical devices with the ability to operate as a functional unit. An example of this was the ability of the operating system to make the hardware of a wireless phone, which included the keypad, the screen, the address book, the phone dialer, the battery and the network connection work effectively to transmit information. It provided a stable, consistent way for applications to deal with the hardware without having to know all the details of the hardware. The Palm OS and Windows Mobile, CDMA (Code Division Multiple Access) and GSM (Global System for Mobile communication) for wireless devices were other examples of operating systems. CDMA was a better technology than GSM because GSM was not able to handle both voice and data effectively. It was also important to have an operating system that was equipped enough to handle the transmission of a variety of voice and data, like CDMA.

The key was to have an operating system that could effectively operate on any network, fixed-line, wireless, or fixed-wireless. The operating system determined what functions the devices could perform and how the different parts of devices would interact with each other to perform as a functional unit. It was important that the operating system allowed devices to work regardless of location. Although CDMA was a better technology, GSM was more widely used. It was the world's most popular wireless handset technology used by more than one billion people in more than 200 countries and offered customers unparalleled global roaming capabilities [U.S. Business Reporter, 2001]. It was also important for operating systems to have a high degree of commonality of design worldwide. Interoperability of operating systems led to advantages of compatibility of services and worldwide roaming capability.

Services/Products

Traditionally, the main services provided were voice and data messaging services but these services were expanded to include information/directory publishing services and TV/Video services. Products were mainly telephone handsets which the customers use to transmit data and other electronic materials. Other products included accessories and calling cards.

Services There were three main areas of services offered in the telecommunications industry: voice and data services, information/directory publishing services, and TV/Video services.

Voice and Data Services. Fixed-line voice services were considered to be local, long-distance or international and different charges applied with international services being more expensive than local or long-distance. Customers were able to make calls to other customers in different locations. Local services involved the use of the local central offices where lines from homes and businesses terminated at a central office. These offices were connected to other central offices within a local access and transport area or to long-distance carriers. Long-distance carriers were telephone companies that provided connections between local central offices in different geographic areas. Customers with fixed-line voice calling services were able to make and receive calls from customers with wireless voice calling services and vice versa.

Other voice services provided for fixed-line, wireless and fixed-wireless networks included messaging, caller identification, call waiting, call-forwarding and three-way calling. Messaging such as voicemail allowed a caller to leave a brief message for a customer who was unable to answer the call. Customers were able to determine the name and/or number of an incoming call through caller identification devices. Call waiting, call forwarding and three-way calling were calling features that customers were able to use. Customers who were on the phone were alerted that another call was coming in by the call waiting feature. If a customer wished to have his or her calls transferred to another telephone number (fixed-line-or wireless), that customer was able to activate the call-forwarding feature. Similarly, a customer was able to speak to two other customers simultaneously by using the three-way calling feature. These services were interoperable for both fixed-line and wireless networks.

Data services provided customers with the ability to send information to each other. Through the use of facsimile devices, customers were able to transmit data using fixed-lines. The main data service used in transmission over any network was the Internet. The Internet was accessed over fixed-line networks through the use of desktop computers or over wireless networks through the use of wireless handsets and laptops. The Internet provided the ability to send short messages through instant messaging applications, unlike messaging services for fixed-line voice services; this was essentially a conversation over the Internet. Customers were able to send documents, pictures, graphics and other data to other customers through electronic mail or email. Recently, the Internet has been used to transmit voice conversations as data packets. An example of this transmission of conversations over the Internet was known as Voice over Internet Protocol (VoIP). The increasing popularity of the Internet has also caused product manufacturers to develop innovative wireless handsets through which customers could access the Internet. Manufacturers were producing handsets and other electronic devices built with advanced equipment that would facilitate the services a customer wished to have.

Information/Directory Publishing Services. These services included all search prints and directory services offered by companies. Traditionally, this consisted of print directories, which were hard copies of contact information for individuals or businesses who gave permission to have their information printed. Customers were able to search for the address or telephone number of any person or entity listed in alphabetical order in the directory. With advancing technologies, these services were extended to include fixed-line and wireless Internet searches used for shopping and information. Customers were able to perform searches for contact information for individuals and businesses that were usually listed in the print directories. They were also able to search for maps and directions, shopping centers, points of interest and many other things based on location, type of business, and several other categories.

TV/Video Services. TV/Video services included not only area TV stations, but dozens of other programming services which consisted of FM radio, movie and special interest channels on a subscription or fee basis. Many cable companies produced their own programs to serve local needs and interests. Cable companies used fixed-lines to transmit television and other programming services to customers. TV/Video was transmitted directly from the company to the customer's television set. Satellite companies used wireless transmission to deliver television and other programming services directly to the customer's television set. For cable companies, the fixed-lines ran directly into a customer's premises but for satellite companies, customers used specific equipment, satellite, provided by the company to receive the services. Deregulation in the industry and the ability of cable TV and satellite companies to offer telephone services began a trend of telephone companies entering the video-delivery technology and vice versa. "The new holy grail of the communications industry is the triple play: the ability to offer customers data, video, and voice" [Bensinger, 2005].

The keys to success were to offer services that were required by customers, those that were either not offered or least likely to be offered by competitors. Customers chose companies based on the ability of the company to appeal to most or all of their needs, a "one stop and shop" deal. "Nearly two thirds of all American homes now subscribe to both wireless and wireline [fixed-line] services, and wireless calls now outnumber calls from traditional wireline [fixed-line] telephones" [Verizon Communications Inc., 2004].

Services were designed to appeal to a customer's need to converse with anyone—locally, long-distance, or internationally; to be able to access information such as driving directions, to retrieve contact information for businesses or the meaning of a word; to be entertained by music, games, or video; to send pictures or short messages; to shop, e-commerce, conduct meetings through video-conferencing and other needs. Companies were also expected to provide additional wireless services to keep up with the industry trend, wireless services such as being able to perform banking transactions, or manage personal account information through the use of the wireless device, or even the ability to be entertained by music or video. It was important that companies provided such a wide variety of services to suite any type of customer. In addition to this, companies offered bundled services which could include local, long-distance, wireless, Internet, and cable TV and satellite services. According to a study done in 2001 by the U.S. Business Reporter, companies in this industry who were not full service providers were at a substantial disadvantage; therefore offering bundles services was a crucial key to success.

Products Products offered by the telecommunications product manufacturers were mainly telephone handsets, corded and cordless. Other products included calling cards and accessories.

Handsets. Handsets were mostly sold with accompanying services provided by telecommunications services providers. However, a customer could purchase only a handset but that customer would have to pay for the services needed to use the handset for telecommunication purposes. Handsets had to be attractive to entice the customers. Product design was especially important with regards to appearance, size and weight. For wireless handsets, smaller, lighter-weight handsets with better display capabilities and a wider range of functions were becoming more popular. It was important for telecommunications services providers to gain exclusive access to "hot" new products, particularly handsets as this gave them a competitive advantage. Products should be designed to perform all requirements needed by customers based on the services they desired; that is, if a customer wished to take pictures and send those pictures to another customer then products should be equipped with a camera and Internet access. "The high-end cellphone [handset] is rapidly gaining functionality formerly reserved for the laptop. [They] have full keyboards, and are getting better . . . at email, instant messaging, Web browsing, and even displaying and editing office documents. Other companies, like Motorola and Nokia, are racing to market with new entries in this category of do-it-all phones" [Mossberg, 2005].

Accessories. Accessories were other electronic or non-electronic devices that enhanced the use of communications systems. Accessories consisted of caller identification devices used to determine the origination of incoming calls; answering machines used to record voice messages; headsets, amplifiers, protective cases and many other devices that enhanced the use of handsets. Companies offered a wide variety of accessories that enhanced the use of telecommunications products.

Calling Cards. Calling cards were specific to each customer and had a unique identification number attached to them. Customers were capable of making calls from anywhere whether it was local, long-distance or international. The customer dialed a toll free number, entered the unique identification number from any phone and the calls were billed to the customer's account. Calling cards could have been customized or personalized to attract customer's attention. Calling cards had different prints based on the season or holiday and they could have been used as marketing tools to advertise the company; this provided companies with an effective way to promote brand recognition.

Customers

Anyone who wanted to be connected to the world was a potential customer. Customers were broken down into two groups: Individuals, and Business, Government, and Other Institutions. Individuals required telecommunications services based on personal use and interest. Business customers included small, medium, and large businesses or enterprises. These business customers along with government and other institutions obtained telecommunications services on the basis of having a secure, faster, reliable network with the services leading to increased productivity and efficiency of business operations among other things.

Individuals As of 2005, 95% of U.S. homes and businesses had a fixed-line telephone [The Insight Research Corporation, 2005]. As innovative technologies reshaped customer behavior around convenience, ease of use and instant gratification, there was a need for faster transmission, improved content and services that enticed individuals. Network speed and reliability were important factors as customers' expectations of the kind of information that could be transmitted increased. Companies with a wide variety of services that provided individuals with the ability to send and receive vast amounts of data at fast rates, be entertained, and be better able to manage all the telecommunications services and devices were in a better position to attract these customers. Companies needed to ensure strong market presence and brand recognition. While wireless services were not a replacement for fixed-line services, they provided customers with a good substitution. Customers favored wireless services mainly because of the mobility, convenience and comparative rates in calling patterns and pricing of local and long-distance calls. "Nearly 65% of Americans, or 195 million people, are expected to be mobile phone subscribers by the close of 2005" [The Insight Research Corporation, 2005]. Individuals increasingly utilized wireless services more than fixed-line services and this shift caused a reduction in the number of fixed-line subscribers. It was necessary that companies offered competitive pricing plans and packages.

Customers that favored wireless-only services were young, single people living in urban areas, typically college students. More mature customers were familiar with the traditional fixed-line services and were more reluctant to part with such services. A study performed by The Insight Research Corporation showed that 51.6% of households had both fixed-line and wireless telephone services, while only 6% of households had only wireless telephone services. In addition to this, wireless transmission was not as fast as fixed-line and many customers preferred both types of services to fit their needs. The Latino market has been a steadily growing market in the U.S. Two factors have driven Hispanic spending growth: higher population growth among Hispanics and the expected growth of Hispanic household incomes. Hispanic household incomes are expected to grow from 77% of the national average in 2000 to 82% by 2020. It was expected that Hispanic spending would grow way above the nation's average in most consumer sectors. Online Hispanic customers outpaced the general online population in several areas of Internet usage, particularly entertainment. In addition to this, about 61% of online Latinos were 34 or under, compared to 37% of Whites and 54% of African Americans [Jordan, 2004].

Business, Government, and Other Institutions Businesses, government and other institutions obtained telecommunications services on the basis of having a secure, faster, reliable network with services that led to increased productivity and efficiency of business operations. Business customers included small businesses (fewer than 20 employees), medium businesses (between 20 and 500 employees or 2 to 25 locations), large businesses and enterprises. Customers required networks that were fast and reliable to facilitate the efficiency of business operations. "They all realize that promotions, cool new handsets and promises of data services won't get them anywhere if users can't get a reliable, clear connection" [Marks, 2001]. It was those companies with a reputation for reliable networks offering fast transmission rates that attracted this market. These customers proved to be profitable because unlike individual customers who could frequently change providers, they could not easily switch to a new telecommunications services provider as they would be forced to buy and implement tons of new equipment, an expensive and time-consuming venture.

Telecommunications services providers offered business, government and other institutions a complete range of basic and advanced communications services and products to meet the voice, video, data and Internet related needs of the customers. It was important that companies provided a wide variety of services suited to the needs of these customers such as video-conferencing, on-hold services for their customers, automatic call back or response systems. Business, government and other institutions chose telecommunications services providers that provided seamless integration of all services needed by these customers. Services providers generally managed the design, operation and maintenance of end-to-end integrated network solutions for these customers. Network security was a paramount factor as many of these customers had e-commerce and dealt with private information. Their systems needed to be able to withstand hackers and prevent unwanted intrusions.

Customer Service

Customer service was an important aspect of the telecommunications industry as this played an essential part in customer retention. Customer service was based on new customers and existing customers.

New Customers Customer service played a major role in which company was chosen by a customer. It was important for a company to gain the confidence of new customers for them to purchase the services. To achieve this the company had to have transparency, which referred to the ability of a company to be open and honest about aspects of the company most important to the customer, things like privacy, speed of processing and quality of services so that customers would more likely trust the company. Strong brand recognition was important because if customers remembered the company's name and business, they were more likely to acquire the services of that particular company. To ensure that customers recognized and remembered a company's name and business, many companies used catchy slogans and logos, and some even had distinct affiliation with particular colors like AT&T whose thematic color was blue. It was important to have friendly and helpful staff that was better able to assist customers in making more informed decisions. The company website had to be user-friendly, that is, it should not be confusing or difficult to navigate as a customer would be unlikely to return to that website. Similarly, the website had to provide interesting and informative content to hold the customer's attention.

Existing Customers Customer service was measured by the churn rate, which is the turnover of existing customers, a closely watched metric measuring the average monthly percentage of customers who left a company in a given quarter. Changes in churn rate provided feedback for a company as it was a good measure for the average length of time an individual remained a customer based on reaction to services provided and pricing. Companies strove to achieve the lowest churn rates possible, which indicated that customers were satisfied with the services they were receiving.

Key factors that affected churn rate were usability of website, good web content, customer satisfaction, customer support, and operational excellence. The website was expected to be secure as many e-commerce activities were performed through the website. Customers were able to view and pay bills online and they could shop for new plans, handsets or packages. Customer satisfaction was determined by how well services and products provided by a company fit the needs of customers; customers demanded high quality of services provided. A company that provided good customer support through the website, 24-hour call support or other means attended to customers' concerns more efficiently and improved customer loyalty; these customers were more likely to stay with that company. It was also important to have a reputation for operational excellence, which could be reflected through simplified billing to customers.

Geographic Region

With national and international coverage it was important to understand what was roaming and the effect it had on coverage. Roaming is the ability to get access to another company's network when away from "home" access. Wireless services providers generally gave customers access to their cell system, which was essentially local. When traveling out of the range of this cell system, the cell system enabled you to be transferred to a neighboring company's cell system without you being aware of it. The use of a neighboring company's cell system caused a customer to be roaming. Geographic region referred to the coverage area of a particular company's wireless network. Networks provided national or international coverage.

National National coverage was the ability of a company to provide services across the United States. Due to Federal Communications Commission (FCC) regulation on fixed-lines, licenses had to be obtained before companies could utilize access lines to operate within a specific area. For companies to expand coverage nationally, they were expected to obtain licenses to operate in specific areas. Wireless coverage depended on several key factors: the number of cell sites, the amount of spectrum band covering an area and roaming agreements between neighboring companies for use of their cell systems. The more cell sites a company had, the larger the national network. Spectrum band referred to the range of frequencies that could be used to transmit wireless signals. The more spectrum band a company acquired, the greater its ability to cover a wider area. Companies were expected to obtain licenses for spectrum bands in different geographic areas. It was also necessary that companies obtained roaming agreements with neighboring companies to allow each other's customers to utilize the cell systems. For example, if a customer normally got access to the company's network from a provider such as Cingular in Brooklyn, New York, and was traveling to Miami, Florida, the customer would get wireless access through a designated provider in Florida such as Verizon, only if the customer's company (Cingular) did not have cell sites in that area.

International International coverage was the ability of a company to provide services in different geographic areas. Customers were able to send and receive calls and data from others in different countries. Telecommunications services providers were expected to obtain necessary roaming agreements with other countries for wireless networks. Roaming was made possible through service providers who had cooperative agreements to grant each other's customers access to their network. For example, if a customer normally got access to the company's network from a provider in Brooklyn, New York, and was traveling to Hong Kong, the customer would get wireless access through a designated provider in Hong Kong. Instead of paying long-distance charges to the telecommunications services provider in Brooklyn, the customer would pay the local phone connection charge in Hong Kong and possibly a modest additional charge for the service. The access to designated providers was dependent on agreements made between the customer's services provider and the designated services provider.

Distribution/Marketing

Companies distributed services and products through various channels discussed below. These products and services were priced competitively and marketed through all forms of media. Each of the sections, distribution, pricing and marketing, is discussed in detail in the following sections.

Distribution and Sales Companies in the telecommunications industry sold their products and services through sales distribution channels such as company-owned retail stores or through independent retail stores, which included agent resellers and electronic stores. Most companies also sold their products and services through their own websites. Company-owned retail stores catered primarily to individual customers seeking more information about services and products provided. Setting up their own distribution channels to sell services and products gave those direct sellers more exclusivity with the search-sale-service-support process to the customers. It was important for these stores to have knowledgeable, friendly and helpful staff that made customers feel welcomed, comfortable and better informed to make decisions. This enabled the development of good customer relationships with current and potential customers. It was also necessary to have a user-friendly, attractive and informative website. With growing e-commerce and the ability of customers to pay bills online, it was important to ensure a secure website. By utilizing all distribution channels companies were able to ensure brand recognition of their services. In addition to this, an increased number of distribution channels provided companies with mass market presence.

Pricing The growing popularity of wireless services, which were far less regulated and hence less expensive, made it increasingly difficult for fixed-line services providers. For companies to survive such pricing competitiveness, pricing plans and packages were implemented. Companies that provided many different services offered bundled packages at more affordable prices to attract customers and thus obtain competitive advantage. Bundling generally referred to the inclusion of two or more services or products sold as a single package. The price of a bundled package was usually less than the cost of acquiring the bundled products or services separately. An example of such bundled packages was the ability of a customer to purchase a wireless handset, wireless services such as network connection, text messaging, voicemail and call forwarding and possibly accessories for a lower price than the combined cost of each individual item.

Bundled packages also consisted of family plans where services and products were offered to families at a discounted rate. As the dynamics of the industry changed it was important for the existing companies to revise packaged rates as new services were added and as packages offered may have also changed.

Apart from bundled packages, another method of pricing was to offer competitive plans to customers. Plans consisted of flat rates for services that may have included voice services with charges for local and long-distance calls on a monthly basis for a certain number of minutes, or voice and data services. With the introduction of new services such as TV/Video services, flat rate services would be revised to offer customers value-added services. Companies with different networks and thus a wider variety of services were better able to offer customers discount rates. An example of this would be to offer customers discount rates for calls made to one of the customer's designated fixed-line phones.

Marketing Companies used all media through which to market their services and products. They spent large sums of money per year on print media and television advertising. Many companies also advertised by sponsoring programs geared toward community involvement such as grants programs, nonprofit projects that used technology to build stronger communities, and sponsorship of sports events. Companies were also able to effectively advertise through the distribution channels by offering promotions such as introductory discounted packages for new customers. By having mass market presence companies strengthened brand recognition. As the Latino market continued to increase at a constant rate, it was important that companies focus on target marketing. About 45% of online Hispanic customers said they wished that more advertisements were in Spanish. One-third of that 45% said they would pay more attention to Spanish ads and 23% said that they would more likely buy a service or product that was advertised in Spanish [Jordan, 2004]. New York was one of the top ten states with the fourth largest Latino market (California, Texas and Florida being the top three) and ranked as the seventh state with the largest shares of total buying power that was Latino.

Mergers and Acquisitions

Changes in technology and the industry as a whole led to the consolidation of companies specialized in different networks transmissions and associated services.

Telecommunication giants got bigger by merging with one another, resulting in less and less competition. This made it harder for new entrants to gain a toehold in the market [Consumer Federation of America, 2005]. Deal making was seen as the best way to grow quickly. Through mergers and acquisitions, companies were able to offer a wider variety of services to a larger group of customers. Since there were significant barriers to entry for local fixed-line networks, consolidation gave companies an avenue to offer and bundle disparate services together. It was thought that this would be an effective way to gain market share and ". . . offer customers the industry's coveted "triple play"—voice, video and data [services] . . ." [Senia, 2004].

A company needed to merge or acquire companies that would provide the most benefits, benefits such as large customer base, new or different technological services, and licenses to operate in more regions. This was particularly important because of the high cost of establishing new territories. A good example of this was the recent acquisition of AT&T Corp. by SBC Communications, which increased its customer base with the addition of AT&T's 30 million customers, including its Fortune 1000 customers. It also gained AT&T's wireless services and strong name brand, one of the most recognized brand names worldwide [Hoovers, 2005]. This is the main reason that SBC Communications has changed its name to AT&T. Companies that were considered long-distance companies such as AT&T Corp. and MCI, Inc. consisted of nearly 100% fiber optic cables [U.S. Business Reporter, 2001]. This was an added advantage for telecommunications services provider as fiber optic connections meant more information could be transferred at faster rates. In addition to this, companies that wished to upgrade network connection to fiber optic cables gained the fiber optic networks of long-distance companies. The deals also expanded the national and international presence of companies that merged or acquired other companies. Mergers and acquisitions were also expected to provide more financial resources for innovation and investment in new technology.

Competition

Competition in this industry was quite intense. Competitors included companies that provided fixed-line and wireless voice and data services, companies that provided primarily wireless voice and data services, companies that provided fixed-line data and TV/Video services only and those that provided wireless data and TV/Video services. Companies such as AT&T Inc. and Verizon Communication Inc. provided voice and data services, using both fixed-line and wireless networks while companies such as Sprint Nextel Corporation provided primarily wireless voice and data services. Time Warner Cable was an example of a provider of fixed-line TV/Video services while Direct TV provided wireless TV/Video services.

TV/Video services providers such as Time Warner Cable and Direct TV offered high-speed data and digital voice services to compete directly with the broadband services offered in the telecommunications industry. While these companies increased competition in this industry, they posed no major threat to telecommunications services providers as TV/Video services providers lacked the necessary equipment (switching equipment) and were ". . . generally seen as not having much technological nor networking experience" when compared to the telecommunications services providers [Anonymous, 2005].

The main competitors discussed here were those who maintained the highest market share and were key players in the telecommunications industry. Wireless services constituted a significant source of competition to any company's fixed-line telecommunications services since more end users were substituting wireless services for basic fixed-line services. TV/Video services providers fell under the category of other services providers. The major competitors were fixed-line and wireless voice and data services providers such as AT&T Inc., mainly wireless voice and data services providers such as Sprint Nextel and other telecommunications services providers such as voice and data broadband services providers, fixed-line or wireless TV/Video services providers or any combination of the above. AT&T Inc., Sprint Nextel and other telecommunications services providers are discussed in detail in the following section.

AT&T Inc. (formerly SBC) SBC Communications was the number two provider of fixed-line voice and data services in the U.S., behind Verizon. It had 52 million local access lines and 22 million long distance customers. Its wireless division known as Cingular Wireless held the position as the number one wireless voice and data services provider with more than 50 million customers [Hoovers, 2005]. The company

operated fixed-line and wireless networks and maintained the facilities and equipment used to create these networks. It is also considered one of the major telecommunications resellers. In 2005 for $16 billion, SBC acquired AT&T Corp., a long-distance, fixed-line services provider and a provider of wireless voice and data services (AT&T Wireless) with valuable business customers who included all of the Fortune 1000, particularly those within its major markets (California, Illinois and Texas which account for 60% of its lines) [Hoovers, 2005]. AT&T was the long-distance voice services leader in the U.S. with more than 30 million customers and it boasted the largest and most advanced global network. SBC gained one of the world's most recognized brand names and it is because of this SBC has changed its name to AT&T Inc.

It planned to deploy fiber optic lines to customers' premises in an effort to improve network speed, a $6 billion in investment for the new network. The project, expected to be completed by the end of 2007, would allow the company to offer video over the Internet and voice and data services simultaneously over these new and improved methods of transmission. The company was the market leader in providing fixed-line broadband services transmitted over coaxial cables. The acquisition of AT&T and the fiber-optic network that came with it helped to improve transmission but this only affected a small number of the customers. The company planned to build 142 new cell sites at a cost of $130 million in an effort to expand network coverage and capacity. In an effort to improve capital spending the company was driven to cut expenses, including deep cuts in its workforce in 2002 and 2003 and it also sold off stakes it held in many other companies to raise money for the necessary upgrades. AT&T Inc. reported net revenues of $40.7 billion, which exhibited the financial resourcefulness of the company as a result of the acquisition. This provided the company sufficient resources necessary for upgrades.

The wireless division, Cingular, used the GSM operating system which provided customers with limited information transmission capacity; however, it was strong for operation in any location due to its popularity and strong roaming capabilities and also had a high degree of commonality. With respect to operating systems, the effectiveness of operation on different networks was comparable for all companies. AT&T offers fixed-line and wireless voice and data services and information/directory publishing services.

The company also made an agreement with EchoStar Communications, a satellite TV services provider, to market satellite TV services as part of its services bundle. It was strong at offering customers bundled services. It was strong at offering services not offered or least likely to be offered by competitors such as TV services and providing a wide variety of services. As the leader in wireless services, the company was strong at gaining exclusive access to "hot" new products. Also it provided a wide variety of accessories and customized calling cards.

AT&T was good at network reliability for individual customers; it provided a wide variety of services to attract customers and cater to their needs. The company had strong market presence and brand recognition. It had competitive pricing plans and packages offering customers unlimited calls to other customers and rollover minutes where unused minutes can be transferred to next month. As a provider of services for the Fortune 1000 companies, the company was strong in providing a fast and reliable network with a wide variety of services such as business solutions and network maintenance that were seamlessly integrated. Network security was a main concern for all telecommunications services providers and AT&T was as good as its competitors in providing such security.

AT&T had a user-friendly website that was easy to navigate; it provided information on its services and products for both individual and business customers. The company's website allowed customers to make purchases and pay bills online. Similar to other telecommunications services providers it maintained a secure website that was interesting and an informative way to alert customers to new products. Similar to other companies, it maintained a good degree of transparency through honesty with customers of business processes, services and ventures. The company was good with respect to having a knowledgeable, friendly and helpful staff to assist customers seeking to purchase services and those requesting support for services already purchased. The company was considered to be operating efficiently and had a churn rate of 2.2% in the first quarter of 2005.

AT&T, namely Cingular, was good at obtaining necessary licenses to operate fixed-line networks in other areas and those licenses required for spectrum band to operate wireless network in other areas. It was also good at obtaining roaming agreements with neighboring companies to utilize cell systems nationally and was strong on an international level. AT&T distributed and sold its products through company-owned retail stores, which gave them more exclusivity. The company used all distribution channels available such as independent retail stores and electronic stores and the company website to ensure brand recognition and had many distribution channels to provide mass market presence. AT&T was very strong at pricing by offering bundled packages such as fixed-line and wireless data services, and affordable pricing plans like flat rates for local, long-distance and international calls and offering discount rates to customers who require many services provided by the different networks. It was also strong at revising package rates and plans to reflect changes. With respect to marketing, AT&T used all forms of media to advertise including sponsorship programs and community involvement and they both offered promotions through the various distribution channels. The company marketed to college students and families as well as business individuals.

Sprint Nextel Corporation   In 2005, Sprint Corp., the number three U.S wireless services provider and Nextel Corp., the number five U.S. wireless services provider, merged companies to form the overall third largest wireless services provider in the U.S., behind Cingular and Verizon. Sprint Nextel's main business operations were wireless voice and data services and fixed-line broadband data services using coaxial cables. It operated both wireless and fixed-line networks and it was a telecommunications reseller, which meant that it did not own the facilities and equipment used in transmission. In September 2005, Sprint and Nextel merged to form the third largest wireless services provider in the U.S. Its combined wireless operations served approximately 44 million customers and the fixed-line business served more than 750,000 customers with both fixed-line broadband services in the United States. Sprint Nextel reported net revenues of $27.4 billion and expressed no immediate plans to build new cell sites.

It used CDMA operating systems for wireless devices, which allowed a large number of users to utilize services on the same frequency and it planned to introduce new technology, EvDo (Evolution Data Optimized), which provided faster wireless data speeds. Sprint Nextel was the first in the telecommunications industry to offer wireless services that allowed customers to listen to live TV and download songs to their wireless devices. It was also excellent at providing a wide variety of wireless services that allowed customers to browse the Internet and check email, play games, utilize text messaging and instant messaging services and customize their wireless devices such as customers could choose from a variety of screen savers and they were also able to assign ring tones to specific telephone numbers of callers in their address book. These services were all seamlessly integrated.

It offered a wide range of fixed-line services for business, government and other institutions such as email protection and Centrex services that directed calls, managed voicemail and set up conference calls. In a joint venture with fixed-line broadband company, Sunflower Broadband, Sprint Nextel offered bundled fixed-line broadband voice and data services, wireless voice and data services and cable TV services. Sprint Nextel made agreements with the four largest cable TV companies in the U.S. to offer customers the convergence of video entertainment, fixed-line and wireless data and communications products and services beginning in 2006. The joint venture is believed ". . . to deliver to consumers a comprehensive portfolio of entertainment and communication services . . ." [RCR Wireless News, 2004].

Sprint Nextel had agreements with product manufacturers such as Samsung to gain access to advanced new products. The wireless devices allowed customers to receive the benefits of many of Sprint Nextel's services such as video mail, picture mail, games, ringers, Internet browsing and email access. It was comparable to its competitors in providing a wide variety of accessories but it did not provide calling cards. It was good at providing reliable networks for all customers. Like many of its competitors, the company placed great emphasis on network security. Like other competitors, the website was user-friendly, easy to navigate and listed newsworthy information and reviews of the company's services and product providing interesting content for customer's reading pleasure. Like many of its competitors, Sprint Nextel maintained a secure website through which customers performed e-commerce transactions.

Similar to other competitors it maintained a good degree of transparency through honesty with customers of the company's business processes, services and ventures and it was good with respect to having a knowledgeable, friendly and helpful staff to assist customers seeking to purchase services and those requesting support for services already purchased. It operated

a nationwide wireless network and had roaming agreements with some international countries and most major Caribbean islands. Its ability to obtain necessary licenses for spectrum band was weak compared to other competitors as this would cause regulatory issues. As the third largest wireless services provider in the U.S., Sprint Nextel maintained strong brand recognition. It had a limited number of company-owned retail stores but it distributed and sold its services and products through many independent stores.

The company offered bundled packages that included fixed-line broadband voice and data and cable TV services. Customers purchased competitively priced plans similar to that of Cingular. Sprint was good at using all forms of media to advertise and offered customers promotions such as discounted prices for upgrades of handsets or get $25 if you refer a friend to use the company's services. The company is an active participant in sponsorships of program such as NASCAR racing and the Emmy Awards. It marketed to college students and families, as well as business customers who utilized the wireless "walkie-talkie" technology that allowed customers to communicate with the push of a button. It was used mainly for business purposes and was a cheap and easy form of communication.

Other Telecommunications Services Providers Other telecommunications services providers included Time Warner Cable and Direct TV, which were providers of TV/Video services and fell under the category of other services providers. Their services were primarily TV/Video services and fixed-line broadband voice and data services. Other telecommunications services providers operated fixed-line networks that used fiber-optic connections and had transmission rates that were very fast. Since they lacked telecommunications equipment, to build the facilities and acquire the necessary switching equipment would have been a very expensive venture. They formed joint ventures with many telecommunications services providers as a way to compete in the market without having to purchase telecommunications equipment. This meant that these companies did not have to worry about licenses and other factors that affected wireless business. These companies were weak in operating multiple networks as companies provided either fixed-line services only or wireless services only. The networks were fast and reliable and had good level of security.

With the introduction of VoIP, these companies were able to provide voice services using fixed-line broadband network. This development gave these companies the ability to offer a wider variety of services but they were still limited because of the lack of switching equipment. With a limited variety of services there was not much of a bundled service to offer customers. These bundled services often included data services which were mostly Internet-related, VoIP services and cable TV services. Since these services used the same network, they had to be seamlessly integrated for efficiency. These new competitors into the telecommunications industry had little bargaining power for exclusive products, limited accessories and offered no calling cards. The idea of TV/Video services providers being providers of voice and data services was a fairly new concept for customers and was not as easily accepted. These companies had to ensure a high quality of services provided to gain customers' business in such a competitive industry. The company websites were user-friendly, easy to navigate and provided necessary information for customers. The websites were also secure as many customers performed e-commerce transactions. Staff was friendly, knowledgeable and helpful; they provided good customer support.

Many of these companies utilized a limited number of independent retailers such as Best Buy and Circuit City since they did not have company-owned retail stores. Given limited services compared to services providers like AT&T, they offered limited bundled packages at competitive prices. It was difficult to have revised package rates and affordable pricing plans as TV/Video services were quite expensive. These companies were good at utilizing various forms of media through which to advertise to all customers but they were not known for partaking in sponsorships or community programs.

The Company

History

Verizon Communications Inc. was a telecommunications services provider of fixed-line and wireless services primarily in the Americas and Europe. It also provided Information/Directory Publishing, which consisted of yellow pages and search services in print, over the Internet and on cell phones. In 2000, Bell Atlantic and Vodofone combined their U.S. wireless operations to form Verizon Wireless. Verizon Communications Inc.

was formed later that year upon approval for acquisition of the non-Bell local phone company, GTE. In 2001, the Company received permission to offer long-distance in Massachusetts, Connecticut, and Pennsylvania; in 2002, it received permission for Delaware, New Hampshire, and Rhode Island; and in 2003, it received permission for Maryland, West Virginia, and Washington, D.C. The company, being based in New York City, felt severe effects from the terrorist attack on lower Manhattan in 2001. Verizon reported damage to its central office facility adjacent to the World Trade Center and the loss of eleven cell sites in the surrounding area of the destruction. The company also provides phone services to the Pentagon and suffered damage in that attack. As part of an effort to reduce debt, in 2002 Verizon divested many of its non-core assets, which included several wireless holdings, access lines and its European based directory businesses.

Led by Ivan Seidenburg, chairman and chief executive officer, Verizon achieved the 2005 top ranking position in *Fortune's* list of most admired telecommunications companies and had the enviable position of attaining a reputation for operational excellence and having the most satisfied customers in the wireless industry. As Mr. Seidenburg expressed, "Our commitment to network quality and customer service has made us the industry leader in customer growth, loyalty and profitability" [Verizon Communications Inc., 2005]. Verizon Communications Inc. was a provider of telecommunications services and operated fixed-line and wireless networks. The focus of the company was to transform the networks to provide additional fixed-line and wireless services. In 2004, Verizon experienced strong revenue growth with revenues up 5.7% from 2003. Fueling this growth was a 23% gain in revenues from the wireless division and growth in high-speed data services in fixed-line [Verizon Communications Inc., 2005]. Verizon's operations are shown in Figure 2.

Transmission

Verizon operated two types of networks: fixed-line and wireless networks.

Fixed-Line The fixed-line division accounted for 54% of total revenues. Verizon has nearly 145 million access line equivalents in 29 states and Washington, D.C. The company offered fixed-line broadband network, which provided customers with improved content and

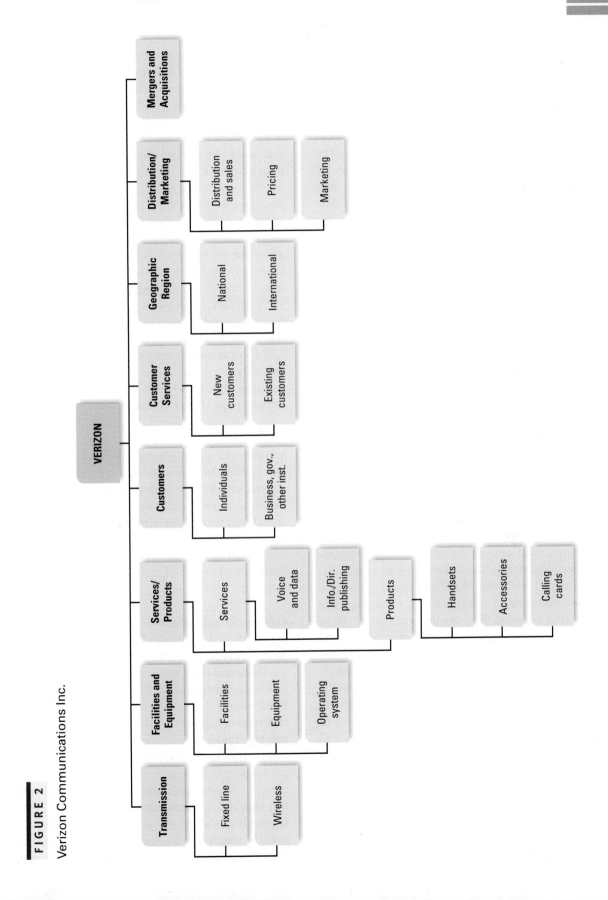

FIGURE 2

Verizon Communications Inc.

great service at an affordable price. In 2004, its broadband network served 3.6 million customers, which was a significant improvement from 2.3 million customers in 2003.

Wireless The wireless network was national and served 47.4 million customers across the United States, a dramatic increase from 37.5 million in 2003. This division accounted for 38% of total revenues for the company. In 2004, Verizon's wireless data revenues increased by almost 60% while fixed-line data revenues increased by a mere 6% from 2003. This was a good indicator of the industry trend towards wireless operations. Verizon operated and maintained fixed-line and wireless networks and provided any and all services for each network that allowed customers to communicate.

Facilities and Equipment

Verizon owned its facilities and equipment used for its networks and intended to expand services through its use. It also leased its facilities and equipment to other telecommunication resellers that generated additional revenues. With the revenues received from leasing its facilities and equipment and that generated from business operations, Verizon was a very sound company with approximately $71 billion in revenues in 2004, which provided the company with sufficient resources to make the upgrades possible.

Facilities Verizon owned most its central offices and equipment used in fixed-line transmission. The Verizon fixed-line network used two types of coaxial cables, twisted pair and shielded twisted pair. This formed the basis of transmission for the fixed-line broadband network. Transmission rates were not as fast as that of fiber optic cables since most of Verizon's customers were connected to the network with the much slower copper wires that had limited bandwidth. It was the second largest wireless network in the United States. Verizon has undergone many improvements to its wireless network and was determined to increase transmission capacity by building new cell sites. Verizon planned to expand its national network by building 280 cell sites at the cost of $200 million.

Equipment As mentioned earlier, Verizon's fixed-line network used two types of coaxial cables, twisted pair and shielded twisted pair with limited bandwidth and slower transmission speeds when compared to

that of fiber optic cables. By setting up more cell sites, Verizon's wireless network improved in the areas of coverage, reliability and transmission rates. More cell sites meant more transmitters, which in turn allowed voice and data to be transferred more easily between company-owned transmitters. This was also cheaper as customers would not have to pay roaming charges that would be applied for the use of another company's network.

Operating Systems Verizon used CDMA operating system, which was similar to GSM in that it effectively operated on any of the company's networks to allow the exchange of voice and data between the same networks such as wireless to wireless, and different networks such as wireless to fixed-line or vice versa. While CDMA was a better operating system, it was not as widely installed as GSM, and this limited the ability to use devices in any location. While the CDMA operating system had a good degree of commonality, its limited use worldwide restricted the roaming capability, which affected the ability of customers to use the services anywhere.

Services/Products

The services and products offered by Verizon Communications Inc. are discussed in detail in the following sections. Verizon won the Frost & Sullivan's 2005 Product Innovation Award for developing and launching two technologically advanced products that made it easier for businesses and consumers to manage all of their communications. These were the Verizon iobi family of services and the Verizon One integrated device.

Services Verizon offered voice and data services, and information/directory publishing services for both fixed-line and wireless networks.

Voice and Data Services. Its fixed-line voice services were considered to be local, long-distance and international. Customers were able to make calls to and receive calls from other customers in the same neighborhood, region, country, or even a foreign country. Verizon benefited because in June 2000 its predecessor company, Bell Atlantic, merged with the nation's largest independent telecommunications company, GTE, which offered long-distance services. It was through this merger that Verizon has grown over the past five years, and became one of the largest long-distance providers in the nation. The company offered all its customers a wide variety of other voice services for fixed-line and wireless networks. These services included voice, text and picture messaging, caller identification, call waiting, call forwarding and three-way calling. It also offered speed-dialing where customers could store the most frequently dialed numbers and use a one digit number to reference that number when dialing and it offered customers a "Gold Telephone Number," which was a customized telephone number using letters and digits that were meaningful and easy to remember. These features added value for customers and were often sold as part of bundled services.

Its data services consisted primarily of Internet services to customers in two-thirds of the top 100 U.S. markets. Customers accessed the Internet using fixed-line or wireless devices to exchange information. Customers sent short messages to each other through instant messaging applications and they sent documents, pictures, graphics and other data through email. It also offered "VoiceWing," which was VoIP, where customers were able to make calls over any broadband Internet connection. The Verizon iobi family of services allowed customers to email voicemail, have the computer hold calls or schedule call forwarding to any phone. It provided customers with an integrated service that made it easier to stay connected. Customers were not only capable of speaking to other customers but their wireless devices allowed them to be able to play games, download ring tones, and take, send and receive pictures as messages.

Information/Directory Publishing Services. Verizon provided its customers with yellow pages and search services in print, over the Internet and on wireless devices. It was the leading print and online directory publisher and content provider with revenues of $3.6 billion in 2004 with 134 million monthly searches on SuperPages.com. These information services were expanded in new electronic markets allowing customers the luxury of searching and retrieving information as well as shopping. It was good at developing and introducing innovative services to the market quickly. A good example of this was the development of the high-speed EvDO (Evolution Data Only) network which allowed Palm's Treo smartphones to access wireless services and the Internet, posing many advantages for corporate IT as a less costly alternative for mobile email. Another example was the development of the fixed-line product known as Verizon

One, which was the simplicity of a telephone combined with the richness of the Internet and this provided customers with an all-in-one information touch-point. It was also a major services provider offering a variety of services for both fixed-line and wireless networks.

Products   Verizon sold accompanying products such as handsets, accessories and calling cards. These products were discussed in detail in the following sections.

Handsets. Verizon was not as good as its competitors in obtaining exclusive access to new, impressive and attractive products. The company found it difficult to work out cost and pricing issues with manufacturers and so has not made any agreements with any manufacturer [Business Week, 2005]. Its competitors were very good at obtaining exclusive access to such products.

Accessories. It provided accessories like caller id devices, answering machines, headsets, battery packs, amplifiers for wireless devices, protective cases, adaptors, car chargers and many other accessories that gave customers the convenience of utilizing communications services.

Calling Cards. Verizon offered calling cards that allowed customers to make calls from their fixed-line or wireless handsets that were conveniently billed to the customers' home phone bill. It allowed customers to use one number, 800-255-CALL, to make calls from any phone to anywhere in the world. The company also offered calling cards known as the Verizon Phone-In Card that permitted calls to be made to a customer's home phone from anywhere in the world. This was used by customers as an alternative to collect calls. These cards were usually customized with the company's logo and used as marketing tools to advertise the company and promote brand recognition.

Customers

Verizon provided network services and products for a variety of customers ranging from individuals, small and medium-sized businesses to large businesses, government, and other institutions.

Individuals   It was voted as the number one provider of telecommunications services in the United States and had an excellent reputation for network speed and reliability. It was strong at providing a wide variety of fixed-line and wireless services and products that fit the needs of its customers. While the company maintained strong market presence and brand recognition through which it attracted most of its competitors, the services and products offered were quite costly.

Business, Government and Other Institutions Verizon provided a wide variety of services for all types of businesses, government and other institutions. These services included voice and data services, network security services, and wireless services, which included Global Phone where business customers could access to the Internet and voice services anywhere in the world through international roaming capabilities. It also offered business solutions services that managed the design, operation and maintenance of end-to-end integrated network services for large business, government, and other institutions such as educational institutions, across the U.S. Verizon was strong in providing services that appeared seamlessly integrated on and between networks. This promoted network reliability for which Verizon had an excellent reputation. Verizon believed that its strongest market segment was individual customers. There was tremendous competition for the business, government and other institutions market, in which AT&T was the dominant telecommunications services provider. In 2005, the business segment, though an $85 billion market, was fading fast and revenues were shrinking about 10% a year. It is because of this, Verizon was not convinced "... that the potential for such gains is worth the high price of buying into the [business] market" [Rosenbush, 2005]. This meant that the company would focus its energies on more profitable markets but it was not going to neglect the business segment. Verizon felt that it was necessary to have faster networks that allow for high-speed Internet connections and services to compete for the business market share.

Customer Service

In 2004, Verizon achieved a reputation for having the best customer service. Customer service was based on that for new customers and that for existing customers.

New Customers Verizon's goal was to operate with the highest level of integrity, responsibility and accountability that led to an increased level of trust the company has earned over the years. It maintained a good level of transparency. Verizon was excellent at making sure that customers recognized and remembered

its name. The company's logo was its name Verizon, with an emphatic red V and Z, symbolic of network speed and also echoed the origin of the company name: veritas, which was a Latin word for certainty, reliability, and horizon, signifying forward-looking and visionary. Its slogan was "We never stop working for you" and this was reflected in the quality of staff. Verizon was strong at having a knowledgeable, friendly and helpful staff. The company also maintained a user-friendly, easy-to-navigate website that contained information on all services and products offered by Verizon.

Existing Customers The company placed great emphasis on providing the best possible quality of service. In the first quarter of 2005, Verizon posted a churn rate of 1.33% compared to 1.5% at the end of 2004. This was a new low for the industry. Verizon maintained a reputation for having operational excellence by providing the highest quality of services to customers, offering a wide variety of services to fit customers' needs, maintaining a secure and interesting website for customers and by having excellent customer support staff. The company has a 24-hour customer support telephone number that customers could call and it also maintained a quick reference and easy to understand customer support section on the company website. According to Mr. Seidenberg, it provided the best customer service because of "... the commitment of our ... dedicated Verizon employees who constantly find new ways to serve customers ..." [Verizon Communications Inc., 2004].

Geographic Region

Verizon's wireless network provided national and limited international coverage.

National Verizon has national presence in fixed-line and wireless markets, with approximately 100 million Americans connecting to a Verizon network daily. It was good at obtaining necessary licenses to operate fixed-line networks in other areas and it was also good at obtaining wireless spectrum bands in different geographic areas. In 2005, Verizon acquired a significant portion of spectrum band covering central Arkansas from other companies within the area [RCR Wireless News, 2005]. It planned to increase the number of cell sites which would allow the company to provide better network coverage over a larger area. As mentioned earlier, the company had the resources necessary to do this. It was one of the largest wireless services providers that owned and operated its facilities and equipment. Verizon had more than 23,000 cell sites nationally, which made it less dependent on roaming agreements; however it also made it easier for the company to obtain roaming agreements with neighboring companies to utilize each others' cell systems.

International It also provided international services using both fixed-line and wireless networks primarily in the Americas and Europe. Verizon's international coverage was limited as it did not possess the necessary roaming agreements with many international telecommunications services providers to utilize their networks to facilitate transmission and a greater coverage area.

Distribution/Marketing

Verizon distributed through various channels and offered competitively priced services and products using all forms of media to market its services and products. Distribution and sales, pricing, and marketing were discussed in detail in the following sections.

Distribution and Sales The company's main distribution channel was its company-owned retail stores. This gave Verizon more exclusivity with the search-sale-service support process to customers. Verizon also sold its services and products through independent retail stores, which included agent resellers and other electronic stores such as RadioShack, Best Buy and Circuit City. It was necessary that staff was knowledgeable, friendly and helpful to make the customer feel welcomed, comfortable and better informed to make decisions. This allowed the customers and staff to develop trusting relationships. Verizon also used its website to sell its services and products. The company had a strong website with interesting and informative content for both potential and existing customers. Its website was also designed for e-commerce and provided customers with the convenience and ease of access to account information, hassle-free online billing and payment methods, shopping and informational resources. Many existing customers performed such activities through the company's very secure website. Verizon offered promotions such as free phones when customers signed up for particular pricing plans of services, or additional features supplied as part of a package, through

its distribution channels as a way to ensure brand recognition. All of its channels boasted the company's logo and slogan. Verizon sold its services and products through a limited number of distribution channels and only those channels that sold Verizon services and products exclusively; however, it still maintained good mass market presence because of the large number of company-owned retail stores.

Pricing It offered customers a wide variety of bundled packages such as wireless handset, a few pieces of accessories and wireless voice and data services, and plans such as flat monthly rates for the use of the services and products. Many of these packages and plans were varied combinations of services and products that gave customers the feeling of added value. The company was strong at revising package rates as packages changed and it was also strong at revising the plans as new services were added or as value was added to the services. However, Verizon's services and products were more expensive than most companies in the industry and discount rates to customers were minimal.

Marketing Verizon was extremely successful at mass marketing its services and products. It utilized all forms of media through which to advertise. It advertised using television advertisements, print, billboards, flyers and in-store promotions to effectively grab customers' attention. In 2005, Verizon won the "Stevies Award," presented by the American Business Awards, for its national literacy program, Verizon Reads, and also that year, the Verizon Foundation won a "Gold Award" from the Council on Foundations for its website, www.verizon.com/foundation, which was honored for excellence in communication. Verizon was instrumental in sponsorship programs and community involvement. The company had mass market presence and strong brand recognition. It used its distribution channels to offer customers promotions like special packages, an example of which included voice and data services, the handset, a headset, and the protective case at a combined discounted price. It marketed its products to all customers but was not as effective in target marketing to the Latino population.

Mergers and Acquisitions

In December 2005, Verizon acquired MCI Inc., one of its major competitors. The merger was expected "... to enhance the base of business customers . . . and also expand their national and international presence" [Information Week, 2005]. Verizon saw the acquisition as an opportunity to expand its services to large corporate business. MCI, Inc. was a leading global communications provider, delivering innovative, cost-effective, advanced communications connectivity to businesses, governments and consumers. MCI also had similar business values to those of Verizon, "To serve customers with innovation, value and integrity" [MCI, 2005]. MCI offered an advanced VoIP service in the business VoIP market and was one of the nation's largest long-distance voice services providers. This meant that MCI owned and operated fiber optic networks and had the most robust set of converged communications services in the industry, including integrated voice, data, and Internet services. In addition to this, MCI was expected to provide Verizon with additional financial resources; it brought with it revenues of $20 billion to Verizon.

Finances

In response to the general industry decline in the early part of the decade, most other telecommunications companies sharply reduced capital spending on network infrastructure. During this time, Verizon emphasized overall expense control as newer technologies made networks and operations more efficient. Verizon also sold non-strategic assets, both domestically and internationally, and the company maintained strong, consistent cash flows from operating activities ($21.8 billion in 2004). This enabled the company, unlike its peers, to maintain a healthy level of network spending in growth areas—investing more in wireless and fixed-line broadband networks than anyone else in the industry. In 2004, Verizon experienced strong revenue growth with revenues up 5.7% from 2003. Fueling this growth was a 23% gain in revenues from the wireless division and growth in high-speed data services in fixed-line [Verizon Communications Inc., 2005]. Verizon reported consolidated revenues of $71.3 billion. In 2005, Verizon planned to sell or spin-off its information/directory publishing services in a deal valued at more than $17 billion. "Some analysts questioned the wisdom of giving up the strong, profitable cash flows from directories despite Verizon's need to bolster its finances . . ." [Los Angeles Times, 2005]. The company explored different means of acquiring additional financial resources to concentrate more on providing wireless, data and phone services.

Management and Strategy

With increasing competition in the telecommunications industry, Mr. Seidenberg, chairman and chief executive officer, was faced with the challenge of raising the standards for performance and redefining the growth possibilities for the telecommunications industry. Mr. Seidenberg aimed to transform Verizon into a full-service provider of video, Internet, wireless, and other services by improving the equipment used in transmission. He perceived that the best way to expand and thrive in the telecommunications world was by focusing on growth in the profitable wireless and broadband markets while building up in the business, government and other institutions market. He saw the acquisition of MCI Corp. as an opportunity to expand services and increase market share by acquiring MCI's customers. Under his leadership, Verizon maintained the position as the largest telecommunications provider; however, it ranked second to Cingular in providing wireless services. While the company maintained an advantageous position as the largest telecommunications provider, Mr. Seidenberg realized that in a dynamic industry such as this, standing still meant falling behind and it was therefore necessary to focus on the opportunities ahead.

Looking Towards the Future

Mr. Seidenberg was faced with many decisions that affected the future of Verizon. The major decisions included a drastic redesign of the equipment used in the transmission of an increasing variety of data, allowing for an array of services the company offered that were better suited to the needs of its customers, retention of the customers the company had and the ability to increase market share. Verizon believed that it was more important to be the best network operator than the biggest.

The decision revolved around two alternatives. The first was the drastic upgrade of the wireless network and the fixed-line broadband network providing services for business, government and other institutions only, while the second was the drastic upgrade of the wireless network and the fixed-line network providing services for all customers but target marketing to the Latino population.

The first alternative proposed that Verizon built new cell sites to increase the wireless network and that it would also improve the fixed-line broadband networks by drastically upgrading the coaxial cables to fiber optic cables. Verizon's upgrades to the networks were expected to attract the lucrative businesses, government and other institutions market.

The company was expected to expand its services to include necessary business services such as video conferencing, business network solutions, VoIP services and network equipment maintenance services and it would increase international coverage for business customers utilizing wireless services. Pricing strategies for these customers such as plans for long-distance calls or cheaper international calls were to be implemented to compete with other companies that dominated this market niche.

The implementation of fiber optic cables was expected to provide increased bandwidth, faster transmission and the ability to transmit additional information that was necessary for businesses, government and other institutions. By upgrading the networks and offering a wider variety of services tailored to these customers, Verizon would put itself in a more competitive position to gain market share and increase profitability in this $85 billion market.

This alternative was feasible because the company had more financial resources than its competitors. It also maintained a good reputation for network reliability and customer satisfaction. Verizon had a long history of providing services and products that enabled efficiency and productivity of businesses, which contributed to its reputation. Verizon was good at developing and introducing innovative services and products to the market quickly; a good example of this is the development of the high-speed EvDO (Evolution Data Only) network, which allowed Palm's Treo smartphones to access wireless services and the Internet, posing many advantages for corporate IT as a less costly alternative for mobile email. By building new cell sites, national coverage would be improved. The company had to obtain roaming agreements with other countries to improve international coverage; the benefit of this greater coverage was that the brand would become internationally recognized and that would provide great opportunity for international expansion.

Verizon was an industry leader and maintained notable positions for customer satisfaction and network reliability. Its merger with MCI placed it in a better position than its competitors with sufficient scale and presence to be a major supplier to national and global business entities, governments and other institutions. MCI was the industry leader and better than AT&T in the VoIP market, which was an increasingly popular voice and data service business used. Verizon had more financial resources compared to its competitors and was capable of financing the drastic upgrade of both networks simultaneously; it could do this much more easily than its competitors. Verizon also had a stronger reputation for operational excellence and customer satisfaction. It was better than its competitors at providing the highest quality of services and having excellent customer support. Verizon had stronger brand recognition than most of its competitors and was the only company to offer services that were specifically for network security, its network security solutions.

A drawback to this alternative was that upgrading the fixed-line and wireless networks simultaneously, expanding services significantly and also expanding coverage internationally would place a tremendous strain on finances. One way around this drawback would be to merge with or acquire a company that offers either of these technological services and would provide additional licenses, therefore expanding the coverage area.

The second alternative proposed was that Verizon would focus on the drastic upgrade of fixed-line coaxial cables to fiber optic cables, and simultaneously build new cell sites to improve the wireless network. To facilitate this upgrade the company was expected to sell or spin-off its information/directory publishing services. Upgrades in fixed-line and wireless networks would allow the company to expand its services to include TV/Video services, enhanced data services, particularly Internet, and offer a wider variety of bundled services. Verizon was expected to target all customers with special focus on the potential Latino population. It was expected to improve national coverage but maintain a limited international coverage.

By replacing all copper lines with fiber optic links the amount of bandwidth would be dramatically increased. This would lead to best overall values in broadband, with improved content, faster speeds and allow for a host of next-generation services to be delivered, services such as fast Internet access and high definition and quality of video. The fiber infrastructure was expected to reduce operating costs and allow for new revenue streams from high-capacity applications like video and music. The sale or spin-off of the information/directory publishing services was expected to generate $17 billion which would be used towards the upgrade of the networks to offer a faster, more reliable network with greater information carrying capacity and hence position itself as a wireless and fixed-line broadband competitor. Focusing on the individual customers, specifically target marketing the Latino population, would give Verizon first mover advantage and secure its position within the Latino community. The U.S. market was also the company's strongest market and by improving national coverage, Verizon stands to gain significant market share.

This alterative was feasible because the company was financially strong and with the additional resources provided from the sale of the information/directory publishing services, it would be able to cover this massive investment. It also maintained a good reputation for network reliability and had excellent customer service. Verizon offered an already wide variety of services and had a long history of offering services and products that enabled efficiency and productivity for business customers and convenience for its individual customers. Verizon was good at developing and introducing innovative services and products to the market quickly.

Verizon had more financial resources than its competitors and it stood to gain considerable financial leverage from the sale of its information/directory publishing services to cover the cost of financing the drastic upgrade of both networks simultaneously. Its merger with MCI placed it in a better position than its competitors with sufficient scale and presence to be a major supplier to national and global business entities, governments and other institutions. MCI was the industry leader and better than AT&T in the VoIP market, which was an increasingly popular voice and data service business used. Verizon also had a stronger reputation for operational excellence and customer satisfaction. It was an industry leader and maintained notable positions for customer satisfaction and network reliability. It was better than its competitors at providing the highest quality of services and having excellent customer support. Verizon had stronger brand recognition than most of its competitors and was the only company to offer services that were specifically for network security, its network security solutions. To improve national coverage, Verizon was better than its competitors at obtaining roaming agreements with neighboring companies to use their cell systems and they had significant resources necessary to build more cell

sites that improved the wireless transmission and coverage; it had more cell sites than its competitors.

A drawback was that Verizon could potentially harm itself from the sale of its industry leading information/directory publishing services and end up spreading its financial resources too thinly by drastic upgrades in all networks. A way around this drawback would be to drastically upgrade the fixed-line network and gradually expand the wireless network. Another drawback was that Verizon would experience tremendous competition from other companies particularly in the wireless services area that offer cheaper services and products. A way around this drawback would be to promote brand recognition, network reliability, and revise pricing plans and packages bundling services and products that provide customers with value added services and products in contrast to its competitors.

Both alternatives seemed reasonable. Deciding among the two alternatives under consideration and other strategic decisions areas was now the problem Verizon Communications Inc. was faced with resolving.

REFERENCES

Anonymous (2005). "The Communications Industry: Past, Present and Future." [Online]. *http://www.sims.berkely.edu.* Accessed November 11, 2005.

Bensinger, A. (2005). "IPTV: Big Potential—but When?" [Online]. *http://www.businessweek.com.* Accessed October 11, 2005.

Bureau of Labor Statistics (2004). "Telecommunications." [Online]. *http://www.bls.gov/oco/cg/cgs020.htm.* Accessed October 18, 2005.

Business Week (2005). "Verizon Wireless' Wizard." *Business Week,* June 21, 2005, p.N1.

Consumer Federation of America (2005). "Review and Denial of the Plan for Merger." [Online]. *http://consumerfed.org.* Accessed October 24, 2005.

Coustan, D., and Franklin, C. (2005). "How Operating Systems Work." [Online]. *http://howstuffworks.com.* Accessed October 10, 2005.

Cybercollege (2004). "Mass Media Course: Cable and Satellite TV Services." [Online]. *http://www.cybercollege.com/frtv/frtv029.htm.* Accessed October 10, 2005.

FCC (2005). "Broadband." [Online]. *http://www.fcc.gov/cgb/broadband.html#broadband.* Accessed October 15, 2005.

FCC (2005). "Statistical Trends in Telephony." [Online]. *http://www.fcc.gov/wcb/iatd/trends.html.* Accessed October 15, 2005.

FCC (2005). "Wireless Communication Service." [Online]. *http://wireless.fcc.gov/wcs/.* Accessed October 15, 2005.

Hoovers (2005). "AT&T Corp." [Online]. *http://premium.hoovers.com/subscribe/co/overview.xhtml?ID=10103.* Accessed October 24, 2005.

Hoovers (2005). "SBC Communications Inc." [Online]. *http://premium.hoovers.com/subscribe/co/overview.xhtml?ID=11379.* Accessed October 24, 2005.

Jordan, M. (2004). "Latinos Embrace Web Entertainment; Hispanics Are Outpacing General Online Population for Internet Music Usage." *Wall Street Journal,* April 14, 2004, p.B3.

Los Angeles Times (2005). "Verizon May Sell or Spin Off Directory Unit to Raise Cash." *Los Angeles Times,* December 6, 2005, p.C7.

Marks, A. (2001). "Local Carriers Bolster Service for Edge." *Crain's New York Business*, September 24, 2001, p.16.

MCI (2005). "About MCI." [Online]. *http://global.mci.com/about/company/facts*. Accessed November 24, 2005.

Mergent Online (2005). "Verizon Communications Inc. (United States)." [Online]. *http://www.mergentonline.com/compdetail.asp?company=-1&company_mer=36979&Page=business*. Accessed October 29, 2005.

Mossberg, W. (2005). "Imagine It: The Sun, Some Ancient Ruins, You With No Laptop." *Wall Street Journal*, November 10, 2005, p.B1.

RCR Wireless News (2004). "Broadband Company Offers Sprint PCS in Bundle." *RCR Wireless News*, March 22, 2004, p.1

RCR Wireless News (2005). "Verizon Plans Ark. Expansion in November." *RCR Wireless News*, August 15, 2005, p.9.

Rosenbush, S. (2005). "Telecom: To Buy or To Build." *Business Week*, February 21, 2005, p.38.

Rulison, L. (2005). "Verizon Adds Cell Sites to Increase Coverage." *Knight Ridder Tribune Business News*, September 13, 2005, p.1.

Senia, A. (2004). "Smart Spending Spells Transformation." *America's Network*, June 15, 2005, p.25.

The Insight Research Corporation (2005). "Fixed Mobile Convergence: Single Phone Solutions for Wireless, Wireline, and VoIP Convergence 2005-2010." [Online]. *http://www.insight-corp.com/reports/fixmobcon.asp*. Accessed November 2, 2005.

U.S. Business Reporter (2001). "Industry Trends." [Online]. *http://www.activemediagiude.com/smp_telecos.htm*. Accessed November 2, 2005.

Verizon Communications Inc. (2004). "Verizon Communications Annual Report 2004." [Online]. *http://www22.verizon.com*. Accessed October 10, 2005.

Wireless Review (2005). "Deals and Deployments." *Wireless Review*, August 2005, p.16.

Procter & Gamble: The Beauty/Feminine Care Segment of the Consumer Goods Industry

This case was prepared by Dr. Robert J. Mockler.

Introduction

In 2005, A.G. Lafley, chairman, president, and chief executive of Procter & Gamble (P&G), told the shareholders that since 2000 sales had grown more than 40% to $57 billion and profit had more than doubled [P&G Annual Report, 2005]. P&G was a global manufacturing, distribution, and marketing company focusing on providing branded products with superior quality and value. Two billion times a day, P&G brand products touched the lives of people around the world. The company provided over 300 brands reaching consumers in about 140 countries.

P&G was formed in 1837 by William Procter and James Gamble. It all started by making and selling soaps and candles. On August 22, 1837, they formalized their business relationship by pledging $3,596.47 a piece; in early 2006, the company made approximately $68 billion annually in sales. In 1862, during the civil war, the company was awarded several contracts to supply soap and candles to the Union armies. These orders kept the factory busy day and night, building the company's reputation as soldiers returned home with their P&G products. Since then P&G had continued to grow in sales and in the introduction of new products [P&G Company Information, 2006].

Over the years P&G has acquired new product brands and companies such as Iams, Clairol, and Wella. The most recent one was on October 1, 2005, when P&G added Gillette to expand the Company's product mix to 22 brands. The Gillette Company was a manufacturer and distributor of various types of

consumer goods in the following five areas/brands: Blades and Razors, Duracell (batteries), Oral Care, Braun (small appliances), and Personal Care. The merger with Gillette made P&G a more balanced company in terms of brands, employees, and sales against its competitors over the intermediate and long-term future.

The consumer goods industry was changing drastically in the last few years leading up to 2006. Retail power was increasing and today's consumers were more confidently deciding when, where, and how to shop, and at what price to buy. There were various reasons for these changes, such as more variety of products in the market place. In addition, according to the Bureau of Economic Analysis (BEA), personal income increased to $41.1 billion and disposable personal income (DPI) increased to $35.5 billion, in December 2005 [BEA, 2006].

P&G, as illustrated in Figure 1, was structured into four organizational units: Market Development Organization (MDO), Global Business Services (GBS), Corporate Functions (CF), and Global Business Unit (GBU).

- **Market Development Organizations (MDO)** studied consumers to build local understanding which was used as a foundation for marketing campaigns. Interacting with consumers helped ensure that the company's marketing plans and campaigns were structured to change the game to favor P&G at the point of purchase.

- **Global Business Services (GBS)** provided business technology and services that drove business success and won customers and consumers. This unit provided services and solutions that enabled the company to operate efficiently around the world, collaborate effectively with business partners, and help employees to become more productive.

FIGURE 1

Procter & Gamble's Structure Division

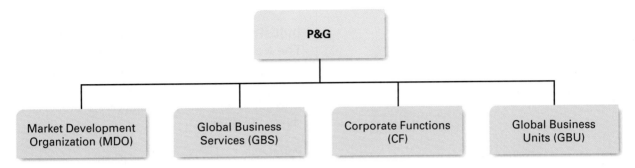

- **Corporate Functions (CF)** worked to maintain P&G's place as the leader of the consumer good's industries. This unit ensured that the functional capability integrated into the rest of the company remained on the cutting edge of the industry.

- **Global Business Unit (GBU)** created strong brand equities, robust strategies, and ongoing innovation in products and marketing to build major global brands [P&G Corporate Information, 2006]. The main philosophy of the GBU was to think globally instead of locally. This case study will concentrate on this unit to get a better understanding of the global operations of P&G. In early 2006, P&G had 5 divisions in its GBU: Baby/Family care, Fabric/Home care, Snacks and Beverage, Health care, and Beauty/Feminine care.

With the acquisition of Gillette, P&G's product mix of billion-dollar brands was well-balanced. In early 2006, the company had 12 billion-dollar brands in Baby/Family care and Fabric/Home care, and 10 billion-dollar brands in Beauty/Feminine care and Health care [P&G Annual Report, 2005]. The effects on the Beauty/Feminine care segment due to the acquisition of Gillette and the natural fast growth nature of this segment will be further discussed in detail later in this case. It is also important to note that even though this division is named Beauty/Feminine care, most people would assume it focuses just on products for females, but in reality quite a few products in this division are geared towards men.

P&G was always creating and acquiring new products. To make the public aware of these products, the company had high advertising and marketing expenses. It also had a very good distribution channel that acted as a revenue source for the company, when it partnered with other companies to help distribute its products. Some of the threats facing P&G were the increase in commodity costs and competition in the consumer goods industry. There were a couple of strategic business decisions that P&G could focus on: it could produce more products with natural ingredients and more men's products because these were the growing trends in the industry; or it could focus on one of its product segments such as skin products for a while and then later introduce its other products. All these were possible alternatives, but the main question to be resolved was how to differentiate P&G from its competition, and so achieve a winning edge over competitors within intensely competitive, rapidly changing immediate, intermediate, and long-term time frames.

The Overall Industry and Competitive Market Analysis: The Consumer Goods Industry

Consumer goods companies were those that provided services primarily to consumers. The industry, as shown in Figure 2, was divided into durable goods and nondurable goods.

Durable Goods

Durable goods were items with a normal life expectancy of three years or more, such as furniture, household appliances, jewelry, and mobile homes. Due to the nature of these goods, the durable good industry was sensitive to business cycles. Business cycles were predictable long-term patterns of alternating periods of economic growth (recovery) and decline

FIGURE 2

The Consumer Goods Industry

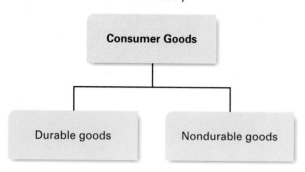

(recession), characterized by changing employment, industrial productivity, and interest rates [Webster's Dictionary, 2006].

Nondurable Goods

On the other hand, nondurable goods were items that generally lasted for only a short time (three years or less), such as petroleum, beverages, apparel, tobacco, pharmaceutical, and beauty/feminine care products. Nondurable goods were not responsive to any economic conditions such as interest rate, inflation, business cycle, and the like. They were not responsive, because some of these products met the needs of people. Consumers had to buy these products such as food, medicine, and apparel to survive. They also bought these goods when they needed them because of their short life span; they did not want to buy a lot in bulk and then would not be able to use them. In the United States, the Bureau of Economic Analysis (BEA) released reports stating

that nondurable goods manufacturing turned up in 2004—increasing 2.7% after decreasing 1.2% in 2003 [BEA, 2006].

Industry and Market Segment: The Nondurable Goods Industry

As mentioned earlier, examples of nondurable goods were petroleum, beverages, apparel, tobacco, pharmaceutical, and beauty/feminine care products, as shown in Figure 3.

Petroleum

Petroleum products were divided into three major categories: fuels, finished nonfuel products, and feedstocks.

- **Fuels**—These are products such as motor gasoline and distillate fuel oil (diesel fuel).

- **Finished Nonfuel Products**—These are products such as solvents and lubricating oils.

- **Feedstocks**—These products were for the petrochemical industry such as naphtha and various refinery gases.

Petroleum products were used by everyone: from gasoline used to fuel cars to heating oil used to warm homes. The demands for these products varied dramatically, but the greatest demand was for products in the fuels category, especially motor gasoline [EIS, 2005]. In the United States (U.S.), petroleum products contributed about 40.2% of the energy used, more than that of natural gas, coal, nuclear, and hydroelectric. It was estimated that by 2025, the U.S. would increase its consumption of these products to 27.9 million barrels per day [EIS, 2005].

FIGURE 3

The Nondurable Goods Industry

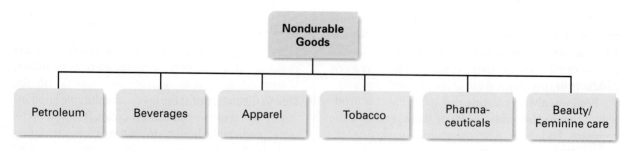

Beverages

This industry group included alcoholic beverage and non-alcoholic beverage products.

- **Alcoholic Beverage**—These were drinks that contained ethanol. There were two types, those that included low-alcohol-content, which were produced by the fermenting of sugar of starch-containing products, and high-alcohol-content beverages produced by distillation of the low-alcohol-content beverage [Wikipedia, 2006]. Examples of these products were beer, wine, ale, and cider.

- **Non-alcoholic Beverage**—These were drinks that did not contain ethanol, such as coffee, juice, tea, and soda water.

Apparel

This industry group included products for men, women, children, and infants. The products consisted of both inner and outerwear clothes.

Tobacco

This industry group included products that were made from tobacco, which was a plant that grew in a wide range of soil and climate conditions. Its nonedible leaf was dried and used to manufacture products such as cigarettes, pipe tobacco, cigars, chewing tobacco, and snuff. Companies who produced these products constantly had problems because of the health risk associated with using their products. According to the World Health Organization (WHO), tobacco killed more than two and a half million people prematurely every year.

Pharmaceuticals

This industry group included companies that researched, developed, produced, and sold chemical or biological substances for medical or veterinary use. These substances included prescription, generic, and OTC drugs; vitamins and nutritional supplements; drug delivery systems; and diagnostic substances [Hoovers, 2006].

The Beauty/Feminine care industry, the focus of this study, is discussed in detail in the following section.

Industry and Competitive Market: Beauty/Feminine Care Goods

The desire to be beautiful is as old as civilization. This desire created an industry which generates $160 billion a year. Americans spent more each year on beauty than they did on education [Economist, 2006]. The industry, as shown in Figure 4, encompassed some of the following products: hair products, skin products, feminine products, fine fragrances, cosmetics, and personal cleansing.

Companies that produced beauty/feminine care products were influenced by fashion, seasons, and culture. The latest trends to affect this market were the movement by consumers towards natural products and the increased interest by men to look clean and well groomed, creating a large emerging men's market. From 2003 to 2008, as shown in Figure 5, the sale of most beauty/feminine care products, such as hair products, cosmetics, and skin products increased. Each of these beauty/feminine care products are further described in the following section.

FIGURE 4

Beauty/Feminine Care Goods Segment

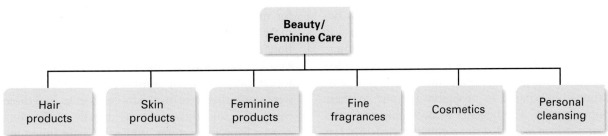

FIGURE 5

Projected U.S. Retail Dollar Sales of Ethnic Specific Cosmetics (in millions), 2003–2008

Year	Hair Care		Cosmetics		Skin Care		Total
	$	% Change	$	% Change	$	% Change	$
2003	$1,030	−4.0%	$367	5.6%	$118	3.3%	$1,515
2004	$1,009	−2.0%	$387	5.5%	$121	2.5%	$1,517
2005	$1,019	1.0%	$410	6.0%	$124	2.5%	$1,553
2006	$1,035	1.5%	$437	6.5%	$129	4.0%	$1,601
2007	$1,055	2.0%	$463	6.0%	$132	2.3%	$1,650
2008	$1,030	2.5%	$493	6.5%	$137	3.6%	$1,712

Source: Packaged Facts (2005). "The U.S. Market for Ethnic HBC Products." [Online]. http://cpprod.stjohns.edu/cp/tag.b9b5fA3031868bbe.render. userLayoutRootNode.uP?uP_root=root&uP_sparam=activeTab&activeTab=U11l1S39&uP_tparam=frm&frm=fram. Accessed January 25, 2006.

How Industry Segment Works: The Business Process Model

The beauty/feminine care industry was comprised of various segments as shown in Figure 6. This industry included companies that manufactured goods that were used to fulfill the needs of consumers.

The products these companies produced included hair products, skin products, feminine products, fine fragrances, cosmetics, and personal cleansing products.

Consumers used each product for their own personal reasons, but the main purposes were to make people look beautiful and feel clean. The consumers for these products included both females and males from all age groups. Even though it was called beauty/feminine care, males were actually a large part of the consumer base because they used a lot of beauty products. Consumers also included people from different ethnic groups, marital status, and also low income consumers.

Consumers seemed to be more confident about what they wanted and this played a major role in determining what products were manufactured. In early 2006, a national survey of consumer goods executives showed that a majority of respondents believed that their organizations were well on the way to becoming demand-driven. Demand-driven enterprises were defined as those that not only identified real-time changes in demand, but were also organizationally prepared to profitably respond to these opportunities. The benefits of becoming more demand-driven were that the companies had 15% less inventory, a 17% better perfect-order performance,

and a 35% shorter cash-to-cash cycle time [Findarticles, 2006]. So as consumers changed, the companies also changed in order to remain in the competitions with their competitors.

These products were produced in factories all over the world with raw materials ranging from materials as simple as water to chemicals such as stearic acid and sodium hydroxide. These materials were mixed in unique ways to make each product. Regardless of the raw materials or procedures used to make them, each product had to meet regulatory standards. In the United States of America, an example of such a regulatory body was the U.S. Food and Drug Administration (FDA). These standards varied by country, and they helped to ensure that these products were safe enough to be used by the consumers.

After production, these products were packaged and distributed to consumers through various distribution channels such as distribution companies, individual stores, and chain store outlets. Packaging was another important factor in selling products, for example, male products had to be packaged in a different way to attract them. Most times, the packets for men's products were normally dark colored to make the products look more masculine. Distribution companies were companies that bought and sold large amounts of products to various retailers, which then sold to the consumers. Individual stores were stores that were owned by companies, and these companies sold their products directly to the consumers from these stores. While the chain store outlets included some multinational companies such as

FIGURE 6

Beauty/Feminine Care Goods Industry

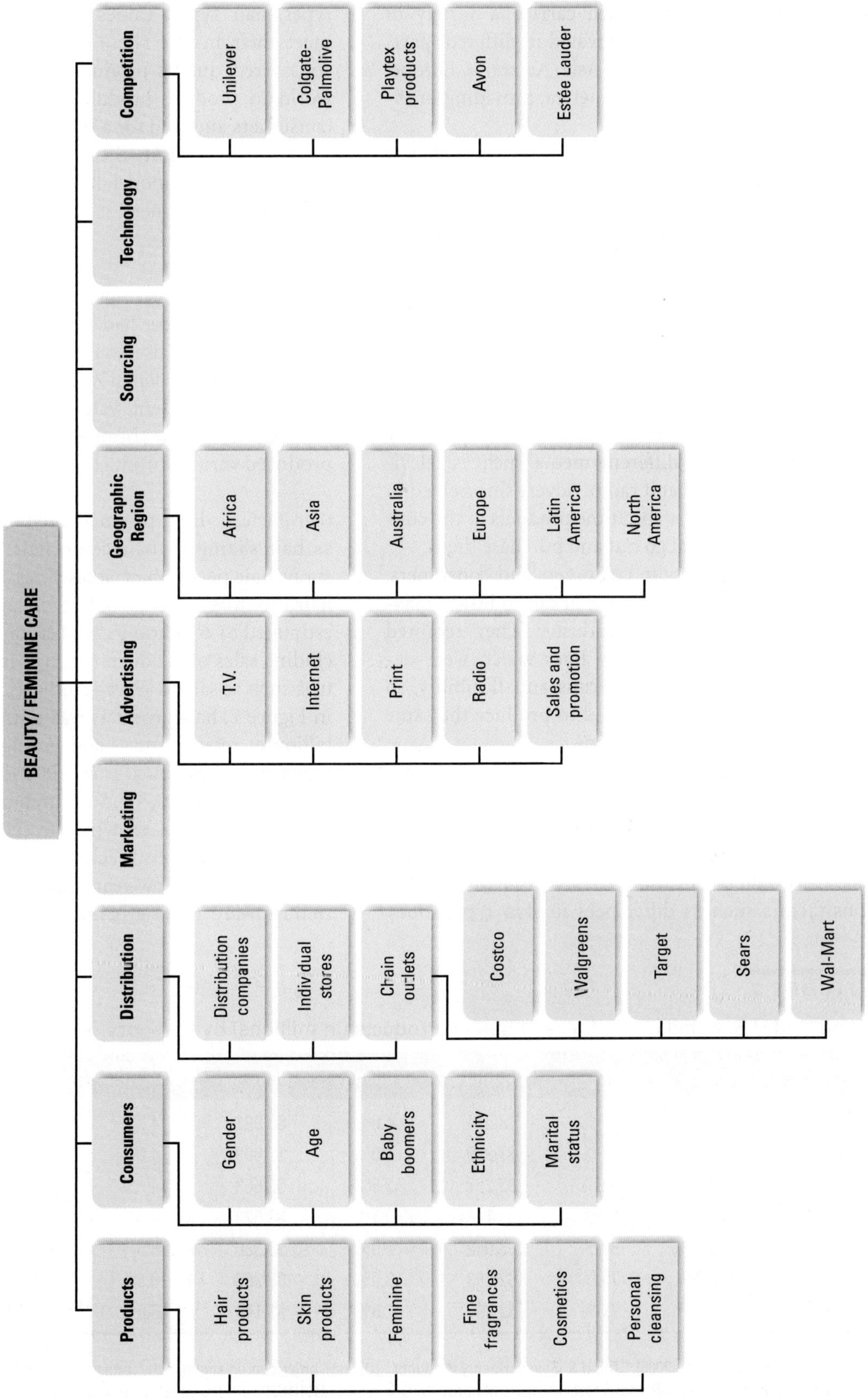

BEAUTY/FEMININE CARE

- Products
  - Hair products
  - Skin products
  - Feminine
  - Fine fragrances
  - Cosmetics
  - Personal cleansing

- Consumers
  - Gender
  - Age
  - Baby boomers
  - Ethnicity
  - Marital status

- Distribution
  - Distribution companies
  - Individual stores
  - Chain outlets
    - Costco
    - Walgreens
    - Target
    - Sears
    - Wal-Mart

- Marketing

- Advertising
  - T.V.
  - Internet
  - Print
  - Radio
  - Sales and promotion

- Geographic Region
  - Africa
  - Asia
  - Australia
  - Europe
  - Latin America
  - North America

- Sourcing

- Technology

- Competition
  - Unilever
  - Colgate-Palmolive
  - Playtex products
  - Avon
  - Estée Lauder

Costco and Wal-Mart, which carried a variety of products, these stores were located in different parts of the world, such as Africa, Asia, Australia, Europe, Latin America, and North America, providing products to consumers there.

Manufacturing companies had to decide if they wanted to make or buy their manufacturing materials. If they decided to buy any item they usually looked for the cheapest and most efficient source to buy from. This process was called Sourcing and it was a process that had to be continuously reviewed in order to maintain the best deals that suited the company.

Advertisement was the promotion of goods, services, companies and ideas, usually by an identified sponsor. Companies used advertisement as part of an overall promotional strategy for their products. They advertised through different media such as television, Internet, print, and radio. Advertising helped to bring some awareness about the products to the consumers, so they could go out and purchase them.

Due to the variety in customers and consumers, technology played a major role in this industry, making it a capital intensive industry. They required highly mechanized assembly lines which were designed for long production runs and flexibility, so that it could be easily changed to produce the same products with minor alterations.

Some of the companies that produced beauty/feminine care products were Unilever, Colgate-Palmolive, Playtex products, Avon, and Estée Lauder. Since they produced products that appealed to people all over the world, they had to take into consideration various factors such as differences in skin types, body types, hair types, values and beliefs, to efficiently meet their needs. These differences were seriously considered during production in each part of the world to produce products that could be used by consumers and sold for a profit.

Figure 6 illustrates the beauty/feminine care goods segment business model. It serves as the framework in discussing this segment.

Products

The life span of these products were three years or more. This industry had a wide variety of products and they could be used on different parts of the body, by either males or females. Each product had its own brand with different value, quality, and quantity. Companies in the beauty/feminine care segment produced various products, as illustrated in Figure 6.

Hair Products Hair products included products such as hair shampoo, hair color, hair conditioner, hair spray, hair perms, hair accessories, and the like. The hair care market was a billion dollar market, with an estimated $7.6 billion in 2004 from retail market, excluding sales of products through professional channels such as salons [Packaged Facts, 2005]. As shown in Figure 7, hair products was estimated to top $3.5 billion at retail in mass and prestige channels combined, as of 2010. Also from 2004–2010, the category would gain 22.9%, or $657 million. The resultant compound annual growth rate (CAGR) for the six years would be 3.5% [Packaged Facts, 2005].

Over the past few years, there has been a growing trend toward natural hair remedies and treatments.

FIGURE 7

Projected U.S. Retail Dollar Sales of Beauty Products (in millions) by Category, 2004–2010

Year	Skincare	% Change	Haircare	% Change	Make-up	% Change	Total	% Change
2010	$8,949	5.0%	$3,524	4.0%	$3,981	4.5%	$16,454	4.7%
2009	$8,523	5.0%	$3,389	4.0%	$3,809	4.0%	$15,721	4.5%
2008	$8,117	5.0%	$3,258	3.5%	$3,663	4.0%	$15,038	4.4%
2007	$7,730	5.5%	$3,148	3.5%	$3,522	4.0%	$14,400	4.7%
2006	$7,327	6.5%	$3,042	3.0%	$3,386	4.0%	$13,755	5.1%
2005	$6,880	7.0%	$2,953	3.0%	$3,256	3.5%	$13,089	5.2%
2004	$6,430	7.3%	$2,867	2.8%	$3,146	3.9%	$12,443	5.4%

Source: Packaged Facts (2005). "The U.S. Sale of Beauty Products." [Online]. http://cpprod.stjohns.edu/cp/tag.b9b8fA3031868bbe.render. userLayoutRootNode.uP?uP_root=root&uP_sparam=activeTab&activeTab=U11l1S39&uP_tparam=frm&frm=fram. Accessed January 25, 2006.

Consumers were more aware of, and growing wary of chemicals that could be in some mass market hair treatment products. The other trend mentioned above about men's interest was also obvious in the hair care industry, because there was an increased effort by men to keep their hair well groomed.

The keys to success included several factors. The hair products had to be competitively priced and affordable. There had to be a wide selection of these products available to the consumers. The quality of these products had to be considered during production to maintain the company's brand quality reputation. Brand recognition was also an important factor because consumers had to feel as if they could relate with the brand and its attributes. Location and distribution were also important to ensure that these products had a mass market presence. They also had to frequently introduce new products. The packaging for the products had to be designed to attract the right consumer.

Skin Products Skin products were further divided into two product classes: mass market products, which were generally lower priced and sold in such mass outlets as drugstores, discount stores, and food stores, and prestige products, which were higher priced, usually packed stylishly and contained special ingredients, and often sold in department and specialty stores. Skin products included moisturizers, cleansers, gels, conditioners, toners, and the like. Factors that affected this segment of this industry were the aging U.S. consumers and technological development; mass market went upscale, and new products were introduced into the market. As illustrated in Figure 7, it was estimated that the sale of skin care products would reach $8.9 billion in combined mass and prestige channels in 2010. This segment would grow a total of 39.2%, or $2.5 billion, during 2004–2010. That translated into a highly desirable 5.7% CAGR over the six years [Packaged Facts, 2005]

The way people looked after their skin was often dictated by the degree of affluence. In rural parts of Africa, men and women still made crude bars of soap using crude potassium hydroxide produced from burnt tree bark. Many used coconut oil as a moisturizer. In addition many people tried to lighten their skin by using skin creams containing certain drugs. Steroid creams were freely available for sale in some places, as were creams containing skin-lightening ingredients called hydroquinone. In the developed world, these ingredients could legally be incorporated in low concentrations in well-formulated cosmetic preparations [P&G Skin Care, 2003].

The keys to success included several factors. The skin products had to be competitively priced and affordable. There had to be a wide selection of these products available to the consumers. The quality of these products had to be considered during production to maintain the company's brand quality reputation. Brand recognition was also an important factor because consumers had to feel like they could relate with the brand and its attributes. Location and distribution were also important to ensure that these products had a mass market presence. They also had to develop these products according to fashion trends. The packaging for the products had to be designed to attract the right consumer.

Feminine Products Feminine products were the only products under the beauty/feminine care segment that were used only by females. They included products such as sanitary pads, tampons, heat patches, and disposable cups. In early 2006, the trends were that consumers wanted products that were more comfortable and easy to use. Some of these products affected the health of the consumers, so companies who produced them had to warn consumers about the possible side effects from using these products. An example of a product that came with such warnings was tampons. A possible side effect from using these products was Toxic Shock Syndrome, which was caused by a particularly virulent and penicillin resistant strain of bacterium.

The keys to success included several factors. There had to be a wide variety of these products available to the consumers. These products had to be competitively priced and affordable. The quality of these products had to be considered during production to maintain the company's brand quality reputation. Brand recognition was also an important factor. Location and distribution were also important to ensure these products had a mass market presence. The packaging for the products had to be designed to attract the right consumer.

Fine Fragrances The fragrance industry was a growing industry with companies like Estée Lauder, Calvin Klein, Tommy Hilfiger, and the like. It was a billion dollar industry and it was constantly changing due to the trends in fashion. In early 2006, many people enjoyed using these fragrances so they could smell clean and attractive.

The keys to success included several factors. Quality of these products had to be maintained to retain the company's brand quality reputation. These products had to be competitively priced. Brand recognition was also important. Location and distribution were also important to ensure these products had a mass market presence. They also had to develop these products according to fashion trends. The packaging for the products had to be designed to attract the right consumer.

Cosmetics The cosmetic industry was constantly changing according to its customer's need, but in early 2006, the growth in the industry was tremendous. Cosmetics have a temporary benefit and effect, so they have to be reapplied on a regular basis depending on the particular customer. This temporariness of the product made the market a continuous and strong one, because customers had to constantly go out and purchase new products. There were various products in this industry, which included concealers, powders, blushers, and the like, which were for the skin, and those for the lips, which included lip gloss, lip sticks, lip liner, and the like. It was estimated, as shown in Figure 7, that cosmetics (for face, lips, and eyes) should be worth just under $4 billion in 2010, in mass and prestige channels combined. From 2004–2010, this segment would expand by 26.5%, or $835 million. Cosmetic's CAGR for the same span was therefore calculated at 4% [Packaged Facts, 2005].

The cosmetic industry was also divided based on the customer's skin type. An example was the ethnic color-specific cosmetics, which were the best in this category and were predicted, as shown in Figure 5, to push to $493 million at retail by 2008.

The keys to success included several factors. The cosmetics products had to be competitively priced. Brand recognition was also an important factor because consumers needed to feel like they could relate with the brand and its attributes. Availability of a variety of these products was required to suit all consumers' needs. Location was also important, so that the companies manufacturing these products could maintain their brand quality reputation. New products had to be frequently developed according to fashion trends. Location and distribution were also important to ensure these products had a mass market presence. The packaging for the products had to be designed to attract the right consumer.

Personal Cleansing The personal cleansing products included products such as soap bars, body wash, body scrubbers, and the like. This segment of the industry had witnessed tough times as it sales declined by 11.9% from 2000 to 2004. This decline was largely due to consumers substituting bath products with higher multi-benefit skin care products at comparatively lower prices. The sales of personal cleansing products were projected to continue to decline by $210.3 million, from an estimated $2.4 billion in 2005, to $2.2 billion in 2010 [Packaged Facts, 2005].

The keys to success included several factors. The personal cleansing products had to be competitively priced. Availability of a variety of these products was required to suit all consumers' need. Brand recognition was also an important factor. Location and distribution were also important to ensure these products had a mass market presence. The manufacturing companies had to maintain their brand quality reputations. They had to also frequently introduce new products. The packaging for the products had to be designed to attract the right consumer.

Consumers

Consumers were those that ultimately used the products. Consumers made better purchasing decisions when they were aware of the products in the market. When they knew about the products, such as their price and quality, they had the choice to make a better purchase. The common mistakes that some consumers made were instinctive purchases and ignorantly following trends that did not necessarily affect them. There was a wide variety of products in the market place so most consumers could easily get the products they wanted. Consumers for this industry's products could be segmented into gender, age, ethnicity, marital status, and low income consumers.

Gender While most people thought that beauty/feminine care products were just for females, this was not the case because most of the products in this division were also used by males. Both groups needed these products to meet their basic needs such as cleansing products to keep their bodies clean. For many years, women represented a larger part of the customer and consumer base because of several factors, such as women were usually the ones that bought products for their homes and families, and some segments of this industry, like the feminine care, manufactured products that could be used only by women. But in early 2005, there was a trend for men to beautify themselves. This trend made manufacturing companies increase their production of men's products.

The keys to success included several factors. The beauty/feminine care products had to be competitively priced and affordable. There had to be a wide selection of these products available to the consumers, distributed through various channels. The quality and value had to be high for each of the products. Brand loyalty was also an important factor because some consumers had always used these products and wanted to continue using them. Location and distribution of these products were also important because these products had to have mass market presence. The packaging for the products had to be designed to attract the right consumer. Consumers had to have promotions targeted at them. An example of a promotion that attracted male consumers was to get a popular male celebrity to promote products.

Age   Age was another major factor that companies considered when analyzing the market. What was the age for their consumers? The answer was everyone, from infants to senior citizens. Everyone used beauty/feminine products. The manufacturing companies addressed each age group differently. For example, the baby boomers age group, which included consumers who were born during the period of an increased birth rate when economic prosperity arose in many countries following World War II. This term was commonly used to refer to the generation which demographic popularizers had identified as people who were born between 1946 and 1964 [Wikipedia, 2006].

In the United States the baby boomers made up the lion's share of the cultural, political, academic leadership and industrial class. They therefore were a group of people that had significant influence on the beauty/feminine care products. An example of their effect on a particular product can be seen using the hair care products. The number of men in the 55–64 age group, which represented half of the baby boomers, was expected to grow from 11.39 million in 1999 to 17.39 million in 2010, thus increasing

as percentage of the total male population from 8.3% to 11.5% [Packaged Facts, 2005]. As men grew older they were faced with issues like loss and dryness of hair. This forced them to spend more on hair care products. Companies were aware of this trend and were willing to produce these products because of the increase in that particular target age group.

The keys to success included several factors. The beauty/feminine care products had to be competitively priced and affordable. There also had to be a wide selection of these products available to the consumers. Brand recognition was also an important factor because consumers needed to feel like they could relate with the brand and its attributes. Location and distribution of these products were also important because these products had to have mass market presence. These products had to have a strong brand image. Brand loyalty was also an important factor because some consumers had always used their products.

Ethnicity   An ethnic group was a human population whose members identified with each other, usually on the basis of a common genealogy or ancestry. Ethnic groups were also usually united by common cultural, linguistic, religious, and behavioral practices [Wikipedia, 2006].

Each ethnic group had distinct tastes looks, and needs. It was important that the companies manufactured products that were suitable for them to use. To meet these different ethnic needs, the manufacturers had to perform in-depth research into each group. For example, in the United States, the population of the African American and Hispanics, which were big buyers of the hair care products, was very high. The Hispanics were estimated to increase from 12.6% in 2000 to 15.5% in 2010, while the African Americans would increase from 12.7% in 1999 to 13.1% in 2010. On the other hand, non-Hispanic whites were estimated to decline from 69.4% to 50.1% of the total population during 2000–2050 [U.S. Census Bureau, 2004].

Although ethnicity was an issue for manufacturers in the United States, it was not necessarily an issue for manufacturers in countries with one main ethnic group like Ghana. Consumers in countries like Ghana generally had the same hair type, skin types, beliefs, and the like. These differences in countries were issues that manufacturing companies had to take into consideration before manufacturing and promoting any products.

The keys to success included several factors. The beauty/feminine care products had to be competitively priced and affordable. There also had to be a wide selection of these products, tailored to meet the needs of each ethnic group. The products had to be of high quality and value. Brand loyalty was also an important factor because some consumers had always used their products. Brand recognition was also an important factor because consumers needed to feel like they could relate with the brand and its attributes. They also always had to be the development of products according to fashion trends.

Marital Status In 1998, 110.6 million adults (56% of the adult population) were married and living with their spouses [USCB, 1998]. This meant that there was a bigger part of the adult population which was buying things in bulk because they had to buy for the family. If 56% of the adult population was married, it meant that the remaining 44% were single. Single consumers had more disposable income, because they had more to spend on themselves. These consumers also spent a lot on beauty care products, because they wanted to keep themselves looking good and probably attract people to them.

The keys to success included several factors. The beauty/feminine care products had to be competitively priced and affordable. There also had to be a wide selection of these products available to the consumers that were tailored to meet their needs. The products had to be of high quality and value. Brand recognition was also an important factor because consumers needed to feel like they could relate with the brand and its attributes. The products had to be distributed properly to ensure that there was mass market presence. Brand loyalty was also an important factor because some consumers had always used their products.

Low Income Consumers The indebtedness of American households grew substantially in the last decade. The outstanding balance of all consumer credit, excluding mortgage debt, was $800 billion at the end of 1990 [Wikipedia, 2006]. This group of consumers was a very large part of the beauty/feminine care industry. Companies in this industry had to manufacture products that would be affordable for them. Some of the methods used to reduce the costs of the

products were reducing the size of the package and reducing the quality of the packaging.

The keys to success included several factors. The beauty/feminine care products had to have a wide selection of these products available to the consumers that were tailored to meet their needs. Brand recognition was also an important factor because consumers needed to feel like they could relate with the brand and its attributes. Brand loyalty was also an important factor because some consumers had always used their products. There also had to be mass market presence. The packaging for the products had to be designed to attract the right consumer.

Distribution

Distribution was the act of dispersing products from the point of production to the final consumer. Most distribution channels had a designated sales force which was in charge of selling and promoting their products. The sales force included individuals who were recruited to move from place to place encouraging customers to purchase their products. These individuals were encouraged to do a better job by offering them incentives such as days off and monetary incentives. Companies had various channels of distributions, such as distribution companies, individual stores, and chain store outlets.

Distribution Companies These were the middlemen that purchased directly from the manufacturers and resold them to the retailers for a profit. They were experts at moving things into the market. To do this most of them generally had a good transportation system. These companies normally bought in bulk to control their inventory and increase their profits.

The keys to success included several factors. Distribution companies had to offer competitive pricing. Prices they set were not only competitive with that of their competitors but also that of the manufacturing companies, which sold directly to the outlet store chains. Distributors had to also establish good relationships with the store managers to get good product display and shelf space. Some companies also incorporated supply chain technology with their retailers to ensure proper distribution of their products. Distribution companies had to recruit good employees and offer incentives for them to work hard.

Individual Stores Individual stores were stores that were owned by companies, where consumers could walk into and purchase the product they wanted. An advantage of this kind of service provided by companies was that they were able to remove the extra price allocated by the middlemen. It also gave them a chance to relate with their consumers and learn what they liked and disliked about their products, especially the male consumers who were generally not thought to purchase beauty/feminine care products. They also learned trends amongst their consumers and were able to educate them on their products. Also the presence of these stores in different communities helped to build a household name amongst the consumers.

The keys to success included several factors. Individual stores had to competitively price their products. Employees in these stores had to be willing to interact with customers to get their opinion about the products. The companies had to offer incentives to their employees to do a good job. These stores had to have a variety of products. Brand recognition was also an important factor. These stores had to be located in prime locations to attract more consumers.

Chain Store Outlets All over the world, the numbers of chain outlets were growing. In Taiwan the total number of chain store outlets grew 11% to 62,637 in 2004, according to a survey released in late April by the Taiwan Chain Store and Franchise Association. These were stores that sold a variety of products. In the United States, a large percentage of the population purchased beauty/feminine products in these types of stores. There were different types of chain stores outlets; some were specialized chain stores, where they sold a wide variety of products and offered very good customer service. Another kind of store was the discount store that offered a limited variety of products and did not spend too much of its resources on customer services. These stores had to pay special attention to their customers, especially the male customers, by offering sales and promotions on products that they thought these customers might be interested in. Some of these chain store outlets were Costco, Walgreens, Target, Sears, and Wal-Mart.

Costco. Costco was the largest membership warehouse club chain in the world. It was a discount chain store with about 456 locations worldwide. In 2004, the company's store sales rose 13% to $47.1 billion and its main competitor was Wal-Mart-owned Sam's Club [Wikipedia, 2006]. Since it was a discount chain store, it sold very high volume products for low prices, by keeping overhead low and using idiosyncratic inventory practices. It also bulk-packaged its products and sold primarily to large families and small businesses [Costco Services, 2006].

Walgreens. Walgreens was the nation's leading drugstore chain. It was a specialized chain store with about 4,000 locations. In January of 2005, its sales increased by 11.8% [Walgreens Corporate News, 2006]. It provided a wide array of products and was totally geared to providing its customers with complete satisfaction.

Target. Target was an upscale discounter that provided high-quality, on-trend merchandise at attractive prices in clean, spacious and guest-friendly stores. In addition, Target operated an online business, Target.com [Target Corporate News, 2006]. It had 1397 locations and had revenue of $15.2 billion for the last quarter of 2005.

Sears. Sears was a specialty outlet stores that provided a wide variety of services to its customers. It had revenues in 2004 of $36.1 billion. It had more than 2,400 Sears-branded and affiliated stores in the U.S. and Canada, which included approximately 870 full-line and 1,100 specialty stores in the U.S. Sears also offered its services through sears.com, landsend.com, and specialty catalogs [Aboutsears, 2006]. It was also the only retailer where consumers could find each of the Kenmore, Craftsman, DieHard, and Lands' End brands together.

Wal-Mart. Wal-Mart was a discount store outlet that sold to more than 138 million customers worldwide each week, with more than 1,500 locations. The company was growing constantly and had over $56 billion in international sales in 2005. It operated like Costco, which is described above [Wikipedia, 2006].

The keys to success included several factors. Chain store outlets had to be competitively priced. The stores had a variety of products for each consumer. They offered sales and promotions that attracted more consumers. They also provided free samples and trials for their consumers. The companies also provided websites that made it more convenient for consumers to shop from home. These stores were located in prime locations to attract more consumers. These stores had to recruit and maintain quality employees. Also they had to offer incentives to their employees. Manufacturers had to build strong relationships with these retailers to get shelf space, store promotion, and product display area.

Advertising

Advertising was used in the beauty/feminine care product industry to make consumers aware of the products that were available. It was done through various forms, but companies had to be careful in choosing the form that would be suitable to convey their message to their target consumers. Advertising could be done through television, Internet, print, radio, and sales and promotions.

Television Television was a very good form for advertising products because it had a large audience. Companies advertised through different methods; some would produce commercials that focused on their products while some would introduced their products in shows that they thought their target audience regularly watched. An example of a show that companies spent a lot of money on advertising was the Super Bowl in 2006. Some companies paid $3.5 million for 30 seconds to advertise their products. They believed that advertising their product during the show would help create awareness of their product.

The keys to success included several factors. Television stations had to be competitively priced. Manufacturers had to choose the appropriate channels and shows to advertise on. To do this successfully, they had to choose the audience they wanted to target for each product. The rating of the shows was an important factor that most companies considered before advertising on them. Sales promotions, coupons, and free products were good ways to attract the consumers.

Internet Globally, the Internet was quickly becoming the most popular form of advertising because it was accessible to potential customers all over the world. The Internet affected many aspects of consumers' lives: the way they worked, played, and communicated, etc. The keys to success included several factors. Websites had to be competitively priced. Manufacturers had to choose the appropriate sites to advertise on. To do this successfully, they had to choose the audience they wanted to target for each product. Sales promotions, coupons, and free products were good ways to attract the consumers.

Print This advertisement included those in the newspapers, magazines, and the like. In early 2006, companies were gradually reducing the use of newspaper for advertising. They were moving to other forms of advertising, because in the United States, studies showed that people were reading less. These made some companies change from this form of advertising to others so that they were sure their products' information would reach their target audience. The keys to success included several factors. Printing media had to be competitively priced. Manufacturers had to choose the appropriate books, magazines, and newspapers to advertise in. To do this successfully, they had to choose the audience they wanted to target for each product. Sales promotions, coupons, and free products were good ways to attract the consumers.

Radio Radio was another effective form of advertising. There were no visuals in radio advertising, just vocal information of the products. It had a large audience, especially people listening at work or in their cars. In 2005, the XM satellite radio was launched, and it offered a variety of channels including commercial free music channels. These features would encourage more people to listen to radio, creating a better channel for advertisement. The keys to success included several factors. Radio stations had to be competitively priced. Manufacturers had to choose the appropriate channels and shows to advertise on. To do this successfully, they had to choose the audience they wanted to target for each product. The rating of the shows was an important factor that most companies considered before advertising on them. Sales promotions, coupons, and free products were good ways to attract the consumers.

Advertisement was important to this industry. It helped educate the consumers on their products. It made them aware of the products, informed them of the uses, and encouraged them to go out and purchase them.

Sales and Promotions Various sales and promotions such as free samples, coupons, and discounts were used by companies to attract more consumers. These methods were especially effective for new products. Sales and promotions for these products normally encouraged the consumers to take the risk and try the new product. Chain store outlets also used these methods to attract more customers. The keys to success included several factors. Customers and consumers had to be aware of the sales and promotions. They also had to be easy to use and be available to the consumers and customers.

Geographic Region

A geographic region was a term used to refer to a separated place on earth, such as Africa, Asia, Australia, Europe, Latin America, and North America.

- **Africa**—Africa was a continent with countries like Botswana, which had a population of 1,640,115 people, and Nigeria, which had a population of 128,771,988 as of January, 2006 [CIA, 2006].

- **Asia**—Asia was a continent with countries like China, which had a population of 1,306,313,812 people, and Taiwan, with a population of 22,894,384 people [CIA, 2006].

- **Australia**—Australia was the sixth largest country in the whole world with about 20,090,437 people [CIA, 2006]. It was known for its uniqueness.

- **Europe**—Europe was a continent with countries like the United Kingdom, which had a population of about 60,441,457 people, and Spain, with about 40,341,462 people [CIA, 2006].

- **South America**—South America included countries like Brazil, with about 186,112,794 people, and Colombia, with about 42,954,279 people [CIA, 2006].

- **North America**—This was a continent with countries like the United States of America, which had a population of about 295,734,134 people, and Canada, with about 32,805,041 people [CIA, 2006].

These geographical regions had people who consumed beauty/feminine care products. So they were important for the existence of this industry. The keys to success included several factors. They had to be tailored to meet the needs of the consumers; for example, in Asia, manufacturers had to produce hair products that were suitable for straight, not curly hair. Brand recognition was also an important factor because consumers needed to feel like they could relate with the brand and its attributes. Products had to be competitively priced, and companies had to have a mass market presence in these regions.

Sourcing

Sourcing was a systematic procurement process that continuously improved and re-evaluated the purchasing activities of a company. It was a form of supply chain management. It involved various processes, such as formally selecting a vendor to supply a particular product or service that was routinely purchased by the company. This process included the definition of product and service requirements, identification of qualified suppliers, negotiation of pricing, service, delivery and payment terms, and supplier selection. Most times, the end result of the sourcing process was a negotiated contract with a preferred supplier [ICG Commerce, 2006].

Some manufacturing companies chose to outsource some or all of their processes to other companies in the same country they operated in or in another country. There were various reasons why companies outsourced; some did it because it was cheaper, while others did it because they lacked the expertise required to make their products better.

The keys to success included several factors. Sources who wanted to sell to these manufacturing companies had to make their products competitively priced. They also had to be conveniently located to the manufacturing companies. Lastly they had to have a good transportation system to move these materials to and from the manufacturing company.

Technology

The beauty/feminine care industry was a capital intensive industry. The companies that manufactured these products required highly mechanized assembly lines which were designed for long production runs and flexibility. These companies constantly manufactured the same products over and over again, so they had to have machines that could run for long periods of time. Also, due to the differences in their consumers, products sometimes had to be manufactured with some differences. An example was in the production of moisturizers; some consumers had oily skin while some had dry skin. During production, the companies had to make slight changes in the ingredients for their products to suit these differences in their consumers. In order to achieve this, the machineries used had to be designed in a way that it allowed such changes and flexibility.

The Internet made business easier for some companies because it provided a fast and efficient way for them to communicate amongst themselves, with their customers, suppliers, and distributors. It also gave them the opportunity to research and get more information that helped to make their products better. With the introduction of the Internet, companies created and designed websites that helped their consumers and customers learn more about them; it gave them an opportunity to purchase things from the companies without leaving their homes.

The keys to success included several factors. The companies had to use high quality machines and technology systems, so they continuously had problems with them. These equipments also had to be flexible in their functions so they could be used to manufacture different products. They also had to be competitively priced so that it was affordable by these companies. The websites had to be designed properly so that they were easy to use.

Competition

Competition in the beauty/feminine product was based on price, brand quality reputation, mass market presence, variety of products, brand recognition, and introduction of new products. Some of the companies in the beauty/feminine care industry were Unilever, Colgate-Palmolive, Playtex products, Avon, and Estée Lauder.

Unilever Unilever was founded in 1930 in England; it was an international manufacturer of leading brands in foods, home care and personal care, such as Axe, Dove, Lux, Pond's, Rexona, Sunsilk, and Vaseline. Every day 150 million people in over 150 countries used one of its products. Unilever believed that most of its brands gave the benefits of feeling and looking good. The trends the company addressed in early 2006 were aging populations, urbanization, changing diets, and lifestyles [Unilever Annual Report, 2005].

In regard to hair products, Unilever was strong in brand quality reputation, price competition, mass market presence, variety of products, and brand recognition. It was moderately competitive in frequently introducing new products. In regard to skin product, Unilever was also strong in all keys to success except for development of products according to fashion trends, in which the company was only moderately competitive. Lastly, in regard to the company's cleansing product, it was strong in all keys to success except for frequent new product introduction, in which the company was only moderately competitive. In early 2006, Unilever did not manufacture feminine products, fine fragrances, and cosmetics.

In regard to gender and age, it was strong in all keys to success. In regard to ethnicity, Unilever was

strong in all keys to success except for manufacturing products that were tailored to meet their needs and developing products according to trends, in which the company was a weak competitor. In regard to marital status, it was strong in all keys to success except for manufacturing products that were tailored to meet their needs, high quality and value, and mass market presence, in which the company was only moderately competitive. In regard to low income consumers, Unilever was strong in all keys to success except for manufacturing products that were tailored to meet their needs, in which it was only moderately competitive.

In regard to distribution companies, it was moderately competitive in all keys to success except for competitive price, in which the company was strongly competitive. In regard to chain store outlets, Unilever was strong in all keys to success except for recruiting quality employees, offering them incentives, and developing strong relationship with the store managers, in which it was only moderately competitive.

In regard to television advertising, the company was strong in all keys to success. The company was strong in all keys to success relating to Internet advertising. In regard to print advertising, the company was strong in all keys to success. The company was strong in all keys to success relating to radio advertising. In regard to geographic regions, it was strong in all keys to success except for mass market presence, in which it was moderately competitive. And in regard to sourcing, operations, and technology, Unilever was strong in all keys to success.

Colgate-Palmolive Colgate-Palmolive was a $10.6 billion global consumer goods company, operating in more than 200 countries, with approximately 70% of its sales coming from international operations. The Company focused on strong global brands in its core businesses—Oral Care, Personal Care, Home Care, and Pet Nutrition. Its worldwide sales were up 5.5% on unit volume growth of 4.5%, on top of 9.0% volume growth in the 2005 [Colgate Corporate News, 2006]. Worldwide it sold more than 40 different products and encouraged customers to try products by offering an array of sales promotions, such as coupons, free products, and discounts. Its beauty/feminine care products were Irish Spring, Palmolive, Softsoaps, Colgate, Protex, Speed Sticks, and Lady Sticks.

In regard to skin products, Colgate-Palmolive was strong in brand recognition, variety of products, brand quality reputation, price competition, and mass market presence. The company was moderately competitive in the development of products according to fashion trends. Also in regard to the company's cleansing products, Colgate-Palmolive was strong in all keys to success except for frequent new product introduction, in which the company was only moderately competitive. In early 2006, Colgate-Palmolive did not manufacture hair products, feminine products, fine fragrances, and cosmetics.

In regard to gender, age, and marital status, it was strong it all keys to success. In regard to ethnicity, the company was strong in all keys to success except for manufacturing products that were tailored to meet their needs and development of products according to fashion trends, in which it was a weak competitor. And in regard to low income consumers, it was moderately competitive in all keys to success.

In regard to distribution companies, it was strong in all keys to success. In regard to chain store outlets, Colgate-Palmolive was strong in all keys to success except for developing strong relationship with the store managers, in which it was only moderately competitive.

In regard to television advertising, the company was strong in all keys to success. The company was strong in all keys to success relating to Internet advertising. In regard to print advertising, the company was strong in all keys to success. The company was strong in all keys to success relating to radio advertising. In regard to geographic regions, it was strong in all keys to success except for mass market presence, in which it was moderately competitive. And in regard to sourcing, operations and technology, the company was strong in all keys to success.

Playtex Products Playtex Products was a leading manufacturer and distributor of personal care products. It was founded in 1932 as the "International Latex Corporation" in Rochester, New York, selling latex products under the "Playtex" name. In January 1994, the Company went public as Playtex Products, Inc. Since then, Playtex has acquired many leading consumer brands, including Banana Boat, Wet Ones, Mr. Bubble, Ogilvie, Binaca, Diaper Genie and Baby Magic. Approximately 98% of the Company's net sales were from products that were number one or two in their respective markets. Net sales for the company from October 1, 2004 to October 1, 2005 were $651 million, continuing the Company's upward trend in sales of non-divested brands [Playtex Products Corporate News, 2006].

The company's Feminine Care products were leading the plastic applicator and deodorant tampon categories with brands like Gentle Glide, Beyond, and Portables. Also its skin care segment included Banana Boat sun care, Wet Ones hand and face wipes and Playtex Gloves. The Banana Boat brand offered a full spectrum of sun block, tanning, sunless tanning, and after-sun products. Banana Boat was the number two brand overall and the number one brand in after-sun care. Wet Ones and Playtex Gloves were both leaders in their markets [Playtex Products Corporate News, 2006].

In regard to skin products, Playtex Products was strong in brand quality reputation and price competition. It was moderately competitive in its variety of products and mass market presence, and it was competitively weak in terms of brand recognition and development of products according to fashion trends. In regard to feminine products, the company was strong in all keys to success except for brand recognition and variety of products, in which the company was only moderately competitive. In early 2006, Playtex Products did not manufacture hair products, fine fragrances, cosmetics, and personal cleansing products.

In regard to gender, it was strong in all keys to success except for various distribution channels and mass market presence, in which the company was only moderately competitive. In regard to age, Playtex Products was moderately competitive in all keys to success except in competitive pricing, in which it was strongly competitive. In regard to marital status, it was moderately competitive in all keys to success. And in regard to low income consumers, it was moderately competitive in all keys to success except for brand recognition, in which it was a weak competitor.

In regard to distribution companies and chain stores outlets, it was moderately competitive in all keys to success. In regards to television advertising, the company was strong in all keys to success. The company was strong in all keys to success relating to Internet advertising. In regard to print advertising, the company was strong in all keys to success. The company was strong in all keys to success relating to radio advertising. In regard to geographic regions, it was moderately competitive in all keys to success, except for competitive pricing, in which it was strongly competitive. And in regard to sourcing, operations and technology, Playtex Products was strong in all keys to success.

Avon   Avon was the world's largest direct seller with almost 5 million representatives. Its products were available to consumers in 100 countries, with its representatives earning about $3 billion annually. It all started in 1886 in the United States. In 2005, it became the world leader in anti-aging skin care products [Avon Annual Report, 2005].

The company's skin care brands included Anew—a ground-breaking line of anti-aging skincare products. This brand contained popular products like Anew Retroactive+ and Anew Ultimate. Other products were the new blockbuster, Anew Clinical brands, a brand of targeted skin treatments that offered at-home alternatives to professional cosmetic treatments, and also Avon solutions—which was a full line of products that simplified the process of buying skincare without compromising results. Its hair care brands included Advance Techniques—which offered high performance hair products for every hair type, age group, and ethnic background to accommodate a diverse worldwide consumer base, and all of the products were formulated with conditioning ingredients that prevented long-term damage to hair. Avon was also the world's largest sellers of perfumes, with brands like Treselle, Perceive, Today, Tomorrow, and Always Trilogy. In early 2006, Avon did not manufacture hair products and feminine products.

In regard to skin products, Avon was strong in brand quality reputation, price competition, and mass market presence. The company was moderately competitively in terms of brand recognition, variety of products, and development of products according to fashion trends. In regard to fine fragrances, the company was strong in brand quality reputation, price competition, and mass market presence. It was moderately competitive in brand recognition and development of products according to fashion trends. In the cosmetics segment of Avon, the company was strong in brand quality reputation, price competition, and mass market presence. It was moderately competitive in the variety of products, brand recognition, development of new products according to fashion trends. The cleansing products manufactured by Avon were strong in all keys to success except for brand recognition and frequent introduction of new products, in which it was moderately competitive.

In regard to gender, it was strong in all keys to success except for various distribution channels and mass market presence, in which the company was only moderately competitive. In regard to age, Avon was moderately competitive in all keys to success except in competitive pricing, in which it was strongly competitive. In regard to ethnicity, the company was strongly competitive in price competition and high quality and value; it was moderately competitive in tailoring products to meet their needs, brand recognition, and brand loyalty, and weakly competitive when it came to the development of products according to fashion trends. In regard to marital status, it was moderately competitive in all keys to success except for competitive pricing and high quality and value, in which it was strongly competitive. And in regard to low income consumers, it was moderately competitive in all keys to success.

In regard to distribution companies and chain stores outlets, it was moderately competitive in all keys to success, except for competitive pricing, in which it was strongly competitive. In regard to television advertising, the company was strong in all keys to success. The company was strong in all keys to success relating to Internet advertising. In regard to print advertising, the company was strong in all keys to success. The company was strong in all keys to success relating to radio advertising. In regard to geographic regions, it was moderately competitive in all keys to success, except for competitive pricing, in which it was strongly competitive. And in regard to sourcing, operations and technology, Avon was strong in all keys to success.

Estée Lauder   Estée Lauder was founded in 1946; this technologically advanced, innovative company has gained a worldwide reputation for elegant, luxurious products in over 100 countries. The Company distributed its various products through department and specialty stores. The company was very involved in the breast cancer awareness program, being the largest corporate sponsor of The Breast Cancer Research Foundation, founded by Evelyn H. Lauder in 1993 [Estée Lauder Annual Report, 2005].

Its skin care segment included brands such as Re-Nutriv—which was an anti-aging cream for the eyes, Self-Tan—an air-brush self-tan spray for body, and Perfectionist—an anti-aging product for skin and lips. The cosmetics segments also included brands such as Pure Color Crystals, Graphic Color Eye

Shadow Quad, Double Wear, and Prime FX. Lastly its fragrance segment included brands like Beautiful, Pleasure, Intuitions, and Paradise. In early 2006, Estée Lauder did not manufacture hair products, feminine products, and personal cleansing products.

In regard to skin products, Estée Lauder was strong in brand quality reputation and price competition. It was moderately competitive in its variety of products and mass market presence, and it was competitively weak in terms of brand recognition and development of products according to fashion trends. In regard to fine fragrances, the company was strong in brand quality reputation, price competition, and mass market presence. It was moderately competitive in brand recognition and development of products according to fashion trends. In the cosmetics segment of Estée Lauder, the company was strong in brand quality reputation and price competition. It was moderately competitive in the variety of products and brand recognition. In terms of mass market presence and the frequent development of new products according to fashion trends, the company was competitively weak.

In regard to gender, it was moderately competitive in all keys to success except for high quality and value and promotion targeted to them, in which Estée Lauder was strongly competitive. In regard to age and marital status, it was moderately competitive in all keys to success. And in regard to low income consumers, it was a weak competitor in all keys to success, except for brand recognition, in which it was moderately competitive.

In regard to distribution companies and chain stores outlets, it was moderately competitive in all keys to success. In regard to television advertising, the company was strong in all keys to success. The company was strong in all keys to success relating to Internet advertising. In regard to print advertising, the company was strong in all keys to success. The company was strong in all keys to success relating to radio advertising. In regard to geographic regions, it was moderately competitive in all keys to success. And in regard to sourcing, operations, and technology, Estée Lauder was strong in all keys to success.

The Company

P&G was a company that manufactured, distributed and marketed consumer goods products. It was established in 1837 in the United States. It later started expanding to other countries, and in early 2006 it was one of the global leaders in the consumer goods industry. It acquired its first overseas subsidiary with the purchase of Thomas Hedley & Sons Company, UK, in 1930. Also in 1915, P&G built a manufacturing facility in Canada, its first outside the U.S. [Datamonitor, 2006].

In early 2006, the company had its headquarters in Cincinnati, Ohio. In the United States, the company owned and operated 35 manufacturing facilities, which were located in 21 different states. Worldwide, the company owned and operated 83 manufacturing facilities in 42 countries. P&G provided branded products and services of superior quality and value that improved the lives of consumers all over the world. And as a result, it believed that the consumers rewarded it with leadership sales, profit, and value creation. These results allowed its people, shareholders, and the communities in which they lived and worked to prosper [P&G Company Information, 2006].

P&G's top 10 customers were Ahold, Albertson's, Carrefour, Costco, Kmart, Kroger, Metro, Target, Tesco, and Wal-Mart. The company always acquired new brands and products, either by creating them or by merging with other companies. An example of these mergers was in 1985, P&G expanded its over-the-counter and personal health care business with the acquisition of Richardson-Vicks, owners of Vicks respiratory care and Oil of Olay product lines. Also in 1988, the company announced a joint venture to manufacture products in China. This marked the company's foray into the largest consumer market in the world [Datamonitor, 2006].

One of the threats that P&G faced was intense competition. It operated in an industry with rivals such as Unilever, Colgate-Palmolive, Playtex Products, Avon, and Estée Lauder. These companies operated and sold their products worldwide. Their presence in the same industry put pressure on P&G to competitively price its products and continually strive to develop innovative products. Another threat was the increase in prices of raw materials. These prices were subject to price volatility caused by weather, supply conditions, and other unpredictable factors.

Lastly, the risk associated with merger integration was another threat for this company. In September 2003, P&G acquired Wella, owning 79.2 percent of the company's total shares. This acquisition contributed about $3.3 billion in sales to P&G's overall beauty business—around $1.6 billion in the professional hair care segment, $1 billion in the retail hair care segment, and $800 million in fragrances. However, Wella's results (as of October 2003) were falling below P&G's stated long-term targets, giving an early indication of disruptions post its takeover [Datamonitor, 2006]. Other brands acquired by P&G were Clairol from Bristol-Myers Squibb in 2001 and Gillette in 2005.

In 2004, P&G did not manufacture products that were specifically for different ethnic groups, such as Hispanic and African American, and products that were made with natural ingredients. There was a high demand for these types of products because some consumers wanted to use products that were made from natural ingredients and some consumers wanted products that were made for their ethnic group.

In the United States it was virtually impossible to calculate the absolute number of companies that produced and marketed beauty/feminine care products. The field of competition was highly fragmented, for example, between those companies active in mass channels (supermarkets, chain drugstores, and mass merchandisers) and prestige channels, not to mention those active in the natural food and beauty care channel. The company size was another factor, between globally-oriented mega-corporations like P&G and kitchen table-based entrepreneurs limited to regional or even local distribution.

Although it was impossible to calculate the number of companies that produced and marketed beauty/feminine care products, it was obvious that P&G was one of the leaders in this industry because, as illustrated in Figure 8, P&G was well ahead of the industry.

P&G faced various challenges in 2006, such as consumers' interest in natural products. This trend was as a result of consumers questioning the ingredients used in making products and their effects. Some activists claimed that these products contained toxic chemicals known to cause cancer, fertility problems, and birth defects. Another challenge was the stagnant sales of some products due to low product development and innovation. Duane Reade Inc.'s Divisional Merchandise Manager, Mike Cirilli, said, "The market's poor sales will only turn around with the launch of dramatically different products. We need the leaders in these categories, such as P&G and L'Oreal, to come out with some revolutionary products, spend $100 million on them in advertising and get all the

FIGURE 8

Financial Information of P&G and the Industry

	P&G	Industry
Market Capital	202.67B	275.79M
Employees	110,000	2.81K
Quarterly Revenue Growth	26.90%	10.40%
Revenue	61.68B	1.74B
Gross Margin	51.05%	36.68%
EBITDA	14.42B	262.13M
Operating Margins	19.95%	7.40%
Net Income	7.77B	13.16M
EPS	2.733	1.23
P/E	22.55	22.50
PEG (5 yr expected)	2.02	2.02
P/S	3.28	2.05

Source: Yahoo Finance (2006). "Procter & Gamble 2006." [Online]. *http://finance.yahoo.com/q/co?s=PG*. Accessed March 17, 2006.

consumers excited again. We need excitement. Excitement and advertising spending will bring sales dollars to these categories" [Packaged Facts, 2005].

The emerging men's market was another trend that was affecting the industry. The number of men spending time in front of the mirror, grooming themselves had increased. The acquisition of Gillette helped P&G to start to address this trend with products like Gillette's complete skin care for men and Gillette's Fusion. This was some of the steps that P&G decided to take to remain at the top in the beauty/feminine care segment. Following were detailed analyses of P&G's business model, as illustrated on the next page in Figure 9. It serves as the framework in discussing the company's strategy on business development.

Products

When the company started in 1837, it was producing only two products, candles and soap. In early 2006, P&G was manufacturing, marketing, and distributing close to a hundred different brands. These brands and products were sold to consumers worldwide.

In 2005, the beauty/feminine care segment of P&G delivered its third consecutive year of double digit growth in volume, sales, and profit. Volume increased 12%, sales increased 14%, and net earnings

FIGURE 9

Procter & Gamble (P&G)

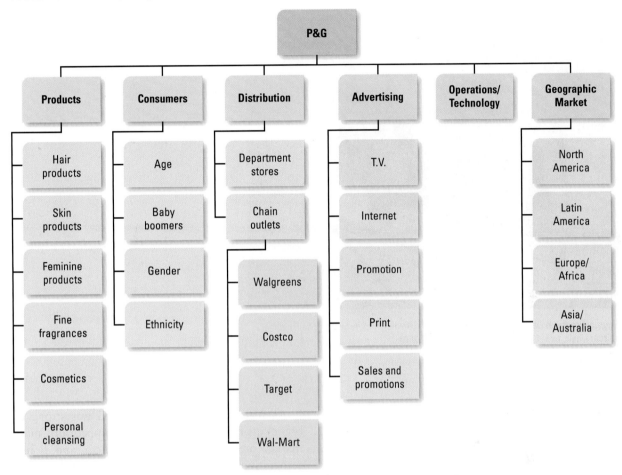

increased 22%. The industry leading performance was driven mainly by broad-based organic growth across geographies and brands. Each of its top 10 countries delivered higher sales than 2004, with solid gains in both developed and developing markets. Global market shares continued to grow, with most of its leading brands at record highs [P&G Annual Report, 2005].

P&G produced products that were used by male and females. With the growing trend for men to use beauty products, the company started manufacturing more products for them. They designed the products so that they would attract male consumers, by using dark colors for the packaging so that it looked more masculine. Some of P&G's products were hair products, skin products, feminine products, fine fragrances, cosmetics, and personal cleansing products.

Hair Products P&G offered a variety of hair products. These products passed through different processes before they reached the consumers. A major process was the testing phase. These products were developed for different types of hair—normal, dry, greasy, permed, bleached, and so on. So each product had to be tested, not only as a formulation that was to be stored for months in a bottle or tube and then sold, but also as a product that was to be used on human hair and scalp.

The process started in the laboratory; the experimental formulation was thoroughly tested on cut lengths of human hair, as shown in Figure 10, before production was considered.

The product under test was applied to the hair and rinsed off, and an experienced technician judged the amount of tangling, stretching, perming, and coloring

FIGURE 10

Cut Lengths of Human Hair

Source: Procter & Gamble (2006). "Hair product." [Online]. http://www.pg.com/science/haircare/hair_twh_116.htm. Accessed March 17, 2006.

that resulted. After that, a complex computer-assisted technology assessed many aspects of the product's performance. If all went well, the products were evaluated in real life conditions, on the hair of clients in salons. This was an essential part of testing, because it was the only way to judge whether the new product was acceptable to consumers. Only when these tests were completed safely and satisfactorily did the products go on the open market for the consumers to try. This whole process might have involved thousands of tests and took up to a couple of months or even years to complete [P&G Hair Care, 2003].

Some of the hair products brands which were produced by P&G were: Herbal Essences—this brand offered a variety of shampoo, conditioners and styling aids; Infusium 23—this brand included shampoos, conditioners, specialty care products, leave-ins; Physique—these products included cutting-edge technology formulas; Pantene—these products included amino pro-v complex; Aussie—these products were produced using Australian ingredients; and Head and Shoulders—products used to eliminate dryness, irritation, and itchiness of the scalp.

In regard to hair products, P&G was strong in brand quality reputation, price competition, mass market presence, variety of products, and brand recognition. It was moderately competitive in frequently introducing new products.

Skin Products P&G tried to address the three main types of skin, which were oily, normal, and dry. Some of the skin care products brands it produced were: Noxzema—this included facial cleansers in the form of creams, pads, and astringents; Gillete—this included shave multigel, facial moisturizers, razors, shaving sticks, and skin soothing after shave; and Olay—this brand offered products that provided multiple benefits that were designed for women of all ages.

Each product was made for a different function. The skin cleanser was used to remove surface dirt, make-up, top layer of dead skin cells and potentially harmful micro-organisms (bacteria). Skin toner was used after cleansing to ensure complete removal from the skin of all cleansing preparations, and also after a face mask to remove all traces of the mask. These products were based on plant extracts and sometimes contained alcohol. Skin moisturizers hydrated the skin, and/or protected the skin from dehydration. That is, they were designed to improve water retention in the skin. They could be in the form of creams, lotions or serums [P&G Skin Care, 2003].

In regard to skin products, P&G was strong in brand recognition, variety of products, brand quality reputation, price competition, and mass market presence. It was moderately competitive in the development of products according to fashion trends.

Feminine Products Some of the feminine products brands produced by P&G were: Tampax—this brand included different sizes of tampons. Another brand was Always, which included different styles and sizes of sanitary pads. Always was the world's leading feminine care brand; it grew in volume by 11% and reached record-high global market share of 22% [P&G Annual Report, 2005]. Feminine products were specifically for females to use during their menstrual cycles. The target consumers for these products were generally females from the ages of 12 to 50 years old.

In regard to feminine products, P&G was strong in brand quality reputation, price competition, mass market presence, variety of products, and brand recognition.

Fine Fragrances P&G was a major distributor of fine fragrances brands such as: Giorgio Beverly Hills—this included products such as Giorgio, G and Red. Another brand was Hugo Boss—which included Hugo Deep Red, Hugo Woman and Hugo Energise, which were used by either men or women. Hugo Boss, along with Lacoste—which was now 10 times bigger than when P&G acquired the license in 2001—further strengthened its global leadership position in men's fine fragrances [P&G Annual Report, 2005].

In regard to fine fragrances, P&G was strong in brand quality reputation, price competition, brand recognition, and mass market presence. It was moderately competitive in the development of products according to fashion trends.

Cosmetics P&G's target consumer for cosmetics were women of all ages. The cosmetics included those for lips, face, nails, eyes, etc. P&G had two major brands for cosmetics. First was CoverGirl, which was for women who wanted to have a clean, fresh, and natural look. It included foundation, loose powder, eye shadow, mascara, etc. The other brand was the Max Factor, which gave women a more edgy look, making them look more like celebrities. This brand also included various products, such as lip gloss, mascara, eye shadow, etc.

In regard to cosmetics, P&G was strong in variety of products, brand quality reputation, brand recognition, price competition, and mass market presence. It was moderately competitive in the development of products according to fashion trends and in frequently introducing new products.

Personal Cleansing P&G had a couple of brands that included personal cleansing products. These products included bar soaps, body wash and cleansing bars that were used for cleaning the body. The target consumers for these products were everybody. People needed to stay clean to reduce infections, illness, and smell that were related to dirt. One of the brands that P&G provided was Zest. It believed that this product was refreshingly different from ordinary soap. It rejuvenated the consumer with a combination of great, refreshing scent and clean-rinsing lather that would not dry skin like soap [P&G Product Information, 2006]. Other products were Camay, which was a moisturizing bar soap enriched with perfumes of French inspiration that P&G believed would leave skin feeling fresh, soft and sensual, and Noxzema, which included creams, astringents, and pads used for deep cleaning.

In regard to personal cleansing products, P&G was strong in brand recognition, price competition, variety of products, brand quality reputation, and mass market presence. It was moderately competitive in frequently introducing new products.

Consumers

Consumer goods were used by everyone. Consumers for P&G's products could be segmented into age, gender, ethnicity, and low-income consumers.

Age P&G addressed each age group differently and produced products that were suitable for them to use. An example was the group of people who were showing signs of aging. P&G understood that as people aged, their skin's vitality and radiance were reduced. So in the skin care segment, the company produced products that would address these issues. One of the products it produced was Olay's Total Effects, which it believed would fight seven signs of aging. These products diminished the appearance of fine lines and wrinkles, smoothed skin texture, evened skin tone, improved surface dullness, gave skin a radiant, healthy glow, minimized the appearance of pores, visibly reduced the appearance of blotches and age spots, and soothed dry skin [P&G Product Information, 2006].

When it came to the company's hair products, an example of the group of people it considered was the baby boomers and senior citizens. These people had similar issues such as loss and dryness of hair. P&G produced products like Head and Shoulders, which eliminated dryness, itchiness, and irritations. Another product which P&G produced that could be used by these age groups was the Pantene Sheer Volume, because it increased hair volume and made it look healthier.

In regard to age, P&G was strong in brand image, brand recognition, price competition, variety of products, brand loyalty, and mass market presence.

Gender P&G manufactured products that could be used by both men and women. Some products could be used by both groups, while others were specifically for either one of them.

In 2005, the men's beauty market was emerging and growing at a very fast rate. Men were more interested in grooming themselves and looking good. Some people called this group of men metrosexuals because they liked to groom and take care of themselves. P&G acknowledged this trend and in late 2005, the company acquired Gillette. This acquisition put P&G at the top of this market. It produced products like Gillette Fusion, Gillette Complete Skin Care, and Gillette MacH3, which were used by men to keep themselves looking good.

Women, on the other hand, have always been interested in looking beautiful. P&G had various products that satisfied their needs, from Olay's base moisturizers that smoothed and softened skin to CoverGirl cosmetics that were used to put on the most beautiful face possible [P&G Product Information, 2006]. The P&G Beauty segment was focused on delivering consumer understanding that reached beyond functional needs to connect at a deeper emotional level. It was a leader in innovation that went beyond science to include sophisticated design that created a total beauty experience and delight for consumers [P&G Annual Report, 2005]. These processes

made the consumers connect with the company and its attributes, building consumer loyalty and brand recognition.

In regard to gender, P&G was strong in price competition, high quality and value, brand loyalty, promotion targeted to them, various distribution channels, and mass market presence.

Ethnicity P&G understood that its consumers belonged to different ethnic groups. It produced products that would suit their different needs. To be very effective in reaching these groups, P&G set up strategies to market these groups. In 2005, P&G was one of the leaders in multicultural marketing and was awarded for its jobs by agencies. An example of an agency that awarded the company was the Association of Hispanics Advertising Agencies.

Another ethnic group that P&G was actively involved with was the African Americans. In 2005, Anne Sempowski Ward, the Associate Marketing Director for the African American Marketing team of P&G, released the following statement:

> P&G's commitment to African-Americans is stronger today than ever before. It has spanned more than a century and is still growing—a collective accomplishment rooted in the vision and actions of our leadership, the involvement of our local plants, and the interest of individual employees. African-American ideas, experiences, customs and lifestyles are represented throughout our advertising and packaging and have inspired several product innovations. We look forward to the next 100 years, and thank you for your support as P&G continues to make journeys of hope, freedom and success possible. [P&G Ethnic Echoes, 2005]

An example of how P&G incorporated ethnicity into its products was in the hair care segment for ethnic groups such as Caucasians, which included people who had different colors of hair. The company produced Clairol's highlighting and blonding, which helped to color and maintain the color of hair.

In regard to ethnicity, P&G was strong in products tailored to meet their needs, brand recognition, developing products according to fashion trends, price competition, high quality and value, and brand loyalty.

Low Income Consumers P&G was constantly innovating ways to reach more consumers. The low income consumers were a group that the company really wanted to target. It understood that these people had low disposable income and decided to manufacture products that they could afford. Some ways it reduced the prices of its products were to reduce the sizes of these products. It also changed some of its packages, so that the product was cheaper and easier to store. An example was changing the package from boxes to bags.

In regard to low income consumers, P&G was strong in products tailored to meet their needs, brand recognition, mass market presence, and brand loyalty.

Distribution

P&G had a very effective distribution system. It was used to distribute its products to its consumers. This function was also a form of capital for the company, when it helped other companies distribute their products. P&G had various distribution centers all over the world. In June 2005, P&G built a new Canadian Distribution Center in Brantford, Ontario. This center was built to serve the company's $2 billion national business. The site employed more than 150 people and the total investment was estimated to be $70 million [P&G Annual Report, 2005].

In the United States, a major distribution center was the Brown Summit, which was located in Greensboro, North Carolina. The center held over 1,000 different products. Most of these products were from U.S. plants and were shipped when orders were made

by the customers. The distribution channels of P&G included department stores, such as Macy's and JCPenney, and discount stores, such as Wal-Mart and Costco. P&G's biggest customer is Wal-Mart. In the 1980s, the two giants built a software system that linked P&G up to Wal-Mart's distribution centers. This system was called the Supply Chain System (SCS). It was used to facilitate the coordination with outside business entities. In the case of P&G and Wal-Mart, whenever the inventory level of P&G's products at Wal-Mart's distribution centers reached re-order point, the system automatically alerted P&G to ship more products. This process helped to manage inventory and increase profit. P&G distributed its products through distribution companies and chain store outlets.

In regard to distribution, P&G was strong in all keys to success, such as price competition, variety of products, recruiting good employees, offering incentives to employees, strong relationship with store manager, and store sales and promotion.

Advertising

With over 300 brands to market, P&G was specialized in advertising its products. For the past 5 years, the company has constantly increased its advertising cost, as shown in Figure 11, to accommodate its growing brands. The company used various media to reach its consumers, such as the television, Internet, radio and print. It offered sale promotions, such as free trials, discounts and coupons. These advertisements

FIGURE 11

Advertising Expenses

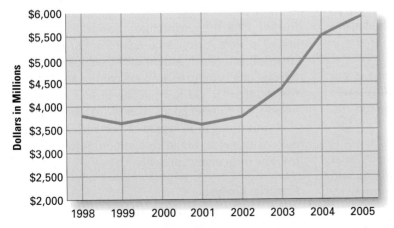

Source: P&G Annual Report (2005). [Online]. *http://www.pg.com/annualreport/2005/pdf/ pG2005annualreport.pdf.* Accessed March 17, 2006.

served different purposes for the company. First they made consumers aware of the products. These advertisements were sometimes made to be interactive, so that they held the consumer's attention. They also served to make the consumers aware of sale promotions that were going on at a particular time. And lastly they helped to convince consumers that they needed the products, so they actually went out and purchased them.

In each segment of the company, P&G hired employees who were responsible for marketing its products. These representatives would move from store to store, selling its products to the store managers. These interactions helped to build a better relationship with the store managers, because these managers helped increase and maximize shelf space and also provided better displays for P&G's products. P&G advertised on television, Internet, print, and radio.

Television P&G created commercials and it was careful to choose the right channels and shows that it hoped its target consumers viewed. Most of its commercials showed people using its products and their experiences after using them.

Internet P&G used the Internet to advertise because it could reach its consumers worldwide. It did this advertisement through various methods, such as posters on websites, emailing codes for samples and discounts, and the like.

Print In 2000, advertising in prints such as newspapers, magazines, and the like was declining. In early 2006, P&G still used this form of advertising to reach those consumers that read these prints. It advertised its products by showing pictures of people using its products or just by showing its products and explaining their uses.

Radio P&G also advertised on radio because it was effective in reaching some consumers. Since radio was audio, P&G did not have to spend money on creating and directing visual commercials.

Sales and Promotions P&G also used various sales and promotions such as free samples, coupons, and discounts. These methods were used by the company to attract more consumers. These methods were especially effective for new products. Sale and promotion for these products normally encouraged the

consumers to take the risk and try the new product. P&G's consumers had to be made aware of the sales and promotions so they could go out and use them to purchase the products.

In regard to advertising, P&G was strong in all keys to success, such as ratings, audience, price of advertisement, offering coupons and samples, availability, easy to use, and awareness.

Operations/Technology

P&G was a manufacturing company that prided itself on the quality of its products. To achieve such high quality, the company had to ensure it had the right machines and facilities required to manufacture its products. When the company could not effectively manufacture parts of its product, it outsourced that function to another company to help it do it better.

With the introduction of the Internet, P&G moved to greater heights. It created numerous ways for the company to do business in a faster and more efficient way. It was easier for it to communicate with its customers, suppliers, and distributors. It also gave P&G the opportunity to research and get more information that helped to make its products better. With the introduction of the Internet, P&G created and designed its website that helped its consumers and customers learn more about the company; it gave them an opportunity to purchase things from the company without leaving their homes.

In regard to operations/technology, P&G was strong in all keys to success, such as high quality machines and technology, flexibility, competitive price, affordability, and properly designed websites.

Geographical Regions

In early 2006, the geographical regions that P&G operated in were Africa, Asia, Australia, Europe, South America, and North America. The company did not operate in all countries in these continents. Some of the countries it did not operate in had a high demand for consumer goods such as Togo in Africa.

It was strong in all keys to success such as products tailored to needs, brand recognition, price competitive, and mass market presence.

Financial Analysis

For the past 5 years, P&G's net sales have grown, as shown in Figure 12a and Figure 12b. The company was a global leader with sales growth of more than 40%,

FIGURE 12

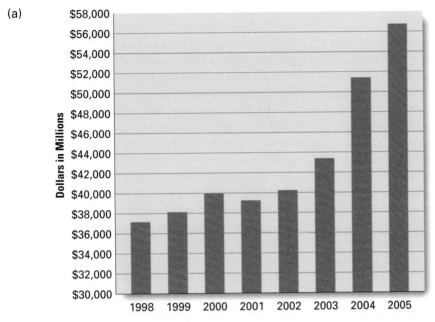

P&G's Financial Data—Net Sales

(a)

(b)

Amounts in millions except per share amounts	Years Ended June 30					
	2005	**2004**	**2003**	**2002**	**2001**	**2000**
Net sales	$56,741	$51,407	$43,377	$40,238	$39,244	$39,951
Operating income	10,927	9,827	7,853	6,678	4,736	5,954
Net earnings	7,257	6,481	5,186	4,352	2,922	3,542
Net earnings margin	12.8%	12.6%	12.0%	10.8%	7.4%	8.9%
Basic net earnings per common share	$2.83	$2.46	$1.95	$1.63	$1.08	$1.30
Diluted net earnings per common share	2.66	2.32	1.85	1.54	1.03	1.23
Dividends per common share	1.03	0.93	0.82	0.76	0.70	0.64

Source: P&G Annual Report (2005). [Online]. *http://www.pg.com/annualreports/2005/pdf/ pG2005annualreport.pdf.* Accessed March 17, 2006.

increasing to $57 billion. P&G's profit also more than doubled in 2005, and it generated more than $30 billion in free cash flow. Shareholders received $11 billion in cash through dividends, and this increased their value with another $60 billion by nearly doubling the price of P&G stock. The company has increased sales per employee nearly 40% over the past five years, and even though Research and Development (R&D) investment has increased over the past years, R&D as a percentage of sales has declined from 4.8% in 2000 to 3.4% in 2005. More than 80% of initiatives succeeded in creating shareholder value,

an improvement of 25% over the past three years. The productivity of P&G's product supply organization has increased at a high single-digit rate since 2000, and there had been a decrease in P&G's Global Business Services (GBS) costs by more than 15% on base business services since 2000.

Companies tried to increase profit by various methods. One of these methods was to reduce cost. P&G reduced capital spending as a percentage of sales since 2000 from nearly 8% to less than 4%, without forgoing any strategic investment in growth. They also added an incremental growth point to the company's top line over the past two years with marketing Return on Investment (ROI) initiatives [P&G Annual Report, 2005].

Management Strategy

One of P&G's strategies was to build existing core businesses into stronger global leaders. In 2005, the company grew market share, profit, and sales in all its core categories, such as its beauty and health segments. These increases were achieved by the decision to reach more consumers, especially low income consumers and the acquisition of Gillette. This acquisition increased the brands, products, and consumers of the company. Another strategy was to develop faster-growing, higher-margin, more asset efficient businesses with global leadership potential. In 2005, this was evident in the beauty segment, where sales nearly doubled to $19.5 billion and profit more than doubled to $2.9 billion. This growth was also noticed in the Health Care segment, where sales doubled to $7.8 billion and profit more than tripled to $1 billion. These two segments made up 47% of P&G's sales and 50% of the company's profit [P&G Annual Report, 2005].

Internationally, P&G tried to regain growth momentum and leadership in Western Europe, by introducing new products and increasing advertisements. In 2005, the Western Europe volume went up mid-single digit and on average it went up twice the rate of Western Europe Gross Domestic Profit (GDP) growth. At the end of the year, the company's brands growing share in categories accounted for more than half of Western Europe sales. Another major strategy for P&G was to increase growth among lower-income consumers in developing markets, such as Nigeria and Ghana. To attract these consumers, P&G changed the package, making it small and reducing the quality of the packaging, so it was more affordable for these consumers. This strategy has delivered mid-teens volume growth, on average, in these countries.

Looking Towards the Future

Since 2000, A.G. Lafley and his colleagues have been successful in trying to maximize the strengths of the company, while also reducing its weaknesses. They have worked to increase P&G's brands, net sales, and profit. In 2005, male consumers became more interested in beauty products, and to satisfy this need and other issues the company were facing, P&G acquired

Gillette. It also entered a major multimedia marketing partnership with Viacom Plus in 2001, to create more ways to reach its consumers.

On various occasions, the executives and employees of P&G discussed strategies that would make P&G a better company and put it ahead of its competitors, such as Unilever, Colgate-Palmolive, Playtex Products, Avon, and Estée Lauder. Some of the strategies they discussed are as follows:

The first alternative was for P&G to expand and build existing core businesses, such as the health and beauty segments. It decided to do this by reaching more consumers, especially the low income consumers. These segments would be expanded to include new brands and products which would attract such consumers. The already existing products would be altered by reducing their sizes and changing their packages to reduce their prices. Doing this would make it easier for consumers to buy them.

The benefit of this strategic alternative was that P&G would only have to expand on products and services it already had. It would not have to spend a lot of money on research and development, reducing the cost for the company. At the same time it would reach more customers just by altering some of its products.

This alternative was feasible because P&G had already built strong brand recognition and loyalty with its consumers. Consumers would need little conviction to buy another product from the same company. P&G had also already built a strong relationship with most of the large chain stores outlets, such as Wal-Mart. So the distribution process would remain effective for the new products that would be introduced into the market. The company already had the expertise within each of its segments required to support the introduction of new brands. From 2000 to 2005, P&G's net income increased, so the company had the financial resources to create or acquire new brands. It would also be able to afford the costs that would be attributed to these brands, and at the same time maintain its position as the global leader in the Consumer goods industry.

This alternative would win against the competition such as multinational firms like Unilever, Colgate-Palmolive, Playtex Products, Avon, and Estée Lauder, because P&G would increase its brands and products to reach more consumers. The company would do this by merging with other companies to create more products and specifically targeting the low income consumers. These consumers represented a large part of the consumer base, and changing its products by reducing the packaging size and quality would reduce the price of the products, making it more attractive and affordable for these consumers. These changes would increase its sales and make its products more price competitive.

The drawback of this alternative was the reduction in its expertise in one particular product. P&G had so many products that it was difficult to appropriately manage each and every one of them. Another drawback was the lack of enough prestigious products, such as very expensive fragrances. There was not enough attention given to high earning consumers who were able to afford such products. This alternative also did not address consumers who were interested in products that contained natural ingredients. The current trend was to use products with natural ingredients because of the uncertainty that came with using products manufactured with chemicals. People feared that using such products resulted in health problems, such as cancer and infertility. A way around this drawback was to get more qualified employees so P&G could continue to appropriately manage each product. The company also needed to manufacture products that incorporated the trends as mentioned above.

The second alternative was for P&G to focus and expand just on its skin care segment of the beauty/feminine care segment. The company would focus and specialize just on these products. It would produce different types of products for each ethnic group, products that had natural ingredients (such as herbs), and more skin products for men. It would have to sell all its other products, such as its hair products, cosmetics, feminine products and fine fragrances. The money from the sale of these products would be used to acquire more brands and products in the skin care segment.

The benefit of this alternative was that it would enable the company to focus just on one segment of the beauty/feminine care division and do it well. P&G would be able to apply all its resources and skills to this segment. Its employees would all be working in the same field, making it easier to share information between each other. The marketing team would only need to collect information from its consumers about skin products, making it easier to market and advertise these products.

This alternative was feasible because P&G already had a skin care segment. It just had to expand its products to incorporate every trend. P&G was financially capable of doing this, especially after selling off its other segments. The company already had a strong relationship with most of the large chain stores outlet, such as Costco and Wal-Mart. So the distribution process would remain effective for the new products that would be introduced into the market. P&G's employees already had the expertise within this segment required to support the introduction of new brands.

This alternative would win against the competition because P&G would increase its products and expertise in the skin care segment. The company would offer a wider variety of skin care products that would satisfy more consumers' needs. Satisfying more consumers would increase the company's sale and number of consumers, allowing P&G to win against its competitors such as Unilever, Colgate-Palmolive, Playtex Products, Avon, and Estée Lauder. Concentrating on this segment would also create a better environment for P&G to create more innovative products according to trends and this would keep it ahead of its competitors.

The drawback of this alternative was the loss of its other segments. The company would lose those consumers who wanted other products, such as hair products, cosmetics, fine fragrances, and feminine products. P&G's employees would also lose the flexibility of moving from one segment to the other. This flexibility would have allowed them to learn about different segments in the consumer goods industry. A way around this drawback was to allow another company such as Unilever that sold products in these other segments to use P&G's name to sell its products. This would satisfy the needs of those consumers who would prefer to use products associated with P&G. And also those employees who wanted to get more experience and flexibility could go to this other company and work for a while.

Lafley and his colleagues had a tough choice to make. These and other alternatives needed to be considered very carefully before reaching a decision which will impact the Company's future substantially.

REFERENCES

Aboutsears (2006). [Online]. *http://www.aboutsears.com/*. Accessed February 15, 2006.
Avon Annual Report (2005). [Online]. *http://www.avoncompany.com/investor/annualreport/index.html*. Accessed February 15, 2006.
BEA (2006). "News release." [Online]. *http://www.bea.gov/bea/newsrel/pinewsrelease.htm*. Accessed January 25, 2006.

CIA (2006). "The World Fact Book." [Online]. *http://www.cia.gov/cia/ publications/factbook/fields/2119.html*. Accessed March 21, 2006.

Colgate Corporate News (2006). [Online]. *http://www.colgate.com/ app/Colgate/US/Corp/ChairmansMessage.cvsp*. Accessed February 15, 2006.

Costco Services (2006). [Online]. *http://www.costco.com/*. Accessed February 15, 2006.

Datamonitor (2006). "Procter and Gamble." [Online]. *http://cpprod. stjohns.edu/cp/tag.b9b8fA3031868bbe.render.userLayoutRootNode .uP?uP_root=root&uP_sparam=activeTab&activeTab=U1l1lS39& uP_tparam=frm&frm=frame*. Accessed March 17, 2006.

Economist (2006). "Pots of Promise." [Online]. *http://www.economist .com/printedition/displayStory.cfm?Story_ID=1795852*. Accessed January 25, 2006.

EIS (2005). [Online]. *http://www.eia.doe.gov/neic/infosheets/ petroleumproducts .htm*. Accessed February 12, 2006.

Estée Lauder Annual Report (2005). [Online]. *http://www.esteelauder .com/home.html*. Accessed February 15, 2006.

Hoovers (2006). "Companies Information." [Online]. *http://www.hoovers .com/company-information/—HICID__1486—/free-ind-factsheet .xhtml*. Accessed February 12, 2006.

ICG Commerce (2006). "Strategic Sourcing." [Online]. *http://www .icgcommerce.com/corporate/doc/html/resource/procurement_terms. htm*. Accessed March 17, 2006.

Packaged Facts (2005). A division of marketresearch.com. "The U.S. Market for Hair Products." [Online]. *http://cpprod.stjohns.edu/ misc/timedouT2.html*. Accessed January 25, 2006.

Playtex Products Corporate News (2006). [Online]. *http://www .playtexproductsinc.com/index.htm*. Accessed February 15, 2006.

Procter & Gamble 2005 Annual Report (2006). [Online]. *http://www.pg.com/annualreports/2005/pdf/pG2005annualreport.pdf*. Accessed January 22, 2006.

Procter & Gamble Company Information (2006). [Online]. *http:// www.pg.com/company/index.jhtml*. Accessed February 22, 2006.

Procter & Gamble Corporate News (2006). [Online]. *http://pg.com/ news/index .jhtml*. *http://ccbn.mobular.net/ccbn/7/1142/1201/*. Accessed January 22, 2006.

Procter & Gamble Product Information (2006). [Online]. *http://www.pg .com/product_card/brand_overview.jhtml*. Accessed February 27, 2006.

Procter & Gamble Ethnic Echoes (2005). [Online]. *http://www.pg com/images/ company/who_we_are/diversity/multi/echo_feb_april05 .pdf*. Accessed March 5, 2006.

Procter & Gamble Hair Care (2003). [Online]. *http://www .pg.com/ science/haircare/hair_twh_116.htm*. Accessed February 27, 2006.

Procter & Gamble Skin Care (2003). [Online]. *http://www.pg.com/ science/skincare/Skin_tws_toc.htm*. Accessed February 27, 2006.

Target Corporate News (2006) [Online]. *http://sites.target.com/site/ en/corporate/page.jsp?contentId=PRD03-000482*. Accessed February 15, 2006.

Unilever Annual Report (2005). [Online]. *http://www.unilever.com/ ourcompany/investorcentre/*. Accessed February 22, 2006.

U. S. Census Bureau (2004). "U. S. Interim Projections by Age, Sex, Race and Hispanic Origin." [Online]. *http://www.census.gov/prod/ 99pubs/P20-514u.pdf*. Accessed February 12, 2006.

Walgreens Corporate News (2006). [Online]. *http://investor.walgreens .com/home.cfm*. Accessed February 15, 2006.

Wal-Mart Corporate News (2006). [Online]. *http://www.walmartstores .com/GlobalWMStoresWeb/navigate.do?catg=316*. Accessed February 15, 2006.

Webster's Dictionary (2006). [Online]. *http://www.webster.com/*. Accessed February 10, 2006.

Wikipedia (2006). [Online]. *http://en.wikipedia.org/wiki/Main_Page* .*http://en.wikipedia.org/wiki/Baby_boomer*. Accessed January 30, 2006.

28

3M in 2006

This case was prepared by Charles W. L. Hill, the University of Washington.

Established in 1902, by 2006 3M was one of the largest technology driven enterprises in the United States with annual sales of $23 billion, 61% of which were outside the United States. Throughout its history, 3M's researchers had driven much of the company's growth. In 2006, the company sold some 50,000 products, including Post-it Notes, Flex Circuits, Scotch tape, abrasives, specialty chemicals, Thinsulate insulation products, Nexcare bandage, optical films, fiber-optic connectors, drug delivery systems, and much more. Around 6,500 of the company's 69,000 employees were technical employees. 3M's annual R&D budget exceeded $1.25 billion. The company had garnered over 7,000 patents since 1990, with 487 new patents awarded in 2005 alone. 3M was organized into thirty-five different business units in a wide range of sectors including consumer and office products; display and graphics; electronics and telecommunications; health care; industrial; safety, security, and protection services; and transportation (see Exhibit 1 for more details).

The company's one-hundred-year anniversary was a time for celebration, but also one for strategic reflection. During the prior decade, 3M had grown profits and sales by between 6 to 7% per annum, a respectable figure but one that lagged behind the growth rates achieved by some other technology-based enterprises and diversified industrial enterprises like General Electric. In 2001, 3M took a step away

from its past when the company hired the first outsider to become CEO, James McNerney Jr. McNerney, who joined 3M after heading up GE's fast-growing medical equipment business (and losing out in the race to replace legendary GE CEO, Jack Welch), was quick to signal that he wanted 3M to accelerate its growth rate. McNerney set an ambitious target for 3M—to grow sales by 11% per annum and profits by 12% per annum. Many wondered if McNerney could achieve this without damaging the innovation engine that had propelled 3M to its current stature. The question remained unanswered, as McNerney left to run the Boeing Co. in 2005. His successor, however, George Buckley, seemed committed to continuing on the course McNerney had set for the company.

The History of 3M: Building Innovative Capabilities

The story of 3M goes back to 1902 when five Minnesota businessmen established the Minnesota Mining and Manufacturing Co. to mine a mineral that they thought was corundum, which is ideal for making sandpaper. The mineral, however, turned out to be low-grade anorthosite, nowhere near as suitable for making sandpaper, and the company nearly failed. To try and salvage the business, 3M turned to making the sandpaper itself using materials purchased from another source.

In 1907, 3M hired a twenty-year-old business student, William McKnight, as assistant bookkeeper. This turned out to be a pivotal move in the history of the company. The hardworking McKnight soon made his mark. By 1929, he was CEO of the company, and in 1949, he became chairman of 3M's board of directors, a position that he held until 1966.

EXHIBIT 1

3M Financial Facts—Year-End 2005[a]

Sales

Worldwide	$21.167 billion
International	$12.900 billion
	61% of company's total

Net Income

Net Income	$3.199 billion
Percent to sales	15.1%
Earnings per share—diluted	$4.12

Taxes

Income tax expense	$1.694 billion

Dividends (Paid every quarter since 1916)

Cash dividends per share	$1.68
One original share, if held, is now . . .	3,072 shares

R&D and Related Expenditures

For 2005	$1.242 billion
Total for last five years	$5.814 billion

Capital Spending

For 2005	$943 million
Total for last five years	$4.3 billion

Employees

Worldwide	69,315
United States	33,033
International	36,282

Organization

● More than 35 business units, organized into 6 businesses: Consumer and Office; Display and Graphics; Electro and Communications; Health Care; Industrial and Transportation; Safety, Security and Protection Services
● Operations in more than 60 countries—29 international companies with manufacturing operations, 35 with laboratories
● In the United States, operations in 22 states

Contributions

Cash and gifts-in-kind (3M and 3M Foundation)	Nearly $39 million

Patents

U.S. patents awarded	487

3M Values

● Provide investors an attractive return through sustained, quality growth.
● Satisfy customers with superior quality, value, and service.
● Respect our social and physical environment.
● Be a company employees are proud to be part of.

[a] 3M is one of 30 companies in the Dow Jones Industrial Average and also is a component of the Standard & Poor's 500 Index.

Source: 3M website, http://www.3m.com.

From Sandpaper to Post-it Notes

It was McKnight, then 3M's president, who hired the company's first scientist, Richard Carlton, in 1921. Around the same time, McKnight's interest had been peaked by an odd request from a Philadelphian printer by the name of Francis Okie for samples of every sandpaper grit size that 3M made. McKnight dispatched 3M's East Coast sales manager to find out what Okie was up to. The sales manager discovered that Okie had invented a new kind of sandpaper that he had patented. It was waterproof sandpaper that could be used with water or oil to reduce dust and decrease the friction that marred auto finishes. In addition, the lack of dust reduced the poisoning associated with inhaling the dust of paint that had a high lead content. Okie had a problem, though; he had no financial backers to commercialize the sandpaper. 3M quickly stepped into the breach, purchasing the rights to Okie's Wetodry waterproof sandpaper and hiring the young printer to come and join Richard Carlton in 3M's lab. Wet and dry sandpaper went on to revolutionize the sandpaper industry and was the driver of significant growth at 3M.

Another key player in the company's history, Richard Drew, also joined 3M in 1921. Hired straight out of the University of Minnesota, Drew would round out the trio of scientists, Carlton, Okie and Drew, who under McKnight's leadership would do much to shape 3M's innovative organization.

McKnight charged the newly hired Drew with developing a stronger adhesive to better bind the grit for sand paper to paper backing. While experimenting with adhesives, Drew accidentally developed a weak adhesive that had an interest quality—if placed on the back of a strip of paper and stuck to a surface, the strip of paper could be peeled off the surface it was adhered to without leaving any adhesive residue on that surface. This discovery gave Drew an epiphany. He had been visiting auto-body paint shops to see how 3M's wet and dry sandpaper was used, and he noticed that there was a problem with paint running. His epiphany was to cover the back of a strip of paper with his weak adhesive and use it as "masking tape" to cover parts of the auto body that were not to be painted. An excited Drew took his idea to McKnight and explained how masking tape might create an entirely new business for 3M. McKnight reminded Drew that he had been hired to fix a specific problem and pointedly suggested that he concentrate on doing just that.

Chastised, Drew went back to his lab, but he could not get the idea out of his mind, so he continued to work on it at night, long after everyone else had gone home. Drew succeeded in perfecting the masking tape product, and then went to visit several auto-body shops to show them his innovation. He quickly received several commitments for orders. Drew then went to see McKnight again. He told him that he had continued to work on the masking tape idea on his own time, had perfected the product, and got several customers interested in purchasing it. This time it was McKnight's turn to be chastised. Realizing that he had almost killed a good business idea, McKnight reversed his original position, and gave Drew the go-ahead to pursue the idea.[1]

Introduced into the market in 1925, Drew's invention of masking tape represented the first significant product diversification at 3M. Company legend has it that this incident was also the genesis for 3M's famous 15% rule. Reflecting on Drew's work, both McKnight and Carlton agreed that technical people could disagree with management and should be allowed to go and do some experimentation on their own. The company then established a norm that technical people could spend up to 15% of their own workweeks on projects that might benefit the consumer, without having to justify the project to their managers.

Drew himself was not finished. In the late 1920s, he was working with cellophane, a product that had been invented by DuPont, when lightening struck for a second time. Why, Drew wondered, couldn't cellophane be coated with an adhesive and used as a sealing tape? The result was Scotch Cellophane Tape. The first batch was delivered to a customer in September 1930, and Scotch Tape went on to become one of 3M's best-selling products. Years later, Drew noted: "Would there have been any masking or cellophane tape if it hadn't been for earlier 3M research on adhesive binders for 3M™ Wetordry™ Abrasive Paper? Probably not!"[2]

Over the years, other scientists followed Drew's footsteps at 3M, creating a wide range of innovative products by leveraging existing technology and applying it to new areas. Two famous examples illustrate how many of these innovations occurred—the invention of Scotch Guard and the development of the ubiquitous Post-it Notes.

The genesis of Scotch Guard was in 1953 when a 3M scientist named Patsy Sherman was working on a new kind of rubber for jet aircraft fuel lines. Some of the latex mixture splashed onto a pair of canvas tennis shoes. Over time, the spot stayed clean while the rest of the canvas soiled. Sherman enlisted the help of fellow chemist Sam Smith. Together they began to investigate polymers, and it didn't take long for them to realize that they were onto something. They discovered an oil and water repellant substance, based on the fluorocarbon fluid used in air conditioners, with enormous potential for protecting fabrics from stains. It took several years before the team perfected a means to apply the treatment using water as the carrier, thereby making it economically feasible for use as a finish in textile plants.

Three years after the accidental spill, the first rain and stain repellent for use on wool was announced. Experience and time revealed that one product could not, however, effectively protect all fabrics, so 3M continued working, producing a wide range of Scotch Guard products that could be used to protect all kinds of fabrics.[3]

The story of Post-it Notes began with Spencer Silver, a senior scientist studying adhesives.[4] In 1968, Silver had developed an adhesive with properties like no other; it was a pressure-sensitive adhesive that would adhere to a surface, but it was weak enough to easily peel off the surface and leave no residue. Silver spent several years shopping his adhesive around 3M, to no avail. It was a classic case of a technology in search of a product. Then one day in 1973, Art Fry, a new product development researcher who had attended one of Silver's seminars, was singing in his church choir. He was frustrated that his bookmarks kept falling out of his hymn book, when he had a Eureka moment. Fry realized that Silver's adhesive could be used to make a wonderfully reliable bookmark.

Fry went to work the next day and, using 15% time, started to develop the bookmark. When he started using samples to write notes to his boss, Fry suddenly realized that he had stumbled on a much bigger potential use for the product. Before the product could be commercialized, however, Fry had to solve a host of technical and manufacturing problems. With the support of his boss, Fry persisted, and after eighteen months, the product development effort moved from 15% time to a formal development effort funded by 3M's own seed capital.

The first Post-it Notes were test marketed in 1977 in four major cities, but customers were lukewarm at best. This did not gel with the experience within 3M, where people in Fry's division were using samples all the time to write messages to each other. Further

research revealed that the test-marketing effort, which focused on ads and brochures, didn't resonate well with consumers, who didn't seem to value Post-it Notes until they had the actual product in their hands. In 1978, 3M tried again, this time descending on Boise, Idaho, and handing out samples. Follow-up research revealed that 90% of consumers who tried the product said they would buy it. Armed with this knowledge, 3M rolled out the national launch of Post-it Notes in 1980. The product subsequently went on to become a bestseller.

Institutionalizing Innovation

Early on, McKnight set an ambitious target for 3M—a 10% annual increase in sales and 25% profit target. He also indicated how he thought that should be achieved with a commitment to plow 5% of sales back into R&D every year. The question, though, was how to ensure that 3M would continue to produce new products?

The answer was not apparent all at once, but rather evolved over the years from experience. A prime example was the 15% rule, which came out of McKnight's experience with Drew. In addition to the 15% rule and the continued commitment to push money back into R&D, a number of other mechanisms evolved at 3M to spur innovation.

Initially research took place in the business units that made and sold products, but by the 1930s, 3M had already diversified into several different fields, thanks in large part to the efforts of Drew and others. McKnight and Carlton realized that there was a need for a central research function. In 1937, they established a central research laboratory that was charged with supplementing the work of product divisions and undertaking long-run basic research. From the outset, the researchers at the lab were multidisciplinary, with people from different scientific disciplines often working next to each other on research benches.

As the company continued to grow, it became clear that there was a need for some mechanism to knit together the company's increasingly diverse business operations. This led to the establishment of the 3M Technical Forum in 1951. The goal of the Technical Forum was to foster idea sharing, discussion, and problem solving among technical employees located in different divisions and the central research laboratory. The Technical Forum sponsored "problem solving sessions" at which businesses would present their most recent technical nightmares in the hope that somebody might be able to suggest a solution—and that often was the case. The forum also established an annual event in which each division put up a booth to show off its latest technologies. Chapters were also created to focus on specific disciplines, such as polymer chemistry or coating processes.

During the 1970s the Technical Forum cloned itself, establishing forums in Australia and England. By 2001, the forum had grown to 9,500 members in eight U.S. locations and nineteen other countries, becoming an international network of researchers who could share ideas, solve problems, and leverage technology.

According to Marlyee Paulson, who coordinated the Technical Forum from 1979 to 1992, the great virtue of the Technical Forum is to cross-pollinate ideas:

> 3M has lots of polymer chemists. They may be in tape; they may be medical or several other divisions. The forum pulls them across 3M to share what they know. It's a simple but amazingly effective way to bring like minds together.[5]

In 1999, 3M created another unit within the company, 3M Innovative Properties (3M, IPC) to leverage technical know-how. 3M IPC is explicitly charged with protecting and leveraging 3M's intellectual property around the world. At 3M there has been a long tradition that while divisions "own" their products, the company as a whole "owns" the underlying technology, or intellectual property. One task of 3M IPC is to find ways in which 3M technology can be applied across business units to produce unique marketable products. Historically, the company has been remarkably successful at leveraging company technology to produce new product ideas (see Exhibit 2 for some recent examples).

Another key to institutionalizing innovation at 3M has been the principle of "patient money." The basic idea is that producing revolutionary new products requires substantial long-term investments, and often repeated failure, before a major payoff occurs. The principle can be traced back to 3M's early days.

EXHIBIT 2

Recent Examples of Leveraging Technology at 3M[6]

Richard Miller, a corporate scientist in 3M Pharmaceuticals, began experimental development of an antiherpes medicinal cream in 1982. After several years of development, his research team found that the interferon-based materials they were working with could be applied to any skin-based virus. The innovative chemistry they were working with was applied topically and was more effective than other compounds on the market. They found that the cream was particularly effective in interfering with the growth mechanism of genital warts. Competitive materials on the market at the time were caustic and tended to be painful. Miller's team obtained FDA approval for its Aldara (imiquimod) line of topical patient-applied creams in 1997.

Miller then applied the same Aldara-based chemical mechanism to basal cell carcinomas and found that, here too, it was particularly effective to restricting the growth of the skin cancer. "The patient benefit is quite remarkable," says Miller. New results in efficacy have been presented for treating skin cancers. His team recently completed phase III clinical testing and expects to apply later this year for FDA approval for this disease preventative. This material is already FDA-approved for use in the treatment of genital warts. Doctors are free to use it to treat those patients with skin cancers.

Andrew Ouderkirk is a corporate scientist in 3M's Film & Light Management Technology Center. 3M has been working in light management materials applied to polymer-based films since the 1930s, according to Ouderkirk. Every decade since then 3M has introduced some unique thin film structure for a specific customer application from high-performance safety reflectors for street signs to polarized lighting products. And every decade, 3M's technology base has become more specialized and more sophisticated. Their technology has now reached the point where they can produce multiple-layer interference films to 100-nm thicknesses each and hold the tolerances on each layer to within +/-3 nm. "Our laminated films are now starting to compete with vacuum-coated films in some applications," says Ouderkirk.

Rick Weiss is technical director of 3M's Microreplication Technology Center, one of 3M's twelve core technology centers. The basic microreplication technology was discovered in the early 1960s when 3M researchers were developing the fresnel lenses for overhead projectors. 3M scientists have expanded on this technology to a wide variety of applications including optical reflectors for solar collectors, and adhesive coatings with air bleed ribs that allow large area films to be applied without having the characteristic "bubbles" appear. Weiss is currently working on development of dimensionally precise barrier ribs that can be applied to separate the individual "gas" cells on the new high-resolution large screen commercial plasma displays. Other applications include fluid management where capillary action can be used in biological testing systems to split a drop of blood into a large number of parts.

It took the company twelve years before its initial sandpaper business started to show a profit, a fact that drove home the importance of taking the long view. Throughout the company's history, similar examples can be found. Scotchlite reflective sheeting, now widely used on road signs, didn't show much profit for ten years. The same was true of flurochemicals and duplicating products. Patient money doesn't mean substantial funding for long periods of time, however. Rather, it might imply that a small group of five researchers is supported for ten years while they work on a technology.

More generally, if a researcher creates a new technology or idea, he or she can begin working on it using 15% time. If the idea shows promise, the researcher may request seed capital from his or her business unit managers to develop it further. If that funding is denied, which can occur, the researcher is free to take the idea to any other 3M business unit. Unlike the case in many other companies, requests for seed capital do not require that researchers draft detailed business plans that are reviewed by top management. That comes later in the process. As one former senior technology manager has noted:

> In the early stages of a new product or technology, it shouldn't be overly managed. If we start asking for business plans too early and insist on tight financial evaluations, we'll kill an idea or surely slow it down.[7]

Explaining the patient money philosophy, Ron Baukol, a former executive vice president of 3M's international operations and a manager who started as a researcher, has noted:

> You just know that some things are going to be worth working on, and that requires technological patience. . . . [Y]ou don't put too much money into the investigation, but you keep one to five people working on it for twenty years if you have to. You do that because you know that, once you have cracked the code, it's going to be big.[8]

An internal review of 3M's innovation process in the early 1980s concluded that despite the liberal process for funding new product ideas, some promising ideas did not receive funding from business units or the central research budget. This led to the establishment in 1985 of Genesis Grants, which provide up to $100,000 in seed capital to fund projects that do not get funded through 3M's regular channels. About a dozen of these grants are given every year.

One of the recipients of these grants, a project that focused on creating a multilayered reflective film, has subsequently produced a breakthough reflective technology that may have applications in a wide range of businesses, from better reflective strips on road signs to computer displays and the reflective linings in light fixtures. Company estimates in 2002 suggested that the commercialization of this technology might ultimately generate $1 billion in sales for 3M.

Underlying the patient money philosophy is recognition that innovation is a very risky business. 3M has long acknowledged that failure is an accepted and essential part of the new product development process. As former 3M CEO Lew Lehr once noted:

> We estimate that 60% of our formal new product development programs never make it. When this happens, the important thing is to not punish the people involved.[9]

In an effort to reduce the probability of failure, in the 1960s, 3M started to establish a process for auditing the product development efforts ongoing in the company's business units. The idea has been to provide a peer review, or technical audit, of major development projects taking place in the company. A typical technical audit team is composed of ten to fifteen business and technical people, including technical directors and senior scientists from other divisions. The audit team looks at the strengths and weaknesses of a development program and its probability of success, both from a technical standpoint and a business standpoint. The team then makes nonbinding recommendations, but they are normally taken very seriously by the managers of a project. For example, if an audit team concludes that a project has enormous potential but is terribly underfunded, managers of the unit would often increase the funding level. Of course, the converse can also happen, and in many instances, the audit team can provide useful feedback and technical ideas that can help a development team to improve its project's chance of success.

By the 1990s, the continuing growth of 3M had produced a company that was simultaneously pursuing a vast array of new product ideas. This was a natural outcome of 3M's decentralized and bottom-up approach to innovation, but it was problematic in one crucial respect: The company's R&D resources were being spread too thinly over a wide range of opportunities, resulting in potentially major projects being underfunded. To try to channel R&D resources into projects that had blockbuster potential, in 1994, 3M introduced what was known as the Pacing Plus Program.

The program asked business to select a small number of programs that would receive priority funding, but 3M's senior executives made the final decision on which programs were to be selected for the Pacing Plus Program. An earlier attempt to do this in 1990 had met with limited success because each sector in 3M submitted as many as two hundred programs. The Pacing Plus Program narrowed the list down to twenty-five key programs that by 1996 were receiving some 20% of 3M's entire R&D funds (by the early 2000s, the number of projects funded under the Pacing Plus Program had grown to sixty). The focus was on "leapfrog technologies," revolutionary ideas that might change the basis of competition and lead to entirely new technology platforms that might, in typical 3M fashion, spawn an entire range of new products.

To further foster a culture of entrepreneurial innovation and risk taking, over the years 3M established a number of reward and recognition programs to honor employees who make significant contributions to the company. These include the Carton Society award, which honors employees for outstanding career scientific achievements, and the Circle of Technical Excellence and Innovation Award, which recognizes people who have made exceptional contributions to 3M's technical capabilities.

Another key component of 3M's innovative culture has been an emphasis on duel career tracks. Right from its early days, many of the key players in 3M's history, people like Richard Drew, chose to stay in research, turning down opportunities to go into the management side of the business. Over the years, this became formalized in a dual career path. Today, technical employees can choose to follow a technical career path or a management career path, with equal advancement opportunities. The idea is to let researchers develop their technical professional interests without being penalized financially for not going into management.

Although 3M's innovative culture emphasizes the role of technical employees in producing innovations, the company also has a strong tradition of emphasizing that new product ideas often come from watching customers at work. Richard Drew's original idea for masking tape, for example, came from watching workers use 3M wet and dry sandpaper in auto-body shops. As with much else at 3M, the tone was set by McKnight who insisted that salespeople needed to "get behind the smokestacks" of 3M customers, going onto the factory floor, talking to workers, and finding out what their problems were. Over the years this theme has become ingrained in 3M's culture, with salespeople often requesting time to watch customers work and then bringing their insights about customer problems back into their organization.

By the mid-1990s, McKnight's notion of getting behind the smokestacks had evolved into the idea that 3M could learn a tremendous amount from what were termed "lead users," who were customers working in very demanding conditions. Over the years, 3M had observed that in many cases, customer themselves can be innovators, developing new products to solve problems that they face in their work settings. This was most likely to occur for customers working in very demanding conditions. To take advantage of this process, 3M has instituted a lead user process in the company in which cross-functional teams from a business unit observe how customers work in demanding situations.

For example, 3M has a $100 million business selling surgical drapes, which are drapes backed with adhesives that are used to cover parts of a body during surgery and help prevent infection. As an aid to new product development, 3M's surgical drapes business formed a cross-functional team that went to observe surgeons at work in very demanding situations—including on the battlefield, hospitals in developing nations, and in vets' offices. The result was a new set of product ideas, including low-cost surgical drapes that were affordable in developing nations, and devices for coating a patient's skin and surgical instruments with antimicrobial substances that would reduce the chance of infection during surgery.[10]

Driving the entire innovation machine at 3M has been a series of stretch goals set by top managers. The goals date back to 3M's early days and McKnight's ambitious growth targets. In 1977, the company established "Challenge 81," which called for 25% of sales to come from products that had been on the market for less than five years by 1981. By the 1990s, the goal had been raised to the requirement that 30% of sales should come from products that had been on the market less than four years.

The flip side of these goals were that over the years, many products and businesses that had been 3M staples were phased out. More than twenty of the businesses that were 3M mainstays in 1980, for example, had been phased out by 2000. Analysts estimate that sales from mature products at 3M generally fall by 3 to 4% per annum. The company has a long history of inventing businesses, leading the market for long periods of time, and then shutting those businesses down or selling them off when they can no longer meet 3M's own demanding growth targets. Notable examples include the duplicating business, a business 3M invented with Thermo-Fax copiers (which were ultimately made obsolete by Xerox's patented technology) and the video and audio magnetic tape business. The former division was sold off in 1985, and the latter in 1995. In both cases, the company exited these areas because they had become low-growth commodity businesses that could not generate the kind of top-line growth that 3M was looking for.

Still, 3M was by no means invulnerable in the realm of innovation and on occasion squandered huge opportunities. A case in point was the document copying business. 3M invented this business in 1951 when it introduced the world's first commercially successful Thermo-Fax copier (which used specially coated 3M paper to copy original typed documents). 3M dominated the world copier business until 1970, when Xerox overtook the company with its revolutionary xerographic technology that used plain paper to make copies. 3M saw Xerox coming, but rather than try to develop its own plain paper copier, the company invested funds in trying to improve its (increasingly obsolete) copying technology. It wasn't until 1975 that 3M introduced its own plain paper copier, and by then it was too late. Ironically, 3M turned down the chance to acquire Xerox's technology twenty years earlier, when the company's founders had approached 3M.

Building the Organization

McKnight, a strong believer in decentralization, organized the company into product divisions in 1948, making 3M one of the early adopters of this organizational form. Each division was set up as an individual profit center that had the power, autonomy, and resources to run independently. At the same time, certain functions remained centralized, including significant R&D, human resources, and finance.

McKnight wanted to keep the divisions small enough that people had a chance to be entrepreneurial and retained their focus on the customer. A key philosophy of McKnight's was "divide and grow." Put simply, when a division became too big, some of its embryonic businesses were spun off into a new division. Not only did this new division then typically attain higher growth rates, but the original division had to find new drivers of growth to make up for the contribution of the businesses that had gained independence. This drove the search for further innovations.

At 3M, the process of organic diversification by splitting divisions became known as "renewal." The examples of renewal within 3M are legion. A copying machine project for Thermo-Fax copiers grew to become the Office Products Division. When Magnetic Recording Materials was spun off from the Electrical Products division, it grew to become its own division, and then in turn spawned a spate of divisions.

However, this organic process was not without its downside. By the early 1990s, some of 3M's key customers were frustrated that they had to do businesses with a large number of different 3M divisions. In some cases, there could be representatives from ten to twenty 3M divisions calling on the same customer. To cope with this problem, in 1992, 3M started to assign key account representatives to sell 3M products directly to major customers. These representatives typically worked across divisional lines. Implementing the strategy required many of 3M's general managers to give up some of their autonomy and power, but the solution seemed to work well, particularly for 3M's consumer and office divisions.

Underpinning the organization that McKnight put in place was his own management philosophy. As explained in a 1948 document, his basic management philosophy consisted of the following values:

> As our business grows, it becomes increasingly necessary to delegate responsibility and to encourage men and women to exercise their initiative. This requires considerable tolerance. Those men and women to whom we delegate authority and responsibility, if they are good people, are going to want to do their jobs in their own way.
>
> Mistakes will be made. But if a person is essentially right, the mistakes he or she makes are not as serious in the long run as the mistakes management will make if it undertakes to tell those in authority exactly how they must do their jobs.
>
> Management that is destructively critical when mistakes are made kills initiative. And it's essential that we have many people with initiative if we are to continue to grow.[11]

At just 3% per annum, employee turnover rate at 3M has long been among the lowest in corporate America, a fact that is often attributed to the tolerant, empowering, and family-like corporate culture that McKnight helped to establish. Reinforcing this culture has been a progressive approach toward employee compensation and retention. In the depths of the Great Depression, 3M was able to avoid laying off employees while many other employers did because the company's innovation engine was able to keep building new businesses even through the worst of times.

In many ways, 3M was ahead of its time in management philosophy and human resource practices. The company introduced its first profit sharing plan in 1916, and McKnight instituted a pension plan in 1930 and an employee stock purchase plan in 1950. McKnight himself was convinced that people would be much more likely to be loyal in a company if they had a stake in it. 3M also developed a policy of promoting from within and of giving its employees a plethora of career opportunities within the company.

Going International

The first steps abroad occurred in the 1920s. There were some limited sales of wet and dry sandpaper in Europe during the early 1920s. These increased after 1929 when 3M joined the Durex Corp., a joint venture for international abrasive product sales in which 3M was involved along with eight other U.S. companies. In 1950, however, the Department of Justice alleged that the Durex Corp. was a mechanism for achieving collusion among U.S. abrasive manufacturers, and a judge ordered that the corporation be broken up. After the Durex Corp. was dissolved in 1951, 3M was left with a sandpaper factory in Britain, a small plant in France, a sales office in Germany, and a tape factory in Brazil. International sales at this point amounted to no more than 5% of 3M's total revenues.

Although 3M opposed the dissolution of the Durex Corp., in retrospect it turned out to be one of the most important events in the company's history, for it forced the corporation to build its own international operations. By 2002, international sales amounted to 55% of total revenues.

In 1952, Clarence Sampair was put in charge of 3M's international operations and charged with getting them off the ground. He was given considerable

strategic and operational independence. Sampair and his successor, Maynard Patterson, worked hard to protect the international operations from getting caught up in the red tape of a major corporation. For example, Patterson recounts:

> I asked Em Monteiro to start a small company in Colombia. I told him to pick a key person he wanted to take with him. "Go start a company," I said, "and no one from St. Paul is going to visit you unless you ask for them. We'll stay out of your way, and if someone sticks his nose in your business you call me."[12]

The international businesses were grouped into an International Division that Sampair headed. From the get go, the company insisted that foreign ventures pay their own way. In addition, 3M's international companies were expected to pay a 5 to 10% royalty to the corporate head office. Starved of working capital, 3M's International Division relied heavily on local borrowing to fund local operations, a fact that forced those operations to quickly pay their own way.

The international growth at 3M typically occurred in stages. The company would start by exporting to a country and working through sales subsidiaries. In that way, it began to understand the country, the local marketplace, and the local business environment. Next 3M established warehouses in each nation and stocked those with goods paid for in local currency. The next phase involved converting products to the sizes and packaging forms that the local market conditions, customs, and culture dictated. 3M would ship jumbo rolls of products from the United States, which were then broken up and repackaged for each country. The next stage was designing and building plants, buying machinery and getting them up and running. Over the years, R&D functions were often added, and by the 1980s, considerable R&D was being done outside of the United States.

Both Sampair and Patterson set an innovative, entrepreneurial framework that according to the company, still guides 3M's International Operations today. The philosophy can be reduced to several key and simple commitments: (1) Get in early (within the company, the strategy is known as FIDO—"First in Defeats Others"). (2) Hire talented and motivated local people. (3) Become a good corporate citizen of the country. (4) Grow with the local economy. (5) American products are not one-size-fits-all around the world; tailor products to fit local needs. (6) Enforce patents in local countries.

As 3M stepped into the international market vacuum, foreign sales surged from less than 5% in 1951 to 42% by 1979. By the end of the 1970s 3M was beginning to understand how important it was to integrate the international operations more closely with the U.S. operations and to build innovative capabilities overseas. It expanded the company's international R&D presence (there are now more than 2,200 technical employees outside the United States), built closer ties between the U.S. and foreign research organizations, and started to transfer more managerial and technical employees between businesses in different countries.

In 1978 the company started the Pathfinder Program to encourage new product and new business initiatives born outside the United States. By 1983, products developed under the initiative were generating sales of over $150 million a year. 3M Brazil invented a low-cost, hot-melt adhesive from local raw materials, 3M Germany teamed up with Sumitomo 3M of Japan (a joint venture with Sumitomo) to develop electronic connectors with new features for the worldwide electronics industry, 3M Philippines developed a Scotch-Brite cleaning pad shaped like a foot after learning that Filipinos polished floors with their feet, and so on. On the back of such developments, in 1992 international operations exceeded 50% for the first time in the company's history.

By the 1990s 3M started to shift away from a country-by-country management structure to more regional management. Drivers behind this development included the fall of trade barriers, the rise of trading blocks such as the European Union and NAFTA, and the need to drive down costs in the face of intense global competition. The first European Business Center (EBC) was created in 1991 to manage 3M's chemical business across Europe. The EBC was charged with product development, manufacturing, sales, and marketing for Europe, but also with paying attention to local country requirements. Other EBCs soon followed, such as EBCs for Disposable Products and Pharmaceuticals.

As the millennium ended, 3M seemed set on transforming the company into a transnational organization characterized by an integrated network of businesses that spanned the globe. The goal was to get the right mix of global scale to deal with competitive pressures, while at the same time maintaining 3M's traditional focus on local market differences and decentralized R&D capabilities.

The New Era

The DeSimone Years

In 1991, Desi DeSimone became CEO of 3M. A longtime 3M employee, the Canadian-born DeSimone was the epitome of a twenty-first-century manager—he had made his name by building 3M's Brazilian business and spoke five languages fluently. Unlike most prior 3M CEOs, DeSimone came from the manufacturing side of the business rather than the technical side. He soon received praise for managing 3M through the recession of the early 1990s. By the late 1990s, however, his leadership had come under fire from both inside and outside the company.

In 1998 and 1999, the company missed its earnings targets, and the stock price fell as disappointed investors sold. Sales were flat, profit margins fell, and earnings slumped by 50%. The stock had underperformed the widely tracked S&P 500 stock index for most of the 1980s and 1990s.

One cause of the earnings slump in the late 1990s was 3M's sluggish response to the 1997 Asian crisis. During the Asian crisis, the value of several Asian currencies fell by as much as 80% against the U.S. dollar in a matter of months. 3M generated a quarter of its sales from Asia, but it was slow to cut costs there in the face of slumping demand following the collapse of currency values. At the same time, a flood of cheap Asian products cut into 3M's market share in the United States and Europe as lower currency values made Asian products much cheaper.

Another problem was that for all of its vaunted innovative capabilities, 3M had not produced a new blockbuster product since Post-it Notes. Most of the new products produced during the 1990s were just improvements over existing products, not truly new products.

DeSimone was also blamed for not pushing 3M hard enough earlier in the decade to reduce costs. An example was the company's supply-chain excellence program. Back in 1995, 3M's inventory was turning over just 3.5 times a year, subpar for manufacturing. An internal study suggested that every half point increase in inventory turnover could reduce 3M's working capital needs by $700 million and boost its return on invested capital. But by 1998, 3M had made no progress on this front.[13]

By 1998, there was also evidence of internal concerns. Anonymous letters from 3M employees were sent to the board of directors, claiming that DeSimone was not committed to research as he should have been. Some letters complained that DeSimone was not funding important projects for future growth, others that he had not moved boldly enough to cut costs, and still others that the company's duel career track was not being implemented well, and that technical people were underpaid. Critics argued that he was a slow and cautious decision maker in a time that required decisive strategic decisions. For example, in August 1998, DeSimone announced a restructuring plan that included a commitment to cut 4,500 jobs, but reports suggest that other senior managers wanted 10,000 job cuts, and DeSimone had watered down the proposals.[14]

Despite the criticism, 3M's board, which included four previous 3M CEOs among its members, stood behind DeSimone until he retired in 2001. However, the board began a search for a new top executive in February 2000 and signaled that it was looking for an outsider. In December 2000, the company announced that it had found the person they wanted, Jim McNerney, a fifty-one-year-old General Electric veteran who ran GE's medical equipment businesses and, before that, GE's Asian operations. McNerney was one of the front runners in the race to succeed Jack Welsh as CEO of GE, but lost out to Jeffrey Immelt. One week after that announcement, 3M hired him.

McNerney's Plan for 3M

In his first public statement days after being appointed, McNerney said that his focus would be on getting to know 3M's people and culture and its diverse lines of business:

> I think getting to know some of those businesses and bringing some of GE here to overlay on top of 3M's strong culture of innovation will be particularly important.[15]

It soon became apparent that McNerney's game plan was exactly that: to bring the GE playbook to 3M and use it to try to boost 3M's results, while simultaneously not destroying the innovative culture that had produced the company's portfolio of 50,000 products.

The first move came in April 2001 when 3M announced that the company would cut 5,000 jobs, or about 7% of the work force, in a restructuring effort that would zero in on struggling businesses. To cover severance and other costs of restructuring, 3M announced that it would take a $600 million charge against earnings. The job cuts were expected to save $500 million a year. In another effort to save costs, the company streamlined its purchasing processes, for example, by reducing the number of packaging suppliers on a global basis from fifty to five, saving another $100 million a year in the process.

Next, McNerney introduced the Six Sigma process, a rigorous statistically based quality control process that was one of the drivers of process improvement and cost savings at GE. At heart, Six Sigma is a management philosophy, accompanied by a set of tools, that is rooted in identifying and prioritizing customers and their needs, reducing variation in all business processes, and selecting and grading all projects based on their impact on financial results. Six Sigma breaks every task (process) in an organization down into increments to be measured against a perfect model.

McNerney called for Six Sigma to be rolled out across 3M's global operations. He also introduced a 3M-like performance evaluation system at 3M under which managers were asked to rank every single employee who reported to them.

In addition to boosting performance from existing business, McNerney quickly signaled that he wanted to play a more active role in allocating resources between new business opportunities. At any given time, 3M has around 1,500 products in the development pipeline. McNerney believed that was too many and indicated that he wanted to funnel more cash to the most promising ideas, those with a potential market of $100 million a year or more, while cutting funding to weaker looking development projects.

In the same vein, he signaled that he wanted to play a more active role in resource allocation than had traditionally been the case for a 3M CEO, using cash from mature businesses to fund growth opportunities elsewhere. He scrapped the requirement that each division get 30% of its sales from products introduced in the past four years, noting that:

> To make that number, some managers were resorting to some rather dubious innovations, such as pink Post-it Notes. It became a game, what could you do to get a new SKU?[16]

Some long-time 3M watchers, however, worried that by changing resource allocation practices, McNerney might harm 3M's innovative culture. If the company's history proved anything, they said, it's that it is hard to tell which of today's tiny products will become tomorrow's home runs. No one predicted that Scotch Guard or Post-it Notes would earn millions. They began as little experiments that evolved without planning into big hits. McNerney's innovations all sound fine in theory, they said, but there is a risk that he will transform 3M into "3E" and lose what is valuable in 3M in the process.

In general, though, securities analysts greeted McNerney's moves favorably. One noted that "McNerney is all about speed" and that there will be "no more Tower of Babel—everyone speaks one language." This "one company" vision was meant to replace the program under which 3M systematically spun off successful new products into new business centers. The problem with this approach, according to the analyst, was that there was no leveraging of best practices across businesses.[17]

McNerney also signaled that he would reform 3M's regional management structure, replacing it with a global business unit structure that would be defined by either products or markets.

At a meeting for investment analysts, held on September 30, 2003, McNerney summarized a number of achievements.[18] At the time, the indications seemed to suggest that McNerney was helping to revitalize 3M. Profitability, measured by return on invested capital, had risen from 19.4% in 2001 and was projected to hit 25.5% in 2003. 3M's stock price had risen from $42 just before McNerney was hired to $73 in October 2003 (see Exhibit 3 for details).

Like his former boss, Jack Welsh at GE, McNerney seemed to place significant value on internal executive education programs as a way of shifting to a performance-oriented culture. McNerney noted that some 20,000 employees had been through Six Sigma

training by the third quarter of 2003. Almost 400 higher level managers had been through an Advanced Leadership Development Program set up by McNerney and offered by 3M's own internal executive education institute. Some 40% of participants had been promoted on graduating. All of the company's top managers had graduated from an Executive Leadership Program offered by 3M.

McNerney also emphasized the value of five initiatives that he had put in place at 3M: indirect cost control, global sourcing, e-productivity, Six Sigma, and the 3M Acceleration program. With regard to indirect cost control, some $800 million had been taken out of 3M's cost structure since 2001, primarily by reducing employee numbers, introducing more efficient processes that boost productivity, benchmarking operations internally, and leveraging best practices. According to McNerney, internal benchmarking highlighted another $200 to $400 million in potential cost savings over the next few years.

On global sourcing, McNerney noted that more than $500 million had been saved since 2000 by consolidating purchasing, reducing the number of suppliers, switching to lower cost suppliers in developing nations, and introducing duel sourcing policies to keep price increases under control.

The e-productivity program at 3M embraces the entire organization and all functions. It involves the digitalization of a wide range of processes, from customer ordering and payment, through supply-chain management and inventory control, to managing employee process. The central goal is to boost productivity by using information technology to more effectively manage information within the company and between the company and its customers and suppliers. McNerney cited some $100 million in annual cost savings from this process.

EXHIBIT 3

Selected Financial Data, 1996–2006

	1996	1997	1998	1999	2000	2001	2002	2003	2004	2005	2006
Sales (billion)	$14.2	$15.1	$15.0	$15.7	$16.7	$16.1	$16.3	$18.2	$20.0	$21.0	$22.9
Operating margin	23.7%	23.5%	22.6%	24.7%	23.3%	20.3%	24.5%	26.5%	30.6%	31.1%	31.0%
ROIC	21.7%	23.9%	20.7%	22.5%	25.2%	19.4%	25.1%	25.5%	27.3%	28.5%	28.0%
EPS	$1.82	$1.94	$1.87	$2.11	$2.32	$1.79	$2.50	$3.02	$3.75	$4.12	$4.55

Source: 3M Company, Value Line Investment Survey, November 17, 2006.

The Six Sigma program overlays the entire organization and focuses on improving processes to boost cash flow, lower costs (through productivity enhancements), and boost growth rates. By late 2003, there were some 7,000 Six Sigma projects in process at 3M. By using working capital more efficiently, Six Sigma programs had helped to generate some $800 million in cash, with the total expected to rise to $1.5 billion by the end of 2004. 3M has applied the Six Sigma process to the company's R&D process, enabling researchers to engage customer information in the initial stages of a design discussion. According to Jay Inlenfeld, the vice president of R&D, Six Sigma tools

> Allow us to be more closely connected to the market and give us a much higher probability of success in our new product designs.[19]

Finally, the 3M Acceleration program is aimed at boosting the growth rate from new products through better resource allocation, particularly by shifting resources from slower growing to faster growing markets. As McNerney noted:

> 3M has always had extremely strong competitive positions, but not in markets that are growing fast enough. The issue has been to shift emphasize into markets that are growing faster.[20]

Part of this program is a tool termed 2X/3X. 2X is an objective for two times the number of new products that were introduced in the past, and 3X is a business objective for three times as many winning products as there were in the past (see Exhibit 4). 2X focuses on generating more "major" product initiatives, and 3X on improving the commercialization of those initiatives. The process illustrated in Exhibit 4 is 3M's "stage gate" process, where each gate represents a major decision point in the development of a new product, from idea generation to post-launch.

Other initiates aimed at boosting 3M's organization growth rate through innovation include the Six Sigma process, leadership development programs, and technology leadership (see Exhibit 5). The purpose of these initiatives was to help implement the 2X/3X strategy.

As a further step in the Acceleration program, 3M decided to centralize its corporate R&D effort. Prior to the arrival of McNerney, there were twelve technology centers staffed by 900 scientists that focused on core technology development. The company is replacing these with one central research lab, staffed by 500 scientists, some 120 of whom will be located outside the United States. The remaining 400 scientists will be relocated to R&D centers in the business

---

EXHIBIT 4

The New Product Development Process at 3M

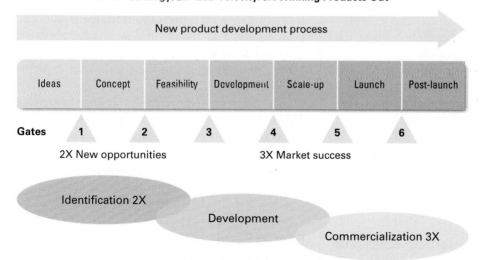

Source: Adapted from a presentation by Jay Inlenfeld, 3M Investor Meeting, September 30, 2003, archived at http://www.corporate-ir.net/ireye/ir_site.zhtml?ticker=MMM&script=2100.

EXHIBIT 5

R&D's Role in Organic Growth

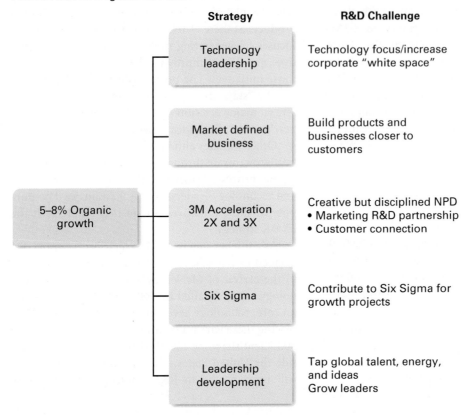

	Strategy	R&D Challenge
	Technology leadership	Technology focus/increase corporate "white space"
	Market defined business	Build products and businesses closer to customers
5–8% Organic growth	3M Acceleration 2X and 3X	Creative but disciplined NPD • Marketing R&D partnership • Customer connection
	Six Sigma	Contribute to Six Sigma for growth projects
	Leadership development	Tap global talent, energy, and ideas Grow leaders

Source: Adapted from a presentation by Jay Inlenfeld, 3M Investor Meeting, September 30, 2003, archived at http://www.corporate-ir.net/ireye/ir_site.zhtml?ticker=MMM&script=2100.

units. The goal of this new corporate research lab is to focus on developing new technology that might fill high-growth "white spaces," which are areas where the company currently has no presence, but where the long-term market potential is great. An example is research on fuel cells, which is currently a big research project within 3M.

Responding to critics' charges that changes such as these might impact on 3M's innovative culture, vice president of R&D Inlenfeld noted:

> We are not going to change the basic culture of innovation at 3M. There is a lot of culture in 3M, but we are going to introduce more systematic, more productive tools that allow our researchers to be more successful.[21]

For example, Inlenfeld repeatedly emphasized that the company remains committed to basic 3M principles, such as the 15% rule and leveraging technology across businesses.

By late 2003, McNerney noted that some 600 new product ideas were under development and that collectively, they were expected to reach the market and generate some $5 billion in new revenues between 2003 and 2006, up from $3.5 billion eighteen months earlier. Some $1 billion of these gains were expected to come in 2003.

The Acceleration program was helping to increase 3M's organic growth rate in earnings per share, which hit an annual rate of 3.6% in the first half of 2003, up from 1% a year earlier and a decline in 2001. To complement internally generated growth, McNerney signaled that he would make selected acquisitions in business that 3M already had a presence in.

George Buckley Takes Over

In mid-2005, McNerney announced that he would leave 3M to become CEO and chairman of Boeing, a company on whose board he had served for some time. He was replaced in late 2005 by another out-sider, George Buckley, the highly regarded CEO of Brunswick Industries. Over the next year in several presentations Buckley outlined his strategy for 3M, and it soon became apparent that he was essentially sticking to the general course laid out by McNerney, albeit with some minor corrections.[22]

Buckley does not see 3M as an enterprise that needs radical change. He sees 3M as a company with impressive internal strengths, but one that has been too cautious about pursuing growth opportunities.[23] Buckley's overall strategic vision for 3M is that the company must solve customer needs through the provision of innovative and differentiated products that increase the efficiency and competitiveness of customers. Consistent with long-term 3M strategy, he sees this as being achieved by taking 3M's multiple technology platforms and applying them to different market opportunities.

Controlling costs and boosting productivity through Six Sigma continue to be a major thrust under Buckley. This was hardly a surprise, since Buckley had pushed Six Sigma at Brunswick. By late 2006, some 55,000 3M employees had been trained in Six Sigma methodology, 20,000 projects had been completed, and some 15,000 were still under way. 3M was also adding techniques gleaned from Toyota's lean production methodology to its Six Sigma tool kit. As a result of Six Sigma and other cost control methods, between 2001 and 2005 productivity measured by sales per employee increased from $234 to $311, and some $750 million were taken out of overhead costs.

In addition to productivity initiatives, Buckley has stressed the need for 3M to more aggressively pursue growth opportunities. He wants the company to use its differentiated brands and technology to continue to develop core businesses and extend those core business into adjacent areas. In addition, like McNerney, Buckley wants the company to focus R&D resources on emerging business opportunities, and he too seems to be prepared to play a more proactive role in this process. Areas of focus include filtration systems, track and trace information technology, energy and mineral extraction, and food safety. 3M made a number of acquisitions during 2005 and 2006 to achieve scale and acquire technology and other assets in these areas. In addition, it increased its own investment in technologies related to these growth opportunities, particularly nanotechnology.

In addition to focusing on growth opportunities, 3M under Buckley has made selective divestures of businesses not seen as core. Most notably, in November 2006, 3M reached an agreement to sell its pharmaceutical business for $2.1 billion. 3M took this step after deciding that slow growth combined with high regulatory and technological risk made the sector an unattractive one that would dampen the company's growth rate.

Finally, Buckley is committed to continuing internationalization at 3M. The goal is to increase foreign sales to 70% of total revenues by 2011, up from 61% in 2006. 3M plans to double its capital investment in the fast-growing markets of China, India, Brazil, Russia, and Poland by 2009. All of these markets are seen as expanding two to three times as fast as the U.S. market.

Judged by the company's financial results between 2001 and 2006, the McNerney and Buckley eras do seem to have improved 3M's financial performance. Most notably, return on invested capital increased from 19.4% to 28%, earning per share from $1.79 to $4.55, operating margins from 20.3% to 31%, and sales from $16 billion to $23 billion. Despite this improvement, the company's stock price had remained mired in the $70 to $80 range since 2003, raising the question of what Buckley needs to do to deliver value to shareholders.

ENDNOTES

1. M. Dickson, "Back to the Future," *Financial Times*, 1994, May 30, page 7. http://www.3m.com/profile/looking/mcknight.jhtml.
2. http://www.3m.com/about3M/pioneers/drew2.jhtml.
3. http://www.3m.com/about3M/innovation/scotchgard50/index.jhtml.
4. 3M, "A Century of Innovation, the 3M Story." 3M, 2002. Available at http://www.3m.com/about3m/century/index.jhtml.
5. 3M, "A Century of Innovation, the 3M Story." 3M, 2002, page 33. Available at http://www.3m.com/about3m/century/index.jhtml.
6. Tim Studt, "3M—Where Innovation Rules," *R&D Magazine*, April 2003, Vol. 45, pages 20–24.
7. 3M, "A Century of Innovation, the 3M Story." 3M, 2002, page 78. Available at http://www.3m.com/about3m/century/index.jhtml.
8. 3M, "A Century of Innovation, the 3M Story." 3M, 2002, page 78. Available at http://www.3m.com/about3m/century/index.jhtml.
9. 3M, "A Century of Innovation, the 3M Story." 3M, 2002, page 42. Available at http://www.3m.com/about3m/century/index.jhtml.
10. Eric Von Hippel et al., "Creating Breakthroughs at 3M," *Harvard Business Review*, September–October 1999.
11. From 3M website at http://www.3m.com/about3M/history/mcknight.jhtml.
12. 3M, "A Century of Innovation, the 3M Story." 3M, 2002, pages 143–144. Available at http://www.3m.com/about3m/century/index.jhtml.
13. Michelle Conlin, "Too Much Doodle?" *Forbes*, October 19, 1998, pages 54–56.
14. De'Ann Weimer, "3M: The Heat Is on the Boss," *Business Week*, March 15, 1999, pages 82–83.

15. Joseph Hallinan, "3M's Next Chief Plans to Fortify Results with Discipline He Learned at GE Unit," *Wall Street Journal*, December 6, 2000, page B17.

16. Jerry Useem, "(Tape) + (Light bulb) = ?" *Fortune*, August 12, 2002, pages 127–131.

17. Rick Mullin, "Analysts Rate 3M's New Culture," *Chemical Week*," September 26, 2001, pages 39–40.

18. 3M Investor Meeting, September 30, 2003, archived at http://www.corporate-ir.net/ireye/ir_site.zhtml?ticker=MMM&script=2100.

19. Tim Studt, "3M—Where Innovation Rules," *R&D Magazine*, April 2003, page 22.

20. 3M Investor Meeting, September 30, 2003, archived at http://www.corporate-ir.net/ireye/ir_site.zhtml?ticker=MMM&script=2100.

21. Tim Studt, "3M—Where Innovation Rules," *R&D Magazine*, April 2003, page 21.

22. Material here drawn from George Buckley's presentation to Prudential's investor conference on "Inside Our Best Ideas," September 28, 2006. This and other relevant presentations are archived at http://investor.3m.com/ireye/ir_site.zhtml?ticker=MMM&script=1200.

23. Jeffery Sprague, "MMM: Searching for Growth with New CEO Leading," *Citigroup Global Markets*, May 2, 2006.

GE's Growth Strategy: The Immelt Initiative

This case was prepared by Christopher A. Bartlett, Harvard Business School.

In February 2006, after four and a half years in the CEO role, Jeff Immelt felt General Electric (GE) was finally poised for the double-digit growth for which he had been positioning it. Having just announced an 11% increase in revenues for 2005 (including 8% organic growth), he was now forecasting a further 10% revenue increase in 2006. And following 12% growth in earnings from continuing operations in 2005 (with all six businesses delivering double-digit increases), he committed to leveraging the 2006 revenues into an even greater 12% to 17% earnings increase. It was a bold pledge for a $150 billion global company. (See Exhibit 1 for GE financial data, 2001–2005.)

Yet, for the past year GE's share price had been stuck at around $35, implying a multiple of around 20 times earnings, only half its price-to-earnings (P/E) ratio in the heady days of 2000. (See Exhibit 2 for GE's 10-year share price history.) It frustrated Immelt that the market did not seem to share the belief that he and his management team had in his growth forecasts. "The stock is currently trading at one of the lowest earnings multiples in a decade," he said. "Investors decide the stock price, but we love the way GE is positioned. We have good results and good governance. . . . What will it take to move the stock?"[1]

Professor Christopher A. Bartlett prepared this case from published sources. HBS cases are developed solely as the basis for class discussion. Cases are not intended to serve as endorsements, sources of primary data, or illustrations of effective or ineffective management.

Taking Charge: Setting the Agenda

On Friday, September 7, 2001, Immelt took over the reins of GE from Jack Welch, the near-legendary CEO who preceded him. Four days later, two planes crashed into the World Trade Center towers, and the world was thrown into turmoil. Not only did 9/11 destabilize an already fragile post-Internet-bubble stock market, but it also triggered a downturn in an overheated economy, leading to a fall in confidence that soon spread into other economies worldwide.

After the chaos of the first few post-9/11 days during which he checked on GE casualties, authorized a $10 million donation to the families of rescue workers, and dispatched mobile generators and medical equipment to the World Trade Center, on September 18 Immelt finally focused on reassuring the financial markets by purchasing 25,000 GE shares on his personal account. Three days later, he appeared before a group of financial analysts and promised that 2001 profits would grow by 11% and by double digits again in 2002. As impressive as such a performance might have appeared, it was less than Welch's expansive suggestion in the heady days of 2000 that GE's profits could grow at 18% per annum in the future.[2] The net result was that by the end of Immelt's first week as CEO, GE's shares had dropped 20%, taking almost $80 billion off the company's market capitalization.

To make matters worse, as the year wore on, a scandal that had been engulfing Enron finally led to that company's bankruptcy. Soon, other companies were caught up in accusations of financial manipulation, including Tyco, a company that had billed itself as a "mini GE." Again, the market punished GE stock, concerned that its large and complex operations were too difficult to understand.

EXHIBIT 1

GE's Performance, 2001–2005: Selected Financial Data

General Electric Company and Consolidated Affiliates (in millions, per share amounts in dollars)

Selected Financial Data	2005	2004	2003	2002	2001
Revenues	$149,702	$134,481	$112,886	$113,856	$107,558
Earnings from continuing operations before accounting changes	18,275	16,285	13,766	15,798	12,948
Earnings (loss) from discontinued operations, net of taxes	−1,922	534	2,057	−616	1,130
Earnings before accounting changes	16,353	16,819	15,823	15,182	14,078
Cumulative effect of accounting changes	—	—	−587	−1,015	−287
Net earnings	16,353	16,819	15,236	14,167	13,791
Dividends declared	9,647	8,594	7,759	7,266	6,555
Return on average shareowners' equity (a)	17.60%	17.60%	19.60%	27.20%	24.70%
Per share					
Earnings from continuing operations before accounting changes—diluted	$ 1.72	$ 1.56	$ 1.37	$ 1.58	$ 1.29
Earnings (loss) from discontinued operations—diluted	−0.18	0.05	0.2	−0.06	0.11
Earnings before accounting changes—diluted	1.54	1.61	1.57	1.51	1.4
Cumulative effect of accounting changes—diluted	—	—	−0.06	−0.1	−0.03
Net earnings—diluted	1.54	1.61	1.51	1.41	1.37
Earnings from continuing operations before accounting changes—basic	1.73	1.57	1.37	1.59	1.3
Earnings (loss) from discontinued operations—basic	−0.18	0.05	0.21	−0.06	0.11
Earnings before accounting changes—basic	1.55	1.62	1.58	1.52	1.42
Cumulative effect of accounting changes—basic	—	—	−0.06	−0.1	−0.03
Net earnings—basic	1.55	1.62	1.52	1.42	1.39
Dividends declared	0.91	0.82	0.77	0.73	0.66
Stock price range	37.34–32.67	37.75–28.88	32.42–21.30	41.84–21.40	52.90–28.25
Year-end closing stock price	35.05	36.5	30.98	24.35	40.08
Total assets of continuing operations	626,586	618,241	503,610	441,768	373,550
Total assets	673,342	750,507	647,828	575,236	495,012
Long-term borrowings	212,281	207,871	170,309	138,570	77,818
Shares outstanding—average (in thousands)	10,569,805	10,399,629	10,018,587	9,947,113	9,932,245
Shareowner accounts—average	634,000	658,000	670,000	655,000	625,000
Employees at year-end					
United States	161,000	165,000	155,000	161,000	158,000
Other Countries	155,000	142,000	150,000	154,000	152,000
Total Employees	316,000	307,000	305,000	315,000	310,000

Source: GE 2005 Annual Report.

EXHIBIT 2

GE Stock Price and P/E Multiple vs. S&P 500 Performance, 1995–2005

GE Price and P/E vs. S&P 500
1995–2006 (indexed 1/1995 = 100)

GE P/E —— S&P 500 —— GE Price ——

Source: Thomson Datastream International.

Beyond all this immediate market pressure, Immelt was acutely aware that he stood in the very long shadow cast by his predecessor, Welch. During his 20 years as CEO, Welch had built GE into a highly disciplined, extremely efficient machine that delivered consistent growth in sales and earnings—not only through effective operations management that resulted in organic growth (much of it productivity-driven) of 5% annually, but also through a continuous stream of timely acquisitions and clever deal making. This two-pronged approach had resulted in double-digit profit increases through most of the 1990s.

The consistent reliability of GE's growth had created an image in shareholders' minds of a powerful machine that could not be stopped and earned the company a significant premium over price/earnings multiples in the broad stock market. As a result, over two decades, GE had generated a compound annual total return to shareholders of more than 23% per annum through the 1980s and 1990s. (See Exhibit 3 for summary GE financials, 1981–2000.) But Immelt was very conscious that he could not hope to replicate that performance by simply continuing the same strategy. "I looked at the world post-9/11 and realized that over the next 10 or 20 years, there was not going to be much tailwind," he said. "It would be more driven by innovation, and a premium would be placed on companies that could generate their own growth."[3]

Building on the Past, Imagining the Future

While recognizing the need for change, Immelt saw little need to challenge the basic business model on which GE had operated for decades. Like his predecessor, he bristled at the characterization of GE as a conglomerate, preferring to see it as a well-integrated, diversified company. On taking charge, he explained:

> Our businesses are closely integrated. They share leading edge business initiatives, excellent financial disciplines, a tradition of sharing talent and best practices, and a culture whose cornerstone is absolute unyielding integrity. Without these powerful ties, we could actually merit the label "conglomerate" that people often inaccurately apply to us. That word just does not apply to GE. . . . What we have is a company of diverse benefits whose sum is truly greater than the parts; a company executing with excellence despite a brutal global economy. . . . We believe GE is different, and one of the things that makes us different is that—in good times and in bad—we deliver. That is who we are. [4]

Immelt committed to building on what he saw as the core elements of the company's past success: a

EXHIBIT 3

GE and Consolidated Affiliates' Financial Performance: 1981–2000 ($ millions)

	2000	1999	1998	1997	1996	1991	1986	1981
Revenues	$129,853	$111,630	$100,469	$90,840	$79,179	$51,283	$36,725	$27,240
Earnings from continuing operations	12,735	10,717	9,296	8,203	7,280	3,943	3,689	N/A
Loss from discontinued operations	—	—	—	—	—	492	N/A	N/A
Net earnings	12,735	10,717	9,296	8,203	7,280	2,636	2,492	1,652
Dividends declared	5,647	4,786	4,081	3,535	3,138	1,808	1,081	715
Earned on average shareowners' equity	27.5%	26.8%	25.7%	25.0%	24.0%	12.2%	17.3%	19.1%
Per share:								
Net earnings	3.87	3.27	2.84	2.50	2.20	2.55	2.73	N/A
Net earnings—diluted	3.81	3.21	2.80	2.46	2.16	1.51	N/A	N/A
Dividends declared	1.71	1.47	1.25	1.08	0.95	1.04	1.18	N/A
Stock price range[a]	181.5–125.0	159.5–94.3	103.9–69.0	76.6–47.9	53.1–34.7	78.1–53.0	44.4–33.2	69.9–51.1
Total assets of continuing operations	437,006	405,200	355,935	304,012	272,402	166,508	84,818	20,942
Long-term borrowings	82,132	71,427	59,663	46,603	49,246	22,602	100,001	1,059
Shares outstanding—average (in thousands)	3,299,037	3,277,826	3,268,998	3,274,692	3,307,394	1,737,863	912,594	227,528
Employees at year-end:								
United States	168,000	167,000	163,000	165,000	155,000	173,000	302,000	N/A
Other countries	145,000	143,000	130,000	111,000	84,000	62,000	71,000	N/A
Discontinued operations (primarily U.S.)	—	—	—	—	—	49,000	N/A	N/A
Total employees	313,000	310,000	293,000	276,000	239,000	284,000	373,000	404,000

Source: GE Annual Reports, various years.

[a]Price unadjusted for four 2-for-1 stock splits during the period.

portfolio of strong businesses, bound through a set of companywide strategic initiatives and managed by great people in a culture that was performance driven and adaptive. It was a source of competitive advantage that Immelt felt was not easily imitated. "It requires financial and cultural commitments over decades," he said.

Having committed to GE's fundamental business model, Immelt wasted little time in articulating a new vision of growth based on using GE's size and diversity as strengths rather than weaknesses. He wanted to take the company into "big, fundamental high-technology infrastructure industries," places where he felt GE could have competitive advantage and where others could not easily follow. He elaborated this into a vision of a global, technology-based, service-intensive company by defining a growth strategy based on five key elements:

- **Technical leadership:** Believing that technology had been at GE's core since the day Thomas Edison founded the company, Immelt committed to technical leadership as a key driver of future growth.

- **Services acceleration:** By building service businesses on its massive installed base of aircraft engines, power turbines, locomotives, medical devices, and other hardware, Immelt believed GE could better serve customers while generating high margins and raising entry barriers.

- **Commercial excellence:** Reflecting his own sales and marketing background, Immelt committed to creating a world-class commercial culture to overlay the engineering bias and financial orientation of GE's dominant business approach under Welch.

- **Globalization:** Building on an old Welch initiative, Immelt committed to expanding GE's sourcing strategy and market access worldwide, in particular focusing on its underexploited opportunities in developing world countries such as China and India.

- **Growth platforms:** Finally, he recognized that significant resource reallocation would be necessary to build new business platforms capitalizing on "unstoppable trends" that would provide growth into the future.

Because plans at GE always came with measurable goals attached, Immelt committed to increasing the company's organic growth from its historical 5% annual rate to 8% and, beginning in 2005, to generating consistent double-digit earnings growth.

Investing through the Down Cycle

Perhaps predictably, the press was skeptical of the notion that a $130 billion company could grow at two to three times the global gross national product (GNP) rate. Still, there was no shortage of advice for the new CEO in his attempt to make the company do so. Some suggested he should sell off the mature lighting and appliances businesses.[5] Others proposed bold expansions—into the hospital business, for example.[6] And as always, there were calls for GE to break up the company and sell off its component businesses.[7] But Immelt insisted GE had great businesses that provided a strong foundation for the future. All he planned to do was rebalance and renew the portfolio, then drive growth from the revitalized base.

Within weeks of taking charge, he started making significant investments to align GE's businesses for growth. Seeing opportunities to expand its NBC broadcast business to capture the fast-growing Hispanic advertising market, for example, the company acquired the Telemundo and Bravo networks. And its power-generation business acquired Enron's wind energy business as a new platform that management felt was positioned for long-term growth and high returns in the future.

In addition to these and other natural business extensions, management identified whole new segments that provided a stronger foundation for innovation and where future market opportunities would drive rapid growth. For example, in security systems, GE acquired Interlogix, a medium-sized player with excellent technology, and in water services, it bought BetzDearborn, a leading company with 2,000 sales engineers on the ground.

Internally, Immelt also lost little time in making big financial commitments to the growth strategy. Within his first six months, he committed $100 million to upgrade GE's major research and development (R&D) facility at Nishayuna in upstate New York. In addition to building new laboratories, the investment provided for new meeting centers on Nishayuna's 525-acre campus, creating an environment where business managers and technologists could meet to discuss priorities. Scott Donnelly, a 40-year-old researcher who led GE's overall R&D activity, said, "GE is not the place for scientists who want to work on a concept for years without anybody bothering them. Here scientists can do long-term research, but they have to be willing to spar with the marketing guys. This is the best of both worlds."[8]

Although Immelt was willing to increase his commitment to R&D, he pushed to change the balance of work being done. In addition to developing technologically sophisticated new products, he wanted to commit more resources to longer-term research that might not pay off for a decade or more. In the past, limited commitment to such long-term research had frustrated many of the center's science and engineering Ph.Ds. ("Science was a dirty word for a while," said Anil Duggal, a project leader on the advanced lighting project. "Now it's not.")[9] In selecting the long-term projects for funding, Donnelly whittled down more than 2,000 proposals and then worked with researchers to come up with the technologies that could transform a business. From the 20 big ideas his staff proposed, Donnelly had them focus on a group of five, representing fields as diverse as nanotechnology, advanced propulsion, and biotechnology.

Beyond its historic Nishayuna R&D facility, in 2000 the company had established a center in Bangalore, India. To build on that global expansion, in 2002 Immelt authorized the construction of a new facility in Shanghai, China. And as the year wore on, he began talking about adding a fourth global facility, probably in Europe.[a] Despite the slowing economy, he upped the R&D budget from $286 million in 2000 to $327 million in 2002. When asked about this increase in spending during such a difficult time for the company, he said, "Organic growth is the driver. Acquisitions are secondary to that—I can't see us go out and pay a start-up $100 million for technology that, if we had just spent $2 million a year for 10 years, we could've done a better job at. I hate that, I just hate that."[10]

Reflecting on his extensive investments in 2002, a year in which the stock dropped a further 39% from its 2001 close, Immelt said:

> Financial strength gives us the ability to invest in growth and we have viewed this economic cycle as a time to invest. We've increased the number of engineers, salespeople, and service resources. We will invest more than $3 billion in technology, including major investments in our global resource centers. We've strengthened our commitment to China, increasing resources there 25% in 2002, and we've increased our presence in Europe. Acquisitions are a key form of investment for us and we have invested nearly $35 billion in acquisitions over the past two years. They are a key way for us to redeploy cash flow for our future growth.[11]

Ongoing Operations: Rigor and Responsiveness

To fund his strategy, Immelt drew his first source of capital from the sale of underperforming businesses, and the company's struggling insurance business was his prime target for divesture. But in the depths of an economic downturn, getting good prices for any business was not easy. So the investments needed to drive the company's growth still relied primarily on funds generated by ongoing operations, and Immelt drove the organization to deliver on the market's expectations for current-year performance. Picking up on initiatives launched years earlier, he harnessed well-embedded capabilities such as Six Sigma and digitization to drive out costs, increase process efficiency, and manage resources more effectively.

In this tough environment, Immelt's primary operating focus was on cash flow, and he realigned all the powerful tools in GE's toolbox to meet that objective. For example, Six Sigma discipline was applied to reducing the cash tied up in inventory and receivables, while process digitization was focused on sourcing economies and infrastructure efficiencies. By 2002, digitization alone was generating savings of almost $2 billion of savings a year. As always at GE, initiatives were tied to metrics, with 60% of incentive compensation dependent on cash flow generation. So, despite a tough 2002 economy that held GE's revenue growth to 5%, its cash flow from operations was $15.2 billion, up 10% on the previous year.

Although this disciplined approach was reminiscent of GE in decades past, Immelt's management style contrasted with Welch's in many ways. First, he recognized that in a post-Enron world, corporate executives faced a more skeptical and often cynical group of critics. For example, an article in *Business-Week* suggested, "Increasingly, the Welch record of steady double digit growth is looking less like a miracle of brilliant management and more like clever accounting that kept investors fat and happy in boom

---

[a] In 2003, GE opened its Shanghai research center and broke ground for another center in Siemens's backyard in Munich, Germany. In 2004, its 2,500 researchers worldwide filed for more than 450 patents.

times."[12] And *The Economist* opined, "Immelt has had a torrid time since taking over from Jack Welch, GE's former boss, in 2001. Waking from the dreamy 1990s, investors discovered that GE was not, after all, a smooth earnings machine that pumped out profit growth of 16 to 18% a year."[13]

Immelt understood that in such a skeptical environment, there was a need for a CEO to establish much more openness and trust. Since his natural style tended to be open and communicative, he was perfectly comfortable with the idea of increasing the transparency of GE's often complex operations. In July 2002, to make the performance of GE's financial businesses easier to understand, he broke GE Capital into four separate businesses, each with its own balance sheet and explicit growth strategy. He also committed to communicating more frequently and in more detail with investors. "We have the goal of talking about GE externally the way we run it internally," he said. After his first analysts meeting, where everyone got an advance bound copy of the data and forecasts, *BusinessWeek* commented, "That's already a break with the Welch regime where, some say, you were scared to blink in case you missed a chart."[14]

The new CEO also wanted to create a more open and less hard-edged environment within the company. He asked the 2002 class of GE's Executive Development Course (EDC) to study where GE stood in its approach to corporate responsibility.[b] Historically, this was not an issue that had received much attention at GE. Although Welch had always emphasized the importance of integrity and compliance, he had shown little interest in reaching beyond that legal requirement. The several dozen participants in the 2002 EDC visited investors, regulators, activists, and 65 companies in the U.S. and Europe to understand how GE was performing in terms of corporate responsibility. They reported to top management that although the company was ranked in the top five for its financial performance, investment value, and management talent, it was number 72 for social responsibility.

One outcome of the EDC group's report was that Immelt appointed GE's first vice president for corporate

citizenship. He tapped Bob Corcoran, a trusted colleague from his days running GE Medical Systems, to lead an effort to ensure that the company was more sensitive and responsive to its broader societal responsibilities. Ever the pragmatist, Immelt saw this as more than just an altruistic response. He believed it was important for the company to remain effective:

> To be a great company today, you also have to be a good company. The reason people come to work for GE is that they want to be involved in something bigger than themselves. They want to work hard, they want to get promoted, they want stock options. But they also want to work for a company that makes a difference, a company that's doing great things in the world.... It's up to us to use our platform to be a good citizen. Because not only is it a nice thing to do, it's a business imperative.[15]

Rebuilding the Foundation: Beginning a Marathon

As 2003 began, Immelt was not sorry to see the end of his first full year as CEO. Despite all his efforts, 2002 had been a terrible year for the company. Revenues were up only 5% after a 3% decline the prior year. And rather than the double-digit growth he had promised, 2002 earnings increased by only 7%. By year's end the stock was at $24, down 39% from the year before and 60% from its all-time high of $60 in August 2000. Having lived through a struggling economy, the post-9/11 chaos, new regulatory demands following the corporate scandals, and an unstable global political situation, Immelt commented, "This was a not a great year to be a rookie CEO."[16]

In the midst of the turmoil, however, he reminded himself of advice he received from his predecessor. "One of the things Jack said early on that I think is totally right is: It's a marathon, it's not a sprint," Immelt recalled. "You have to have a plan, and you have to stick with it. You have to modify it at times, but every day you've got to get out there and play it hard."[17] Entering 2003 with that thought in mind, Immelt continued to drive his growth-strategy agenda.

Rebalancing the Portfolio

The year turned out to be an important one in the new CEO's efforts to rebuild the business portfolio on which he would drive GE's growth. Even after

---

[b] EDC was the top-level course at GE's renowned Crotonville training center and was reserved for those destined for the most senior echelons of management at GE. As part of their studies, each EDC class was assigned a major corporate issue to study in teams and then report back to GE's Corporate Executive Council.

completing $35 billion worth of acquisitions in the previous two years, 2003 became the biggest acquisition year in GE's history with total commitments exceeding $30 billion. The first megadeal came when the company decided to bid for the Universal entertainment business of French conglomerate Vivendi. Defying those who suggested that GE should exit the volatile media business, Immelt pushed ahead with the acquisition, which included Universal's film library, film studio, cable services, and theme park. "This is about stuff we know how to do," he said. "We understand the nuances of this industry and where it's going."[18]

Immelt's vision was to create a media business that was better positioned for a digital future. The NBC franchise, although strong, was being buffeted by changes in media distribution that saw the share of broadcast television's market shrinking. Universal added content, production facilities, cable distribution, and a strong management team—all assets that Immelt felt could greatly strengthen GE's core business. On top of that, the $5.5 billion up-front purchase price for assets valued at $14 billion was seen as an excellent buy.

Two days after announcing final terms in its purchase of Vivendi-Universal Entertainment (VUE), GE announced an agreement to purchase Amersham, a British life sciences and medical diagnostic company that Immelt had been pursuing for many months. He believed that health care was moving into an era of biotechnology, advanced diagnostics, and targeted therapies, and combining GE's imaging technology with Amersham's pharmaceutical biomarkers, for example, could create whole new ways of diagnosing and treating diseases. At $10 billion, this was a more expensive acquisition but one that he believed could boost GE's $9 billion medical products business to a $15 billion business by 2005. More important, he saw it as an engine of growth that would continue for years and even decades into the future. In his mind, it was a classic "growth platform."

The real issue that many saw in the deal, however, was less about strategic fit than organizational compatibility. The concern was that the highly innovative, science-oriented talent that Amersham had developed in the U.K. would not thrive when swallowed up by GE. It was the same criticism that Immelt had heard when critics wondered whether the creative talent in Universal's film studios would tolerate the management discipline for which GE was so well-known. But the idea of bringing creative and innovative outsiders into GE was part of the appeal to Immelt. He saw people like Sir William Castell, Amersham's CEO, as major assets who could help develop in GE the culture of innovation that he longed to build. To emphasize the point, he put U.K.-based Castell in charge of the combined $14 billion business renamed GE Health Care and made him a vice chairman of GE. For the first time, one of the company's major businesses would be headquartered outside of the United States, a move that Immelt felt fit well with his thrust of globalization.

The other great challenge in the ongoing task of portfolio rebalancing was that GE was finding it difficult to dispose of some of the assets it no longer regarded as vital. While the recession provided lots of buying opportunities if one was willing to step up and invest, it was hardly an ideal environment in which to be selling businesses. For GE, the biggest challenge was to find buyers for the struggling insurance businesses. Although its 2003 sale of three of its major insurance entities had freed up $4.5 billion in cash, the company was still trying to find a buyer for Employers Reinsurance Company (ERC), a business generating huge ongoing losses due to its poor underwriting in the late 1990s.[c] And several other GE businesses from motors to super adhesives remained on the blocks with no bidder offering a price the company was willing to accept. Part of the problem was that bidders felt that if GE had run the business for years, most of the potential savings had already been extracted, making the units being offered less attractive for a company that wanted to squeeze out costs.

To communicate the major portfolio transformation he had undertaken to date, in 2003 Immelt began describing GE's businesses as "growth engines" and "cash generators" (see Exhibit 4). He characterized the former, which accounted for 85% of earnings, as market leaders that could grow at 15% annually through the business cycles with high returns. The latter were acknowledged as being more cyclical in nature but with consistently strong cash flows.

Focusing on Customers, Emphasizing Services

In addition to his portfolio changes, the new CEO kept working on his internal growth initiatives. As an

---

[c] After taking a $1.4 billion write-off in 2004 due to claims relating to asbestos and September 11, the company finally sold ERC for $8.5 billion in 2005, but only after booking another $2.9 billion insurance loss.

EXHIBIT 4

GE Portfolio: Growth Engines and Cash Generators

GROWTH ENGINES

Commercial Finance
GE Commercial Finance offers businesses an array of financial services and products worldwide. With particular expertise in the mid-market segment, Commercial Finance also offers loans and financing leases for major capital assets, including aircraft fleets, industrial facilities and equipment, and energy-related facilities; real estate loans and investments; and loans to and investments in public and private entities in diverse industries.

Consumer Finance
GE Consumer Finance is a leading provider of credit services to consumers, retailers and auto dealers in over 38 countries around the world. The business offers a range of financial products, including private label credit cards, personal loans, bank cards, auto loans and leases, residential mortgages, corporate travel and purchasing cards, debt consolidation, home equity loans and credit insurance.

Energy
GE Energy is one of the world's leading suppliers of technology to the energy industry, providing a comprehensive range of solutions for oil and gas, traditional and renewable power generation and energy management.

Healthcare
GE Healthcare is a global leader in diagnostic and interventional medical imaging, information and services technology. The pending acquisition of Amersham plc, a world leader in diagnostic imaging agents and life sciences, will transform GE Healthcare into the world's most comprehensive medical diagnostics company.

Infrastructure
GE Infrastructure is a high-technology platform comprising some of GE's fastest-growing businesses. They offer a set of protection and productivity solutions to some of the most pressing issues that industries face: pure water, safe facilities, plant automation and sensing applications for operating environments.

NBC
America's first broadcast network, NBC is a diverse, international media company with the Number One-ranked U.S. television network, 29 owned and operated stations, cable channels CNBC, MSNBC, and Bravo, and Spanish-language broadcaster Telemundo. NBC and Vivendi Universal Entertainment have agreed to merge and form NBC Universal, creating one of the world's fastest-growing media companies.

Transportation
GE Transportation comprises Aircraft Engines and Rail, two industry-leading business units whose products and services span the aviation, rail, marine and off-highway industries with jet engines for military and civil aircraft, freight and passenger locomotives, motorized systems for mining trucks and drills, and gas turbines for marine and industrial applications.

Leading with PORTFOLIO TRANSFORMATION

CASH GENERATORS

Advanced Materials
GE Advanced Materials is a world leader in providing customers in a wide range of industries with materials solutions through engineering thermoplastics, silicon-based products and technology platforms, and fused quartz and ceramics.

Consumer and Industrial
GE Consumer and Industrial serves customers in more that 100 countries with appliances, lighting products and integrated industrial equipment, systems and services sold under the Monogram®, Profile™, GE®, Hotpoint®, SmartWater™, and Reveal® consumer brands, and the Entellisys™ industrial brand.

Equipment Services
GE Equipment Services helps medium- and large-sized businesses around the world manage, finance and operate a wide variety of business equipment. Products and services include operating leases, loans, sales and transportation asset management services.

Insurance
GE Insurance offers a wide range of insurance and investment products. For businesses, GE Insurance provides insurance and reinsurance products to insurance companies, Fortune 1000 companies, self-insurers and healthcare providers. It helps consumers create and preserve personal wealth, protect assets and enhance their lifestyles.

As of January 1, 2004, GE has reorganized its 13 businesses into 11 focused on markets and customers—seven Growth Engines, which generate about 85% of earnings and are market leaders with strengths in technology, cost, services, global distribution and capital efficiency; and four Cash Generators, which consistently generate strong cash flow and grow earnings in an expanding economy.

This chart reflects the most significant changes: the combination of Aircraft Engines and Rail into GE Transportation; the combination of Industrial Systems and Consumer Products into Consumer & Industrial, with portions of Industrial Systems moving to other businesses; and the formation of Infrastructure from portions of Industrial Systems and Specialty Materials. Results for 2003 in this annual report are reported on the 13-business basis in effect in 2003.

Source: GE 2003 Annual Report, p. 6.

ex-salesman, Immelt had always directed attention toward the customer, and one of his priorities was to redirect GE's somewhat internal focus—an unintended by-product of Welch's obsession with operating efficiency and cost-cutting—toward the external environment. "In a deflationary world, you could get margin by working productivity," he said. "Now you need marketing to get a price."[19]

In 2001, among his first appointments had been Beth Comstock, named as GE's first chief marketing officer. Next, to drive the change deeper, he redeployed most of GE's extensive business development staff into marketing roles, then asked each of GE's businesses to appoint a VP-level marketing head, many of whom had to be recruited from the outside. "We hired literally thousands of marketers," he said. "For the best, we created the Experienced Commercial Leadership Program, the kind of intensive course we've long offered in finance. That's 200 people a year, every year."[20]

In 2003, with strong marketing capabilities now embedded in the businesses, he formed a Commercial Council to bring GE's best sales and marketing leaders together in a forum that could transfer best practice, drive initiatives rapidly through the organization, and develop a world-class commercial culture. Chaired by Immelt personally, the council's agenda included developing world-class marketing capabilities, taking Six Sigma to customers, and driving sales force effectiveness. As always, metrics were attached. Using a tool called Net Promoter Score (NPS), the company began to track changes in customer attitudes and loyalty, tying compensation to improvements in NPS scores. "If we can create a sales and marketing function that's as good as finance at GE, I'll change this company," he said. "But it will take ten years to drive these changes."[21]

Immelt also believed GE could significantly strengthen its customer relationships by becoming more of a services provider. In 2002, $23 billion of the company's $132 billion revenue came from services, but with its massive installed base of more than 100,000 long-lived jet engines, locomotives, power generators, and medical devices in the field, the CEO saw the potential service annuity stream. As someone who had increased GE Medical Systems' share of service business from 25% to 42% in the three and a half years he headed that operation, Immelt was convinced that services could grow much faster than hardware and at much higher profit levels. To underscore his belief, whenever businesses developed important service

contracts—GE Transportation's sale of its IT-based dispatch system to railroad customers to increase locomotive utilization, for example—he celebrated them very publicly.

Yet despite all these efforts, the reality was that just as many of GE's products were becoming commodities, its service contracts were increasingly going to the lowest bidder and not providing the barriers to entry they once did. GE's solution was to make itself indispensable by building enduring relationships based not only on offering its products and services but also its expertise.

One initiative, dubbed "At the Customer, For the Customer" (ACFC, as it soon became known), was designed to bring GE's most effective internal tools and practices to bear on its customers' challenges. Immelt used health care as an example of what GE could offer. With cost control being a major concern as health-care expenditures headed toward 20% of GDP, Immelt felt that GE could help its customers, only 50% of which were profitable. "Through our health care services agreements, we are the hospitals' productivity partner," he said. "We completed more than 6,000 Six Sigma projects with health care providers in 2002 and these projects are improving the quality of patient care and lowering costs."[22] In addition, the company began bundling its services and linking its products to clinical information technology. It also added a health-care financial services business to the GE Health Care organization to provide it with specialized financing support. "The phrase 'solutions provider' is so overused it makes us all snore," said Immelt. "I want GE to be essential to those whom we serve, a critical part of the profit equation, a long-term partner, a friend."[23]

Driving for Growth: New Platforms, New Processes

Beginning in 2002, Immelt had challenged his business leaders to identify growth business platforms with the potential to generate $1 billion in operating profit within the next few years. In response, six opportunities had emerged: health-care information systems, security and sensors, water technology and services, oil and gas technology, Hispanic broadcasting, and consumer finance. By the end of 2002, these businesses represented $9 billion in revenue and $2 billion in operating profit. But, as Immelt pointed out, at a 15% annual organic growth rate, they were on track to become a much larger portion of GE's future business portfolio.

With 2003's major acquisitions such as Amersham and VUE, the company added new growth platforms such as biosciences and film/DVD to its list. Through other acquisitions, renewable energy (wind, solar, biomass), coal gasification, and supply chain financing became elements of GE's new growth platform. And the emphasis on services built a series of businesses in environmental services, nondestructive testing, and asset optimization that were also seen as having high growth potential.

In defining and then building these growth platforms, GE followed its normal disciplined approach. First, management segmented the broad markets and identified the high-growth segments where they believed they could add value. Then, they typically launched their initiative with a small acquisition in that growth platform. After integrating it into GE, the objective was to transform the acquisition's business model by applying GE growth initiatives (services and globalization, for example) that could leverage its existing resources and capabilities. As a final step, the company applied its financial muscle to the new business, allowing it to invest in organic growth or further acquisitions. The objective was to grow it rapidly while simultaneously generating solid returns.

GE's expansion into Hispanic broadcasting provides an example of the process. After identifying this as a fast-growth segment in its broadcast business, the company acquired Telemundo, the number two player in the Hispanic entertainment segment. Believing that the Hispanic demographic would drive growth, management felt that it would be able to apply GE's capabilities to fix Telemundo's struggling business model. Through 2002 and 2003, NBC offered its management and programming expertise, helping Telemundo to evolve from purchasing 80% of its content to producing two-thirds of its own broadcast material. In the second half of 2003, Telemundo grew its ratings by 50% over the first half and captured 25% of the Hispanic advertising market. The company expected revenues to grow more than 20% in 2004.

As Immelt summarized, "A key GE strength is our ability to conceptualize the future, to identify unstoppable trends, and to develop new ways to grow. The growth platforms we have identified are markets that have above average growth rates and can uniquely benefit from GE's capabilities. . . . Growth is *the* initiative, *the* core competency that we are building in GE."[24]

Aligning Management: New People Profiles

The biggest challenge Immelt saw in implementing his agenda was to make growth the personal mission of every one of the company's 310,000 employees worldwide. "If I want people to take more risks, solve bigger problems, and grow the business in a way that's never been done before, I have to make it personal," he said. "So I tell people, 'Start your career tomorrow. If you had a bad year, learn from it and do better. If you had a good year, I've already forgotten about it.'"[25]

As the company began to implement its new growth strategy, the CEO worried that some of his current management team might not have the skills or abilities to succeed in the more entrepreneurial risk-taking environment he was trying to create. Realizing that this implied a massive challenge to develop a new generation of what he termed "growth leaders," he said:

> Historically, we have been known as a company that developed professional managers . . . broad problem solvers with experience in multiple businesses and functions. However, I wanted to raise a generation of *growth leaders*—people with market depth, customer touch, and technical understanding. This change emphasizes depth. We are expecting people to spend more time in a business or a job. We think this will help leaders develop "market instincts" so important for growth, and the confidence to grow global businesses.[26]

Beyond changes in career path development that emphasized more in-depth experience and fewer job rotations, GE's HR professionals wanted to identify the new personal competencies that growth leaders would need to exhibit. Benchmarking GE against best practice, they researched the leadership profiles at 15 large global companies—Toyota and Dell among them—that had grown for more than a decade at three times GDP rates or better. In late 2004, they arrived at a list of five action-oriented leadership traits they would require: an *external focus* that defines success in market terms; an ability to *think clearly* to simplify strategy into specific actions, make decisions, and communicate priorities; the *imagination and courage* to take risks on people and ideas; an ability to energize teams through *inclusiveness and connection with people*, building both loyalty and commitment; and an *expertise* in a function or domain, using depth as a source of confidence to drive change.

To help develop these characteristics, each business created 20 to 30 "pillar jobs": customer-facing, change-oriented assignments in which growth leaders could be developed in assignments of at least four to five years. The new leadership competencies also became the criteria for all internal training programs and were integrated into the evaluation processes used in all management feedback.

Immelt was also quite involved personally in developing growth leaders on his team. In response to a question about his time utilization, he said, "I'm probably spending 20% of my time with customers, 30% of my time on people, teaching and coaching . . . [and] 10% of my time on governance, working with the board, and meeting with investors. The rest would be time spent on the plumbing of the company, working on operating reviews and strategy sessions."[27] But, as he regularly pointed out, the time he spent on the "plumbing" in operating reviews and strategy sessions—"touch points," he called them—was primarily about people development. He was committed to make "every moment a learning opportunity, every activity a source of evaluation."[28]

Funding the Growth: Operating Excellence

While driving growth, Immelt never forgot that he inherited a great operating company. He did not want long-term growth to distract managers from current performance. "I've always worried about a jailbreak," he said. "How do we make sure people don't say 'Jeff doesn't care about productivity'?"[29] So he insisted that innovation be "funded with an intent to lead, but paid for by increasing productivity."[30] During 2003, for example, about one-third of the Six Sigma specialists were focused on a new initiative called "cash entitlement." The target was for GE to be twice as good as competitors on a number of benchmarks such as accounts receivable or inventory turnover. At full potential, Immelt told his team, it would free up an additional $7 billion in cash.

By 2004, while the drives for cash generation and cost reduction were still in place, Immelt added a new initiative called Lean Six Sigma, which borrowed the classic tools of lean manufacturing and set them to new applications. In its industrial businesses, the focus was on reducing working capital and improving return on equity, while in its commercial finance business it was on margin expansion, risk management, and cost reduction. Through these efforts, in 2003–2004, the company achieved $2.7 billion in improvement in working capital and expected that kind of progress to continue.

Yet another operating initiative called "simplification" aimed at reducing overhead from 11% of revenue to 8%. Targeting reductions in the number of legal entities, headquarters, "rooftops," computer systems, and other overhead-type costs not directly linked to growth, the company set a goal of removing $3 billion of such costs over three years. In the first year, the commercial finance business consolidated into three customer service/operations centers and expected to save $300 million over three years. In another simplification move, the consumer and industrial business brought its three existing headquarters into one, saving more than $100 million in structural costs. And the transportation and energy businesses began sharing some IT and operational assets that also reduced structural costs by some $300 million annually.

Preparing for Liftoff: Innovation and Internationalization

As 2004 progressed, the worldwide economy gradually started to turn around, and GE began showing signs of more robust growth. By year's end, nine of its 11 businesses had grown their earnings by double digits. For the first time, Immelt sounded confident that the company was finally moving beyond the disappointing results of the previous three years and onto the growth trajectory for which he had been preparing it. In his annual letter to stakeholders in February 2005, he recalled his time as a college football player to draw a sports analogy to GE's recent performance:

> GE has "played hurt" for the last few years. . . . So we went to the "training room." These difficult years triggered a critical review of our capabilities, and as a result, we initiated an exciting transformation. We invested more than $60 billion to create a faster-growing company. We committed to divest $15 billion of slow-growth assets. We built new capabilities, launched new products, expanded globally and invested in the GE brand. Now the company has begun an era of strong performance. . . . We're back at full strength. This is our time.[31]

To underscore the point, he predicted that GE's "growth engines"—businesses whose earnings growth since 1999 had averaged 15% annually—would generate 90% of the company's earnings in 2005, compared with only 67% in 2000. (See Exhibit 5 for a representation of the shift.) Due to this transformation of the

EXHIBIT 5

GE's Representation of Its Portfolio Transformation, 2000–2005

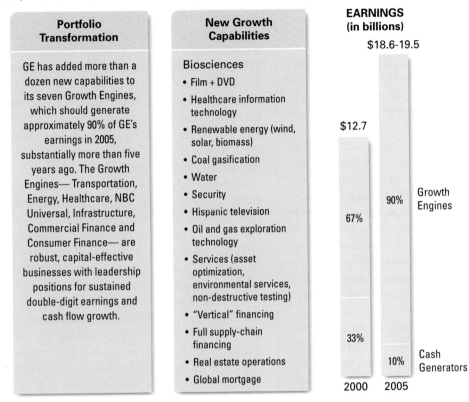

Portfolio Transformation

GE has added more than a dozen new capabilities to its seven Growth Engines, which should generate approximately 90% of GE's earnings in 2005, substantially more than five years ago. The Growth Engines— Transportation, Energy, Healthcare, NBC Universal, Infrastructure, Commercial Finance and Consumer Finance— are robust, capital-effective businesses with leadership positions for sustained double-digit earnings and cash flow growth.

New Growth Capabilities

Biosciences
- Film + DVD
- Healthcare information technology
- Renewable energy (wind, solar, biomass)
- Coal gasification
- Water
- Security
- Hispanic television
- Oil and gas exploration technology
- Services (asset optimization, environmental services, non-destructive testing)
- "Vertical" financing
- Full supply-chain financing
- Real estate operations
- Global mortgage

EARNINGS (in billions)

$18.6-19.5

$12.7

2000: 67% / 33%
2005: 90% Growth Engines / 10% Cash Generators

Source: GE 2004 Annual Report, p. 4.

business portfolio and also the addition of more than a dozen new capabilities from biosciences to renewable energy, Immelt claimed that for the first time in 20 years, GE was positioned to grow its industrial earnings faster than its financial services earnings.

Imagination Breakthroughs

To drive his earlier growth platform challenge deep into the organization, the CEO launched a process he called "imagination breakthroughs," quickly abbreviated to IBs. These were projects—technological innovations, market expansion opportunities, product commercialization proposals, or ideas to create value for customers—that had the potential to generate, over a three-year horizon, at least $100 million in incremental earnings. The process required each business leader to submit at least three breakthrough proposals a year for review by the Commercial Council. "Imagination Breakthroughs are a protected class of ideas—safe from budget slashers because I've

blessed each one," said Immelt. "What we're trying to do is take risks, using my point of view. I have the biggest risk profile and broadest time horizon in the company . . . so I can bring to bear the right risk-taking and time horizon tradeoffs."[32]

A year into the program, 80 IB initiatives had been identified and qualified—half technically based programs and half commercial innovations. Immelt had assigned the company's best people to drive them and had committed $5 billion over the next three years to fully fund them. In that time, they were expected to deliver $25 billion of additional revenue growth. By 2005, 25 IBs were generating revenue. "The big difference is that the business leaders have no choices here," Immelt explained. "Nobody is allowed not to play. Nobody can say, 'I'm going to sit this one out.' That's the way you drive change."[33]

Believing that the businesses could initiate 200 such projects over the next year or two, Immelt said, "Our employees want to live their dreams. It is up to me to give them that platform. I can help them take smart risks that will win over time. . . . We aim to be the best in the world at turning small ideas into huge businesses."[34]

Of Town Halls and Dreaming

To stimulate ideas that would drive the imagination breakthroughs, Immelt continued to push his leaders to get out in the field and in touch with the market. Setting the example himself by spending at least five days a month with customers, he began creating forums he called "town hall meetings." Here, several hundred customers would gather together to hear where GE's CEO wanted to take his company, to provide input on that direction, and to suggest how GE could be more helpful to them.

As an outgrowth of these meetings, Immelt decided to create another forum that he described as "dreaming sessions." In these sessions, he engaged in intensive conversations with a group of senior executives drawn from key customers in a particular industry to try to identify major industry trends, their likely implications for them, and how GE might be able to help them. Immelt understood the importance of his own role in these meetings. "If I show up, we'll get six CEOs to show up," he said. "So you don't have to cut through anything else if we all do it together. We can make some high-level tradeoffs that way."[35]

For example, in one meeting with the CEOs and key operating managers of companies in the railroad industry, Immelt spent an afternoon listening to their view of their industry situation, the key trends, and its five- to 10-year outlook. GE's CEO then asked them to think through a number of scenarios including higher fuel prices, a growth in east-west rail shipments due to increasing Chinese imports, and so on. He then challenged them to think through how they would spend $200 million to $400 million on R&D at GE. The ensuing debate highlighted, for example, the relative importance of spending on fuel efficiency versus information technology to optimize rail movement planning. But Immelt was careful to note that while the company listened carefully to the input, GE always made its own choices on these investments. "I love customers. I get great insight from them, but I would never let them set our strategy for us," he said. "But by talking to them, I can put it in my own language. Customers always pay our bills, but they will never pick our people or set our strategies."[36]

Infrastructure for Developing Countries: A New Growth Market

In 2004, Immelt's push for globalization also began bearing fruit with revenues from outside the U.S. growing 18% to $72 billion. Of this, the developing world accounted for $21 billion, an even more impressive 37% increase on the previous year, leading Immelt to predict that over the next decade, 60% of GE's international growth would come from developing countries. China represented the most visible growth opportunity, but he also planned to expand aggressively into India, Russia, Eastern Europe, Southeast Asia, the Middle East, and South America.

Through the imagination breakthrough program, proposals for improving GE's ways of doing business in the developing world began bubbling up. For example, one plan that would quickly generate $100 million in sales involved shipping unassembled locomotives to Russia, India, and China, where they would be assembled in local factories and workshops.

Furthermore, through an initiative known as "one GE," the company began creating vertical teams to deliver what it called enterprise selling. For example, companywide enterprise teams had targeted the Olympics in Beijing, Vancouver, and London and were aiming to deliver additional sales of $1 billion in energy, security, lighting, and health-care products to those venues. And increasingly GE was adopting "company-to-country relationships" in selling infrastructure projects. It was an approach that had helped it book $8 billion in Middle East orders in 2005, twice the level of 2003.

Reorganizing for Efficiency—and Growth

Driven by such developments, in July 2005, Immelt announced a major reorganization that consolidated GE's 11 businesses into six large units, one of which was GE Infrastructure. Integrating aircraft engines, rail products, water energy, oil and gas, and some financial services, the unit was headed by GE veteran David Calhoun, who aimed to offer one-stop shopping for all infrastructure products and services. Immelt's expectation was that by focusing on the needs of an underserved customer group—the governments of developing countries—GE could tap into investments in developing country infrastructure predicted to be $3 trillion over the next 10 years.

While one objective of the reorganization was to create savings (expected to be $400 million in administrative costs alone), Immelt emphasized that a more important goal was to better align the businesses with customer and market needs. But he also made clear that he wanted to create an organization that gave more opportunity for younger growth leaders to drive their businesses. The six new macrobusiness groups—GE Industrial, GE Commercial Financial Services, NBC Universal, GE Health Care, GE Consumer Finance, and GE Infrastructure—would each be led by one of GE's most experienced top executives. But these individuals would be forced to step back more from operations and spend most of their time coaching, developing, and supporting the younger managers who were to be pulled up into the 50-odd profit-responsible units directly under them. It was all part of the company's commitment to developing its growth leaders and the businesses they ran.

Going Forward: Immelt's Challenges

In 2006, Immelt felt that GE was well placed on the growth path he had laid out over four years earlier. Between 2002 and 2005, he had put $30 billion of divestitures on the block, completed $65 billion in acquisitions, and made major investments in new capabilities in technology, marketing, and innovation. He now represented GE's growth engine as a linked six-part process (see Exhibit 6). While the components varied little from his original 2001 list

---

EXHIBIT 6

GE Growth Strategy: Core Elements, 2005 Version

Growth Is the GE Initiative. After growing historically at an average of 5% revenue growth, in 2004, we launched this initiative to achieve 8% organic growth per year. This is about twice the rate of our industrial and financial peers. We want to make organic growth a process that is predictable and reliable.

Source: GE 2005 Annual Report.

of growth elements, he explained the difference: "You've got to have a process. Investors have to see it is repeatable. . . . It took time, though, to understand growth as a process. If I had worked out that wheel-shaped diagram in 2001, I would have started with it. But in reality, you get these things by wallowing in them awhile."[37]

His main challenge now as he saw it was to maintain the growth in this $150 billion global giant. But to those who felt GE was too big to grow so fast, he had a clear response:

> The corporate landscape is littered with companies that allowed themselves to be trapped by size. But GE thrives because we use our size to help us grow. Our depth allows us to lead in big markets by providing unmatched solutions for our customers; our breadth allows us to spread concepts across the company, leveraging one small idea to create big financial gains; and our strength allows us to take the risks required to grow. . . . Our goal is not just to be big, but to use our size to be great.[38]

All he had to do now was convince the financial markets that the changes he had initiated would enable this global giant to deliver on his promise of continued double-digit growth.

ENDNOTES

1. GE Annual Report, pp. 4, 12.
2. "Solving GE's Biggest Problems," *The Economist*, October 26, 2002, p. 55.
3. Jeffery R. Immelt, "Growth as a Process," *Harvard Business Review*, June 2006, p. 62.
4. GE 2001 Annual Report.
5. Rachel Silverman, "GE Goes Back to the Future," *The Wall Street Journal*, May 7, 2002, p. B1.
6. Holman W. Jenkins, Jr., "Why GE Should/Shouldn't Go Into the Hospital Business," *The Wall Street Journal*, November 20, 2002, p. A21.
7. "Solving GE's Biggest Problems," *The Economist*, October 26, 2002, p. 55.
8. "GE Goes Back to the Future—R&D Grows in Importance," *The Wall Street Journal*, May 7, 2002, p. B1.
9. Ibid.
10. Robert Buderi, "GE Finds Its Inner Edison," *Technology Review*, October 2003, pp. 46–50.
11. Amy Stone, "GE Investors Saying 'Jack Who?'" BusinessWeek On-Line, May 9, 2003.
12. Ibid.
13. "Business: The Hard Way; General Electric," *The Economist*, October 18, 2003, p. 60.
14. Diane Brady, "Welcome to the Frying Pan, Jeff," *BusinessWeek*, October 8, 2001, p. 82.
15. Mark Gunther, "Money and Morals at GE," *Fortune*, November 15, 2004, pp. 176–182.
16. GE 2002 Annual Report, p. 5.
17. John A. Byrne, "The Fast Company Interview: Jeff Immelt," *Fast Company*, July 2005, pp. 60–65.
18. Diane Brady, "Why GE Went For a Little Glitz," *BusinessWeek*, September 15, 2003, p. 44.
19. Jeffery R. Immelt, "Growth as a Process," *Harvard Business Review*, June 2006, p. 64.
20. Ibid.
21. Ibid.
22. Ibid.
23. GE 2002 Annual Report, p. 13.
24. GE 2003 Annual Report, p. 9.
25. Jeffery R. Immelt, "Growth as a Process," *Harvard Business Review*, June 2006, p. 70.
26. Ibid.
27. John A. Byrne, "The Fast Company Interview: Jeff Immelt," *Fast Company*, July 2005, pp. 60–65.
28. GE 2005 Annual Report, p. 11.
29. Jeffery R. Immelt, "Growth as a Process," *Harvard Business Review*, June 2006, p. 64.
30. GE 2005 Annual Report, p. 7.
31. GE 2002 Annual Report, p. 4.
32. Jeffery R. Immelt, "Growth as a Process," *Harvard Business Review*, June 2006, p. 69.
33. John A. Byrne, "The Fast Company Interview: Jeff Immelt," *Fast Company*, July 2005, pp. 60–65.
34. GE 2005 Annual Report, p. 10.
35. Ibid.
36. Ibid.
37. Jeffery R. Immelt, "Growth as a Process," *Harvard Business Review*, June 2006, pp. 63–64.
38. GE 2005 Annual Report, p. 4.

This case was prepared by Gareth R. Jones, Texas A&M University.

CBS Broadcasting established Viacom as an independent company in 1970 to comply with regulations set forth by the U.S. Federal Communications Commission (FCC) barring television networks from owning cable TV systems or from syndicating their own programs in the United States. The increasing spread of cable television and the continuing possibility of conflicts of interest between television networks and cable television companies made the spinoff necessary, and Viacom separated formally from CBS in 1971 when CBS distributed Viacom's stock to its shareholders at the rate of one share for every seven shares of CBS stock.

Viacom quickly became one of the largest cable operators in the United States, with over 90,000 cable subscribers. It also owned the syndication rights to a large number of popular, previously run CBS television series that it made available for syndication to cable TV stations. Revenue from these rights accounted for a sizable percentage of Viacom's income. In 1976, to take advantage of Viacom's experience in syndicating programming to cable TV stations, its managers decided to establish the Showtime movie network to compete directly with HBO, the leading outlet for films on cable television. In 1977, Viacom earned $5.5 million on sales of $58.5 million. Most of its earnings represented revenues from the syndication of its television series, but they also reflected

growth of its own cable TV systems, which at this time had about 350,000 subscribers. Recognizing that both producing and syndicating television programming could earn greater profits, Viacom's managers decided to produce their own television programs in the late 1970s and early 1980s. Their efforts produced only mixed results, however, no hit series resulted from their work, and the Big Three television networks of ABC, NBC, and CBS continued to dominate the airwaves.

During the early 1980s, the push to expand the cable television side of its business became Viacom's managers' major priority. Cable television is a highly capital-intensive business, and Viacom made a large investment to build its cable infrastructure; for example, it spent $65 million on extending its customer base in 1981 alone. By 1982, Viacom had added 450,000 subscribers to the 90,000 it inherited from CBS, making it the ninth largest cable operator in the United States. Also, by 1982 Viacom sales had grown to $210 million, with about half its revenues coming from program syndication and about half from its cable operations.

Viacom's managers, however, continued to feel that its cable operations were not a strong enough engine for future growth. One reason was that cable TV prices were regulated at this time, and cable companies were limited in how much they could charge customers. Its managers continued to believe that real growth in earnings would come not from providing cable television service but providing the *content* of cable programming—television programs. Given their previous failure in making their own programs, Viacom's managers sought to make acquisitions in the content side of the business—in companies that made entertainment programs. In 1981,

Viacom started in a small way by buying a minority stake in Cable Health Network, a new advertiser-supported television network. Then, in September 1985, in a stroke of fortune, it made the acquisition that would totally change the company's future. Viacom purchased the MTV Networks from Warner Bros., a company that desperately needed cash because Warner's own cable TV system needed a lot of capital to keep it viable.

The MTV Networks included MTV, a new popular music video channel geared toward the fourteen-to-twenty-four-age group; Nickelodeon, a channel geared toward children; and VH-1, a music video channel geared toward an older twenty-five-to-forty-four-age audience. MTV was the most popular property in the MTV Network. Its quick pace and flashy graphics were popular among young television viewers, and its young audience was a major target of large advertisers. The popularity of a station's programming determines how many advertisers it will attract and how much it can charge them. While MTV was performing well, Nickelodeon had been less successful and had not achieved any notable following among young viewers, which limited the revenues it could earn from advertisers. Viacom moved quickly to revamp Nickelodeon, giving it the slick, flashy look of MTV and developing unique programming that appealed to children, programming that was very different from that offered by competitors like the Disney Channel. In the next few years, Nickelodeon went from being the least popular channel on basic cable among children to being the most popular, and Viacom's managers were confident that they had in place the beginning of a new programming strategy to complement Viacom's cable TV interests and to guide the company to long-term profitability.

Enter Sumner Redstone

Viacom's hopes were shattered when its Showtime channel lost about 300,000 customers between March 1985 and March 1986 because of intense competition from HBO. HBO, under its then CEO Frank Biondi, was making itself the dominant pay movie channel by producing its own innovative programming and by forming exclusive agreements with major movie studios like Paramount to offer their movies to HBO first. As a result of the loss of customers, Viacom's cash flow dropped dramatically,

and the company lost $9.9 million on sales of $919.2 million in 1986. Further weakened by the $2 billion debt load it had incurred to fund its cable expansion program and make its programming acquisitions, Viacom became a takeover target.

After a competitive six-month battle to acquire the company, Sumner M. Redstone bought Viacom for $3.4 billion in March 1986. Redstone was the owner of a closely held corporation, National Amusements Inc. (NAI), that owned and operated 675 movie screens in fourteen states in the United States and the United Kingdom. Redstone became chairman of Viacom's board and moved quickly to take control of the company. He had built NAI from fifty drive-in movie theaters to a modern theater chain. He is credited with pioneering the development of the multiplex movie theater concept, which offers moviegoers a choice of a dozen or more screens to choose from. However, running a chain of movie theaters was very different from running a debt-laden media conglomerate as complicated as Viacom.

Many analysts felt that Redstone had overpaid for Viacom, but he saw a great potential for growth. Besides its cable television systems and syndication rights, which now included the popular TV series *The Cosby Show,* Redstone recognized the potential of its MTV and Nickelodeon channels. Moreover, over the years Viacom had acquired five television and eight radio stations in major markets, which he saw as valuable investments. Redstone moved quickly to solve Viacom's problems, and with the "hands-on" directive management style for which he is well known, he fired Viacom's top managers and began the search for capable managers who would be loyal and obedient to him. To turn Showtime around, he immediately hired Frank Biondi, the chief executive who had made HBO the dominant movie channel, as CEO of Viacom.

Frank Biondi was just a few days away from moving to Hollywood to run Columbia Pictures when Redstone called and asked him to take over as CEO of Viacom. The forty-nine-year-old Biondi was known for his strong financial, deal-making, and strategic skills and a knack for managing a diverse group of young executives and building them into a cooperative unit. Unlike Redstone, who likes to be directly involved in the day-to-day operations of a business, however, Biondi felt that his job was to set challenging goals, find the resources—both capital and people—to achieve them, and then get out of the way to let his managers achieve them. His approach was to decentralize control to his managers and to let them get the job done. Analysts felt the combination of Redstone's hands-on approach and Biondi's future thinking style made them a very effective team to head the growing entertainment conglomerate.

Viacom Speeds Up

Redstone's takeover of Viacom was fueled by his belief that cable television programming would become the dominant means of providing consumers with their entertainment content in the future. With the acquisition of Viacom, Redstone now owned 76% of MTV and Nickelodeon, which together gave Viacom access to millions of viewers aged two to twenty-four. Redstone believed Viacom's cable networks were its "crown jewels" because they provided half the company's revenues and profits, which came both from subscribers (the cable companies that bought the programming) and from advertisers (who advertised on these channels). To strengthen the cable channel franchise and build its brand name, Redstone restructured MTV and installed a more aggressive advertising and sales staff. Against the expectations of many industry analysts, MTV and Nickelodeon experienced continued growth and profitability. In 1989, for example, the MTV Networks won 15% of all dollars spent on cable advertising. MTV was expanding throughout the world, broadcasting to Western Europe, Japan, Australia, and large portions of Latin America.

Despite the success of the MTV channels, Redstone still faced the problem of paying off the debt that he had incurred to acquire Viacom—debt that amounted to $450 million in interest in the first two years following the takeover. Several fortuitous events aided him. First, shortly after the buyout, Viacom began to earn millions of dollars from television stations wanting to show reruns of the blockbuster *Cosby Show*. Second, in 1987 Congress deregulated cable television and allowed cable television companies to charge what they liked for their programming. The result was that the prices charged for cable television service soared, and so did the price of cable television franchises. Redstone took full advantage of this situation to sell off some of Viacom's cable assets to help reduce debt. In February 1989, Viacom's Long Island and suburban Cleveland cable systems were sold to Cablevision Systems Corp. for $545 million,

or about twenty times their annual cash flow. Cablevision also bought a 5% stake in Showtime for $25 million, giving it an interest in promoting the channel to Cablevision's customers and helping Showtime get back in competition with HBO. These events enabled Redstone to significantly cut Viacom's debt and negotiate more favorable terms on its loans. However, it was rough going, and Viacom lost $154.4 million in 1987, even though its sales increased to almost $1 billion.

With Viacom's finances on a firmer footing and Showtime showing some renewed vigor, Redstone and Biondi began to plan how to make Viacom a leader in the production of creative entertainment. In a strategic alliance with the Hearst Corp. and Capital Cities/ABC Inc., Viacom introduced Lifetime, a channel geared toward women. Viacom Pictures was started in 1989 so that the company could make its own movies. Viacom Pictures produced ten feature films in its first year at a cost of about $4 million a film—a very low cost compared to the money the major studios like Paramount and Universal spent. Under Biondi, Viacom's television production operations, which had always achieved mixed results, started to achieve great success with programs like *Matlock* for NBC and *Jake and the Fatman* for CBS. To increase subscribers to the important Showtime channel, Redstone sold 50% of Showtime to TCI, a major cable systems operator, for $225 million in 1989. In November of 1989, Viacom bought five more radio stations for $121 million to add to the nine it already owned.

Together with the five television stations and the fourteen cable systems it owned, Viacom's many different properties and assets earned revenues of $1.4 billion in 1989 and generated profits of $131 million. In 1990 and 1991, however, while Viacom's sales continued to increase, Viacom experienced losses of $89 million and $49 million on sales of $1.6 billion and $1.7 billion, respectively, because of increased costs associated with developing new programming and the lackluster performance of its Showtime network.

Viacom in the Early 1990s

The problem facing Redstone and Biondi was how to position Viacom for profitable growth in the 1990s. Both executives felt that developing and expanding Viacom's strengths in content programming—often referred to as entertainment software—were the key to its future success, despite how costly such programming was. They believed that the message or content that is sent is what really matters, not the medium or distribution channels that carry it. As Biondi put it, "In the end, a pipe is just a pipe. The customer doesn't care how the information is obtained; all that matters is the message."

To build its content programming strengths, Biondi worked hard to build and expand on the success of Viacom's MTV channels. His goal was to promote the MTV networks as global brands that were perceived as having something unique to offer. Since MTV's viewers dominate the record-buying audience, Biondi sought to negotiate exclusive contracts that give MTV the first crack at playing most major record companies' music videos—thus making it unique. At the same time, under Redstone and Biondi's control MTV went from being a purely music video channel to a channel that championed new kinds of programming to appeal to a young audience. The result was innovative programming such as *Beavis and Butthead, Road Stories,* and other kinds of youth-oriented programming interspersed with music videos.

In developing its programming strategy, however, Viacom's interest was not in promoting certain specific programs or stars—all of which may have short-lived popularity of fame—but in building its networks as unique brands. For example, on the MTV channel, the goal was to attract viewers because of what the channel as a whole personifies—an appeal to youth. Its success is based not on any particular person but on what MTV stands for. Under its new management, MTV prospered and its franchise was extended into Europe, Asia, and Latin America. Soon, MTV reached 250 million households in seventy-four countries. Viacom began to perform much better: in 1992 it made profits of $48 million on sales of $1.86 billion, and in 1993 it made profits of $70 million on sales of $2 billion.

While the development of innovative new programming was one reason for Viacom's return to profitability, a second, very important reason was Redstone's emphasis on keeping costs under control. Redstone is well known for his frugal way of doing business. He runs Viacom in a cost-conscious manner, and this trend is evident throughout the organization, from the top executives to the lower levels of management. For example, Redstone has his office not in a prestigious Park Avenue, New York, location like the large networks, but in a small unimposing building a couple of blocks from New York's "red light" district. Despite his huge personal net worth, he was walking to work every morning.

Redstone tried to instill his cost-conscious attitude down through the organization and across its many properties into specific business projects. For example, in the last decade costs soared in many Hollywood studios and television networks because the producers were at the mercy of talent agencies that demanded high prices for their stars, writers, and production companies. Not so with Viacom. Redstone insisted that its own programming be produced by its own employees using low-cost, homegrown talent. An example of this is the production of its MTV shows. All of its hosts are virtually unknown and are paid little relative to well-known network hosts who are paid millions of dollars a year.

Changes in the Media and Entertainment Industry

In their efforts to build their companies' programming strengths, Redstone and Biondi realized that the environment around them was rapidly changing and that it was not at all clear how programming would be delivered to customers in the future. First, by the mid-1990s the U.S. cable television industry was in a state of flux. Emerging technologies such as wireless satellite TV and then Internet broadband threatened to bypass traditional cable systems, rendering Viacom's investment in wired cable much less valuable. Second, pressures were building to deregulate the telecommunications industry, and eventually companies in different industries, for example, cable companies, telephone companies, and Internet service providers (ISPs), were allowed to enter each other's markets. These changes reinforced Redstone and Biondi's belief that during the coming decade the most successful companies would not be those that offered customers a channel into the home by cable, telephone wire, or wireless transmission.

Instead, they believed that to prosper in this fast-changing environment an entertainment company should be the provider of the entertainment to all these channels. In other words, the most successful companies would be those that could offer the programming to go on the channels—*the software providers,* not the hardware providers who provided the infrastructure to bring the entertainment into peoples' homes. With its MTV, Nickelodeon, Showtime, and Cinemax channels, as well as its syndicated programming, and its ability to make its own programming, Viacom was in a good position to form alliances with the companies that provided the channels into peoples' homes. It would provide the software (the programming) to the companies that provided the hardware (the wired and wireless cable companies and telephone companies). Viacom's revenues would come both from the fees it charged to the hardware providers for its entertainment channels and, most importantly, from the advertising revenues it would obtain from selling spots on its many channels—revenues that are determined by the extent of the viewing audience. However, Redstone and Biondi had discovered how expensive it is to develop innovative programming and how devastating the effects of a flop of several movies or programs can be for profitability. The question was how to obtain high-quality programming at the right price, especially in an entertainment and media industry in which the value of companies was rocketing as stock prices increased.

The Paramount and Blockbuster Mergers

Viacom now had a new mission: it should become a software-driven company with a goal of driving its entertainment software through every distribution system, to every multimedia application, and to every region on earth. To achieve Viacom's mission, Redstone began to search for a company that possessed the software strengths that could produce the programming content for worldwide distribution. In particular, he went looking for an entertainment company that had an already established film studio that would round out Viacom's programming portfolio by supplying feature films and TV shows to its television channels. Paramount Pictures provided Redstone with his opportunity.

Paramount's many businesses include both entertainment and publishing. Its entertainment businesses include the production, financing, and distribution of motion pictures, television programming, and prerecorded videocassettes; and the operation of motion picture theaters, independent television stations, regional theme parks, and Madison Square Garden. Paramount also owned a large library of movies. Its publishing interests included Simon & Schuster, which publishes and distributes hardcover and paperback books for the general public and textbooks for elementary schools, high schools, and colleges; it also provides information services for businesses and professions.

Redstone and Biondi began to picture the extensive synergies that a merger with Paramount would provide Viacom in the future. As Redstone told reporters, "This merger is not about two plus two equaling four, but six, or eight, or ten." Redstone believed that together Viacom and Paramount would be a much more efficient and profitable organization. He had a vision, for example, of Paramount making films that featured MTV characters like Beavis and Butthead and new cable TV channels supported by Paramount's library of 1,800 films and 6,100 television programs. Both Redstone and Biondi believed that Paramount was a priceless asset for an entertainment company hoping to provide a broad range of programming content for future distribution to global customers. With its strengths not just in visual programming but also in publishing books and magazines, Viacom would become a multimedia entertainment powerhouse that could redraw the competitive map in the entertainment industry.

On September 12, 1993, after behind-the-scene talks between Redstone and Paramount executives, Paramount announced an $8.2 billion merger with Viacom. Soon, however, a bidding war for Paramount started. Barry Diller, the CEO of QVC Network Inc., another large entertainment company and the owner of the home shopping network, recognized the logic behind Viacom's strategy and announced a hostile bid for Paramount. On September 20, 1993, QVC announced an $80 per share or $9.5 billion bid for Paramount, and the battle between Viacom and QVC for ownership of Paramount Communications Inc. was on.

This unwelcome bid from QVC presented a significant problem for Redstone: Viacom still had substantial debt because of his original 1987 acquisition of Viacom and the rapid development of its own television programming. Redstone could not afford to counter QVC's bid unless he obtained other sources of financing, and he had to search around for partners to support his bid. After a career of financing deals with his own pocketbook, including the 1987 Viacom takeover, the seventy-year-old tycoon was forced to turn to other companies to rescue the Paramount deal. Redstone found two potential partners in Nynex and Blockbuster.

Nynex, one of the Baby Bell companies, anticipated that deregulation would allow it to enter the cable television market and wanted an alliance with a company that could supply it with programming content. Blockbuster, under its own energetic CEO Wayne Huizinga, had grown to become the largest chain of video stores in the nation. Blockbuster was cash rich as a result of its recent rapid growth. Huizinga, recognizing the threat that the growth in electronic movie mediums (such as video pay-per-view, wireless cable, and videos through fiber-optic phone lines) could pose to the sale and rental of videocassettes, was on the lookout for a way to reduce this risk. He agreed to support Redstone's bid for Paramount as a way to diversify Blockbuster's interests.

Redstone was not anxious to forge alliances with these companies, commenting that alliances are tricky: "No one who is not a hypocrite or a liar can guarantee how a relationship will look in the future." Moreover, Redstone also saw that Blockbuster's future was in doubt as a result of the growth in electronic means of providing home movie videos. However, his need for cash to outbid QVC for ownership of Paramount was stronger than his worries about forming the alliances. On October 21, 1993, after having aligned himself with these partners, Redstone obtained $600 million cash from Blockbuster and a $1.2 billion commitment from Nynex Corp. He then used this money to match QVC's offer of $80 per share for 51% of Paramount stock with the rest in Viacom stock. Furthermore, anticipating a higher offer by QVC, Viacom raised its bid to $85 a share for 51% of the stock. Many analysts argued that this bidding war had become a personal battle between Redstone and QVC chairman Barry Diller and that whoever was the winner was doomed to pay much too much for Paramount—so much for low-cost programming.

On December 20, QVC raised its offer to $92 a share in cash for 50.1%, topping Viacom, which asked for more time to raise cash. On December 22, Paramount signed a merger agreement with QVC, but the bidding could continue, with a deadline for final bids on February 1, 1994. Redstone, desperate for more cash, went to Blockbuster CEO Wayne Huizinga for more money. Huizinga, increasingly convinced that it was in Blockbuster's shareholders' best interests to merge with Viacom, suggested that Viacom should take over Blockbuster for a hefty stock price. Redstone, recognizing the value of Blockbuster's cash reserves and huge cash flow from current operations, agreed.

On January 7, 1994, Viacom announced an $8.4 billion merger with Blockbuster; it also announced a new bid for Paramount for $105 a share in cash. After the bruising battle with QVC, Viacom gained full ownership of Paramount on July 7, 1994. Redstone hailed the new Viacom as an "entertainment colossus" and "a massive global media company."

Explosive Growth

In a few short years, Redstone had gone from controlling several hundred movie theaters to controlling the properties and franchises of three *Fortune 500* companies; Viacom, Blockbuster, and Paramount. By engineering the three-way merger of Viacom, Paramount, and Blockbuster Entertainment, Redstone created one of the three largest media empires in the United States (the others being the Disney/Capital Cities ABC, and AOL Time Warner), with annual revenues in excess of $10 billion. This was a large jump from the $2 billion revenue that Viacom had just before these mergers. However, Redstone and Biondi faced several major challenges in managing Viacom's new entertainment empire.

Engineering Synergies

To justify the expensive purchase of Paramount and Blockbuster, it became essential that Redstone and Biondi engineer synergies between Viacom's different entertainment properties, each of which was organized as a separate business division. Several efforts were immediately begun. Paramount executives were instructed to evaluate the potential of new shows developed by MTV for sale to television networks and TV stations. Viacom launched its new channel, the United Paramount Network (UPN), in January 1995 to take advantage of all the programming resources across its entertainment divisions. For example, MTV executives were instructed to quickly begin developing programming for the new network channel, which in 1996 was on the air only a few hours a day but today is on the air five days a week and through its TV broadcasting affiliates can reach almost all U.S. television households.

In another attempt to create synergies, Paramount executives were instructed to make their moviemaking skills available to the MTV Network and to help it make inexpensive movies that could be distributed through Paramount. One result of this was a Beavis and Butthead movie produced by Paramount and scheduled for late 1996. This was a first step in Redstone's strategy to boost the output of movies at the Paramount studio without having to finance a big increase in the studio's own movie budget and to find ways of making low-budget movies. Redstone and Biondi also searched for synergies between Blockbuster and Viacom's other divisions. They hoped that Blockbuster could link its retail stores with Viacom's cable networks and Paramount's extensive film library. Perhaps Blockbuster could sell copies of Paramount's vast library of movies to encourage people to create their own video collections. Also, the release of a new Paramount movie on video could be timed to coincide with a major advertising campaign in Blockbuster stores to promote the launch. In addition, Viacom's publishing division, Simon & Schuster, would be able to release paperback books to coincide with the release, and perhaps even a multimedia CD-ROM product could be introduced to boost sales. Finally, the launch of new movies could be timed to coincide with a major advertising blitz on the MTV channel—something that happened when Paramount released *Mission Impossible,* in the summer of 1996. As Redstone said, "Viacom through its new combination of assets is poised to participate in, and in many ways define, the entertainment and information explosion about to engulf the globe." As things turned out, however, there was little potential for synergies to emerge between Viacom's various divisions.

Structure and Management Challenges

Sumner Redstone has always enjoyed hands-on control of the day-to-day running of the company and is constantly involved in managing the problems facing the various divisions. To jump-start the process of leveraging competencies across divisions and reducing costs, he moved quickly to develop a hand-picked team of executives across Viacom's new divisions to install his cost-conscious frugal values in divisional managers. Before being acquired, Paramount was run by an all-powerful boss, Martin S. Davis, and a group of executives who flew corporate jets and spent company funds lavishly. Redstone sold Paramount's two corporate jets and installed his own cost-conscious managers to change Paramount's free-spending habits. Also in 1994 Viacom dismissed Richard E. Snyder, the chairman of Simon & Schuster, who was known for his free-spending ways.

Media and Entertainment Industry Challenges

The fast-changing entertainment and media industry also created many new challenges for Redstone and Biondi. The major Hollywood players were changing rapidly. In the old Hollywood, seven major studios dominated film and the three Big Three networks—ABC, CBS, and NBC—delivered TV programming to mass audiences. Now, the number of distribution channels was exploding. Government regulations preventing broadcast networks from owning TV programming companies were phased out, and the competitive dynamics of the industry changed. Viacom's strategy to develop a full line of entertainment programming fitted well with the changes occurring in the industry. The media and entertainment industry was also experiencing rapid globalization as U.S. movies, news, and TV shows spread around the world. A major challenge facing Viacom was to obtain access to the global marketplace—with a potential market of 900 million viewers in India and a billion-plus in China. As an example of Viacom's global push, in March 1995 Viacom won a cable television license to launch its Nickelodeon and VH-1 channels in Germany, Europe's biggest and potentially most lucrative media market, to complement the MTV pop music network, which has operated in Europe since 1987.

Technology challenges also confronted the media industry. Advances in digital and information technology, including streaming audio and video, began to offer viable new ways to distribute software content to customers. Just as the dominance of the Big Three networks—ABC, NBC, and CBS—has been eroded by the growth of companies like Viacom with its assorted networks, so now many new avenues for distributing content to consumers were emerging with the growth of the Internet and advances in broadband technology. Digital piracy was also becoming evident, as websites were springing up to exchange digital files, and companies like Napster were just a few years away.

Finally, the growing strength of Viacom spurred the consolidation of the entertainment industry. In 1995, Time Warner announced that it would merge with Turner Broadcasting, and Disney announced that it would merge with Capital Cities/ABC. As a result, the industry was now composed of four major players: Disney, Viacom, AOL Time Warner, and News Corp., which owns the Fox channel.

Problems for Viacom

Soon after Redstone's expensive decision to buy Paramount, the Paramount movie *Forrest Gump* became a surprise hit, generating over $250 million for Viacom and silencing those Redstone critics who had argued that he had spent too much to buy the movie company. Viacom's managers began to feel like Forrest Gump, with his philosophy that "life is like a box of chocolates: You never know what you're going to get." It seemed that Redstone and Viacom had been in the right place at the right time and had made a profitable acquisition. Just as Redstone had sensed the potential of MTV, so too had he sensed the potential of Paramount and Blockbuster.

By summer 1995, however, the selection of chocolates in Viacom's box did not seem as good as in 1994. Many of the hoped-for synergies had not been obtained. For example, before the merger Redstone claimed that Blockbuster would be valuable to Viacom as a distributor of its creative programming; however, few benefits of this kind had been achieved. Similarly, analysts argued that Paramount had to cooperate much more closely with Viacom's cable TV channels and with Blockbuster Video if synergies were to be forthcoming. Moreover, the performance of both the Paramount and Blockbuster divisions had been disappointing. The Gump smash hit had been followed by a string of expensive failures. Redstone and Biondi had begun to realize that making movies is a very risky business and that past successes are no indication of future success. Paramount's share of the box office dropped from 14% in 1994 to 10% in 1995. Moreover, Redstone was annoyed about the high marketing and production costs of the movies that Paramount was making, and after a string of failures, he wanted to know what the studio was doing. Hit movies are vital to a movie studio because they provide the cash flow that pays for the flops and bankrolls the future. Paramount's poor performance was hurting Viacom's cash flow and ability to service its debt. Moreover, box-office hits are crucial because they drive the rest of a movie studio's profits from international markets to home video and television.

To compound the Paramount problem, the Blockbuster division was also not doing well. Viacom had bought Blockbuster at the peak of its success—when its revenues were doubling every year and its free cash flow was a valuable asset. After the acquisition Blockbuster began to run into intense competition from two sources. First, a number of new rival video chains such as Hollywood Video had recently sprung up that were giving it intense competition and creating a price war in some markets. Second, pay-per-view on demand television was spreading rapidly in large urban markets. Blockbuster's revenues were flat, and the hoped-for growth in cash flow to help service Viacom's debts had not occurred.

To make matters worse, Redstone had a falling-out with the top management teams of Paramount and Blockbuster whom he thought were doing a poor job. He forced the resignations of many key executives and went in search of new leadership talent. Then, in January 1996 he stunned the entertainment world when he announced that he was firing his second-in-command Frank Biondi, who was well respected throughout Hollywood, because he believed Biondi did not have the "hands-on skills" needed to manage the kinds of problems that Viacom was facing. Redstone felt that Biondi's decentralized management style was out of place in a company actively searching for synergies and cost reductions. In place of Biondi he promoted his two lieutenants, Phillipe Dauman and Tom Dooley, to orchestrate Viacom's strategy, even though they had little direct experience with the entertainment business.

Viacom's New Moves

In March 1996, Redstone hired William Fields, a senior Wal-Mart manager who had extensive experience in running efficient retail operations through advanced IT, to be the CEO of Blockbuster. Redstone hoped he could find a way to transform the Blockbuster Video stores into broader based entertainment-software stores, given that it currently seemed likely that the video rental business would be swept away by the new wireless cable and direct broadcasting technologies.

Redstone himself became more involved in the day-to-day running of Paramount, spending more time with its marketing and production executives to understand the workings of the business. Many analysts wondered how good a job the seventy-year-old Redstone would do without the aid of a seasoned entertainment executive. Analysts also pointed to Viacom's lack of a strong global presence or any executives who had experience globally. They noted that Redstone did not have any personal international experience.

In the spring of 1996 Viacom's stock price plunged from a high of $54.50 to $35 as investors fled the stock because of problems at Blockbuster and Paramount. In the summer of 1996, after a string of flops (with the exception of *Mission Impossible*), Redstone announced plans to cut back the number of movies Paramount would make and to reduce its production costs as he searched for a new strategy. Chief among Viacom's problems was its huge debt, which had to be pruned by more asset sales. In addition, Redstone and his managers had to find ways to reduce rising operating costs and overheads as well as to find new ways of leveraging resources and competences across divisions to increase revenues and build cash flow.

On the cost side, flat revenues and soon-to-be losses at Blockbuster and Paramount were pulling down the performance of the whole corporation. Blockbuster was now a growing liability, and Field's efforts were not bearing quick results. In fact, Blockbuster's revenues were falling. In 1997, Fields left and Redstone brought in a new CEO, John Antioco. In 1998 they streamlined Blockbuster's operations and sold off its new music store business for $115 million in cash. (Case 13 on Blockbuster provides detailed information on Blockbuster's new strategy.) They also introduced the radical idea of video-rental revenue sharing with the movie studios, and within a few years Blockbuster's revenues were increasing again. Also, in 1998 Redstone sold off all the rest of Paramount Studios' publishing interests, except for its lucrative consumer publishing group, to Pearson for $4.6 billion and used this money to reduce debt.

On the revenue side, there were signs that some potential synergies were emerging. For example, an alliance between MTV and Simon & Schuster resulted in a successful line of "Beavis and Butthead" titles, and Paramount did produce a successful Beavis and Butthead movie. Also, Viacom's global presence was widening as Redstone formed alliances overseas and as its television studios were developing new channels, including a second MTV channel to be called MTV2, which would focus exclusively on music videos, since the regular MTV channel had become more involved in regular programming. In 1997, growing demand for its entertainment content led Viacom to offer to buy the rest of Spelling entertainment with its Star Trek franchise and Big Ticket Television Unit. Its content was perfect for Viacom's growing UPN network, although that network had yet to make a profit. Redstone integrated Spelling into Paramount's television operations to obtain economies of scale and scope in the production of new television programming. He was clearly focused on reaping the long-term benefits from his entertainment empire, although the poor performance of Viacom's stock was a big personal embarrassment to him as his acquisitions were continually being criticized.

By 1999, Blockbuster's recovering revenues and cash flow allowed Redstone to announce an initial offering of Blockbuster stock so that the performance of that division could be separated from the rest of the company. Redstone believed it was impossible to assess Viacom's true value until a real market value was put on this unit. About 18% of Blockbuster's stock was sold at $16 to $18 a share, and the over $250 million raised was used to pay off its debt.

Also in 1999, Redstone hired the experienced media and entertainment manager and former head of CBS, Mel Karmazin, as Viacom's chief operating officer to help solve its ongoing problems. Karmazin was well known for his ability to select and manage hit programming and for his hands-on ability to find ways to leverage resources to improve operational effectiveness. He set to work restructuring Viacom's businesses to engineer cross-divisional synergies, create new programming content, and enhance its revenue and earnings stream.

Both Redstone and Karmazin also understood that one of the most important reasons to build an entertainment empire was to achieve economies of scale that arise from being able to offer potential advertisers the opportunity to advertise their products across multiple channels that attract different kinds of viewers. In other words, a potential advertiser could produce one or more themed commercials to run across all of Viacom's different TV networks as well as with its movies or in its books, theme parks, and so on. Redstone had also watched Disney merge with the ABC networks to provide it with a major new distribution channel for its Disney franchise, a move that also had made DisneyABC the biggest entertainment and media company in the world.

Since the majority of Viacom's future revenue stream would come from advertising, Redstone established a new unit, Viacom Plus, to provide a centralized advertising service that deals directly with large advertisers and handles advertising for *all* of Viacom's divisions. For example, in 2001 Procter & Gamble and Viacom Plus negotiated a groundbreaking cross-platform deal whereby P&G would pay $300 million for advertising spread across nine of Viacom's major divisions; the success of this deal led it to pay $350 million in 2002 for advertising spread across fourteen of Viacom's divisions. P&G obtained a better deal than if it had negotiated with each Viacom property individually, and Viacom Plus reduced the costs associated with managing the vital advertising process. In 2002, Monster.com, the online job site, signed a $15 million deal with Viacom Plus to put all its "scatter money"—the money a company has to scatter across different channels and demographic groups—into the Viacom platform.

The CBS Acquisition

A new opportunity arose in 1999. CBS networks were in trouble because CBS ratings were dropping, and the company was interested in a merger in the consolidating entertainment industry. Redstone realized that with CBS's assets Viacom would reach the greatest number of viewers and listeners (CBS-owned Infinity Radio Broadcasting) of any media enterprise, spanning all ages and demographics from "cradle to cane." As such, it would become a premier outlet for advertisers around the world because it could now offer them the opportunity to achieve huge economies of scale and scope in their advertising efforts. Advertising content could be driven and promoted across virtually all media segments, including broadcast and cable television, radio, and outdoor advertising and new digital media. Also, channels such as MTV, MTV2, VH-1, and CMT could now be broadcast over Trinity's radio stations and over the Internet, and CBS's high-quality content, such as its news and sports programming, could be broadcast over all Viacom's properties. The huge scale would also give the combined company bargaining power with programming suppliers and allow it to maximize the effectiveness of its sales force across all its divisions—a major source of potential extra revenue and cost savings. Perhaps a part of Viacom's problems was that it was simply not big enough?

In September 1999, Viacom and CBS Corp. announced that they would merge the two companies in the largest media transaction to that date. All operations of the company would report to Mel Karmazin. The range of Viacom's properties was now staggering in its scope, especially because at the time of the merger CBS was in the process of taking control of radio station owner Infinity Broadcasting and King World productions, which syndicated such shows as *Jeopardy* and the *Oprah Winfrey Show*. Moreover, the merger was achieved through a stock swap so that no debt needed to be incurred to fund it, something

Viacom could not afford because its revenues and performance were still slowly increasing.

Karmazin now gave his full attention to structuring and managing Viacom's assets to realize the gains from sharing and leveraging the competencies of its division across all its operations. It began to seem that with the CBS acquisition Viacom had achieved the critical mass that made such gains realizable. In May 2000, Karmazin announced the integration of the company's theme parks, Paramount Parks, into the Viacom Entertainment Group. This move would grow the parks faster by linking them to Viacom's other properties, such as its Nickelodeon and MTV cast of characters. In 2000, Karmazin integrated Paramount's and CBS's television groups, and the new division consisted of thirty-five television stations reaching eighteen of the top twenty television markets in the United States. The hope was that this would lead to major operational and sales efficiencies, especially because all advertising and promotion could be linked to the company's Infinity radio stations and outdoor advertising operations, creating the "advertising bundle" mentioned above. CBS would now function as a local as well as a national broadcaster and it could leverage its news, sports, and other programming across many more markets. In 2000, Viacom's television studios also formed a unit called MTV Films to produce movies for Paramount. Some of its low-budget movies, which generally cost around $30 million to make, half the normal Hollywood budget, made a profit, including the Rugrats and *Beavis and Butthead Do America*.

In 2001, in yet another move to make it the number 1 advertising platform in the world for advertisers with programming that appealed to every demographic category, Viacom acquired Black Entertainment Television (BET) for $3 billion. The BET network reaches 63.4 million U.S. households, and its other channels, like BET on Jazz and BET International, reach thirty countries in Europe and thirty-six in Africa. The BET acquisition was just one part of Viacom's push to become the dominant global media company. Continuing its strategy of leveraging value from its properties, BET is seeking more ways to integrate its activities with other Viacom properties, both by customizing various Viacom TV programming for BET's channels and vice versa, not only popular shows but also news and sports.

All of Viacom's networks were also instructed to follow MTV's lead and develop a global strategy to produce content locally in each country in which they were broadcast to increase the company's global viewing audience. MTV, for example, has a presence in most of the world's major markets; it reaches 125 million households and is a major revenue generator for Viacom. And, while it broadcasts its U.S. programming in countries abroad, it had also produced successful shows in countries abroad that are customized to local tastes; these have proved so popular that they have been transferred successfully to the United States and other countries. In 2001, Redstone met China's president Jaing in Beijing to affirm Viacom's commitment to China, and in May 2001 channels such as MTV and Nickelodeon started to be broadcast in China, also with extensive programming customized to the Chinese market.

Viacom's stock climbed in the spring of 2002, despite the huge fall in advertising revenues caused by the recession in 2000 and the following September 11 tragedy—a fall that caused the earnings of its broadcast networks to drop by 20%. The over 10% fall in advertising revenues affected all entertainment and media companies and caused a plunge in the stock price of companies like Yahoo and AOL Time Warner. Indeed, the latter's stock price fell so far that Viacom became the number 2 global media company in 2002. Analysts felt that Viacom was the best-positioned media company to benefit from the upswing in advertising that was expected in the latter half of 2002 because of its combination of large-scale operations, leading brands, and diverse revenue streams. While the broadcast groups' earnings fell by 20%, for example, the earnings of the cable network division rose by 12%, largely because of greater broadcasting in the United States and abroad. Redstone claimed in the summer of 2002 that the worst was over.

Still reeling from the downturn in advertising, Redstone and Karmazin continued to seek ways to counter future threats to the Viacom empire, particularly because now the threat from digital and broadband technology was hurting its Blockbuster unit and might in the future threaten Viacom's distribution channels as TVs and computers merged as broadband connections to the Internet increased. Indeed, there have been many reports since the hiring of Mel Karmazin that he and Redstone have locked heads on many occasions about major strategic issues. Karmazin was especially critical of Redstone's expensive acquisitions, which increased debt but had no clear future benefits, and he also made strong suggestions that Viacom should increase its online presence. However, in June 2002 with the positive results from the CBS merger and BET acquisition suggesting the value of Redstone's growth-by-acquisition strategy, Karmazin was joking that their management styles were complementary and that he was in no rush to assume leadership of Viacom, especially since the seventy-nine-year-old Redstone was "good for another thirty to forty years—at least!" Redstone, however, joked that when Karmazin's contract expired in 2003, Karmazin "might want to retire." Karmazin's response? "Never, never, never."

New Problems for Viacom: The Growing Use of the Internet

Viacom made no significant acquisitions in 2002 or 2003. Redstone felt his company has all the right pieces of entertainment property in place and that the main issue for Karmazin was to manage them to realize the stream of advertising revenues and profits locked up in its entertainment assets. Operating revenues from its entertainment division, which included Paramount Pictures and theme parks, rose by 46% during 2003 and its operating income was up 15% to $66 million as a result of higher movie ticket sales and—paradoxically—much stronger sales of DVDs. Its Viacom Plus unit continued to aggressively market its "one-stop-shopping approach across all marketing channels," and, as the economy picked up in 2003, advertising revenues at the national level rebounded. In the spring of 2004, Viacom was happy to announce that the company's overall revenues were up 11% and that 46% of its 2003 revenues came from advertising.

While national advertising revenues on Viacom's many cable channels rebounded, however, local advertising revenues from its TV stations, including the CBS network, and from its radio stations were now lagging behind and hurting the company's performance—Viacom only just met analysts' earnings expectations. The reason local advertising revenues were not keeping pace with national advertising was that fewer and fewer people were watching or listening to local channels, preferring to watch their favorite cable channels or to surf the Web. Slowly but steadily the growing use of the Internet and new online digital media properties were cutting into available advertising revenues. Redstone and Karmazin were slow to pick up on the dangers the Internet posed, not just as a competitor for advertising revenues but also as an important emerging media asset that could complement its existing businesses. And major online companies such as Yahoo were now expensive, and these too were suffering from new competition from upstart websites that began to offer specialist services, such as www.rottentomatoes, the movie review website, and soon Flickr and YouTube, which offered photograph and video content now made possible by the rapidly expanding use of broadband Internet connections. Karmazin and Redstone preferred to regard falling revenues as a temporary phenomenon and announced that they expected revenue increases in 2004 of 5 to 7% and operating profits to increase by 12 to 14%.

At the same time, however, Viacom has always been alert to the threat downloading movies through the Internet or by pay-per-view cable posed for its Blockbuster unit, so Redstone and Karmazin also announced that despite Blockbuster's considerable contributions to its revenues and free cash flow, they believed the business models of both companies had drifted so far apart that the lack of fit between them would hurt Viacom's future profitability. Viacom's business model is based on growing the value of its properties and the advertising revenues they generate. Blockbuster's business model is to increase its presence in the movie DVD rental and retail sales market. The was especially true by 2004 when the prospect of increasing competition from movie downloads through broadband channels started to increase, and so in the future falling revenues from DVD rentals might offset any increase in advertising revenues that Viacom might enjoy. However, divesting Blockbuster and losing its revenues would make Viacom even more dependent on advertising revenues.

Another problem by 2004 was that Viacom's acquisition of CBS was now causing major problems because the anticipated synergies were not forthcoming—buying more media properties also results in a company facing more sets of competitive threats. Investors were becoming increasingly wary of Viacom's stock because they found it more and more difficult to evaluate the real value of each of its many media properties and its cash flow. Spinning off Blockbuster would help eliminate the uncertainty this unit's future performance was having on its stock price. So in January 2004, when Blockbusters stock was trading at a high of $20, Viacom announced that it would divest its remaining shareholding in Blockbuster by

allowing holders of Viacom shares to swap them for shares in Blockbuster. New Blockbuster shareholders would also receive a substantial once-and-for all dividend for swapping their Viacom stock for Blockbuster's. This made the deal attractive, and enough Viacom shareholders took advantage of the offer for Redstone to finally spin off the unit into a fully independent company controlled by its current CEO, John Antioco.

The Big Split

At the same time Viacom was failing to build strong Internet and online media assets, it was now also encountering many other problems with its empire of media assets. First, even after the Blockbuster spinoff, the company's erratic performance failed to reassure investors about the value of Viacom's remaining assets. Five years after Redstone bought the CBS television network in 2000, adding its television stations and Infinity Broadcasting radio stations to his movie studio, theme parks, and Blockbuster video stores, it was clear that bigger is not always better. Redstone had learnt the hard way that the different units of a company grow at different rates, and the performance of the weakest unit pulled down the performance of the whole company—and Viacom's growth was slowing fast. Its theme parks, radio stations, and CBS assets had not met Viacom's aggressive growth goals, and Redstone was frustrated that Viacom's slowest growing units were dragging down its stock price, which by 2004 was almost half its 2000 high of nearly $70 per share. Karmazin had warned Redstone about this, and the personal relationship between Redstone and Karmazin continued to deteriorate. Although in 2003 it was announced that Karmazin's contract would be renewed for two more years, Redstone now had other plans for his company, and in 2004 Karmazin was fired (he is now the CEO of Sirius Satellite Radio).

In March 2005 Redstone announced that Viacom would split the steadier, slow-growth units, the CBS side, from the faster-growth side, MTV and the film studio. The $60 billion conglomerate would be split into two smaller, separately traded companies, one running CBS and the stations and the other the movie studio and cable channels, such as MTV and Comedy Central. He also announced the company was looking to sell its slow-growth, expensive Paramount theme parks and buy growing Internet and videogame companies, and that it might also divest its 856 movie screens in Canada—the original Redstone media property.

The split was approved by Viacom's board June 14, 2005, took effect December 31, 2005, and effectively undid the Viacom/CBS merger. The existing Viacom was renamed CBS Corp. and was headed by Les Moonves, its long-time CEO. It now includes Viacom's "slow-growth businesses," namely CBS, the CW network (formerly UPN), CBS Radio, Simon & Schuster, CBS Outdoor (formerly Viacom Outdoor), Showtime, and most television production assets. In addition, CBS Corp. was given Paramount Parks, which it later sold to amusement park operator Cedar Fair, L.P., on June 30, 2006.

Then, a new spin-off company was created called Viacom, which was headed by Tom Freston, the long-time head of MTV networks. It comprises MTV Networks, BET Networks, Paramount's movie studio, and Paramount Pictures' home entertainment operations. Redstone still controls 71% of the voting stock of both companies and is the chairman of both companies—he still earns $27 million a year as its chairman, and he and his family members are a major drain on its cash flow.

Do Media Empires Create Value and Profit?

After a decade of growth by acquisition, media conglomerates such as Viacom, Sony, and Time Warner all began to reconfigure their business models, pushed by new Internet technologies and changing customer viewing habits that had altered the mix of advertising revenues on which media content companies depend. The 1990s cookie-cutter model of a media giant where one could just add different media properties, such as a television network, to others, such as a movie studio, theme parks, music company, or pro sports team, had been shown to be a failure—at least in terms of generating consistent increases in a company's stock price. Nevertheless, in December 2005, Viacom's Paramount Pictures sealed a deal to buy movie studio DreamWorks for $1.6 billion, thwarting rival NBC-Universal's five-month-long attempt to acquire the independent movie studio. "The acquisition of DreamWorks is an enormous step forward in our ongoing work to unlock the full potential of Viacom's brands and businesses," said Redstone. But how the acquisition would actually do this was left unsaid.

Redstone's focus on fixing the ongoing problems with his media empire also made him very late to recognize the growing importance of the Internet and the World Wide Web and the threat of competition from digital video downloading and streaming media. In 2005, Viacom moved to acquire some small Internet media properties; for example, in June 2005 it acquired Neopets, a virtual pet website, and in 2006 it acquired Xfire, iFilm, Quizilla.com and Harmonix Music Systems, and Atom Entertainment. These companies serve niche markets, such as virtual pets, or make music gaming titles. However, these acquisitions had nothing like the reach of a MySpace or YouTube, and despite this progress Viacom was much slower to react to the changes in Internet technology taking place than its rivals, and its stock price suffered.

New threats were also emerging; Disney, which had always had a strong interest in developing media websites, was rebuilding a strong Disney Internet property and announced it was pioneering movie downloading through the Internet. In 2005 it claimed it had a proprietary new technology for delivering movies over the Internet, and in 2006 it formed a close alliance with Apple to download its movies and TV programs over the Internet to iPods. Similarly, after its disastrous start with AOL, Time Warner was also developing a new business model, based on free user access, to build its AOL channel into a major Internet property and so share in the billions of dollars of advertising revenues that were up for grabs. But the company that showed the best developed strategy was News Corp., whose CEO, Rupert Murdock, had pushed early for a strong Internet strategy, and the result was early important strategic Internet acquisitions. The most important of these acquisitions was MySpace.com in 2004, one of the fastest-growing social networking websites ever. It also bought several other specialist websites such as RottenTomatoes.com, a movie review website, and it developed these into major websites to increase advertising revenues and also to advertise its other media assets, such as the movies it made through its Fox Studios.

More Changes at the Top

As the names of its Internet acquisitions suggest, Viacom was failing in its attempt to develop a strong, coherent Internet strategy. In particular, it had lost the battle with News Corp. to acquire MySpace.com, and now this strategic failure too began to hurt its stock price. Its stock, which had been around $45 after the 2005 split, plunged to $35 by the summer of 2006, and Redstone, as usual, responded by firing Viacom's CEO, Freston, blaming him for the company's poor performance. Redstone named Philippe Dauman as the new head of Viacom. Dauman has been a Viacom board member since 1987 and, as mentioned earlier, had been a top Viacom executive from 1994 to 2000.

In his first public announcement, Dauman claimed he had free reign to run things and develop a new business model, and that he wasn't simply a pawn for Redstone to use. Redstone himself had been getting negative attention from analysts who believed he had undermined Freston's authority and was grooming his own children to take over the company when he decides to retire (he turns eighty-four in May 2007). If Redstone attempts to micromanage or meddle in operational issues, Dauman said, "I can push back," but he also indicated he would work to continue Freston's legacy, "creative excellence," while focusing on strategic Internet acquisitions—an area that led to Freston's downfall. However, given the frugal Redstone, he optimistically said that he does not anticipate any acquisition as big as News Corp.'s $580 million MySpace purchase. He will look for companies under $100 million that have the potential to become the next MySpace—companies that will not be easy to find in today's competitive digital environment.

At the same time, Dauman said the company has untapped organic growth, meaning that it could achieve more innovation and product development internally so that the company could make better use of its media resources. He cited BET and Comedy Central as lynchpins with huge future potential and said that even with established brands, such as MTV and Nickelodeon, Viacom could bring in more advertising revenues by offering advertisers opportunities to reach both targeted and mass audiences. Once again, a corporate group focused on selling the aggregated reach of Viacom's cable network assets is being formed, something similar to Viacom's former centralized marketing unit that was disbanded after the split. If advertising revenues don't increase in the next few years, it seems that more divestitures may be likely.

In November 2006, the first financial reporting period under Dauman's leadership, Viacom reported a 16% fall in third-quarter profit, as weakness at the box office from unprofitable movies offset strength in cable and higher advertising revenues. Viacom's share price, which had been recovering, closed down 3.3% at $38.37. As usual, Redstone fired someone, this time Viacom's chief financial officer, and Redstone once again announced that his company would "move rapidly to the forefront of emerging digital markets, keeping us on the path to outstanding long-term financial performance and free cash flow generation" and backed its full-year target to deliver double-digit growth in revenue and operating income. Clearly, even managing a smaller, more focused media company to achieve profitable growth is a difficult task—especially when its units each face complex problems and agile competitors. Only time will tell if the new Viacom will succeed or if, once again, the company may be split apart to realize the value in its assets. Clearly its top executives face difficult choices in figuring out the best corporate and business strategies to pursue to create a highly profitable business model. Having an eighty-three-year-old owner in charge may not be the best thing for its shareholders, apart from Redstone himself, of course.

REFERENCES

Frank Biondi, "A Media Tycoon's Take on the 21st Century," *Business Week*, 21st Century Capitalism, November 18, 1994, p. 190.

Shirley Brady, "BET Seeks More Ways to Work with Viacom Family," *Cable World*, June 10, 2002, p. 24.

"Deals Give Viacom Even More Muscle," *Wall Street Journal*, September 30, 1994, p. B1.

"The Ending of Paramount's Script May Not Be Written Yet," *Business Week*, September 27, 1993, pp. 38–39.

Wayne Friedman, "Viacom Snares Monster TV Deal," *Advertising Age*, April 29, 2002, p. 1.

"Gump Happens—and Viacom Is Thanking Its Lucky Stars," *Business Week*, August 8, 1994, p. 29.

Marc Gunther, "MTV Films: It's a Sleeper," *Fortune*, April 29, 2002, pp. 24–28.

Nancy Hass, "The Message Is the Medium," *Financial World*, June 8, 1993, pp. 24–25.

"Hollywood Scuffle," *Business Week*, December 12, 1994, p. 38.

"IBM Thrusts into Entertainment via Viacom," *Communications Today*, May 8, 2002, p. 1.

International Directory of Company Histories, vol. 7 (St. James Press, 1994,) pp. 560–562.

Dyan Machan, "Redstone Rising," *Forbes*, May 13, 2002, pp. 46–48.

Steve McClellan, "Viacom: Flat and Happy," *Broadcasting & Cable*, February 18, 2002, p. 8.

"The MTV Tycoon—Sumner Redstone Is Turning Viacom into the Hottest Global TV Network," *Business Week*, September 21, 1992, pp. 56–62.

Jack Neff and Wayne Friedman, "P&G Broadens Deal with Viacom Plus," *Advertising Age*, June 17, 2002, p. 3.

"Paramount: Do I Hear $11 Billion?" *Business Week*, November 8, 1993, p. 36.

"The Paramount Takeover: The Drama Ended, Two Stars Get New Scripts; Viacom's Biondi Has to Stretch to Fill Big Role," *Wall Street Journal,* February 16, 1994, p. B1.

"The Paramount Takeover: Wall Street's Final Analysis: Might Made Right," *Wall Street Journal,* February 16, 1994, p. B1.

Martin Peers, "Viacom Passes AOL in Market Value—CBS Acquisition Has Brought Shareholder Value to Media Company," *Wall Street Journal,* June 6, 2002, p. B3.

Martin Peers, "Viacom Posts $1.11 Billion Loss Largely Due to Goodwill Charge," *Wall Street Journal,* April 26, 2002, p. B4.

"Redstone in Motion," *Financial World,* December 6, 1994, pp. 36–38.

"Remaindered at Simon & Schuster," *Business Week,* June 27, 1994, p. 32.

Matthew Schifrin, "I Can't Even Remember the Old Stars' Names," *Forbes,* March 16, 1992, pp. 44–45.

"Sumner at the Summit," *Business Week,* February 28, 1994, p. 32.

"Sumner Redstone Gets a Little Help from His Friends," *Business Week,* October 11, 1993, p. 36.

Viacom, http://www.viacom.com, 1991–2007.

Viacom Annual Reports and 10Ks, 1991–2001.

"Viacom Firms Up Plans for Movies Produced by MTV," *Wall Street Journal,* Jun 14, 1994, p. B8.

"Viacom Inc.: Paramount Gets 'First Look' at MTV Unit's TV Shows," *Wall Street Journal,* November 11, 1994.

"Viacom Inc. Wins German License for Nickelodeon," *Wall Street Journal,* March 1, 1995, p. B10.

"Viacom Now Is a Full Owner of Paramount After Vote," *Wall Street Journal,* July 8, 1994, p. B9.

"Viacom Unit Continues Sell-off of Businesses That Don't Fit Strategy," *Wall Street Journal,* November 22, 1994, p. B4.

Karissa S. Wang, "Mel Sez: CBS 'Pretty Darn Good,'" *Electronic Media,* June 3, 2002, p. 37.

From Silver Halide to Digital Imaging Technology at Eastman Kodak: The Challenges Ahead

This case was prepared by Gareth R. Jones, Texas A&M University.

In February 2007, Antonio Perez, the chief executive officer (CEO) of the Eastman Kodak Co., was reflecting on Kodak's current situation since he took over almost two years ago. After eight quarters of losses, his revamped digital strategy seemed to be finally starting to pay off. His efforts to cut costs while investing heavily to develop new digital products resulted in a slender profit of $16 million on sales of $3.8 billion and were expected to rise further in 2007.

Following several billion dollars of losses and tens of thousands of job cuts, the news gave Kodak shares a boost. But could Kodak maintain its momentum in the face of its digital rivals that were all introducing new and improved products? Had Kodak finally achieved a distinctive competence in digital imaging? Was its new digital business model—based on strategies to counter the threats posed to Kodak's traditional silver halide-based technology by the convergence of imaging and digital information technology—really working? Did the company have the digital products in place to rebuild its profitability and fulfill its "You press the button, we do the rest" promise? Or, after ten years of declining sales and profits, was the company just on the verge of another downward slope in the face of intense global competition on all product fronts?

Kodak's History

Eastman Kodak Co. was incorporated in New Jersey on October 24, 1901, as successor to the Eastman Dry Plate Co., the business originally established by George Eastman in September 1880. The Dry Plate Co. had been formed to develop a dry photographic plate that was more portable and easier to use than other plates in the rapidly developing photography field. To mass-produce the dry plates uniformly, Eastman patented a plate-coating machine and began to manufacture the plates commercially. Eastman's continuing interest in the infant photographic industry led to his development in 1884 of silver halide paper-based photographic roll film. Eastman capped this invention with his introduction of the first portable camera in 1888. This camera used his own patented film, which was developed using his own proprietary method. Thus Eastman had gained control of all the stages of the photographic process. His breakthroughs made possible the development of photography as a mass leisure activity. The popularity of the "recorded images" business was immediate, and sales boomed. Eastman's inventions revolutionized the photographic industry, and his company was uniquely placed to lead the world in the development of photographic technology.

From the beginning, Kodak focused on four primary objectives to guide the growth of its business: (1) mass production to lower production costs, (2) maintaining the lead in technological developments, (3) extensive product advertising, and (4) the development of a multinational business to exploit the world market. Although common now, those goals were revolutionary at the time. In due course, Kodak's yellow boxes could be found in every country in the world.

Preeminent in world markets, Kodak operated research, manufacturing, and distribution networks throughout Europe and the rest of the world. Kodak's leadership in the development of advanced color film for simple, easy-to-use cameras and in quality film processing was maintained by constant research and development in its many research laboratories. Its huge volume of production allowed it to obtain economies of scale. Kodak was also its own supplier of the plastics and chemicals needed to produce film, and it made most of the component parts for its cameras.

Kodak became one of the most profitable American corporations, and its return on shareholders' equity averaged 18% for many years. To maintain its competitive advantage, it continued to invest heavily in research and development in silver halide photography, remaining principally in the photographic business. In this business, as the company used its resources to expand sales and become a global business, the name *Kodak* became a household word signifying unmatched quality. By 1990, approximately 40% of Kodak's revenues came from sales outside the United States.

Starting in the early 1970s, however, and especially in the 1980s, Kodak ran into major problems, reflected in the drop in return on equity. Its preeminence was being increasingly threatened as the photographic industry and industry competition changed. Major innovations were taking place within the photography business, and new methods of recording images and memories beyond silver halide technology, most noticeably digital imaging, were emerging.

The New Industry Environment

In the 1970s, Kodak began to face an uncertain environment in all its product markets. First, the color film and paper market from which Kodak made 75% of its profits experienced growing competition from Japanese companies, led by Fuji Photo Film Co. Fuji invested in huge, low-cost manufacturing plants, using the latest technology to mass-produce film in large volume. Fuji's low production costs and aggressive, competitive price cutting squeezed Kodak's profit margin. Finding no apparent differences in quality and obtaining more vivid colors with the Japanese product, consumers began to switch to the cheaper Japanese film, and this shift drastically reduced Kodak's market share.

Besides greater industry competition, another liability for Kodak was that it had done little internally to improve productivity to counteract rising costs. Supremacy in the marketplace had made Kodak complacent, and it had been slow to introduce productivity and quality improvements. Furthermore, Kodak (unlike Fuji in Japan) produced film in many different countries in the world rather than in a single country, and this also gave Kodak a cost disadvantage. Thus the combination of Fuji's efficient production and Kodak's own management style allowed the Japanese to become the cost leaders—to charge lower prices and still maintain profit margins.

Kodak was also facing competition on other product fronts. Its cameras had an advantage because of their ease of use as compared with complex 35-mm single-lens reflex models. They were also inexpensive. However, the quality of their prints could not compare with those of 35-mm cameras. In 1970 Kodak had toyed with the idea of producing a simple-to-use 35-mm camera but had abandoned it. In the late 1970s, however, the Japanese did develop an easy-to-use 35-mm pocket camera featuring such innovations as auto flash, focus, and rewind. The quality of the prints produced by these cameras was far superior to the grainy prints produced by the smaller Instamatic and disk cameras, and consumers began to switch to these products in large numbers. This shift led to the need for new kinds of film, which Kodak was slow to introduce, thus adding to its product problems.

Shrinking market share due to increased competition from the Japanese was not Kodak's only problem. In the early 1980s, it introduced several less-than-successful products. In 1982, it introduced a new disk camera as a replacement for the pocket Instamatic. The disk camera used a negative even smaller than the negative of the Instamatic and was smaller and easier to use. Four and a half million units were shipped to the domestic market by Christmas, but almost a million of the units still remained on retailers' shelves in the new year. The disk cameras had been outsold by pocket 35-mm cameras, which produced higher-quality pictures. The disk camera also sold poorly in the European and Japanese markets. Yet Kodak's research showed that 90% of disk camera users were satisfied with the camera and especially liked its high "yield rate" of 93% printable pictures, compared with 75% for the pocket Instamatic.

A final blow on the camera front came when Kodak lost its patent suit with Polaroid Corp. Kodak had forgone the instant photography business in the 1940s when it turned down Edwin Land's offer to develop his instant photography process. Polaroid developed it, and instant photography was wildly successful, capturing a significant share of the photographic market. In response, Kodak set out in the 1960s to develop its own instant camera to compete with Polaroid's. According to testimony in the patent trial, Kodak spent $94 million perfecting its system, only to scrub it when Polaroid introduced the new SX-70 camera in 1972. Kodak then rushed to produce a competing instant camera, hoping to capitalize on the $6.5 billon in sales of instant cameras. However, on January 9, 1986, a federal judge ordered Kodak out of the instant photography business for violating seven of Polaroid's patents in its rush to produce an instant camera. The cost to Kodak for closing its instant photography operation and exchanging the 16.5 million cameras sold to consumers was over $800 million. In 1985 Kodak reported that it had exited the industry at a cost of $494 million. However, the total costs of this misadventure were finally realized on July 15, 1991, when Kodak agreed to pay Polaroid a sum of $925 million to settle out of court a suit that Polaroid had brought against Kodak for patent infringement.

On its third product front, photographic processing, Kodak also experienced problems. It faced stiff competition from foreign manufacturers of photographic paper and from new competitors in the film-processing market. Increasingly, film processors were turning to cheaper sources of paper to reduce the costs of film processing. Once again the Japanese had developed cheaper sources of paper and were eroding Kodak's market share. At the same time, many new independent film-processing companies had emerged and were printing film at far lower rates than Kodak's own official developers. These independent laboratories had opened to serve the needs of drugstores and supermarkets, and many of them offered twenty-four-hour service. They used the less expensive paper to maintain their cost advantage and were willing to accept lower profit margins in return for a higher volume of sales. As a result, Kodak lost markets for its chemical and paper products—products that had contributed significantly to its revenues and profits.

The photographic industry surrounding Kodak had changed dramatically. Competition had increased in all product areas, and Kodak, while still the largest producer, faced increasing threats to its profitability as it was forced to reduce prices to match the competition. To cap the problem, by 1980 the market was all but saturated: 95% of all U.S. households owned at least one camera. Facing increased competition in a mature market was not an enviable position for a company used to high profitability and growth.

The second major problem that Kodak had to confront was due not to increased competition in existing product markets but to the emergence of new industries that provided alternative means of producing and recording images. The introduction of videotape recorders, and later video cameras, gave consumers an alternative way to use their dollars to produce images, particularly moving images. Video basically destroyed the old, film-based home movie business on which Kodak had a virtual monopoly. After Sony's introduction of the Betamax machine in 1975, a video industry grew into a multibillion-dollar business. VCRs and 16-mm video cameras became increasingly hot-selling items as their prices fell with the growth in demand and the standardization of technology. The development of compact 8-mm video cameras that were much smaller than the 16-mm version, and then the later introduction of laser disks, compact disks, and, in the 1990s, DVDs were also significant developments. The vast amount of data that can be recorded on these disks gave them a great advantage in reproducing images through electronic means. It was increasingly apparent that the whole nature of the imaging and recording process was changing from chemical methods of reproduction to electronic, digital methods. Kodak's managers should have perceived this transformation to digital-based methods as a disruptive technology because its technical preeminence was based on silver halide photography. However, as is always the case with such technologies, the real threat lies in the future.

These changes in the competitive environment caused enormous difficulties for Kodak. Between 1972 and 1982, profit margins from sales declined from 15.7 to 10.7%. Kodak's glossy image lost its luster. It was in this declining situation that Colby Chandler took over as chairman in July 1983.

Kodak's New Strategy

Chandler saw the need for dramatic changes in Kodak's businesses and quickly pioneered four changes in strategy: (1) he strove to increase Kodak's control of its existing chemical-based imaging businesses; (2) he aimed to make Kodak the leader in electronic imaging; (3) he spearheaded attempts by Kodak to diversify into new businesses to increase profitability; and (4) he began on major efforts to reduce costs and improve productivity. To achieve the first three objectives, he began a huge program of acquisitions, realizing that Kodak did not have the time to venture new activities internally. Because Kodak was cash rich and had low debt, financing these acquisitions was easy.

For the next six years, Chandler acquired businesses in four main areas, and by 1989 Kodak had been restructured into four main operating groups: imaging, information systems, health, and chemicals. In a statement to shareholders at the annual meeting in 1988, Chandler announced that with the recent acquisition of Sterling Drug for $5 billion the company had achieved its objective: "With a sharp focus on these four sectors, we are serving diversified markets from a unified base of science and manufacturing technology. The logical synergy of the Kodak growth strategy means that we are neither diversified as a conglomerate nor a company with a one-product family."

The way these operating groups developed under Chandler's leadership is described in the following text.

The Imaging Group

Imaging comprised Kodak's original businesses, including consumer products, motion picture and audiovisual products, photo finishing, and consumer electronics. The unit was charged with strengthening Kodak's position in its existing businesses. Kodak's strategy in its photographic imaging business has been to fill gaps in its product line by introducing new products either made by Kodak or bought from Japanese manufacturers and sold under the Kodak name. For example, in attempting to maintain market share in the camera business, Kodak introduced a new line of disk cameras to replace the Instamatic lines. However, in addition, Kodak bought a minority stake and entered into a joint venture with Chinon of Japan to produce a range of 35-mm automatic cameras that would be sold under the Kodak name. This arrangement would capitalize on Kodak's strong brand image and give Kodak a presence in this market to maintain its camera and film sales. That venture succeeded; Kodak sold 500,000 cameras and

gained 15% of the market. In addition, Kodak invested heavily in developing new and advanced film. It introduced a whole new range of "DX" coded film to match the new 35-mm camera market film that possesses the vivid color qualities of Fuji film. Kodak had not developed vivid film color earlier because of its belief that consumers wanted "realistic" color.

Kodak also made major moves to solidify its hold on the film-processing market. It attempted to stem the inflow of foreign low-cost photographic paper by gaining control over the processing market. In 1986 it acquired Texas-based Fox Photo Inc. for $96 million and became the largest national wholesale photograph finisher. In 1987, it acquired the laboratories of American Photographic Group. In 1989, it solidified its hold on the photo-finishing market by forming a joint venture between its operations and the photo-finishing operations of Fuqua industries. The new company, Qualex Inc., had ninety-four laboratories nationwide. These acquisitions provided Kodak with a large, captive customer for its chemical and paper products as well as control over the photo-finishing market. Also, in 1986 Kodak introduced new improved one-hour film-processing labs to compete with other photographic developers. To accompany the new labs, Kodak popularized the Kodak "Color Watch" system that requires these labs to use only Kodak paper and chemicals. Kodak hoped that this would stem the flow of business to one-hour mini-labs and also establish the industry standard for quality processing.

New and improved film products, including Kodak Gold Label film and Ektachrome film, were announced during 1988, as were new types of 35-mm cameras. Kodak also formed a battery venture with Matsushita to produce a range of alkaline batteries for Kodak. A gold-topped battery was introduced to compete with Duracell's copper-top battery. Moreover, Kodak internally ventured a new lithium battery that lasted six times as long as conventional batteries. As a result of these moves, Kodak regained control over the processing end of the market and made inroads into the camera, film, and battery ends as well. In 1988, Kodak earnings were helped by the decline in value of the dollar, which forced Fuji Photo, its main competitor, to raise its prices. Consequently, Kodak was able to increase its prices. All these measures increased Kodak's visibility in the market; Kodak was protecting its mission of "You push the button, we do the rest."

Kodak also engaged in a massive internal cost-cutting effort to improve the efficiency of the photographic products group. Beginning in 1984 it introduced more and more stringent efficiency targets aimed at reducing waste while increasing productivity. In 1986, it established a baseline for measuring the total cost of waste incurred in the manufacture of film and paper throughout its worldwide operations. By 1987 it had cut that waste by 15%, and by 1989 it announced total cost savings worth $500 million annually.

Despite these strategic moves, the net earnings of Kodak's photographic business dropped dramatically in 1989. Although Kodak's volume and sales of its products were up, profit margins were down. Polaroid with its new One Film product was advertising aggressively to capture market share. Fuji, realizing the strong threat posed by Kodak's price cutting, responded in kind, and a price war ensued. Both Fuji and Kodak were spending massive amounts to advertise their products in order to increase market share. In 1989, Kodak had 80% of the $7 billion film market while Fuji had 11%, but Fuji increased its advertising budget by 65% in 1989 to increase its market share and simultaneously offered discount coupons on its film products. Moreover, Fuji announced plans for a major new filmmaking plant in Europe—a plant the size of its Japanese plant, which by itself can produce enough film for one-quarter of the world market. The result was a huge amount of excess capacity in global film production as Fuji, the cost leader, went all out to build global market share through aggressive pricing.

Kodak's losses mounted as it was forced to reduce prices to counter Fuji's attempts to build market share and to give multipack discounts on its products. Also to fight back, Kodak announced a fifteen-year agreement with the Walt Disney Co. to use Disney characters in its advertising. However, these moves were very expensive for Kodak and slashed profits. They also offset most of the benefits from Kodak's cost-cutting effort, and the slow growth in Kodak's core photographic imaging business meant that there was little prospect of increasing profitability.

It was because of this slow industry growth that Chandler saw the need for diversification. Because sales increased only 5% a year and Kodak already had 80% of the market, it was tied to the fortunes of one industry. While this made Kodak cash-rich when competition was weak, it made Kodak poor when competition increased. This fact, plus the increasing use and growing applications of digital imaging techniques, led to Chandler's second strategic thrust: an immediate policy of acquisition and diversification into the electronic imaging business with the stated goal of being "first in both industries"—imaging and digital.

The Information Systems Group

In 1988, when Sony introduced an electronic camera that could take still pictures and then transmit them back to a television screen, it became increasingly obvious that the threat to Kodak from new electronic imaging techniques would continue to increase. Although pictures taken with video film could not match the quality achieved with chemical reproduction, the advent of compact disks offered the prospect of an imaging medium that could meet such standards in the future. For the company to survive and prosper in the imaging business, Kodak's managers began to realize that it required expertise in a broad range of technologies to satisfy customers' recording and imaging needs—they began to see the threat posed by the disruptive technology. Kodak's managers saw that a large number of different types of electronic markets were emerging. Electronic imaging had become important in the medical sciences and in all business, technical, and research activities, driven by the advent of powerful personal computers. However, Kodak's managers did not choose to focus on imaging products and markets close to "photographs." They began to target any kind of imaging applications in communications, computer science, and various hard-copy-output technologies that they believed might be important in the imaging markets of the future. Since Kodak had no expertise in digital imaging, it began to buy companies its managers perceived did have these skills, and then pursued its strategy of marketing the products of these companies under its own famous brand name—for instance, an electronic publishing system for corporate documents and an automated microfilm-imaging system.

Kodak thus began a strategy of acquisitions and joint ventures to invest its excess cash in new imagining technologies that it hoped, somehow, would lead to increased future profitability. In the new information systems group, several acquisitions were made, including Atex Inc., Eikonix Corp., and Disconix Inc. Atex, acquired in 1981, made newspaper and magazine electronic publishing and text-editing systems to newspapers and magazines worldwide as well as to government agencies and law firms. Eikonix Corp. was a leader in the design, development, and production of precision digital imaging systems. Further growth within the information systems group came with the development of the Ektaprint line of copier-duplicators. The copiers achieved good sales growth and reached new standards for quality, reliability, and productivity in the very competitive high-volume segment of the copier marketplace. In 1988, Kodak announced another major move into the copier service business. It purchased IBM's copier service business and copier sales agreements in the United States. Kodak also announced that it would market copiers manufactured by IBM while continuing to market its own Ektaprint copiers. This service agreement was eventually extended to sixteen countries outside the United States.

Kodak also announced two new image management packages: the Kodak Ektaprint Electronic Publishing System (KEEPS) and the Kodak Imaging Management System (KIMS). KIMS electronically scans, digitizes, and stores film images and transmits image information electronically. The system enables users with large, active databases to view and manipulate information stored on microfilm and magnetic or optical disks. KEEPS was a high-quality electronic publishing package that had the ability to edit, print, and update text and graphics for publications. However, the KEEPS package included a computer made by Sun Microsystems, software produced by Interleaf Inc. and just enhanced by Kodak, and a printer manufactured by Canon. In 1988, Kodak announced that it would begin marketing a "VY-P1" printer developed in a joint venture with Hitachi to make high-quality still images from VCRs and camcorders. Although Kodak had begun to spend more and more of its R&D budget on digital imaging, it still had not internally ventured any important new products.

Moreover, these new markets did not overlap much with its core photography business. With these moves, Kodak extended its activities into the electronic areas of artificial intelligence, computer systems, consumer electronics, peripherals, telecommunications, and test and measuring equipment. Kodak was hoping to gain a strong foothold in these new businesses to make up for losses in its traditional business—not to strengthen its core business.

Soon, Kodak's managers began to purchase imaging companies that made products as diverse as computer workstations and floppy disks. It aggressively acquired companies to fill in its product lines and obtain technical expertise in information systems. After taking more than a decade to make its first four acquisitions, Kodak completed seven acquisitions in 1985 and more than ten in 1986. Among the 1985 acquisitions—for $175 million—was Verbatim Corp., a major producer of floppy disks. This acquisition made Kodak one of the three big producers in the floppy disk industry.

Entry into the information systems market, like the expansion in its core photographic products business, produced new competitive problems for Kodak. In entering office information systems, Kodak entered areas where it faced strong competition from established companies such as IBM, Apple, and Sun. The Verbatim acquisition brought Kodak into direct competition with 3M. Entering the copier market brought Kodak into direct competition with Japanese firms such as Canon that competitively marketed their own lines of advanced, low-cost products. Kodak was entering new businesses where it had little expertise, where it was unfamiliar with the competitive problems, and where there was already strong competition.

Thus Kodak was forced to retreat from some of these markets. In 1990, it announced that it would sell Verbatim to Mitsubishi. (Mitsubishi was immediately criticized by Japanese investors for buying a company with an old, outdated product line.) Kodak was soon forced to withdraw from many other areas of business by selling assets or closing operations and taking a write-off. For example, to reduce costs it sold Sayett Technology, Kodak Video programs and videocassettes, and Aquidneck Data Corp. The decline in the performance of the information systems group, attributed to increased competition, a flat office systems market, and delays in bringing out new products, reduced earnings from operations from a profit of $311 million in 1988 to a loss of $360 million in 1989.

The Health Group

Kodak's interest in health products emerged from its involvement in the design and production of film for medical and dental x-rays. The growth of imaging in medical sciences offered Kodak an opportunity to apply its skills in new areas, and it began to develop such products as Kodak Ektachem—clinical blood analyzers. It developed other products—Ektascan laser imaging films, printers, and accessories—for improving the display, storage, processing, and retrieval of diagnostic images.

However, Kodak did not confine its interests in medical and health matters to imaging-based products. In 1984, it established within the health group a life sciences division to develop and commercialize new products deriving from Kodak's distinctive competencies in chemistry and biotechnology. One of the division's objectives was to focus on product opportunities in markets with relatively few competitors and high profit potential—products such as nutritional supplements that can be delivered orally or intravenously, as well as nutrition products for sale over the counter to consumers. Another objective was to develop innovative ways to control the absorption of pharmaceutical drugs into the body so that a drug would remain therapeutically effective for the optimum amount of time. A third objective involved developing new applications for existing products and processes. Kodak had in its files about 500,000 chemical formulations on which it could base new products.

Within life sciences was the bioproducts division, which engaged in joint research with biotechnology companies such as Cetus Corp., Amgen, and Immunex. Bioproducts pursued an aggressive strategy to scale up and commercialize products based on biotechnology derived from in-house as well as outside contract research. Ventures entered into by the bioproducts division included an agreement with Advanced Genetic Sciences for the commercial production of SNOW-MAX, a product useful in making artificial snow for ski areas.

Kodak began to enter into joint ventures in the biotechnical industry, both to build its business and to enter new businesses. In April 1985 Kodak and ICN Pharmaceuticals jointly announced the formation of a research institute that would explore new biomedical compounds aimed at stopping the spread of viral infections and slowing the aging process. Kodak and ICN were to invest $45 million over six years to form and operate the Nucleic Acid Research Institute, a joint venture located at ICN's Costa Mesa, California, facility. The institute would dedicate much of its research exclusively to preclinical studies of new antiviral and anti-aging substances.

However, these advances into biotechnology proved expensive, and the uncertainty of the industry caused Kodak to question the wisdom of entering this highly volatile area. In 1988, to reduce the costs of operating the bioproducts division, a joint venture incorporating bioproducts was formed between Kodak and Cultor Ltd. of Finland, and Kodak essentially left the market. The remaining parts of the life sciences division were then folded into the health group in 1988, when Chandler completed Kodak's

biggest acquisition, the purchase of Sterling Drug for more than $5 billion.

The Sterling acquisition once again totally altered Kodak's strategy for the health group. Sterling Drug is a worldwide manufacturer and marketer of prescription drugs, over-the-counter medicine, and consumer products. It has such familiar brand names as Bayer aspirin, Phillips' milk of magnesia, and Panadol. Chandler thought this merger would provide Kodak with the marketing infrastructure and international drug registration that it needed to become a major player in the pharmaceuticals industry. With this acquisition, Kodak's health group became pharmaceutically oriented, its mission being to develop a full pipeline of major prescription drugs and a world-class portfolio of over-the-counter medicine.

Analysts, however, questioned the acquisition. Once again Chandler was taking Kodak into an industry where competition was intense and the industry itself was consolidating because of the massive cost of drug development. Kodak had no expertise in this area, despite its forays into biotechnology, and the acquisition was unrelated to the other activities of the health group. Some analysts claimed that the acquisition was aimed at deterring a possible takeover of Kodak and that it was too expensive.

The acquisition of Sterling dramatically increased the sales of the health group but dampened Kodak's earnings and helped lead to a reversal in profits in 1989. Moreover, by purchasing Sterling, Kodak had obtained Sterling's Lehn & Fink products division, which produced products as diverse as Lysol and Minwax wood-care products. Far from wishing to sell this division, Kodak believed that this acquisition would lead to long-term profits. Analysts asked whether this was growth without profitability.

The Chemicals Group

Established more than sixty-five years ago as a supplier of raw materials for Kodak's film and processing businesses, the Eastman Chemical Co. has been responsible for developing many of the chemicals and plastics that have made Kodak the leader in the photographic industry. The company has also been a major supplier of chemicals, fibers, and plastics to thousands of customers worldwide. Kodak has been enjoying increased growth in its plastic material and resins unit because of outstanding performance and enthusiastic customer acceptance of Kodak PET (polyethylene terephthalate), a polymer used in soft-drink bottles and other food and beverage containers. The growth in popularity of 16-ounce PET bottles spurred a record year for both revenue and volume in 1985. Kodak announced the opening of a major new PET facility in England in 1988. In 1986, three new businesses were established within the chemicals group: specialty printing inks, performance plastics, and animal nutrition supplements. They all had the common objective of enabling the chemicals group to move quickly into profitable new market segments where there is the potential for growth.

In its chemical business, too, Kodak ran into the same kinds of problems experienced by its other operating groups. There is intense competition in the plastics industry, not only from U.S. firms like DuPont but also from large Japanese and European firms like Imperial Chemical Industries PLC and Hoech, which compete directly with Kodak for sales. In specialty plastics and PET, for example, volume increased but Kodak was forced to reduce prices by 5% to compete with other firms in the industry. This squeeze in profit margins also contributed to the reversal in earnings in 1989.

Logical Synergies?

With the huge profit reversal in 1989 after all the years of acquisition and internal development, analysts were questioning the existence of the "logical synergy" that Chandler claimed for Kodak's businesses. Certainly, the relative contributions of the various operating groups to Kodak's total sales differed from the past, and Kodak was somewhat less dependent on the photographic industry. But was Kodak positioned to compete successfully in the 1990s? What was the rationale for Kodak's entry into different businesses? What were the synergies that Chandler was talking about? Wasn't the improvement on profits in 1990 due to corporate restructuring to reduce costs?

Corporate Restructuring and Cost Reduction

As Chandler tackled changes in strategy, he also directed his efforts at reshaping Kodak's management style and organizational structure to (1) reduce costs and (2) make the organization more flexible and attuned to the competitive environment. Because of its dominance in the industry, in the past, Kodak had not worried about outside competition. As a result, the organizational culture at Kodak emphasized

traditional, conservative values rather than entrepreneurial values. Kodak was often described as a conservative, plodding monolith because all decision making had been centralized at the top of the organization among a clique of senior managers. Furthermore, the company had been operating along functional lines. Research, production, and sales and marketing had operated separately in different units at corporate headquarters and dispersed to many different global locations. Kodak's different product groups also operated separately. The result of these factors was a lack of communication and slow, inflexible decision making that led to delays in making new product decisions. When the company attempted to transfer resources between product groups, conflict often resulted, and the separate functional operations also led to poor product group relations, for managers protected their own turf at the expense of corporate goals. Moreover, there was a lack of attention to the bottom line, and management failed to institute measures to control waste.

Another factor encouraging Kodak's conservative orientation was its promotion policy. Seniority and loyalty to "mother Kodak" counted nearly as much as ability when it came to promotions. Only twelve presidents had led the company since its beginnings in the 1880s. Long after George Eastman's suicide in 1932, the company followed his cautious ways: "If George didn't do it, his successors didn't either."

Kodak's technical orientation also contributed to its problems. Traditionally, its engineers and scientists had dominated decision making, and marketing had been neglected. The engineers and scientists were perfectionists who spent enormous amounts of time developing, analyzing, testing, assessing, and retesting new products. Little time, however, was spent determining whether the products satisfied consumer needs. As a result of this technical orientation, management passed up the invention of xerography, leaving the new technology to be developed by a small Rochester, New York, firm named Haloid Co. (later Xerox). Similarly, Kodak had passed up the instant camera business. Kodak's lack of a marketing orientation allowed competitors to overtake it in several areas that were natural extensions of the photography business, such as 35-mm cameras and video recorders.

Kodak's early management style, while profitable throughout the 1960s because of the company's privileged competitive position, was thus creating difficulties. With its monopoly in the photographic film and paper industry gone, Kodak was in trouble. Chandler had to alter Kodak's management orientation. He began with some radical changes in the company's culture and structure.

Firmly committed to cost cutting, Chandler orchestrated a massive downsizing of the work force to eliminate the fat that had accumulated during Kodak's prosperous past. Traditionally, Kodak had prided itself on being one of the most "Japanese" of all U.S. companies, hiring college graduates and giving them a permanent career. Now it had to go against one of its founding principles and reduce its work force. Kodak's policy of lifetime employment was swept out the door when declining profitability led to a large employee layoff. Chandler instituted a special early retirement program, froze pay raises, and ordered the company's first layoffs in more than a decade. By 1985, the "yellow box factory" had dropped 12,600 of its 136,000 employees. To further reduce costs in 1986, divisions were required to cut employment by an additional 10% and to cut budgetary expenditures by 5%. These measures helped, but because of Kodak's deteriorating performance, new rounds of cost cutting came in 1988 and 1989. Additional 5% reductions in employment aimed at saving $1 billion. The effect of these huge cuts was seen in 1990 when profits rebounded; however, it was not clear whether their effect on earnings would be short run or long run.

Although these measures had an effect on Kodak's culture, Chandler still needed to reshape Kodak's structure. In 1985 he began by shedding the old, stratified corporate structure for what he called an "entrepreneurial" approach. The first step was to reorganize the imaging group into seventeen operating units. Each of the seventeen lines of business contained all the functions necessary for success, including marketing, financial, planning, product development, and manufacturing. Each unit was treated as an independent profit center and was managed by a young executive with authority over everything from design to production. All units had the common goal of improving quality and efficiency and eliminating problems in the transfer of resources and technology among operating groups. The purpose behind this change was to eliminate the old divisional orientation, which had led to competition and reduced integration within the company. Chandler hoped the changes in organizational control and structure would promote innovation, speed reaction time, and establish clear profit goals. With this restructuring,

Chandler also reduced Kodak's top-heavy management to decentralize decision making to lower levels in the hierarchy. This reorganization was a sign that the company was at last shedding its paternalistic approach to management.

With its new risk-taking attitude, Kodak also attempted to create a structure and culture to encourage internal venturing. It formed a "venture board" to help underwrite small projects and make conventional venture capital investments. In addition, the company created an "office of submitted ideas" to screen outside projects. Kodak received more than three thousand proposals, but only thirty survived the screening process. This aggressive research program led to a breakthrough in tubular silver halide grains, which improve the light-gathering capability of film. The discovery resulted in the new line of 35-mm products. However, Kodak's attempts at new venturing were generally unsuccessful. Of the fourteen ventures that Kodak created, six were shut down, three were sold, and four were merged into other divisions. One reason was Kodak's management style, which also affected its new businesses. Kodak's top managers never gave operating executives real authority or abandoned the centralized, conservative approach of the past. One example is Kodak's managing of Atex Inc., the manufacturer of desktop publishing systems that Kodak bought in 1981. Because of Kodak's overbearing management style, the top executives and employees of Atex resigned, creating serious management problems for Kodak. The Atex executives claimed that Kodak executives were hardworking but bureaucratic and did not understand the competitive nature of computer technology. Kodak managers should have been reacting to the computer marketplace weekly. They did not, and Atex executives could not handle Kodak's slow pace.

Another reason for the failure at managing new ventures and acquisitions was that Kodak did not give managers an equity stake in the new ventures, so they felt that they had no stake in the ventures' success. Having learned its lesson, Kodak announced that throughout the company pay would be more closely related to performance. For example, in 1990 up to 40% of a manager's annual compensation was to be based on corporate performance. Even at the middle-manager level, 15% of compensation was to be linked to company results. Kodak hoped by these measures to make the company more entrepreneurial and to move it along the cost reduction path.

Kodak also reorganized its worldwide facilities to reduce costs. International divisions were turning out identical products at higher cost than their counterparts in the United States. In a plan to coordinate worldwide production to increase productivity and lower costs, Kodak streamlined European production by closing duplicate manufacturing facilities and centralizing production and marketing operations, and it also brought some foreign manufacturing home. As a result, Kodak gained $55 million in productivity savings. However, Fuji's new European facility posed a severe challenge. Starting from scratch and employing production techniques learned from low-cost Japanese operations, Fuji remained the clear cost leader with the ability to start a price war to increase market share.

George Fisher Changes Kodak

Chandler retired as CEO in 1989 and was replaced by his chief operating officer, Kay Whitmore, another Kodak veteran. Whitmore immediately was forced to confront the problem of dealing with the poor performance of Chandler's misguided acquisitions. As Kodak's performance continued to plunge under his leadership, however, he came under intense scrutiny from analysts, who began to question the whole logic behind Kodak's aggressive diversification efforts. Whitmore responded by hiring managers from outside Kodak to help him restructure the company, but when they proposed selling off most of Kodak's new acquisitions and laying off many more thousands of employees to reduce costs, Whitmore resisted. He, too, was entrenched in the old Kodak culture and was unwilling to take such drastic steps. Finally, after continued criticism from analysts, Kodak's board of directors ousted Whitmore as CEO, and in 1993 George Fisher, the first outsider to lead Kodak in 117 years, became the new CEO. Fisher left his job as CEO of Motorola to join Kodak. At Motorola, he had been credited with leading that company into the digital age, and it was his expertise in the digital sector that led to his appointment. Fisher was given 2 million Kodak stock options at around $90 a share, Kodak's then stock price, to reward him for what many felt would be a fast turnaround in Kodak's fortunes.

Fisher's strategy was to reverse Chandler's diversification into any industry in the digital sector. Kodak's principal thrust, Fisher decided, should be to strengthen its competencies in the digital photography industry. However, given that Kodak had spent so much money on making its acquisitions, the question was what to do about its other businesses, especially as the company was now burdened with increasing debt from its acquisitions and falling profits. Fisher's solution was dramatic.

Looking at Kodak's four business groups, he decided that the over-the-counter drugs component of the health products group was doing nothing to add value to Kodak's profitability, and he decided to divest Sterling Drugs and use the cash to pay off debt. Soon, all that was left of this group was the health imaging business. Fisher also decided that the chemicals group, despite its expertise in the invention and manufacture of chemicals, no longer fitted with his new digital strategy. Henceforth Kodak would buy its chemicals in the open market, and in 1995 he spun this group off and gave each Kodak shareholder a share in the new company, Eastman Chemicals, whose stock price soon increased rapidly. The information systems group with its diverse businesses was a more difficult challenge; the issue was which components would help promote Kodak's new digital strategy and which were superfluous and could be sold off. In the end, Fisher decided that Kodak would focus on building its presence in the document imaging industry with a focus on photocopiers, commercial inkjet printers, and commercial digital imaging and either sold or closed down the various other parts of the business that did not fit this theme. However, he also decided to outsource the sales and service end of the business, and in 1995 Kodak announced an agreement with Danka Business Systems for it to sell and service Kodak's high-volume copiers throughout the United States and Canada.

With these actions, within two years Fisher had pared down Kodak's debt by $7 billion, dumped chemicals and health, and boosted Kodak's stock price—all this signaled good times ahead. However, Fisher still had to confront the problems inside Kodak's core photographic imaging group, and here the solution was neither easy nor quick. Kodak was still plagued by high operating costs that were still 27% of annual revenue, and Fisher knew he needed to get these costs down to about 15 to 20% to compete effectively in the digital world. Kodak's work force had shrunk to 95,000 by 1993, and he wanted to avoid further layoffs, which would demoralize an already shaken work force. But with Kodak's current revenue in 1995 of $16 billion, this would mean finding ways to squeeze another couple of billion out of operating costs.

At the same time, Fisher also knew that Kodak had to invest more and more of its R&D budget into digital imaging. Kodak had no particular competency in making either digital cameras or the software necessary to allow them to operate efficiently. Soon Kodak was spending over $400 million a year on digital projects. However, new digital products were slow to come on line. Also, consumers were slow to embrace digital photography, the cameras were expensive and bulky, the software was complicated to use, and printing digital photographs was both expensive and difficult at this time. Neither Kodak nor its customers had ramped up the digital photography learning curve, and by 1997 its digital business was still losing over $100 million a year.

To compound matters, in 1995 Fuji Film decided to open up a state-of-the-art filmmaking operation in the United States to further attack the $6 billion film market with "home-grown" products. Fuji also snatched the biggest photo-finishing contract in the United States, the Wal-Mart account, away from Kodak in 1995, and soon after sales of Fuji film in Wal-Mart started to rocket. Through 1995–1997 Fuji also lowered its prices and started a price war, and by 1997 Kodak's share of the U.S. film market had fallen to 78%, down a further 4% from 1996, while Fuji's had risen to 14%. This loss of four points cost Kodak about $125 million in lost sales, and sales of private-label film were beginning to increase, putting more pressures on revenues and costs.

To speed product development, Fisher reorganized Kodak's product groups into fourteen autonomous business units based on serving the needs of distinct groups of customers, such as those for its health products or commercial products. The idea was to decentralize decision making, thus putting managers closer to their major customers and escaping from Kodak's suffocating centralized style of decision making. Fisher also changed the top managers in charge of the film and camera units; however, he did not bring in many outsiders to spearhead the new digital efforts. This new emphasis on customer groups also meant that overhead costs rose because each unit had its own complement of functions; thus sales forces and so on were duplicated.

Fisher had been performing the roles of Kodak's chairman, CEO, president, *and* COO—something that analysts now started to complain about bitterly.

How could Kodak get rid of its centralized decision-making style when its new leader apparently wanted to centralize all important decision making in his own hands? The reorganization into fourteen autonomous business units had not decentralized control to business unit leaders, and Fisher and his top management team were still overseeing all important strategy decisions. This explained the slow pace of change at Kodak. Thus while Fisher had brought Kodak's focus back to its core photography business, he had not put in place the infrastructure that would allow its managers to achieve its new digital mission.

In 1996, Fisher finally realized his dilemma, and with pressure from the board, Daniel A. Carp was named Kodak's president and COO, the appointment to COO meaning that he was Fisher's heir apparent as Kodak's CEO. Carp was a Kodak veteran who had spearheaded the global consolidation of its operations and its entry into major new international markets such as China. He was widely credited with having had a major impact on Kodak's attempts to fight Fuji on a global level and help it to maintain its market share. Henceforth, Kodak's digital and applied imaging, business imaging, and equipment manufacturing—almost all its major operating groups—would now report to Carp. Carp also retained control of the Greater China region, where potential future film sales were seen as crucial to Kodak's future in its battle with arch-rival Fuji.

However, Kodak's revenues and profits continued to decline during the mid to late 1990s. It was slowly but steadily losing market share in its core film business to Fuji, but now generic film brands were also attracting customers and putting squeezes on profit margins. By 2000 analysts estimated it had only 66% of the U.S. market. Although the major price war with Fuji was over, sales of private-label film were still rising, and Kodak was periodically forced to use tactics such as multipack price discounts and rebates to prevent even further erosions to its market share, even at the cost of profits. Fisher knew that Kodak must preserve its market share to protect its future profitability and to give time both for it to develop its own digital competencies and for customers to develop an understanding and appetite for digital cameras. Meanwhile, the quality of the pictures taken by digital cameras was advancing rapidly as more and more pixels were being crammed into them. Also, at the low end, the price of a basic digital camera was falling rapidly because of economies of scale in production. Perhaps, finally, the digital photography market was taking off, but would Kodak be able to meet the challenge?

Despite early enthusiasm from analysts, Kodak's slow progress on all fronts and Fisher's leadership had become a major disappointment. When in July 1997 Fisher announced poor second-quarter results, analysts and shareholders who had bought into his new strategy for Kodak began to bail out. Its share price soon tumbled to below $70 from $90, and Fisher's stock options that had been granted at $90 were now valueless at this price. Many analysts wondered if Kodak's board had been right in February 1997 to extend Fisher's contract for three more years to December 31, 2000.

Carp's Growing Influence

With Carp now in control of both Kodak's digital and global operations, the pace of change started to quicken. In 1997, Kodak announced it would open an office of the COO in Hong Kong to capitalize on trends in emerging markets, especially because of China's low-cost manufacturing advantages. Also in 1997, Kodak increased its stake in the Japanese camera manufacturer Chinon to 50.1%, effectively taking control of the company that now was making its advanced digital cameras and scanners. In 1998, Kodak announced its lowest-priced-yet digital camera with "megapixel" (million pixels per inch) image quality. This camera looked and operated like a conventional point-and-shoot camera. Kodak also bought Picture-vision Inc., whose digital Photonet online network products, combined with Kodak's brand name, would attract more customers who could now scan their pictures into its digital network, transmit the images and share them with others, and also receive outputs ranging from reprints to enlargements. Photo retailers also named Kodak's digital picture-maker kiosks the "top product of the year." Customers could take their ordinary photographs and use the kiosks to remove red eye, do quick and easy color corrections, and zoom or crop to select and print the best part of a photo. Essentially, Kodak was using these kiosks to help customers learn about the advantages of digital photography and to help develop the market. Kodak and Intel also formed an agreement to use Intel digital scanning equipment in Kodak's Qualex photo-finishing labs to make it easy for customers to put photos onto CD-ROM for use in home computers. In 1998, AOL and Kodak announced a strategic alliance to offer AOL members an exclusive online service, "You've Got Pictures," whereby AOL members could have their regular processed pictures delivered in digital format to their AOL mailboxes. Customers were becoming increasingly familiar with how the new digital products worked, and Kodak was in the forefront of online efforts to capture customers and promote the Internet for transmission of digital images.

Thus Kodak was beginning to make steady progress in its digital mission; its digital cameras were growing in popularity, in large part because of its developing competencies in making easy-to-use camera-printer software. Also, its digital kiosks and photo-finishing operations were being increasingly visited by customers, and their number was increasing rapidly both in the United States and globally. In recognition of his progress, in June 1999 Kodak's board named Carp as new CEO of Kodak, and he was to keep his other roles of president and COO. Fisher was to remain chairman until January 2001.

In the next few years, Kodak's developing digital skills led to new products in all its major businesses. In 1999, its health imaging group announced the then fastest digital image management system for echocardiography labs. It also entered the digital radiography market with three state-of-the-art digital systems for capturing x-ray images. Its document imaging group announced several new electronic document management systems. It also teamed up with inkjet maker Lexmark to introduce the stand-alone Kodak Personal Picture Maker by Lexmark, which could print color photos from both compact flash cards and Smart Media. Its commercial and government systems group announced advanced new high-powered digital cameras for uses such as in space and in the military.

With these developments, Kodak's net earnings shot up between 1998 and 2000, and its stock price recovered somewhat. However, one reason for the increase in net revenues was that the devastating price war with Fuji that had raged from 1979 to 1999 had ended as both companies saw that continuing to offer price discounts simply reduced both companies' profits. Kodak also was still not getting quickly to the market the range of new digital imaging products it needed to drive its future profitability, since there was intense competition in the core film businesses, which had traditionally given it 30 to 40% of its profits. Here, as in film products, Kodak's high operating costs overwhelmed the benefits it obtained from its new product introductions and hurt its bottom line—its profits were not increasing.

Kodak in the Early 2000s

New digital product developments and changing industry conditions in most of its markets began to punish Kodak afresh as it entered the 2000s. In the consumer imaging group, for example, Kodak launched a new camera, the EasyShare, in 2001. Over 4 million digital cameras were sold in 2000 and over 6 million in 2001, and over a half-million of the easy-to-use new Kodak camera were sold in 2001. However, given the huge development costs and intense competition from Japanese companies like Sony and Canon, which also make advanced cameras and "digicams," Kodak has not yet made any money from its digital cameras—profit margins are razor thin because of intense competition. Moreover, every time it sells a digital camera, it reduces demand for its high-margin film; so Kodak is cannibalizing a profitable product for an unprofitable one—with no choice in the matter. As a result, its profitability has plunged.

Kodak argued that it would make more money in the future from sales of the paper necessary to print these images and from its photo-finishing operations. However, it is becoming increasingly obvious that consumers are not printing out many of the photographs they take, preferring to save many in disk form and only selecting and printing out the few best ones to send to relatives and friends. With chemical films, one could not pick and choose; the whole roll had to be developed. So revenues are not increasing on this front. Moreover, it is the ink sellers such as Hewlett-Packard and Lexmark that have been charging monopoly prices for ink cartridges, which have been making the money in printing images, and Kodak has failed to use its strengths in chemicals to get into the printer ink business.

On the photo-finishing end, Kodak's future revenues and profits depend on it maximizing the number of its in-store kiosks or the number of photo-finishing contracts with large chain stores. After Kodak lost the Wal-Mart contract to Fuji, it signed new agreements with Walgreens (the second largest U.S. film processor, with over 3,000 stores) and with Kmart. It also operated its own Fox and Qualex photo-finishing labs. However, in 2001, Kmart declared Chapter 11 bankruptcy, and the Fox photo store chain, which was primarily finishing traditional

roll film, went bankrupt, causing a large loss to Kodak. To compound matters, in June 2002 it was reported that Walgreens was testing Fuji's new photo-finishing laboratory system in thirty of its stores and that it might award this important contract to Fuji when it came up for renewal sometime in 2002. In June 2002, recognizing that Fuji was gaining a competitive edge in the vital photo-finishing systems market, Kodak announced that it was buying key components of its new digital system from Agfa, a European imaging firm, since it did not have the time to develop them itself. This suggests that Kodak's technology was no better than that of competitors, and it might be even behind that of competitors like Fuji. Thus it was not clear that Kodak had a lead in all the activities—cameras, software, paper, and photo finishing—necessary to dominate the photography market as it had in the past. It did have its powerful brand name going for it, however, which is why it has been so concerned to protect its market share at any cost to its profits.

At the industry level, the emergence of powerful buyers in many markets also seriously hurt Kodak's performance. In photo finishing, large store chains like Wal-Mart and Walgreens are in strong bargaining positions and can threaten Kodak's profitability (it has been estimated that 10% of Kodak's photo-finishing operations are with Walgreens). This same situation occurred in the health imaging industry. Here, Kodak's state-of-the-art imaging products were widely expected to generate large revenues and boost its profitability. However, after a good start, in 2000 Kodak faced the problem of bargaining over prices with Novation Group Purchasing organization, a major buyer of health equipment and therefore a powerful buyer as well. Kodak was forced to slash its prices to win the contract against agile competitors, and this experience was repeated with many other large health care providers. So intense was competition in this segment that in 2001 sales of laser printers and health-related imagining products, which make up Kodak's second biggest business, fell 7% while profit in the segment fell 30%, causing a large drop in Kodak's share price. In 2000, after its profits fell drastically, it announced another 2,000 job cuts, and in 2001 it announced another 5,000, for a total of 7,000, bringing Kodak's work force down to about 78,000.

Also, in 2001 Carp announced another major reorganization of Kodak's businesses. To give it a sharper focus on its products and customers, Kodak announced that it was moving from a structure based on customer groups to one based on strategic product lines, and it created four distinct product groups: the film group, which now contained all its silver halide activities; consumer digital imaging; health imaging group; and growing commercial imaging group, which continued to develop its business imaging and printing applications. Nevertheless, revenues plunged from $19 billion in 2001 to only $13 billion by 2002, its profits almost disappeared, and analysts now wondered if Kodak under Carp was really faring any better than Kodak under Fisher. There was no real change taking place, and Carp was avoiding the massive downsizing that still needed to take place to make Kodak a viable company. Analysts attributed this to Kodak's entrenched, inbred, and unresponsive top management that persisted in doing everything possible to frustrate real efforts to reduce costs and streamline operations. For despite all the advances in its digital skills, Kodak was still burdened with high operating costs, well out of proportion with its declining revenues. Would the layoffs or reorganization be enough to turn Kodak's performance around?

Amazingly, despite its problems, Kodak still paid its shareholders one of the top ten dividends of all companies in the *Fortune 500*. Analysts argue that it should be run for profit now, not in the future. But Kodak's managers replied that the economic recession and events of 2000–2002 were to blame for a large part of its problems and that it had all the pieces in place for a sustained recovery and for dominance in the digital arena using its powerful brand name once the market recovered. Investors didn't believe this story. Kodak's stock price plunged in 2002 and was selling in the $30s by June—a far cry from the $90s when Fisher took over and a continuing sign of the fall of this once economic powerhouse.

The year 2002 proved to be a turning point in the photographic imaging business as sales of digital cameras and other products soared. The result for Kodak's film business was disastrous because not only did sales of Kodak film start to fall sharply, but what analysts had expected was true—photographers printed only a fraction of the pictures they took, so demand for Kodak's paper also fell. In 2003, this trend accelerated as digital cameras became the camera of choice of photographers worldwide and Kodak's film and paper revenues continued to fall. This was very serious for Kodak because sales of film

and paper are its most profitable product and generate most of its cash. Kodak's fourth-quarter net income was only $19 million in 2003, compared with a net income of $113 in 2002. This huge fall in Kodak's profitability was somewhat ironic given that Kodak's line of EasyShare digital cameras were the best-selling cameras in the United States by 2003. Sales rose by 87% in 2003, and Kodak now was the number 2 global seller with about 18% of the market. However, rising sales of digital products were not enough to offset losses in film since profit margins remained tight in digital products because of intense competition from companies such as Canon, Olympus, and Nikon.

In the fall of 2003, CEO Daniel Carp announced Kodak's cash-cow yellow box business was in "irreversible decline" and that it was withdrawing from the Advanced Photo Systems camera business and stopping sales of reloadable film cameras, the old silver halide kind. However, Carp also announced a major change of strategy; Kodak would stop investing in its traditional business and pour all its resources into developing new digital products, such as cameras and accessories, to improve its competitive position and margins. It bought the remaining 44% of Chinon, its Japanese unit that designed and made its digital cameras, to protect its competency in digital imaging and ensure the long-term flow of profits from this unit. Kodak began a major push to develop new camera models and also to develop skills in inkjet printing to create digital photo printing systems so its users could directly print from its cameras. Also, Carp announced Kodak would try to grow its digital health imaging business, which was enjoying increased success, and announced a new initiative to make inroads in the digital commercial printing business.

However, analysts and investors reacted to this news badly. Xerox had tried to enter the digital printer business years before with no success against HP, the market leader. Moreover, they wondered how new revenues from digital products could ever make up for the loss of Kodak's film and paper revenues. Carp also announced that to fund this new strategy, Kodak would reduce its hefty dividend by 72% from $1.80 to 50 cents a share, which would raise $1.3 billion for investment in digital products. Investors had no faith in Carp's new plan, and Kodak's stock, which had been around $27, plunged to $22, its lowest price in decades. Analysts argued that Kodak should have funded its new strategy by reducing operating costs to increase business efficiency, pointing out that a 5%

increase in efficiency would have raised the $1.3 billion. Kodak's top management came under intense criticism for not reducing its cost structure, and Kodak's stock price continued to fall as it became clearer that its new strategy would do little to raise its falling revenues.

Finally, in the spring of 2004, Carp announced another change of strategy for Kodak—a strategy that it should have implemented at least a decade ago and probably two decades ago, when competition from Fuji in its film business began to bite into its profits. Announcing that it "was smart business in a business that's shrinking," Carp said Kodak would cut its work force by 21% by the end of 2006 and take charges of $1.5 billion against revenues to cover the cost of this new round of huge layoffs. This would mean that another 12,000 to 15,000 Kodak employees would lose their jobs, but that operating costs would drop by about $1 billion a year. Jobs would be lost in film manufacturing, at the support and corporate levels, and from global downsizing as Kodak reduced its total facilities worldwide by one-third and continued to shutter photo-finishing labs that served retailers.

This news sent Kodak's share price up by 20% in 2004 as investors finally hoped Kodak would be able to take the profits from its new streamlined film business and invest them successfully in new digital imaging technology ventures. However, Kodak was late building the distinctive competences that might give it a competitive advantage in many digital imaging research areas. With so many agile competitors, and a fast-changing digital technology, there were many challenges still facing the company—could it do it?

A New Kodak CEO Takes Control

By 2003 it had become clear that Carp was not the right person to take on the hard job of radically restructuring Kodak's operations. He was too politically involved in the present status quo, and he would never make the changes necessary. So Kodak's board of directors hired Antonio Perez, a former HP executive, as its new president and COO, to take charge of the reorganization effort. Perez was the person who made the hard choices about which divisions Kodak would close and orchestrated the termination of thousands of Kodak's managers and employees. In 2004, Carp realized he had lost the support of the board, and Perez's success at restructuring the company led to his appointment as Kodak's new CEO. He

was now in charge of implementing the downsized, streamlined company's new digital imaging strategy. Perez announced a major three-year restructuring plan in 2004 to continue to 2007 to transform the company into a leader in digital imaging.

Lowering the Cost Structure

On the cost side, Perez announced that Kodak needed "to install a new, lower-cost business model consistent with the realities of a digital business. The reality of digital businesses is thinner margins—we must continue to move to the business model appropriate for that reality." His main objectives were to reduce operating facilities by 33%, divest redundant operations, and reduce its labor force by 20%, and to achieve this Kodak made many strategic changes. In January 2004, it stopped all its traditional camera and film activities except for the Advanced Photo System and 35-mm film. Also in 2004, Kodak implemented SAP's ERP system to link all segments of its value chain activities together and to its suppliers in order to reduce costs. Kodak had benchmarked its competitors and found it had a much larger cost of goods sold than them; using SAP, its goal was to reduce cost of goods sold from 19% to 14% by 2007 and so significantly boost profit margins.

Since 2004 Kodak has steadily laid off more than 25,000 employees, shut down and sold units, and moved to a more centralized structure with all four heads of Kodak's main operating groups reporting directly to Perez. In September 2006, Kodak announced the closing of its synthetic chemicals operation, which seemed to signal one of the last steps in its current drive to lower costs and move from its traditional operations to focus on the digital side of its business. Also, in 2006, Kodak signed deal with Flextronics, a Singapore-based company, to outsource its camera manufacturing and so trim excess capacity and focus on developing new digital core competences.

The costs of this transformation have been huge. It created losses of $900 million in 2004, $1.1 billion in 2005, and around $1 billion in 2006. Because of this transformation, its ROIC was a negative 20% compared to its main digital rival, Canon, which enjoys a positive 14% ROIC.

Building Differentiated Products

Kodak was still organized into four main business units; now the push was on to develop innovative new products in three of these imaging units—consumer, business graphics, and health, while reducing costs in the fourth, film products. The main problem facing Kodak continued to be that profit margins were by far the highest in the declining film unit; digital products result in profit margins 50 to 70% lower than film products, so increasing profit margins in digital sales was vital. Kodak had to increase profit margins in all its consumer, commercial graphics, and health imaging units, and Perez's new goal was to eliminate any digital business in which Kodak was not number 1 or 2 in terms of market share.

In the consumer unit, Perez put the focus on developing new improved digital cameras and bringing out new products several times a year—and to increase profit margins at the expense of increasing market share. It already was the market leader in the United States. Now its goal was to keep its prices and profits high in consumer imaging. So it needed differentiated products, and in 2004, Kodak announced it had developed the world's smallest ultrawide-angle optical zoom digital camera, the Kodak EasyShare V705, and other innovations. But competition from manufacturers like Canon and Nikon came quickly, and in 2005, Kodak brought out a new line of more powerful EasyShare cameras to fight back. However, Kodak gained the number 1 spot in digital camera sales in the United States in the second quarter of 2005, and digital imaging product sales and revenues increased sharply, which seemed to be a boon to the company. As an example, Kodak said sales of its EasyShare line of digital cameras rose 87% compared with the previous year.

At the same time, however, growing consumer acceptance of digital cameras accelerated the decline of Kodak's traditional film business. And, in 2006, the company's prospects deteriorated further as growth in its consumer digital cameras and photo printers came to a standstill because of increased competition and a mature market. This resulted in intensified price pressure in consumer digital products, which forced it to lower prices and so its revenues and profit margins. At the same time, this led to a major decline in its film business, which was still Kodak's major profit maker. Nevertheless, in 2006, the company brought out new products such as its dual-lens cameras and cameras with WiFi that could connect wirelessly to PCs to download and print photographs, and it used these innovations to once again raise prices.

Improving its other consumer digital imaging products and services was also a continuing part of Kodak's new strategy. Perez was determined to make Kodak the leader in digital processing and printing in the United States and even globally. Kodak's EasyShare Internet service that allows customers to download their images to its website and receive back both printed photographs and the images on a CD soared in popularity, for example. EasyShare revenues increased by 55% from 2003 to 2004, and it reached a customer base of 30 million by 2006. However, profit margins were still slim since this is an expensive business.

In another major move to attract and reach customers, Kodak put all its efforts into developing and extending its empire of digital processing kiosks, installing them into stores, pharmacies, and other outlets as fast as possible because it sensed the importance of establishing its brand name in this arena. It configured these kiosks to give customers total control over which pictures to develop at what quantity, quality, and size. Kodak discovered that putting two kiosks in one store reduced customer waiting time significantly and that customers often shopped in stores while waiting for their images to be processed. This led to increased store sales—something that led to more demand for kiosks. In 2005, for example, Kodak and Wal-Mart signed an alliance to put 2,000 kiosks into 1,000 Wal-Mart store. By 2006, Kodak had over 65,000 kiosks worldwide and was the global leader in this business—far ahead of its nearest competitor. Retailers increasingly discovered how Kodak kiosks offer an attractive digital processing alternative at a much lower cost than managing their own onsite digital mini-labs. Kodak, of course, also receives a larger percentage of the photo printing revenues when it controls in-store kiosks, and in 2005 revenues grew by 60% and printing volume by 400%—this looked good for the future.

Kodak also has made major attempts to penetrate the mobile imaging market because of the huge growth in the use of camera phones in the 2000s. Around 600 million camera phones were sold globally in 2006 alone. The Kodak Mobile Imaging Service offers camera phone users several options to view, order, and share prints of all the digital photos on their phones. Users can upload and store pictures from their cameras in their personal EasyShare accounts; then after editing, they can send their favorite photos back to their mobile phones or to anybody else's, and they can be used as photo wallpaper or caller ID. Launching this service required many partnerships and collaborations with wireless providers like Verizon and Cingular and also handset manufacturers such as Nokia, Motorola, and many others that have integrated imaging capability into mobile devices. Kodak benefits from the revenues it receives when camera users take advantage of its processing and printing services as users upload, share, and enjoy pictures via mobile phone capability. In January 2006, Kodak and Motorola announced a ten-year global product cross-licensing and marketing agreement. By combining Motorola's expertise in mobile devise technology and Kodak's experience in digital imaging, the two companies plan to improve the digital capturing feature of the phone.

As a result of its substantial investment in R&D, Kodak is now number 1 in sales of digital cameras and snapshot printing systems in the United States, and second or third globally, and number 1 in online services and in physical digital kiosks in stores. This rosy picture is hampered by the fact that the digital imaging market has intense competition and thin profit margins, however, and Perez decided to keep prices high and sacrifice market share for higher margins. Thus R&D seemed especially important given the progress being made by all digital competitors in improving technology. The costs of research and marketing and selling the new, improved products that need to be continually introduced are high, and all competitors needed to protect their margins. Nevertheless, even though Kodak was now competitive in the consumer digital market segment, it still was not able to make enough profit to offset the losses it incurred from the rapid decline of its cash-cow film business. All its efforts in consumer digital products staved off bankruptcy but contributed little or nothing to increasing its profitability.

Graphic Communications Group

In fact, although its consumer digital business is its most visible unit, Kodak has been putting forth major efforts to increase its strengths and distinctive competencies in its graphic communications group (GCG)—this seemed to be the best bet for increasing its future profitability because profit margins are much higher. In 2005, for example, sales of the graphic communications group more than doubled, and the profit margins of products sold by this unit are three times as high as in its consumer unit because the primary users of these products are companies with large budgets. In this segment, Kodak has also been able to increase sales and profits by keeping its prices high and refusing to lower prices—even during price wars with aggressive competitors like Xerox, Canon, and HP—because of the innovative features of its new imaging products.

The six main customers groups served by the GCG are commercial printers, in-plant printers, data centers, digital service providers, packaging companies, and newspapers. Within each of these segments, Kodak has developed digital products that offer customers a single solution to deliver the products and services they need to compete in their business. Kodak solutions extend from up-front workflow and professional services, to digital pre-press, to print—in other words, all the way from initial composition to final product printing. Kodak was able to develop this end-to-end solution because of its acquisition in the 2000s of specialist digital printing companies such as KPG, CREO, Versamark, and Express. By 2006, it had successfully integrated all these new companies and their employees into the GCG.

From each acquisition Kodak gained access to more products and more customers along with more services and solutions to offer them. No single solution will work for every customer because each business customer uses some combination of traditional offset printing and new digital printing, which is why GCG assembled the broadest product portfolio in the industry. Kodak claims that no other competitor can offer the same breadth of products and solutions that it offers. Kodak's product line includes image scanners and document management systems, the industry's leading portfolio of digital proofing solutions. It also includes offset, flexo, digital plates and CTP award-winning wide-format inkjet printing, including the most robust toner-based platforms for four-color and monochrome printing. Kodak also claims to have the leading continuous inkjet technology for high-speed, high-volume printing, as well as imprinting capabilities that can be combined with traditional offset printing for those customers still in the process of making the transition to digital printing.

The Medical Imaging Group

By 2006 the costs of research and marketing digital products in its consumer and commercial units was putting intense pressure on the company's resources—and Kodak still had to invest large amounts of capital to develop a lasting competitive advantage in its medical imaging unit. Here too in the 2000s, Kodak had made many strategic acquisitions to strengthen its competitive advantage in several areas of the medical imaging segment, such as digital mammography and advanced x-rays. It had developed one of the top five medical imaging groups in the world. However, in May 2006 Kodak put its medical imaging unit up for sale. It realized that this unit required too much future investment in its own right if it was to succeed—and its consumer and commercial groups were not providing the revenue enough for this investment. In addition, Kodak could realize capital from the sale of this unit to reduce its long-term debt and provide some capital to pursue new initiatives in its two remaining digital units. Also, although the medical unit accounted for nearly one-fifth of Kodak's overall sales in 2005, its operating profit had plunged 21% as profit margins fell because of increased competition from major rivals such as GE.

Each of Kodak's digital business units was encountering its own set of competitive threats, and Kodak still lacked a secure "core" digital group on which to base its future success, although now all bets seemed to be on its commercial imaging unit—given its high profit margins. At the same time, profits from its old profitable film unit were declining sharply; Kodak needed more cash, so something had to be done to find a buyer for its medical unit.

In January 2007, Kodak announced that its medical imaging unit had been sold to the Onex Corp., Canada's biggest buyout firm, which owned a small but profitable medical imaging unit in its portfolio, for $2.35 billion. In addition, if the acquisition resulted in substantial synergies that met certain profit targets, Kodak would get another $200 million. Kodak plans to use the proceeds to repay about $1.15 billion of debt and to fund its digital research program. All 8,000 health group employees, who make x-ray film, medical printers, and information management software and storage systems, will now be employed by Onex. Perez said, "We now plan to focus our attention on the significant digital growth opportunities within our businesses in consumer and professional imaging and graphic communications."

In 2007, Kodak entered the fourth year of its digital makeover under Perez. It has accumulated $2 billion in net losses over the last eight quarters and piled up $2.6 billion in restructuring charges since January 2004. However, its losses narrowed to $37 million in the July-to-September quarter as digital profits surged above $100 million. Just a year ago, the film group's gross profit exceeded the consumer digital unit's by $86 million, but now the consumer unit earned a gross profit of $323 million, a 31% increase from the fourth quarter of 2005, versus a $243 million profit for the film unit, a 27% decrease. Also, by disposing of its health imaging unit, trimming manufacturing operations, and cutting 27,000 more jobs, Kodak's global work force is now under 50,000 from a peak of 145,300 in 1988.

After the sale, industry analysts wondered if Kodak was hoping to find a buyer for the rest of its assets because it will be even more exposed to fluctuations in sales without health imaging, previously its second largest revenue earner. But because its competitive position is so uncertain, it is not clear that private equity bidders or even industry buyers would be interested in the company. Another scenario would be for Kodak to use the money it raises from the sale of its medical imaging group to make a takeover attempt of the newly reborn Xerox Corp., which is one of its major competitors in the commercial digital graphic business, a merger that might be welcomed by the stockholders of both companies. Certainly Kodak's stockholders have taken an optimistic view of its future, either as an independent company, as a takeover target, or as an acquirer of another major digital company—its share price rose by 30% in the second half of 2006.

It rose again on February when Kodak announced that it was introducing a revolutionary new line of color digital printers using an advanced Kodak ink that would provide brighter pictures that would keep their clarity for decades. Apparently Perez, who had been in charge of HP's printer business before he left Kodak, had made developing the line a major part of his turnaround strategy, and he and a research team had been working on the new project codenamed "Goya." The new printers will arrive in stores in March priced at $149 to $299, and Kodak is targeting consumers who print loads of photos and are willing to pay full price for high-quality printers. However, Perez's printer strategy is based upon charging a higher price for the printer than competitors like HP and Lexmark, but then charging a much lower price for the ink cartridge to attract a bigger market share. Black ink cartridges will cost $9.99 and color $14.99, which will be about 10 cents a print, far lower than the current 20 to 25 cents per print. Kodak's strategy is that consumers will be willing to buy the printers and then print more pictures, which will give it a share of the market that will make this a multibillion revenues generator in the years ahead. Perez expects inkjet printing to produce Kodak's best profit—in double digits after a three-year investment phase.

At the same time, in a clear sign the U.S. market has matured, shipments of digital cameras fell 3% in the fourth quarter to 12.1 million units from 12.4 million units a year ago, a sharp contrast from double-digit gains in previous years, when the attraction of filmless cameras swelled as consumers replaced their traditional film devices; now much demand is in the direction of upgrading to better digital cameras. As noted earlier, Perez kept prices high to protect profit margins and so for years Canon had a 20% market share, followed by Sony with 17% and Kodak with 16%. But Perez's strategy seems to be the correct one because also in February Panasonic announced a totally new line of advanced digital cameras that will further cut profit margins unless companies drop price competition. So with its paper, kiosk, Internet, and now printer business growing, Kodak might be able to generate profits in the consumer unit too, so that combined with the profits from its commercial graphics unit, it will indeed have turned the corner and will emerge as a digital leader in the coming decade.

REFERENCES

"Agfa to Supply Kodak with Lab Equipment," Yahoo.com, Friday, June 7, 2002.

James Bandler, "Kodak Advances in Market Share of Digital Cameras," *Wall Street Journal*, December 21, 2001, p. B2.

James Bandler, "Kodak Net Plummets 77% on Weak Sales," *Wall Street Journal*, October 25, 2001, p. B9.

James Bandler, "Kodak, Sanyo Agree to Make New Type of Screen Display," *Wall Street Journal*, December 4, 2001, p. B7.

James Bandler, "Kodak Slashes Earnings Forecast, Citing Weak Sales," *Wall Street Journal*, September 20, 2001, p. B4.

James Bandler, "Kodak's Net Fell 93% in Second Quarter on Weakness in Film, Medical Divisions," *Wall Street Journal*, July 18, 2001, p. B4.

James Bandler, "Kodak Stock Falls on Credit Downgrade, Signs Film Market Share Is Decreasing," *Wall Street Journal*, November 1, 2001, p. B8.

James Bandler, "Kodak Will Acquire Ofoto in a Move to Expand Services," *Wall Street Journal*, May 1, 2001, p. B9.

James Bandler, "Kodak Will Offer Its Staff a Chance to Upgrade Options," *Wall Street Journal*, November 30, 2001, p. B7.

James Bandler and Joann Lublin, "Russo's Departure Is a Blow to Kodak as It Seeks to Move into the Digital Age," *Wall Street Journal*, January 8, 2002, p. B4.

Barbara Buell, "A Gust of Fresh Air for the Stodgy Giant of Rochester," *Business Week*, June 10, 1985, p. 93.

Barbara Buell, "Kodak Is Trying to Break Out of Its Shell," *Business Week*, June 10, 1985, pp. 92–95.

Barbara Buell, "Kodak Scrambles to Fill the Gap," *Business Week*, February 8, 1986, p. 30.

"Business Brief—Eastman Kodak Co.: Photo Concern Is Shutting Its Picture Vision Operation," *Wall Street Journal*, November 20, 2001.

"Business Brief—Eastman Kodak Co.: Suit Is Filed Charging Sun with Infringement of Patents," *Wall Street Journal*, February 15, 2002, p. B8.

"Business Brief—Kmart Corp.: Retailer Teams with Kodak in an On-line Photo," *Wall Street Journal*, May 9, 2001.

Adrienne Carter, "Kodak's Promising Developments," *Money*, February 2002, p. 39.

"Citigroup Moves to Stress Global Products," Yahoo.com, Tuesday, June 11, 2002.

"Eastman Kodak Rating May Fall a Rung Lower," *Wall Street Journal*, July 24, 2001.

"Eastman Kodak to Acquire Encad," *Daily Deal*, November 16, 2001.

Daniel Eisenburg, "Kodak's Photo Op," *Time*, April 30, 2001, p. 46.

John Greenwald, "Aiming for a Brighter Picture," *Time*, January 9, 1984, p. 49.

John Hechinger, "Kodak to Reorganize Its Business Again," *Wall Street Journal*, November 15, 2001, p. B12.

Laura Heller, "PMA Highlights Print Kiosks, but Digital Imaging Steals Show," *DSN Retailing Today*, March 11, 2002, p. 6.

James S. Hirsch, "Kodak Effort at 'Intrapreneurship' Fails," *Wall Street Journal*, August 17, 1990, p. 32.

Kodak, http://www.Kodak.com, 2002, 2003, 2004, 2005, 2006, 2007.

Kodak Annual Reports, 1980–2007.

"Kodak's New Image: Electronic Imaging," *Electron Business*, January 1986, pp. 38–43.

"Kodak's New Lean and Hungry Look," *Business Week*, May 30, 1983, p. 33.

"Kodak, Walt Disney Sign Multiyear Alliance Agreement," Yahoo.com, Tuesday, May 28, 2002.

"Moody's Downgrades Kodak's Debt Rating on Digital Concerns," *Wall Street Journal*, March 20, 2002, p. B5.

Thomas Moore, "Embattled Kodak Enters the Electronic Age," *Fortune*, August 22, 1983, pp. 120–128.

Fauziah Muhtar, "Kodak Zooms In with New Digital Cameras," *Computimes Malaysia*, May 2, 2002, p. 1.

Emily Nelson and Joseph B. White, "Blurred Image: Kodak Moment Came Early for CEO Fisher, Who Takes a Stumble—Bet on Digital Photography Has Been a Money Loser; Fuji Is Gaining Ground—Dennis Rodman's Film Flop," *Wall Street Journal*, July 25, 1997, p. A1.

Doug Olenick, "Kodak, Sanyo Plan to Produce OEL Flat-Panel Displays," *Twice*, December 17, 2001, p. 90.

Daniel P. Palumbo, "Kodak Embraces Disruptive Technology," *Journal of Business Strategy*, July–August 2001, p. 11.

Franklin Paul, "Kodak Digital Camera, Software Sims to Ease Printing," Yahoo.com, Tuesday, May 21, 2002.

Franklin Paul, "Sony to Muscle into Kodak's Digital Printing Arena," Yahoo.com, Wednesday, June 5, 2002.

Charles K. Ryan, Eastman Kodak, Company Outline, Merrill Lynch, Pierce, Framer & Smith Incorporated, May 7, 1986.

Andy Serwer, "Kodak: In the Noose," *Fortune*, February 4, 2002, pp. 147–148.

Geoffrey Smith and Faith Keenan, "Kodak Is the Picture of Digital Success," *Business Week*, January 14, 2002, p. 39.

"Yellow at the Edges," *Economist*, December 7, 1984, p. 90.

Philips versus Matsushita: A New Century, a New Round

This case was prepared by Christopher A. Bartlett, Harvard Business School.

Throughout their long histories, N.V. Philips (Netherlands) and Matsushita Electric (Japan) had followed very different strategies and emerged with very different organizational capabilities. Philips built its success on a worldwide portfolio of responsive national organizations while Matsushita based its global competitiveness on its centralized, highly efficient operations in Japan.

During the 1990s, both companies experienced major challenges to their historic competitive positions and organizational models, and at the end of the decade, both companies were struggling to reestablish their competitiveness. At the start of the new millennium, new CEOs at both companies were implementing yet another round of strategic initiatives and organizational restructurings. Observers wondered how the changes would affect their long-running competitive battle.

Philips: Background

In 1892, Gerard Philips and his father opened a small light-bulb factory in Eindhoven, Holland. When their venture almost failed, they recruited Gerard's brother, Anton, an excellent salesman and manager. By 1900, Philips was the third largest light-bulb producer in Europe.

From its founding, Philips developed a tradition of caring for workers. In Eindhoven it built company houses, bolstered education, and paid its employees so well that other local employers complained. When Philips incorporated in 1912, it set aside 10% of profits for employees.

Technological Competence and Geographic Expansion

While larger electrical products companies were racing to diversify, Philips made only light-bulbs. This one-product focus and Gerard's technological prowess enabled the company to create significant innovations. Company policy was to scrap old plants and use new machines or factories whenever advances were made in new production technology. Anton wrote down assets rapidly and set aside substantial reserves for replacing outdated equipment. Philips also became a leader in industrial research, creating physics and chemistry labs to address production problems as well as more abstract scientific ones. The labs developed a tungsten metal filament bulb that was a great commercial success and gave Philips the financial strength to compete against its giant rivals.

This case derives from an earlier case, "Philips versus Matsushita: Preparing for a New Round," HBS No. 399-102, prepared by Professor Christopher A. Bartlett, which was an updated version of an earlier case by Professor Bartlett and Research Associate Robert W. Lightfoot, "Philips and Matsushita: A Portrait of Two Evolving Companies," HBS Case No. 392-156. The section on Matsushita summarizes "Matsushita Electric Industrial (MEI) in 1987," HBS Case No. 388-144, by Sumantra Ghoshal (INSEAD) and Christopher A. Bartlett. Some early history on Philips draws from "Philips Group—1987," HBS Case No. 388-050, by Professors Frank Aguilar and Michael Y. Yoshino. This version was also prepared by Professor Bartlett. HBS cases are developed solely as the basis for class discussion. Cases are not intended to serve as endorsements, sources of primary data, or illustrations of effective or ineffective management.

Holland's small size soon forced Philips to look beyond its Dutch borders for enough volume to mass produce. In 1899, Anton hired the company's first export manager, and soon the company was selling into such diverse markets as Japan, Australia, Canada, Brazil, and Russia. In 1912, as the electric lamp industry began to show signs of overcapacity, Philips started building sales organizations in the United States, Canada, and France. All other functions remained highly centralized in Eindhoven. In many foreign countries Philips created local joint ventures to gain market acceptance.

In 1919, Philips entered into the Principal Agreement with General Electric, giving each company the use of the other's patents. The agreement also divided the world into "three spheres of influence": General Electric would control North America; Philips would control Holland; but both companies agreed to compete freely in the rest of the world. (General Electric also took a 20% stake in Philips.) After this time, Philips began evolving from a highly centralized company, whose sales were conducted through third parties, to a decentralized sales organization with autonomous marketing companies in 14 European countries, China, Brazil, and Australia.

During this period, the company also broadened its product line significantly. In 1918, it began producing electronic vacuum tubes; eight years later its first radios appeared, capturing a 20% world market share within a decade; and during the 1930s, Philips began producing X-ray tubes. The Great Depression brought with it trade barriers and high tariffs, and Philips was forced to build local production facilities to protect its foreign sales of these products.

Philips: Organizational Development

One of the earliest traditions at Philips was a shared but competitive leadership by the commercial and technical functions. Gerard, an engineer, and Anton, a businessman, began a subtle competition where Gerard would try to produce more than Anton could sell and vice versa. Nevertheless, the two agreed that strong research was vital to Philips' survival.

During the late 1930s, in anticipation of the impending war, Philips transferred its overseas assets to two trusts, British Philips and the North American Philips Corporation; it also moved most of its vital research laboratories to Redhill in Surrey, England, and its top management to the United States. Supported by the assets and resources transferred abroad, and isolated from their parent, the individual country organizations became more independent during the war.

Because waves of Allied and German bombing had pummeled most of Philips' industrial plants in the Netherlands, the management board decided to build the postwar organization on the strengths of the national organizations (NOs). Their greatly increased self-sufficiency during the war had allowed most to become adept at responding to country-specific market conditions—a capability that became a valuable asset in the postwar era. For example, when international wrangling precluded any agreement on three competing television transmission standards (PAL, SECAM, and NTSC), each nation decided which to adopt. Furthermore, consumer preferences and economic conditions varied: in some countries, rich, furniture-encased TV sets were the norm; in others, sleek, contemporary models dominated the market. In the United Kingdom, the only way to penetrate the market was to establish a rental business; in richer countries, a major marketing challenge was overcoming elitist prejudice against television. In this environment, the independent NOs had a great advantage in being able to sense and respond to the differences.

Eventually, responsiveness extended beyond adaptive marketing. As NOs built their own technical capabilities, product development often became a function of local market conditions. For example, Philips of Canada created the company's first color TV; Philips of Australia created the first stereo TV; and Philips of the United Kingdom created the first TVs with teletext.

While NOs took major responsibility for financial, legal, and administrative matters, fourteen product divisions (PDs), located in Eindhoven, were formally responsible for development, production, and global distribution. (In reality, the NOs' control of assets and the PDs' distance from the operations often undercut this formal role.) The research function remained independent and, with continued strong funding, set up eight separate laboratories in Europe and the United States.

While the formal corporate-level structure was represented as a type of geographic/product matrix, it was clear that NOs had the real power. NOs reported directly to the management board, which Philips enlarged from 4 members to 10 to ensure that top management remained in contact with and control of the highly autonomous NOs. Each NO also regularly sent envoys to Eindhoven to represent its interests. Top management, most of whom had careers that included multiple foreign tours of duty, made frequent overseas visits to the NOs. In 1954, the board established the International Concern Council to formalize regular meetings with the heads of all major NOs.

Within the NOs, the management structure mimicked the legendary joint technical and commercial leadership of the two Philips brothers. Most were led by a technical manager and a commercial manager. In some locations, a finance manager filled out the top management triad that typically reached key decisions collectively. This cross-functional coordination capability was reflected down through the NOs in frontline product teams, product-group-level management teams, and at the senior management committee of the NOs' top commercial, technical, and financial managers.

The overwhelming importance of foreign operations to Philips, the commensurate status of the NOs within the corporate hierarchy, and even the cosmopolitan appeal of many of the offshore subsidiaries' locations encouraged many Philips managers to take extended foreign tours of duty, working in a series of two- or three-year posts. This elite group of expatriate managers identified strongly with each other and with the NOs as a group and had no difficulty representing their strong, country-oriented views to corporate management.

Philips: Attempts at Reorganization

In the late 1960s, the creation of the Common Market eroded trade barriers within Europe and diluted the rationale for maintaining independent, country-level subsidiaries. New transistor- and printed circuit-based technologies demanded larger production runs than most national plants could justify, and many of Philips' competitors were moving production of electronics to new facilities in low-wage areas in East Asia and Central and South America. Despite its many technological innovations, Philips' ability to bring products to market began to falter. In the 1960s, the company invented the audiocassette and the microwave oven but let its Japanese competitors capture the mass market for both products. A decade later, its R&D group developed the V2000 videocassette format—superior technically to Sony's Beta or

Matsushita's VHS—but was forced to abandon it when North American Philips decided to outsource, brand, and sell a VHS product which it manufactured under license from Matsushita.

In the following pages, we will see how over three decades, seven chairmen experimented with reorganizing the company to deal with its growing problems. Yet, entering the new millennium, Philips' financial performance remained poor and its global competitiveness was still in question. (See Exhibits 1 and 2.)

Van Reimsdijk and Rodenburg Reorganizations, 1970s

Concerned about what one magazine described as "continued profitless progress," newly appointed CEO Hendrick van Riemsdijk created an organization committee to prepare a policy paper on the division of responsibilities between the PDs and the NOs. Their report, dubbed the "Yellow Booklet," outlined the disadvantages of Philips' matrix organization in 1971: "Without an agreement [defining the relationship between national organizations and product divisions], it is impossible to determine in any given situation which of the two parties is responsible. . . . As operations become increasingly complex, an organizational form of this type will only lower the speed of reaction of an enterprise."

On the basis of this report, van Reimsdijk proposed rebalancing the managerial relationships between PDs and NOs—"tilting the matrix towards the PDs" in his words—to allow Philips to decrease the number of products marketed, build scale by concentrating production, and increase the flow of goods among national organizations. He proposed closing the least efficient local plants and converting the best into International Production Centers (IPCs), each supplying many NOs. In so doing, van Reimsdijk hoped that PD managers would gain control over manufacturing operations. Due to the political and organizational difficulty of closing local plants, however, implementation was slow.

In the late 1970s, his successor CEO, Dr. Rodenburg, continued this thrust. Several IPCs were established, but the NOs seemed as powerful and independent as ever. He furthered matrix simplification by replacing the dual commercial and technical leadership with single management at both the corporate and national organizational levels. Yet the power struggles continued.

EXHIBIT 1

Philips Group—Summary Financial Data, 1970–2000 (millions of guilders, unless otherwise stated)

	2000	1995	1990	1985	1980	1975	1970
Net sales	F83,437	F64,462	F55,764	F60,045	F36,536	F27,115	F15,070
Income from operations (excluding restructuring)	NA	4,090	2,260	3,075	1,577	1,201	1,280
Income from operations (including restructuring)	9,434	4,044	-2,389	N/A	N/A	N/A	N/A
As a percentage of net sales	11.3%	6.3%	-4.3%	5.1%	4.3%	4.5%	8.5%
Income after taxes	12,559	2,889	F-4,447	F1,025	F532	F341	F446
Net income from normal business operations	NA	2,684	-4,526	n/a	328	347	435
Stockholders' equity (common)	49,473	14,055	11,165	16,151	12,996	10,047	6,324
Return on stockholders' equity	42.8%	20.2%	-30.2%	5.6%	2.7%	3.6%	7.3%
Distribution per common share, par value F10 (in guilders)	F2.64	F1.60	F0.0	F2.00	F1.80	F1.40	F1.70
Total assets	86,114	54,683	51,595	52,883	39,647	30,040	19,088
Inventories as a percentage of net sales	13.9%	18.2%	20.7%	23.2%	32.8%	32.9%	35.2%
Outstanding trade receivables in month's sales	1.5	1.6	1.6	2.0	3.0	3.0	2.8
Current ratio	1.2	1.6	1.4	1.6	1.7	1.8	1.7
Employees at year-end (in thousands)	219	265	273	346	373	397	359
Wages, salaries and other related costs	NA	NA	F17,582	F21,491	F15,339	F11,212	F5,890
Exchange rate (period end; guilder/$)	2.34	1.60	1.69	2.75	2.15	2.69	3.62
Selected data in millions of dollars:							
Sales	$35,253	$40,039	$33,018	$21,802	$16,993	$10,098	$4,163
Operating profit	3,986	2,512	1,247	988	734	464	NA
Pretax income	5,837	2,083	-2,380	658	364	256	NA
Net income	5,306	1,667	-2,510	334	153	95	120
Total assets	35,885	32,651	30,549	19,202	18,440	11,186	5,273
Shareholders' equity (common)	20,238	8,784	6,611	5,864	6,044	3,741	1,747

Source: Annual reports; Standard & Poors' Compustat, Moody's Industrial and International Manuals.

Note: Exchange rate 12/31/00 was Euro/US$: 1.074

EXHIBIT 2

Philips Group—Sales by Product and Geographic Segment, 1985–2000 (millions of guilders)

	2000		1995		1990		1985	
Net sales by product segment:								
Lighting	F11,133	13%	F8,353	13%	F7,026	13%	F7,976	12%
Consumer electronics	32,357	39	22,027	34	25,400	46	16,906	26
Domestic appliances	4,643	6	—		—		6,644	10
Professional products/Systems	—		11,562	18	13,059	23	17,850	28
Components/Semiconductors	23,009	28	10,714	17	8,161	15	11,620	18
Software/Services	—		9,425	15	—		—	
Medical systems	6,679	8	—		—		—	
Origin	1,580	2	—		—		—	
Miscellaneous	4,035	5	2,381	4	2,118	4	3,272	5
Total	83,437	100%	64,462	100%	F55,764	100%	F64,266	100%
Operating income by sector:								
Lighting	1,472	16%	983	24%	419	18%	F910	30%
Consumer electronics	824	9	167	4	1,499	66	34	1
Domestic appliances	632	7	—		—		397	13
Professional products/Systems	—		157	4	189	8	1,484	48
Components/Semiconductors	4,220	45	2,233	55	-43	-2	44	1
Software/Services	—		886	22	—		—	
Medical systems	372	4	—		—		—	
Origin	2,343	25	—		—		—	
Miscellaneous	-249	-3	423	10	218	10	200	7
Increase not attributable to a sector	-181	-2	(805)	(20)	-22	-1	6	0
Total	9,434	100%	4,044	100%	2,260	100%	F3,075	100%

Source: Annual reports.

Notes:

Conversion rate (12/31/00): 1 Euro: 2.20371 Dutch Guilders

Totals may not add due to rounding.

Product sector sales after 1988 are external sales only; therefore, no eliminations are made. Sector sales before 1988 include sales to other sectors; therefore, eliminations are made.

Data are not comparable to consolidated financial summary due to restating.

Wisse Dekker Reorganization, 1982

Unsatisfied with the company's slow response and concerned by its slumping financial performance, upon becoming CEO in 1982, Wisse Dekker outlined a new initiative. Aware of the cost advantage of Philips' Japanese counterparts, he closed inefficient operations—particularly in Europe where 40 of the company's more than 200 plants were shut. He focused on core operations by selling some businesses (for example, welding, energy cables, and furniture) while acquiring an interest in Grundig and Westinghouse's North American lamp activities. Dekker also supported technology-sharing agreements and entered alliances in offshore manufacturing.

To deal with the slow-moving bureaucracy, he continued his predecessor's initiative to replace dual leadership with single general managers. He also continued to "tilt the matrix" by giving PDs formal product management responsibility, but leaving NOs responsible for local profits. And, he energized the management board by reducing its size, bringing on directors with strong operating experience, and creating subcommittees to deal with difficult issues. Finally, Dekker redefined the product planning process, incorporating input from the NOs, but giving global PDs the final decision on long-range direction. Still sales declined and profits stagnated.

Van der Klugt Reorganization, 1987

When Cor van der Klugt succeeded Dekker as chairman in 1987, Philips had lost its long-held consumer electronics leadership position to Matsushita, and was one of only two non-Japanese companies in the world's top ten. Its net profit margins of 1% to 2% not only lagged behind General Electric's 9%, but even its highly aggressive Japanese competitors' slim 4%. Van der Klugt set a profit objective of 3% to 4% and made beating the Japanese companies a top priority.

As van der Klugt reviewed Philips' strategy, he designated various businesses as core (those that shared related technologies, had strategic importance, or were technical leaders) and non-core (standalone businesses that were not targets for world leadership and could eventually be sold if required). Of the four businesses defined as core, three were strategically linked: components, consumer electronics, and telecommunications and data systems. The fourth, lighting, was regarded as strategically vital because its cash flow funded development.

The non-core businesses included domestic appliances and medical systems which van der Klugt spun off into joint ventures with Whirlpool and GE, respectively.

In continuing efforts to strengthen the PDs relative to the NOs, van der Klugt restructured Philips around the four core global divisions rather than the former 14 PDs. This allowed him to trim the management board, appointing the displaced board members to a new policy-making Group Management Committee. Consisting primarily of PD heads and functional chiefs, this body replaced the old NO-dominated International Concern Council. Finally, he sharply reduced the 3,000-strong headquarters staff, reallocating many of them to the PDs.

To link PDs more directly to markets, van der Klugt dispatched many experienced product-line managers to Philips' most competitive markets. For example, management of the digital audio tape and electric-shaver product lines were relocated to Japan, while the medical technology and domestic appliances lines were moved to the United States.

Such moves, along with continued efforts at globalizing product development and production efforts, required that the parent company gain firmer control over NOs, especially the giant North American Philips Corp. (NAPC). Although Philips had obtained a majority equity interest after World War II, it was not always able to make the U.S. company respond to directives from the center, as the V2000 VCR incident showed. To prevent replays of such experiences, in 1987 van der Klugt repurchased publicly owned NAPC shares for $700 million.

Reflecting the growing sentiment among some managers that R&D was not market oriented enough, van der Klugt halved spending on basic research to about 10% of total R&D. To manage what he described as "R&D's tendency to ponder the fundamental laws of nature," he made the R&D budget the direct responsibility of the businesses being supported by the research. This required that each research lab become focused on specific business areas (see Exhibit 3).

Finally, van der Klugt continued the effort to build efficient, specialized, multi-market production facilities by closing 75 of the company's 420 remaining plants worldwide. He also eliminated 38,000 of its 344,000 employees—21,000 through divesting businesses, shaking up the myth of lifetime employment at the company. He anticipated that all these

EXHIBIT 3

Philips Research Labs by Location and Specialty, 1987

Location	Size (Staff)	Specialty
Eindhoven, The Netherlands	2,000	Basic research, electronics, manufacturing technology
Redhill, Surrey, England	450	Microelectronics, television, defense
Hamburg, Germany	350	Communications, office equipment, medical imaging
Aachen, W. Germany	250	Fiber optics, X-ray systems
Paris, France	350	Microprocessors, chip materials, design
Brussels	50	Artificial intelligence
Briarcliff Manor, New York	35	Optical systems, television, superconductivity, defense
Sunnyvale, California	150	Integrated circuits

Source: Philips, in *Business Week*, March 21, 1988, p. 156.

restructurings would lead to a financial recovery by 1990. Unanticipated losses for that year, however—more than 4.5 billion Dutch guilders ($2.5 billion)—provoked a class-action law suit by angry American investors, who alleged that positive projections by the company had been misleading. In a surprise move, on May 14, 1990, van der Klugt and half of the management board were replaced.

Timmer Reorganization, 1990

The new president, Jan Timmer, had spent most of his 35-year Philips career turning around unprofitable businesses. With rumors of a takeover or a government bailout swirling, he met with his top 100 managers and distributed a hypothetical—but fact-based—press release announcing that Philips was bankrupt. "So what action can you take this weekend?" he challenged them.

Under "Operation Centurion," headcount was reduced by 68,000 or 22% over the next 18 months, earning Timmer the nickname "The Butcher of Eindhoven." Because European laws required substantial compensation for layoffs—Eindhoven workers received 15 months' pay, for example—the first round of 10,000 layoffs alone cost Philips $700 million. To spread the burden around the globe and to speed the process, Timmer asked his PD managers to negotiate cuts with NO managers. According to one report, however, country managers were "digging in their heels to save local jobs." But the cuts came—many

from overseas operations. In addition to the job cuts, Timmer vowed to "change the way we work." He established new performance rules and asked hundreds of top managers to sign contracts that committed them to specific financial goals. Those who broke those contracts were replaced—often with outsiders.

To focus resources further, Timmer sold off various businesses including integrated circuits to Matsushita, minicomputers to Digital, defense electronics to Thomson and the remaining 53% of appliances to Whirlpool. Yet profitability was still well below the modest 4% on sales he promised. In particular, consumer electronics lagged with slow growth in a price-competitive market. The core problem was identified by a 1994 McKinsey study that estimated that value added per hour in Japanese consumer electronic factories was still 68% above that of European plants. In this environment, most NO managers kept their heads down, using their distance from Eindhoven as their defense against the ongoing rationalization.

After three years of cost-cutting, in early 1994 Timmer finally presented a new growth strategy to the board. His plan was to expand software, services, and multimedia to become 40% of revenues by 2000. He was betting on Philips' legendary innovative capability to restart the growth engines. Earlier, he had recruited Frank Carrubba, Hewlett-Packard's director of research, and encouraged him to focus on developing 15 core technologies. The list, which included interactive compact disc (CD-i), digital compact cassettes (DCC), high definition television (HDTV), and multimedia software, was soon dubbed "the president's projects." Over the next few years, Philips invested over $2.5 billion in these technologies. But Timmer's earlier divestment of some of the company's truly high-tech businesses and a 37% cut in R&D personnel left it with few who understood the technology of the new priority businesses.

By 1996, it was clear that Philips' analog HDTV technology would not become industry standard, that its DCC gamble had lost out to Sony's Minidisc, and that CD-i was a marketing failure. And while costs in Philips were lower, so too was morale, particularly among middle management. Critics claimed that the company's drive for cost-cutting and standardization had led it to ignore new worldwide market demands for more segmented products and higher consumer service.

Boonstra Reorganization, 1996

When Timmer stepped down in October 1996, the board replaced him with a radical choice for Philips—an outsider whose expertise was in marketing and Asia rather than technology and Europe. Cor Boonstra was a 58-year-old Dutchman whose years as CEO of Sara Lee, the U.S. consumer products firm, had earned him a reputation as a hard-driving marketing genius. Joining Philips in 1994, he headed the Asia Pacific region and the lighting division before being tapped as CEO.

Unencumbered by tradition, he immediately announced strategic sweeping changes designed to reach his target of increasing return on net assets from 17% to 24% by 1999. "There are no taboos, no sacred cows," he said. "The bleeders must be turned around, sold, or closed." Within three years, he had sold off 40 of Philips' 120 major businesses—including such well known units as Polygram and Grundig. He also initiated a major worldwide restructuring, promising to transform a structure he described as "a plate of spaghetti" into "a neat row of asparagus." He said:

> How can we compete with the Koreans? They don't have 350 companies all over the world. Their factory in Ireland covers Europe and their manufacturing facility in Mexico serves North America. We need a more structured and simpler manufacturing and marketing organization to achieve a cost pattern in line with those who do not have our heritage. This is still one of the biggest issues facing Philips.

Within a year, 3,100 jobs were eliminated in North America and 3,000 employees were added in Asia Pacific, emphasizing Boonstra's determination to shift production to low-wage countries and his broader commitment to Asia. And after three years, he had closed 100 of the company's 356 factories worldwide. At the same time, he replaced the company's 21 PDs with 7 divisions, but shifted day-to-day operating responsibility to 100 business units, each responsible for its profits worldwide. It was a move designed to finally eliminate the old PD/NO matrix. Finally, in a move that shocked most employees, he announced that the 100-year-old Eindhoven headquarters would be relocated to Amsterdam with only 400 of the 3,000 corporate positions remaining.

By early 1998, he was ready to announce his new strategy. Despite early speculation that he might abandon consumer electronics, he proclaimed it as the center of Philips' future. Betting on the "digital revolution," he planned to focus on established technologies such as cellular phones (through a joint venture with Lucent), digital TV, digital videodisc, and web TV. Furthermore, he committed major resources to marketing, including a 40% increase in advertising to raise awareness and image of the Philips brand and de-emphasize most of the 150 other brands it supported worldwide—from Magnavox TVs to Norelco shavers to Marantz stereos.

While not everything succeeded (the Lucent cell phone JV collapsed after nine months, for example), overall performance improved significantly in the late 1990s. By 2000, Boonstra was able to announce that he had achieved his objective of a 24% return on net assets.

Kleisterlee Reorganization, 2001

In May 2001, Boonstra passed the CEO's mantle to Gerard Kleisterlee, a 54-year-old engineer (and career Philips man) whose turnaround of the components business had earned him a board seat only a year earlier. Believing that Philips had finally turned around, the board challenged Kleisterlee to grow sales by 10% annually and earnings 15%, while increasing return on assets to 30%.

Despite its stock trading at a steep discount to its breakup value, Philips governance structure and Dutch legislation made a hostile raid all but impossible. Nonetheless, Kleisterlee described the difference as "a management discount" and vowed to eliminate it. "Our fragmented organization makes us carry costs that are too high," he said. "In some production activities where we cannot add value, we will outsource and let others do it for us."

The first sign of restructuring came within weeks, when mobile phone production was outsourced to CEC of China. Then, in August, Kleisterlee announced an agreement with Japan's Funai Electric to take over production of its VCRs, resulting in the immediate closure of the European production center in Austria and the loss of 1,000 jobs. The CEO acknowledged that he was seeking partners to take over the manufacturing of some of its other mass-produced items such as television sets.

But by 2001, a slowing economy resulted in the company's first quarterly loss since 1996, and by year's end the loss had grown to 2.6 billion euros compared to the previous year's 9.6 billion profit. Many felt that these growing financial pressures—and shareholders' growing impatience—were finally leading Philips to recognize that its best hope of survival was to outsource even more of its basic manufacturing and become a technology developer and global marketer. It believed it was time to recognize

that its 30-year quest to build efficiency into its global operations had failed.

Matsushita: Background

In 1918, Konosuke Matsushita (or "KM" as he was affectionately known), a 23-year-old inspector with the Osaka Electric Light Company, invested ¥100 to start production of double-ended sockets in his modest home. The company grew rapidly, expanding into battery-powered lamps, electric irons, and radios. On May 5, 1932, Matsushita's 14th anniversary, KM announced to his 162 employees a 250-year corporate plan broken into 25-year sections, each to be carried out by successive generations. His plan was codified in a company creed and in the "Seven Spirits of Matsushita" (see Exhibit 4), which, along with the company song, continued to be woven into morning assemblies worldwide and provided the basis of the "cultural and spiritual training" all new employees received during their first seven months with the company.

In the postwar boom, Matsushita introduced a flood of new products: TV sets in 1952; transistor

---

EXHIBIT 4

Matsushita Creed and Philosophy (excerpts)

> **Creed** Through our industrial activities, we strive to foster progress, to promote the general welfare of society, and to devote ourselves to furthering the development of world culture.
>
> **Seven Spirits of Matsushita**
>
>   Service through Industry
>
>   Fairness
>
>   Harmony and Cooperation
>
>   Struggle for Progress
>
>   Courtesy and Humility
>
>   Adjustment and Assimilation
>
>   Gratitude
>
> **KM's Business Philosophy (Selected Quotations)**
>
>   "The purpose of an enterprise is to contribute to society by supplying goods of high quality at low prices in ample quantity."
>
>   "Profit comes in compensation for contribution to society. . . . [It] is a result rather than a goal."
>
>   "The responsibility of the manufacturer cannot be relieved until its product is disposed of by the end user."
>
>   "Unsuccessful business employs a wrong management. You should not find its causes in bad fortune, unfavorable surroundings or wrong timing."
>
>   "Business appetite has no self-restraining mechanism. . . . When you notice you have gone too far, you must have the courage to come back."

Source: "Matsushita Electric Industrial (MEI) in 1987," Harvard Business School Case No. 388-144.

radios in 1958; color TVs, dishwashers, and electric ovens in 1960. Capitalizing on its broad line of 5,000 products (Sony produced 80), the company opened 25,000 domestic retail outlets. With more than six times the outlets of rival Sony, the ubiquitous "National Shops" represented 40% of appliance stores in Japan in the late 1960s. These not only provided assured sales volume, but also gave the company direct access to market trends and consumer reaction. When postwar growth slowed, however, Matsushita had to look beyond its expanding product line and excellent distribution system for growth. After trying many tactics to boost sales—even sending assembly line workers out as door-to-door salesmen—the company eventually focused on export markets.

The Organization's Foundation: Divisional Structure

Plagued by ill health, KM wished to delegate more authority than was typical in Japanese companies. In 1933, Matsushita became the first Japanese company to adopt the divisional structure, giving each division clearly defined profit responsibility for its product. In addition to creating a "small business" environment, the product division structure generated internal competition that spurred each business to drive growth by leveraging its technology to develop new products. After the innovating division had earned substantial profits on its new product, however, company policy was to spin it off as a new division to maintain the "hungry spirit."

Under the "one-product-one-division" system, corporate management provided each largely self-sufficient division with initial funds to establish its own development, production, and marketing capabilities. Corporate treasury operated like a commercial bank, reviewing divisions' loan requests for which it charged slightly higher-than-market interest, and accepting interest-bearing deposits on their excess funds. Divisional profitability was determined after deductions for central services such as corporate R&D and interest on internal borrowings. Each division paid 60% of earnings to headquarters and financed all additional working capital and fixed asset requirements from the retained 40%. Transfer prices were based on the market and settled through the treasury on normal commercial terms. KM expected uniform performance across the company's 36 divisions, and division managers whose operating profits fell below 4% of sales for two successive years were replaced.

While basic technology was developed in a central research laboratory (CRL), product development and engineering occurred in each of the product divisions. Matsushita intentionally under-funded the CRL, forcing it to compete for additional funding from the divisions. Annually, the CRL publicized its major research projects to the product divisions, which then provided funding in exchange for technology for marketable applications. While it was rarely the innovator, Matsushita was usually very fast to market—earning it the nickname "Manishita," or copycat.

Matsushita: Internationalization

Although the establishment of overseas markets was a major thrust of the second 25 years in the 250-year plan, in an overseas trip in 1951 KM had been unable to find any American company willing to collaborate with Matsushita. The best he could do was a technology exchange and licensing agreement with Philips. Nonetheless, the push to internationalize continued.

Expanding Through Color TV

In the 1950s and 1960s, trade liberalization and lower shipping rates made possible a healthy export business built on black and white TV sets. In 1953, the company opened its first overseas branch office—the Matsushita Electric Corporation of America (MECA). With neither a distribution network nor a strong brand, the company could not access traditional retailers, and had to resort to selling its products through mass merchandisers and discounters under their private brands.

During the 1960s, pressure from national governments in developing countries led Matsushita to open plants in several countries in Southeast Asia and Central and South America. As manufacturing costs in Japan rose, Matsushita shifted more basic production to these low-wage countries, but almost all high-value components and subassemblies were still made in its scale-intensive Japanese plants. By the 1970s, an East-West trade war mentality forced the company to establish assembly operations in the Americas and Europe. In 1972, it opened a plant in Canada; in 1974, it bought Motorola's TV business and started manufacturing its Quasar brand in the United States; and in 1976, it built a plant in Cardiff, Wales, to supply the Common Market.

Building Global Leadership Through VCRs

The birth of the videocassette recorder (VCR) propelled Matsushita into first place in the consumer electronics industry during the 1980s. Recognizing the potential mass-market appeal of the VCR—developed by Californian broadcasting company, Ampex, in 1956—engineers at Matsushita began developing VCR technology. After six years of development work, Matsushita launched its commercial broadcast video recorder in 1964, and introduced a consumer version two years later.

In 1975, Sony introduced the technically superior "Betamax" format, and the next year JVC launched a competing "VHS" format. Under pressure from MITI, the government's industrial planning ministry, Matsushita agreed to give up its own format and adopt the established VHS standard. During Matsushita's 20 years of VCR product development, various members of the VCR research team spent most of their careers working together, moving from central labs to the product division's development labs and eventually to the plant producing VCRs.

The company quickly built production to meet its own needs as well as those of OEM customers like GE, RCA, Philips, and Zenith, who decided to forego self-manufacture and outsource to the low-cost Japanese. Between 1977 and 1985, capacity increased 33-fold to 6.8 million units. Increased volume enabled Matsushita to slash prices 50% within five years of product launch, while simultaneously improving quality. In parallel, the company aggressively licensed the VHS format to other manufacturers, including Hitachi, Sharp, Mitsubishi and, eventually, Philips. By the mid-1980s, VCRs accounted for 30% of total sales—over 40% of overseas revenues—and provided 45% of profits.

Changing Systems and Controls

In the mid-1980s, Matsushita's growing number of overseas companies reported to the parent in one of two ways: wholly owned, single-product global plants reported directly to the appropriate product division, while overseas sales and marketing subsidiaries and overseas companies producing a broad product line for local markets reported to Matsushita Electric Trading Company (METC), a separate legal entity. (See Exhibit 5 for METC's organization.)

Throughout the 1970s, the central product divisions maintained strong operating control over their offshore production units. Overseas operations used plant and equipment designed by the parent company, followed manufacturing procedures dictated by the center, and used materials from Matsushita's domestic plants. By the 1980s, growing trends toward local sourcing gradually weakened the divisions' direct control so instead of controlling inputs, they began to monitor measures of output (for example, quality, productivity, inventory levels).

About the same time, product divisions began receiving the globally consolidated return on sales reports that had previously been consolidated in METC statements. By the mid-1980s, as worldwide planning was introduced for the first time, corporate management required all its product divisions to prepare global product strategies.

Headquarters-Subsidiary Relations

Although METC and the product divisions set detailed sales and profits targets for their overseas subsidiaries, local managers were told they had autonomy on how to achieve the targets. "Mike" Matsuoko, president of the company's largest European production subsidiary in Cardiff, Wales, however, emphasized that failure to meet targets forfeited freedom: "Losses show bad health and invite many doctors from Japan, who provide advice and support."

In the mid-1980s, Matsushita had over 700 expatriate Japanese managers and technicians on foreign assignment for four to eight years, but defended that high number by describing their pivotal role. "This vital communication role," said one manager, "almost always requires a manager from the parent company. Even if a local manager speaks Japanese, he would not have the long experience that is needed to build relationships and understand our management processes."

Expatriate managers were located throughout foreign subsidiaries, but there were a few positions that were almost always reserved for them. The most visible were subsidiary general managers whose main role was to translate Matsushita philosophy abroad. Expatriate accounting managers were expected to "mercilessly expose the truth" to corporate headquarters; and Japanese technical managers were sent to transfer product and process technologies and provide headquarters with local market information. These expatriates maintained relationships with senior colleagues in their divisions, who acted as career mentors, evaluated performance (with some input

EXHIBIT 5

Organization of METC, 1985

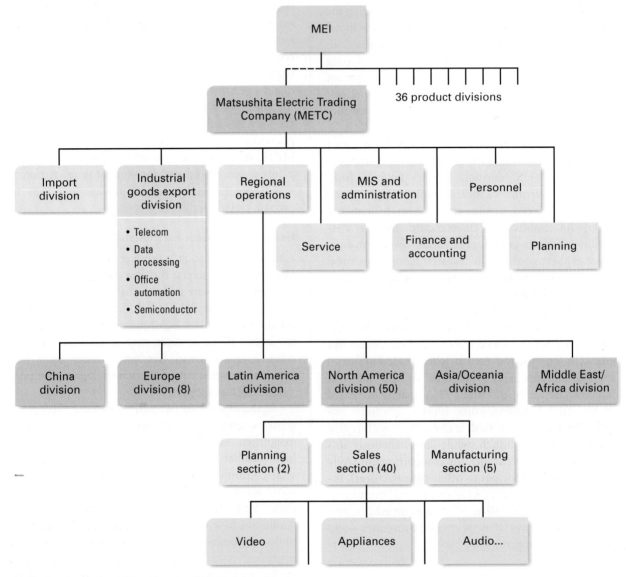

Source: Harvard Business School Case No. 388-144.

Note: ( ) = number of people.

from local managers), and provided expatriates with information about parent company developments.

General managers of foreign subsidiaries visited Osaka headquarters at least two or three times each year—some as often as every month. Corporate managers reciprocated these visits, and on average, major operations hosted at least one headquarters manager each day of the year. Face-to-face meetings were considered vital: "Figures are important," said one manager, "but the meetings are necessary to develop judgment." Daily faxes and nightly phone calls between headquarters and expatriate colleagues were a vital management link.

Yamashita's Operation Localization

Although international sales kept rising, as early as 1982 growing host country pressures caused concern about the company's highly centralized operations.

EXHIBIT 6

Matsushita—Summary Financial Data, 1970–2000[a]

	2000	1995	1990	1985	1980	1975	1970
In billions of yen and percent:							
Sales	¥7,299	¥6,948	¥6,003	¥5,291	¥2,916	¥1,385	¥932
Income before tax	219	232	572	723	324	83	147
As % of sales	3.0%	3.3%	9.5%	13.7%	11.1%	6.0%	15.8%
Net income	¥100	¥90	¥236	¥216	¥125	¥32	¥70
As % of sales	1.4%	1.3%	3.9%	4.1%	4.3%	2.3%	7.6%
Cash dividends (per share)	¥14.00	¥13.50	¥10.00	¥9.52	¥7.51	¥6.82	¥6.21
Total assets	7,955	8,202	7,851	5,076	2,479	1,274	735
Stockholders' equity	3,684	3,255	3,201	2,084	1,092	573	324
Capital investment	355	316	355	288	NA	NA	NA
Depreciation	343	296	238	227	65	28	23
R&D	526	378	346	248	102	51	NA
Employees (units)	290,448	265,397	198,299	175,828	107,057	82,869	78,924
Overseas employees	143,773	112,314	59,216	38,380	NA	NA	NA
As % of total employees	50%	42%	30%	22%	NA	NA	NA
Exchange rate (fiscal period end; ¥/$)	103	89	159	213	213	303	360
In millions of dollars:							
Sales	$68,862	$78,069	$37,753	$24,890	$13,690	$4,572	$2,588
Operating income before depreciation	4,944	6,250	4,343	3,682	1,606	317	NA
Operating income after depreciation	1,501	2,609	2,847	2,764	1,301	224	NA
Pretax income	2,224	2,678	3,667	3,396	1,520	273	408
Net income	941	1,017	1,482	1,214	584	105	195
Total assets	77,233	92,159	49,379	21,499	11,636	4,206	2,042
Total equity	35,767	36,575	20,131	10,153	5,129	1,890	900

Source: Annual reports; Standard & Poors' *Compustat*; Moody's Industrial and International Manuals.

[a]Data prior to 1987 are for the fiscal year ending November 20; data 1988 and after are for the fiscal year ending March 31.

In that year, newly appointed company President Toshihiko Yamashita launched "Operation Localization" to boost offshore production from less than 10% of value-added to 25%, or half of overseas sales, by 1990. To support the target, he set out a program of four localizations—personnel, technology, material, and capital.

Over the next few years, Matsushita increased the number of local nationals in key positions. In the United States, for example, U.S. nationals became the presidents of three of the six local companies, while in Taiwan the majority of production divisions were replaced by Chinese managers. In each case, however, local national managers were still supported by senior Japanese advisors, who maintained a direct link with the parent company. To localize technology and materials, the company developed its national subsidiaries' expertise to source equipment locally, modify designs to meet local requirements, incorporate local components, and adapt corporate processes and technologies to accommodate these changes. And by the mid-1980s, offshore production subsidiaries were free to buy minor parts from local vendors as long as quality could be assured, but still had to buy key components from internal sources.

One of the most successful innovations was to give overseas sales subsidiaries more choice over the products they sold. Each year the company held a two-week internal merchandising show and product planning meeting where product divisions exhibited the new lines. Here, overseas sales subsidiary managers described their local market needs and negotiated for change in features, quantities, and even prices of the products they wanted to buy. Product division managers, however, could overrule the sales subsidiary if they thought introduction of a particular product was of strategic importance.

President Yamashita's hope was that Operation Localization would help Matsushita's overseas companies develop the innovative capability and entrepreneurial initiatives that he had long admired in the national organizations of rival Philips. (Past efforts to develop such capabilities abroad had failed. For example, when Matsushita acquired Motorola's TV business in the United States, the U.S. company's highly innovative technology group atrophied as American engineers resigned in response to what they felt to be excessive control from Japan's highly centralized R&D operations.) Yet despite his four localizations, overseas companies continued to act primarily as the implementation arms of central product divisions. In an unusual act for a Japanese CEO, Yamashita publicly expressed his unhappiness with the lack of initiative at the TV plant in Cardiff. Despite the transfer of substantial resources and the delegation of many responsibilities, he felt that the plant remained too dependent on the center.

Tanii's Integration and Expansion

Yamashita's successor, Akio Tanii, expanded on his predecessor's initiatives. In 1986, feeling that Matsushita's product divisions were not giving sufficient attention to international development—in part because they received only 3% royalties for foreign production against at least 10% return on sales for exports from Japan—he brought all foreign subsidiaries under the control of METC. Tanii then merged METC into the parent company in an effort to fully integrate domestic and overseas operations. Then, to shift operational control nearer to local markets, he relocated major regional headquarters functions from Japan to North America, Europe, and Southeast Asia. Yet still he was frustrated that the overseas subsidiary companies acted as little more than the implementing agents of the Osaka-based product divisions.

Through all these changes, however, Matsushita's worldwide growth continued generating huge reserves. With $17.5 billion in liquid financial assets at the end of 1989, the company was referred to as the "Matsushita Bank," and several top executives began proposing that if they could not develop innovative overseas companies, they should buy them. Flush with cash and international success, in early 1991 the company acquired MCA, the U.S. entertainment giant, for $6.1 billion with the objective of obtaining a media software source for its hardware. Within a year, however, Japan's bubble economy had burst, plunging the economy into recession. Almost overnight, Tanii had to shift the company's focus from expansion to cost containment. Despite his best efforts to cut costs, the problems ran too deep. With 1992 profits less than half their 1991 level, the board took the unusual move of forcing Tanii to resign in February 1993.

Morishita's Challenge and Response

At 56, Yoichi Morishita was the most junior of the company's executive vice presidents when he was tapped as the new president. Under the slogan "simple, small, speedy and strategic," he committed to cutting headquarters staff and decentralizing responsibility. Over the next 18 months, he moved 6,000 staff to operating jobs. In a major strategic reversal, he also sold 80% of MCI to Seagram, booking a $1.2 billion loss on the transaction.

Yet the company continued to struggle. Japan's domestic market for consumer electronics collapsed—from $42 billion in 1989 to $21 billion in 1999. Excess capacity drove down prices and profits evaporated. And although offshore markets were growing, the rise of new competition—first from Korea, then China—created a global glut of consumer electronics, and prices collapsed.

With a strong yen making exports from Japan uncompetitive, Matsushita's product divisions rapidly shifted production offshore during the 1990s, mostly to low-cost Asian countries like China and Malaysia. By the end of the decade, its 160 factories outside Japan employed 140,000 people—about the same number of employees as in its 133 plants in Japan. Yet, despite the excess capacity and strong yen, management seemed unwilling to radically restructure its increasingly inefficient portfolio of production facilities or even lay off staff due to strongly-held commitments to lifetime employment. Despite Morishita's promises, resistance within the organization prevented his implementation of much of the promised radical change.

In the closing years of the decade, Morishita began emphasizing the need to develop more of its technology and innovation offshore. Concerned that only 250 of the company's 3,000 R&D scientists and engineers were located outside Japan, he began investing in R&D partnerships and technical exchanges, particularly in fast emerging fields. For example, in 1998 he signed a joint R&D agreement with the Chinese Academy of Sciences, China's leading research organization. Later that year, he announced the establishment of the Panasonic Digital Concepts Center in California. Its mission was to act as a venture fund and an incubation center for the new ideas and technologies emerging in Silicon Valley. To some it was an indication that Matsushita had given up trying to generate new technology and business initiatives from its own overseas companies.

Nakamura's Initiatives

In April 2000, Morishita became chairman and Kunio Nakamura replaced him as president. Profitability was at 2.2% of sales, with consumer electronics at only 0.4%, including losses generated by one-time cash cows, the TV and VCR divisions. (Exhibit 6 provides the financial history for Matsushita and key product lines.) The new CEO vowed to raise this to 5% by 2004. Key to his plan was to move Matsushita beyond its roots as a "super manufacturer of products" and begin "to meet customer needs through systems and services." He planned to flatten the hierarchy and empower employees to respond to customer needs, and as part of the implementation, all key headquarters functions relating to international operations were transferred to overseas regional offices.

But the biggest shock came in November, when Nakamura announced a program of "destruction and creation," in which he disbanded the product division structure that KM had created as Matsushita's basic organizational building block 67 years earlier. Plants, previously controlled by individual product divisions, would now be integrated into multi-product production centers. In Japan alone 30 of the 133 factories were to be consolidated or closed. And marketing would shift to two corporate marketing entities, one for Panasonic brands (consumer electronics, information and communications products) and one for National branded products (mostly home appliances).

In February, 2001, just three months after raising his earnings estimate for the financial year ending March 2001, Nakamuta was embarrassed to readjust his estimate sharply downward. As Matsushita's first losses in 30 years accelerated, the new CEO announced a round of emergency measures designed to cut costs. When coupled with the earlier structural changes, these were radical moves, but in a company that even in Japan was being talked about as a takeover target, observers wondered if they were sufficient to restore Matsushita's tattered global competitiveness.

Merck, the FDA, and the Vioxx Recall

This case was prepared by Anne T. Lawrence, San Jose State University.

In 2006, the pharmaceutical giant Merck faced major challenges. Vioxx, the company's once best-selling prescription painkiller, had been pulled off the market in September 2004 after Merck learned it increased the risk of heart attacks and strokes. When news of the recall broke, the company's stock price had plunged thirty percent to $33 a share, its lowest point in eight years, where it had hovered since. Standard & Poor's had downgraded the company's outlook from "stable" to "negative." In late 2004, the Justice Department had opened a criminal investigation into whether the company had "caused federal health programs to pay for the prescription drug when its use was not warranted."[1] The Securities and Exchange Commission was inquiring into whether Merck had misled investors. By late 2005, more than 6,000 lawsuits had been filed, alleging that Vioxx had caused death or disability. From many quarters, the company faced troubling questions about the development and marketing of Vioxx, new calls for regulatory reform, and concerns about its political influence on Capitol Hill. In the words of Senator Charles Grassley, chairman of a Congressional committee investigating the Vioxx case, "a blockbuster drug [had become] a blockbuster disaster."[2]

Merck, Inc.[3]

Merck, the company in the eye of this storm, was one of the world's leading pharmaceutical firms. As shown in Exhibit 1, in 2005 the company ranked fourth in sales, after Pfizer, Johnson & Johnson, and

GlaxoSmithKline. In assets and market value, it ranked fifth. However, Merck ranked first in profits, earning $7.33 billion on $30.78 billion in sales (24 percent).

Merck had long enjoyed a reputation as one of the most ethical and socially responsible of the major drug companies. For an unprecedented seven consecutive years (1987 to 1993), *Fortune* magazine had named Merck its "most admired" company. In 1987, Merck appeared on the cover of *Time* under the headline, "The Miracle Company." It had consistently appeared on lists of best companies to work for and in the portfolios of social investment funds. The company's philanthropy was legendary. In the 1940s, Merck had given its patent for streptomycin, a powerful antibiotic, to a university foundation. Merck was especially admired for its donation of Mectizan. Merck's scientists had originally developed this drug for veterinary use, but later discovered that it was an effective cure for river blindness, a debilitating parasitic disease afflicting some of the world's poorest people. When the company realized that the victims of river blindness could not afford the drug, it decided to give it away for free, in perpetuity.[4]

In 1950, George W. Merck, the company's longtime CEO, stated in a speech: "We try never to forget that medicine is for the people. It is not for the profits. The profits follow, and if we have remembered that, they never fail to appear. The better we have remembered that, the larger they have been."[5] This statement was often repeated in subsequent years as a touchstone of the company's core values.

Merck was renowned for its research labs, which had a decades-long record of achievement, turning out one innovation after another, including drugs

EXHIBIT 1

The World's Top Pharmaceutical Companies, 2005

Company	Sales ($bil)	Profits ($bil)	Assets ($bil)	Market Value ($bil)
Pfizer	40.36	6.20	120.06	285.27
Johnson & Johnson	40.01	6.74	46.66	160.96
Merck	**30.78**	**7.33**	**42.59**	**108.76**
Novartis	26.77	5.40	46.92	116.43
Roche Group	25.18	2.48	45.77	95.38
GlaxoSmithKline	34.16	6.34	29.19	124.79
Aventis	21.66	2.29	31.06	62.98
Bristol-Myers Squibb	19.89	2.90	26.53	56.05
AstraZeneca	20.46	3.29	23.57	83.03
Abbott Labs	18.99	2.44	26.15	69.27

Source: Forbes 2000, available online at www.forbes.com. Listed in order of overall ranking in the Forbes 2000.

for tuberculosis, cholesterol, hypertension, and AIDS. In the early 2000s, Merck spent around $3 billion annually on research. Some felt that the company's culture had been shaped by its research agenda. Commented the author of a history of Merck, the company was "intense, driven, loyal, scientifically brilliant, collegial, and arrogant."[6] In 2006, although Merck had several medicines in the pipeline—including vaccines for rotavirus and cervical cancer, and drugs for insomnia, lymphoma, and the effects of stroke—some analysts worried that the pace of research had slowed significantly.

Estimating the company's financial liability from the Vioxx lawsuits was difficult. Some 84 million people had taken the drug worldwide over a five-year period from 1999 to 2004. In testimony before Congress, Dr. David Graham, a staff scientist at the Food and Drug Administration, estimated that as many as 139,000 people in the United States had had heart attacks or strokes as a result of taking Vioxx, and about 55,000 of these had died.[7] Merrill Lynch estimated the company's liability for compensatory damages alone in the range of $4 to $18 billion.[8] However, heart attacks and strokes were common, and they had multiple causes, including genetic predisposition, smoking, obesity, and a sedentary lifestyle. Determining the specific contribution of Vioxx to a particular cardiovascular event would be very difficult.

The company vigorously maintained that it had done nothing wrong and vowed to defend every single case in court. By early 2006, only three cases had gone to trial, and the results had been a virtual draw—one decision for the plaintiff, one for Merck, and one hung jury.

Government Regulation of Prescription Drugs

In the United States, prescription medicines—like Vioxx—were regulated by the Food and Drug Administration (FDA).[9] Before a new drug could be sold to the public, its manufacturer had to carry out clinical trials to demonstrate both safety and effectiveness. Advisory panels of outside medical experts reviewed the results of these trials and recommended to the FDA's Office of Drug Safety whether or not to approve a new drug.[10] After a drug was on the market, the agency's Office of New Drugs continued to monitor it for safety, in a process known as postmarket surveillance. These two offices both reported to the same boss, the FDA's director of the Center for Drug Evaluation and Research.

Once the FDA had approved a drug, physicians could prescribe it for any purpose, but the manufacturer could market it only for uses for which it had been approved. Therefore, companies had an incentive to continue to study approved drugs to provide data that they were safe and effective for the treatment of other conditions.

In the 1980s, the drug industry and some patient advocates had criticized the FDA for being too slow to approve new medicines. Patients were concerned that they were not getting new medicines fast enough, and drug companies were concerned that they were losing sales revenue. Each month an average drug spent under review represented $41.7 million in lost revenue, according to one study.[11]

In 1992, Congress passed the Prescription Drug User Fee Act (PDUFA). This law, which was supported by the industry, required pharmaceutical companies to pay "user fees" to the FDA to review proposed new medicines. Between 1993 and 2001, the FDA received around $825 million in such fees from drug makers seeking approval. (During this period, it also received $1.3 billion appropriated by Congress.) This infusion of new revenue enabled the agency to hire 1,000 new employees and to shorten the approval time for new drugs from 27 months in 1993 to 14 months in 2001.[12]

Despite the benefits of PDUFA, some felt that industry-paid fees were a bad idea. In an editorial published in December 2004, the *Journal of the American Medical Association (JAMA)* concluded: "It is unreasonable to expect that the same agency that was responsible for approval of drug licensing and labeling would also be committed to actively seek evidence to prove itself wrong (i.e., that the decision to approve the product was subsequently shown to be incorrect)." *JAMA* went on to recommend establishment of a separate agency to monitor drug safety.[13] Dr. David Kessler, a former FDA Commissioner, rejected this idea, responding that "strengthening post-marketing surveillance is certainly in order, but you don't want competing agencies."[14]

Some evidence suggested that the morale of FDA staff charged with evaluating the safety of new medicines had been hurt by relentless pressure to bring drugs to market quickly. In 2002, a survey of agency scientists found that only 13 percent were "completely confident" that the FDA's "final decisions adequately assess the safety of a drug." Thirty-one percent were "somewhat confident" and 5 percent lacked "any confidence." Two-thirds of those surveyed lacked confidence that the agency "adequately monitors the safety of prescription jobs once they are on the market." And nearly one in five said they had "been pressured to approve or recommend approval" for a drug "despite reservations about [its] safety, efficacy or quality."[15]

After the FDA shortened the approval time, the percentage of drugs recalled following approval increased from 1.56% for 1993–1996 to 5.35% for 1997–2001.[16] Vioxx was the ninth drug taken off the market in seven years.

Influence at the Top

The pharmaceutical industry's success in accelerating the approval of new drugs reflected its strong presence in Washington. The major drug companies, their trade association PhRMA (Pharmaceutical Research and Manufacturers of America), and their executives consistently donated large sums of money to both political parties and, through their political action committees, to various candidates. The industry's political contributions are shown in Exhibit 2.

Following the Congressional ban on soft money contributions in 2003, the industry shifted much of its contributions to so-called stealth PACs, nonprofit organizations which were permitted by law to take unlimited donations without revealing their source. These organizations could, in turn, make "substantial" political expenditures, providing political activity was not their primary purpose.[17]

In addition, the industry maintained a large corps of lobbyists active in the nation's capital. In 2003, for example, drug companies and their trade association spent $108 million on lobbying and hired 824 individual lobbyists, according to a report by Public Citizen.[18] Merck spent $40.7 million on lobbying between 1998 and 2004.[19] One of the industry's most effective techniques was to hire former elected officials or members of their staffs. For example, Billy Tauzin, formerly a Republican member of Congress from Louisiana and head of the powerful Committee on Energy and Commerce, which oversaw the drug industry, became president of PhRMA at a reported annual salary of $2 million in 2004.[20]

Over the years, the industry's representatives in Washington had established a highly successful record of promoting its political agenda on a range of issues. In addition to faster drug approvals, these had more recently included a Medicare prescription drug benefit, patent protections, and restrictions on drug imports from Canada.

EXHIBIT 2

Pharmaceutical/Health Products Industry: Political Contributions, 1990–2006

Election Cycle	Total Contributions	Contributions from Individuals	Contributions from PACs	Soft Money Contributions	Percentage to Republicans
2006	$5,187,393	$1,753,159	$3,434,234	N/A	70%
2004	$18,181,045	$8,445,485	$9,735,560	N/A	66%
2002	$29,441,951	$3,332,040	$6,957,382	$19,152,529	74%
2000	$26,688,292	$5,660,457	$5,649,913	$15,377,922	69%
1998	$13,169,694	$2,673,845	$4,107,068	$6,388,781	64%
1996	$13,754,796	$3,413,516	$3,584,217	$6,757,063	66%
1994	$7,706,303	$1,935,150	$3,477,146	$2,294,007	56%
1992	$7,924,262	$2,389,370	$3,205,014	$2,329,878	56%
1990	$3,237,592	$771,621	$2,465,971	N/A	54%
Total	$125,291,328	$30,374,643	$42,616,505	$52,300,180	67%

Source: Center for Responsive Politics, online at www.opensecrets.org.

The Blockbuster Model

In the 1990s, 80 percent of growth for the big pharmaceutical firms came from so-called "blockbuster" drugs.[21] Blockbusters have been defined by *Fortune* magazine as "medicines that serve vast swaths of the population and garner billions of dollars in annual revenue."[22] The ideal blockbuster, from the companies' view, was a medicine that could control chronic but usually non-fatal conditions that afflicted large numbers of people with health insurance. These might include, for example, daily maintenance drugs for high blood pressure or cholesterol, allergies, arthritis pain, or heartburn. Drugs that could actually cure a condition—and thus would not need to be taken for long periods—or were intended to treat diseases, like malaria or tuberculosis, that affected mainly the world's poor, were often less profitable.

Historically, drug companies focused most of their marketing efforts on prescribing physicians. The industry hired tens of thousands of sales representatives—often, attractive young men and women—to make the rounds of doctors' offices to talk about new products and give out free samples.[23] Drug companies also offered doctors gifts—from free meals to tickets to sporting events—to cultivate their good will. They also routinely sponsored continuing education events for physicians, often featuring reports on their own medicines, and supported doctors financially with opportunities to consult and to conduct clinical

trials.[24] In 2003 Merck spent $422 million to market Vioxx to doctors and hospitals.[25]

During the early 2000s, when Vioxx and Pfizer's Celebrex were competing head-to-head, sales representatives for the two firms were hard at work promoting their brand to doctors. Commented one rheumatologist of the competition between Merck and Pfizer at the time: "We were all aware that there was a great deal of marketing. Like a Coke-Pepsi war."[26] An internal Merck training manual for sales representatives, reported in *The Wall Street Journal*, was titled "Dodge Ball Vioxx." It explained how to "dodge" doctors' questions, such as "I am concerned about the cardiovascular effects of Vioxx." Merck later said that this document had been taken out of context and that sales representatives "were not trained to avoid physician's questions."[27]

Direct-to-Consumer Advertising

Although marketing to doctors and hospitals continued to be important, in the late 1990s the focus shifted somewhat. In 1997, the FDA for the first time allowed drug companies to advertise directly to consumers. The industry immediately seized this opportunity, placing numerous ads for drugs—from Viagra to Nexium—on television and in magazines and newspapers. In 2004, the industry spent over $4 billion on such direct-to-consumer, or DTC, advertising. For example, in one ad for Vioxx, Olympic figure skating champion Dorothy Hamill glided gracefully across an outdoor ice rink to the tune of "It's a Beautiful Morning" by the sixties pop group The Rascals, telling viewers that she would "not let arthritis stop me." In all, Merck spent more than $500 million advertising Vioxx.[28]

The industry's media blitz for Vioxx and other drugs was highly effective. According to research by the Harvard School of Public Heath, each dollar spent on DTC advertising yielded $4.25 in sales.

The drug companies defended DTC ads, saying they informed consumers of newly available therapies and encouraged people to seek medical treatment. In the age of the Internet, commented David Jones, an advertising executive whose firm included several major drug companies, "consumers are becoming much more empowered to make their own health care decisions."[29]

However, others criticized DTC advertising, saying that it put pressure on doctors to prescribe drugs that might not be best for the patient. "When a patient comes in and wants something, there is a desire to serve them," said David Wofsy, president of the American College of Rheumatology. "There is a desire on the part of physicians, as there is on anyone else who provides service, to keep the customer happy."[30] Even some industry executives expressed reservations. Said Hank McKinnell, CEO of Pfizer, "I'm beginning to think that direct-to-consumer ads are part of the problem. By having them on television without a very strong message that the doctor needs to determine safety, we've left this impression that all drugs are safe. In fact, no drug is safe."[31]

The Rise of Vioxx

Vioxx, the drug at the center of Merck's legal woes, was known as "a selective COX-2 inhibitor." Scientists had long understood that an enzyme called cyclooxygenase, or COX for short, was associated with pain and inflammation. In the early 1990s, researchers learned that there were really two kinds of COX enzyme. COX-1, it was found, performed several beneficial functions, including protecting the stomach lining. COX-2, on the other hand, contributed to pain and inflammation. Existing anti-inflammatory drugs suppressed both forms of the enzyme, which is why drugs like ibuprofen (Advil) relieved pain, but also caused stomach irritation in some users.

A number of drug companies, including Merck, were intrigued by the possibility of developing a medicine that would block just the COX-2, leaving the stomach-protective COX-1 intact. Such a drug would offer distinctive benefits to some patients, such as arthritis sufferers who were at risk for ulcers (bleeding sores in the intestinal tract).[32] As many as 16,500 people died each year in the United States from this condition.[33]

In May 1999, after several years of research and testing by Merck scientists, the FDA approved Vioxx for the treatment of osteoarthritis, acute pain in adults, and menstrual symptoms. The drug was later approved for rheumatoid arthritis. Although Merck, like other drug companies, never revealed what it spent to develop specific new medicines, estimates of the cost to develop a major new drug ran as high as $800 million.[34]

Vioxx quickly became exactly what Merck had hoped: a blockbuster. At its peak in 2001, Vioxx generated $2.1 billion in sales in the United States alone, contributing almost 10 percent of Merck's total sales revenue worldwide, as shown in Exhibit 3.

EXHIBIT 3

Vioxx Sales in the United States, 1999–2004

	U.S. Prescriptions Dispensed	U.S. Sales	U.S. Sales of Vioxx as % of Total Merck Sales
1999	4,845,000	$372,697,000	2.2%
2000	20,630,000	$1,526,382,000	7.6%
2001	25,406,000	$2,084,736,000	9.8%
2002	22,044,000	$1,837,680,000	8.6%
2003	19,959,000	$1,813,391,000	8.1%
2004*	13,994,000	$1,342,236,000	5.9%

*Withdrawn from the market in September 2004.

Sources: Columns 1 and 2: IMS Health (www.imshealth.com); Column 3: Merck Annual Reports (www.merck.com).

The retail price of Vioxx was around $3.00 per pill, compared with pennies per pill for older anti-inflammatory drugs like aspirin and Advil. Of course, Vioxx was often covered, at least partially, under a user's health insurance, while over-the-counter drugs were not.

Safety Warnings

Even before the drug was approved, some evidence cast doubt on the safety of Vioxx. These clues were later confirmed in other studies.

Merck Research

Internal company emails suggested that Merck scientists might have been worried about the cardiovascular risks of Vioxx as early as its development phase. In a 1997 email, reported in *The Wall Street Journal*, Dr. Alise Reicin, a Merck scientist, stated that "the possibility of CV (cardiovascular) events is of great concern." She added, apparently sarcastically, "I just can't wait to be the one to present those results to senior management!" A lawyer representing Merck said this email had been taken out of context.[35]

VIGOR

A study code-named VIGOR, completed in 2000 after the drug was already on the market, compared rheumatoid arthritis patients taking Vioxx with another group taking naproxen (Aleve). Merck financed the research, which was designed to study gastrointestinal side effects. The study found—as the company had expected—that Vioxx was easier on the stomach than naproxen. But it also found that the Vioxx group had nearly five times as many heart attacks (7.3 per thousand person-years) as the naproxen group (1.7 per thousand person-years).[36] Publicly, Merck hypothesized that these findings were due to the heart-protective effect of naproxen, rather than to any defect inherent in Vioxx. Privately, however, the company seemed worried. In an internal email dated March 9, 2000, under the subject line "Vigor," the company's research director, Dr. Edward Scolnick, said that cardiovascular events were "clearly there" and called them "a shame." But, he added, "there is always a hazard."[37] At that time, the company considered reformulating Vioxx by adding an agent to prevent blood clots (and reduce CV risk), but then dropped the project.

The FDA was sufficiently concerned by the VIGOR results that it required Merck to add additional warning language to its label. These changes appeared in April 2002, after lengthy negotiations between the agency and the company over their wording.[38]

Kaiser/Permanente

In August 2004, Dr. David Graham, a scientist at the FDA, reported the results of a study of the records of 1.4 million patients enrolled in the Kaiser health maintenance organization in California. He found that patients on high doses of Vioxx had three times the rate of heart attacks as patients on Celebrex, a competing COX-2 inhibitor made by Pfizer. Merck discounted this finding, saying that studies of patient records were less reliable than double blind clinical studies.[39] Dr. Graham later charged that his superiors at the FDA had "ostracized" him and subjected him to "veiled threats" if he did not qualify his criticism of Vioxx. The FDA called these charges "baloney."[40]

APPROVe

In order to examine the possibility that Vioxx posed a cardiovascular risk, Merck decided to monitor patients enrolled in a clinical trial called APPROVe to see if they those taking Vioxx had more heart attacks and strokes than those who were taking a placebo (sugar pill). This study had been designed to determine if Vioxx reduced the risk of recurrent colon polyps (a precursor to colon cancer); Merck hoped it would lead to FDA approval of the drug for this condition. The APPROVe study was planned before the VIGOR results were known.

Merck Recalls the Drug

On the evening of Thursday, September 23, 2004, Dr. Peter S. Kim, president of Merck Research Labs, received a phone call from scientists monitoring the colon polyp study. Researchers had found, the scientists told him, that after 18 months of continuous use individuals taking Vioxx were more than twice as likely to have a heart attack or stroke than those taking a placebo. The scientists recommended that the study be halted because of "unacceptable" risk.[41]

Dr. Kim later described to a reporter for *The New York Times* the urgent decision-making process that unfolded over the next hours and days as the company responded to this news.

> On Friday, I looked at the data with my team. The first thing you do is review the data. We did that. Second is you double-check the data, go through

it and make sure that everything is O.K. [At that point] I knew that barring some big mistake in the analysis, we had an issue here. Around noon, I called [CEO] Ray Gilmartin and told him what was up. He said, "Figure out what was the best thing for patient safety." We then spent Friday and the rest of the weekend going over the data and analyzing it in different ways and calling up medical experts to set up meetings where we would discuss the data and their interpretations and what to do.[42]

According to later interviews with some of the doctors consulted that weekend by Merck, the group was of mixed opinion. Some experts argued that Vioxx should stay on the market, with a strong warning label so that doctors and patients could judge the risk for themselves. But others thought the drug should be withdrawn because no one knew why the drug was apparently causing heart attacks. One expert commented that "Merck prides itself on its ethical approach. I couldn't see Merck saying we're going to market a drug with a safety problem."[43]

On Monday, Dr. Kim recommended to Gilmartin that Vioxx be withdrawn from the market. The CEO agreed. The following day, Gilmartin notified the board, and the company contacted the FDA. On Thursday, September 30, Merck issued a press release, which stated in part:

> Merck & Co., Inc. announced today a voluntary withdrawal of VIOXX®. This decision is based on new data from a three-year clinical study. In this study, there was an increased risk for cardiovascular (CV) events, such as heart attack and stroke, in patients taking VIOXX 25 mg compared to those taking placebo (sugar pill). While the incidence of CV events was low, there was an increased risk beginning after 18 months of treatment. The cause of the clinical study result is uncertain, but our commitment to our patients is clear. . . . Merck is notifying physicians and pharmacists and has informed the Food and Drug Administration of this decision. We are taking this action because we believe it best serves the interests of patients. That is why we undertook this clinical trial to better understand the safety profile of VIOXX. And it's why we instituted this voluntary withdrawal upon learning about these data. Be assured that Merck will continue to do everything we can to maintain the safety of our medicines.

ENDNOTES

1. "Justice Dept. and SEC Investigating Merck Drug," *New York Times*, November 9, 2004.
2. "Opening Statement of U.S. Senator Chuck Grassley of Iowa," U.S. Senate Committee on Finance, Hearing—FDA, Merck, and Vioxx: Putting Patient Safety First?" November 18, 2004, online at http://finance.senate.gov.
3. A history of Merck may be found in Fran Hawthorne, *The Merck Druggernaut: The Inside Story of a Pharmaceutical Giant* (Hoboken, NJ: John Wiley & Sons, 2003).
4. Merck received the 1991 Business Enterprise Trust Award for this action. See Stephanie Weiss and Kirk O. Hanson, "Merck and Co., Inc.: Addressing Third World Needs" (Business Enterprise Trust, 1991).
5. Hawthorne, op. cit., pp. 17–18.
6. Hawthorne, op. cit., p. 38.
7. "FDA Failing in Drug Safety, Official Asserts," *New York Times*, November 19, 2004. The full transcript of the hearing of the U.S. Senate Committee on Finance, "FDA, Merck, and Vioxx: Putting Patient Safety First?" is available online at http://finance.senate.gov.
8. "Despite Warnings, Drug Giant Took Long Path to Vioxx Recall," *New York Times*, November 14, 2004.
9. A history of the FDA and of its relationship to business may be found in Philip J. Hilts, *Protecting America's Health: The FDA, Business, and One Hundred Years of Regulation* (New York: Alfred A. Knopf, 2003).
10. Marcia Angell, *The Trust About the Drug Companies* (New York: Random House, 2004), Ch. 2.
11. Merrill Lynch data reported in "A World of Hurt," *Fortune*, January 10, 2005, p. 18.
12. U.S. General Accounting Office, *Food and Drug Administration: Effect of User Fees on Drug Approval Times, Withdrawals, and Other Agency Activities,* September 2002.
13. "Postmarketing Surveillance—Lack of Vigilance, Lack of Trust," *Journal of the American Medical Association* 92(21), December 1, 2004, p. 2649.
14. "FDA Lax in Drug Safety, Journal Warns," *www.sfgate.com*, November 23, 2004.
15. 2002 Survey of 846 FDA scientists conducted by the Office of the Inspector General of the Department of Health and Human Services, online at www.peer.org/FDAscientistsurvey.
16. "Postmarketing Surveillance," op. cit.
17. "Big PhRMA's Stealth PACs: How the Drug Industry Uses 501(c) Non-Profit Groups to Influence Elections," *Congress Watch*, September 2004.
18. "Drug Industry and HMOs Deployed an Army of Nearly 1,000 Lobbyists to Push Medicare Bill, Report Finds," June 23, 2004, www.citizen.org.
19. Data available online at www.publicintegrity.org.
20. "Rep. Billy Tauzin Demonstrates that Washington's Revolving Door Is Spinning Out of Control," *Public Citizen*, December 15, 2004, press release.
21. "The Waning of the Blockbuster," *Business Week,* October 18, 2004.
22. "A World of Hurt," *Fortune*, January 10, 2005, p. 20.
23. In 2005, 90,000 sales representatives were employed by the pharmaceutical industry, about one for every eight doctors. The *New York Times* revealed in an investigative article ("Give Me an Rx! Cheerleaders Pep Up Drug Sales," November 28, 2005) that many companies made a point of hiring former college cheerleaders for this role.
24. The influence of the drug industry on the medical professional is documented in Katharine Greider, *The Big Fix: How the*

Pharmaceutical Industry Rips Off American Consumers (New York: Public Affairs, 2003).

25. "Drug Pullout," *Modern Healthcare*, October 18, 2004.

26. "Marketing of Vioxx: How Merck Played Game of Catch-Up," *New York Times*, February 11, 2005.

27. "E-Mails Suggest Merck Knew Vioxx's Dangers at Early Stage," *Wall Street Journal*, November 1, 2004.

28. IMS Health estimate reported in "Will Merck Survive Vioxx?" *Fortune*, November 1, 2004.

29. "With or Without Vioxx, Drug Ads Proliferate," *New York Times*, December 6, 2004.

30. "A 'Smart' Drug Fails the Safety Test," *Washington Post*, October 3, 2004.

31. "A World of Hurt," *Fortune*, January 10, 2005, p. 18.

32. "Medicine Fueled by Marketing Intensified Troubles for Pain Pills," *New York Times*, December 19, 2004.

33. "New Scrutiny of Drugs in Vioxx's Family," *New York Times*, October 4, 2004.

34. This estimate was hotly debated. See, for example, "How Much Does the Pharmaceutical Industry Really Spend on R&D?" Ch. 3 in Marcia Angell, op. cit., and Merrill Goozner, *The $800 Million Pill: The Truth Behind the Cost of New Drugs* (Berkeley: University of California Press, 2004).

35. "E-Mails Suggest Merck Knew Vioxx's Dangers at Early Stage," *Wall Street Journal*, November 1, 2004.

36. "Comparison of Upper Gastrointestinal Toxicity of Rofecoxib and Naproxen in Patients with Rheumatoid Arthritis," *New England Journal of Medicine*, 2000: 323.

37. "E-Mails Suggest Merck Knew Vioxx's Dangers at Early Stage," *Wall Street Journal*, November 1, 2004.

38. At one of the early Vioxx trials, the plaintiff introduced a Merck internal memo that calculated that the company would make $229 million more in profits if it delayed changes to warning language on the label by four months (*New York Times*, August 20, 2005). The FDA did not have the authority to dictate label language; any changes had to be negotiated with the manufacturer.

39. "Study of Painkiller Suggests Heart Risk," *New York Times*, August 26, 2004.

40. "FDA Official Alleges Pressure to Suppress Vioxx Findings," *Washington Post*, October 8, 2004.

41. "Painful Withdrawal for Makers of Vioxx," *Washington Post*, October 18, 2004. Detailed data reported the following day in the *New York Times* showed that 30 of the 1287 patients taking Vioxx had suffered a heart attack, compared with 11 of 1299 taking a placebo; 15 on Vioxx had had a stroke or transient ischemic attack (minor stroke), compared with 7 taking a placebo.

42. "A Widely Used Arthritis Drug Is Withdrawn," *New York Times*, October 1, 2004.

43. "Painful Withdrawal for Makers of Vioxx," *Washington Post*, October 18, 2004.

34

Mired in Corruption—Kellogg, Brown and Root in Nigeria

This case was prepared by Charles W. L. Hill, the University of Washington.

In 1998, the large Texas-based oil and gas service firm, Halliburton, acquired Dresser Industries. Among other businesses, Dresser owned M. W. Kellogg, one of the world's largest general contractors for construction projects in distant parts of the globe. After the acquisition, Kellogg was combined with an existing Halliburton business and renamed Kellogg, Brown and Root, or KBR for short. At the time, it looked like a good deal for Halliburton. Among other things, Kellogg was involved in a four-firm consortium that was building a series of liquefied natural gas (LNG) plants in Nigeria. By early 2004, the total value of the contracts associated with these plants had exceeded $8 billion.

In early 2005, however, Halliburton put KBR up for sale. The sale was seen as an attempt by Halliburton to distance itself from several scandals that had engulfed KBR. One of these concerned allegations that KBR had systematically overcharged the Pentagon for services it provided to the U.S. military in Iraq. Another scandal centered on the Nigerian LNG plants and involved KBR employees, several former officials of the Nigeria government, and a mysterious British lawyer named Jeffrey Tesler.

The roots of the Nigerian scandal date back to 1994 when Kellogg and its consortium partners were trying to win an initial contract from the Nigerian government to build two LNG plants. The

contract was valued at around $2 billion. Each of the four firms held a 25% stake in the consortium, and each had veto power over its decisions. Kellogg employees held many of the top positions at the consortium, and two of the other members, Technip of France and JGC of Japan, have claimed that Kellogg managed the consortium (the fourth member, ENI of Italy, has not made any statement regarding management).

The KBR consortium was one of two to submit a bid on the initial contract, and its bid was the lower of the two. By early 1995, the KBR consortium was deep in final negotiations on the contract. It was at this point that Nigeria's oil minister had a falling out with the country's military dictator, General Abacha, and was replaced by Dan Etete. Etete proved to be far less accommodating to the KBR consortium, and suddenly the entire deal looked to be in jeopardy. According to some observers, Etete was a tough customer who immediately began to use his influence over the LNG project for personal gain. Whether this is true or not, what is known is that the KBR consortium quickly entered into a contract with Tesler. The contract, signed by a Kellogg executive, called on Tesler to obtain government permits for the LGN project, maintain good relations with government officials, and provide advice on sales strategy. Tesler's fee for these services was $60 million.

Tesler, it turned out, had long-standing relations with some twenty to thirty senior Nigerian government and military officials. In his capacity as a lawyer, for years Tesler had handled their London affairs, helping them to purchase real estate and set up financial accounts. Kellogg had a relationship with Tesler that dated back to the mid-1980s, when it had employed him to broker the sale of Kellogg's minority interest in a Nigerian fertilizer plant to the Nigerian government.

What happened next is currently the subject of government investigations in France, Nigeria, and the United States. The suspicion is that Tesler promised to funnel big sums to Nigerian government officials if the deal was done. Investigators base these suspicions on a number of factors, including the known corruption of General Abacha's government; the size of the payment to Tesler, which seemed out of all proportion to the services he was contracted to provide; and a series of notes turned up by internal investigators at Halliburton. The handwritten notes, taken by Wojciech Chodan, a Kellogg executive, document a meeting between Chodan and Tesler in which they discussed the possibility of channeling $40 million of Tesler's $60 million payment to General Abacha.

It is not known whether a bribe was actually paid. What is known is that in December 1995, Nigeria awarded the $2 billion contract to the KBR consortium. The LNG plant soon became a success. Nigeria contracted to build a second plant in 1999, two more in 2002, and a sixth in July 2004. KBR rehired Tesler in 1999 and again in 2001 to help secure the new contracts, all of which it won. In total, Tesler was paid some $132.3 million from 1994 through to early 2004 by the KBR consortium.

Tesler's involvement in the project might have remained unknown were it not for an unrelated event. Georges Krammer, an employee of the French company Technip, which along with KBR was a member of the consortium, was charged by the French government for embezzlement. When Technip refused to defend Krammer, he turned around and aired what he perceived to be Technip's dirty linen. This included the payments to Tesler to secure the Nigeria LNG contracts.

This turn of events led French and Swiss officials to investigate Tesler's Swiss bank accounts. They discovered that Tesler was "kicking back" some of the funds he received to executives in the consortium and to sub-contractors. One of the alleged kickbacks was a transfer of $5 million from Tesler's account to that of Albert J. "Jack" Stanley, who was head of M. W. Kellogg

and then Halliburton's KBR unit. Tesler also transferred some $2.5 million into Swiss bank accounts held under a false name by the Nigerian oil minister, Dan Etete. Other payments include a $1 million transfer into an account controlled by Wojciech Chodan, the former Kellogg executive whose extensive handwritten notes suggest the payment of a bribe to General Abacha, and $5 million to a German subcontractor on the LNG project in exchange for "information and advice."

After this all came out in June 2004, Halliburton promptly fired Jack Stanley and severed its long-standing relationship with Jeffrey Tesler, asking its three partners in the Nigeria consortium to do the same. The U.S. Justice Department took things further, establishing a grand jury investigation to determine if Halliburton, through its KBR subsidiary, had been in violation of the Foreign Corrupt Practices Act. In November 2004, the Justice Department widened its investigation to include payments in connection with the Nigerian fertilizer plant that Kellogg had been involved with during the 1980s under the leadership of Jack Stanley. In March 2005, the Justice Department also stated that it was looking at whether Jack Stanley had tried to coordinate bidding with rivals and fix prices on certain foreign construction projects. As of late 2006, the investigation was still ongoing. As for Halliburton's plans to sell KBR, these too had come to naught. In April 2006, Halliburton announced that it would spin off KBR to investors, but a lack of interest in the offering resulted in a delay, and it was not clear when Halliburton would be able to complete the planned transaction.

REFERENCES

R. Gold, "Halliburton to Put KBR Unit of Auction Block," *New York Times*, January 31, 2005, page A2.

R. Gold and C. Flemming, "Out of Africa: In Halliburton Nigeria Inquiry, a Search for Bribes to a Dictator," *Wall Street Journal*, September 29, 2004, page A1.

Halliburton 10K and 10Q documents for 2005 and 2006, filed with the Securities and Exchange Commission.

D. Ivanovich, "Halliburton: Contracts Investigated," *Houston Chronicle*, March 2, 2005, page 1.

T. Sawyer, "Citing Violations, Halliburton Cuts Off Former KBR Chairman," *ENR*, June 28, 2004, page 16.

Index